JOSEPHUS' STORY OF THE LATER MONARCHY

BIBLIOTHECA EPHEMERIDUM THEOLOGICARUM LOVANIENSIUM

CXLV

JOSEPHUS' STORY OF THE LATER MONARCHY (*AJ* 9,1–10,185)

BY

CHRISTOPHER BEGG

LEUVEN
UNIVERSITY PRESS

UITGEVERIJ PEETERS
LEUVEN

2000

ISBN 90 6186 966 8 (Leuven University Press)
D/1999/1869/31
ISBN 90-429-0785-1 (Uitgeverij Peeters)
D/1999/0602/74

Leuven University Press / Presses Universitaires de Louvain
Universitaire Pers Leuven
Blijde-Inkomststraat 5, B-3000 Leuven-Louvain (Belgium)

© Peeters, Bondgenotenlaan 153, B-3000 Leuven (Belgium)

FOREWORD

As I bring to completion this, my second monograph on Josephus, I am especially conscious of all I owe to so many people who have supported me through the years of my writing it. Those persons represent a wide variety of groups and settings. My gratitude goes in first place to all members of my family, George and Catherine Begg, Joseph and Teresa Begg, and Joseph and Susan Fantom, in particular. As a priest of the Archdiocese of Washington, I am thankful to my Ordinary, James Cardinal Hickey, as well as to my long-time priest friends Rev. Michael Murray and Rev. Msgr. Paul Langsfeld for their interest in my scholarly endeavors. I appreciate too the hospitality of the people of St. Joseph's Church, Washington, D.C. and their pastor, Rev. Paul Lavin, who have afforded me a place to exercise my priestly ministry for many years. Each summer for over a decade and a half Edna and Ida Fecker of Sigmaringen, Germany have generously opened their home and their hearts to me during my European wanderings; notwithstanding the physical distance between us, they are often in my thoughts. All of the above persons are ones whom I have known for a long time now, and most of them appeared by name in the foreword of my earlier volume. To that list I would like to add here a newer friend and source of great inspiration to me, i.e. Rev. Daniel B. Gallagher of Gaylord, Michigan ("Amico fideli nulla est comparatio et non est digna ponderatio auri et argenti contra bonitatem fidei illius", Sir 6,15).

Among my colleagues at Catholic University, Washington, D.C. where I have taught since 1982, I would like to single out Profs. Frank Matera and John Galvin for their daily companionship and counsel. Prof. Louis H. Feldman of Yeshiva University has been of great assistance in my project, both through his prolific writings and his numerous acts of personal kindness.

I am also grateful to Prof. em. Frans Neirynck, general editor of *Bibliotheca Ephemeridum Theologicarum Lovaniensium*, for accepting my new volume in the series and to the publishers of BETL, Leuven University Press and Uitgeverij Peeters, for making this publication possible. Finally, I wish to thank Mr. James Hornecker for his help in preparing the indexes.

Washington, D.C., March, 1999   Christopher BEGG

TABLE OF CONTENTS

ACKNOWLEDGEMENTS

The text and translation of *Jewish Antiquities* 9,1–10,185 cited in this volume
are reprinted by permission of the publishers and Loeb Classical Library from
Josephus, vol. VI, translated by R. Marcus, Cambridge, MA, Harvard University
Press, 1937. Other, shorter portions of the text and/or translation of Josephus'
writings cited in this volume are reprinted by permission of the publishers and
Loeb Classical Library from *Josephus*, vols. I-X, translated by H. St.J. THACKE-
RAY, *et al.*, Cambridge, MA, Harvard University Press, 1926-1965. Scripture
quotations are from the Revised Standard Version of the Bible, copyright 1946,
1952, 1971 by the Division of Christian Education of the National Council of
the Churches of Christ in the USA. Used by permission.

INTRODUCTION

In an earlier study I investigated Josephus' treatment, in his *Antiquitates Judaicae* (hereafter *AJ*) 8,212-420, of the period extending from
the death of Solomon through that of Ahab[1]. The present volume picks
up where that previous one left off: it examines the historian's account
of the epoch running from the later years of Jehoshaphat's reign through
the immediate sequels to the Babylonian capture of Jerusalem as found
in *AJ* 9,1–10,185[2]. Also in its mode of procedure this volume represents
a continuation of its predecessor. Here too, I make a detailed comparison between Josephus' presentation and its various Biblical sources as
represented by the following major textual witnesses: MT (BHS), the
Dead Sea Scrolls[3], Codex Vaticanus (hereafter B)[4] and the Lucianic

1. C. BEGG, *Josephus' Account of the Early Divided Monarchy (AJ 8,212-420):
Rewriting the Bible* (BETL, 108), Leuven, University Press / Peeters, 1993 (hereafter
Early Divided Monarchy). For more details concerning the matters touched on here (e.g.,
the Biblical text-forms used by Josephus in *AJ*) I refer the reader to the introduction of
this work, pp. 1-6.
2. For the text and translation of Josephus' writings I base myself on: H. ST.J. THACKE-
RAY, R. MARCUS, A. WIKGREN, L.H. FELDMAN, *Josephus* (LCL), Cambridge, MA, Harvard
University Press; London, Heinemann, 1926-1965 (*AJ* 9,1–10,185 appears in Vol. VI,
1937, pp. 2-261, ed. by R. MARCUS). I have likewise consulted the following editions/
translations of Josephus' writings: G. DINDORF, *Flavii Josephi Opera*, Paris, Didot, 1845-
1847; I. BEKKER, *Flavii Iosephi Opera Omnia*, Leipzig, Teubner, 1855-1856; B. NIESE,
Flavii Josephi Opera: Editio maior, Berlin, Weidmann, [2]1955 (= 1885-1895); S.A. NABER,
Flavii Josephi Opera Omnia, Leipzig, Teubner, 1888-1896; T. REINACH (ed.), *Œuvres
complètes de Flavius Josèphe*, Paris, Leroux, 1900-1932 (the translation of *AJ* 9,1–10,185
in Vol. II is by J. WEILL); A. SCHALIT (tr.), *Joseph ben Mattijahu Kadmoniot ha-jehudim*,
Jerusalem, Bialik Institute, 1944-1963. For the sigla used to designate the various textual
witnesses for *AJ*, see the list of abbreviations at the end of this volume.
3. The Qumran textual evidence for Josephus' two main Biblical sources in
AJ 9,1–10,185, i.e. 2 Kings 1–25 and 2 Chronicles 19–36, is quite meager. 2 Chronicles
is not represented at all among the Qumran MSS finds; see the "Index of Biblical Pas-
sages" in J.A. FITZMYER, *The Dead Sea Scrolls: Major Publications and Tools for Study*
(SBL Resources For Biblical Study, 20), Atlanta, Scholars, 1990 (rev. ed.), 205-227.
As for 2 Kings, portions of 5,26; 6,32; 7,8-10; 7,20–8,5; 9,1-2; 10,19-21 (which do not
differ significantly from MT) appear in the MS designated 6Q4 (6Q6). For the text, see
M. BAILLET, *et al.* (eds.), *Les 'Petites Grottes' de Qumrân. Textes* (DJD, 3), Oxford,
Clarendon, 1962, pp. 108-112. I shall make reference to the Qumran evidence for other of
the Biblical books used by Josephus in 9,1–10,185 at the appropriate points.
4. For the B text of Josephus' two main Biblical sources in *AJ* 9,1–10,185, i.e. Kings
and Chronicles, I use A.E. BROOKE, N. MCLEAN, H. ST.J. THACKERAY, *The Old Testament
in Greek according to the Text of Codex Vaticanus*, II:II: *I and II Kings*, Cambridge, University Press, 1930; II:III: *I and II Chronicles*, 1932. For the various books of the "Latter
Prophets" also used by Josephus in our segment and of which the Cambridge edition never

(hereafter L)[5] or Antiochene MSS of the LXX, the *Vetus Latina* (hereafter *VL*)[6] and the Targums[7].

Again as in my earlier work, this comparison aims to determine what can be learned about the following overarching questions: Which of the Biblical (and non-Biblical) sources relating to the period covered by this study did Josephus actually use? What considerations influenced his use or non-use of a given body of source material? In which text-form(s) did he have available the Biblical sources used by him? What sort of rewriting techniques has Josephus applied to the source data, and what were the reasons for and effects of his employing these procedures? In which respects might Josephus' account of the later monarchical period be called a distinctive one? Finally, what messages might Josephus'

appeared, I use the diplomatic text of the Göttingen edition of the LXX. I shall make reference to the relevant volumes of that edition at the appropriate point in my discussion.

5. For the L text of Kings and Chronicles I use N. FERNÁNDEZ MARCOS and J.R. BUSTO SAIZ, *El texto antioqueno de la Biblia griega, II. 1-2 Reyes* (TECC, 53), Madrid, Instituto de Filología del CSIC, 1992; ID., *III. 1-2 Crónicas* (TECC, 60), 1996. For a comparison of the L and Josephan texts of Chronicles, see Mª V. Spottorno, *The Books of Chronicles in Josephus' Jewish Antiquities*, in B.A. TAYLOR (ed.), *IX Congress of the International Organization for Septuagint and Cognate Studies* (SBLSCS, 45), Atlanta, Scholars, 1995, 381-390. For additional bibliography on L, see BEGG, *Early Divided Monarchy*, p. 4, n. 12.

6. The *VL* text of those portions of Kings and Chronicles corresponding to *AJ* 9,1–10,185 is found scattered among various *VL* MSS as well as in the marginal notes of certain Vulgate MSS. For its readings I use: R. WEBER, *Les anciennes versions latines du deuxième livre des Paralipomènes* (CBL, 8), Rome, Abbaye Saint-Jérôme - Liberia Vaticana, 1945, pp. 41-79; B. FISCHER (with the collaboration of E. ULRICH and J.E. SANDERSON), *Palimpsestus Vindobonensis: A Revised Editon of L 115 for Samuel-Kings*, in *BIOSCS* 16 (1983) pp. 13-87, esp. 82-87; J. TREBOLLE BARRERA, *Centena in Libros Samuelis et Regum. Variantes Textuales y Composición literaria en los Libros de Samuel y Reyes* (TECC, 47), Madrid, Instituto de Filología del CSIC, 1989, pp. 155-206; A. MORENO HERÁNDEZ, *Las glosas marginales de Vetus Latina en las biblias vulgatos españolas* (TECC, 49), Madrid, Instituto de Filología del CSIC, 1992; N. FERNÁNDEZ MARCOS, *Scribes & Translators: Septuagint & Old Latin in the Books of Kings* (VTSup, 54), Leiden, Brill, 1994. On *VL*'s text of Kings and Chronicles in relation to those of the other Biblical witnesses (and to Josephus) see FERNÁNDEZ and BUSTO, *1-2 Reyes*, pp. lxi-lx; ID., *1-2 Crónicas*, pp. xxxiv-xlviii; N. FERNÁNDEZ MARCOS, *The Old Latin of Chronicles between the Greek and the Hebrew*, in B.A. TAYLOR (ed.), *IX Congress of the International Organization for Septuagint and Cognate Studies* (SBLSCS, 45), Atlanta, Scholars, 1997, pp. 123-136.

7. For the Aramaic text of the relevant targums I use A. SPERBER, *The Bible in Aramaic*, II-III, Leiden, Brill, 1959; R. LE DÉAUT and J. ROBERT, *Targum des Chroniques*, I (AB, 51), Rome, P.B.I., 1971. For their translation I use D.J. HARRINGTON and A.J. SALDARINI, *Targum Jonathan of the Former Prophets* (The Aramaic Bible, 10), Wilmington, DE, Glazier, 1987; B.D. CHILTON, *The Isaiah Targum* (The Aramaic Bible, 11), Wilmington, DE, Glazier, 1987; R. HAYWARD, *The Targum of Jeremiah* (The Aramaic Bible, 12), Wilmington, DE, Glazier, 1987; K.J. CATHCART and R.P. GORDON, *The Targum of the Minor Prophets* (The Aramaic Bible, 14), Wilmington, DE, Glazier, 1989; J.S. MCIVOR, *The Targum of Chronicles* (The Aramaic Bible, 19), Collegeville, MN, Liturgical Press / Glazier, 1994.

retelling of the Biblical material in *AJ* 9,1–10,185 be intended to convey to his double audience, i.e. cultivated Gentiles and fellow Jews[8]?

A considerable portion of the material to be studied here has already been treated by me in the form of journal articles; references to these earlier publications will be made at the appropriate points in the course of the subsequent study. The present work has given me the opportunity to update, correct, and integrate them into a larger whole. The updating aspect of this study involves especially utilization of a series of relevant investigations which have appeared in the last few years[9].

To facilitate my comparison of them (and the reader's task!) I have divided up the material of *AJ* 9,1–10,185 and its Biblical parallels into the 24 longer, more or less self-contained, segments cited in the table of contents of this volume[10].

8. On Josephus' two-fold intended audience for his *Ant.*, see L.H. FELDMAN, *Josephus's Interpretation of the Bible*, Berkeley, CA, University of California Press, 1998, pp. 46-50 (hereafter *Interpretation*).

9. Such works include L.H. FELDMAN, *Studies in Josephus' Rewritten Bible* (JSJSup, 58), Leiden, Brill, 1998 (hereafter *Studies*; this volume comprises revised versions of twenty-five articles published by Feldman in the years 1968-1997; a number of them deal with Biblical figures featured in *AJ* 9,1–10,185) and ID., *Interpretation* (revised versions of an additional fifteen articles on Biblical figures from the years 1968-1995). In my references to Feldman's treatments of a given Biblical figure I shall make mention both of his original article and the *Studies* or *Interpretation* version. See also P. SPILSBURY, *The Image of the Jew in Flavius Josephus' Paraphrase of the Bible* (TSAJ, 69), Tübingen, Mohr Siebeck, 1998; and S. MASON (ed.), *Understanding Josephus* (JSPSup, 32), Sheffield, Academic Press, 1998.

10. These divisions are based primarily on content considerations – many of them, e.g., coincide with the reign of a given king of Israel or Judah – and are designed to make the component chapters of this study of manageable length. I recognize, of course, that in some instances alternative divisions of both the Biblical and Josephan material might well be proposed.

I

JEHOSHAPHAT AT MID-CAREER[1]
(9,1-17)

Josephus cites the accession of Jehoshaphat, Judah's fourth king, during the period of the divided monarchy, in *AJ* 8,315 (= 1 Kgs 15,24b // 2 Chr 17,1a). Thereafter, following the Northern-centered segment 8,316-392, he returns to the figure of Jehoshaphat, recounting his early achievements (8,393-397 = 2 Chr 17,1b-19) and disastrous involvement with his Israelite counterpart Ahab (8,398-420 = 1 Kgs 22,1-40 // 2 Chr 18,1-34)[2]. Aligning himself with the Chronicler's sequence Josephus next reproduces (*AJ* 9,1-17) the *Sondergut* segment 2 Chr 19,1–20,30 which features events from the middle part of Jehoshaphat's reign. I divide up the material to be studied in this chapter into 8 parallel segments: 1. Jehu's rebuke (*AJ* 9,1 = 2 Chr 19,1-3); 2. Jehoshaphat's judicial initiatives (9,2-6 = 19,4-11); 3. Enemy advance & Jerusalem assembly (9,7-8a = 20,1-4); 4. Jehoshaphat's prayer (9,8b-9 = 20,5-13); 5. Jahaziel's word & hearers' response (9,10-11 = 20,14-19); 6. Judean advance & overthrow of the enemy (9,12-13 = 20,20-23); 7. Battle sequels (9,14-16 = 20,24-30); and 8. Jehoshaphat's maritime venture (9,17 = 20,35-37[3]; cf. 1 Kgs 22,47-49).

1. *Jehu's Rebuke*

2 Chr 19,1-3 (= *AJ* 9,1) relates the immediate sequel to the death of Ahab in battle against the Syrians as told in 2 Chr 18,34 (// 1 Kgs 22,35

---

1. This chapter represents a revision of my *Jehoshaphat at Mid-Career according to AJ 9,1-17*, in *RB* 102 (1995) 379-402 which I use here by permission of the publisher. It likewise draws on C.T. BEGG, *Josephus' Portrait of Jehoshaphat Compared with the Biblical and Rabbinic Portrayals*, in *BN* 78 (1995) 39-48; and FELDMAN, *Studies*, pp. 307-321 (= ID., *Josephus' Portrait of Jehoshaphat*, in *SCI* 12 [1993] 159-175).

2. On this material see BEGG, *Early Divided Monarchy*, pp. 147-149, 236-269.

3. In 2 Chronicles 20 there supervenes between vv. 24-30 (= *AJ* 9,14-16: battle sequels) and 35-37 (= 9,17: Jehoshaphat's maritime venture) a series of standard framework notices for the king, vv. 31-34, these corresponding to 1 Kgs 22,41-43.45. Josephus redistributes to other points in his work that portion of the latter material which he does take over (he has no equivalent to the "source reference" of 20,34 // 22,45), see 8,315 (= 20,31b-32 // 22,42b-43: Jehoshaphat's mother and the evaluation of his reign); 9,44 (= 20,31a // 22,42a: Jehoshaphat's 25-year reign).

= *AJ* 8,415)[4]. In that sequel Jehoshaphat, Ahab's ally in the battle, returns to Jerusalem where he is confronted by the prophet Jehu for his association with the reprobate Northern king. In line with 19,1 Josephus commences his version of this incident with mention of Jehoshaphat's arrival back in Jerusalem. He proceeds, however, to expand (9,1a) this notice with an elaborate *Rückverweis* – appropriate here at the start of a new "book" of *AJ* – to the story of the Syrian campaign related by him in 8,398-420: "Now when King Josaphat returned to Jerusalem *after having made an alliance* (συμμαχίας, cf. συμμαχῆσαι, 8,398) *with Achab, the king of the Israelites, and furnished him help in the war against Adados* (Ἀδάδῳ)[5], *the Syrian king, as we have previously related*[6]...".

In 19,2a (MT) the returning king is met by "Jehu the son of Hanani the seer[7]". As is his practice with lesser Biblical figures, Josephus leaves aside the name of the father of "Jeūs" (Ἰηοῦς, compare B Ἰού, L Ἰηού), just as he follows BL in designating this personage as a "prophet" rather than a "seer" (so MT)[8]. Thereafter, Josephus transposes Jehu's opening rhetorical question of 19,2bα ("should you help the wicked and love those who hate [BL the one hated by] the Lord?") into a narrative notice (9,1b) which likewise identifies the referent of the Biblical allusions by name: "(Jeūs)... found fault with him for making an alliance (συμμαχίας, see 9,1a) with an impious and wicked (ἀσεβῆ καὶ πονηρόν)[9] man *like*

---

4. Between *AJ* 8,415 (= 2 Chr 18,35) and 9,1 (= 2 Chr 19,1, i.e. the immediate continuation of 18,35 in Chronicles) there stands, in Josephus' presentation, a segment (8,416-420) consisting of the following items: a version (8,416-417) of the *Sondergut* passage 1 Kgs 22,36-38 (the Israelite retreat and Ahab's burial), appended reflections by the historian (8,418-420a), and notice on the accession of Ahab's son Ahaziah (8,420b = 1 Kgs 22,40b).

5. This is the conjecture of Dindorf, Bekker, and Naber, and Marcus, based on Lat's "Adadum". Niese reads Ἀδερι with several codices. (In the story of 1 Kings 22 // 2 Chronicles 18 the Syrian king against whom Ahab and Jehoshaphat campaign remains nameless, whereas in 8,414 Josephus calls him "Adados" [Ἀδαδος], i.e. the name read by Dindorf *et al.* in 9,1.)

6. Throughout this monograph I shall indicate elements of Josephus' presentation like the above which have no direct equivalent in his Biblical sources by means of italics. I shall likewise use italics to highlight Biblical items without parallel in Josephus.

7. The Chronicler apparently derived this figure from 1 Kgs 16,1-4.7 where "Jehu, the son of Hanani" pronounces judgment on Baasha of Israel. Josephus' parallel to that Kings passage is *AJ* 8,299-300.

8. Compare *AJ* 7,321 where Josephus calls Gad simply "the prophet" in contrast to the various witnesses to 2 Sam 24,11 // 1 Chr 21,9 which (also) use the term "seer" of him: "the prophet... David's seer" (MT B 24,11); "David's seer" (L 24,11; MT BL 21,9).

9. The above collocation, in this or the reverse order, recurs in *AJ* 8,243.299; 12,252.385;13,34. In making "Jehu" refer to a single figure here, i.e. Ahab, Josephus goes together with BL against the plural form ("those who hate the Lord") of MT; see above.

Achab". In his reproduction of the remainder of Jehu's speech (19,2bβ-3), Josephus, as so often elsewhere, recasts direct as indirect discourse[10]. Jehu's word of doom for Jehoshaphat in 19,2bβ reads: "because of this, wrath has gone out against you from the Lord". Josephus "softens" this reference to divine wrath, having Jeūs merely state that "God[11] was displeased (ἀηδῶς)[12] at this (act)[13]". Jehu's address to the king concludes in 19,3 with the acknowlegement that there is, after all, "some good" (BL λόγοι ἀγαθοί) to be found in him, this consisting in Jehoshaphat's having eliminated the "Asherahs" (BL τὰ ἄλση, "the groves") and his resolute "seeking" of the Lord. Josephus (9,1c) replaces the source's double specification concerning Jehoshaphat's "goodness" with a word of promise which foreshadows the divine response to the invasion of the enemy coalition in what follows. The historian's version of Jehu's closing word reads thus: "... (God would, nevertheless), *despite his having sinned, deliver him from his enemies* (ῥύσασθαι ... ἐκ τῶν πολεμίων) because of his own good (ἀγαθήν)[14] character (φύσιν)[15]".

2. *Jehoshaphat's Judicial Initiatives*

2 Chronicles 19 does not a record a direct response by Jehoshaphat to Jehu's rebuke. Rather, v. 4 opens by noting that the king "dwelt in Jerusalem" and then, somewhat abruptly, proceeds to relate his tour throughout his domains. Josephus (9,2a), on the contrary, takes care to have Jehoshaphat give due recognition to the prophetic word he has just received, substituting mention of this for the (superfluous) Biblical remark about his dwelling in Jerusalem: "And thereupon the king

10. On this feature, see BEGG, *Early Divided Monarchy*, pp. 12-13, n. 38 and the literature cited there.

11. On Josephus' virtually total avoidance of "(the) Lord" as a divine title (so 19,2), see BEGG, *Early Divided Monarchy*, p. 45, n. 218 and the literature cited there.

12. This is Josephus' only use of ἀηδής in reference to the Deity.

13. Commenting on the above "softening", FELDMAN, *Studies*, p. 317 (= ID., *Jehoshaphat*, 171) suggests that it reflects Josephus' concern with intra-Jewish unity, this prompting him to play down the Bible's strong condemnations of Jehoshaphat's cooperation with the Northern kingdom; cf. nn. 86, 89. For the opposite Rabbinic tendency, see the references cited in BEGG, *Josephus' Portrait of Jehoshaphat*, 48.

14. Compare the λόγοι ἀγαθοί attributed to Jehoshaphat in BL 19,3. Note too Josephus' verbal contrast between the "impious and wicked" Ahab and Jehoshaphat with his "good character".

15. With regard to Josephus' non-utilization of the source's mention of Jehoshaphat's elimination of the "Asheras" (MT)/ "groves" (BL) in the above rendition of 19,3, FELDMAN, *Studies*, pp. 318-319 (= ID., *Jehoshaphat*, 172-173) sees this as reflective of the historian's general apologetic tendency to play down Biblical statements concerning Jewish aggressivity towards pagan religion.

betook himself to (τρέπεται)[16] giving thanks and offering sacrifices (εὐχαριστίας καὶ θυσίας)[17] to God (τοῦ θεοῦ)[18]".

Following the above interjected notice, Josephus (9,2b) rejoins 19,4aβ in recounting Jehoshaphat's tour of his territory, omitting the source's mention that this extended "from Beersheba to the hill country of Ephraim[19]". According to 19,4b the king on his tour "brought the people back to the Lord...". Josephus cites a double, more specific purpose for Jehoshaphat's initiative: "... to teach the people thoroughly (ἐκδιδάσκειν) both the laws (τὰ ... νόμιμα) given by God through Moses and the piety to be shown Him (τὴν εὐσέβειαν τὴν πρὸς αὐτόν)[20]".

2 Chr 19,5-7 relates Jehoshaphat's appointment of "judges" in the cities of Judah (v. 5) and his charge to them (vv. 6-7). The latter item, in turn, comprises a double series of directives with attached motivations. Josephus (9,3) reworks the content and sequence of the king's speech rather markedly. He begins by having Jehoshaphat urge his appointees "... not to take thought for anything so much as for justice (τοῦ δικαίου προνοουμένους)[21] in judging the multitude" (compare the king's rather indeterminate opening directive in 19,6aβ: "consider what you do"). To this initial, positive injunction Josephus' king then attaches a negative admonition ("without regard to gifts [δώρων] or the rank [ἀξιώματος] of those who were held to be superior by reason of wealth or birth [διὰ πλοῦτον ἢ διὰ γένος][22]") which appears to represent a "de-theologized" version of the motivation adduced for Jehoshaphat's second exhortation (19,7a) in v. 7b ("*for* there is no perversion of justice with

16. Note the historic present. On Josephus' frequent use of this form, often in place of past forms of the LXX, see BEGG, *Early Divided Monarchy*, pp. 10-11, n. 32 and the literature cited there.

17. This nominal collocation occurs only here in Josephus.

18. NABER, *ad loc.*, tentatively proposes the emendation τῷ θεῷ.

19. Josephus likewise has no equivalent to 19,4aβ's mention of Jehoshaphat's "again" (BL πάλιν) traversing his territory. Here, the reference is apparently to the mission that Jehoshaphat dispatched to teach the people in 2 Chr 17,7-9 (= AJ 8,395). Josephus' omission of the indication may reflect the consideration that, in fact, this is the first time that Jehoshaphat in person is recorded as going out among his people.

20. With this indication concerning Jehoshaphat's purpose Josephus echoes his earlier statement about the objectives of the mission dispatched by the king at the start of his reign in 8,395 (= 2 Chr 17,9): "(the royal delegates were) to teach (διδάξαι) all the people... the laws (τοὺς ... νόμους) of Moses, both to keep them and to be diligent in worshipping God (περὶ τὴν θρησκείαν τοῦ θεοῦ)".

21. The above construction recurs in AJ 9,186; 10,104. On terms of the δικαι-stem as a *Leitwort* of Josephus' presentation of Jehoshaphat, see FELDMAN, *Studies*, pp. 312-313 (= ID., *Jehoshaphat*, 165).

22. This is Josephus' only use of this precise collocation; variants of it appear in AJ 4,14; 20,100.147.

the Lord..., or partiality... or taking bribes [BL δῶρα]")²³. The Josephan Jehoshaphat then concludes his charge by calling on his appointees to "deal equal justice to all (βραβεύειν... τὸ ἴσον)²⁴; compare 19,7a: "... let the fear of the Lord (BL [ὁ] φόβος Κυρίου) be upon you²⁵; take heed what you do". To this reiterated call for just judging Josephus then has the king attach a "theological" motivation – the first and only evocation of the Deity in his version of the royal speech –: "... in the knowledge that God sees everything that is done even in secret" (compare 19,6bβ: "he [God] is with you in giving judgment").

In 19,8 the Chronicler shifts, somewhat abruptly, to relating an additional judicial initiative undertaken by Jehoshaphat, i.e. his appointment of judges in Jerusalem itself. Josephus (9,4) takes care to provide a smoother transition between this item and what precedes: "*after giving these instructions* (διδάξας, cf. ἐκδιδάσκειν, 9,3a) *in every city of the two tribes, he returned to Jerusalem*, in which place he also appointed (κατέστησε = BL) judges (κριτάς, compare δικαστάς, 9,3; cf. n. 23)". In line with the continuation of 19,8 Josephus has Jehoshaphat draw his Jerusalem judges from both the clerical (priests and Levites)²⁶ and lay ("those holding the chief places among the people"; compare 19,8: "heads of families of Israel") orders. On the other hand, he leaves aside the double indication concerning the task envisaged for these judges, i.e. to give judgment for the Lord and to decide disputed case(s), found at the end of 19,8. Rather, he passes immediately to the charge (= 19,9-11) Jehoshaphat addresses to them. As does 19,9 ("thus you shall do in the fear of the Lord [see n. 25], in faithfulness, and with your whole heart"), the historian opens this new royal charge with a general exhortation, i.e.

23. The above opening of Jehoshaphat's speech in 9,3 seems patterned on the Mosaic directives concerning judges (Deut 16,19-20a) in their Josephan version (*AJ* 4,216): "... (the judges) must be influenced neither by lucre (κέρδει) nor by rank (ἀξιώματι) in declaring judgement, but must set justice (τὸ δίκαιον) above all". Note too that in 9,3 Josephus uses the same term, i.e. δικασταί, to designate the "judges" appointed by Jehoshaphat as he does in 4,216.218 for Moses' appointees (compare κριτάς, BL 2 Chr 19,5).

24. This construction occurs only here in Josephus.

25. This element has no equivalent as such in Josephus' version of Jehoshaphat's address. As A. SCHLATTER, *Wie sprach Josephus von Gott?* (BFCT, 14.1), Gütersloh, Bertelsmann, 1910, p. 60; ID., *Die Theologie des Judentums nach dem Bericht von Josefus* (BFCT, 2.26), Gütersloh, Bertelsmann, 1932, p. 155, points out, the historian consistently avoids the key Biblical expression "fear of God". In fact, the only passage where he associates the term φόβος with God as object is *AJ* 1,114 (Nimrod "held that the only way to detach men from the fear of God [τοῦ φόβου τοῦ παρὰ τοῦ θεοῦ] was by making them continuously dependent upon his own power").

26. Josephus cites these two groups in the same order as does B 19,8, whereas MT, L and the Targum of Chronicles (hereafter TC) have the reverse sequence.

"(he exhorted them) to decide all cases with care and justice (ἐπιμελεῖς καὶ δικαίας)²⁷". Thereafter, following 19,10, he has (9,5) Jehoshaphat address the Jerusalem judges concerning those cases that could not be resolved at the local level. The Bible speaks of such cases being transmitted by "your brethren who live in their cities"; Josephus substitutes "if any of their fellow-citizens (ὁμοφύλων)²⁸... should send to them from other cities...". The Chronicler (19,10) uses five terms ("concerning bloodshed, law or commandment, statutes or ordinances", RSV) to specify the kind of cases envisaged. Josephus simplifies with his reference to the provincials' "having differences about matters of great importance". Conversely, he elaborates on the Bible's lapidary "you shall instruct them" (v. 10aβ): the Jerusalem judges are "to take very great pains (σπουδῆς) to render them a just (δικαίως) decision about these matters". Josephus likewise markedly modifies 19,10b's indication that the judges are to act as directed lest both those approaching them and they themselves incur "guilt" and divine "wrath". In the historian's formulation (9,5c) the motivation for the foregoing injunction becomes rather: "for it was proper that in the city in which was the temple of God and where the king had his residence, judgement should be given (προσῆκε)²⁹ with special care and with the utmost justice (σπουδαίας ... καὶ δικαιοτάτας³⁰)".

In 2 Chr 19,11 Jehoshaphat's discourse continues with the king first designating various legal officers for the Jerusalem court and then pronouncing a final exhortation, "deal courageously, and may the Lord be with the upright". Josephus leaves the latter element aside completely. He likewise (9,6a) turns the words with which the king appoints the officers into a narrative notice about the fact of his doing this. The first of the officers cited in the Bible is "Amariah the chief priest" (BL Ἀμαρίας ὁ ἱερεὺς ἡγούμενος) who is to be "over you in all matters of the Lord". Josephus calls "Amasias" (Ἀμασίαν)³¹ simply "the priest"

---

27. This adjectival collocation recurs in *AJ* 9,236 (reverse order).

28. On Josephus' use of this and other related designations for his people in preference to the Biblical term "brethren", see SCHLATTER, *Theologie*, pp. 80-81. The historian employs the term ὁμόφυλος *ca.* 100 times, virtually always to refer to Jews; see K.H. RENGSTORF, *A Complete Concordance to Flavius Josephus*, III, Leiden, Brill, 1979, s.v.

29. This is the reading adopted by Niese and Marcus. Dindorf and Bekker follow the προσήκει of MSP, while Naber reads προσήκειν (so apparently Lat).

30. This collocation occurs only here in Josephus. Compare σπουδῆς ... δικαίως, 9,5b.

31. J. Hudson conjectures Ἀμαρίαν based on the BL reading (see above). Dindorf, Bekker, Niese, Naber, and Marcus retain the reading of the codices, as do A. SCHLATTER, *Die hebräischen Namen bei Josephus* (BFCT, 17.3), Gütersloh, Bertelsmann, 1913, p. 19 and A. SCHALIT, *Namenwörterbuch zu Flavius Josephus*, Leiden, Brill, 1968, p. 9 both of whom suggest that Josephus found the form Ἀμασίας in his Greek text of Chronicles.

(τὸν ἱερέα) and does not indicate which specific competence he is to exercise as "officer" of the court. The historian effects a similar "reduction" with respect to the other figure cited in 19,11, i.e. "Zebadiah" (so MT, B Ζαβδείας, L Ζαβαδίας [= Josephus], TC "Zechariah"), passing over the name of his father ("Ishmael", MT), his status ("the governor of the house of Judah"), and area of competence ("all the king's matters"). In the same line he also leaves aside the source's further reference to the "Levitical officers" (so MT; compare BL οἱ γραμματεῖς καὶ [> L] οἱ Λευεῖται)[32]. In place of this last item, Josephus has the (curiously careless) indication – based, it would seem, on Chronicles' designation of Zebadiah as "governor of the house of *Judah*" – that both "Amasias" and "Zabadias" were "from the tribe of Judah[33]". Thereafter, in line with his frequent practice, he rounds off his whole account of Jehoshaphat's judicial initiatives (9,2-6 = 19,4-11) with the appended closing notice "in this fashion, then, did the king order affairs".

3. *Enemy Advance & Jerusalem Assembly*

2 Chr 20,1 makes the transition to the story of the foreign coalition's advance against Jehoshaphat with the vague chronological indication "after this". Josephus (9,7) represents the assault as simultaneous with the king's judicial initiatives: "... at this same time there marched against him...". According to MT 20,1 the peoples comprising the hostile coalition were "the Moabites, the Ammonites, and with them some of the Ammonites". The versions diverge with regard to the third of these groups: B reads καὶ μετ' αὐτῶν ἐκ τῶν Μειναίων (= RSV: "and with them some of the Meunites"), L the composite καὶ μετ' αὐτῶν ἐκ τῶν υἱῶν Ἀμμανιεὶμ (= MT) τῶν υἱῶν Σηείρ (i.e. the Edomites), and TC "some of the Edomites (cf. L) who were allied with the

---

32. On the priest Josephus' tendency to downplay the role assigned the Levites by the Bible throughout his account of Jehoshaphat (and *AJ* generally), see FELDMAN, *Studies*, p. 308 (= ID., *Jehoshaphat*, 161). See further U. GLESSMER, *Leviten in spät-nachexilischen Zeit. Darstellungsinteressen in den Chronikbüchern und bei Josephus*, in M. ALBANI and T. ARNDT (eds.), *Gottes Ehre erzählen. Festschrift für Hans Seidel zum 65. Geburtstag*, Leipzig, Thomas Verlag, 1994, 127-151, esp. pp. 139,148-151. Cf. n. 52 and chap. XV concerning Josephus' similar handling of the Chronicler's highlighting of the Levites' involvement in Hezekiah's cultic reform (2 Chronicles 29-31) in his own version of that reform in *AJ* 9,260-276.

33. As MARCUS, *Josephus*, VI, p. 5, n. d remarks, one would certainly presume that Amariah, the "chief priest" according to 2 Chr 19,11, was rather of the tribe of Levi. It seems that Josephus' attempt to drastically compress the data of the Biblical verse (see above) has led him into a misstatement on the matter.

Ammonites". Josephus, for his part, has the "Moabites" and the "Ammanites" take along a "large division of Arabs (Ἀράβων)³⁴". In 20,2 Jehoshaphat is informed that the enemy is advancing against him "from beyond the sea of Aram (so MT = BL ἀπο Συρίας)³⁵", being presently situated at "Hazazon-tamar" (compare the transliterations of B [Ἀσάμ Θαμαρά] and L [Ἀσασὰν Θαμάρ]), a site that is itself, in turn, identified with "Engedi" (B Ἐνγάδει, L Ἐγγάδδι). Josephus recasts the Biblical "report" into a notice that continues his previous narrative concerning the enemy's advance: "... they encamped at Engadē (Ἐγγάδη)³⁶, a city situated on Lake (λίμνη) Asphaltis³⁷...". To his mention of "Engadē" Josephus further appends mention of two points of interest about the site, i.e. its lying 300 stades from Jerusalem and the outstanding "palm-trees (φοίνιξ)³⁸ and opobalsamum³⁹" it produced.

2 Chr 20,3 cites the "fear" the report made him in 20,2 inspired in Jehoshaphat. Josephus, who has not previously cited that report as such

34. MARCUS, *Josephus*, VI, p. 5, n. e points out that in 2 Chr 26,7 where there is mention of the "Meunites", i.e. the reading of B (which both BHS and RSV adopt) as against MT's (second) mention of the "Ammonites" in 20,1 (see above), the "Arabs" are cited together with these. Perhaps, then, given the association between them in 26,7, Josephus here in 9,7 opts to replace the unfamiliar "Meunites" with the name of a better-known allied people, i.e. the Arabs (this proposal presupposes, of course, that Josephus had B's reading before him in his text[s] of 20,1). Note that in his version of 2 Chr 26,7 itself in *AJ* 9,217 Josephus speaks only of the "Arabs", making no mention of the "Meunites" (so MT; BL "Mineans").

35. Generally (so BHS, RSV), "Aram" here is emended to "Edom", a reading found in one Hebrew MS and various witnesses of the *VL*, see FERNÁNDEZ, *Old Latin*, p. 127. Josephus simply omits MT and LXX's problematic reference to "Syria" as the coalition's point of origin in his version of 20,2; see above.

36. This is the emendation of Niese which Marcus follows. Dindorf, Bekker, and Naber adopt the reading of J. Hudson, i.e. Ἐγγάδδί (cf. L 20,2). SCHALIT, *Namenwörter-buch*, pp. 44-45 reads Ἐγγαδδαί.

37. Compare 20,2: "from beyond the sea" (BL ἐκ τοῦ πέραν τῆς θαλάσσης) where the reference is to the "Dead Sea". In *AJ* 1,174 Josephus states that "Lake Asphaltis" got its name from the fact that it covers the site of the valley where "bitumen (ἀσφάτου) pits" were once worked. In *Bellum Judaicum* (hereafter *BJ*) 4,476 he provides a description of the lake's features. Both Josephus' name for the sea and the description he gives of it have classical parallels, see, e.g., Diodorus of Sicily, *Library of History*, 19.98 (R.M. GREER, tr., *Diodorus of Sicily*, X [LCL], Cambridge, MA, Harvard University Press; London, Heinemann, 1954, pp. 98-103) and Pliny, *Natural History*, 5.15.72 (H. RACK-HAM, tr., *Pliny, Natural History*, II [LCL], Cambridge, MA, Harvard University Press; London, Heinemann, 1947, p. 271).

38. One might see this item as an allusion to the other name of Engedi, i.e. "Hazazon-tamar" (literally "sand dunes of *palm trees*", MT) cited in 20,2 but not utilized by Josephus as such.

39. In *AJ* 8,174 Josephus affirms that the "root of the opobalsamon" was first introduced into the land of Israel by the queen of Sheba in Solomon's time. In *BJ* 1,138.361; *AJ* 14,54;15,96 he speaks of the outstanding palm trees and balsam found at another site, i.e. Jericho.

(see above), introduces (9,8a) his reference to the king's "fearing" with a long transitional formula which picks up on the Biblical notice concerning the report made to the king: "*now when Josaphat heard that the enemy had crossed the lake and had already invaded the country ruled by him*, he was afraid (δείσας; BL ἐφοβήθη)...". Thereafter, Josephus passes over two additional indications concerning Jehoshaphat's reaction to the report as enumerated in 20,3, i.e. "he set himself to seek the Lord[40], and proclaimed a fast throughout all Judah". In their place he transposes subsequent elements of the Biblical presentation (all Judah's assembling, 20,4; Jehoshaphat's standing in the house of the Lord, 20,5) into the statement that, in his fear, the king "called together the people of Jerusalem[41] to meet in the temple (εἰς τὸ ἱερόν; compare BL 20,5 ἐν οἴκῳ Κυρίου)". The Chronicler (20,5) introduces Jehoshaphat's prayer with mention of the king's "standing... in the house of the Lord, before (BL κατὰ πρόσωπον) the new court...". Generalizing this place indication, Josephus represents him as "standing before (κατὰ πρόσωπον) the sanctuary (τοῦ ναοῦ)".

4. *Jehoshaphat's Prayer*

2 Chr 20,6-12 relates a lengthy prayer by Jehoshaphat which Josephus (9,8b-9) markedly shortens, even while rearranging its components (and recasting it in indirect address). Specifically, he makes Jehoshaphat begin (9,8b) with an appeal to the Deity which utilizes elements of 20,6c ("in thy [the Lord's] hand are power and might [L ἰσχὺς καὶ δυναστεία]") and 12a ("wilt thou [God] not execute judgment upon them [the enemy coalition]?"): "(he began to pray and call upon God) to grant him the power and strength (δύναμιν καὶ ἰσχύν) to punish those who had marched against him...[42]". Thereafter (9,9a) he has the king associate his current petition with the prayer of the Temple's

40. Recall Josephus' non-utilization of the similar word addressed by Jehu to the king in 2 Chr 19,3: "you have set your heart to seek God".

41. In 20,4 the reference is to an assembly drawn from "all the cities of Judah", while in 20,5 Jehoshaphat stands "in the assembly of Judah and Jerusalem". Josephus' limiting of the king's summons to "the people of Jerusalem" might be inspired by the consideration that the urgency of the situation would not allow time for "all Judah" to come together. Cf. nn. 49,73.

42. Note that while in 20,6.12 Jehoshaphat prays that the God of "power and might" will himself "execute judgment" on the coalition, in Josephus he (initially) asks to be empowered by God to himself punish the enemy. This difference should not be pressed, however, since in what follows Josephus has the king use expressions in which God is the subject of the (hoped-for) overthrow of the hostile force; see below.

original builders: "… for, he said, this had been the prayer of those who had built His temple…". The historian's inspiration for this item is 20,8-9 where the king alludes to the appeal once made by the sanctuary's builders. 2 Chr 20,9 formulates Jehoshaphat's "quotation" of the Temple-builders' prayer as a reminiscence of the words of Solomon on the occasion of the Temple's dedication (see, e.g., 1 Kgs 8,37-40 // 2 Chr 6,28-31) with their allusion to many possible calamities in the face of which the Lord's intervention might be implored. Josephus, by contrast, so words the "citation" that it appears more closely oriented towards the crisis at hand: "… that He should protect (ὑμερμάχηται)[43] this city and should repel (ἀμύνηται)[44] those who dared to come against the temple and were now there to take away from them the land He had given them for a habitation (εἰς κατοίκησιν[45])[46]". In this formulation particularly the concluding reference to the coalition's coming to seize the land given his people by God has its counterpart in 20,10-11 where Jehoshaphat affirms that the enemy is advancing "to drive us out of thy (MT, BL our) possession (BL κληρονομίας), which thou hast given us to inherit" (see also 20,7: "Didst thou not, O our God, drive out the inhabitants of this land before thy people Israel, and give it for ever to the descendants of Abraham…?")[47].

One of the elements of Jehoshaphat's prayer as cited in Chronicles which Josephus omits from his version is the closing words of v. 12b: "… we are powerless against this great multitude that is coming against us. We do not know what to do, but our eyes are upon thee". In their place Josephus inserts (9,9b) a transitional notice, i.e. "having made this prayer, he began to weep…". As Marcus points out, while the reference here to the king's "weeping" lacks a Biblical equivalent as such, it

43. The verb ὑπερμαχέω/ὑπερμάχομαι appears twice elsewhere in Josephus' writings: AJ 3,309 (with God as subject, as in 9,9); contra Apionem (hereafter c. Ap.) 1,242 (in a quotation from Manetho).

44. Elsewhere in Josephus the verb ἀμύνω is used with God as subject in BJ 5,407; AJ 1,114; 2,293; 9,266.

45. This is the reading of RO adopted by Niese and Marcus. Dindorf, Bekker, and Naber read κατάσχεσιν ("possession") with MSP. The nominal form read by Niese and Marcus (κατοίκησιν) might have been inspired by the related verb κατῴκησαν used of the ancestors' "dwelling" in the Promised Land in BL 20,8.

46. This portion of Jehoshaphat's prayer likewise harks back to the words which Josephus places on the lips of Solomon at the dedication of the Temple in AJ 8,114 (cf. 1 Kgs 8,29 // 2 Chr 6,20): "… I pray Thee to guard it [the Temple] for ever from sacking by our enemies, as Thine own temple, and to watch over it as Thine own possession".

47. Josephus leaves aside the historical reminiscence of 20,10-11 about Israel's having avoided the territories of the three peoples (Ammon, Moab, Mount Seir = Edom) now advancing against it on its own march towards the promised land – a good deed which those peoples are now "repaying" by invading Judah.

perhaps does reflect Jehoshaphat's final statement in v. 12b: "our eyes are upon thee" understood in the sense "we implore Thee with tears[48]". In any case, Josephus rounds off the scene of Jehoshaphat's appeal with the notice, inspired by 20,13, that "the entire multitude (σύμπαν ... τὸ πλῆθος)[49], together with their wives and children, made supplication (ἱκέτευεν)[50]".

5. *Jahaziel's Word & Hearers' Response*

2 Chr 20,14-17 relates the pivotal moment of the story of the coalition's assault on Jehoshaphat, i.e. the salvation oracle delivered in response to the king's appeal by a certain Jahaziel; Josephus' parallel is 9,10-11. In 20,14 "Jahaziel" (B Ὀζειήλ, L Ἰεζιήλ) is introduced by means of a four-member genealogy and designated as a Levite of the sons of Asaph. Josephus (9,10) leaves aside both of these items, calling "Jaziēlos" (Ἰαζίηλος)[51] simply "a certain prophet[52]". Of Jahaziel 20,14 further states that "the Spirit of the Lord came (literally was) upon (TC the spirit of prophecy from before the Lord rested upon) him in the midst of the assembly". Josephus passes over this reference to the "spirit's" action upon Jahaziel; his doing so is in line with his overall tendency to avoid

48. MARCUS, *Josephus*, VI, pp. 6-7, n. d. FELDMAN, *Studies*, p. 315 (= ID., *Jehoshaphat*, 168) points out that the historian's depiction of the king's "weeping" heightens his appeal to the reader by "showing... true sincerity and sympathy for his people...". I would add that the reference accentuates the pathos of the scene – a frequent feature in Josephus' rewriting of Biblical history.

49. In 20,13 itself the reference is to "all the men of Judah". Recall that in 9,8, in contrast to 20,4-5, Josephus limited those assembled by Jehoshaphat to "the people of Jerusalem". Cf. nn. 41, 73.

50. In 20,13 the assembly simply "stands before the Lord"; Josephus gives them a more active role in the face of the enemy threat. On the theme of "prayer" in the Biblical portion of *AJ* overall, see: M. HARDING, *Making Old Things New. Prayer Texts in Josephus'* Antiquities *1-11: A Study in the Transmission of Tradition*, in J.H. CHARLESWORTH et al. (eds.), *The Lord's Prayer and other Prayer Texts from the Greco-Roman Period*, Valley Forge, PA, Trinity, 1994, pp. 54-72.

51. This is the form of the name read by the *ed. pr.* and followed by Dindorf, Bekker, Niese, Naber, Marcus and SCHALIT, *Namenwörterbuch*, p. 56. (The *ed. pr.* as well as Dindorf, Bekker, Niese, Naber, and Marcus likewise place a period after the preceding verb ἱκέτευεν, thus making the subject of this action "the entire multitude" – cf. Marcus's rendering of the final words of 9,9 above – rather than the prophet named immediately thereafter, as in the reading of MSPE, i.e. ἱκέτευεν ἰναζίηλος.) Compare RO ἱκέτευε τὸν θεὸν ἵνα ὑπερμαχήσῃ αὐτοῖς Ζῆλος (On this reading see NIESE, *Opera*, I, p. xxxviii who, even though he generally follows the witness of RO, identifies this as a instance where the text of these MSS is secondary) and Lat (suplicabant [i.e. the entire multitude]. quo facto quidam Iazel...).

52. Compare his designation of Elijah in *AJ* 8,319 as "a certain prophet of the most high God". On Josephus' tendency to omit Biblical mentions of the Levites; see n. 32.

Biblical mentions of the human and especially the divine "spirit[53]". In the historian's presentation then Jaziēlos simply "came into the midst of the assembly (εἰς μέσην τὴν ἐκκλησίαν, BL 20,14 ἐν τῇ ἐκκλησίᾳ)".

The citation of Jahaziel's actual words begins in 20,15 with his calling both "all Judah and inhabitants of Jerusalem" as well as Jehoshaphat himself to pay heed; the transition to the body of his message is then made via the standard *Botenformel*. Josephus transposes the prophet's opening call to attention into the narrative notice that he addressed "both the people (τῷ ... πλήθει, see σύμπαν ... τὸ πλῆθος, 9,9) and the king"; as is his wont, he omits the Biblical "messenger formula". In 20,15b Jahaziel exhorts king and people "fear not, and be not dismayed...", motivating this appeal with the affirmation "the battle is not yours, but God's". Josephus replaces the prophetic exhortation with the explicit announcement that "God had hearkened to their prayers" (ἐπακοῦσαι τῶν εὐχῶν[54], coupling this with his version of 20,15bβ: "... and promised that He would fight (πολεμήσειν) against their foes".

Jahaziel next (20,16) instructs the assembly concerning its upcoming advance: "tomorrow go down against them; behold they will come up by the ascent of Ziz (B κατὰ τὴν ἀνάθασιν Ἀσᾶε, L κατὰ τὴν ἀνάθασιν τῆς ἐξοχῆς Ἀσεῖς; TC the slope of Odiquth-Kelila); you will find them at the end of the valley, east of the wilderness of Jeruel (BL Ἰεριήλ)". Josephus' version omits the added specification concerning the enemy's whereabouts found in v. 16b. His parallel to 20,16a (9,10b-11a) highlights the king's status as commander: "the prophet also instructed him to lead his army out on the morrow to meet the enemy, saying that he would find them on the ascent (ἐπὶ τῆς ... ἀναβάσεως; cf. κατὰ τὴν ἀνάθασιν, BL) between Jerusalem and Engadē[55], called Prominence (Ἐξοχῆς)[56]".

---

53. Cf., e.g., *AJ* 8,285 where for the reference in 2 Chr 15,1 to the "spirit of God" coming upon Azariah, Josephus simply states that "a prophet named Azarias" met Asa's party on the road. On the question, see E. BEST, *Use and Non-Use of Pneuma by Josephus*, in *NovT* 3 (1959) 218-233; J.R. LEVISON, *Josephus' Interpretation of the Divine Spirit*, in *JJS* 47 (1996) 234-55, esp. 252-254 ("Omissions").

54. This precise phrase occurs only here in Josephus; cf. the variant expressions (likewise with God as subject) in *AJ* 10,41 (14,24).

55. This insertion harks back to Josephus' likewise interjected remark in 9,7 that "Engadē" lies "three hundred stades distant from Jerusalem".

56. The use of this term would seem to indicate Josephus' dependence on a L-like text of 20,16 with its plus τῆς ἐξοχῆς (Ἀσεῖς); cf. MARCUS, *Josephus*, VI, p. 7, n. f. Note, however, that whereas in L the word in question is a common noun which is itself coupled with a proper place name (i.e., Ἀσεῖς), Josephus takes it as the actual name of the site.

Jahaziel's discourse concludes in 20,17 with a further series of assurances and exhortations. From this sequence Josephus (9,11b) reproduces the content of v. 17a, while leaving aside the (repetitive) v. 17b: "they were not, he added, to engage the enemy, but only to stand still (στάν-τας)[57] and see (ὁρᾶν, BL ἴδετε) how the Deity (τὸ θεῖον; compare 20,17 the salvation of the Lord)[58] would fight (μάχεται; cf. πολεμή-σειν – also with God as subject – in 9,10) against them".

2 Chr 20,18-19 recounts the hearers' immediate response to Jahaziel's word: king and people prostrate themselves while the Levites loudly praise the Lord. Josephus (9,11c) introduces his notices on the audience's response with a transitional phrase, "when the prophet [cf. a certain prophet, 9,10] had said these things...". He then relates that "the king and the multitude (τὸ πλῆθος, see 9,10.11a; compare 20,18 all Judah and the inhabitants of Jerusalem), falling upon their faces, *gave thanks to God* (ηὐχαρίστουν ... τῷ θεῷ; cf. εὐχαριστίας ... τοῦ θεοῦ, 9,2)[59] and did obeisance to Him (προσεκύνουν, BL τοῦ προσκυνῆσαι τῷ Κυρίῳ)". In their doing this they are accompanied by "the Levites[60]" who "continued praising (ὑμνοῦντες, BL αἰνεῖν) [God] with their instruments (ὀργάνοις)[61]".

6. *Judean Advance & Enemy Overthrow*

2 Chr 20,20-23 (= *AJ* 9,12-13) recounts how when, as directed, Judah advances against the enemy (vv. 20-22a), God routs the hostile force (vv. 22b-23).

In 20,20a "they" (the people as a whole) "go out (BL ἐξῆλθον) into the wilderness of Tekoa (BL εἰς τὴν ἔρημον Θεκῶε)", Jehoshaphat taking his stand to speak to them as they do so. Josephus, in line with his presentation in 9,10 where Jahaziel instructs Jehoshaphat to "lead out his army on the morrow", makes the king the subject of the advance

---

57. As MARCUS, *Josephus*, VI, p. 7, n. g points out, Josephus' verb corresponds to that of MT and L (στῆτε) in 20,17 whereas B reads σύνετε ("look on").

58. On Josephus' use of the term "the Deity" (frequently as a substitute for Biblical references to "God" or "the Lord"), see R.H.J. SCHUTT, *The Concept of God in the Works of Flavius Josephus*, in *JJS* 31 (1980) 171-189, esp. 173-179.

59. This element has no equivalent as such in 20,18 where king and assembly are portrayed as responding to Jahaziel's assurances with a wordless act of worship.

60. Josephus leaves aside the specification of 20,19 that these Levites were "of the Kohathites and the Korahites".

61. For similar references to the Levites' "making praise with their instruments", see *AJ* 7,305; 8,176; 11,62; cf. 9,269. In 20,19 the reference is to their praising "with a very loud voice".

which he reports in 9,12a: "as soon as it was day the king went out into the wilderness below the city of Thekoa (εἰς τὴν ἔρημον τὴν ὑποκάτω Θεκωᾶς πόλεως)...". 2 Chr 20,20b cites Jehoshaphat's exhortation to his advancing forces. This consists of a call to attention (directed to "Judah and inhabitants of Jerusalem", cf. 20,15) followed by a double appeal-promise, i.e. "believe in the Lord... and you will be established; believe his prophets (so MT and L; B has his prophet, i.e. Jahaziel), and you will succeed". The Chronicler then (20, 21a) reverts to narrative in recounting that, upon consultation with the people, the king designated those who were to go in front of the army, singing in praise of the Lord, with v. 21b supplying the words – a quotation of the opening verse of Psalm 136 – which they are to recite. From the royal word of v. 20b Josephus takes over only its closing call to trust in the prophet(s). In so doing, he (9,12b) aligns himself with the singular reading of B (see above), making the king's exhortation – even more clearly than in the B reading – an allusion to Jahaziel whose message the assembly has just heard: "(Jehoshaphat told the people) that they must have faith (πιστεύειν, cf. B ἐνπιστεύσατε, L ἐμπιστεύσατε)⁶² in what the prophet *had said*". To this admonition Josephus has the king append a (Biblically unparalleled) reminiscence of Jahaziel's actual instruction: "(the people are not) to draw themselves up for battle" (compare 9,11 where Jahaziel tells the assembly that they are "not to engage the enemy"). Thereafter, Josephus (9,12c) recasts 20,21's narrative notice about the king's appointing singers to precede the army into a continuation of Jehoshaphat's (indirect discourse) address, likewise varying the source's wording quite markedly. His version (with elements peculiar to himself italicized) thus reads: "(the people are to) place at their head *the priests with their trumpets*⁶³ *and the Levites*⁶⁴ with the singers (τῶν ὑμνούντων)⁶⁵

62. On the term "believe/belief" in Josephus, see SCHLATTER, *Gott*, pp. 27-28; ID., *Theologie*, pp. 104-105; D.R. LINDSEY, *Josephus and Faith: πίστις and πιστεύειν as Faith Terminology in the Writings of Flavius Josephus and the New Testament* (AGJU, 19), Leiden, Brill, 1993.

63. Josephus may have found inspiration for this reference in 20,28 which speaks of the victorious Judeans returning to Jerusalem "with trumpets". An alternative (or additional) inspiration for the item might be the account of Abijah's battle against Jeroboam in 2 Chronicles 13 where vv. 12 and 14 (= AJ 8,283) make reference to the *priests* blowing trumpets on that occasion. In any event, the inserted reference to the priests here reflects the priest Josephus' tendency to accentuate his group's role in Biblical history, on which see FELDMAN, *Studies*, pp. 545-546.

64. See this same binomial ("priests and Levites") in 9,3; cf. also the mention of the Levites praising God with their instruments in 9,11.

65. Cf. ὑμνοῦντες of the Levites in 9,11; compare BL's double designation for those who are to precede the army in 20,21 ψαλτῳδούς καὶ αἰνοῦντας [+ τὸν Κύριον, L]. Josephus leaves aside the specification of 20,21 that the singers are to praise the Lord "in

and to give thanks (εὐχαριστεῖν, BL 20,21b ἐξομολογεῖσθε)[66] to God *as if he had already delivered our country from the enemy* (ῥυσαμένῳ ... παρὰ τῶν πολεμίων)[67]". Josephus (9,13a) rounds off this expanded word which he attributes to Jehoshaphat with a narrative notice on its reception by the hearers: "the king's plan (γνώμη) met with their approval, and they did just as he had counseled (συνεβούλευσε) them[68]".

2 Chr 20,22 makes the transition to the account of the Lord's overthrow of the enemy forces by noting that this occurred "when they (i.e. those designated by Jehoshaphat in 20,21) began to sing and praise...". Josephus leaves aside this "fulfillment notice" for the king's directives in 20,21 in favor of immediate mention of the divine intervention itself. The continuation of 20,22 (MT) speaks of the Lord's "setting ambushers" (MT מְאָרְבִים)[69] against the three enemy peoples (the third of these now being called "the men of Mount Seir"; compare above on 20,1) with the result that "they were routed". Thereafter, 20,23 explicates the enemy's self-destruction process: the Ammonites and the Moabites first dispatch the inhabitants of Mount Seir, whereupon they turn on each other. Josephus' version (9,13b) clarifies (while also compressing) these Biblical notices: "Then God sent fear and confusion (εἰς φόβον ἐνέβαλε καὶ ταραχήν)[70] into the midst of the Ammanites[71], and they, *mistaking one another for the enemy*[72], killed (their own men)...". He

holy array" (BL αἰνεῖν τὰ ἅγια). (In place of the Greek underlying Marcus's above rendition ["the Levites with the singers"], i.e. Ληουίτας μετὰ τῶν ὑμνούντων, Niese reads simply Ληουίτων with RO.)

66. Compare εὐχαριστίας (9,2); ηὐχαρίστουν (9,11).

67. The above phrase clearly echoes the ("un-Biblical") word which Josephus attributes to the prophet Jehu in 9,1, i.e. God "would deliver (ῥύσασθαι) him [Jehoshaphat] from his enemies (ἐκ τῶν πολεμίων)". The king's directive here in 9,12 is thus indicative of his confidence in that prophetic announcement. Note in the above formulation also the historian's self-identification with his people, via use of the word "our" in relation to them. Compare, e.g., *AJ* 8,261 where he refers to "*our* nation" as the one to which Herodotus was referring.

68. The foregoing notice represents Josephus' (re-positioned) version of 20,21aα: "he took counsel (B ἐβουλεύσατο, L συμβουλευσάμενος) with the people".

69. BHS proposes emending to מַאֲרְבִים or מִרְהֵבִים; cf. L ἔδωκε ... ἔνεδρον (> B; compare *VL* insidias) τοῦ πολεμεῖν.

70. This construction recurs in *AJ* 9,87 (the Syrian king learns that it was the Deity "who had thrown... his army into all that terror and confusion") and 11,175 (the Ammonites, Moabites [cf. 9,7] and Samaritans [so 11,174] "instilled fear and alarm into them [the Jews of Nehemiah's time, see 11,174]"). Cf. 11,141.

71. Josephus here uses this term as a general designation for the whole enemy force, leaving aside the Biblical mention of its two other components.

72. With this item, unparalleled in the Biblical account, Josephus picks up on his previous mention of the "confusion" God brought upon the enemy. Thereby, he likewise provides a response to the question, not as such addressed in 20,22-23, as to why the enemy forces turned on each other as they are said to do.

then rounds off this description with a notice anticipated from the end of 20,24 ("none had escaped"): "... so that out of so great an army not one escaped alive".

7. Battle Sequels

2 Chr 20,24-30 (= *AJ* 9,14-16) relates the sequels to the Lord's triumph over Judah's enemies. According to 20,24 it was "Judah" which ascertained the annihilation of the foe upon arriving at "the watchtower of the wilderness", this geographical specification being taken over from Jahaziel's announcement in 20,16 (see above). Josephus (9,14a), with an eye to the continuation of the account in which the people will be assembled in "the valley of Beracah" (see 20,26), makes "the valley in which the enemy had encamped" the site where their "corpses" are seen. He likewise highlights, in line with a previously noted tendency, Jehoshaphat's stature in the narrative by making him – rather than "Judah" (so 20,24)[73] – subject of the "seeing" of the enemies' remains: "and when Josaphat looked out over the valley (φάραγγα) in which the enemy had encamped and saw it full of corpses (νεκρῶν, BL 20,24 νεκροί)...". Jehoshaphat's standing is then still further accentuated by the following inserted notice (9,14b) on the king's fitting response to his "vision": "... he rejoiced[74] at the wonderful way in which God had helped (ἐπὶ τῷ παραδόξῳ τῆς τοῦ θεοῦ βοηθείας)[75] (his side) and that, with no effort on their part, He had by Himself given them the victory".

2 Chr 20,25 recounts a joint plundering of the enemy's possessions on the part of Jehoshaphat and his men which extends over three days and which leaves them unable to carry anything more. Josephus' version (9,14c) evidences a concern with upholding both the royal dignity and direction of the proceedings; rather than join his men in their plunder-taking, Jehoshaphat "... gave his army leave to plunder the camp of the enemy and strip the dead bodies (σκυλεῦσαι τοὺς νεκρούς)[76]". His

73. Recall that throughout his version Josephus consistently avoids the Biblical mentions of Judah's involvement in the episode; for him Jehoshaphat and the inhabitants of Jerusalem (see 9,8) alone confront the enemy advance; cf. nn. 41,49.

74. This reference to Jehoshaphat's immediate response of "rejoicing" at the sight of the enemy's corpses represents an anticipation (and reapplication to the king personally) of the notice of 20,27: "Then they returned... Jehoshaphat at their head... to Jerusalem *with joy*, for the Lord *had made them rejoice* over their enemies".

75. With the above phrase "(God's) wonderful help", compare the equivalent expression παραδόξου τῆς σωτηρίας used in *AJ* 2,345 (here this prompts the Hebrews to "rejoice", just as Jehoshaphat is said to do in 9,14); 3,1; 6,290.

76. This phrase recurs in *AJ* 4,93; 6,374.

account dispenses as well with the Chronicler's catalogue (20,25) of the various items taken[77], noting simply (9,15a) that the despoiling of the slain by Jehoshaphat's forces went on for three days, by which point they had become "weary", given the number of bodies involved.

The plundering process concludes (so 20,26) on the fourth day with an assembly which "blesses the Lord"; this takes place in a "valley" which, accordingly, receives the name "Valley of Blessing" (BL κοιλὰς εὐλογίας). The historian (9,15b) situates the happening "in a certain hollow place like a valley (εἴς τινα κοῖλον καὶ φαραγγῶδη [cf. εἰς τὴν φάραγγα, 9,14][78] τόπον; compare B εἰς τὸν αὐλῶνα [L κοιλάδα] τῆς εὐλογίας)". In addition, he explicates Chronicles' reference to the assembly's "blessing the Lord", making this "they blessed the power of God and His assistance (δύναμιν καὶ ... συμμαχίαν)[79]". His designation for the resultant name of the site corresponds to that of BL; see above.

2 Chr 20,27-28 narrates the people's joyful return, led by Jehoshaphat, to Jerusalem and their proceeding to the Temple with assorted musical instruments. Whereas 20,27 speaks first of the return of "every man of Judah and Jerusalem" and only then of Jehoshaphat proceeding them, Josephus (9,16a) once again throws into relief the royal initiative: "from there [the just-mentioned Valley of Blessing] the king led his army[80] back to Jerusalem...". As noted above, 20,28 mentions the returned forces' coming to the Temple with their instruments, but leaves unspecified what happened then. Josephus, continuing to focus on the royal initiative, clarifies matters: "(in Jerusalem Jehoshaphat) "gave himself up (τρέπεται) to feasting (εὐωχίας) and offering sacrifice (θυσίας) for many days". The wording of this notice introduces a verbal echo of Josephus' earlier account of the king's return from his campaign against Syria as Ahab's ally in 9,2: "and thereupon the king betook himself (τρέπεται) to giving thanks (εὐχαριστίας) and offering sacrifices (θυσίας) to God".

The account of the sequels to the Lord's overthrow of the enemy reaches its conclusion in 2 Chr 20,29-30: "fear of God" (MT; BL ἔκτα-

77. The textual witnesses differ among themselves regarding these; see FERNÁNDEZ, Old Latin, p. 127.

78. The adjective φαραγγῶδης occurs twice elsewhere in Josephus: AJ 5,162; 13,227.

79. This collocation recurs – in reverse order – once elsewhere in Josephus, i.e. AJ 7,122 where the reference is to "the confederacy and Ammanite force" arrayed against David. Compare Jehoshaphat's prayer as cited in 9,8 for divine "power and strength" (δύναμιν καὶ ἰσχύν) against the enemy coalition. The use of (partially) identical terminology here in 9,15 underscores the fact of the realization of the king's prayer.

80. With this generalizing expression, Josephus once again avoids the source's mention of "Judah"; see nn. 41,49,73.

σις Κυρίου) befalls the surrounding nations when they hear of the Lord's having "fought" (BL ἐπολέμησεν) on behalf of "Israel" with the result that Jehoshaphat's kingdom enjoys a time of quiet and "rest". Josephus (9,16b) represents the "foreign nations" learning of "his" (i.e. Jehoshaphat's) "destruction of the enemy" and so being "struck with terror of him (Jehoshaphat)[81]". The reason for the nations' "terror", in turn, is the realization evoked by the coalition's destruction, i.e. "God would henceforth fight (τοῦ θεοῦ ... συμμαχοῦντος; see τὴν τοῦ θεοῦ ... συμμαχίαν, 9,15)[82] on his (Jehoshaphat's) side[83]". For 20,30's mention of the "quiet" and "rest" that result for Jehoshaphat, Josephus (9,16c) then substitutes a more exalted reference to the "splendid fame" (λαμπρᾶς δόξης)[84] enjoyed by the king in virtue of "his righteousness and his piety toward the Deity" (ἐπὶ ... δικαιοσύνῃ καὶ τῇ πρὸς τὸ θεῖον εὐσεβείᾳ). With this alternative formulation which – it will be noted – represents yet another positive enhancement of the figure of Jehoshaphat – Josephus echoes wording used by him in account of the beginnings of the king's reign in 8,394 (compare 2 Chr 17,3-6): "he had the favour and assistance of the Deity since he was upright (δίκαιος) and pious (εὐσεβής)... and acquired the greatest glory (δόξαν)".

8. *Maritime Venture*

At this point (2 Chr 20,31-21,1 // 1 Kgs 22,41-51), the Chronicler gives his standard royal framework notices for Jehoshaphat; included within these is a summary account of the king's ill-fated maritime venture (20,35-37 // 1 Kgs 22,49-50). From this sequence, Josephus exacts for use at this point, i.e. the conclusion (9,17) of his "Jehoshaphat bloc",

81. This formulation once again highlights the figure of Jehoshaphat by making him – rather than God – the one responsible for destroying the enemy, just as the nations are said to "fear" – not God (compare "fear of God", 20,29; on Josephus' avoidance of this Biblical expression, see n. 25) – but the king. In the context, of course, Josephus does follow the Bible in depicting the coalition's overthrow as brought about directly by God.

82. Josephus uses the verb συμμαχέω with God as subject also in AJ 1,313 (19,233).

83. Note that, here, after the foregoing references to Jehoshaphat's destroying the enemy and the nations' resultant terror of him, Josephus (re-)invokes the divine agency responsible for the king's success. Note as well, however, the continued accentuation of the figure of the king: God "fights", not against the enemies of "Israel" (so 20,29), but "on his (Jehoshaphat's) side". Finally, whereas in 20,29 the reference is to God's fighting for his people in the (recent) past, Josephus' formulation looks to his continuing military support for Jehoshaphat – something that can only increase the nations' consternation.

84. This phrase is hapax in Josephus. Compare the similar expression used of Jehoshaphat in 8,394, i.e. δόξαν ... μεγίστην.

9,1-17, only those items relating to the king's ship-building initiative[85]. Before considering Josephus' own version of the happening, it is necessary to say a word about the two, quite divergent Biblical accounts concerning it. In 1 Kgs 22,49-50 Jehoshaphat, on his own, constructs "ships of Tarshish"; these are intended to carry gold from Ophir, but end up being wrecked at Ezion-geber. Only at that point does Ahaziah of Israel suggest that his servants join those of Jehoshaphat in manning the ships; for reasons unspecified the Judean turns down his proposal. 2 Chr 20,35-37, by contrast, represents Jehoshaphat and Ahaziah ("who did wickedly", v. 35) as cooperating from the start in the building, at Ezion-geber, of ships which are to go to Tarshish (compare 1 Kgs 22,49: ships of Tarshish to go to Ophir). In response to this joint initiative, a prophet named Eliezer announces to Jehoshaphat that the Lord will punish his entanglement with Ahaziah by destroying the ships that have been made (v. 37a; no parallel in Kings), and this, in fact, happens so that the ships are unable to proceed to Tarshish (v. 37b; compare 1 Kgs 22,49b).

Josephus' account (9,17) of the maritime episode of 20,35-37 (which he appends directly to his version of 2 Chr 20,30, see above) starts off in close parallel to the opening of the Chronicler's account: "And he (Jehoshaphat) was also friendly (φίλος) with Achab's son [i.e. 'Ochozias' = Ahaziah whose demise Josephus will relate in 9,18-27 = 2 Kgs 1,1-18][86]... and joined (κοινωήσας, BL ἐκοινώησεν) with him in building ships...". Thereafter, however, he begins going his own way in recounting the episode. Thus, unlike both 1 Kgs 22,49 and 2 Chr 20,36, he makes no mention of the site of Jehoshaphat's ship-building, i.e.

---

85. Josephus has already "anticipated" the mention (2 Chr 20,31b // 1 Kgs 22,42b) of Jehoshaphat's mother in his notice on the king's accession in 8,315. He will present the remaining data of 20,31-21,1 (minus its source notice, which, in line with his usual practice, he omits – presumably because he is basing himself on the Bible itself rather than its sources) in 9,44-45, following his account of the final Biblical incident involving Jehoshaphat, i.e. his participation in the campaign against Moab initiated by Joram of Israel (9,29-43 = 2 Kgs 3,4-27; see chap. III). That account, in turn, represents the continuation of Josephus' parallel (9,18-28) to 2 Kings 1-2, dealing with the end-phase of Elijah's ministry (see chap. II).

86. Throughout his presentation of Jehoshaphat, Josephus, as here, accentuates the cordial relations between the Judean king and his Northern counterparts. See 8,398 (Ahab gives Jehoshaphat a friendly [φιλοφρόνως] "welcome", "splendidly entertaining" his entourage "with an abundance of grain and wine and meat"; compare the more restrained notice of 2 Chr 18,2 where Ahab "kills an abundance of sheep and oxen" for his Judean visitors); 9,30 (Joram of Israel turns to Jehoshaphat as a potential ally in his campaign against Moab because "he had from the first been his father's" [Ahab's] friend [φίλος, see 9,17]; no parallel in 2 Kings 3); 9,31 (Jehoshaphat "splendidly entertains" the Israelite force in Jerusalem [compare 8,398]; no parallel in 2 Kings 3). Note, conversely, that Josephus leaves aside 2 Chr 20,35's negative characterization of Jehoshaphat's "partner" as one "who did wickedly". Cf. n. 13.

Ezion-geber. Similarly, his double indication concerning the ships' intended designation, i.e. "Pontus and the trading-stations of Thrace (Θράκης)[87]", diverges from that given in both Kings (Ophir) and Chronicles (Tarshish). Still more remarkable is the fact that Josephus – his tendency to accentuate the role of prophets in Biblical history notwithstanding[88] – passes over in complete silence the prophet Eliezer and his condemnatory announcement as cited in 2 Chr 20,37a[89]. In place thereof, Josephus proceeds directly to the fact of the ships' being destroyed (= 1 Kgs 22,49b // 2 Chr 20,37b). To that indication he then appends two brief notices, neither of which has a parallel in either Kings or Chronicles as such: the ships' destruction was "due to their great size[90]", while their loss caused Jehoshaphat to be "no longer keen about ships[91]". Thereupon, Josephus, in anticipation of his shift to a focus on Northern figures and events beginning in 9,18, rounds off the whole "Jehoshaphat sequence" (9,1-17) with the closing formula "Such, then, was the state of affairs under Josaphat, the king of Jerusalem[92]".

Conclusions: Josephus' Rewriting of 2 Chronicles 19–20

By way of conclusion to this chapter, I shall now briefly sum up on my findings with regard to: 1) the text-form(s) of 2 Chronicles 19–20

87. MARCUS, *Josephus*, VI, pp. 10-11, n. b suggests that here in 9,17 Josephus "connects (or confuses)" the ships' destination as cited in 20,36, i.e. "Tarshish" with the name of Japheth's son "Tiras" in Gen 10,2. He makes this suggestion in view of the fact that in his parallel to the Genesis text in *AJ* 1,125 (Marcus incorrectly reads 1,127 here) Josephus states that "Theires (Θείρες) called his subjects Theirians, whom the Greeks have converted into Thracians (Θρᾳκας)". In the same note Marcus mentions that in 1,127 (see also 9,208) Josephus identifies the "Tarshish" of Gen 10,4 (rendered by him θάρσος) rather as the ancient name of "Cilicia" in Asia Minor (see further below on *AJ* 9,208). Josephus' conjunction of "Pontus" and "Thrace" as the fleet's intended destination here might reflect the fact that the regions bearing these names faced each other across the Bosphorus in his own time.
88. On this tendency, see L.H. FELDMAN, *Prophets and Prophecy in Josephus*, in *JTS* 41 (1990) 386-422, pp. 388-391.
89. FELDMAN, *Studies*, p. 317 (= ID., *Jehoshaphat*, 171) attributes this "omission" to the fact that in the Bible Eliezer appears to censure that intra-Jewish cooperation Josephus is eager to promote via his retelling of Biblical history; see nn. 13,86. (On the other hand, recall that he does retain – even while softening this – the similar condemnation by the prophet Jehu of Jehoshaphat's involvement with Ahab of Israel; see 9,1 = 2 Chr 19,2.)
90. With this statement Josephus "resolves" a question left unelucidated in the sources, i.e. what (secondary) cause was responsible for the "wrecking" of the ships?
91. Conceivably, Josephus found inspiration for this last notice in the statement of 1 Kgs 22,50b, i.e. "but Jehoshaphat was not willing", i.e. to have Ahaziah's crews join his own in manning the ships; see v. 50a.
92. Josephus uses the above alternative expression for the Biblical title "king of Judah" also in *AJ* 8,314.393.411.412; 9,95; 10,229.

utilized by Josephus in 9,1-17 and 2) the rewriting techniques applied by him and their effect in generating a distinctive version of the events of Jehoshaphat's mid-carreer.

On the textual question, our reading uncovered various indications of Josephus' greater affinity with the text of B and/or L as against that of MT. Thus, he calls Jehu a "prophet" (so 9,1 = BL 19,2) rather than a "seer" (thus MT), while in 9,4 one finds the sequence "priests and Levites" of B 19,8 as opposed to the reverse order found in MT and L. Similarly, Josephus' use of the term Ἐξοχή (9,11) accords with the L plus in 20,17, just as his having Jehoshaphat refer to "the prophet" (i.e. Jahaziel) in 9,12 goes together with B 20,20 *contra* the plural form of MT and L. Finally, in the exhortation he attributes to Jahaziel in 9,11, i.e. that his hearers "stand still", Josephus agrees with MT and L 20,17 against B's "look on". These findings suggest that Josephus knew 2 Chronicles 19–20 in a form like that represented by BL.

Turning now to Josephus' rewriting techniques in 9,1-17, I distinguish four (overlapping) such techniques, i.e. omissions, additions, re-arrangements, and modifications.

a) *Omissions*: Overall, it may be said that Josephus compresses the presentation of 2 Chronicles 19-20, its discourse sections in particular. A case in point in his treatment of Jehoshaphat's judicial directives in Jerusalem itself (9,4-6 = 19,5-11). From the source's account here Josephus leaves aside numerous points of detail: the tasks envisaged for the Jerusalem judges (19,5), the five-fold specification of the kind of cases that may be referred to them and the "negative motivation" of 19,10; the differentiation of functions between Amariah and Zebadiah, the supporting role of the Levites, and the summary exhortation cited in 19,11. In general, Josephus' omissions in 9,1-17 seem motivated by a simple concern to streamline the source's narrative by eliminating its repetitive and/or obscure elements (see, e.g., the five types of cases which are enumerated in 19,10 without the distinction among them being made clear). His non-mention of the intervention of the prophet Eliezer (20,37a) in his version of Jehoshaphat's maritime venture (9,17) on the other hand, is, perhaps, prompted by the desire not to lend credibility to centrifugal tendencies within contemporary Judaism (see nn. 13, 86, 89).

b) *Additions*: Josephus in 9,1-17 does not, however, only delete elements of the source; he also adds items of his own. These additions are themselves of various sorts. A first category may be called stylistic, being designed to enhance the narrative flow of the account and the demarcation of its component sections. Under this heading can be mentioned, e.g., the extended *Rückverweis* linking up what follows to the previous narrative of Jehoshaphat's Syrian adventure (8,398-420) in 9,1, the concluding formulas at the end of 9,6 and 17 which serve to round off the account of the king's judicial initiatives (9,2-6) and the entire "Jehoshaphat bloc", respectively, and the transitional phrase "when the prophet had said these things..." of 9,11. A second category of Josephan additions in 9,1-17 elucidates matters which the source leaves unresolved: the foes' mutual slaughter results from their "mistaking one another for the enemy" (9,13; compare 20,23), while Jehoshaphat's ships are wrecked "due to their great size" (9,17; compare 20,37b // 1 Kgs 22,49b). Yet another category of additions provides further information of interest concerning a given matter, see, e.g., the notices on the location of Engedi and its trees which Josephus introduces in 9,7. Still other additions function as foreshadowings of coming events (Jehu announces that "God will deliver Jehoshaphat from his enemies" [9,3], this looking forward to the subsequent divine overthrow of the hostile coalition, see 9,13), or introduce "verbal echoes" of previous formulations (Jehoshaphat instructs the singers to "give thanks to God as if He had already delivered our country from the enemy" [9,12], this picking up on the wording of the historian's earlier addition to Jehu's speech in 9,3). Finally to be distinguished here are those additions intended to accentuate the stature of the story's hero, Jehoshaphat, see, e.g., "the thanks and sacrifices" with which the king responds to Jehu's admonition (9,2); the people's approval of and acting on the royal battle plan (9,13); and the invocation of Jehoshaphat's "righteousness and piety towards the Deity" as the grounds for the "splendid fame" which he came to enjoy (9,16; compare 20,30).

c) *Re-arrangements*: On occasion, Josephus also re-arranges the sequence of his Biblical material. In 9,1-17 the most obvious example of this technique is the fact of his "repositioning" the bulk of the Chronicler's framework notices for Jehoshaphat (20,35-37) to either an earlier (see 8,315) or a later (see 9,44-45) point in his own narration. Other, smaller-scale re-arangements within the context of 9,1-17 itself may also be noted, however. Thus, the notice of 20,24 on the total extermination of the hostile forces is "anticipated" to an earlier moment in Josephus' account (see 9,13), as is also the mention (20,29) of the "rejoicing" evoked by the enemy's overthrow (see 9,14). Recall also Josephus' version of Jehoshaphat's prayer (9,8-9a) in which elements of the Biblical *Vorlage* (20,6-12) are cited in the sequence vv. 6c,12a,8-10a,11 (see above).

d) *Modifications*: Josephus' modifications of his Biblical source in 9,1-17 involve both matters of style/terminology and content.

Stylistic/terminological modifications are represented, e.g., by his (invariable) substitution of indirect for direct discourse, preference for hypotaxis over parataxis, and characteristic reformulation of various Biblical expressions, i.e. "(divine) spirit" (see 20,14 and compare 9,10; cf. n. 53), "Lord" as a divine title (see n. 11), and "fear of God" (compare 19,7 and 9,3; 19,9 and 9,4; 20,29 and 9,16; see n. 25). The contentual modifications introduced by Josephus in his version are themselves of different kinds. In 9,1, e.g., the specific "merits" of Jehoshaphat as cited in 19,2 (destruction of the Asherahs, seeking the Lord) are generalized into a reference to the king's "good character". Conversely, Josephus "specifies" (9,12) the undifferentiated mention (20,21) of "those appointed to sing and to praise the Lord": his Jehoshaphat positions "the priests with their trumpets and the Levites with the singers" at the head of his forces. The third member of the enemy coalition (i.e. Ammonites, Edomites, Meunites according to the various witnesses of 20,2) is identified rather as "a large division of Arabs" (9,7). Jehoshaphat's affirmation "our eyes are upon thee (God)" at the end of his prayer in 20,12 becomes (9,9) the notice "having made this prayer, he began to weep" (see n. 48). References to Judah's involvement in the campaign against the enemy coalition are systematically eliminated in favor of mentions of "the people of Jerusalem" (9,8) and "the multitude" (9,9.11.12), likely on the consideration that Judah as a whole would not have had time to assemble in the face of the enemy advance (see n. 41). Looking ahead to the later mention of the people's assembling in a "valley", after their plundering of the enemy (20,26), Josephus (9,14) has the foes' corpses seen by Jehoshaphat "in the valley", rather than "at the watchtower in the wilderness" (so 20,24). He assigns a destination for Jehoshaphat's ships ("Pontus and the trading-stations of Thrace", 9,17) different from those cited in either 1 Kgs 22,49 (Orphir) or 2 Chr 20,36 (Tarshish). The notice about the people's coming to the Temple with musical instruments in hand (20,28) is reworked (9,16) into a verbal reminiscence of the king's "turning to sacrifice" (9,2). This last instance, in turn, serves to recall another characteristic Josephan modification in our pericope, i.e. his recasting of the source's formulations so as to accentuate Jehoshaphat's stature (the same tendency is also at work in various of Josephus' additions in 9,1-17; see above). Under this latter head, I would note, e.g., Josephus' downplaying of features of the source's presentation which reflect negatively on the king: Jehu announces not that "wrath has gone forth against you from the Lord" (so 19,2), but more blandly, that "God was displeased" at his involvement with Ahab (9,1), while the Biblical qualification of Jehoshaphat's later partner Ahaziah as "one who did wickedly" (20,35) is replaced by a ("non-judgmental") reference to the Judean's being "friendly" with him (9,17). Elsewhere and more positively, Josephus takes pains to underscore the king's preeminence and initiative vis-à-vis his subjects: it is not "Judah" but Jehoshaphat himself who first "sees" the enemy corpses (9,14; compare 20,24), just as the king does not undignifiedly join his men in plundering the foe himself, but instead "gives them leave to do so" (9,14; compare 20,25).

Summing up on the effect of Josephus' application of the above rewriting techniques, I would draw attention especially to their impact on his presentation of the story's various characters. The role of the king – and to a lesser extent – that of the priests in the events is accentuated. By contrast two other groups, i.e. the Levites and the prophets (see the omission of Eliezer, 20,37), receive less attention than they do in the source. On the other hand, the (miraculous) divine involvement in the proceedings is not notably diminished – contrary to what happens in other portions of *AJ*[93].

Finally, on the question of what Josephus' account in 9,1-17 might be intended to offer his double audience, his elimination of the source reference to Jehoshaphat's destruction of the Asherahs/ groves (19,3) perhaps has Gentile religious sensibilities in mind (see n. 15). On the other hand, his downplaying of the Chronicler's emphasis on the wrongfulness of Jehoshaphat's involvement with the North could be inspired by a concern to further contemporary Jewish unity (see nn. 13,86,89).

---

93. On Josephus' general – though by no means invariable – tendency to diminish the divine/miraculous role in Israel's Biblical history in his retelling of that history in *AJ*, see FELDMAN, *Interpretation*, pp. 205-213; ID., *Studies*, pp. 568-570. Cf. the additional literature on the topic cited in BEGG, *Early Divided Monarchy*, p. 165, n. 1076.

II

AHAZIAH AND JEHORAM; ELIJAH AND ELISHA[1]
(9,18-28)

In *AJ* 9,1-17 Josephus, as we have seen, reproduces the *Sondergut* passage 2 Chronicles 19–20 with its focus on the Judean king Jehoshaphat. Thereafter, he reverts to his other Biblical source, presenting his version of its Northern-centered bloc, 1 Kgs 22,51–2 Kgs 8,15, in 9,18-94. Within the later segment, a first sub-unit which may be distinguished is 9,18-28. This passage corresponds to 1 Kgs 22,51–2 Kgs 3,3* and features the earthly ends of one king-prophet pair (i.e. Ahaziah and Elijah) plus an initial presentation of a second such pair (i.e. Jehoram and Elisha). The material of 1 Kgs 22,51–2 Kgs 3,3 and *AJ* 9,18-28, in turn, may be broken down into the following component sections: 1. Ahaziah Presented (1 Kgs 22,51–2 Kgs 1,1 = 9,18-19a); 2. Ahaziah's Fall & Inquiry (1,2 = 9,19b); 3. Double Commissioning (1,3-4a = 9,20); 4. King-Messenger Exchange (1,4b-8 = 9,21-22a); 5. Ahaziah's Triple Sending (1,9-15a = 9,22b-26a); 6. Elijah before Ahaziah (1,15b-18 = 9,26b-27a); 7. Jehoram Introduced (3,1-3 [MT] = 9,27b); and 8. Elijah-Elisha Transition (2,1-25 = 9,28).

1. *Ahaziah Presented*

Josephus has twice made passing mention of "Ochozias" (= Biblical Ahaziah), son and successor of Ahab, king of Israel, in what precedes, see 8,420 (= 1 Kgs 22,40b: his accession) and 9,17 (= 1 Kgs 22,46 // 2 Chr 20,35: his ship-building venture with Jehoshaphat). Now in 9,18-19a (= 1 Kgs 22,51–2 Kgs 1,1) he finally comes to give this king more

---

1. This chapter represents a reworking of my article *Ahaziah's Fall (2 Kings 1): The Version of Josephus*, in *Sef* 55 (1995) 35-40 which I use with permission here; see also my *"Josephus's Portrayal of the Disappearances of Enoch, Elijah and Moses": Some Observations*, in *JBL* 109 (1990) 691-693. It likewise draws on the treatments of Elijah and Jehoram found, respectively, in FELDMAN, *Studies*, pp. 291-306 (= ID., *Josephus' Portrait of Elijah*, in *SJOT* 8 [1994] 61-84) and 322-333 (= ID., *Josephus's Portrait of Jehoram, King of Israel*, in *BJRL* 76 [1994] 3-20) as well as J.D. TABOR, *"Returning to the Divinity": Josephus' Portrayal of the Disappearances of Enoch, Elijah, and Moses*, in *JBL* 108 (1989) 225-238.

sustained attention. He begins with mention of Ochozias' reigning "in Samaria", an item drawn from 22,51[2]. Next he reproduces – employing quite similar terms – the negative evaluation of Ahaziah given in 22,52: "he was a wicked man (πονηρός)[3] and in all respects like both his parents[4] and like Jeroboam, *who was the first to transgress the laws* (παρανομήσαντι)[5] and who began the leading astray of the people (τὸν λαὸν ἀπατᾶν)[6]". Thereafter, he passes over the further, more specific charges against Ahaziah set out in 22,53[7]. Instead, he proceeds immediately (9,19a) to the the Moabite revolt against Israel as reported in 2 Kgs 1,1, combining this with the additional, related data on the matter given in 3,(4-)5: "But after he had been reigning for two years[8], the king of the Moabites[9] revolted (ἀφίσταται; BL 1,1 and 3,5 ἠθέτησε[ν])[10] from him [i.e. Ahaziah][11] *and ceased to pay the tribute*[12] which he had formerly been paying to his father Achab[13]".

2. From 1 Kgs 22,51 Josephus leaves aside its double chronological indication, i.e. Ahaziah's accession in Jehoshaphat's 17th (so MT B; L 24th) year and reign of two years (he will, however, make use of the latter item subsequently; see 9,19a).

3. Compare 22,52aα: "he did what was evil (BL τὸ πονηρόν) in the sight of the Lord".

4. Compare 22,52aβ: "he walked in the way of his father and in the way of his mother".

5. On terms of the παρανομ – root as a *Leitwort* of Josephus' accounts of both Jeroboam and of the contemporary Zealots of whom the Josephan Jeroboam appears the prototype, see FELDMAN, *Studies*, pp. 230-243, esp. 239 (= ID., *Josephus' Portrait of Jeroboam*, in *AUSS* 31 [1993] 29-52, pp. 45-46).

6. This phrase echoes the formulation used of Jeroboam in *AJ* 8,229: ἐξηπάτησε τὸν λαόν. Compare 22,52b: "(Ahaziah walked) in the way of Jeroboam... who made Israel to sin (BL ἐξήμαρτε)".

7. These read: "He served Baal (so MT; BL pl.) and worshiped him (MT; BL them) and provoked the Lord... to anger in every way that his father had done". With Josephus' non-mention of Ahaziah's "Baal-worship", compare his like non-use of the prophet Jehu's reference to Jehoshaphat's having "destroyed the Asherahs" (2 Chr 19,3) in 9,1.

8. For this indication concerning the moment of the Moabite revolt, Josephus draws on the notice of 22,51b, earlier passed over by him (see n. 2) – that Ahaziah ruled two years. The dating given in 1,1 (and 3,5) is vaguer, i.e. "after the death of Ahab". As MARCUS, *Josephus*, VI, p. 11, n. e points out, the Biblical sequence suggests that the revolt took place at the beginning – rather than the end (so Josephus) – of Ahaziah's two-year reign.

9. In 2 Kgs 1,1 the reference is to "Moab" (MT BL). Josephus draws his mention of the Moabite "king" as the subject of the revolt from 3,5.

10. Note Josephus' use of an historic present in place of the aorists of BL.

11. 2 Kgs 1,1 has Moab revolting "against Israel". Here again (see n. 9) Josephus follows the parallel text 3,5 where the "king of Moab" rebels against "the king of Israel".

12. Neither 1,1 nor 3,5 mention this "concretization" of Moab's revolt as such. Josephus found inspiration for it, rather, in the notice of 3,4 concerning the "tribute" which Mesha king of Moab had been required to pay the Israelite king; see below.

13. In 9,29, Josephus, basing himself on 2 Kgs 3,4, will spell out the nature of this "tribute"; see previous note.

2. *Ahaziah's Fall & Inquiry*

The one incident of Ahaziah's short reign which the Bible relates *in extenso* is the king's (ultimately) fatal fall, 2 Kgs 1,2-18. Josephus recounts the episode in comparable detail in 9,19b-27a.

The happening is set in motion when Ahaziah falls through "the lattice in his upper chamber in Samaria" (RSV), this causing him to become "sick" (1,2a). Josephus (9,19b) gives a somewhat different picture of the royal accident: Ahaziah "fell down" when "descending from the roof of his house"; the Biblical localization of this ("in Samaria") is omitted by him. 2 Kgs 1,2b cites, in direct discourse, the commission which the injured Ahaziah entrusts to the messengers dispatched by him: "go inquire, whether I shall recover from this sickness". Josephus' version incorporates the words of Ahaziah's commission into his notice on the fact of the royal initiative: "he sent... to inquire about his chances of recovery". The source (1,2b) designates the deity to whom Ahaziah dispatches his messengers as "Baalzebub (BL Βάαλ μυῖαν), the god (so MT B [θεόν]; Targum Jonathan [hereafter TJ] "the idol", טעות; L προσόχθισμα θεόν) of Ekron (MT; BL Ἀκκαρών)". Josephus conflates this double designation with his phrase "the Fly-God of Akkarōn" (Ἀκκάρων θεὸν Μυῖαν), omitting the element "Baal" common to all the biblical textual witnesses[14]. He likewise underscores the peculiarity of the divine name in question ("Fly-God") with his inserted phrase "this was the god's name".

3. *Double Commissioning*

In 2 Kgs 1,3 Elijah "the Tishbite" receives his commission from "an angel (MT מַלְאַךְ; BL ἄγγελος) of the Lord" who "speaks" to him. Josephus' wording (9,20) of this development differs significantly: "The God of the Hebrews (ὁ τῶν Ἑβραίων θεός)[15]

---

14. Compare his non-reproduction of 22,53 with its mention of Ahaziah's worship of "Baal" in 9,18; see n. 7. Note too that he has no equivalent to the pejorative terms used of the one to whom Ahaziah sends found in TJ and L 1,2b; see above.

15. This designation for the Deity appears only here in Josephus. On the historian's use of "the Hebrews" as one of several denominations for his people at various points of their history, see G. HARVEY, *The True Israel: Uses of the Names Jew, Hebrew and Israel in Ancient Jewish and Early Christian Literature* (AGJU, 35), Leiden, Brill, 1996, pp. 124-129; SPILSBURY, *Image*, pp. 36-42.

Also elsewhere Josephus substitutes a mention of God himself for Biblical references to an "angel"; see, e.g., *AJ* 1,233-235 ("God" addresses Abraham in connection with the

appeared (φανείς)[16] to the prophet (τῷ προφήτῃ)[17] Elijah and bade him...".

2 Kgs 1,3b-4a cites the angel's direct discourse word to Elijah; this consists of: commissioning of the prophet (v. 3bα), accusation against Ahaziah in question form (v. 3bβ) and announcement of doom for the king (v. 4a). In line with his frequent practice elsewhere, Josephus transposes the whole complex into indirect discourse. In formulating the rhetorical question of v. 3bβ ("is it because there is no God in Israel [so MT B; L is it because there is no prophet in Israel] that you [Ahaziah] are going to inquire of Baalzebub...?"), the historian introduces a contrast between the people of Israel's "own god" (θεόν... ἴδιον) and "the foreign (god)" (τὸν ἀλλότριον)[18] to whom Ahaziah is having recourse. By means of this (re-) formulation Josephus imparts a more general character to the opposition expressed in the source's question: Israel's "own god" is now contrasted, not with a particular rival deity (Baalzebub), but with any "foreign god[19]". Finally, in anticipation of 1,6 where the messengers report to Ahaziah that Elijah had enjoined them to "go back to

sacrifice of his son; compare Gen 22,11.15 where there is twice mention of an "angel of the Lord" doing so); and 8,239 (the Bethel prophet claims that "God" has sent him to offer hospitality to his Judean colleague; compare 1 Kgs 13,18 where the Bethelite states that "an angel spoke to me by the word of the Lord"). Such substitutions are by no means universal in the historian's handling of the relevant Biblical texts; they do, however, point to a certain reserve on his part with regard to Scripture's mentions of angelic figures, who could seem to call into question the fundamental Jewish doctrine of monotheism. For more on Josephus' angelology, see M. MACH, *Entwicklungsstadien des jüdischen Engelglaubens in vorrabbinischer Zeit* (TUAJ, 34), Tübingen, Mohr Siebeck, 1992, pp. 300-322; FELDMAN, *Studies*, p. 300 (= ID., *Elijah*, 77-79); ID., *Interpretation*, pp. 212-213.

16. In 1,3 the supernatural communication to Elijah involves only speech. Josephus' addition of a (divine) "appearance" is in line with a practice attested also elsewhere in his retelling of Biblical "commission accounts", a practice inspired, in part at least, by Greek religion's emphasis on divine epiphanies as opposed to the Bible's greater stress on revelation via the word (alone). For further examples of the phenomenon in *AJ* and bibliographical references, see BEGG, *Early Divided Monarchy*, pp. 53-54, n. 300. See further the comprehensive monograph of R.K. GNUSE, *Dreams & Dream Reports in the Writings of Josephus: A Traditio-Historical Analysis* (AGJU, 36), Leiden, Brill, 1996.

17. In 1,3 the reference is rather to Elijah as "the Tishbite". In *AJ* 8,360 Josephus makes the same substitution as here for the "Elijah the Tishbite" of his source text, i.e. 1 Kgs 21,17 (he does, however, cite Elijah's place of origin in his initial mention of him in 8,319 = 1 Kgs 17,1). FELDMAN, *Prophets and Prophecy*, p. 390 and n. 27 points out that in no less than 17 instances Josephus uses the terms "prophet/prophesy" in reference to Elijah where the Bible itself does not.

18. Elsewhere Josephus designates the Lord as Israel's "own God" in *AJ* 8,192.194.290.335.338. The above phrase "foreign god" recurs in *AJ* 9,98; 10,68 (both times in the plural).

19. A similar generalizing tendency may be noted in Josephus' version of the contest between the Lord and Baal (1 Kgs 18,17-40) in *AJ* 8,335-343 on which see BEGG, *Early Divided Monarchy*, p. 187 and n. 1235.

the king... and say to him", Josephus, already here, has God instruct Elijah to "command them (the messengers) to return and tell the king...".

4. King-Messengers Exchange

2 Kgs 1,4b-5a comprises two, paratactically-linked sentences which
effect – a rather abrupt – transition between the commissioning of the
royal messengers Elijah is instructed to undertake (1,3-4a) and the resultant conversation between the king and those messengers (1,5b-8). This
reads: "and Elijah went (+ and he spoke to them [Ahaziah's messengers],
BL) and the messengers returned to the king". Josephus (9,21a) creates
a smoother transition with his use of a series of participial phrases: "so
Elijah did (ποιήσαντος) as God had ordered, *and when the messengers
heard* (ἀκούσαντες) *his words*, they *at once*[20] returned to the king". In
1,5b Ahaziah's first word to the messengers is a question: "why have
you returned?" Such a question might appear odd – addressed as it is to
messengers who, after all, would be expected to return to their sender.
Josephus, accordingly, takes care to preface the king's query with a motivation, one which, at the same time, picks up on his previously inserted
reference to their returning "at once" (see n. 20): "*and he wondered at
the speediness of their return*, and, when he inquired the reason...".

The messengers commence their reply to Ahaziah in 1,6 with mention
of a "man" (BL ἀνήρ) who had come to "meet" them. Josephus too
(9,21b) has the messengers cite their meeting "a certain man (ἄνθρωπον)". He adds, however, a further qualification of Elijah which – like his
earlier insertion of the term "at once", see above – serves to accentuate the
prophet's irresistible authority: "(he) had... prevented them from going
further". Having mentioned their encounter with the "man" at the start of
v. 6, the messengers proceed, in the remainder of the verse, to relate his
words to them. These comprise a (re-)commissioning of them as envoys to
Ahaziah, plus the content of the message they are to convey. The latter
item is introduced by a *Botenformel* and essentially reproduces the wording of the judgment speech of vv. 3b-4a with its sequence of rhetorical
question/accusation and announcement of punishment for the king[21]. Jose-

20. Josephus' insertion of this indication underscores the authority of Elijah's word. It
likewise prepares his – also inserted – notice concerning Ahaziah's wondering at the
"speediness" of the messengers' return; see below.

21. In L 1,6 there is a plus following the announcement of Ahaziah's coming demise
(= 1,6bβ MT) in which, in language reminiscent of 1 Kgs 21,21, etc., Ahaziah is charged
with doing evil and so evoking the divine decision to annihilate the house of Ahab. Like
MT, B and TJ, Josephus has no equivalent to this plus.

phus, somewhat exceptionally, does retain the direct address of the messengers' report. On the other hand, he also shortens it considerably, omitting the repetition of the accusation of v. 3bβ (= v. 6bα) and varying the wording of the announcement of doom from that cited by him in 9,20. His version of the messengers' report thus reads: "(Elijah bade them) return and tell you by the command (ἐξ ἐντολῆς) of the God of Israel [literally the Israelites, τοῦ Ἰσραηλιτῶν θεοῦ][22] that your illness (νόσος) will grow worse (κάκιον ἕξει)[23]".

The dialogue between king and messengers continues in 1,7 with the former asking about the "manner" (MT מִשְׁפַּט, B ἡ κρίσις, L τὸ δικαίωμα) of the man they had encountered. Josephus (9,22a) employs equivalent terminology: Ahaziah bids the messengers "describe" (σημαίνειν) the one whose words they have just reported. In reply to the king's new question the messengers (1,8a) supply a two-fold characterization of the unknown figure: he was a "hairy man" (MT בַּעַל שֵׂעָר, BL ἀνὴρ δασύς)[24] and was "girded with a belt of leather around his loins" (B ζώνην δερματίνην [L ζώνη δερματίνη] περιεζωσμένος τὴν ὀσφὺν αὐτοῦ = L). Josephus' version of this double description is quite reminiscent of the wording of BL: ἄνθρωπον [see 9,21]... δασὺν καὶ ζώνην περιειλημμένον δερματίνην. The king-messengers exchange concludes in 1,8b: Ahaziah reacts to the envoys' description with the declaration: "it (is) Elijah the Tishbite". Josephus makes his equivalent to this item the introduction to the king's dispatch of a force against the prophet (= 1,9a), see below.

5. Ahaziah's Triple Sending

The core of our episode is the account of Ahaziah's dispatch of three groups of soldiers against Elijah, their dealings with the prophet, and fate at his hands (1,9-15a = 9,22b-26a). In 1,9a the first of these "missions" is paratactically juxtaposed to the king's declaration of 1,8b: "and he [Ahaziah] said... and he sent to him...". Josephus (9,22b) uses participial phrases to fashion a more flowing transition between the two items: "understanding (συνείς) that the man... was Elijah (= 1,8b),

22. The designation "God of the Israelites" recurs in AJ 9,60; compare "God of the Hebrews", 9,20. The entire above phrase takes the place of the Botenformel of 1,6 which Josephus regularly avoids.

23. Compare the wording of Elijah's directive to the messengers as cited in 9,20: (they are to inform the king) "that he would not recover from his illness (νόσον)".

24. Contrast the RSV rendering of the MT phrase: "he wore a garment of haircloth". On the translation question here, see the commentaries.

sending (πέμψας) an officer after him… he ordered (ἐκέλευσεν, compare κελεῦσαι used with Elijah himself as subject in 9,20)…". The Bible designates those sent by Ahaziah as "a captain of fifty men (MT שַׂר־חֲמִשִּׁים, BL πεντηκόνταρχον) and his fifty". Josephus formulates the reference using contemporary Greek military terminology: "an officer (ταξίαρχον)[25] with fifty soldiers (ὁπλίτας)". To the mention of the force's dispatch by Ahaziah the historian likewise adds a clarification as to its objective: "… ordering that he (Elijah) *be brought to him*[26]".

In 1,9b the captain ascends[27] to Elijah who had seated himself "on the top of *the* hill[28]" and there speaks to him. In Josephus (9,23a) as well, Elijah is said to be sitting "on the top of the hill" (ἐπὶ τῆς κορυφῆς τοῦ ὄρους = BL 1,9bα). On the other hand, he does not refer to the officer's "going up" to Elijah. In his presentation then the commander appears to shout up to the prophet above him on the hill. The lack of respect implicit in such a procedure goes together with the content of his words which, in Josephus, are considerably more peremptory and threatening than in the Bible. Thus, the biblical officer first (1,9bβ) addresses Elijah with the honorable title "man of God" (BL ἄνθρωπε τοῦ θεοῦ) and then continues "the king says, 'Come down'". His Josephan counterpart dispenses with any form of address[29]. Conversely, he "orders" (ἐκέλευε) Elijah "to come down *and go to the king*[30], saying that he [Ahaziah] had so ordered (κελεύειν; compare ἐκέλευσεν, of Ahaziah, 9,22), *and, if he refused, he would force* (βιάσεσθαι)[31] *him to go against his will*". By thus accentuating the "threat quotient" in the officer's address, Josephus, at the same time, makes Elijah's violent reaction (see below) seem better motivated than in the source where his response appears out of all proportion to the captain's actual offense.

25. This term is the Greek equivalent of the Latin *centurio*; see RENGSTORF, *Concordance*, IV, s.v.

26. Like MT, B and TJ, Josephus has no equivalent to the L plus after 1,9a which states that the force did in fact go to Elijah as directed.

27. In L his fifty soldiers go up as well.

28. Commentators generally suggest that the (unnamed) hill referred to here is Mount Carmel with which Elijah is associated in 1 Kings 18.

29. On Josephus' tendency to avoid the Biblical title "man of God" of 1,9, frequently (like the Targums) replacing this with the term "prophet", see BEGG, *Early Divided Monarchy*, pp. 24-25, n. 129; FELDMAN, *Studies*, p. 301 (= ID., *Elijah*, 79-80 [Feldman tentatively suggests that Josephus' avoidance of the title may be in reaction to Christian claims for Jesus as "the man of God" *par excellance*]).

30. Recall Josephus' inserted specification concerning the reason for Ahaziah's sending his force to Elijah, i.e. "that he be brought to him", 9,22.

31. This is the emendation of Dindorf which Bekker, Niese, Naber, and Marcus follow; the codices and E have the aorist βιάσασθαι. On Josephus' use of this verb and other terms of the *Wortfeld*, see E. MOORE, ΒΙΑΖΩ, ΑΡΠΑΖΩ *and Cognates in Josephus*, in *NTS* 21 (1974-75) 519-543.

Elijah's initial response in 1,10a picks up on the officer's addressing him as "man of God" in 1,9; it begins "if I am a man of God...". As noted above, Josephus' commander omits any title or address for Elijah. In reporting – in indirect address – the protasis of Elijah's reply, the historian (9,23b) accordingly has him employ an alternative self-designation: "But Elijah said to him that to prove whether he was a true prophet (προφήτης ἀληθής)[32]...". The apodosis of the biblical Elijah's reply constitutes a kind of curse: "... let fire come down from heaven (BL καταβήσεται πῦρ ἐκ τοῦ οὐρανοῦ) and consume you and your fifty". Josephus substitutes a statement of intention by the prophet: "... he would pray (εὔξεσθαι)[33] for fire to fall from heaven (πῦρ ἀπ' οὐρανοῦ πεσόν) and destroy (ἀπολέσαι) both his soldiers and himself[34]".

2 Kgs 1,10b describes the realization of Elijah's "curse", utilizing the same language as that employed in the curse itself (see above): "and fire came down from heaven and consumed him and his fifty". After noting that Elijah did in fact "pray" (εὔχεται) as announced, Josephus describes the outcome in wording varied from the prophet's earlier statement: "... a whirlwind of fire (πρηστήρ)[35] came down (κατενεχθείς, cf. κατενεχθῆναι, used of Ahaziah's 'fall' in 9,19; compare κατέβη, BL 1,10b) and consumed (διαφθείρει, BL κατέφαγεν)[36] both the officer and those with him".

In 1,11a Ahaziah's second mission is rather abruptly juxtaposed with the disastrous conclusion to his first one: "again the king sent to him another captain of fifty men with his fifty". Josephus (9,24a) supplies an

32. In having Elijah refer to himself here as a "(true) prophet" – rather than as a "man of God", Josephus goes together with TJ in its rendering of 1,10a ("if I am a *prophet of the Lord*"); see n. 29. Elsewhere Josephus uses the expression "true prophet" in *AJ* 6,47 (Samuel) and 8,296 (of the figure Israel will lack in the future should it turn apostate); cf. 9,34 where it is employed ironically by Elisha in reference to the "prophets" of Ahab and Jezebel.

33. This is the emendation of Dindorf, followed by Bekker, Niese, Naber, and Marcus, for the aorist form εὔξασθαι read by the codices and E.

34. With this inserted reference to Elijah's "prayer" Josephus makes clear that the prophet does not have the celestial fire at his own disposal (as might appear to be the case in the Bible); he can only request, not command, its activation. In addition, Josephus' wording here in 9,23 serves to accentuate the parallelism between the present episode and a previous incident involving Elijah and "heavenly fire", i.e. the Carmel contest; compare *AJ* 8,342 (= 1 Kgs 18,36-37 [here, in contrast to 2 Kgs 1,10, there is mention of Elijah's "praying"]) where, having prepared his sacrifice, Elijah "began to pray (εὔχεσθαι) to God and entreat Him", with the result that "fire fell from heaven" (πῦρ ἐξ οὐρανοῦ... ἔπεσε; see πῦρ ἀπ' οὐρανοῦ πεσόν, 9,23). In both cases Elijah, in Josephus' presentation, has no magical control over the heavenly fire; he must pray God to send it.

35. This term is hapax in Josephus.

36. Note here again (see n. 10), Josephus' use of an historic present for the past form found in BL.

expansive transition between the two items: *"when the destruction* (ἀπωλείας; see ἀπολέσαι in Elijah's prayer, 9,23) *of these men was reported to the king, he became very angry* (παροξυνθείς)[37] and sent against Elijah another officer with the same number of soldiers as he had sent with the first one". The Biblical account (1,11b) recounts the initiative of the second captain in language largely similar to that used of the first in v. 9b: he too "goes up[38] to Elijah to whom he conveys the royal directive that he is to "come down". This time, however, that directive is formulated in somewhat more emphatic terms: the simple "the king says" of 1,9 now becomes a *Botenformel*, "thus says the king", just as Elijah is enjoined to descend "quickly". As with the first officer, Josephus here makes no mention of his colleague's ascending to Elijah or addressing him by title. Rather, he simply reports of him: "… this one also threatened [compare 9,23 he ordered him] the prophet that he would seize him by force (βία; cf. βιάσεσθαι, 9,23) and take him away if he did not come down willingly (βουλόμενος)…".

2 Kgs 1,12 repeats 1,10 virtually verbatim: Elijah calls for heavenly fire which falls and annihilates the second force. This time (compare 9,23b), Josephus (9,24b) refrains from citing the actual words of the prophet's response to his summoner; rather, he merely notes that Elijah "prayed (εὐξαμένου; see εὔχεται, 9,23) against him" with the result that "fire" (πῦρ; compare πρηστήρ, 9,23) destroyed the company.

In 1,13a the third royal mission is once again simply juxtaposed paratactically to the preceding notice (1,12b) on the annihilation of the previous force. Here too, Josephus (9,25a) introduces a transitional mention of Ahaziah's "learning of" the latter event. Vv. 13b-14 portray the third captain as displaying a very different demeanor in his dealings with Elijah than had his two predecessors: he kneels before the prophet and pleads for his life and those of his men. Josephus sets up the shift in question with a double characterization of the third captain with which he prefaces the report of his exchange with Elijah: "… being a prudent man and of a very mild (φρόνιμος … ἐπιεικής)[39] disposition[40]…". In

37. This inserted mention of the king's emotional state is an example of Josephus' tendency to psychologize the Biblical account. In particular, in a whole series of cases, he uses the above participle in reference to a character's "rage" at some state of affairs; see BEGG, *Early Divided Monarchy*, pp. 46-47, n. 234.
38. Thus L followed by RSV. MT (= TJ) reads "he answered" (וַיַּעַן); cf. B "he spoke" (ἐλάλησεν).
39. This collocation occurs only here in Josephus.
40. Such inserted characterizations which provide readers with advance perspective on what to expect of a given figure and how they are to regard that figure are a regular feature of Josephus' rewriting of the Biblical record; see, e.g., *AJ* 8,236 where, prior to his reporting the initiatives taken by the Bethel prophet with regard to the Judean "man

the same line he qualifies the officer's speaking to Elijah (= 1,13b-14) as "friendly" (φιλοθρόνως)[41].

The discourse which the Biblical third captain addresses to Elijah comprises a double appeal that his life and that of his fellows "be precious in the eyes of" the prophet (vv. 13bβ, 14b), with a reference to the fate of the two previous groups supervening (v. 14a). In this formulation what it is the captain in fact wants of Elijah remains rather indeterminate, just as it is not immediately clear how his evocation of his colleagues' end is supposed to relate to his present appeal. Josephus clarifies matters in his version of the third officer's speech. This begins (9,25b) with the commander's citing a reason why Elijah should pay heed to his following appeal, i.e. the fact that both he and his hapless colleagues had approached Elijah not "willingly" (βουλόμενος)[42], but under royal compulsion[43]. Having thus presented himself and his colleagues as the king's reluctant agents, the Josephan captain next proceeds to formulate a two-fold appeal. First, in a clarification of the Biblical phrase about his and his men's lives being "precious in the eyes of" Elijah, he asks the prophet "to have pity (ἐλεῆσαι) on him and on the soldiers who were with him". Secondly, he requests, without a basis in the words attributed to the captain in 1,13b-14 as such (although see the continuation of the story), that he "come down and accompany him to the king".

2 Kgs 1,15a rounds off the exchange between prophet and third officer with mention of a new (see 1,3) intervention by an "angel of the Lord" who instructs Elijah to descend with his interlocutor whom he is "not to fear". As will be recalled, Josephus' version of 1,3 (see 9,20)

---

of God" (see 1 Kgs 13,11ff.), the historian qualifies the former as "a wicked old man, a false prophet".

41. As in the case of his two colleagues, Josephus does not take over the Biblical indication that the third officer "went up" (so MT 1,13; BL came) to Elijah. Accordingly, he likewise leaves aside 1,13's further mention of his "kneeling" before the prophet. Like his Biblical counterpart, Josephus' third captain remains nameless. In the *Lives of the Prophets* 9.3 (first cent. A.D.?) the figure is identified with the future prophet Obadiah; see A.M. SCHWEMER, *Vitae Prophetarum* [hereafter *VP*] (JSHRZ, I.7), Gütersloh, Gütersloher Verlagshaus, 1997, p. 616.

42. This participle picks up the same term used (9,24) by the second officer who threatens to take Elijah by force if he will not come "willingly". As it now turns out, all three officers – as well as Elijah himself – are united in their "unwillingness" to do as directed by the king.

43. The third commander's assertion about his two colleagues here comes as something of a surprise since nothing in Josephus' own previous depiction (or that of the Bible) of their exchanges with Elijah has suggested any reluctance on their part to carry out their royal mandates. In any case, this reference to them represents Josephus' replacement for the allusion to their fate attributed to the third officer in 1,14a.

replaces its reference to the angel with an appearance by God himself to Elijah. Here in 9,26a, Josephus goes a step further in his reworking of the Bible's reference to an angel. As the historian presents things, Elijah makes his response to the officer's appeal without any kind of supernatural guidance, angelic or divine, but solely on the basis of the impression made upon him by the latter's speech: "so Elijah, approving of [the tactfulness (δεξιότητα)[44] of] his words and the courtesy (ἀστεῖον)[45] of his manner, came down...". Why does Josephus proceed as he does here? I suggest that he may have concluded that a supernatural directive to the prophet was really not called for at this juncture. After all, Elijah had dealt with the first two captains entirely at his own discretion – why should he not do so with the third as well? In addition, the Biblical angel's injunction that Elijah "not fear" the last officer appears somewhat odd: Elijah, who had shown no fear in the face of the first two commanders' peremptory summons, certainly has no reason to be "afraid" of their suppliant colleague. In view of these considerations, Josephus, I propose, opted not to tax the credulity of his sophisticated Gentile audience with a second recourse to a *deus/ angelus ex machina* within a single story. What he offers them in its stead is an illustration of the efficacy of "tactful" speech – a lesson which that audience, in whose educational system rhetorical training was a key component, would surely have found more congenial[46].

6. *Elijah before Ahaziah*

Our episode concludes with Elijah coming before the king (v. 15b) to whom he delivers his word of doom (v. 16), whereupon Ahaziah dies (v. 17a) and is succeeded by his brother (so L) J(eh)oram (v. 17b MT L; B has no equivalent to this item in its version of 1,17, but does mention it subsequently), the whole complex being rounded off with the standard source notice for Ahaziah (v. 18)[47]. In v. 16 the angel's initial announcement to Elijah is repeated – now by the prophet himself – largely verbatim for the

44. Josephus' other uses of the term δεξιότης are in *AJ* 2,41; 17,207; 19,88. The phrase enclosed within brackets above ("the tactfulness of") has no equivalent in the translation of Marcus, *ad loc.* who renders simply "approving of his words..."; compare Weill's rendition "touché de *l'habilité de* ces paroles...".

45. Josephus' other uses of the adjective ἀστεῖος are in *AJ* 7,147; 12,177.

46. Also elsewhere, it might be noted, Josephus eliminates Biblical references to the supernatural impetus behind characters' initiatives; see, e.g., *AJ* 8,319, where, in contrast to the source's reference (1 Kgs 17,2) to "the word of the Lord" that prompts Elijah to retire to the brook, the prophet acts on his own volition in doing this.

47. Thus the sequence of MT (and L) 1,17-18. In B the source notice for Ahaziah (1,18) precedes – rather than follows – mention of Jehoram's accession (1,17b).

third time in the story (see vv. 3 and 6b). Here again, Josephus' version
(9,26b) avoids the source's verbal repetitions. The variation introduced by
him begins already with the opening formula for Elijah's address to the
king. In 1,16 this is the standard *Botenformel*. Josephus previously (see
9,21) substituted the phrase "at the command of the God of Israel" for the
"thus says the Lord" of 1,6. Here in 9,26 he makes a comparable substitution, indicating the supernatural origin of Elijah's words with the expression "he prophesied (προεφήτευσεν)[48] to him and revealed (ἐδήλου) that
God had said...". In next citing the content of God's word for Ahaziah,
Josephus, exceptionally, retains the source's direct discourse (cf. 9,21). In
the judgment speech of 1,16 the accusation element (v. 16a) comprises a
charge about Ahaziah's consulting Baalzebub to which is attached (so MT,
> BL) a rhetorical question about whether there is no God in Israel of
whom the king might have inquired (= vv. 3,6)[49]. Josephus reformulates
MT's rhetorical question as a direct charge against the king: "because you
have scorned me (κατέγνως... αὐτοῦ)[50] as though I were not God *and
were not able to foretell the truth* (τἀληθὲς προειπεῖν; cf. προφήτης
ἀληθής, 9,23)[51] *concerning your illness...*". Reversing the (MT) sequence
of 1,16a, he has Elijah then continue "... but have sent to the god of
Akkarōn (τὸν Ἀκκαρωνιτῶν; compare τὸν Ἀκκάρων θεὸν Μυῖαν,
9,19) to inquire of him *what the end of this illness will be...*". Thereafter,
he reproduces ("... know that you shall die") the death announcement from
the end of v. 16, passing over (as previously in his renderings of vv. 3 and
6) the preceding statement that Ahaziah "will not come down from the bed
to which he had gone up" as something self-evident and superfluous.

2 Kgs 1,17a narrates Ahaziah's death in accordance with the Lord's
"word" (BL τὸ ῥῆμα Κυρίου) as spoken by Elijah. Josephus (9,27a)
begins his parallel notice with the inserted chronological indication "a
very short time thereafter". As is his wont, Josephus likewise has
recourse to alternative terminology for the source's mention of the
divine "word", stating that Ahaziah died "as Elijah had foretold
(προεῖπεν; cf. ταληθὲς προειπεῖν, used of God in 9,26)[52]".

48. This verb occurs a total of 58x in Josephus (only once in *BJ*, i.e. 1,69).
49. In these two previous instances accusation and rhetorical question stand in reverse
order to their sequence in 1,16a.
50. This is Josephus' only use of the above construction with God as (genitival) object
of the verb καταγινώσκω (= "to scorn"). Note Marcus's above rendering of the pronoun
αὐτοῦ by "me"; compare Weill "(puisque tu as dédaigné) le Seigneur...".
51. Josephus' one other use of the above expression is in *AJ* 2,209 where he employs
it of the Egyptian "sacred scribe" whose predictions about the future achievements of
Moses did come about.
52. On Josephus' general tendency to avoid Biblical references to the divine "word",
see BEGG, *Early Divided Monarchy*, p. 20, n. 90.

Ahaziah's death, in turn, results (1,17b) in the accession of "Jehoram" (MT; BL Ἰωράμ) whom MT does not further identify, but whom B calls "son of Achab" and L "the brother of Ochozeias". This last development occurs "in the second year of Jehoram the son of Jehoshaphat, king of Judah" (so MT 1,17bα and L [1,19]; B in the 18th year of Jehoshaphat = MT 3,1, see below) and is due to the fact that Ahaziah himself "had no son" (1,17bβ). Josephus' rendition leaves aside the problematic – given the discrepancy between MT 1,17 and 3,1 on the matter – source synchronistic notice[53]: "... and was succeeded in the kingdom by his brother[54] Joram (Ἰώραμος; see BL Ἰωράμ)[55], for he [Ahaziah] had died childless (ἄπαις)". In line with his usual practice, he leaves aside the source notice for Ahaziah of 1,18.

7. *Joram Introduced*

At this juncture in 2 Kings their occurs a noteworthy divergence in sequence between MT and BL. The former witness moves immediately from its closing framework notices for Ahaziah (1,17-18) to an account of the "translation" of Elijah and his succession by Elisha (2,1-25) and only then gives its opening framework notices for Jehoram, 3,1-3. BL, by contrast, append their parallel to the content of MT's 3,1-3 (B 1,18a-c; L 1,19-22) to their version of MT 1,17-18, placing the matter of 2,1-25 after this. Josephus' sequence, in this case, follows that of BL against MT[56].

The Biblical opening framework notices for Joram (MT 3,1-3) begin with a double chronological indication in 3,1 (his accession in Jehoshaphat's 18th year [so MT and B; L in the second year of Jehoshaphat's son Joram = MT 1,17b; see above] and reign of twelve years in Samaria). There follows an expansive, qualifiedly negative judgment notice in 3,2-3: "He did what was evil in the sight of the Lord, though not like his father (so MT; BL his brothers) and mother, for he put away the pillar (MT מַצְּבַת; BL τὰς στήλας) which his father had

---

53. Recall that he likewise passed over the synchronistic notice for Ahaziah cited in 1 Kgs 22,51a.

54. This indication corresponds to the L plus in 1,17; see above.

55. In what follows I shall refer to the king with this shorter (BL) form of his name rather than by the "Jehoram" of MT 1,17. On Josephus' ("rehabilitative") portrayal of this king overall, see the discussion(s) of him by Feldman cited in n. 1.

56. A. RAHLFS, *Septuaginta-Studien I-III*, Göttingen: Vandenhoeck & Ruprecht, 1965², p. 467 (= p. 107 in the original edition of 1911) comments on this fact: "... daraus können wir nicht sicher auf Abhängigkeit von der LXX schliessen, denn da Josephus das Ende Elias nicht ausführlich erzählt, sondern nur ganz kürz erwähnt [see below on 9,28], so lag es nahe, erst einiges über den König [Joram] zu bemerken, in dessen Regierungszeit das Ende Elias fiel".

made (BL + καὶ συνέτριψεν αὐτάς). Nevertheless he clung to the sin of Jeroboam... which he made Israel to sin: he did not depart from it (BL + καὶ ἐθυμώθη ὀργῇ Κύριος [L + ἐπ' αὐτῷ καὶ] εἰς [so B; ἐπὶ, L] τὸν οἶκον 'Αχαάβ)".

Just as he did with the synchronistic notice of MT 1,17b, Josephus leaves aside that of 3,1a, likewise passing over the reference to Joram's capital ("in Samaria) of 3,1b[57]. As for the indication of 3,1b about Joram's length of reign, Josephus incorporates this into his evaluation of the king (9,27b) to which, in turn, he gives his own distinctive wording: "Now this Joram, who was *very like his father Achab in wickedness* (πονηρίαν, cf. πονηρός used of Ahaziah in 9,18)[58], reigned twelve years [so 3,1b], *showing every form of lawlessness* (παρανομία; cf. παρανομήσαντι of Jeroboam in 9,18) *and impiety* (ἀσεβείᾳ)[59] *toward God, for he neglected His service* (παρεὶς... θρησκεύειν)[60] *and worshipped strange gods* (τοὺς ξενικοὺς ἐσέβετο)[61]; *he was also a man of bold action* (δραστήριος)[62] *in other respects*[63]".

57. In both instances, his procedure corresponds to his handling of the similar data for Ahaziah; see on 9,18.

58. Compare 3,2a: "he did what was evil (BL τὸ πονηρόν) in the sight of the Lord, though *not like his father* (so MT; BL his brothers)...". Josephus' reversal of the Biblical contrast between Joram and Ahab reflects the fact that he will not reproduce the notice of 3,2b concerning Joram's "removing (+ breaking in pieces, BL) the pillar(s) of Baal which *his father* had made". That omission, in turn, may reflect Josephus' concern to avoid offending pagan sensibilities by reporting aggressive measures on the part of Jews against specific, named foreign gods; see above on 9,1.18.

59. The above collocation "lawlessness and impiety" recurs – in reverse order and in the plural – one other time in Josephus, i.e. 10,104 (of King Zedekiah).

60. This expression occurs only here in Josephus.

61. Compare the reference (*AJ* 8,192) to Moses' warning the Hebrews not to marry foreign women lest... τοὺς ἐκείνων σέβωνται θεούς παρέντες τιμᾶν τὸν ἴδιον. Cf. also the contrast (9,20) made in the case of Joram's brother Ahaziah, between "their own (i.e. the Israelites') God" and "this foreign god (τὸν ἀλλότριον)". The entire sequence italicized above with its additional accusations against Joram takes the place of that made in 3,3 where Joram is charged with persisting in "the sin of Jeroboam". On the significance of Josephus' non-reproduction of the charge of 3,3 which links Joram with the historian's *bête noire*, Jeroboam, as indicative of his concern to (partially) "rehabilitate" the figure of Joram, see FELDMAN, *Studies*, p. 328 (= ID., *Jehoram*, 15-16). (Recall that in 9,18 Josephus does take over the connection made in 1 Kgs 22,52 between Joram's brother Ahaziah and their ancestor Jeroboam.)

62. This characterization of Joram is without Biblical basis as such. As FELDMAN, *Studies*, p. 328 (= ID., *Jehoram*, 16) points out, the above word is more often than not used by Greek writers (and by Josephus himself), in a positive sense, i.e. in reference to the "boldness" or "energy" of those so qualified (see, e.g., *AJ* 5,182 where Josephus applies it to the judge "Keniaz" (Biblical Kenaz) whom he calls "vigorous [δρασστήριος] and noblehearted"). See also BEGG, *Early Divided Monarchy*, p. 153, n. 991.

63. Like MT, Josephus has no equivalent to the plus with which BL conclude their rendering of 3,1-3, i.e. "and the wrath of the Lord burned against (+ him [Joram] and, so L, > B) the house of Ahab"; see above.

8. *Elijah-Elisha Transition*

Continuing to follow the BL sequence (see above), Josephus (9,28) appends to his opening notices for Joram (9,27b // MT 2 Kgs 3,1-3) a version of the segment (MT 2,1-25) dealing with the prophetic transition from Elijah to Elisha. Within the latter passage, one might distinguish two longer units, i.e. the circumstantial account of Elijah's removal from the earth (vv. 1-12a) and the sequels to this portraying Elisha as Elijah's power-filled, prophetic successor (vv. 12b-25). The historian reduces both these units to their core content, namely, the "vanishing" of Elijah (= 2,12aβ) and Elisha's remaining behind, ready to undertake the initiatives which will be attributed to him in what follows[64]. Josephus' condensed version of 2 Kings 2 reads:

> *Now about that time*[65] Elijah disappeared (ἠφανίσθη)[66] from among men, and to this day no one knows his end[67]. He left behind him a disciple (μαθητήν) Elisha, as we have already related[68]. However, concerning Elijah and Enoch, who lived before the Flood[69], it is written (ἀναγέγραπται)[70] in the sacred books (ἐν ταῖς ἱεραῖς... βίβλοις)[71] that

64. On the historian's procedure here, see FELDMAN, *Studies*, pp. 301-302, 306 (= ID., *Elijah*, 77, 80-81) and especially the article of Tabor and my response to this cited in n. 1.

65. This inserted indication supplies a temporal connection between Joram's accession and Elijah's "disappearance" which is lacking in the Bible itself.

66. The verb ἀφανίζω is one of those used in Hellenistic literature in connection with the *Entrückung* of some famous figure, see G. LOHFINK, *Die Himmelfahrt Jesu* (SANT, 26), München, Kosel, 1971, p. 41, n. 57. It is likewise the term twice used by Josephus when relating the end of Moses' life on earth; see *AJ* 4,323.326. The term might be seen as Josephus' equivalent to the notice of 2 Kgs 2,11aβ: "and he (Elisha) saw him (Elijah) no more".

67. FELDMAN, *Studies*, p. 301 (= ID., *Elijah*, 80) points out that the above formulation recalls the statement of the messenger in Sophocles' *Oedipus at Colonus* (1655-1656) that no one but Theseus could tell how Oedipus had disappeared. I would further note that the phrase is reminiscent of the notice of Deut 34,6b concerning Moses' end: "no man knows the place of his burial to this day".

68. The *Rückverweis* here is to Josephus' account of Elijah's call of Elisha in *AJ* 8,353-354 (= 1 Kgs 19,19-21). That account culminates in the statement "... so long as Elijah was alive he (Elisha) was his disciple (μαθητής) and attendant" which Josephus echoes here in 9,28. The above, non-descript notice takes the place of the sequence devoted to Elisha's exploits following Elijah's ascent in 2,12b-25.

69. Josephus' account of Enoch's departure from the earth stands in *AJ* 1,85: "Anoch lived 365 years and then returned to the divinity (ἀνεχώρησε πρὸς τὸ θεῖον), whence it comes that there is no record in the chronicles (ἀναγεγράφασι) of his death". Compare Gen 5,24: "Enoch walked with God; and he was not, for God took him".

70. This verbal form echoes the term ἀναγεγράφασι used by Josephus in connection with Enoch in *AJ* 1,85; see previous note.

71. This same phrase occurs in *AJ* 4,326 where Josephus reports that "(Moses) has written of himself in the sacred books (ἐν ταῖς ἱεραῖς βίβλοις) that he died, for fear lest they should venture to say that by reason of his surpassing virtue he had gone back to the Deity (πρὸς τὸ θεῖον ... ἀναχωρῆσαι, i.e. the phrase used of Enoch in 1,85; see n. 69)".

they became invisible (γεγόνασιν ἀφανεῖς)[72], and no one knows of their death.

The question that naturally arises here is why Josephus would have so drastically abridged the source's presentation, notwithstanding its dramatic potential and the centrality of prophetic figures throughout it – features which the historian elsewhere shows himself eager to exploit? I suggest that a variety of factors came into play in Josephus' proceeding as he did here: the sheer length and circumstantiality of the Biblical account, its many unresolved perplexities (e.g., how do the sons of the prophets and Elisha "know" that Elijah is about to be taken up, as they are said to do in 2,3.5?), the emphasis on the (divine) "spirit" (see 2,9,16) which Josephus generally downplays (see on 9,10), the cascade of miraculous happenings which skeptical Gentile readers would likely find offputting and – in the case of the "bear miracle" of 2,23-25 grotesque and offensive-[73], the desire not to make Elijah appear superior to Moses (whose end, as reported in both the Bible and Josephus himself, does not involve a spectacular removal to heaven as described in 2 Kgs 2,11), monotheistic concerns about giving too much play to ideas of "apotheosis", as well as his possible awareness of the ridicule of these notions attested in the writings of such enlightened (near) contemporaries as Seneca, Lucian and Plutarch[74]. On the other hand, in the case of all three figures, Enoch, Moses and Elijah, via the terminology used by him ("return to the divinity", disappear", "become invisible") Josephus, in his own understated way, wants to make clear to Gentile readers that his people too had its heroes whose earthly lives ended in the same mysterious and awe-inspiring ways that tradition reported for many great figures of Greco-Roman antiquity[75].

72. Like ἀφανίζω (see n. 66) this phrase is used in Hellenistic *Entrückung* accounts; see LOHFINK, *Himmelfahrt*, p. 41, n. 59.

73. In this connection it should be pointed out that whereas here in 9,28 Josephus leaves aside the miracle of Elisha's "healing" of the Jericho spring as recounted in 2,19-22, he does relate the story of that miracle *in extenso* in *BJ* 4,460-464 in the context of a description of Jericho. His non-mention of the story in 9,28 is then no indication that his Bible text lacked the passage (or the rest of 2 Kings 2). On Josephus' version of 2 Kgs 2,19-22 in *BJ* 4,460-464 and a possible reason for his including there while leaving it aside in his version of 2 Kings 2 in *AJ*, see FELDMAN, *Studies*, pp. 344-345 (= ID., *Josephus' Portrait of Elisha*, in *NovT* 36 [1994] 1-28, p. 21).

74. On the point, see A.S. PEASE, *Some Aspects of Invisibility*, in *Harvard Studies in Classical Philology* 53 (1924) 17-21.

75. For more on the question of Josephus' handling of the earthly ends of Elijah, Enoch and Moses, see the article of Tabor and my response to this cited in n. 1. See further FELDMAN, *Studies*, pp. 337-338, 339, 341 (= ID., *Elisha*, 6-7, 12, 14-15) on the many problems 2 Kings 2 would have posed for Josephus (as it did for the Rabbis) and his characteristic way of dealing with these, i.e. simple omission of the offending material.

Conclusions: Josephus' Rewriting of 1 Kgs 22,51–2 Kgs 3,3

With regard, first of all, to the question of Josephus' Biblical text for *AJ* 9,18-28, the following findings are of relevance. In line with the BL sequence and against that of MT, the historian gives his initial presentation of Joram before relating Elijah's disappearance (cf. n. 56). His qualification (9,27) of Joram as Ahaziah's "brother" parallels the L plus of 1,17b. On the other hand, like MT, he lacks an equivalent to various of the B and/or L plusses scattered throughout the Biblical segment (see nn. 21, 27, 63).

The pre-eminent Josephan rewriting technique evidenced by *AJ* 9,18-28 is abridgement. This procedure is conspicuous above all in his handling of 2 Kgs 2,1-25. He also, however, eliminates or compresses a whole series of other source items: the synchronistic notices of 1 Kgs 22,51b; 2 Kgs 1,17b (MT); 3,1, the "additional charges" made against Ahaziah in 22,53, the going up and address to Elijah by the three captains, as also the "prostration" on the part of the third (1,9b, 11b, 13), the source notice for Ahaziah (1,18), and Joram's removal of the Baal pillar (3,2), even as he persists in Jeroboam's sin (3,3).

Also noteworthy in Josephus' rewriting of 1 Kgs 22,51–2 Kgs 3,3 are his varied sorts of modification of Biblical data: The double mention of angelic interventions (1,3 and 15a) are both replaced with alternative presentations concerning what caused Elijah to act as he did, i.e. a divine appearance (9,20) and the good impression made on him by the third captain's words (9,26), respectively. The verbal repetitions which figure so prominently throughout 1,2-18 (see, e.g., the threefold reiteration of the word of doom for Ahaziah, vv. 3b-4a,6,16) are consistently attentuated via the use of varied terminology. Mostly, though not always (see 9,21.26) direct address is converted into indirect (see, e.g., 9,20; compare 1,3-4a). Several times (see nn. 10,36) the historian employs an historic present where the source reads a past form. Elijah does not refer to himself as a "man of God" (so 1,10), but instead as a "true prophet" (9,23), just as he does not call down fire from heaven on his own, but "prays" for this to happen (9,23, compare 1,10; 9,24, compare 1,12). The third captain's request of Elijah is clarified (9,25b; compare 1,13b.14b). The source's uses of the *Botenformel* (1,5, compare 9,21; 1,16, compare 9,26) and its references to the divine "word" (1,17a; compare 9,27) yield to alternative formulations. Rather than being "not like" his father (so 3,2), Joram is said to be "very like" him (9,28).

For all his abridgement of the Biblical segment overall, Josephus does, conversely, interject various small-scale expansions throughout 9,18-28. Examples include: the messengers' "immediate" return to the king and the latter's "wondering" at this (9,21, compare 1,5); Ahaziah's command that Elijah be brought to him (9,22, compare 1,9a); the first captain's threat (9,23, compare 1,9b); the king's hearing of and angry reaction to the initial contingent's destruction (9,24, compare 1,11); the opening characterization of the third captain (9,25, compare 1,13); this figure's claim about himself and his colleagues (9,25, compare 1,14a); Elijah's reference to Ahaziah's acting as though God were unable to "foretell the truth" (9,26, compare 1,16); and the chronological linking of Joram's accession and Elijah's disappearance (9,28, compare 2,1). The source's sequence likewise undergoes occasional re-arrangement at Josephus' hands in 9,18-28. Having, e.g., cited the notice on the Moabite revolt from 2 Kgs 1,1, he proceeds to "anticipate" the related material of 3,4-5 (see 9,19a), introducing the whole complex with a "delayed" use of 1 Kgs 22,51b (Ahaziah's length of reign). Similarly, he works the Biblically distinct notice of 3,1b (Joram's twelve year reign) into his version of 3,2-3 (the evaluation of Joram) in 9,27b.

The Josephan rendering of 1 Kgs 22,51 – 2 Kgs 3,3 which results from the application of the historian's varied rewriting techniques is a distinctive one in several respects. Specifically, his version relates the source happenings in streamlined fashion, with attenuation of the verbal repetitions, complete elimination of the "angelic element", and marked lessening of the miraculous factor. Conversely, the narrative takes on a smoother flow via the use of hypotaxis and inserted transitional elements. Characters' emotions and motivations receive greater attention (see Ahaziah's "anger", 9,24; the third captain's qualities, 9,25; and the effect of his words upon Elijah, 9,26). The negative "Baal-focus" running through the Biblical segment gives way to a more generalized opposition between Israel's "own" God and "foreign" deities of all sorts. God's control of events is accentuated via the way in which Josephus presents the heavenly fire's double descent. Elijah's "disappearance" is implicitly or explicitly linked with the historian's account of the earthly ends of two earlier figures, i.e. Enoch and Moses, such that he appears as part of a Biblical trio accorded the benefit of a "rapture".

Josephus' rewriting of 1 Kgs 22,51–2 Kgs 3,3 clearly seems intended, in first place, to cater to Gentile readers (e. g., in its downplaying of the miraculous and of Biblical references to Jewish aggression against pagan gods and their cults), while also endeavoring to teach them appropriate lessons concerning the historian's people (e.g., the Jews too have their heroes who "disappeared" back to the Deity). As for Jewish readers, the Josephan version inculcates the urgent, yet timeless message that the religiously "foreign" is to be avoided and that they must look instead to their "own" God (and his prophets) for guidance in all circumstances.

III

THE CAMPAIGN OF THE THREE KINGS[1]
(9,29-45)

Josephus continues drawing on the *Sondergut* of 2 Kings, specifically 3,4-27, in his next section, i.e. *AJ* 9,29-45, which relates the campaign of three allied kings against rebellious Moab and features a set of characters who have already figured in what precedes, i.e. Joram of Israel, Jehoshaphat of Judah, and the prophet Elisha. I divide up the parallel material for the section into five sub-units: 1. Background (9,29-31b = 3,4-8); 2. Water crisis en route (9,31c-32 = 3,9-10); 3. Prophetic consultation (9,33-36 = 3,11-19); 4. Elisha's Words Fulfilled (9,37-43 = 3,20-25); and 5. Sacrifice & Sequels (9,42-45 = 3,26-27).

1. *Background*

The story told in 2 Kings 3 opens with a revolt on the part of the king of Moab against his overlord, the king of Israel (vv. 4-5), itself harking back to 1,1 = 9,19a (see above), and Joram's initial response to that rebellion. In recounting this *casus belli*, Josephus (9,29) rearranges the sequence 3,4-6a in the order 3,6a. 5.4 so as to highlight the initiative of Joram[2]:

> *When Joram took over the throne* (see 9,27), he decided to march against the Moabite king named Meisa (Μεισάν)[3], *for, as we have said before*[4],

---

1. This chapter is a reworking of my article *Filling in the Blanks: Josephus' Version of the Campaign of the Three Kings, 2 Kings 3*, in *HUCA* 64 (1993) 89-109, which I use by permission here.
2. Recall his qualification of the king as "a man of bold action" in 9,28. Subsequently as well, Josephus will accentuate Joram's role within the episode related in 3,4-27; see on 9,32.34.
3. Thus Niese and Marcus; Dindorf, Bekker, Naber, and Weill read Μισᾶν with the codices MSP. Cf. מֵישַׁע (MT 3,4); Μωσά (BL). Josephus leaves aside the further qualification of "Mesha" found in 3,4, i.e. his being a "sheep breeder" (so RSV; MT נֹקֵד), perhaps because, like BL which simply transliterate it, he did not understand the designation. With the above notice on Joram's initiative compare 3,6a: "So King Jehoram marched out of Samaria at that time and mustered all Israel".
4. The referent of this inserted *Rückverweis* is to Josephus' expanded rendering of 1,1 in 9,19a; see there.

he had revolted (ἀποστάς) ·from Joram's brother[5] *after paying tribute* (φόρους τελῶν) *to his father Achab*[6] amounting to two hundred thousand sheep with their wool[7].

2 Kgs 3,7-8 relates the negotiations between Joram and Jehoshaphat of Judah regarding their projected campaign against rebellious Moab. Josephus (9,30) makes the preceding reference in 3,6b to Joram's mustering of Israel the transition to this exchange: "And so, collecting (συναθροίσας, BL ἐπεσκέψατο) his own force, he sent to Josaphat (= 3,7aα)...". He likewise supplies a motivation for Joram's approach specifically to the Judean king, i.e. "since he (Jehoshaphat) had from the first been his father's (Ahab's) friend (φίλος)...[8]". Joram's (direct discourse) message to Jehoshaphat in 3,7aβ consists of a mention of Mesha's revolt and a question concerning the Judean's willingness to join his proposed expedition. Josephus reverses the sequence of Joram's communication, likewise recasting it in indirect address: Joram "asks" (παρακαλῶν) Jehoshaphat "to be his ally (συμμαχῆσαι)[9] in the war (πόλεμον) which he was about to wage on the Moabites who had revolted (ἀποστάντας) from his rule[10]".

5. Compare 3,5: "But when Ahab died, the king of Moab revolted (BL ἠθέτησεν) against the king of Israel". Cf. Josephus' earlier notice on this happening in 9,19a (= 1,1): "(But after he [Ahaziah] had been reigning for two years), the king of the Moabites revolted (ἀφίσταται) from him...".

6. The above formulation closely echoes Josephus' wording in 9,19a: "(the king of Moab ceased to) pay the tribute which he had formerly been paying (τοὺς φόρους ... ἐτέλει) to his father Achab".

7. In 3,4 (MT BL) the figure is "one hundred thousand lambs and the wool of one thousand rams". Josephus' rendering – according to which Mesha has to hand over 200,000 ovines plus their wool – represents a *Steigerung* of the Biblical requirement. It has a certain parallel in TJ where the figure given is "100,00 fatted cattle and 100,000 rams of the pasture", i.e. a total of 200,00 beasts that are to be delivered by Mesha as in Josephus. (Like MT and BL 3,4 Josephus has no equivalent to TJ's additional specification that Mesha's tribute had to be paid "annually".) See also VL 3,4 where Mesha's tribute is specified as "centum millia modium tritici, et centum hordei et lanas," cf. FERNÁNDEZ, *Scribes & Translators*, pp. 57-58.

8. With the use of this term, Josephus echoes his statement in 9,17 that Jehoshaphat was "friendly" (φίλος) with Ahaziah; see above. In content the above notice further recalls Josephus' account of Jehoshaphat's marriage and military alliance with Ahab in AJ 8,398-420 (= 1 Kings 22 // 2 Chronicles 18). On Josephus' accentuation of the cordial, cooperative relations between Jehoshaphat and the northern royal house throughout his version of 2 Kings 3, see FELDMAN, *Studies*, pp. 317-318 (= ID., *Jehoshaphat*, 171) who sees this as part of the historian's overall effort to promote the ideal of Jewish unity.

9. The above formulation echoes AJ 8,397: "Achab invited (παρεκάλεσε) [Jehoshaphat] to become his ally (συμμαχῆσαι)". Cf. also 9,1 where the noun συμμαχία is twice used of Jehoshaphat's "alliance" with Ahab. Compare Joram's equivalent question to Jehoshaphat as cited in 3,7aβ: "will you go with me to battle (BL εἰς πόλεμον) against Moab"?

10. Compare the Israelite king's opening statement to Jehoshaphat in 3,7aβ: "The king of Moab has rebelled (BL ἠθέτησεν) against me".

Jehoshaphat's response in 3,7b begins with the avowal "I will go up". Thereafter, in language reminiscent of his own earlier words to Ahab in 1 Kgs 22,4 (// 2 Chr 18,3), the Judean affirms his solidarity with Joram by means of a triple formula: "I am as you are, my people as your people, my horses as your horses". Josephus (9,30b) summarizes Jehoshaphat's threefold claim in a single statement, i.e. "he promised to assist him (βοηθήσειν ὑπέσχετο)[11]". To that statement he then appends an element proper to himself, i.e. (Jehoshaphat also promised) "to compel the Idumaean king, who was under his authority, to join in the campaign". Josephus introduces this item with a view to accounting for a subsequent, rather unexpected feature of the Biblical narrative, i.e. the fact that when Joram and Jehoshaphat eventually do set out against Moab the (previously unmentioned) "king of Edom[12]" is said to accompany them; see 3,9. In Josephus this anamoly is resolved in advance: the king of Edom will accompany the expedition at the direction of Jehoshaphat, his overlord. Josephus' "solution" here is not, however, it might be noted, without a certain Biblical warrant. In MT 1 Kgs 22,48, first of all, one reads a notice which RSV renders "there was no king in Edom [i.e. during the reign of Jehoshaphat, see 22,41ff.], a deputy (וְנִצָּב) was king[13]". Also to be noted is 2 Kgs 8,20 which states that in the reign of Jehoshaphat's son J(eh)oram, "Edom revolted from the rule of Judah and set up a king of their own[14]". With this appended notice here in 9,30 Josephus thus pulls together and harmonizes the discordant indications of MT 1 Kgs 22,48a (Edom had "no king" in Jehoshaphat's time) and 2 Kgs 3,9 (a "king of Edom" appears as ally of Jehoshaphat and Joram). Inspired – it would

11. This formulation echoes that which Josephus attributes to Jehoshaphat in *AJ* 8,399 (= 1 Kgs 22,4): τοῦ δὲ Ἰωσαφάτου τὴν βοήθειαν ἐπαγγειλαμένου.

12. Josephus designates the third ruler here in 9,30 rather as "king of the Idumaeans", while subsequently he will use the place name "Idumaea" (see 9,31) in place of MT and BL's "Edom". Josephus' designation is inspired by the wider usage of the LXX which, on occasion, does employ Ἰδουμαία in place of Ἐδώμ, sometimes juxtaposing the two forms in the same context (see, e.g., 3 Rgns 11,14-16). In *AJ* 2,3 the historian comments as follows when making his first reference to "Idumaea" in the work: whereas Esau called the country over which he ruled by his own nickname, i.e. "Adom" (Ἄδωμος), "the more dignified (σεμνότερον) name of Idumaea (Ἰδουμαίαν) it owes to the Greeks". On the whole subject, see C.H.J. DE GEUS, *Idumaea*, in *JEOL* 26 (1979-80) 53-74, p. 55.

13. In BL, whose parallel to MT 1 Kgs 22,48 follows MT 16,28, the reference is to there being no king in "Syria" (= MT "Aram", a misreading of Hebrew "Edom") and the term נִצָּב is simply transliterated as ναο(ε)ιβ. (Josephus himself has no equivalent to the content of 22,48 – whether in its MT or BL position.)

14. Compare Josephus' version of this notice in *AJ* 9,96 with its echo of his reference here in 9,30 to the Idumaean king being "under Jehoshaphat's authority": "the Idumaeans revolted from him [Joram] and, *after killing their former king who had been submissive to Joram's father* [i.e. Jehoshaphat], set up a king of their own".

seem – by the reference in 1 Kgs 22,48b to the "deputy" who ruled
Edom in Jehoshaphat's day, the historian gives us the figure of an
"Idumaean king" who stands under the Judean's "authority".

Throughout 2 Kgs 3,7-8 Joram and Jehoshaphat communicate, apparently, via messengers, with their actual coming together being simply
presupposed rather than related as such; see 3,9. Josephus (9,31a) fills
this narrative lacuna by way of the notice he interjects between his version of the first (3,7) and second (3,8) Biblical royal exchanges. This
notice reads: "Joram, after receiving such assurances of assistance
(συμμαχίας; cf. συμμαχῆσαι, 9,30) from Josaphat, took his army and
came to Jerusalem and was splendidly entertained (ξενισθεὶς λαμπρῶς)
by the king of Jerusalem[15]". Josephus' inspiration for this inserted item
is clearly his own earlier account (AJ 8,398) – itself based on 2 Chr 18,2
– of the reception given Jehoshaphat by Ahab prior to their joint campaign against Syria: "when... he (Jehoshaphat) went to Samaria, Achab
gave him a friendly welcome and, after splendidly entertaining (ἐξένισε
λαμπρῶς) the army which had accompanied him, with an abundance of
grain and wine and meat...". In Josephus' presentation here in 9,31
Jehoshaphat reciprocates, in his own capital, the hospitality once offered
him by Joram's father in Samaria. By means of this insertion, then, Josephus accentuates the implicit parallelism – already discernible in the
Bible itself – between the episodes of 1 Kings 22 // 2 Chronicles 18 and
2 Kings 3. In addition, the insertion allows Josephus to underscore, for
the benefit of Greco-Roman readers, that one of their fundamental values, i.e. hospitality, is equally cherished by Jews[16].

The "background section" 2 Kgs 3,4-8 concludes in v. 8 with
Jehoshaphat asking Joram – apparently still via messengers – about their
march route, the latter replying that they will proceed "by way of the wilderness of Edom". Josephus, for his part (9,31b), represents the determination
of the line of march as a joint decision by the two kings present together in
Jerusalem ("it was decided by them"), rather than as something simply dictated by Joram[17]. In addition, he provides a rationale for the choice of this
particular (indirect) route towards the kings' destination: "for these [the

15. Literally: "king of the Jerusalemites" (τῶν Ἰεροσολυμιτῶν). Josephus uses this
title in place of the Bible's "king of Judah" also in AJ 9,112.117.130.177.246.278. Cf. the
related designation "king of Jerusalem" (τῶν Ἰεροσολύμων) in 8,314.393.411. 412;
9,17.95; 10,229.

16. On the point, see FELDMAN, Studies, p. 333 (= ID., Jehoram, 14).

17. Compare Josephus' rewording of the item about what Jehoshaphat and Ahab are
to wear into battle against the Syrians of 1 Kgs 22,30 // 2 Chr 18,29. In the Biblical
text(s), Ahab issues the following pre-battle instruction to Jehoshaphat: "I will disguise
myself and go into battle, but you wear your [so MT; BL 3 Rgns and 2 Par my] robes".

Moabites] would not expect them to attack by this road". In place of the Bible's silence on the matter, Josephus here offers readers a plausible explanation (i.e. the hoped-for benefit of surprise) for the kings' choice of route.

2. *Water crisis en route*

Following the above preliminaries, Josephus next (9,31c) relates the advance of the three kings (= 3,9a)[18]. In his presentation, however, mention of the "king of Edom" accompanying the other three rulers on their march does not come as the surprise it does in the Bible; this item has been carefully "set up" by Josephus in what precedes (see above). Basing himself on 3,9b, the historian (9,32a) goes on to cite the critical water shortage that developed seven days into the kings' advance. Once again, however, Josephus takes it upon himself to provide an answer to a question suggested by the Biblical account, i.e. how did it come to such an emergency on a route deliberately chosen by the kings themselves? In his reponse to that question Josephus informs us that the expedition found itself unexpectedly bereft of water "because their guides had lost the way".

2 Kgs 3,10 proceeds directly to Joram's despairing statement in the face of the water crisis: "Alas, the Lord has summoned us, three kings, only to be handed over to Moab". Josephus prefaces the Israelite's word with a remark accentuating the urgency of the situation (and thus accounting for Joram's vehement reaction to it): "and so they were all in torment (ἀγωνιᾶν), Joram most of all[19]". Josephus further expatiates on Joram's word itself: "*... in his distress*, he cried out to God, *asking what bad deed He charged them with that* He had led out the three kings to deliver them *without a fight* into the hands of the Moabite king[20]".

In *AJ* 8,412 this becomes: "Now *Achab and Josaphat had agreed...* that the king of Jerusalem should take his (Achab's) place in the line of battle with the other's [so LXX] robe on...". In both instances (8,412 and 9,31) Josephus is intent then on emphasizing the equality and harmony existing between the allied kings. See FELDMAN, *Studies*, p. 323 (= ID., *Jehoram*, 8-9); ID., *Studies*, 310-311 (= ID., *Jehoshaphat*, 171).

18. In the text of 9,31 printed by Niese and Marcus (which reproduces the reading of the codices RO), the title used of Joram is "king of the Israelites" (compare 3,9 "king of Israel"). In the codices MSP (which Dindorf, Bekker, Naber and Weill follow) he is called rather "king of Samaria".

19. The particular intensity of the Josephan Joram's distress here is, one might suppose, due to his feeling responsible for initiating an expedition which has ended up in such a predicament for all concerned; see n. 2.

20. Joram's accusatory question addressed to God here takes on a certain irony in view of Josephus' earlier characterization of him (9,27) as "showing every form of lawlessness and impiety towards God". Given that characterization, readers, at any rate know that God "has something against" Joram, even if the king does not (or feigns not to). Cf. further FELDMAN, *Studies*, p. 329 (= ID., *Jehoram*, 17).

3. Prophetic Consultation

In 2 Kgs 3,11a Jehoshaphat responds to Joram's word by asking about the availability of a prophet for consultation. Josephus (9,33a) introduces the Judean's query with mention of his "comforting" the distressed Joram and a characterization of Jehoshaphat as "righteous" (δίκαιος). This characterization accords with Josephus' recurring emphasis on Jehoshaphat's "righteousness/justice" throughout his presentation of him[21].

In formulating Jehoshaphat's actual suggestion to Joram (cf. 3,11a), Josephus makes the Judean king echo his own earlier words to Ahab prior to their Syrian campaign. Specifically, 9,33 states: "(Jehoshaphat) told (ἐκέλευσε) him (Joram)... to find out whether any prophet of God (εἴ τις ... τοῦ θεοῦ προφήτης) had come along with them, 'in order that (ἵνα) through him we may learn (μάθωμεν) from God what we must do'". This formulation recalls the language employed by him in 8,400: "(Jehoshaphat) bade (ἐκέλευσεν) him (Ahab) call the prophets if there were any (εἴ τινές εἰσι προφῆται)..." and 402 "(Jehoshaphat asks Ahab whether there was some other prophet of God (τίς ἐστι προφήτης τοῦ θεοῦ) in order that (ἵνα) we may know (μάθωμεν) more clearly what is going to happen". Once again, then, Josephus underscores the parallelism between the two Israelite-initiated military adventures in which Jehoshaphat became involved.

2 Kgs 3,11b records the report of one of Joram's "servants" about the presence of Elisha with the expedition. In reproducing this notice, Josephus (9,33b) replaces the figurative Biblical qualification of Elisha as one "who poured water on the hands of Elijah"[22] with a more definite designation: "the disciple (μαθητήν)[23] of Elijah".

According to 2 Kgs 3,12 Jehoshaphat responds to the servant's report by affirming that "the word of the Lord is with him". Josephus, who consistently avoids Biblical mentions of the divine word, reformulates so as to eliminate the expression also here. At the same time he gives Jehoshaphat's utterance a more directive character: "the three kings, *at Josaphat's urging* went to him (Elisha)[24]".

---

21. See AJ 8,394; 9,16.35; cf. p. 8, n. 21.

22. FELDMAN,, *Studies*, p. 338 (= ID., *Elisha*, 7) qualifies the image evoked by the Biblical phrase as "a rather degrading picture" which would account for Josephus' reformulation of it. Compare the paraphrase of TJ: "who served (דשמיש) Elijah".

23. Josephus has used this term twice previously of Elisha; see AJ 8,394; 9,28.

24. Compare the more assertive Jehoshaphat in Josephus' version of the death of Ahab. In the source (1 Kgs 22,8b // 2 Chr 18,7b) the Judean responds to Ahab's charge that Micaiah "never prophecies good concerning me, but evil" (22,8a // 18,7a) with a soothing interjection, "let not the king say so". In Josephus (8,403) Jehoshaphat replies to Ahab's word about Micaiah by "asking (κελεύσαντος, literally bidding) that he (Micaiah) be brought".

2 Kgs 3,13 has Elisha addressing himself immediately to Joram, giving his royal visitors no chance even to state their business. Josephus (9,34a) provides a more flowing transition between the kings' approach (3,12) and Elisha's outburst against Joram (3,13). In so doing, he first specifies where the encounter takes place: "when they came to the prophet's tent – he had, as it happened, pitched his tent outside the camp...". Thereafter, he has the royal callers be the ones to initiate the exchange: "... they inquired what would befall the army...". In this connection, Josephus further highlights – with a view to what follows where Elisha directs himself precisely to him – the Israelite king's role in the inquiry: "... Joram in particular asking this (μάλιστα δὲ ὁ Ἰώραμος)[25]".

Following the above – interjected – interlude, Josephus (9,34b) comes to relate Elisha's word to Joram (= 3,13a). The Biblical version of this word opens with an obscure question ("what to me and to you?", RSV) which Josephus, as is his wont in such cases, transposes into a clear statement: "... he told him not to trouble (διοχλεῖν)[26] him". In 3,13aβ Elisha proceeds to sarcastically urge the king to betake himself to "the prophets of your father and the prophets of your mother" (thus MT and L; B lacks a reference to Jezebel's "prophets"). Josephus expands on Elisha's injunction, appending an ironic "motivation", to it: "(he told him) to go to the prophets of his father and mother [so MT L] *for they... were true* (ἀληθεῖς) [prophets][27]".

In 3,13b Joram responds to Elisha's invective by simply reverting to his earlier despairing assertion (see 3,10) about the Lord's intended

---

25. Compare 9,32 μάλιστα δὲ τὸν Ἰώραμον where the reference is to the expedition's "agony" at the lack of water. See n. 19.

26. This is the reading adopted by Niese, Naber and Marcus. Dindorf and Bekker read διενοχλεῖν with SP.

27. On Josephus' use of the term "true" in reference to prophets, see on 9,23. On the Biblical Elisha's "outburst" in 3,13, see FELDMAN, *Studies*, pp. 339-340 (= ID., *Elisha*, 12-13) who notes that this is one of several instances of bad-temper recorded of Elisha in the Bible which came in for censure by the Rabbis (see, e.g., *b. Pes.* 66b; *b. Sanh.* 39b where it is affirmed that, in punishment for his outburst against Joram, Elisha was deprived by God of his capacity to prophesy, and so had to have recourse to the aid of a minstral as described in 3,15). Feldman goes on to state (*Elisha*, 13): "In Josephus' version... the sarcasm is completely omitted; indeed he [Elisha] explicitly says, in recommending that Jehoram go to the prophets of Ahab and Jezebel, that those prophets were true prophets" (note: this remark is not taken over in Feldman's treatment of Elisha's response to Joram in *Studies*, pp. 339-340). Surely, however, Elisha's designation of his "colleagues" – who were his master Elijah's rivals in the sacrificial contest on Mount Carmel and whom Elijah subsequently (had) butchered (see 1 Kings 18 = *AJ* 8,328-346) – as "true" is intended ironically. I suggest then that the Biblical Elisha's "sarcasm" is not "omitted", but rather heightened by Josephus. See further the historian's explicit qualification of the prophets of both Jezebel (*AJ* 8,318) and Ahab (8,402) as ψευδοπροφῆται.

doom for the three kings. Josephus (9,34c) provides the king with a response that seems more appropriate, given the urgency of the situation and Elisha's initial rebuff: "he begged him to prophesy (προφητεύειν; see 9,26) and save (σώζειν) them[28]".

Responding in his turn to Joram, Elisha (3,14) swears: "As the Lord of hosts lives, were it not that I have regard for Jehoshaphat... I would neither look at you, nor see you". Characteristically avoiding the wording of the above "oath formula[29]", Josephus' prophet responds (9,35a) with words that both spell out the meaning of the figurative phrase "neither look at nor see[30]", while also motivating Elisha's "regard" for the Judean king: "Then he swore before God that he would not answer him if it were not for the sake of Josaphat *who was a holy* (ὅσιον) *and righteous* (δίκαιον; see δίκαιος, 9,33)[31] man".

2 Kgs 3,15 consists of two elements: Elisha's directive that a "minstrel" (MT מְנַגֵּן, BL ψάλλοντα) be brought to him, plus the notice that the "hand of the Lord" came upon the prophet when the former played. Josephus (9,35b) incorporates the directive of 3,15a into the narrative of its sequels, also substituting alternative language for the Bible's anthropromorphic reference to the divine "hand". His version reads thus: "... *when there had been brought to him* a man who could play the harp (ψάλλειν ... πρὸς τὸν ψαλμόν)[32] – the prophet himself had asked for him (see 3,15a) – he became divinely inspired (ἔνθεος γενόμενος)[33] at the playing of the harp...".

28. Compare TJ's rather similar rewording of Joram's response in 3,13b: "Please do not recall sins in this hour. Beg for mercies upon us".

29. Josephus regularly passes over the actual wording of the oaths which the Bible attributes to its characters. Behind that procedure likely lies a concern with precluding any possible violation of the Decalogue's prohibition of taking God's name in vain.

30. Compare his similar handling of the figurative reference to Elisha's "pouring water on the hands of Elijah" (3,11) in 9,33.

31. The above collocation recurs in *AJ* 6,87; 8,245.295 (reverse order); 15,138. On Josephus' recurrent coupling of Jehoshaphat's "righteousness" and "piety" as the king's characteristic virtues, see FELDMAN, *Studies*, pp. 314-315 (= ID., *Jehoshaphat*, 167-168).

32. Thus the reading of RO followed by Niese and Marcus. Dindorf, Bekker, and Naber read (πρὸς τὸν) ψάλλοντα (= BL 3,15a) with MSPE and Lat, a reading which MARCUS, *Josephus*, VI, p. 20, n. 2 qualifies as "forte recte".

33. Compare TJ's substitution for the "hand of the Lord" of MT 3,15b, i.e. "a spirit of prophecy from before the Lord". Josephus likewise substitutes the above phrase for the Biblical "hand of the Lord" in his version of 1 Kgs 18,46 ("the hand of the Lord was upon Elijah" in his running before Ahab to Jezreel) in *AJ* 8,346. He uses the term ἔνθε(ε)ος a further five times in his writings: *BJ* 3,353 (in reference to himself); 4,33 (of Vespasian). 388 ("an ancient saying of inspired men"); *AJ* 6,56 (= 1 Sam 10,6 "the spirit of the Lord is to come upon" Saul), 76 (= 1 Sam 11,6 "the spirit of God came upon" Saul). The term does not occur in the LXX, but is much used in profane Greek to denote divine "possession/inspiration; see, e.g., Plato, *Ion* 534B; Dionysius of Halicarnassus, *Roman Antiquities* 2.48.1. Josephus' introduction of the term thus serves to heighten the

Elisha's prophetic announcements to the three kings are cited in 3,16-19. The first of these (v. 16, MT) comprises a *Botenformel* coupled with a formulation that reads literally "making this wadi, pools, pools" (compare RSV: "I [the Lord] will make this dry stream-bed full of pools"). Josephus, once again, omits the Bible's "messenger formula". He likewise (9,35c) follows (while also elucidating) BL 3,16 (literally: "make [pl.] this stream pools, pools") in formulating the "announcement" of MT rather as a directive to his hearers: "(Elisha) ordered the kings to dig *many pits* in the (bed of) the stream (τῷ χειμάρρῳ; BL τὸν χειμάρρουν)". In 3,17 Elisha goes on to explicate the promise (MT)/ directive (BL) of v. 16: though neither wind nor rain will be seen, the wadi is about to be filled with enough water to satisfy the expedition's men and beasts. Josephus (9,36a) amplifies, attaching Elisha's announcement to his preceding directive as its motivation: "*For...* though there will be neither *cloud* nor wind (πνεύματος, BL πνεῦμα) nor downpour of rain (ὑετοῦ; BL ὑετόν), you shall see the stream (literally river, ποταμόν)[34] full of water, so that both your army and your beasts of burden will be saved (διασωθῆναι; cf. σώζειν, 9,34) by drinking".

In 2 Kgs 3,18 Elisha, after calling the promised advent of the water "a light thing in the eyes of the Lord", further announces that the kings will achieve a complete subjugation of Moab. Josephus (9,36b) makes the transition to this sequence with a phrase that avoids the Bible's anthropomorphic reference to the "eyes of the Lord[35]": "nor will this be the only thing you shall receive from God, but you shall also conquer your enemies...".

The prophet concludes his discourse in 3,19 with an enumeration of four acts of devastation which God will enable the kings to perpetrate on Moab. Josephus too (9,36c) has Elisha cite four destructive initiatives that the kings will perform. Of these, the first two agree with the opening items in the Biblical list (capturing the Moabite cities[36],

Hellenistic coloration of his presentation, even as it eliminates a Biblical anthropomorphism. On his use of the word, see SCHLATTER, *Theologie*, p. 60; C.H. HOLLIDAY, *Theios Aner in Hellenstic Judaism* (SBLMS, 40), Missoula, MT, Scholars, 1977, p. 65; and LEVISON, *Spirit*, 248.

34. Note the variation – which will recur in the continuation of the account – in Josephus' designation for the body of water in question here and in 9,35. BL use the identical term, i.e. ὁ χείμαρρους, in both vv. 16 and 17. The same alternation, exemplifying Josephus' proclivity for verbal variation, occurs in his version of 1 Kgs 17,1-6. In *AJ* 8,319 the body of water from which Elijah drinks is called χειμάρρῳ τινι, while 8,320 speaks of τοῦ ποταμοῦ (the LXX parallel text uses the former term twice; see 3 Rgns 17,5.6).

35. Compare his handling of the reference to the Lord's "hand" (3,15) in 9,35.

36. Like MT 3,19 ("every fortified city and every choice city"), Josephus has a double qualification of the Moabite sites the kings are to capture: "the fairest and strongest cities". BL read simply "every fortified city".

felling of trees[37]). In the case of the third and fourth items on the source list (stopping up the springs of water, ruining the land's good portions with stones), Josephus re-arranges and modifies: "(you shall) lay waste their country and stop up their springs (πηγὰς ... ἐμφράξετε = BL) *and rivers*". Finally, as he does frequently elsewhere, Josephus supplies a concluding/ transitional formula, rounding off Elisha's extended speech ("so spoke the prophet"), at the opening of 9,37.

4. *Elisha's Words Fulfilled*

2 Kgs 3,20-25 (= 9,37-41) recounts the realization of Elisha's double announcement, first the advent of the water (v. 20; cf. 3,17) and then the devastation of Moab (v. 25; cf. 3,18-19) with the battle account of vv. 21-24 supervening.

The source (3,20) gives a quite concise account of the arrival of the needed water on the day following Elisha's announcement. For the verse's chronological indication ("about the time of the morning offering") which would not have been readily understood by Gentile readers, Josephus (9,37) substitutes the phrase "before the sun arose[38]". He likewise elaborates on 3,20's brief reference to the source of the arriving water ("from the direction of Edom") with his notice "the stream (ὁ χειμάρρους, see 9,35) flowed with much (water)[39], *for it came about that* in this region of Idumaea, *which was three days' journey away, God had sent a heavy rain[40]...*". Finally, the historian explicitly notes the ful-

---

37. In 3,19 the reference is to "good tree(s)". Josephus has Elisha announce that the kings are to "cut down their (the Moabites') fruit-bearing trees" (δένδρα ... ἥμερα κόψετε; compare ἥμερα δένδρα κόπτοντας in the historian's version [*AJ* 4,299] of the law of Deut 20,19 prohibiting the felling of fruit trees during a siege).

38. SCHALIT, *Kadmoniot, ad loc.* suggests an alternative explanation for the divergence beteen the Biblical and Josephan chronological indications, i.e. the historian read the המנחה ("the offering") of MT 3,20 rather as החמה, "the sun".

39. Compare Elisha's prediction in 9,36: "you shall see the stream (τὸν ποταμόν) full of water". Cf. the Biblical account where prophetic announcement ("*this wadi* will be filled with water", 3,17) and realization ("*the country* was filled with water", 3,20) are not so closely aligned verbally.

40. S. RAPPAPORT, *Agada und Exegese bei Flavius Josephus*, Wien, Alexander Kohut Foundation, 1930, p. 132, n. 251a cites Rashi's similar affirmation, made in his commentary on 2 Kgs 3,20, that the "water" mentioned in that verse originated in a rain that had fallen on Edom. (Rappaport goes on to state "Raschis Quelle konnte ich nicht ermitteln".) WEILL, *Josèphe*, II, p. 253, n. 4 comments concerning Josephus' above wording: "Josèphe rationalise suivant son habitude"; similarly FELDMAN, *Studies*, p. 345 (= ID., *Elisha*, 21-22). It is not so clear to me, however, that Josephus' formulation – with its explicit, Biblically unparalleled mention of *God* sending the rainfall (and of the distance it travels to reach the designated spot) – really constitutes a "rationalization" of the Bible's presentation.

fillment also of Elisha's promise (see 3,17bβ = 9,36) about the expedition's participants getting sufficient drink: "... so that the army and the beasts of burden found an abundance of water to drink".

2 Kgs 3,21 (MT) prepares the following battle account with its notice that the Moabites, upon "hearing" of the allies' advance, were "mustered at the frontier". In Josephus (9,38) the Moabites "hear" specifically of the kings' "making their advance through the wilderness" (διὰ τῆς ἐρήμου ποιουμένους τὴν ἔφοδον)[41]. Whereas 3,21 (MT) speaks impersonally of the Moabites' "being mustered" (MT וַיִּצָּעֲקוּ)[42], Josephus' formulation assigns a more active role to the Moabite ruler: "... their king at once collected an army and ordered them to pitch camp on the frontier (ἐπὶ τῶν ὅρων)[43]...". To his mention of the stationing of the Moabites "on the frontier", the historian then appends a rationale for this initiative: "... in order that the enemy might not invade their country unperceived".

In 3,22 one hears of the Moabites beholding the water on which the early morning sun is shining "red as blood". Once again, Josephus (9,39) embellishes in several respects: the "water" is "in the stream" (see 9,38) which itself "was not far from Moabite territory" (and hence, one understands, readily visible to the Moabites). Their perception of the blood-colored water further takes place specifically "at sunrise" (cf. "before the sun arose", 9,37) since "... just at this time the water looks especially red in the rays of the sun...".

2 Kgs 3,23a notes the Moabites' inference from what they see: "this is blood; the kings have surely fought together, and slain one another". Josephus inserts an advance qualification concerning the mistakenness of their supposition: "they received a false impression (ψευδῆ δόξαν) concerning the enemy...". In then reporting what the Moabites (wrongfully) supposed, the historian supplies a motivation for the allied kings' (presumed) mutual slaughter which picks up on his earlier mention (9,32) of the water crisis confronting them: "... supposing they had

---

41. This phrase echoes Josephus' wording in 9,31: (the kings decide) "to make their advance upon the enemy through the wilderness (διὰ τῆς ἐρήμου) of Idumaea, for these would not expect them to attack (ποιήσεσθαι τὴν ἔφοδον) by this road".

42. BL 3,21bα, reading the above form with a different vocalization, represent the Moabites rather as "crying out" (ἀνεβόησαν, B; ἐβόησαν, L). Josephus has no equivalent.

43. Thus the conjecture of Niese, followed by Naber and Marcus; see MT 3,21 עַל-הַגְּבוּל = BL ἐπὶ τοῦ ὁρίου. The codices (retained by Dindorf and Bekker) read ἐπὶ τῶν ὁρῶν, a reading which WEILL, Josèphe, II, p. 254, n. 1 views as possibly correct. From 3,21 Josephus leaves aside the specification concerning the makeup of the Moabite force, i.e. "all who were able to put on armor from the youngest to the oldest" (so MT; B and L differ somewhat here).

slain one another *because of thirst*". He likewise spells out the cryptic statement attributed to the Moabites in 3,23a ("this [is] blood") via his notice "… (they supposed) *that the river was running with* their blood (αἷμα αὐτοῖς ῥέοντος)[44]". The Moabites' word concludes in 3,23b with their cry: "Now then, Moab, to the spoil"! Here again, Josephus (9,40) amplifies, highlighting their misapprehensions about the enemy's state, while also underscoring the Moabite king's active and authoritative role (see above on 9,38): "… and so, *imagining this to be the case, they asked their king to send them out* to plunder the enemy…[45]".

2 Kgs 3,24 recounts the Moabites' approach to the "Israelite" camp and Israel's counter-assault upon them[46]. Josephus' version continues to insist upon the Moabites' deluded state: "… all rushing out *as if* upon booty that waited to be seized, they came to the camp of the *supposedly* dead enemies. And then their hopes *proved false* (διαψεύδεται; cf. ψευδῆ δόξαν, 9,39), for the enemy…"[47].

2 Kgs 3,25a records the four destructive measures carried out by the allies in the territory of Moab in accordance with Elisha's announcement in 3,19. Josephus (9,41) cites the same four initiatives. He does, however, reverse the sequence of the third (stopping up the springs) and fourth (felling of trees)[48]. He likewise introduces mention of the "source" of the "stones" with which the invaders cover the Moabite fields: they obtain these "from the streams".

MT and BL 3,25b differ markedly. The former reads (so RSV) "… till only its stones were left in Kir-hareseth and the slingers surrounded it and conquered it". As Marcus points out[49], BL apparently took the two components of MT's phrase בַּקִּיר חֲרָשֶׂת as respectively a common noun and a participial form modifying this, and so renders: "… until

44. H. SCHRECKENBERG, *Einige Vermutungen zum Josephustext*, in *Theokratia* 1 (1967-68) 64-75, 69-70, with reference to *AJ* 2,294 (ὁ γὰρ ποταμὸς αὐτοῖς [i.e. the Egyptians] αἱματώδης … ἐρρύη), proposes emending the above phrase to αἱματώδους ῥέοντος. He reiterates the proposal in his *Untersuchungen zu Flavius Josephus* (ALGHJ, 10), Leiden, Brill, 1977, p. 109.

45. With the above accentuation of the royal authority, compare, e.g., *AJ* 9,14. In that text Josephus rewords the reference of 2 Chr 20,25 to Jehoshaphat and his men engaging together in plundering the fallen enemy as follows: "… he (Jehoshaphat) gave his army leave to plunder the camp of the enemy" which they then proceed to do.

46. On the textual problem at the end of v. 24, see BHS.

47. 2 Kgs 3,24 speaks of the Moabites' advancing against the camp "of Israel" and of "the Israelites" rising up against them. Josephus' generalizing double reference to "the enemy" (see above) implicitly "corrects" the Biblical wording which seems to leave out of account the fact that Moab's attackers consisted also of Judeans and Edomites.

48. Compare 9,36 where, in accord with 3,19, Josephus has Elisha mention the felling of the trees before the measure against the streams.

49. *Josephus*, VI, pp. 24-25, n. a.

they left *the stones of the wall cast down* (τοὺς λίθους τοῦ τοίχου καθηρημένους), and the slingers surrounded and smote it" (so B)[50]. In this instance, Josephus (9,41 *in fine*) does align himself with the reading of BL against that of MT (see, however, below): "(the invaders) *razed their walls to the ground* (τὰ τείχη καθεῖλον ἕως ἐδάφους)[51]".

5. *Sacrifice & Sequels*

The conclusion of 2 Kings 3 (vv. 26-27 = 9,42-43 [44-45]) tells of a double initiative undertaken by the Moabite king in the face of the enemy assault, the first unavailing, the second efficacious. 2 Kgs 3,26a attributes the king's initial measure to his "seeing the battle going against him". Given this realization he attempts, unsuccessfully, to "break through opposite the king of Edom", accompanied by 700 "swordsmen". Josephus (9,42a) modifies the Biblical formulation in several respects. What the Moabite king "sees" becomes "the city in danger of being taken by storm". In speaking of "the city" here where 3,26 itself does not, Josephus seems to be evidencing his familiarity (also) with MT 3,25b's "Kir-hareseth" understood as a proper place name, see above. The source gives no reason for the Moabite's attempting to break through precisely at the point where he does, i.e. "opposite the king of Edom". Josephus, for his part, substitutes a different indication as to where the attempted breakout occurs, while likewise interjecting a motivation for the choice of this particular site: the king and his 700 men try "to ride through the enemy's camp at a place *where he thought the guards would let them get through*". In the same line, he goes on (9,42b) to supply an explanation for the failure of the venture (compare 3,26bβ's simple "but they could not") as well: "... but was unable to escape, *for he happened on a place that was carefully guarded*".

In the Bible, the notice on the Moabite king's failure (3,26bβ) is followed directly by mention of his "taking his oldest son" (3,27aα). Josephus (9,43a) introduces an element of transition between the two Biblical items which, at the same time, alerts readers to the portentous character of what is to follow: "Then he returned to the city [see above] and performed an act of despair and terrible necessity (ἔργον ἀπογνώσεως καὶ δεινῆς ἀνάγκης)[52]".

50. Compare TJ: "... until the stone was not left in the wall (בכותלא); whatever they did not overthrow (בגרשהא) the slingers surrounded and struck down".

51. On the other hand, Josephus has no equivalent to the reference – common to both MT and BL – to the role of the "slingers" in the siege.

52. The above phrases "act of despair" and "terrible necessity" occur only here in Josephus.

2 Kgs 3,27aβ describes the "sacrifice" (MT עֹלָה, B ὁλοκαύτωμα, L ὁλακαύτωσιν) of the Moabite crown prince who is "offered up" by his father "on the wall". This formulation leaves undetermined to whom the prince is being sacrificed: is it the Lord or rather the Moabite god Chemosh (see, e.g., 1 Kgs 11,7)[53]? Josephus, with a view to explaining how it was that the allies became aware of the Moabite's sacrifice and so respond as they do (see below), emphasizes (9,43b) the visibility of the proceedings: "His oldest son... he led up on to the wall (ἐπὶ τὸ τεῖχος = L 3,27aβ) *so that he was visible to all his enemies*, and consecrated him as a whole burnt offering (ἱερούργησεν εἰς ὁλοκαύτωσιν; cf. L 3,27aβ ἀνήνεγκεν... ὁλοκαύτωσιν)...". The historian further introduces the specification that the sacrifice was offered τῷ θεῷ. The ambiguity of this indication is pointed up by the divergent renditions of it in the respective translations of Marcus ("to his [Moabite] god") and Weill ("à Dieu"). Thus in Josephus too the intended "recipient" of the sacrifice remains finally unclear.

According to MT 3,27b the immediate sequel to the sacrifice of v. 27a is that "great wrath (קֶצֶף) came upon Israel" with the result that the allies withdraw "to the land" (לָאָרֶץ). Ambiguity attaches to this formulation as well: whose "wrath" overtakes Israel – the Lord's or Chemosh's? In any case, with their rendering of קֶצֶף by μετάμελος ("repentance") BL seem to transpose into the subjective realm what MT envisages as an extra-mental happening having its source in some deity, whether the Lord or Chemosh. In addition, BL speak, in more differentiated terms, of the allies returning to "their land" as opposed to MT's generalizing "the land". Josephus' version (9,43c) of these developments aligns itself with that of BL for both of their above differences with MT. At the same time, the historian broadly embellishes BL's allusion to the allies' "repentance": "... when the kings saw him, *they felt*

---

53. In subsequent Jewish and Christian tradition the dominant opinion is that the sacrifice was offered to the Lord. See L. GINZBERG, *Die Haggada bei den Kirchenvätern. Erster Theil: Die Haggada in den pseudo-hieronymianischen "Quaestiones"*, Amsterdam, 1899, pp. 83-86; ID., *The Legends of the Jews* (6 vols.), Philadelphia: Jewish Publication Society of America, 1909-1925, IV, p. 90; VI, p. 314. As representative of these extra-Biblical traditions on the matter, see *Midr. Tanhuma – Yelammedenu* Exod. 9.5 (*Midrash Tanhuma-Yelammedenu*, trans. S.A. Berman, Hoboken, NJ, Ktav, 1996, p. 575) which reports the pronouncement of R. Abba son of Kahana according to which Mesha was prompted to offer his son to the Lord when he heard from his astrologers of Abraham's near sacrifice of his first-born and concluded that, if God had done miracles for Abraham's people even though the patriarch had not actually carried out the sacrifice, that the Lord would do still greater miracles for him if he were, in fact, to offer his own son to him. Compare, however, the (anonymous) opinion cited in the same passage, i.e. the use of the term חֹמָה ("wall") in 3,27 indicates that Mesha bowed down to the חַמָּה ("sun") in offering his sacrifice, this evoking the divine "wrath" against Israel spoken of in the verse.

pity for him in his necessity (κατῷκτειραν τῆς ἀνάγκης [cf. δεινῆς ἀνάγκης, 9,43a])[54], and, being moved by a feeling of humanity and compassion (ἀνθρώπινον ... καὶ ἐλεεινόν)[55], they raised the siege...". Josephus' emphasis here on the kings' compassionate response to the Moabite monarch's act of desperation serves, as L.H. Feldman has pointed out, as an implicit response to contemporary anti-Semitic claims that Jews lacked concern for other peoples[56]. Contrary to such allegations, his Joram and Jehoshaphat appear as Jewish leaders who are indeed touched by the plight of a non-Jew – and a rebel vassal and military opponent at that[57]. In line with the BL ending of 3,27 (see above) Josephus conludes his account of the expedition with the notice that the three kings "... returned, each to his home (εἰς τὴν οἰκείαν)". This statement, in turn, serves as the point of attachment for the historian's notices (9,44-45) on Jehoshaphat's death and burial and succession of his son Joram which occur once that monarch "came to Jerusalem". This latter complex, for its part, draws (very selectively) on the data of 1 Kgs 22,41-50 (MT = BL 3 Rgns 16,28a-h) // 2 Chr 20,31-21,3), the Biblical framework notices for Jehoshaphat. It reads:

> (44) *So Josaphat came to Jerusalem and dwelt in peace* (μετ' εἰρήνης)[58], *but lived on only a little while after that campaign*[59], dying at the age of sixty years[60], for twenty-five of which he had reigned (= 1 Kgs 22,42b // 2 Chr 20,31b). And he received a *magnificent* burial (ταφῆς ... μεγαλοπρεποῦς)[61] in Jerusalem[62], *for he had, indeed, been emulous* (μιμητής) *of the acts of David*[63].

54. The above phrase has a counterpart in *AJ* 7,193 τὴν ἀνάγκην ... κατοικτείρας (Joab of Absalom).

55. The above collocation occurs only here in Josephus.

56. See FELDMAN, *Studies*, p. 326 (= ID., *Jehoram*, 12-13).

57. Josephus similarly accentuates Ahab's kindly treatment of his defeated foe Benhadad of Syria in his version of the story of 1 Kings 20 in *AJ* 8,363-392; see my *Early Divided Monarchy*, pp. 226-230.

58. This indication about the "peacefulness" of the end of Jehoshaphat's reign echoes Josephus' notice about his early reign in *AJ* 8,396, i.e. "the neighboring peoples also continued to cherish Josaphat and remained at peace (πρὸς ... εἰρήνην) with him".

59. The author of Kings (who mentions the fact of Jehoshaphat's death already in 1 Kgs 22,50) gives no indication as to the length of time that elapsed between the expedition of 2 Kings 3 and the monarch's demise.

60. Josephus arrives at this figure for Jehoshaphat's life-span by combining the data of 1 Kgs 22,42 // 2 Chr 20,31: Jehoshaphat acceded at age 35 and ruled for 25 years (see above).

61. The above phrase recurs in *AJ* 9,182 (of Elisha); comparable formulations, involving the use of the word "magnificent" in connection with a burial, occur in *AJ* 3,210; 7,42; 10,177.

62. The above notice represents an embellishment of the non-descript statements of 1 Kgs 22,50aβ // 2 Chr 21,1aβ: "(Jehoshaphat) was buried with his father in the city of David".

63. This appended indication as to why Jehoshaphat was accorded a "magnificent" burial recalls Josephus' opening remark concerning him in *AJ* 8,315: "That [Jehoshaphat]

(45) Now he left behind a good number of sons[64], but as his successor he had named the eldest (πρεσβύτατον)[65], Joram ('Ιώραμον)[66], *who thus had the same name as his wife's* (γυναικός)[67] *brother, the ruler of the Israelites and the son of Achab*[68].

Conclusions: Josephus' Rewriting of 2 Kings 3

Our reading of *AJ* 9,29-45 yielded a variety of indications regarding the text-forms of 2 Kgs 3,4-27 utilized by Josephus. His having Elisha issue a directive rather than make a announcement about the coming water (9,36; compare 3,13), mention of the Moabite "razed walls" (9,41 = 3,25b) and reference to the kings' change of heart and return to their individual homelands (9,43 = 3,27b), e.g., all correspond to the distinctive readings of BL against MT. On the other hand, like MT and in contrast to BL, Josephus gives a double qualification of the Moabite cities whose overthrow Elisha announces (9,36 = 3,19; see n. 36). Similarly, his reference to "the city" in 9,42-43 seems to reflect knowledge of MT's proper place name ("Kir-hareseth") in 3,25b, just as his form of the Moabite king's name ("Meisa", 9,29) stands closer to that of MT ("Mesha") than to BL's Μωσά. In addition, we encountered a series of

imitated (μιμητήν) his [great great-] great grandfather David in courage and piety, all men have recognized from his deeds". (In his rendering of this sequence MARCUS, *ad loc.* takes the reference to be to Jehoshaphat's father Asa, wrongly in my view; see *Early Divided Monarchy*, pp. 148-149, n. 968.)

64. Josephus' formulation here has in view 2 Chr 21,2 which lists by name six sons of Jehoshaphat in addition to his successor, Jehoram. In accord with his frequent practice, Josephus leaves aside the names of these other sons.

65. This is the reading of ROEZon which Niese, Naber and Marcus follow. Dindorf and Bekker read πρεσβύτερον with MSP, cf. Lat seniorem.

66. This is the declined form of the name as read by LXX, i.e. 'Ιωράμ; compare MT "Jehoram". Josephus handles the name of the Judean king's Northern namesake in the same way, see on 9,27. The above notice represents Josephus' anticipation of 2 Chr 21,3 according to which, whereas Jehoshaphat awarded his other sons a variety of "gifts" (this point is nowhere mentioned by Josephus), he "gave the kingdom to Jehoram because he was the oldest (BL ὁ πρωτότοκος)".

67. This is the reading of RO which Niese, Naber and Marcus follow. Dindorf and Bekker read μητρός with MSP Zon Lat. As MARCUS, *Josephus*, VI, p. 26, n. b points out, while the former reading is in accord with Scripture (see 2 Kgs 8,18 // 2 Chr 21,6; cf. *AJ* 8,398) which states that the woman to whom the Judean Joram was married was the "daughter of Ahab", i.e. the sister of King Joram of Israel, whose name was Athaliah (see 2 Kgs 8,26 // 2 Chr 22,2), the latter is not.

68. The above appendix to the data of 2 Chr 21,1-3 points up the "coincidence" of the contemporary kings of Judah and Israel having identical names, thereby precluding possible reader suspicion that Josephus might have gotten his kings confused. Josephus resumes his account of Joram of Judah, based in first place on 2 Chr 21,4-20 in *AJ* 9,95-104; see Chap. V of this work.

instances where a given feature of Josephus' presentation appears closer to the wording of TJ than to that of either MT or BL (see nn. 28,33). It thus would seem that Josephus based himself on a number of different text-forms of the 2 Kings 3 story.

Josephus' predominant rewriting technique throughout *AJ* 9,29-45 proved to be his expansions of source data. Many of these expansions, as we have seen, serve to respond to questions left unanswered by the Bible itself, e.g., why does Joram turn precisely to Jehoshaphat as a possible ally? (9,30, compare 3,7); how is that these two kings end up being accompanied also by the king of Edom/ Idumaea? (see 9,30, compare 3,9); why do the allies choose the route they do? (9,31, compare 3,8) and why does a water crisis befall them on that chosen route? (9,32, compare 3,9)?; where do the kings encounter Elisha? (9,34, compare 9,12); why should Joram go to his parents' "prophets" as Elisha tells him to do? (9,34, compare 3,13); what (or who) was the "cause" of the water that reached the expedition? (9,37, compare 3,20); why does the Moabite king station his men on the frontier? (9,38, compare 3,21); why does the water look "blood-red" to the Moabites (9,39, compare 3,22) and why do they think the three kings have slain one another? (9,39, compare 3,23); where did the allies obtain the stones with which they cover the Moabite fields? (9,41, compare 3,25); why did the Moabite king attempt to breakout at the point where he did? (9,42, compare 3,26a) and why did the attempt fail? (9,42, compare 3,26b); how do the kings become aware of the Moabite's sacrifice? (9,43, compare 3,27a); to whom was the crown-prince offered? (9,43, compare 3,27a); and what became of Jehoshaphat upon his return home? (9,44, compare 3,27bβ). Others of them function to heighten the narrative profile of the two kings, i.e. Joram (see, e.g., his being afflicted "most of all" by the water crisis [9,32, compare 3,9] and taking the lead in the prophetic consultation [9,34, compare 3,13]) and Jehoshaphat (see, e.g., his "splendid entertainment" of Joram's force [9,31]; his being a "righteous" man who "comforts" the afflicted Joram [9,33, compare 3,11]; "urging" recourse to Elisha [9,33, compare 3,12]; Elisha's qualification of him as "holy and righteous" [9,35, compare 3,14]; his "magnificent" burial [9,44, compare 1 Kgs 22,51 // 2 Chr 21,1] and the reason for this, i.e. his "emulation" of David). Still other serve to accentuate the drama/ emotional quality of the happenings recounted: the expedition's "torment" (9,32, compare 3,9), the prefatory characterization of the Moabite king's sacrifice as "an act of despair and terrible necessity" (9,43a, compare 3,27a), and the *Ausmalung* of the allies' emotional response to his deed (9,43b, compare 3,27b BL).

As compared with the above, all-pervasive elaborations, Josephus'
omissions/ abridgements in 9,29-45 appear minor both in extent and significance. Under the latter head we may, however, recall the following
instances: Mesha's status as a "sheep-breeder" (3,4, compare 9,29); the
specification concerning the makeup of the Moabite force (3,21, compare 9,38); and the mention of the "slingers'" role in the siege (3,25,
compare 9,41). Far more conspicuous are the terminological and contentual modifications/ adaptations which Josephus introduces into his
retelling of the story of 2 Kings 3. These concern such points as:
Mesha's tribute (9,29, compare 3,4); the decision about the march route
(9,31, compare 3,8); Joram's initial response to the water crisis (9,32,
compare 3,10); the designation of Elisha in relation to Elijah (9,33, compare 3,11); Joram's response to Elisha's rebuff (9,34, compare 3,13b),
the prophet's "oath" (9,35, compare 3,14), the "hand of the Lord" coming upon him (9,35, compare 3,15); the time of the water's arrival (9,37,
compare 3,20); the role of their king in the mustering of the Moabites
(9,38, compare 3,21) and subsequently in their (intended) plundering of
the allied camp (9,40, compare 3,24) and the (un)reality of the Moabites'
surmises (9,39-40, compare 3,22-24).

Finally, Josephus also re-arranges the source sequence in a series of
instances within 9,29-45: Mesha's revolt and Joram's response thereto
(9,29, compare 3,4-6); Elisha's four announcements about what the
kings will accomplish against Moab (9,36, compare 3,19); and the realization of these (9,41, compare 3,25a).

Josephus' re-writing techniques as applied to the material of 3,4-27
give rise to a version of the episode evidencing many distinctive features
vis-à-vis the *Vorlage(n)*. Overall, many of the source's "blanks" are filled
in. The kings Joram, Jehoshaphat, and Mesha all assume a heightened
stature in his presentation. The Israelite-Judean bond is accentuated,
as is the Jewish kings' empathy with their Gentile colleague in distress
(see 9,43). Anthropomorphic wording is replaced with alternative language. The (verbal) parallelism between the current joint Israelite-Judean
campaign against Moab and the earlier one against Syria (see *AJ* 8,398-
420) is underscored.

In its peculiarities, Josephus' version of the 2 Kings 3 story functions,
first of all, as an *apologia* for the historian's people, one designed to
counteract the prejudices and suspicions of Gentile readers by portraying
Jewish leaders who, e.g., are effective military leaders, hospitable, and
compassionate in the face of the distress of their non-Jewish opponents
– all qualities which had been denied to Jews by their detractors. Such
readers would further find the story in its Josephan form more congenial

given its use of such familiar phrases of their own literary tradition as "become divinely inspired" (9,35) in place of the Bible's anthropomorphic reference to the "hand of the Lord coming upon" Elijah (3,15); see n. 33. For his own compatriots the historian's retelling offers above all an accentuated picture of intra-Jewish cooperation, this leading to a spectacular victory over a Gentile foe. Such a presentation would serve to bring home to Jewish readers the realization that their only hope of achieving like success against their current Gentile enemies lay in their working together as harmoniously as had Joram and Jehoshaphat, rather than continuing the disastrous internecine conflicts of the recent past.

IV

ELISHA'S GREAT DEEDS[1]
(9,46-94)

Within the Book of Kings, 2 Kgs 4,1-8,15 constitutes a rather distinct section, focussed as it is on the memorable words and deeds of the prophet Elisha[2]. In this chapter I shall examine Josephus' (partial, see below) rendition of this segment in *AJ* 9,46-94. For purposes of my comparison I divide up the material into four longer segments as follows: 1. Elisha's Oil Miracle (*AJ* 9,(46)47-50 = 2 Kgs 4,1-7); 2. Elisha Preserved (9,51-59 = 2 Kgs 6,9-23); 3. Elisha's Word Fulfilled (9,60-86 = 2 Kgs 6,24–7,20); and 4) Elisha in Damascus (9,87-94 = 2 Kgs 8,7-15).

1. *Elisha's Oil Miracle*

The Biblical "Elisha Complex" (2 Kgs 4,1–8,15) begins rather abruptly in 4,1 with mention of the embattled widow's approach to the prophet who, for his part, has not been on the scene since 3,19. Josephus takes care (9,46) to provide his version of the complex with a more elaborate transition which prepares readers for the character of the following segment, i.e. 9,47-94. It reads: "And when the king of the Israelites came from Moab to Samaria[3], he had with him the prophet Elisha[4], whose acts I wish to relate – for they are glorious (λαμπραί) and worthy

---

1. This chapter represents a revised version of my article *Elisha's Great Deeds according to Josephus (AJ 9,47-94)*, in *Henoch* 18 (1996) 69-109 and is used by permission here.

2. Elisha, of course, is not absent either in what precedes (see 1 Kgs 19,19-21; 2 Kings 2-3) or follows (see 2 Kgs 9,1-3; 13,14-21) this segment. In this other material, however, he does not have the same sustained prominence as he does in 4,1–8,15, being either more or less overshadowed by other figures (Elijah, various kings) or making (as in 2 Kgs 2,19-25; 13,14-21), only a rather brief appearance.

3. This formulation harks back, following the account of Jehoshaphat's death and the accession of his son Joram in 9,44-45, to the end of 9,43 (= 2 Kgs 3,27b) where Josephus relates the three kings' return to their own lands. After the "Judean interlude" of 9,44-45, Josephus now (9,46) redirects attention to the North and its great prophet, Elisha.

4. Recall that in 2 Kings 3 (see vv. 11-19 = 9,33-36) Elisha accompanies the expedition against Moab, being "consulted" by the kings when water runs out. Accordingly, Josephus here represents the prophet as "returning" to Israel along with his king, Joram, now that the expedition has ended.

of record (ἱστορίας ἄξιαι)[5] – as we discover them in the sacred books (ἐν ταῖς ἱεραῖς βίβλοις; see 9,28)[6]".

In both Josephus (9,47-50) and the Bible (2 Kgs 4,1-7) the first miraculous deed to be related in their respective "Elisha complexes" is the prophet's multiplication of oil for a woman in need. 2 Kgs 4,1 (MT, BL) introduces that woman as "the wife of "one of the sons (TJ: students, *tlmydy*) of the prophets", and then has her inform Elisha that her "husband" has died. Josephus presents her rather as "the wife of Obedias, the steward of Achab…". In making the woman the spouse of "Obadiah" here, Josephus aligns himself with a tradition attested in TJ 2 Kgs 4,1 as well as elsewhere in both Jewish and Christian literature[7]. As Marcus suggests[8], the likely Biblical inspiration for this identification is the parallelism between the woman's word to Elisha in 2 Kgs 4,1 ("you know that *your servant feared the Lord*") and Obadiah's own statement about himself to Elijah in 1 Kgs 18,12 ("… I *your servant have feared the Lord* from my youth"). Having thus identified Elisha's interlocutor, Josephus rewords her general invocation of her husband's "fear of the Lord" (so 4,1)[9] into a more specific reminiscence of his good deed as related in 1 Kgs 18,4.13 = *AJ* 8,330.334: "(she said that he [Elisha] was not ignorant) of how her husband had saved the lives of the prophets who were to have been slain by Achab's wife Jezabela, for, she said, a hundred of them had been fed by him *with money he had borrowed* and had been kept in hiding…". In the above formulation note especially the italicized phrase which has no parallel either in the above-cited verses of 1 Kings 18 nor in Josephus' reproduction of these in 8,330.334. That Obadiah did go so

5. The above phrase occurs only here in Josephus.

6. This closing formulation in 9,46 is echoed in the notice which Josephus introduces into his account of Elisha's death (= 2 Kgs 13,14-19) in 9,182: "he was a man renowned for righteousness and one manifestly held in honour by God; for through his prophetic power he performed astounding and marvelous deeds, which were held in glorious (λαμπρᾶς) memory by the Hebrews".

7. Other attestations of this tradition are, e.g.: *Pesik. Rab. Kah.* 2.5 (W.G. BRAUDE & I.J. KAPSTEIN, trs., *Pĕsiḳta dĕ-Rab Kahāna*, Philadelphia, Jewish Publication Society of America, 1975, p. 28); *Midr. Prov.* 21.27 (A. WÜNSCHE, tr., Leipzig, Pfeiffer 1885, p. 86); *Midr. Tanhuma-Yelammedenu* Exod. 9.5 (Berman, *Midrash Tanhuma-Yelammedenu*, p. 575); and THEODORET, *Quaest. in IV. Regum* 14 (PG 80, c. 754). It might be noted here that, in contrast to all these references which retain the Biblical designation of the deceased as "one of the sons (TJ students) of the prophets" (whom they then name as Obadiah), Josephus has the widow refer to her husband simply as "Obedias the steward of Achab". His reason for doing so may be the fact that in 1 Kings 18 (and in Josephus' own account in *AJ* 8,330) Obadiah is portrayed as a protector of the prophets, rather than as a "(son of the) prophet(s)" himself.

8. *Josephus*, VI, pp. 26-27, n. d.

9. On Josephus' avoidance of the Biblical idiom "fear (of) the Lord/God", see p. 9, n. 25.

far as to borrow money in order to provide for the threatened prophets is not, however, an affirmation unique to Josephus here. Rather, one finds this same action being credited to him in several other Jewish sources as well[10]. After this amplification of the Biblical widow's words, Josephus does – finally – reproduce her statements from 4,1b: her husband has died; her children and she herself face enslavement by their creditors[11]. Thereafter, he rounds off the woman's report with an explicit appeal by her, unparalleled in the Bible, which itself picks up on her previous evocation of her husband's meritorious initiative: "... and she besought him, *because of this good deed* (εὐεργεσίαν)[12] of her husband, to pity (ἐλεῆσαι)[13] her and give her some assistance".

In 2 Kgs 4,2a Elisha responds to the woman's address with a double question: "what shall I do for you?; what have you in the house?" Josephus (9,48a) dispenses with the first of these questions, thereby having the prophet come directly to the key point, i.e. the resources available to the woman: "... he inquired what she had in the house". The widow's reply as cited in MT contains a *hapax legomenon* which RSV takes as a noun: "your maidservant has nothing in the house, except a jar (אָסוּךְ) of oil". Alternatively, the MT term might be seen as a verbal form (from סוּך, "to anoint"); compare B's ὃ ἀλείψομαι ἔλαιον and cf. the conflate rendering of L (ἀγγεῖον ἐλαίου ὃ ἀλείψομαι). Josephus' rendition has her speak of "a very little oil in a jar" (ἔλαιον... ἐν

10. Thus *Midr. Pss.* on Ps 15,5 (W.G. Braude, tr., *The Midrash on Psalms* I, New Haven, Yale University Press, 1959, p. 194) states that Obadiah exemplifies the reference in the Psalm verse to "the man who does not put out his money at interest". *Exod. Rab.* 31.4 (S.M. LEHRMAN, tr., *Midrash Rabbah Exodus*, London-New York, Soncino, 1983, pp. 381-382) makes the same application of Ps 15,5. In addition, these authorities aver that the one who lent Obadiah the money was none other than Joram, son and successor of Ahab, doing this, however, at interest. Joram, who thereby violated the Torah (cf. Exod 22,25), was subsequently shot by Jehu "between his arms" with a arrow that "pierced his heart" (see 2 Kgs 9,24) because he had "hardened his heart and stretched out his hand to receive usury". Thus did Joram, the interest-taker, lose his life in accordance with the threat against usurers of Ezek 18,13. See also TJ on 2 Kgs 4,1 "(Obadiah) *was borrowing* and feeding them *in order not to feed them from the revenues of Ahab on account of those who were the oppressor*".

11. Josephus' report of the woman's words here differs in two points of content from those of her Biblical counterpart (it is likewise formulated in indirect rather than direct address). In both instances one has a kind of *Steigerung* of the woman's predicament: it is not only her children, but she as well who are about to be taken into slavery and this not by one "creditor" but by several (compare 9,47 ὑπὸ τῶν δανειστῶν and BL 4,1 ὁ δανεσιστής). In further contrast to the Bible, Josephus does not have the woman specify the number ("two") of her children facing enslavement.

12. This is the conjecture of Ernesti which Dindorf, Bekker, Naber and Marcus follow. Niese reads ἐργασίαν with the codices.

13. This term echoes 9,25 where the same form is used by the third captain in his appeal to Elijah for "pity" on him and his men.

κεραμίῳ), a reading corresponding to that of TJ מנא דמשחא (and the initial element of L's double expression; see above)[14]. 2 Kgs 4,3-4 relates Elisha's instructions to the woman: she is to borrow "not a few" vessels from her neighbors, shut herself in with her children, pour oil into the borrowed vessels, and set the full ones aside. Josephus' version (9,48b) of these directives[15] eliminates the references to the widow's children and the setting aside of the full vessels, but adds a word of assurance about the procedure enjoined. His version thus reads: "(the prophet bade her) go and borrow from her neighbors (παρὰ τῶν γειτόνων; BL παρὰ πάντων τῶν γειτόνων [L + σου]) many empty (κενά, so BL) vessels (ἀγγεῖα, so L) and then shut (ἀποκλείσασαν; BL ἀποκλείσεις) the doors (τὰς θύρας, BL τὴν θύραν) of her chamber and pour some of the oil into all of them, *for God, he said, would fill them* [the vessels][16]".

The woman's execution of Elisha's directives is recounted in 2 Kgs 4,5-6, while 4,7a relates her reporting the outcome to Elisha. Josephus (9,49) compresses and modifies: "and the woman did (ποιησάσης) as he had bidden[17], and instructed her children to bring every one of vessels; and when all were filled and not a single one was left empty...[18]".

14. In stating categorically that Josephus' above rendition agrees with that of L against LXX (B) and MT, MARCUS, *Josephus*, VI, p. 27, n. h fails to take into account several relevant considerations: MT's term אסוך could itself have the meaning "jar"; L's reading is in fact conflate, containing also a reference to the woman's "anointing" herself to which Josephus has no parallel; and finally, the Greek words for "jar" used by Josephus and L differ.

15. In 4,3 Elisha's words are introduced simply "and he said". Josephus has a more specific introductory formula: "the prophet bade her...". FELDMAN, *Prophets and Prophecy*, 390 and n. 28 points out that Josephus employs the terms "prophet" and "prophesy" of Elisha in no less than 28 instances where the Bible itself does not do so explicitly.

16. With the above italicized words Josephus introduces an explicit theological reference into a story which, in its Biblical version, does not mention God as such. His expansion here might be compared with the similar case of *AJ* 8,326. In that passage Josephus amplifies Elijah's directive to the Phoenician woman that she hand over to him the body of her dead son as found in 1 Kgs 17,19a with the assurance "for he would, he said, restore him to her alive". Both Josephan additions serve to accentuate the respective prophet's self-assurance in situations calling for a miraculous solution.

17. This general notice corresponds to the L plus in 4,5 καὶ ἐποίησεν οὕτως.

18. This formulation represents Josephus' "conflation" of the double indication of 4,5-6a, i.e. "as she poured they (the sons) brought the vessels to her. When the vessels were full, she said to her son, 'Bring me another vessel'. And he said to her, 'There is not another'". By means of his conflation, Josephus eliminates the Bible's odd-seeming reference to the woman's asking for another vessel when all of these have just been said to be already full. Josephus' version of 4,5-6 likewise dispenses with the closing words of v. 6 ("then the oil ceased"). Note further that Josephus rendering does away with the source's oscillation as to whether one or more of the women's sons was involved in the jar-filling process, see above.

In 2 Kgs 4,7a the woman comes and tells "the man of God" (so MT, BL). Josephus (9,49b) has her report "to the prophet" – see his previous use of this designation for Elisha in 9,48[19]. The Biblical story concludes in 4,7b with Elisha's double word to the woman: she is to sell the oil and pay off her debts, and then she and her sons may live off the remainder. Josephus (9,50a) reproduces both these items, introducing as well a reference to her "creditors" which echoes the reference to them in 9,47, while eliminating mention of the woman herself being supported by the surplus along with her children[20]. He then (9,50b) rounds off the episode with a notice that highlights the figure of Elisha and his beneficent, efficacious initative: "In this way, then, did Elisha free the woman of her debts and deliver (ἠλευθέρωσεν) her from the harsh treatment (ὕβρεως)[21] of her creditors (τῶν δανειστῶν, see 9,47)".

2. Elisha Preserved

The story of 2 Kgs 4,1-7 is followed by a long segment, 4,8–6,8[22] which has no parallel in our codices of AJ. Since J. Hudson[23] it has been generally recognized by editors and translators that a Josephan parallel to – at least some part – of the latter Biblical segment did once exist, but has fallen out in the course of the text's transmission[24]. For one thing,

19. Compare TJ 2 Kgs 4,7a: "the prophet of the Lord". On Josephus' (and TJ's) tendency to replace the Bible's phrase "man of God" with the more determinate designation "prophet", p. 35, n. 29.

20. Compare 9,47 where Josephus goes beyond the parallel 4,1 in having the woman represent herself too as being threatened with enslavement by her creditors.

21. This is Josephus' only use of the above construction "deliver from harsh treatment".

22. The content of this segment is as follows: 4,8-37 (Elisha's interactions with the Shunemite woman); 4,38-41 (Elisha detoxifies the pottage); 4,42-44 (Elisha multiplies bread); 5,1-27 (Elisha cures Naaman and afflicts Gehazi with leprosy); 6,1-7 (Elisha raises the axe head); 6,8 (introduction to the story of Elisha's preservation from the Syrians, 6,8-23).

23. Hudson's statement on the point is incorporated as a note to AJ 9,51 in J. HUDSON and S. HAVERCAMPUS, Flavii Josephi Opera Omnia I, Amsterdam, apud R. and G. Wetstenios, 1726.

24. Compare, however, the following statements on the matter: G. DELLING, Josephus und das Wundebare, in NovT 2 (1958), 291-309, p. 299, n. 4 "… ist es möglich, dass Josephus…. einige Wunder des Elisa gestrichen hat, weil sie ihm zu massiv oder sonst bedenklich erschienen, 2 Kön. 4,8-44; 5,1-27; 6,1-7…"; O. BETZ, Das Problem des Wunders bei Flavius Josephus im Vergleich zum Wunderproblem bei den Rabbinen und im Johannesevangelium, in O. BETZ, K. HAAKER, and M. HENGEL (eds.), Josephus-Studien (FS O. MICHEL), Göttingen, Vandenhoeck & Ruprecht, 1974, 23-44, p. 25 "… die meisten der in kleineren Kreisen spielenden Elisawunder lässt er einfach aus"; cf. similarly FELDMAN, Studies, p. 346 (= ID., Elisha, 22). These authors seem simply not to reckon with the possibility of a text-critical explanation for the absence of (some part of)

there would seem to be no reason for Josephus – who earlier (9,46) inserted a announcement of his intention of relating Elisha's acts as deeds "glorious and worthy of record" (see above) – to leave aside a whole series of such noteworthy performances by the prophet. In addition, the abrupt beginning of 9,51 in its extant form ("... Elisha sent word to Joram, warning him to beware of *that place*" = 2 Kgs 6,9) clearly presupposes that, at the least, something corresponding to the notice of 2 Kgs 6,8 (the Syrian king designates a certain "place" as his camp) once stood before it in *AJ*.

As just noted, Josephus' version of the story of Elisha's preservation from the Syrians begins (9,51a), at present, quite abruptly with mention of Elisha[25] warning Joram[26] "to beware of that place" (τὸν τόπον ἐκεῖνον; compare L τὸν τόπον τοῦτον). In 2 Kgs 6,9 this warning is motivated with reference to the fact of the "Syrians hiding (MT נְחִתִּים, B κέκρυπται) there". Josephus accentuates and clarifies the danger facing Joram: "for there... were some Syrians (Σύρους)[27] there lying in wait (λοχῶντας; compare L ἐνεδρεύουσιν) *to kill him*". 2 Kgs 6,10a represents the Israelite king "sending to the place of which the man of God (MT L; B Elisha; TJ the prophet of the Lord) told him". This formulation involves the seeming difficulty that the king "sends to" the very site of which he has just been told to "beware". Accordingly, Josephus (9,51b) words the king's response to Elisha's warning differently: "and so the king did not again start out for the hunt [which, one might understand, would have taken him to the ambush site][28], in obedience to the prophet (τῷ προφήτῃ πειθόμενος)". Streamlining matters, he has no equivalent to the notice of 6,10b: "Thus he (Elisha) used to warn him (the Israelite king), so that he saved himself there more than once or twice".

2 Kgs 6,11 recounts the consternation over the preceding developments on the part of the king of Syria who addresses his "servants" with

the material in question from Josephus' account. In this connection it might be noted as well that Josephus would have had every reason to make use, e.g., of 2 Kings 5's story of Elisha's cure of Naaman, the Syrian enemy of his people, given his interest throughout *AJ*, in counteracting contemporary claims that the Jews lacked concern for non-Jews, on which point see FELDMAN, *Studies*, pp. 557-558.

25. Josephus' use of the prophet's name here corresponds to the reading in B 6,9; MT and L have rather "the man of God" (compare TJ "the prophet of the Lord").

26. The "king of Israel" is nameless throughout the whole of 2 Kgs 6,8-7,20. Josephus derives the name "Joram" from 2 Kings 3 where it is this Israelite king (see vv. 12-13) who functions as Elisha's *Nebeneinander*.

27. Josephus' mention of the "Syrians" here agrees with L against the "Aram" of MT and "Syria" of B.

28. As MARCUS, *Josephus*, VI, p. 29, n. b points out, there is no mention of a "hunt" in the Bible itself. Perhaps, however, such a mention did stand in the material that once preceded 9,51 in Josephus' own presentation; see above.

the provocative question "will you not show me who of us (so MT
מִשֶּׁלָּנוּ; BL προδίδωσιν με) is for the king of Israel?" Josephus (9,52)
elaborates on the mental state which prompts the Syrian ruler's outburst:
"Then Adados[29], *having been unsuccessful in his plot, and thinking that
his own men had betrayed the plan of the ambush to Joram*, was enraged
(ὠργίζετο; compare 6,11: the mind of the king...was greatly troubled)...". In his presentation the king's question to his entourage (see
above) becomes a direct accusation of them, one with a threat attached
as well: "... he called them betrayers (προδότας, see BL προδίδωσιν
με) of his secrets, *and threatened them with death for having let the
attempt (on Joram's life), which he had entrusted to them alone, become
known to the enemy*".

In 2 Kgs 6,12 the Syrian king is answered by one of his servants as
follows: "None [are for the king of Israel]...; but Elisha the prophet
who is in Israel tells the king of Israel the words that you speak in your
bedchamber". Here again, Josephus (9,53) expatiates, while rewording
the (somewhat obscure) reference to the king's "bedchamber discourse": "But one of those present said *that he [Adados] was under a
false impression* (ψευδοδοξεῖν)[30] *and that he should not suspect them
of having told his enemy* (τὸν ἐχθρόν, i.e. Joram) *of the sending out of
the men who were to kill* (τῶν ἀναιρησόντων) *him*[31], but should know
that it was Elisha the prophet who had informed him (Joram) of everything and had revealed to him the things plotted by Adados".

At this point (6,13a) the Syrian king gives the directive "go and see
where he (Elisha) is, that I may send and seize him". Thereupon (6,13b),
"they" tell him that he is in "Dothan" (BL Δωθάειμ). In reporting
the king's order, Josephus leaves for a later point 6,13a's mention of
his intention in ascertaining the prophet's whereabouts. Conversely
(9,54a) he specifies that those who "tell" Adados of Elisha's being in
"Dothaein" (Δωθαείν)[32] are "the men who were sent". 2 Kgs 6,14 con-

---

29. The Syrian king is nameless throughout 2 Kgs 6,8-23. Josephus derives his name
from 2 Kgs 6,24 where MT calls him "Ben-hadad", BL υἱὸς Ἀδέρ. This monarch has
already figured in Josephus' account, i.e. in 8,363-392 (= 1 Kings 20, MT) and 8,398-420
(= 1 Kings 22 // 2 Chronicles 18). In his mention of him in 8,363 Josephus gives the king
his full name, i.e. "the son of Adados", while thereafter he uses the shortened form
"Adados" as here in 9,52.

30. This is Josephus' only use of the verb ψευδοδοξέω (MSPE Lat, followed by Dindorf and Bekker, read μὴ ψευδοδοξεῖν).

31. See Josephus' (inserted) reference to the Syrians lying in wait "to kill (ἀνελεῖν)
him (Joram)" in 9,51.

32. Thus the reading of the codices RO (which Niese, Marcus and SCHALIT, *Namenwörterbuch*, p. 40 follow); the other codices (as well as Dindorf, Bekker, and Naber) read
"Dothaeim" (Δωθαῖμ), cf. Δωθάειμ (BL).

cludes the exchange between the Syrian king and his retainers with the former dispatching horses (so MT L; B sg.) and chariot (so MT, B; L pl.) plus a "weigthy army" (BL δύναμιν βαρεῖαν) who surround "the city" (i.e. Dothan) by night. Josephus' version (9,54b) of the Syrian initiative is quite parallel: "... Adados sent (πέμπει)[33] to that city a great force (δύναμιν πολλήν) with horses (so MT L) and chariots (so L)[34] *in order to take Elisha*[35]. These surrounded the whole city by night (νυκτός, so BL) *and kept it under guard*".

In 2 Kgs 6,15a "the servant (BL ὁ λειτουργός) of the man of God (so MT L; B of Elisha; TJ of the prophet of the Lord)" sees "an army surrounding the city and horse(s) and chariot(s)" when he goes forth at dawn. 6,15b then relates the word with which "his (Elisha's) young man" (MT נַעֲרוֹ, BL τὸ παιδάριον) reacts to the sight: "Alas, my master! What shall we do"? In Josephus' version (9,54c) this figure is designated initially as "the servant (ὁ διάκονος) of the prophet (see TJ)[36]". Rather than reiterating the wording of 6,14 about the enemy force in describing what the servant "sees" (as does 6,15a), Josephus has him, in a reprise of the indication concerning the purpose of the Syrian expedition which he drew from 6,13a in 9,54b (see above), discover that "the enemy were seeking to take Elisha". He dramatizes as well the servant's reaction to his discovery: "... he came running to him (Elisha) with cries of alarm (μετὰ βοῆς καὶ ταραχῆς)[37] and informed him of these things[38]".

2 Kgs 6,16-17a narrates a double initiative by Elisha in response to the servant's outburst: he urges the other not to fear (v. 16) and then prays that God will "open his eyes that he may see" (v. 17a). In his version of this sequence ("but the prophet *encouraged* his servant, telling him not to be afraid [μὴ δεδιέναι; compare μὴ φοβοῦ, BL 6,16a]"), Josephus (9,55a) eliminates the reason Elisha cites in urging the servant not to fear as cited in v. 16b ("for those who are with us are more than

33. Here, as often, Josephus' historic present stands in contrast with the past form of BL, *in casu* ἀπέστειλεν.
34. Note that Josephus, like L 6,14, and against MT and B, uses pl. forms in designating both the Syrian horse and chariotry.
35. This specification concerning the purpose of the Syrian expedition has been "held over" by Josephus from 6,13a; see above.
36. Compare Josephus' same substitution of "the prophet" for the Biblical (MT BL) "man of God" in 9,49 (= 4,7).
37. This collocation occurs only here in Josephus.
38. The servant's informing Elisha of what he has seen (so Josephus) seems to make more sense in the context than does his question in 6,15b ("what shall we do?") since the prophet, who is not said to have "gone out" with the servant, would not know to what he is referring with the question.

those who are with them")[39]. Conversely, he expatiates on 6,17's reference to the prophet's prayer: "... he besought God, *with whom as ally* (συμμάχῳ)[40] *he was scornful of danger and without fear* (καταφρονῶν[41] ἀδεής)[42], to reveal, *so far as was possible,* His power and presence (ἐμφανίσαι τὴν αὐτοῦ δύναμιν καὶ παρουσίαν)[43] to his servant *in order that he might take hope and courage* (εὔελπι θάρσος)[44]". Josephus (9,55b) goes on to introduce his report of the positive divine response to Elisha's appeal (= 6,17b) with the transitional phrase "then God, hearkening to the prophet's prayers (ὁ δὲ θεὸς ἐπήκοος τῶν εὐχῶν ...)...[45]". The Biblical report itself speaks of the servant's seeing "the mountain full of horses and chariot(s) of fire round about Elisha". From this formulation, Josephus eliminates mention of both "the mountain" (this has not been cited previously) and the qualification of the "chariot(s)" as "of fire[46]". His version thus reads: "... (God) permitted his servant to behold a host of chariots and horses[47] in a circle around Elisha". To this notice he adds the indication that the vision did have its

39. Perhaps, Josephus passes over this element on the consideration that at this point, prior to the divine intervention, it might appear as a mere assertion on the prophet's part which, as such, would do nothing to remove the servant's fear. In any case, note that here in 9,55 Josephus employs a different term for "servant" (i.e. θεράποντα) than in 9,54 (διάκονος); compare the alternation between "servant" and "young man" in 2 Kgs 6,15.

40. Josephus uses the term σύμμαχος over 20x to designate God (the Deity) as the "ally" either of a whole people (the Jews, the Romans) or of an individual. Other key Biblical personages whom Josephus states had God as their "ally" are, e.g., Abraham (*AJ* 1,129), Moses (2,278), and David (6,189).

41. This is the reading adopted by Niese, Naber, and Marcus; Dindorf and Bekker read χρώμενος with P.

42. The above phrase occurs only here in Josephus; it serves to underscore the contrast between Elisha and his servant who must be admonished "not to be afraid".

43. With the above phrase compare *AJ* 8,109 where Solomon, in his address to the people on the occasion of the dedication of the Temple, employs the expression ἐμφανίζων τοῦ θεοῦ τὴν δύναμιν ... καὶ τὴν πρόνοιαν. On Josephus' use of the term παρουσία in reference to a divine self-manifestation, see SCHLATTER, *Theologie*, pp. 30-31.

44. The above construction occurs only here in Josephus. The historian's version of the prophet's prayer (compare 6,17a: "open his eyes that he may see") thus introduces an elaboration/ clarification both of what God is being asked to do ("reveal his power and presence") and the reason why he is being asked to do this ("in order that he [the servant] might take hope and courage").

45. In *AJ* Josephus uses the term ἐπήκοος 12x with God as subject. With the above construction compare especially 6,25 ἐπήκοος δὲ γίνεται τῶν εὐχῶν ὁ θεός (i.e. of Samuel).

46. With this elimination Josephus gives the servant's vision a less "fantastic" character. (Compare his – greatly abridged – version of Elijah's "translation" in 9,28 where he leaves aside the similar mention, in 2 Kgs 2,11, of the "chariot and horses of fire" which separate Elijah and Elisha.) See FELDMAN, *Studies*, p. 346 (= ID., *Elisha*, 23).

47. This sequence is the reverse of that in 6,17b (and also of 9,54 where Josephus refers to the Syrian "horses and chariots"; see above). Note too that while the Bible has the sg. "chariot", Josephus reads a pl. form in line with his mention of "horses".

intended effect: "... so that he [the servant] lost his fear (τὸ δέος; cf. μὴ δεδιέναι, 9,55a) and took new courage (ἀναθαρσῆσαι; cf. θάρσος, 9,55a) at the sight of what seemed a host of allies (συμμαχίας)[48]".

2 Kgs 6,18a speaks of the Syrians "coming down against" Elisha who responds by praying that God will smite them with blindness. Josephus passes over – for the moment (but see below) – the source's mention of the Syrian advance, proceeding immediately to the prophet's appeal; thereby, he highlights the stature of Elisha as the one who takes the initiative at this juncture. In his version of the prophet's prayer itself (9,56a), Elisha requests God (Bible: the Lord) "to blind (ἀμαυρῶσαι, BL πάταξον ... ἀορασίᾳ)[49] the eyes of the enemy (Bible: this people) *and throw a mist (ἀχλύν)*[50] *about them through which they would be unable to see him*". 2 Kgs 6,18b notes that the Lord did act "in accordance with the word of Elisha". Between his corresponding fulfillment notice ("when this too was done...") and his parallel to Elisha's address to the Syrians in 6,19, the historian (9,56b) inserts mention of the prophet's "coming into the midst of the foe". This item might be regarded as the historian's (delayed) replacement for 6,18a's reference to the Syrians' "coming down against" Elisha: given their blinded state, they are in no condition to advance towards him, so he goes out to them. Here again, Josephus contrives to assign the initiative to Elisha.

In his word to the Syrians in 6,19a Elisha begins by informing them that "this is not the way, and this is not the city". Josephus substitutes for this formulation – with its indeterminate reference to "the (which?) way" and "the (which?) city" – an opening dialogue between prophet and the Syrians: "he asked them whom they had come in search of (ἐπιζητοῦντες)[51]. When they said it was the prophet Elisha...". He then continues (9,56c) with his version of Elisha's word (6,19aβ) urging the Syrians to "come after" (BL δεῦτε ὀπίσω) him as he brings them to their query. This reads: "... he promised to deliver him if they would follow him (ἀκολουθήσειαν αὐτῷ)[52] to the city (τὴν

48. This term picks up the reference to God as Elisha's "ally" (συμμάχῳ) in 9,55a.

49. Josephus' wording here consitutes a verbal echo of *AJ* 1,202: "God blinded" (ἠμαύρωσεν) the Sodomites. The historian's one remaining use of the verb ἀμαυρόω is in *AJ* 8,268 where the eyes of the prophet Ahijah are said to be "blinded" with age.

50. Josephus' only two uses of the word ἀχλύς are here in 9,56 and immediately thereafter in 9,57. MARCUS, *Josephus*, VI, p. 31, n. c qualifies this item as "a rationalistic detail added by Josephus"; similarly FELDMAN, *Studies*, p. 346 (= ID., *Elisha*, p. 23).

51. Josephus' inspiration for this element appears to be the prophet's word as cited in 6,19ba: "I will bring you to the man whom you seek (BL ζετεῖτε)".

52. G. KITTEL, ἀκολουθέω κτλ, in *TWNT* 2 (1935), 210-216, p. 211 notes that Josephus, in line with non-Biblical Greek usage, regularly avoids the "Semiticizing" phrase "come after" of 2 Kgs 6,19 in favor of ἀκολουθέω + dative, the construction one finds above.

πόλιν)[53] where he happened to be". 2 Kgs 6,19b laconically notes the result of Elisha's proposal: "and he led them to Samaria". Once more, Josephus (9,57a) expatiates, adding a remark as to how it was that the Syrians, in the country of their enemies, do as suggested without misgiving: "*And so, with their eyes and understanding beclouded* (ἐπεσκοτημένοι) *by God*[54], they *eagerly* went with the prophet, who led the way".

2 Kgs 6,20a records the prayer pronounced by Elisha immediately upon arriving in Samaria; in it, he asks, in language reminiscent of his earlier petition on behalf of his servant (see 6,17a), that the Lord "open" the Syrians' eyes that they might "see". Josephus accentuates (9,57b) the prophet's foresight and authority by having him, in first place, issue instructions about the necessary precautionary measures to be taken with regard to the Syrian force: "When Elisha had brought them to Samaria, *he ordered King Joram*[55] *to shut the gates* (πυλάς)[56] *and place his own army around the Syrians*[57]". His version of the prophet's prayer (9,57c) then picks up on Elisha's earlier (Biblically unparalleled) request (see 9,56) that God envelop the Syrians in a "mist": "then he prayed to God to clear the eyes of the enemy *and remove the mist* (ἀχλύν; see 9,56) *from before them*". In 6,20b the Lord does as Elisha had asked with the result that the Syrians realize that they are "in the midst of Samaria". Josephus' parallel (9,57d) runs: "... when they were freed from their blindness (ἀμαυρώσεως)[58], they saw that they were in the midst of their foes[59]".

53. Compare 6,19aα: "this is not the city (BL ἡ πόλις)".

54. Josephus uses the verb ἐπισκοτέω with God as subject also in *BJ* 5,343 (object: "counsels"); its other occurrences in his corpus are in *BJ* 5,246; *AJ* 5,205; 8,106; *c. Ap.* 1,214. Note the emphasis on the divine involvement in the affair introduced by this insertion. Compare the (also non-Biblical) affirmation Josephus attributes to Elisha in 9,48 "God, he said, would fill them [the vessels]".

55. Recall Josephus' (Biblically unparalleled) mention of the king by name already in 9,51.52.

56. This is the reading adopted by Niese, Naber and Marcus. Dindorf and Bekker read θύρας with MSP.

57. On the above sequence as indicative of Elisha's heightened military acumen in Josephus' presentation, see FELDMAN, *Studies*, p. 339 (= ID., *Elisha*, 11).

58. Compare ἀμαυρῶσαι (9,56). The noun form ἀμαύρωσις here in 9,58 is hapax in Josephus.

59. This reference to the Syrians being "in the midst of their enemies" (ἐν μέσοις τοῖς ἐχθροῖς) accentuates the danger facing them vis-à-vis the more "neutral" expression of 6,20, i.e. "in the midst of Samaria". Josephus' formulation here likewise echoes his previous mention (9,56) of Elisha's own "coming into the midst of the foe (εἰς μέσους τοὺς ἐχθρούς)". In this connection it might be noted that throughout his version of 2 Kgs 6,8-23 in 9,51-59, Josephus constantly underscores the hostility existing between the Israelites and Syrians via his (non-Biblical) designation of one or other group as the "enemies" and "foes" (see 9,54.56.57) of the other. Given this emphasis, Israel's eventual sparing of the defenceless Syrians (see below) appears all the more remarkable.

To this notice he appends (9,58a) a remark of his own on the Syrians'
emotional reaction to their "realization" which, at the same time, insists
on the miraculous character of what has befallen them: "Then, while the
Syrians, as was natural, were in dire consternation and helplessness (ἐν
ἐκπλήξει ... δεινῇ καὶ ἀμηχανίᾳ)⁶⁰ at so divine and marvelous (θείῳ
καὶ παραδόξῳ)⁶¹ an event...". Following this inserted transitional
phrase, Josephus proceeds to recount the Israelite king's request for
instructions from Elisha (compare 6,21 "[My, so MT] father, shall I slay
[BL πατάξω] them? Shall I slay them? [L lacks the double use of the
same verb as found in MT and B])". His wording of this item reads: "...
King Joram [Bible: the king of Israel] asked the prophet [MT L said to
Elisha; B lacks this specification of the addressee] whether it was his bidding that they be shot down (κατακοντισθῆναι)⁶²". Elisha's answer to
the king's query in 6,22 comprises three elements: prohibition of killing
the Syrians, rhetorical question expecting a negative answer ("would you
slay those whom you have [L + not] taken captive with your sword and
with you bow?"), and positive injunctions about provisioning and releasing the captives. Josephus substitutes (9,58b) a narrative notice for the
prophet's opening prohibition ("you shall not slay them"): "... Elisha
prevented (ἐκώλυσε)⁶³ him from doing this". He goes on to turn the
Bible's following rhetorical question into an expanded statement by
Elisha whose initial content reverses the thrust of that question (i.e. not
even prisoners taken in battle are to be put to death), while its (un-Biblical) continuation supplies a motivation for the special treatment of the
Syrian enemy recommended by the prophet on this occasion: "... it was
right to kill those who were captured by the law of war (compare the
rhetorical question of 6,22 as cited above)⁶⁴, *but that these men had done*

60. This is Josephus' only use of the above collocation; the expression "dire consternation" recurs in *BJ* 2,538; 6,180.
61. This same collocation "divine and marvellous" is used by Josephus with reference to the manna in *AJ* 3,30 and of God's "providence" in 10,214.
62. This verb is more definite than the "smite" of 6,21. Note that his reference to the
presence of Joram here as well as the king's invocation of the military force available to
him has been "set up" by Josephus via his insertion in 9,57 where Elisha "ordered King
Joram to... place his own army around the Syrians". In the Bible, by contrast, these items
seem to surface abruptly in 6,21 since in what precedes there has been no mention of
either the Israelite king himself or his forces being on hand in Samaria for the Syrians'
arrival.
63. With this reference to Elisha's "preventing" a king from doing something, compare
AJ 7,371 ("God through the prophet Nathan prevented [ἐκώλυσε] David" from building
the Temple) and 8,223 (Rehoboam was "prevented (κωλυθείς) by God through the
prophet [Shemaiah] from undertaking the campaign" [i.e. against the rebel Jeroboam]).
64. Perhaps, Josephus read Elisha's (unpunctuated) question of 6,22 as a statement:
"... you do slay those whom you have taken captive...". Another possibility is that he is
conforming Elisha's word to the practice of his own time with regard to prisoners of war.

no harm to his country and, without knowing it, had come to them by the power of God (θεία[65]... δυνάμει)". Finally, for the conclusion of Elisha's reply, Josephus (9,59a) aligns himself more closely with the Biblical wording: "He also counselled him to offer them hospitality (ξενίων) and food and send them away unhurt (ἀβλαβεῖς)".

2 Kgs 6,23a recounts the Israelite king's preparing the Syrians "a great feast", his dismissal of them, and their return to their "master". Josephus (9,59b) introduces his parallel with an inserted transitional phrase which underscores, yet again (see n. 63) the king's submission to the prophet: "And so Joram, in obedience to the prophet's advice (τῷ προφήτῃ πειθόμενος)...[66]". He then goes on to accentuate the hospitality provided the Syrians by Joram: ".... he entertained the Syrians very splendidly and lavishly (ἑστιάσας λαμπρῶς πάνυ καὶ φιλοτίμως[67])[68] and sent them back to *Adados* their king (τὸν αὐτῶν βασιλέα, BL τὸν κύριον αὐτῶν)". The Biblical account of Elisha's preservation (6,8-23) concludes with the notice of 6,23b: "and the Syrians came no more into the land of Israel". Josephus works his version of this item into his introduction to the following episode, see below.

3. *Elisha's Word Fulfilled*

2 Kgs 6,24–7,20 (= *AJ* 9,60-86) constitutes an extended narration of the fulfilment of a word spoken by Elisha on the occasion of the Syrian siege of Samaria. In Kings the juxtaposition of the opening of this account with the conclusion of the preceding one generates a certain

65. This term echoes Josephus' reference to the "divine (θείῳ) and marvelous event" earlier in 9,58 (Josephus' other uses of the phrase "divine power" are in *AJ* 18,288; 19,69). Note the continued emphasis on God's involvement in the episode.

66. This is the same phrase used in 9,51 in reference to Joram's "not starting out for the hunt" in response to Elisha's warning. Josephus' double use of the phrase within our pericope serves to depict Joram as one who is ready to obey Elisha in all matters.

67. The above collocation "spendidly and lavishly" is used by Josephus also in *AJ* 9,272; 15,194 (reverse order).

68. The wording used by Josephus in reference to Joram's entertaining of the Syrians here in 9,59 echoes that employed by him in recounting the hospitality shown each other by the kings of Israel and Judah; see 8,398 (= 2 Chr 18,2: Ahab gave Jehoshaphat "a friendly [φιλοφρόνως] welcome and splendidly entertained [ἐξένισε λαμπρῶς] the army which had accompanied him...") and 9,31 (no Biblical parallel: Joram "is splendidly entertained [ξενισθεὶς λαμπρῶς]" by Jehoshaphat in Jerusalem); cf. also 7,30 and 10,168. This similarity of language between 9,58 on the one hand and 8,398; 9,31 on the other serves to underscore the point that the Jewish kings treated their hapless captive enemies with the same largess they displayed to one another. That point, in turn, represents an implicit rebutal of contemporary claims that the Jews confined their benefactions to their own people; see FELDMAN, *Studies*, p. 333 (= ID., *Jehoram*, 14).

tension: whereas 6,23b (see above) affirms the end of Syrian invasions of Israel, immediately thereafter in 6,24 one hears of Ben-hadad besieging Samaria with his entire army. As Weill[69] and Marcus[70] point out, Josephus, seemingly aware of the difficulty, attempts to resolve it by means of the lengthy transitional remark (9,60) which he introduces prior to his reproduction of the notice of 6,24 in 9,61. This remark reads:

> But, when they [the released Syrians] came and informed him of what had happened, Adados was amazed at the marvel (τὸ παράδοξον; cf. παραδόξῳ πράγματι, 9,58) and the manifestation (ἐπιφάνειαν)[71] of the God of the Israelites (τοῦ θεοῦ τῶν Ἰσραηλιτῶν)[72] and His power (δύναμιν; see θείᾳ ... δυνάμει, 9,58)[73], and also at the prophet, with whom the Deity was so evidently (ἐναργῶς)[74] present (παρῆν)[75]; and so, because of his fear (δεδοικώς) of Elisha[76], he determined to make no more secret attempts on the life of the Israelite king, but decided to fight openly, in the belief that he would overcome the enemy by the numbers and strength of his army.

In the above formulation, it will be noted, Josephus disposes of the discrepancy between 6,23b and 6,24 by means of a distinction between "secret" (i.e. like that described in 6,8-12 = 9,51-53a) and "open" Syrian attacks on Israel, its king in particular. Adados' shift from the one tactic to the other is, in turn, motivated, on the one hand, by his "fear of Elisha" and, on the other, by his confidence in the superiority of his own forces. In addition, the Josephan insertion serves, as do so many other elements of his presentation, to accentuate the status of Elisha as one "with whom the Deity was so evidently present".

69. *Josèphe*, II, p. 258, n. 2.

70. *Josephus*, VI, p. 34, n. a.

71. On Josephus' use of the term ἐπιφάνεια (ἐμφάνεια) in connection with Biblical "miracles", see G. MacRae, "*Miracle in the* Antiquities *of Josephus*, in C.F.D. Moule (ed.), *Miracles: Cambridge Studies in their Philosophy and History*, Cambridge, Cambridge University Press, 1965, pp. 129-147, esp. 144-147.

72. Josephus uses this same designation for the Deity in 9,21; see there. Compare ὁ τῶν Ἑβραίων θεός, 9,20. The expression "manifestation of God" recurs in *AJ* 2,339; 3,310 (18,286).

73. The above collocation "manifestation and power" recurs once elsewhere in Josephus, i.e. in *AJ* 17,96.

74. Elsewhere Josephus uses the term ἐναργής in reference to God in *AJ* 1,279; 2,345; 18,286; *c. Ap.* 2,190.

75. Note the verbal reminiscences in the above formulation of the prayer Josephus attributes to Elisha on behalf of his servant in 9,55 where he requests God ἐμφανίσαι τὴν αὐτοῦ δύναμιν καὶ παρουσίαν.

76. Compare 9,55 where Elisha himself is said to be "without fear (ἀδεής)" in the face of the forces sent against him by Adados.

In 2 Kgs 6,24 Ben-hadad (BL υἱὸς Ἀδέρ)[77] musters his whole army and "besieges Samaria". In line with his previous notice on Adados' shift of approach in his effort to destroy Joram (see above), Josephus here (9,61a) initially (but see below) "personalizes" the target of the Syrian advance: "he marched with a great force *against Joram* (στρατεύει[78]... ἐπὶ τὸν Ἰώραμον)[79]". Josephus' wording here echoes that used by him in describing an earlier incursion by Adados directed against Joram's father; see 8,363: "he marched against Achab" (ἐστράτευσεν ἐπὶ τὸν Ἄχαβον; contrast 1 Kgs 20 (BL 21),1: "he besieged Samaria"); in both instances Josephus replaces a Biblical reference to a Syrian siege of Samaria with mention of the reigning Israelite king as Adados' specific target. The historian proceeds to introduce a further echo of that earlier account of his with the insertion of the following ("non-Biblical") notice here in 9,61: "... (Joram) not thinking himself a match for the Syrians, shut himself up in Samaria, relying on the strength of its walls"; compare 8,364 (likewise no Biblical parallel): "(Ahab) not having a army equal to his (Adados')... remained in Samaria, for this city was surrounded by exceedingly strong walls...". I would suggest then that in both 9,61 and 8,364 Josephus introduces a reference to an Israelite king's deliberately taking up a position in strongly-walled Samaria in order to counter an impression that the respective Biblical parallels might evoke, i.e. the Syrian army was allowed to penetrate all the way to Israel's capital without resistance due to negligence and/or cowardice on the part of the Israelite king[80]. Thereafter, he does, finally, present his parallel (9,61b) to 6,24, amplifying its notice on the Syrian siege of Samaria, however, with mention of the considerations that influenced Adados to venture a siege of that well-fortified site: *"But Adados, who counted on capturing the city, if not by engines* (μηχανήμασι)[81],

---

77. Recall that the name of the Syrian king is nowhere mentioned in the preceding narrative of 2 Kgs 6,8-23. Josephus, by contrast, has cited the name "Adados" several times over the course of his parallel to 6,8-23 in 9,51-59(60).

78. Note the historic present; see n. 33.

79. Josephus' specification that it was precisely "against Joram" that Adados set out puts the latter in all the more reprehensible a light in that it was this same Joram who, immediately before this, had sent back unharmed to Adados a mass of captive Syrians. Here then, it is not the Jews (so the contemporary canard) who appear to lack any sense of fellow-feeling in their dealings with other peoples, but rather the Gentile Syrians in their response to Joram's good deed in their regard.

80. In so doing Josephus would be providing an implicit response to contemporary claims that the Jews were a people of no military aptitude or distinction; see FEDLMAN, *Studies*, p. 323 (= ID., *Jehoram*, 8-9).

81. Josephus' reference to siege "engines" here might reflect military practice of his own time – note the frequent mention of such engines in *BJ*. Note too his repeated reference to the "engines" employed by the Babylonians in their siege of Jerusalem in 10,132-133 of which the Biblical sources (2 Kings 25 // 2 Chronicles 36) know nothing.

at any rate by bringing the Samaritans (τοὺς Σαμαρεῖς)[82] *to terms through famine and the lack of provisions* (λιμῷ ... καὶ σπάνει τῶν ἐπιτηδείων)[83], moved up his men and besieged (ἐπολιόρκει)[84] the city".

2 Kgs 6,25 speaks of the "great famine" which ravaged Samaria "until an ass's head was sold for eighty (so MT; BL 50) (L + shekels) of silver, and the fourth part of a kab of dove's dung for five (L + shekels) of silver". Josephus, who has already "anticipated" the verse's reference to "famine" (see n. 83), elaborates (9,62) its opening formulation as follows: "And Joram's supply of necessities (ἡ τῶν ἀναγκαίων εὐπορία)[85] was reduced to such an extent that through the excessive lack of food (δι' ὑπερβολὴν τῆς ἐνδείας)...[86]". In accordance with the higher MT figure he then goes to mention an "ass's head" (κεφαλὴν ὄνου = L) being sold for eighty (BL fifty) pieces of silver. In citing thereafter the "dove's dung" (κόπρου περιστερῶν = BL) for which "the Hebrews"[87] paid "five pieces of silver (ἀργυρῶν νομίσματος, L σίκλων ἀργυρίου)", he converts the Biblical measure of quantity (i.e. MT "the fourth part of a kab"; BL transliterates) into one more familiar to his audience, i.e. "a sextarius" (ξέστην)[88]. He likewise appends an indication as to the intended use of the dove's dung, i.e. "for salt".

In 2 Kgs 6,26 "the king of Israel" makes an abrupt first appearance in our episode; while "passing by on the wall", he is accosted by a woman who appeals for his help. Josephus (who has already introduced Joram by name at the start of his version of 6,24–7,20; see 9,61) amplifies

82. According to MARCUS, *Josephus*, VI, p. 55, n. c this designation is "more appropriate to the inhabitants of Samaria after the Babylonian Exile". R. EGGER, *Josephus Flavius und die Samaritaner* (NTOA, 4), Freiburg, Universitätsverlag; Göttingen, Vandenhoeck & Ruprecht, 1986, p. 117, n. 316 points out, however, with reference to *BJ* 1,65; *AJ* 9,61.125f.; 13,275.276.277, that the above form is the one invariably used by Josephus when referring to the inhabitants of the city of Samaria of whatever period, whereas he never employs Σαμαρεῖται in this sense.

83. Josephus' invocation here of the prospect of "famine" as that on which Adados relies in besieging Samaria is inspired by 2 Kgs 6,25 which speaks of the "great famine" that ravaged the city as the siege proceeds. The above collocation "famine and lack" recurs in *AJ* 4,127; 5,212; 14,475 (here with the full phrase "lack of provisions" as in 9,61).

84. This term represents another verbal echo of Josephus' description of Adados' earlier siege of Samaria, the same form occurring in 8,364.

85. This expression is hapax in Josephus.

86. This expression is hapax in Josephus.

87. Here, as, e.g., in *AJ* 8,381, Josephus uses this designation specifically in reference to the inhabitants of the Northern kingdom (= "the Israelites").

88. In *AJ* 8,57 in his version of 3 Rgns 5,14 which speaks of the 20,000 "baths" (MT [5,25] has "twenty cors") of oil Solomon gave Hiram, Josephus states that the Biblical "bath" contained "seventy-two *sextarii* (ξέστας)".

(9,63) the Biblical reference to the king's "passage" with mention of the reasons prompting his presence on the wall:

> And Joram was in constant fear (ἐν φόβῳ)[89] that, because of the famine (λιμόν; see λιμῷ, 9,61), someone might betray (προδῷ)[90] the city to the enemy, and every day he would walk all around the walls to the guards, spying out (σκεπτόμενος) whether any of the enemy were within the city, and by his appearance and precautions preventing any (citizen) even from wishing such a thing, or from acting on it if he had already formed such a plan[91].

Following this expansion, Josephus (9,64a) comes to relate the content of 6,26b, i.e. the woman's "crying out" to the king. In the Bible her word runs "help (so MT; B σῶσον, L σωσόν με), my lord, O king"! Josephus renders "have pity (ἐλέησον)[92], my lord (δέσποτα)[93]". 2 Kgs 6,27 moves immediately to the words with which the king responds to his suppliant. Josephus inserts a reference to the emotional affect of her words upon Joram and the reason for his feeling as he does towards her: "... he was angered (ὀργισθείς), thinking that she was about to beg for food or the like...[94]". According to 6,27 the king begins his response "if the Lord (will) not help you (thus RSV, MT אַל־יוֹשִׁעֵךְ יְהוָה[95]; L μὴ σῶσαι σε ὁ κύριος), whence shall I help you?". Josephus turns the king's words into the notice that "... he called down God's curse (ἐπηράσατο ... τὸν θεόν) upon her[96]". The continuation of the king's response in 6,27 is a further (rhetorical) question, alluding to two

---

89. Joram's "fear" here recalls that of Adados regarding Elisha (9,60). In their fear both kings stand in contrast with the prophet himself who is said to be "without fear" (9,55).

90. This term echoes the formulation in 9,52 where Adados accuses his retine of being "betrayers (προδότας) of his secrets".

91. With the above elaboration of the Biblical datum about the king's walking on the walls, Josephus, in line with his previous insertion about Joram's shutting himself up in strong-walled Samaria (9,61), continues his portrayal of the king as a careful, alert commander who takes a range of deliberate initiatives in the face of the Syrian threat. See FELDMAN, *Studies*, p. 324 (= ID., *Jehoram*, 9); cf. n. 80.

92. In attributing this word to the woman, Josephus echoes his notice on the widow of Obadiah in 9,47: "she besought him (Elisha) to pity (ἐλεῆσαι) her". See also 9,25 where the third captain begs Elijah to "have pity (ἐλεῆσαι) on him and his men".

93. The codices MSP add κύριε. Compare BL κύριε βασιλεῦ.

94. This supposition on the king's part as to what the woman will be asking of him is, of course, a natural one given what Josephus has previously described of the progress of the famine. Compare Josephus' – likewise interjected – qualification of Adados as "enraged" (ὠργίζετο) at the (supposed) betrayal of his secrets to the Israelites, 9,52.

95. On the problem of the grammatical understanding of the Hebrew and its translation here, see the commentaries.

96. As usual, Josephus avoids actually citing the actual wording of a personage's curse or oath here; see p. 54, n. 29.

sources of "help" that, at present, are unavailable to him: "… from the threshing floor (ἅλωνος, B) or from the wine press (BL ληνοῦ)"? Josephus rewords the question into an emphatic assertion by Joram: "… saying that he had neither threshing-floor (ἅλως)[97] nor wine-press (ληνούς) from which he might give her something at her entreaty". In 6,28a the king passes directly from the reproachful questions of 6,27 to asking the woman about her "trouble" which she then begins immediately to present in detail (6,28b). Josephus (9,65a) smooths the movement from one part of Joram's response to the other by introducing mention of the woman's assurance that she is not, in fact, asking for the "impossibilities" to which he has just alluded: "she said that she needed none of these things nor was she troubling him about food". Thereupon, he reverses the sequence of 6,28: it is only once the woman has first alluded in a general way to what it is she does want from the king ("she begged, however, that her case against another woman be judged"; cf. 6,28b), that he "bade her speak and inform him of what she wanted" (= 6,28a)[98].

2 Kgs 6,28b-29 constitutes the woman's presentation of her case. She begins by quoting the words of the other woman she is accusing: "Give your son, that we may eat him today, and we will eat my son tomorrow" (v. 28b). Josephus (9,65b) amplifies this report of the "defendant's" proposal in several respects: "… *she had made an agreement with the other woman, who was her neighbor and friend* (γειτνιώσης καὶ φίλης)[99], *that, since the conditions of famine and need* (λιμοῦ [see 9,61.63] καὶ … ἐνδείας [see 9,62]) *had become impossible to bear*[100], they should make an end of their children – *each had a son* – and 'we[101] were each in turn to feed the other for one day'". The speaker continues in 6,29a, stating "we boiled (BL ἡψήσαμεν) and ate him". Josephus (9,66a) renders:

97. Thus the conjecture of Niese, followed by Naber and Marcus, for the ἅλωας of the codices and the Epitome which Dindorf and Bekker adopt.

98. By means of this reversal of the Biblical sequence, Josephus provides a further motivation for the king's allowing the woman – whose initial intervention so upset him – to continue, i.e. he already has some idea of what is going to be told him.

99. With his introduction of the two items italicized above, Josephus underscores the injustice done to the plaintiff by the other woman in withholding her son from her: there was an actual "agreement" between them which the latter was all the more bound to honor given their intimate relationship. The above collocation "neighbor and friend" occurs once elsewhere in Josephus, i.e. AJ 1,176 where it used in the plural (and in reverse order) of Abraham's relationship to the people of Sodom.

100. With this insertion Josephus supplies a motivation for the woman's so "unmaternal" initiative, one which itself picks up on his earlier accentuation of the severity of the famine.

101. Note the shift from initial indirect to direct discourse here within the woman's single speech.

"'I first slaughtered (κατέσφαξα) my son[102], and we both made a meal of him yesterday'". The speaker's testimony concludes in 6,29b with her charge that, when summoned the next day to hand over her son to be eaten, the other women "hid" him. Josephus' version (9,66b) expatiates on this concluding charge, once again invoking the "agreement" between the two women: "... *and now she will not do the same, but has broken the agreement* (παραβαίνει τὴν συνθήκην)[103] and put her son out of sight'". 2 Kgs 6,30 describes the king's reaction to his hearing of the woman's case: he rends his clothes with the result that, given his position on the wall (see 6,26), the people observe the "sackcloth" which he has under them. In view of the fact that the latter item represents a "blind motif" of which nothing further is said in the course of the narrative, it is not surprising that Josephus leaves it aside without more ado. Conversely, however, he elaborates (9,67a) on the king's reaction to what he has just heard, noting both its inner and external dimensions: "This *grieved Joram sorely* (ἐλύπησε σφοδρῶς)[104] when he heard it, and he tore his garment in pieces (περιρρηξάμενος τὴν ἐσθῆτα; BL διέρρηξεν τὰ ἱμάτια αὐτοῦ) *and cried out fearfully* (δεινόν)[105]". In 2 Kgs 6,31 the king shifts, quite abruptly, from rending his garments (6,30) to pronouncing a conditional self-curse ("May God do so to me, and more also...") should he allow Elisha's head "to remain on his shoulders that day". Josephus supplies (9,67b) both an indication of the king's mental state at this juncture and an elaborate motivation for Joram's sudden outburst against Elisha: "then, *being filled with wrath* (ὀργῆς ... πληρωθείς; see ὀργισθείς, 9,64) against the prophet Elisha, he was bent on doing away with him[106] *because he did not ask God* (δεῖται τοῦ θεοῦ)[107] *to give them*

102. In 6,29a the "preparation" of the first son is a joint effort by the two women. Josephus has the boy's mother act alone, thereby underscoring how readily she carried out her side of the agreement. Also in contrast to the Bible, Josephus appears to represent the mothers as eating the child "raw" rather than "cooked", a *Steigerung* of the horror of the episode which might, in turn, have been suggested by the consideration that, given the severity of conditions in the city, there would not have been sufficient water and/or fuel available to "boil" the lad's body.

103. The above expression recurs in *BJ* 6,320 (with the genitive); *AJ* 2,253; 4,118.

104. Compare Josephus' – also inserted – reference to Joram's being "angered" at the woman's opening words to him in his version of 2 Kgs 6,27 in 9,64.

105. With this term Josephus echoes his reference (9,58) to the Syrians' "dire (δεινῇ) consternation" at finding themselves in the hands of the Israelites at Samaria. Now their one-time captor, Joram, has been reduced to a similar state.

106. With the above formulation Josephus, once again (see n. 96), avoids reproducing the words of a Biblical oath, *in casu* that of 6,31.

107. The above genitival construction is used in *AJ* 5,201 of the prophetess Deborah who is besought by the Israelites "to pray God to take pity on them and not to suffer them to be destroyed by the Canaanites". It recurs in 10,12 where Hezekiah asks the prophet Isaiah "to pray God" in view of the Assyrian threat. In light of these parallels,

a way out and an escape from the ills (διαφυγὴν ... τῶν κακῶν)[108] *that surrounded them...*". Following this inserted remark, the historian converts the king's statement of his resolve to have Elisha's head forthwith as reported in 6,31 into a narrative notice, which, in turn, he combines with an anticipated version of the parenthetical remark of 6,32aβ (see below) about the king's "dispatch" of the executioner (L 6,32 specifies the king as the subject of the "sending" while MT and B do not). This conflated formulation (9,67c) reads: "... he at once sent out a man to cut off (ἀποτεμοῦντα) his head. And so this man hurried off to make away with the prophet".

In 6,32a the scene shifts to Elisha's house where "the elders" are sitting with him. Prior to the appearance of the king's messenger, the prophet asks these elders if they realize that "this murderer" (i.e. the king) has sent to behead him, and then directs them to shut the door against the messenger whose master's "feet" are following him (v. 32b). Josephus (9,68) rearranges the elements of the lengthy Biblical verse so as to throw into relief the prophet's clairvoyance: "But Elisha was not unaware (οὐκ ἔλαθεν)[109] of the king's wrath (ὀργή)[110]..."; compare 6,32bα: "before the messenger came to him, Elisha said to the elders...". To this statement he then attaches 6,32's opening reference to the "session" at Elisha's house; in his version the "elders" who are keeping the prophet company become his "disciples" (μαθηταῖς)[111]. In addressing these "disciples", Elisha, in virtue of his clairvoyance, begins by "warning" them that "Joram, the son of the murderer (ὁ τοῦ φονέως υἱός)[112], had sent someone to take off (ἀφαιρήσοντα; BL ἀφελεῖν)[113] his head". For the continuation of the prophet's discourse,

the anger Josephus attributes to Joram towards the prophet Elisha here during the Syrian siege appears more understandable (and justified) than in the Bible itself in that he (Elisha) has failed to do the thing expected of prophets in such circumstances, i.e. "pray God".

108. The expression "way out of evil(s)" recurs in *AJ* 18,175.

109. This construction echoes *AJ* 8,269 where the prophet Ahijah says to the wife of Jeroboam "your coming here is not unknown (οὐ λανθάνεις) to God".

110. This reference picks up on Josephus' previous statement (9,67) that Joram was "full of wrath (ὀργῆς)" at Elisha for his failure to petition God.

111. Earlier (see 8,354; 9,28.33) Josephus qualified Elisha as Elijah's "disciple". Now Elisha has "disciples" of his own.

112. In 6,32 "this son of the murderer" (BL ὁ υἱὸς τοῦ φονευτοῦ [L + οὗτος]) is a Semitic idiom meaning "this murderer" (so RSV) and designates Joram himself. Josephus, whether by design or not, takes the phrase in its "literal" sense; thereby, Joram becomes, not himself a "murderer" but the "son of" one, i.e. Ahab who was responsible for the judicial murder of Naboth; see 1 Kings 21 and cf. MARCUS, *Josephus*, VI, p. 37, n. d.

113. Note the variation in the participles used for the "removal" of Elisha's head in 9,67 (ἀποτεμοῦντα) and 68 (ἀφαιρήσοντα).

Josephus (9,69a) has him switch to direct address[114]: "'But you (the disciples)', he said, 'when the man [6,32: the messenger] arrives who has been given this order, be on guard as he is about to enter, and press him back against the door (προσαποθλίψατε τῇ θύρᾳ; B παραθλίψατε αὐτὸν ἐν τῇ θύρᾳ) and hold him there, *for* the king will follow him and come to me[115], *having changed his mind* (μεταβεβουλευμένος)[116]'".

2 Kgs 6,33a relates that while Elisha is still speaking, "the messenger" (MT הַמַּלְאָךְ [= L; B "a messenger"]; BHS proposes to emend MT's form to הַמֶּלֶךְ, "the king", see 7,17) does arrive. He (or the king himself?) then pronounces the words of 6,33b: "behold this evil is from the Lord! Why should I wait for the Lord any longer?". In Josephus (9,69b), this presentation undergoes significant alteration and expansion. Specifically, we are first informed that that when the king's man arrived, the prophet's "disciples" (see 9,68) dealt with him as Elisha had directed. Next, Josephus (9,70a) relates the fulfillment also of Elisha's closing prediction about the coming of the king (see above), expanding this with mention of the motivation for his coming: "But Joram, *repenting* (καταγνούς) *of his wrath against the prophet* (τῆς ἐπὶ τὸν προφήτην ὀργῆς; compare ὀργῆς ἐπὶ τὸν προφήτην ... πληρωθείς, 9,67)[117] *and fearing* (δείσας) *that the man who had been ordered to kill him might already be doing so*, hastened to prevent the murder (φόνον)[118] and save (διασῶσαι) the prophet[119]". Finally, the historian also supplies (9,70b) the king with a word to Elisha[120] upon his arrival which picks up on his earlier indications concerning the former's stance towards the latter: "And, when he came to Elisha, he reproached him for not having asked of God a deliverance from

114. Compare the same phenomenon in his reproduction of the woman's speech to the king (= 6,28b-29) in 9,65b-66.

115. This statement is Josephus' clarifying equivalent for the rhetorical question with which Elisha's words in 6,32 conclude: "Is not the sound of his master's feet behind him?".

116. With this addition to Elisha's address, Josephus provides a motivation for Joram's own "coming" as foreseen by the prophet. Josephus' one remaining use of the verb μεταβουλεύω is in *AJ* 10,42.

117. The above expression "repent of wrath" occurs only here in Josephus.

118. The use of this term echoes Elisha's characterization of Joram as "the son of the murderer (φονέως)", i.e. Ahab in 9,67. Whereas, however, Ahab was, in fact, guilty of murder, his son now acts "to prevent the murder" of Elisha. See FELDMAN, *Studies*, p. 329 (= ID., *Jehoram*, 11).

119. Josephus' wording here puts Joram in parallel with Obadiah whom he likewise represents as acting to "save" the prophets (see 8,334; 9,47), while contrasting the king with his own mother, Jezebel, who had tried to destroy the prophets whom Obadiah intervened to rescue.

120. In the Biblical sequence of 6,33-7,2 the king does not speak as such (unless one adopts the BHS emendation in 6,33; see above in the text). Josephus enhances Joram's stature by giving him something to say at this point.

their present misfortunes (μὴ παρὰ τοῦ θεοῦ λύσιν[121] αὐτοῖς τῶν παρόντων αἰτεῖται κακῶν, compare 9,67: μὴ δεῖται τοῦ θεοῦ πόρον ... αὐτοῖς ... τῶν περιεχόντων κακῶν δοῦναι)[122], and for looking on so indifferently (ὑπερορᾷ) while they were being destroyed by them". In 2 Kgs 7,1 Elisha announces (to whom?) the surplus of meal and barley starving Samaria will enjoy the next day. In formulating the prophetic announcement (9,71), Josephus, in line with his regular practice, dispenses with the verse's opening summons "hear the word of the Lord" and following *Botenformel*. Conversely, he prefaces the two specific promises of 7,1 with a more general one: "on the morrow at the very same hour (κατ᾽ ἐκείνην τὴν ὥραν; BL ὡς ἡ ὥρα αὕτη) *at which the king had come to him*[123] *there would be a great abundance of food* (εὐπορίαν τροφῆς; compare ἡ τῶν ἀναγκαίων εὐπορία, 9,62)...". Coming then to the Elisha's particular promises, Josephus reverses their Biblical order (fine meal, barley) while also "converting" the quantities indicated in 7,1 into more contemporary ones[124]. His version concerning the two items thus reads: "... two *sata* (MT סָאתַיִם, L μέτρα)[125] of barley (κριθῆς, L κριθῶν)[126] would be sold in the market (Bible: in the gate(s) of Samaria) for a shekel (σίκλου, so L), while a *saton* (BL μέτρον) of fine flour (σεμιδάλεως, so BL) would be bought for a shekel".

In 7,2 the king's adjutant responds with skepticism to Elisha's promises. Josephus precedes (9,72) his negative reaction with mention of a positive one on the part of the king and Elisha's other hearers:

> These words changed the feelings of Joram and those present to one of joy (εἰς χαράν), for they did not hesitate to believe (πιστεύειν) the prophet, having been convinced of his truthfulness (ἀλήθειαν)[127] by earlier experiences; moreover the expected day (of plenty) made the want and distress (τὸ ... ἐνδεὲς ... καὶ ταλαίπωρον)[128] of that day seem light to them[129].

---

121. In the Josephan corpus the noun λύσις occurs only twice elsewhere, both times as a variant reading: *BJ* 1,428; *AJ* 8,148.

122. The wording of Joram's "reproach" here with its reference to "their present misfortunes (κακῶν)" has a vague parallel in the words of the messenger (or the king himself?; see above in the text) in 6,33: "This trouble (BL κακία) is from the Lord".

123. Recall that, unlike MT and LXX, Josephus previously (9,70) did make explicit mention of the king's "coming" to Elisha.

124. Cf. 9,63 where he converts the "fourth part of a qab" of 6,25 into a *sextarius*.

125. In 9,85 Josephus will state that the *saton* is equivalent to "one and a half Italian *modii*". On the former unit of measure, see further MARCUS, *Josephus*, VI, p. 39, n. 6.

126. Note that B lacks the "barley promise" of MT L 7,1 which Josephus is reproducing here.

127. Compare Elijah's reference to himself as προφήτης ἀληθής in 9,23.

128. The above collocation "want and distress" occurs only here in Josephus.

129. With the above insertion, Josephus, once again, highlights the (positive) stature of Joram, making his the first reaction to Elisha's promises to be mentioned. In addition,

Following the above insertion, Josephus (9,73a) comes to report the officer's reaction as cited in 7,2a. In the MT that figure is designated as הַשָּׁלִישׁ (RSV "the captain"; compare ὁ τριστάτης, BL) "on whose hand the king leaned". Josephus presents him as "the commander of the third division (ὁ ... τῆς τρίτης μοίρας ἡγεμών)[130], *who was a friend* (φίλος) *of the king*[131] and who was just then supporting the king as he leaned (ἐπερηρεισμένον, BL ἐπανεπαύετο) on him". In reproducing the officer's actual words, Josephus (exceptionally) retains the source's direct address: "*Incredible* (ἄπιστα)[132] *are the things you are saying*, O prophet[133]. And, as impossible (ἀδύνατον) as it is for God (7,2 the Lord) to rain down (ἐκχέαι)[134] from heaven torrents (καταρράκτας)[135] of barley or fine flour[136], just so impossible (ἀμήχανον, cf. ἀμήχανα, 9,65) is it for the things which you have now spoken to happen[137]". In 7,2b Elisha replies to the officer with the announcement that while he will "see" the things promised, he will not "eat" of them. Josephus (once again using direct address) formulates (9,73b) equivalently: "you shall see (ὄψει, BL ὄψῃ) these things come to pass in this way, but you shall have no share in any of the things that are to be".

the insertion throws into relief the groundlessness and reprehensibility of the officer's subsequent rejection of the prophet's word.

130. In 9,119 Josephus uses this same expression where MT 2 Kgs 9,25 has שָׁלִשׁה.

131. As here, Josephus frequently introduces the Hellenistic court term "friend(s)" to designate the associates of his Biblical kings; see BEGG, *Early Divided Monarchy*, p. 16, n. 54. The Josephan officer's status as the royal "friend" would explain why the king would be leaning precisely on him (so 7,2).

132. In placing this (Biblically unparalleled) term on the officer's lips, Josephus highlights the contrast between him and the king (as well as Elisha's other hearers) who are to said to "believe (πιστεύειν) the prophet" in 9,72.

133. Compare TJ 2 Kgs 7,2 "(he answered) the prophet of the Lord". Contrast MT L "the man of God" (B Elisha).

134. This is Josephus' only use of the verb ἐκχέω with God as subject.

135. Josephus' two other uses of the noun καταρράκτης/ καταράκτης are in *BJ* 4,608.611 where, both times, the meaning is a literal one as opposed to the metaphorical usage here in 9,73.

136. Compare 7,2: "If the Lord himself should make windows (B καταράκτας) in heaven...". Marcus, *Josephus*, VI, pp. 40-41 n. b comments that "Josephus seems to have confused LXX καταράκτας 'windows' with καταρράκτας ... 'torrents'". Marcus further notes that TJ too has a word other than "windows" in its rendition, i.e. טובא ("good [things]"). I would add that the Josephan officer's reference to "(torrents of) barley and fine flour" picks up on the wording of Elisha's promises as cited in 9,71 = 7,1.

137. In his formulation of the officer's response, Josephus magnifies its "unbelieving" character. Thus whereas in 7,2 the officer employs a rhetorical question ("if the Lord himself should make windows in heaven, could this thing be?"), Josephus makes his words an actual assertion, one employing the emphatic terms "incredible" and "impossible". Such an accentuation of the officer's unbelief, in turn, underscores the appropriateness of the severe punishment that will befall him.

Within the Biblical account there is a abrupt shift at 7,3a from the circle at Elisha's house (6,32-7,2) to the four lepers at the city gates. Around the Biblical reference to the latter group of figures[138] which he takes over from the source, Josephus (9,74a) weaves an elaborate transitional notice concerning them:

> And, indeed, the things which had been foretold by Elisha (τὰ ὑπὸ Ἐλισσαίου προειρημένα)[139] came to pass in this manner[140]. There was a law in Samaria that those who had leprosy (λέπραν) and whose bodies (σώματα) were not clean from such diseases should stay outside the city (ἔξω τῆς πόλεως)[141]. Now there were four men (ἄνδρες, so BL 7,3) who for this reason were dwelling before the gates (πρὸ τῶν πυλῶν; BL παρὰ τὴν θύραν).

2 Kgs 7,3b-4 cites the reflections that prompt the lepers' going out to the Syrian camp (v. 5). Josephus (9,74b-75a) introduces his (indirect discourse) version of these reflections with a remark of his own about the dilemma which provoked their cogitations: "… but, as no one any longer brought food out to them because of the extremity of the famime (διὰ τὴν ὑπερβολὴν τοῦ λιμοῦ; compare δι' ὑπερβολὴν τῆς ἐνδείας, 9,62)[142], and as they were prevented by law from entering the city, they reflected that…". In their reflections the Biblical lepers allude to two possibilites open to them neither of which, however, offers them any prospect of survival, i.e. remaining where they are (this posssibility is, in fact, cited twice by them; see 7,3b and 4aβ) and entering the city. Josephus passes over the question of 7,3b ("why do we sit

138. In both the Bible and Josephus the four remain anonymous throughout. In Rabbinic tradition they are identified with Gehazi (whom Elisha smote with leprosy according to 2 Kgs 5,27) and his three sons. See y. Sanh. 10.29b (M. SCHWAB, Talmud de Jérusalem, XI, Paris, 1889, p. 56); b. Sanh. 107b (trans. I. EPSTEIN, Sanhedrin, London, Soncino, 1935, II, p. 734); b. Sot. 47a (trans. A. COHEN, Sotah, London, Soncino, 1936, p. 247).

139. Compare τὰ ὑπὸ τοῦ Μιχαία προειρημένα, 8,412.

140. With this opening element of his expansion of 7,3, Josephus confirms his earlier reference to Elisha's "truthfulness" (9,72). At the same time, the insertion eliminates, in advance, any element of suspense, such as one does have in the Bible itself, as to how the dispute between prophet and officer will turn out.

141. With his evocation of this "law", Josephus provides an explanation for the lepers' presence outside the besieged city. Its Biblical inspiration is Lev 13,46 which enjoins that the "leper" is to "dwell alone in a habitation outside the camp" to which Josephus' equivalent is AJ 3,261: "He (Moses) banished from the city (τῆς πόλεως; compare ἔξω τῆς πόλεως, 9,74)… those whose bodies (σώματα; see 9,74) were afflicted with leprosy (λέπρᾳ; compare λέπραν, 9,74)…".

142. Compare Josephus' – likewise inserted – remark about the occasion for the women deciding to eat their children in 9,65 "… since the conditions of famine and need had become impossible to bear…". In both contexts Josephus goes beyond the Bible in underscoring the severity of the famine (and, conversely, the magnitude of the miracle whereby the famine will be lifted).

here until we die?"), formulating the two possibilities envisaged by the lepers as follows: "... (they reflected that) *even if it were permitted them*[143] to enter they would perish miserably (κακῶς; cf. κακῶν, 9,67.70; compare 7,4a: we shall die) through the famine (7,4a: the famine is in the city), and that they would suffer the same fate if they remained there...". The lepers' reflections terminate in 7,4b with their resolving to go over to the Syrians on the consideration that they might be spared by them, but if not they will simply die – as they would in any case. Josephus (9,75b) uses equivalent language in reporting the plan they devise: "... so they decided to give themselves up to the enemy (παραδοῦναι τοῖς πολεμίοις; cf. προδῷ ... τοῖς ἐχθροῖς, 9,63 [7,4b: let us go over to the camp of the Syrians])[144], in the hope that if these spared their lives they would be able to live (ζησόμενοι; BL ζησόμεθα), and that if they were put to death they would die without suffering greatly (εὐθανατήσοντες[145]; BL ἀποθανούμεθα)".

2 Kgs 7,5 relates the carrying out of the lepers' plan: they betake themselves "at twilight" to the Syrian camp (v. 5a) where there is no one to be found (v. 5b). At this juncture (9,76a) Josephus does reproduce the content of v. 5a: "*having firmly agreed on this plan*, they went by night (νυκτός; BL ἐν τῷ σκότει) to the enemy's camp (7,5a: the camp of Syria)". Before, however, mentioning the emptiness of the camp as encountered by the lepers (= v. 5b), he "anticipates" the explanation for this state of affairs cited in 7,6-7, i.e. the panic-inducing auditory illusion the Lord had brought upon the Syrians. In so doing, he expatiates (9,76b) on 7,6a's description of the divine deception of the besiegers: "Now God (7,6: the Lord) *had already begun to frighten and disturb* (ἐκφοβεῖν καὶ ταράττειν)[146] *the Syrians* and to cause the noise of chariots and horses (ἁρμάτων καὶ ἵππων[147])[148], as if an army (στρατιᾶς) were advancing (7,6a: the sound of a great army [BL δυνάμεως]), to

143. This counterfactual formulation becomes necessary given Josephus' previous references to the lepers being legally barred from Samaria.

144. Josephus' substitution of "the enemy" here for the neutral Biblical mention of "the Syrians" recalls his procedure in 9,57 as compared with its parallel, 2 Kgs 6,20; see n. 59.

145. The verb εὐθανατέω is hapax in Josephus.

146. The above collocation occurs also in *AJ* 2,82; Josephus' one other use of the verb ἐκφοβέω is in *BJ* 1,492.

147. This is the reading adopted by Niese, Naber and Marcus. The codices MSPE (and Lat) read ὅπλων here (as do Dindorf and Bekker); cf. also Zon which gives the conflate reading ἵππων τε καὶ ὅπλων.

148. Josephus' pl. forms correspond to those of L 7,6a. MT and B read the sg. in both instances. The sequence here in 9,76 is the opposite of that of 9,54 ("horses and chariots"), but corresponds to the one found in 9,55.

resound (ἐνηχεῖν)[149] in their ears, *and this suspicion* (ὑπόνοιαν) *He brought ever closer to them*". 2 Kgs 7,6b "quotes" the word which the Syrians exchange among themselves about what they have been hearing, whereupon they all flee, abandoning everything (7,7). In this sequence, there is, curiously, no mention of any role for the Syrian king in the unfolding of events. Josephus' version (9,77-78) fills this lacuna, making "Adados" the one to whom the Syrians express their surmise: "*Finally they were so much affected by this means that they left their tents and ran to Adados*, saying that Joram, the Israelite king (7,6b: the king of Israel) had hired (μισθωσάμενος, same verb as in BL) *as allies* (συμμάχους) both the king (7,6b: kings) of Egypt and the king (7,6b: kings) of the islands (τῶν νήσων)[150], and was leading these against them, *for, they said, they could hear the noise they made as they approached. As they were speaking, Adados listened carefully – his own ears, indeed, were already being assailed by the same sounds as were those of the people –...*". One might have expected Josephus to continue the above sequence with some reference to Adados' reaction to what he is told (and hears for himself). Instead of this, however, the historian now, rather abruptly, picks up 7,7's account of the Syrian flight: "... and then, abandoning their horses (ἵππους, so BL)[151] and beasts of burden (τὰ ὑποζύγια, BL τοὺς ὄνους) *and uncounted wealth* (πλοῦτον ἄφθονον)[152] in their camp (ἐν τῇ παρεμβολῇ, so BL), they turned to flee in great disorder and confusion (ἀταξίας καὶ θορύβου[153]; compare 7,7: for their lives)".

Only at this point does Josephus (9,79-80a) finally come to narrate the lepers' entry into the Syrian camp (in the Bible their arrival there has

149. The verb ἐνηχέω is hapax in Josephus.

150. MT 7,6b speaks of "(the kings of) the Hittites (הַחִתִּים)", BL, transliterating, of (τῶν) Χετταίων. Marcus, *Josephus*, VI, p. 43, n. b avers that Josephus has confused the BL form with Χεττιείμ (= Hebrew *Kittim*), the Biblical designation for the Greek islands. Note further that Josephus reverses the sequence of 7,6b where the "kings of the Hittites" are cited before the "kings of the Egyptians".

151. In thus beginning his description of the Syrians' flight with mention of their abandoning their "horses", Josephus passes over the indications of 7,7 that their flight occurred "at twilight" and that they forsook their "tents" as well.

152. The above phrase recurs in *AJ* 5,96; 7,392; 9,191. This item has no equivalent in the Biblical list (7,7) of things abandoned by the fleeing Syrians (although see 7,8 which speaks of the lepers carrying off the "silver and gold" left behind by them). It does, however, reflect Josephus' tendency to accentuate the riches acquired by the Jews from their defeated enemies. FELDMAN, *Interpretation*, p. 543 (= ID., *Josephus' Portrait of David*, in HUCA 60 [1989] 129-174, 138-139) sees this emphasis as intended to rebut contemporary charges that the Jews were an impecunious nation of beggars. See further BEGG, *Early Divided Monarchy*, p. 122, n. 766.

153. This construction occurs only here in Josephus. His other uses of the noun ἀταξία are in *BJ* 3,74; 5,79; *AJ* 16,297; 19,241.

already been mentioned in 7,5b, this notice being resumed in 7,8 after the intervening account of the flight of the Syrians in 7,6-7). He recounts this development as follows: "But the lepers who had left Samaria for the camp of the Syrians, *as we mentioned a little while ago* (see 9,76a)[154], came to the camp and observed the great quiet and silence (ἡσυχίαν καὶ ἀφωνίαν[155]; compare 7,5b: when they came to the edge of the camp of the Syrians, behold, there was no one there)". He then proceeds to reproduce 7,8's description of the double act of plundering perpetrated by the lepers in the camp: "... when they had gone inside (i.e. the camp), they hastened to one of the tents [7,8 they went into a tent][156], *but, seeing no one there*[157], they hurriedly ate (ἐμφαγόντες)[158] and drank and carried off garments and much gold (7,8: they carried off silver and gold [so MT B; L has the reverse order] and clothing) from the camp, which they buried (ἔκρυψαν; L κατέκρυψαν). Then they went to another tent and again in the same way carried out what was in it". Josephus lacks an equivalent to the words concluding 7,8b's account of the lepers' second despoliation ("they went and hid them") which repeat those used in reference to the first (note: while MT and L 7,8 do have such a double mention of the lepers' "concealing" their booty, B lacks the first of these). Instead, he indicates that the lepers were able to carry out still further acts of spoil-taking with total impunity: "and this they did four times without meeting anyone at all".

2 Kgs 7,9 relates the lepers' decision to report matters in the city. Josephus (9,80b) introduces his rendition of their deliberations on the matter with a notice inspired by his immediately preceding indication about their "not seeing anyone at all" in the camp: "surmising, therefore, that the enemy had withdrawn...[159]". Thereafter, he markedly compresses

---

154. Such *Rückverweise* are frequently interjected by Josephus; they serve to tie together more closely the different moments of a given narrative.

155. The above collocation is hapax in Josephus; his two remaining uses of the noun ἀφωνία are in *AJ* 2,139; 14,292.

156. Josephus' use of the word "hastened" for the Bible's colorless "went into" accentuates the tension of the moment for the lepers who, as yet, know nothing of the Syrians' previous flight.

157. This element has no equivalent at this point in the Biblical narrative. Josephus may, however, be "anticipating" the item from the lepers' report in 7,10b where they state that "there was no one to be seen" in the Syrian camp.

158. This is the form adopted by Niese and Marcus (Josephus' two remaining uses of the verb ἐμφαγεῖν are in *AJ* 3,321; 17,62). The codices MSP (followed by Dindorf, Bekker, and Naber) read ἐν μέσῳ φαγόντες here. SCHRECKENBERG, *Untersuchungen*, pp. 109-110 argues for the originality of the form φαγόντες as well.

159. Josephus has prepared for this "surmise" on the lepers' part by having them plunder undisturbed not merely two (so 7,8), but no less than four Syrian tents. At the end of this process they are indeed in a position to "surmise" that the enemy has withdrawn.

the words attributed to the lepers in 7,9 itself, taking over only their opening and closing elements: "... they reproached (κατεγίνωσκον; cf. καταγνούς, of Joram, 9,70) themselves (7,9: we are not doing right [literally thus]) for not having reported this to Joram and the citzens (cf. 7,9: let us go and tell the king's household)[160]". Josephus next (9,81a) recounts the realization of the lepers' decision (= 7,10): "And so they came *to the wall of Samaria*[161] and, shouting up (ἀναβοήσαντες; BL ἐβόησαν) to the guards (φύλακας)[162], informed them of what had become of the enemy...[163]".

In 7,11 the "gatekeepers" are said to "cry out" following the lepers' report, relaying the matter to the king's house(hold). According to Josephus (9,81b) the guards on the walls convey the news to "the king's guards". The upshot of the chain of reports according to 7,12 is that the king arises and addresses his "servants". Josephus has Joram summon his "friends" (φίλους)[164] and "commanders" (ἡγεμόνας)[165], making the transition to the royal words to them with the notice "and when they came...". He then goes on to considerably modify the king's statement to the assembly as cited in 7,12b. His version (9,82) which begins in indirect and then shifts to direct discourse (cf. 9,68) reads:

> ... he told them that he suspected (ὑπονοεῖν; cf. ὑπόνοιαν, of the Syrians in 9,76) the retreat of the Syrian king to be a snare and a trick (ἐνέδραν καὶ τέχνην)[166]; 'giving up hope that we shall perish through

160. Josephus thus omits the middle section of the lepers' words in 7,9: "This day is a day of good news; if we are silent and wait until the morning light, punishment will overtake us...". By the omission of these words, Josephus makes their reflections appear less self-interested than they do in the Bible.

161. In 7,10 the lepers are said simply to "come"; Josephus, however, may have found inspiration for his specification concerning their destination in the continuation of that verse where they cry "to the gate (so BL; MT gatekeeper) of the city".

162. Recall Josephus' (non-Biblical) mention of the presence of "guards" (φύλακας) on the wall in 9,63.

163. This formulation picks up on the references to the lepers' "surmising that the enemy had withdrawn" in 9,80. It replaces the detailed enumeration given by the lepers of what they had encountered in the camp as found in 7,10b: "We came to the camp of the Syrians, and behold, there was no one to be seen or heard there, nothing but the horses tied, and the asses tied, and the tents as they were". Recall that Josephus does "antici-pate" one item of the sequence of 7,10b, i.e. the lepers' reference to their seeing no one in the camp in 9,80; see n. 157.

164. Recall that in 9,73 Josephus introduced the term φίλος to qualify the officer who contradicts Elisha; see n. 131.

165. Like "friend" (see previous note), this term too is used by Josephus in 9,73 to designate Elisha's opponent, the "commander (ἡγεμών) of the third division".

166. The above collocation is hapax in Josephus. Th affirmation attributed to Joram here renders more definite the king's opening word in 7,12b: "I will tell you what the Syrians have prepared against us".

famine[167], he has done this[168] in order that, when we go out (ἐξελθόντων; BL ἐξελεύσονται) *to plunder their camp in the belief that they have fled*[169], he may suddenly fall upon our men *and kill them* and take the city without a battle[170]. *Wherefore I urge you to keep it well guarded and by no means to attack, being careless of danger* (καὶ μηδαμῶς προϊέναι καταφρονήσαντας [cf. καταφρονῶν, used of Elisha's "scorning danger" in 9,55])[171] *because of the enemy's withdrawal*[172].

2 Kgs 7,13 cites the response of "one of his servants" to the king's foregoing address. Here too, Josephus (9,83) both expands and modifies:

> But someone said that, *while the king was suspicious* (ὑπονοήσειε; see ὑπονοεῖν, 9,82) *with the best reason and most wisely* (ἄριστα ... καὶ συνετώτατα)[173], he would at least advise him[174] to send two of his horsemen (ἱππέων)[175] to search all the country as far as the Jordan[176] *in order that, if they were captured by the enemy lying in ambush* (λοχώντων; see λοχῶντας, 9,51) *and were slain, they might be a protection to the army*

167. Contrast 7,12b where the king attributes the Syrian ruse precisely to their "knowing that we are hungry". Perhaps, Josephus' modification here is motivated by the consideration that, given Joram's close surveillance of Samaria's population (see 9,63), the Syrians could not be expected to have "known" the situation of the city's food supply.

168. Compare 7,12b: "therefore they have gone out of the camp to hide themselves in the open country...".

169. Compare 7,12b: "(the Syrians) thinking, 'when they come out of the city...'".

170. Compare 7,12b: "'... we [the Syrians] shall take them alive and get into the city'". Note that in contrast to 7,12b which speaks in general terms of what the "Syrians" have devised, Josephus' version focusses attention on the person of Adados; cf. his earlier accentuation of that figure in 9,77-78.

171. The above reading of MSPELat is adopted by Dindorf, Bekker, Naber and Marcus. Niese, *ad loc.* reads simply μὴ καταφρονήσαντας with RO (cf. ID., *Opera*, I, p. xxxvi where he qualifies the reading favored by Marcus *et al.* as "aperte corrupta et interpolata").

172. With this addition, Josephus supplies the missing "practical conclusion" to the king's address. On the historian's version of the king's discourse overall as designed to accentuate Joram's military acumen, see FELDMAN, *Studies*, pp. 324-325 (= ID., *Jehoram*, 10).

173. The above collocation occurs only here in Josephus. In 2 Kgs 7,13 the speaker begins immediately by presenting his own proposal, without addressing the king's statement as such. With the above expansion, Josephus represents the speaker as commencing with more of a *captatio benevolentiae*, i.e. an acknowledgement of the appropriateness of Joram's concerns. See following note.

174. Note the respectfulness with which the speaker's proposal is couched here – he is simply "advising" the king, rather than dictating to him as his Biblical counterpart seems to do, just as he proposes only a minimal modification ("at least") of the king's directive that they (all) remain on guard within the city.

175. In 7,13 the proposal is that "five of the remaining horses (BL ἵππων)" be dispatched. Josephus' reading has in view the divergent indication of 7,14 where, in fact, "two riders (ἐβιβάτας) of horses" (thus BL [and TJ]; MT "two chariot(s) of horses") are sent out.

176. Compare 7,13: "let us send and see". Josephus incorporates into the proposal itself the notice of 7,15 that those dispatched by the king (7,14) went "as far as the Jordan".

against suffering a like fate through an incautious advance (ἀνυπόπτως προελθοῦσαν)¹⁷⁷. "And," he added, "if they are captured by the foe and put to death, you will (merely) be adding the horsemen to those who have perished in the famine¹⁷⁸".

2 Kgs 7,14 comprises a double notice: "they (who?) took two mounted men (so LXX, TJ; MT chariot(s) of horses)¹⁷⁹ and the king sent them after the Syrians...". Josephus (9,84a) conflates these indications, thereby focussing attention on the initative of Joram: "Thereupon the king, *approving of this plan* (ἀρεσθεὶς ... τῇ γνώμῃ)¹⁸⁰, sent out the scouts (κατοψομένους)¹⁸¹". 2 Kgs 7,15a next reports on the expedition's find, i.e. as far as the Jordan the way is littered with abandoned Syrian garments and equipment. Josephus (9,84b) leaving aside the Biblical reference to the extent of the reconnaissance¹⁸², words his parallel as follows: "and these (the scouts) found the road which they covered *bare of enemies*¹⁸³ but full of abandoned provisions and arms (σιτίων καὶ ὅπλων; BL ἱματισμοῦ καὶ σκευῶν) which they had

177. The above phrase "incautious advance" occurs only here in Josephus. With this (added) indication as to what the proposed reconnaissance is expected to achieve, Josephus continues to have the speaker address himself to the king's previously expressed concerns: Joram warned his hearers about "being careless of danger"; his respondent suggests a way to ensure that the whole Israelite army not be destroyed "through an incautious advance".

178. Note once again the shift from indirect to direct discourse in the course of the above speech. The speaker's resumptive comment on the (possible) fate of those to be sent out here in 9,83b represents Josephus' version of the servant's statement in 7,13 where it serves to motivate the proposed expedition: "... seeing that those who are left here will fare like the whole multitude of Israel that have already perished". Both speakers thus invoke the fate of the many who have already perished in the siege. Whereas, however, the Biblical figure warns that all the surviving Israelites face a like death should they simply remain in the city, his Josephan counterpart refers, less drastically, to the two spies joining those already dead. Thereby, he tones down the accusation against the king implicit in the Biblical speaker's proposal, i.e. his proposed "do nothing" policy will result in the death of all surviving Israelites. Note too that while the speaker of 7,13 adduces the depressing subject of the losses Israel has already incurred right at the start of his speech, Josephus' orator more tactfully reserves that item to the very end of his remarks.

179. On the discrepancy between this indication and the proposal as made in 7,13, see n. 175.

180. This phrase echoes *AJ* 9,13 where it is said of the Jerusalemites in face of the threat from the enemy coalition ἤρεσε ἥ ... τοῦ βασιλέως [i.e. Jehoshaphat] γνώμη.

181. Note that in Josephus' formulation here the "contradiction" between 7,13 and 14 as to the number of those being sent out disappears.

182. Recall that he had previously incorporated this indication into his formulation of the speaker's proposal in 9,83.

183. In the Biblical account this point about the absence of the Syrian forces on the route taken by those sent out is left implicit; Josephus makes it explicit given that this was, in fact, the primary matter the expedition was intended to ascertain.

thrown away in order to be unimpeded (τὸ κοῦφοι; cf. κοῦφον, 9,72) in their flight".

In 7,15b the returning messengers report back to the king, whereupon (7,16a) the people venture out, on their own initiative, to plunder the Syrian camp. Once again, Josephus (9,84c) conflates with a view to accentuating royal control over developments: "when the king heard of this, he let the people loose to plunder (ἐπὶ διαρπαγήν; cf. εἰς διαρπαγήν, 9,82) the things in the camp[184]". 2 Kgs 7,16b moves directly from the people's plundering of the camp (v. 16a) to a "fullfillment notice" for Elisha's word of 7,1. Josephus prefaces his parallel to the latter item with an elaborate enumeration of the booty taken (9,85):

> And they acquired no slight or small amount of gain[185], but took (ἐλάμβανον)[186] much gold and silver (πολὺν ... χρυσόν, πολὺν ... ἄργυρον)[187] and herds and flocks of all kinds (ἀγέλας ... παντοδαπῶν κτηνῶν)[188]; moreover, they came upon such untold quantities of wheat (σίτου)[189] and barley as they had not even dreamed of, and so they were delivered from their former sufferings (κακῶν; see 9,67.70) and had such plenty (ἀφθονίαν) that....

Josephus' conclusion to the above sequence makes the transition to his parallel to 7,16b's fulfillment notice which he now gives: "... two *sata* of barley could be bought for a shekel[190], and a *saton* of fine flour for a shekel, in accordance with the prophecy of Elisha (κατὰ τὴν Ἐλισσαίου προφητείαν)[191]". He rounds off this notice, in turn, with a

184. Compare Josephus' similar reworkings of the "plunder notices" of 2 Chr 20,25 and 2 Kgs 3,23 in 9,14.40, respectively, there too in the interest of underscoring a king's control over booty-taking operations.

185. This opening indication picks up on Josephus' notice about the "untold wealth" left behind by the Syrians in 9,78. See also n. 152.

186. This verbal form is read by Dindorf, Bekker, Naber and Marcus on the basis of the codices SP; it is omitted by ROM.

187. Recall that in his version of 7,8 in 9,79 Josephus passes over the reference to the "silver" taken by the lepers; in his (non-Biblical) listing here in 9,85 he now makes use of that item.

188. With the above enumeration of Israel's booty, compare Josephus' listing of the plunder taken from the Ethiopian camp by Asa in *AJ* 8,294 (= 2 Chr 14,14) πολὺν ... χρυσὸν πολὺν ... ἄργυριον ... καὶ ἀγέλας.

189. Mention of this commodity helps set up Josephus' subsequent statement (= 7,16b) about the abundance of "fine flour" available to the Israelites.

190. Just as in his reproduction of Elisha's word itself (see 9,71 = 7,1), Josephus here reverses the sequence of the Biblical fulfillment notice, speaking first of "barley", then of "fine flour".

191. Compare 7,16: "... according to the word (B κατὰ τὸ ῥῆμα/ L κατὰ τὸν λόγον) of the Lord (+ which Elisha spoke, L)". Josephus makes a like substitution in *AJ* 8,309 where the "according to the word of the Lord which he spoke by... Jehu the prophet..." of 1 Kgs 16,12 becomes "in accordance with the prophecy (κατὰ τὴν ... προφητείαν) of Jēūs". See n. 194.

parenthetical indication concerning the *saton*'s equivalency: "Now the *saton* is equal to one and a half Italian *modii*".

2 Kgs 7,17 describes the realization of Elisha's further announcement of 7,2b, i.e. that the officer who had doubted his word (7,2a) will not share in the promised abundance. Josephus (9,86a) introduces his reference to the officer's fate with the transitional formula "the only one who did not enjoy any of these goods things was...". As in 9,73, he designates the personage in question as "the commander of the third division" (see above), while leaving aside, at this point, the Bible's renewed qualification of him as the one "on whose hand the king leaned" (which he did utilize in 9,73; see above). In line with 7,17a he has (9,86b) the king place the officer at the gate (κατασταθεὶς ... ἐπὶ τῆς πύλης; compare BL κατέστησεν ἐπὶ τῆς πύλης), going on, however, to add a double reason for his doing so, i.e. "... to hold back the rush of the crowd and prevent the danger of their pushed around by one another and trampled to death...[192]". Following 7,17bα, Josephus then records that "... he himself (the captain) suffered this (fate)[193] and died (ἀποθνήσκει; BL ἀπέθανεν) in this way...".

2 Kgs 7,17bβ notes that the captain's death occurred "as the man of God (TJ the prophet of the Lord) had said when the king (BL the messenger, τὸν ἄγγελον) came down to him (see 6,33)". 7,18-19 then goes on to cite the exchange between prophet and captain from 7,1-2 verbatim, while 7,20 reiterates (see 7,17b) that the latter died in accordance with the former's word of 7,2b. Josephus' conclusion (9,86c) to the episode drastically compresses this highly repetitious Biblical sequence. It reads simply: "(the officer died) as Elisha had prophesied (προφητεύσαντος Ἐλισσαίου, compare κατὰ τὴν Ἐλισσαίου προφητείαν, 9,85)[194] when this man alone of them refused to believe (ἐπίστευσεν)[195] what he said concerning the abundance of provisions (εὐπορίας τῶν ἐπιτηδείων)[196] that was to be".

192. Josephus "anticipates" this item from 7,17b which states that "the people trod upon him (the captain) in the gate".

193. With the above formulation Josephus underscores the irony of the officer's death: stationed to keep people from trampling each other, he has this happen to himself.

194. Note here too Josephus' characteristic substitution of other language for the Biblical (see 7,17bβ) reference to the divine "word". See n. 191.

195. This term echoes Josephus' use of "belief terminology" earlier in the pericope, see 9,72 (Joram and the others "did not not hesitate to believe (πιστεύειν) the prophet" and 73 (the captain says to Elisha) "incredible (ἄπιστα) are the things you are saying, O prophet". Josephus' renewed reference here to the captain's being the only one of Elisha's hearers who failed to "believe" his promises serves, at the same time, to underscore the deservedness of the punishment that now befalls him.

196. This phrase occurs only here in Josephus; compare τῶν ἀναγκαίων εὐπορία (9,62) and εὐπορίαν τροφῆς (9,71).

4. *Elisha in Damascus*

The final component of Josephus' segment (9,46-94) dealing with Elisha's mighty deeds is the narrative of the prophet's encounter with Hazael in Damascus, 9,87-94 (= 2 Kgs 8,7-15). In the Bible this pericope is preceded by the account of the Shunemite woman's regaining her property after being forced to vacate it during a seven-year famine (2 Kgs 8,1-6) which itself alludes back to the story of Elisha's dealings with the woman in 4,8-37. Josephus lacks all parallel to 8,1-6; his narration precedes directly from the end of 2 Kings 7 to 8,7 (recall that in our MSS of Josephus, 4,8-37, along with the whole of 4,8–6,8, is likewise unparalleled). On the assumption that Josephus' text(s) of Kings did in fact contain the narrative of 8,1-6, how might the historian's total omission of that unit be explained? I suggest that several considerations might have influenced Josephus in leaving the passage aside. For one thing, whereas throughout 9,47-94 he is, according to the introductory remark in 9,46, presenting us with the "glorious and worthy of record acts" of Elisha, the prophet's role in 8,1-6 is a rather minimal, unmemorable one, his only initiative there being to announce to the woman the coming of a seven-year famine at the beginning (see 8,1). In addition, it might be noted that 8,1-6 appears somewhat disruptive in its context in Kings in that, unlike the preceding 6,8–7,20 and the following 8,7-15, it lacks any mention of the Syrians[197]. In passing over the unit, Josephus is able then to keep together in a continuous sequence (9,51-94) the Biblical materials dealing with "Elisha and the Syrians".

The story of 2 Kgs 8,7-15 opens in v. 7a with mention of two happenings, i.e. Elisha's coming to Damascus and the sickness of King Benhadad. Josephus (9,87) reverses the order of these items, prefacing the notice on the royal illness with a lengthy indication on its "cause" which itself explicitly harks back to the previous episode. This reads:

> *Now, when the Syrian king Adados, who had escaped* (διασωθείς; cf. διασῶσαι, 9,70) *to Damascus*[198], *learned that it was the Deity who had thrown both him and all his army into all that terror and confusion* (τὸ

---

197. On the other hand, the unit does have in common with the preceding 6,24-7,20 its "famine motif" (see 8,1). (A further possibility with regard to Josephus' omission of the unit 8,1-6 would be that having earlier passed over the passage, 2 Kgs 4,8-37, on Elisha's initial dealings with the Shunemite (see above) to which the former alludes back, he likewise opted to leave aside the story of 8,1-6 itself.)

198. With this indication, Josephus accounts for the king's presence back in the city in time for Elisha's visit, following his abortive siege of Samaria. Note further that the above participial form διασωθείς is the same one used by Josephus in *AJ* 8,379 for Adados' "saving" himself following his earlier rout before Samaria in the time of Ahab.

θεῖον ... εἰς τὸ δέος καὶ τὴν ταραχὴν ἐκείνην ἐνέβαλεν)[199], *and that it had not arisen from the advance of the enemy, he was greatly disheartened* (ἀθυμήσας) *at having incurred God's displeasure* (τῷ δυσμενῆ τὸν θεὸν ἔχειν)[200], and fell ill (εἰς νόσον κατέπεσεν; compare ἠρρώστησεν, B 8,7).

Whereas 8,7a leaves the temporal relationship between Elisha's arrival and Ben-hadad's sickness quite indeterminate (MT: "and Elisha came to Damascus and Ben-hadad... was sick"), Josephus (9,88) closely coordinates the two events by means of the formula with which he introduces the former: "But at that very time the prophet Elisha had left home (ἐκδημήσαντος)[201] for Damascus...[202]". In 8,7b-8 Ben-hadad, informed of Elisha's presence in Damascus, dispatches (the not-further identified) "Hazael" who, "present" in hand, is go to meet the prophet and inquire about the outcome of the royal sickness. Josephus' rendition introduces a characterization of "Azaēlos" which accounts for the choice precisely of him as Adados' envoy: "... and, when Adados knew of it, he sent Azaēlos (Ἀζάηλον; BL Ἀζαήλ), *the most trusted of his servants* (τὸν πιστότατον τῶν οἰκετῶν)[203], to meet him, bringing him gifts (δῶρα, so L; compare MT מִנְחָה, B μαννά), and he ordered him to inquire [of the prophet] (ἔρεσθαι; BL ἐπιζήτησον τὸν Κύριον δι' αὐτοῦ)[204] and [ask] whether he would escape (διαφεύξεται)[205] the danger it threatened".

199. The reference here is to the description of God's making the Syrians (including Adados himself) hear the sound of advancing enemies in 9,77-78 (= 2 Kgs 7,6). With the above formula, compare Josephus' reference to the divine discomfiture of the coalition which had come up against Jehoshaphat in 9,13 (= 2 Chr 20,22): ὁ δε θεὸς εἰς φόβον ἐνέβαλε καὶ ταραχήν. The above collocation "terror and confusion" occurs also in *BJ* 5,91; *AJ* 6,24 (both times in reverse order).

200. This is Josephus' only use of the construction δυσμενῆ ἔχειν with "God" as object.

201. Josephus uses ἐκδημέω twice elsewhere, i.e. *AJ* 19,332; *Vita* 388.

202. In both the Bible and Josephus no reason is given for Elisha's going to the enemy capital. Rabbinic tradition does supply the missing motivation: Elisha went there in order to try (unsuccessfully in the event) to bring his former servant Gehazi – who had fallen into idolatrous ways – to repentance, thus *y. Sanh.* 10,29b; *b. Sot* 47a; *b. Sanh.* 107b (see n. 138). Alternatively, Theodoret (*Quaestio* 23, PG 80, c. 763) has Elisha going to Damascus in order to anoint Hazael in accordance with the divine directive given his master Elijah in 1 Kgs 19,15.

203. Compare *AJ* 8,384 where Josephus refers to the defeated Adados fleeing with "some of his most faithful servants" (τινῶν πιστοτάτων οἰκετῶν). The above characterization of "Azaēlos" further serves, of course, to accentuate the treachery and reprehensibility of his later assassination of his master.

204. Conceivably, Josephus, in employing the above formulation, is deliberately avoiding placing the name of (the true) God on the lips of a pagan king the way the Bible does here.

205. This is the same term used by Josephus in *AJ* 8,267 (= 1 Kgs 14,3) in formulating Jeroboam's dispatch of his wife to inquire of the prophet Ahijah whether their child Abijah would "survive" his illness. The term also echoes the participle διασωθείς used of Adados in 9,87.

2 Kgs 8,9 relates Hazael's appearance before Elisha with "forty camel loads" of gifts in tow and his posing of the king's question. Josephus' version (9,89) amplifies the honor shown the prophet by the Syrian envoy in several respects: "Thereupon Azaēlos, with forty camels bearing the *most beautiful and costly* (κάλλιστα καὶ τιμιώτατα)[206] gifts (δῶρα; BL μαννά) to be found in Damascus *and in the palace*, went to meet Elisha, and, *after greeting him in a friendly manner* (προσαγορεύσας αὐτὸν φιλοφρόνως)[207], said that he had been sent to him by King Adados *to bring him gifts* and to inquire about his illness, whether he would recover from it". The prophet's reply in 8,10 seems to involve a contradictory message for Hazael who, on the one hand, is told to inform his master that he will certainly recover[208], but who, on the other hand, is also made privy to God's "showing" Elisha that Ben-hadad is surely going to die. Josephus' parallel (9,90a) "resolves" the contradiction (and the problem of a prophet instructing his inquirer to lie), while also dispensing with Elisha's appeal to a divine revelation about Adados' fate. It reads: "Then the prophet bade Azaēlos not to announce the bad news (κακόν) to the king[209], but said that he would die". In 8,11 there follows an interlude of non-verbal communication between prophet and caller, rendered rather obscure by the uncertainty as to the subject of v. 11a. RSV translates "he (Hazael? Elisha?) fixed his gaze and stared at him (Elisha? Hazael?) until he (Hazael? Elisha?) was ashamed. And the man of God wept". Josephus (9,90b) clarifies matters, motivating as well the prophet's "weeping" (v. 11b): "And, while the *king's servant* (οἰκέτης)[210] was grieving (ἐλυπεῖτο)[211] *at what he heard*, Elisha (MT BL 8,11 the man of

206. The above adjectival collocation is hapax in Josephus.
207. This phrase echoes that used of the third captain's approach to Elijah in *AJ* 9,25, i.e. φιλοφρόνως προειπεῖν αὐτόν.
208. Thus MT *qere* (לוֹ), LXX, TJ; MT *ketiv* reads rather "go say you will not (לֹא) recover". Cf. C.J. LABUSCHAGNE, *Did Elisha Deliberately Lie? A Note on II Kings 8:10*, in *ZAW* 77 (1965) 327-328.
209. Also elsewhere, Josephus takes pains to disassociate Biblical prophets from any connection with "falsehood". Thus in his account of Ahab's death (*AJ* 8,398-420), he passes over 1 Kgs 22,15 // 2 Chr 18,14 a verse wherein Micaiah begins his response to the king by (ironically) echoing the words of the false prophets about his (Ahab's) coming triumph. The MT *ketiv* in 8,10 (see preceding note) seems to represent another such attempt at protecting Elisha from the suspicion that he had incited Hazael to lie.
210. Recall Josephus' previous characterization of Azaēlos as "the most trusted of his [Adados'] servants (οἰκετῶν)" in 9,88.
211. MARCUS, *Josephus*, VI, p. 48, n. a suggests that Josephus' rendering here has been influenced by TJ 2 Kgs 8,11 whose term אוֹרִיךְ he takes to mean that Hazael "lengthened (his face) greatly", i.e. adopted a mournful expression. Compare, however, the translation of the Aramaic term in question of HARRINGTON and SALDARINI, *Targum Jonathan*, p. 279: "(he [Hazael] turned his face) *and waited for a long time*".

God, TJ the prophet of the Lord) began to cry (ἔκλαιε; BL ἔκλαυσεν) *and shed many tears, foreseeing the great ills* (κακά; cf. κακόν, 9,90a) *which the people was to suffer after the death of Adados*[212]".

In 8,12 the exchange between them continues with Hazael asking the reason for the prophet's weeping (v. 12a), and Elisha responding by enumerating the fourfold disaster he "knows" the Syrian will bring on Israel (v. 12b). Josephus (9,91) words this moment of their dialogue thus: "... when Azaēlos asked him the reason of his distress (συγχύσεως), he said, '*I am crying out of pity* (ἐλεῶν)[213] for the Israelite people (8,12: to the sons of Israel) because of the misfortunes (δεινῶν; Β κακά) which it will suffer at your hands. For you will slay (ἀποκτενεῖς, so BL [+ with the sword]) their best men (ἀρίστους; BL ἐλεκτούς) and burn their strongest cities (τὰς ὀχυρωτάτας πόλεις ἐμπρήσεις; L τὰς πόλεις αὐτῶν τὰς ἐστερεωμένας ἐμπρήσεις ἐν πυρί)[214], and you will kill their children (παιδία; BL νήπια) by dashing them against the rocks (ἀπολεῖς προσρηγνὺς[215] πέτραις; 8,12: dash in pieces [MT וְעָרֵיהֶם, Β ἐνσείσεις, L ἐδαφιεῖς]) and will rip up their women with child (τὰς ... ἐγκύους ἀναρρήξεις γυναίκας[216]; Β τὰς ἐν γαστρὶ ἐχούσας αὐτῶν ἀναρήξεις)".

In 8,13a Hazael poses a new question to Elisha: "What is your servant, who is but a (BL + dead) dog, that he should do this great thing?" Josephus' Hazael formulates (9,92a) his question without recourse to such self-deprecation: "what power (ἰσχύν) has been given to me, so great that I can do (ποιῆσαι, Β ποιήσει) these things"? Elisha responds to this further question in 8,13b by stating "The Lord has shown me (BL ἐδειξέν) that you are to be king over Syria (thus MT L; B Israel)". Josephus (9,92b) words the prophet's response quite similarly: "... God

212. Josephus has likely anticipated this explanation concerning the reason for Elisha's "weeping" from 8,12b where the prophet answers Hazael's question about why he is crying by invoking the disasters which he (Hazael) will bring upon Israel; see below.

213. This element, which has no parallel in the Biblical Elisha's answer to Hazael, serves to underscore the prophet's solidarity with his threatened people. It echoes too the woman's appeal to the prophet in 9,47 that he "pity (ἐλεῆσαι) her".

214. Note that Josephus here reverses the sequence of Hazael's first two future measures according to 8,12 where his burning of the cities precedes mention of his killing of the Israelite military elite.

215. Josephus' remaining uses the verb προσρήγνυμι are in *BJ* 1,271; *AJ* 6,182; the term occurs as a variant in 14,367. Josephus' wording here ("kill their children by dashing them against the rocks") was perhaps influenced by the macarism of Ps 137,8 ("Happy shall he be who takes your [Babylon's] little ones and dashes them against the rock!").

216. The above construction occurs only here in Josephus. His remaining uses of the verb ἀναρρήγνυμι are confined to *BJ* (1,20; 2,56.434; 6,279.429; 7,310).

had revealed (δεδηλωκέναι)[217] to him that Azaēlos was to be king (βασιλεύειν; BL βασιλεύοντα) of Syria".

The episode concludes in 8,14-15 with the realization of Elisha's announcement (8,13b) about Hazael's becoming king of Syria. This closing sequence opens with the three-fold notice of 8,14: Hazael leaves Elisha and repairs to Ben-hadad; the king asks him what Elisha had said; Hazael replies that he was told that the king is to recover. Josephus (9,92c) compresses: "So Azaēlos came to Adados and gave him a good report as to his illness... [218]". 2 Kgs 8,15 juxtaposes Hazael's reassuring word with the measures he undertakes the next day, i.e. suffocating his master with a dampened "covelet" (so RSV; MT הַמַּכְבֵּר; B transliterates τὸν χαββά; L translates with τὸ στρῶμα, TJ גונכא), and then making himself king. Josephus' description of these initiatives reads: "But the next day he spread (ἐβιβαλών; L ἐπέβαλεν) a mesh-cloth (δίκτυον)[219] dipped in water (διάβροχον[220], BL ἔβαψεν τῷ ὕδατι) over him and killed (διέφθειρε; BL ἀπέθανεν) him by suffocation (στραγγάλη)[221]. Then he took over the royal power himself (ἀρχὴν ... παρέλαβε; BL ἐβασίλευσεν ... ἀντ᾽ αὐτοῦ)...".

In Kings, mention of Hazael's coup (8,15) is followed immediately (and abruptly) by the notice on the accession of J(eh)oram of Judah (8,16). Josephus' parallel to the latter notice comes only in 9,95. Between it and his version of 8,15 he interposes (9,93-94) a lengthy set of appended notices which have no Biblical equivalent as such:

> (93)... (Azaēlos) being a man of action (δραστήριος)[222] and in great favour (εὔνοιαν) with the Syrians and the people of Damascus, by whom Adados and Azaēlos who ruled after him are to this day honoured as gods

217. Here, Josephus thus does have Elisha appeal to a divine "revelation" in contrast to 9,90 where, in his parallel to 8,10b, he leaves aside the Biblical prophet's invocation of such a revelation. Josephus uses the verb δηλόω with God/the Deity as subject also in AJ 2,235; 8,240.269.321; 10,195.242.

218. Here, in his lie to the king, Azaēlos exceeds the instructions given him by Elisha who (see 9,90) tells him simply "not to announce the bad news to the king" (by contrast in the Biblical account there is a correspondence between the prophet's directive [8,10] and Hazael's "execution" of this [8,14]). In Josephus' presentation, the Syrian's lie is thus something he does on his own initiative, rather than in accordance with the prophet's directive; thereby, Elisha's prophetic veracity remains unimpaired; see n. 209.

219. According to WEILL, Josèphe, II, p. 263, n. 3 this term corresponds to the Hebrew mkbr ("network", see LXX Exod 27,4 where δίκτυον translates that word) of MT 8,15. MARCUS, Josephus, VI, p. 49, n.c favors rather either mkmr or mkmrt as its Hebrew equivalent.

220. The adjective διάβροχος is hapax in Josephus.

221. This specification about the manner of Azaēlos' killing Adados corresponds to the Biblical notice about his spreading the wet covelet over the king's face. The word στραγγάλη occurs twice elsewhere in Josephus, i.e. AJ 6,166; 16,394.

222. This is the same term used by Josephus in 9,28 in introducing Joram of Israel; see there.

because of their benefactions (εὐεργεσίας; see 9,47) and the building of temples with which they adorned the city of Damascus[223]. (94) And they have processions every day in honour of these kings and glory in their antiquity (σεμνύνονται τὴν ... ἀρχαιότητα)[224], not knowing that these kings are rather recent and lived less eleven hundred years ago[225]. Now, when Joram, the Israelite king[226], heard of Adados's death, he breathed again more freely (ἀνέπνευσεν)[227] after the alarms and the terror (ἐκ τῶν φόβων καὶ τοῦ δέους[228] [compare εἰς τὸ δέος καὶ τὴν ταραχήν, 9,87]) which he had felt on his account, and gladly (ἀσμένως) welcomed peace (εἰρήνης)[229].

223. MARCUS, *Josephus*, VI, pp. 50-51, n. b suggests that Nicolas of Damascus, whom Josephus cites by name on several occasions in his work (see, e.g., *AJ* 7,100), "may be the source" for Josephus' statement here. Marcus likewise notes that in speaking of king "Adados" as a "god" among the Syrians, Josephus (or Nicolas) appears to confound that historical figure with his divine namesake "Hadad", whereas "a god Hazael seems to be unknown". In this connection Marcus cites as well T. Reinach's reference, in WEILL, *Josèphe*, II, p. 264, n. 1, to Justin (36,2.3) who speaks of two ancient, pre-Abrahamic kings of Damascus with names similar to those mentioned by Josephus in 9,93, i.e. "Azelus" and "Adores" as a possible parallel to Josephus' evocation of "Adados" and "Azaēlos" as divinized rulers.

224. The above construction occurs only here in Josephus; he uses the noun ἀρχαίοτης once elsewhere in *AJ* (14,2), twice in *BJ* and 12(13) times in *c. Ap*.

225. MARCUS, *Josephus*, VI, p. 51, n.c points out that the correct figure for the interval between the reigns of the two kings (*ca*. 850 B.C.) and the moment at which Josephus is writing (*ca*. 100 A.D.) would be "less than 1000 years". In any case, the above remark is in line with Josephus' penchant for pointing out the errors in the Gentile traditions drawn on by him in *AJ*; see, e.g., his critical comments on Herodotus' *History* (2,102ff.) in 8,260-262 in connection with his own account of the Egyptian invasion of Judah at the time of Rehoboam.

With the above deprecation of the "antiquity" of the Syrian kings, compare Josephus' emphasis on the "antiquity" of his own people in *c. Ap*.; see, e.g., his opening statement (1,3) that he has written this work, *inter alia*, "to instruct all who desire to know the truth concerning the antiquity (ἀρχαιότητος; see ἀρχαιότητα, 9,94) of our race". On the great importance attached to a people's "antiquity" by Josephus' (Gentile) contemporaries, see A.J. DROGE, *Josephus between Greeks and Barbarians*, in L.H. FELDMAN, and J.R. LEVISON (eds.), *Josephus' Contra Apionem: Studies in its Character & Context with a Latin Concordance to the Portion Missing in Greek* (AGJU, 34), Leiden, Brill, 1996, pp. 115-142.

226. "Joram" is nowhere mentioned in 2 Kgs 8,7-15. Perhaps, Josephus was inspired to "reintroduce" the Israelite king at this point given the reference to him in the synchronic notice on his Judean namesake's accession in 8,16 (which in Kings follows immediately upon the episode of 8,7-15; see above in the text).

227. Josephus' other uses of the verb ἀναπνέω are in *BJ* 4,131; 5,265; *AJ* 5,198.

228. The above two words are collocated also in *AJ* 6,151.

229. With this notice Josephus provides an appropriate conclusion to his long segment (9,51-94) featuring the conflict between Syria and Israel which now, finally, reaches a (provisional) resolution. On the notice as indicative of Josephus' concern to portray Joram, his military acumen notwithstanding as ultimately a man of peace on the model of Augustus, see FELDMAN, *Studies*, p. 325 (= ID., *Jehoram*, 10-11). Josephus will resume his account of the Israelite Joram in 9,105, following the interlude devoted to his Judean namesake in 9,95-104.

Conclusions: Josephus' Rewriting of 2 Kgs 4,1–8,15

After the foregoing detailed comparison of *AJ* 9,46-94 and 2 Kgs 4,1–8,15*, I shall now try to summarize my findings with regard to the two segments.

Ultimately, given the large measure of content agreement between the witnesses for 2 Kgs 4,1–8,15 examined (MT, B, L, TJ) on the one hand and Josephus' own ubiquitous paraphrasing tendency on the other, it does not seem possible to say anything too definite about the Biblical text(s) utilized by him in 9,46-94. Recall, however, that he does agree with MT 2 Kgs 6,25 against BL on the number of silver pieces (80 vs. 50) paid for an ass's head during the siege of Samaria; see 9,62. Also noteworthy is the historian's citation of items peculiar to TJ (and Rabbinic tradition) in his version of Elisha's multiplication miracle, i.e. the identification of the widow's husband with Obadiah, her reminiscence of his saving the prophets from the hands of Jezebel, and his borrowing money to do this (9,47 = TJ 2 Kgs 4,1). Nor, certainly, is Josephus' use of "LXX" in our segment to be excluded, especially given the recurrent (if limited) verbal contacts between them, compare, e.g., ἀγγεῖα ... παρὰ τῶν γειτόνων (9,48) and ἀγγεῖα παρὰ πάντων γειτόνων σου (L 4 Rgns 4,3). On the other hand sustained evidence for Josephus' primary dependence on L in our segment is not forthcoming, *pace* a long-standing scholarly concensus that (proto-L) was *the* Biblical text used by Josephus from the books of Samuel on[230].

In summing up on Josephus' rewriting techniques in 9,46-94, I distinguish the following (often overlapping) categories: 1) stylistic/terminological modifications; 2) re-arrangements; 3) omissions/condensations; and 4) expansions. I shall now consider each of these categories in turn. 1) Stylistic/Terminological Modifications: Under the "stylistic" rubric, it might be noted first of all that Josephus consistently replaces the Biblical narrative's monotonous parataxis with a more flowing (and better Greek) hypotaxis. With considerable frequency as well, he substitutes indirect for the source's standard direct discourse (see, e.g., 9,47 = 2 Kgs 4,1: the widow's word to Elisha). In our segment, however, as we have seen, Josephus does on occasion retain the Biblical direct address (see,

---

230. For advocates of this view, see BEGG, *Early Divided Monarchy*, pp. 3-4, n. 6. In this connection it might also be pointed out that in 2 Kgs 4,1–8,15 one frequently finds L agreeing with MT against B; see, e.g., 7,1 where B lacks the reference to the coming abundance of "barley" found in the two former witnesses (as also in Josephus; see 9,71). In cases where Josephus does have an equivalent to the item shared by MT and L (but absent in B), one is left uncertain as to which of those witnesses he was, in fact, drawing upon.

e.g., 9,66 = 2 Kgs 6,28b-29: the woman's presentation of her case to the king), just as he also mixes the two forms in a single utterance (see, e.g., Elisha's announcement to his disciples, 9,68 = 2 Kgs 6,32b, which begins in indirect, but then goes over to direct discourse). A further such stylistic modification is Josephus' supplying of proper names – drawn from the wider context – for Biblical figures who lack these, see, e.g., his mention of "Joram" (compare 2 Kgs 6,9: "the king of Israel") and "Adados" (compare 2 Kgs 6,10 "the king of Syria") in 9,51. Thereby, he gives his presentation a more determinate historical character. Finally, Josephus is wont to reword in clearer, more explicit terms Biblical formulations that could appear obscure. E.g., while 2 Kgs 6,12b has the Syrian king informed that Elisha relates to the king of Israel "the words that you speak in your bedchamber", Josephus specifies that the prophet "informed him (Joram) of everything and had revealed to him the things plotted by Adados" (9,53). Another example of such a Josephan "clarification" is his identification of the figure whose facial contorsions are described in 2 Kgs 8,11a. The Biblical verse leaves it unclear whether the subject here is Elisha or rather Hazael. Josephus (9,90) resolves all doubt on the matter by specifying that "the king's servant (i.e. Azaēlus) was grieving at what he had heard".

On the terminological level, we noted that Josephus, in accordance with his standard practice throughout *AJ*, avoids certain Biblical terms or expressions, replacing these with alternative formulations. Thus, "the Lord" becomes "(the) God (e.g., 9,55 = 2 Kgs 6,20); "the man of God" yields (as also in TJ) to "the prophet" (e.g., 9,50 = 2 Kgs 4,7); "the word (of God)" gives way to "prophecy" (e.g., 9,85 = 2 Kgs 7,16) or "prophesy" (e.g., 9,86 = 2 Kgs 7,17), while 2 Kgs 4,1's reference to the deceased's "fearing the Lord" gets replaced by mention of his protecting the prophets (9,47). Beyond these instances of "verbal preference", we noted as well Josephus' replacement of Biblical units of measure with more familiar contemporary ones, see 9,62 ("a *xeste*") for 2 Kgs 6,25's "a fourth part of a *qab*". In addition, Josephus avoids citing the actual wording of curses/oaths as found in his source, see his substitution "(Joram) called down God's curse upon her" (9,64) for "may the Lord not save thee; how shall I save thee?" of 6,27 (see also his elimination of the king's self-curse from his version of 6,31 in 9,67). A further remarkable feature to Josephus' rewording of the Bible's presentation is his repeated introduction of the terms "enemies" or "foes" to qualify the relationship between the Syrians and Israelites. As noted, one function of this terminological insistence is to underscore the chivalry of the Israelite treatment of the Syrian captives (see 9,59 = 2 Kgs 6,23).

2) Re-arrangements: In a whole series of instances, Josephus re-arranges the order of items within a given Biblical verse reproduced by him. Examples are: the future price of barley is cited before that of flour (9,71 = 7,1; 9,85 = 7,16); "the king(s) of Egypt" precede(s) "the king(s) of the islands (Hittites)" (9,77 = 7,6); the lepers carry off "garments and gold" (9,79) while in 7,8 it is the reverse; Ben-hadad's sickness is mentioned before rather than after the coming of Elisha to Damascus (9,87-88 = 2 Kgs 8,7); while Hadad will kill Israel's best warriors and fire its strongholds (9,91) instead of the other way round (thus 8,9). Under this heading might also be mentioned Josephus' "anticipations" of elements from a later point in the particular Biblical narrative he is retelling. One such anticipation occurs in the historian's account of Israel's pursuit of the fleeing Syrians. 2 Kgs 7,15 states that the pursuit extended "as far as the Jordan". Josephus incorporates this specification at a previous point, i.e. the courtier's proposal that the Syrians be pursued (9,83 = 7,13). Conversely, the Bible's indication concerning the reason for Ben-hadad's dispatching an expedition to ascertain Elisha's whereabouts, i.e. in order that he might might seize him (6,13) is "delayed" by Josephus until a later moment, i.e. the Syrian's sending of a force to actually apprehend the prophet whom, he has been informed, is dwelling at Dothan (9,54 = 6,14). Such transpositions seem primarily to reflect Josephus' tendency to vary the wording of the source as much as possible, even while leaving the sense intact. Note too that in 9,46-94 one does not find Josephus re-arranging the sequence of whole pericopes as he does on occasion elsewhere; see, e.g., *AJ* 8,246-273 where he reverses the order of 1 Kgs 14,1-20 and 21-31.

3) Omissions/Condensations: Josephus' ommissions within 9,46-94 involve both whole pericopes of the source as well as shorter elements from those units of it which he does reproduce. With regard to the former category, we noted that the absence of all parallel to 2 Kgs 4,8-6,8 in Josephus' account of Elisha's great deeds is likely due, in part at least, to text-critical factors. On the other hand, the story of 2 Kgs 8,1-6 is also unrepresented in Josephus' presentation. Here, one would seem to have a case of a deliberate omission by Josephus himself for reasons I attempted to indicate above.

Josephus does reproduce the remaining material of 2 Kgs 4,1–8,15, i.e. 4,1-7; 6,9–7,20; 8,7-15, and does so *in extenso*. Occasionally, however, he passes over some particular item also in this material. A case in point is his omission (see 9,67) of the reference to the people's seeing the sackcloth the king is wearing when he rends his outer garments in response to the woman's story in 2 Kgs 6,30b. Here, Josephus' procedure would seem inspired by the fact of the item's "functionlessness" in the further course of the story. He drops as well 6,10b's reference to the multiple warnings given Joram by Elisha about Syrian designs against him; in this case, his motivation is, perhaps, simply the desire to condense the narrative to the extent possible. Elsewhere, Josephus does not completely dispense with the Biblical data. Rather, he significantly reduces elements that appear superfluous or repetitious. Two examples may illustrate this feature of Josephus' rewriting. In 2 Kgs 7,10 the lepers enumerate for the gatekeepers (BL) what they had encountered at the Syrian camp; their "catalogue" re-utilizes items from the description of the enemy's retreat in 7,7. Josephus (9,81) compresses their report into a single, generalized phrase, "they informed them of what had become of the enemy". An even more egregious instance of repetitiousness in the Biblical account is the sequence of 7,18-20 with its verbatim quotation of the exchange between prophet and captain from 7,2 and its duplication of the latter's death notice (7,17b) in 7,20. In Josephus (9,86) this whole complex gets compacted into the words attached to his version of the fulfilment notice at the end of 7,17: "he himself (the captain) suffered this fate, as Elisha had prophesied when this man alone of them all had refused to believe what he said concerning the abundance of provisions that was to be".

4) Additions/Expansions: Of all Josephus' rewriting techniques in 9,46-94, it is, however, his expansions of the Biblical account which predominate. The historian's additions here very greatly in length, character and purpose, as the following catalogue will illustrate (some of the types of additions distinguished in it do, naturally, overlap). In 9,86 he introduces a brief aside concerning the Biblical *saton* equaling 1 and 1/2 Italian *modii*, while in 9,62 (= 6,25) he specifies, with like brevity, that the high-prized dove's dung was to be used "for salt". Many of Josephus' shorter additions in our segment aim at generating a smoother-reading text than its Biblical counterpart with its frequently abrupt juxtapositions of component sections. In 9,46, e.g., Josephus provides a kind of "thesis statement" in which he alerts readers to the topic of the whole segment (9,47-94), i.e. Elisha's mighty deeds (compare the very loose linkage between the end of 2 Kings 3 and the opening of the "Elisha bloc" in 4,1). He rounds off the account of Elisha's multiplication miracle (9,47-50 = 2 Kgs 4,1-7) with the summary statement at the end of 9,50: "in this way, then, did Elisha free the woman of her debts and deliver her from the harsh treatment of her creditors". At the opening of 2 Kings 7 there is a abrupt shift from the dialogue between prophet and captain in 7,1-2 in the house of the former with Elisha's announcement of the

latter's demise to mention of the lepers stationed at the gate in 7,3. Josephus (9,74) inserts an element of transition between the two scenes: "And indeed the things which had been foretold by Elisha came to pass in this manner". Another such transitional insertion is the phrase "as we mentioned a little while ago" of 9,79 which serves to "reintroduce" the subject of the lepers' movements which Josephus breaks off at the beginning of 9,76 in order to describe the Syrians' abandonment of their camp (9,76b-78).

Other of Josephus' insertions serve to accentuate the drama, pathos, and/or reprehensibility of what is being related. The woman who refuses to make her son available to be eaten is the complainant's "neighbor and friend" (9,65 = 2 Kgs 6,29). Joram not only rends his garments at hearing the case, but "cries out fearfully" (9,67 = 6,30). Azaēlos, Adados' future assassin, is the king's "most trusted servant" (9,88; compare 8,8).

In 9,93-94 Josephus appends to his notice on Azaēlos' coup (= 8,15) an extended reference to a Syrian tradition concerning the divinized kings Adados and Azaēlos. His citation of this tradition reflects yet another factor at work in the historian's additions, i.e. his interest in reminding his sophisticated audience of both the breath of his culture and his critical acumen (the Syrians are, he points out, mistaken about the antiquity of their kings).

One may further distinguish within Josephus' additions those made with a view to resolving problems or answering questions suggested by the Biblical text. He disposes, e.g., of the "contradiction" between 6,23 (the Syrians cease their incursions into Israel) and 24 (Ben-hadad's army advances against Samaria) by differentiating between distinct modes of attacking Israel adopted successively by the Syrian ruler; see 9,60. The directive he has Elisha issue Joram about shutting the gates of Samaria and positioning his army before the Syrians' eyes are opened (9,57) serves to prepare – as the Bible itself fails to do – the subsequent mention of the king's presence at the scene and the military capacity which he mentions as available to him (9,58 = 6,21). 2 Kgs 7,3 leaves unexplained what the lepers are doing at the gate of the besieged city; Josephus (9,74) attributes their presence there to a "law" forbidding such persons entry into Samaria. Similarly, he accounts for the illness that overtakes Ben-hadad (2 Kgs 8,7): it comes as a reaction to the king's realization that it was God who in his displeasure at him had brought panic on the Syrian force (9,87).

Closely related to the preceding category is a further one, i.e. the historian's numerous inserted indications concerning characters' mental/ emotional states and the roles assumed by the various personages, the kings Joram and Adados in particular. The Syrian king is "amazed" at God's power and "fearful of Elisha" (9,60; compare 6,24), and becomes "greatly disheartened" in the face of God's displeasure (9,87; compare 8,7). Recall too that whereas in 7,6-7 the Syrian retreat transpires without any mention of Ben-hadad, Josephus (9,77) has the Syrians first report to their king who himself "hears" the noise of the purportedly advancing enemies. Joram undergoes a like magnification in Josephus' presentation. The Israelite king opts to take his stand at Samaria given the strength of the city's walls (9,61), whereas in 6,24 all initiative seems to rest with the Syrians, Joram being nowhere mentioned. Joram is obsessed with fear lest Samaria be betrayed (9,63; recall that with this mention of the king's emotional state Josephus "motivates" the Biblical datum of Joram's walking on the city walls, 6,26). Later, he is "angered" by the woman's initial appeal (9,64 = 6,26), "sorely grieved" at her report (9,67 = 6,30), wrath-filled at Elisha's failure to intercede (9,67 = 6,31), "repents" of this wrath (9,70), "rejoices at" and "believes" Elisha's announcement of coming abundance (9,72 = 7,1), and is relieved at the news of his enemy Adados' death (9,94). In addition, Josephus gives the Israelite king more to say and do than is the case with his Biblical counterpart. Thus while in our witnesses for 2 Kgs 6,33b, it is the "messenger" who addresses Elisha, Josephus (9,70) identifies Joram as the speaker there. Similarly, he assigns the king a longer (and more directive) discourse concerning the Syrian retreat in 9,82-83 than one finds in the Biblical parallel, 7,12. In his presentation, furthermore, the people do not commence plundering the Syrian camp on their own initiative (thus 7,16), but only when "let loose" by Joram (9,84).

Josephus fills out the Biblical portrayal of other personages as well. Elisha, he notes, "with God as his ally was scornful of danger and without fear" (9,55); the directives he gives Joram prior to effecting the Syrians' cure (9,57; see above) underscore his foresight and sense for military realities. The prophet's "truthfulness" is explicitly affirmed in connection with his promise of Samaria's imminent change of fortune (9,72; compare 7,1), while Adados recognizes that "the Deity is so evidently present" with him (9,60). The Syrians sent against him, for their part, "eagerly" follow the prophet to Samaria "with eyes and understanding beclouded by God" (9,57). The restoration of their sight throws them "as was natural, into dire consternation and helplessness at so divine and marvelous an event". The "unbelief" of Joram's captain is accentuated (9,73.86; compare 7,2a.17) – all the more so given the ready acceptance accorded Elisha's announcement by Joram and his other hearers (9,72; no Biblical parallel). Both the lepers (9,75 = 7,3b-4) and Joram's respondent

(9,83 = 7,13) are assigned more expansive reflections by Josephus as well. Finally, Azaēlos, the new king of Syria, is qualified as "a man of action and in great favour with the Syrians" in 9,93 (compare 8,15).

Having reviewed Josephus' various rewriting techniques in 9,46-94, I wish now to address a further question: how does the Josephan version of Elisha's exploits which those techniques help generate compare overall with the Biblical one and what might the distinctive features of his presentation be intended to convey to his Gentile and Jewish readers? In responding to this question, I would note, first of all, that Josephus reproduces those portions of the Biblical sequence 2 Kgs 4,1-8,15 which he does include in great detail. Why should he do this rather than simply summarize the component episodes as he does, e.g., with the story of Elijah's translation (2 Kgs 2,1-18) in 9,28 (see chap. 2)? I suggest that Josephus' willingness to allot the Bible's Elisha material so much space in his own composition reflects the historian's realization that this material could well further various of his apologetic aims. Specifically, utilization of the Elisha stories, in their detailed content, enabled him to counteract a range of contemporary allegations against his people, i.e. the Jews lack great men of the stature of the Greek and Roman heroes (on the contrary, Elisha's deeds are "glorious and worthy of note", 9,46), just as they are militarily undistinguished, impoverished and devoid of concern for other peoples (the story of Samaria's deliverance gives the lie to all such charges).

For the rest, Josephus, in 9,46-94, presents the Biblical content to Gentile readers in a smoother-reading form. He anticipates and resolves questions and difficulties of various sorts the original might pose for (Gentile) readers. The psychological and dramatic element is accentuated. The kings Joram and Adados receive a degree of attention that puts them almost on a par with Elisha himself. On the other hand, Josephus does not downplay the source stories' theological and miraculous dimensions to any noticeable degree – this in contrast to his procedure in other portions of AJ. Indeed, the opposite is the case: God's involvement in and the supernatural character of the events recorded undergoes an intensification in his version: it is God, Elisha is made to aver, who will fill the vessels (9,48, no Biblical parallel); the Syrians accompany Elisha with "eyes and understanding beclouded by God" (9,57); their ending up in the midst of the enemy capital is "a divine and marvellous event" (9,58); Adados is confounded by the manifestation of God's power (9,60), and overwhelmed to learn that it was the Deity who had panicked his forces (9,87), etc. Such an emphasis on God's helpful interventions in the troubles facing their ancestors in Elisha's time

would offer a message of hope to contemporary Jewish readers, themselves confronting analogous difficulties. Thus, it might finally be said
that while Josephus clearly adapts the Elisha material with an eye to
the interests, tastes (and correction-needing prejudices) of his Gentile
readers, he does not do so at the cost of that material's Jewish-religious
message.

V

JORAM OF JUDAH[1]
(9,95-104)

Throughout the long segment *AJ* 9,18-94 Josephus' focus – in line with that of his primary source, i.e. 2 Kgs 2,1–8,15, has been on the Northern figures (Kings Ahaziah and Joram, the prophets Elijah and Elisha). Only in 9,44-45 was there a brief interlude featuring the end of the Judean King Jehoshaphat (9,44) and the succession of his son Joram (9,45), this latter paragraph drawing – selectively – on the more expansive presentation of 2 Chr 21,1b-3 (compare 1 Kgs 22,50b). Now in 9,95-104 Josephus resumes his account of the Judean Joram from 9,45, basing himself here on the detailed narration of 2 Chr 21,4-22,1 as opposed to the schematic Joram narrative of 2 Kgs 8,16-24. I divide up the material to be analyzed in this chapter into four segments: 1. Joram's Crimes (*AJ* 9,95-96 = 2 Kgs 8,18-19 // 2 Chr 21,4-7); 2. Revolts (9,97-98 = 8,20-22 // 21,8-10); 3. Elijah's letter (9,99-101 = 21,11-15); and 4. Joram's End (9,102-104 = 8,23-24 // 21,16-22,1).

1. *Joram's Crimes*

Following the long "Northern interlude" of 9,46-94 which ends up with mention of his Israelite namesake (see 9,94), Josephus, at the beginning of 9,95, reintroduces the Judean Joram with a *Rückverweis* to his initial presentation of him in 9,45 (see there): "But Joram, *the king of Jerusalem*[2] – *he bore this same name* [i.e. as Joram of Israel, see 9,94], *as we stated earlier* –…[3]". Thereafter, he picks up the thread of the Chronicler's story of Joram's dealings with his brothers (21,2-4) held over by him from 9,45. 2 Chr 21,4 states that, once in power, Joram

---

1. This chapter represents a reworking of my article *Joram of Judah according to Josephus (Ant. 9.45, 95-104)*, in *JSQ* 1 (1993-1994) 323-339 which I use here by permission; cf. ID., *Constructing a Monster: The Chronicler's* Sondergut *in 2 Chronicles 21*, in *ABR* 37 (1989) 35-51.

2. Compare the title "king of the Jerusalemites" used of Joram's father Jehoshaphat in 9,31.

3. Compare 9,45 where Josephus states of the Judean Joram that he "had the same name as his wife's [i.e. Athaliah] brother [i.e. Joram of Israel]".

killed both "all his brothers" and "some of the princes (BL ἀρχόντων) of Israel (so MT B; L Judah)". Josephus' rendition changes the designation of the second group of Joram's victims and appends a commentary upon his deed: "... (he) *no sooner* came into power[4] than he proceeded to slay (ἐπὶ σφαγὴν ... ἐχώρησε; compare ἀπέκτεινεν... ἐν ῥομφαίᾳ, BL)[5] his brothers and *his father's friends* (τῶν πατρῴων φίλων)[6] *who were also* chiefs (ἡγεμόνες)[7], *making this the beginning and outward sign of his wickedness* (τὴν ἀρχὴν καὶ ... ἐπίδειξιν[8] τῆς πονηρίας[9])...".

As the continuation of their respective chronological notices for Joram (2 Kgs 8,17 // 2 Chr 21,5)[10], Josephus' Scriptural sources give a similarly worded evaluation of him (8,18// 21,6), both coupling this with the remark that, despite the king's depravity, the Lord maintained Judah/ the Davidic line for the sake of his commitment to David (8,19 // 21,7). Josephus' rendition of the latter sequence is 9,95b-96. It begins (9,95b) with a formulation that explicates the opening charge of 8,18aα // 21,6aα ("he walked in the way of the kings of Israel, as the house of Ahab had done"): "... and in no way did he differ from the kings (μηδὲν διενεγκὼν τῶν ... βασιλεών)[11] of the people (του λαοῦ)[12] who first transgressed against the

4. Compare the opening words of 21,4: "when Jehoram (so MT, BL Joram) had ascended the throne of his father and was established...". Josephus' rendering underscores that Joram's very first royal act ("as soon as") was the crime of fratricide.

5. The above phrase is used by Josephus in connection with Saul's butchering of the Amalekite women and children in *AJ* 6,136. This terminological parallelism serves to underscore the enormity of Joram's deed: what Saul did to the reprobate Amalekites, Joram does to his own brothers.

6. This inserted qualification of Joram's other set of victims (compare 21,4 "some of the princes") likewise underscores the reprehensibility of Joram's deed: the persons killed by him were officials who had a special status and bond to his own house as "friends of his father" (elsewhere in Josephus this phrase occurs in *BJ* 2,104; *AJ* 8,215.264).

7. The above collocation "friends and chiefs" echoes 9,81 where Joram of Israel summons the same two groups upon hearing of the lepers' report.

8. This collocation occurs only here in Josephus.

9. Josephus employs the above phrase "outward sign of wickedness" also of Gessius Florus in *AJ* 20,254.

10. Josephus leaves aside the first component of these notices (Joram's age, i.e. 32, at accession); he will reproduce the second of them (Joram's length of reign: 8 years) at the end of his account of the king in 9,104. His procedure with respect to both items is in accord with his standard practice vis-à-vis such data. In dealing with the elements of 21,5 (= 8,17) in this way, Josephus further avoids the seeming disruptiveness of that verse within the Chronicler's account of Joram's crimes in 21,4 and 6-7; in his own presentation the data of these two passages stand together in a continuous sequence, i.e. 9,95-96.

11. Compare Josephus' similar characterization of Omri in *AJ* 8,313 διέφερε δ' οὐδὲν τῶν πρὸ αὐτοῦ βασιλευσάντων.

12. This is the reading of RO (cf. Lat *populi*) which Niese and Marcus adopt. Dindorf, Bekker, and Naber follow MSP's τοῦ Ἰσραήλ.

ancient customs (παρηνόμησαν εἰς τὰ πάτρια ... ἔθη)[13] of the Hebrews and the worship of God (τὴν τοῦ θεοῦ θρησκείαν)". 2 Kgs 8,18aβ // 2 Chr 21,6aβ attribute Joram's wickedness to the influence ("for") of his wife, the (nameless) daughter of Ahab. Josephus (9,96a) supplies this figure with a name already at this point, also spelling out the nature of her influence: "The one who taught him to do wrong (κακόν)[14], *and especially in worshipping foreign gods* (ξενικοὺς θεοὺς προσκυνεῖν; cf. τοὺς ξενικοὺς ἐσέβετο [of Joram of Israel], 9,27)[15], was Achab's daughter *Othlia* (᾽Οθλία)[16] who was married to him[17]".

The "qualifying notice" which the sources attach to their negative judgment on Joram (8,18 // 21,6) differs somewhat in its first half. 2 Kgs 8,19a speaks of the Lord's unwillingness "to destroy *Judah, for the sake of David his servant*", while 2 Chr 21,7a makes this "destroy *the house of David, because of the covenant* (BL διαθήκην) *which he had made with David*". Both verses conclude, however, with a reference to the Lord's promise of an everlasting "lamp" (so RSV; MT נִיר, BL λύχνον; compare TJ and TC both of which render with a non-figurative term, i.e. מַלְכוּ, "kingship"). The wording of Josephus' parallel (9,96b) stands closer to that of 21,7a than to 8,19a: "But God (21,7: the Lord) because of His covenant with David (τὴν πρὸς Δαυίδην ὁμολογίαν)[18] did not

13. This precise construction occurs only here in Josephus; cf., however, *AJ* 12,286 (without ἔθη). For the occurrences of the phrase "ancestral customs" in Josephus (some 25 times), see BEGG, *Early Divided Monarchy*, p. 171, n. 1161. On the term "ancestral" as a key, positive qualifier of laws, customs, etc. in the Josephan corpus, see SCHLATTER, *Theologie*, pp. 51-52 and the monograph of B. SCHRÖDER, *Die 'väterlichen Gesetze'. Flavius Josephus als Vermittler von Halachah an Griechen und Römer* (TSAJ, 53), Tübingen, Mohr Siebeck, 1996.

14. Josephus' reference to Athaliah as "teaching" her husband to do wrong here is perhaps inspired by the mention of the queen as the "counselor" (BL σύμβουλος) of her son Ahaziah "in doing wickedly" in 2 Chr 22,2.

15. The above phrase recurs in *AJ* 9,133 (where, as in 9,95-96, it stands in opposition to "the service of God"), cf. 8,271. On the contrast made in 9,95-96 between "ancestral (customs)" and "foreign (gods)", see SCHLATTER, *Theologie*, pp. 51-52.

16. This is the emendation of Niese which Marcus follows; the codices (as well as Dindorf, Bekker, and Naber) read Γοθολία. Josephus anticipates the queen's name from 2 Kgs 8,26 // 2 Chr 22,3 where MT has "Athaliah", BL Γοθολία, i.e. the form found in the codices of 9,96.

17. This concluding indication harks back to *AJ* 8,398 where, following 2 Chr 18,1, Josephus states: "Now Josaphat married his son Joram to the daughter of Achab... her name being Othlia", here too supplying the name of Joram's consort where the source lacks it.

18. The above phrase is used by Josephus also in *AJ* 8,207 (= 1 Kgs 11,36) in reporting Ahijah's word to Jeroboam that God will leave two tribes to Solomon's son "because of the promise (ὁμολογίαν) he had made to David". Josephus' avoidance of the BL term διαθήκη (= "covenant") of 21,7 here in 9,96 is in accord with his regular practice (he uses the term only in its standard secular sense of "last will, testament"). On the point, see BEGG, *Early Divided Monarchy*, pp. 100-101, n. 609 and the literature cited there.

wish (οὐκ ἐβούλετο = BL 21,7) utterly to destroy his line (τὸ γένος ἐξαφανίσαι)...[19]". Josephus has no equivalent to the evocation of the divine promise of an everlasting "lamp" (MT BL)/ "kingship" (TJ, TC) for the Davidids cited in 8,19b // 21,7b. The reason for this "omission" is likely the historian's concern over Roman sensibilities regarding ongoing Jewish "messianism" to which such language might seem to lend credence[20]. In place thereof he introduces a notice which highlights both the depravity of Joram and the divine forebearance in sparing – for the time being – the Davidic line: "... although Joram did not let a day go by (οὐ διέλιπεν ἑκάστης ἡμέρας) without devising some new form (καινουργῶν)[21] of impiety and violation (ἀσεβείᾳ καὶ λύμῃ)[22] of his country's traditions (τῶν ἐπιχωρίων ἐθισμῶν)[23]".

2. Revolts

2 Kgs 8,20-22 // 2 Chr 21,8-10 relate revolts by several subject regions against Joram, i.e. Edom (8,20-22a // 21,8-10a) and Libnah (8,22b // 21,10b). The above Biblical sequences begin with the notice that "Edom" revolted from Judean rule and set up its own king. Josephus (9,97a) amplifies this notice with an item peculiar to himself: "Now, when, about that time [Bible: in his (Joram's) days], the Idumaeans[24] revolted (ἀποστάντων; compare ἀπέστη BL 21,8) from him, *and, after killing their former king who had been submissive to Joram's father*[25], set up a king of their own choosing". 2 Kgs 8,21-22a

19. The above construction recurs in *AJ* 3,213; 6,146,291; 9,140. Only in the first of these instances, however, is it used with God as subject, as here in 9,96.

20. This concern makes itself felt throughout Josephus' reworking of the Biblical material concerning David, see FELDMAN, *Interpretation*, pp. 537-539, 567-569 (= ID., *David*, 130-131, 173-174).

21. Josephus' two remaining uses of the verb καινουργέω are in *AJ* 12,76; 15,303 (it is also conjectured by Niese in *BJ* 4,591). Only here in 9,96, however, is is used with negative connotations of cultic "innovating".

22. This collocation occurs only here in Josephus.

23. The above expression is hapax in Josephus; compare τὰ πάτρια ... ἔθη in 9,95. The whole of the above formulation echoes Josephus' earlier statements concerning Jeroboam I; see *AJ* 8,245: "every day (καθ' ἡμέραν) he sought to commit some new (καινόν) act more heinous than the reckless acts he was already guilty of" and 8,265: "he did not cease (οὐ διέλιπεν) nor desist from outraging God, but all the time (καθ' ἑκάστην ἡμέραν) continued...". Like Jeroboam, Josephus' *bête noire*, Joram is guilty, in the historian's presentation, of the "mortal sin" of religious "innovation", i.e. failing to respect his people's ancestral, native customs.

24. On Josephus' characteristic replacement of Biblical mentions of Edom/the Edomites with Idumaea/ the Idumaeans, see on 9,30.

25. The above insertion harks back to *AJ* 9,30 where, in an anticipation of 2 Kgs 3,7, Josephus has Jehoshaphat promise Joram of Israel that he would "compel the Idumaean

// 2 Chr 21,9-10a recount, somewhat obscurely and with differences in detail, Joram's (ultimately abortive) response to the Edomite revolt. Matters begin with Joram and his forces "passing over" (+ to Zair, 8,21). Surrounded by the Edomites, Joram arises by night and "smites" them. 2 Kgs 8,21bβ (as also BL 21,9bβ) couples this last notice with the rather surprising statement, lacking in MT 21,9, "but the people [i.e. of Joram] fled to their tents". The upshot of these developments is that Edom has been in revolt against Judah "to this day" (8,22a // 21,10a). Josephus (9,97b) offers a clearer picture of events: Joram along with his "horsemen (ἱππέων; cf. ἡ ἵππος, BL 21,9) and chariots (ἀρμάτων; cf. ἅρματα, BL 8,21 and L 21,9)" invades Idumaea "by night[26]". Having done so, he "... destroyed those people who were near the borders of his kingdom (τοὺς ... πέριξ τῆς αὐτοῦ βασιλείας)[27], *but did not proceed farther[28]*".

In line with 8,22a // 21,10a Josephus next (9,98) rounds off his presentation with a renewed reference to Edom's "revolt" (cf. 8,20a // 21,8a = 9,97a). At the same time, however, he so generalizes the reference as to include under it the defection of Libnah (which in 8,22b // 21,10b appears as a kind of afterthought) as well, just as he leaves aside the Biblical indication about Edom's revolt perduring "to this day[29]".

king, who was under his authority, to join in the campaign," this indication in turn picking up on the reference to the "deputy" who ruled Edom in Jehoshaphat's time of 1 Kgs 22,48; see chap. 3. The purpose of the insertion here in 9,97 is to resolve the seeming discrepancy between 2 Kgs 3,7 (= 9,30) where Edom already has a "king" in Jehoshaphat's day and 2 Kgs 8,20 // 2 Chr 21,8 according to which Edom set itself up a king in the days of Joram, i.e. as though it had not had one up until that point. Josephus' solution to the problem is to have the Idumaeans "kill" their previous (puppet) king and install one chosen by themselves at this juncture.

26. In the Biblical accounts what happens "at night" is that Joram "smites" the encircling Edomites. Josephus turns this into a night-time "invasion" of Idumaea by Joram (compare the Bible's chronologically indeterminate reference to the king's "passing over").

27. The above phrase might be understood as Josephus' adaptation of the Biblical references to the Edomites "surrounding" Joram.

28. This item has no equivalent in the Biblical accounts as such (compare 8,21bβ's reference to the "flight" of Joram's army subsequent to his smiting of the Edomites); it does, however, make explicit what is implied by them, i.e. Joram's "smiting" of the Edomites did not, in fact, lead to his (re-)subjugation of their entire territory.

29. This "omission" might reflect the fact that neither Judah nor Edom existed as independent states in Josephus' time. In might further have to do with the use of "Edom" as a code word for Rome on the part of the Rabbis – given his Roman sponsorship Josephus would not wish to represent the antagonism between Judah and Edom/Rome as still continuing in his own day. A like concern manifests itself in Josephus' retelling of the Biblical story of the (putative) ancestors of the Jews and Romans, i.e. Jacob and Esau (the original settler of Edom), respectively. See FELDMAN, *Interpretation*, pp. 304-334, 322-324, 333-334 (= ID., *Josephus' Portrait of Jacob*, in *JQR* 79 [1988-1989] 101-151, 130-133, 148-149).

His version of 8,22 // 21,10 thus reads: "*By this act* [i.e. Joram's destruction of the Edomites living near his borders; see above], *however, he gained nothing at all*, for they *all* revolted (ἀπέστησαν; see ἀποστάντων, 9,97) from him[30], *including those who inhabited the region called* Labina (Λαβίναν)[31]". Like 2 Kgs 8,22b, Josephus has no equivalent to the "theological motivation" attached to the mention of Libnah's revolt in 2 Chr 21,10b, i.e. "because he [Joram] had forsaken the Lord, the God of his fathers".

Following their shared account of the revolts of Edom and Libnah, Kings and Chronicles go their separate ways. Whereas the former proceeds immediately to its closing notices for Joram (8,23-24), the latter first gives a long section of *Sondergut* (21,11-18) which Josephus reproduces in 9,98b-103a. The first component of the Chronicler's "special material" is a notice (21,11) on Joram's constructing "high places in the hill country (MT, BL in the cities) of Judah" and "leading astray" both the Jerusalemites and Judah. This notice functions, together with 21,6-7, as a "frame" around the "revolt narrative" of 21,8-10, just as it prepares the condemnatory letter of Elijah to be cited in 21,12-15. Josephus' parallel (9,98b) to 21,11 explicates the nature of the king's "misleading" of his subjects: "*And he was so far out of his mind* (ἐμμανής)[32] that he forced (ἠνάγκαζεν) the people to go up to the highest parts of the mountains (τὰ ὑψηλότατα[33] τῶν ὀρῶν)[34] and worship strange gods (προσκυνεῖν τοὺς ἀλλοτρίους θεούς)[35]".

30. Here again, as in 9,97, Josephus represents the Edomite revolt as directed against Joram personally rather than against Judah (so the Bible). His doing so further serves to play down the sources' presentation of a continuing antagonism between the nations "Judah" and "Edom"; see previous note.

31. MT 8,22b // 21,10b designate the site as "Libnah"; B 8,22b has Σεννά, L 8,22b and BL 21,10b Λοβνά. SCHLATTER, *Namen*, p. 70 suggests that Josephus' above form may go back to a Hebrew לִבְנָה, while SCHALIT, *Namenwörterbuch*, p. 78 proposes a derivation from לְבוֹנָה which had been corrupted to לְבִינָה. In 10,81 where Josephus is reproducing the reference of 2 Kgs 23,31 to "Libnah" as the hometown of the mother of King Jehoahaz, Marcus follows J. Hudson in conjecturing Λοβάνης for the Τομάνης, etc. of the codices; see there.

32. Josephus' two other uses of this adjective are in *BJ* 4,233; 7,57, both times in the plural. Compare *AJ* 9,244 where Josephus speaks of Ahaz "acting like a madman" (ἔχοντος ... μεμηνότος).

33. This is the reading adopted by Niese and Marcus. The codices MSP (followed by Dindorf, Bekker, and Naber) read ὑψηλά, i.e. the BL reading in 21,11.

34. The above phrase constitutes another verbal link between the Josephan Joram and Jeroboam I; see *AJ* 8,265 where the latter is said to continue to erect altars "on the high mountains" (ἐπὶ τῶν ὑψηλῶν ὀρῶν). Note too that with his mention of "mountains" here in 9,98 Josephus aligns himself with MT (בְּהָרֵי [יְהוּדָה]) as against BL (ἐν πόλεσιν) 21,11.

35. This phrase echoes that of 9,96 where Athaliah teaches Joram ξενικοὺς θεούς προσκυνεῖν. On the phrase "strange gods" of 9,98, see on 9,20.

3. *Elijah's Letter*

The Chronicler's next *Sondergut* item in his account of Joram is his "citation" of a "letter" to the king from the prophet Elijah (21,12-15), this consisting of: introductory formula (v. 12aα), *Botenformel* (v. 12aβ), accusation (vv. 12b-13), and announcement of punishment for Joram's people and household (v. 14) and the king himself (v. 15). Josephus (9,99) precedes his parallel to this sequence with a transitional phrase which accentuates Joram's guilt that calls forth the prophetic condemnation of him: "while he was acting in this fashion and completely disregarding his country's laws (τὰ πάτρια νόμιμα[36]; cf. τὰ πάτρια ... ἔθη, 9,95)...". Thereafter, he picks up on the opening of the Chronistic segment (21,12a) with his notice "a letter (ἐπιστολή, B [ἐν] γραφῇ, L ἐγγραφή) was brought to him from the prophet Elijah (παρ' Ἡλίου τοῦ προφήτου = L)[37]".

In reproducing the text of Elijah's letter itself, Josephus follows his usual practice in recasting the content in indirect address and omitting its opening *Botenformel*. In place of the latter item he introduces a preliminary, global announcement concerning Joram's fate which he will have Elijah flesh out subsequently: (Elijah's letter) "informed him that God would inflict severe punishment (μεγάλην ... δίκην) on him...".

The accusation component of Elijah's letter begins in 21,12b with the charge that Joram has not "walked in the ways" of the good Judean kings Asa and Jehoshaphat. Josephus' generalizing parallel omits the names of Joram's father and grandfather: "... because, instead of having imitated (μιμητής)[38] his own fathers...". Elijah's indictment of Joram continues in 21,13a where the latter is accused of having "walked in the way of the kings of Israel" and of having "led Judah and the inhabitants

36. On Josephus' use of this phrase see the work of Schröder cited in n. 13 (on its occurrence here in 9,99 see ibid., p. 78).

37. The codices SP (followed by Dindorf, Bekker, and Naber) append to the above words the parenthetical phrase ἔτι γὰρ ἐπὶ γῆς ἦν. This "plus" attempts to explain how it was that Joram could get a letter from Elijah (who according to 9,28 has already been removed to heaven). On the other hand, it seems to conflict with the sequence of Josephus' own earlier chronology wherein Elijah's "translation" to heaven takes place around the time of the accession of Joram of Israel (9,28 = 2 Kgs 2,1-18) which itself occurs while the Judean Joram's father Jehoshaphat is still reigning (see 9,29-45). Conversely, the text printed by Marcus with its vague passive formulation ("a letter was brought to him from the prophet Elijah"; compare 21,12a: "there came to him a letter from Elijah...") leaves open the possibility that Elijah is indeed already in heaven at the moment of his letter reaching Joram; compare *Seder 'Olam Rabbah* (hereafter *SOR*) 17.12 (L.-F. GIRÓN BLANC, tr., *Seder 'Olam Rabbah El Gran Orden del Universo. Una Cronología judía*, Estella (Navarra), Verbo Divino, 1996, p. 86) which states that the letter arrived seven years after the prophet's "translation".

38. Contrast *AJ* 8,315 and 9,44 where this same term is used of Jehoshaphat's being an "imitator" of David.

of Jerusalem into unfaithfulness [note the echo of 21,11 here], as the house of Ahab led Israel into unfaithfulness". Josephus too has Elijah charge Joram with adopting the apostate ways of the Northern rulers, while also specifying in what these consisted (see on 9,95-96 above): "... he had followed the impious example (κατηκολούθησεν ἀσεβή-μασι [cf. ἀσεβεία, 9,96])[39] of the Israelite kings and had compelled (συνηνάγκασε; cf. ἠνάγκαζεν, 9,98) *the tribe of* Judah and the citizens (πολίτας; compare τοὺς κατοικοῦντας, BL 21,13) of Jerusalem *to give up the holy service* (ἀφέντας τὴν ὁσίαν ... θρησκείαν[40])[41] *of their national God* (τοῦ ἐπιχωρίου θεοῦ)[42] and to worship idols (σέβειν τὰ εἴδωλα)[43], just as Achab had forced the Israelites to do...".

The charges leveled against Joram conclude in 21,13b with a reminiscence of the king's murder of his brothers (see 21,4) who are qualified as "better (BL ἀγαθούς) than" himself. Josephus (9,100a) expands this fratricide charge with a reference to the other category of Joram's victims as cited in 21,4, i.e. "some of the princes of Judah" (compare 9,95 "his father's friends who were also chiefs"), likewise transferring to this second group the ethical qualification 21,13 uses of the king's brothers: "... and also because he had done away with his brothers *and had slain* (ἀπέκτεινεν; BL ἀπέκτεινας) the good *and righteous* (ἀγαθοὺς [so BL of the brothers]... καὶ δικαίους) *men*[44]".

2 Chr 21,14 opens the prophetic sentence upon Joram with the announcement "the Lord will bring a great plague (BL πληγὴν μεγα-λήν) on your people, your children, your wives, and all your possessions". The Josephan version (9,100b) eliminates explicit mention of the Deity as the author of the coming catastrophe[45].

---

39. The above phrase occurs also in *AJ* 8,271 where it is used of the subjects of Jeroboam I.

40. This word is absent in RO and omitted by Niese; it is retained by Dindorf, Bekker, Naber, and Marcus.

41. A variant of the above expression "giving up (God's) service", employing the preposition περί, occurs in *AJ* 12,253. The phrase "holy service" of 9,99 is hapax in Josephus.

42. This expression occurs only here in Josephus; compare τῶν ἐπιχωρίων ἐθισμῶν, 9,96. With the above phrase "give up the service of their national God" compare παρ-ηνόμησαν εἰς ... τὴν τοῦ θεοῦ θρησκείαν of 9,95.

43. The above expression "worship idols" recurs in *AJ* 9,205 in reference to Jeroboam II. Compare the equivalent expressions ξενικοὺς θεοὺς προσκυνεῖν of 9,96 and προσκυνεῖν τοὺς ἀλλοτρίους θεούς of 9,98.

44. With the above appended item Josephus resolves a question suggested by the Bible's presentation, i.e. why does Elijah's letter fail to mention also Joram's killing of the "princes"?

45. Recall, however, that Josephus does speak of divine involvement in Joram's punishment in the opening component of Elijah's letter in 9,99: "*God* would inflict a severe (μεγάλην, the same adjective used in BL 21,14) punishment upon him".

In addition, it reverses the source's (unusual) sequence "children-wives", while also prefacing the actual announcement of punishment with an extended transitional phrase: "... *and the penalty which he* [Joram] *was to pay* (τὴν ... τιμωρίαν ... ὑφέξειν; compare ληψόμενον δίκην, 9,99) *for these offences the prophet indicated in his letter*, namely the destruction (ὄλεθρον) of his people (τοῦ λαοῦ; BL ἐν τῷ λαῷ) and the death of his wives (γυναικῶν[46]; BL γυναιξίν) and children (τέκνων; BL τοῖς υἱοῖς σου)...". In 21,15 Joram is further informed that he will fall victim to a severe disease of the bowels which will eventuate "in their coming out day by day". Josephus (9,101a) expatiates on this graphic announcement: "... and that *he should die* of a disease of the intestines (νόσῳ τῆς νηδύος; BL ἐν νοσῷ κοιλίας) *after a long period of torment, when, from the excessive corruption of his inward parts*, his bowels would fall out, *so that he would look on* (ὁρῶντα)[47] *at his own misery* (συμφοράν) *without being able to help himself at all, and finally would die in this manner*". As we shall see, several of the elements introduced by Josephus into this announcement will recur in his subsequent description of its fulfillment. Finally, Josephus "rounds off" the prophetic letter segment (9,99-101) with a closing formula, comparable to those he inserts at many other points in his retelling of the Biblical account with a view to smoothing the transition from one narrative element to another. This reads (9,101b): "Such were the things which Elijah told him in his letter (ἐδήλου διὰ τῆς ἐπιστολῆς ὁ Ἠλίας; compare παρ' Ἠλίου ... ἐπιστολή, ἥ ... ἐδήλου, 9,99)".

4. *Joram's End*

2 Chr 21,16-19a relates the fulfillment of Elijah's word of doom, first for Joram's people and household (vv. 16-17), then for the king himself (vv. 18-19a); the Josephan parallel is 9,102-103a.

2 Chr 21,16-17aα introduces the first of Joram's punishments with the notice that "the Lord stirred up against Jehoram the anger of (so MT; BL lacks the anger of) the Philistines (BL ἀλλοφύλους) and of the Arabs (BL + and those) who are near the Ethiopians. And they came up against Judah, and invaded it". Here again (see 9,101), Josephus (9,102) passes over the source's explicit reference to a divine involvement. His formulation is further of interest as suggesting his familiarity with both

---

46. MARCUS, *ad loc.*, (mis-) translates with the sg. "wife".

47. This is the reading, adopted by Niese and Marcus, of the codices other than SP (which have ἐπιδόντα, a reading which Dindorf, Bekker, and Naber follow).

the BL and MT readings of 21,16. It runs: "*Not long after*[48], an army of those Arabs who lived near Ethiopia[49] and the Philistines (ἀλλοφύλων)[50] invaded the kingdom of Joram". The remainder of 21,17 narrates the devastation perpetrated by the invaders: "they carried away all the possessions they found that belonged to the king's house[51], and also his sons[52] and his wives (thus MT; BL daughters), so that no son was left to him except Jehoahaz[53] (BL Ὀχοζείας), his youngest son". Josephus' version (9,102b) evidences various peculiarities: "they plundered *the country*[54] and the king's residence (τὸν οἶκον τοῦ βασιλέως; BL ἐν οἴκῳ τοῦ βασιλέως)[55], and moreover slew (κατέσφαξαν)[56] his sons (υἱούς, so BL) and wives (so MT, see above; BL daughters). Only one of his sons, named Ochozias (Ὀχοζίας; cf. BL Ὀχοζείας), was left to him, *having escaped from the enemy*[57]".

48. Josephus introduces this chronological indication in order to smooth the transition from Elijah's words to the account of their fulfillment (and to underscore the immediacy of the latter).

49. With this formulation Josephus aligns himself with MT 21,16 as against BL where "the Arabs" and "those living near Ethiopia" are distinguished as two separate peoples; see above in the text.

50. This term for "the Philistines" corresponds to that of BL. His use of this designation here is of note (and indicative of his acquaintance also with BL 2 Chr 21,16) in that elsewhere (see, e.g., *AJ* 8,288. 308) Josephus regularly employs another Greek term, i.e. Παλαιστῖνοι in rendering Biblical references to the "Philistines". See R. DE VAUX, *Les Philistins dans la Septante*, in J. SCHREINER (ed.), *Wort, Lied und Gottesspruch. Beiträge zur Septuaginta*, I (*Festschrift* J. ZIEGLER, FzB, 1), Würzburg, Echter, 1972, 185-194.

51. It is not clear whether the reference here is to the palace in Jerusalem (which would entail that the invaders got possession of the city itself) or to some other site(s) where the king's goods and household had been assembled in the face of the enemy assault, see the commentaries.

52. In its allusion to the fate of Joram's other sons 2 Chr 22,1 speaks of their being actually "slain" by the invaders. Inspired by this indication, Josephus will speak of the sons' being killed in his version of 21,17 itself; see above in the text, and cf. n. 56.

53. Elsewhere in Kings and Chronicles this figure, Joram's eventual successor, is called "Ahaziah".

54. This Josephan plus serves to accentuate the damage done by the invaders who do not (so 21,17) limit their depradations to the king's own property.

55. As in 21,17 (see n. 51), Josephus leaves unclear whether or not the "house" here is to be understood as the royal palace in Jerusalem.

56. In substituting this word for the "they carried away" of 21,17 (MT and BL), Josephus would seem to have in view the wording of 22,1 which states "the band of men who had come with the Arabs to the camp had *slain* (BL ἀπέκτεινεν) all the older sons [i.e. of Joram]"; see n. 52. Josephus' specification that the invaders "slew" Joram's sons and wives likewise corresponds to Elijah's announcement in 9,100 of the "death" (φθοράν) of the king's family members. It further echoes the noun σφαγήν used of Joram's own "slaying" of his brothers and the friends of his father in 9,95, thereby underscoring the correspondence between the royal misdeed and the penalty this evoked.

57. This indication replaces the Biblical specification that "Jehoahaz" (MT) was Joram's youngest son.

2 Chr 21,18-19a recounts the realization of Elijah's word of doom for Joram personally (see v. 15): he is smitten by the Lord with an incurable disease of the bowels which, after some time[58], fall out, whereupon Joram dies "in great agony[59]". Just as he did with Elijah's prediction itself, Josephus (9,103a) considerably embellishes the account of its fulfillment. His version of vv. 18-19a runs: *"and after this misfortune* (συμφοράν; see 9,101) he himself suffered *for a very long time* (ἐπὶ πλεῖστον ... χρόνον)[60] from the disease *which the prophet had foretold to him*[61] – for the Deity (the Lord, 21,18) had struck at his stomach (εἰς τὴν γαστέρα; BL εἰς τὴν κοιλίαν) *in His wrath* (τὴν ὀργήν)[62] – and so perished (ἀπέθανεν = BL) miserably (ἐλεεινῶς; B ἐν μαλακίᾳ πονηρᾷ, L ἐν ἀρρωστίαις πονηραῖς), looking on while his entrails fell out (ἐπιδὼν αὐτοῦ τὰ ἐντὸς ἐκρυέντα; compare τῶν ἐντέρων αὐτοῦ ... ἐκρυέντων ... αὐτὸν ὁρῶντα, 9,101)".

2 Chr 21,19b begins the account of Joram's burial, noting that his "people" (BL ὁ λαός) refrained from making the customary royal "burning" (so MT; BL ἐκφοράν, "burial") for him. Apparently utilizing the BL reading of v. 19b, Josephus (9,104a) amplifies the item, making it a "lead-in" to the continuation of his burial account: "And the populace (ὁ λαός = BL) treated even his dead body with indignity (περιύβρισε ... τὸν νεκρόν)[63]; *as they reasoned, I suppose* (οἶμαι)[64], *that one who had died in this manner through the wrath of God* (κατὰ μῆνιν

---

58. The double chronological indication at the beginning of 21,19a (RSV "in the course of time, at the end of two years [literally days, לְיָמִים]") is obscure; see the commentaries.

59. With 2 Chr 21,18-19a's description of Joram's gruesome death, compare 2 Kgs 8,24aα whose formulaic phrase ("so Jehoram slept with his fathers") gives no hint as to the circumstances of the king's demise. Here, as consistently elsewhere in his Joram account, Josephus aligns himself with the presentation of Chronicles; see above. In this connection note that Josephus also goes together with Chronicles in omitting the "source notice" for Joram of 2 Kgs 8,23 (it should, however, be kept in mind that the historian invariably passes over, as we have been seeing, such notices even when these are shared by both Kings and Chronicles).

60. This phrase clarifies the obscure Biblical chronological indications; see n. 58. It likewise picks up on Elijah's announcement of 9,101 that Joram will undergo "a long period of torment" (ἐπὶ πολὺ βασανισθείς).

61. This inserted *Rückverweis* points up, in line with a consistent tendency of Josephus' retelling of Biblical history, the veracity of Elijah's prediction in 9,101.

62. Here, in contrast to several previous instances in his reproduction of the Chronicler's Joram story, Josephus does take over a source reference to the divine involvement in the king's fate (cf. "the Lord smote him...", 21,18), adding to this an allusion to the emotional state which prompted God's smiting of Joram.

63. This phrase occurs only here in Josephus.

64. Josephus frequently employs this verbal form in introducing his editorial asides; see, e.g., *AJ* 8,216.409.

θεοῦ)⁶⁵ *was not worthy to obtain a form of burial* (κηδείας, see BL above) *befitting kings...*".

2 Chr 21,20aα interjects into the account of Joram's burial (21,19b,20aβb) chronological data on his reign which have already been cited in 21,5 (= 2 Kgs 8,17). Josephus (who has not previously utilized the sources' chronological indications; see above) reverses this sequence so as to keep together material relating to Joram's burial. 2 Chr 21,20aβ states that Joram "departed to no one's regret (MT בְּלֹא חֶמְדָּה; compare BL οὐκ ἐν ἐπαίνῳ, "not with praise"). V. 20b then continues: "they buried him in the city of David, but not in the tombs of the kings" (compare 2 Kgs 8,24aβ which simply notes that Joram "was buried with his fathers in the city of David"). Josephus' presentation re-arranges as well the above elements of 21,20aβb: "... they neither laid him to rest in the sepulchres of his fathers (οὔτε ταῖς πατρῴαις ... θήκαις; BL οὐκ ἐν τάποις τῶν βασιλέων), nor did they grant him any other honour (τιμῆς; see BL 21,20aβ above), *but buried him like a commoner* (ἰδιώτην)...". To this burial notice for Joram, Josephus then appends his version of the chronological indications of 21,20aα (= 21,5 // 8,17): Joram died at age forty⁶⁶ after a reign of eight (so the Bible) years.

2 Kgs 8,24b // 2 Chr 22,1 narrate the accession of Joram's son Ahaziah. Whereas Kings simply records that Ahaziah "reigned in his [Joram's] stead", Chronicles provides an elaborate account, inspired by its own earlier *Sondergut* presentation, of Ahaziah's accession according to which he, as Joram's youngest son, was installed by "the inhabitants of Jerusalem" since all Joram's older sons had been killed by the foreign raiders; cf. 21,17⁶⁷. Once again, Josephus (9,104c) aligns himself with the distinctive reading of Chronicles, which, however, he reduces to its core datum: "And the people (ὁ δῆμος; compare ὁ λαός, 9,103) of Jerusalem gave the royal power to his son Ochozias (Ὀχοζίᾳ; cf. Ὀχοζίας, 9,102)⁶⁸".

---

65. This phrase (which occurs five times elsewhere in Josephus: *AJ* 1,164; 2,344; 4,8; 9,246; 15,243) picks up on Josephus' earlier mention of the divine displeasure with Joram in 9,103: "God had struck at his stomach in his wrath (τὴν ὀργήν)".

66. This item has no equivalent as such in the sources which speak rather of Joram's age at accession. Josephus obtains the figure by tallying the Biblical indications of his age at accession (32) and length of reign (8).

67. Recall that in this latter verse Joram's surviving son is called "Jehoahaz" (so MT, BL Ὀχοζείας); here in 22,1 MT switches to the name "Ahaziah" which it will use in the continuation of its account. The "discrepancy" between MT 21,17 and 22,1 is absent in BL and Josephus which use the same name, i.e. Ὀχοζείας (BL)/ Ὀχοζίας (Josephus) in both instances.

68. Here in 9,104, as in 9,102 (compare 21,17) Josephus avoids Chronicles' specification that Joram's successor was his youngest son (Kings lacks this specification as well). As for the Chronicler's allusion to the killing of Joram's other sons in 22,1,

Conclusions: *Josephus' Rewriting of* 2 Kgs 8,16-24 // 2 Chr 21,4–22,1

I conclude this short chapter with a summary statement of my findings on the questions that inform this monograph overall. Of the two Biblical accounts, Josephus, in 9,95-104, consistently follows that of Chronicles in preference to Kings' briefer presentation. Specifically, not only does he reproduce (much of) the Chronicler's extensive *Sondergut* in 21,4–22,1, he also omits material peculiar to Kings (e.g., the synchronism of 2 Kgs 8,16; the flight of Joram's force, 8,21bβ; and the source notice of 8,23). Similarly, he aligns himself with Chronicles where it diverges in some way from the parallel verse(s) of Kings (e.g., the presentation of Joram's death, burial and succession by Ahaziah, 8,24 // 21,19–22,1; see 9,103-104). As to the text-form(s) of Chronicles available to Josephus for his treatment of Joram, we noted, first of all, indications that he was acquainted with items peculiar to our MT (e.g., Joram compels apostate worship on "the highest part of the *mountains*" [rather than in the "cities", so BL], 21,11 = 9,98; the "Arabs" [instead of some other unspecified people, so BL] are those bordering on the Ethiopians, 21,16 // 9,102; while Joram suffers loss of his wives [rather than his daughters, so BL], 21,17 = 9,102). At the same time, we found pointers towards his familarity with a "BL-like" text as well (e.g., Joram is denied a kingly "burial" [rather than a "burning", so MT], BL 21,19b = 9,104; and shown "no honor", BL 21,20 = 9,104 [compare MT "he departed to no one's regret"]).

Summing up here on the rewriting techniques applied by Josephus to the Chronicler's Joram account, we can identify the same four general (and overlapping) categories distinguished in previous chapters. Certain of Josephus' *modifications* are terminological (e.g., "the Lord" of 21,7 and 18 becomes, respectively, "God" [9,96] and "the Deity" [9,102]; ὁμολογία [9,96] substitutes for διαθήκη [BL 21,7), or stylistic (the direct discourse of Elijah's letter in 21,12-15 is rendered in indirect discourse in 9,99-101). Others of them are more contentual in nature (e.g., it is the "princes" slain by Joram who are qualified as "good" rather than his "brothers", 9,100, compare 21,13; the manner of Joram's "misleading" the people is specified in 9,98b = 21,11 and 9,99 = 21,13a; Joram's family members are "killed" rather than "carried off", 9,102 [compare 22,1] vs. 21,17; the king's age at accession is replaced by his age at death, 9,104, compare 21,5.20). Several of these "contentual modifications" involve a clarifying rewording of obscure source formu-

Josephus has "anticipated" this in his version (9,102) of 21,17 where the reference is rather to their being "carried off"; see nn. 52,56.

lations; compare 9,97 and 21,8-10a (Edom's revolt) and 9,103 and 21,19 (the chronology of Joram's affliction). Among Josephus' (minor) *re-arrangements* in 9,95-104, we noted his positioning (9,104) of the chronological data at the end of – instead of in the middle of (so 21,19b-20) – his account of Joram's burial[69] and his anticipation of the reference to the killing of Joram's sons (22,1), employing this in his version of 21,17 in place of that verse's mention of the sons' being "carried off" (see nn. 52,56,67).

Josephus' *omissions* of items present in the Chronistic Joram narrative are of various sorts. He passes over, e.g., source repetitions (e.g., the duplication of the chronological data of 21,5 in 21,20aα) and seeming "contradictions" (e.g., the discrepancy between 21,17 and 22,1 concerning the fate of Joram's other sons). He likewise leaves aside items that lack significance for the further course of the narrative, e.g., the names of Jehoshaphat's other sons and his benefactions to them (21,2-3; compare 9,95). In several instances too he jettisons the Chronicler's "theological notations" (see 21,10b, compare 9,98; 21,12, the *Botenformel*, compare 9,99; 21,14, compare 9,100-101; and 21,16, compare 9,102).

The most noteworthy of the Josephan rewriting techniques in 9,95-104 are, however, his many and varied *additions/amplifications*. Of these, some serve stylistic purposes, e.g., linking this segment of *AJ* with other portions of the work (see the interjected *Rückverweis* to 9,45 in 9,95), rounding off a given section (see the closing formula appended to the "quotation" of Elijah's letter in 9,101), or giving the presentation a more definite character (see the insertion of the name of Joram's wife, i.e. "Othlia" in 9,96). Other, longer additions are designed to obviate apparent Biblical discrepancies (e.g., the interpolated notice on the Idumaeans' killing of their former king, Jehoshaphat's vassal, in 9,97 this inspired by the reference to that figure in 9,30 [compare the seeming discordance between 2 Kgs 3,9 and 8,20 // 2 Chr 21,8 on the matter). Another group of additions/amplifications functions to accentuate the depravity of Joram (see 9,95 vs. 21,4; 9,99a vs. 21,12), the torments that befell him (see 9,101 vs. 21,15; 9,103 vs. 21,19a), and the circumstances surrounding his ignoble burial (see 9,103b-104a vs. 21,19b, 20aβb).

What now is the cumulative impact of the above rewriting techniques on Josephus' portrait of Joram vis-à-vis the Biblical one(s)? Overall, the Josephan Joram appears even more depraved than does his Chronistic

---

69. Under this heading I recall as well Josephus' separation of the component elements of 2 Chr 21,1-4 concerning Joram's accession and murder of his brothers. Josephus' parallel to this sequence begins in 9,45, but only concludes in 9,95a, following the long interlude of 9,46-94 focussed on the deeds of Elisha.

counterpart, a veritable Judean version of the prototypical Josephan bad king, Jeroboam I (see nn. 23,34,39)[70]. Accordingly then it is not suprising to see him come, in Josephus' version, to a still more dramatically bad end. Features of the source story likely to ruffle Roman sensibilities (the everlasting Davidic dynasty, 21,7; the ongoing antagonism between "Edom [Rome]" and Judah, 21,10) are played down, even as the divine involvement in Joram's story is somewhat diminished. The above features of Josephus' presentation clearly reflect his concern with retaining the interest and sympathy of Gentile readers. On the other hand, his version of the Joram story has something to offer Jewish readers as well, i.e. an emphatic warning concerning the disastrous consequences of infidelity to the "ancestral" (see 9,95) and "native" (see 9,99) ways of their religion[71].

---

70. By contrast, Josephus plays down the Biblical linkage of Joram's Israelite namesake with Jeroboam, see p. 42, n. 61.

71. On such warnings as a *Leitmotif* of *Ant.* in so far as it is addressed also to a Jewish audience, see, e.g., FELDMAN, *Interpretation*, pp. 570-628, 615-618 (= ID., *Josephus' Portrait of Solomon*, in *HUCA* 66 [1995] 103-167, 154-157).

VI

JEHU OF ISRAEL[1]
(9,105-139)

Following his presentation concerning Joram of Judah in 9,95-104 based on 2 Chr 21,4–22,1, Josephus, in the next segment of *AJ* 9, i.e. 105-139, resumes his account of events in the North from 9,94, at the same time reverting to 2 Kings (8,25–10,36) as his (main) source[2]. I divide up the material for study in this chapter into nine segments: 1. Jehu's Royal Antagonists (2 Kgs 8,25-29 = *AJ* 9,105-106a [cf. 112b,121b]); 2. Jehu Anointed (9,1-13 = 9,106b-111); 3. Jehu's Advance to Jezreel (9,14-20 = 9,112-116); 4. Joram & Ahaziah Assassinated (9,21-29 = 9,117-121); 5. Jezebel Executed (9,30-37 = 9,122-124); 6. Massacre of Ahab's Family (10,1-11 = 9,125-129); 7. Jehu's Advance to Samaria (10,12-17 = 9,130-134a); 8. The Baalists Exterminated (10,18-27 = 9,134b-138); and 9. Closing Notices for Jehu (10,28-30[31-36] = 9,139)[3].

1. *Jehu's Royal Antagonists*

2 Kings rounds off its account of Jehoram of Judah (8,16-24) with mention of the accession of his son Ahaziah (v. 24b // 2 Chr 22,1 = *AJ*

---

1. This chapter represents a reworking of my article *Josephus's Version of Jehu's Putsch (2 Kgs 8,25-10,36)*, in *Anton* 68 (1993) 450-484 and is used by permission. It draws on, as well, the following contributions: M. MULZER, *Jehu schlägt Joram. Text-literar-und strukturkritische Untersuchung zu 2 Kön 8,25-10,36* (ATSAT, 37), St. Ottilien, EOS Verlag, 1992; M. MULZER and K.-S. KRIEGER, *Die Jehuerzählung bei Josephus (Ant.Jud. IX. 105-139, 159f.)*, in *BN* 83 (1996) 54-82 (this article, in fact, consists of two distinct pieces, i.e. MULZER, *Josephus' Bearbeitung der biblischen Jehuerzählung*, pp. 54-70 and KRIEGER, *Die Jehu-Erzählung im Gesamtkontext der Ant. Jud.*, pp. 70-79 [a joint bibliography, 79-82 concludes the article]); and FELDMAN, *Studies*, pp. 352-362 (= ID., *Josephus' Portrait of Jehu*, in *JSQ* 4 (1997) 12-32).

2. The Chronicler, in accord with his Judean-centered approach, gives only a very summary version of the events related in 2 Kgs 8,25-10,36, in the context of his account (2 Chr 22,2-9) of King Ahaziah of Judah who became fatally entangled in those events. It is unclear whether or not Josephus has made (subsidiary) use of the Chronicler's parallel in 9,105-139, see below.

3. Josephus begins his reproduction of the Biblical segment 2 Kgs 10,28-36 in 9,139 (= 10,28-30), but then "delays" his parallel to the remainder of the passage (10,31-36) until 9,159-160 which stands within the context of his account of the Judean King Joash, 9,157-172. Accordingly, I reserve treatment of 9,159-160 until chap. VIII.

9,104). It then continues with various initial data concerning Ahaziah (8,25-27 // 2 Chr 22,2-4), these leading into an account of the Judean's entanglement in the Syrian (mis-)adventure of Joram of Israel (8,28-29 // 2 Chr 22,5-6). For his part, Josephus, immediately after mention of Ahaziah's accession at the end of 9,104, relates Joram's initiative against Syria (9,105-106 = 2 Kgs 8,25-26), but making no reference to Ahaziah's involvement therein. In his presentation then Ahaziah does not (re-)appear until a later point, i.e. 9,112b.121b where Josephus will fill in (part of) the source data on this king from 8,25-27; see below.

In focussing, as he does initially, exclusively on Joram and his Syrian campaign, Josephus likewise takes the opportunity to elaborate on this event. The Bible itself furnishes no background for Joram's initiative, its occasion, or objective. Josephus (9,105a) interjects various indications on these points: "Joram... *hoped, after the death of Adados* ('Αδάδου; MT Ben-hadad)[4], *to take* (ἀφαιρήσεσθαι) *the city of* Aramathē in Galaaditis ('Αραμάθην[5]... τῆς Γαλααδίτιδος; compare MT 8,28 "Ramothgilead", B Ῥεμμὼθ Γαλαάδ, L Ῥαμαὼθ Γαλαάδ) from the Syrians[6], *and marched against it with a great army* (στρατεύει ... ἐπ' αὐτὴν μετὰ μεγάλης παρασκευῆς)".

Josephus elaborates as well (9,105b) on the circumstances of Joram's "wounding" as narrated in 2 Kgs 8,28b // 2 Chr 22,5. Thus, he specifies that the wounding occurred during the "siege" of Aramathē. In further specifying that Joram was "shot by one of the Syrians" (τοξευθεὶς ὑπό τινος τῶν Συρῶν), Josephus, conceivably, is drawing on BL 2 Chr 22,5 which states that "the archers (οἱ τοξόται) wounded Joram"; compare 2 Kgs 8,28 (MT BL) // MT 22,5 where "the Syrians" are simply said to "wound" the king, the manner of their doing so being left indeterminate[7].

4. Josephus describes the assassination of Adados by "Azaēlos" (Biblical Hazael) in *AJ* 9,87-94 (= 2 Kgs 8,7-15); see chap. IV.

5. This is the reading of MSP which Dindorf, Bekker, Naber, and Marcus follow; Niese reads 'Αραμώθα with RO.

6. Josephus' inserted reference to Joram's "objective" here recalls what he tells of that king's father Ahab in *AJ* 8,399 (= 1 Kgs 22,3): (Ahab was planning war against Benhadad) "in order to recover (ἀφέληται; see ἀφαιρήσεσθαι, 9,105) the city of Aramatha in Galadēnē, for it had first belonged to his (Ahab's) father but had been taken away (ἀφῃρῆσθαι) from him by the Syrian's father". Ahab's assault on the city, of course, failed; accordingly, his son Joram now makes a new attempt.

7. An alternative source of inspiration for the above indication would be the BL plus in 2 Kgs 9,16: "(Joram) was being (+ in Jezreel, L) healed of the *arrow-wounds* (τῶν τοξευμάτων) with which the Syrians (BL οἱ 'Αραμιείν) had wounded him at Ramoth in the battle with Hazael king of Syria...". Thus MULZER, *Bearbeitung*, 55, n. 9. In any event, Josephus' wording here in 9,105 serves to associate Joram's wounding with that of two other kings, i.e. Ahab (who, according to *AJ* 8,414 = 1 Kgs 22,34 // 2 Chr 18,33, was

Finally, Josephus makes clear from the start that Joram's wound was "not mortal" (οὐ καιρίως)[8].

In common with 2 Kgs 8,29a // 2 Chr 22,6a Josephus (9,105c) relates Joram's withdrawal to "Jezreel" (Ἰεζαρήλην[9]; cf. Ἰεζραήλ, BL 8,29 // L 22,6; Ἰσραήλ, B 22,6) in order to recuperate from his wound. As noted above, he leaves aside, at this juncture, the Biblical mention (8,29b // 22,6b) of Ahaziah's "coming down" to see Joram at Jezreel. In place thereof, he substitutes (9,105d-106a) a series of notices that both clarify what happened with Joram's force when the king departed for Jezreel and prepare what follows where the Israelite commanders, among them Jehu, are assembled in Ramoth-Gilead. This "replacement sequence" reads: "... (Joram) left his whole army behind in Aramathē with their commander Jehu (Ἰηοῦν), the son of Nemesaios (Νεμε-σαίου)[10], for he had already taken it by storm[11]. And it was his intention, after being cured, to continue the war with the Syrians[12]".

2. Jehu Anointed

The Biblical account of Jehu's seizure of the Israelite kingship begins with the prophet Elisha commissioning Jehu's "anointer" for his task, 2 Kgs 9,1-3. The group to which Elisha's (nameless)[13] agent pertains is

wounded by a "page of the Syrian king" who was "shooting" [τοξεύσας] at the enemy) and Josiah (whom, so *AJ* 10,77 = 2 Chr 35,23, "one of the Egyptians shot" [τοξεύσας τις ... τῶν Αἰγυπτίων]). See next note.

8. In this respect Joram's wounding differs from that of Ahab (who is said in *AJ* 8,415 to have been "gravely and even mortally [καιρίως] wounded") and Josiah (who died from the wound he had received, 10,77). See previous note.

9. This is the reading proposed by Niese and followed by Marcus. Dindorf, Bekker, and Naber read Ἰεσράελαν.

10. This is the reading of the name proposed by Niese and followed by Marcus, harmonizing the form with that given in *AJ* 8,352 (= 1 Kgs 19,16). Dindorf, Bekker, and Naber read Νεμεσσί in accord with the conjecture of J. Hudson. By mentioning only one ancestor for Jehu in both *AJ* 8,352 and 9,105 Josephus eliminates the problem of the discrepancy between 2 Kgs 9,2 MT and B (Jehu is the son of Jehoshaphat and grandson of Nimshi) and L 9,2 (and 1 Kgs 19,16) according to which Nimshi was Jehu's father, Jehoshaphat his grandfather. On Josephus' anticipated mention of Jehu here as a heightening of his stature in view of the role he will assume in the following anointing scene, see MULZER, *Bearbeitung*, 55; FELDMAN, *Studies*, pp. 353-354 (= ID., *Jehu*, 17).

11. By means of this indication – which lacks an explicit Biblical basis – about the Israelite capture of Ramoth-gilead, Josephus accounts for the further course of the narrative where (see 2 Kgs 9,2.4) the Israelite officers appear to be present inside the city.

12. With this appended remark Josephus supplies a rationale for Joram's leaving his forces behind in (what had been) Syrian territory, even as he himself returns to the land of Israel: he plans to rejoin them there at some time in the future.

13. In *SOR* 18.2 (GIRÓN BLANC, *Seder 'Olam Rabbah*, p. 88) he is identified with the prophet Jonah.

designated in 9,1a with the (ambiguous) expression "one of the sons of
the prophets". Josephus (9,106b) clarifies with his designation, i,e. "one
of his [Elisha's] disciples (μαθητῶν)[14]"; cf. TJ's מתלמידי נבייא. In 9,3a
Elisha's envoy is told to "take a flask (MT פַּךְ) of oil" and to pour this
on Jehu's head to the accompaniment of the words "I (the Lord) anoint
(BL κέχρικα) you king... over Israel". Josephus' (indirect discourse)
version of the prophetic mandate runs: "(Elisha sent one of his disciples), to whom he gave the *holy* oil (ἅγιον ἔλαιον), to Aramathē to
anoint (χρίσοντα)[15] Jehu and tell him that the Deity had chosen him
king (τὸ θεῖον αὐτὸν ᾕρηται βασιλέα)". This formulation serves to
associate the Josephan Jehu with Saul (*AJ* 6,83), David (6,157) and
Solomon (7,355), all of whom were likewise "anointed" with "holy oil"
according to him[16].

In 9,3b Elisha's envoy is directed to "flee" and "tarry not" once he
has anointed Jehu with the prescribed word of v. 3a. Subsequently, however, this figure will address Jehu with an expansive discourse which has,
as such, no basis in Elisha's words to him and which also seems out of
line with the prophet's insistence (see 9,3b) on his departing quickly from
the scene. Josephus resolves the discrepancy with his appendix to
Elisha's directives, i.e. "... having instructed him to say other things in
addition...". After thus preparing the envoy's subsequent, extended discourse, Josephus goes on to modify Elisha's directive about the immediacy of his departure as well. In his reformulation what is emphasized is
now the "inconspicuousness" with which the entire mission is to be carried out and the rationale for this: "... (he told him) to make the journey
as if he were a fugitive (τρόπῳ φυγῆς; compare φεύξῃ, BL 9,3b), *in
order that he might get away from there without being seen by anyone*[17]".

2 Kgs 9,4-5aα makes the transition from Elisha's giving of his
commission to its execution with mention of the agent's coming to

14. Compare *AJ* 8,389 where Josephus substitutes "a certain prophet, whose name
was Michaias" for the phrase "a certain man of the sons of the prophets" of 1 Kgs 20,35.
Cf. also his replacement, of the "elders" (so 2 Kgs 6,32) by "his [Elisha's] disciples
(μαθηταῖς)" in 9,68.

15. Note how this formulation avoids making God himself the subject of the verb
"anoint" (as one finds in 9,3).

16. In thus assimilating Jehu's "anointing" to those of all three kings of the united
monarchy, Josephus diverges from the Talmudic passages *b. Meg.* 14a; *b. Hor.* 12a and
b. Ker. 6a which contrast Saul (see 1 Sam 10,1) and Jehu (see 2 Kgs 9,3.6) who were
anointed from a "flask" (פַּךְ) and whose lines ruled for only a limited period, with David
(see 1 Sam 16,13) and Solomon (see 1 Kgs 1,39) whose anointing was from a "horn"
(קֶרֶן) and who were promised an everlasting dominion. See GINZBERG, *Legends*, VI, p.
353, n. 2.

17. On the above sequence as Josephus' heightening of the drama/suspense surrounding the anointing scene, see FELDMAN, *Studies*, p. 360 (= ID., *Jehu*, 30).

Ramoth-gilead where he finds Jehu seated among the Israelite officers. Josephus' version (9,107) underscores, as so often, the accuracy of the prophetic prediction: the envoy finds things "as Elisha had foretold (προεῖπε) to him[18]". According to 9,5aβb Elisha's legate twice states that he desires a word with Jehu (whom he addresses as "O commander"), with Jehu's question as to whether he is, indeed, the one intended supervening. Josphus compresses this whole exchange; there is no need for a clarifying question by Jehu since his interlocutor begins by "going up to him" and then states that "he wished to speak with him about certain matters".

2 Kgs 9,6aα has Jehu and his caller retiring "to the house" (BL εἰς τὸν οἶκον) for their interview. In his designation for the site Josephus (9,108a) has recourse to the term used for this by Elisha when commissioning his envoy in 9,2b: the two men betake themselves to "the inner chamber (τὸ ταμιεῖον; compare BL 9,2b [εἰς] τὸ ταμ(ι)εῖον ἐν ταμείῳ)[19]". At this point as well, Josephus makes use of his equivalent, i.e. ὁ νεανίσκος, for the designation "the young man" used by the Bible for Elisha's envoy already earlier, i.e. in 9,4[20].

The envoy's words to Jehu begin in 9,6b with a (virtually) verbatim quotation of the anointing formula given him by Elisha in 9,3bα. Josephus varies the wording of the formula he attributes to Elisha in 9,106 ("... the Deity had chosen [ᾕρηται] him king"); here in 9,108b Jehu is told that "God had elected him king" (τὸν θεὸν ... βασιλέα χειροτονεῖν)[21]. Having anointed Jehu, the young man goes on (v. 7a) – therein exceeding his actual instructions by Elisha (see above) – to commission him to exterminate the line of Ahab. Through Jehu's doing this, he states, God will avenge (so MT 9,7b; in BL the subject is Jehu himself, ἐκδικήσεις) "on Jezebel the blood of my servants the prophets and the blood of all the servants of the Lord". The verbal form used by Josephus (9,108b) in his (indirect dis-

18. This phrase echoes 9,27 where Ahaziah dies "as Elijah had foretold (προεῖπεν)", as also 9,74 ("the things which had been foretold [προειρημένα] by Elisha came to pass in this manner"). Cf. the phrases, underscoring the prophet's veracity, "in accordance with the prophecy of Elisha" and "as Elisha had prophesied" of 9,80.

19. Josephus has no equivalent to this element in his rendering of Elisha's words in 9,106 (= 9,1-3). He now, however, makes delayed use of it in his version of 9,6 here in 9,108.

20. In 9,4 our witnesses employ, in fact, a (varying) double designation for the figure: "the young man, the young man, the prophet" (MT); "the young man, the student of the prophet" (TJ; cf. TJ 9,1 "one of the students of the prophets"); "the prophet, the young man (τὸ παιδάριον)" (B); "the young man (τὸ παιδάριον) the prophet" (L). Josephus, who previously (9,106) spoke of "one of Elisha's disciples", here in 9,108 has no equivalent to the alternative designation, i.e. "the prophet" used of him in 9,4.

21. This formula establishes another link (see above on 9,106) between Jehu and Saul and David in Josephus' presentation; it is used by him of Saul in AJ 6,54.312; and of David in 7,27.57; cf. 4,66 where God "elects" Aaron to the priesthood.

course) parallel to this sequence, i.e. ἐκδικήσῃ, leaves it ambiguous whether God or Jehu is the subject of the envisaged "avenging"[22]. In any case, the historian compresses the two Biblical groups whose blood is to be avenged into a single one, i.e. the prophets, just as he reworks Kings' mention of Jezebel as the object of the intended "vengeance" into a reference to the avenging of the blood of "the prophets who had "unlawfully (παρανόμως)[23] been put to death by Jezabela[24]". Further according to 9,109a, the intent of God/Jehu's act of vengeance is that Ahab's "house" (οἶκος), like those of Jeroboam and "Basa" (Βασά)[25], "might be destroyed root and branch because of their impiety" (πρόρριζος διὰ τὴν ἀσέβειαν αὐτῶν ἀφανισθῇ)...[26]". With this comparison between the fate of Ahab's dynasty and those suffered by the two earlier Israelite ruling houses, Josephus "anticipates" 2 Kgs 9,9. To that notice he then appends his parallel to 9,8 which speaks of the total extermination of all male members of Ahab's line: "... and that no seed might be left of Achab's family (μηδὲν ὑπολεφθῇ σπέρμα τῆς Ἀχάβου γενεᾶς)[27]". Elisha's envoy concludes his address to Jehu in 9,10a with a word about Jezebel's upcoming fate (being eaten by dogs) which itself echoes the word of Elijah on the matter cited in 1 Kgs 21,23. Josephus has no parallel to this last item, just as in his version of 1 Kings 21 Jezebel and her fate do not receive separate mention à la 21,23, but are simply cited along with Ahab and his line as part of Elijah's general word of doom in 8,361[28].

22. FELDMAN, Studies, p. 355, 362 (= ID., Jehu, 19, 23) opts for latter possibility (though without noting that BL 2 Kgs 9,7 also – and more unambiguously – make Jehu the subject of the action). In any case note that Josephus' verb for "avenge" (ἐκδιήσῃ) is the same used by BL (ἐκδικήσεις).

23. On terms of the παρανο – root as a key negative component of Josephus' vocabulary, see p. 30, n. 5.

24. Jezebel's execution of the (Yahwistic) prophets has been mentioned previously by Josephus in AJ 8,334 (= 1 Kgs 19,3, cf. 19,4) and 9,47 (no Biblical parallel).

25. In his earlier references to this king (Biblical "Basha") in AJ 8,288.298-309 (= 1 Kgs 15,27-16,8) Josephus calls him "Basanēs".

26. With this formulation compare AJ 8,309 "... because of his (Basha's) impiety, his house perished root and branch" (τὸν οἶκον ... πρόρριζον ἀπολέσθαι διὰ τὴν ἀσέβειαν); cf. 8,314 "God destroys the wicked root and branch" (προρρίζους ... ἀπόλλυσιν).

27. Compare AJ 8,314: God caused the successive Northern rulers to "leave none of their [predecessors'] family alive (μηδένα τοῦ γένους ὑπολιπεῖν)". With the above formulation Josephus tones down the graphic language of 9,8 with its reference to those "pissing against the wall" (= males) of Ahab's house; compare TJ's euphemism "him who knows knowledge".

28. MULZER, Bearbeitung, 56 notes that while Josephus lacks an equivalent to the prophetic announcements concerning Jezebel's fate of either 21,23 or 9,10a, he does recount the fact of her being consumed by dogs in accordance with those announcements in 9,124 (compare 2 Kgs 9,35 where this happening is not recounted in so many words). He concludes that Josephus wants to avoid tracing Jezebel's ignominious end back to a divine announcement.

2 Kgs 9,10b terminates the interview between Jehu and his anointer with mention of the latter "opening the door and fleeing" in accordance with Elisha's directive to him in v. 3. Josephus expatiates (9,110b) on the point with wording drawn from his own previous account: "*and, when he had said these things,* he darted out of the inner chamber (ἐκ τοῦ ταμιείου; see εἰς τὸ ταμιεῖον, 9,108), *taking care not to be seen* (μηδενὶ ... ὁραθῆναι) *by any of those in the army* (compare: Elisha "told him to make the journey as if he were a fugitive, in order that he might get away from there without being seen (ἀπιών) by anyone", 9,106)[29]".

2 Kgs 9,11-13 narrates the second stage in the process of Jehu's becoming king, i.e. his acclamation by his fellow officers. Preceding that acclamation, there is an exchange between him and them which opens with his colleagues – to whom Jehu has now returned – querying him (v. 11a): "Is all well (MT הֲשָׁלוֹם) [+"and he said to them 'it is peace'. And they said to him...", L). Why did this mad fellow (MT הַמְשֻׁגָּע, B ὁ ἐπίλημπτος, L ὁ ἐπίληπτος) come to you"? Josephus (9,110a) passes over the officers' initial question, having them come right to the point with a query about the caller for whom they use a double designation: "... they questioned him [Jehu] and urged him to tell them why *the youth* (ὁ νεανίσκος; see 9,106) had come to him, adding that he was a madman (μαίνεσθαι)...".

Jehu seeks (9,11b) to deflect his colleagues' question by joining in their denigration of his visitor: "you know the fellow and his talk (MT שִׂיחוֹ; BL ἀδολεσχίαν)". Josephus (9,110b) aligns query and response even more closely: "... he [Jehu] replied, 'you have, indeed, guessed right, for the words he spoke were those of a madman (μεμηνότος)". Jehu's fellows bluntly qualify (9,12a) his response as a "lie" (MT שֶׁקֶר; BL ἄδικον) and demand that he inform them of what has happened. Josephus' version (9,111a) considerably tones down the sharpness of the Biblical officers' response to the just-anointed king: "but they were eager to hear them [the visitor's words] and begged him to speak...[30]". Jehu concludes (9,12b) the dialogue between himself and his colleagues by repeating to them the "anointing formula" previously cited in vv. 3 and 6. Josephus (9,111b) makes the new king respond with a (slightly varied) quotation of the formula which Elisha had enjoined his envoy to use when anointing Jehu: "... (he said that the youth had told him) that

29. On the above sequence as another instance of Josephus' heightening the drama of the Biblical episode, see FELDMAN, *Studies*, p. 361 (= ID., *Jehu*, 30).

30. On Josephus' reworking of the officers' word with its accusation of "lying" by Jehu as part of the historian's rehabilitation of that Biblical figure (and more generally of the Jewish people as a whole) in view of contemporary charges about Jews' lack of truthfulness, see FELDMAN, *Studies*, pp. 355,362 (= ID., *Jehu*, 20,31).

God had chosen him king (τὸν θεὸν αὐτὸν ἡρῆσθαι βασιλέα; compare τὸ θεῖον αὐτὸν ἥρηται βασιλέα, 9,106; cf. τὸν θεὸν ... βασιλέα χειροτονεῖν αὐτόν, 9,108)".

Following the above exchange, Jehu's colleagues proceed to acclaim him king (9,13). Their doing so involves two initiatives on their part. First, they lay their garments beneath Jehu. In MT this takes place "on the bare (גֶּרֶם) steps" (so RSV). BL appear not to have understood the term in question which they simply transliterate (TJ renders "smooth [דרג] step"). Josephus, for his part, lacks a clear equivalent to the Biblical localization; his rendering (9,111c) of 9,13a reads: "... every man took off his cloak and spread it under Jehu's feet (ὑπερστρώννυεν[31] αὐτῷ τὸ ἱμάτιον)...[32]".

The officers' "divesting" themselves (9,13a) goes together with their blowing the trumpet and saying "Jehu is king" (9,13b). Josephus too speaks of the blowing of trumpets which accompanies the officers' "proclaiming Jehu king (ἐσήμαινον ... βασιλέα)".

3. Jehu's Advance to Jezreel

The next segment of the Jehu narrative (9,14-20 = 9,112-116) relates events that transpire between Jehu's acclamation as king (9,13) and his encounter with Joram and Ahaziah at Jezreel (9,21). The section opens with a summary statement (9,14a) that sets up the following account of Jehu's initiatives against the Israelite ruling house in accord with his divine mandate: "Thus Jehu... conspired (MT וַיִּתְקַשֵּׁר; BL συνεστράφη) against Joram". Josephus (9,112a) expatiates, while likewise eliminating the source's "conspiracy language"[33]: "*then he collected the army and*

31. This is the emendation of Coccejus, inspired by Lat, which Dindorf, Bekker, Niese, Naber and Marcus adopt. RSPE(O) read ἐπεστρώννυεν, M ἐπεστόρευεν.

32. Compare the very similar construction used of Agrippa's retainers in *AJ* 18,204 ἱμάτια ... ὑπέστρώνυσαν αὐτῷ. Marcus, *Josephus*, VI, p. 60, n. a commenting on his above translation ("under Jehu's feet"), affirms: "Josephus apparently takes [MT] *gerem*, which regularly means 'bone' in Aramaic in the sense of 'foot'". Note, however, that the term "feet" in Marcus's translation has no equivalent in the Greek itself, which speaks literally simply of a "spreading out under him (αὐτῷ)". Hence I agree with Mulzer, *Jehu*, p. 78, n. 195 that Marcus's suggestion should be dismissed and that Josephus simply has no equivalent to the localization of 9,13a – perhaps because he – like BL see above – did not understand the relevant phrase of his Hebrew and/or Greek texts (this last proposal is rejected by Mulzer, *Bearbeitung*, 57 who avers that Josephus would at least have known the word "stairs" of the phrase in question. His non-reproduction of the item would be due rather – so Mulzer – to his considering it "dispensible" for the further course of the narrative).

33. On this feature, see Feldman, *Studies*, pp. 358-359 (= Id., *Jehu*, 27) who suggests that, by not speaking of Jehu's initiatives as a "conspiracy", Josephus is trying to disassociate him from such reprobate fomenters of civil unrest as the Zealots and Jeroboam I. Here too, then, we would have an indication of the historian's overall "rehabilitative" treatment of Jehu.

prepared to set out against Joram *to the city of Jezarēla* [compare 9,16a: Jehu went to Jezreel, for Joram lay there]". To his "anticipated" specification concerning Jehu's destination Josephus then attaches a compressed version, in reverse sequence, of the parenthetical information given in 9,14b-15a which itself recapitulates the data of 8,28-29a (= 9,105a)[34]. In line with his frequent practice, Josephus re-introduces his reference to Jezreel as Joram's place of convalescence with a *Rückverweis* ("as we have said before"; see 9,105). The Biblical sequence in 9,14-16 contains a further recapitulation of previous data, i.e. mention of Ahaziah's visit to the wounded Joram (v. 16b = 8,29b) which, however, is separated from the notices of vv. 14b-15a (= 8,28-29a) concerning Joram himself by the intervening mention of Jehu's initiative in vv. 15b-16a (see above). In the continuation of 9,112 Josephus brings together all the recapitulated matter of 9,14b-15a,16b in a continuous sequence which precedes (the remainder of) his parallel to 9,15b-16a concerning Jehu's preparatory measures against Joram (which he introduces at the start of 9,112; see above). Further, in now citing Ahaziah's visit to Joram – not previously mentioned by him, see above – from 9,16b (= 8,29b), the historian interjects specifications concerning the motivation and purpose of that visit. In so doing, he begins by recalling ("as we have said before")[35] his previous mention of the marriage between Ahaziah's father Joram of Judah and Athaliah ("Othlia"), daughter of Ahab (see 8,398; 9,96) this resulting in Ahaziah himself being the "son of his [i.e. Joram of Israel's] sister" (cf. 9,45 where Joram of Judah is said to have "the same name as his wife's [Athaliah's] brother"). This fact of the Israelite Joram's being Ahaziah's uncle suggests, in turn, an obvious rationale for his visiting the former, i.e. "because of their kinship" (compare 8,29b: "because he [Joram] was sick"). Josephus likewise motivates the fact of Ahaziah's undertaking the visit in person: "to see for himself how his [Joram's] wound was doing[36]".

---

34. Compare MULZER, *Bearbeitung*, 57-58 and n. 33 who argues that Josephus simply omits 9,14b.

35. This is Josephus' second such *Rückverweis* in 9,112, the first one relating to Joram's current presence in Jezreel; see above.

36. Recall that 9,112 is Josephus' first mention of Ahaziah since the notice on his accession in 9,104, given that he leaves aside the previous Biblical mentions of the Judean's accompanying Joram against Ramoth-gilead (8,28) and his visit to the wounded Israelite at Jezreel (8,29b = 9,16b). Here in 9,112, he now does make mention of the latter point, even while continuing to pass over the former in silence (the Biblical presentation leaves unanswered the question of what Ahaziah did in the interlude between Joram's being wounded at Ramoth-gilead – where Ahaziah himself had been on hand (so 8,28) – and his "going down" to visit the recovering king at Jezreel (so 8,29; Josephus' omission of any mention of Ahaziah's involvement in the Ramoth-gilead campaign disposes of the problem).

Having now informed readers of the whereabouts of Joram and Ahaziah in 9,112, Josephus proceeds (9,113-114a) to present his (amplified) version of 9,15b-16a on Jehu's opening moves against the royal pair, resuming his initial mention of the matter from the start of 9,112 (see above). In 9,15b Jehu addresses a conditional command to an unspecified audience about their not leaving Ramoth-gilead to divulge what has just happened there in Jezreel. The protasis of this command differs somewhat in MT ("if this in your mind [נַפְשְׁכֶם]...") and B ("if your mind [ψυχήν] is [L if you have your mind] with me..."). Josephus' version (9,113) of Jehu's word seems to reflect the wording of BL in this instance, while at the same time elaborating on the considerations which prompt Jehu to make his appeal (and reversing the sequence of its component parts). It runs: "But Jehu, *wishing to fall* (προσπεσεῖν)[37] *suddenly upon Joram and his men*, asked that none of his soldiers [recall Josephus' inserted reference to Jehu's "collecting his army", 9,112] and inform Joram of these plans, *saying that if they observed this request*, it would be a clear proof of their loyalty (εὐνοίας; cf. B if your mind is with me...) *and that they had declared him king* (ἀποδεῖξαι αὐτὸν βασιλέα; compare ἐσήμαινον Ἰηοῦν εἶναι βασιλέα, 9,111) *because of their friendly feeling toward him*". The Bible does not, as such, relate the response of Jehu's hearers to his word. Josephus fills this lacuna with his notice (9,114a): "And so, approving (ἡσθέντες)[38] of what he said, they guarded the roads in order that no one might escape to Jezarēla and betray him to those who were there[39]". Thereafter, he reproduces the notice of 9,16a about Jehu "mounting" (his chariot) and proceeding towards Jezreel[40]. Within it he inserts, with a view to subsequent source references to Jehu's entourage, mention of his "taking along the pick of his horsemen (ἱππέων)".

2 Kgs 9,17-20 comprises a double sequence consisting of: watchman's report, dispatch of an envoy by Joram, exchange between the envoy and Jehu which ends with the former joining the latter, and report

37. This is the reading adopted by Niese, Naber and Marcus. Dindorf and Bekker read ἐμπεσεῖν with MSP.
38. This is the reading of the codices which Dindorf, Bekker, Niese, and Marcus follow. Naber conjectures πεισθέντες.
39. As FELDMAN, *Studies*, p. 359 (= ID., *Jehu*, 28) points out, the above, Biblically unparalleled, notice (9,114) – along with the preceding appeal (9,113) by Jehu for a show of "loyalty" to himself to which it refers back – heightens Jehu's stature as one who enjoys the devotion of his men.
40. In BL 9,16a there is a long plus attached to MT's mention of Joram's "laying" at Jezreel, this explaining the circumstances of his going there, i.e. his having been wounded by the Syrians at Ramoth-gilead. Josephus' rendering of 9,16a here in 9,114 shows no familarity with this plus; see, however, n. 36.

on this development by the watchman. The first of these sequences commences in v. 17a with the watchman on the Jezreel tower espying an approaching "company" (RSV, see below) and announcing this – to whom is not said. Josephus (9,114b), already here, highlights the role/initiative of King Joram: he "... had stationed the watchman (ὁ σκοπός = BL) to watch for those entering the city[41]", and it is to him specifically that the announcement is made. The historian likewise clarifies the Biblical designation for what the watchman sees (MT אֶת־שִׁפְעַת יֵהוּא, B τὸν κονιορτὸν Εἰού, L τὸν κονιορτὸν τοῦ ὄχλου Ἰού) and then announces. In his version the watchman sees "Jehu advancing with a host of men (μετὰ πλήθους)", while his report speaks of a "troop of horsemen" (ἱππέων ἴλην; cf. the inserted reference to Jehu's taking along "the pick of of his horsemen [ἱππέων]" in 9,114a). Joram (9,17b) responds to the watchman's report by dispatching a "horseman" who is to ask of the approaching company "Is it peace"? (cf. the officers' query to Jehu in 9,11). Josephus (9,115a) notes that Joram dispatched "one of his horsemen (τινα τῶν ἱππέων; compare L ἐπιβάτην ἵππου [> B]) at once", likewise having him being instructed to ascertain – not the company's intentions (so 9,17b) – but a prior matter, i.e. "who it was that was coming".

The "approach sequence" continues in 9,18a with the messenger repeating the question given him by the king (9,17b) verbatim to Jehu, this prefaced by a *Botenformel*. Josephus, who (9,115a) substituted another question for that of the Biblical Joram (see above), in his version of 9,18 (= 9,115b) has the messenger pose a question which sounds more like the one cited in that verse than the query which he himself has just placed on the lips of Joram: "... he asked him about the state of affairs in the camp[42], saying that the king wanted to know". Jehu replies (v. 18bα) to the messenger's query with an obscurely laconic question of

41. This inserted reference to the precautionary measures taken by Joram at Jezreel recalls what Josephus relates of the same king's provident initiatives in the face of Syrian siege of Samaria in 9,63 (cf. 2 Kgs 6,26): "And Joram was in constant fear that... someone might betray the city to the enemy, and every day he would walk all around the walls to the guards, spying out whether any of the enemy were within the city...".

42. This formulation might be taken as Josephus' adaptation of the source question "Is it peace"? (9,17b), understood as an inquiry about whether things are "peaceful" at Ramoth-gilead where Jehu had been left by Joram (see 9,106). As for the "switch" between the question prescribed to be asked by Joram and the one actually put to Jehu by the messenger in Josephus' presentation, I suggest that this might be understood as follows: the messenger upon encountering Jehu recognizes him, this making it unnecessary for him to pose the king's question. Accordingly, he shifts to another question – itself suggested by Joram's query as cited in 9,17b – designed to elicit information he does not already know.

his own (literally: "what to you and to peace"?) together with the command that his interlocutor "turn round after me". Josephus (9,115c) recasts Jehu's opening question as an initial command by him: "But Jehu told him not to trouble himself about these matters [i.e. the conditions in the camp about which he had just asked], but to follow him". 2 Kgs 9,18 concludes with the watchman reporting (once again, the addressee is left unspecified) that the messenger is "not returning" from his encounter with the advancing party. Josephus' rendering (9,116a) introduces a transitional reference to the lookout's "seeing" what has just transpired, here too (cf. 9,114), specifying that his report was made to Joram. The source verse 9,19, re-utilizing the wording of vv. 17b-18bα largely verbatim, relates the sequels to the lookout's new announcement: Joram's dispatch of a second messenger, the latter's question ("is it peace"?) to Jehu, and Jehu's counter-question and command that the messenger join him. Josephus (9,116b) avoids such verbal repetition in his drastically compressed version of v. 19: "... when the king sent a second man, Jehu ordered him to do the same (as the first)". The double sequence of vv. 17-20 concludes in v. 20a with the lookout reporting the non-return of the second messenger, using virtually the same formula as he had employed in v. 18bβ. To that report the lookout adds (v. 20b) a remark on the "furious" (so MT) driving of the one approaching, calling this similiar to that of Jehu. Josephus, for his part, incorporates the content of v. 20 into the following segment of his narrative; see below.

4. Joram & Ahaziah Assassinated

A new segment of the Biblical narrative opens in 9,21 with Joram and Ahaziah mounting their chariots to go to meet Jehu whom they encounter at the one-time property of Naboth (see 1 Kings 21). The historian (9,117) introduces an extended *Rückverweis* into his rendering of this verse: "But, when the look-out informed Joram of this also[43], he himself mounted his chariot with Ochozias, the king of Jerusalem [literally of the Jerusalemites; see 9,95] – *he too was there, as we have said before* [see 9,112][44], *because of their kinship* (διὰ συγ-

---

43. The above transitional phrase, introducing the content of 9,21, represents Josephus' rendering of 9,20a ("again the watchman reported, 'he [Joram's second envoy] reached them, but he is not coming back'"); see above.

44. This is the third such *Rückverweis* within Josephus' Jehu narrative; see the two previous ones in 9,112.

γένειαν), *to see how Joram's wound was getting on* (ὀψόμενος αὐτὸν πῶς ἐκ τοῦ τραύματος ἔχοι)[45] – and went out to meet him". Prior to the king's setting out in 9,21 the watchman of 9,20b had stated "the driving is like the driving of Jehu, for he drives furiously (MT בְּשִׁגָּעוֹן, BL ἐν παραλλαγῇ, "careeningly"; contrast TJ בניח, "with gentleness")". In Josephus this report becomes an appended note (9,117b) to his preceding account of the kings' sally (9,117a): "Now Jehu was going along rather slowly (σχολαίτερον)[46] and in good order (μετ' εὐταξίας)[47]". The agreement between TJ and Josephus here against MT and BL in their characterization of Jehu's driving is striking and could point to the historian's familiarity with a interpretative tradition that finds expression in the Targum. In any case, the Targumic/Josephan reading does have the effect of casting Jehu in a more favorable light, i.e. as both self-controlled[48] and the "Herr der Lage[49]". In addition, Josephus' presentation on the point helps dispose of a difficulty suggested by the MT/BL reading in 9,20b, i.e. how is that Joram, having been informed that someone driving "like a madman" is approaching, ventures out (so 9,21) of the security of the Jezreel citadel accompanied only by Ahaziah to meet that "madman"? In the historian's rendition, by contrast, there is nothing to incite caution or suspicion on Joram's part: Jehu's "ambling approach" would not have appeared at all threatening.

In 9,21bβ the two kings encounter Jehu "at the property (MT בְּחֶלְקַת, BL ἐν τῇ μερίδι) of Naboth the Jezreelite". Josephus (9,118a) designates the site as Naboth's "field" (ἐν ἀγρῷ), thereby establishing a terminological link with *AJ* 8,355 where, at the start of his version of 1 Kings 21, this is the first term he uses to designate Naboth's inheritance. Joram initiates the exchange between Jehu and himself in 9,22a by reiterating the question of his earlier messengers, i.e. "is it peace?". In Josephus the king echoes the question the first messenger had attributed to him (see 9,115), i.e. "he inquired whether all was well with the camp". Jehu's response (9,22b) is formulated as a (hostile) rhetorical question: "what peace (can there be) as long as...?" Josephus (9,118b) reformulates this question as a statement in indirect discourse itself intro-

---

45. Josephus' wording in the above italicized phrase closely echoes that used by him in 9,112: (Ahaziah was visiting Joram) ἐπισκέψασθαι δὲ πῶς ἐκ τοῦ τραύματος ἔχοι διὰ τὴν συγγένειαν.

46. Josephus' one other use of the adjective σχολαῖος is in *BJ* 7,98, where it refers to a river whose current is "far from slow".

47. On Josephus' usage of the word εὐταξία, see MULZER, *Bearbeitung*, 59, n. 50.

48. So FELDMAN, *Studies*, pp. 354-355 (= ID., *Jehu*, 18-19).

49. So MULZER, *Bearbeitungen*, 59.

duced by a phrase that already makes clear the animosity of the speaker towards Joram: "but Jehu reviled (βλασφημήσαντος)[50] him bitterly...". According to the Biblical Jehu what precludes "peace" between himself and Joram are (so 9,22) the many "harlotries and sorceries" (BL πορνεῖαι ... καὶ φάρμακα) of the queen mother Jezebel. Josephus personalizes the charge, having Jehu call the queen herself, in a reversal of the Biblical sequence "a witch and a harlot" (φαρμακὸν καὶ πόρνην)[51].

2 Kgs 9,23 relates Joram's reaction to Jehu's invective: he "turns his hands" (RSV reined about) and flees, saying "treachery" (MT מִרְמָה, BL δόλος) to Ahaziah[52]. Josephus interjects (9,118c) a note on the psychological effects of Jehu's outburst upon Joram which prompt the latter's attempted flight: "... fearing (δείσας) his intentions and suspecting that he meant no good...". He likewise elaborates on the king's exclamation to his Judean counterpart: "(he told Ochozias) that they had been manoeuvred into a trap and tricked (ἐνέδρᾳ καὶ δόλῳ [cf. δόλος, BL] κατεστρατηγῆσθαι[53])[54]".

The story now (9,24) reaches its culmination with the assassination of Joram: Jehu fills his hand with his bow, "smites" Joram between the shoulders, the arrow passing through his heart, whereupon the king sinks "in his chariot" (so MT, בְּרִכְבּוֹ; compare BL ἐπὶ τὰ γόνατα αὐτοῦ = עַל־בִּרְכָּיו)[55]. Josephus' rendition (9,118d) begins with Jehu shooting

50. The use of this term effects another link between the Jehu narrative and Josephus' version of the Naboth incident of 1 Kings 21 in AJ 8,355-362 where it is twice used (see 8,358.359) in reference to the (false) accusation that Naboth had "blasphemed" (in the source texts, i.e. 1 Kgs 21,10.13, one reads a euphemism, i.e. "he blessed") King Ahab. In the earlier episode Naboth is put to death by Ahab whom, in fact, he had not "blasphemed"; here in 9,118 Ahab's son Joram is not only "blasphemed" by Jehu, but assassinated by him as well in punishment for his father's crime against Naboth.

51. The words καὶ πόρνην are absent in RO and omitted by Niese. They are retained by Dindorf, Bekker, Naber, and Marcus in accordance with the readings of MSPLat. Both terms of the above collocation occur only here in the Josephan corpus.

52. The VL reading in 9,23 differs in several respects from that of MT and BL; it runs: "Et circumagens Joram currum suum dixit ad Ochoziam: Iaculare, Ochozia!". See FERNÁNDEZ, Scribes & Translators, p. 77. With his reference to Joram's "turning his chariot" (στρέψας ... τὸ ἅρμα) in his version of 9,23 Josephus goes together with this VL reading against MT and BL (where what Joram "turns" are his "hands").

53. Josephus' two remaining uses of the verb καταστρατηγέω are in Vita 320,372.

54. On Josephus' above reworking of Joram's word of 9,23 which eliminates its mention of a "conspiracy" by Jehu, replacing this with a verb which translates "out-general", as intended to highlight the military stature of Jehu, see FELDMAN, Studies, p. 354 (= ID., Jehu, 17); cf. n. 33.

55. Here again (cf. n. 52) VL goes its own way, its version of 9,24 reading "Et percussit Ioram... et decidens in terram mortuus est residens in genua sua (cf. BL)". See FERNÁNDEZ, Scribes & Translators, p. 57.

(τοξεύσας)⁵⁶ and "hitting" Joram – without specification of where he does so (compare 9,24: "between the shoulders"). Joram's arrow, Josephus continues, went through Joram's heart (τοῦ βέλους διὰ τῆς καρδίας; compare BL τὸ βέλος ... διὰ τῆς καρδίας), with the result (9,119a) that Joram "*immediately* fell on his knees (πεσὼν ἐπὶ γόνυ)⁵⁷". He then rounds off the sequence by explicitly noting, as the Bible (MT BL) itself does not⁵⁸, the fact of Joram's demise: "he breathed his last" (τὴν ψυχὴν ἀφῆκεν).

2 Kgs 9,25-26 relates the disposition of Joram's corpse. The segment begins (v. 25a) with Jehu directing "Bidkar" (B Βαδεκά, L Βαδέκ), his "aide" (so RSV, MT שָׁלִשׁה, BL τριστάτην) to cast the king's body onto "the plot of ground (BL τοῦ ἀγροῦ) belonging to Naboth the Jezreelite". Josephus (9,119b) designates "Badakos" (Βαδάκῳ) as "the commander of the third division" (τῷ τῆς τρίτης μοίρας ἡγεμόνι)⁵⁹; he is enjoined to "throw" (ῥῖψαι, so BL) Joram's corpse "into the field (εἰς τὸν ἀγρόν, cf. ἐν ἀγρῷ, 9,118) of Naboth". Jehu (9,25b-26a) motivates his directive to Bidkar by reminding him of the divine "burden" (MT הַמַּשָּׂא, BL τὸ λῆμμα) pronounced as they were riding behind Ahab (v. 25b) which he then proceeds to quote (v. 26a). Josephus' rendition (9,119c) rearranges the component elements of vv. 25b-26a. It first (= 9,25bβ-26a) has Jehu "recall" (ἀναμήσας) the content of "*Elijah's*⁶⁰ prophecy (προφητείας)⁶¹" made against Ahab "*who had killed (ἀποκτείναντι) Naboth*⁶²", i.e. "... both he [Ahab] *and his line* (τὸ γένος) should perish in Ahab's field (ἐν τῷ ... χωρίῳ; compare ἐν τῇ μερίδι ταύτῃ, BL 9,26a)⁶³". Only thereafter (9,120a) does the Josephan Jehu

56. This term, absent in 9,24 itself, echoes the form τοξευθείς used of Joram's wounding by the Syrians in 9,105. The king's not-fatal "shooting" there foreshadows his mortal shooting here in 9,119.

57. For this detail Josephus clearly aligns himself with the reading of BL (cf. *VL*, n. 55) against that of MT (see above in the text). As MULZER, *Jehu*, p. 99, n. 280 points out, MARCUS, *Josephus*, VI, p. 64, n. a misleadingly states that Josephus' reference to Joram's "falling on his knees" accords with the joint reading of MT and LXX 9,24.

58. See, however, *VL*'s "mortuus est" (n. 55).

59. Josephus uses this same designation in *AJ* 9,73 where the parallel, i.e. MT 2 Kgs 7,2, has הַשָּׁלִישׁ; see there.

60. 2 Kgs 9,25b-26 nowhere names the bearer of the oracle cited there by Jehu. Josephus derives the name from 1 Kings 21 (cf. v. 19) where Elijah is directed to deliver an announcement whose wording approximates that cited by Jehu in 9,26a.

61. With this substitution for the term "burden" used in MT BL 9,25b (see above), compare TJ's "the burden *of this prophecy*" (מטל נבואתא הדין).

62. This Josephan expansion of 9,25's reference to the oracle "against him (Ahab)" reminds readers of the historian's Naboth story. In particular it echoes *AJ* 8,360 where God instructs Elijah to ask Ahab why he has "killed" (κτείνας) Naboth.

63. With this rendition of Jehu's "quotation" of Elijah's word from 9,26a, Josephus eliminates its opening, first-person reference to God's "having seen the blood of

mention (= 9,25bα) that he had "... heard the prophet [Elijah] say [these things], when seated behind Achab's chariot[64]".

In 9,26b Jehu reiterates his previous injunction to Bidkar (see 9,25a), qualifying this as being "in accordance with the word of the Lord (BL κατὰ τὸ ῥῆμα Κυρίου)". Josephus does not have Jehu repeat his directive. He does, however, pick up on that directive's closing phrase with a fulfillment notice (9,120b) which, in accord with his standard practice, substitutes alternative language for the source's mention of the divine "word": "And indeed it fell out in accordance with Elijah's prophecy (κατὰ τὴν πρόρρησιν)[65]".

2 Kgs 9,27-28(29) records the murder of Jehu's second royal victim, i.e. Ahaziah of Judah. In v. 27aα Ahaziah, seeing Joram's demise, flees towards "Beth-haggan". Josephus (9,120c) elaborates on this flight notice, while omitting its place name: "When Joram fell, Ochozias, being fearful (δείσας)[66] for his own safety, turned his chariot aside to another road, thinking to elude Jehu". Here too, Josephus' characteristic concern with highlighting the motivations and feelings behind figures' actions comes to the fore. The remainder of v. 27a proceeds to relate Jehu's pursuit of Ahaziah, this ending with the latter's being smitten[67] in

Naboth and his sons". That omission is understandable given that neither the story of 1 Kings 21 itself nor Josephus' version of this in AJ 8,355-362 makes mention of Naboth's "sons". In addition, the historian inserts into the closing words of the quoted source prophecy ("I [the Lord] will requite you [sg., Ahab] on this plot of ground...") the notation that the "requital" will extend also to Ahab's "line"; see above. Thereby, he brings the prophecy's wording here in 9,119 into line with his citation of Elijah's own prediction in 8,361 (compare 1 Kgs 21,19) according to which not only will the blood of Ahab and Jezebel be shed at the site of Naboth's murder, but also "all his family" (τὸ γένος) are to perish there. See further MULZER, Bearbeitung, 59-60.

64. In Josephus then it is only Jehu who was so positioned as to hear the prophetic word against Ahab. In 9,25b, by contrast, Jehu speaks of both Bidkar and himself having ridden behind Ahab and so also both hearing the word in question. The difference highlights the stature of Jehu, who alone had the privilege of riding behind Ahab.

65. The term πρόρρησις occurs 18x in Josephus (never in LXX). The above formula appears also in AJ 1,258; 2,229. The Josephan formula serves to underscore that Elijah's prophecy uttered to Ahab years before did indeed find fulfillment – a point about (true) prophecy which the historian insistently underscores; see, e.g., 9,74.

66. This is the same term used of Joram's reaction when confronted by Jehu in 9,118. By means of the common term (in both instances inserted by him) Josephus accentuates the fear-inducing character of Jehu's initiatives.

67. The Biblical witnesses leave the identity of Ahaziah's "smiter" uncertain. In MT 9,27 Jehu orders "smite (pl.) him", but the execution of this order is not cited as such. In BL Jehu's word is simply "and him too", followed by a plus, i.e. "and he smote (ἐπά-ταξεν) him". Similarly, the L plus following MT 2 Kgs 10,36 (10,42) states that "Jehu shot (ἐτόξυσεν) Ahaziah". The same ambiguity regarding the identity of Ahaziah's killer can also be noted in MT 2 Chr 22,9 as compared with BL; in the former Jehu's retainers both bring the Judean king to Jehu and put him to death themselves, while in the latter it is Jehu who "kills" the captive Ahaziah.

his chariot "at the ascent of Gur (BL Γαί) which is by Ibleam". Josephus (9,121a), eliminating any role for Jehu's retainers, has Jehu himself "shooting" (τοξεύσας)[68] and "wounding" (ἔτρωσε)[69] Ahaziah, doing so after "overtaking him at a certain rise of ground[70]". V. 27b relates, quite summarily, the sequels to Ahaziah's smiting: "he fled to Megiddo and died there". As with Ahaziah's attempted escape (see above), Josephus (9,121b) elaborates considerably here as well: "... *thereupon Ochozias abandoned his chariot and, mounting* (ἐπιβάς)[71] *a horse*[72], fled *from Jehu* to Mageddo, where (κἀκεῖ), *although he received treatment* (θεραπευόμενος)[73], he died (τελευτᾷ; compare ἀπέθανεν, BL 9,27b) *from the wound* (ἐκ τῆς πληγῆς)[74]".

2 Kgs 9,28 rounds off the narrative of Ahaziah's demise with mention of the transport of his corpse to Jerusalem[75], where he is buried "in his tomb with his fathers in the city of David". In contrast to his treatment of Ahazi-

68. This is the same form used of Jehu's "shooting" of Joram in 9,118, see also the L plus following MT 2 Kgs 10,36 (cf. n. 67). Josephus' presentation thus underscores, by the use of common terminology, the parallelism between the ends of both Joram and Ahaziah at Jehu's hands: both kings "fear" (see n. 66) Jehu, who, for his part, personally "shoots" the two of them.

69. Via this inserted indication Josephus, with the continuation of the story in view, makes clear, from the start, that Ahaziah's "smiting" did not lead to his immediate death, this in contrast to what happened with Joram; see 9,118.

70. With this generalized localization Josephus avoids (as in the case of "Beth-haggan" earlier in 9,27a; see above) the (obscure) Biblical place names, *in casu* "(the ascent of) Gur" and "Ibleam" of 9,27b.

71. This is the reading of MSP which Dindorf, Bekker, Naber, and Marcus follow. Niese reads ἀναβάς with RO.

72. According to MULZER, *Bearbeitung*, 60 this inserted item would be intended to explain how Ahaziah was able to make his escape at this point, i.e. he transferred from his slower chariot to a faster horse.

73. This indication corresponds to that in BL 2 Chr 22,9 where Ahaziah is captured while "being treated" (ἰατρευόμενον) in Samaria; compare MT which speaks rather of the king's "hiding" (מִתְחַבֵּא) in that city. On the supposition that Josephus is dependent on BL 22,9 for the item, he has at the same time, adapted it in accordance with the wording of 2 Kgs 9,28b, making the king's treatment site, not Samaria, but rather the Megiddo of the latter verse. Josephus' utilization of 22,9 (BL) is, however, rejected by MULZER, *Bearbeitung*, 60 who suggests rather that via his inserted "treatment notice" Josephus here in 9,121 would be assimilating Ahaziah's end to the earlier situation of Joram of whom he states in 9,105 that he was having his wound "healed" (ἰαθησόμενος) in Jezreel.

74. With the above phrase κἀκεῖ ... ἐκ τῆς πληγῆς τελευτᾷ of 9,121, compare Josephus' notice on the end of Josiah in 10,77: τελευτᾷ ... ἐκ τῆς πληγῆς ἐκεῖ. In this connection note too that, like Ahaziah, Josiah is "shot" (τοξεύσας) but only dies some time afterwards. Thus in Josephus' presentation Ahaziah's death foreshadows that of Josiah, notwithstanding their divergent status as respectively "bad" and "good" kings.

75. MT speaks of Ahaziah's servants "riding" (וַיַּרְכִּבוּ [RSV "they carried him in a chariot"]; see L ἀνήνεγκαν) the dead Ahaziah to Jerusalem. B is more expansive: "his servants *placed him on the chariot and* brought him...".

ah's assassination (see above), Josephus (9,121c) abridges the Biblical burial notice for the king, simply stating: "then he was brought to Jerusalem
and there received burial...[76]". Attached to 9,27-28 is the notice (9,29)
about Ahaziah's acceding in Joram's eleventh year which appears both out
of place at this juncture with Ahaziah already dead and buried, and which
further repeats, even while deviating from, the datum of 8,25 dating Ahaziah's accession in Joram's *twelfth* year. Accordingly, it is not surprising that
Josephus makes no use of the indication of 9,29. In its place, he presents
two items from the opening framework notices for Ahaziah (8,25-27; cf. 2
Chr 22,2-3) previously passed over by him (see above) i.e. his reign of
only one year (so 8,26aβ // 22,2aβ)[77] and the qualification of him as a
"bad" (πονηρός) king, "even worse than his father[78]".

5. Jezebel Executed

At this juncture in the Biblical account, Jehu "rounds off" his assassination of Joram and Ahaziah (9,21-29) with yet another act of regicide,
i.e. his bringing about the death of Jezebel, the Israelite queen mother,
9,30-37 (recall the mentions of her in 9,10b.22). The Biblical Jezebel,
true to character, takes the initiative even in precipitating her own death;

76. In representing Ahaziah as being buried in Jerusalem (by his own retainers) Josephus aligns himself with the account of 2 Kgs 9,28 against that of 2 Chr 22,9 where the
king, subsequent to his execution, is buried by Jehu's men at an unspecified site
(Jezreel?) in consideration of his being "the grandson of Jehoshaphat who sought the
Lord with all his heart".

77. This same datum appears in the plus which follows 9,29 in L; MULZER, *Bearbeitung*, 60-61 suggests that it was this plus which inspired Josephus to mention Ahaziah's length of reign at this point in his presentation. In any event, Josephus, in accord
with his standard practice, has no equivalent to the Bible's further, divergent indications
about Ahaziah's age at accession, i.e. 22 (so 8,26aα) vs. 42 (22,2aα).

78. Compare 8,27 // 22,4 where the stereotyped charge against Ahaziah is that he "did
evil (BL τὸ πονηρόν) in the sight of the Lord", this under the influence of his consort
Athaliah. Given the detailed catalogue of crimes with which he charges Joram, Ahaziah's
father, in 9,95-104 (see chap. V) and to which his (and the Bible's) account of the latter
have no counterpart, Josephus' ("un-Biblical") claim here that Ahaziah was "even worse
than his father" comes as a surprise. Conceivably, this characterization of Ahaziah
reflects the fact of his having given active "aid and comfort" to Joram, king of the rebel
Northern kingdom (something that is not "credited" to Joram of Judah). With regard to
this suggestion, it should, however, be borne in mind that Josephus, in fact, diminishes
the extent of Ahaziah's involvement with Joram in that he does not mention his participation in the latter's campaign against Ramoth-gilead (so 2 Kgs 8,28 // 2 Chr 22,5). In
any case, it is of interest to note that also Rabbinic tradition evidences a tendency to magnify Ahaziah's wrongdoing; see *b. Sanh.* 102b which, in connection with the notice of 2
Chr 22,9 about Ahaziah's fleeing to Samaria after his encounter with Jehu, states that he
spent his time there substituting the names of idols for that of the Lord in the Torah. On
the whole problem; see further KRIEGER, *Jehu-Erzählung*, 73-75.

v. 30 portrays her beautifying herself and looking out of the window in expectation of Jehu's arrival in Jezreel. In Josephus' version (9,122a) Jezebel "stands on the tower" (στᾶσα ἐπὶ τοῦ πύργου) to await Jehu, an indication perhaps inspired by 9,17 where the "lookout" is depicted as "standing (so MT L [εἰστήκει]) on the tower [L ἐπὶ τοῦ πύργου])" of Jezreel as Jehu's party advances. Jezebel (9,31) greets Jehu with a sarcastic question which picks up (for the last time) the *Leitwort* of 2 Kings 9: "Is it peace, you Zimri, murderer (B ὁ φονευτής, L ὁ φονεύς) of your master (BL τοῦ κυρίου αὐτοῦ)"? Josephus reformulates, eliminating both the "peace question" and the mention of Zimri, assassin of King Elah of Israel (see 1 Kgs 16,10 = AJ 8,307)[79] from the queen's word, even while retaining its sarcastic tone: "... a fine servant, who has killed (ὁ ἀποκτείνας)[80] his master (τὸν δεσπότην)"! Looking up "to the window" [+ "and he saw her", BL] (see v. 30), Jehu (v. 32a) responds to Jezebel's provocation with words that differ in MT and BL. In the former his question is: "Who is with me? Who?", while in the latter, addressing himself specifically to Jezebel, he says: "Who are you? Come down to me". In this instance, Josephus (9,122b) clearly aligns himself with the distinctive reading of BL: "... but he looked up at her [see BL's plus: and he saw her] and asked who she was, and commanded her to come down (καταβᾶσαν; BL κατάβηθι) to him". Josephus passes over the reference in 9,32b to the "two or three (so MT; BL specifies two) eunuchs" who "look down" at Jehu. Instead, he moves immediately to the main point, i.e. Jehu's command that Jezebel be thrown down (= v. 33aα, here without specification of the addressee): "... *finally* he ordered the eunuchs[81] to throw her *from the tower* (ἀπὸ τοῦ πύργου)[82]". The remainder of v. 33 recounts the sequels to Jehu's order: the queen is thrown down; her blood splatters both the wall and the horses, while the latter trample her (so various Hebrew MSS, the *qere*, BL, TJ; in MT's *ketiv* the verb is singular, with Jehu himself

79. Josephus might well have adjudged the Biblical Jezebel's designation of Jehu with the name of this earlier, rather obscure, regicide as an over-subtlety which would likely puzzle his readers – after all, the man being addressed by Jezebel is named Jehu, not Zimri – and so omitted it.

80. This is the reading of ME which Naber and Marcus follow. Dindorf reads ὃς ἀπέκτεινε with P², Bekker ὃς ἀπέκτεινας with SP¹, and Niese ὃς ἀποκτείνει with O.

81. In specifying these persons as the addressees of Jehu's order, Josephus makes delayed use of the mention of them in 9,32b. In so doing, he passes over, however, the source figure(s) for their number, perhaps in view of the witnesses' diversity on the point (see above).

82. This appended specification concerning the place from which Jezebel is to be thrown down echoes Josephus' mention of the queen's "standing on the tower (ἐπὶ τοῦ πύργου)" at the opening of 9,122.

as subject (?))[83]. Josephus (9,123a) specifies, *inter alia*, the upshot of the process: "*And, behold, as she fell*[84], the wall was splattered (περιέρρανε)[85] with her blood[86], and she was trampled by the horses (συμπατηθεῖσα ὑπὸ τῶν ἵππων; compare BL συνεπάτησαν [i.e. the horses] αὐτήν)[87], *and so died* (ἀπέθανε)[88]".

Jehu's studied indifference to Jezebel's appalling fate finds expression in his "going in to eat and drink" (v. 34) immediately thereafter. Josephus (9,123b) expatiates with various minor details concerning Jehu's action: "*After these happenings*, Jehu came *to the palace*[89] *with his friends* (φίλοις)[90], and refreshed himself *after his ride* with food and other things". It is only thereafter (v. 34b) that Jehu orders, using a second person plural verb, the burial of Jezebel in consideration of her royal lineage. In reproducing this directive Josephus (9,123c) specifies who is to do the burying ("the servants who had sent Jezebel to her death", i.e. the "eunuchs" cited in 9,122), while omitting the Biblical Jehu's derogatory qualification of her as "that cursed woman".

2 Kgs 9,35 relates that Jehu's burial order could not, in fact, be carried out since only Jezebel's skull, feet and palms were to be found. To his version of this notice (9,124a) Josephus appends an explanation of what happened with the remainder of Jezebel's corpse: "But the men *who had been ordered to bury her* found nothing more of her body than the extremities (ἀκρωτήρια)[91] alone; *all the rest had been devoured by dogs* (ὑπὸ κυνῶν ... δεδαπανημένον)". The historian found his inspiration for this explanation in the continuation of the Biblical narrative which (vv. 36-37) quotes the prediction of Elijah (see 1 Kgs 21,23): "(in the territory of Jezreel) the dogs shall eat the flesh

83. On the difference between the witnesses here, see MULZER, *Jehu*, pp. 123-124.

84. This transitional phrase takes the place of the (self-evident) execution notice of 9,33aβ: "so they threw her down".

85. Josephus' one remaining use of the verb περιρραίνω is in *AJ* 13,243.

86. In 9,33 the horses are splattered with her blood as well.

87. In making the horses the subject of the "trampling" Josephus agrees with BL etc. against the MT *ketiv*; see above.

88. With this appended indication specifying that Jezebel did in fact "die", compare the explicit mention of Joram's "breathing his last" following his shooting by Jehu introduced by Josephus in his rendering of 9,24 in 9,119.

89. According to 9,34 Jehu simply "went/entered"; Josephus' above indication specifies his destination.

90. Mention of these persons recalls Josephus' – likewise inserted – reference to Jehu's "taking along the pick of his horsemen" as he advances against Jezreel in 9,114 (compare 9,16a).

91. This is Josephus' generalization for the three remains that are said to be found in 9,35; see above. The historian's one remaining use of the word ἀκρωτήριον is in *AJ* 8,344 where it refers to the "peak" of Mount Carmel.

of Jezebel[92]". Having thus "anticipated" 9,36's reference to the dogs' consumption of Jezebel, Josephus (9,124b) compresses Jehu's extended quotation of Elijah's prediction into the statement that Jehu "... marvelled (ἐθαύμαζε) at the prophecy (προφητείαν; see 9,119)[93] of Elijah[94], for he had foretold (προεῖπε; see 9,107) that she would perish (ἀπολεῖσθαι, see ἀπολεῖται, of Ahab's line in 9,119) in this manner at Jezarēla[95]".

6. *Massacre of Ahab's Family*

2 Kings 10 opens with an account (vv. 1-11) of Jehu's contriving the destruction of Ahab's 70 male relatives in Samaria. In making reference to the 70, Josephus (9,125 = 10,1a) specifies that they were "being brought up" (τρεφομένων) in the city, thereby anticipating the allusion in 10,6 to "the great men of the city who were "bringing them [the 70] up (BL ἐξέτρεφον)". MT 10,1b speaks of "letters"(סְפָרִים; compare, however, 10,2 "this letter") which Jehu wrote to three groups of persons in Samaria, i.e. the rulers of Jezreel (*sic!*), the elders, and the "guardians [RSV inserts of the sons] of Ahab". BL 10,1b, on the contrary, speak of "a letter" (βιβλίον) dispatched by Jehu to "the rulers of the city (so L, B of Samaria), the elders, and the guardians of the sons of (so L, > B) Ahab". Josephus' account (9,125a) of Jehu's initiative seems to reflect a mixture of several of the above readings: "Jehu sent *two* letters (ἐπιστολάς)[96], one to their tutors (παιδαγωγοῖς), and the other to the

92. Josephus' own version of this prediction comes in *AJ* 8,361 (the language of which is closely echoed by him here in 9,124): "... in that very place where Naboth's body had been devoured by dogs (ὑπὸ κυνῶν δαπανηθῆναι [compare ὑπὸ κυνῶν ... δεδαπανημένον, 9,124]), his own blood and his wife's should be shed...". In using the same phrase to speak of the fate of the corpses of both Naboth and Jezebel, Josephus underscores the operation of the talion-principle in the latter's end.

93. The construction "marvel at prophecy" occurs only here in Josephus.

94. Cf. 9,120: "and indeed it fell out in accordance with Elijah's prophecy (πρόρρησιν)". Here too, Josephus' formulation replaces a source reference to the divine "word"; compare 9,36aβ: "this is the word of the Lord which he spoke by his servant Elijah...".

95. In reproducing the content of Elijah's prophecy in the vague fashion above Josephus avoids the problem that in 9,37 ("and the corpse of Jezebel shall be as dung upon the face of the field in the territory of Jezreel, so that no one can say, This is Jezebel") Jehu claims to be citing a previous word of Elijah which, however, is not recorded as such elsewhere in the Bible.

96. According to MULZER, *Bearbeitung*, 69, n. 136 Josephus' reference to "(two) letters" here need not entail the historian's dependence on the MT as opposed to the BL reading in 10,1b. Rather, the Josephan plural could be derived by him from the wider context wherein two distinct groups of addressees figure.

magistrates of Samaria (τοῖς ἄρχουσι τῶν Σαμαρέων; see B τοὺς ἄρχοντας Σαμαρείας, compare L τοὺς στρατεγοὺς τῆς πόλεως)...".
His omission of a third group of addressees common to all the above wit-nesses, i.e. "the elders" is in line with the continuation of his narrative where this group – in contrast to the source (see 10,6) – will play no role.

2 Kgs 10,2-3 cites the content of Jehu's "letter(s)" in which he, after reminding the recipients of the varied resources at their disposal (v. 2), urges them to designate the "best and fittest (MT וְהַיָּשָׁר הַטּוֹב, BL τὸν ἀγαθὸν καὶ [τὸν] εὐθῆ) as their king" and to "fight for" their master's (Ahab's) house (v. 3). Josephus (9,125b) re-arranges the sequence of the letters' content in his reproduction of Jehu's message: "... telling them to appoint the bravest (ἀνδρειότατον)[97] of Achab's sons as king (ἀποδεῖξαι Βασιλέα[98]; cf. 10,3a), *for*, he said, they had *an abundance of* chariots, horses, arms, *soldiers* and fortified cities (πόλεις ὀχυράς = BL; MT has the singular, i.e. a fortified city)[99], *and, when they had done this* [i.e. appoint themselves a king], to take vengenance (εἰσπράττεσθαι δίκην) for their master's death (ὑπερ τοῦ δεσπότου; cf. Jezebel's refer-ence to Jehu as the servant who killed "his master" [τὸν δεσπότην] in 9,122)[100]". Having thus reproduced, in re-arranged form, the content of Jehu's "letter(s)", Josephus goes on to append a explanation (9,126a) of his rationale for sending them: "This he wrote (δὲ γράφει)[101] because he wished to test the feelings of the Samarians (Σαμαρέων) towards him-self[102]".

2 Kgs 10,4 recounts the "terror" inspired by Jehu's letter, the Samar-itans asking themselves how they could "stand before" him when two

97. This quality for the king-designate seems more appropriate than the Biblical ones ("best and fittest") given that his primary role will be to lead the resistance against Jehu.

98. This phrase ironically echoes the same construction used in 9,113 where Jehu refers to his men's having "declared him king (ἀποδεῖξαι ... βασιλέα) because of their friendly feelings towards him". Jehu, who has himself already been "appointed king", now mockingly invites the Samarian notables to "appoint" one of their own – if they dare.

99. The above list of the Samarians' resources differs from that of 10,2b in several respects: it consists of five items rather than four (the Biblical enumeration lacks "sol-diers") and reverses the source order fortified cities – weapons. In addition, in Josephus' presentation the list (= 10,2b) is made to function as a motivation ("for") of Jehu's preceding exhortation about appointing a king (= 10,3a).

100. With this formulation Josephus renders more specific the exhortation of 10,3b, i.e. "and fight for your master's (BL τοῦ κυρίου ὑμῶν) house".

101. This is the reading of E which Niese, Naber and Marcus follow. Dindorf and Bekker read δ' ἐγεγράφει with RO.

102. On Josephus' penchant for supplying motivations like the above for characters' actions in his Jehu-story, see FELDMAN, *Studies*, p. 360 (= ID., *Jehu*, 28-29). Compare 9,113 (cf. 9,15b) where Jehu devises a test of his men's loyalty, i.e. they will show them-selves loyal if none of them goes off to report to King Joram of the approach of his rival, Jehu.

kings had already failed to do so. Josephus' rendition (9,126b) accentuates the addressees' awareness of the futility of resistance given Jehu's past accomplishments: "*but, when they read the letters*[103] the magistrates and the tutors[104] were terrified (κατέδεισαν; BL 10,4 ἐφοβήθησαν σφόδρα) and, reflecting that they could do nothing against one who had overcome two *very great* (μεγίστων) kings …[105]". 2 Kgs 10,5 complements the preceding reference to the Samarians' inner state with mention of their actual reply to Jehu. That reply emanates (v. 5a) not only from the "elders and the guardians" (see 10,1b), but also from two important individual figures, i.e. "he who was over the palace, and he who was over the city". Josephus (9,126c) leaves the two latter figures unmentioned given their abrupt appearance in the narrative at this juncture (and absence in its continuation). In their reply (v. 5b) those enumerated in v. 5a affirm themselves to be Jehu's "servants". As such, they are, they continue, ready to do his bidding, rather than make themselves a king (as urged by him, see 10,3a); they only ask that Jehu do whatever appears "good" to him. Josephus gives the Samarians a comparable, though shorter, answer: "… they wrote back [10,5: they sent to Jehu, saying…], agreeing to have him for their master (δεσποτήν)[106] and to do whatever he commanded (κελεύῃ)".

The exchange between Jehu and the Samarian worthies comes to a conclusion in 10,6a with a "second letter" being dispatched by him to them. In this new letter, Jehu issues a conditional command to the recipients: if they are indeed ready "to hear his voice", they are to "take" the heads of Ahab's sons and repair to him (so MT; BL bring [i.e. the heads]) at Jezreel the next day. Josephus (9,127a) eliminates the conditionality from Jehu's reply; in accord with their own pledge to "do whatever he commanded" (see above), he "commands (κελεύων) them to obey him". He likewise spells out the meaning of Jehu's injunction

103. This inserted transitional notice makes explicit mention of a matter which the source's presentation simply takes for granted.

104. In 9,125 these two groups are mentioned in the reverse order; compare 10,4 where the identity of those who "fear" before Jehu is left unspecified.

105. Note how Josephus' formulation here accentuates Jehu's stature by speaking of him as one who "overcame" the kings, rather than of the kings' inability to "stand before" him (so 10,4). The inserted qualification of Jehu's opponents as "great" has the same effect.

106. This acknowledgement by the Samarians of Jehu as their "master" might be seen as Josephus' positive equivalent to the negative declaration of 10,5b, i.e. "we will not make any one king". Its use of the word "master" echoes, while also negating, Jehu's proposal in 9,125 that they "take vengeance for their *master*'s death". By acknowledging Jehu as their "master", the Samarians make clear that they have no intention of avenging their former "master", Joram.

about the "taking" of the youths' heads, i.e. they are to "cut these off". Finally, he aligns himself with the BL reading (see above) in having Jehu enjoin the "sending" of the heads to him, although unlike both MT and BL, he leaves unspecified the whither and when of the recipients' doing this. At the end of 10,6 there stands the notice "now the king's sons were with the great men (BL οἱ ἁδροί) of the city, who were bring-ing them up". Josephus has no equivalent as such to this notice which introduces a new, not previously cited, entity, i.e. the Samarian "great men" whose relationship to the previously mentioned "guardians" of Ahab's sons remains unclear[107].

According to the presentation of 10,7a the various groups to whom Jehu has just written act in undifferentiated concert in carrying out his murderous directive. Josephus, who has already accentuated the distinc-tion among Jehu's Samarian correspondents by having him write sepa-rate letters to the "tutors" and the "magistrates" (see 9,125), picks up on (9,127b) that distinction at this juncture at well. Specifically, he portrays the "tutors" beheading the youths at the order of the "magistrates[108]". He further underscores the horror of a deed perpetrated by those espe-cially charged with the victims' care via his interjected comment that the tutors "showed them no mercy at all[109]". The youths' killers next (v. 7b) put their heads "in baskets" and send these, as directed (see v. 6, BL), to Jehu at Jezreel. Josephus words equivalently: "... putting their heads in *woven* baskets, (they) sent them off to Jezarēla".

V. 8a records Jehu's being informed of the heads' arrival at Jezreel. Josephus (9,128a) specifies the circumstances in which this happened, i.e. "as he was dining with his friends (μετὰ τῶν φίλων)". This notation picks up on the reference (9,123; cf. 9,34b) to Jehu's entering the palace at Jezreel immediately following Jezebel's dramatic death "with his friends" (σὺν τοῖς φίλους)[110], there to "refresh himself after his ride with food and other things". In both instances, the historian's picture of Jehu participating in a convivial banquet underscores his callousness towards those who have just been brutally done away with at his orders. The king responds (v. 8b) to the report made him by directing that the

---

107. Recall, however, that he seems to anticipate its term "bring up" in 9,125 where he speaks of the royal youths' "being brought up in Samaria"; see above.

108. With this formulation Josephus clarifies the "power relationship" between the two groups in question, making clear the subordination of the "tutors" to the "magis-trates".

109. Compare, however, MULZER, *Bearbeitung*, 62 who denies such a function to the above notice, claiming that it is simply inspired by the term "slaughter" (MT וַיִּשְׁחֲטוּ, BL ἔσφαξαν) used of the Samarians' action against the youths in 10,7.

110. Neither of the above references to Jehu's "friends" has a Biblical basis.

heads be piled in two heaps at the city gateway until morning. In relating Jehu's order Josephus (9,128b) leaves aside its specification that the piles are to remain "until morning"; conversely, he has the king enjoin that the "heaps" (βουνούς, so BL) are to be erected "on either side" before the gate.

2 Kgs 10,9aα cites Jehu's "going out in the morning", taking his stand (L + in the gate of the city), and addressing "all the people (BL λαόν)". Josephus (9,129a) provides a motivation for Jehu's dawn "exit": *"and, after this was done, he went out at dawn to see them, and, when he had looked at them, he began to speak to the people* (λαόν, so BL) *there present...".* Thereafter, he leaves aside Jehu's opening statement (v. 9aβ) to his hearers, "you are innocent" (so RSV; MT צַדִּקִים, BL δίκαιοι) whose import/ basis is not immediately apparent. In its place he proceeds immediately to Jehu's further acknowledgement in 10,9b of his having "conspired" against and slain his "master (BL κύριον), wording this as follows: "... (saying that) he had indeed marched against[111] his master (δεσπότην; see 9,122.125.126) and killed (ἀποκτείνειε; BL ἀπέκτεινα) him". Jehu's address in v. 9b terminates with a question which remains as such without an answer, i.e. "but who struck down all these (the sons of Ahab)?" Josephus reformulates the question which the Bible "leaves hanging" as a negative statement corresponding to Jehu's previous affirmation: "... but these youths he himself had not slain (ἀνέλοι; cf. ἀνελομένοις, of the eunuchs who kill Jezebel, 9,123)". In 10,10 Jehu asks his hearers to learn a lesson from the fate of Ahab's sons to which they are now witnesses, i.e. God's not "letting fall to earth" anything of the "word" against the house of Ahab which he had pronounced through Elijah. Josephus' version (9,129b) reformulates Jehu's affirmation in line with the language of his own previous presentation: "He also asked them to recognize (γινώσκειν)[112] that all these things had happened to Achab's family (γενεᾶς), in accordance with God's prophecy (κατὰ τὴν τοῦ θεοῦ προφητείαν)[113], *and his house had perished* (ὁ οἶκος ...

111. This verbal form represents Josephus' substitution for that used by the Biblical Jehu, i.e. "I have conspired" (BL συνεστράφην) in 10,9b. On Josephus' avoidance of "conspiracy language" in reference to Jehu, see nn. 33,54.

112. This term echoes Josephus' formulation in *AJ* 8,417 where the Israelites are said to have "acknowledged (ἐπέγνωσαν) the truth of Elijah's prophecy [i.e. about dogs licking up Ahab's blood in the field of Naboth in Jezreel; see 1 Kgs 22,38]", this being the "first installment" in the realization of Elijah's prophecy about Ahab's house which finds its final fulfilllment with Jehu's extermination of that king's entire line.

113. Josephus uses the above expression only twice elsewhere: *AJ* 6,136 (God's promise that Saul will defeat the Amalekites is fulfilled) and 8,289 (Jeroboam's family meets the destruction announced by God). Compare the alternative expression of 9,120:

ἀπόλωλε)[114], just as Elijah had foretold (προεῖπεν; see 9,107.124)". 2 Kgs 10,11 rounds off the Biblical account of Jehu's dealings with the house of Ahab with mention of his killing members of the house resident in Jezreel. Josephus makes his parallel to this notice the transition to the following segment of his Jehu story; see below.

7. *Jehu's Advance to Samaria*

Having accomplished his purposes in Jezreel, Jehu now proceeds to advance towards the Israelite capital. The narrative concerning that advance, 2 Kgs 10,12-17, recounts two incidents which occurred during it, i.e. Jehu's slaughter of the relatives of Ahaziah (vv. 12b-14)[115] and his encounter with Jehonadab (vv. 15-17).

As noted above, Josephus (9,130a) "leads into" his narrative of the king's march on Samaria with a condensed version of 10,11: "Then, having also destroyed (προσδιαφθείρας; compare ἐπάταξεν, BL 10,11)[116] the nobles (ἱππεῖς)[117] related to Achab, who were found among the people of Jezarēla[118], he set out for Samaria".

2 Kgs 10,12b-13aα tells how Jehu, while *en route* to Samaria, came upon Ahaziah's "kinsmen" (MT אֲחֵי, BL ἀδελφούς)[119] at "Beth-eked of the Shepherds". Josephus (9,130b) leaves the site of the encounter unspecified[120]: "But on the way he fell in with some relatives (οἰκείοις)

κατὰ τὴν πρόρρησιν τὴν ἐκείνου (Elijah). Thrice within his Jehu narrative Josephus replaces a source mention of the divine "word" with the term "prophecy", see 9,120 (= 9,26).124 (= 9,36).129 (= 10,10).

114. This inserted reminder of the content of Elijah's "prophecy" echoes the words which Josephus has Elijah address to Ahab in *AJ* 8,361: πᾶν ... τὸ γένος ἀπολείσθαι; see also 9,119 where Jehu reminds Bidkar of Elijah's word "that both he (Ahab) and his line should perish (ἀπολεῖται ... τὸ γένος) in Naboth's field".

115. In 2 Chr 22,8-9 Jehu's encounter (at an unspecified locale) with a Judean group (// 2 Kgs 10,12b-14) seems to take place prior to his execution of Ahaziah (// 2 Kgs 9,27-28). Josephus follows the sequence of Kings on the point.

116. Josephus uses the compound verb προσδιαφθείρω twice elsewhere: *BJ* 4,128.405.

117. This word is absent in M and bracketed by Niese; cf. Lat cum equis ("with horses"). MULZER, *Bearbeitung*, 62, n. 86 contests Marcus's above translation of the word ἱππεῖς by "nobles", arguing that the meaning is rather "riders" (*Reiter*), as in 9,115.116. (Weill's rendering, *ad loc.*, i.e. "cavaliers" encompasses both these meanings.)

118. The above designation for Jehu's victims takes the place of the three particular categories cited in 10,11, i.e. "(all that remained of the house of Ahab in Jezreel), all his great men [see Josephus' "nobles"; but cf. previous note] and his familiar friends, and his priests".

119. 2 Chr 22,8 distinguishes two groups within the Judean party: "the princes of Judah and the sons of (> BL) Ahaziah's brothers". Like Kings, Josephus does not make this distinction.

120. Recall his omission of all but one of the place names of 9,27 in his account of Ahaziah's assassination in 9,121.

of Ochozias[121], the king of Jerusalem (literally the Jerusalemites; see 9,112. 117)...". In 10,13aβb Jehu inquires about the identity of those he meets, the latter replying that they are kinsmen ("brothers") of Ahaziah. They then proceed to inform Jehu concerning the purpose of their journey – a point about which he not yet asked – i.e. to visit (literally "for the peace of") the sons of the king (Joram) and those of the queen mother (Jezebel). Josephus drops the "identification question", making Jehu ask immediately about the purpose of their coming. In the Biblical Judeans' response to Jehu it seems odd that they should speak of coming to visit the sons of the king and those of Jezebel, while making no mention, as such, of a visit to the kings Joram and his earlier caller Ahaziah (see 9,29) who, one might suppose, would be owed such a courtesy call in first place. Accordingly, Josephus reformulates their response, having them state (9,131a) that they had come "to greet Joram and their own king, Ochozias". Another question prompted by, though left unanswered in, the Biblical presentation is why the Judeans make no attempt in their answer to conceal the dangerous truth about their identity from the blood-drunk Jehu. Josephus has a response to this question as well: they spoke so candidly because "they were not aware that both kings had been done to death by him".

The incident of 10,12-14 concludes in v. 14 with Jehu ordering the seizure of the Judeans, their slaughter by his retainers, and the notation that those killed numbered 42. Josephus' rendition (9,131b) leaves aside the source's mention of the massacre site ("the pit of Beth-eked"), as well as its repetitious closing formula, "he spared none of them[122]".

2 Kgs 10,15 makes the transition to the following episode of Jehu's meeting with Jehonadab with the words "and when he departed from there (i.e. Beth-eked, 10,12; cf. the pit of Beth-eked, 10,14)...". Josephus, who has not reproduced the place names of 10,12-14, substitutes (9,132a) another transitional formula: "after these men (had been disposed of)...". V. 15 continues with mention of Jehu's "finding" (so MT L, B taking) "Jehonadab (BL Ἰωναδάβ) son of Rechab" who was "(coming to) meet him". As he not infrequently does with (minor) Bib-

---

121. Josephus' use of this designation in preference to the "brothers" of 10,13a might reflect the fact that, according to 2 Chr 22,1 (= 9,102) all the sons of Joram of Judah other than Ahaziah himself had been killed by the enemy invaders; cf. the name used for the group, i.e. "the sons of Ahaziah's brothers", i.e. his nephews in MT 2 Chr 22,8.

122. As MULZER, Bearbeitung, 63-64 points out, Josephus further smooths over a seeming discrepancy in the Biblical presentation (10,14) where Jehu first orders that the Judeans be "taken alive", but once this is done, "they" (i. e. Jehu's men) proceed – without express orders from Jehu – to "slay" them. The Josephan Jehu simply commands the seizing and slaying of the 42.

lical characters, Josephus omits the name of the father of "Jonadabos" (Ἰωνάδαβος). Conversely, he introduces a double qualification of this figure. First, he characterizes him as a "good and just (ἀγαθὸς καὶ δίκαιος) man". Secondly, Josephus further informs us that Jonadabos was Jehu's long-time "friend" (φίλος)[123]. These two indications concerning the person of Jehonadab inserted here by Josephus serve a variety of purposes with regard to the continuation of the narrative. They, e.g., help explain why Jehu is so ready to "pick up" Jehonadab and why the latter is unhesitatingly willing to accompany him, as also to endue Jehu's coming bloody deed with the "goodness and righteousness" of Jehonadab who will witness it without demur[124].

In 10,15aβ it is Jehu who takes the initiative by "greeting" (literally "blessing") Jehonadab and then asking whether his "heart" is as attached to his as is his own heart towards Jehonadab (see n. 123), a query which the latter answers affirmatively, but minimalistically with "it is". In Josephus' presentation (9,132b) on the contrary, it is Jonadabos who gets the first (as well as) much expanded a word: "... after greeting him [Jehu], *he began to commend him for having done everything in accordance with the will of God* (κατὰ βούλησιν τοῦ θεοῦ)[125] *in extirpating the house of Achab* (τὴν οἰκίαν ἐξαφανίσας[126] τὴν Ἀχάβου)". By attributing such a statement to "a good and just man" (see above), Josephus further underscores the legitimacy of Jehu's murderous measures.

V. 15b ends up with Jehu, responding to Jehonadab's affirmative reply to his own preceding question (see above), directing the other to "give him his hand"; Jehonadab does so, whereupon Jehu takes him up into his chariot. Josephus (9,133a) reduces this whole sequence to the notice "then Jehu asked him to come up into his chariot...". To that request by the king he then attaches a further one, this representing a much expanded (and concretized) version of Jehu's word to Jehonadab as reported in 10,16a ("Come with me and see my zeal [BL τῷ ζηλῶσαι

---

123. Recall his two previous – likewise inserted references – to the "friends" accompanying Jehu in 9,123.128. MARCUS, *Josephus*, VI, p. 71, n. d suggests that Josephus' identification of Jehonadab as Jehu's "friend" might have been inspired by the (BL) wording of Jehu's question to Jehonadab in 10,15b, i.e. "is your heart true to my heart as mine is to yours?" (so RSV, translating BL).

124. On the point, see FELDMAN, *Studies*, p. 357 (= ID., *Jehu*, 24).

125. The above expression is a Josephan favorite, occurring with slight variations some 30 times in his corpus; see BEGG, *Early Divided Monarchy*, p. 20, n. 88 and the literature cited there.

126. This is the reading adopted by Dindorf, Niese, and Marcus. The *ed. pr.* (as well as Bekker and Naber) read ἐξαφανίσαντα, "forte recte" according to Marcus.

με] for the Lord")[127]. In its Josephan version the request reads: "... (he asked him) to come along with him to Samaria, saying that he would show him how he would spare (φείσεται; cf. φεισάμενοι, 9,127) no wicked man (πονηροῦ)[128], but would punish the false prophets (ψευδο-προφήτας)[129] and the false priests (ψευδιερεῖς)[130] and those who had seduced the people (τοὺς ἐξαπατήσαντας τὸ πλῆθος)[131] into abandoning the worship (τὴν ... θρησκείαν ἐγκαταλιπεῖν)[132] of the most high God (τοῦ μέγιστου θεοῦ)[133] and bowing down to strange gods (τοὺς ... ξενικοὺς προσκυνεῖν; see 9,96)...[134]". Josephus rounds off (9,133b) the foregoing statement of Jehu's intentions by having the king further inform Jehonadab that it is "... the most desirable and pleasant (κάλ-λιστον ... καὶ ἥδιστον)[135] of sights for a good and upright (χρηστῷ καὶ δικαίῳ)[136] man to see (ἰδεῖν)[137] the wicked (πονηρούς, cf. πονηροῦ, 9,133a) punished (κολαζομένους)[138]".

Josephus attributes the above extended discourse to Jehu with a view to reassuring Jehonadab (and even more the reader) that he, as a "good and just man" (9,132) has nothing to fear at the king's bloody hands.

127. Josephus' rewording of this statement eliminates its reference to Jehu's Jahwistic "zeal". On the historian's avoidance of Biblical "zeal" language in light of its appropriation/ arrogation by the contemporary "Zealots", see: BEGG, *Early Divided Monarchy*, p. 183, n. 1209, p. 195, n. 1209; FELDMAN, *Studies*, pp. 358-359 (= ID., *Jehu*, 28); KRIEGER, *Jehu-Erzählung*, 75-77.

128. This term stands in negative contrast to the designation used of Jehonadab himself in 9,132, i.e. ἀγαθός καὶ δίκαιος.

129. On Josephus' usage of this term (16 times in his corpus), see BEGG, *Early Divided Monarchy*, p. 50, n. 270 and the literature cited there as well KRIEGER, *Jehu-Erzählung*, 70-72.

130. Josephus uses this term only once elsewhere, i.e. in *AJ* 8,232 (in reference to the clergy of Jeroboam's Bethel sanctuary).

131. Compare the similar phrases used in *AJ* 8,229 (ἐξηπάτησε τὸν λαόν, of Jeroboam) and *BJ* 4,228 (ἐξαπατήσας τὸν δῆμον, of Ananas).

132. This phrase recurs in *AJ* 12,269 where Mattathias states that he and his sons will never allow themselves to be compelled to "abandon their ancestral religion". See KRIEGER, *Jehu-Erzählung*, 72.

133. Josephus uses this designation a total of 14 times: *AJ* 6,86; 7,353; 8,343; 9,133.211.288.289; 10,68; 11,3.90; 12.257; 13,64.65; 15,385.

134. Both parts of the above charge ("abandoning the worship of God/ bowing down to strange gods") are paralleled in *AJ* 8,271 where God, speaking through the prophet Ahijah, accuses the Israelites as follows: προσκυνεῖ θεοὺς τὴν ἐμὴν θυσίαν ἐγκαταλιπόν.

135. This collocation is hapax in Josephus.

136. This collocation is used by Josephus in reference to Samuel (*AJ* 6,294, reverse order); Jehoiada (9,166); Hezekiah (9,260); Jehoiachin (10,100); Nehemiah (11,183); and Ptolemy Philometer (13,114). Recall his characterization of Jehonadab himself as ἀγαθὸς καὶ δίκαιος in 9,132.

137. This word is lacking in ROM and omitted by Niese and Naber. Dindorf, Bekker, and Marcus read it with SP.

138. On Jehu's statement above, see KRIEGER, *Jehu-Erzählung*, 72 who calls attention to its reminiscence of the overall "moral" of *AJ* as articulated in 1,14.

Having done so, he introduces (9,134a) a transitional reference to the inner effect of Jehu's words upon Jehonadab ("being persuaded by these arguments"), before noting (= 10,16b-17a) that he "got up into Jehu's chariot and came to Samaria".

In 10,17b Jehu marks his entry into Samaria by "wiping out all that remained to Ahab", thereby fulfilling "the word of the Lord which he spoke to Elijah". Josephus does speak of the king's "seeking out and killing all of Achab's relatives", but leaves aside the attached Biblical "fulfillment notice", perhaps because in his version of Elijah's word against Ahab (see 8,361) Jezreel, not Samaria (compare 10,17), is designated as the site where all members of Ahab's house are to meet destruction.

8. The Baalists Exterminated

The account of Jehu's putsch culminates (10,18-27 = 9,134b-138) with the new king's ridding Samaria of Baal worship and its adherents. He does so by means of a stratagem in which the Baalists are deceived into thinking that Jehu is one of them; see v. 19b ("but Jehu did it with cunning [BL ἐν πτερνισμῷ] in order to destroy the worshipers of Baal"). Josephus (9,134b) "anticipates" this "delayed" parenthetical remark, beginning his account with a statement that makes clear, right from the start, that Jehu was indeed no Baalist: "then, resolving that none of the false prophets or priests (ἱερέων[139]; compare false prophets and false priests [ψευδιερεῖς], 9,133) of Achab's gods [cf. strange gods, 9,133][140] should escape punishment (τιμωρίαν; cf. τιμωρήσεται, 9,133), he caught them all by deceit and cunning (ἀπάτῃ καὶ δόλῳ)[141]".

Having thus clarified Jehu's motivation at the outset, Josephus now (9,135a) proceeds to give his parallel to 10,18a, the king's gathering of the people of Samaria. In v. 18b Jehu informs the assembly that, whereas

139. Lat reads "sacerdotibus idolorum" here; on its reading see MULZER, *Bearbeitung*, 64, n. 102.

140. This generalized designation replaces the mention of the individual deity "Baal" of 10,19b. In his version of the "Carmel contest" (1 Kings 18) in *AJ* 8,335-343, Josephus similarly repeatedly substitutes generalizing expressions (e.g., "foreign gods") for the Bible's mention of "Baal", thereby giving the contest a more comprehensive character; see BEGG, *Early Divided Monarchy*, p. 187 and n. 1235. See also chap. II on Josephus' treatment of the references to "Baal-zebub" of 2 Kings 1.

141. This collocation recurs in *AJ* 7,32; 12,4 (reverse order); 18,326 (reverse order); *c. Ap.* 2,200. With Josephus' accentuation of Jehu's "deceitfulness" here, compare TJ 10,19b which has Jehu acting "with wisdom" (בחכמה) and cf. the comment of HARRINGTON and SALDARINI, *Targum Jonathan*, p. 284, n. 26: "Tg uses a clearly positive word to describe Jehu".

Ahab had served Baal "a little", he intends to serve that deity "much". Once again avoiding the proper name "Baal", Josephus has Jehu affirm that he proposes to "worship twice as many gods (διπλασίονας ... θεῶν προσκυνεῖν)[142] as Achab had introduced...".

In 2 Kgs 10,19abα Jehu enumerates three groups of Baalists (the prophets of Baal, his worshipers [BL δούλους], and priests) whose presence at his "great sacrifice" for Baal he requires under penalty of death. The Josephan Jehu cites (9,135b) three groups as well, likewise embellishing on the intended sacrifice: "... and he asked the priests of these gods[143] and their prophets (προφήτας)[144] and servants (δούλους, so BL) to be present, for, he said, he intended to offer *costly and* great sacrifices (θυσίας ... πολυτελεῖς καὶ μεγάλας; compare θυσία μεγάλη, BL 10,19)[145] to Achab's gods [see 9,134], and he would punish with death any *of the priests* who might be absent[146]". To his version of Jehu's address (9,135b = 10,19a), Josephus attaches (9,135c) an appendix[147] concerning its mention of "Achab's gods": "now the god (ὁ ... θεός note the shift to the singular here) of Achab was called Baal (Βαάλ)[148]".

Jehu's directives continue in 10,20a with the king enjoining that a solemn assembly be "sanctified" for Baal; once this is done (v. 20b), the entire body of Baalists assembly at Jehu's summons (10,21a) and enter their god's "house" filling this completely (10,21b). Josephus (9,136a) compresses: "and so, having set a day on which he intended to offer the sacrifices[149],

142. Compare τοὺς ξενικοὺς [i.e. gods] προσκυνεῖν, 9,133.

143. In 10,19a "all his [Baal's] priests" are cited only in third place. Josephus has Jehu mention them first since they would be the group whose attendance at a sacrifice would be needed above all; see n. 146. Once again here (see n. 140), Josephus substitutes a generalizing reference ("these gods") for a source mention of Baal. Compare TJ's rendering, i.e. "all his [Baal's] idol priests" (וכל כמרוהי זמינו).

144. In Josephus' previous editorial comments the reference has been to "*false* prophets" (9,133.134). In having Jehu address himself to the Baalists here in 9,135, Josephus naturally avoids attributing that derogatory designation to him.

145. Josephus' one remaining use of the phrase "costly sacrifice" is in *AJ* 9,165.

146. Compare 10,19aβ: "whoever is missing shall not live". Josephus' singling out of the "priests" for special mention is in line with his citing this group in first place earlier in Jehu's speech; see n. 143.

147. This appendix takes the place of the notice of 10,19b concerning the "cunning" with which Jehu acted against the Baalists, anticipated by him in 9,134b; see above.

148. Here for the first time in his Jehu narrative Josephus makes use of the proper name of the deity whose worship Jehu will exterminate from Israel. In his initial reference to that god in *AJ* 8,318 Josephus called him "Belias".

149. The above formulation involves a conflation of 10,20 where an unspecified "they" proclaim the assembly at Jehu's direction. It likewise elucidates, in light of what precedes, the intended character of the "solemn assembly" spoken of in the source, while avoiding 10,20a's (peculiar) use of the term "sanctify" in reference to this (note that TJ substitutes the word "summon" for this in its rendition of Jehu's order).

Jehu sent (διέπεμπεν)¹⁵⁰ men throughout the Israelites' country to bring to him the *priests* of Baal¹⁵¹". In 10,22a Jehu proceeds to charge the "wardrobe keeper" (MT לַאֲשֶׁר עַל־הַמֶּלְתָּחָה; BL transliterates: τῷ ἐπὶ τοῦ οἴκου μεσθαάλ) to bring out the "vestments" for the assembled Baalists, with the latter being said to comply in v. 22b. Josephus' rendition (9,136b) specifies the identity of the recipient of the royal command in line with his previous highlighting of the role of the Baalistic "priests": "... he also ordered the (chief) priest (τῷ ἱερεῖ)¹⁵² to give vestments (ἐνδύματα, so L; compare B ἔνδυμα) to all". The compliance notice of 10,22b becomes the transition to the following moment of the story; see below.

2 Kgs 10,23 has Jehu, along with Jehonadab, entering the Baal temple where he commands a search be made to determine that only Baalists and no Yahwists are present. The Josephan Jehu (9,136c) gives a plausible motivation to his command: "And when they had taken them [the vestments, 10,22b], he went into the temple (οἶκον; 10,23 the house [BL οἶκον] *of Baal*) with *his friend* (τοῦ φίλου; see 9,132) Jonadab, and ordered a search to be made (ἐρευνῆσαι; BL ἐρευνήσατε) that there might be no foreigner nor stranger (ἀλλόφυλος ... καὶ ξένος)¹⁵³ among them, *saying that he did not wish any outsider* (ἀλλότριον) *at their rites* (τοῖς ἱεροῖς)".

2 Kgs 10,24 (MT and B) juxtaposes two initiatives taken by Jehu at this point: his (so B; in MT L and *VL* the subject is – ambiguously – plural, with the reference being either to the Baalists addressed by Jehu in v. 23b or to the king and Jehonadab whose entry into the temple is cited in v. 23a) going in to offer the "sacrifices and burnt offerings" (v. 24a) and his (prior) stationing of eighty (so MT B; L 3,000) outside the temple with orders – reinforced by the threat of death – to let no one escape. L and *VL* 10,24, on the contrary, present the two items in reverse order. Josephus (9,137) follows the MT B sequence, while also elaborating on the measure attributed to Jehu in 10,24b: "And, when they [the assembled Baalists] said that there was no stranger (ξένον; see 9,136c)

150. This is the reading adopted by Niese and Marcus; Dindorf, Bekker, and Naber read διέπεμψεν with MSP.

151. Once again (see nn. 143,146), Josephus focusses attention on the Baalistic "priests"; in 10,21aα (MT L) the reference is more generally to "all the worshipers of Baal" (compare, however, B 10,21 which, in a plus reminiscent of 10,19, has Jehu summoning, not only Baal's worshipers, but also "all his priests [so Josephus] and all his prophets"). He leaves aside as something self-evident the notice of 10,21aβ that all those summoned by Jehu did in fact assemble, as well as the mention of their entry into "the house of Baal" (10,21b) which anticipates the notice on the king's own entering the Baal temple in 10,23a.

152. This is the reading of ROLat which Niese and Marcus follow. Dindorf, Bekker, and Naber read τοῖς ἱερεῦσι with MSPE (and perhaps Zon).

153. This collocation occurs only here in Josephus. It replaces the source reference to "the servants of the Lord".

present[154] and began the sacrifices (θυσιῶν, see θυσίας, 9,135.136; compare τὰ θύματα καὶ τὰ ὁλοκαυτώματα, BL 10,24)[155], he placed outside (ἔξωθεν; compare ἔξω, B; ἐν τῷ κρυπτῷ, L)[156] the temple some of his men (ἄνδρας, so BL) eighty [= MT B] in number, whom he knew to be most faithful (πιστοτάτους) to him[157], and commanded them to kill the false prophets (ψευδοπροφήτας; see 9,133.134)[158] and now avenge (τιμωρεῖν, see 9,133.134) their fathers' customs (πατρίοις ἔθεσι)[159] which had for so long a time been set at naught (ὠλιγωρ-ημένοις)[160], and he threatened that their own lives (ψυχάς; BL ἡ ψυχή) should be forfeit (ἀφαιρεθήσεσθαι)[161] for any who escaped".

2 Kgs 10,25a records a new directive by Jehu once he (so MT B, L "they," i.e. the Baalists; VL lacks an equivalent) had "completed the sacrifice"; he now enjoins the "runners and the officers" to enter and slay the Baalists, allowing no one to escape[162]. This item, coming as it does immediately after Jehu's instructions to the 80 in v. 24b, seems rep-

154. MULZER, Bearbeitung, 65 points out that this transitional phrase has a certain parallel in the L plus in 10,23e, i.e. καὶ ἐξαποστείλατε [i.e. the Baalists] αὐτοὺς καὶ εἶπον οὐκ ἐστίν. See also the plus of VL 10,24 "et factum est sicut locutus est ieu rex". On the VL version of Jehu's extermination of the Baalists in relation to the other Biblical witnesses, see: J. TREBOLLE, Textos "Kaige" en la Vetus Latina de Reyes (2 Re 10,25-28), in RB 89 (1982) 198-209; ID., From the "Old Latin" through the "Old Greek" to the "Old Hebrew" (2 Kings 10.23-25), in Textus 11 (1984) 17-36.

155. In making the Baalists – rather than Jehu himself – the ones to sacrifice – Jose-phus aligns himself with the reading of MT and L 10,24 against B, even while eliminat-ing the ambiguity concerning the identity of the sacrificers present in MT and L; see above. He thereby leaves no doubt about Jehu's non-participation in the Baalistic sacri-fices.

156. This word is absent in RO and omitted by Niese. It is read by Dindorf, Bekker, Naber, and Marcus following MSPE, cf. Zon (ἔξω) and Lat ("a foris").

157. The above indication concerning the 80 lacks a Biblical parallel. It helps explains why these men in particular are chosen for their assignment and why Jehu can feel confi-dent in assigning the task to so small a group, i.e. his knowing of their outstanding loy-alty to him. Compare Josephus' – also inserted – characterization of "Hazael" as "the most trusted" (πιστότατον) of Ben-hadad's servants in 9,88.

158. The above formulation makes more definite the wording of Jehu's directive to the 80 as cited in 10,24b (MT B): "the man who allows any of those whom I give into your hands to escape...". It likely reflects the king's subsequent order reported in 10,25, i.e. "go in and slay them; let not a man escape".

159. The above expression "avenge ancestral customs" occurs only here in Josephus.

160. The above component of Jehu's command to the 80 lacks a Biblical equivalent. It serves to make clear that the king's massacre of the Baalists is motivated by something beyond mere bloodlust. On the sequence, see: FELDMAN, Studies, p. 358 (= ID., Jehu, 24-25) and KRIEGER, Jehu-Erzählung, 72-73.

161. This is the reading adopted by Dindorf, Bekker, Niese and Marcus. MSP (and perhaps Lat) read ἀφαιρήσεσθαι. Naber reads ἐφαιρήσεσθαι.

162. In L 10,25 there follows at this juncture a long plus which states that, in accor-dance with Jehu's directive in 10,23b, there were, at this moment, no adherents of the Lord in the Baal temple, but only those of Baal.

etitious of the latter, just as it leaves unclear how the groups spoken of in v. 25a relate to those 80. Josephus (9,138a) circumvents these difficulties by passing over the content of 10,25a, proceeding immediately to the initiatives undertaken by the previously mentioned 80 (see 9,137). In so doing, he markedly compresses the series of measures against the Baal cult attributed to the "runners and officers" (10,25a) in 10,25b-27, i.e. killing of the assembled Baalists, casting out of their corpses (v. 25b) removal, burning and demolishing of the Baal pillar(s) (vv. 26-27a), and demolishing of the Baal temple and making it a latrine "to this day". Of all these measures, Josephus has an equivalent only to the first and penultimate ones[163]: "So they slew (κατέσφαξαν; see 9,102) all the men and burnt down (ἐμπρήσαντες)[164] the temple of Baal, *thus purging* (ἐκάθηραν) *Samaria of strange rites* (ξενικῶν ἐθισμῶν[165])[166]".

In place of the additional "iconoclastic" measures cited in 10,25b-27, Josephus rounds off his account of Jehu's extermination of Baalism (9,134b-138) with a notice that recalls the introduction of that reprobate cult into Israel. The notice (9,138b) – itself harking back to the historian's initial mention of Baal in *AJ* 8,317-318 – reads: "This Baal was the god of the Tyrians, to whom Achab, wishing to please his father-in-law Ithōbalos, king of the Tyrians and Sidonians, had built a temple (ναόν) in Samaria and had appointed prophets (προφήτας; see 9,135) and honoured him with every manner of cult (θρησκείας; see 9,133)[167]".

163. Josephus' compression of the "iconoclastic sequence" 10,25b-27 accords with his general tendency to minimalize such Biblical items which Gentile readers would likely find offensive. On his omission of the "latine notice" of v. 27bβ in particular, see FELDMAN, *Studies*, pp. 355-356 (= ID., *Jehu*, 21-22).

164. In MT L 10,27bα the "house of Baal" is said to be "demolished" (L καθεῖλον); B lacks an equivalent. Josephus' specification on the point might have been inspired by the reference to the "burning" (BL ἐνέπρησαν) of the Baal "pillar(s)" in 10,26b. See further MULZER, *Bearbeitung*, 66 and n. 125.

165. This is the reading adopted by Dindorf, Bekker, Niese, Naber, and Marcus. ROM have θεῶν.

166. This generalizing remark on the import of Jehu's anti-Baal measures echoes the – likewise inserted – reference to the "avenging of the ancestral customs (πατρίοις ἔθεσι)" which Josephus attributes to the king in 9,137.

167. With the above sequence compare Josephus' introductory remarks concerning Ahab in *AJ* 8,317b-318: "And he took to wife the daughter of Ithōbalos, the king of Tyre and Sidon, whose name was Jezabelē, and from her he learned to worship her native gods. ... she built a temple (ναόν) to the Tyrian god whom they call Belias... she also appointed priests and false prophets (ψευδοπροφήτας) to this god". Note that in his recapitulation of 8,317b-318 here in 9,138b Josephus omits mention of the role of Jezebel, attributing the reprobate measures there ascribed to the queen (building a Baal temple, appointing [false-] prophets) to Ahab himself and his desire to please his father-in-law. The two presentations need not, of course, be considered contradictory, in that Ahab's Baalistic initiatives (9,138) would have been done at Jezebel's instigation, such that she could be credited with these herself (so 8,318)

9. *Closing Notices for Jehu*

The Biblical treatment of Jehu concludes in 10,28-36 with a series of summary remarks. As noted above, Josephus begins his reproduction of this sequence in 9,139 (= 10,28-30), but then reserves the remainder of it for a later point, i.e. 9,159-160 (= 10,31-36). Accordingly, we limit ourselves to a consideration of the former passage at this juncture.

The opening element of the complex 10,28-36, v. 28, epitomizes Jehu's religious achievement: "Thus Jehu wiped out Baal [+ and his house, L] from Israel". Immediately thereafter, however, v. 29 invokes Jehu's failure to "turn aside from" Jeroboam's calf-cult. The historian's version (9,139a) of this source juxtaposition appears to play down Jehu's personal involvement in the calf-worship[168]: "When this god [Baal] had been removed (ἀφανισθέντος [see 9,109]; BL ἠφάνισεν), Jehu permitted (ἐπέτρεψε) the Israelites to bow down before the golden heifers (τὰς χρυσᾶς δαμάλεις [compare B 10,29 αἱ δαμάλεις αἱ χρυσαῖ] προσκυνεῖν)[169]".

2 Kgs 10,30 rather abruptly attaches to the preceding mention of Jehu's participation in the calf-cult a divine promise that the king's line would perdure for four generations in reward for his carrying out the Lord's will by exterminating Ahab's house. Josephus (9,139b) turns the Deity's motivation for his promise to Jehu (v. 30a) into a transitional, editorial remark. He likewise represents the divine promise as having been mediated by a prophet: "But, since he had carried out these reforms, and had provided for the punishment of these impious men (τῆς κολάσεως τῶν ἀσεβῶν)[170], God foretold (προεῖπεν) *through the prophet*[171] that his

168. On the point, see FELDMAN, *Studies*, p. 358 (= ID., *Jehu*, 25).

169. The above wording recalls that used by Josephus with regard to Jeroboam and his calf cult; see *AJ* 8,225 where Jeroboam reflects on the negative consequences for himself should he "permit the people to go to Jerusalem to worship (προσκυνεῖν ... ἐπέτρεψε) God" and 8,248 where the historian mentions those Israelites who would not submit to being forced to "worship the heifers (προσκυνεῖν ... τὰς δαμάλεις) which Jeroboam had made".

170. The above phrase echoes 9,133 where Jehu addresses Jehonadab about the pleasantness of seeing "the wicked punished (κολαζομένους πονηρούς)". With the whole above formulation compare the divine word as cited in 10,30a: "because you [Jehu] have done well in carrying out what is right in my eyes and have done to the house of Ahab according to all that was in my heart...".

171. Josephus' introduction of a prophetic intermediary here has a number of counterparts elsewhere in his rewriting of Biblical history; see e.g., *AJ* 8,197 (= 1 Kgs 11,11) where the divine rebuke of the apostate Solomon is conveyed by "a prophet". See further C.T. BEGG, *Solomon's Apostasy (1 KGS. 11,1-13) according to Josephus*, in *JSJ* 28 (1997) 294-313, pp. 306-307, nn. 82-83 and the literature cited there. More generally, it reflects his insertion of explicit prophetic terminology in contexts where the Bible lacks such. *SOR* 19.1 too represents the promise of 10,30 as being delivered by a prophet to

sons should rule (βασιλεύσειν; see 9,107.124.129)[172] over the Israelites for four generations[173]. Before next proceeding to switch (9,140) to events in the Southern Kingdom, Josephus (9,139c) provides a temporary conclusion to his account of Jehu: "Such, then, was the state of affairs under Jehu".

Conclusions: Josephus' Rewriting of 2 Kgs 8,25-10,30(36)

It is, first of all, clear that, faced with the difference between the expansive account of Jehu's putsch in 2 Kgs 8,25-10,30(36) and the allusive references to this event in the Judean-centered narrative of 2 Chr 22,2-9, Josephus opts to base his presentation in 9,105-139 (+ 159-160) on the former, just as he generally follows whichever Biblical source offers him the more detailed treatment of a given happening. The historian's dependence on Kings rather than Chronicles is especially obvious in those instances where the two narratives somewhat parallel each other; see, e.g., their respective depictions of the deaths of Ahaziah and of the 42 Judean princes where Josephus (9,121.130-131) aligns himself with 2 Kgs 9,27-28; 10,12-14 against 2 Chr 22,8-9[174].

Our findings on the further question of the text-form(s) of Kings' Jehu narrative employed by Josephus were more ambiguous. On occasion, Josephus agrees with MT where this diverges from BL, e.g., his referring (9,125) to the "letters" Jehu sends the Samarian leaders (so MT 10,1 vs. BL "a letter"). On the other hand, the words, e.g., he has Jehu address to Jezebel (9,122) clearly reflect those cited in BL 9,32 as opposed to MT, just as his reference to the wounded Joram's "falling to his knees" (9,119) coheres with the reading of BL 9,24 *contra* MT's "in his chariot". We noted further that the Josephan reference (9,117) to Jehu's driving "rather slowly and in good order" parallels TJ 9,20 ("with gentleness"), these readings representing the opposite of the "frenzy" with which Jehu is said to drive in both MT and BL. It thus

whom, however, it, in contrast to Josephus, gives a name, i.e. Jonah (see GIRÓN BLANC, *Seder 'Olam Rabbah*, p. 91).

172. This is the emendation of J. Hudson, based on Lat, and followed by Dindorf, Bekker, Niese, Naber, and Marcus for the βασιλεύειν of the codices and E.

173. Compare the divine promise of 10,30b: "your sons of the fourth generation shall sit on the throne of Israel".

174. One possible instance of Josephus' (secondary) use of 2 Chronicles comes in 9,121 where his mention of Ahaziah's "undergoing treatment" following his wounding by Jehu has a parallel in BL 22,9, but not in either MT 22,9 or in the account of the Judean's death found in 10,12-14. See n. 73. Cf. also n. 7.

appears that Josephus knew the Jehu narrative of Kings in a variety of textual forms[175].

The foregoing comparison has likewise made clear that Josephus does reproduce the material of the Jehu story *in extenso*. His doing so is readily understandable given the fact that this story features dramatic political and military events which could be counted on to elicit the interest of Gentile readers. On the other hand, throughout his rendition, Josephus does takes various sorts of liberties with source data. Thus, he, now and again, "re-arranges" the Biblical sequence, reserving, e.g., the opening notices of 8,25-27 concerning Ahaziah for a considerably later point in his own presentation (see 9,121), even as he re-positions the reference in 9,20 to Jehu's driving (see on 9,117) and gives his own order to the material of 9,14b-16 in 9,112. Moreover, Josephus either simply eliminates or significantly reduces various source items (see, e.g., the mention of Ahaziah's participation in Joram's Syrian campaign [8,28], the stray reference to the Judean's accession [9,29], and the catalogue of iconoclastic measures making up 10,25b-27; compare 9,138a). Conversely, he also amplifies the Biblical record. Such additions involve inserted characterizations (see 9,132, Jehonadab), personages' motivations and inner states (see, e.g., the interpolated allusions to the "fear" experienced by both Joram [9,118] and Ahaziah [9,120] upon encountering Jehu, or the explanatory clarification that the Judean party who volunteered their identity to Jehu knew nothing of his previous assassinations, so 9,131; compare 10,13b), expansion of characters' words (see his amplification of the "speeches" of both Jehonadab and Jehu in 9,132-133 as compared with those of 10,15-16), preparations of subsequent developments (e.g., mention of Joram's having captured Aramathē/Ramoth-gilead and leaving Jehu in charge there [9,105], this serving to set up the latter's status and location in the later course of the story), *Rückverweise* (see the two-fold occurrence in 9,112) and closing formulae (see, e.g., 9,139c). Finally, Josephus also introduces modifications/adaptations of Kings' Jehu story, e.g., the two (distinct?) groups of the 80 men (10,24b) and the "guard and the officers" (10,25) are conflated into a single one (9,137b-138a), while God speaks to Jehu, not directly (so 10,30), but through a prophet (9,139b).

The Josephan account of Jehu's putsch stands out from its *Vorlage* above all in its positive retouchings of the image of the story's protagonist, this with a view to furthering the historian's aims regarding both his

---

175. See also nn. 52 and 55 regarding points of contact between Josephus' Jehu story and the distinctive readings of *VL* 9,23. Cf. the conclusions of MULZER, *Bearbeitung*, 68 on Josephus' *Textvorlage* in 9,105-139.159-160.

Gentile and Jewish audiences. Josephus' Jehu is no "zealot" (see 9,133; compare 10,16), nor is his uprising qualified as a "conspiracy" (compare 9,14.23), both features which might put his two categories of readers in mind of the Jewish rebels of the recent past. The king's self-control is manifest even in his mode of driving (see 9,117; compare 9,20 MT BL), even as the accusation of "lying" made against him by his fellow officers is eliminated (9,111; compare 9,12a). For the benefit of Jewish readers Josephus makes absolutely clear – as the Bible itself does not – that Jehu himself took no part in the Baal rites (9,137; compare 10,23-25). With the sensibilities of Roman readers in mind he strives to give Jehu's bloody elimination of the Baal cult a greater legitimacy by having him accompanied to Samaria by a "good and just man", i.e. Jehonadab (9,132) and by making his action there a matter of "avenging ancestral customs" (9,137) and "purging strange rites" (9,138). In the same line the historian takes care (9,138a) to compress and tone down the graphic iconoclastic details of 10,25b-27. In sum Josephus goes beyond the Bible in making Jehu the bearer of messages and values appropriate to both his readerships[176].

---

176. See further the concluding remarks of FELDMAN, *Studies*, p. 302 (= ID., *Jehu*, 31-32).

VII

ATHALIAH OF JUDAH[1]
(9,140-156)

As indicated in chap. VI, Josephus breaks off his reproduction of the Biblical Jehu story at 9,139 (// 2 Kgs 10,28-30) in order to relate, in 9,140-156, contemporaneous events in the Southern kingdom. Those events feature the Northern-born queen mother Athaliah, her usurpation of the Davidic throne, and eventual overthrow by the priest Jehoiada. In Josephus' Biblical sources the happenings in question are related twice with various differences of detail, i.e. in 2 Kgs 11,1-20 and 2 Chr 22,10–23,21. I divide up the three Athaliah narratives to be compared in this chapter into four parallel segments: 1. Preliminaries (*AJ* 9,140-142 = 2 Kgs 11,1-3 // 2 Chr 22,10-12); 2) Jehoiada's Measures (9,143-149 = 11,4-12 // 23,1-11); 3) Athaliah's Death (9,150-152 = 11,13-16 // 23,12-15); and 4. Sequels (9,153-156 = 11,17-20 // 23,16-21).

1. *Preliminaries*

In all three of its versions (2 Kgs 11,1-3 // 2 Chr 22,10-12 = *AJ* 9,140-142) our story begins by relating the opposing initiatives of two women, i.e. Athaliah, mother of the slain King Ahaziah, and a member of the Judean royal house to whom 2 Kgs 11,2 gives the name "Jehosheba".

2 Kgs 11,1 // 2 Chr 22,10 cite the occasion for Athaliah's "destroying all the royal family", i.e. her "seeing" that "her son [Ahaziah] was dead" (on his assassination by Jehu see 2 Kgs 9,27-28 // 2 Chr 22,9; cf. *AJ* 9,121). Josephus (9,140a) elaborates on the background to her murderous initiative: "When Othlia ('Οθλία; BL Γοθολία), *the daughter of Achab*[2], heard *of the death of her brother Joram*[3] and her son Ochozias and of the destruction of the royal family (τοῦ γένους τῶν βασιλέων

---

1. This chapter represents a reworking of my article *Athaliah's Coup and Overthrow according to Josephus*, in Anton 71 (1996) 192-210 and is used by permission.

2. Josephus has mentioned the queen by name as daughter of Ahab previously in *AJ* 8,398; 9,96 (see there).

3. On Jehu's assassination of Joram King of Israel, see 2 Kgs 9,24 = *AJ* 9,119.

τὴν ἀπώλειαν)...[4]". The historian likewise expatiates (9,140b) on Athaliah's response to what she "hears": "... she took steps to leave no one of the house of David (ἐκ τοῦ Δαυίδου ... οἴκου)[5] alive and to extirpate his family (ἐξαφανίσαι τὸ γένος)[6], *in order that there might never again be a single* (εἷς) *king of his line*[7]".

Josephus' sources move directly from Athaliah's initiative (11,1 // 22,10) to Jehosheba's counter-measure (11,2 // 22,11). Josephus (9,141a) inserts a transitional notice between these two items which makes clear, from the start, that Athaliah did not, in fact, fully accomplish her murderous objective: "And this plan, as she thought, she carried out, but one (εἷς, note the echo of the same word used in the statement of Athaliah's purpse in 9,140 above) son of Ochozias was saved (διεσώθη), and this was the way in which he escaped death". Thereafter (9,141b) he introduces the story's savior figure, conflating the personal data concerning her found in 11,2 // 22,11: "Ochozias had a sister by the same father[8], whose name was Ōsabethē (Ὠσαβέθη)[9], who was married to the high priest (ὁ ἀρχιερεύς)[10] Jōdas (Ἰώδας)[11]".

In 2 Kgs 11,2aα // 2 Chr 22,11aα Jehosheba's intervention begins with her "stealing away" the prince Joash "from among the king's sons who were about to be slain". Josephus' elaborated rendition (9,142a) anticipates mention of the infant's "nurse" from 11,2aβ // 22,11aα:

4. The reference here is to the killing of the "seventy sons" of Ahab resident in Samaria at Jehu's direction (2 Kgs 10,1-11 = AJ 9,125-129) and/or to Jehu's execution of the "kinsmen of Ahaziah" recounted in 2 Kgs 10,12-14 // 2 Chr 22,8 = AJ 9,130b-131.

5. Compare the plus, unparalleled in 2 Kgs 11,1, at the end of 2 Chr 22,10: "(Athaliah destroyed all the royal family) of the house of Judah (BL ἐν οἴκῳ Ἰούδα)".

6. This same construction appears in AJ 9,96: (in virtue of his covenant with David God did not wish) "utterly to destroy his [David's] line (τὸ γένος ἐξαφανίσαι)". The terminological parallel points up the opposition between God's intentions and those of the queen with respect to the Davidic line. Cf. also 9,132 where Jehonadab commends Jehu for "extirpating the house of Achab" (τὴν οἰκίαν ἐξαφανίσας τὴν Ἀχαβοῦ). Here, the verbal echo highlights Athaliah's intention of doing to the Davidic dynasty what Jehu had done to her father's house.

7. With this inserted purpose clause, Josephus spells out, as his sources do not, the intention behind Athaliah's initiative.

8. I.e. King J(eh)oram of Judah who is mentioned by name in 11,2 // 22,11.

9. This is the emendation of Niese which Marcus follows for the varied readings of the codices. SCHLATTER, *Namen*, p. 58 and SCHALIT, *Namenwörterbuch*, p. 68 propose rather Ἰωαβεθή. In MT 11,2 the woman's name is יְהוֹשֶׁבַע, while MT 22,11 calls her יְהוֹשַׁבְעַת. In B 11,2 and 22,11 the name is Ἰωσαβεέ, in L 11,2 // 22,11 Ἰωσαβεαί (many LXX MSS in both 11,2 and 22,11 read Ἰωσάβεθ).

10. In MT L 22,11 "Jehoiada" is called simply "the priest" (L ὁ ἱερεύς; > B *prima manu*); 2 Kgs 11,2 makes no mention of Jehosheba's husband. Subsequently, Josephus will call "Jehoiada" both "high priest" and simply "priest".

11. Compare MT יְהוֹיָדָע, BL Ἰωδᾶε.

"*When she entered the palace*¹², and found Joas ('Ἰώασον)¹³ – *this was the name of the child, who was a year old*¹⁴ – concealed (ἐγκεκρυμ-μένον)¹⁵ with his nurse (τῆς τρεφούσης; compare τὴν τροφόν, BL 11,2 // 22,11) among those who had been slain (τοῖς ἀπεσφαγμένοις; compare τῶν θανατουμένων, BL 11,2 // 22,11)...". The sources (11,2aβb // 22,11aβb) continue with Jehosheba putting prince and nurse "in a bedchamber" where she keeps him "hidden" so that he escapes death. Josephus (9,142b) formulates equivalently: "... she carried him with her to a private bedchamber (εἰς τὸ ταμιεῖον ... τῶν κλινῶν [Lat lacks an equivalent to these last two words]; compare B 22,11 εἰς ταμεῖον κλινῶν) and shut him up there".

2 Kgs 11,3 // 2 Chr 22,12 round off their respective introductions to the Athaliah episode with a notice about Joash's being hid in the house of the Lord/God for six years while Athaliah ruled "the land". The Josephan parallel (9,142c) reproduces this item as follows: "and secretly she [Jehosheba] and her husband [Jehoiada]¹⁶ brought him up in the temple (ἐν τῷ ἱερῷ) for six years, during which time Othlia ruled over (ἐβασίλευσεν = L 11,3 // BL 22,12) Jerusalem and the two tribes¹⁷".

2. *Jehoiada's Measures*

2 Kgs 11,4-12 // 2 Chr 23,1-11, dealing with Jehoiada's preparations for his coup against Athaliah, constitute the longest unit within our episode. They are also that portion of the narrative where the two Biblical versions diverge most strongly from each other. Those divergences surface already at the outset of the respective segments. According to 2 Kgs 11,4 Jehoiada set matters in motion "in the seventh year" by assembling a group of officers in the Temple, whereupon he makes a covenant

12. The sources lack an equivalent indication as to where Jehosheba encountered Joash.

13. MT וַיִּשָׂא, BL Ἰωάς.

14. The sources do not specify the child's age at the moment of his rescue. Josephus calculates the above figure by subtracting the chronological indication of 11,3 // 22,12 (*six* years supervened between Joash's rescue and his acclamation as king at the instigation of Jehoiada) and 12,1 // 24,1 (Joash began to reign at age *seven*).

15. In introducing the specification that Joash (along with his nurse) was "concealed" among the slain, Josephus suggests an explanation as to how the pair survived the general massacre, i.e. this was due to their "concealment".

16. In making reference to both Jehosheba and Jehoiada here, Josephus aligns himself with MT (and most MSS of LXX) 2 Chr 22,12 against 2 Kgs 11,3 which refers only to the former and B 22,12 which alludes solely to Jehoiada.

17. Josephus uses the above phrase also in *AJ* 8,314 in reference to Asa, "the king of Jerusalem and the two tribes".

with them, puts them under oath, and finally exhibits Joash to them. The corresponding account of Jehoiada's initial measures in 2 Chr 23,1-3 is more complicated. Here, the priest, having "taken courage", begins by making a covenant – of unspecified content – with five named "commanders of hundreds" (v. 1, MT). Those officers, in turn, proceed to summon "the Levites and the heads of fathers' houses" from the cities of Judah and Jerusalem (v. 2). Thereafter, the whole assembly concludes a covenant with the king in the Temple (v. 3a); Jehoiada then shows them Joash[18], and urges that he should reign in accordance with the Lord's word concerning the Davidids (v. 3b).

The opening of Josephus' account of Jehoiada's measures (9,143-149) clearly aligns itself with the more expansive presentation of 2 Chr 23,1-3 as opposed to the shorter account of 2 Kgs 11,4. Specifically, in 9,143a Josephus relates that "in the seventh year[19] Jōdas took into his confidence some of the captains of hundreds (ἑκατοντάρχοις; BL 23,1 ἑκατονάρχους)[20], five in number[21], and persuaded them[22] *to join in the plot formed against Othlia and to secure the royal power for the child...[23]*".

Next, however, Josephus turns to 2 Kgs 11,4 in presenting (9,143b) an expanded version of its *Sondergut* reference to Jehoiada's putting the commanders under oath[24]. This reads: "... and, having obtained

---

18. This item (corresponding to the end of 11,4) is lacking in MT 23,3b but is present in BL. BHS suggests that its absence in MT is due to homoioteleuton.

19. With this indication Josephus agrees with 2 Kgs 11,4 (MT and BL) and MT L 2 Chr 23,1 against B 23,1 which reads "eighth". In accord with MT 23,1, but in contrast to 11,4 (MT and BL) and BL 23,1, Josephus does not specify where the encounter between Jehoiada and the commanders took place, i.e. the Temple.

20. In line with 2 Chr 23,1, Josephus lacks the indication of 11,4 concerning the two bodies of troops commanded by these officers, i.e. "the Carites and the guards (literally runners, MT רָצִים)".

21. 2 Chr 23,1 gives the names of the five. As often elsewhere, Josephus here leaves aside a source catalogue of Biblical names that would have sounded strange and off-putting to Gentile readers. Cf., e.g., *AJ* 8,395 where he omits the names of the sixteen members of Jehoshaphat's teaching delegation cited in 2 Chr 17,7-8.

22. The above reference to Jehoiada's "persuading" the commanders is his equivalent to the notice of 2 Chr 23,1 (MT L; cf. 2 Kgs 11,4) that the priest "took them into a covenant (L διαθήκη)". On the historian's systematic avoidance of the LXX's usage of the word διαθήκη in the sense of "covenant", see pp. 115-116, n. 18.

23. The above specification concerning what it was Jehoiada "persuaded" the commanders to do has no equivalent in either 23,1 or 11,4 where the content of the priest's "covenant" with them is left indeterminate. Josephus may have found (partial) inspiration for the item in 23,3b where Jehoiada urges "let him (Joash) reign". See n. 25.

24. In 2 Kgs 11,4 mention of Jehoiada's taking the commanders' oath is followed, in turn, by the notice "he showed them the king's son". In line with 2 Chr 23,3b (BL; see n. 18), Josephus has Jehoiada present Joash only at a later point, i.e. to the assembled religious and political leaders of Judah, see on 9,145 below.

oaths (λαβὼν ὅρκους; BL 11,4 ὥρκισεν [+ αὐτούς]) *by which he was assured that in future he would have nothing to fear from the conspirators*[25], *he felt hopeful of success* (ἐθάρρει ταῖς ... ἐλπίσιν) *in the attempt against Othlia*[26]".

Following his conflation of data drawn from both 2 Chr 23,1 and 2 Kgs 11,4 in 9,143, Josephus now (9,144) presents his parallel to the notice, peculiar to 2 Chr 23,2, concerning the gathering of the Judean notables to Jerusalem. His version runs: "Then the men *whom the priest* (ὁ ἱερεύς)[27] *Jōdas had taken as his partners in the deed*[28] went out through the entire country[29] and, having gathered together *the priests and* Levites[30] therein and the chiefs of the tribes (τοὺς τῶν φυλῶν προεστηκότας; BL 23,2 τοὺς ἄρχοντας τῶν πατριῶν Ἰσραήλ), *brought them to the high priest* (τὸν ἀρχιερέα)[31] when they returned to Jerusalem".

In 2 Chr 23,3a, following the gathering of the Judean notables (v. 2), "the whole assembly", acting on its own, "makes a covenant (BL διαθήκην) with the king". Josephus (9,145a) attributes this new development rather to Jehoiada's initiative, likewise making the priest – rather than the king – the other party to the agreement[32]: "Thereupon he demanded of them [i.e. the Judean notables, 9,144] a sworn pledge (πίστιν ... ἔνορκον)[33] *that they would surely guard whatever secret*

25. Just as he spells out the content of Jehoiada's agreement with the commanders where the sources do not (see n. 23), so here Josephus goes beyond 11,4 in specifying the purpose of the priest's taking the officers' oath, i.e. to assure that they would not, e.g., betray his plan to Athaliah.

26. The above indication concerning Jehoiada's "confidence" once he has formalized the agreement with the officers has no parallel in the sources. It might, however, be seen as Josephus' delayed version of the opening reference in 23,1 to Jehoiada's "taking courage" (BL ἐκραταίωσεν). Such a notice might seem better in place after rather than before (so 23,1) the support of the officers has been secured.

27. Compare Josephus' designation of Jehoiada as ὁ ἀρχιερεύς in 9,141; cf. n. 10.

28. With the above resumption of the content of 9,143 Josephus specifies the identity of the "they" who summon the Judean notables according to 23,2.

29. In 23,2 the commanders go about "through Judah" and gather "the Levites from all the cities of Judah". Josephus' more generalized wording disposes of the question as to why the messengers did not go also to the other southern tribe, i.e. Benjamin; compare his reference to Athaliah ruling over "Jerusalem and the two tribes" in 9,142.

30. 2 Chr 23,2 speaks only of Levites. Josephus' introduction of the "priests" as well has in view Jehoiada's addressing himself to both groups in 23,4. Also subsequently in his version of the Athaliah episode, Josephus will introduce mention of "the priest(s)" where the sources lack such. On Josephus' overall tendency to accentuate the priestly role in biblical history, while downplaying that of the Levites, see p. 11, n. 32.

31. Note the double designation for Jehoiada within the single paragraph 9,144: "the priest... the high priest".

32. Thereby he disposes of the seemingly odd sequence of 23,3 where the assembly's covenant with the king (v. 3a) precedes his presentation by Jehoiada (v. 3b).

33. With this phrase Josephus, once again (see n. 22), substitutes alternative language for source mention of a "covenant" (διαθήκη).

they might hear from him which required equally their silence and their co-operation[34]. *And when they had sworn and it was safe for him to speak...*[35]*"*. Following the above, highly modified rendition of 23,3a, Josephus in 9,145b aligns himself more closely with the wording of 23,3b: "... he brought forward the child of David's line (ἐκ τοῦ Δαυίδου γένους; compare ἐκ τοῦ Δαυίδου ... οἴκου, 9,140)[36] *whom he had raised* (ἔτρεφεν)[37], and said, 'This is your king [23,3b: behold, the king's son] from that house, which, *as you know*[38], God foretold (προφητεύσαντα)[39] to us should rule (βασιλεύσειν)[40] *for all time to come*[41]*"*.

2 Kgs 11,5-8 // 2 Chr 23,4-7 recount various security measures promulgated by Jehoiada. Not only do these two passages differ in detail, each also has its own obscurities as to, e.g., the placement of the various groups of guards, see the commentaries. Josephus (9,146a), following 2 Kgs 11,5-6 // 2 Chr 23,4-5a, begins by having Jehoiada first assign three sets of guards to various points in the Temple-palace complex: "I now advise (παραινῶ)[42] that a third of your

34. With the above sequence, spelling out the content of the "pledge" exacted by Jehoiada from the "notables", compare Josephus' specification as to what the priest "persuaded" the officers to do in 9,143. By contrast, 23,3a says nothing concerning the content of the "covenant" which the assembly makes with the king.

35. This inserted transition between Josephus' rendition of the two parts of 23,3 picks up on the reference to the "sworn pledge" required by Jehoiada in what precedes. The whole of the sequence italicized above with its reference to the need for silence accentuates the drama surrounding the proceedings.

36. In making explicit mention of Jehoiada's "presentation" of Joash here, Josephus goes together with BL 23,3b (and 11,4, *in fine*) against MT 23,3b; see n. 18.

37. This inserted phrase harks back to 9,142c which speaks of Jehosheba and Jehoiada "bringing Joash up (ἀνέθρεψαν) for six years".

38. This inserted phrase serves to call to mind the earlier divine prophecy which Jehoiada will now go on to cite.

39. Elsewhere in Josephus' corpus God appears as (grammatical) subject of the verb προφητεύω also in *AJ* 6,261; 10,126. Compare 9,139 where a similar verb, i.e. προεῖπεν is used with God as subject.

40. This verb echoes that used in 9,142 of Athaliah's "rule" (ἐβασίλευσεν). The verbal echo underscores the wrongfulness of the non-Davidic queen's assumption of rule.

41. The above specification concerning the (unlimited) duration of the Davidids' divinely intended rule has no parallel as such in Jehoiada's words according to 23,3bβ ("let him [Joash] reign, as the Lord spoke concerning the sons of David"). It does, however, hark back to Nathan's promise to David in 2 Sam 7,13.16 // 1 Chr 17,12.14 that his descendants would rule "for ever" (in his actual rendering of the prophecy in *AJ* 7,93-97 Josephus edits out these references, likely out of deference to Roman sensibilities about Jewish Messianism; here in 9,145, however – i.e. at a less prominent juncture of his presentation – he makes use of them where the Bible itself does not).

42. Compare the more peremptory Jehoiada of 11,5 ("he commanded them...") and 23,4 ("this is the thing you must do"). See n. 59.

(ὑμῶν)⁴³ force *guard him* [i.e. Joash] *in the temple*⁴⁴, and that another third (τρίτην)⁴⁵ be stationed at all the gates (πύλαις) of the sacred precinct (τοῦ τεμένους)⁴⁶, while the remaining third keeps watch over the gate that opens and leads into the palace (εἰς τὸ βασίλειον)⁴⁷". Following 2 Chr 23,5b (no parallel in Kings), he rounds off (9,146b) the above catalogue of assignments with Jehoiada's exhortation: "and let the rest of the people (τὸ … ἄλλο πλῆθος; BL πᾶς ὅ λαός) stay *unarmed* (ἄοπλον)⁴⁸ in the temple (ἐν τῷ ἱερῷ)⁴⁹".

In 2 Chr 23,6 (no parallel in Kings) Jehoiada, having assigned the first three divisions of guards and the people their positions, enjoins the former not to admit anyone to the Temple except the "holy" priests and Levites, while the latter are directed to "keep the charge of the Lord". Josephus' version (9,146c) of the priest's additional directives omits the second of these injunctions⁵⁰, while likewise rewording the first: "But allow *no sol-*

43. The referent of this pronoun is the priests and Levites plus the tribal leaders cited in 9,144-145 as having been assembled in Jerusalem and as the addressees of Jehoiada's discourse. In 2 Chr 23,4-5a Jehoiada gives his orders to "the priests and Levites who come off duty on the sabbath" (so RSV), i.e. the regular Temple personnel. According to 2 Kgs 11,5-6 he directs himself rather to those of the "captains of hundreds" (see v. 4) who are (due to be) off duty on the sabbath. Josephus does not take over the sources' specification that the three contingents whom Jehoiada sets in place were normally those who did not have sabbath duty.

44. In 2 Kgs 11,5 the first "third" is assigned to "guard the king's house (+ in the gateway, B)", while according to 2 Chr 23,4 its task is to act as "gatekeepers of (at) the thresholds". Josephus' alternative formulation on the matter might reflect the consideration that Jehoiada's first concern would surely have been the protection of Joash's person.

45. This is the reading of RO which Niese and Marcus follow. Dindorf, Bekker, and Naber read τετάρτην with MSP Lat.

46. According to 2 Kgs 11,6 the second contingent is to position itself at the gate "Sur" (MT; BL at the gate of the ways), while 2 Chr 23,5a has it stationed "at the king's house", i.e. the position of the first unit according to 11,5-6.

47. Compare 2 Kgs 11,6 (the third contingent is directed to place itself "at the gate behind the guards [runners]") and 2 Chr 23,5aβ (the third division's designated post is "the gate of the Foundation [so MT; BL the middle gate]"). In his version of 11,5-6 // 23,4-5a as cited above, it would appear that Josephus has modified and rearranged the source data so as to have Jehoida assign the three divisions according to a clear order of priorities: first guards for Joash himself in the Temple building, then those for the Temple area, and finally those for the palace.

48. This specification concerning the "people" has no equivalent in 23,5b. Josephus may have introduced here it as a way of explaining how it was that Athaliah would later suicidally venture alone into the Temple, i.e. the crowd she encountered there was "unarmed".

49. Compare 23,5b: "in the courts of the house of the Lord (BL ἐν αὐλαῖς οἴκου Κυρίου)". Josephus' wording here may have in view 2 Kgs 11,13 // 2 Chr 23,12 (MT): "(Athaliah) went into the house of the Lord to the people".

50. His reason for this may be the vagueness of that directive which, as such, in contrast to Jehoiada's preceding command about who may enter the Temple, will have no impact on the subsequent course of the story.

dier (ὁπλίτην)⁵¹ to enter (εἰσελθεῖν; BL 23,6 μὴ εἰσελθέτω), nor anyone but a priest (ἱερέα)⁵²".

Jehoiada's security directives conclude in 2 Chr 23,7 with his enjoining the Levites to keep armed watch over the king at all times⁵³. Josephus (9,147a) transposes the priest's direct address to the Levites into the following narrative notice: "He also arranged that *in addition to these* [i.e. the guard contingents cited in 9,146] *a body of priests and* Levites⁵⁴ should be with the king himself and with drawn swords (μαχαίραις ἐσπασμέναις; B ἀνδρὸς σκεῦος ἐν χειρὶ αὐτοῦ) serve as his bodyguard and *immediately* kill anyone who should venture to enter the temple (εἰς τὸ ἱερόν; BL εἰς τὸν οἶκον) *armed* (ὡπλισ-μένον)⁵⁵". He rounds off (9,147b) this notice with an indirect address version of Jehoiada's further word to the Levites as cited in 23,7b ("be with the king when he comes in and goes out"): "and he told them *to fear nothing* (δείσαντας ... μηδέν) and remain on guard over the king".

2 Kgs 11,9 // 2 Chr 23,8 note the (positive) response of Jehoiada's hearers to his preceding instructions⁵⁶. Josephus' parallel (9,148a) simplifies, omitting the sources' distinction (11,9b // 23,8b) between those due to be on and off duty on the sabbath⁵⁷: "so these men⁵⁸ followed the counsel which the high priest (ὁ ἀρχιερεύς; see 9,142.144) gave them

51. In having Jehoiada specifically prohibit "soldiers" from entering the Temple here, Josephus is preparing his own subsequent presentation in 9,150 where he reports – without Biblical basis – that, while the guards allowed Athaliah to enter the Temple, they, in accordance with Jehoiada's directive here in 9,146, kept "the armed men (ὁπλίτας) accompanying her" from doing so.

52. In 2 Chr 23,6, not only the priests, but also "the ministering Levites" (so MT, BL the Levites and those ministering of the Levites), are allowed to enter. Josephus' omission of the latter group in favor of exclusive mention of the former reflects a tendency seen already in 9,144 (see n. 30). In addition, Josephus leaves aside the (self-evident) source rationale as to why the cultic officers are to be allowed to enter, i.e. "for they are holy" (23,6αβ).

53. In 2 Kgs 11,7 this task is assigned, not to the Levites, but rather to the two contingents who have duty on the sabbath and who are to guard the Temple.

54. With his insertion of "priests" alongside the Levites who are the sole addressees of Jehoiada's directive in 23,7, Josephus once again accentuates the role of the former at the expense of the latter, see nn. 30,52.

55. With this inserted specification Josephus echoes the directive he attributes to Jehoiada in 9,146c, i.e. "allow no soldier (ὁπλίτην) to enter..."; see n. 51.

56. In Kings those responding are "the captains of hundreds" cited in 11,4, whereas in Chronicles it is "the Levites and all Judah".

57. This distinction is introduced in the report of Jehoiada's instructions as cited in 2 Kgs 11,5 (// 2 Chr 23,4) and 7. Likewise Josephus' preceding version of those instructions (9,146-147) makes no mention of the distinction.

58. With this generalized reference to Jehoiada's hearers, Josephus resolves the divergence between the sources as to their identity, see n. 56.

(συνεβούλευσεν; BL 11,9 // 23,8 ἐνετείλατο)⁵⁹, *and made plain their intentions by their deeds*".

2 Kgs 11,10 // 2 Chr 23,9 narrate a new initiative by Jehoiada, i.e. his arming "the captains of hundreds" with various Temple objects which had once belonged to David. Josephus (9,148b) amplifies: "Then Jōdas *opened the armoury* (ὁπλοθήκην) in the temple (ἐν τῷ ἱερῷ), *which* (ἥν, referring to ὁπλοθήκην) *David had built*⁶⁰, and distributed to the captains of hundreds (τοῖς ἑκατοντάρχοις = BL 11,10) *and, at the same time, to the priests and Levites*⁶¹ all the spears and quivers (δόρατα ... καὶ φαρέτρας)⁶² he found in it and whatever kind of weapon (ὅπλου)⁶³ he came upon...".

Thus armed, the conspirators now (2 Kgs 11,11 // 2 Chr 23,10) assume their positions in a circle "from the south side of the house to the north side of the house, around the altar and the house to the king". Josephus (9,148c) simplifies the sources' place indications: "*and when they were armed* (καθωπλισμένους; compare ὡπλισμένον, 9,147), he placed (ἔστησεν) them⁶⁴ in a circle (ἐν κύκλῳ; BL 11,11 // 23,10

---

59. Josephus' above substitution of a less "authoritarian" verb for that found in the sources is in line with his previous reference to Jehoiada's "advising" his hearers (9,146) where 11,5 // 23,4 use rather the language of command; see n. 42.

60. With the above formulation Josephus specifies from where within the Temple Jehoiada procured the objects he will distribute. Previously in *AJ* there has been no mention of David's building such a Temple "armoury" (although cf. *AJ* 1,226 with its reference to "that mount whereon king *David* afterwards erected the temple"). Note further the difference between the sources' presentation where Jehoiada distributes David's weapons which had been stored in the Temple and that of Josephus who connects David, not with the weapons themselves, but rather with their storage site; see above. Josephus' reformulation here likely reflects the fact that in *AJ* 8,259, following the LXX plus in 1 Kgs 14,26, he mentions Shishak's removing from the Temple, during the reign of Rehoboam, the "golden quivers" which David had earlier dedicated. Given this indication, the question arises whether there would still have been weapons of David in the Temple for Jehoiada to distribute. Josephus resolves the matter by avoiding the Biblical qualification of the weapons as having actually belonged to David.

61. Josephus' inserted notice here that Jehoiada armed also "the priests and Levites" has in view his earlier (9,147; cf. 2 Chr 23,7) reference to Jehoiada's directing these two groups to guard Joash "with drawn swords". By means of the insertion he explains where they obtained the weapons they had been directed to have ready.

62. This same collocation, in reverse order, occurs in L 2 Kgs 11,10. The MT of that verse reads אֶת־הַחֲנִית וְאֶת־הַשְּׁלָטִים (RSV "the spears and shields"), B τοὺς σειρομάστας καὶ τοὺς τρισσούς. MT 2 Chr 23,9, for its part, lists three items distributed by Jehoiada, i.e. אֶת־הַחֲנִיתִים וְאֶת־הַמָּגִנּוֹת וְאֶת־הַשְּׁלָטִים (RSV "the spears and the large and small shields"); compare B (τὰς μαχαίρας καὶ τοὺς θυρεοὺς καὶ τὰ ὅπλα) and L (τὰ δόρατα καὶ τὰς ἀσπίδας καὶ τὰ ὅπλα).

63. This item corresponds to the third object in the enumeration of BL 23,9; see previous note. In his wording of the list of objects distributed by Jehoiada Josephus thus in effect conflates the peculiar readings of L 11,10 and BL 23,9.

64. In having Jehoiada take the initiative in placing the guards here, Josephus follows 2 Chr 23,10 ("he set [BL ἔστησε(ν)] all the people [as a guard for the king]") as opposed to 2 Kgs 11,11 ("the guards stood...").

κύκλῳ) round the temple *with their hands joined*[65] *so as to bar entrance to any who did not belong there*[66]".

The account of Jehoiada's measures (2 Kgs 11,4-12 // 2 Chr 23,1-11) culminates in 11,12 // 23,11 with Joash being made king. This happening begins when Jehoiada "brings out" (so MT BL 11,12 and BL 23,11; in MT 23,11 the subject is an indefinite "they") the royal child. Next, the priest (MT 23,11: "they") places the "crown" upon him and gives him "the testimony" (so RSV, MT אֶת־הַנֵּזֶר וְאֶת־הָעֵדוּת, BL 11,12 // L 23,11 τὸ μαρτύριον, B 23,12 τὰ μαρτύρια). Like MT 23,11 Josephus (9,149a) attributes the bringing forward and crowning of Joash to an unspecified collectivity rather than to Jehoiada alone: "then they set the boy in their midst and placed (ἐπέθεσαν) the royal crown (τὸν στέφανον τὸν βασιλικόν)[67] on his head…". In contrast to both his sources he omits mention of Joash's also being given "the testimony", perhaps because he – like many interpreters after him – was unclear as to what this object might have been. The source verses continue with Joash being proclaimed king and anointed. Here too, the witnesses diverge as to the subject of these actions: in MT 11,12 it is an unspecified "they", in BL Jehoiada alone (in B and MT [*contra* L] Joash's "being made king" is mentioned prior to his "anointing"); the witnesses to 23,11 agree in making the subject "Jehoiada and his sons". In this instance Josephus (9,149b) aligns himself with the reading of BL 11,12: "and Jōdas, having anointed him *with oil* (τῷ ἐλαίῳ χρίσας; BL ἔχρισεν αὐτόν)[68],

---

65. This indication has no equivalent in the sources as such. MARCUS, *Josephus*, VI, p. 81, n. b., does, however, note that the term which RSV twice renders "side" in its translation of 11,11 // 23,10 (see above) is literally "shoulder" (MT כָּתֵף, BL τῆς ὠμίας), and so suggests that Josephus' reference to "hands" here represents a "misunderstanding of the Biblical text".

66. Also this indication concerning the purpose of Jehoiada's positioning of the guard has no equivalent in 11,11 // 23,10. It does, however, pick up on the priest's directive as cited in 9,146c ("allow no soldier to enter, nor anyone who is not a priest"). See too 9,147 where Jehoiada enjoins the priests and Levites to dispatch "anyone who should enter the temple armed". This recurrent emphasis on the question of who may (not) enter the Temple serves to prepare Josephus' ("un-Biblical") presentation in 9,150 according to which Athaliah is admitted to the Temple, while her armed retinue is excluded.

67. Compare BL 23,11 τὸ βασίλειον. B 11,12 reads ἰέζερ, transliterating MT's הַנֵּזֶר, while L renders τὸ ἁγίασμα. TC 23,11 has a long plus concerning Joash's "crown", identifying this with the one David took from the king of the Ammonites according to 2 Sam 12,30 // 1 Chr 20,2 = AJ 7,61. The Targum further declares, e.g., that this crown would only fit a descendant of David. A similar tradition is cited in *b. 'Abod. Zar.* 44a. Josephus gives no evidence of familiarity with this particular targumic/Rabbinic tradition.

68. Josephus uses the above phrase "anoint with oil" also in AJ 6,159 (David); 7,357.382 (Solomon); cf. 9,106 (Jehu). In speaking of Joash's "anointing" before his designation as king, Josephus agrees with L (and MT) against B 11,12.

proclaimed him king (ἀπέδειξε βασιλέα; BL ἐβασίλευσεν αὐτόν)[69]".
2 Kgs 11,12 // 2 Chr 23,11 both terminate with the acclamation of
Joash[70]; in the former verse reference to "applause" precedes. Josephus' version (9,149c) reflects – with a slight dramatic heightening – the
more expansive conclusion of 11,12: "whereupon the multitude (τὸ
πλῆθος)[71] *with rejoicing* (χαῖρον)[72] and clapping of hands (κροταλίζον;
L 11,12 ἐκρότησαν ... ταῖς χερσὶν αὐτῶν) cried out (ἐβόα)[73], 'Long
live the king (σώζεσθαι τὸν βασιλέα; BL 11,12 // 23,11 ζήτω ὁ
βασιλεύς)'".

3. *Athaliah's End*

The Athaliah episode culminates in 2 Kgs 11,13-16 // 2 Chr 23,12-15
with the account of the queen's violent death at the hands of the conspirators. 2 Kgs 11,13 // 2 Chr 23,12 re-focus attention on Athaliah herself,
unmentioned in the preceding segment: hearing noise[74], she goes into the
Temple to the people (BL to the king). Josephus (9,150) greatly embellishes the scene of the queen's re-appearance: "When Othlia heard the
tumult (θορύβου, BL 11,13 // 23,12 φωνήν) and the acclamations (τῶν
ἐπαίνων, cf. αἰνούντων τὸν βασιλέα, BL 23,12), *which were so unexpected, she was thrown into great confusion* (τεταραγμένη) *of mind*[75],
and jumped up and ran out (ἐξεπήδησε)[76] *of the palace with her private*

---

69. In making Jehoiada alone the subject of this action, Josephus goes together with
BL 11,12 against MT where "they proclaim him king"; see above.
70. In MT 11,12 "they" acclaim Joash, L specifying the subject as "the people",
while in B it is Jehoiada who does this. According to 23,11 (MT and BL) the apparent
subject is Jehoiada and his sons (as in the case of the king's preceding "anointing" and
"appointment"). See next note.
71. This identification of those who applaud (and subsequently acclaim Joash) corresponds to the specification concerning the subject of these actions in L 11,12 as ὁ λαός;
see previous note.
72. Josephus may have found inspiration for this indication in the subsequent course
of the Biblical stories, see 11,14 // 23,13 where Athaliah observes the people "rejoicing"
(BL 11,14 χαίρων).
73. Compare the non-descript "said" of the sources.
74. In MT 11,13 the "noise" is that of "the runners, the people"; L has "of the guards
and of the people", B "of the runners of the people". MT 23,12 reads "(the sound) of the
people running and praising the king", while BL renders "of the people running and
acknowledging and praising the king".
75. This remark on the queen's emotional response to what she hears has no counterpart in the sources. It does, however, serve to account for Athaliah's failure to take due
precautions in what follows.
76. With the above description of Athaliah "thrown into confusion and running out",
compare *AJ* 8,273 where Josephus narrates the reaction of the wife of Jeroboam to the
prophet Ahijah's announcement that her son will die: ἐπηδήσασα ἡ γυνὴ τεταραγμένη.

force of soldiers (στρατιᾶς)[77]. And, when she came to the temple, *the priests*[78] *admitted her, but the armed men* (ὁπλίτας) *who accompanied her were prevented from entering* (εἰσελθεῖν) *by those stationed in a circle* (ἐν κύκλῳ), *who had been given this order by the high priest*[79]".

2 Kgs 11,14a // 2 Chr 23,13a narrate what Athaliah sees and hears once she enters the Temple, i.e. Joash by (or upon) "the pillar", flanked by "the captains (BL 11,14 οἱ ᾠδοί) and trumpeters", while the "people of the land rejoice and blow trumpets (+ and the singers with their musical instruments leading in the celebration, 23,13)". Having greatly embellished the queen's entry into the Temple (9,150), Josephus now (9,151a) drastically compresses[80] the sources' report of what she encountered there: "But Othlia saw the boy standing (ἑστῶτα; BL 11,14 εἰστήκει) on the platform (ἐπὶ τῆς σκηνῆς)[81] *and wearing the royal crown* (τὸν βασιλικὸν περικείμενον[82] στέφανον)[83]". In 11,14b // 23,13b Athaliah reacts to what she sees and hears by rending her clothes and crying "treason, treason" (BL σύνδεσμος, σύνδεσμος). Josephus (9,151b) retains the sources' indication concerning the queen's gesture,

77. Josephus' mention of the "soldiers" accompanying Athaliah here responds to a difficulty suggested by the Biblical accounts, i.e. is it conceivable, as they seem to indicate, that the queen would have gone alone to investigate the uproar she heard coming from the Temple?

78. Note Josephus' continued emphasis on the role of the priests; whereas in 9,147 Jehoiada designates both "priests and Levites" to control access to the Temple, only the former group is mentioned here as granting access to the queen.

79. The above *Rückverweis* in 9,150 underscores the paragraph's various verbal echoes of 9,146 ("allow no soldier [ὁπλίτην] to enter [εἰσελθεῖν]"), 147 (the priests and Levites are to "kill anyone who who should venture to enter the temple armed [ὡπλισμένον]"), and 148 (he [Jehoiada] placed them [the priests and Levites] "in a circle" [ἐν κύκλῳ]). Josephus' inserted reference to Athaliah's retainers being kept from accompanying her into the Temple goes together with his previous – likewise "un-Biblical" – mention of the queen's taking soldiers with her. The former notice, in turn, explains how it was that, as the sources record, Athaliah could later be seized and executed without a fight.

80. The effect of this compression is to keep attention focussed on the two royal rivals, Athaliah and Joash, whereas in the sources these figures seem to take second place to the description of Joash's adherents and their activities.

81. This is the reading adopted by Dindorf, Niese, Naber, and Marcus. The codices RO (followed by Bekker) read ἐπὶ τῆς στήλης (cf. Lat tribunal) in line with the ἐπὶ τοῦ στύλου of BL 11,14 (BL 23,13 renders ἐπὶ τῆς στάσεως αὐτοῦ). In *AJ* 10,63 Josephus makes a similar modification of the Biblical text, having Josiah stand "on the tribune (ἐπὶ τοῦ βήματος)" rather than "on/by the pillar" as in 2 Kgs 23,3 // BL 2 Chr 34,31 (MT has "in his place").

82. This is the reading adopted by Dindorf, Bekker, Naber, and Marcus. Niese reads τὸν βασίλειον ἐπικείμενον with RO.

83. This Josephan insertion recalls his mention of the people's placing "the royal crown" (τὸν στέφανον τὸν βασιλικόν) upon Joash's head in 9,149 (= MT 23,11). Seeing Joash thus "crowned", Athaliah can have no doubt about his status as her rival, this prompting her outcry in what follows.

while supplying her with a quite different verbal response: "... rending her garments (περιρρηξαμένη; compare διέρρηξεν ... τὴν στολὴν αὐτῆς, BL 23,13) and with a fearful outcry (δεινὸν ἀνακραγοῦσα; BL 11,14 // 23,13 ἐβόησεν), *she commanded* (ἐκέλευε) *her men to take the life of the man* who had plotted (ἐπιβουλεύσαντα) against her[84] *and had worked to deprive her of the royal power* (ἀρχήν)[85]".

2 Kgs 11,15 // 2 Chr 23,14 shift attention from Athaliah to her nemesis, Jehoiada, who now issues commands to the military leaders concerning the queen's fate. Josephus reproduces the source data in more expansive form and with one noteworthy deviation in content (i.e. concerning the site of Athaliah's prescribed execution) in 9,151c-152a: "Thereupon Jodas called[86] the captains of hundreds (τοὺς ἑκατονάρχους [see 9,143]; BL 11,15 // 23,14 τοῖς ἑκατοντάρχαις) and commanded (ἐκέλευσεν; BL 11,15 // 23,14 ἐνετείλατο)[87] them to lead Othlia away *to the valley of Kedron*[88] *and there put her to death* (ἀνελεῖν)[89], saying that he did not wish to defile (μιᾶναι) the temple by punishing the guilty wretch (τὴν ἀλιτήριον)[90] on the

84. The above characterization of Jehoiada might be seen as as a reminiscence of Athaliah's cry "treason, treason" in the sources.

85. With the above mention of Athaliah's "commanding her men" Josephus harks back to his ("un-Biblical") notice (9,150a) that the queen exited the palace "with her private force of soliders". At the same time, the reader is left wondering how Athaliah, inside the Temple, can issue commands to her retainers who, according to 9,150b, were made to remain outside. Are we to suppose that in her "great confusion of mind" (9,150a) Athaliah failed to notice that her entourage had not been allowed to follow her into the Temple?

86. This reference to Jehoiada's first "calling" the officers might be seen as Josephus' equivalent to the opening plus of 2 Chr 23,14: "Jehoiada... brought out captains of hundreds" (so MT; BL: Iōdae brought out).

87. Note the verbal contrast set up by Josephus in 9.151 where Athaliah vainly "commanded" (ἐκέλευε) her men while Jehoiada efficaciously "commands" (ἐκέλευσεν) his.

88. In MT 2 Kgs 11,15 Jehoiada directs that Athaliah be led out אֶל־מִבֵּית לַשְּׂדֵרֹת, MT 2 Chr 23,14 reading אֶל־מִבֵּית הַשְּׂדֵרוֹת (RSV: "between the ranks" in both instances). B 11,15 renders with a (partial) transcription of the Hebrew phrase i.e. ἔσωθεν τὸν ἀσηρώθ (L τῶν σαδηρώθ), while BL 23,14 gives ἐκτὸς τοῦ οἴκου. MARCUS, *Josephus*, VI, p. 83, n. b avers that Josephus' "Kedron" "seems to be based on a corruption", i.e. either of the Hebrew הַשְּׂדֵרוֹת (MT 23,14) or of Greek σαδηρώθ (so L 11,15). Alternatively, it might be suggested that Josephus' reading represents a reminiscence of the status of "the brook Kidron" as *the* Biblical site for the disposition of everything connected with idol-worship (see 1 Kgs 15,13; 2 Kgs 23,4.6.12). As such the spot would be an appropriate place for the execution of Athaliah to whom Josephus will subsequently (9,154) attribute, in an extra-Biblical addition, the building of the Baal temple in Jerusalem.

89. This part of Jehoiada's order has a counterpart in the plus of L 11,15: "and bring her (Athaliah) out behind the house of the commanders and put her to death (θανατώσατε) with the sword". Cf. n. 92.

90. Josephus uses the term ἀλιτήριος a total of 12 times in his writings, but only here in 9,152 in reference to a woman.

spot⁹¹. He also ordered them to put to death anyone who might come forward to help her⁹²".

2 Kgs 11,16 // 2 Chr 23,15 recount the fulfillment of Jehoiada's direc-tives: Athaliah is seized and conducted to "the entrance (+ of the gate, 23,15 MT) of the horses of the king's house" (11,16) where she is put to death. Here again (see on the "valley of Kedron", above), Josephus' version (9,152b) involves a topographical indication peculiar to himself: *"Accordingly those who had been ordered to put Othlia to death⁹³* took hold of her and led (ἤγαγον)⁹⁴ her to the gate of the king's *mules* (ἐπὶ τὴν πύλην τῶν ἡμιόνων τοῦ βασιλέως)⁹⁵, where they made an end of her".

4. Sequels

The Athaliah episode finds its dénouement in 2 Kgs 11,17-20 // 2 Chr 23,16-21 = AJ 9,153-156 which relate a series of initiatives, mostly instigated by Jehoiada, following the queen's demise. In the sources (11,17 // 23,16) these measures begin with a covenant-making activity on the part of the priest. Josephus' parallel (9,153) opens with an elabo-rate introductory formula (9,153a) which smooths the transition between what precedes and follows: "when the fate of Othlia had been skilfully determined in this manner, Jōdas summoned the people (τὸν ... δῆμον)⁹⁶

91. The above component of the Josephan Jehoiada's directive spells out the motiva-tion behind his ordering that "she not be slain in the house of the Lord" in 11,15 // 23,14.

92. In having Jehoiada address the handling of Athaliah's possible supporters only after he has finished his directives as to what is to be done with the queen herself, Jose-phus aligns himself with the sequence of L 11,15, whereas in the other witnesses, the for-mer order (11,15bα // 23,14bα) supervenes between the two components of the priest's instructions regarding Athaliah (11,15aβ // 23,14aβ [her being led away] and 11,15bβ // 23,14bβ [her not being slain in the Temple]). Cf. n. 89.

93. In 11,16 // 23,15 the subject of the actions in question is simply "they", i.e. the "captains" to whom Jehoiada addresses his orders in 11,15 // 23,14. Cf. 9,144 where Josephus specifies that it was "the men whom the priest Jōdas had taken as his partners in the deed" who assembled the notables from outside Jerusalem (compare 2 Chr 23,2 where the "collecting" is attributed to a "they").

94. In thus having Athaliah "led" by the officers, Josephus agrees with L 11,16 against the other witnesses where the queen is said rather to "go" on her own.

95. The sources speak rather of "(the gate of) the horses". Perhaps, Josephus' refer-ence to mules here reflects previous Biblical mentions of the mule as *the* royal mount; see 1 Sam 21,8 (LXX = 6,244); 22,9 (LXX = 6,254); 2 Sam 18,8 (= 7,239); 1 Kgs 1,33 (= 7,355). 38 (= 7,357).

96. Mention of Jehoiada's summoning "the people" here harks back to 9,146b where he directs that "the rest of the people (τὸ ... πλῆθος) stay unarmed in the temple", i.e. until Athaliah is disposed of. The waiting people will now be given a role of their own.

and the soldiers (τοὺς ὁπλίτας)[97] to the temple...". Following this insertion, Josephus proceeds (9,153b) to give his version of the sources' mention of Jehoiada's covenant-making(s)[98]: "... (he) made them take an oath (ἐξώρκωσεν; cf. λαβὼν ὅρκους, 9,143)[99] *to be loyal* (εὐνοεῖν) *to the king and watch over his safety* (προνοεῖν ... τῆς σωτηρίας)[100] *and the continuance of his rule* (ἀρχῆς)[101]. *He then compelled* (ἠνάγκασε)[102] the king himself *to honour God* (τιμήσειν τὸν θεόν)[103] *and to give his pledge* (δοῦναι πίστιν; cf. πίστιν ... ἔνορκον, 9,145) *not to transgress the laws of Moses* (παραβῆναι τοὺς Μωυσέος νόμους)[104]".

The next sequel to Athaliah's execution as narrated in 2 Kgs 11,18a // 2 Chr 23,17 is the people's destruction of the Baal temple and killing of its priest, Mattan. Josephus (9,154) underscores the reprehensibility of the pagan temple, thereby giving added legitimacy to its destruction: "*and after that they ran to* (εἰσδραμόντες)[105] *to the temple of Baal* (τὸν

97. The reference here would seem to the various guard contingents to whom Jehoiada assigns their tasks in 9,146a, prior to his stationing the people in 9,146b.

98. In MT B 2 Kgs 11,17 Jehoiada mediates a double covenant, the first involving the Lord, the king and the people and having as its content the people's status as the Lord's people, the second between Joash and the people. L 11,17 omits mention of the second of these covenants. In 23,16 (MT and BL) there is likewise a single, three-way covenant with Jehoiada himself, the people and Joash as parties and with the same content as the first covenant spoken of in MT B 11,17. In line with MT B 11,17, Josephus speaks of Jehoiada's mediating a double "agreement" among the various parties; see above.

99. With this use of this verb, Josephus continues his characteristic avoidance of the term διαθήκη employed by BL 11,17 // 23,16 in translation of Hebrew בְּרִית. See nn. 22,33.

100. Elsewhere Josephus employs the above expression in *AJ* 6,10; 8,334; 11,231; *Vita* 301.

101. This term both echoes, while also contrasting, with 9,151 where Athaliah commands the killing of the one (Jehoiada) who had "worked to deprive her of the royal power (ἀρχήν)". Having successfully stripped Athaliah of her "power", Jehoiada now effects the conferral of that power on Joash. The entire sequence italicized above spells out the content of the covenant between people and king spoken of in the plus of MT B 11,17b (see n. 98). At the same time, in making this the first of the "agreements" concluded by Jehoida, Josephus reverses the sequence of MT B 11,17.

102. With the use of this verb Josephus underscores Jehoiada's authority over the boy-king.

103. Elsewhere Josephus uses the verb τιμέω with God/the Deity as object also in *AJ* 3,250; 4,130.318; 8,22.192.418; 9,256; 12,323; 14,41; 16,42.55.

104. Elsewhere Josephus uses the above expression "transgress the laws of Moses" in *AJ* 8,191; 10,59. The above notice on the second "agreement" concluded by Jehoiada represents Josephus' adaptation of what in 11,17 (MT B) is the first (and in L 11,17 and 23,16 the sole) "covenant" mediated by the priest. From that "covenant" Josephus eliminates the sources' mention of both God and the people as parties, thereby focussing attention on Joash as the sole party to the agreement. In addition, he gives a new content to the agreement, i.e. not that the people will be God's people – a matter which might seem to have been determined long prior to this time – but the king's committing of himself to God and the Mosaic law.

105. This verb, which recalls Athaliah's "running out" (ἐξεπήδησε) of the palace to the Lord's Temple in 9,150, replaces the non-descript terms "go to/enter into" used in the

τοῦ Βαάλ οἶκον; compare εἰς τὸν οἶκον τοῦ Βαάλ, BL 11,18 // 23,17), *which Othlia and her husband [Joram] had built* (κατεσκεύασεν)[106] *in contempt of the nation's god* (ἐφ᾽ ὕβρει ... τοῦ πατρίου θεοῦ)[107] *and in honour* (τιμῇ)[108] *of the god of Achab* [see 9,135: Now the god of Achab was called Baal][109], and razed it to the ground (κατέσκαψαν; BL 11,18 // 23,17 κατέσπασαν)[110] and killed (ἀπέκτειναν = BL 11,18) Mathan (Μάθαν)[111] who held the office of priest (ἱερωσύνην) of Baal[112]".

2 Kgs 11,18b // 2 Chr 23,18 next record Jehoiada's instituting "watches/ watchmen" for the Temple, the Chronicler adding "under the direction of the Levitical priests and the Levites whom David had organized to be in charge of the house of the Lord, to offer burnt offerings to the Lord, as is written in the law of Moses, with rejoicing and singing according to the order of David" (RSV). Josephus' rendition (9,155a) represents a condensed, simplified version of Chronicles' more expansive wording: "The care (ἐπιμέλειαν καὶ φυλακήν; compare ἐπισκοπήν, L 23,18)[113] of the temple Jōdas committed to the priests and Levites[114] in

sources. Josephus leaves unspecified the identity of those who proceed to the Baal temple; compare "all the people of the land" (11,18 MT and BL // BL 23,17)/ "all the people" (MT 23,17).

106. This is the same verb used in 9,138 where the reference is to Ahab's "building (κατεσκεύασεν) a temple to Baal in Samaria" (compare 8,318 where the "building" is attributed rather to Jezebel).

107. The above genitival expression "contempt of God" occurs also in *AJ* 1,113; cf. the comparable phrases using ὕβρις + a preposition + God/ the Deity in the accusative in 6,61; 8,316; 10,241. The above expression "ancestral God" recurs in *AJ* 10,50.68, and in the plural in *BJ* 6,127; *AJ* 18,211; it is further conjectured in *AJ* 9,254; 18,198 (pl.).328 (pl.).

108. This noun form employed in reference to Baal here in 9,154 both recalls and contrasts with the verb τιμήσειν used of Joash's required "honouring" of God in 9,153.

109. The whole italicized sequence above has no equivalent in the sources; the insertion serves to account for the fact of the presence of a Baal temple in Jerusalem which is simply presupposed in the Bible.

110. Josephus uses the verb κατασκάπτω in a similar "iconoclastic" sense in *AJ* 10,52 (Josiah "razed [κατέσκαψεν] the altars of the foreign gods"). Here in 9,154 he leaves aside the further indication of 11,18 // 23,17 that the people "broke in pieces his [Baal's] altars and images". Compare his similiar compression of the Biblical account concerning Jehu's measures against the Baal cult (2 Kgs 10,25b-27) in 9,138a.

111. This is the reading proposed by Niese on the basis of Lat. The codices RO read Νάθαν, MSP (followed by Dindorf, Bekker, and Naber) Μααθάν. In MT 11,18 // 23,17 the priest's name is מַתָּן; B 11,18 calls him Μααθάν, L 11,18 and BL 23,17 Ματθάν.

112. Josephus leaves asides the sources' specification that "Mattan" was killed "before the altars", just as he passes over their earlier reference to the Baalistic "images and altars" smashed by the people; see n. 110.

113. The above collocation recurs in *AJ* 11,50; 16,167.

114. This phrase corresponds to that found in BL 23,18; compare MT "the Levitical priests and the Levites". On the other hand Josephus has no equivalent to the plus (Jehoiada "established the courses of the priests and Levites") which follows in BL 23,18.

accordance with the ordinance (διάταξιν) of King David [cf. καθὼς διέστειλε Δαυίδ, L 23,18], and ordered them to offer the customary sacrifice of the whole burnt-offerings (ἐπιφέρειν τὰς νεομισμένας τῶν ὁλοκαυτώσεων θυσίας)¹¹⁵ *twice a day*¹¹⁶ *and burn incense* (θυμιᾶν)¹¹⁷ in conformity with the law (ἀκολούθως τῷ νόμῳ, BL 23,18 καθὼς γέγραπται ἐν νόμῳ Μωυσῆ)". Josephus likewise (9,155b) draws on the *Sondergut* notice of 2 Chr 23,19 concerning Jehoiada's appointment of "gatekeepers" to bar access to the Temple to "unclean persons". His rendering of this item runs: "He also appointed (ἀπέδειξε)¹¹⁸ *some of the Levites*¹¹⁹ and porters (πυλωρούς; BL 23,19 οἱ πυλωροί) to guard the sacred precinct (τοῦ τεμένους; BL ἐπὶ τὰς πύλας οἴκου Κυρίου)¹²⁰, that no impure person (μεμιασμένον; BL 23,19 ἀκάθαρτος)¹²¹ might enter it *unseen*".

2 Kgs 11,19a // 2 Chr 23,20a relate a final, culminating initiative by Jehoiada following the elimination of Athaliah: he leads a procession consisting of officers, people and Joash himself to the palace. Josephus (9,156a) follows the sources' presentation quite closely for this item: "*when he had arranged these several matters*¹²², he and the captains of

115. Compare BL 23,18: ἀνανέκγαι ὁλοκαυτώματα Κυρίῳ. The above phrase has a close parallel in *AJ* 9,257 where King Ahaz forbids τὰς νενομισμένας ... θυσίας ἐπιφέρειν.

116. This Josephan specification has no equivalent in 23,18. It reflects the prescription of Num 28,3-4 concerning the *tāmîd*.

117. In 23,18 there is no mention of "incense"; rather, the prescribed sacrifices are to be offered "with rejoicing and singing". Josephus' above coupling of "holocausts" and "incense" recalls 2 Chr 13,10-11 where King Abijah of Judah, in his address to the Israelites, cites Judah's having Aaronite priests and their helper Levites who "offer... every morning and every evening burnt offerings (LXX ὁλοκαυτώματα) and incense (LXX θυμίαματα)". The phrase δὶς τῆς ἡμέρας ... θυμιᾶν used here in 9,155 occurs also Josephus' notice on the incense offering in *AJ* 3,199.

118. Josephus' active singular form with Jehoiada as subject here corresponds to the וַיַּעֲמֵד of MT 23,19 as opposed to the plural construction of BL (ἔστησαν οἱ πυλωροί).

119. 2 Chr 23,19 makes no mention of the Levites. Josephus' inserted reference to them here reflects David's assignment of gate-keeping duties precisely to the Levites in 1 Chr 26,1-19.

120. Josephus' reference here in 9,155 to the guarding of the "sacred precinct" recalls 9,146 where Jehoiada advises that a third of the assembled force "be stationed at all the gates of the sacred precinct (τοῦ τεμένους)".

121. Josephus' use of the participle μεμιασμένον here echoes the statement he attributes to Jehoiada in 9,152: "he did not wish to defile (μιᾶναι) the temple by punishing the guilty wretch [Athaliah] on the spot". By appointing (permanent) guards for the "sacred precinct", Jehoiada is now acting to definitively preclude future "defilement" of the Temple.

122. With this inserted Josephan transitional phase, compare that prefaced by him to his version of 11,17 // 23,16 in 9,153: "when the fate of Othlia had skilfully been determined in this manner...".

hundreds (τῶν ἑκατοντάρχων)[123] and the officers (ἡγεμόνων)[124] and all the people (τοῦ λαοῦ παντός)[125] conducted (παραλαβὼν ἄγει)[126] Joas from the temple to the palace[127]". Following his arrival at the palace Joash is enthroned. In MT 11,19b he "takes his seat" (וַיֵּשֶׁב) upon the throne, while in 23,20b (MT BL) as well as in BL 11,19b "they" (Jehoiada and the assembly) "set him" there. Josephus' version reflects the former reading: "... and when he (Joash) had taken his seat (καθίσαντος) on the royal throne (ἐπὶ τὸν βασιλικὸν θρόνον; cf. ἐπὶ τοῦ θρόνου τῶν βασιλέων, BL 11,19; BL 23,20 ἐπὶ τοῦ θρόνου τῆς βασιλείας)".

2 Kgs 11,20 // 2 Chr 23,21 conclude the Athaliah episode with a double notice on the situation following the queen's demise: "rejoicing" by "the people of the land" and "quiet" in Jerusalem. Josephus (9,156b) amplifies the first of these items, while simply reproducing the second as such: "... the multitude (τὸ πλῆθος; see 9,146)[128] *acclaimed him with shouts, and then turned to feasting* (πρὸς εὐωχίαν τραπέντες) *and celebrated for many days* (ἐπὶ πολλὰς ... ἡμέρας)[129]. The city (ἡ ... πόλις = BL 11,20 //

123. This designation corresponds to the "captains of hundreds" cited at the opening of 11,19a (MT and BL) and MT L 23,20 (B reads τοὺς πατριάρχας).

124. This term might be seen as Josephus' generalizing equivalent to the two further military/political groupings mentioned in the sources, i.e. "the Carites and the guards (runners)" (11,19a)/ "the nobles (BL τοὺς δυνατούς) and the governors of the people (BL τοὺς ἄρχοντας τοῦ λαοῦ)" (23,20).

125. In 11,19a // 23,20 the reference is to "all the people *of the land*" (BL πάντα τὸν λαόν τῆς γῆς). Also elsewhere Josephus rewords the Biblical expression "the people of the land", perhaps because of the negative connotations it was coming to take on among the Rabbis in his time (= the ignorant, non-observers of the Law). On the subject see *EI*, s.v. AM HA-AREZ.

126. The subject of this singular verbal phrase would be Jehoiada (alone). In the sources Jehoiada is likewise the subject of their initial verb ("he took"). Thereafter, however, there is a divergence among the witnesses as to who it was who "conducted" Joash from the Temple to the palace: in MT BL 11,19a "they" (Jehoiada and those accompanying him) "brought the king down from the house of the Lord" and "came (L caused him [Joash] to enter)... to the king's house". MT 23,20 makes Jehoiada the subject of the "bringing down", but "they" of Joash's "coming" to the palace, while BL reads "they conducted the king into the house of the Lord and he (Joash) entered... into the king's house". Vis-à-vis all these presentations, Josephus' version emphasizes the active role of Jehoiada.

127. Josephus leaves aside the sources' divergent indications concerning the "gate" (11,19 "of the guards [runners]" vs. MT 23,20 "the upper", BL "the inner" [τῆς ἐσωτέρας]) through which the procession proceeds on its way from the Temple to the palace.

128. Here again (see n. 125), Josephus avoids the sources' expression "people of the land".

129. With the above sequence Josephus spells out in dramatic detail what was involved in the people's "rejoicing" spoken of in 11,20 // 23,21. Its wording recalls *AJ* 9,16: (having led his army back to Jerusalem) King Jehoshaphat "gave himself up to

23,21), *on the other hand* (μέντοι γε)[130], had been calm (ἡσυχίαν ἤγαγεν; cf. ἡσύχασε[ν] BL 11,20 // 23,21) at the death of Othlia[131]".

Conclusions: Josephus' Rewriting of 2 Kings 11 // 2 Chr 22,10–23,21

Of the two Biblical narrations of the Athaliah episode, Josephus clearly draws, overall, more on that of Chronicles than on Kings' less expansive version[132]. On the other hand, he does, on occasion, make use of elements peculiar to Kings as well, e.g., Jehoiada's putting the commanders under oath (11,4 = 9,143; compare 23,1) and the "clapping" at Joash's coronation (11,12 = 9,149; compare 23,11). As to the specific text-form(s) of the Biblical narratives employed by Josephus in retelling the Athaliah narrative, we noted, first of all, evidence of his familiarity with distinctive readings of both MT Kings (Joash takes his own seat on the throne, 9,156 = 11,19b) and Chronicles (an unspecified "they" brings Joash forward and crowns him, 9,149 = 23,11; Jehoiada "stations" the porters, 9,155 = 23,19; cf. n. 118). We likewise, however, saw instances where the historian aligns himself with readings distinctive of B and/or L Kings (e.g., Jehoiada alone anoints Joash and designates him king, 9,149 = BL 11,12; see also his use – in reverse order – of the phrase "quivers and spears" proper to L 11,10 in 9,148; cf. n. 62)[133] and Chronicles (in common with BL 23,9, he cites, 9,148, "weapons" as the third of the items which Jehoiada distributes to the forces; cf. n. 63). On the other hand, there is no indication that Josephus knew the traditions about Joash's crown preserved in TC 23,11 (and elsewhere in Rabbinic tradition); see n. 67.

In his rewriting of the source materials in 9,140-156, Josephus, first of all, does introduce a fair number of insertions and expansions. These

feasting (τρέπεται πρὸς εὐωχίας)... for many days (ἐπὶ πολλὰς ἡμέρας)".

130. With this phrase Josephus introduces a contrast between the two component elements of 11,20 // 23,21 (the people's rejoicing, Jerusalem's quiet) which in the sources are simply joined paratactically.

131. Compare the phrase "after Athaliah had been slain with the sword [+ in the king's house, 11,20]" with which the source verses conclude.

132. Recall, e.g., the following items of Chronistic *Sondergut* used by him: the five commanders with whom Jehoiada initiates the conspiracy (23,1 = 9,143); the commanders' assembling of the provincial religious and civil notables to Jerusalem (23,2 = 9,144); Jehoiada's prohibition of anyone other than cultic officials being allowed to enter the Temple (23,6 = 9,146); the reference to the cultic directives given by David to the priests and Levites, themselves grounded in the Mosaic Law (23,18 = 9,155a); and Jehoiada's stationing guards to prevent "unclean" persons from entering the Temple (23,19 = 9,155b).

133. Under this head recall as well the several points of contact between 9,149 and

additions are of varying length and serve a range of purposes. Some are inspired by stylistic considerations: specification of the subject(s) of actions which the sources leave indeterminate (see, e.g., the opening of 9,144 and compare 23,2) or smoothing the transition between one part of the story and another (see, e.g., the openings of 9,153 and 156). Others aim to accentuate the role of the priests in the Athaliah episode (see the inserted reference to them in 9,144 [compare 23,2]. 148 [here in conjunction with the Levites [compare 11,10 // 23,9]. and 150). Still others expatiate on the link between Athaliah's opening initiatives and the preceding events which occasion the former (see the expansion of the reference to Athaliah hearing of the death of her son, 11,1 // 22,10, in 9,140). With his inserted reference to Athaliah's coming to the Temple with her retinue (9,150), Josephus "resolves" the implausibility of the queen's setting out alone – as she seems to do in 11,13 // 23,12 – to investigate the suspicious clamor emanating from the Temple[134]. Similarly, the notice about the Baal temple having been built by Joram and Athaliah which he introduces in 9,154 provides an explanation of the origins of this edifice which in 11,18 // 23,17 appears – for the first time – without any such indication. Above all, however, Josephus' additions in 9,140-156 are designed to accentuate the dramatic character of the episode. Under this heading, we might recall, e.g., Jehoiada's portentous oath-taking of the assembly before presenting Joash to them (9,145), Athaliah's mental confusion upon hearing the noise from the Temple and her "running out" of the palace (9,150), her "fearful outcry" and (unavailing) directive to her entourage (9,151), as well as the people's "feasting and celebrating for many days" following Joash's enthronement (9,156)[135].

    While Josephus thus embellishes the sources' Athaliah story in many ways, he also, conversely, for a variety of reasons, simplifies and compresses certain elements of their presentation(s): e.g., the actual names of the five commanders whom Jehoiada takes into his confidence are passed over (9,143; compare 23,1); details concerning Jehoiada's placing of the guard contingents (9,146-147; compare 11,5-8 // 23,4-7) omitted; the Biblical accounts of the scene which Athaliah encounters in the

L 11,12 and between 9,151-152 and L 11,15 pointed out in nn. 68 and 89 and 92, respectively.

    134. As will be recalled, this Josephan addition, in turn, gives rise to another one, i.e. the notice that Athaliah's retainers were barred from entering the Temple (9,150) with the result that, as in the sources, the queen dies alone with no resistance being offered on her behalf.

    135. In the same line as these "dramatizing additions" to the Biblical story stand Josephus' replacement of the sources' non-descript verbs with more colorful ones: the people "cry out" (9,149) their acclamation of Joash rather than simply "saying" (so 9,149; compare 11,12 // 23,11) this, and their "running" (9,154) – instead of merely

Temple abbreviated (9,151; compare 11,13 // 23,12), as are the source narratives of the destruction of the Baal temple (9,154; compare 11,18 // 23,17); and the allusion to the "gate" through which Joash is conducted to the palace left aside (9,156; compare 11,19 // 23,20).

Re-arrangement of the source sequences within 9,140-156 is exemplified by the historian's presenting the "agreements" spoken of in MT B 11,17 in reverse order in 9,153. As for modifications/adaptations of the Biblical Athaliah stories, Josephus' version is notable especially for its systematic rewording of all source uses of the term "covenant" (διαθήκη); see nn. 22,33,99, and for the new content which it gives to the two "agreements" mediated by Jehoiada (see 9,153; compare MT B 11,17).

The Athaliah story presented by Josephus, while not diverging from its Biblical prototypes in any major way, does evidence a number of distinctive features generated by the above rewriting techniques. These include a certain streamlining and dramatization of the episode, filling in of its "gaps", and hightening of the role of the priests at the expense of the Levites in the proceedings. Otherwise, Josephus is content to reproduce the Biblical narrative – especially in its Chronistic form – largely as he found it. His doing so doubtless reflects the realization that the source story of the usurper queen whose misdeeds are so spectacularly requited could, of itself, very well serve to inculcate the (negative side of the) moral set out at the opening of *AJ* in 1,14: "... in proportion as they [men] depart from the strict observance of these [God's] laws... whatever imaginary good thing they strive to do ends in irretrievable disasters".

"going" (so 11,18 // 23,17) – to the Baal temple.

VIII

JOASH OF JUDAH[1]
(9,157-172)

Both of Josephus' Biblical sources follow their respective narratives of the overthrow of the usurper Athaliah (2 Kgs 11,1-20 // 2 Chr 22,10–23,21) with accounts (2 Kgs 12,1-22 [MT whose numbering I follow = BL; Eng. 11:21-12:20] // 2 Chr 24,1-27) of the reign of her legitimate, Judean successor, i.e. Joash which, however, differ rather notably in what they tell of this king. Josephus adopts this sequence as well, giving his presentation of Joash in 9,157-172, immediately following his presentation of Athaliah's downfall in 9,140-156 (see chap. VII), inserting therein (9,159-160) the conclusion of his Jehu story (see chap. VI) broken off by him in 9,139.

To facilitate my comparison of the three Joash accounts, I divide up the material as follows: 1. Joash Introduced (*AJ* 9,157-158(159-160) = 2 Kgs 12,1-4 (MT) [+ 2 Kgs 10,31-36] // 2 Chr 24,1-3); 2. Temple Repair (9,161-165 = 12,5-17 // 24,4-14); 3. Joash's Defection (9,166-169 = 24,15-22); 4. Syrian Incursion (9,170-171a = 12,18-19 // 24,23-24); and 5. Closing Notices (9,171b-172 = 12,20-22 // 24,25-27).

1. *Joash Introduced*

Josephus' sources commence their respective introductions of Joash (2 Kgs 12,1-4 // 2 Chr 24,1-3) with chronological indications (12,1-2a // 24,1a): he accedes at age seven (+ in the seventh year of Jehu, 12,2aα) and reigns forty years. They go on to note the name of his mother (Zibiah of Beersheba, 12,2b // 24,1b), and conclude with a summary evaluation of the king, stating that Joash "did right in the Lord's eyes" due to the influence of the priest Jehoiada (12,3 // 24,2). Thereafter, 2 Kgs 12,4 mentions the continuation of worship on the high places under Joash, while 2 Chr 24,3 speaks rather of the king's familial situation (Jehoiada provides him with two wives [see below]; he has sons and daughters).

---

1. This chapter represents a reworking of my article *Joash of Judah according to Josephus*, in M.P. GRAHAM et al. (eds.), *The Chronicler as Historian* (JSOTSup, 238), Sheffield, Sheffield Academic Press, 1997, pp. 301-320 and is used by permission here.

Josephus' introduction to Joash's reign in 9,157-158 first (9,157a) reproduces the data of 12,1-2 // 24,1 on the king's age at accession plus the name of his mother ("Sabia", Σαβία)[2] and her birthplace ("Bērsabee", Βηρσαβεέ = BL 12,2 // B 24,1). In line with his usual practice, Josephus "delays" the sources' mention of Joash's length of reign until the end of his own account (see 9,172). Like Chronicles, he offers no equivalent to 12,2aα's synchronization; see above. In place of the stereotyped Biblical expression about Joash's doing "right in the Lord's eyes", he affirms (9,157b) that the king "kept strict observance of the ordinances (τῶν νομίμων[3] φυλακήν)[4] and was zealous (φιλοτιμίαν) in the worship of God (περὶ τὴν τοῦ θεοῦ θρησκείαν)...[5]". In line with 2 Chr 24,2 the historian qualifies this assessment via the appended phrase "all the time Jōdas lived" (compare 12,2: Joash did right "all his days because Jehoaida... instructed him", RSV). Josephus (9,158a) likewise follows Chronicles for its *Sondergut* item (24,3a)[6] about Joash's marriages: "... *when he came of age*[7], he married two women whom the high priest had given him". This notice is of interest for its indication concerning the text-form of 2 Chronicles 24 utilized by Josephus. MT 24,3a reads the ambiguous וַיִּשָּׂא־לֹו יְהֹויָדָע נָשִׁים שְׁתָּיִם which leaves unclear the referent of the pronoun לֹו – is it Joash or rather Jehoiada himself? BL resolves the matter with their rendering, i.e. καὶ ἔλαβεν ἑαυτῷ Ἰωδᾶε γυναῖκας δύο. It would seem that in this instance Josephus had before him, not the unambiguous reading of LXX, but rather the MT one which he "clarifies" in his own way[8]. In any case, he does not reproduce the reference in

---

2. This form of the name corresponds to that found in L 24,1. Compare צִבְיָה (MT 12,2 // 24,1); Ἀβιά (BL 12,2 // B 24,1).

3. This is the reading adopted by Bekker, Niese, Naber, and Marcus; Dindorf reads νόμων with MSP Lat.

4. The above phrase "observance of the ordinances" recurs in *AJ* 8,195.290.

5. The above double notice concerning Joash recalls the pledge exacted of him by Jehoiada in *AJ* 9,153, i.e. "to honour (τιμήσειν) God... and not to transgress the laws (νόμους) of Moses". In so doing, it underscores the efficacy of Jehoiada's initiative on the king.

6. As noted above, this notice takes the place of the statement found in 2 Kgs 12,4 about the "high places" continuing to function during Joash's (early) reign. In opting to following Chronicles against Kings on the matter, Josephus may have reckoned that the content of 12,4 might seem to negate his own earlier affirmation about the young Joash's "strict observance of the ordinances" and "zeal for the worship of God" – both of which would have disallowed such toleration of the high places and their cult. In any case, like the Chronicler, he regularly omits the "high places notice" with which Kings qualifies its positive assessment of a whole series of "good" Judean rulers.

7. Josephus' insertion of the above indication might reflect the fact that Joash was only seven (12,1 // 24,1 = 9,157a) at his accession.

8. The ambiguity of MT 2 Chr 24,3a (which is paralleled in TC and *VL*) continued to generate controversy in Jewish tradition concerning which man married the two wives, see Ginzberg, *Legends*, VI, p. 354, n. 11.

24,3b to the children begotten by Joash (or Jehoiada). In place thereof he introduces (9,158b) an expansive, provisional closing formula for his whole preceding account concerning Joash's rescue, accession and early reign (*AJ* 9,140-158a = 2 Kgs 11,1-12,4 // 2 Chr 23,1-24,3). It reads: "This much, then, concerning King Joas and how he escaped (διέφυγε)[9] the plot (ἐπιβουλήν)[10] of Othlia and succeeded to the throne is all that we have to relate at this point". Josephus' insertion of this formula has in view the immediately following "interruption" of his Joash story in 9,159-160. This latter sequence represents the historian's "delayed" conclusion to the reign of Jehu (= 2 Kgs 10,31-36) last mentioned by him in 9,139 (cf. the closing formula "such, then, was the state of affairs under Jehu" at the end of that paragraph)[11].

In his handling of the data of the complex 2 Kgs 10,31-36 here in 9,159-160, Josephus re-arranges the source sequence. In particular, he begins (9,159) his version with immediate mention of the Syrian incursion that occurred during Jehu's latter reign as cited in 10,32b-33: "Now Azaēlos[12], *the king of Syria*, made war on the Israelites *and their king Jehu*[13], *and ravaged* (διέφθειρε) the eastern parts (τὰ πρὸς τὴν ἀνατολήν) of the country across the Jordan belonging to the Reubenites and Gadites and Manassites, and also Galaaditis and Batanaia[14], *spreading fire* (πυρπολῶν) *everywhere and plundering* (διαρπάζων) *everything and inflicting violence* (βίαν προσφέρων) *on all who fell into his hands*[15]". Having

9. This verb harks back to Josephus' initial allusion to Joash in 9,141 where he refers to the infant's "escaping" (διέφυγεν) death at Athaliah's hands.

10. This noun echoes the verbal form used in 9,151 where Athaliah commands her men "to take the life of the man who had plotted (ἐπιβουλεύσαντα) against her...".

11. By thus reversing the sequence of 2 Kgs 10,31-36 (= *AJ* 9,159-160: Jehu's latter reign and death) and 11,1-12,4 (= *AJ* 9,140-158 with the accession of Joash occurring in Jehu's seventh year; see 12,2), Josephus presents events in their proper chronological order, whereas the Biblical account "gets ahead of itself".

12. Josephus reported this king's seizure of power for himself in *AJ* 9,87-94 (= 2 Kgs 8,7-15); see chap. IV.

13. Compare 10,32b: "Hazael defeated them [the Israelites] throughout the territory of Israel".

14. The above catalogue of the five specific areas seized by Hazael east of the Jordan represents Josephus' re-arranged and shortened version of the enumeration given in 10,33 (elements without parallel in 9,159 are italicized): "from the Jordan eastward, *all the land of Gilead*, the Gadites, and the Reubenites [in Josephus these two tribes appear in the reserve order], and the Manassites, *from Aroer, which is by the valley of Arnon, that is Gilead* [L + and Jabbok (Ἰαβόκ)] and Bashan (BL Βασάν; cf. Josephus' Βαταναίαν)".

15. The above italicized words, accentuating the damage done to Israel by Hazael, lack a parallel in 10,32b-33. They do, however, serve to provide an implicit fulfillment for Elisha's announcement to Hazael as cited in *AJ* 9,91 (= 2 Kgs 8,12): "I [Elisha] am crying out of pity for the Israelite people because of the misfortunes which it will suffer at your hands. For you will slay their best men and burn (ἐμπρήσεις) their strongest cities, and you will kill their children by dashing them against the rocks and will rip up their women with child".

related these developments on the basis of 10,32b-33, Josephus now proceeds to suggest the reason for their occurrence, this (partially) derived from 10,31 ("But Jehu was not careful to walk in the law [BL νόμῳ] of the Lord... with all his heart; he did not turn from the sins of Jeroboam, which he made Israel to sin"). His rendering (9,160a) of the latter verse runs: *"For Jehu had not been prompt to oppose him when he began to devastate* (κακοῦντα) *the country*[16], but had become careless of his duties toward the Deity (εἰς τὸ θεῖον ὑπερόπτης)[17] and contemptuous of holiness and the laws (καταφρονήσας τῆς ὁσίας καὶ τῶν νόμων)[18]".

Following his re-arranged rendition (9,159-160a) of the content of 10,31-33, Josephus comes in 9,160b to relate the concluding indications concerning Jehu found in 10,34-36[19]: "he died after ruling over the Israelites for twenty-seven years[20], and was buried in Samaria [= 10,35aβ), after leaving his son Jōazos (Ἰωάζον)[21] as his successor on the throne [= 10,35b][22]".

16. This reference to Jehu's military "inactivity" which allowed Hazael to achieve the successes he did lacks a parallel in 10,31-36. It might, however, be seen as Josephus' transposition into "non-theological" terms of the anthropromorphic notice of 10,32a: "In those days the Lord began to cut off parts of Israel".

17. With this construction compare those used in *AJ* 1,73 (many of the angels were "distainful [ὑπερόπτας] of every virtue") and 10,103 (Zedekiah was "contemptuous [ὑπερόπτης] of justice and duty").

18. This is Josephus' only use of the above expression. Elsewhere, however, he does use similar phrases involving the verb καταφρονέω with God or things related to God as (genitival) object with some frequency; see, e.g., *AJ* 1,43; 3,16; 4,181.215; 6,150; 7,151; 8,251; 9,173; 12,357. With the above nominal collocation "holiness and the laws", compare *AJ* 9,290 where the Assyrian king sends priests to instruct the population of Samaria in "the ordinances (τὰ ... νόμιμα) and religion (τὴν ὁσίαν) of this God".
FELDMAN, *Studies*, p. 358 (= ID., *Jehu*, 25) points out that in his above rendition of 2 Kgs 10,31 (as also in his version of 10,29 in 9,139) Josephus does not reproduce the explicit Biblical linkage of Jehu with the renegade Jeroboam. He sees the historian's procedure in this regard as part of his overall rehabilitation of the former figure. On the other hand, the above double characterization of Jehu as "careless" with regard to God and "contemptuous of the laws" clearly does set him in negative contrast to his contemporary, Joash of Judah, whom Josephus, just previously in 9,158, has described as "keeping strict observance of the ordinances and zealous in the worship of God".

19. From this complex he omits, as is his invariable practice, the source notice of 10,34.

20. In this formulation Josephus brings together the data of 10,35aα ("Jehu slept with his fathers") and 36 ("the time that Jehu ruled over Israel in Samaria was twenty-eight years"). On the discrepancy between Josephus' figure for the length of Jehu's reign (27 years) and the Biblical one (28 years), see MULZER, *Bearbeitung*, 67, n. 131 who points out that the former has a counterpart in several *VL* MSS.

21. Compare יְהוֹאָחָז (MT 10,35b); Ἰωαχάς (B); Ἰωαχάζ (L).

22. Josephus will resume his account of Joash of Israel in 9,173 (= 2 Kgs 13,1), once he has concluded his treatment of Joash of Judah (9,157-158.161-172) which he "interrupted" to relate the end of Jehu and the accession of his son Joash in 9,159-160. Josephus has no equivalent to the long plus (10,37-43), recapitulating elements of the preceding complex 8,25-9,28, which follows mention of Jehu's length of reign (MT 10,36) in L.

2. *Temple Repair*

2 Kgs 12,5-17 and 2 Chr 24,4-14 both describe Joash's (financial) initiatives for the repair of the Temple in considerable detail, though also
with numerous divergences. The latter sequence opens (24,4) with a
statement concerning the king's intentions: "after this Joash decided to
restore the house of the Lord". Josephus' Temple repair account (9,161-
165) commences (9,161a) with an amplification of this Chronistic plus:
"As for Joas... he was seized by a strong desire to renovate (ἀνακαινίσαι) the temple of God..." (cf. the reference to the king's being "zealous in the worship of God" in 9,157).

2 Kgs 12,5-6 and 2 Chr 24,4-5a recount a directive by Joash addressed
respectively to "the priests" and "the priests and the Levites". Here too,
Josephus (9,161b) aligns himself with the Chronicler's presentation,
while also representing the king as using Jehoiada, the head of the clerical hierarchy, as his intermediary: "... summoning the high priest Jōdas,
he commanded him to send Levites and priests [compare priests and
Levites, 2 Chr 24,5]". Subsequently as well Josephus will highlight
Jehoaida's role in the episode. The content of the royal directive differs
markedly in the source accounts. In Kings Joash enjoins the priests to
collect, at the Temple itself, various categories of monies[23] and to repair
the edifice. In Chronicles, on the contrary, the priests and Levites are dispatched to "the cities of Judah" to there gather funds [BL 24,5:
ἀργύριον] for the Temple repairs and are further called on to "hasten the
matter". Josephus agrees with the Chronicler in reporting a "mission"
undertaken by the two groups of cultic officials "to the entire country".
Into his wording of the charge given the delegation by the king via the
high priest, he, at the same time, incorporates language "anticipated"
from Joash's rebuke of Jehoiada in 24,6-7; see below. Specifically, in
Josephus' narration, those sent out are told "to ask *a half shekel* of silver
(ἀργύρου) *for each person*[24] for the repairing (ἐπισκευήν) and renovation (ἀνανέωσιν, see ἀνακαινίσαι, 9,161a) of the temple [compare
24,5: money to repair the house of your God], which had been left crumbling (καταλυθέντος) by *Joram* and Othlia and her sons[25]".

---

23. On the terminology used for these, see L.S. WRIGHT, *mkr in 2 Kings xii 5-17 and
Deut xviii 8*, in *VT* 39 (1989) 438-448.
   24. This specification is inspired by 24,6 where Joash asks why the "tax levied by
Moses... for the tent of testimony" has not been collected by the Levites. The "tax" in
question is the one prescribed in Exod 30,11-16 (compare *AJ* 3,194-196) i.e. "half a
shekel... for the service of the tent of meeting".
   25. This concluding reference to the damage done the the Temple by Joash's predecessors represents an anticipation and adaptation of the editorial comment of 2 Chr 24,7:

Both Biblical sources note that the disregard of Joash's instructions on the part of their respective addressees. 2 Chr 24,5bβ states that "*the Levites* did not hasten it", while 2 Kgs 12,6 records that "by the twenty-third year of King Joash *the priests* had made no repairs on the house". Josephus, who earlier made Jehoaida the (direct) recipient of the royal injunction, likewise represents him (9,162a) as the one who ignores this, just as he also supplies a reason for his doing so: "The high priest, how-ever, did not do this, *realizing that no one would be well affected enough to offer the money...*". To this notice, in turn, he appends the dating indi-cation peculiar to 2 Kgs 12,6; see above. In Josephus' presentation (9,162b) the date is associated with the confrontation between Joash and his heedless officials (see 2 Kgs 12,7-8 // 2 Chr 24,6-7) as follows: "when in the twenty-third year of his reign the king summoned...". According to 2 Kgs 12,7 those called to account by Joash at that moment are "Jehoaida and the (other) priests", while 2 Chr 24,6 has the king confront Jehoaida alone regarding the latter's failure to compel the Levites to collect the Mosaic tax; see above. The Josephan Joash's sum-mons are extended to Jehoiada and the Levites. In both Kings and Chron-icles Joash's confrontation of the hearers opens with the question of "why" they have not done as directed. Josephus turns this question into an accusatory statement formulated in indirect address: "... after charg-ing them with having disobeyed his orders...". He couples this accusa-tion with a renewed directive ("he commanded them in future to look after the repair [ἐπισκευῆς; cf. ἐπισκευήν, 9,161] of the temple") somewhat reminiscent of Joash's word to the priests cited in 12,8bβ: "hand it [i.e. the money they are no longer to collect, v. 8bα] over for the repair of the house". On the other hand, he has no equivalent to the notice of 12,9 about the priests' "agreeing" henceforth neither to collect money nor to "repair the house", the latter part of which would conflict with the injunction just issued by Joash in his own account[26]. Rather, he proceeds immediately to his version of the Biblical notices on the "collection chest". In 2 Kgs 12,10 it is Jehoaida, acting on his own initiative, who takes measures regarding this chest, whereas in 2 Chr 24,8 an unspecified

"For the sons of Athaliah, that wicked woman, had broken into (RSV; MT פָּרְצוּ, BL κατέσπασαν) the house of God; and had also used all the dedicated things of the house of the Lord for the Baals". In his rewording of this statement Josephus has Joash accuse not only Athaliah's sons, but also the queen herself and her husband Joram, of abusing the Temple. This rendering echoes 9,154 where Josephus refers to "the temple of Baal which Othlia and her husband Joram had built in contempt of the nation's God...".

26. Recall in this connection that Josephus has already "anticipated" (elements of) Joash's address to Jehoiada of 2 Chr 24,6-7 in his version of the king's opening directive to the high priest in 9,161b.

"they" does so at the command of the king. In accord with his highlighting the role of Jehoiada throughout our episode, Josephus follows Kings' presentation on the point. At the same time, however, he introduces the priest's initiative with an elaborate transitional phrase which itself picks up on, while also reversing, his earlier mention of Jehoiada's awareness of the people's unwillingness to contribute to the Temple's repair (see 9,162a). This inserted formulation (9,162c) runs: "... the high priest employed the following device for collecting the money, which the people willingly accepted". Thereafter (9,163a), he enumerates, with various minor embellishments, Jehoaida's measures regarding the chest as cited in 12,10a: "he made a *wooden* chest and, *having closed it on all sides*, made a *single* opening in it. Then he placed it in the temple[27] beside the altar (παρὰ τὸν βωμόν)[28]". In what follows, Josephus seems to rejoin the Chronicler's account, i.e. its 24,9 where "proclamation is made" to Judah and Jerusalem to bring the Mosaic tax (cf. 24,6); compare 2 Kgs 12,10b: "and the priests who guarded the threshold put in it (the chest) all the money that was brought into the house of the Lord". He does, however, specify the subject/source of the "proclamation" as Jehoiada himself: "... he told everyone to throw into it, through the opening, as much as he wished, for the repair (ἐπισκευήν; see 9,161.162) of the temple". In this presentation, Jehoaida's initiative as cited in Kings (12,10a) is further accentuated. On the other hand, in contrast to Kings, but in the line of Chronicles, Josephus here represents ordinary Temple visitors depositing their offerings directly into the chest rather than having the priests do this for them.

Josephus rounds off (9,163b) his mention of Jehoiada's "command"[29] with a notice on its effect inspired by 2 Chr 24,10: "To this request all the people (πᾶς ὁ λαός = BL 24,10) were well disposed[30] [contrast 9,161: Jehoiada realized that no one would be well affected enough to offer the money], *and they collected much gold and silver, vying with one another in bringing it in*". 2 Kgs 12,11 // 2 Chr 24,11 describe, with divergent details, what was done with the contents of the collection chest. Josephus' parallel (9,164a) reads like an expanded conflation of

27. Compare the more complicated localizations cited in 2 Kgs 12,10 ("on the right side as one enters the house of the Lord") and 2 Chr 24,8 ("outside the gate of the house of the Lord").

28. Compare L 4 Rgns 12,10 παρὰ τὸ θυσιαστήριον (B παρὰ ἰαμειβείν).

29. Josephus uses the same verbal form, i.e. ἐκέλευσεν, for Joash's "commanding" Jehoiada to dispatch the priests and Levites to collect the Temple tax (9,161) and for the latter's "commanding" the people to deposit their offerings in the chest (9,163). The usage accentuates the priest's stature.

30. Compare 2 Chr 24,10: "all the princes and all the people rejoiced (so MT L; B gave)".

elements from both source presentations. It goes: "Then, when the scribe[31] and the priest of the treasury (ἱερεὺς τῶν γαζοφυλακείων)[32] had emptied the chest (κενοῦντες ... τὸν θησαυρόν)[33] *and in the presence of the king*[34] had counted (ἀριθμοῦντες; BL 12,11 ἠρίθμησαν) the sum that had been collected[35], they put the chest back in the same place. And this they would do every day[36]".

The Biblical accounts (12,12-13a // 24,12) continue with mention of a two-stage process of distribution of the collected funds to those working on the repair of the Temple. In 2 Kgs 12,12 those initiating the process would appear to be the two officials cited in 12,11, whereas 2 Chr 24,12 specifies that it was rather "the king and Jehoaida (+ the priest, BL)". Josephus (9,164b) follows Chronicles on the point, incorporating its reference into a transitional phrase of his own composition: *"when the people had put in what seemed a sufficient amount of money*[37], *the high priest* Jōdas and King Joas[38] *sent...".* In both 2 Kgs 12,12 and 2 Chr 24,12 those initiating the distribution of the money to the Temple workers act through "middlemen" ("those who had charge of the work of the house of the Lord", Chronicles) to whom they confide the sums to be used in hiring various categories of artisans. Jose-

---

31. 2 Kgs 12,11 // 2 Chr 24,11 specify the "scribe *of the king*". In beginning immediately with mention of this official, Josephus leaves aside the respective transitional phrases of Kings ("and whenever they saw that there was much money in the chest..." [see, however, 9,164b and cf. n. 37]) and Chronicles ("and whenever the chest was brought to the king's officers by the Levites, when they saw there was much money in it...").

32. Josephus' designation for this second official reflects the title used in 2 Chr 24,11, i.e. "the officer of the chief priest (BL ὁ προστάτης τοῦ ἱερέως τοῦ μεγάλου)" as opposed to 2 Kgs 12,11 ("the high priest [BL ὁ ἱερεὺς ὁ μέγας]"), i.e. Jehoiada himself.

33. Compare BL 24,11: καὶ ἐξεκένωσαν τὸ γλωσσόκομον. 2 Kgs 12,11 does not mention an "emptying" of the chest as such.

34. This reference to Joash's involvement in the disposition of the funds collected has no counterpart in either source; it underscores the king's continued concern with the Temple repair project.

35. For this mention of the officials' "counting" the money, Josephus draws on Kings after following Chronicles for its *Sondergut* item concerning the "emptying" of the chest; see above. On the other hand, he leaves aside Kings' further reference, peculiar to itself, about the officials "tying up the money".

36. These last two items of Josephus' notice here in 9,164a are drawn from the *Sondergut* conclusion of 2 Chr 24,11. He does, however, omit the closing words of that verse: "(the two officials) collected money in abundance"; cf. his anticipation of this in 9,163, i.e. "(the people) collected much silver and gold".

37. This phrase might be seen as Josephus' "delayed" equivalent to the expression "whenever they saw that there was much money in the chest" at the opening of 2 Kgs 12,11 which he passed over earlier; see n. 31.

38. Note Josephus' reversal here of the sequence in which 2 Chr 24,12 mentions the two figures. Note too that he adds the name "Joas" to Chronicles' title "the king". His designation of "Jōdas" as "the high priest" corresponds to the BL plus ("the priest") in 24,12; see above.

phus dispenses with the Biblical intermediaries; the high priest and king themselves "... hire (μισθούμενοι; BL 24,12 ἐμισθοῦντο) stone-cutters (λατόμους, so BL 24,12) and carpenters (οἰκοδόμους, so BL 12,12)[39]". Following their respective shared notices on the hiring of Temple workers, Kings and Chronicles diverge once again. 2 Kgs 12,13b speaks of additional uses of the collected monies, i.e. "to buy timber and quarried stone for making repairs on the house of the Lord, and for any outlay upon the repairs of the house". 2 Chr 24,13, on the contrary, proceeds immediately to describe the workers' efforts and their results: "so those who were engaged in the work labored, and the repairing went forward in their hands, and they restored the house of God to its proper condition and strengthened it". Josephus, for his part, follows Kings here, even while condensing its wording markedly: "(Jehoaida and Joas, see above) ordered *great* timbers (ξύλα, so BL 12,13b) *of the finest wood*[40]".

As this juncture Josephus' sources evidence an apparent "contradiction": 2 Kgs 12,14 states that no money was used to make vessels of any sort for the Temple; rather all money collected was distributed to the workmen (12,15), no accounting being asked of the supervisors because of their honesty (12,16). By contrast, 2 Chr 24,14a affirms that, once the Temple repairs were complete, the money left over was utilized in fabricating liturgical vessels. Faced with this discrepancy, Josephus (9,165a) opts to follow Chronicles[41]. His version of 24,14 reads: "And, when the temple had been repaired[42], they spent the money[43] that was left over – *it was no small amount* – for bowls (κρατῆρας) and pitchers (οἰνοχόας) and cups (ἐκπώματα) and other vessels (σκεύη)[44]".

39. Josephus speaks of only two categories of artisans; by contrast 2 Kgs 12,12b-13a mentions four (RSV: "carpenters and builders... masons and stone cutters") and 2 Chr 24,12 three (or four): "masons and carpenters... and workers in iron and bronze" (RSV).

40. Note Josephus' embellishment of Kings' simple mention of "timber" here.

41. Josephus' option for Chronicles over Kings in this instance could reflect the consideration that the former's presentation underscores the magnitude of the sums collected – there was so much left over from the repair of the Temple that a variety of vessels could be fabricated from the remainder. As such, the Chronicler's notice points up the Jews' devotion to their Temple in still more impressive fashion than does Kings.

42. Josephus omits the indication of 2 Chr 24,14 about the surplus money being "brought before the king and Jehoiada".

43. Literally: "gold and silver" (χρυσὸν καὶ ἄργυρον; see the same phrase in reverse order in 9,163 where the people collect "much silver and gold"). Compare τὸ κατάλοιπον τοῦ ἀργυρίου, BL 24,14a.

44. Of the four Greek terms in the above sequence, only the final, general one has an equivalent in BL 24,14a. With the three previous, more specific terms of the sequence, compare, however, Josephus' (Biblically unparalleled) enumeration of the items that Josiah directs the high priest Hilkiah to make from the money left over after the repair of the Temple in *AJ* 10,57: κρατῆρας καὶ σπονδεῖα καὶ φιάλας.

Kings and Chronicles go their own way also in their respective conclusions to the Temple repair episode. 2 Kgs 12,17 ends its account with the notice that the monies generated by the guilt and sin offerings remained the property of the priests rather than being "brought into" the Temple. 2 Chr 24,14b concludes rather: "and they offered burnt offerings in the house of the Lord all the days of Jehoiada". Here again, Josephus (9,165b) aligns himself with the Chronicler's formulation: "... and they continued *day by day* to enrich the altar with costly sacrifices. Thus, so long as Jōdas lived (ἐφ᾽ ὅσον Ἰώδας χρόνον ἔζη)[45], these things were done with the required care".

3. *Joash's Defection*

In Kings, Joash's initiative on behalf of the Temple (12,5-17) is abruptly juxtaposed with his humiliation in having to buy off the Syrians (12,18-19). The Chronicler interposes between these two happenings an account of Joash's defection which provides a characteristic theological rationale ("immediate retribution") for what befalls him. This Chronistic insertion stands in 24,15-22; Josephus' parallel is 9,166-169.

The Chronicler's account of Joash's defection (24,17) opens (24,15-16) with a preparatory notice on the death (at age 130) and burial among the Judean kings of his mentor Jehoaida. In Josephus (9,166) an expanded version of this notice is incorporated into his mention of the royal apostasy itself. It reads as follows: "But, after Jōdas died at the age (see 24,17aα) of one hundred and thirty years, *having been an upright man and good* (δίκαιος ... καὶ ... χρηστός)[46] *in all ways*, and was buried in the royal sepulchres at Jerusalem [24,16: in the city of David with the kings] because he had restored the kingdom to the line of David[47], King Joas proved faithless...".

According to 2 Chr 24,17 Joash was induced to defect by "the princes of Judah" who, following Jehoiada's death, appeared before the king to do him homage and to whom Joash "hearkened". Josephus, on the contrary, represents Joash going astray on his volition: "(after the death of Jōdas)... Joas proved faithless to the service of God (προέδωκεν ...

---

45. Note the echo of 9,157: παρὰ πάντα τὸν χρόνον ὄν Ἰώδας ἐβίωσεν.
46. For this collocation see on 9,133.
47. This motivation for Jehoiada's burial among the kings represents a specification of that given in 2 Chr 24,16b ("because he had done good in Israel, and toward God and his house"), recalling the high priest's initiative in re-establishing the legitimate dynasty; see 2 Kings 11 // 2 Chronicles 23 = AJ 9,140-156.

τὴν ἐπιμέλειαν τὴν πρὸς τὸν θεόν)⁴⁸". Thereby, he excludes the "extenuating circumstances" Chronicles posits for the apostate Joash (just as he makes the severity of the king's subsequent punishment appear all the more deserved). In 2 Chr 24,18a the outcome of Joash's heeding the "princes" is that "they" together forsake the Temple and begin serving "the Asherim and the idols". Josephus' presentation continues to portray Joash himself as the instigator of the defection which, in turn, the historian describes in much more general terms than does the Chronicler. His statement (9,167a) on the matter runs: "and together with him [Joash] were corrupted (συνδιεφθάρησαν) the leaders of the people (οἱ τοῦ πλήθους προτεύοντες; BL 24,17 οἱ ἄρχοντες Ἰούδα)⁴⁹ so that they transgressed against what was right (τὰ δίκαια; compare δίκαιος of Jehoiada, 9,166) and held among them to be the highest good⁵⁰".

2 Chr 24,18b-19 juxtaposes two notices concerning the sequels to Joash's defection: "wrath comes upon" Judah and Jerusalem (v. 18b) and the Lord sends prophets of repentance whose "testimony" goes unheeded (v. 19). Josephus effects (9,167b) a smoother linkage between the two items: "Thereupon God, being displeased (δυσχεράνας)⁵¹ *at this change of heart in the king*⁵² *and the others*, sent (πέμπει; BL 24,19 ἀπέστειλεν) *the* prophets (τοὺς προφήτας)⁵³ to protest solemnly (διαμαρτυρησομένους; BL 24,19 διεμαρτύραντο) *against their actions* and to make them leave off their wrong-doing [24,19: to bring them

48. Contrast Josephus' statement (9,157) that Joash, when under Jehoiada's tutelage, περὶ τὴν τοῦ θεοῦ θρησκείαν φιλοτιμίαν. With the construction of 9,166 above, compare Samuel's accusation of the people in *AJ* 6,90: προδεδώκατε τὴν θρησκείαν καὶ τὴν εὐσέβειαν.

49. Josephus' statement about the king's self-corruption influencing the leaders (rather than vice versa as in Chronicles) echoes his remark concerning the defection of Rehoboam in *AJ* 8,252 (= 2 Chr 12,1): "... the morals of subjects are corrupted simultaneously (συνδιαφθείρεται) with the characters of *their rulers*...".

50. With the above "generalization" of 2 Chr 24,18's reference to the king and princes' "serving the Asherim and the idols", compare 9,161, where for Joash's statement of 2 Chr 24,7b about the sons of Athaliah using dedicated Temple objects "for the Baals", Josephus has him simply aver that Athaliah's family "had left the Temple crumbling".

51. Josephus' other uses of δυχεραίνω with God as subject are *AJ* 3,218; 4,107; 5,14; 6,91; cf. 9,87 where Ben-hadad is said to be "greatly disheartened at having incurred God's displeasure (δυσμενῆ)". With this reference to God's "displeasure" with Joash, Josephus elucidates the indeterminate Biblical mention of "wrath" coming upon nation and capital (24,18b).

52. In this inserted Josephan specification of the object of the divine "displeasure", note the continued emphasis on Joash as the primary guilty party.

53. 2 Chr 24,19 (MT and BL) speaks of "prophets" without the definite article; contrast *AJ* 10,39 where Josephus reads "(God) sends prophets" in place of 2 Kgs 21,10's "the Lord spoke through the hand of his servants *the* prophets".

back (BL ἐπιστρέψαι) to the Lord]". He then goes (9,168a) to greatly amplify the Chronicler's concluding reference (24,19) to the inefficacy of (the) prophets' words ("they would not give heed"):

> But they indeed were seized with so strong a love (ἔρωτα) and so terrible a desire (δεινὴν ἐπιθυμίαν)[54] for it [i.e. their wrong-doing; see 9,167][55] that, heeding neither the punishment which those before them had suffered together with all their house for outraging the ordinances (ἐξυβρίσαντες εἰς τὰ νόμιμα)[56], nor what the prophets [see 9,167] had foretold, they refused to repent (μετανοῆσαι)[57] and turn back (μετελθεῖν) from the lawless course (παρανομήσαντες) which they had taken.

2 Chr 24,20-22 (= AJ 9,168b-169) exemplifies Joash's persistence in apostasy with its story of his execution of Zechariah, the son of his mentor Jehoiada. That story commences in v. 20 with the spirit of God "clothing" Zechariah who addresses the people with an accusatory question and announcement of retribution. Zechariah's initiative, in turn, prompts an unspecified "they" to "conspire against him", this eventuating in their stoning him in the Temple court at the command of Joash (v. 21) who thus shows himself completely "unmindful" of the benefits done him by Zechariah's father (v. 22a). Josephus rearranges (9,168b) the sequence of 24,20-21, thereby throwing into relief the king's reprobate directive: "Moreover the king even ordered Zacharias, the son of the high priest Jōdas, to be stoned to death in the temple...[58]". To this mention of Joash's command drawn from 24,21b, Josephus next appends an anticipated version of 24,22a: "... unmindful of the good works (τῶν ... εὐεργεσιῶν ... λαθόμενος; BL οὐκ ἐμνήσθη ... τοῦ ἐλέους) of his father...". Only thereafter, does he come (9,169a) to relate the content of 24,20, making this the motivation for Joash's directive: "... *because*, when God appointed him [Zechariah] to prophesy

54. Josephus' one other use of the above phrase "terrible desire" is in AJ 17,169 (of Herod's urge to scratch himself); cf. the related expressions in 6,279; 7,168. See n. 56.

55. With the above reference to Joash and the others having "so terrible a desire" for their wrongful deeds, compare the mention in 9,161 of the king's being "seized by a strong desire (ὁρμή) to renovate the Temple...". The reminiscence of that earlier formulation here in 9,168 underscores the extent of Joash's moral degeneration. See next note.

56. This precise expression occurs only here in Josephus; cf. AJ 4,13. With it compare Josephus' mention (9,157) of the youthful Joash "keeping strict observance of the ordinances (νομίμων)". Once again (see n. 55) a verbal reminiscence serves to underscore the king's moral decline.

57. On this term and its *Wortfeld* in Josephus, see the literature cited in BEGG, *Early Divided Monarchy*, pp. 31-32, n. 162.

58. With the above formulation Josephus turns the "execution notice" of 2 Chr 24,21b ("they stoned him... in *the court of* the house of the Lord") into the content of Joash's "command" alluded to there.

(προφητεύειν)[59], he stood in the midst of the people (στὰς ἐν μέσῳ τῷ πλήθει)[60] and counselled (συνεβούλευεν)[61] both them *and the king*[62] to do right (τὰ δίκαια πράττειν)[63], and warned them that they would suffer heavy punishment if they disobeyed[64]". The episode of Zechariah's martyrdom concludes in 24,22b with the victim's dying appeal "may the Lord see and avenge". Josephus (9,169b) elaborates: "As he died, however, Zacharias made God the witness (μάρτυρα; see διαμαρτυρησομένους, 9,167) and judge (δικαστήν; BL κρινάτω, compare MT וְיִדְרֹשׁ) *of what he had suffered in being so cruelly and violently* (βιαίως) *put to death for all his good counsel* (συμβουλίας; see συνεβούλευεν, 9,169a) *and for all that his father had done for Joas* [cf. unmindful of the good works of his father, 9,168b][65]".

4. *Syrian Incursion*

2 Kgs 12,18-19 and 2 Chr 24,23-24 converge in their basic story line of a Syrian incursion which results in ignominious losses for Joash. At the same time, the two accounts differ markedly in their particulars. Josephus' version (9,170-171a) eclectically combines elements of both presentations – compare his handling of the Temple repair episode above.

In line with 2 Chr 24,23aα ("at the end of the year the army of the Syrians came up against Joash"), Josephus' narrative (9,170a) opens with a transitional phrase that insists on the speed with which Joash's

59. This expression is Josephus' substitution for the mention of God's spirit (BL πνεῦμα θεοῦ) "clothing" Zechariah in 24,20a. On Josephus' tendency to avoid Biblical uses of πνεῦμα in reference to either the divine or human "spirit", see on 9,10.

60. This phrase is very similiar to the one used in *AJ* 8,231 in Josephus' version of 1 Kgs 13,1 where a "man of God" (called "Jadōn" by Josephus) from Judah confronts Jeroboam I, i.e. σταθεὶς ἐν μέσῳ τῷ πλήθει. Compare BL 24,20a: καὶ ἀνέστη ἐπάνω τοῦ λαοῦ.

61. In introducing his reproduction of Zechariah's words with this verb, Josephus, in accord with his standard practice, leaves aside the *Botenformel* of 24,20b.

62. In 2 Chr 24,20b Zechariah's words are directed to the people globally; Josephus' singling out Joash for explicit mention here is in line with his consistent highlighting of the king's responsibility for the negative course taken after Jehoiada's death.

63. This phrase echoes (positively) the negative formulation of 9,167 πλημμελεῖν εἰς τὰ δίκαια; cf. the qualification of Jehoaida as δίκαιος in 9,166.

64. This phrase represents Josephus' (more determinate) version of Zechariah's closing words according to 24,20: "because you have forsaken the Lord, he has forsaken you".

65. Josephus lacks the embellishments on the circumstances of Zechariah's murder (e.g., its occurring on Yom Kippur; for this detail, see, e.g., TC 2 Chr 24,20) and the "seething" of his shed blood until the Babylonians finally avenged his slaying by executing many of the surviving Jews found in Jewish (and Christian) tradition. On the tradition, see S.H. BLANK, *The Death of Zechariah in Rabbinic Literature*, in *HUCA* 12-13 (1937-1938) 327-346.

previous crimes were requited: "It was not long, however, before the
king paid the penalty (δίκην, see δικαστήν; 9,169) for his unlawful
acts (παρηνόμησεν; see παρανομήσαντες, 9,168)". He then goes
on to cite several items peculiar to 2 Kgs 12,18 (name of the king
of Syria, his capture of "Gath"). His notice (9,170b) on the Syrian
incursion itself thus reads: "For Azaēlos, king of Syria[66], invaded his
(Joash's) country[67] and, after subduing Gitta (Γίτταν; BL 12,18 Γέθ)
and despoiling it, he prepared to march against *him* [Joash; see 24,23a
supra] to Jerusalem [cf. 2 Kgs 12,18: Hazael set his face to go up
against Jerusalem]...[68]".

Josephus likewise follows Kings' distinctive presentation in his
account of Joash's "buying off" the Syrians with the palace and Temple
treasures. In so doing, he introduces (9,170c) his parallel to 2 Kgs 12,19a
with mention of the psychological state which prompts Joash to do as
he does, i.e. "Joas, fearing (φοβηθείς) this [i.e. Hazael's advance on
Jerusalem]...[69]". He then continues: "... (Joash) emptied [12,19: took]
all the treasures of God and of the palace (βασιλείων; the codices
MSPE read βασιλέων)[70] and, taking down the dedicatory offerings (τὰ
ἀναθήματα; BL 12,19: τὰ ἅγια)[71], sent them to the Syrian *to buy himself off* (ὠνούμενος) *with these from being besieged and endangering*

66. This figure (called "Hazael" in 2 Kgs 12,18) was previously cited by Josephus in
9,159 as the devastator of Jehu's kingdom; in his presentation then both the contemporary
kings, Jehu and Joash, have their lands overrun by the same Syrian ruler in punishment
for their disregard of God's laws; see 9,160.170.

67. Cf. 2 Chr 24,23aβ: "The Syrians came to Judah and Jerusalem".

68. Josephus lacks an equivalent as such to the *Sondergut* sequence of 2 Chr 24,23b-
24: "(the Syrians) destroyed all the princes of the people from among the people, and
sent all their spoil to the king of Damascus. Though the army of the Syrians had come
with few men, the Lord delivered into their hand a very great army, because they had forsaken the Lord God of their fathers. Thus they executed judgment on Joash". In so
doing he downplays the "theological component" of the episode which the Chronicler
here highlights.

69. Also elsewhere, Josephus inserts references to the "fear" which causes a king to
either surrender Jerusalem to an advancing enemy or "buy off" that enemy; see *AJ* 8,258
("out of fear" Rehoboam admits Shishak).304 ("fearing" [φοβηθείς] Baasha's invasion,
Asa sends silver and gold to the king of Syria); 10,96 ("in fear of" Jeremiah's prophecies, Jehoiakim opens Jerusalem to Nebuchadnezzar).

70. Compare 2 Kgs 12,19: "all the gold that was found in the treasuries (BL θησαυροῖς)
of the house of the Lord and the house of the king".

71. Josephus omits the specification of 2 Kgs 12,19 that the "votive gifts" in question
were those dedicated by Jehoshaphat, Jehoram and Ahaziah. Josephus' omission here is
readily understandable given the Biblical (and his own) presentation of the last two of
these three rulers as "bad" kings. He passes over as well the source verse's mention of
Joash's own "votive gifts" – likewise understandably given his immediately preceding
portrayal of Joash's defection borrowed by him from the Chronicler's *Sondergut*. Note
too that Josephus reverses the sequence of 2 Kgs 12,19 where Joash's handling of the
"votive gifts" is cited before his dispatch of gold from the treasuries.

his entire power[72]". 2 Kgs 12,19 ends with a laconic notice on the result of Joash's desperate initiative: "Then Hazael went away from Jerusalem". Here again, Josephus (9,171a) elaborates: "Accordingly the other [Hazael], *being persuaded by the very large amount of money* (τῇ τῶν χρημάτων ὑπερβολῇ)[73], did not lead his army against Jerusalem".

5. *Closing Notices*

2 Kgs 12,20-22 first gives the standard source notice for Joash (v. 20) and then its account of his violent death (v. 21), along with appended mention of his two named assassins (v. 22a), plus his burial and succession by his son Amaziah (v. 22b). 2 Chr 24,25-27 rearranges the sequence of these items as follows: Joash's death (v. 25a), burial (v. 25b), names of his assassins (v. 26), source notice (v. 27a), and accession of Amaziah (v. 27b). In his own conclusion for Joash (9,171b-172), Josephus, in accord with his regular practice, simply dispenses with the "source notice" of 12,20 // 24,27a. He introduces (9,171b) his account of the king's death with what seems like a reminiscence of the *Sondergut* notice of 24,25aα (the Syrians depart from Joash "leaving him severely wounded", BL ἐν μαλακίαις μεγάλαις), i.e. "but Joas, being stricken by a very severe illness (νόσῳ ... χαλεπῇ)...[74]". In that condition, Josephus goes on to record, the king "was attacked by some of his friends (τῶν φίλων)[75], who had plotted (ἐπεβούλευσαν; BL 24,25 ἐπέθεντο)[76] against the king to avenge the death of Zacharias, the son

72. This inserted explication of the purpose of Joash's initiative underscores as well the humiliation involved for the king.

73. Also this embellishment accentuates the enormity of Joash's loss and humiliation; compare *AJ* 8,305 where in his narrative of Asa's "buying" Syrian assistance against Israel (= 1 Kgs 15,18-20 // 2 Chr 16,2-4) Josephus introduces mention that the Syrian king's "gladly accepted the large sum of money (τῶν χρημάτων τὸ πλῆθος)".

74. Josephus' formulation here, it will be noted, leaves the "source" of Joash's "malady" quite indeterminate; contrast 2 Chr 24,25 which certainly seems to suggest that the Syrians were responsible for the king's "wounds" (recall in this connection that Josephus has no parallel to the notice of 24,23 about the Syrians "destroying all the princes of the people"). In Josephus' (and Kings') presentation(s), in contrast to the Chronicler's, then the Syrians, having been "paid off" by Joash, do no actual harm to either him or his retinue.

75. Some codices read rather "the friends of Zacharias"; see MARCUS, *Josephus*, VI, p. 92, n. 4; p. 93, n. a. Josephus' substitution of "friends" for the Biblical designation of Joash's assassins as his "servants" (so 2 Kgs 12,21 // 2 Chr 24,25aβ) is in line with a recurrent tendency in his rewriting of Biblical history, see BEGG, *Early Divided Monarchy*, p. 115, n. 708.

76. The above verb ironically echoes the reference in 9,158 to Joash's "escaping the plot (ἐπιβουλήν)" made against him by Athaliah. Having survived the usurper's plot, Joash now falls victim to one initiated by his own "friends".

of Jōdas[77], and was done to death by them". In limiting his narrative of Joash's assassination to the above points, Josephus leaves aside several further, though divergent, particulars found in the Biblical sources: the site of the murder ("in the house of Millo, on the way that goes down to Silla", 2 Kgs 12,21/ "on his bed", 2 Chr 24,25) and the names of his killers, i.e. Jozacar and Jehozabad (12,22a // 24,26)[78]. Rather, he proceeds immediately (9,172a) to the burial of the murdered king. On this point as well, Josephus was faced with a divergence between his sources. 2 Kgs 12,22bα avers simply that Joash was "buried with his fathers in the city of David", i.e. he received the regular burial accorded deceased Judean monarchs. By contrast, 2 Chr 24,25bβ informs us that the apostate king – as he ends up being in the Chronicler's account – was buried "in the city of David", but "not in the tombs of the kings". As might be expected given his earlier inclusion of the Chronicler's *Sondergut* account of Joash's defection, Josephus aligns himself with Chronicles on the point: "... though he was buried (θάπτεται, 2 Par ἔθαψαν) in Jerusalem (12,22b // 24,25b in the city of David), it was not in the sepulchres of his forefathers (ἐν ταῖς θήκαις ... τῶν προγόνων)...[79]". To this burial notice taken over from Chronicles Josephus appends a final, brief invocation of Joash's defection, this explaining why he was denied a proper royal interment: "... because of his impiety (ἀσεβὴς γενόμενος)".

In 2 Kgs 12,22b notice of Joash's burial is followed immediately by mention of Amaziah's succession. The Chronicler, on the other hand, interposes other material (24,26-27a; see above) between his rendition of these two items which stand in 24,25b and 27b, respectively. Josephus (9,172b) follows the Chronicler also in this regard, although his interposed material has a content peculiar to himself. Specifically, in between his notices on Joash's burial and the accession of "Amasias" at the very end of 9,172 he pauses to make use of a source chronological datum he had earlier passed over; see above. Whereas, however, 2 Kgs 12,1-2a // 2 Chr 24,1 cite Joash's age at accession (7 years) and length of reign (40 years), Josephus, who has already adduced the former item (see 9,157),

---

77. Compare 2 Chr 24,25aβ: "... because of the blood of the son (so BL; MT sons) of Jehoiada the priest".

78. 2 Chr 24,26 supplies as well ethnic designations for (what it takes to be) the mothers of the two assassins as cited by Kings, making one an "Ammonitess", the other a "Moabitess". Josephus' non-mention of the Biblical names is in accord with his tendency not to overburden his account with the names of minor characters whose peculiarities might prove offputting to Gentile readers.

79. Compare 9,166: (Jehoaida is buried) ἐν ταῖς βασιλικαῖς θήκαις ἐν Ἱεροσολύμοις.

here in 9,172b, in line with his regular practice, combines these two figures into the statement that Joash lived 47 years.

Conclusions: *Josephus' Rewriting of 2 Kings 12 // 2 Chronicles 24*

The presence of *Sondergut* items from both 2 Kings 12 and 2 Chronicles 24 in *AJ* 9,157-172 as noted above makes clear, first of all, that for his Joash account Josephus drew on both these sources, rather than using one to the exclusion of the other. Given the overall agreement among the textual witnesses for the two chapters (MT, BL, Targum), as well as Josephus' own paraphrasing tendencies, it is does not, however, seem possible to determine with any assurance which particular text-form(s) of the two sources Josephus was in fact working with in our passage. I would recall, noneless, several of our negative findings on the question: Josephus either did not know or opted against the distinctive reading of BL regarding the husband of the "two wives" cited in 2 Chr 24,3 (= 9,158; see n. 8), just as he gives no evidence of familiarity with the various peculiarities of TC (e.g., on Zechariah's intervention; see TC 2 Chr 24,20 and compare 9,169; cf. n. 65).

How then does Josephus deal with his sources for Joash? Most notably, perhaps, he freely alternates between Kings and Chronicles for the details of his presentation in those instances (i.e. the Temple repair, the Syrian incursion and Joash's demise) where those sources generally parallel each other but go their own ways in many particulars. In so doing, Josephus evidences his intention of "making room" for some special material of each *Vorlage*. In addition, Josephus modifies both the style/wording and content of his sources. Biblical parataxis becomes a better Greek hypotaxis; direct discourse is consistently turned into indirect. Twice, he introduces historic present forms (πέμπει, 9,167; θάπτε-ται, 9,172). The names of minor characters (i.e. Joash's two assassins) are avoided, as is 2 Chr 24,20's mention of "the Spirit of God". Chronicles' cultic particulars give way to more general formulations, while Joash's killer "servants" are Hellenized into royal "friends" (9,171; compare 12,20 // 24,25). Joash's reference to the Mosaic "tax for the tent of testimony" in 2 Chr 24,6.8 is specified, on the basis of the earlier Biblical text to which the king is alluding (Exod 30,13), as "half a shekel" (9,161). Instead of Joash's length of reign (so 2 Kgs 12,2 // 2 Chr 24,1), Josephus (9,172) reports his age at death.

On occasion, Josephus re-arranges the sequence of source material, see, e.g., his "anticipation" of elements of Joash's second discourse on the repair of the Temple (2 Chr 24,6-7) in his version of the king's first pronouncement on the subject (9,161; compare 24,5abα). See also his re-arrangement of the components of 2 Chr 24,20-22a in 9,168b-169a. Under the heading of "re-arrangements" one might also recall Josephus' insertion of his parallel to 2 Kgs 10,31-36 (closing notices for Jehu), i.e. 9,159-160, within the body of his Joash narrative, as also his re-ordering of the content of the Kings passage itself.

Josephus omits relatively little material common to both his sources (or of the extended *Sondergut* segment, 2 Chr 24,15-22). In accord with his standard practice, he does, however, pass over the "source notice" of 2 Kgs 12,20 // 2 Chr 24,27a. Occasionally, too, Josephus simply omits items about which the sources differ, e.g., the place of Joash's assassination (2 Kgs 12,21a vs. 2 Chr 24,25a; compare 9,171b). Under the "omission rubric", we might also mention Josephus' simplification of his sources' presentation, e.g., high priest and king hire the Temple workers directly, rather than going through overseers (9,164b; compare 2 Kgs 12,11 // 2 Chr 24,12).

Josephus' additions to the Biblical accounts are also rather minor; see, e.g., the (provisional) concluding formula of 9,158b, the reason for the disregard of Joash's initial instructions (9,161; compare 2 Kgs 12,7 // 2 Chr 24,5bβ), and the characterization of Jehoiada as "upright and good in all ways" (9,166). Beyond such instances of actual "addition" to the sources' record, we also noted Josephus' more frequent practice of elaborating upon some bare Biblical datum, e.g., the wood procured for the Temple (9,164; compare 2 Kgs 12,13), the people's (eventual) enthusiastic response to the collection (9,162-163; compare 2 Chr 24,10), the hearers' disregard of Zechariah's admonition (9,168; compare 2 Chr 24,19), and the prophet's dying words (9,169; compare 24,24b).

Having reviewed Josephus' various rewriting techniques in *AJ* 9,157-172, we might now raise the wider question: given the application of those techniques, how does the Josephan presentation of Joash differ from the Biblical one(s)? Overall, it might be said that Josephus goes beyond the Bible in accentuating the stature and activity of the two main characters, i.e. Jehoiada and Joash. This is particularly the case for the latter figure whose initial zeal for God's law and Temple he highlights, just as he does his subsequent, self-initiated (compare 2 Chr 24,17-18) defection. In its concentration on the personage of Joash as a good man who comes to a bad end at the hands of an outraged Deity Josephus' story of this king is one that both Gentile and Jewish readers could readily appreciate in light of their individual literary traditions.

IX

JEHOAHAZ AND JOASH OF ISRAEL[1]
(9,173-185)

2 Kgs 11,1–12,21 // 2 Chr 22,10–24,27 constitute a "Judean bloc" focussed on the reigns of Athaliah and Joash in the South. Thereafter, however, the two works diverge: 2 Kings 13 shifts to a presentation of the two Northern kings whose reigns overlapped those of Joash of Judah, while 2 Chronicles 25 proceeds immediately to the next Southern ruler, i.e. Amaziah, whom Kings will treat only subsequently; see 14,1-22. Josephus follows the sequence of Kings in this instance, his account of the Israelite monarchs Jehoahaz and Joash (9,173-185) coming directly after his portrayal of Joash of Judah in 9,157-172. I divide up the parallel material of 2 Kings 13 and *AJ* 9,173-185 as follows: 1. Jehoahaz Introduced (9,173 = 13,1-2); 2. Syrian Invasion (9,174-175a = 13,7 [cf. 13,22a]); 3. Appeal & Delivery (9,175b-176 = 13,4-6 [+ 13,23]); 4. Framework Notices for Joash (9,177-178a = 13,[8]9-13); 5. The Arrows Episode (9,178b-181 = 13,14-19); 6. The Grave Incident (9,182-183 = 13,20-21); and 7. Joash's Triumph (and Death) (9,184-185 = 13,24-25).

1. *Jehoahaz Introduced*

Jehoahaz is (re-)introduced[2] in 2 Kgs 13,1 with a double chronological notice: acceding in the twenty-third year of Joash of Judah, Jehoahaz ruled seventeen years. The latter of these indications poses a problem in that according to 2 Kgs 13,10 Jehoahaz' son Joash succeeded his father in the *thirty-seventh* year[3] of his Judean namesake, whereas a tally of the chronological data of 13,1 (Jehoahaz acceded in Joash's 23th year and ruled 17 years himself) would place the Israelite Joash's accession in the

---

1. This chapter represents a reworking of my articles *Jehoahaz, King of Israel according to Josephus*, in *Sef* 55 (1995) 227-238 and *Joash and Elisha in Josephus*, ANT. *9.177-185*, in *Abr-Nahrain* 32 (1994) 28-46 which are used here by permission.

2. Jehoahaz' succession has been already mentioned (see 2 Kgs 10,35b) in passing as part of the closing notices for his father Jehu (10,31-36). Josephus' parallel to this initial mention of the former king comes in the context of his "displaced" parallel (9,159-160) to 10,31-36 at the end of 9,160; see there.

3. Thus MT and BL*. Other LXX MSS read 40, 36, and 39; see BHS.

fortieth regnal year of Joash of Judah. Josephus (9,173a) disposes of the difficulty by having "Jōazos" (Ἰωάζος, so 9,160)[4] accede in Joash's *twenty-first* (rather than twenty-third) year[5].

2 Kgs 13,2 pronounces an unqualified, stereotyped judgment on Jehoahaz:

> "He did what was evil in the sight of the Lord, and followed the sins of Jeroboam... which he made Israel to sin; he did not depart from them".

Josephus begins (9,173b) his evaluation of the king with an attenuating remark: "... although he was no imitator (μιμητής)[6] of his father...". This qualification concerning Jehoahaz' (cultic) depravity has no basis in the Biblical account as such[7]. It likely has in view the subsequent portrayal, common to both the Bible (see 2 Kgs 13,4) and Josephus himself (9,175), of Jehoahaz' imploring divine assistance in the face of Syrian aggression – something which his father Jehu is not described as doing in like circumstances; see 2 Kgs 10,32-33 = *AJ* 9,159-160a. Having thus mitigated the Biblical censure of Jehoahaz, Josephus next proceeds, nonetheless, to cite (a generalized version of) the charge of 2 Kgs 13,2b about the former's persistence in the sins of Jeroboam: "... he committed as many impieties (ἀσεβήσας; cf. the adjective ἀσεβῆς used of Joash of Judah in 9,172) as did the first (kings) who held God in contempt (τοῦ θεοῦ καταφρονήσαντες)[8]".

---

4. B 13,1 has Ἰωαχάς, L Ἰωαχάζ.

5. On the point see M. COGAN and H. TADMOR, *II Kings* (AB, 11), Garden City, NY, Doubleday, 1988, p. 143. (Josephus' subsequent chronology raises a problem of its own in that he dates, 9,177 [= 2 Kgs 13,10], the accession of Joash of Israel, following the seventeen year reign of his father Jehoahaz in the *thirty-seventh* year of Joash of Judah, whereas the figures he cites in 9,173 [21 + 17] would place Joash's accession rather in his Judean namesake's *thirty-eighth* year; possibly, the discrepancy relates to the difference among the witnesses regarding the synchronism of 13,10; see below.) On Josephus' monarchical chronology in relation to the Biblical one(s) in general; see E.R. THIELE, *The Mysterious Numbers of the Hebrew Kings*, Chicago, Chicago University Press, 1951, pp. 204-227.

6. The terminology of "(non-)imitation" figures prominently in Josephus' versions of the royal judgment notices of Kings and Chronicles; see, e.g., *AJ* 10,37 (Manasseh "imitating" [μιμούμενος] the lawless deeds of the Israelites...").47 (Amon "imitated [μιμησάμενος] the deeds of his father..."). Cf. also Josephus' remark on Jehoahaz' own son Joash: "he was a good man and in no way like his father in character" (*AJ* 9,178).

7. Rabbinic tradition likewise has nothing good to say of Jehoahaz (I owe this observation to Prof. L.H. Feldman).

8. Elsewhere Josephus uses the above construction καταφρονέω + "(the) God" as genitival object in *AJ* 3,15 (the Israelites); 4,215 (men); 12,357 (Antiochus). Compare *AJ* 1,43 (Eve is misled by the serpent to "scorn the commandment of God"); 7,151 ("God had been disregarded [καταφρονηθέντος] and impiously treated" [ἀσεβηθέντος – note the collocation of the same two verbs used of Jehoahaz in 9,173 here] by David); 8,251 (Rehoboam "showed disrespect for the worship of God"); 9,160 (Jehu "became contemptuous [καταφρονήσας] of holiness and the laws").

2. Syrian Invasion

2 Kgs 13,3 recounts the divine response to Jehoahaz' impiety (13,2): in his anger against Israel, the Lord hands it into the power of the Syrian rulers Hazael and Ben-hadad. This notice is subsequently picked up, following the parenthetical sequence of 13,4-6[9] in 13,7, which relates the drastic reduction of the Israelite forces effected by the (unnamed) king of Syria. Passing over the theological indication of 13,3[10], Josephus (9,174) moves immediately to his version of 13,7: "But the king of Syria *humbled* (ἐταπείνωσε) *him* [Jehoahaz] and reduced his force (δυνάμεως)[11] *from the very great one it was* to ten thousand foot soldiers (ὁπλίτας; BL πεζών) and fifty horsemen (πεντήκοντα ἱππεῖς = BL)[12] *when he marched against him and took from him many great cities* (πόλεις ... μεγάλας καὶ πολλάς)[13] and destroyed (διαφθείρας; L ἀπώλεσεν, B καταπάτησεν) his army[14]". To his parallel to 13,7 Josephus appends (9,175a) a *Rückverweis* which represents the Syrian devastation of Israel in the time of Jehoahaz as the fulfillment of an earlier announcement by the prophet Elisha; see *AJ* 9,90-92 (= 2 Kgs 8,10-13): "These (misfor-

9. This complex consists of the following items: Jehoahaz' appeal (v. 4a), the Lord's favorable response and the motivation for this (v. 4b), the sending of a "savior" to Israel (v. 5), and Israel's persistence in the sin of Jeroboam (v. 6). It is often regarded as a secondary insertion within 13,1-10; see the commentaries. It has as well a partial parallel in the displaced Jehoahaz segment 13,22-23. Josephus will present his version of 13,4-6 in 9,176, following his rendering of 13,7 in 9,174(-175); see below.

10. Compare his non-reproduction of the similar notice of 2 Kgs 10,32a ("in those [Jehu's] days the Lord began to cut off parts of Israel") in his rendering of 10,31-36 in 9,159-160.

11. This term is Josephus' precising substitute for the word "people" (MT עַם, BL λαός) of 2 Kgs 13,7.

12. 2 Kgs 13,7 also speaks of the (mere) "ten chariots" left to Jehoahaz. By omitting this item, while conversely inserting a reference to the "very great" force Israel earlier possessed (see above in the text), Josephus accentuates the extent of Israel's losses at the hands of the Syrians.

13. This "un-Biblical" indication continues Josephus' accentuation of the damage inflicted by the Syrians (see previous note). He likely found inspiration for this insertion in the prophecy of Elisha to Hazael, the future king of Syria, as cited by him in *AJ* 9,91 (= 2 Kgs 8,12): "you will burn their strongest cities (πόλεις)", to which he will introduce an explicit allusion in 9,175; see below. Another inspiration for Josephus' mention of the Syrian conquest of Israelite "cities" here might be 2 Kgs 13,25 (= *AJ* 9,184) which states, without the reader having been previously informed of the matter, that Joash of Israel regained from Ben-hadad "the cities" which the latter's father Hazael had seized from Jehoahaz. Unlike the Bible then Josephus "sets up" this later item via his inserted reference to the Syrian seizure of Israelite cities during Jehoahaz' reign.

14. Josephus leaves aside the image with which 2 Kgs 13,7 concludes, i.e. (the king of Syria had made the Israelite forces) "like the dust at threshing". The participle διαφθείρας as used here in 9,174 echoes the form διέφθειρε employed in 9,159 of Hazael's "ravaging" the Trans-jordan in the time of Jehoahaz' father Jehu.

tunes) the Israelite people (ὁ ... λαός)[15] suffered (ἔπαθεν)[16] in accordance with the prophecy (κατὰ τὴν ... προφητείαν) of Elisha[17], who had foretold (προεῖπε) that Azaēlos [= Biblical Hazael] would kill (ἀποκτείναντα) his master [i.e. Ben-hadad][18] and become king (βασιλεύσειν) of Syria and Damascus (τῶν Σύρων καὶ Δαμασκηνῶν)[19]".

3. *Appeal & Delivery*

Having presented his parallel to 2 Kgs 13,(3).7 in 9,174-175a, Josephus now (9,175b) gives his amplified version 13,4a ("Jehoahaz besought [BL ἐδεήθη] [the face of] the Lord"). This reads: "But Jōazos, *being (helpless) before such great difficulties* (κακοῖς)[20], had recourse to prayer and supplication (ἐπὶ δέησιν καὶ ἱκετείαν ... κατέφυγε)[21] to God (τοῦ θεοῦ)[22] *and begged Him to save him from the*

15. The codices SP (followed by Dindorf and Bekker) read rather βασιλεύς, the reference being to Jehoahaz.

16. Note the verbal echo here of 9,90 where Elisha, speaking to Hazael, refers to "the great ills which the [Israelite] people (ὁ λαός) was about to suffer (πάσχειν)..." because of him.

17. For the phrase "according to the prophecy of Elisha" see on 9,85. It will recur in 9,185.

18. In both the Bible (2 Kgs 8,10) and Josephus himself (9,90) all Elisha actually predicts to Hazael is that the reigning king Ben-Hadad will, in fact, "die" of his current sickness. Here in 9,175 Josephus transposes into a prophecy by Elisha the action subsequently undertaken by Hazael who according to 2 Kgs 8,15 = 9,92 took it upon himself to ensure the fulfillment of the prophet's announcement by suffocating the hapless Ben-hadad.

19. Compare the wording of Elisha's announcement to Hazael in 9,92 (= 2 Kgs 8,13b) "(he [Elisha] replied) that God had revealed to him that Azaēlos was to be king of Syria (τῆς Συρίας ... βασιλεύειν)". The above double designation, literally "(king of) the Syrians and the Damascenes" has its equivalent in the notice which Josephus attaches to his version of the encounter between Elisha and Hazael in 9,93 "(Hazael) was in great favour with the Syrians and the people of Damascus (τῶν Σύρων καὶ τοῦ δήμου τῶν Δαμασκενῶν)". Josephus' insistence, via the above inserted *Rückverweis*, on the realization of Elisha's announcements to Hazael is in line with his recurrent concern to underscore the "truth" of Biblical prophecies understood as accurate "predictions". The insertion here in 9,175 further has a counterpart in Josephus' expanded rendering of 2 Kgs 10,32b-33 in 9,159b which, as we noted in our discussion of that passage, functions as an implicit fulfillment of Elisha's prediction about Hazael's future depredations cited in 9,91.

20. With this inserted transitional phrase, Josephus continues to accentuate the gravity of Israel's plight; see above on his version of 2 Kgs 13,7 in 9,174.

21. This is Josephus' only use of the above phrase "have recourse to prayer...". Likewise the collocation of the above two terms for "appeal" occurs only here in his writings; cf. the similar formulations in *AJ* 10,242; 15,188.

22. Josephus' reference to "(the) God" here substitutes for "the Lord" of 2 Kgs 13,4. His formulation "prayer and supplication to God" likewise avoids the anthropomorphism of the phrase "besought *the face* of the Lord" found in MT and BL 2 Kgs 13,4; compare TJ "he prayed before (קדם) the Lord".

hands (τῶν χειρῶν) *of Azaēlos*[23] *and not suffer him to fall into his power*[24]".

2 Kgs 13,4b relates the Lord's initial reaction to the king's appeal, i.e. he "hearkened to" Jehoahaz, doing so because "he saw the oppression of Israel, how the king of Syria oppressed them". 2 Kgs 13,5 then continues: "Therefore the Lord gave Israel a savior (so MT [מוֹשִׁיעַ], BL σωτηρίαν), so that they escaped from the hand of the Syrians; and the people of Israel dwelt in their homes as formerly". These notices, in turn, has a contentual parallel in the seemingly displaced indication of 13,23 (MT B): "But the Lord was gracious to them and had compassion on them, and he turned towards them because of his covenant (B διαθήκην) with Abraham, Isaac, and Jacob and would not destroy (B διαφθεῖραι); nor has he cast them from his presence [literally: face] until now [these final two words are absent in B][25]". Here again (see on 9,174 in relation to 2 Kgs 13,3.7) Josephus brings together (9,176) in a single sequence matter that in the source stands in separate contexts notwithstanding its contentual affinities. His version of 13,4b-5 // 13,23 thus runs: "Thereupon God accepted his [Jehoahaz'] repentance (τὴν μετάνοιαν ... ἀποδεχόμενος)[26] as a virtue (ἀρετήν)[27] and, because He saw fit (δοκοῦν αὐτῷ) to admonish the powerful and not completely destroy (ἀπολλύειν) them[28], gave him (αὐτῷ, Jehoahaz) security (δίδ-

23. This formulation is likely inspired by the reference to the "*hand(s)* (L τῶν χειρῶν) of Syria" from which the Israelites are said to "go forth" in 13,5. Cf. also "the *hand(s)* of Hazael king of Syria and the *hand(s)* of Ben-hadad" in 13,3.

24. With the above expansion of 2 Kgs 13,4a ("Then Jehoahaz besought the Lord") Josephus supplies a content for Jehoahaz' prayer, one likely inspired by the account of the Lord's actual response in 13,5; see below.

25. The notice on the Lord's compassion for Israel in 13,23 (MT B; L gives its parallel to this verse after 13,7) is introduced by the statement of 13,22: "Now Hazael king of Syria oppressed Israel all the days of Jehoahaz" which itself – oddly – follows after the presentation of Jehoahaz' son Joash in 13,10-21 (in L what follows 13,22 is not 13,23, but rather an extended *Sondergut* sequence, i.e. "and Hazael took Philistia from his [Jehoahaz'] hand, from the sea of the West to Aphek"; Josephus has no equivalent either to this item or to 13,22 [MT B]).

26. This is Josephus' only use of the phrase "accept repentance". His explicit mention of such "repentance" on Jehoahaz' part serves to further the historian's (partial) rehabilitation of this king whom he earlier described as "no imitator of his [reprobate] father"; see 9,173b. The μετάνοια attributed to the Israelite Jehoahaz here in 9,176 sets up a contrast between him and his Judean contemporaries Joash and the "leaders of the people" who, in 9,168, are said to "refuse to repent (μετανοῆσαι) and turn back" from their lawless ways when urged to do so by the prophets; see there.

27. This is the reading adopted by Dindorf, Bekker, Niese, Naber, and Marcus. The codices MSP read ἀρίστην.

28. This reference to God's seeing fit not to completely "destroy" the powerful was perhaps inspired by the words "he (God) would not *destroy* (B διαφθεῖρα) them" of 13,23; see above. In any case, the "didactic" motivation which Josephus supplies ("*because He saw*

ωσιν ... ἄδειαν) from war and its dangers. And so, when the country had obtained peace, it was restored to its former condition (τὴν προτέραν κατάστασιν)[29] and began to flourish[30]".

Josephus' account of Jehoahaz (9,173-176) terminates at this point. In 9,177a he begins his presentation of the next Northern king, Joash, juxtaposing data drawn from 2 Kgs 13,9aαb (Jehoahaz' death and Joash's succession) and 10. In so doing, he simply passes over the remaining items of the source narrative concerning Jehoahaz, i.e. the statement of 13,6 that, notwithstanding the Lord's intervention on their behalf "they" (the Israelites) persisted in the sins of Jeroboam, even as the Asherah was allowed to remain in Samaria[31]; the reduction of the Israelite forces by the Syrians (13,7; recall that he has anticipated the content of this verse in 9,174); the "source notice" for Jehoahaz (13,8); and mention of that king's burial in Samaria (13,9aβ).

4. Joash Introduced

2 Kgs 13,10-13 (MT and B) applies the standard data used in the Book of Kings for an Israelite ruler to Joash: accession and length of reign (v. 10), (negative) evaluation (v. 11), source notice (v. 12), death, burial, and successor (v. 13). L, by contrast, has no equivalent to

fit... to admonish... and not completely destroy") here for God's intervention on Israel's behalf substitutes for those given in both 2 Kgs 13,4b ("*for* he saw the oppression of Israel...") and 13,23 ("*because* of his covenant [BL διαθήκην] with Abraham...").

29. Josephus' one other use of the expression "former condition" is in *AJ* 6,35.

30. According to MARCUS, *Josephus*, VI, p. 95, n. d, Josephus' formulation in 9,176 (see above) represents an "amplification" of 2 Kgs 13,23 as opposed to 13,5. It seems, however, that the wording of 9,176 has also -and even more – been influenced by that of 13,4b-5. In particular, its reference to God's "giving security" (δίδωσιν ... ἄδειαν) to Jehoahaz might be seen as Josephus' equivalent to the BL reading in 13,5a, i.e. ἔδωκεν ... σωτηρίαν. Note too that, whereas 13,23 speaks only of God's solicitude for Israel as a whole, Josephus, *à la* 13,4b ("he hearkened to him [Jehoahaz]"), has the Deity "give security *to him*", i.e. Jehoahaz. Similarly, the mention of the country's being "restored to its former condition" echoes the phrase "the people of Israel dwelt in their homes as formerly (MT literally: as yesterday and the day before)" of 13,5b. Thus while 9,176 might be seen as a conflation of 13,4b-5 and 13,23 (with which the paragraph shares a reference to God's "not destroying" the afflicted; see n. 28), its verbal/contentual contacts are, *pace* Marcus, more with the former than the latter passage.

31. Josephus' non-utilization of these items is likely inspired by the consideration that to mention them would detract from Jehoahaz' "repentance" which, following 13,4a, he has just highlighted in 9,176 (just as it would point up the inefficacy of the divine "admonition" – the purpose for God's intervention on Israel's behalf according to Josephus; see n. 28). The historian's option not to associate Jehoahaz with the arch-renegade Jeroboam I (so 13,6a) further has an equivalent in his non-reproduction of the explicit link made between Jeroboam and Jehu in 2 Kgs 10,29.31 (compare 9,138.160); see p. 192, n. 18.

13,12-13 in their MT B position, supplying the content of these two verses for the first time after 13,25. As noted above Josephus, for his part, gives a conflated version of 13,9aαb + 10 in 9,177. It runs: "After the death of Jōazos[32], the royal power came to his son Joas ('Ιώασος)[33] (= 13,9b). In the thirty-seventh[34] of Joas's reign over the *tribe of* Judah, this Joas – *he had the same name as the king of Jerusalem[35]* – took over the government of the Israelites at Samaria and held it for sixteen years (= 13,10)". While Josephus thus does reproduce the chronological data of 13,10 for Joash, he diverges markedly from 13,11's evaluation of that king as one who, like his father (see 13,2) did evil in the Lord's sight and persisted in the sin of Jeroboam. Josephus, on the contrary, affirms (9,178a) that Joash "was a good man (ἀγαθός) and in no way like his father in character[36]". This "contradiction" is all the more glaring given that elsewhere Josephus does regularly follow (the main thrust of) the Biblical judgments on the Israelite/Judean kings[37]. How is it to be explained? I suggest that Josephus has "reversed" the Biblical evaluation of Joash in view of what follows where the king appears to be on good terms with the prophet Elisha whom he calls "father" and who, for his part, shows no hesitation in receiving Joash on his deathbed. In other words the historian would have found problematic

32. Compare 13,9aα: "So Jehoahaz slept with his fathers"; Josephus regularly avoids this metaphorical expression.

33. In MT 13,9b (and 13,12ff.) the new king is called יוֹאָשׁ (13,10 uses the longer form יְהוֹאָשׁ). BL name him 'Ιωάς.

34. This synchronism for the start of the Israelite Joash's reign corresponds to that found in MT B L* TJ 13,10. The Biblical witnesses' datum poses a problem in that, according to 2 Kgs 13,1 Jehoahaz, Joash's father, began to reign in the *23th* year of Joash of Judah and ruled for 17 years, this entailing that Joash's rule over Israel would have begun rather in the Judean Joash's 40th year (the figure actually found in the L MS 127/ c_2). Josephus, as noted above (see n. 5), has Jehoahaz acceding in the Judean Joash's *21st* year (9,173). Just like the Biblical ones, however, his subsequent chronological indications pose problems of internal consistency in that, following 13,1b, he allots Jehoahaz a 17-year reign with the result that his son's accession would be expected to fall in the *38th* regnal year of his Judean counterpart, rather than in his *37th*, as Josephus, basing himself on 13,10, reports here in 9,177.

35. This interjected indication recalls the similar notices introduced by Josephus concerning the Judean Joram in 9,45 ("he thus had the same name as his wife's brother, the ruler of the Israelites and the son of Achab") and 95 ("he bore the same name [i.e. as Joram of Israel; see 9,94], as we stated earlier"). Such indications make clear to readers that Josephus has not gotten his names "mixed up".

36. Recall that, in fact, Josephus tones down the unrelievedly negative judgment of 13,2 concerning Jehoahaz himself; see 9,173b: "although he was no imitator of his father [Jehu], he committed as many impieties as did the first (kings) who held God in contempt".

37. Cf., however, below on his treatment of Jehoiachin and Zedekiah of Judah; in both their cases the historian introduces positive characterizations of them which are at variance with the unqualifiedly negative evaluations found in Kings and Chronicles.

the Biblical sequence in which the Lord's prophet seems so accepting of a "godless" king, whereas earlier that same prophet had sharply rebuffed an equally wicked Israelite king, i.e. Joash's predecessor Joram (see 2 Kgs 3,11 = AJ 9,34) and indeed instigated a bloody revolt against him (see 2 Kings 9-10 = AJ 9,105-139). Josephus accordingly resolves the Biblical "discrepancy" regarding Elisha's dealings with the two "bad" Israelite kings Joram and Joash by making the latter a "good man" to whom, as a result, the prophet can grant a favorable reception without difficulty[38].

The framework notices for Joash continue in 13,12-13 (MT B) with a standard source reference for him (v. 12) and then mention of the monarch's death, burial, and succession by Jeroboam II (see v. 13) Of these items, Josephus, in line with his regular practice, leaves the former aside completely. He does, on the other hand, reproduce the content of 13,13, but reserves this for the very end of his account concerning Joash; see 9,185b. In so doing, Josephus aligns himself with L whose rendering of 13,12-13 (MT and B) stands after 13,25, as noted above. This state of affairs does not, however, necessarily entail the historian's dependence on a (proto-) L text here. Rather, it is equally conceivable that Josephus, having before him a text or texts in which the material of 13,12-13 stood in its MT/B position, shifted the data of 13,13 to the end of his account simply on his own initiative in view of the curious sequence of the MT/B narration in which Joash, dead and buried in 13,13, appears as very much alive in what follows; see below.

5. The Arrows Episode

The story of the joint royal/prophetic symbolic act(s) involving arrows in 2 Kgs 13,14-19 (= AJ 9,178b-181) opens (13,14) with mention of Elisha's mortal illness which occasions Joash's "coming down" to him. Josephus' version passes over, for the moment (but see below), the Biblical specification concerning the severity of the prophet's illness;

---

38. On Josephus' "rehabiliation" of Joash, see further FELDMAN, *Studies*, pp. 437-49 (= ID., *Josephus' Portrait of Jehoiachin*, in *Proceedings of the American Philosophical Society* 139 [1995] 11-31, pp. 18-19) and S.J.D. COHEN, *Josephus in Galilee and Rome: His Vita and Development as a Historian* (Columbia Studies in the Classical Tradition, 8), Leiden, Brill, 1979, p. 39 and n. 64 (Cohen proposes an explanation of the discrepancy between the Biblical and Josephan evaluations of Joash of Israel along the above lines; in addition, however, he calls attention to an alternative possibillity, i.e. Josephus has simply confused the Israelite king with his Judean namesake – whom both he and the Bible represent as an [initially] good king).

conversely, it prefaces (9,178b) its notice about Elisha taking sick "about this time" (i.e. of Joash's accession) with mention of his being "now an old man". This inserted indication is quite appropriate given that there has been no mention of Elisha, in either the Bible or in Josephus himself, since his instigation of the coup perpetrated by Jehu, the grandfather of Joash (see 2 Kgs 9,1-3 = AJ 9,106) some 45 years before[39]. Like Kings, Josephus gives no indication as to where Joash's encounter with the sick prophet took place; he does, however, replace the source's somewhat indeterminate reference to the king's "going down to him (Elisha)" with a specification concerning the purpose of the royal initiative: "he came to visit him".

2 Kgs 13,14bα has Joash "weeping before" Elisha. Josephus (9,179a) accentuates the pathos of the moment, just as he supplies a "motivation" for the king's emotional outburst: "... finding him near his end [compare 13,14aα's reference to Elisha's having fallen sick with the illness of which he was to die], he began to lament (κλαίειν), *as Elisha looked on, and to wail* (ποτνιᾶσθαι)...". In 2 Kgs 13,14bβ the grieving Joash addresses Elisha with the title "my father, my father!. The chariot(s) of Israel and its horsemen[40]". For the latter part of this designation Josephus substitutes another term, thereby setting up his own subsequent presentation; see below: "... (he began to) call him 'Father' and 'armour' (ὅπλον)'".

In 2 Kgs 13,15 Elisha responds, rather abruptly, to Joash's tearful address by directing him to take bow and arrows. Josephus, by contrast (9,179b-180a), interjects a lengthy additional word by the king which serves to elucidate his previous use of the designation "armour" in reference to the prophet:

(179b) Because of him, he said, they had never had to use arms (ὅπλοις; see ὅπλον, 9,179a) against the foe, but through his prophecies (ταῖς ἐκείνου προφητείαις) they had overcome the enemy without a battle[41]. But

39. This figure results from combining the chronological indications for the reigns of Joash's two immediate predecessors, Jehu (28 years, so 2 Kgs 10,36 [AJ 9,160 reads 27]) and Jehoahaz (2 Kgs 13,1 = AJ 9,173).

40. In 2 Kgs 2,12 these same words are addressed by Elisha himself to Elijah at the moment of the latter's translation. In Josephus' very compressed version of the "translation story" of 2 Kgs 2,1-18 in AJ 9,27-28 that address is left aside. See chap. II.

41. This generalizing assertion which Josephus places on the lips of Joash here certainly appears exaggerated given his previous mention of the Syrian devastations of Israel under both Jehu (9,159 = 2 Kgs 10,32-33) and Jehoahaz (9,174 = 2 Kgs 13,3.7). Note too that neither the Bible nor Josephus himself records any initiative by Elisha on Israel's behalf in the face of the dire Syrian threat at the time of those of two kings (in fact, in a non-Biblical insertion Josephus asserts, 9,175, that the misfortunes Israel suffered in the time of Jehoahaz were the fulfillment of the announcement made by Elisha to the Syrian

now he was departing this life[42] and leaving him unarmed (ἐξωπλισ-μένον)[43] before the Syrians and the enemies under them[44]. (180) It was, therefore, no longer safe (ἀσφαλές) for him to live, but he would do best to join him in death and depart this life together with him[45].

Following the above amplification of Joash's address Josephus further introduces (9,180b) a transitional phrase leading into his version of the prophet's "arrows directive" to the king (= 13,15): "... as the king was bemoaning (ὀδυρόμενον; cf. κλαίειν ... καὶ ποτνιᾶσθαι, 9,179a) in these words, Elisha comforted (παρεμυθεῖτο) him...[46]".

In what precedes Josephus has significantly embellished the end of 2 Kgs 13,14 and the opening of 13,15. At this point, however, the histo-rian has recourse to a drastic compression of the source account. Specif-ically, he condenses into a single sequence (9,180b-181) the double symbolic act involving a use of arrows and attached interpretation related in 2 Kgs 13,15-19. Why does Josephus proceed in this way? I suggest that he does so primarily in view of the seeming discrepancy between the interpretative announcements attached to the Bible's first and second "arrow signs". Thus in 13,17b, following Joash's shooting

Hazael; see 2 Kgs 8,10-13 = AJ 9,90-92). On the other hand, the Josephan Joash's state-ment here in 9,179 does have a (partial) basis in the episode of Elisha's delivering a whole force of hapless Syrians into the hand of Joram of Israel; see 2 Kgs 6,18-23 = AJ 9,56-58.

42. This phase picks up on the reference to Joash's "finding him (Elisha) near the end" in 9,179a; cf. the mention of Elisha having "fallen sick with the illness of which he was to die" in 2 Kgs 13,14aα.

43. This accusative singular participle used by Joash in reference to himself represents a further play on the "armour" terminology employed by the king twice previously in 9,179. The reading in question is found in the codices RO and adopted by Niese, Weill, and Marcus. The codices (M)SP, followed by Dindorf, Bekker, and Naber, read rather the dative plural participle ἐξωπλισμένοις with the "Syrians" as referent (in this reading Joash would assert that Elisha is "leaving him to the *fully armed* Syrians" rather than "leaving him *unarmed* before the Syrians" as in Marcus's translation above).

44. The intended referent of this phrase is not immediately clear. Perhaps, Josephus has in view the 32 allied kings whom Ben-hadad, Hazael's predecessor, brought against Samaria in Ahab's time; see AJ 8,363 = 1 Kgs 20,1.

45. MARCUS, *Josephus*, VI, p. 97, n. c points out that TJ also amplifies Joash's address to Elisha as cited in MT 13,14. The Targum renders that address as follows: "My master, my master [Aramaic *rabbi*, replacing MT father], *to whom there was more good for Israel in his prayer than* chariots and horsemen". Note, however, that whereas TJ thus attributes Elisha's preeminent assistance to his "prayer", Josephus, characteristically, ascribes it rather to his "prophecies"; see above.

46. Josephus' inserted reference to Elisha's "comforting" Joash here accentuates the emotional bond between them, a bond which, in turn, is only understandable given the latter's status as a "good man" (so 9,177) rather than an "evildoer" (so 2 Kgs 13,11); see above. The reference further recalls the historian's – also interjected – notice (AJ 9,33; compare 2 Kgs 3,11) that Jehoshaphat "comforted" (παρεθάρρυνε) the northern King Joram in his distress at the failure of the water supply during their joint campaign against Moab.

of the arrow at his command (v. 17a), Elisha states that he (Joash) will fight with the Syrians "until you have made an end of them". Thereafter, however, in 13,19b, once the king has ceased striking the ground with the arrows after having done so only three times (v. 18), this earlier promise is (implicitly) abrogated and Joash is now informed by Elisha that he will defeat Syria a mere three times. Josephus resolves the difficulty as to the extent (total vs. partial) of the promised Israelite victory over Syria by conflating into a single account the source's first arrow sign (13,15-17a) with the interpretation of the second sign act (13,19b). In so doing, he leaves aside both the interpretation appended to the first sign in 13,17b and the description of the second sign (Joash's striking the ground with the arrows) in 13,18.

The account of the first arrow sign of 13,15-17a utilized by Josephus in 9,180b-181a itself consists of a four-fold series of (paratactically-linked) directives by Elisha and corresponding notices of their execution by Joash. These concern: 1) the king's taking a bow and arrows (v. 15), 2) drawing the bow (+ Elisha's placing his hands over those of Joash, v. 16), 3) opening the window towards the east (v. 17aα), and 4) "shooting" (v. 17aβ, MT L, > B). Josephus compresses this sequence (eliminating, e.g., the window-opening of v. 17aα), likewise replacing its parataxis with hypotaxis and direct with indirect discourse: "... Elisha told him to have a bow [13,15a mentions arrows as well] brought to him and to bend it; when the king had made the bow ready, the prophet took hold of his hands (= v. 16) and bade him shoot (τοξεύειν; compare τόξευσον, L 13,17aβ)". In formulating his equivalent to the continuation of 13,17aβ (MT L) where Joash "shoots" as directed, Josephus already begins drawing on elements of the second sign account of 13,18-19. In particular, whereas 13,17aβ seems to suggest that Joash "shot" only one arrow, the historian, in clear dependence on 13,18bβ (Joash "struck [the ground with the arrows; see v. 18bα] *three times, and stopped*), words the item as follows: "he then let fly *three arrows and ceased...*".

As noted above, Josephus attaches to his version of the first arrow sign of 13,15-17a, not the associated prophetic interpetation of 13,17b, but rather the announcement (13,19) appended to the Bible's second arrow sign (13,18), which is not reproduced as such by him. Hence, after the above notice that Joash ceased after shooting three arrows, Josephus continues immediately (9,181b) with his expanded version of 13,19[47]:

---

[47]. From 13,19 Josephus eliminates its opening words "the man of God was angry with him (Joash)". In so doing, he avoids having the deathbed exchange between king and prophet end up with a statement of the latter's negative feelings towards the former.

"... whereupon the prophet said, 'if you had sent more arrows[48], you would have destroyed the kingdom of Syria to its foundations [13,19bα: you would have struck down Syria until you made an end of it], *but, since you were satisfied with only three* [i.e. arrows, see 9,181a], you shall meet the Syrians in as many battles and defeat them [13,19bβ: but now you will strike down Syria only three times], *that you may recover the territory which they cut off from your father's possessions*[49]'".

In Kings the episode of 13,14-19 concludes with no indication concerning Joash's response to Elisha's (second) announcement in v. 19. As a result, it remains unclear whether or not the king was present for what follows next, i.e. Elisha's death, burial, and the incident involving his grave (13,20-21), and if so why he did not intervene in the face of the Moabite advance related in v. 20b. Josephus clarifies matters with the notice he attaches to his rendering of Elisha's word of 13,19 at the end of 9,181, i.e. "and the king, having heard these words, departed".

6. *The Grave Incident*

The brief incident centered on Elisha's grave (13,20-21 = 9,182-183) begins in v. 20a with the laconic notice that Elisha died and was buried. Josephus (9,182) expands these jejune data into a elaborate epithet for the departed prophet:

> But not long *afterward*[50], the prophet [13,20a: Elisha] died; *he was a man renowned for righteousness* (ἐπὶ δικαιοσύνῃ διαβόητος)[51] *and one manifestly held in honour by God* (φανερῶς σπουδασθεὶς ὑπὸ τοῦ θεοῦ)[52];

---

48. Note Josephus' retention of the direct address of 13,19 here. In 13,19 itself Elisha's opening words run "you should have struck [the ground] five or six times", this relating back to the prophet's bidding Joash to "strike the ground with them [the arrows]" in v. 18aβ. Josephus' modified rendering of the start of Elisha's announcement reflects the fact of his combining the first Biblical arrows sign (i.e. Joash's shooting of these, so 13,17) with the prophet's interpretation (= 13,19) of the second such sign (i.e. Joash's striking the ground with the arrows, 13,18).

49. This Josephan appendix to the prophetic word of 13,19 looks ahead to the notice of 2 Kgs 13,25 (= 9,184) about Joash's regaining the cities which Hazael "had taken from Jehoahaz in war". It likewise picks up on Josephus' earlier expansion of 13,7 in 9,174 where he speaks of Hazael's "taking many great cities (cf. 13,25) from him (Jehoahaz)"; see above.

50. The Bible itself gives no indication as to how long an interval elapsed between the king-prophet exchange related in 13,14-19 and the latter's death as cited in 13,20a.

51. This expression is hapax in Josephus.

52. This is Josephus' sole use of the phrase "held in honour by God". The phrase is, however, reminiscent of his earlier (also non-Biblical) notice in 9,60 that Adados (Benhadad) of Syria was "amazed... at the prophet (Elisha) with whom God was so evidently present". Both notices accentuate the stature of Elisha as one enjoying an especially close relationship to God.

for through his prophetic power (διὰ τῆς προφητείας)[53]; *he performed astounding and marvelous* (θυαμαστὰ ... καὶ παράδοξα)[54] *deeds, which were held as a glorious memory* (μνήμης λαμπρᾶς)[55] *by the Hebrews.* He was given a *magnificent* (μεγαλοπρεποῦς)[56] burial, *such as it was fitting for one so dear to God* (θεοφιλῆ)[57] *to receive.*

Following 13,20a's summary notice on Elisha's death and burial, v. 20b makes the transition to the miracle story of v. 21 with mention of "Moabite bands" who "invaded the land in the spring of the year" (so RSV; MT בָּא שָׁנָה, BL ἐλθόντος τοῦ ἐνιαυτοῦ). Next, v. 21a speaks of a man being buried on this occasion whose corpse is "thrown" – apparently by the (Israelite) burial party[58] – when one such "band" makes its appearance. Josephus (9,183a) conflates these data: "Now it happened just as that time[59] that some robbers (ληστῶν; BL 13,20 μονόζωνοι)[60]

---

53. This phrase echoes the (non-Biblical) words Josephus attributes to Joash in his speech to Elisha in 9,179: "... through his prophecies (ταῖς ἐκείνου προφητείαις) they had overcome the enemy without a battle".

54. This collocation occurs only here in Josephus.

55. This phrase is hapax in Josephus. It is, however, reminiscent of his introductory notice concerning the prophet in 9,46: "he [King Joram of Israel] had with him the prophet Elisha whose acts I wish to relate – for they are glorious (λαμπραί) and worthy of record – as we discover them in the sacred books". FELDMAN, *Studies*, pp. 335-336 (=·ID., *Elisha*, 5) points out that Josephus' only other uses of the adjective λαμπρός of 9,46.182 are in reference to David (7,65) and to that king's heroes (7,307).

56. On Josephus' other (likewise inserted) uses of this term in reference to the burials of Biblical characters, see on 9,44.

57. Josephus uses the term θεοφιλής a total of 11 times. The other figures to whom he applies it are: the Hebrews (*BJ* 5,381); the Patriarchs (*AJ* 1,106); Isaac (1,346); David (6,280); Solomon (8,49), Daniel's relatives (10,215); Daniel himself (10,264); the high priest Onias (14,22); and Herod (in popular opinion, *BJ* 1,331 // *AJ* 14,455).

58. As MARCUS, *Josephus*, VI, pp. 98-99, n. a points out, the text of 13,21a might, however, be construed as saying that the mauraders were the ones who "dumped" the body – as Josephus unambiguously represents them as doing; see below.

59. I.e. of Elisha's burial (see 9,182). In thus modifying the chronological indication of 13,20b (see above) which seems to presuppose an extended interlude between Elisha's burial and the appearance of the Moabite "bands", Josephus is attempting to account for the immediate availability of Elisha's grave as a dumping place for the corpse as presupposed by the presentation of 13,21a, i.e. the grave was still open since the prophet's burial was in progress "just at the time" the robbers made their appearance.

60. Josephus omits the source's specification of their homeland, i.e. Moab, perhaps on the consideration that this was situated at quite a distance from Israel, Elisha's country. Another such consideration could be the fact that the last mention of Moab in both the Bible and his own presentation concerned its being overrun by the three allied kings, Joram of Israel at their head (2 Kings 3 = 9,29-45). That earlier happening might raise questions as to whether the "Moabites" would be now in a position to range throughout Israel as they are represented as doing in 13,20b.

threw (ῥιψάντων; BL ἔρριψαν) into the grave of Elisha[61] a man *whom they had murdered...*[62]".

2 Kgs 13,21b relates the miraculous outcome of the "toss" cited in v. 21a: "the man (MT; > B; L + being buried) went and touched (TJ drew near, קריב[63]) the bones of Elisha and he revived and stood upon his feet". In contrast to his handling of the data of 13,20b-21 (see above) Josephus renders this notice without significant modification: "... when the corpse came into contact with his body (σώματι)[64], it was restored to life". He then rounds off his whole presentation of Elisha, first introduced by him in 8,353, with an appended remark (9,183b) which, like the embellishments of the death and burial notice of 13,20a in 9,182, serves to accentuate the prophet's stature. It reads: "This much, then, concerning Elisha, both as to what he foretold (προεῖπε; see 9,175) in his lifetime and how after death he still held divine power (δύναμιν εἶχε θείαν)[65], we have now related".

61. In 13,21a it is – apparently – the (Israelite) burial party who toss the corpse into Elisha's grave; see n. 58. Josephus simplifies matters by eliminating all mention of this group or of the burial they were conducting, in favor of having the maurauders themselves dispose of the corpse. Thereby he reduces the series of coincidences presupposed by the Biblical account where an Israelite group happens to be burying a corpse in proximity to Elisha's grave at the very moment when the Moabites come on the scene.

62. This inserted indication suggests an explanation both for the fact of the robbers' having a body on their hands and of their unceremonial dumping it into the open grave of Elisha, i.e. to avoid discovery of their "murder". Josephus' indication on the matter has a counterpart in Pseudo-Tertullian's *Carmen adversus Marcionem* 3.173 which, in the context of an encomium on Elisha (cf. *AJ* 9,182) refers to the one tossed into the prophet's tomb as "mactatus caede latronum"; see R. WILLEMS (ed.), *Tertulliani Opera*, II (CC SL, II:II), Turnhout, Brepols, 1954, p. 1438. Neither the Bible nor Josephus attach a name to the dead man of 13,21. In Rabbinic tradition he is variously identified, i.e. as the false prophet Zedekiah of 1 Kgs 22,24 (so *Eccl. Rab.* 8.10.1; see A. COHEN, tr., *Midrash Rabbah Ecclesiastes*, London/New York, Soncino, 1983, p. 222); the son of the Shunammite woman previously revived by Elisha (see 2 Kgs 4,34-35) but who turned wicked in later life (so *Midr. Pss.* on Ps 26.9; see BRAUDE, *Midrash on Psalms*, I, p. 363) and Shallum, the husband of the prophetess Huldah according to 2 Kgs 22,14 (thus *Pirqe R. El.* 33.4; see M. PÉREZ FERNÁNDEZ, tr., *Los Capítulos de Rabbí Eliezer* [Biblioteca Midrásica, 1], Valencia, Institución San Jerónimo, 1984, p. 232).

63. HARRINGTON and SALDARINI, *Targum Jonathan*, p. 290, n. 28 see TJ's reading here as reflecting the Talmudic prohibition of burying the wicked and the righteous together.

64. In 13,21b it is "the bones" of Elisha which the dead man "touches", this implying that the prophet had already been in the grave a considerable time. Josephus' substitution of a reference to Elisha's "body" goes together with his previous indication that the grave incident occurred "just at this time", i.e. of Elisha's own burial when his body would still have been intact.

65. With this expression compare 8,408 (no Biblical parallel) where Zedekiah, the false prophet, proposes a test to see whether his rival Micaiah "has the power of the divine spirit" (τοῦ θείου πνεύματος ἔχει τὴν δύναμιν). The above phrase likewise echoes Elisha's own statement in 9,58 that the Syrian captives have come to Samaria "by the power of God" (θεία ... δυνάμει).

7. Joash's Triumph (and Death)

As noted above, Jehoahaz, father of Joash, makes an unexpected return in 13,22-23 (MT and B) which juxtaposes mention of the Syrian oppression of Israel during his time (v. 22) and of the Lord's compassion for them, prompted by his covenant with the patriarchs (v. 23). Given the seemingly displaced character of this sequence – recall that L offers its equivalent to 13,23 following 13,7[66] – as well as its repetition of what has already been reported in 13,4-7 (= 9,174-176), it is not surprising to find that Josephus has no parallel to the material of 13,22-23 in its MT B position, i.e. subsequent to the "grave incident" of 13,20-21. Instead, the historian proceeds immediately to the following, final component of 2 Kings 13, i.e. its notices on Joash's successes against the Syrians (vv. 24-25). This last sequence commences with mention (13,24) of the death of Hazael, Israel's long-time nemesis, and the succession of his son Ben-hadad (BL υἰὸς ᾿Αδέρ). Josephus relates this preliminary happening at the opening of 9,184: "On the death of Azaē̄-los, the king of Syria, the kingship came to his son Adados (῎Αδαδον)[67]".

2 Kgs 13,25 (MT and B) recounts the sequel to the change of leadership in Syria: Joash thrice defeats Ben-Hadad and recovers "cities" lost by his father Jehoahaz to Hazael, this "recovery" being cited twice, first in v. 25a and then again in v. 25b. L amplifies the MT and B content of the verse with a variety of further particulars, i.e. an opening transitional phrase ("and it came to pass after the death of Azaēl"); specification that Joash's triple "smiting" of the "son of Ader" transpired "in the war in Aphek according to the word of the Lord"[68]; and the addition "as many as he [i.e. Hazael] took" to v. 25b's mention of Joash's recovering "the cities of Israel". Josephus too presents (9,184b-185a) a more expansive, while also re-arranged, version of the content of MT 13,25. His rendition starts off

---

66. Recall further that in L the place of 13,23 (MT B) is taken by a *Sondergut* item about Hazael capturing Philistia from Jehoahaz (see n. 25) to which Josephus has no parallel.

67. This is the emendation proposed by J. Hudson and followed by Dindorf, Bekker, Naber, Marcus and SCHALIT, *Namenwörterbuch*, p. 4. Niese and Weill read rather ᾿Αδδάν with the codices RO (and Lat). The form read by Marcus *et al.* represents a shortened form of MT's "Ben-Hadad", whose initial element it omits. In the case of the earlier Syrian king Ben-hadad, the enemy of Ahab and Joram, Josephus starts off (8,363 = 1 Kgs 20,1) calling him ὁ τοῦ ᾿Αδάδου υἱός, but thereafter consistently uses "Adados" (so 9,184) for him.

68. With this plus L provides a fulfillment notice for/ verbal echo of Elisha's "arrow word" of 13,17bβ ("you shall fight the Syrians *in Aphek* until you have made an end of them") that likewise specifies the site of Joash's victories. Recall that Josephus lacks a parallel to Elisha's "arrow word" of 13,17b.

with the introductory notice that Joash "began war" against Adados which has no source counterpart as such. It continues with the datum of v. 25b about the Israelite king's "thrice defeating" (τρισὶ μάχαις νικήσας) – this echoing Elisha's announcement in 9,181 (τοσαύταις [τρισίν] μάχαις κρατήσεις) – his Syrian counterpart. Thereafter, Josephus compresses into one the Bible's double mention of the recovery of the Israelite cities. At the same he words this item, like the foregoing, in accordance with the announcement he attributes to Elisha in 9,181 ("... you may recover the territory [τὴν χώραν] which they cut off from your father's possessions"): "(Joash) got back from him [Adados] all *the territory* (τὴν χώραν) [and as many (see L 13,25 above) cities (πόλεις = BL) *and villages* (καὶ κώμας)][69] which his father Azaēlos had taken from the Israelite kingdom [13,25: from Jehoahaz]". To this description of Joash's triumph Josephus further appends a "fullfilment notice" (9,185a) which serves to explicitly relate that triumph to Elisha's prediction as cited in 9,181: "This, moreover, came about in accordance with the prophecy (κατὰ τὴν προφητείαν; see 9,175) of Elisha [compare the L plus in 13,25: Joash smote the son of Ader "according to the word of the Lord[70]]".

The Biblical segment (MT B) 13,10-25 concerning Joash concludes in v. 25 with mention of the king's successes against the Syrians. As pointed out above, L, for its part, positions its equivalent to the closing notices for Joash of 13,12-13 (MT B) after 13,25. As has also already been noted, Josephus, while lacking a parallel to the "source reference" of 13,12 (= L 13,25) cites the data of 13,13 (= L 13,26) in the same position as does L, however this "agreement" be explained; see above. His rendition of 13,13 (MT) reads: "... when the time came for Joash to die[71], he was buried (κηδεύται; L θάπτεται) in Samaria (so MT L, > B) and the royal power fell to his son Jeroboam (Ἰεροβόαμον)[72]". For this sequence with its mention of Jeroboam's accession *after* the burial of his father, Josephus goes together with L (13,26) against MT (13,13; B does

---

69. Note that Marcus's translation of 9,184 passes over the sequence rendered above as "and as many cities and villages" in his rendering of 9,184 (even though his text does give the corresponding Greek words). Compare WEILL, *ad loc.*: "(il lui enleva tout le pays) *et toutes les villes et bourgades...*".

70. Given the historian's characteristic insistence on the realization of "true" prophecy – exemplified, e.g., in his interjected fulfillment notice in 9,175 – one need not assume that it was under the influence of the above L plus that Josephus devised his evocation of Elisha's "prophecy" here in 9,185.

71. Josephus' reference to Joash's "dying" here substitutes for the metaphorical expression of 13,13 ("he slept with his fathers"); compare his similar substitution (9,177) for the same formula used of Jehoahaz in 13,9.

72. Josephus will resume his presentation of this king in 9,205, following the interlude devoted to Amaziah of Judah in 9,186-204.

not mention Joash's burial at all) which cites those two happenings in the reverse order. Once again, however, the question arises as to whether this communality necessarily betokens the historian's dependence on a L-like text of 2 Kings 13. That question suggests itself here given the fact that the MT order in 13,13 is not the expected one nor that normally found in Kings[73]. Hence it remains possible that Josephus' sequence reflects, not his use of a L-like text, but rather his own, independent re-arrangement of the odd sequence attested by MT 13,13.

Conclusions: Josephus' Rewriting of 2 Kings 13

On the question of Josephus' textual affinities in 9,173-185, the most noteworthy finding to emerge from the above discussion concerned the various points of contact between his account of Jehoahaz and Joash and that of L against MT (and B). Such contacts include the following items: placing of the data of 13,(12-)13 at the very end of the segment (see 9,185b = L 13,26); positioning of the content of MT 13,23 at a earlier point in the narrative (see 9,176 = L 13,8); the inserted fullfillment notice in connection with Joash's recovery of the Israelite cities (9,185a = L 13,25); and mention of Jeroboam's accession after rather than before (so MT 13,13) Joash's burial (9,185b = L 13,26). Still, as I have argued above, none of these four cases necessarily entails Josephus' dependence on a L-like text of 2 Kings 13 since they can be alternatively explained in terms of the historian's own authorial tendencies or of problems posed by the MT presentation to which the historian could, independently, have been reacting[74]. Conversely, however, our reading did not turn up clear-cut indications of the historian's familiarity with the distinctive readings of MT (B) 2 Kings 13 either.

Despite its relatively brief compass (and the minor status of the two kings who are its subject), AJ 9,173-185 does evidence the range of characteristic Josephan rewriting techniques. Among the segment's longer instances of expansion/addition are: the interjected fulfillment notice of 9,175a; the elaboration of Joash's word to Elisha (9,179-180a; compare 13,14b), the epithet for Elisha grafted onto the summary notice of his death and burial (13,20a) in 9,182; and the closing notice (9,183a) for his entire career appended to 13,21b. On the other hand, Josephus notably compresses both the source's double "arrows sequence" (13,15-

---

73. In the duplicate of 13,13 in 2 Kgs 14,16 one does, in fact, find the expected sequence: burial of Joash – accession of Jeroboam.

74. In this connection recall too that Josephus has no equivalent to the L plus of 13,22 with its mention of Hazael's seizure of Philistine territory.

19; compare 9,180b-181), and the grave episode (13,20b-21; compare 9,183a). Among the segment's (smaller-scale) omissions we noted his non-utilization of the following items: the theological notice of 13,3, the affirmation about Israel's persistence in Jeroboam's sin and the continuation of the Asherah in Samaria (13,6), the mention of Elisha's "anger" against Joash of 13,19, and the source references of 13,8 (Jehoahaz) and 13,12 (Joash). Modifications/adapations of source data permeate 9,173-185 as well. Jehoahaz' accession comes in Joash's 21st (9,173) rather than in his 23rd year (so 13,1). The unqualifiedly negative judgment on Jehohaz given in 13,2 is attenuated (9,173b), while that of 13,11 concerning Joash is completely reversed in 9,177. God's motivation for hearing Jehoahaz' plea is a different one in 9,176 than in either 13,4 or 13,23; see n. 28. Joash designates Elisha with the term "armour" rather than "horses and chariots" (9,179; compare 13,14). It is the marauders themselves, rather than an Israelite burial party, who toss the man's corpse into the grave of Elisha where it comes into contact with the prophet's "body" instead of his "bones" (9,183a; compare 13,21). Finally, Josephus' version evidences a "re-arrangement" in its working together of the data of 13,9aαb and 10 into the opening of his presentation of Joash, whereas in the source the former verse pertains to the conclusion of its account of Jehoahaz, 13,8-9.

As a result of his application of the foregoing rewriting techniques, Josephus presents readers with an account of Jehoahaz and Joash manifesting a number of distinctive features. The unfolding of events in accordance with past prophetic announcements is accentuated; see 9,175a.184b. Problems posed by the source's presentation are resolved or mitigated, e.g., God's "hearing" the wicked Jehoahaz (13,2.4; compare 9,173b) and the welcome accorded the evil Joash by Elisha (13,11.14-19; compare 9,177); the discrepancy between 13,17b and 19 as to the extent of Joash's promised victory over Syria (compare 9,181); and the designation of the marauders as "Moabites" (13,21; compare 9,183). Josephus' "solution" to the first two of these problems involves his giving a more positive characterization of the kings Jehoahaz and Joash than does his source. In the same line, he interjects (9,182.183b) an elaborate commendation of the prophet Elisha who finally departs the scene at this point. Thus all three of the characters featured in 2 Kings 13 take on more positive features in his presentation of them. Their doing so, in turns, helps account for the good things accomplished or experienced by them in accord with the moral – equally relevant to Gentile and Jewish readers – set out in 1,14: "men who conform to the will of God... prosper in all things beyond belief, and for their reward are offered by God felicity...".

X

AMAZIAH OF JUDAH[1]
(9,186-204)

Having disposed of the two Northern kings Jehoahaz and Joash in 9,173-185, Josephus now (9,186-204) reverts to the Judean contemporary of the latter, i.e. Amaziah ("Amasias") whose succession to his father Joash he had mentioned at the end of 9,172. The Bible gives both a shorter (2 Kgs 14,1-22) and more expansive (2 Chr 25,1-26,2) account of this Southern ruler. I divide up the relevant material into five segments: 1. Amaziah Introduced (*AJ* 9,186b = 2 Kgs 14,1-4 // 2 Chr 25,1-2); 2. Joash Avenged (9,186c-187 = 14,5-6 // 25,3-4); 3. Edom Conquered (9,188-195 = 14,7 // 25,5-16); 4. Judah vs. Israel (9,196-202 = 14,8-14[15-16] // 25,17-24); and 5. Amaziah Assassinated (9,203-204 = 14,17-22 // 25,25-26,2).

1. *Amaziah Introduced*

In all three accounts under consideration here the initial presentation (9,186 = 14,1-4 // 25,1-2) of Amaziah consists of three items: 1) chronological indications; 2) mention of the queen mother; and 3) evaluation. In common with 14,1 Josephus (9,186a) synchronizes Amaziah's accession with the second regnal year of Joash of Israel; as usual, Chronicles, with its Judean focus, lacks an equivalent. 2 Kgs 14,2a and 2 Chr 25,1 both supply a double figure for the reign of Amaziah here at the outset: acceding at age 25, he ruled 29 years. Josephus, following his usual practice, delays these data until the end of his Amaziah account; see 9,204. The next component in the three introductions is a notice on Amaziah's mother. MT 14,2b calls her "Jehoadin" (BL Ἰωαδείν), MT 25,1b "Jehoaddin" (B Ἰωναά, L Ἰωαδείμ); both texts further note that she was "of Jerusalem". Josephus names the woman "Jōadē" (Ἰωάδης) and designates her "a citizen (πολίτιδος)[2] of that city [Jerusalem]".

---

1. This chapter represents a reworking of my article *Amaziah of Judah according to Josephus (ANT. 9.186-204)*, in *Anton* 70 (1995) 3-30 and is used by permission.

2. Josephus' two other uses of this feminine form are likewise both employed in reference to Jerusalemite queen mothers, i.e. "Epsiba" (*t.e.*), mother of Manasseh (*AJ* 10,37) and "Noostē", mother of Jehoiachin (10,98).

All three introductions of Amaziah end up with an evaluation of the king. In both Biblical passages that evaluation is qualifiedly positive. The wording of their respective judgment formulas does differ considerably, however. According to 14,3 while Amaziah did what was right in the Lord's eyes, he did not match the preeminent standard fixed by David, but only the lesser one set by his father Joash. 2 Kgs 14,4, reprising the words of 12,4 concerning Joash, then goes on to specify the religious failure common to both father and son, i.e. their toleration of worship on the "high places". The Chronicler, in line with his regular procedure, dispenses with 14,4's remark about the high places. Moreover, in place of 14,3's comparison of Amaziah with David and Joash, 2 Chr 25,2 simply states without further specification: "he did what was right in the eyes of the Lord, *yet not with a blameless heart*". Josephus' own introductory evaluation of the new king (9,186b) avoids the element of qualification common to both sources' judgment of him: "he was remarkably observant of justice (τοῦ δικαιοῦ προυνόει)[3], *even though a youth*[4]". The wording of this notice clearly has in view the immediately following episode in which Amaziah's concern precisely for "justice" will be made manifest.

2. *Joash Avenged*

The first event of Amaziah's reign to be reported in both the Biblical sources (14,5-6 // 25,3-4) and in Josephus (9,186c-187) is the king's avenging the murder of his father Joash in accordance with Mosaic law. 2 Kgs 14,5 // 2 Chr 25,3 relate the fact of Amaziah's executing the "servants" who had slain his father (on this see 2 Kgs 12,20-21 // 2 Chr 24,25-26 = *AJ* 9,171), once he (Amaziah) had the kingdom firmly in hand. Josephus (9,186c) introduces the royal initiative – which he has already adumbrated by way of his notice on the king's precocious "observance of justice" (see above) – with mention of the "first decision"

---

3. For this phrase see on 9,3 where it is used of the judges appointed by Jehoshaphat.

4. Recall that according to 14,2 // 25,1 Amaziah was 25 years old at the moment of his accession. Elsewhere as well Josephus inserts wording highlighting the "precocious" justice/piety displayed by various Biblical kings; see *AJ* 8,21 (Solomon was "not hindered *by his youth* from dealing justice and observing the laws... but performed all tasks with as great scrupulousness as do those of advanced age and mature wisdom") and 10,50 (already at age twelve Josiah, "reviewing the acts of his forefathers, ... wisely corrected the errors they had made, just as if he were a very old man and quite competent to see what needed to be done..."). On this feature of Josephus' presentation as inspired by the emphasis on the hero's precocity common to Hellenistic biographies, FELDMAN, *Interpretation,* pp. 381-384 (= ID., *Josephus' Portrait of Moses,* in *JQR* 82 [1992] 285-328, pp. 303-307).

taken by Amaziah "when he came into office and held power". Thereby, he underscores the deliberateness with which the young king proceeds in the matter. What Amaziah "decided" (ἔγνω) to do at this point was to "avenge (τιμωρῆσαι) his father Joas and to punish (κολάσαι) his friends (φίλους)[5] who had laid violent hands on him". Thereafter, Amaziah, as Josephus goes on to report at the start of 9,187 (= 14,5b // 25,3b), "having seized them,... put them all to death (ἐφόνευσε; BL 14,5 ἐπάταξεν, BL 25,3 ἐθανατωσε[ν])[6]".

2 Kgs 14,6 // 2 Chr 25,4 append a clarification to the preceding notice on Amaziah's deed of vengeance: he spared the regicides' children in accord with the law of Deut 24,16 prohibiting "transgenerational punishment" which these texts proceed to quote in full. Josephus' rendition (9,187b) confines itself to an allusion to that portion of the law which is directly relevant to the case at hand: "... but did no harm (δεινόν) to their children, for he was acting in accordance with the laws of Moses (ἀκόλουθα ... τοῖς Μωυσέος νόμοις)[7], who declared it unjust (οὐκ ἐδικαίωσε)[8] to punish children for the sins of their fathers (διὰ πατέρων ἁμαρτίας τέκνα κολάζειν [cf. κολάσαι, 9,186])[9]".

3. Edom Conquered

As this point in their respective accounts of Amaziah, Kings and Chronicles evidence their greatest divergence. 2 Kgs 14,7 disposes of

5. In 14,5 // 25,3 the regicides are designated as Joash's "servants"; Josephus' substitute designation for them here picks up on his earlier reference (9,171) to Joash's killers as "some of his friends (φίλων)"; compare 2 Kgs 12,20 // 2 Chr 24,25 which attribute the deed to Joash's "servants". In both instances the substitution serves to heighten the pathos surrounding Joash's assassination, just as it reflects the historian's characteristic practice of introducing references, inspired by contemporary Greco-Roman court language, to royal "friends" into his rewriting of Biblical history.

6. Josephus' use of the form ἐφόνευσε in reference to Amaziah's initiative is perhaps inspired by the participle φονεύσαντες employed in BL 25,3 of the regicides' own action.

7. This phrase echoes that used by Josephus in 9,155 in reference to the cultic provisions laid down by the high priest Jehoiada, i.e. ἀκολούθως τῷ νομῷ. It takes the place of the more elaborate formulation common to 14,6 // 25,4 (MT), i.e. "according to what is written in the book of the law of Moses (BL 14,6 ἐν βιβλίῳ νόμων [B; L νόμου] Μωσῆ; B 25,4 κατὰ τὴν διαθήκην τοῦ νόμου Κυρίου; L 25,4 ἐν νομῷ Μωσῆ), where the Lord commanded...".

8. This verbal form echoes Josephus' characterization of Amaziah as "remarkably observant of justice (τοῦ δικαίου)" in 9,186.

9. With the formulation compare Josephus' version of Deut 24,16aβ in AJ 4,289 (παίδας ὑπὲρ ἀδικίας πατέρων μὴ κολάζειν). Josephus leaves aside the remaining portions of Deut 24,16 as cited in 14,6 // 25,4 ("the fathers shall not be put to death for the children [24,16aα]... but every man shall die for his own sin [24,16b]") as not directly relevant to the case at hand.

Amaziah's triumph over Edom in a single verse, whereas the Chronicler devotes 11 verses (25,5-16) to the happening, its background and immediate sequels. As is his wont in such cases, Josephus bases himself (9,188-195) on Chronicles' more expansive narrative.

2 Chr 25,5-10 recounts a series of events preceding Amaziah's actual devastation of Edom that is itself cited only in 25,11 // 14,7. This introductory sequence begins in v. 5 with mention of Amaziah's mustering of 300,000 picked troops from Judah and Benjamin (so MT L; B: Judah and Jerusalem). Josephus (9,188a) reproduces the Chronicler's notice with relatively minor variations: "Thereafter he raised an army from the tribes of Judah and Benjamin [so MT L 25,5] of such as were in their prime [25,5: picked men, fit for war, able to handle spear and shield] and about twenty years of age [25,5: from twenty years and above], and, having collected some three hundred thousand, appointed captains of hundreds (ἑκατοντάρχους = BL 25,5)[10] over them".

In 2 Chr 25,6 Amaziah "hires (BL ἐμισθώσατο) from Israel" an additional 100,000 troops at the cost of 100 talents of silver. Josephus' parallel report (9,188b) specifies that Amaziah procured these mercenaries from "the king of Israel" himself. To his version of Amaziah's double initiative according to 25,5-6 Josephus appends (9,188c) a statement of his own concerning the purpose behind it: "for he had decided (διεγνώκει; cf. ἔγνω, 9,186) to undertake a campaign against the nations of the *Amalekites* and Edomites (Ἰδουμαίων) and *Gabalites*". With this indication Josephus is, of course, anticipating (and preparing) the subsequent Biblical statements about the king's massacre of "Edom" (2 Kgs 14,7; TJ men of Edom)/ "men of Seir" (2 Chr 25,11). On the other hand, Josephus' formulation also, one notes, makes mention of two additional peoples, neither of them cited in the sources, as the target of Amaziah's projected campaign, i.e. the Amalekites and the Gabalites. How is this state of affairs to be explained? R. Marcus[11] points out that elsewhere as well Josephus associates the Edomites/Idumaeans with the other two peoples listed here in 9,188. Specifically in *AJ* 2,6 he states that the grandsons of Esau born to his son "Aliphaz", among them the bastard "Amalek(os)" (see Gen 36,12), "occupied the region of *Idumaea*[12] termed *Gobolitis* and that called, after Amalek, *Amalekitis*". Subsequently, in his parallel to the account of Israel's battle with

10. In 25,5 mention of these officers is preceded by reference to "the commanders of thousands" also appointed by Amaziah.

11. *Josephus*, VI, pp. 101-102, n. e.

12. For "Idumaea" as Josephus' standard name for the country called "Edom" in MT and alternatingly "Edom" and "Idumaea" in the LXX, see on 9,30.

Amalek (Exod 17,8-16) he designates (*AJ* 3,40) those who took the lead in the attempt to repulse the advancing Hebrews in the desert as "the inhabitants of *Gobolitis* and Petra who are called *Amalekites…*". Josephus' association of these other peoples with the "Edomites/Idumaeans", in turn, has a Biblical basis in Ps 83,6 where "Edom… Gebal… and Amalek" figure in a list of Israel's enemies[13]. I would further suggest that by thus introducing mention of the Amalekites in first place in his enumeration of Amaziah's "targets", Josephus intends to intimate a legitimation for the king's projected campaign – which in both Kings and Chronicles remains completely unmotivated – i.e. the divine injunction of Deut 25,17-19 (= *AJ* 4,309) that Amalek be exterminated for its sneak attack on Israel in the desert[14].

2 Chr 25,7-10 relates the intervention by "a man of God" which results in Amaziah's dismissing the just hired Israelite mercenaries. Josephus (9,189a) provides a smoother transition to this development – in the Bible Amaziah's interlocutor surfaces quite abruptly in 25,7a – by means of his inserted phrase "when he [Amaziah] had made his preparations for the campaign and was about to set out…". The historian likewise designates the one who admonishes Amaziah rather as "*the* prophet" (ὁ προφήτης). His use of the designation "prophet" in preference to the source's title ("man of God") is in line with Josephus' regular practice[15]; it likewise has a parallel in TC 2 Chr 25,7 which speaks of "a prophet" (נבא). On the other hand, Josephus' use of the definite article with the title is somewhat curious. As Weill remarks, this would suggest "… il s'agissait d'un personnage connu: cependant ni la Bible ni Josèphe ne donnent son nom[16]". In 25,7b the man of God tells Amaziah not to allow the Israelite army to accompany him on the grounds that the Lord is "not with Israel, with all these Ephraimites".

13. Also of interest here is TC 2 Chr 25,14 which, in place of MT's reference to Amaziah's carrying off "the gods of the men of *Seir*", has him remove "the idols of the men of *Gebal*".

14. On Josephus' treatment of the Amalekites see further: J. MAIER, *Amalek in the Writings of Josephus*, in F. PARENTE & J. SIEVERS (eds.), *Josephus & the History of the Greco-Roman Period: Essays in Memory of Morton Smith* (SPB, 41), Leiden, Brill, 1994, pp. 109-126; C.T. BEGG, *Israel's Battle with Amalek according to Josephus*, in *JSQ* 4 (1997) 201-216.

15. On the point, see BEGG, *Early Divided Monarchy*, pp. 24-25, n. 129.

16. *Josèphe*, II, p. 282, n. 4. Recall the comparable case of *AJ* 9,167 where for the reference in 2 Chr 24,19 to "prophets", Josephus speaks of "*the* prophets" whom God sent to the reprobate Joash and his people; cf. p. 195, n. 53. Rabbinic tradition does give a name to the prophetic figure of 2 Chr 25,7-10. Specifically, *SOR* 20.21 (see GIRÓN BLANC, *Seder 'Olam Rabbah*, p. 99) identifies him with Amoz, the father of Isaiah (see Isa 1,1) and brother of Amaziah himself (this last identification has no Biblical basis; it is, however, cited also in *b. Meg.* 10b and *b. Sot.* 10b as an old tradition deriving from R. Levi).

Josephus' prophet – whose words he relates in indirect discourse – is less peremptory in his speech to the king; he (9,189b) "advises" (συνεβούλευσεν) Amaziah to "dismiss (ἀπολῦσαι)[17] the Israelite army". The prophet then motivates this "advice" with a double affirmation which might be seen as an adaptation of the grounds adduced by his Biblical counterpart in 25,7b-8. The first reason cited by the Josephan prophet in support of his advice is that the Israelites are "impious men" (ἀσεβῆ), this charge representing the converse of the speaker's assertion of 25,7b that the Lord is "not with" them. Thereafter, the prophet goes on to warn the king about what awaits him should he ignore his advice: "... God foretold (προλέγειν)[18] a defeat (ἧτταν) for him if he employed them as allies (συμμάχοις)...". With this added warning compare the more emphatic threat issued Amaziah in 25,8: "If you suppose that in this way [i.e. with the support of the Israelite mercenaries] you will be strong for war, God will cast you down before the enemy, for God has the power to help or to cast down". To the prophet's foregoing evocation of the possibility of "defeat" for Amaziah inspired by 25,8, Josephus has him add (9,189c) a positive promise, itself an amplification of that verse's allusion to God's ability to "help" as well as to "cast down" (see above). This concluding element of the prophet's speech according to Josephus runs: "... but... he would overcome the enemy, even if he fought with only a few men, if God so willed (βουλομένου τοῦ θεοῦ)[19]".

Amaziah responds to his interlocutor in 25,9a with a question about the money he has already distributed to the hired Israelite forces. Josephus' version of this reply (9,190a) accentuates the king's "resistance" to the prophet's urgings: Amaziah "objected to this because of already (δυσφορούντος ... ἐπὶ τῷ φθῆναι)[20] having given the Israelites their pay...". Their dialogue then terminates in 25,9b with the man of God assuring Amaziah that "the Lord is able to give you much more than

17. The above expression "advised to dismiss" has a parallel in Josephus' account of another prophetic intevention, i.e. that of the prophet Oded who, in the reign of Amaziah's great-grandson Ahaz "advised" (συνεβούλευε) the Israelites "to release" (ἀπολύσαι) the Judean captives they had taken (9,249 = 2 Chr 28,11). This verbal correspondence serves to underscore the reverse parallelism of the situations described in 9,189 and 9,249; in the former text it is a Judean king who is being called on to "dismiss" an Israelite army, while in the latter it is the victorious Israelite forces who are urged to "release" the Judean troops they had captured.

18. Josephus' other uses of the verb προλέγω with God as subject are AJ 7,72; 8,232.319.406; 10,33.178; 11.96.

19. Other Josephan uses of this genitival construction are AJ 1,223.229.233; 3,45; 4,237.288; 8,237; 15,135. On the "will of God" as a key Josephan concept in AJ, see on 9,132.

20. This datival construction recurs in AJ 1,86; 2,163; 5,276; 6,2.38; 7,82.154.276.

this". Josephus (9,190b) amplifies with a renewed directive by the prophet to which he attaches a (specifying) rendition of the promise of 25,9b: "... whereupon the prophet *exhorted him to do what was pleasing to God* (παρῄνει ... ὅ τι τῷ θεῷ δοκεῖ)²¹, and said that he should have much wealth (χρήματα ... πολλά) from Him".

2 Chr 25,10 relates the sequels to the exchange of vv. 7-9: Amaziah does dismiss the Israelite force (v. 10a) to the latter's intense indignation (v. 10b). Josephus reserves the latter item to a subsequent point in his own presentation; see below. On the other hand he now gives (9,190c) an expanded version of 25,10a: "And so he dismissed (ἀπολύει; BL 25,10 διεχώρισεν)²² the Israelites, *saying that he would make them a present* (χαρίζεσθαι) *of their pay...*". The italicized phrase in this formulation has no equivalent in the source verse. Marcus²³ accordingly raises the question of whether Josephus' plus might not be due to his (mis-) reading of the BL form used in 25,10, i.e. διεχώρισεν ("he [Amaziah] separated [i.e. the Israelites from his force]") as διεχάρισατο ("he distributed gifts"). Alternatively, I would suggest that the item in question represents a free "invention" by Josephus designed to respond to a question left unclarified in the Bible itself, i.e. what became of the money which Amaziah states (25,9a) he had already handed over to the Israelites – were they allowed to retain this or not?

Following the elaborate preliminaries he relates in 25,5-10 (= 9,188-190c), the Chronicler narrates Amaziah's actual campaign more summarily in 25,11-13 (= 9,190d-192). The latter account begins in 25,11a with Amaziah's "strengthening himself" and then leading "his people to the Valley of Salt", this place name being derived from 2 Kgs 14,7a. Josephus' version (9,190d) omits mention of both the king's "self-strengthening" and of the specific destination of his advance. Conversely, in line with the indication of 9,188 about the king's plan to take on, not only the Edomites, but two other peoples as well, it speaks of Amaziah "with his own force marching *against the afore-mentioned nations*". The historian likewise elaborates (9,191a) on the enemy casualty figures cited in 25,11b // 14,7a: "*and, having defeated them in battle, he killed ten thousand of them...*²⁴".

21. On δοκέω with God as dival object (= "it pleased God"), see 9,176.

22. Josephus' use of the above verb serves to underscore the comformity between the king's action and the exhortation made him by the prophet who (9,189) "advised him to dismiss (ἀπολῦσαι συνεβούλευσεν) the Israelite army". Note too the historic present form of the verb here in 9,190 in place of the aorist employed by BL 25,10.

23. *Josephus*, VI, p. 101, n.g.

24. In 14,7 those whom Amaziah slays are called "Edomites", while 25,11 designates them as the "men of Seir". In line with his notice of 9,188 about Amaziah's intended

The Chronicler, who momentarily rejoined the sequence of 2 Kings in
25,11b (// 14,7a; see above), diverges again already in v. 12 from the
second half of the Kings verse. 2 Kgs 14,7b records that Amaziah captured "Sela" (so MT; BL understands the term as a common noun, i.e.
τὴν πέτραν) and renamed it "Jokthel" (so MT; BL Καθοήλ). 2 Chr
25,12 recasts Kings' reference to "Sela/the rock" into a notice on the
fate of an additional 10,000 Edomites whom the Judeans had captured
alive: the victors convey their captives to "the top of the rock (הַסֶּלַע,
MT; BL τοῦ κρημνοῦ)" whence they toss them down with the result
that the Edomites are all "dashed to pieces". Josephus, for his part, does
clearly (9,191b) follow the presentation of 25,12 against that of 14,7b.
On the other hand, he makes, not the Judeans *en bloc* (so Chronicles),
but Amaziah himself the perpetrator of the "rock massacre" (as also of
the previous slaughter of the 10,000, so 14,7a // 25,11b): "... he took
alive as many more [i.e. as the just-mentioned 10,000 slain by him in
battle], whom he then led to the great rock (τὴν μεγάλην ... πέτραν;
cf. τὴν πέτραν, BL 14,7b) *which is over against Arabia*[25], and hurled
(κατεκρήμνισεν, BL 25,12 κατεκρήμνιζον) them from it...". He then
rounds off (9,191c) his battle account with mention of the realization of
the prophet's promise ("... he should have much wealth") of 9,190 =
25,9b: "... he [Amaziah] also carried off much booty (λείαν πολλήν)
and untold wealth (πλοῦτον ἄφθονον) from these nations [i.e. those
cited in 9,188]". This item has no Biblical parallel as such. By means
of it, Josephus, in accord with a recurrent tendency, does make clear,
first of all, that the prophetic promise cited by him 9,190 indeed came
to realization. In addition, such inserted notices on the magnitude of
the booty acquired by his people from their defeated foes are a characteristic feature of Josephus' rewriting of Biblical battle accounts, one
designed, as pointed out by L.H. Feldman, to counteract contemporary
claims about the Jews being an impecunious people[26].

three targets (Amalekites, Edomites, Gabalites), Josephus represents the king as defeating
and killing (representatives of) all three of those nations.

25. This localization of "the great rock" where Amaziah perpetrates his massacre has
no parallel in 25,12. It does, however, hark back to *AJ* 4,82 where Josephus locates the
site of Aaron's death as "a place *in Arabia*, today named *Petra* (Πέτραν)"; see also the
above-cited 3,40 with its reference to the threat to Israel from "those inhabitants of
Gobolitis and Petra (Πέτραν) who are called Amalekites", i.e. the peoples against whom
Amaziah decides to war in 9,188. Josephus is perhaps then thinking of "the rock in
Arabia" at which he locates the massacre in 9,191 as the site of the future city of Petra,
cf. MARCUS, *Josephus*, VI, p. 102, n.a.

26. On the point, see FELDMAN, *Interpretation*, p. 543 (= ID., *David*, 138-139) and
BEGG, *Early Divided Monarchy*, p. 122, n. 765. To the examples cited in that note I would
here add that in *AJ* 3,57 where Josephus introduces a lengthy enumeration of the booty

It is only at this point, now that he has recounted Amaziah's victorious campaign, that Josephus comes (9,192) to speak, for the first time (compare 25,10b), of the Israelites' reaction to the king's "dismissal" of them (9,190b = 25,10a; see above). In so doing, he brings together in a continuous sequence data which appear separately in Chronicles, i.e. the mercenaries' anger at their dismissal (25,10b) and their expression of this anger by ravaging Judean cities (25,13), the account of Amaziah's campaign supervening in 25,11-12. Josephus introduces (9,192a) his "delayed" mention of the Israelites' negative emotional reaction to their dismissal by noting that they gave vent to this "while Amasias was so engaged [i.e. in his war against the three peoples]". By means of this indication he provides an implicit answer to a difficulty the Biblical presentation might evoke, i.e. how was it that the Israelite mercenaries could devastate Amaziah's domains with apparent impunity (as they are depicted as doing in 25,13), i.e. they could do so because the king was not on hand to hinder them. Josephus then proceeds to expatiate on 25,10b's reference ("they became very angry at Judah, and returned home in a fierce rage") to the Israelites' emotional state by noting the reason for their feeling as they do: "... the Israelites *whom he had dismissed* (ἀπέλυσε; cf. ἀπολῦσαι, 9,189; ἀπολύει, 9,190) *after hiring* (μισθωσάμενος; cf. μισθοῦται, 9,188; μισθόν, 9,190) *them*[27] showed resentment at this act (ἀγανακτήσαντες ἐπὶ τούτῳ)[28], *and, considering their dismissal* (ἀπολύσιν)[29] *an insult* (ὕβριν) – *for, they said, they would not have experienced this treatment had they not been held in contempt* (κατεγνωσμένους) – ...". Thereafter, he relates (9,192b) the Israelites' "expression" of their "resentment" (// 25,13): "... they fell upon his [Amaziah's] kingdom and advancing as far as Bethsemēra (Βηθσεμήρων)[30], ravaged

taken by Israel from the defeated Amalekites which lacks all parallel in the source text, i.e. Exod 17,8-16. Perhaps then that earlier text – along with the prophetic promise of 25,9b = 9,190 – has influenced Josephus in appending a "booty notice" to his account of Amaziah's victory over, *inter alia*, the Amalekites (see 9,188). Thereby, the parallelism between his presentation of the two Amalekite war episodes is accentuated.

27. The above inserted qualification concerning the Israelites here in 9,192 with its reminiscences of terminology employed in reference to them in 9,188-190c (see above) is appropriate given the fact that they are now being re-introduced, following the intervening campaign account of 9,190d-191.

28. Other instances of the above construction (ἀγανακτέω) + ἐπὶ + dative in Josephus are *BJ* 4,162; 5,5; *AJ* 1,202; 4,126; 7,206 (same phase as in 9,192); 19,307; 20,120 (same phase); *c. Ap.* 1,306.

29. By means of this noun Josephus creates a wordplay with his previous uses of the verb ἀπολύω in our pericope; see 9,189.190.192.

30. This curious form (compare Lat's Bethoron) would seem to represent a conflation of the two place names, i.e. "Samaria" and "Beth-horon", which in 25,13 mark the limits of the Israelites' devastation. In addition, it may be that the reference to "Beth-shemesh"

the country and took many cattle (πολλὰ ... ὑποζύγια)³¹ and killed (ἀπέκτειναν) three thousand men"³².

2 Chr 25,15-16 (= AJ 9,194-195) relates the sequel to Amaziah's Edomite triumph, i.e. his run-in with "prophet(s)". This second interaction between king and a divine envoy (see 25,7-9) is, in turn, provoked by Amaziah's misdeed as related in 25,14, i.e. his bringing back the Edomite gods and offering worship to these. Josephus (9,193) recasts the notice of 25,14, preceding mention of the king's actions with a reference to the royal mental state that prompted these. His version thus reads: "But Amasias, *elated at his victory* (τῇ νίκῃ ... ἐπαρθείς)³³ *and achievements* (κατορθώμασιν)³⁴, *began to neglect God* (θεὸν ... ὑπερορᾶν)³⁵, *who had been the cause* (αἴτιον) *of them*³⁶, and persisted in worshipping (σεβόμενος διετέλει)³⁷ (the gods) whom he had brought from the country of the Amalekites³⁸". In the above formulation Josephus "anticipates", in this his opening reference to Amaziah's reaction to his victory, the comment of King Joash of Israel (14,10 // 25,19) about the Judean's "heart being lifted up (in boastfulness)" as a result of his conquest of Edom.

as the site of the subsequent battle between Amaziah and Joash in 2 Kgs 14,11.13 (// 2 Chr 25,21.23) has affected the above form. See MARCUS, *Josephus*, VI, p. 103, n. d.

31. This phrase is Josephus' specification of the more general reference to the "much spoil" (BL σκῦλα πολλά) which the Israelites are said to carry off in 25,13.

32. In 25,13b the Israelites' deeds are cited in the reverse order, i.e. first their killings, then their plundering. Note the verbal parallelism which Josephus sets up between Amaziah's own initiatives and those of the Israelites. Amaziah himself "killed" (ἀπέκτεινε) 10,000 enemies and then carried off "much (πολλήν) booty", 9,191. While he is so occupied, the Israelites took "many (πολλά) cattle" and "killed" (ἀπέκτειναν) 3,000 Judeans (9,192).

33. The above construction ἐπαίρω + dative occurs also in *BJ* 3,9; 4,27.42; 7,371; *AJ* 8,209; 11,311; 13,186; 15,27; 17,96. In all these instances, as above, the construction relates to a person's "over-confidence", this prompted by some success, promise, or hope.

34. The noun κατόρθωμια occurs 27 times in *BJ*, but only three times in *AJ* (6,213.272; 9,193).

35. This is Josephus' only use of the verb ὑπερορἀω with "God" as object. The historian's inserted reference to Amaziah's "neglect of (his own) God" here is the corrollary to his worshipping the Edomite divinities as cited in 25,14 (and the continuation of 9,193).

36. This inserted reference to God as the "cause" of Amaziah's triumph implicitly underscores the wrongfulness of the king's "(self-)elation" over this and his "neglect" of the one to whom he owed it.

37. Compare 25,14: (Amaziah) "set them up as gods and worshiped (BL προσκυνεῖν) them, making offerings (BL ἔθυεν) to them".

38. In 25,14 (MT and BL) Amaziah's new "gods" are called those "of the sons of Seir". Josephus' alternative designation for the people in question accords with the fact that, throughout his presentation (see 9,188.198), he highlights the "Amalekites" among the three peoples attacked by Amaziah. Recall that in its 25,14 TC refers to "the idols of the sons of *Gebal*", i.e. a people who in Ps 83,6 (as well as in *AJ* 2,6; 3,40) are associated with the Amalekites; see n. 13).

By moving this item to an earlier point in his presentation, Josephus high-lights the perspective in which the whole disastrous sequel to Amaziah's victory is to be seen, i.e. as an instance of the well-known sequence of Greek tragedy in which success breeds a hubris which itself evokes divine punishment[39]. In addition, the historian's emphasis on Amaziah's "elation" here in 9,193 accentuates the contrast between him and the dis-missed Israelites of 9,192 who regarded their dismissal as an "insult" (ὕβριν) and themselves as having been treated with "contempt"[40].

2 Chr 25,15a notes that the Lord became "angry" with the idolator Amaziah to whom he sent "a prophet" (so MT TC; BL προφήτας). Josephus (9,194a), leaving aside both the divine anger and resultant "sending", has "the prophet" (ὁ προφήτης)[41] approach Amaziah on his own initiative. The prophet(s) of v. 15a proceeds in v. 15b to address the king with a reproachful question which points up the folly of his idola-trous deed: "Why have you resorted to the gods of a people, which did not deliver their own people from your hand?" Josephus (9,194), once again transposing into indirect discourse, expands:

(the prophet said that) he wondered (θαυμάζειν)[42] how he could consider those beings as gods who had neither given any help to their own people, *by whom they were honoured*, nor saved them from his hands (μηδ' ἐκ χειρῶν ἐρρύσαντο; BL 25,15: οὐκ ἐξείλαντο ... ἐκ χειρός σου), *but had looked on while many of them were perishing, and had allowed themselves to be taken captive* (αἰχμαλωτισθέντας) *for they had, he said, been brought to Jerusalem in the same manner one might bring enemies whom one had taken alive* (ζωγρήσας; cf. ζῶντας ἔλαβεν, of the persons seized by Amaziah, 9,191).

With the above elaboration of the prophetic word of 25,15b Josephus still further accentuates the foolishness of Amaziah's action by insisting

39. On Josephus' application of this pattern to other Biblical episodes (e.g., his retelling of the Tower of Babel episode in *AJ* 1,103-109), see FELDMAN, *Interpretation*, pp. 180-181; ID., *Studies*, p. 563; and BEGG, *Early Divided Monarchy*, p. 70, n. 401 with the literature cited there.

40. Note in this connection that Josephus' highlighting of the ("over-) elation" which Amaziah's success evokes in him has a counterpart in his (Biblically unparalleled) notice on the outcome of the Israelite triumph over Amalek in *AJ* 3,57: "the Hebrews now [after the battle] began to plume themselves on their valour and to have high aspirations to heroism...".

41. Given the use of the definite article here, Josephus likely intends the figure of 9,194 to be identified with "the prophet" of 9,189-190. Neither the Bible nor Josephus give a name to the prophet who confronts Amaziah at this juncture. The *VL* version of 25,15 cited by Lucifer Calaritanus (*De non parcendo in Deum delinquentibus* 5.36, ed. G. DIERCKS, *Luciferi Calaritani Opera quae supersunt* [CC SL, 36], Turnhout, Brepols, 1978, p. 203) calls him "Baneas".

42. Other Josephan orators as well begin their discourses by expressing their "won-der" at some state of affairs; see *BJ* 1,198. 501.628; 3,405; 4,93.238; 5,462; *AJ* 1,57; 8,272; 12,205.

that the gods taken over by him had shown themselves, not only impotent and indifferent in the face of their worshippers' plight, but had even been unable to prevent their own humiliating capture and display. With this last notice Josephus put readers in mind of the contemporary Roman practice of the triumph in which booty seized from the foe was exhibited in the capital. He likewise (ironically) foreshadows the fate awaiting the gods' captor himself; see below.

Amaziah responds to the prophet's intervention in 25,16a by first challenging his right to speak ("Have we [BL: I] made you a royal counselor?"), and then by threatening him with execution ("why should you be put to death [MT; BL: beware lest you be scourged]?"). Josephus (9,195a), characteristically, precedes the king's response with mention of the emotional state that prompts it: "but these words moved the king to anger (ὀργὴν ἐκίνησε)...[43]". He then continues with Amaziah's actual reply: "and he ordered the prophet to hold his peace (ἡσυχίαν ἄγειν), threatening to punish (ἀπειλήσας ... κολάσειν)[44] him if he meddled in these affairs". 2 Chr 25,16b recounts the prophet's reaction to the king's rejection of his warning: he does desist, though not before informing Amaziah "I know that God (MT; > B; the Lord, L) has determined to destroy you because you have done this and not listened to my counsel". Once against replacing direct with indirect discourse, Josephus (9,195b) makes the source notice on his desisting part of the prophet's reply itself: "and the other, though he said he would hold his peace (ἡσυχάζειν; cf. ἡσυχίαν ἄγειν, 9,195a), foretold (προύλεγεν)[45]

43. Variants of this construction, employing a preposition ("to"), occur in *AJ* 6,186; 12,158.

44. Amaziah's threatening to "punish" the prophet here echoes language used by Josephus earlier in reference to the king; see 9,187 (Amaziah "decided... to punish [κολάσαι]" his father's murderers) and 188 (in so doing, Amaziah acted "in accordance with the laws of Moses, who declared it unjust to punish [κολάζειν] children for the sins of their fathers"). In these earlier passages the "punishment" resolved upon and executed by Amaziah was, of course, a righteous one, whereas, now in 9,195, the "punishment" he threatens is an unjustified one and hence indicative of his moral decline. With the above wording compare also Josephus' formulation (9,224) regarding Amaziah's son and successor Uzziah when confronted by the priests over his intended cultic transgression: "he became angry (ὀργισθείς) and threatened (ἠπείλησεν) them with death if they did not hold their peace (τὴν ἡσυχίαν ἄξουσι)". In Josephus' presentation the parallels between Amaziah and Uzziah are even more far-reaching, however: both kings' achievements cause them to become puffed up, this showing itself in their turning to wrongful cultic measures. When rebuked concerning those measures, they both respond with threatening words (see above), but ultimately end up themselves as the ones who are punished. It seems clear than that readers are intended to see the pattern of success-hubris – (disregarded) warning – punishment as playing itself out from father to son in the case of the Josephan Amaziah and Uzziah; see further chap. XII.

45. Compare 9,189 where the prophet informs Amaziah τὸν θεὸν ... προλέγειν.

that God [cf. MT 25,16b] would not overlook (ἀμελήσειν)⁴⁶ the strange and unlawful practices (νεωτερίζων)⁴⁷ to which he had set his hand".

4. *Judah vs. Israel*

Following the Chronicler's long expansion of the "Edom notice" of 2 Kgs 14,7 in 25,5-16, the two Biblical accounts once again converge in 14,8-14(15-16) // 25,17-24, the story of Amaziah's disastrous provocation of Joash of Israel. Josephus' version of this new episode is 9,196-202.

2 Kgs 14,8 // 2 Chr 25,17 record Amaziah's "sending" to Joash with the challenge "come let us look one another in the face". Josephus (9,196a) precedes his parallel to this notice with an elaborate reference to the mental state that prompts Amaziah's initiative: "Amasias, however, was not able to contain himself at this good fortune (κατέχειν ἑαυτὸν ἐπὶ ταῖς εὐπραγίαις οὐ δυνάμενος)⁴⁸, but outraged God (εἰς αὐτὸν ἐξύβριζεν)⁴⁹ from whom he had received it⁵⁰, and in his presumption (φρονηματισθείς)... ⁵¹". This introductory description of Amaziah's state of mind as he challenges Joash clearly harks back to

46. Josephus' three remaining uses of the verb ἀμελέω with God/the Deity as subject are: *AJ* 4,13 (God does not "suffer" the rebellious Israelites altogether to escape disaster); 5,31 (the realization of the curse pronounced over any who would attempt to rebuild Jericho is not left "unregarded" by the Deity); and 11,300 (the Deity was "not indifferent" to the high priest's murder of his brother in the Temple).

47. The verb νεωτερίζω (along with its various nominal and adjectival cognates) is used with considerable frequency by Josephus particularly in reference to the "agitation" and "sedition" of the Jewish rebels against Rome as described in *BJ*; see RENGSTORF, *Concordance*, III, s.v. As such the term has highly negative connotations for Josephus, denoting as it does the antithesis of the ideal of fidelity to established ways in religion and society cherished by him.

48. The above formulation echoes that of *AJ* 6,63 where Josephus, as part of an extended extra-Biblical reflection, contrasts the "restraint and modesty" displayed by Saul at the outset of his career with the behavior of "most people" in similarly auspicious circumstances who οὐδ' ἐπὶ ... εὐπραγίαις ... τὴν χαρὰν κατασχεῖν δυναμένων.

49. The above verb echoes Josephus' reference to the dismissed mercenaries "considering their dismissal an insult (ὕβριν)" in 9,192; Amaziah's "insults", it now emerges, extend to God himself. Elsewhere Josephus uses the construction ἐξυβρίζω + εἰς with God as object in *BJ* 2,230 (a Roman soldier); 5,394 (Antiochus Epiphanes); *AJ* 1,100 (humanity as a whole); 8,245 (Jeroboam I). 265 (Jeroboam I). 299 (Baasha); 10,39 (the Israelites). The application to the Judean Amaziah by Josephus here in 9,196 of a formula thrice used by him of notorious Northern kings accentuates the former's godlessness (and prepares for the bad end to which he will come); see n. 56.

50. This appended characterization of God, insisting on his role as the giver of Amaziah's victory harks back to Josephus' reference in 9,193 to the Deity as "the cause" of the king's triumphs. In both instances, the qualification serves to underscore the wrongfulness of the king's treatment of the one who had so assisted him.

51. Josephus' one remaining use of the verb φρονηματίζομαι is in *AJ* 5,222 where Gideon's men are "elated" (φρονηματισθέντες) when he tells them of his dream.

Josephus' (likewise Biblically unparalleled) reference to the king's immediate reaction to his triumph in 9,193 ("But Amasias, elated at his victory and achievements, began to neglect God, who had been the cause of them..."). Here in 9,196, however, the king's continued self-delusion appears all the more reprehensible in that, in the interlude, he has been warned by the prophet.

Only after the preceding psychological preface does Josephus come to relate (9,196b) Amaziah's actual challenge, the obscurely laconic Biblical wording of which ("come let us look one another in the face", 14,8 // 25,17) he elaborates and clarifies:

> (Amaziah)... wrote (14,8 // 25,17 sent) to Joas, the king of the Israelites, commanding him to submit to him with all his people *just as formerly they had submitted to his forefathers David and Solomon; if he refused to be reasonable* (εὐγνωμονεῖν)[52], let him understand that the question of supremacy (ἀρχῆς) would have to be decided by war.

The above version of Amaziah's message does indeed give evidence of that "presumption" Josephus had attributed to him just previously: the king thinks he can "command" the "submission" of Joash and his people, just as he has an altogether misplaced confidence in his own military superiority – as events will soon prove.

In 2 Kgs 14,9a // 2 Chr 25,18a Joash, in turn, "sends" to Amaziah. Josephus (9,197) substitutes he "wrote back", matching his earlier "he wrote" for Amaziah himself. The content of Joash's message is a fable (14,10 // 25,18b) for which Josephus' version is 9,197-198 and which he prefaces with a formal letter opening "King Joas to King Amasias[53]".

According to the Biblical fable the two plant characters are a "cedar" (BL 14,9b // 25,18: τὴν κέδρον) and a "thistle" (B 14,9: ὁ ἀκάν [L ἀκχάν]; BL 25,18 uses first ὁ χοζεί, then τὸν ἀχούχ). Josephus' word for "thistle" is (ἡ) ἄκανος (compare B 14,9), the two occurrences of this term in 9,197 being its only uses in his corpus. In addition, he turns the sources' "cedar" into a "*very great* cypress" (κυπάρισσος παμμεγέθης)[54].

---

52. Josephus' only other use of the verb εὐγνωμονέω is in *AJ* 17,240 ("they compelled men of conciliatory spirit [τῶν εὐγνωμονεῖν] to defend themselves by fighting").

53. This salutation echoes that of the letter sent by Hiram to Solomon as cited in *AJ* 8,53 (= 1 Kgs 5,22, MT): "King Eirōmos to King Solomon". We shall note further verbal reminiscences of that earlier letter in Josephus' version of Joash's communication in 9,197-198.

54. Apart from 9,197, Josephus' only mention of the "cypress" is in *AJ* 8,54 (= 1 Kgs 5,22, MT) where, in the context of Hiram's letter to Solomon, one reads the phrase ξύλα ... μεγάλα κέδρου ... καὶ κυπαρίσσου which Josephus is perhaps deliberately echoing here in 9,197 with his reference to a "*great* cypress"; see n. 53. In any case, his inserted qualification of the cypress as "great" does serve to accentuate the contrast between it and the upstart thistle.

The Biblical fable continues with the thistle summoning the cedar to "give your daughter to my son for a wife". Josephus does reproduce this speech of a talking plant, though rendering it in indirect discourse. Thereafter, he makes the transition to the description of the thistle's fate (14,9bβ // 25,18bβ) with the inserted phase "... but meanwhile, as she was asking this...". What befalls the thistle at this juncture is that a passing "beast of the field" (MT; BL 14,9 // 25,18 read the plural τὰ θηρία) "tramples it down". With MT Josephus speaks of "a beast" (θηρίον), while at the same time using the same verbal form (κατεπάτησε) of the beast's action as does L* 25,18 (B 25,18 reads the plural, while B 14,9 has συνεπάτησαν [L* sg.])[55].

2 Kgs 14,10 // 2 Chr 25,19 report Joash's "application" of his fable as addressed by him to Amaziah with minor variations: the latter's victory over the Edomites, Joash avers, has resulted in his heart's lifting him up (+ in boastfulness, 25,19). He then goes on to urge the Judean to "stay at home", motivating this exhortation with the warning question "why should you provoke trouble, so that you fall, you and Judah with you"? Josephus' version (9,198) of Joash's admonition – where for once in our pericope he retains the Biblical direct discourse – opens with an explicit summons to Amaziah to draw a lesson from what he has heard, just it accentuates the sources' reference to the Judean king's current self-exaltation:

> Let this therefore be an example (παράδειγμα) to you not to reach for what is beyond you (τοῦ μὴ μειζόνων ἐφίεσθαι)[56], nor, because you were lucky (εὐτύχησας)[57] in battle against the *Amalekites*[58], need you take so much pride (γαυρούμενος)[59] in that and bring down danger upon yourself and your kingdom.

55. TC appends to its rendering of 25,18 a long plus, in which Joash, continuing to address himself to Amaziah, recalls the foregoing "mercenary affair" (25,6-10.13 = 9,188b-190a.192). Josephus has no equivalent to this plus in his rendition of Joash's fable. Joash's statement in the course of this plus that Amaziah had sent to himself to hire the mercenaries does, however, correspond to Josephus' notice on the point in 9,188 (compare 25,6 where Amaziah is said to hire them "from Israel", with no mention of Joash personally).

56. Josephus' two other uses of the above construction – in these instances without the negation – are in *BJ* 2,590 (John of Gischala, Josephus' great rival, "had yet higher ambitions"); and *AJ* 5,251 (Abimelech "was aspiring higher"). The terminological link Josephus makes here between Amaziah and these two notorious figures serves to place the former in very bad company; see n. 49.

57. This verbal form echoes the phrase ἐπὶ ταῖς εὐπραγίαις in Josephus' description of the mental state which prompts Amaziah to challenge Joash in 9,196.

58. Note, here again, Josephus' substitution of this people for the one cited in the sources (14,10 // 25,19), i.e. "Edom". See on 9,193.

59. The verb γαυρόομαι is hapax in Josephus.

2 Kgs 14,11a and 2 Chr 25,20 both report that Amaziah "would not listen"; the Chronicler goes on to evoke a theological motivation for his heedlessness, i.e. "for it was of God (BL the Lord) in order that he might give them into the hand of their enemies, because they had sought the gods of Edom [cf. 25,14]". Josephus (9,199a) follows the Chronicler's expanded version, likewise accentuating Amaziah's disregard of Joash's warning: *"When Amasias read this letter* [cf. the reference to Joash's "writing back" to him in 9,197], he was still further provoked (παρωξύνθη) into making war; it was God, *I think* (οἶμαι), who urged him on (τοῦ θεοῦ παρορμῶντος)⁶⁰ to it, in order that he might suffer punishment (ἵνα ... δίκην ἀπολάβῃ)⁶¹ for his transgressions against Him (παρανομηθέντων εἰς αὐτόν)⁶²".

2 Kgs 14,11b // 2 Chr 25,21 narrate the two kings' coming face to face for battle "at Beth-shemesh which belongs to Judah". Josephus' parallel (9,199b) leaves aside the Biblical place name⁶³: "But, after he had marched out with his force (μετὰ τῆς δυνάμεως)⁶⁴ against Joas, and

60. Elsewhere Josephus uses the verb παρομάω (*in bonam partem*) with God as subject in *AJ* 4,111 (God "exhorted" Balaam to pursue his way) and 11,3 (God "stirred up" the spirit of Cyrus). With the above statement of Josephus' "opinion" as to the supernatural agency active in Amaziah's (self-destructive) decision to proceed against Joash, compare his similar formulations in *AJ* 8,409 ("It was Fate, I suppose, that prevailed [ἐνίκα ... οἶμαι τὸ χρεών]", i.e. in causing Ahab to lend credence to the false prophets and so suffer loss of his own life); and 10,76 ("It was Destiny, I believe, that urged him [Josiah] on [τῆς πεπρωμένης, οἶμαι, ... παρομησάσης] to this course [i.e. his fatal attempt to block Neco's advance]"). These two passages further have in common with 9,199 the fact that the supernatural power in question overrides the good advice given an Israelite/Judean king by some "prophet-like" figure (Micaiah, Joash, Neco), thereby acting to bring disaster on the former. At the same time, it should be noted that whereas in 9,199 Josephus follows 25,20 in evoking God as the cause of Amaziah's ill-conceived decision, in 8,409 and 10,76, he "Hellenizes" his language, attributing the disastrous royal resolve to the operation of "Fate" or "Destiny", respectively.

61. The other Josephan uses of the above construction "suffer punishment" are *AJ* 6,117.124 (both times in connection with the battlefield penalty prescribed by Saul which becomes a threat to his son Jonathan). With the above purpose clause specifying why God "urged Amaziah on" compare that appended to the parallel notices of 8,409: "(fate prevailed)... in order to hasten Achab's end (ἵνα λάβῃ τὴν ἀφορμὴν τοῦ τέλους)" and 10,76: "(Destiny urged Josiah on) in order to have a pretext for destroying him (ἵνα λάβῃ πρόφασιν κατ' αὐτοῦ)"; see previous note.

62. The above phrase has a counterpart in Josephus' account of Amaziah's son Uzziah in *AJ* 9,224: "(the priests clamoured for Uzziah) not to transgress against God (παρανομεῖν εἰς τὸν θεόν)". See n. 44. Note further the contrasting wordplay between the above statement about Amaziah's "transgressions (παρανομηθέντων) against God" and Josephus' earlier reference to the king's "acting in accordance with the laws (νόμοις) of Moses" (9,187).

63. Compare his omission of the sources' localization of Amaziah's Edomite massacre in "the Valley of Salt" (so 14,7 // 25,11) in 9,191.

64. This phrase echoes that used in 9,190 in connection with Amaziah's advance against the three foreign peoples ("... he himself with his own force [μετὰ τῆς οἰκείας

they were about to join battle…". In 2 Kgs 14,12 // 2 Chr 25,22 the battle itself is narrated with almost anti-climactic brevity: "And Judah was defeated (MT וַיִּנָּגֶף; BL 14,12 ἔπταισεν; BL 25,22 ἐτροπώθη) by Israel, and every man fled to his home". Josephus takes care to dramatize these minimalistic data, likewise calling attention to the divine involvement in Judah's debacle[65]: "… there came upon the army of Amasias such a sudden terror (φόβος αἰφνίδιος)[66] and consternation (κατάπληξις)[67] *as God inspires when He is unpropitious* (οὐκ εὐμενής)[68], and turned them to flight".

The continuation of the Biblical accounts, i.e. 14,13a // 25,23a, simply juxtaposes the fact of Amaziah's own being captured at Beth-shemesh with the flight of all his men as reported in 14,12 // 25,22. Josephus (9,200a), continuing to elaborate the sources' summary indications (though once again omitting their place name "Beth-shemesh"), points up the causal nexus between the two happenings: "*and, when they were dispersed in alarm before even a blow was struck, the result was that* Amasias, *being left alone*, was taken captive (αἰχμάλωτον)[69] by the enemy (πρὸς τῶν πολεμίων)[70]".

2 Kgs 14,13b // 2 Chr 25,23b relate the sequels to Joash's capture of Amaziah: the two kings come to Jerusalem, whereupon Joash "broke down the wall of Jerusalem for four hundred cubits, from the Ephraim Gate to the Corner Gate". Josephus (9,200b-201a) prefaces the Bible's notices on Joash's initiative with an extended sequence explaining how the Israelite king was able to do what he did given that nothing has been said of a previous conquest of the city by him. This reads:

δυνάμεως] marched against the afore-mentioned nations"). Whereas, however, that earlier advance resulted in a triumph for Amaziah, the current one will end in ignominious defeat.

65. In this connection see the remark of MARCUS, *Josephus*, VI, p. 106, n. a: "The account of the battle is amplified [by Josephus]. Josephus, however, seems rightly to have recognized that the Heb. verb *yinnāgeph* [of 14,12 // 25,22; see above]… applied to Judah, really means 'was seized by divinely inspired terror in battle'".

66. This is Josephus' only use of the above phrase.

67. This noun occurs 19 times in *BJ*; elsewhere in *AJ* its only other uses are in 5,63 and 8,177 (= "dazzlement").

68. Compare 9,258 where Josephus states that Hoshea, Israel's last king "did not have God propitious (οὐκ εἶχεν … εὐμενῆ) to him…".

69. This participial form ironically echoes the anonymous prophet's use of the term αἰχμαλωτισθέντας for the Amalekite gods who "had allowed themselves to be taken captive" by Amaziah in 9,194. There, Amaziah was the captor, while here in 9,200 he becomes himself a captive.

70. The referent of this plural form is the Israelites as a whole. In 14,13a // 25,23a the capture of Amaziah is attributed to Joash personally.

(200) And Joas threatened him with death (ἠπείλησε ... αὐτῷ θάνατον)[71] unless he persuaded the people of Jerusalem to open their gates to him and to admit him with his army into their city. (201) And so Amasias from necessity (ἀνάγκης) and fear for his life (τοῦ περὶ τὸ ζῆν δέους)[72] caused the enemy to be admitted[73].

Only after the above "interlude" does Josephus come to relate (9,201b) the Biblical datum (14,13b // 25,23b) of Joash's wall-demolition, leaving aside, however, the source specifications concerning the starting and end points ("from the Ephraim Gate to the Corner Gate") of this process: "... Joas then broke down (διακόψας)[74] the wall for a distance of about four hundred cubits...". To this notice he then appends a reference to the use made by the Israelite king of the space thus created: "... and in his chariot rode through the breach (διακοπῆς)[75] into Jerusalem, leading Amasias captive (αἰχμάλωτον; see 9,200)[76]".

2 Kgs 14,14 // 2 Chr 25,24 conclude the episode of the conflict between Joash and Amaziah by enumerating a further series of measures perpetrated by the former: taking the gold and silver, as well as the vessels of the Temple[77] and the palace, along with "hostages", he returned to Samaria. Josephus both re-arranges and elaborates in his rendition (9,202): "*And, having become master* (κύριος) *of Jerusalem in this*

71. Here again (see n. 44) there is an ironic echo of wording employed by Josephus earlier in his account of Amaziah. See 9,195 where to the prophet's admonitions, the king responds by "threatening to punish him" (ἀπειλήσας αὐτὸν κολάσειν). Having disregarded the prophet's warning, Amaziah now finds himself being "threatened with death".

72. The above collocation "necessity and fear" appears also in *BJ* 5,427.

73. Elsewhere as well Josephus goes beyond the Bible in specifying that it was "out of fear" that a given Judean king admitted an enemy ruler into Jerusalem; see *AJ* 8,258 (Rehoboam) and 10,96 (Jehoiakim).

74. This is Josephus' only use of the verb διακόπτω in *AJ*; it occurs 12 times in *BJ*. The same verb is read by a number of LXX MSS in 14,13b; compare BL 14,13 and L 25,23 (καθεῖλε[ν]); B 25,23 (κατέσπασεν).

75. This noun form echoes the participle διακόψας used earlier in 9,201.

76. The ironic echoes of Josephus' earlier presentation of Amaziah continue here. In 9,194 he has the prophet refer to the king's having brought the captive (αἰχμαλωτισθέντας) gods to Jerusalem "in the same manner as one might bring enemies whom one had taken alive". Now (9,201) this very fate befalls the heedless king who is dragged into his own capital behind the chariot of his captor. In both instances, Josephus might well have in view the contemporary Roman custom of the triumph. In 9,218 he will introduce a (Biblically unparalleled) *Rückverweis* to Joash's deed here in 9,201: "(Uzziah rebuilt those portions of the Jerusalem wall) which had been thrown down by the king of Israel when, after taking his father Amasias captive (αἰχμάλωτον, so 9,200.201), he entered the city".

77. MT (and L) 25,24 append the words "of Obed-Edom" (> B) to their mention of the "house of the Lord". TC expatiates on this reference, recalling that Obed-Edom had dedicated the vessels in question at the time when David took the Ark from his house (cf. 2 Samuel 6 // 1 Chronicles 13-16). Josephus' rendition lacks mention of Obed-Edom; see above.

way[78], he carried off the treasures of God (τοὺς ... τοῦ θεοῦ θησαυρούς)[79], and took out all the gold and silver *that Amasias had in his palace*[80], *then having released him from captivity* (ἀπολύσας τῆς αἰχμαλωσίας)[81] *under these conditions*[82], he departed for Samaria (εἰς Σαμάρειαν = BL 14,14 // 25,24)".

Following their common mention of Joash's return to Samaria (14,14 // 25,24), the sources diverge once again. 2 Kgs 14,15-16 (MT and B) appends closing notices for Joash which recapitulate those already given in 13,12-13[83]. 2 Chr 25,25, by contrast, proceeds immediately to the chronological indication concerning Amaziah's surviving Joash by fifteen years (= 2 Kgs 14,17). Josephus, for his part, follows (9,203a) mention of Joash's withdrawal at the end of 9,202 with a chronological notation of his own, i.e.: "these things [i.e. the series of calamities related in 9,200-202] happened to the people of Jerusalem in the fourteenth year of the reign of Amasias...". This dating of Amaziah's debacle is not, as such, Biblically paralleled. For it, Josephus seems to have based himself, however, on the disparate chronological data of 2 Kgs 14,2 // 2 Chr 25,1 (Amaziah reigned a total of 29 years) and 14,17 // 25,25 (Amaziah outlived Joash by 15 years). In utilizing these data, Josephus apparently assumed that Joash's triumph over Amaziah was

78. With this inserted transitional phrase Josephus harks back to his – likewise interjected – account of Joash's compelling Amaziah to secure him entry into Jerusalem in 9,200-201a.

79. Both BL 14,14 and 25,23 employ the term θησαυρούς as well, doing so, however, in reference to the "treasuries/treasures" of the palace rather than those of the Temple as Josephus does. Josephus' other uses of the above phrase "treasur(i)es" of God are *BJ* 2,231; *AJ* 7,367; 8,95.258. The last of these texts uses the phrase in a context quite similar to that of 9,202, i.e. Shishak "emptied the treasuries of God", having been "admitted" to Jerusalem by Rehoboam "because he feared him"; see n. 73.

80. In the above sequence Josephus rearranges the order of 14,14 // 25,23 which speak of silver and gold (from an indeterminate source) prior to the Temple treasures, likewise conflating this with the source references to the "treasures of the king's house". Thereby, he highlights the Temple treasures as the most significant component of Joash's booty.

81. Once again, Josephus' wording of the above phrase (which is intended to clarify, in light of subsequent events, what Joash ended up doing with his royal captive) echoes language used previously in his Amaziah story. Thus, the participle ἀπολύσας harks back to 9,189.190 where Amaziah himself is the subject of the verb ἀπολύω as the one who "dismisses" the Israelite mercenaries; here in 9,202 he now becomes the object of a "release" by Joash. Similarly, the noun αἰχμαλωσία here recalls the uses of the participle αἰχμαλωτισθέντες in 9,194 and of the adjective αἰχμάλωτος in 9,200.201.

82. The above italicized phrase is Josephus' substitution for the sources' mention of the "hostages" carried off by Joash. The substitution underscores the magnanimity of the Israelite king who, in Josephus' presentation, takes no hostages back to Samaria with him. On the contrary, he "releases" the Judean king.

83. L lacks a parallel to the "source reference" of MT B 14,15 for Joash. On the other hand, it does have an equivalent to 14,16 (= 13,13) with its sequence concerning Joash's death, burial and succession by Jeroboam II. See chap. VIII.

the former's final act – the Bible, in fact, has nothing more to say of him
thereafter – and so assigned the Israelite's victory to the year just before
the 15 years that Amaziah is said by his sources to have survived Joash,
i.e. the fourteenth of Amaziah's twenty-nine regnal years[84].

5. *Amaziah Assassinated*

Amaziah's misfortunes did not end with his humiliating defeat by
Joash. On the contrary, 2 Kgs 14,17-22 // 2 Chr 25,25-26,2 conclude
their respective accounts of his reign by recounting how the hapless king
died at the hands of a conspiracy fomented in Jerusalem itself. This final
source segment opens with mention of Amaziah's outliving Joash by fifteen years (14,17 // 25,25) whose utilization by Josephus we treated
above. It then continues with the standard "source reference" for
Amaziah (14,18 // 25,26) which Josephus, in line with his invariable
practice, leaves aside. Thereafter, the sources report the conspiracy made
against Amaziah in Jerusalem and the king's resultant flight to Lachish
(14,19a // 25,27a), the Chronicler prefacing these developments with the
theological notation that they occurred "from the time when he
[Amaziah] turned away from the Lord". Reserving this last item for a
later point (see below), Josephus (9,203b) introduces his account of
Amaziah's end with a temporal transitional note of his own: "... *and
when, after these events,* his friends (τῶν φιλῶν) conspired (ἐπιβουλευθείς) against him[85], he fled (φεύγει; BL 14,19 // 25,27 ἔφυγεν)
to the city of Lacheisa (Λάχεισαν; BL 14,19 // 25,27 Λαχείς)...".

In 2 Kgs 14,19b // 2 Chr 25,27b Amaziah's misfortunes continue: the
conspirators "send after" him to Lachish, his place of refuge, and slay
him there. Josephus' parallel (9,203c) attributes the assassination, not
directly to the conspirators, but rather to their agents: "... but was put to
death by the men whom the conspirators (τῶν ἐπιβουλῶν; cf. ἐπιβουλευθείς, 9,203b) had sent there to kill him".

---

84. Cf. Marcus, *Josephus*, VI, p. 107, n. e. *SOR* 19.10 (Girón Blanc, *Seder 'Olam
Rabbah*, p. 93) sees in the wording of 2 Kgs 14,22 // 2 Chr 26,2 (Azariah/Uzziah "built
Elath and restored it to Judah, after the king [Amaziah] slept with his fathers") an indication that Uzziah had already served as regent for his father during the last fifteen years
of the latter's reign.

85. In the sources the "conspiracy" against Amaziah emanates from an indeterminate
"they". By attributing the plot to the royal "friends", Josephus accentuates the pathos of
the king's end – he is not even safe from his "friends". In addition, this specification
serves to parallel the ends of the Josephan Amaziah and his father Joash, the latter too
falling victim, in the historian's presentation, to his "friends"; see 9,171.186.

2 Kgs 14,20 // 2 Chr 25,28 go on to report the sequels to Amaziah's murder: "they brought him upon horses, and he was buried in Jerusalem (> 25,28) with his fathers in the city of David". From this report Josephus (9,203d) leaves aside its (extraneous) mention of the "horses" as well as the specification concerning "the city of David": "Then they[86] brought his body (σῶμα) to Jerusalem and gave him a royal burial (βασιλικῶς ἐκήδευσαν)[87]". To this burial notice drawn from the sources, he appends (9,204a) an editorial comment which might be seen as his "delayed" adaptation of the theological remark of 25,27 (see above). It runs: "Thus, then, did Amasias meet his end because of his innovations (διὰ τὸν νεωτερισμόν[88] which led him to show contempt of God (τῆς πρὸς τὸν θεόν ὀλιγωρίας)[89]".

In 2 Kgs 14,21 // 2 Chr 26,1, mention of the succession of Azariah/ Uzziah, Amaziah's son, follows directly upon the accounts (14,20 // 25,28) of the latter's burial. Josephus interposes (9,204b) between these two items the chronological data concerning Amaziah's reign "held over" by him, in accord with his regular practice, from 14,2 // 25,1. Whereas, however, those source texts cite the king's age at accession (25) and length of reign (29 years), Josephus, again in line with his usual procedure, substitutes for the first of these items the king's age at death (54), calculating this figure by adding up the above two Biblical indications (25 + 29). Thereafter, he concludes his account of Amaziah with

86. Josephus' formulation leaves the identity of the subject indeterminate here – was it the king's actual killers or the conspirators for whom the former acted (see 9,203c)?

87. This is Josephus' only use of the above phrase. Compare 10,154 where the expression θάψας ... βασιλικῶς is employed of Zedekiah's burial. On the historian's tendency to accentuate the pomp surrounding the burials of Biblical characters, see on 9,44.182.

88. The above noun echoes the language of the prophetic prediction made to Amaziah as cited in 9,195, i.e.: "... God would not overlook the strange and unlawful practices (νεωτερίζων) to which he had set his hand". The verbal link serves to remind readers that this earlier prophecy did indeed find its fulfillment.

89. Josephus' other uses of the noun ὀλιγωρία are AJ 3,19 (= "negligence"); 4,190 (= "disdain for virtue"); 5,179 (the Israelites' "neglect of the Divinity"); 9,218 ("neglect of the walls of Jerusalem" by Uzziah's predecessors). 257 (Ahaz' "despite [of God]"); c. Ap. 2,273 (the Lacedaemonians' "contempt for marriage"). The terminological linkage which Josephus establishes between Amaziah and his great-grandson Ahaz as fellow "scorners of God" is of interest given the fact that Rabbinic tradition as well parallels these two figures. In particular, b. Sanh. 103 preserves a tradition, which it traces back to R. Simeon b. Yohai, concerning Prov 29,9 ("if a wise man contend with a foolish man, whether he rage or laugh, there is no rest"). According to Simeon, God applied this word to his dealings with Ahaz and Amaziah. Angered at the former, he effected his defeat by the Syrians, whereupon Ahaz began worshipping the Syrian gods (see 2 Chr 28,23). Well-disposed towards Amaziah, the Deity brought about his victory over Edom whose gods the king thereafter adopted as his own (2 Chr 25,21). In other words, God's dealing in opposite ways with the two "fools", Ahaz and Amaziah, had the same deleterious result, i.e. idolatry in which he could find no rest/satisfaction.

mention of the accession of his son "Ozias" ('Οζίας; compare BL 26,1 'Οζίαν)[90]. From the source accession notices Josephus leaves aside their mention of the role of "the people of the land" (so 26,1)/ "the people of Judah" (14,21) in bringing "Ozias" to the throne[91]. Similarly, he retains until the end of his account of Uzziah (see 9,227) their further datum that the new king was 16 years old at his accession. Finally, he also "delays" the appended notice of 2 Kgs 14,22 // 2 Chr 26,2 about Uzziah's "(re-)building" of Elath/Eloth and restoring it to Judah. The historian's parallel to this last item will appear (9,217) in the context of his subsequent presentation of Uzziah (9,216-227), following a section devoted to the Israelite king Jeroboam II and his contemporary, the prophet Jonah (9,205-215) to which we turn in the following chapter.

Conclusions: Josephus' Rewriting of 2 Kings 14 // 2 Chronicles 25

It is clear first of all that Josephus did draw on both Biblical accounts of Amaziah in composing AJ 9,186-204. That this is the case appears from the presence in his version of Sondergut items from each Biblical segment, e.g., the synchronistic notice of 2 Kgs 14,1 (= AJ 9,186) and 2 Chr 25,5-16's elaboration of 2 Kgs 14,7's narrative of Amaziah's triumph over Edom; see 9,188-195.

On the other hand, there do not seem to be decisive indications as to which text-form(s) of his two sources Josephus employed. An example may illustrate the uncertainty surrounding the matter. In 2 Chr 25,15 MT reads "the Lord sent a prophet to him (Amaziah), and he said", whereas BL speak of "prophets" and what "they said". Josephus aligns himself (9,194) in this instance with MT's singular; see his opening reference to "the prophet". That "agreement" is not, however, a compelling reason for postulating Josephus' dependence on MT 25,15. Militating against

90. MT 14,21 calls him "Azariah", BL 'Αζαρίαν. In MT 26,1 the name is rather "Uzziah".

91. Compare AJ 10,48 where Josephus does make use of the reference in 2 Kgs 21,24 // 2 Chr 33,25 to the "people of the land" executing the killers of Amon and installing his son Josiah as king. His version of this notice reads: "But when the people (τὸ πλῆθος) punished his (Amon's) murderers... and gave the kingship to his son Josiah...". Perhaps, Josephus' difference of procedure in the two cases has to do with the kings' ages at their respective accessions. According to 2 Kgs 14,21 // 2 Chr 26,1 Uzziah was 16 at his accession, whereas 2 Kgs 22,1 // 2 Chr 34,1 state that Josiah was only 8 at his. The former figure, Josephus may have reasoned then, was already at an age when he could be expected to act on his own in securing the throne, whereas the latter would require others to take the initiative on his behalf (cf. the case of the six-year old Joash who comes to the throne via a coup instigated by the high priest Jehoiada, 2 Kings 11 // 2 Chronicles 23).

such a supposition is the fact that in 25,16 BL too speak, like MT and Josephus (see 9,195), of "the prophet" in the singular. One might then very well suppose that Josephus, having a BL-like text of 2 Chronicles before him and noting the discrepancy between its vv. 15 and 16, harmonized matters on his own initiative, without necessarily knowing MT's (self-consistent) readings. Given too that MT and BL do not differ markedly from each other in either source, it seems best to acknowledge that the text-form(s) of the Biblical Amaziah stories utilized by Josephus eludes our determination.

Much more readily identifiable are the various rewriting techniques employed by Josephus in 9,186-204. I confine myself here to recalling several representative examples of the various categories of these. Instances of outright *additions* are: Amaziah's intention in mustering his forces (9,188; compare 25,5), the booty taken by him (9,191), and Joash's triumphal entry into Jerusalem (9,200). More often, however, Josephus *expatiates* on a point present in the Biblical account(s), but only summarily cited there. Thus, e.g., he repeatedly accentuates Amaziah's success-provoked hubris (see 9,193.196.198; compare 14,10 // 25,19). He likewise elaborates on Amaziah's message to Joash, highlighting its bombastic self-delusion (see 9,196; compare 14,8 // 25,17). He offers as well a more expansive narration (9,199-200) of the actual battle between the two kings, as compared with the minimalistic references to Judah's defeat and flight found in 14,12 // 25,22. Finally, recall too Josephus' large-scale embellishment (9,200-201) of the sequels to the battle, i.e. Amaziah's capture by Joash, the latter's coming to Jerusalem, and demolition of part of the city wall; compare 14,13 // 25,23.

In his version of the Amaziah story, Josephus simply *omits* certain Biblical items, e.g., the continuation of worship on the high places under Amaziah (14,4), the reference to "Obed-edom" in 25,24, the source references of 14,18 // 25,26, mention of the king's body being carried "on horses" (14,20 // 25,28), and the involvement of the "people of the land/Judah" in Uzziah's accession (14,21 // 26,1). The historian dispenses as well with a number of the place names found in his sources, i.e. the valley of Salt (14,7 // 25,11), Beth-semesh as the site of the Israelite-Judean battle and of Amaziah's capture (14,11.13 // 25,21.23), and the two Jerusalem gates marking the limits of the portion of the city wall demolished by Joash (14,13 // 25,23).

Josephus' version also exhibits *modifications/adaptations*. Stylistically, he regularly substitutes hypotaxis for parataxis (compare, e.g., 2 Chr 25,27-28 and 9,203) and indirect for direct discourse, just as he sometimes reads an historic present where BL has a past form (see, e.g., φεύγει, 9,203, vs. ἔφυγεν, BL 14,19 // 25,27). He also, however, modifies the sources' presentation with respect to content. E.g., he cites Amaziah's age at death (9,204) rather than at accession (so 14,2 // 25,1). The king's single foe, i.e. the Edomites of 14,7 // 25,11 becomes a trio of enemy nations, with focus on the Amalekites (see 9,189.193.198). The notice of 14,17 // 25,25 about Amaziah surviving Joash by fifteen years is transposed into the statement that the latter's victory over the former occurred in Amaziah's fourteenth regnal year (9,203). Whereas 14,19 // 25,27 attribute the conspiracy against Amaziah to an indeterminate "they", Josephus (9,203) makes the subject the king's own "friends".

In retelling the Amaziah story Josephus occasionally takes the liberty of *re-arranging* the sources' sequence as well. The opening chronological data of 14,2a // 25,1 appear (in modified form; see above) at the very end of his Amaziah story; see 9,204. References to the Israelites' "internal" and "external" reactions to their dismissal are brought together in a continuous sequence (9,192), as against the separate mention of these in 25,10b and 13 with Amaziah's Edomite triumph of 25,11-12 supervening.

The application of the above re-writing techniques yields a Josephan version of the Amaziah story with a number of distinctive nuances. Somewhat uncharacteristically, the historian actually accentuates the divine involvement in Amaziah's fortunes; see, e.g., his inserted reference explicitly attributing the rout of the Judean force to a God-sent "terror and consternation" in 9,199 (compare 14,12 // 25,22; cf. n. 65). With a view to highlighting the story's appeal for Gentile readers, he, e.g., plays up the operation of the familiar "tragic pattern" of Greek literature in the king's career (see nn. 39,44), and introduces allusions to the Roman triumph (9,194.200). Similarly, his interjected mention of the vast booty taken by Amaziah from his defeated foes (9,191) seems designed to counter contemporary Gentile prejudices about Jewish impecuniousness; see n. 26. Finally, in representing the Amalekites (rather than the Edomites of the sources) as Amaziah's primary target, Josephus is perhaps attempting to offer Gentile readers a plausible rationale for what in the Bible appears as an unprovoked act of aggression by the king upon a Gentile nation (and one conducted with egregious brutality by him, see 14,7 // 25,11-12 = 9,191) i.e. the Amalekites' status as the Jews' *Urfeind*, whose extermination was a matter of divine command[92].

92. Josephus' making the Amalekites rather than the Edomites Amaziah's main target might further be intended to avoid antagonizing his Roman readers, given the tradition according to which the Romans were themselves descendants of Esau, the ancestor of the Edomites. On this tradition and its influence upon Josephus' rendition of the Biblical Jacob-Esau conflict, see FELDMAN, *Interpretation*, pp. 322-324 (= ID., *Jacob*, 148-149).

As for Jewish readers, Josephus' accentuation of the ignominy which ultimately befalls Amaziah serves to warn them against a series of transgressions – all of them committed by this king – which rank as especially heinous in the historian's view, i.e. recourse to foreign religious ways, failure to heed prophetic warnings, and disruption of intra-Jewish harmony. If they are to escape coming to the spectacularly bad end that Amaziah himself did, Josephus' Jewish audience must, the king's story intimates, avoid such religious and social deviations in their own contemporary situation.

XI

JEROBOAM II AND JONAH
(9,205-215)

Having recounted the reign of Amaziah of Judah in 9,186-204 (= 2 Kgs 14,1-22 // 2 Chr 25,1–26,2), Josephus, following the sequence of Kings, shifts back to a Northern ruler, i.e. Jeroboam II, in 9,205-208.215 (= 14,23-29). Into this presentation he works (9,209-214) elements drawn from another Biblical source, i.e. the Book of Jonah, doing so given the mention of a "Jonah" in 2 Kgs 14,25. I distinguish three sections within this material: 1. Jeroboam II Introduced (*AJ* 9,205-207 = 2 Kgs 14,23-25[26-27]); 2. The Jonah Story (9,208-214 = Jonah 1,1-3,4[3,5-4,11]); and 3. Jeroboam's End (9,215 = 2 Kgs 14,28-29).

1. *Jeroboam II Introduced*

2 Kgs 14,23 introduces Jeroboam II, the longest-reigning king of the North, with two standard chronological indications (accession in Amaziah's 15th year and 41-year rule). Josephus' equivalent notice (9,205a) "rounds off" the latter figure: "In the fifteenth year of the reign of Amasias (Ἀμασία; BL Ἀμεσσείου)[1], Jeroboam (Ἱεροβόαμος, BL Ἱεροβοάμ), the son of Joas (Ἰωάσου; BL Ἰωάς)[2], began to reign (ἐβασίλευσε; BL ἐβασίλευσεν) over the Israelites (τῶν Ἰσραηλιτῶν)[3] (and reigned) in Samaria (ἐν Σαμαρείᾳ = BL) forty[4] years".

Kings' account continues in 14,24 with a stereotyped evaluation of Jeroboam as one who "did what was evil in the sight of the Lord" and persisted in the sins of his earlier namesake. Josephus' version (9,205b) not only varies the wording of this notice, but also appends a positive qualification of sorts: "This king was shockingly arrogant and lawless

1. Compressing, Josephus leaves aside 14,23's identification of Amaziah as "the son of Joash, king of Judah".
2. Like B 14,23, Josephus has no equivalent to the identification of Joas as "king of Israel" found in MT L.
3. This specification corresponds to the BL plus in 14,23 according to which Jeroboam reigned "over Israel" (ἐπὶ Ἰσραήλ).
4. In all Biblical witnesses under consideration here the figure is rather 41. Josephus repeats his rounded-off figure for Jeroboam's reign in 9,215.

(ὑβριστὴς καὶ παράνομος)[5] (in his conduct) towards God[6], worshipping idols (εἴδωλα ... σεβόμενος)[7] and adopting many unseemly foreign (ἀτόποις καὶ ξένοις)[8] practices[9], *but to the people of Israel he was the cause* (αἴτιος) *of innumerable benefits* (ἀγαθῶν)[10]".

The Biblical narrative next (14,25) gives its only concrete particular for Jeroboam's extended reign: his recovery of Israelite territory (v. 25a) in accordance with the word of the prophet Jonah (v. 25b). In rendering this item, Josephus (9,206-207a) reverses the sequence of its components, citing the prophetic word – together with his editorial comment on this – in first place: "Now *a certain* Jonah (Ἰωνᾶς; BL Ἰωνᾶ) prophesied (προεφήτευσε)[11] *to*

5. This collocation is hapax in Josephus. The combination is reminiscent of the terminology used by the historian in reference to Jeroboam's contemporary Amaziah whom he accuses (9,196) of having "outraged (ἐξύβριζεν) God" and of having committed "transgressions (παρανομηθέντων) against him" (9,199).

6. With the above formulation Josephus, in line with his regular practice, eliminates both the anthropomorphism of the formulation of 14,24a ("he did what was evil in the sight of the Lord") and its use of the divine title "(the) Lord".

7. Josephus' one other use of this phrase is in *AJ* 9,99, there in connection with Joram of Judah; see above.

8. The above hendiadys occurs only here in Josephus.

9. The above phrase is Josephus' generalizing replacement for the reference in 14,24b to "the sins of Jeroboam" which he regularly avoids. In avoiding the Bible's explicit linking of Jeroboam II with his earlier namesake, Josephus follows the same procedure adopted by him in the case of the three preceding Northern kings, Jehu, Jehoahaz, and Joash; see p. 192, n. 18; p. 212, n. 31.

10. Thus the reading of RO followed by Niese and Marcus. Dindorf, Bekker, and Naber, on the contrary, read κακῶν with MSPExc. Suidas. MARCUS, *Josephus*, VI, p. 109, n. e. comments concerning the disputed reading here: "The variant 'evils' is probably a scribal correction to fit the context [see what precedes in 9,205b]; the reading 'benefits' is supported by what Josephus says in §215 [King Jeroboam died after a life of complete prosperity], and by Scripture, 2 Kings xiv.25,27, which speaks of Jeroboam's conquests". The above phrase "cause of benefit(s)" is elsewhere applied by Josephus to events or persons in *BJ* 3,101; *AJ* 3,56; 4,99; 6,290 (David); 8,1 (David); 13,173; 14,254 (sg.). His employing the same phrase of the reprobate Jeroboam II that he had twice earlier used of the exemplary David is noteworthy – as is the fact that it is only these two individual figures in his entire *corpus* who receive this accolade.

11. Compare 14,25b: "according to the word (BL τὸ ῥῆμα) of the Lord, the God of Israel which he spoke by his servant Jonah... the prophet...". See further n. 21.

From the formulation of 14,25b Josephus omits both the name of Jonah's father ("Amittai") and his place of origin ("Gath-hepher," MT). By contrast, other ancient Jewish/ Christian writings expatiate on Jonah's *personalia*, identifying him, e.g., as that (nameless) son of the widow of Zarephath whom Elijah resuscitates in 1 Kgs 17,17-24 (= *AJ* 8,325-327), see *Pirqe R. El.* 33.2 (PEREZ FERNÁNDEZ, *Los capítulos de Rabbí Eliezer*, p. 230); *Midr. Pss.* 26.7 (BRAUDE, *Midrash on Psalms*, I, p. 363); *VP* 10.2-5 (SCHWEMER, *Vitae Prophetarum*, pp. 618-620); Jerome, *in Jonam*, Preface (reporting the tradition of the "Hebrews") (Y.-M. DUVAL, *Jérôme Commentaire sur Jonas* [SC, 323], Paris, Cerf, 1985, p. 164). Elsewhere "Jonah" is identified as a member either of the tribe of Asher or of Zebulon (or both), through his mother and father, respectively, so *Gen. Rab.* 98.11 (H. FREEDMAN, tr. *Midrash Genesis Rabbah*, II, London/New York, Soncino, 1983, p. 959); *y. Suk.* 5.1. See further n. 27.

him[12] *that he should make war on the Syrians and defeat* (κρατῆσαι) *their forces*[13] and extend (πλατῦναι)[14] his (αὐτοῦ)[15] realm *on the north* as far as the city of Amathos ('Αμάθου) *and on the south* as far as Lake Asphaltitis (τῆς 'Ασφαλτίτιδος)[16] – *for in ancient times these were the boundaries of Canaan as the general* (στρατηγός) Joshua[17] had defined them (περιώρισε)[18]". Thereafter (9,207b), he gives his equivalent to the notice of 14,25a on Jeroboam's initiatives, representing these as being carried out, however, in accordance with Jonah's directive of 9,206[19]: "And so, *having marched against the Syrians* [compare he should make war on the Syrians, 9,206a], Jeroboam subdued their entire country

12. The wording of 14,25 does not clearly indicate whether or not Jonah addressed his prophecy to Jeroboam personally – or indeed whether the two were even contemporaries. Josephus' clarification on the point might be seen as part of his wide-going assimilation of the data of 14,25 to the earlier episode involving Jeroboam's father Joash and the prophet Elisha in which the latter announces to the former that he will defeat the Syrians three times (2 Kgs 13,19 = AJ 9,181), as he in fact does do (13,25 = 9,184). See further below.

13. These "preliminary directives" issued Jeroboam by Jonah lack any equivalent in 14,25. They do, however, have a certain counterpart in the word of Elisha to Joash as reported in AJ 9,181 (cf. 2 Kgs 13,19): "... you shall meet *the Syrians* in as many [i.e. three] battles and *defeat* (κρατήσεις) them...". See previous note.

14. The verb πλατύνω is hapax in AJ; it occurs 7 times in BJ.

15. This is the reading adopted by Dindorf, Bekker, Niese, Naber, and Marcus; the codices and E have αὐτοῦ.

16. The above formulation represents a transposition into prophetic directive of the narrative notice of 14,25a: "He (Jeroboam) restored the border of Israel from the entrance of Hamath (BL ἀπὸ εἰσόδου Αἰμάθ) as far as the sea of the Arabah (B ἕως τῆς θαλάσσης τῆς 'Αραβά [L πρὸς ἑσπέραν])". On "Lake Asphaltitis" as Josephus' designation for the Biblical "Sea of the Arabah", see on 9,7.

17. FELDMAN, *Interpretation*, pp. 443-460, 448 and n. 8 (= ID., *Josephus' Portrait of Joshua*, in HTR 82 [1989], 351-376, p. 358 and n. 20) points out that Joshua applies the term "general" to Joshua no less than 10 times, i.e. BJ 4,459; AJ 3,59; 4,165.324; 6,84; 7,68.294; 9,207.280; 11,112.

18. The verb περιορίζω is hapax in Josephus. On Josephus' account of Joshua's fixing of the boundaries of the land, see AJ 5,80-89. The above explanation/ legitimation ("for") of Jonah's directive that Jeroboam "extend his realm" precisely to the points indicated (Hamath... Lake Asphaltitis) has no equivalent in 14,25 as such. Conceivably, however, Josephus found inspiration for it in the reference to Jeroboam's "*restoring* (הֵשִׁיב, MT; ἀπέστησεν, B; ἀπεκατέστησε, L) the border of Israel" in that verse.

19. In thus depicting Jeroboam as carrying out a prophetic directive given him, Josephus provides an implicit answer to the question of how it was that such a reproboate king was able to achieve the successes he did. Compare the "explanation" – to which Josephus has no parallel (see above) – on the matter suggested by 2 Kgs 14,26-27, i.e. the Lord's seeing Israel's "bitter affliction" and the fact of his "not having said that he would blot out the name of Israel from under heaven", with the result that "he saved them by the hand of Jeroboam"; see n. 22. Compare too the Rabbinic tradition cited in *b. Pesaḥ*. 87b; E.R. §17(88) (BRAUDE and KAPSTEIN, *Tanne děbe Eliyyahu*, pp. 193-194); E.Z. §7(184) (ibid., p. 393) according to which God granted the idolator Jeroboam an unprecedented enlargement of Israel's borders in recognition of the king's refusal to act against the prophet Amos when the latter was denounced to him by the priest Amaziah of Bethel (see Amos 7,10-11).

(καταστρέφεται πᾶσαν ... τὴν χώραν)[20], as Jonah had prophesied (προεφήτευσεν; see προεφήτευσε, 9,206a)[21]".

To his notice on Jeroboam's successes as the realization of Jonah's word (14,25) the author of Kings attaches a reflection about the divine motivation for "saving" Israel through the agency of Jeroboam, 14,26-27 (see n. 19). Josephus has no equivalent to this latter sequence[22]. Instead, he proceeds immediately to a digression, inspired by the mention, elsewhere in the Bible, of a prophet with the same name as the "Jonah" of 14,25.

2. The Jonah Story[23]

Josephus makes the shift from the narrative of Kings which he had been following in 9,205-207 to the story told in the Book of Jonah at the open-

20. Here again (see nn. 12 and 13) Josephus introduces a verbal echo of his earlier account of Elisha's prophecy to King Joash and its realization; see 9,184: "he (Joash) got back from him (King Adados of Syria) all the territory (τὴν χώραν ἄπασταν) which his father Azaēlos had taken". Cf. also 8,408 where the false prophet Zedekiah assures King Ahab that he will "subdue (καταστρέψεσθαι) the whole of Syria".

21. This appended "fullfillment notice" might be seen as Josephus' characteristic reformulation/reiteration (see n. 11) of the statement of 14,25b that Jeroboam's conquests were in accordance with "the word of the Lord which he spoke by... Jonah... the prophet". It likewise has a counterpart in the remark which Josephus appends to his account of King Joash's successes against the Syrians in 9,185a, i.e.: "This... came about in accordance with the prophecy (προφητείαν) of Elisha".

22. A variety of reasons may be suggested for his non-utilization of it: the historian's general tendency to "detheologize" Biblical history, the apparent discrepancy between the reference to Israel's "bitter affliction" and lack of anyone to "help" it in Jeroboam's time (14,26) and the account of the successes against the Syrians achieved by Jeroboam's father, Joash (see 2 Kgs 13,25 = AJ 9,184), as well as the problematic character of the reference to the Lord's "not having said that he would blot out the name of Israel from under heaven" in 14,27, given that within a quarter century of Jeroboam's death the Lord would do just that, using Assyria as his instrument. In this connection recall too that Josephus has no equivalent to the somewhat similar notice of 2 Kgs 13,23 (MT B = L 13,8) about the Lord's "having compassion" on Israel because of his covenant with the patriarchs and refraining from "destroying" them and "casting them from his presence until now".

23. Josephus' version of the Book of Jonah in Ant. 9,208-214 has been studied in depth by FELDMAN, Studies, pp. 393-415 (= ID., Josephus' Interpretation of Jonah, in AJS Review 17 [1992] 1-29). For summary treatments of the Josephan Jonah in relation to the wider corpus of Jewish (and Christian) traditions concerning the prophet, see: Y.-M. DUVAL, Le Livre de Jonas dans la littérature chrétienne grecque et latine, I, Paris, Etudes augustiennes, 1973, pp. 69-111, esp. 82-85; S. CHOW, The Sign of Jonah Reconsidered: A Study of its Meaning in the Gospel Traditions (ConB NT, 27), Stockholm, Almqvist & Wiksell, 1995, pp. 27-44, esp. 32-34; A.M. SCHWEMER, Studien zu den frühjüdischen Prophetenlegenden Vitae Prophetarum, II (TSAJ, 50), Tübingen, Mohr Siebeck, 1996, pp. 48-83, esp. 69-70; T.M. BOLIN, Freedom beyond Forgiveness: The Book of Jonah Reexamined (JSOTSup, 236), Sheffield, Sheffield Academic Press, 1997, pp. 14-18, esp. 15; K. HUBER, "Zeichen des Jona" und "Mehr als Jona". Die Gestalt des Jona im Neuen Testament und ihr Beitrag zur bibeltheologischen Fragestellung, in Protokolle zur Bibel 7 (1998) 77-94, pp. 89-92.

ing of 9,208 via an elaborate transition explaining his reason for incorporating the latter work's content. This reads: "But, since I have promised to give an exact account of our history (τὴν ἀκρίβειαν τῶν πραγμάτων), I have thought it necessary (ἀναγκαῖον ... ἡγησάμην)[24] to recount what I have found written (ἀναγεγραμμένα) in the Hebrew books (ἐν ταῖς Ἑβραϊκαῖς βίβλοις)[25] concerning this prophet (προφήτου)[26]".

Following the above introduction, Josephus (9,208b) proceeds to give his – highly modified – version of the prophet's "commissioning" (Jonah 1,1-2): "This man[27], then, having been commanded by God

24. This phrase recurs in *AJ* 9,242 in the conclusion of Josephus' account of the prophet Nahum (9,239-242): "And many more things beside did this prophet prophesy about Nineveh, which *I have* not *thought it necessary* (ἀναγκαῖον ἡγησάμην) to mention, but have omitted in order not to seem tiresome to my readers". Note, however, the different functions given the phrase in the two contexts: in 9,208 it figures within an explanation as to why Josephus felt constrained to include Biblical material that might appear extraneous, while in 9,242 it is part of a formula legitimating, rather, his non-reproduction of a portion of the Biblical record. See further chap. XIII.

25. Josephus' one remaining use of the phrase "the Hebrew books" is in *AJ* 10,218. Cf. the equivalent phrase "the Hebrew records (γραμμάτων)" in the prologue of *AJ*, 1,5.

26. The Book of Jonah itself – Josephus' source in 9,208-214 – nowhere designates Jonah as a "prophet". Josephus would, however, have found inspiration for applying the term to Jonah in 2 Kgs 14,25b where he is so designated. At the same time, he extends this solitary Scriptural usage, employing the title of Jonah no less than four times within the seven paragraphs of 9,208-214, doing this in accord with his recurrent tendency to highlight the prophetic factor in Israel's history. The sixth century A.D. (?) Jewish sermon *De Jona*, earlier, though wrongfully associated with Philo, and originally composed in Greek but extant in Armenian, likewise repeatedly employs the term "prophet" for Jonah. See the translation of F. SIEGERT, *Drei hellenistisch-jüdische Predigten*, I (WUNT, 20), Tübingen, Mohr Siebeck, 1980, pp. 9-50. The terms "prophecy" and "prophesy" (though not "prophet" itself) are also frequent in the Targum's rendering of the Book of Jonah; see A. SPERBER, *The Bible in Aramaic*, III, Leiden, Brill, 1959, pp. 436-439 and the translation of this in K.J. CATHCART & R.P. GORDON, *The Targum of the Minor Prophets* (The Aramaic Bible, 14), Wilmington, DE, Glazier, 1989, pp. 105-108. See finally Tob 14,4.8 (BA) where the dying Tobit twice affirms that what "the prophet" Jonah had announced about Nineveh will come to pass (in codex Sinaiticus 14,4 the reference is to the prophet *Nahum*, while it lacks an equivalent to the prophet reference of 14,8).

As FELDMAN, *Studies*, pp. 394-395 (= ID., *Jonah*, 5-6) points out, Josephus' above statement introducing his reproduction of the Jonah story in terms of a "necessity" imposed by his earlier "promise" to relate what he "found in the Hebrew books" is more than a little disingenuous in that elsewhere Josephus clearly feels no "necessity" to incorporate Scriptural material that does not suit his purposes (including, e.g., any mention of Jonah's contemporaries, the prophets Amos and Hosea, both of whom functioned under Jeroboam as well according to the titles of their respective books). Thus his real/primary motivation for giving relatively extended treatment to the prophet Jonah would seem to be something other than the one alleged by him here in 9,208. On the matter, see further below.

27. As in his reproduction of 2 Kgs 14,25 in 9,206 (see n. 11), Josephus here in 9,208 avoids mentioning the name of Jonah's father ("Amittai") as cited in Jonah 1,1. He nonetheless clearly presupposes that the two Biblical contexts are speaking about one and the same prophet – a presupposition favored above all precisely by the identical patrynomic used for "Jonah" in 2 Kgs 14,25 and Jonah 1,1.

(κελευσθεὶς ... τοῦ θεοῦ)²⁸ to go (πορευθῆναι) to the kingdom of Ninos (Νίνου²⁹)³⁰ and, *when he arrived there*, to preach (κηρῦξαι) in that city (ἐν τῇ πόλει)³¹ that it would lose its power (τὴν ἀρχὴν ἀπολέσαι)...³²".

28. This is Josephus' replacement for the *Wortereignisformel* of Jonah 1,1 "the word (LXX λόγος [for the LXX text of the Book of Jonah I use the edition of J. ZIEGLER, *Duodecim prophetae* (Septuaginta, XIII), Göttingen, Vandenhoeck & Ruprecht, ³1984]) of the Lord came to Jonah..." with its doubly "un-Josephan" reference to a divine "word" and use of "Lord" as a divine title. See n. 11. With the above passive construction compare the more usual active expression (τοῦ) θεοῦ κελεύσαντος used in *AJ* 1,110.154(184).187.259; 2,279.323.337; 4,46.55.112.165; 5,65.230; 6,139; 7,92.

29. This is the reading of the codices MSP which Dindorf, Bekker, Naber, and Marcus adopt. Niese reads Νινύου with RO, while SCHALIT, *Namenwörterbuch*, p. 91 calls the form Νινευή (= the form found in LXX and elsewhere in Josephus as well; see, e.g., *AJ* 9,239-242) the one most likely to represent the original reading. With reference to Marcus's reading ("Ninos"), FELDMAN, *Studies*, p. 412 (= ID., *Jonah*, 26) suggests that this might be intended to remind Josephus' Greco-Roman audience of the name of the first king of Assyria whose exploits are reported by Diodorus of Sicily (first century B.C.) in his *Library of History* 2.1.4-2.7.2 (Diodorus, in turn, based his account of "Ninos" on the fourth century B.C. historian Ctesias of Cnidus); see C.H. OLDFATHER, ed. and tr., *Diodorus of Sicily*, I (LCL), London, Heinemann; New York, Putmans, 1933, pp. 349-371.

30. Compare the direct addresss of the opening divine word as cited in Jonah 1,2aα: "arise, go (LXX πορεύθητι) to Nineveh, that great city..." (in what follows Josephus will make use of the Biblical designation of Nineveh as a "city" here).

31. Compare the continuation of the Lord's directive as cited in 1,2aβ with whose LXX rendering (κήρυξον ἐν αὐτῇ) Josephus' formulation shows a closer affinity than to MT's wording, i.e. וּקְרָא עָלֶיהָ (RSV: "and cry *against* it").

32. The above construction occurs also in *AJ* 6,336; 8,264; 18,345. This divine prescription as to what Jonah is to say in Nineveh takes the place of the Deity's statement about why he is sending Jonah to Nineveh in 1,2b, i.e.: "for (LXX + the noise of) their wickedness has come up to me". (Josephus' non-utilization of the Bible's opening evocation of Nineveh's "depravity" likely holds together with the fact that he will have nothing to say about the related theme of the city's repentance which figures so largely in the continuation of the source story; see below.) His replacement for this item might have been inspired by the words of Jonah's actual address to the Ninevites as cited in 3,4, i.e.: "yet forty (LXX three) days, and Nineveh will be destroyed". Why, though, did Josephus feel the need to modify the wording ("loss of power" vs. actual "destruction") of this announcement as he does? E. BICKERMAN, *Four Strange Books of the Bible*, New York, Schocken, 1967, p. 37 suggests that the modification has in view the fact that a new Greek city of "Nineveh" was in existence in Josephus' time. To this SCHWEMER, *Prophetenlegenden*, I, p. 70, n. 117 rightly objects that, subsequently, Josephus has Nahum announce the "downfall (καταστροφῆς, i.e. the noun cognate of the verb καταστραφῆται used in the LXX rendering of Jonah's announcement in 3,4) of Assyria and Nineveh" (see 9,239). Schwemer herself proposes that Josephus, in line with his overall conception of the prophet as a "true predictor", reworded the announcement of Jonah 3,4 in more general terms with a view to eliminating any suggestion that Jonah was a "false prophet" – as might appear to be the case in the Biblical Jonah story where, in fact, Nineveh does not end up being destroyed at all – much less within the time period foretold by Jonah. Finally, note that Josephus' supplying of a divine directive as to what Jonah is to say in Nineveh here at the outset of his account has a counterpart in *De Jona* (§19) where the Lord instructs the prophet "Verkündige dieser Stadt den Untergang, dass ein qualvoller Tod über (sie) kommen wird" (the translation is that of SIEGERT, *Predigten*, I, p. 11).

Jonah 1,3 relates the prophet's response to his commission, doing so with considerable repetition (triple mention of "Tarshish" as his intended destination, double use of the phrase "from the presence [face] of the Lord"). Josephus' rendition (9,208c) eliminates the source's repetitions, while also introducing a variety of new elements: "... (he) *was afraid* (δείσας)[33] *and did not set out* (οὐκ ἀπῆλθεν), but fled from God (ἀποδιδράσκει τὸν θεόν)[34] to the city of Jopē ('Ιόπην)[35], where he found a boat (πλοῖον εὑρών; compare LXX εὗρε πλοῖον)[36] and embarked in it to sail (ἐμβὰς ... ἔπλει; LXX

---

33. At this juncture (1,3-4) the Bible offers no indication as to what motivated Jonah to try to evade his commission. Only in 4,2b do we read his statement of explanation/self-justification to the Lord: "That is why I made haste to flee to Tarshish; for I knew that thou art a gracious God and merciful, slow to anger, and abounding in steadfast love, and repentest of evil". By contrast, Josephus, right at the start, "motivates" Jonah's flight by invoking the prophet's "fear" (i. e., presumably of how the Ninevites would react to his announcement that they would "lose their power").

Elsewhere in Jewish (and Christian) tradition, one finds much speculation – itself spelling out the implications of his statement in 4,2 – about the grounds for Jonah's prophetic flight. Thus, e.g., this is attributed to his apprehension that he would end up appearing a false prophet in the eyes of the Ninevites who would see the non-fulfillment of his announcement, so, e.g., *Pirqe R. El.* 10.1 (PÉREZ FERNÁNDEZ, *Los capítulos de Rabbí Eliezer*, pp. 100-101); *Midr. Jonah* on Jonah 1,3 (A. WÜNSCHE, tr., *Aus Israels Lehrhallen*, I, Leipzig, Pfeiffer, 1907, pp. 39-40). Alternatively, his flight is connected to Jonah's concern that unrepentant Israel would be placed in a bad light should the Ninevites respond positively to his message (so, e.g., *Mek. Pisha* 1.85-87 (J.Z. LAUTER-BACH, *Mekilta de-Rabbi Ishmael*, I, Philadelphia, Jewish Publication Society of America, 1933, p. 8); Jerome, *in Jonam* (on Jonah 1,3; Y.-M. DUVAL, *Jérôme Commentaire sur Jonas* [SC, 323], Paris, Cerf, 1985, p. 172). Both the above motivations for Jonah's flight are evoked in the homily *De Jona* (see ## 20,62,63,190-191, in the translation of Siegert cited in n. 26).

34. Josephus' one other use of this expression is in *BJ* 3,373 (Josephus' address to his Jewish compatriots at Jotapata). It takes the place of the opening formulation of Jonah 1,3: "But Jonah rose to flee (LXX [τοῦ] φυγεῖν)... from the presence (literally: face, LXX ἐκ προσώπου) of the Lord". Like Josephus, Tg. Jonah eliminates the anthropomorphism of MT's (and LXX's) reference to the divine "face" with its rendering "(and Jonah arose to flee)... before he would prophesy in the name of the Lord (לימא מן קדם דיתנבי בשמא דיוי)".

35. LXX has 'Ιόππην which is also the reading of the codices RMP[2].

36. Josephus leaves aside the Biblical detail about Jonah's "paying the fare" for the boat. This "omission" might have in view the custom cited in *Pirqe R. El.* 10.2 (PÉREZ FERNÁNDEZ, *Los capítulos de Rabbí Eliezer*, p. 101) and *Midr. Jonah* on 1,3 (WÜNSCHE, *Lehrhallen*, p. 40) according to which ship travelers payed when disenmarking rather than embarking: the historian wants to avoid having Jonah act in a way contrary to usual practice (in the above Rabbinic documents his unusual procedure in paying in advance is explained in terms of Jonah's joy at finding a ship to take him away from the Lord's presence). *Midr. Jonah* (on 1,3) and *b. Ned.* 38a further embellish the Biblical datum, claiming that Jonah payed the fares of all the ship's passagers, the amount coming to 4,000 gold *denarii*. Finally, in the version of *De Jona* (§7; SIEGERT, *Predigten*, I, p. 12) Jonah is simply taken on board the ship in accord with his request to the crew, no "payment" by him being mentioned.

ἐνέβη ... τοῦ πλεῦσαι) to Tarsus (Ταρσόν)[37] *in Cilicia* (τῆς Κιλικίας)[38]".

Jonah 1,4-15 comprises a long sequence describing the storm at sea and culminating with Jonah's being tossed overboard (v. 15). The Josephan parallel is 9,209-213; it leaves aside many of the Biblical particulars, while also introducing various new features. The historian begins (9,209a), in line with 1,4-5a, by recounting the onset of the tempest and the crew's initial reaction to this: "But a very severe storm (χειμῶνος) came up[39] and, as the vessel (σκάφους)[40] was in danger of sinking (κινδυνεύοντος καταδῦναι)[41], the sailors (ναῦται; LXX 1,5 ναυτικοί) *and pilots* (οἱ κυβερνῆται)[42] *and even the shipmaster* (ναύκληρος)[43] began to pray (εὐχὰς ἐποιοῦντο; LXX ἀνεβόων [πρὸς

---

37. MT "Tarshish", LXX Θαρσις (Tg. Jonah "translates" with "to sea" [לימא]). This is Josephus' first – and only – mention of Jonah's intended destination, whereas in 1,3 the phrase "to Tarshish" appears no less than three times.

38. Jonah 1,3 provides no indication concerning the location of "Tarshish". Josephus' specification on the point here in 9,208 is in accord with his statement in AJ 1,127 where, in his rendering of Gen 10,4 ("Tarshish" as a son of "Javan"), he states: "... (Javan's son) Tharsos (Τάρσας) gave his name to the Tharsians; the latter was the ancient name of Cilicia [see 9,208], as is proved by the fact that its principal and capital city is called Tarsus (θαρσός), the *Th* having been converted into *T* [see 9,208 where "Tarsus" is spelled with an initial *taw*]". Compare, however, AJ 9,17 where, as noted in chap. I, the reference in 2 Chr 20,36 to the joint venture of Jehoshaphat and Ahaziah in building ships to go "to Tarshish" (compare 1 Kgs 22,48: ships of Tarshish) becomes "(building ships to sail to Pontus) and the trading-stations *of Thrace*".
Josephus' localization of "Tarshish" here in 9,208 is cited by Jerome, *in Jonam* on 1,3 (DUVAL, *Commentaire*, p. 175) who, however, prefers the tradition of the "Hebrews" that "Tarshish" means "sea" (see the rendering of Tg. Jonah, cited in n. 37). On the long-running scholarly controversy concerning the location of Biblical "Tarshish" (Spain?, Carthage?, India?, Asia Minor?), see A. PADILLA MONGE, *Consideraciones sobre el Tarsis bíblicos*, in *AO* 12 (1994) 51-71 who concludes that Josephus' localization is, in fact, the most likely one.

39. Compare 1,4a: "But the Lord hurled a great wind upon the sea and there was a mighty tempest (LXX κλύδων) on the sea". Josephus' non-mention of God's role in generating the storm is part of his wide-going "de-theologizing" of the Biblical Jonah story on which see FELDMAN, *Studies*, pp. 397-399 (= ID., *Jonah*, 8-11). By contrast, Rabbinic tradition, see *Pirqe R. El.* 10.2 (PÉREZ FERNÁNDEZ, *Los capítulos de Rabbí Eliezer*, p. 101); *Midr. Jonah* on Jonah 1,4 (WÜNSCHE, *Lehrhallen*, I, pp. 40-41); *Gen. Rab.* 24.4 (FREEDMAN, *Midrash Rabbah Genesis*, I, p. 201), accentuates the miraculous character of the storm, affirming that it affected only Jonah's ship, leaving all other ships at sea in peace.

40. Compare πλοῖον in 9,208, the term read by LXX throughout Jonah 1.

41. Compare Jonah 1,4b: "the ship threatened to break up (LXX ἐκινδύνευε συντριβῆναι)".

42. This is the reading of the codices RO which Niese and Marcus follow. Dindorf, Bekker, and Naber read the singular with MSPLat.

43. This word is hapax in Josephus. Jonah 1,5 speaks in undifferentiated terms of the "sailors" responding to the storm with prayer. Josephus' formulation makes clear that also the ship's officers joined in the appeal; its inserted references to them might be seen as an anticipation/recasting of the role assigned the ship's "captain" (LXX ὁ πρωρεύς) in 1,6; see below.

τὸν θεόν]) and vow thank offerings (χαριστηρίους)[44] *if they escaped the sea...*[45]".

Jonah 1,5b establishes a contrast between the crews' response to the storm as recounted in v. 5a and that of Jonah himself who repairs to the interior of the ship where he lies down and falls asleep (LXX ἔρρεγχε, "he snored"). This portrayal of a prophet who physically distances himself from his threatened shipmates and sleeps as they struggle to counteract the storm's menace is not one that reflects well on him (or ultimately on the people he represents). Understandably, therefore, Josephus (9,209b) modifies the source's presentation on the point: "Jonah, however, *covered himself up* and lay (there) (ἐβέβλητο; LXX ἐκάθευδε)[46], not imitating (μιμούμενος) any of the things that he saw the others doing[47]".

44. This latter element of the crew's response has no equivalent in 1,5 itself; it might, however, be seen as an anticipation of what is said of their reaction to their ultimate deliverance in 1,16 (no parallel in Josephus; see below), i.e.: "... they offered a sacrifice (LXX ἔθυσαν θυσίαν) to the Lord and made vows (LXX εὐχάς, i.e. the term employed by Josephus here in 9,209)". See on 9,213.

45. This indication concerning the content of the crew's prayer is Josephus' replacement for 1,5aα's specification regarding the recipient(s) of their prayer. In MT this is אֱלֹהָיו (LXX τὸν θεὸν αὐτοῦ). Tg. Jonah renders – *in malam partem* – with "to his idol (דחלתיה, literally: 'his fear'; see CATHCART & GORDON, *Targum of the Minor Prophets*, p. 105, n. 9), adding "but they [the crew] saw that they [the idols] were useless". Josephus' "omission" leaves the question of the sailors' religion completely indeterminate; see FELDMAN, *Studies*, pp. 409-410 (= ID., *Jonah*, 24) who views the historian's procedure here as reflective of his endeavor to assuage Roman concerns about Jewish 'proselytism' throughout his retelling of the Jonah story. Compare *Pirqe R. El.* 10.2 (PÉREZ FERNÁNDEZ, *Los capítulos de Rabbí Eliezer*, pp. 101-102); *Midr. Jonah* on 1,5 (WÜNSCHE, *Lehrhallen*, I, p. 41) which, going further in the line of TJ, aver that the crew consisted of representatives of the 70 nations making up humanity (see the "Table of the Nations" in Genesis 10) and that each had "his idol in his hand".

The Bible proceeds (Jonah 1,5aβ) to speak of a further initiative by the crew in addition to their prayer (1,5aα), i.e. they throw the ship's cargo overboard in order to lighten the vessel. Josephus keeps attention focussed on the crew's religious response to the storm by passing over this latter item (as do also *Pirqe R. El.*, *Midr. Jonah*, and *De Jona* in their respective retellings of the Jonah story; conversely, these documents share with Tg. Jonah its plus [see above in this note] concerning the inefficacy of the sailors' prayer).

46. In contrast to 1,5b, Josephus thus seems to represent Jonah as remaining on deck in the midst of his shipmates. This modification, in turn, leads the historian to introduce the Biblically unparalleled mention of the prophet "covering himself" – something that would be much more necessary on the exposed deck with a storm raging than in the interior of the ship. Compare *De Jona* §7 (SIEGERT, *Predigten*, I, p. 26) which motivates Jonah's "withdrawal" in terms of his wanting thereby to be forgotten by those on the ship, or – on an alternative translation – to forget himself.

47. This indication takes the place of the Biblical reference to Jonah's "sleeping" (LXX "snoring"). As FELDMAN, *Studies*, p. 407 (= ID., *Jonah*, 20) remarks, Josephus' formulation intimates a laudable rationale for Jonah's "failure" to join the others in their prayer, i.e. he did not wish to have any part in pagan religious practices (this on the – possible – understanding that Josephus intends us to identify the sailors as Gentiles; see n. 45). Josephus' version likewise eliminates a difficulty that the Biblical account might suggest – is it conceivable that anyone could actually fall asleep in the midst of such a great storm?;

Having "recast" the sleeping Jonah of 1,5b, Josephus leaves aside entirely the related happening reported in 1,6, i.e. the captain's remonstrance with the sleeper[48]. In place thereof he introduces (9,210) an elaborate transition to the following lot-casting episode of 1,7, this serving to explain why the sailors decided to have recourse to the practice at this juncture: "Then, when the waves rose still higher and the sea became more violent (βιαιοτέρας) in the wind[49], they began to suspect[50], as is natural (ὡς ἐνδέχεται)[51], that one of the passagers (ἐμπλεόντων)[52] was the cause of the storm (αἴτιον ... χειμῶνος)[53] that had come upon them...[54]".

compare Jerome, *In Jonam* 1,5 (DUVAL, *Commentaire*, pp. 190, 192) who expatiates at length on the prophet's state of mind as he settles down to sleep). See further n. 48.

48. This omission is explained by FELDMAN, *Studies*, p. 408 (= ID., *Jonah*, 20) in terms of Josephus' desire to avoid an unflattering depiction of a prophet (and his people) as one who stands in need of religious instruction from one who is – apparently – a Gentile; cf. nn. 45, 47. In addition, Josephus may also have been influenced by the character of 1,6 as a "blind motif" given that Jonah makes no response to the captain's reproaches which, accordingly, have no affect on the subsequent course of the story. At the same time, it should be kept in mind that Josephus does not simply eliminate the figure of the "captain" from his Jonah story; rather, his reference to the "pilot(s)" and "shipmaster" joining the sailors' prayer in 9,208 might be seen as his anticipation/reuse of the content of 1,6; see n. 43.

With Josephus' non-utilization of the captain's initiative as reported in 1,6 contrast *Pirqe R. El.* 10.2 (PÉREZ FERNÁNDEZ, *Los capítulos de Rabbí Eliezer*, p. 102); *Midr. Jonah* on 1,6 (WÜNSCHE, *Lehrhallen*, p. 41) where additional words are attributed to this figure (e.g., the hope that God will act on their behalf as he did "at the Sea of Reeds") and where Jonah does respond to what is said to him, addressing "them" (presumably the crew as a whole) with a confession and a call to throw him overboard anticipated from 1,12. See also *De Jona* §9 (SIEGERT, *Predigten*, I, pp. 13-14) which not only amplifies the captain's reproaches, but also provides an explanation as to how he located the sleeper (he heard Jonah's loud "snoring" [see LXX 1,5b]) and reports (§10) that, in response to the captain's words, Jonah went back on deck where, seeing the storm's fury, he began to suspect that this was due to his sins. Thus while Josephus deals with the "functionlessness" of the Biblical captain's intervention by simply omitting it, these other witnesses adopt another tack, i.e. they depict his words as evoking a response of some sort from Jonah.

49. The above sequence has no equivalent at the corresponding point in the Biblical account, i.e. Jonah 1,7. It might, however, be seen as Josephus' anticipation of the double reference to the sea's growing "more and more tempestuous" in 1,11b and 13b subsequent to the lot-casting of 1,7.

50. In *De Jona* §10 (SIEGERT, *Predigten*, I, p. 14) it is Jonah himself who is led to "suspect" that he is the cause of the storm when beholding the sea's turbulence; see n. 48.

51. This is the reading adopted by Dindorf, Bekker, Naber, and Marcus; Niese conjectures λέγεται, while codex R has δέχεται. Josephus' one other use of the verb ἐνδέχομαι is in *AJ* 19,237 where it has the meaning of "to be possible".

52. Josephus' one other use of the verb ἐμπλέω is in *BJ* 3,523. The term echoes the form ἔπλει of 9,208.

53. Note the verbal contrast established between Jonah and his contemporary, Jeroboam II here: the latter was "the cause (αἴτιον) of innumerable benefits" for his people (9,205), while Jonah was "the cause (αἴτιον) of the life-threatening "storm" to his shipmates.

54. In *De Jona* §11 (SIEGERT, *Predigten*, I, pp. 14-16) the crew's recourse to the lot-casting procedure – itself prompted by their panic and not knowing what to do – is preceded by an interrogation of all persons on board in the course of which Jonah is asked questions inspired by those cited in 1,8 (i.e. after he has been "taken" by the lot, 1,7) to

Following this inserted transition, the historian reconnects (9,211a) with the Biblical account (1,7) in relating the sailors' actual initiative and its outcome: "... and they agreed to draw lots (κλήρῳ) to see who it might be[55]. Accordingly they drew them (κληρωσαμένων; LXX ἔβαλον κλήρους), and it was the prophet (ὁ προφήτης; see 9,208; 1,7: Jonah) who was taken (λαγχάνει)[56]".

Once the lot has "taken" Jonah (1,7), the sailors proceed to address a series of five (so MT)[57] questions to him (1,8). Josephus (9,211b) has them pose only two questions, these corresponding to the double answer Jonah will give in what follows; he likewise recasts the questions in indirect address: "And when they asked him where he came from (πόθεν ... εἴη; LXX πόθεν ἔρχῃ) and what his business was (τί μετέρχεται; LXX τίς σου ἡ ἐργασία ἐστί)...[58]". The historian's rendition (9,211c) of Jonah's response (1,9) is noteworthy especially for its rewording of the prophet's second statement about himself: "... he said that[59] he was a Hebrew *by race* (τὸ γένος)[60],

which he responds by calling himself a "servant of the Lord" (so 1,9 LXX), even while keeping silent about his "sin" which has called forth the storm.

55. Compare the direct discourse "quotation" of the sailors' words in 1,7a: "And they said to one another, 'Come, let us draw lots (LXX κλήρους), that we may know on whose account this evil has come upon us'". (Josephus' previous reference [9,210] to the sailors' "suspecting that one of the passagers was the cause of the storm that had come upon them" might be seen as his "anticipation" of the indication about the purpose of the lot-casting with which their words as cited in 1,7a conclude.)

56. Compare 1,7bβ: "and the lot fell on (LXX ἔπεσεν ὁ κλῆρός ἐπί) Jonah". Note Josephus' use of the historic present where LXX employs a past form.

57. In some Hebrew MSS as well as in codices B and Sinaiticus of LXX the opening question of MT 1,8 ("on whose account has this evil come upon us?", RSV) is missing, likely because the sailors would already appear to know the answer to it, given the wording of 1,7a where the purpose of the lot-casting is precisely to find out "on whose account this evil has come upon us".

58. In 1,8 itself the question about Jonah's occupation precedes that concerning his place of origin. Josephus' reversal of the Biblical sequence might have in view the fact that in 1,9 (as well as in his own presentation) Jonah responds to the latter query in first place.

From the sailors' five questions as quoted in MT 1,8 Josephus omits both the first (see n. 57) and the two final ones ("What is your country? And of what people are you?") which might appear to simply duplicate their previous query, i.e. "whence do you come?".

59. As with the sailors' questions, Josephus reformulates the Biblical Jonah's response in indirect address.

60. In having Jonah represent himself as a "Hebrew" Josephus agrees with MT 1,9 ("I [am] a Hebrew") as against LXX which reads δοῦλος κυρίου ἐγώ εἰμι (on the origin of this reading, see MARCUS, *Josephus*, VI, p. 111, n. e) and Tg. Jonah where Jonah states "I (am) a Jew". On Josephus' added specification "(a Hebrew) *by race*", see FELDMAN, *Studies*, p. 396 (= ID., *Jonah*, 7) who suggests that the addition is intended to downplay the nationalistic connotations of the word "Hebrew" and who further notes that the expression used of Jonah here in 9,211 has a counterpart in *BJ* 1,3 where the historian says of himself "I Josephus... a Hebrew by race" (γένει Ἑβραῖος [these two words are absent in codex P and in Eusebius and are printed in brackets by St.J. Thackeray, while

and a prophet of the Most High God (προφήτης ... τοῦ μεγίστου θεοῦ)⁶¹".

The Biblical narrative continues in 1,10-11 with an extended sequence concerning the crew's reactions to Jonah's statements to them (1,9), this culminating with their question "what shall we do with you that the sea may quiet down for us?" of v. 11a. Josephus leaves this whole sequence aside⁶². In place thereof he has (9,211d) the prophet continue his preceding reply, now drawing on the words attributed to him in 1,12 (where they constitute his response to the sailors' question of 1,11a; see above): "He advised them, therefore, if they wished to escape (ἀποδρᾶναι)⁶³ their present danger (κίνδυνον; cf. κινδυνεύοντος, 9,209), to throw him into the water (ἐκβαλεῖν ... εἰς τὸ πέλαγος), for, he said, he was the cause of the storm (αἴτιον ... τοῦ χειμῶνος [see the same phrase in 9,210]) that had come upon them⁶⁴".

Niese omits them from his text]). Cf. further S.J.D. COHEN, Ἰουδαῖος τὸ γένος and *Related Expressions in Josephus*, in F. PARENTE & J. SIEVERS (eds.), *Josephus & the History of the Greco-Roman Period: Essays in Memory of Morton Smith* (SPB, 41), Leiden, Brill, 1994, pp. 23-38.

61. Jonah's self-identification here echoes that used by Josephus in introducing Elijah in *AJ* 8,319 ("there was a certain prophet of the most high God [προφήτης... τίς τοῦ μεγίστου θεοῦ]"). It takes the place of the statement attributed to Jonah in 1,9b, i.e. "I fear the Lord (LXX τὸν κύριον ... σέβομαι), the God of heaven, who made the sea and the dry land". Josephus' reformulation eliminates the "un-Greek" divine title "the Lord", and likewise avoids the seeming self-illusion/deceit on the part of the run-away prophet claiming to be a "God-fearer". On this last problem, see the reflections of Jerome, *in Jonam* on 1,9 (DUVAL, *Commentaire*, p. 200) who suggests that even sinners "fear the Lord" and that Jonah might be using the term to refer to himself as one who "worships" the Lord, in the cultic sense. Likewise to be recalled here is Josephus' habitual avoidance of the Biblical expression "fear God"; see p. 9, n. 25.

According to Niese *ad loc.*, there is a lacuna in the extant text following the word θεοῦ.

62. In so doing he disposes of a series of problems posed by the wording of 1,10. Thus, whereas that verse begins by stating "then the men were exceedingly afraid", it is not clear what in Jonah's immediately preceding statement would occasion such "fear" on their part (the problem is noted by Jerome, *In Jonam ad loc.* (DUVAL, *Commentaire*, p. 202). The verse then continues with a quotation of the sailors' words ("What is this you have done"?) to which is attached the explanatory comment "for the men knew that he was fleeing from the face of the Lord, because he had told them". Here too, a problem arises, i.e. the fact that in his preceding declaration as cited in 1,9 Jonah makes no mention of his "flight" as such.

63. This term echoes the same verb used of Jonah himself in 9,208 where he is said to "flee (ἀποδιδράσκει) from God".

64. Compare Jonah's words as cited in 1,12: "Take me up and throw me into the sea (LXX ἐμβάλετε ... εἰς τὴν θάλασσαν); then the sea will quiet down for you; for I know that it is because of me that this great tempest has come upon you". As FELDMAN, *Studies*, p. 408 (= ID., *Jonah*, 20-21) notes, Jonah's moral stature is accentuated in Josephus' presentation here where the prophet "volunteers" the information that he must be thrown overboard if the ship is to be saved without previous prompt-

The Biblical crew's initial, negative response to Jonah's proposal that they toss him overboard comes in 1,13 where they try to row back to land, but without success due to the sea's resistance. Thereupon, they address a prayer to the Lord, begging not to be held guilty of "innocent blood" (1,14), before finally (1,15a) doing as directed by Jonah (1,12). Josephus eliminates the sailors' "Yahwistic" prayer with its triple invocation of "the Lord"[65], just as he transposes the reference to their futile "rowing" (1,13) into a account of their motivation, first for not acting immediately on Jonah's proposition and then for eventually doing so. His version of the "preliminaries" to Jonah's removal from the ship (9,212a) thus reads:

> At first they did not dare to do so, regarding it as an impious act (ἀσέ-βημα) to take a man who was a stranger (ξένον)[66] and had entrusted his life to them, and cast him out (ἐκρῖψαι)[67] to so (οὕτως)[68] certain a death (πανερὰν ... ἀπώλειαν)[69]; but finally, as their distress pressed more heavily (ὑπερβιαζομένου τοῦ κακοῦ)[70] upon them and the vessel was on the point of sinking (βαπτίζεσθαι τοῦ σκάφους)[71], and since they were driven to it both by the prophet himself (ὑπὸ ... τοῦ προφήτου παρορμηθέντες;

ing by the crew – as happens in 1,11-12. I would further note that Josephus' omission of the sequence of 1,10-11 has a certain counterpart in *Pirqe R. El.* 10.2 (PÉREZ FERNÁNDEZ, *Los capítulos de Rabbí Eliezer*, p. 102) and *Midr. Jonah* (WÜNSCHE, *Lehrhallen*, I, p. 41) whose retellings of the story move directly from 1,6 (the captain's exhortation to Jonah) to 1,12 (Jonah's words to the crew). Contrast *De Jona* §§11-12 (SIEGERT, *Predigten*, I, pp. 15-17) which develops an extended speech by the sailors on the basis of their question to Jonah as cited in 1,11 in which, e.g., even while affirming that they do not desire his death, they call on him to vacate the ship on his own.

65. Here again, one may see Josephus' sensitivity to Roman's concerns about Jewish proselytism at work; cf. n. 45.

66. FELDMAN, *Studies*, pp. 410,413 (= ID., *Jonah*, 24,27) points out that Josephus' use of this term represents a Hellenizing retouching of Jonah story in that hospitality to "strangers" was a key value in Greek tradition, as seen, e.g., in the *Odyssey*. The term further echoes, though now *in bonam partem*, the mention of Jeroboam's "adopting many unseemly *foreign* (ξένοις) practices" in 9,205.

67. Josephus' other uses of the verb ἐκρίπτω are in *BJ* 3,337; 5,569.

68. This is the reading adopted by Dindorf, Bekker, Naber, and Marcus. Niese follows RO's αὐτούς concerning which reading NABER, *Opera*, II, p. xxxi comments "quod Ns. non debuerat probare".

69. Josephus' one other use of this expression is in *AJ* 2,117 (where it also is associated with the term οὕτως).

70. MARCUS, *Josephus*, VI, p. 113, n. b points out that this phrase occurs in Thucydides 2.52. The verb ὑπερβιάζομαι is hapax in Josephus; compare the cognate adjective βιαιοτέρας in 9,210.

71. This phrase recurs in *BJ* 3,368(403).525 (*Vita* 15). Compare the equivalent expression (κινδυνεύοντος) καταδῦναι τοῦ σκάφους in 9,209. The entire above sequence "as their distress... the point of sinking" is likely inspired by the double reference to "the sea's growing more and more tempestuous" in 1,11b and 13b.

cf. 9,211d)[72] and by fear for their own lives (ὑπὸ τοῦ δέους τοῦ περὶ τῆς αὐτῶν σωτηρίας)...[73]

Having thus elaborated on the "buildup" to the sailors' deed in what precedes, Josephus, in accord with 1,15, next relates (9,212b-213a) that deed itself and its consequences quite concisely: "... they cast him into the sea (ῥίπτουσιν αὐτὸν εἰς τὴν θάλασσαν)[74]. And so the storm was stilled (ὁ ... χειμὼν ἐστάλη)...[75]".

Before proceeding to relate the fate of overboard Jonah, the Bible (1,16) pauses to note the affect of the stilling of the storm (1,15b) upon the crew: they "feared the Lord exceedingly, and they offered a sacrifice to the Lord and made vows". Conscious of Roman sensibilities about Jewish inroads on their traditional religion, Josephus elects not to reproduce this item[76] (although he does seem to have drawn on its context at an earlier point; see 9,209 and n. 44). Instead, he moves immediately (9,213b) to recount Jonah's extraordinary delivery (= 2,1 [MT]; RSV 1,17): "as for Jonah, *the story* (λόγος) *has it*[77] that he was swallowed by

72. With this expression compare *AJ* 8,406 where Micaiah avers that "they were false prophets who led him [King Ahab] on (παρορμήσειαν ... οἱ ψευδοπροφῆται)". Note also the verbal echo of 9,199 where Josephus, in an editorial aside, states of Amaziah's ill-fated provocation of Joash of Israel: "it was God, I think, who urged (παρορμῶντος) him on to it, in order that he might suffer punishment for his transgressions against Him".

73. The above construction is hapax in Josephus. Note that this is Josephus' only reference to the sailors' "fear" whereas the Biblical account mentions it three times (1,5.10,16; cf. Jonah's evocation of his own "fear" of the Lord in 1,9 (MT), likewise eliminated by Josephus). On the other hand, the reference does echo the historian's inserted allusion to Jonah's being "afraid" (δείσας) in 9,208.

74. Compare LXX 1,15a:... ἐξέλαβον αὐτὸν εἰς τὴν θάλασσαν. Here again, Josephus employs an historic present where the LXX reads a past form. In *De Jona* §14 (SIEGERT, *Predigten*, I, p. 18) Jonah takes the initiative in casting himself into the sea.

75. Compare 1,15b: "and the sea ceased (LXX ἔστη) from its raging".

76. Cf. nn. 45,65. In omitting the content of 1,16 Josephus likewise disposes of a further difficulty posed by its (MT) wording, i.e. the sailors' (apparent) offering of their "sacrifice to the Lord" outside the Temple precincts in violation of Deuteronomy's centralization requirement (in Tg. Jonah 1,16 this difficulty is circumvented in that the men are said to "*promise* to offer a sacrifice"; for his part, Jerome, *In Jonam* on 1,16 [DUVAL, *Commentaire*, p. 218], acknowledging that the sailors would not have had the requisite victims on the high seas, spiritualizes their sacrifice as that of a "contrite heart"; cf. Ps 51,17).

With Josephus' omission of the sailors' "conversion" compare *Pirqe R. El.* 10.4 (PÉREZ FERNÁNDEZ, *Los capítulos de Rabbí Eliezer*, pp. 104-105); *Midr. Jonah* on 1,16 (WÜNSCHE, *Lehrhallen*, I, p. 45) which expatiate on the point: throwing their idols overboard, the sailors go to Jerusalem where they are circumcised (this is their "sacrifice") and then return to their homes where they make "God-fearers" out of their families as well. By contrast, *De Jona*, like Josephus, says nothing of any such "conversion" by the crew.

77. FELDMAN, *Studies*, p. 403 (= ID., *Jonah*, 15) notes that this opening disclaimer – likely interjected with the sceptical sensibilities of cultivated Gentile readers in mind – has a counterpart in the formula used by Herodotus (*Histories* 1.24) in presenting the similiar tale of Arion who was rescued by a dolphin when thrown overboard, i.e. "they say (λέγουσι)".

a whale (ὑπὸ τοῦ κήτους καταποθέντα)[78] and after three days and as many nights...[79]".

Jonah 2,2-10 (MT, RSV 2,1-9) constitutes an interlude between Jonah's swallowing by the fish (2,1) and his explusion from it (2,11), featuring an extended prayer by the prophet. Doubtless wishing to be done with the credulity-straining "fish story" (see n. 77) as quickly as possible, Josephus reverses the Biblical sequence of Jonah's prayer and release from the fish, making the former come subsequent to the latter[80]. In reporting then Jonah's release (= 2,11, MT) in first place, Josephus connects this directly with the preceding chronological notice drawn by him from 2,1: "... (and after three days and as many nights Jonah) was cast up (ἐκβρασθῆναι)[81] on the shore of *the Euxine sea*[82], *still living and unharmed in body* (τοῦ σώματος λελωβημένον[83])[84]...". To this notice he attaches (9,214a) his version of the prayer of 2,2-10 (MT)

---

78. Josephus' formulation eliminates the divine role in Jonah's delivery as cited in Jonah 2,1a: "And the Lord appointed a great fish (LXX κήτει μεγάλῳ) to swallow up (LXX καταπιεῖν) Jonah". Compare his similiar elimination of God's involvement in stirring up the storm in his rewriting of 1,4 in 9,208; cf. n. 39. *Pirqe R. El.* 10.3 (PÉREZ FERNÁNDEZ, *Los capítulos de Rabbí Eliezer*, p. 103) *Midr. Jonah* on 2,1 (WÜNSCHE, *Lehrhallen*, I, p. 42) quote R. Tarfon as affirming that the fish in question had been designated for its task already from the sixth day of creation.

79. Compare Jonah 2,1b: "and Jonah was in the belly of the fish three days and three nights".

80. Josephus may have found inspiration for this "reversal" in the wording of Jonah's prayer which, as a "thanksgiving song", speaks of God's delivery of him as a *fait accompli*, and so might seem to come more appropriately after his release from the fish. In contrast to Josephus who has nothing to say about the events of the three days Jonah spent inside the fish, *Pirqe R. El.* 10.3 (PÉREZ FERNÁNDEZ, *Los capítulos de Rabbí Eliezer*, pp. 103-105); *Midr. Jonah* on Jonah 2 (WÜNSCHE, *Lehrhallen*, I, pp. 43-44); and *De Jona* §18 (SIEGERT, *Predigten*, I, p. 20) expatiate on the matter, telling, e.g., of the sights seen by Jonah beneath the sea, his encounter with Leviathan, his being swallowed by a pregnant female fish after his initial "consumption" by a male fish, and his use of the fish as a mouthpiece for his prayer. Obviously, these other sources did not share Josephus' embarassment over the fish episode.

81. Josephus' one remaining use of the verb ἐκβράζω is in *BJ* 3,427. Compare the ἐξέβαλε employed by LXX for Jonah's "expulsion" by the fish in 2,11. SCHWEMER, *Prophetenlegenden*, I, p. 62 points out that Josephus' verb is the same one used by *VP* 10.2 and Justin, *Dialogue* 107.2 when relating the episode.

82. Jonah 2,11 speaks more indeterminately of his being deposited "on dry land (LXX ἐπὶ τὴν ξηράν)". See the comment of MARCUS, *Josephus*, VI, p. 113, n. c: "Josephus apparently assumes that the Black (Euxine) Sea would be the nearest sea to Nineveh".

83. The above phrase ("unharmed in body") recurs in *AJ* 15,181; *c. Ap.* 1,234.253.273.

84. The above indication concerning Jonah's condition at the moment of his emergence from the whale lacks an equivalent in 2,11 itself. It does have a counterpart in Jerome, *In Jonam*, on 2,7 (DUVAL, *Commentaire*, p. 248) who states that in the belly of the fish Jonah "sospes et integer manserit" as well as in *De Jona* §§24,25 and 3 Macc 6,8 ("and Jonah, wasting away in the belly of a huge, sea-born monster, you, Father, watched over and restored *unharmed* [LXX ἀπήμαντον] to all his family").

which he not only drastically shortens[85], but also gives a new, distinctive content: "then, having prayed to God to grant him pardon (συγγνώμην ... παρασχεῖν) for his sins (ἡμαρτημένων)...[86]".

The Jonah story takes a new, positive turn in 3,1-2 where the Lord renews his commission of 1,1 "a second time"[87] and Jonah, this time, does as directed (3,3a). Josephus skips Jonah's "recommissioning", having (9,214b) the prophet take the initiative himself at this juncture[88]: "... he went (ἀπῆλθεν)[89] to *the city of* Ninos (Νίνου, see 9,208; compare LXX 3,2 Νινευη)...[90]".

Jonah 3,3b describes Nineveh, Jonah's destination, as an "exceedingly great city, three days journey in breadth". Given the seeming exaggeration of this description, Josephus leaves it aside[91]. Having done so,

85. This compression of the Biblical Jonah's prayer is in line with Josephus' treatment of other Scriptural prayers which he either notably abridges (see, e.g., his rendition of David's prayer, 2 Sam 7,18-29 in *AJ* 7,95, and his mere allusion to Hezekiah's psalm [Isa 38,9-20; compare 10,29]) or omits entirely (e.g., Hannah's prayer [1 Sam 2,1-10] and the "laments" of Jeremiah).

86. The above construction ("pardon of sins") occurs also in *AJ* 7,193 where Absalom entreats David for such; cf. the related expression using the preposition ἐπὶ + the dative in *AJ* 2,156; 6,208; 7,198. In making a plea for forgiveness the (sole) content of Jonah's prayer Josephus introduces into it a element which one might well expect – given that the speaker is one who has violated a divine order with potentially fatal consequences for many people – to find in Jonah's prayer of 2,2-10 but, in fact, does not. This "lacuna" is similarly filled in the (vastly expanded) prayer attributed to Jonah in *De Jona* §§19-25 (SIEGERT, *Predigten*, I, pp. 20-25).

87. This indication provoked a discussion among the Rabbis seeing that the Bible would appear to record *three* speakings by the Lord to Jonah, i.e. those of Jonah 1,1-2 and 3,1-2, plus that of 2 Kgs 14,25. E.g., in *b. Yeb.* 98a the problem is resolved by means of the claim that the last of these divine communications, like the two former ones, had in view the fate of Nineveh and so is to be subsumed under them.

88. His doing this might be associated with the plea for forgiveness which Josephus represents Jonah as making in what immediately precedes: his acting on his original commission at this juncture without waiting for God to reissue this would provide convincing proof of Jonah's penitence and resolve to make amends for his past disobedience. In this connection it is of interest to note that also *De Jona* makes no mention of Jonah's "re-commissioning", portraying him rather as acting to carry out his original task with great eagerness once he has been released from the fish (see §26; SIEGERT, *Predigten*, I, p. 26). Josephus' omission of the content of 3,1-2a likewise has the effect of doing away with the "counting problem" posed by the reference to the Lord's speaking to Jonah "a second time" in 3:1; see preceding note.

89. This term introduces both an echo of and a contrast with Josephus' formulation in 9,208: "(Jonah was afraid and) did not set out (οὐκ ἀπῆλθεν)" which serves to underscore the prophet's change of behavior. For a similar element in the continuation of Josephus' presentation, see n. 94. *VP* 10.2 (SCHWEMER, *Prophetenlegenden*, II, p. 48) employs the same verb, in the participial form ἀπελθών, to speak of Jonah's "going" to Nineveh following his release from the fish.

90. Having passed over the new commissioning account of 3,1-2a, Josephus likewise leaves aside the fulfillment notice of 3,3aβ: "(Jonah went to Nineveh) *according to the word of the Lord*".

91. Compare the *Ausmalung* of the Biblical notice on Nineveh's extent in *Midr. Jonah* on 3,3 (WÜNSCHE, *Lehrhallen*, I, p. 45).

he likewise modifies the Biblical notice (3,4a) concerning the preliminaries ("Jonah began to go into the city, going a day's journey...") to the prophet's announcement of Nineveh's doom (3,4b): "... and, standing where all could hear him..."[92]. He modifies as (9,214c) well both the form and content of Jonah's announcement as reported in 3,4b ("Yet forty [MT, LXX three] days and Nineveh shall be overthrown [LXX καταστραφήσεται]"): "... (he) proclaimed (ἐκήρυσσεν; cf. LXX ἐκήρυξε and κηρῦξαι, 9,208) that in a very short time (ὀλίγον πάνυ χρόνον)[93] they would lose their dominion over Asia (ἀποβαλοῦσι τὴν ἀρχὴν τῆς ᾽Ασίας)..."[94].

The Biblical Book of Jonah continues with no less than 18 verses (3,5-4,11) subsequent to the prophet's announcement of 3,4. This concluding segment relates, in turn, Nineveh's repentance (3,5-9), God's corresponding relenting (3,10), and a two-fold exchange between God and Jonah concerning the appropriateness of the latter's "anger" at the former's sparing of the city (4,1-5 and 4,6-11). In striking contrast to this drawn-out Biblical finale, Josephus, having presented his parallel to 3,4

92. This indication concerning the "position" from which Jonah makes his announcement has a certain parallel both in *Midr. Jonah* on 3,3 (WÜNSCHE, *Lehrhallen*, I, p. 46: Jonah stands on the street and cries aloud, his voice carrying throughout the city) and *De Jona* §27 (SIEGERT, *Predigten*, I, p. 26: Jonah positions himself at an elevated point). Note, however, that, in contrast to Josephus, both these documents do make previous use of the notice of 3,4a about Jonah's "going a day's journey (in)to Nineveh".

93. This is the reading of ROSPELat which Dindorf, Bekker, Naber, and Marcus follow. Niese reads rather πάλιν with M and the ed. pr. in place of the above words πάνυ χρόνον. The indeterminate chronological indication read by Naber and Marcus takes the place of the definite figures supplied by MT ("forty") and LXX ("three") 3,4. The vagueness of Josephus' indication serves to preclude readers from viewing Jonah as a false prophet for what concerns the "timing" of his announcement; see SCHWEMER, *Prophetenlegenden*, II, pp. 69-70. In this connection mention should, however, be made of Josephus' statement in 9,242: "*all* the things that had been foretold concerning Nineveh [i.e. presumably those announced by Jonah (9,209-214) as well as the later prophet Nahum (see 9,239-241)] came to pass after a hundred and fifteen years [i.e. subsequent to the reign of King Jotham of Judah under whom Josephus dates the prophecy of Nahum, see 9,236-238, who was himself a contemporary of King Pekah of Israel, Jeroboam II's penultimate successor on the throne of Israel]". A period of more than "115 years" hardly seems, however, to match the "very short time" evoked by Jonah in 9,214 for Nineveh's coming fate.

94. The above phrase "lose dominion" recurs in *AJ* 14,491; 20,47. The wording of Jonah's announcement as cited here in 9,214 echoes that of God's directive to him to proclaim that Nineveh "would lose its power (τὴν ἀρχὴν ἀπολέσει)" in 9,208. This verbal parallelism underscores the fact of Jonah's ultimate carrying out of the divine commission (for another such item, see n. 89). The language of 9,208.214 recurs in 10,30 where Josephus states: "now it happened at this time that the empire (ἀρχήν) of the Assyrians was destroyed by the Medes"; cf. 10,74: (Pharoah Neco advances to the Euphrates) "to make war on the Medes and Babylonians who had overthrown the Assyrian empire (ἀρχήν); for he had the desire to rule Asia".

(9,214bc), very quickly "wraps up" (9,214d) his story of Jonah with the following closing notices: "... after giving them this message, he departed (ὑπέστρεψε)[95]. And I have recounted (διεξῆλθον) his story (διήγησιν) as I found (εὗρον) it written down (ἀναγεγραμμένην)[96]".

3. *Jeroboam's End*

The closing words of 9,214 clearly signify the end of Josephus' "excursus" concerning Jonah (9,208-214); see above. In 9,215, accordingly, he returns to Kings' account of Jeroboam which he had begun reproducing in 9,205-207 (= 2 Kgs 14,23-25[26-27]) in order to complete his presentation of that monarch. Of the items constituting 14,28-29, he leaves aside, in line with his invariable practice, the source notice

95. The Bible itself says nothing about such a "return" by Jonah following the completion of his mission. This item does, however, have a parallel both in 3 Macc 6,8 ("and Jonah... you, Father, restored [LXX ἀνέδειξας] to all his family") and *VP* 10.2 ("after he had been thrown out of the fish and had gone to Nineveh, he went back (ἀνακάμ-ψας)..."; see SCHWEMER, *Prophetenlegenden*, II, p. 48). (In this connection it might be pointed out that the bulk of *VP*'s account of Jonah (10.2b-8) is devoted to the period subsequent to his "return" from Nineveh about which neither the Bible nor Josephus say anything, the whole of the Biblical Jonah story being summed up in the opening words of 10.2 as cited above.)

96. The above notice constitutes an inclusion with the introduction to Josephus' Jonah story in 9,208a: "... I have thought it necessary to recount (διεξελθεῖν) what I have found (εὗρον) written (ἀναγεγραμμένα)... concerning this prophet" whose wording it so clearly echoes. Taken together, the notices at the opening of 9,208 and the close of 9,214 serve to set the Jonah story apart as a self-contained unit within the overall flow of Josephus' narrative. At the same time, the reiteration of the historian's assurance here in 9,214 that he has given us the story of the prophet as he "found it written", coming as it does in place of the lengthy omitted sequence 3,5-4,11, only underscores the disingenuousness of Josephus' handling of the Biblical Jonah material; compare n. 26 and see further the conclusion of this chapter.

As for Josephus' reason(s) for omitting the content of Jonah 3,5-4,11, FELDMAN, *Studies*, pp. 393-415 (= ID., *Jonah*, *passim*) has identified a whole series of features in this sequence which Josephus would have found problematic in one or other respect, this prompting him to eliminate the whole: the pagan Ninevites' "conversion" to the Lord and their implied religious superiority to the so often unrepentant Jews (3,5-9), the "bizarre" detail of the Ninevites' beasts joining in their acts of penitence (3,7-8; cf. 4,11), the divine change of mind (3,10) contrary to affirmations about God's "unchangeability" elsewhere in the Bible (see, e.g., 1 Sam 15,29; Hos 11,9), the less than exemplary image of the prophet in 4,1-11, who, after his seeming change of heart in 3,3 (cf. 9,214) reverts to petuantly resisting God's purposes and gives expression to a disturbing xenophobia in 4,2, as well as the (excessive) immediacy of God's operations on natural realities, i.e. the plant, the worm and the east wind (3,6-8), this reminiscent of his earlier dealings with the sea (1,4), and the fish (2,1.11), both of which are also eliminated by Josephus; see above.

In contrast to Josephus, other Jewish (and Christian) traditions expatiate on the episodes related in Jonah 3,5-4,11. For a summary account of this material, see GINZBERG, *Legends*, IV, pp. 250-253 and the references in Vol. VI, pp. 323-325, nn. 34-40.

of v. 28. Conversely, he expatiates in his rendition of the elements making up v. 29: "Now King Jeroboam died (ἐτελεύτησε)[97] *after a life of complete prosperity* (πάσης εὐδαιμονίας)[98] *and a reign of forty years*[99]; he was buried (θάπτεται) in Samaria[100] and was succeeded on the throne by his son Zacharias (Ζαχαρίας = L; compare B ᾿Αζαρίας υἱὸς ᾿Αμεσσείου[101])".

Conclusions: Josephus' Rewriting of 2 Kgs 14,23-29 & the Book of Jonah

In summing up on my findings regarding *AJ* 9,205-215, I shall treat separately Josephus' handling of his two distinct Biblical sources for this segment, i.e. 2 Kgs 14,23-29 and the Book of Jonah.

Textually, Josephus' account of Jeroboam (9,205-207.215) stands somewhat closer to "LXX" (L in particular) than to "MT" 2 Kgs 14,23-29; see nn. 2,3,100. He makes no use of either the theological reflection of 14,26-27 (see n. 22) or the "source notice" of 14,28. On the other hand, he twice introduces references to the welfare brought by Jeroboam's reign (9,205.215), just as he expatiates on the notice of 14,25 concerning the king's military successes. In his handling of 14,25 Josephus likewise re-arranges the sequence of its component parts. The historian's "modifications" of source data involve *inter alia* his (twice) rounding off the figure for Jeroboam's length of reign (9,205.215; compare 14,23), substitution of alternative language (9,205) for the stereotyped judgment formula of 14,24, (updated) renaming of "the Sea of the Arabah" (see n. 16), and representing Jonah's prophecy as having been addressed to Jeroboam himself (9,206; compare 14,25). The most

97. Compare 14,29a: "And Jeroboam slept with his fathers, with the kings of Israel" (so MT B; L "reapplies" the phrase "with the kings of Israel" to Jeroboam's burial; see n. 100).

98. This phrase is hapax in Josephus. On Josephus' use of εὐδαιμονία, a key term of Greek ethics, see: H.-F. WEISS, *Pharisäismus und Hellenismus. Zur Darstellung des Judentums im Geschichtswerk des jüdischen Historikers Flavius Josephus*, in *OLZ* 74 (1979) 421-431, c. 427; S. MASON, *Flavius Josephus and the Pharisees: A Composition-Critical Study* (SPB, 39), Leiden, Brill, 1991, p. 185.

99. The wording of the sequence italicized above recalls that of Josephus' introduction of Jeroboam in 9,205 ("he reigned... forty years... to the people of Israel he was a cause of innumerable benefits").

100. In providing the above burial notice for Jeroboam Josephus goes together with L 14,29: "he was buried (ἐτάφη) in Samaria with the kings of Israel" (see n. 97) against MT and B which lack such. Note, once again, Josephus' use of an historic present where the source has a past form.

101. B's reading here confuses "Zachariah" with his southern contemporary Azariah (= Uzziah), son of Amaziah (see 2 Kgs 15,8).

notable feature to Josephus' rewriting of 2 Kgs 14,23-29 is, however, his intercalation within it of matter drawn from a quite distinct Biblical context, i.e. the Book of Jonah.

With regard, first of all, to the text of the Book of Jonah used by Josephus in 9,208-214, we noted his agreement with a distinctive MT reading in having Jonah designate himself as a "Hebrew" (9,211 = 1,9; see n. 60, cf. n. 31).

Josephus' Jonah story furnishes noteworthy examples of his various rewriting techniques. Most obviously, he drastically abridges the source account, jettisoning not only the whole of 3,5-4,11, but also large portions of 1,1-3,4 itself (see, e.g., the reduction of the nine-verse prayer of 2,2-10 [MT] to a single phrase in 9,214). His additions to/expansions of the Biblical narrative are less conspicuous. They include the framework notices of 208,214; the localization of "Tarsus" (9,208; compare 1,3-4); the rationale for the sailors' recourse to lot-casting (9,210; compare 1,7); the opening disclaimer about the fish story (9,213; compare 2,1); the site of Jonah's explusion from the fish (9,213; compare 2,11); his surviving his ordeal unharmed (9,213; compare 2,11); and "return" following his proclamation in Nineveh (9,214).

Josephus further re-arranges the sequence of the Bible's Jonah story. The most notable instance of this technique in 9,208-214 is his positioning (9,214) of Jonah's prayer after – rather than before – the prophet's explusion from the fish (compare 2,1-11). In addition, however, we noted under this head, e.g., his anticipation of the reference to the crew's sacrificial activity from the very end of the storm scene (so 1,16) to its beginning (so 9,209) and reversal of the source order of the questions put to Jonah (9,211; compare 1,8).

Finally, Josephus' version of the Jonah story features numerous and varied modifications/adaptations of source data. Terminologically, he replaces Biblical uses of "the Lord" title (see 9,208; compare 1,3-4; 9,211; compare 1,9) and mentions of the divine "word" (see 9,208; compare 1,3) with alternative language. The Bible's place name "Nineveh" becomes "Ninos" (9,208; compare 1,2; 9,214; compare 3,3), while no less than four times in the space of seven paragraphs the title "prophet" is applied by him to Jonah. On the stylistic level, he introduces historic presents where the LXX reads rather a past form (see, e.g., n. 74) and substitutes indirect for direct address (see 9,211; compare 1,8-9). Josephus' modifications extend as well to the story's content, with his prophet proclaiming a different message (see 9,208.214; compare 3,4) and addressing a different prayer to God (see 9,213; compare 2,2-10) than does his Biblical counterpart.

As a result of the above rewriting techniques, Josephus' Jonah story ends up differing rather markedly from its Biblical prototype. Overall, he has greatly "streamlined" the source's narration[102]. The roles of all other characters (God, the sailors, the Ninevites) are reduced, while that of Jonah is accentuated[103]. With the sensibilities of sophisticated Gentile readers in mind, Josephus plays down the theological, anthropomorphic, anthropathetic[104], miraculous, "anti-pagan"[105], and "missionary/proselytizing" dimensions of the Scriptural story. On the other hand, he presents Jewish readers with a prophet of enhanced moral stature[106] and unquestioned accuracy as a predictor[107], even as they are spared the provocative self-critique implicit in the Book of Jonah between the Ninevites' eager response to Jonah's preaching (see 3,5-9; no parallel in Josephus) and the negative reaction Israel's prophets so often encountered from their own people.

The foregoing considerations about Josephus' rendition of the Biblical story of Jonah leave one with a final question. Given that story's somewhat extraneous character vis à vis the historian's main story-line, given

102. Such streamlining, in first place, has to do, it would seem, with Josephus' consciousness that his Jonah story does represent a "digression" within its wider context – see his "apology" for introducing the story at all at the opening of 9,208.

103. On this point, see FELDMAN, *Studies*, p. 407 (= ID., *Jonah*, 20).

104. Under this head, recall that Josephus makes no use of the reference (3,10) to God's "repenting" of his earlier decision in the manner of a "fickle" human person. On the point, see FELDMAN, *Studies*, pp. 400-402 (= ID., *Jonah*, 11-14).

105. In this connection recall that Josephus leaves aside the divine reference (1,2) to "the wickedness" of Nineveh which had come before him. In the same line, he passes over the prophet's word of 4,2 ("That is why I made haste to flee to Tarshish; *for* I know that thou art a gracious God...") with its xenophobic implications.

106. Thus, e.g., Josephus' Jonah takes the initiative in suggesting that he be thrown overboard so that the crew may be saved (9,211; compare 1,11-12), explicitly acknowledges his "sins" in praying for forgiveness (9,213; compare 2,2-10) and needs no second order from God to undertake his mission once delivered from the fish (9,213; compare 3,1-2). Josephus' positive retouching of Jonah's image is further served by his omission of the book's closing scenes (4,1-11) featuring a petulant prophet obstinately nursing his anger against God.

107. Compare the "non-fulfillment" of Jonah's announcement of 3,4 in the continuation of the Biblical narrative.

Also the wider Jewish-Christian tradition evidences a concern with upholding Jonah's prophetic credibility in some fashion. Thus *Pirqe R. El.* 43.6 (PÉREZ FERNÁNDEZ, *Los capítulos de Rabbí Eliezer*, p. 307) affirms that his announcement of Nineveh's destruction (3,4) was eventually fulfilled in that, following a forty-year period of good behavior – corresponding to the forty days of Jonah's proclamation – the inhabitants returned to their old ways, whereupon God destroyed them, similarly Jerome, *In Jonam*, Preface (DUVAL, *Commentaire*, p. 166). *De Jona* §48; cf. §2 (SIEGERT, *Predigten*, I, pp. 43-44, 9-10) for its part, has God tell Jonah that he has no reason to regard himself as a false prophet in light of the city's repentence given that the securing of such repentence was the divine intent in dispatching Jonah from the start.

too the many problems posed by it which required so large a measure of reworking of its content on his part, why did Josephus elect to use it at all, when, as noted above, he has no qualms about denying a place in *AJ* to other prophetic books? In other words, what was it about the Jonah story which caused Jonah to feel that he simply could not dispense with it in some form (cf. his phrase "I have thought it necessary" used in introducing the story in 9,208)? In response to this question, I suggest that Jonah's (reliable) announcement as (re-)formulated by Josephus in 9,208.214 i.e. that Ninos' kingdom was to "lose its rule (over Asia)" may provide the key to understanding the historian's perceived "compulsion" to utilize the Book of Jonah. On the one hand, that announcement might be counted on to evoke a positive response from Roman readers in that Ninos' kingdom was situated in an area currently dominated by Rome's major Eastern rival, i.e. the Parthian empire[108]. On the other hand, that same announcement could – on the presumption of another contemporary symbolic value for its cipher "the kingdom of Ninos" – offer Jewish readers a veiled message of hope: their Roman oppressors of today would someday "lose their dominion" just as surely as had Ninos' kingdom[109]. As we have often had occasion to remark over the course of this study, such "twofacedness" is not at all an isolated case in Josephus' retelling of Biblical history.

---

108. On this point, see FELDMAN, *Studies*, p. 397 (= ID., *Jonah*, 8).

109. In this connection I would call attention to Josephus' quotation of his statement to the defenders of Jerusalem in *BJ* 5,367: "Fortune, indeed, had from all quarters passed over to them [the Romans], and God who went the round of the nations, bringing to each in turn the rod of empire (ἀρχήν; see 9,208.214) *now* rested on Italy". Taken in conjunction the affirmations of *BJ* 5,367 and *AJ* 9,208.214 might suggest the thought: "rule" does rest with Rome "now", but that rule will be "lost" as had occurred with Ninos' kingdom.

Also to be noted here in the ambiguity surrounding Josephus' "supression" of the Ninevites' repentance and God's positive reaction to this (Jonah 3,5-10). On one level his procedure in this regard is simply intended to obviate Roman uneasiness about conversions to Judaism and the prosletyizing efforts that gave rise to these. For Jewish readers, however, the same "lacuna" might assume a quite different import: whereas the Ninevites of old had repented of their "wickedness" (1,2) with beneficial results for themselves, there can be no question of their contemporary equivalents, the Romans, doing the same.

In light of the above considerations, I further suggest that Josephus' blatantly disingenuous assertions about his having reproduced the Jonah story as "he found it written" (9,208.214) have, in fact, the character of authorial asides for the benefit of Jewish readers with the following tenor: You and I both know, of course, that there is more to the Jonah story than this, including a saving repentence by the wicked Ninevites. With that in mind, draw your own conclusions from what I had left out in the version of the story I've served up to our Roman masters.

XII

UZZIAH OF JUDAH AND NORTHERN COUNTERPARTS[1]
(9,216-235)

The next longer segment within Josephus' account of the divided monarchy which may be distinguished is 9,216-235 in which he treats, first the long-reigned King Uzziah of Judah (9,216-227), and then his five Northern contemporaries, i.e. Zechariah, Shallum, Menahem, Pekahiah, and Pekah (9,228-235). The former ruler is the subject of 2 Kgs 15,1-7 // 2 Chr 26,3-23, while the latter ones are presented in 2 Kgs 15,8-29(30-31). I divide the material for consideration in this chapter into eight sub-sections: 1. Uzziah Introduced (*AJ* 9,216 = 2 Kgs 15,1-4 // 2 Chr 26,3-5); 2. Uzziah's Achievements (9,217-221 = 26,6-15); 3. Uzziah's Offense (9,222-224 = 26,16-19a); 4. Uzziah Afflicted (9,225-227a = 15,5 // 26,19b-21); 5. Closing Notices for Uzziah (9,227b = 15,6-7 // 26,22-23); 6. Zechariah & Shallum (9,228 = 2 Kgs 15,8-13); 7. Menahem (9,229-233b = 15,14-22); and 8) Pekahiah & Pekah (9,233c-235 = 15,23-29[30-31]).

1. *Uzziah Introduced*

As we noted in the two preceding chapters, Josephus rounds off (9,204b) his account of Amaziah of Judah (9,186-204) with mention of the accession of his son "Ozias" (= Azariah, 2 Kgs 14,21/ Uzziah, 2 Chr 26,1), but then immediately drops him in order to tell the story of King Jeroboam II of Israel (= 2 Kgs 14,23-29) and the contemporary prophet Jonah in 9,205-215. In so doing, he likewise leaves for a latter point, as also mentioned above, the attached, seemingly "stray" notice on the new Judean king's "building" of Elath/Eloth (14,22 // 26,2).

2 Kgs 15,1, picking up the account of "Azariah" after the Jeroboam interlude of 14,23-29, synchronizes his accession (see 14,21) with the *27th* regnal year of Jeroboam. The Chronicler, with his Judean focus, unsurprisingly, has no equivalent. Josephus does give a synchronism for "Ozias'" succession in the context of his "resumed" accession notice of

1. This chapter is a reworking of my articles *Uzziah (Azariah) of Judah according to Josephus*, in *EstBíb* 53 (1995) 5-24 and *The Last Six Kings of Israel according to Josephus*, in *ETL* 72 (1996) 371-384, pp. 372-379 which are used here by permission.

9,216a (cf. 9,204b), but one which, at the same time, differs markedly form that of Kings, i.e. in Jeroboam's *14th* year. Here, one sees Josephus "correcting" a source indication in light of the Bible's (and his own) chronology elsewhere. Specifically, 2 Kgs 14,23 (= 9,205) states that Jeroboam II began to rule in the *15th* year of Azariah's father Amaziah who himself according to 14,1 (= 9,204) ruled *29* years. Subtracting the former from the latter figure, one arrives at Jeroboam's 14th – rather than his 27th (so 15,1) regnal year as the year of Uzziah's accession, just as Josephus reports, thereby eliminating the disrepancy among Kings' data[2].

2 Kgs 15,2a // 2 Chr 26,3a next note Azariah/Uzziah's age at acession (16) and length of reign (52 years). Josephus, here again, reserves these indications until the very end of his Uzziah account; see 9,227. In place thereof he proceeds immediately to the following source item, i.e. the name of the queen mother and her place of origin, designating her as "Achia" (Ἀχίας)[3], "a native of that city [i.e. Jerusalem; 15,2 // 26,3: of Jerusalem]".

The sources conclude their respective introductions of Azariah/ Uzziah with an evaluation of him. 2 Kgs 15,3 // 2 Chr 26,4 agree in stating that the king "did what was right in the eyes of the Lord as his father Amaziah had done". Thereafter, 15,4 qualifies Azariah's commendation by noting that worship on the high places continued during his reign. The Chronicler, who consistently avoids Kings' notices about high place worship, substitutes (26,5) a remark about Uzziah's "seeking the Lord" (who, in turn, made him prosper) throughout the lifetime of "Zechariah" – an otherwise unknown figure – by whom he was instructed in the fear of God. Josephus' own initial encomium of the king (9,216b) takes the form of a four-fold adjectival sequence: "he was a good and just man (ἀγαθὸς ... καὶ δίκαιος)[4] by nature and both magnanimous (μεγαλόφρων) and most industrious (φιλοπονώτατος)[5] in providing for the state". Of these terms, the last was clearly chosen by Josephus in view of Uzziah's many initiatives for Judah's benefit which he will now relate.

2. *Uzziah's Achievements*

At this point, Kings and Chronicles begin going their own ways to a marked degree. The former proceeds forthwith to relate the Lord's

---

2. See further MARCUS, *Josephus*, VI, pp. 114-115, n. a.

3. Compare "Jecholiah" (MT 15,2b // 26,3b); Χαχειά (B 15,2); Ἰεχελειᾶ (L 15,2 // 26,3); Χααιά (B 26,3).

4. For this collocation, see on 9,132.

5. This is Josephus' only use of the collocation "magnanimous and industrious". It is likewise his only employment of the superlative of the adjective φιλόπονος.

afflicting Azariah with leprosy (15,5a), while the Chronicler at this point presents rather his catalogue of Uzziah's accomplishments (26,6-15) to which the Josephan parallel is 9,217-221.

The Chronicler's "catalogue" opens in 26,6-8 with mention of the various neighboring peoples subjugated by Uzziah. Of these, it is the Philistines who receive the most attention. 2 Chr 26,6a records that in the course of his war against that people Uzziah demolished the walls of three cities (Gath, Jebneh, Ashdod). V. 6b then recounts the king's "building of cities" in the territory of Ashdod and elsewhere in Philistine country, while v. 7a attributes his success against the Philistines to divine assistance. Josephus (9,217a) drastically compresses, leaving aside both the "building notice" of 26,6b[6] and the theological comment of v. 7a. He likewise leaves aside the third city name from the listing of 26,6a, i.e. Ashdod. On the other hand, he introduces explicit mention of what is presupposed by the Chronicler's notice on Uzziah's demolition of the Philistine city walls, i.e. his prior defeat of the Philistines and capture of the cities in question (called by him "Gitta" and "Jamneia").

According to 26,7 God assisted Uzziah, not only against the Philistines, but also against two other peoples, i.e. "the Arabs that dwell in Gurbaal (BL ἐπὶ τῆς πέτρας) and the Meunities (B τοὺς Μειναίους, L μιναίους)". Josephus' version (9,217b) makes no mention of the latter people, while placing the "Arabs" rather "on the borders of Egypt" – a localization anticipated from 26,8 (see below). It is to this mention (= 26,7b) of Uzziah's success against the Arabs that Josephus then appends – appropriately so, in the context of an enumeration of Uzziah's achievements in foreign affairs – his equivalent to the "stray" notice (14,22 // 26,2) of Azariah/Uzziah's initiatives regarding the city of Elath/Eloth. The Biblical sources cite the city by name and speak of the king's "building" it and "restoring it to Judah". Josephus, on the contrary, only alludes to it as "a city on the Red Sea" which Uzziah "founds" and where he "stations a garrison[7]".

---

6. Perhaps he does this in view of the seeming discrepancy between 26,6a (Uzziah demolishes Philistine city walls) and 6b (Uzziah builds cities in Philistine territory) – why should the king first "destroy" only thereafter to "(re-) build?"

7. In 9,245 (= 2 Kgs 16,5) Josephus does mention "Elathus" by name as "situated on the Red Sea"; see also 8,163. Josephus' modification of the wording of 14,22 // 26,2 here could reflect the consideration that in Uzziah's time "Elath/Eloth" was an already existent city (and so had no need to be "built" by him). Similarly, the sources' reference to the king's "recovering" the site for Judah might appear problematic in that neither the Bible nor Josephus himself have previously mentioned a loss of the city by Judah (cf. 1 Kgs 9,26 // 2 Chr 8,17 = AJ 8,163 which suggest that it was under Israelite control in Solomon's time).

The last of the foreign peoples to be brought into Judah's orbit by Uzziah are the "Ammonites" (so MT, B οἱ Μειναῖοι, L οἱ μιναῖοι; cf. v. 7b); they "pay him tribute" (v. 8a). Thereafter, v. 8b speaks of the king's "fame" reaching to "the borders of Egypt", this as the result of his being "very strong". With MT 26,8 Josephus (9,218a) designates the final people in his listing as "the Ammanites". He further makes their paying of tribute to Uzziah, not a self-initiated gesture of submission (as it appears to be in 26,8), but rather the outcome of his "subduing" them and imposing such tribute upon them. In the same line, he represents Uzziah as actually "making himself master of all the country as far as the borders of Egypt" (cf. 9,217b), rather than being simply "well-known" within that area (so 26,8b). Both these modifications serve to accentuate the king's military and political stature.

2 Chr 26,9-10 (= 9,218b-220a) next relates Uzziah's building and agricultural initiatives within the territory of Judah itself. First to be mentioned (26,9) among Uzziah's building projects are the fortified "towers" which he erects at various points along the Jerusalem walls (the Corner Gate, the Valley Gate, and "the Angle"). Josephus makes (9,218b) the transition to this new topic with the phrase "(having made himself master of the country as far as the borders of Egypt), he began to take thought (ἐπιμέλειαν) thereafter for Jerusalem". He likewise precedes his mention of Uzziah's "towers" with an extended insertion concerning the king's repair of the city walls, in particular those portions demolished by Joash of Israel following his capture of Uzziah's father Amaziah (see 2 Kgs 14,13 // 2 Chr 25,23 = 9,201; cf. chap. X). This inserted *Rückverweis* responds to the question of whether and when the damage perpetrated by Joash was repaired. It likewise serves to link more closely the figures of Amaziah and Uzziah, a distinctive feature of Josephus' account as we noted already in the case of the former king and will be seeing further here in that of the latter. Only then does Josephus come to relate Uzziah's "tower-building". In so doing, he passes over the precise placements of the towers as given in 26,9 (see above)[8]. Conversely, however, he introduces (9,219a) the precision that the towers were each "fifty cubits high"[9].

2 Chr 26,10 records Uzziah's constructing "towers" and hewing out "cisterns" in the desert. Josephus (9,219b) varies the wording of this

---

8. Compare 9,201 where in his account of Joash's demolition of Jerusalem's wall, Josephus dispenses with the specification that the segment in question extended "from the Ephraim Gate to the Corner Gate" (so 2 Kgs 14,13 // 2 Chr 25,23).

9. On Josephus' penchant for introducing "exact" figures where the Bible lacks such, see BEGG, *Early Divided Monarchy*, p. 72, n. 426.

notice: what Uzziah establishes "in desert regions" are "fortified posts" and "canals for water". The continuation of 26,10 indicates that Uzziah's cisterns were prepared by him in view of the "large herds" he possessed in both the Shephelah and "the plain". Josephus accounts for the king's large livestock holdings with his appended notice "*for* the country was naturally good for pasture", while leaving aside the source reference to the two regions where these holdings were concentrated. At the conclusion of 26,10 one reads that Uzziah had farmers and vinedressers stationed "in the hills and in the fertile fields (so RSV; literally: in the Carmel), his doing so being attributed to his "love of the soil" (B ὅτι γεωργός [L φιλογέωργος] ἦν). Josephus (9,220a) accentuates the king's devotion to agriculture: "... being interested in farming (γεωργικός)[10], he took the greatest care (ἐπεμελεῖτο; cf. ἐπιμέλειαν, 9,218) of the soil and cultivated it with plants and all kinds of seed"[11].

2 Chr 26,11-15a rounds off the catalogue of Uzziah's achievements with the enumeration of the (defensive) military initiatives undertaken by him; the Josephan parallel is 9,220b-221. In Chronicles this segment begins with a reference to the divisions of the royal army devised by three named officials (v. 11a). It then goes on to provide statistics for the army's commanders (2,600, v. 12) and the army itself (307,500, v. 13). Josephus (9,220b) cites the data of 26,11-13 in the following order: number of troops (370,00; compare 26,13: 307,500), and their officers (2000; compare 26,12: 2,600) and divisions of the army (26,11). It will be noted that Josephus' statistics diverge from the Biblical ones in both instances here: he assigns Uzziah more troops but fewer officers than does his source[12]. He likewise (9,221a) attributes the division of the army into "phalanxes" (φάλαγγας) to Uzziah himself, leaving unmen-

---

10. This term is hapax in Josephus.

11. In contrast to both the Chronicler and Josephus, Rabbinic tradition speaks disparagingly of Uzziah's agricultural interests. *Midr. Tanhuma Yelammedu*, Noah 13 (S.A. BERMAN, tr., *Midrash Tanhuma-Yelammedenu*, Hoboken, NJ, Ktav, 1996, pp. 66-69), e.g., associates the king with Cain and Noah as three figures whose attachment to "the soil" brought evil upon themselves. Specifically with respect to Uzziah, this Midrash affirms that the king's agricultural enthusiasms led him to neglect the study of the Torah with the result that, in his arrogance, he attempted to arrogate the priestly prerogative of offering incense, as 2 Chr 26,16 relates. The tradition associating Uzziah with other reprobate lovers of the soil is also found in *Gen. Rab.* 22.3 (FREEDMAN, *Midrash Genesis Rabbah*, I, p. 181); 36.3 (ibid., p. 289).

12. Particularly in the latter case where, not a *Steigerung*, but a diminution of the Biblical figure is involved, one might suppose that Josephus drew his lower number from a text of Chronicles containing that figure. For a comparable case, see *AJ* 8,396 where Josephus specifies that the Arabs supplied Jehoshaphat with *360* lambs plus the same number of kids, whereas 2 Chr 17,11 cites much higher figures, i.e. 7,700 rams and 7,700 he-goats.

tioned the officials to whom 26,11 ascribes the army's mustering/ organization into divisions. Thereby, he accentuates the king's (military)
stature, even while "Hellenizing" the source's wording with his interjection of the Greek military term "phalanx".

2 Chr 26,14 enumerates six pieces of equipment Uzziah provides for
his soldiers: shields, spears (BL δόρατα), helmets, coats of mail, bows,
and stones for slinging. Josephus' own list (9,221b) replaces spears with
"a sword"[13], specifies that the breastplates were made "of bronze",
passes over the source mention of "helmets", and speaks of "a sling"
rather than of "stones for slinging". The Chronicler's record of Uzziah's
military preparedness measures concludes in 26,15a with a notice on his
constructing "engines" (BL μηχανάς) to be mounted on the "towers
and corners of Jerusalem" and designed to cast "arrows and great
stones". Josephus' parallel (9,221c) cites Uzziah's "engines (μηχανήματα) for sieges"; it goes on to differentiate these into "rock-throwers
and spear-throwers and grappling-irons[14], and the like", while omitting
reference to their intended placement(s). Josephus likewise dispenses
with the summarizing notice of 26,15b ("his [Uzziah's] fame spread far,
for he was marvelously helped, till he was strong") with its echoes of
26,7-8 (reworked by Josephus as well; see above).

3. Uzziah's Offense

Chronicles' *Sondergut* on Uzziah continues in 26,16-19a with an
account of the cultic offense which leads to his being stricken with leprosy as recounted in 2 Kgs 15,5a // 26,19b. Josephus gives his expanded
version of this Chronistic sequence in 9,222-224[15]. The Chronicler makes
the transition from Uzziah's first, good period to his later, bad one with
the notice of 26,16a: "but when he was strong [see 26,15b] he grew
proud, to his destruction. For he was false (BL ἠδίκησεν) to the Lord his

13. Josephus' substitution of another weapon for the Bible's mention of "spears" (BL
δόρατα) here is in line with his regular tendency elsewhere; see BEGG, *Early Divided
Monarchy*, p. 66 and n. 372; p. 76 and n. 464.

14. The codices SP (followed by Dindorf, Bekker, and Naber) add καὶ ἀρτῆρας
("and attachments?") at this point.

15. On the Chronicler's account of Uzziah's offense (and its sequels) as well as Josephus' version of this, see: M. RAHMER, *Das biblische Erdbeben*, Magdeburg, Friese,
1881, pp. 6-7; J. MORGENSTERN, *Amos Studies, II. The Sin of Uzziah, the Festival of Jeroboam, and the Date of Amos*, in *HUCA* 12-13 (1938) 1-53; ID., *The King-God among
the Western Semites and the Meaning of Epiphanes*, in *VT* 10 (1960) 138-197, pp. 191-
197; A. ZERON, *Die Anmassung des Königs Uzia im Lichte von Jesajas Berufung. Zu 2.
Chr. 26,16-22 und Jes. 6,1ff.*, in *TZ* 33 (1977) 65-68.

God...". Josephus amplifies, underscoring the success-hubris-doom nexus he had already highlighted in the case of Uzziah's father, Amaziah (see chap. X). His greatly expanded rendition (9,222-223a) reads:

> (222) But, after he had made these arrangements and preparations, *he was corrupted in mind* (διεφθάρη τὴν διάνοιαν)[16] *through pride* (ὑπὸ τύφου)[17] *and, being filled with vanity* (χαυνωθείς)[18] *on account of his mortal prosperity* (θνητῇ περιουσίᾳ)[19], he became contemptuous (ὠλιγώρησεν)[20] of the power (ἰσχύος) *that is immortal* (ἀθανάτου)[21] *and endures* (διαρκοῦς)[22] *for all time, that is, piety towards God* (ἡ πρὸς τὸν θεὸν εὐσέβεια)[23] *and observance of the laws* (τὸ τηρεῖν τὰ νόμιμα)[24]. (223) *And so because of his successes* (ὑπ' εὐπραξίας)[25], he slipped (ὤλισθε) *and became involved in the same sins* (κατηνέχθη πρὸς τὰ ... ἁμαρτήματα)[26] *as those of his father, who had also been led into them by his brilliant good fortune* (ἡ τῶν ἀγαθῶν λαμπρότης)[27] *and the greatness of his power, which he had not been able to direct rightly* (προστῆναι καλῶς)[28].

According to 2 Chr 26,16b Uzziah's prideful unfaithfulness to the Lord (26,16a) found expression in his "entering the temple of the Lord (BL εἰσῆλθεν εἰς τὸν ναόν κυρίου) to burn incense on the altar of incense (BL τοῦ θυμιᾶσαι ἐπὶ τὸ θυσιαστήριον τῶν θυμιαμάτων)". Josephus (9,223b) continues to expatiate: *"Thus, on the occasion of a notable day which was a public festival* (ἐνστάσης δ' ἡμέρας ἐπισήμου καὶ πάνδημον ἑορτὴν ἐχούσης)[29], *he put on the priestly*

---

16. Elsewhere Josephus uses this construction in 9,261 (of the people in Ahaz' time) and 11,332 (of Alexander the Great).

17. The term τῦφος is hapax in Josephus.

18. The verb χαυνόω is hapax in Josephus.

19. This is Josephus' only use of this phrase.

20. Compare the cognate nominal form used by Josephus in reference to Amaziah in 9,204: "... because of his innovations, which led him to show contempt (τῆς ὀλιγωρίας) of God".

21. This adjective is hapax in Josephus.

22. This is Josephus' only use of the phrase "enduring power".

23. For this construction and its variants in Josephus, see on 9,2.

24. This phrase recurs in *AJ* 8,395 (Jehoshaphat's subjects) "loved nothing so much as the observance of the laws". With the above double accusation of Uzziah compare Josephus' positive evaluation, in *AJ* 8,290, of Asa of Judah as one who "showed due regard for piety (εὐσέβειαν) and the observance of the laws (τὴν τῶν νομίμων φυλακήν)".

25. Compare 9,196 where Josephus refers to Amaziah's "not being able to contain himself at his good fortune (ἐπὶ ταῖς εὐπραγίαις)...".

26. This is Josephus' only use of the above construction.

27. Josephus uses the above construction only here.

28. This phrase is hapax in Josephus.

29. With this inserted chronological indication compare Josephus' opening notice on Jeroboam's attempted sacrifice at Bethel in *AJ* 8,230: ἐνστάσης δὲ τῆς ἑορτῆς. We shall note several further terminological links between the historian's accounts of Jeroboam's and Uzziah's cultic transgressions.

garment (ἐνδὺς ἱερατικὴν στολήν)[30] and entered the sacred precinct (εἰσῆλθεν εἰς τὸ τέμενος; compare BL 26,16b above) to offer sacrifice (θυσιάσων)[31] *to God* on the golden altar (ἐπὶ τοῦ χρυσοῦ βωμοῦ)[32]".

2 Chr 26,17 records that Uzziah was followed into the Temple by Azariah "the priest" (BL ὁ ἱερεύς) along with 80 "priests of the Lord", who are further qualified as "men of valor". Josephus (9,224a) designates "Azarias" (᾿Αζαρία; BL ᾿Αζαρίας) as "the high priest" (τοῦ ἀρχιερέως)[33], while dispensing with the Biblical mention of his fellows' "valor". The Chronicler (26,18a) has the whole body of priests "withstand" Uzziah; Josephus makes Azariah alone the subject of his corresponding phrase, i.e. "trying to prevent him" (κωλύοντος αὐτόν); see, however, below. The remainder of 26,18 quotes the priests' words to Uzziah. These begin with the affirmation that the king has no right to "burn incense to the Lord" (see 26,16), this being the prerogative of the "priests, the sons of Aaron" who have been "consecrated" for that purpose. In Josephus too not only Azariah, but the priests as a group remonstrate with the king: "… for, they said, it was not lawful (οὐ … ἐξόν) for any one to offer sacrifice (ἐπιθύειν; compare B θῦσαι, L θυμιάσαι), but to do so was allowed only to those of the line of Aaron (ἐκ τοῦ ᾿Ααρῶνος γένους; compare BL τοῖς υἱοῖς ᾿Ααρών)". The priests' words conclude (26,18b) with a directive to Uzziah, coupled with a condemnatory motivation: "go out of the sanctuary, for you have done wrong, and it will bring you no honor from the Lord God". Josephus' (more dramatic) parallel represents the priests as "… all clamouring

---

30. With Josephus' mention of Uzziah's "vesting" himself in priestly garb here, compare his likewise inserted reference (*AJ* 8,230) to what Jeroboam did prior to undertaking his sacrifice, i.e. γενόμενος δὲ αὐτὸς ἀρχιερεύς; see previous note.

31. This is the reading adopted by Niese and Marcus. Compare ἐπιθυσιάσων (M Exc Suidas); ἐπιθυμιάσων (SP Lat, followed by Dindorf, Bekker, and Naber); θυμιάσων (E Zon).

32. Josephus' "golden altar" here is his equivalent to the "altar of incense" of 26,16; see Exod 30,1-3 which prescribes that the (wooden) incense altar be overlaid with "pure gold". Elsewhere Josephus uses the above phrase "the golden altar" in *AJ* 3,243; 8,90.104; 12,250, cf. *c. Ap.* 1,198. The phrase ἐπὶ τοῦ … βωμοῦ here likewise echoes that of *AJ* 8,230 where Jeroboam, having made himself "high priest" (see n. 30), goes up ἐπὶ τὸν βωμόν. Note further that Josephus' use of the term βωμός in 9,223 in contrast to the θυσιαστήριον of BL 26,16 has a parallel in 8,230 as compared with 3 Rgns 12,32-33 where the same difference may be observed; see BEGG, *Early Divided Monarchy*, p. 42, n. 209.

33. Josephus' designation of Azariah as "high priest" already at this point is likely inspired by the title given him subsequently by the Chronicler in 26,20 where MT calls him כֹּהֵן הָרֹאשׁ, BL ὁ ἱερεὺς ὁ πρῶτος. Note that Theodoret too uses the term ἀρχιερεύς for Azariah in his citation of 26,17; see PG 80, c. 848.

(καταβοώντων) for him to go out and not transgress against God (παρανομεῖν εἰς τὸν θεόν)...[34]".

2 Chr 26,19a redirects attention to Uzziah: the king, censer in hand, "becomes angry". Josephus leaves aside the source's "censer notice". Conversely, he expatiates (9,224b) on its reference to the king's emotional reaction, utilizing for this wording drawn from his account of Uzziah's father: "... he became angry (ὀργισθείς; BL ἐθυμώθη) *and threatened them with death if they did not hold their peace* (ἠπείλησεν αὐτοῖς θάνατον, εἰ μὴ τὴν ἡσυχίαν ἄξουσι)[35]".

4. *Uzziah Afflicted*

2 Chr 26,19b directly juxtaposes Uzziah's becoming angry at the priests (v. 19a) with the "breaking out of leprosy on his forehead" (compare the – unmotivated – notice of 2 Kgs 15,5a: "and the Lord smote the king, so that he was a leper to the day of his death..."). Josephus (9,225a), on the other hand, interposes several additional items between these two source elements: *"but, while he spoke, a great tremor* (σεισμὸς ... μέγας) *shook the earth*[36], *and as the temple was riven*[37], *a bril-*

34. With the above formula Josephus reinforces the parallelism between Uzziah and his father Amaziah; see the phrase τῶν παρανομηθέντων εἰς αὐτόν (God) which he uses of the latter in 9,199. The above verb παρανομέω is likewise employed by him in reference to Jeroboam, Uzziah's "model" as cultic offender; see *AJ* 8,245.

35. Compare Josephus' account of the confrontation between Amaziah and an unnamed prophet over the former's idolatry in *AJ* 9,195: "(the prophet's words) moved the king to anger (ὀργήν), and he ordered the prophet to hold his peace (ἡσυχίαν ἄγειν), threatening to punish him (ἀπειλήσας αὐτόν κολάσειν)...".

36. Josephus' above mention of an "earthquake" on the occasion of Uzziah's attempted sacrilege is one he shares with Rabbinic (and Christian) tradition; it is mentioned as well by, e.g., *y. Ber.* 9.13c; Jerome on Amos 1,1 (see PL 25, c. 992) and Isa 7,3ff. (see PL 24, c. 104 [here Jerome cites the "tradition of the Hebrews" that the earthquake occurred in Uzziah's 25th regnal year]). Cf. F.-M. ABEL, *AŠAL dans Zecharie XIV,5*, in *RB* 45 (1936) 385-400; J.A. SOGGIN, *Das Erdbeben von Amos 1,1 und die Chronologie der Könige Ussia und Jotham von Juda*, in *ZAW* 82 (1970) 117-121, as well as the literature cited in n. 15. The Biblical basis for this particular embellishment of the Chronicler's account is the mention of the "earthquake in the days of Uzziah king of Judah" in Zech 14,5 (cf. Amos 1,1 where the prophet's activity is dated "in the days of Uzziah... two years before the earthquake").

37. Also this (extra-Biblical) element of Josephus' account has Rabbinic parallels; see *'Abot R. Nat.* 9 (J. GOLDIN, tr., *The Fathers According to Rabbi Nathan*, New Haven/London, Yale University Press, 1955, p. 57); *Midr. Tanhuma-Yelammedenu*, Noah 13 (BERMAN, *Midrash Tanhuma-Yelammedenu*, p. 68) (These sources further specify that the two parts of the "riven" Temple were separated by a twelve-mile cleft). Compare also Jerome in his commentary on Isa 7,3ff. (see previous note) who cites the "tradition of the Hebrews" that on the occasion of the earthquake in Uzziah's time "cineres altaris effusi sunt" (this item – which has no parallel in Josephus – recalls the "pouring out of the ashes" when Jeroboam's altar at Bethel was overthrown, as reported in 1 Kgs 13,5).

liant shaft of sunlight gleamed through it and fell upon the king's face[38]
so that leprosy (λέπραν; BL 26,19 ἡ λέπρα)[39] at once smote him...".

2 Chr 26,20 moves immediately from Uzziah's being smitten with
leprosy (26,19b // 15,5a) to the priests' reaction to this occurrence. Here
again, Josephus' rendition (9,225b) interjects a number of additional elements into the source sequence, i.e. "... while before the city at a place
called Erōgē ('Ερωγῇ)[40] half of the western hill was broken off and
rolled four stades till it stopped at the eastern hill and obstructed
(ἐμφραγῆναι) the roads and the royal gardens (παραδείσους)". As is
generally recognized, Josephus (or his tradition) found inspiration for
this embellishment of the Chronistic Uzziah story in Zech 14,4-5 which
speaks of a (future) splitting of the Mount of Olives "from east to west
by a very wide valley (v. 4), and then continues with a mention of the
sequels to this happening that itself concludes with a reminiscence of
"the earthquake in the days of Uzziah" (see n. 36). More specifically,
the MT of Zech 14,5 thrice employs the form (וְ)נַסְתֶּם ("you shall flee/
you fled"), the first time with "the valley of my mountains" as subject.

38. Generally, commentators see this element of Josephus' *Ausmalung* of 26,19b as
inspired by the term זָרְחָה (RSV "broke out") used in connection with the leprosy on
Uzziah's face in that verse, since this verb is customarily used in the MT of the "shining"
of the sun (see, e.g., Exod 22,2). So RAPPAPORT, *Agada*, p. 62, #260; GINZBERG, *Legends*,
VI, p. 358, n. 30; MARCUS, *Josephus*, VI, p. 119, n. f; WEILL, *Josèphe*, II, p. 228, n. 5.
Josephus' above reference to the "brilliant shaft of light" falling on Uzziah's face does
find a certain parallel in TJ on Isa 28,21 which introduces a mention of the revelation of
the "glory (יקרא) of the Lord in the days of Uzziah the king" into its translation of that
verse. See also *Yalqut* on Isa 6,2 which interprets the "seraps" cited in that verse as a
"fire" poised to burn the reprobate Uzziah just as Korah and his company had been consumed by fire (cf. Num 16,35). S. KLEIN, *Talmudische-midraschische Glossen zu Josephus*, in *Jeshurun* 7 (1920) 456-461, pp. 457-458 proposes that both Josephus and *Yalqut*
drew their reference to the shaft of sunlight/fire that confronted Uzziah in the Temple
from Zech 14,6 (i.e. the continuation of Zech 14,5 with its reference to "the earthquake
in the days of Uzziah"; see n. 36) which speaks of the continuous "light" that will pre-
vail in the eschatological period. RAPPAPORT, *Agada*, p. 133, n. 258 calls Klein's suggestion "nicht einleuchtend und zu kompliziert".

39. Josephus' reproduction of the sources' mention of Uzziah's "leprosy" here is
noteworthy given the fact that elsewhere in *AJ* he passes over mentions of the (temporary)
leprosy of such Biblical figures as Moses and Miriam, in order, it would seem, not to lend
credibility to contemporary claims about the Jews being a nation of lepers who originated
with the leper Moses. On the point, see FELDMAN, *Interpretation*, pp. 385-386 (= ID.,
Moses, 309-310).

40. There have been two major proposed identifications for the site designated by this
Greek term. E.g., SCHLATTER, *Namen*, 187, s.v. עין רוגל and MARCUS, *Josephus*, VI, p.
119, n. g (as a possibility) see it as a corruption of the place name "En-rogel" mentioned
in 1 Kgs 1,9. KLEIN, *Glossen*, 458; RAPPAPORT, *Agada*, p. 63, n. 262; MORGENSTERN,
Amos Studies II, 5, n. 7; SCHALIT, *Namenwörterbuch*, pp. 45-46, s.v. Ἐρογή hold that it
derives, via a metathesis of the Hebrew consonants, rather from the reference in Zech
14,5 to the גֵּיא־הָרַי. Given that the continuation of Josephus' addition (see above) does
clearly reflect the language of Zech 14,5, the latter suggestion seems preferable.

By contrast, LXX uses verbs (ἐμφραχθήσεται [bis], ἐνεφράγη) having the sense of "block up" (= Hebrew וְנִסְתַּם)[41], in all three instances; see also TJ which agrees with LXX against MT for the initial verb of 14,5 which it renders "(the valley of the mountains) shall be stopped up (וְיסתתם)". For his reference in the above expansion to the broken-off portion of the hill "obstructing" the roads Josephus would seem then to depend specifically on the LXX reading of Zech 14,5 with which he shares the same verb, i.e. ἐμφράρρω, to denote the "blockage".

After the above insertion Josephus (9,226a) picks up the thread of the Chronicler's account, now relating the priests' (and Uzziah's own) response to the king's affliction (= 26,20). His version downplays the brusqueness of the priests' treatment of the stricken king (in v. 20a they "thrust him out"), while also highlighting Uzziah's emotional response to his condition. It reads: "When the priests[42] saw the king's face smitten with leprosy, *they explained to him the cause of his misfortune*[43], and told him to go out of the city *as an unclean person* (ἐκέλευον ἐξιέναι τῆς πόλεως ὡς ἐναγῆ)[44]. *And so, in his shame* (ὑπ' αἰσχύνης) *at the terrible thing* (δεινοῦ) *that had happened to him and because he no longer had the right to speak out* (παρρησίαν)[45], he did as he was told [26,20b: he himself hastened to go out]". To this version of 26,20 Josephus then appends (9,226b) a comment of his own which, once again, underscores the hubris theme he has been highlighting throughout his account of Uzziah: "so miserable and pitiable (ταλαίπωρον καὶ οἰκτράν)[46] a penalty did he pay for thinking to reach a station higher than man's (τῆς ὑπὲρ ἄνθρωπον διανοίας; cf. διεφθάρη τὴν διάνοιαν, 9,222) and for the impieties towards God (εἰς τὸν θεόν ἀσεβημάτων)[47] which were caused thereby".

2 Kgs 15,5aβb // 2 Chr 26,21 relate the long-term sequels to Uzziah's smiting: he remains a leper until his death, dwelling in a "separate house"

41. Note that the difference between MT and LXX here is a matter of vocalization.

42. Josephus omits the explicit mention of "Azariah the chief priest" found in 26,20a.

43. This "explanation" by the priests might be seen as Josephus' adaptation of the concluding words of 26,20: (Uzziah went out) "because the Lord had smitten him". The adaptation avoids attributing Uzziah's affliction directly to God.

44. With the above formulation compare *AJ* 7,208 where Josephus cites Shimei's word to David fleeing Jerusalem in the face of Absalom's revolt: ἐκέλευε ... τῆς γῆς ὡς ἐναγῆ ... ἐξιέναι. Elsewhere in Josephus the term ἐναγῆ occurs only in *BJ* 2,472 ("cursed wretches").

45. Uzziah's recognition here that he has lost his right to "speak out" stands in ironic contrast with the king's earlier threatening the priests with death "if they did not hold their peace" in 9,224.

46. This collocation occurs only here in Josephus.

47. This phrase is hapax in Josephus; compare παρανομεῖν εἰς τὸν θεόν, 9,224.

(so RSV; MT בְּבֵית הַחָפְשִׁית[48], + because he was excluded from the house of
the Lord, 26,21), while his son Jotham governs "the people of the land". In
agreement with the Targums' paraphrase (see n. 48). Josephus (9,227a) has
Uzziah "dwelling for a time outside the city[49]". There he "lived the life of a
private citizen (ἰδιώτην)[50]", Jotham having "taken over the government[51]".

5. *Closing Notices for Uzziah*

2 Kgs 15,6-7 // 2 Chr 26,22-23 provide the standard closing notices for
Azariah/Uzziah: source reference ("the Book of the Chronicles of the
Kings of Judah", 15,6 vs. "the rest of the acts of Uzziah... Isaiah the
prophet... wrote", 26,22), death, burial, and his succession by Jotham. Josephus, here too, leaves aside the first of these items entirely. In place thereof
he prefaces (9,227b) his death notice for Uzziah (= 15,7aα // 26,23aα) with
an additional reference to the stricken king's emotional state: "*and then,
from grief and despondence* (ὑπὸ λύπης καὶ ἀθυμίας)[52] *at what had happened to him* [compare: in his shame at the terrible thing that had happened
to him, 9,226], he died". To this mention of Uzziah's death, the historian
then appends his equivalent to the chronological data of 15,2 // 26,3 previously left aside by him (see above): "... (Uzziah died) at the age of sixty-
eight years[53], of which he had reigned fifty-two". Leaving aside the
source's accession notice for Jotham (15,7b // 26,23b) until a later point (see
9,236), Josephus rounds off his treatment of Uzziah with the statement (=
15,7aβ // 26,23aβ) "he was buried alone in his own gardens[54]".

---

48. BL 15,5 // 26,21 transliterate the unfamiliar word qualifying "house" in MT. TJ
explicates the term with its "(he dwelt) outside Jerusalem", as does TC: "(he lived) in the
Leprosy House outside Jerusalem, for he had been separated from the men of his house
because of what had been decreed concerning him".
49. This notice is prepared by Josephus' wording in 9,226 where the priests direct
Uzziah to "go out of the city as an unclean person".
50. This term apparently represents Josephus' rendering of the Hebrew word חפשית of
MT 15,5 // 26,21 which generally has the meaning of "free (person)" in the MT; see,
e.g., Exod 21,5. RAPPAPORT, *Agada*, p. 63, #263 cites Rashi's comentary on *b. Hor.* 10a
where he takes the phrase of 15,5 // 26,21 as meaning that Uzziah was "made free from
the kingship like a private person (הדיוט)".
51. Like 15,5 Josephus has no equivalent to the plus of 2 Chr 26,21aβ citing Uzziah's
being "excluded from the house of the Lord" as the grounds for his "dwelling in a separate house".
52. The only other occurrence of this collocation in Josephus in *AJ* 5,36 where it is
used of the Israelites' reaction to their defeat before Ai.
53. Josephus calculates this figure by combining the Biblical indications concerning
Azariah/Uzziah's age at accession (16) and length of reign (52).
54. This burial notice diverges from those of both 15,7aβ ("they buried him with his
fathers in the city of David") and 26,23aβ ("they buried him with his fathers in the burial field which belonged to the kings, for they said, 'He is a leper'"). Josephus' indication

6. *Zechariah & Shallum*

At this juncture, rather than proceeding immediately to the reign of the Judean Jotham, Uzziah's successor, as does 2 Chronicles 27, Josephus, in the line of Kings (2 Kgs 15,8-31) first pauses to "catch up" on the series of Northern monarchs who ruled contemporaneously with Uzziah. Of these, the first two were Zechariah and Shallum to whose short, ill-fated reigns Kings devotes eight verses (15,8-15). Josephus compacts all he has to say about the pair into a single, brief paragraph, 9,228. From 2 Kgs 15,8 he extracts the item that "Zacharias" (Ζαχαρίας = BL) ruled a mere six months[55]. On the other hand, he leaves aside the source's (self-evident) specification that Zechariah reigned "in Samaria". He likewise passes over the "synchronistic indication" of 15,8, i.e. Zechariah acceded in the thirty-eighth year of Azariah (= Uzziah) of Israel. As we shall see, this latter omission is typical of Josephus' procedure throughout our passage where he has no equivalent to any of the Biblical synchronistic notices for the Israelite kings Zechariah-Pekah[56].

2 Kgs 15,9 pronounces a negative judgment on Zechariah, using highly stereotyped language: "he did evil in the sight of the Lord" and "did not depart from the sin of Jeroboam [I]". Josephus, on the contrary, refrains from any evaluation of Zechariah, likely on the consideration that given the brevity of his reign he would not have had an opportunity to do much of anything, whether good or bad[57]. Instead, he procceds

on the matter is perhaps inspired by the burial notices for other, subsequent, "bad" kings of Judah, i.e. Manasseh and Amon both of whom are said (in 2 Kgs 21,18 and 26, respectively) to have been "buried in the garden of Uzza (= Uzziah?)".

55. This king has already been introduced in passing by Josephus in 9,215 where, in parallel to 2 Kgs 14,29b, he mentions his succeeeding his father Jeroboam II.

56. Prior to Zechariah, Josephus does generally reproduce Kings' synchronisms (see, e.g., 9,205 where he cites the notice of 2 Kgs 14,23 that Jeroboam II – the father of Zechariah – acceded in the fifteenth year of Joash of Judah). When, on occasion, he does omit these, his doing so would seem to relate the fact of discrepancies among the textual witnesses regarding a particular synchronism (such an explanation is not applicable in the case of 2 Kgs 15,8 where the witnesses agree in dating Zechariah's accession to Azariah/Uzziah's thirty-eighth year). Thus, e.g., in *AJ* 8,316 he fails to date the start of Ahab's rule by reference to the regnal year of his Judean counterpart as does 1 Kgs 16,29, presumably in view of the divergence on the matter between MT (the thirty-eighth year of Asa) and LXX (the second year of Jehoshaphat). For further examples of Josephus' omission of textually divergent Biblical synchronisms in the earlier monarchical period, see BEGG, *Early Divided Monarchy*, p. 151, n. 976.

57. A similar case occurs in connection with the earlier Israelite ruler Zimri. 1 Kgs 16,15 credits this monarch with a reign of only seven days, but nonetheless the standard Deuteronomistic condemnatory notice for Northern rulers does get applied to him too; see 16,19. Josephus' account of the king (*AJ* 8,307) dispenses with the latter item, doubtless in view of the extreme brevity of Zimri's rule.

immediately to present his parallel to the notice of 15,10 on the assassination of Zechariah by the conspirator Shallum (B Σελλούμ, L Σελλήμ) who thereafter takes power himself. Josephus' version of the assassin's name, i.e. "Sellēmos" (Σελλήμου), represents an inflected form of
that given in L, while his name for this figure's father, i.e. "Jabēsos"
seems closer to the "Jabesh" of MT than to BL's Ἰαβείς. The historian
goes beyond the Biblical evidence in characterizing Shallum as "one of
Zechariah's friends (φίλου)". Thereby, he heightens the pathos of the
latter's end[58]. The textual witnesses for 2 Kgs 15,10 disagree as to the
"site" of Zechariah's assassination. In MT (and TJ) he is killed "before
the people" (MT קׇבׇל־עׇם; compare B's transliteration Κεβλαάμ), while
L localizes his murder "at Ibleam" (ἐν Ἰεβλαάμ; so RSV). In the face
of this discrepancy, Josephus simply leaves the happening "unlocated".

Josephus completes his parallel to 2 Kgs 15,10 (Shallum's murder of
Zechariah and seizure of power for himself) by immediately citing the
chronological datum of 15,13, i.e. Shallum himself reigned but "thirty
days[59]". In thus combining (elements of) 15,10 and 15,13 Josephus skips
over both the standard "source notice" for Zechariah of 15,11 and the
remark of 15,12 according to which the rule of Zechariah – short though
it was – did bring to fulfillment God's promise to Jehu that four generations of his descendants would occupy the throne of Israel[60]. As to 15,13
itself, Josephus confines himself to reproducing its notice on Shallum's
length of reign (see above). Conversely, precisely as with the parallel
indications for Zechariah in 15,8, he leaves unused 15,13's synchronism
(Shallum accedes in Uzziah/ Azariah's thirty-ninth [the L MS 127 reads
thirty-eighth] year) and specification that he ruled "in Samaria".

7. Menahem

2 Kgs 15,14 relates how the usurper Shallum met the same fate he
himself had previously meted out to Zechariah. This happens at the

---

58. See the similar cases of Joash (9,171) and Amaziah (9,203), both of whom end up
being assassinated by their "friends" in Josephus' presentation.

59. MT, TJ and L all speak literally of "a month of days"; B 15,13 has simply "(he
ruled) days".

60. The promise itself of which 2 Kgs 15,12 notes the fulfillment is quoted in 2 Kgs
10,30, God delivering this to Jehu directly. Josephus' version of the latter verse is 9,139
where the promise is mediated by an unnamed prophet; see there. Elsewhere, Josephus
does generally reproduce Biblical "fulfillment notices" in line with his characteristic
stress on "true" prophets as accurate predictors. His failure to utilize the notice of 2 Kgs
15,12 seems then to have to do with Josephus' overall tendency to abridge the Biblical
account concerning Israel's last kings (Menahem and Hoshea excepted); see below.

hands of Menahem, son of Gedi, who comes from Tirzah to Samaria where he kills Shallum[61] and makes himself king. In contrast to his drastic abridgement of the source notices on Zechariah and Shallum, Josephus (9,229a) considerably elaborates on Menahem's initiative (also linking this more smoothly than does the Bible's parataxis to what precedes by making it the explanation ["for"] of the brevity of Shallum's reign). His "Manaēmos" (Μαναῆμος; compare the undeclined Μαναήμ of BL) receives the title "the general" (ὁ στρατηγός) which replaces the Biblical mention of his father's name[62]. Josephus likewise provides an occasion for Menahem's advance from "Tharsē" (Θαρσῆ) to Samaria, i.e. his "hearing" of what had happened to Zechariah. In line with his designation of Menahem as "the general", Josephus further represents him as bringing his "whole army with him" to Samaria and "engaging Sellēmos in battle". With these further added indications he makes, it might be noted, the course of events appear more plausible than they do in 2 Kgs 15,14 where it is left unexplained how Menahem, acting on his own – as the Bible's wording has it – was able to get Shallum within his power – in the latter's own capital, no less; see n. 62.

Appended to the mention of Shallum's overthrow in 15,14 is the standard source notice for this king in 15,15. In accord with his consistent practice Josephus omits the latter item. In its place he introduces (9,229b) a reference, designed to prepare the continuation of the Biblical account in 15,16, concerning Menahem's "going" (παραγίνεται) from Samaria to "the city of Thapsa (Θαψάν)". In the witnesses for 15,16 the latter city is variously denominated: MT reads תִּפְסַח, B Θερσά, and L Ταφῶε; many modern translators (e.g., RSV) and commentators emend to "Tappuah". Concerning the site, the Biblical verse (16a) first reports that Menahem "sacked" it and the surrounding area "from Tirzah (see 15,14) on". It then goes on to cite his reason for doing so, i.e. "because they did not open to him" (v. 16bα) and concludes (v. 16bβ) with mention of Menahem's "ripping up" the pregnant women in the recalcitrant city. Josephus reverses the sequence of 15,16. Specifically, to his "extra-Biblical" mention of Menahem's "going" to Thapsa (9,229b) he immediately appends (9,230a), as his elaborated parallel to 15,16bα, mention

---

61. Some Hebrew MSS as well as L lack the explicit statement of MT and B that Menahem slew Shallum "in Samaria".

62. In giving Menahem this title Josephus provides an implicit explanation of how he was able to undertake the (military) initiatives attributed to him in the Bible, i.e. he could do so given his status as a "commander" with troops as his disposal. Also elsewhere, Josephus ascribes the above Greek title to figures who lack it in the Bible itself (e.g., Joshua; see 9,207), this reflecting his own military background and desire to cater to the interests of Gentile readers of like backgrounds.

of the usurper's (non-) reception there: "but those within the city shut their gates *with bars* and refused to admit the king[63]". Next (9,230b), he presents his – likewise embellished – version of 15,16a: "*Thereupon he avenged himself upon them* by ravaging the country round about[64], *and after a siege took* (λαμβάνει) *the city by storm*[65]". Finally (9,231), Josephus reproduces the content of 15,16bβ, here again with considerable elaboration, e.g., with regard to the emotional state that underlies the king's actions: "*Then, resenting the actions of the inhabitants of Thapsa* (Θαψιατῶν)[66], he did away with all (πάντας) of them[67], *not sparing even infants* (νηπίων)[68]; *and not stopping short of the utmost extremes of cruelty* (ὠμότητος) *and savagery* (ἀγριότητος)[69]; *those things which it would be unforgivable* (οὐδὲ ... συγγνωστόν) *to do even to aliens* (ἀλλοφύλων) *if taken captive, such things did he do to those of his own race* (ὁμοφύλους)[70]".

2 Kgs 15,17-18 provides the standard framework notices for Menahem's reign: synchronization of his accession with Azariah/Uzziah's

63. Like the Bible, Josephus gives no indication as to why the city's inhabitants declined to admit Menahem.

64. This phrase is Josephus' generalized equivalent for the formulation of 15,16a: "(Menahem sacked Tappuach [so RSV])... and its territory from Tirzah on". His omission of the place name "Tirzah" here in his parallel to 15,16a may have to do with the fact that earlier, in dependence on 15,14, he spoke of Menahem leaving this city, apparently his home-base, for Samaria. Hence, one would not expect Menahem's campaign of devastation to include Tirzah itself – as the Biblical formulation might suggest it did.

65. With the above notice Josephus makes explicit what is presupposed in 15,16, i.e. Menahem did, in fact, capture "Tappuah" (RSV) notwithstanding its resistance.

66. This is the reading of SP followed by Dindorf, Bekker, Naber, and Marcus; Niese reads θαψίων with RO.

67. Compare 15,16a: (Menahem sacked Tappuah) "and all (BL πάντα) who were in it".

68. Josephus' formulation here might be seen as a toning down of the brutally explicit language of 15,16bβ: "and he (Menahem) ripped up all the women... who were with child". Compare 9,91 where he does reproduce the announcement made by Elisha to Hazael in 2 Kgs 8,12 that the latter will "rip up" the Israelite women who are with child. (Perhaps the fact that the latter text – in contrast to 15,16 – concerns a non-Israelite would account for Josephus' readiness to utilize its wording.)

69. AJ 9,231 is the only occurrence of the above collocation "cruelty and savagery" in the Josephan corpus. The term ἀγριότης recurs but twice elsewhere in Josephus, i.e. BJ 7,7 (of the Jewish rebels) and AJ 16,363 (of Herod). The fact that Josephus applies to Menahem a term he elsewhere employs for persons whom he depicts as moral monsters (the rebels, Herod) serves to accentuate the depravity of Menahem's deed.

70. The entire sequence italicized above has no equivalent in 2 Kgs 15,16. In it, Josephus supplies an expansive evaluation of Menahem's deed which Scripture is content to relate in "neutral" terms. It might also be noted here that Josephus' highlighting of the fact that Menahem subjected "his own race" to a treatment that would be inexcusable even in the case of foreign captives likely reflects his own experiences of the horrors of intra-Jewish bloodletting during the great revolt. Also elsewhere in AJ one finds reflections of this same preoccupation with the wrongfulness of Jews doing violence to their fellows; see BEGG, *Early Divided Monarchy*, p. 25, n. 133.

thirty-ninth year, Menahem's ten-year rule, and stereotyped negative evaluation of him as one who persisted in Jeroboam's sin. In accord with his practice throughout our segment, Josephus leaves aside the first of these items. He likewise rewords 15,18's judgment notice in line with language previously used by him concerning Menahem. His version (9,232a) of 15,17-18 thus reads: "*having become king in this way*, Man-aēmos continued to reign for ten years as a perverse (σκαιός) and excessively cruel (ὠμότατος)[71] man".

The Bible has only one additional concrete happening to relate for Menahem's ten-year reign, i.e. his tribute-paying to the Assyrian king "Pul"; see 2 Kgs 15,19-20. Here again (9,232b), Josephus both elaborates and modifies. Specifically, he interjects the notice that, in the face of the Assyrian advance under "Phūlos" (Φούλου; BL Φουά), Menahem "would not meet the Assyrians in the contest of battle". This notice, it might be pointed out, adds yet another negative touch to Josephus' portrait of Menahem: for all the "savagery" of his treatment of helpless "infants" (9,231), Menahem shows himself a total coward when faced with a superior foe. Thereafter, Josephus proceeds to reproduce the statement of 15,19bα about Menahem's paying Pul "a thousand talents of silver" (χίλια τάλαντα ἀργυρίου = BL). 2 Kgs 15,19bβ states that Menahem payed this sum in order that Pul "might help him to confirm his hold of the royal power" (so RSV). Josephus, by contrast, assigns a more military motivation to Menahem's initiative which itself picks up on his preceding reference to his unwillingness to engage the Assyrians in battle: "… (he persuaded the king to accept a thousand talents of silver) *and retire*[72], *and so brought the war to an end*". 2 Kgs 15,20a rounds off the "tribute incident" with mention of how Menahem obtained the money he gave Pul, i.e. by a head tax on the wealthy Israelites of fifty shekels a head. Josephus' version (9,233a) "converts" the Biblical figure into one that would be more familiar to his contemporary audience: "This sum was contributed to Manaēmos by the people[73], who were taxed at fifty

---

71. Compare "(Menahem did not stop short of the utmost extremes of cruelty (ὠμότητος)", 9,231. The terms used by Josephus in reference to Menahem in 9,231-232, i.e. "utmost extremes of cruelty" (ὠμότητος ὑπερβολήν) and "perverse" (σκαιός) recur in his characterization of the degenerate Parthian prince Orodes in *AJ* 18,44 whom he charges with responsibility "for acts of extreme cruelty" (καθ᾽ ὑπερβολὰς ὠμότητος) and being "utterly gauche" (σκαιός).

72. This reference to Pul's "retiring" might be seen as Josephus' anticipation of 15,20b which reads "so the king of Assyria turned back, and did not stay there in the land".

73. Josephus leaves aside the Biblical specification that the tribute money was raised "from all the wealthy men" (MT גִּבּוֹרֵי הַחַיִל, BL δυνατὸν ἰσχύϊ); in his presentation it thus appears that the entire Israelite population had to contribute towards Menahem's tribute.

drachmas a head[74]". Having "anticipated" the notice of 15,20b about Pul's "withdrawal" (see n. 72), he breaks off his account of the tribute incident with this parallel to 15,20a (see above).

2 Kgs 15,21 is the standard "source notice" for Menahem. Adhering to his consistent practice, Josephus (9,233b) omits this, passing directly to the data of 15,22, i.e. Menahem's death (τελευτήσας; Bible: "he slept with his fathers") and the accession of his son, "Phakeas" (Φακέαν; compare MT Pekahiah, B Φακεσίας, L Φακεεία). Between these two Biblical items, Josephus inserts one final "plus" into his account of Menahem, i.e. the fact of his being "buried (κηδεύεται) in Samaria".

8. *Pekahiah & Pekah*

The Bible's brief (and largely stereotypical) account of the short-reigned Pekahiah is found in 2 Kgs 15,23-26. This opens in 15,23 with chronological indications (Pekahiah acceded in the fiftieth year of Azariah/Uzziah; he ruled over Israel in Samaria two years). There follows a judgment notice employing the standard Deuteronomistic formulae for the northern kings in 15,24. Josephus appends his version (9,233c) of 15,24 directly to his notice on Pekahiah's accession (= 15,22b) thus: "(Menahem) left as his successor on the throne his son Phakeas who followed his father's example of cruelty (ὠμότητι)...[75]". Thereafter, he presents the chronological datum of 15,23b about Pekahiah's reigning all of two years, joining this, in turn, directly with the content of 15,25 which reports the circumstances of the king's demise. According to the latter Biblical verse Pekahiah fell victim to a plot by his "captain" (RSV), Pekah, son of Remaliah, who, abetted by fifty Gileadites (so MT L; B "fifty of the four hundred"), slew him "in Samaria in the citadel of (so MT, בְּאַרְמוֹן, > BL) the king's house[76]", and seized power for himself. Josephus (9,234a) reproduces these notices with certain omissions (Pekah's fifty Gileadite co-conspirators, the site of the

74. MARCUS, *Josephus*, VI, p. 123, n. e points out that in other contexts (see, e.g., AJ 3,195; 8,189) Josephus equates the Biblical shekel rather with the tetradrachm.

75. This term echoes the forms ὠμότητος and ὠμότατος used of Menahem in 9,231 and 232, respectively. In 2 Kgs 15,24 the wicked Pekahiah is (stereotypically) associated with Jeroboam I; Josephus links him rather with his father whose "cruelty" he imitates. Compare the historian's accentuation of the parallelism between the Judean kings Amaziah and his son Uzziah in his presentations of them.

76. In MT (as well as BL and TJ) there follows the curious phrase "(with) Argob and Arieh". RSV suggests that these words originally stood as part of the list of Israelite cities and territories annexed by the Assyrians in 2 Kgs 15,29. In any case, Josephus has no equivalent to the phrase in question.

assassination), but also with a certain heightening of the pathos. His version reads: "He was then treacherously put to death (δολοφονηθεὶς ... ἀπέθανε), *while at a banquet* (συμποσίῳ)[77] *with his friends* (φίλων)[78], through a conspiracy (ἐπιβουλεύσαντος; see 9,203) formed against him[79] by a certain Phakeas (Φακέου)[80], the son of Romelias (Ῥομελία; BL Ῥομελίου), who was the captain of a thousand (χιλίαρχος)[81]".

2 Kgs 15,26 rounds off the treatment of Pekahiah with a standard source notice. Josephus, once again, leaves this item aside, proceeding immediately to the Biblical chronological indications for (15,27) and evaluation of (15,28) Israel's new king, Pekah. Here too, he disregards the source synchronism of Pekah's accession with the fifty-second year of Azariah/Uzziah. He does, however, reproduce the further datum of 15,27 about Pekah ruling twenty years[82], coupling this with his version

---

77. The use of this term here is an obvious instance of Josephus' Hellenizing the Biblical account for the benefit of Greco-Roman readers.

78. Recall that in Josephus' presentation Zechariah, the first in the series of Israel's six last kings, is killed by "one of his friends" (φίλου), i.e. Shallum; see 9,228. Of like pathos is his version of Pekahiah's end here: the king is assassinated in what would normally be the most relaxed and secure of situations, i.e. "a banquet with friends". By representing Pekahiah's death as coming in these circumstances, Josephus likewise suggests an answer to a difficulty the Biblical account might evoke for readers, i.e. how was Pekah with a mere fifty men (so 15,25) able to penetrate the citadel of the palace of Samaria and slay Pekahiah there? In Josephus' presentation things appear more plausible: he omits the Biblical specification about the small number of Pekah's confederates as well as the reference to the Samaria palace citadel as the site of the assassination (so MT; recall, however, that BL lacks this indication, see above), just as his mention of Pekahiah's being at "a banquet with friends" intimates that the king and his retainers were caught off guard by Pekah at a moment of carefree festivity. See further n. 81.

79. Conceivably, Josephus found inspiration for the above depiction of Pekahiah's sorry end in the account of the assassination of an earlier Israelite king (who like Pekahiah reigned a mere two years) at the hands of one of his officers, i.e. Elah whom Zimri struck down while the former was "drinking himself drunk in the house of Arza, who was over the household in Tirzah" (1 Kgs 16,9; Josephus' parallel in *AJ* 8,308 reads: "(Elah) was treacherously slain... as he was being entertained at table by his steward, whose name was Osa...").

80. Note that in Josephus assassin and victim bear the same Greek name, i.e. "Phakeas". In the MT the former has a shortened form (Pekah) of the latter's name (Pekahiah). Compare B Φακεσίας (15,22)/ Φάκεε (15,25) and L Φακεεία (15,22)/ Φάκεαι (15,25).

81. Compare MT שָׁלִישׁוֹ (RSV "his captain"); LXX ὁ τριστάτης αὐτοῦ. MARCUS, *Josephus*, VI, p. 124, n. c points out that in 9,73 Josephus does give a more literal rendering of the above Hebrew title in his parallel to 2 Kgs 7,2 (the Israelite "captain" [MT הַשָּׁלִישׁ] expresses disbelief in Elisha's prediction of the imminent end of the famine), i.e. ὁ ... τῆς τρίτης μοίρας. The title Josephus uses of Pekah here in 9,234 represents him as a commander of a substantial force (i.e. of 1,000 men); this in turns helps explain how he was able to accomplish the overthrow of his predecessor; compare his treatment of Menahem and his coup above; cf. n. 78.

82. The L MS 127 reads "thirty" here. As is well known, the Biblical indication about Pekah's ruling twenty years seems to be historically impossible; for various attempts at

of the stereotyped judgment notice of 15,28, i.e. he was "an impious (ἀσεβής) and lawless (παράνομος)[83] man".

The one happening of Pekah's two-decade reign which the Bible singles out for mention is the large-scale reduction of Israelite territory and the deportation of the population effected by the Assyrian ruler Tiglath-pileser (= Pul, 15,19) at some point during it. In particular, 2 Kgs 15,29 enumerates no less than five cities (Ijon, Abel-beth-maacah, Janoah, Kedesh and Hazor), plus three regions (Gilead, Galilee, all the land of Naphtali; L adds a fourth area, i.e. Gaddei) which Israel lost to Assyria at this period. Josephus' version of these developments (9,235) runs: "Now the king of Assyria, named Thaglathphallaser (Θαγλαθφαλλάσαρ)[84] marched *against the Israelites*[85] and subdued all of Galadēnē (Γαλαδηνήν; BL Γαλαάδ)[86] *and the country across the Jordan and the adjoining country called* Galilee (τὴν Γαλιλαίαν = L)[87], and Kydisa (Κύδισαν)[88] and Asōra

dealing with the difficulty, see the commentaries. In any case, Josephus takes over the datum without any apparent realization of its problematic character.

83. This is the only occurrence of the above adjectival collocation "impious and lawless" in Josephus. Compare, however, his characterization of Pekah's predecessor Jeroboam II as "shockingly arrogant (ὑβριστής) and lawless (παράνομος) in his conduct towards God", 9,205. See too the priests' admonishing Uzziah not to "transgress (παρανομεῖν) against God in 9,224.

84. As might be expected, both the codices of Josephus and the LXX MSS evidence many variant readings of this un-Greek name. Like the Bible itself, Josephus leaves one uncertain as to whether or not he realized that the "Tiglath-pileser" of 2 Kgs 15,29 (= 9,235) and the "Pul" of 15,19 (= 9,232) were one and the same person, the latter name being Tiglath-pileser's Babylonian throne name.

85. Like 15,29, Josephus offers, at this juncture, no motivatation for Tiglath-pileser's advance against Israel. In 2 Kgs 16,5ff. (cf. 9,244ff.) there is, however, a reference to Pekah's joining forces with Rezin king of Syria in an attack on Jerusalem whose king, Ahaz, responds by appealing to Tiglath-pileser for assistance against the confederate kings. 2 Kgs 15,29 would then be an "anticipation" of the measures taken by the Assyrian monarch in response to this appeal by Ahaz.

86. In *AJ* 1,324 Josephus, in his version of Gen 31,47, which speaks of Laban's calling the memorial stone heap erected by him and Jacob "Galeed", introduces his Hellenized version, i.e. "Galadēnē" of the Biblical place name "Gilead" as follows: "... they erected a monument in the form of an altar; hence comes the name Galad(es) (Γαλάδης) given to the hill, and hence to this day they call the district Galadēnē (Γαλαδηνήν)".

87. Note that in contrast to 2 Kgs 15,29 Josephus lists the regions – rather than the cities – seized by Tiglath-pileser in first place. In addition, he leaves aside the Biblical reference to a third such region, i.e. "all the land of Naphtali", perhaps as one no longer current in his own day. Compare Josephus' treatment (*AJ* 8,395) of the list of Israelite sites ravaged by Ben-hadad of Syria during the reign of Baasha according to 1 Kgs 15,20. In the Biblical text that list ends up (as in 2 Kgs 15,29) with mention of "all the land of Naphtali", which mention Josephus leaves aside – just as he does the equivalent phrase of 2 Kgs 15,29.

88. This is Josephus' equivalent to the name which stands in fourth place in 15,29's list of captured cities, i.e. Kedesh, BL Κένεζ. In *AJ* 5,63 Josephus calls the same city "Kedese" (Κεδέσης). In beginning his enumeration of the conquered cities here in 9,235 with this city, Josephus passes over the first three cities cited in the Biblical list, i.e. Ijon, Abel-beth-maacah and Janoah. Also elsewhere, Josephus freely abbreviates or omits

("Ασωρα; BL 'Ασώρ)[89]; and, having taken the inhabitants captive, he transported them to his own kingdom (15,29: to Assur [MT]/ to the Assyrians [BL])".

At this juncture, following his account of the Assyrian reduction of Israel's territory (= 15,29), Josephus diverges somewhat from the Biblical sequence. In the latter, what follows immediately is the conclusion to the reign of Pekah, i.e. his assassination by Hoshea (15,30) and the usual source notice (15,31) for the former. Thereafter, we are given, back to back, Kings' presentation of the two Southern kings whose reigns overlapped that of Pekah, i.e. Jotham (2 Kgs 15,32-38) and Ahaz (16,1-20), whereupon the account of Hoshea of Israel resumes in 17,1ff. Josephus, here too, has no equivalent to the source notice of 2 Kgs 15,31. As to the mention of Pekah's assassination in 15,30, he reserves this item until 9,258 where he picks up his narrative of Northern history following a "Judean interlude" in which he treats successively of Jotham (9,236-243a) and Ahaz (9,243b-257)[90]. Before, however, commencing his treatment of Jotham in 9,236, Josephus takes care to round off the account of Tiglath-pileser's initiative with a charateristic closing notice at the very end of 9,235, "with these words, then, let us end our account of the king of Assyria".

Conclusions: Josephus' Rewriting of 2 Kgs 15,1-29 & 2 Chronicles 26

In the case of Azariah/Uzziah where two Biblical accounts (2 Kgs 15,1-7 // 2 Chr 26,3-23) were extant, Josephus, in accord with his usual practice, aligns himself with the more expansive of these, reproducing the *Sondergut* of 2 Chr 26,6-19a in 9,217-226. At the same time, his reproduction of the synchronization notice peculiar to 2 Kgs 15,1 in 9,216 points to his secondary usage also of Kings' presentation.

In the course of our study of Josephus' Uzziah story we noted several points of contact between this and the peculiarities of one or other of the textual witnesses for its Biblical parallels. Thus in 9,218 the people who

entirely lists of place names found in the Bible, doing so out of deference to Gentile readers to whom those names would have been unfamiliar (and strange-sounding); see, e.g., *AJ* 8,284 where, in his version of 2 Chr 13,19's list of the Israelite cities captured by Abijah of Judah, he omits that of Ephron/Ephrain.

89. In the list of 2 Kgs 15,29 "Hazor" is the fifth and final city mentioned; in Josephus it is the second of the only two captured sites he enumerates by name.

90. By following this arrangement Josephus contrives to keep together in a continuous sequence the opening data concerning Hoshea which in the Bible are found in two widely separate contexts, i.e. 2 Kgs 15,30 and 17,1ff. (On the other hand, Josephus' own arrangement separates Pekah's assassination [9,258] from the remainder of his account concerning this king [9,234-235].)

pay the king tribute are called the "Ammanites" *à la* MT 26,8's "Ammonites" as compared with the M(ε)ιναῖοι of BL. His reference (9,227) to the stricken king's "dwelling outside the city" corresponds to the Targumic renderings of 2 Kgs 15,5 // 2 Chr 26,21. The mention (9,225) of the broken-off mountain "obstructing" the roads seems to reflect the LXX reading in Zech 14,5. We noted too that the figures given for Uzziah's officers and men in 9,220 diverge from those found in any of the witnesses for 2 Chr 26,12-13; see n. 12. These findings suggest, in any event, that Josephus made use of various Biblical text-forms in composing his own Uzziah story. His narrative concerning the Northern kings in 9,228-235, by contrast, betrays little regarding the text-forms of 2 Kgs 15,8-29(30-31) available to him.

The segment 9,216-235 evidences the range of Josephan rewriting techniques we have been encountering throughout this study. Within the category of *additions/ expansions*, those that serve to accentuate the stature – whether *in bonam* or *malam partem* of two of the six kings treated in the segment, i.e. Uzziah and Menahem, are especially notable. Regarding the former, Josephus, e.g., notes his defeat of the Philistines and storming of their cities (9,217; compare 26,6); interjects notices on his repair of the walls of Jerusalem damaged in his father's time (9,218b); highlights his agricultural interests (9,220a; compare 26,10) and his success-engendered hubris, recalling that of his father (9,222-223a; compare 26,16a); expatiates on his negative reaction to the priests' warning (9,224; compare 26,19); embellishes the dramatic circumstances surrounding his being stricken with leprosy (9,225; compare 26,19 // 15,5a); and elaborates on the gravity of the king's affliction and the emotional distress this causes him (9,226-227; compare 26,20b-21 // 15,5b-6). As for Menahem, the historian inserts (9,229; compare 2 Kgs 15,14) mention of his status as a "general" and details concerning his overthrow of Shallum. In addition, he underscores (9,231; compare 15,16) the reprehensibility of Menahem's dealings with his opponents and his cowardice in face of the Assyrian threat (9,232; compare 15,19).

Over against Josephus' expansions in 9,216-235, as seen especially in his handling of Uzziah and Menahem, stand his *omissions/ reductions* of source data, conspicuous above all in his portrayal of Zechariah and Shallum (9,228; compare 15,8-13). Also within his generally expanded treatment of Uzziah, however, Josephus does leave aside a number of Biblical particulars, e.g., place names (Ashdod, 26,6; the Jerusalem gates, 26,10), minor personages (the royal mentor Zechariah, 26,5; the three officials cited in 26,11), as well as the explicitly theological notices of 26,7.9. 20 (// 15,5a). In the same line, he confines himself to enumerating

(9,235) the names of two of the Israelite cities seized by Tiglath-pileser as opposed to the five cited in 2 Kgs 15,29. Josephus also, occasionally, *re-arranges* his sources' sequence. The opening chronological data of 15,2 // 26,3 are held over to the very end of his account of Uzziah (9,227b). The king's measures with regard to "Elath/Eloth" are integrated into the account of his other conquests (9,217) rather than standing apart from these (so 14,22 // 26,2), while the notices on Uzziah's military organization appear in a different order in 9,220-221a vis-à-vis 2 Chr 26,11-13. Subsequently, Josephus (9,235) reverses the sequence (first cities, then regions) in which 15,29 enumerates Tiglath-pileser's conquests, just as he puts off until a later point (see 9,258) the notice on Hoshea's coup which directly follows mention of these in 15,30.

Josephus likewise introduces many *modifications/adaptations* of the wording and content of his sources throughout 9,216-235. He, e.g., synchronizes Uzziah's accession with the 14th rather than the 27th year of Jeroboam (9,216; compare 2 Kgs 15,1) in light of other Biblical chronological indications. He employs alternative language for Scripture's stereotyped evaluations of Uzziah (9,216; compare 15,3 // 26,4) and Pekah (9,234; compare 15,28) and provides a different localization for the "Arabs" (9,217; compare 26,7). His rendition replaces the name "Elath/Eloth" with an allusion to "a city on the Red sea" and has Uzziah "founding a city and stationing a garrison" there rather than "building and restoring it to Judah" (9,217; compare 14,22 // 26,2). His Uzziah actually subjugates the Ammonites and the territory extending to Egypt (9,218a; compare 26,8). He refers to the "golden altar" instead of "the altar of incense" (9,223; compare 26,16). The priests explain the "cause" of Uzziah's affliction to him, rather than "thrusting him out quickly" (9,226; compare 26,20). The historian gives Uzziah's age at death, not at accession (9,227; compare 15,2 // 26,3), and situates his burial at a spot other than the Biblical one(s), 9,227; compare 15,7 // 26,23. The gory reference to Menachem's ripping up pregnant women (15,16) is somewhat toned down by him (9,231). An updated currency is mentioned for the sum collected by Menahem to pay off Pul (9,232; compare 15,20), and a different aim for its payment cited (9,232; compare 15,19). Finally, the figure of Pekahiah's assassin, Pekah, and the circumstances of his deed undergo various modifications in Josephus' presentation (9,234; compare 15,25).

In consequence of the application of the above rewriting procedures, Josephus' story of Uzziah and his Northern contemporaries does present a number of distinctive features. With his omission of numerous secondary source items he offers a streamlined version of the Biblical narratives. The drama (see, e.g., the "smiting" of Uzziah) and pathos (see, e.g., the killing of both Zechariah and Pekahiah by "friends") of various events is highlighted. His rendition throws into relief the parallel trajectories of the careers of Uzziah and his father Amaziah. Difficulties and implausibilities of the Biblical accounts (e.g., the synchronization for Uzziah's accession, the circumstances under which Menahem and Pekah were able to overthrow their respective predecessors) are disposed of in some fashion.

Josephus' accentuation of the "military element" throughout the segment together with his highlighting of the "hubris pattern" operative in Uzziah's career are designed to appeal to Gentile readers. For Jewish readers the segment offers the warning examples of its two featured kings, Uzziah and Menahem, of whom the former "transgressed against God" with his attempted sacrifice (see 9,224), while the latter engaged in "unforgivable" mistreatment of "those of his own race" (9,231). Contemporary Jews must refrain from both these sorts of behavior; otherwise they will face the same kinds of disasters that befell Uzziah and Menahem's hapless son Pekahiah.

XIII

JOTHAM OF JUDAH AND THE PROPHET NAHUM[1]
(9,236-243a)

Following the "Northern Interlude" of 9,228-235 (= 2 Kgs 15,8-29[30-31]) Josephus returns in 9,236-238 (+ 243a) to the Judean ruler Jotham whose regency for his leprous father Uzziah he had cited *en passant* in 9,227 (= 2 Kgs 15,5b // 2 Chr 26,21b); see chap. XII. The Biblical sources for the former monarch are 2 Kgs 15,32-38 and 2 Chr 27,1-9. The most distinctive feature of the Josephan Jotham narrative is its "interruption" by a segment drawn from a totally different Biblical context, i.e. Nahum 2,9-12 in 9,239-242. Accordingly, I divide up the material for this chapter as follows: 1. Jotham's Reign (*AJ* 9,236-238 = 2 Kgs 15,32-35 // 2 Chr 27,1-6); 2. Nahum Introduced (9,239a; cf. Nahum 1,1); 3. Nahum Quoted (9,239b-241 = Nahum 2,9-14); 4. Editorial Comments (9,242); and 5. Closing Notices for Jotham (9,243a = 15,36-37 // 27,7-9).

1. *Jotham's Reign*

The parallel passages 2 Kgs 15,33 and 2 Chr 27,1 have in common their double chronological indication concerning Jotham: acceding at age twenty-five, he reigned sixteen years[2]. 2 Kgs 15,32 precedes these data with an additional element which synchronizes Jotham's accession with the second year of Pekah of Israel. Like Chronicles, Josephus makes no use of this last item[3]. In addition, however, he reserves, in line with his usual practice, his version of the sources' shared chronological data until the end of his account of Jotham, see 9,243a. From 2 Kgs 15,33 // 2 Chr 27,1 he does, on the other hand, take over at this point (9,236a) the specification that Jotham's reign transpired "in

---

1. This chapter represents a revision of my articles *Jotham and Amon: Two Minor Kings of Judah according to Josephus*, in BBR 6 (1996) 1-13, pp. 2-9 and *Josephus and Nahum Revisited*, in REJ 154 (1995) 5-22 which are used with permission here. It has likewise profited from the comments of Prof. Chaim Milikowsky of Bar-Ilan University.

2. These same data are repeated in 2 Chr 27,8 (no parallel in Kings).

3. On Josephus' general tendency to omit such synchronisms for the later rulers of both Israel and Judah, see p. 285, n. 56.

Jerusalem[4]". To this notice he appends mention of Jotham's mother, i.e. "Jerasē" (Ἰεράσης) which name he draws from 2 Kgs 15,33b // 2 Chr 27,1b (MT יְרוּשָׁא; B 15,33 Ἐρούς; L 15,33 Ἰεροῦσα; BL 27,1 Ἰερουσσά). The sources further record the name of Jerusha's father, i.e. "Zadok" (so MT). In place thereof Josephus qualifies Jotham's mother as "a native (ἀστῆς) of Jerusalem[5]".

2 Kgs 15,34 // 2 Chr 27,2a begin their respective evaluations of Jotham with the stereotyped notice about his doing "what was right in the eyes of the Lord according to all that his father Uzziah had done (Chronicles + only he did not invade the temple of the Lord)[6]". Josephus' parallel (9,236b) varies the wording of this formula (while also leaving aside its evocation of Uzziah[7]): "(Jotham) lacked no single virtue (οὐδεμιάς ἀρετῆς ἀπελείπετο)[8], but was pious toward God (εὐσεβὴς ... τὰ πρὸς τὸν θεόν)[9] and just toward men (δίκαιος ... τὰ πρὸς ἀνθρώπους)[10]". Both Biblical presentations go on to "qualify" their initial commendations of Jotham. 2 Kgs 15,35a notes that under him worship on the high places continued to flourish, while 2 Chr 27,2b speaks in more general

4. Josephus adds the further specification that Jotham ruled "over the tribe of Judah." With this designation of Jotham's domain Josephus leaves out of account the other tribe over which he ruled, i.e. Benjamin. Elsewhere, by contrast, Josephus does employ the title "king of the two tribes" for Judah's rulers; see AJ 8,224.246.298.314.398; 10,1; cf. 8,274; 9,142.216.

5. Twice elsewhere, Josephus interjects a comparable "extra-Biblical" notice about a Judean queen mother being a native of Jerusalem, i.e. 9,260 (compare 2 Kgs 18,1, the mother of Hezekiah [as in 9,236 this notice replaces mention of the royal mother's patronym]); 10,37 (compare 2 Kgs 21,1, the mother of Manasseh). In thus filling in a Biblical lacuna, Josephus was likely inspired by the case of other Judean kings whose mothers are stated in his sources to have haled from Jerusalem; see, e.g., "Jecoliah/Jehoaddan", mother of Azariah/Uzziah, the father of Jotham (2 Kgs 15,2 // 2 Chr 26,3; cf. AJ 9,216 [here Josephus employs the same Greek word, ἀστή, for the queen mother, as he does of Jerasē in 9,236]).

6. The reference here is to the Chronicler's Sondergut episode of Uzziah's attempted offering of incense in the Temple which leads to his being stricken with leprosy in 2 Chr 26,16-20 (compare 2 Kgs 15,5a). Josephus gives his version of the Temple episode in AJ 9,222-226; see chap. XII.

7. Josephus' dispensing with the sources' paralleling of righteous Jotham with Uzziah is understandable given the serious offense into which the latter fell according to 2 Chr 26,16-20 (see n. 6), this neccessitating the Chronicler's qualification (27,2a) of the statement of 15,34 about Jotham doing right as Uzziah had; see above.

8. This construction occurs only here in Josephus.

9. This phrase echoes that used of Jotham's father Uzziah in 9,222: "(he became contemptuous...) of piety towards God (ἡ πρὸς τὸν θεὸν εὐσέβεια)", while also serving to establish a contrast between them.

10. With the above collocation "pious toward God and just toward men" compare AJ 7,384 where David exhorts Solomon "to be just toward your subjects (δικαίῳ ... πρὸς τοὺς ἀρχομένους) and pious toward God (εὐσεβεῖ ... πρὸς τὸν ... θεόν)". David's descendant Jotham realizes that counsel, whereas Solomon himself failed to maintain "piety toward God" over the whole course of his life.

terms of the people still following "corrupt practices" (RSV). By contrast, Josephus leaves his praise of Jotham "unqualified[11]", directly continuing his encomium of the king's virtues with an elaborate transitional notice (9,236c-237a) leading into the account (9,237bc) of the royal building measures he adapts from 2 Kgs 15,35b // 2 Chr 27,3-4. The notice reads: "… he also took care (ἐπιμελής)[12] of the needs of the city[13], for all places that were in need of repair or adornment (ἐπισκευῆς … καὶ κόσμου)[14] he completely reconstructed at great expense (φιλοτίμως)…".

As noted, both Biblical sources follow their evaluations of Jotham with reference to his building activity. Specifically, 2 Kgs 15,35b // 2 Chr 27,3a credit him with "building the upper gate (BL πύλην) of the house of the Lord". Josephus represents Jotham as undertaking more comprehensive construction activities at the Temple site: "… he erected porticos (στοάς)[15] and gateways (προπύλαια)[16] in the temple area (ἐν τῷ ναῷ)". The author of Kings confines himself to the single building notice cited above. The Chronicler, on the contrary, expands (27,3b-4) this with a number of additional items. Of these, the first concerns Jotham's "doing much building on the wall (BL τείχει) of Ophel". Josephus, in reproducing this Chronistic plus once again generalizes: "… he set up those parts of the walls (τειχῶν) that had fallen down…[17]".

In 2 Chr 27,4 the Chronicler widens the perspective beyond Jerusalem itself to speak of Jotham's building cities in the Judean hill country and "forts and towers (BL πύργους) on the wooded hills". In Josephus' presentation the "very large and impregnable (παμμεγέθεις καὶ δυσαλώτους)[18] towers (πύργους)" which Jotham constructs would, like the

11. Compare his similar procedure with regard to the source qualifications (2 Kgs 15,4 // 2 Chr 26,4) of the praise given Jotham's father Azariah/Uzziah (15,3 // 26,3) in 9,216b.

12. This is the reading of RO adopted by Niese and Marcus. Dindorf, Bekker, and Naber follow MSP's ἐπιμελητής.

13. The above formulation is a verbal echo of that used by Josephus of Jotham's father Uzziah in 9,218: "he began to take thought (τὴν ἐπιμέλειαν) thereafter for Jerusalem". Implicitly then, Josephus does link Jotham and his father as his sources (15,34 // 27,2a) do explicitly in their evaluations of the former; see above.

14. This collocation occurs only here in Josephus.

15. Josephus' reference to "porticos" here likely has in view Herod's Hellenized Temple.

16. Josephus' one other use of the nominalized adjective προπύλαιος is in *AJ* 8,78.

17. Josephus' avoidance of the proper name "Ophel" of 2 Chr 27,3b in the above formulation is in line with his tendency to leave aside such topographical particulars that would be unfamiliar (and uninteresting) to Gentile readers. See the comparable case of *AJ* 9,218 where he passes over the various specific sites (the Corner Gate, the Valley Gate and "the Angle") where Uzziah is said to have erected his towers in the source text, i.e. 2 Chr 26,9.

18. This collocation is hapax in Josephus.

"walls" mentioned just previously by him, seem rather to be part of the king's Jerusalem building initiatives[19]. Thereafter, however, Josephus rounds off his account of Jotham the builder with a generalizing notice that does seem inspired by Chronicles' reference to his extra-Jerusalem activities: "... and to any other matters which had been neglected throughout his entire kingdom he gave his constant attention".

The Chronicler's Jotham *Sondergut* continues in 27,5 with notices on the king's subjection of the Ammonites and the tribute paid by them. Josephus' parallel (9,238a) highlights Jotham's initiative in the matter: "he also marched against [27,5: fought with] the Ammanites [27,5: the king of the sons of Ammon] and, having defeated (κρατήσας; BL κατίσχυσεν) them[20] in battle, he imposed upon them [27,5: they (the Ammonites) gave him] a yearly tribute (φόρους ... τελεῖν)[21] of a hundred talent [27,5 + of silver] and ten thousand *kors* (κόρους)[22] of wheat and as many of barley[23]". Chronicles (26,6) rounds off its *Sondergut* segment (27,3b-6) with the following theological reflection on Jotham's achievements: "So Jotham because mighty (BL κατίσχυσεν), because he ordered his ways before the Lord his God". Josephus (9,238b) rewords, eliminating the source's theological component[24]. His version –

19. In thus representing Jotham as (re-) building, it would seem, both "walls" and "towers" in Jerusalem, Josephus aligns his activities with those of his father Uzziah as described in 9,218b-219a: "he began to take thought for Jerusalem... whatever parts of the walls that had fallen... he rebuilt and repaired.... In addition he built many towers (πύργους), each fifty cubits high...".

20. Josephus agrees with MT 2 Chr 27,5a in having Jotham defeat the Ammonites as a whole; in BL Jotham vanquishes "him," i.e. the king of the Ammonites cited at the start of the verse. MT and BL likewise diverge at the end of 27,5; in the former it is the Ammonites who pay Jotham "the same amount in the second and third years", while in the latter the Ammonite king does so. In contrast to both MT and BL Josephus makes no mention of the Ammonite king in his version of 2 Chr 27,5.

21. Josephus' reference to the Ammonites' "yearly tribute" represents a simplification of the circumstantial indications of 2 Chr 27,5 (MT): "they gave him that year a hundred talents of silver... they paid him the same amount in the second and third years".

22. Like BL (κόρων) Josephus transliterates the Hebrew כֹּרִים of MT 27,5.

23. In its divergences from 2 Chr 27,5 the above formulation serves to reinforce the parallelism between Jotham and his father Uzziah; compare 9,218, itself a rewording/expansion of 2 Chr 26,8 ("the Ammonites paid tribute to Uzziah..."): "*Next he subdued the Ammanites* and, having imposed a tribute (φόρους ... τελεῖν) upon them...". Note in particular that Josephus mentions explicitly a subjugation of the Ammonites by both rulers, whereas Chronicles cites this only of Jotham, just as he has both take the initiative in "imposing" tribute on the Ammonites in contrast to 2 Chr 26,8 and 27,5 which speak of that people "giving" their tribute to Uzziah or Jotham, respectively. Finally, while 2 Chr 26,8 has Uzziah subduing the Ammonites and 27,5 depicts Jotham fighting with their king, Josephus refers in both instances simply to a conquest of the "Ammanites" *en bloc*.

24. Compare his similar procedure with regard to Chronicler's "theological comments" on the career of Jotham's father Uzziah in 2 Chr 26,7 (cf. 9,217). 15b (cf. 9,221), 20b (cf. 9,226).

with its highlighting of the stature of Jotham himself – reads: "So greatly did he strengthen his kingdom (ηὔξησε... τὴν βασιλείαν)²⁵ that it was not lightly regarded (ἀκαταφρόνητον)²⁶ by his enemies, while to his own people it brought happiness (εὐδαίμονα)²⁷".

2. *Nahum Introduced*

At this point (9,239-242) Josephus deviates from the sequence of both his narrative sources in order to cite a passage, announcing doom for Nineveh, from the Book of the prophet Nahum (2,9-14, MT) whose activity he vaguely dates, at the beginning of 9,239, with the formula "there was at that time," i.e. in the reign of Jotham. A question which immediately suggests itself here is why Josephus associates Nahum's prophesing with the reign of Jotham, given the fact that the Jotham narratives of Kings and Chronicles do not mention the prophet, while conversely the Book of Nahum itself provides no explicit indication as to when he functioned²⁸. In responding to the question I would begin by noting that Josephus' citation of the Nahum passage (9,239-242) stands in fairly close proximity to his version of the story of Jonah, another "anti-Assyrian" prophet, in 9,208-214 which, inspired by the mention of Jonah in 2 Kgs 14,25, he interjects into his account of Jeroboam II, 9,205-207.215; see chap. XI. Perhaps, then, Josephus' procedure here reflects his knowledge of a tradition, attested in Tg. Nahum 1,1²⁹ and *VP* 11.2³⁰, which explicitly associated the two

25. The expression "strengthen the kingdom" recurs in *AJ* 8,248 (251).393.

26. The term ἀκαταφρόνητος is hapax in Josephus.

27. With this term, Josephus echoes his closing notice on the reprobate Jeroboam II in 9,215, i.e., "he died after a life of complete prosperity (εὐδαιμονίας)"; cf. also 9,205 where he states that "to the people of Israel" Jeroboam "was the cause of innumerable benefits". These terminological reminiscences underscore the anamoly of a bad king like Jeroboam benefitting his people just as much as does a good king like Jotham, the principle set down in *AJ* 1,14 notwithstanding.

28. Note too that *SOR* 20.23 (GIRÓN BLANC, *Seder 'Olam Rabbah*, p. 99) makes Nahum a contemporary of Jotham's great-grandson, Manasseh.

29. TJ gives a greatly amplified version of MT Nahum 1,1 ("an oracle concerning Nineveh. The book of the vision of Nahum of Elkosh"). The relevant section of its rendition reads: "Previously Jonah... prophesied against her [Nineveh] and she repented of her sins; and when she sinned there prophesied once more against her Nahum...". The translation is that of K.J. CATHCART & R.P. GORDON, *The Targum of the Minor Prophets* (The Aramaic Bible, 14), Wilmington, DE, Glazier, 1989, p. 131.

30. This text reads "after Jonah this man (Nahum) gave to Nineveh a portent...". The translation is that of D.R.A. HARE, *The Lives of the Prophets*, in *OTP* 2, Garden City, New York, Doubleday, 1985, 379-399, p. 393.

prophets and represented Nahum as arising at some (indeterminate) point after Jonah[31]. In any case, by positioning his quotation of Nahum's word of doom for Assyria where he does, i.e. not long after his citation of Jonah's similar message, Josephus underscores the certainty of Assyria's demise as something announced by two different prophets[32]. Such a "confirmation" of Jonah's announcement would be all the more in order at this point seeing that in the interval (see 9,235 = 2 Kgs 15,29) Josephus has related the Assyrian king Tiglath-pileser's seizure of large portions of Israelite territory and deportation of their inhabitants. This intervening item could then well cause readers to wonder if Jonah's prediction (9,214) of Assyria's "imminent" loss of its power still holds. By means of his citation of Nahum's similar prophecy just a few paragraphs after the notice of 9,235, Josephus makes clear that Jonah's prediction has not, in fact, lost its validity.

Following the opening dating indication of 9,239 (see above), Josephus proceeds to introduce the figure whose message he will cite in what follows: "... a certain prophet (τις ... προφήτης)[33] named Naum (Ναοῦμος)[34]". Thereafter, he sums up Nahum's message with the phrase "(he) prophesied (προφητεύων)[35] the downfall (καταστροφῆς)

---

31. In this connection it might also be recalled that in the MT Book of the Twelve, Nahum comes after Jonah (with Micah supervening), while in LXX Nahum follows Jonah immediately.

32. Nahum's message of doom for Nineveh as cited by Josephus can function all the more effectively as a confirmation of Jonah's earlier such word given that in his version of the Book of Jonah Josephus omits all mention of Nineveh's positive response to Jonah's preaching and of God's corresponding decision to spare the city (Jonah 3:5-10); see chap. XI. On Josephus' emphasis that "true" prophets agree with one another in their respective messages, see FELDMAN, Prophets, 409-410.

33. The Book of Nahum itself nowhere uses the title "prophet" for Nahum. Josephus' employment of the designation for him corresponds to his fourfold application of the same title to Jonah in his retelling (9,208-214) of the Book of Jonah which never so qualifies its protagonist (cf., however, 2 Kgs 14,25 which does designate Jonah as "the prophet"). More broadly Josephus' use of the prophet title for Nahum reflects his tendency to apply the term to Biblical figures in contexts where his sources do not. For the phrase "a certain prophet", see on 9,10.

34. This is the declined equivalent of LXX's Ναούμ; compare MT נַחוּם. For the LXX text of Nahum I use J. ZIEGLER, Duodecim prophetae (Septuaginta, XIII), Göttingen, Vandenhoeck & Ruprecht, 1984³.

35. Josephus' use of this verb picks up his earlier designation of Nahum as a "prophet". It has a counterpart in TJ's amplification of Nahum 1,1 (see n. 29) which states "when she (Nineveh) sinned again there prophesied (ואתנבי) once more against her Nahum" (for the Aramaic text of Tg. Nahum I use A. SPERBER, The Bible in Aramaic, III, Leiden, Brill, 1959). With Josephus' above introductory formula for Nahum (τις ... προφήτης ... Ναοῦμος ... προφητεύων) compare his initial presentation of Jonah in 9,206 (προεφήτευσε τις Ἰωνᾶς).

of Assyria and Nineveh (Νίνου[36])[37]". With this indication Josephus completes his introduction of the figure of Nahum, while also making the transition to the "quotation" that immediately follows. In so doing, he leaves aside Nahum 1,1's reference – of controverted localization – to the prophet's place of origin, i.e. "Elkosh" (MT הָאֶלְקֹשִׁי; Tg. Nahum דמבית קושי, of Beth Qoshi)[38]".

3. Nahum Quoted

As just mentioned, Josephus' introduction of Nahum (9,239a) leads directly into a rather extended quotation (9,239b-241) of words of the prophet (i.e. Nahum 2,9-14, MT) that serve to exemplify the historian's previous statement concerning the content of his message, i.e. "the downfall of Assyria and Nineveh". The segment of the Book of Nahum which Josephus begins citing in 9,239b opens in 2,9aα with a comparison: "and Nineveh like a pool of water(s)". Josephus' rendition (ὡς ἔσται Νινευὴ[39] κολυμβήθρα ὕδατος, "Nineveh would be like a... pool of water") is quite similar to that of LXX (καὶ Νινευη, ὡς κολυμβήθρα ὕδατος). In MT the continuation of this image is the difficult phrase מִימֵי הִיא ("from the days of... it"?; cf. Tg. Nahum ביומי קדם היא). LXX (τὰ [Codex Alexandrinus τείχη] ὕδατα αὐτῆς) prolongs the previous water imagery. Josephus goes his own way here, reading a participle (κινουμένη, "troubled") qualifying the noun κολυμβήθρα he shares with LXX; see above[40].

---

36. This alternative name for the Assyrian capital (compare Νινευή, LXX Nahum 1,1) echoes that used in Josephus' Jonah story, see 9,208.214; on the form see p. 256, n. 29. In the remainder of 9,239-242 Josephus will employ the LXX form of the city's name. With the above expression "Assyria [literally: Assyrians, 'Ασσυρίων] and Ninos", compare AJ 1,143: "Assyras founded the city of Ninus (Νίνον), and gave his name to his subjects, the Assyrians ('Ασσυρίους)...". Cf. also codex Sinaiticus in Tob 14,4 where Tobit affirms that the divine word spoken by Nahum will indeed befall "Assyria and Nineveh" (the codices AB have Tobit quoting *Jonah* here, thus attesting to the paralleling of/ confusion between the two figures and their messages in the course of the tradition).

37. Compare Nahum 1,1a: "An oracle (MT מַשָּׂא, LXX λῆμμα; Tg. Nahum + of the cup of malediction to be given to) concerning Nineveh (LXX Νινευή)".

38. Josephus' omission of this item consitutes a "negative agreement" with his portrayal of Jonah where he passes over (9,206) the specification of 2 Kgs 14,25 that this prophet came from "Gath-hepher".

39. This is the reading proposed by J. Hudson and followed by Dindorf, Bekker, Naber, and Marcus on the basis of Lat's nineuae. Codex P reads Νινύα, the others Νινύας (the reading adopted by Niese). Compare Νίνου in 9,239a.

40. J. WEILL, *Nahoum II, 9-12 et Josèphe (Ant. IX, XI, #239-241)*, in REJ 76 (1923) 96-98; P. HUMBERT, *Nahoum II, 9*, in REJ 83 (1927) 2-9 and F. LUCIANI, *I Profeti Minori*, III (LSB), Torino, Marietti, 1969, p. 63 (without reference to Weill) all regard Josephus'

Nahum 2,9a continues with a participial construction "and they [who?] (are) fleeing" (MT וְהֵמָּה נָסִים). Josephus expatiates on this item, identifying those "fleeing" and motivating their flight with a reference – itself prolonging his previous characterization of Nineveh as "a troubled pool of water" – to their inner state: "... *so also all the people* [i.e. of Nineveh], *being disturbed and agitated* (παρασσόμενος καὶ κλυδωνιζόμενος[41]), *shall go away and* flee (φεύγων; LXX φεύγοντες)...".

MT (and Tg. Nahum) 2,9b open with a double pl. imperative ("halt, halt", RSV)[42] whose speaker and addressee is, however, left indeterminate. LXX, by contrast, reads a single indicative form (οὐκ ἔστησαν) which it connects with its preceding participle, thus reading "fleeing, they did not stand". In this instance Josephus aligns himself with MT etc., reading a double imperative (στῆτε καὶ μείνατε, "stop and remain")[43], while also supplying the missing indication as to who is speaking and being addressed here: "... one [i.e. of all the people, *vide supra*] saying to another[44]". Nahum 2,9 concludes with the statement "there is no one who turns back" (MT וְאֵין מַפְנֶה). 2,10aα then continues with a double imperatival sequence "plunder the silver, plunder the gold" (here again, LXX reads past indicative forms "they plundered the silver, they plundered the gold"). Josephus re-arranges, reading his version of 2,9bβ after 2,10aα: "(one saying to another 'stop and remain) and seize (ἁρπάσατε; LXX διήρπαζον) gold and silver for yourselves[45]'. (9,240a) But there will be no one willing...[46]". To this last notice he appends a self-devised explanation of the Ninevites' "unwill-

---

above form (= Hebrew הימיה) as preserving Nahum's original reading. This view is rejected by A. HADAR, *Studies in the Book of Nahum* (UUÅ, 1946:7), Uppsala, A.B. Lundequistska Bokhandeln; Leipzig, Harrassowitz, 1946, p. 55 and K.J. CATHCART, *Nahum in the Light of Northwest Semitic* (BibOr, 26), Roma, P.B.I., p. 101, n. 147.

41. The verb κλυδωνίζω is hapax in Josephus.

42. In his reconstruction of the fragmentary Greek text from Naḥal Ḥever, E. TOV, *The Greek Minor Prophets Scroll from Naḥal Ḥever (8 Ḥev XII gr)* (DJD, 5), Oxford, Clarendon, 1990, p. 89, likewise reads a double imperative (στῆτε, στῆτε) corresponding to that of MT.

43. The first of the above imperatives is a literal translation of MT's initial עִמְדוּ (compare also the στῆτε reconstructed by Tov in the Naḥal Ḥever fragment; see n. 42). Whereas, however, MT uses an imperatival form of the same verb (עמד) twice, Josephus employs a different word for his second imperative.

44. As CATHCART and GORDON, *Targum of the Minor Prophets*, p. 137, n. 30 point out, Josephus' specification of the speaker of the above imperatives has a counterpart in the plus of Tg. Nahum MS z which reads "and they say".

45. In the above formulation Josephus compresses MT 2,10aα's double imperative into a single one, likewise reversing the sequence of the two metals cited.

46. This phrase might be regarded as Josephus' clarifying version of the concluding words of 2,9, i.e. "but there is no one who turns back".

ingness" to "remain": "... *for* they will wish to save their own lives rather than their possessions". Conceivably, Josephus' inspiration for this reference to the Ninevites' "possessions" was Nahum 2,10b ("there is no end of treasure or wealth of every precious thing", RSV).

Nahum 2,11 speaks of Nineveh's devastation using three, more or less, synonymous terms (RSV "Desolate! Desolation and ruin!")[47] and then of the four-fold response this evokes from those affected: "hearts faint and knees tremble, anguish is on all loins, all faces grow pale". Josephus' rather loose, compressed parallel (9,240b) to this sequence is formulated as a motivation ("for...") of the Ninevites' previously cited desire to save their lives rather than their possessions; see above. In particular, he reduces to a single expression 2,11aα's triple mention of Nineveh's devastation "*for* terrible strife (δεινὴ ... ἔρις)[48] of one with another[49] will come upon them...". Similarly, in his rendering the four source items speaking of the response to Nineveh's devastation are compacted into three: "... and lamentation (θρήνος; cf. 2,11: hearts faint), and loosening of their limbs [this phrase might be regarded as a conflation of 2,11's knees tremble and anguish is on all loins], and their eyes (ὄψεις [or: faces, thus Weill, *ad loc.*]) will be completely (τελέως)[50] darkened (μέλαιναι)[51] *with fear* (ὑπὸ τοῦ φοβοῦ)". Especially the final phrase in this sequence calls for comment. It corresponds to the last of the four responses by the Ninevites as cited in 2,11. In MT this reads וּפְנֵי כֻלָּם קִבְּצוּ פָארוּר which is variously understood either in the sense that people's faces became "red" or that they lost their color, i.e. became "pale" (so RSV above). The versions all seem to read MT's פָארוּר ("glow, redness" (?), elsewhere only in Joel 2,6) as מָרוּר ("pot"), thus LXX "and the faces of all like the blackening of a pot (ὡς πρόσκαυμα χύτρας)"; Tg. Nahum "all their faces are covered with a coating of black like a pot (אתחפיאו אכרום אוכמין)", cf. Vulgate "... sicut nigredo ollae". Josephus' rendering of the phrase (see above) shares with the versions a reference to the "blackening" of eyes/ faces. On the other hand, it lacks their association of this process with a "pot". Perhaps, then, his wording of the item represents his own attempt at render-

---

47. Tg. Nahum's rendering applies this sequence more specifically to the situation of conquered Nineveh: "she is plundered and spoiled, and the gate is open to the enemy".

48. This phrase is hapax in Josephus.

49. With this inserted indication Josephus represents Nineveh's coming destruction as the result of civil strife, whereas Nahum himself envisages its overthrow as the work of an (unnamed) external enemy.

50. This adverbial intensifier is not reproduced in the translation of Marcus; compare WEILL, *Josèphe*, II, *ad loc.*: "leurs faces deviendront *complètement* noirs".

51. Josephus' two other uses of the verb μελαίνω are in *BJ* 5,273; *AJ* 16,233.

ing a text like that of MT 2,11bβ, rather than reflecting the influence of the versions' reading[52].

In Nahum 2,12-13 the imagery used of Nineveh's anticipated destruction abruptly shifts to a leonine one. This new segment opens with the question, "where is the lions' den?" (so MT, LXX)[53]. Josephus' formulation (9,241) of this question is virtually identical with that of LXX (apart from using the future tense of the verb "to be" for the latter's present)[54]: ποῦ δε ἔσται [LXX ἐστι] τὸ κατοικητήριον τῶν λεόντων.

Nahum 2,12a continues with a phrase that stands in apposition to the preceding question, i.e. "... and (the) pasturage (MT מִרְעֶה, LXX ἡ νομή) to the (young) lions (MT לַכְּפִרִים, LXX τοῖς σκύμνοις)[55]". Such a reference to lions' "pasturage" appears odd, and so many (e.g., BHS) emend MT to מְעָרָה ("cave"), this producing a closer parallel to the מְעוֹן ("den") of the preceding colon. Josephus, for his part, diverges from the MT/LXX reading as well, although in a quite different direction from the emendation proposed by modern scholars. His continuation of the question about the whereabouts of the lions' habitation (see above) reads: "... and *the mother* of the young lions"? (καὶ ἡ μήτηρ σκύμνων; compare LXX τοῖς σκύμνοις). Weill in his article of 1923 (see n. 40) called attention to Josephus' distinctive reading here, suggesting that he may have found it in the Biblical text used by him. He also acknowledges, however, "quelque incohérence" in the juxtaposition of the two Josephan images ("habitation of lions/ mother of young lions"), and ultimately leaves the question of the origin and text-critical status of the reading undecided[56]. I

52. Thus WEILL, *Josèphe*, II, p. 292, n. 2 who says of Josephus' above rendering ("their eyes/ faces will be completely darkened"): "cette traduction de l'hébreu קבצו פארור est indépendante des LXX...".

53. Tg. Nahum's rendition of this opening question replaces image ("lions") with the intended referent: "where are the dwelling-places of the kings, and the princes' residences"? In its interpretation of the opening words of MT 2,12 4QpNah, for its part, seems to equate the "lions' dwelling place" spoken of there with "a dwelling place for the wicked ones of the Gentiles" (מדור לרשעי גוים); see J.M. ALLEGRO and A.A. ANDERSON (eds.), *Qumrân Cave 4 1 (4Q158-4Q186)* (DJD, 5), Oxford, Clarendon, 1968, 37-42, p. 38. In *Exod. Rab.* 29.9 (LEHRMAN, *Midrash Rabbah Exodus*, p. 344) the question of Nahum 2,12a is placed on the lips of God who, following the devastation of Jerusalem by the "lion" Nebuchadnezzar (see Jer 4,7), asks, by means of this question, about what has become of his [God's] own "lions", i.e. the Temple (see Isa 29,1), the dynasty (see Ezek 19,2) and Israel itself (see Gen 49,9).

54. This "substitution" could reflect the consideration that what is being quoted is a prediction of the *future* overthrow of Nineveh.

55. Tg. Nahum would seem to have no equivalent to the above sequence in its (very free) rendering of 2,12.

56. WEILL, *Nahoum II 9-12*, 98. Commenting subsequently on his translation of the above text, WEILL, *Josèphe*, II, p. 292, n. 3 states: "Si l'on maintient le texte d'Josèphe, il faudrait admettre dans la Bible une leçon אם לכפירים".

propose that Josephus may have been inspired to introduce a reference to the "mother of the young lions" here on the basis of another "lion passage" in the Bible, i.e. the elegy on the lioness and her two cubs (= Judah and two of its last kings) in Ezek 19,1-9. In LXX's v. 2 of this text one finds collocated, in fact, the same three "leonine" terms used by Josephus in his rendering of Nahum 2,12a, i.e. "the mother" (ἡ μήτηρ), "lions" (λεόντων, *bis*) and "young lions" (σκύμνους). Such an interpretative rendering of Nahum 2,12 in light of Ezek 19,2 by Josephus seems quite conceivable given the standard Rabbinic practice of explaining one Biblical text on the basis of another which happens to share some term(s) with it[57].

Nahum 2,12b-13 continues the leonine imagery introduced in v. 12a with particular attention to the "prey" which the lion had once so easily acquired for himself and his young. Josephus dispenses with this further elaboration of the Bible's metaphor in order to come immediately to th climatic divine address of v. 14. That verse opens with the words "Behold I am against you[58], says (literally: "oracle", MT נְאֻם; LXX λέγει) the Lord (LXX κύριος) of hosts". Josephus (9,241b), for once, retains the source's direct address: "God (ὁ θεός) says (λέγει = LXX) to thee, *Nineveh* (Νινευή)[59]...". The remainder of 2,14 comprises a four-fold announcement of doom for Nineveh: The Lord will burn its chariots in smoke (Tg. Nahum: fire), devour its (young) lions (MT כְּפִירַיִךְ; LXX λέοντας; compare Tg. Nahum: princes) with the sword, cut off its prey (Tg. Nahum: סהורתיך, your trade) from the earth, while the sound of its messengers (so MT; LXX τὰ ἔργα σου) will be heard no more. Josephus reduces these four items to two, of which the first has no equivalent as such in the Biblical listing: "... I [God] will blot thee out (ἀφανιῶ)[60], and no more (οὐκέτι) shall lions (λέοντες = LXX) go

---

57. Indeed, it seems possible that the wording of Ezek 19,1-9 has influenced Josephus' rendering of Nah 2,9-12 already at an earlier point. As noted above, Josephus' version of 2,11 in 9,240 introduces a reference to the "lamentation" (θρῆνος) which awaits Nineveh. This term has no equivalent in 2,11 itself. It does, however, occur in the title of the poem of Ezek 19,1-9 in v. 1 where the prophet is enjoined to "take up a lamentation (LXX θρῆνον) for the princes of Israel". Note too that Josephus' *simplex* form ἀρπάσατε in his rendering of 2,10 (9,239) as against the compound διήπραζον of LXX has its counterpart in the phrase (τοῦ) ἀρπάζειν of LXX Ezek 19,3.6.

58. Tg. Nahum reads: "Behold I am sending my wrath against you".

59. With this added element, Josephus specifies the identity of the "thou" to whom the divine word of 2,14 is addressed. The term likewise harks back to the opening of Josephus' "quotation" in 9,239 (= Nahum 2,9): "(Nahum said) that *Nineveh* would be a troubled pool of water" with which it constitutes a kind of *inclusio*.

60. Josephus' other uses of ἀφανίζω with God as subject are *AJ* 1,116 (God was not minded to "exterminate" the builders of the tower of Babel) and 203 (God "obliterated" the land of Sodom with a conflagration).

forth from thee to rule the world (ἐπιτάξουσι τῷ κόσμῳ)⁶¹". With this latter notice Josephus does not, it will be observed, have the Deity announce the actual destruction ("devouring") of the "lions" as does the second prediction of 2,14, but rather of their ceasing to go forth to dominate the world. Perhaps, his wording of the item stands under the influence of the fourth item of the source list which speaks (MT) of the voice of Nineveh's "messengers" "no longer" (LXX οὐκέτι) being heard. In any case, the fact that Josephus singles out precisely the source reference to the lions for inclusion in his version is readily understandable given his previous utilization of the lion imagery of 2,12a⁶². It is with this reference to the coming end of the lions' expeditions for purposes of world-domination that Josephus concludes his citation of Nahum's word.

4. *Editorial Comments*

In 9,242 Josephus rounds off his citation of Nahum with a series of editorial remarks, freely created by him. The complex opens (9,242a) with the historian acknowledging his selective use of Nahum's words: "And many more things beside did this prophet prophesy about Nineveh (προεφήτευσεν οὗτος ὁ προφήτης περὶ Νινευῆς)⁶³, which I have not thought it necessary to mention (ἃ λέγειν οὐκ ἀναγκαῖον ἡγησάμην)⁶⁴, but have omitted in order not to seem tiresome (ὀχληρός) to my readers⁶⁵".

Josephus next (9,242b) provides a (Biblically unparalleled) indication concerning the duration of the interval between Nahum's prediction of Nineveh's overthrow and its realization: "But all the things that had been foretold (τὰ προειρημένα; see 9,74) concerning Nineveh came to

61. This is Josephus' only use of the above expression.

62. Conversely, his non-utilization of 2,14's reference to the "cutting off" of Nineveh's "prey" goes together with his earlier passing over of 2,12b-13 with their focus on the lion's prey; see above.

63. The above formulation constitutes an inclusion with that used in Josephus' introduction of Nahum in 9,239 (τις ... προφήτης ... περὶ καταστροφῆς ... τῆς Νίνου προφητεύων).

64. Compare the formula with which Josephus' introduces his account of Jonah in 9,208: "(since I have promised to give an exact account of our history), I have thought it necessary to recount (ἀναγκαῖον δὲ ἡγησάμην ... διεξελθεῖν) what I have found written in the Hebrew books concerning this prophet". Elsewhere Josephus uses the "I have (not) thought it necessary to..." construction in *AJ* 2,177; 7,369; 8,26.155; 10,51; 12,245; *c. Ap.* 2,4.

65. This is the only occurrence of the above formula about not wishing to appear "tiresome" to readers in the Josephan corpus. He employs the word ὀχλήρος thrice elsewhere: *AJ* 15,345; 16,22; 20,162.

pass after a hundred and fifteen years[66]". Thereafter, he clearly signals
the end of his "Nahum interlude" by means of the closing formula "and

66. This statement might, first of all, appear to stand in tension with the announcement
attributed by Josephus to Jonah in 9,214, i.e. "Nineveh would lose its dominion over
Asia *in a very short time*" – 115 years hardly seems to qualify as a "very short time". In
addition, there is the question about the above figure's coherence with the chronological
indications cited elsewhere by him. The problem is complicated by the fact that Josephus
does not indicate when precisely during Jotham's sixteen year reign (see 9,243) Nahum
delivered his announcement; recall the vague chronological formulation with which he
introduces the prophet in 9,239: "there was at this [Jotham's] time…". As for the event
of Assyria's overthrow, Josephus gives an equally vague dating for this in 10,30: "*now
it happened at this time* that the empire of the Assyrians was destroyed by the Medes…"
(cf. the implicit *Rückverweis* to this notice in 10,74: "… the Medes and the Babylonians
who had overthrown the Assyrian empire…"). Via the chronological indication of 10,30
the historian, in turn, refers back to the complex of events (Sennacherib's assault on
Jerusalem, Hezekiah's sickness and the visit of the Babylonian envoys) related by him in
what immediately precedes (10,1-29) and which, following 2 Kgs 18,14, he dates (10,1)
to the 14th regnal year of Jotham's grandson, Hezekiah. If then one tallies the dating indications provided by Josephus between 9,242 (the 115 years from Nahum's prophecy to
its fulfillment) and 10,30 (Assyria's actual fall), i.e. 16 years for Jotham's reign (9,243),
16 for that of Ahaz (9,257), and 14 for the first half of Hezekiah's rule (10,1), one arrives
at a total of 46 years, 69 less for the interlude between Nahum's prediction and its realization according to 9,242 (the discrepancy is still greater if one supposes – as the placing
of Josephus' "Nahum segment" might suggest – that this prophet delivered his announcement of Assyria's fall at the very end of Jotham's reign; in this case the period in question would be a mere 30 years). Such chronological discrepancies occur elsewhere in *AJ*
(see, e.g., below on 9,280) and reflect the protracted process of its composition, during
which such inconsistencies might well have arisen. In any event the statement of MARCUS,
Josephus, VI, p. 128, n. b with regard to the 115 year figure given in 9,242, i.e. "Nineveh
fell in 607/606 B.C. [more recent scholarship generally assigns it to the year 612]. Josephus thus dates the prophecy [i.e. of Nahum] in the last year of the Israelite kingdom (722
B.C.)" appears problematic in several respects. First, the historian (9,239) explicitly associates Nahum's activity with the reign of Jotham, whereas according to both the Bible
(2 Kgs 18,10) and Josephus (9,278) the end of the Northern kingdom came with the fall
of Samaria in the reign of Jotham's grandson Hezekiah (Kings dates the North's fall to
Hezekiah's sixth regnal year, Josephus to his seventh). In addition, Josephus gives no indication of knowing – as Marcus seems to presuppose that he did – the actual date of the fall
of Nineveh, i.e. the end point of the 115 years spoken of in 9,242. Finally, Prof.
Milikowsky (see n. 1) has kindly drawn my attention to the parallelism between Josephus'
figure of 115 years for the interval from Nahum's prophesying to Assyria's fall and the
chronological indications found in *SOR* 22.18 (Samaria fell in Hezekiah's 6th year, so
2 Kgs 18,10 [721 B.C.]) and 24,10 (Nebuchadnezzar conquered Nineveh in Jehoiakim's
4th year [605 B.C.]), i.e. an interval of just about 115 years. Accordingly, Milikowsky
suggests that in 9,242 Josephus has taken over a pre-existing tradition about the moment
of Assyria's overthrow without, however, harmonizing this with the chronological data
elsewhere in his work. Finally, P. HÖFFKEN, *Hiskija und Jesaja bei Josephus*, in *JSJ* 29
(1998) 37-48, esp. pp. 42-44 takes a different tack on the problem of the chronological
indication of 9,242 (and its apparent discrepancy with Jonah's announcement as cited in
9,214). In particular, he would distinguish between Assyria's losing its "dominion over
Asia" (as foretold by Jonah [see 9,214] and realized fairly soon thereafter under Hezekiah
[see 10,30]) and Nineveh's actual destruction as announced by Nahum [see 9,242] and
accomplished only much latter, i.e. under Josiah [cf. 10,74]). On this proposal and the
whole question, see further our discussion of 10,30 in chap. XVIII.

now, concerning these matters, what we have written may suffice (περὶ
... τούτων ἀποχρώντως ... δεδήλωται)⁶⁷".

5. *Closing Notices for Jotham*

Having thus disposed of Nahum at the end of 9,242, Josephus reverts,
at the opening of 9,243, to the figure of King Jotham, last mentioned by
him in 9,238. Of the items making up the concluding notices for this
king in 15,36-38 // 27,7-9, he characteristically omits, first of all, the
source references of 15,36 ("the Book of the Chronicles of the Kings of
Israel") // 27,7 ("the Book of the Kings of Israel and Judah"). In common with 2 Chronicles 27 Josephus likewise has no equivalent to the
"afterthought" remark of 2 Kgs 15,37 according to which during
Jotham's reign "the Lord began to send Rezin the king of Syria and
Pekah the son of Remaliah against Judah". The non-utilization of this
item by both the Chronicler and Josephus is understandable in that it
raises the theodicy question of why God would have thus afflicted a
pious king like Jotham⁶⁸. From 15,38aα // 27,9aα he does take over mention of Jotham's demise, to which he appends a double chronological
indication inspired by 2 Kgs 15,33 // 2 Chr 27,1a (= 27,8): (Jotham died)
"at the age of forty-one years⁶⁹, of which he reigned sixteen". The
sources differ somewhat in their respective burial notices for Jotham:
according to 15,38aβ he "was buried (BL ἐτάφη) with his fathers⁷⁰ in
the city of David his father", while 27,9aβ states: "they buried (MT
וַיִּקְבְּרוּ; compare BL ἐτάφη) him in the city of David". Once again,
Josephus goes his own way: "... he was buried (θάπτεται) in the royal
sepulchres (ἐν ταῖς βασιλικαῖς θήκαις)⁷¹".

The sources (15,38b // 27,9b) round off their accounts of Jotham with
mention of the accession of his son Ahaz, a matter which is then reiter-

---

67. Compare the similar construction in *BJ* 4,475 τὰ ... περὶ Ἱεριχοῦν ... ἀποχρώντως δεδήλωται.

68. The notice of 2 Kgs 15,37 is "duplicated" in 16,5 (// Isa 7,1) where the same two
foes (unsuccessfully) assault Jerusalem in the reign of Jotham's son, Ahaz. Given Ahaz'
reprobate status (see 2 Kgs 16,2b-4), both the Chronicler (see 2 Chr 28,5-7) and Josephus
(9,244) find no difficulty in reproducing the latter notice – likewise reformulating this
into a statement that the allied kings actually defeated Ahaz; see next chapter.

69. In the sources the first figure given is for Jotham's age at accession. In accord
with his regular practice, Josephus substitutes the king's age at death (41) here, calculating this figure by adding the Biblical indications on his age at accession (25) and length
of reign (16).

70. L 2 Kgs 15,38 (like 2 Chr 27,9) lacks the MT and B phrase "with his fathers"
here.

71. For this expression see on 9,166.

ated in what immediately follows, i.e. 2 Kgs 16,1 // 2 Chr 28,1. Josephus avoids this repetition by making his single reference to Ahaz' accession the opening of a new segment of his work, 9,243b-257, devoted to that king; see following chapter.

Conclusions: Josephus' Rewriting of 2 Kings 15 // 2 Chronicles 27 and Nahum 2,9-14

In summing up here on my findings regarding *AJ* 9,236-243a it seems best to treat separately the segment's two distinct components, i.e. 9,236-238.243a (Jotham) and 9,239-242 (Nahum).

With regard to the former material, it is clear that Josephus, as he does regularly in like circumstances, has opted to follow Chronicles' more detailed presentation of Jotham as opposed to the summary account found in Kings. Specifically, he (9,237-238) reproduces the Chronistic *Sondergut* items (2 Chr 27,3b-6) concerning Jotham's additional building activities and subjugation of the Ammonites. Conversely, he has no equivalent to those notices peculiar to Kings' Jotham segment, i.e. the synchronization of 15,32 and the reference to the Syrian-Israelite attack on Judah of 15,37. Given the lack of noteworthy divergences among them (as well as the brevity of the passages in question) it does not seem possible, on the other hand, to determine which text-form(s) of Chronicles Josephus had available in composing his Jotham narrative.

The image of Jotham presented by Josephus is still more positive than that found in the Bible. Thus, whereas 2 Kgs 15,35 and 2 Chr 27,2 both report that cultic abuses did continue among the people throughout Jotham's reign, Josephus affirms (9,236), without any such qualification, that Jotham "lacked no single virtue[72]". Also noteworthy in Josephus' version of Jotham are its various verbal echoes of his account of Jotham's father Uzziah[73], these being his replacement for the explicit contrasting of the two monarchs found in 2 Kgs 15,34 // 2 Chr 27,2a.

---

72. Such a magnification of Jotham's rectitude is in line with scattered comments in Rabbinic tradition. See *Gen. Rab.* 63.1 (FREEDMAN, *Midrash Rabbah Genesis*, II, p. 556) where God responds to the angels' lament at the accession of the wicked Ahaz by stating that, given the righteousness of his father Jotham, he (God) "can do nothing" to his reprobate son. Even more strikingly, in *b. Suk.* 45b the first-century A.D. Rabbi Simeon b. Yohai is quoted as affirming that the combined merits of himself, his son Eliezer, and of King Jotham would suffice to exempt the world from divine judgment from its creation until its final disappearance.

73. Such "echoes" concern especially the two kings' building measures in Jerusalem (compare 9,237 and 9,218b; and cf. nn. 13,17,19) and subjugation of the Ammonites (compare 9,238 and 9,218a; and cf. n. 23).

Such affinities themselves, in turn, serve to heighten the Josephan Jotham's perfection of character in that his achievements did not lead him into a prideful offense against God as did Uzziah's similar accomplishments (see 9,222-224). In this imperviousness to the *hubris* that took hold of Uzziah – as well as of many other characters in *AJ* – Jotham indeed shows himself to "lack no single virtue". The historian's aggrandizement of the figure of Jotham is furthered as well by his modification of the notice of 27,6 attributing the king's "becoming mighty" to his "ordering of his ways before the Lord". In Josephus' version of this notice in 9,238b attention is focussed on Jotham alone: he so strengthens his kingdom that his enemies are intimidated and his people enjoy "happiness".

What distinguishes Josephus' Jotham narrative from its Biblical counterparts is above all, however, his insertion within it of a digression concerning the prophet Nahum who (purportedly) functioned during this king's reign. I thus now turn to a summation of my findings on the "Nahum interlude" of 9,239-242.

From the textual-critical point of view, Josephus' rendering of Nahum 2,9-14 in 9,239b-241 evidences affinities with the distinctive readings of both MT (e.g., the two-fold imperative of 2,9a; see 9,239) and LXX (whose wording for 2,9aα and 12aα he very closely parallels in 2,239 and 241, respectively). At the same time he either omits or significantly reduces elements of the source text (i.e. 2,10b.12b-13.14abα), even as he inserts clarifying additions (e.g., regarding the speaker of the words of 2,9b [see 9,239] and the addressee of those of 2,14aα [see 9,241]) and adapts Nahum's language (see his substitution of a reference to the lions' "mother" for 2,11aβ's allusion to their "pasturage" in 9,241 and replacement of the threat of 2,14 about the lions' being "devoured" with the announcement [9,241] that their expeditions for purposes of world-domination will end). Likewise Josephus' introduction to (9,239a) and concluding remarks (9,242) on the "quotation" of Nahum 2,9-14 in 9,239b-241 evidence a number of distinctive features vis-à-vis the Book of Nahum itself: designation of Nahum as a "prophet" who "prophesies" (9,239a.242a); opening summation of his message ("the downfall of Assyria and Nineveh", 9,239a); statement about its coming true 115 years later (9,242a); and remark about his own selective use of Nahum's words (9,242b).

Josephus' insertion within his Jotham narrative of the "Nahum interlude" of 9,239-242 raises a final, wider question: why has the historian gone to the trouble of thus "making room" for the words of this rather obscure Biblical prophet when, e.g., he passes over in total silence seven of the twelve "minor prophets", i.e. Hosea, Joel, Amos, Obadiah, Habakkuk, Zephaniah, and Malachi? A first answer to this question has already been suggested above: Nahum's announcement of the coming "overthrow of Assyria and Nineveh" serves to reinforce, in line with Josephus' emphasis on the agreement of "true" prophets with one another, the earlier, similar message of Jonah as reproduced by him in 9,208-214. Why, though, should Josephus be so concerned to utilize Biblical predictions of the fall of Assyria in particular? In response to this further question I begin by recalling the suggestion of L.H. Feldman cited in chap. XI about the "Assyria" of Jonah's prophecy functioning as a kind of cipher for Rome's contemporary rival Parthia such that his inclusion of Jonah's words is designed to gratify his Roman patrons who would be pleased to find that a Biblical prophet had announced the over-throw of the "ancestor" of their great present-day foe. But if such con-siderations influenced Josephus to incorporate Jonah's predictions into his presentation, those same considerations would likewise help account for his utilization of Nahum's like announcement – thereby he would provide additional satisfaction to Roman readers.

In chap. XI we likewise suggested, however, that for Jewish readers the cipher "Assyria" of Josephus' version of the Jonah story could have been intended by him to bear another, quite different value, i.e. that of a code-name for their current oppressor Rome itself whose imminent loss of dominion (see 9,214) Jonah would thus be foretelling. Having had this message intimated to them in the case of Jonah, Jewish readers would then find its confirmation via Nahum's prediction of the "over-throw of Assyria and Nineveh" (9,239) an added source of gratification – and of hope.

The words of Jonah and Nahum concerning the fate of Assyria/ Parthia/ Rome thus provided Josephus with a means of presenting both his antagonistic publics with a message they would be well pleased to hear. Accordingly, it does seem so surprising, after all, that the historian has made sure to utilize the words of these two minor prophets in par-ticular even as he leaves aside so many of their Biblical counterparts.

XIV

AHAZ AND HOSHEA[1]
(9,243b-259)

In accordance with the sequence of both his sources, Josephus directly follows his account of Jotham (9,236-243a) with his presentation of that king's unworthy successor, Ahaz of Judah (9,243b-257 = 2 Kgs 16,1-20 // 2 Chr 28,1-27). To the latter passage he attaches, as a kind of appendix (9,258-259), his initial remarks on Ahaz' Northern contemporary, Hoshea, drawing these from two distinct Biblical contexts, i.e. 2 Kgs 15,30(31) and 17,1-3.

I divide up the material to be studied in this chapter as follows: 1. Ahaz Introduced (AJ 9,243b = 2 Kgs 16,1-4 // 2 Chr 28,1-4); 2. Military Developments (9,244-254 = 16,5-9 // 28,5-21); 3. Ahaz' Cultic Measures (9,255-257a = 16,10-18 // 28,22-25); 4. Closing Notices for Ahaz (9,257b = 16,19-20 // 28,26-27); and 5. Hosea's Reign (9,258-259 = 2 Kgs 15,30(31) + 17,1-3).

1. Ahaz Introduced

The Biblical sources begin (2 Kgs 16,1b // 2 Chr 28,1a) their respective introductions of Ahaz with chronological indications: his age at accession (20) and length of reign (16 years). In 2 Kgs 16,1a these items are preceded by a synchronism of Ahaz' accession with the 17th year of Pekah of Israel to which the Chronicler has no parallel. Following his normal practice with regard to the synchronisms of the later kings of both Judah and Israel (see p. 285, n. 56) Josephus leaves aside the datum of 16,1a. Again in line with his usual procedure, he likewise holds over until the very end of his account the sources' shared chronological indications for Ahaz; see 9,257b.

The source narratives commence (16,2b-3a // 28,1b-2a) their (negative) evaluations of Ahaz with the charge that the king failed "to do right

1. This chapter represents a revision of my articles *Ahaz, King of Judah according to Josephus*, in *SJOT* 10 (1996) 28-52 (used by permission of Scandinavian University Press, Oslo, Norway) and *The Last Six Kings of Israel according to Josephus*, in *ETL* 72 (1996) 371-384, pp. 379-380 (which I likewise use with permisson).

in the eyes of the Lord". In so doing, they continue, he diverged from his ancestor David, walking rather "in the ways of the kings of Israel". Josephus' parallel (9,243b) to this opening assessment omits the sources' allusion to David, while conversely introducing a reference to Ahaz' law-breaking: "... (Ahaz) acting most impiously towards God (ἀσεβέστατος εἰς τὸν θεόν)[2] *and violating his country's laws* (τοὺς πατρίους παραβὰς νόμους)[3] imitated (ἐμιμήσατο) the kings of Israel...[4]".

2 Kgs 16,3b-4 // 2 Chr 28,2b-4 "substantiate" the preceding negative judgment of Ahaz by citing various of his cultic misdeeds (burning of his son[s], 16,3b // 28,3b; sacrificing and burning incense at illicit sites, 16,4 // 28,4). To these charges the Chronicler adds (28,2b-3a) those of "making molten images for the Baals (so MT L; B ἐν τοῖς εἰδώλοις) and burning incense (BL ἔθυεν) in the valley of the son of Himmon". Josephus opens his own initial list (9,243c) of Ahaz' cultic crimes with an "anticipation" of an item drawn from a later point in Chronicles. Specifically, his statement that Ahaz "set up altars (βωμούς) in Jerusalem" seems inspired by 2 Chr 28,24bβ, "he made for himself altars (θυσιαστήρια, BL) in every corner of Jerusalem". Upon these altars in Jerusalem, Josephus goes on to state, Ahaz "sacrificed to idols (θύων ... τοῖς εἰδώλοις)". Here, the historian seems to conflate the formulations of 2 Chr (Par) 28,2b and 3; see above.

Common to both 2 Kgs 16,3b and 2 Chr 28,3b is the accusation that Ahaz subjected his son(s) to some sort of procedure involving "fire"; both verses likewise designate his doing this as a following of the "abominable practices" of "the nations whom the Lord had expelled from before his people". In Kings Ahaz is said to make his son (sg., so MT B; L sons) "pass through the fire" (MT הֶעֱבִיר בָּאֵשׁ, BL διῆγεν πυρί), while Chronicles speaks rather of his "burning his son*s* in the fire (וַיַּבְעֵר ... בָּאֵשׁ, MT; both BL and TC use a verb meaning "pass through" in accordance with 16,3b rather than MT's "burn")[5]. Josephus agrees

2. The above construction recurs in *AJ* 1,194 (the Sodomites) and 5,339 (the two sons of Eli); cf. 8,256 (with περί, the Judeans). The phrase echoes that used of Ahaz' grandfather Uzziah in 9,226 (τῶν ... εἰς τὸν θεόν ἀσεβημάτων).
3. The above construction recurs in *AJ* 10,214 where Daniel's relatives are said to be "unwilling to transgress their fathers' laws". On the key Josephan term πάτριους, see p. 115, n. 13.
4. On Josephus' recurrent use of the verb μιμέομαι and the cognate noun μιμητής in his evaluations of the kings, see on 9,44. Here in 9,243 the former term replaces the figurative expression "he walked in the way(s) of the kings of Israel" of 16,3a // 28,2a.
5. For the Targumist, the plural form "sons" of MT 28,3 which he takes over in his translation seems to have suggested that Ahaz destroyed all his (male) children by fire; accordingly, he appends a long expansion to account for the fact that at least one son, i.e.

with MT B Kings against L Kings and Chronicles (MT BL TC) in speaking of only a single son as the object of Ahaz' reprobate measure. In contrast to both sources, however, he designates that measure as a "sacrifice": "... he even offered his own son as a whole burnt offering (ὡλοκαύτωσε)[6]". Josephus likewise specifies the Biblical references to the "abominations of the nations"; Ahaz' deed was "according to the *Canaanite* custom[7]". 2 Kgs 16,4 // 2 Chr 28,4 conclude the catalogue of Ahaz' offenses with mention of his "sacrificing and burning incense on the high places, and on the hills and under every green tree". Josephus, who has already cited the king's (wrongful) sacrificial activity (see above), ends his indictment of Ahaz with the generalizing formula: "he committed other offences similar to these".

2. *Military Developments*

Following their respective introductions of Ahaz, the Biblical sources (2 Kgs 16,5-9 // 2 Chr 28,5-21) begin narrating the military events of his reign. The content of their accounts differs in many details, however. Those differences manifest themselves already at the very start of the two passages. In 2 Kings 16 we hear initially (v. 5) of an (unsuccessful) joint attack on Jerusalem by Syria and Israel[8], and then of a further (successful) initiative by Aram (so MT; see further below) against the Judean-held port of Elath/Eloth (v. 6). 2 Chr 28,5, on the other hand, first relates (seemingly) separate assaults by Syria and Israel upon Ahaz, the latter happening being told quite expansively (vv. 6-16); mention of the Edomite incursion (// 16,6b BL) comes then only in v. 17.

Hezekiah, did survive Ahaz. Here, the Targumist states that Hezekiah was miraculously delivered from the fire in virtue of God's foreknowledge that the boy was to be the ancestor of Daniel's three companions who themselves would be thrown into the fiery furnace for their loyalty to the Lord (see Dan 3,21). The same Targumistic expansion further cites a whole series of other righteous figures who, like Hezekiah, survived their being cast into the fire.

6. Josephus uses the verb ὁλακαυτάω in reference to two other (potential or actual) human "sacrifices", i.e. those of Isaac (*AJ* 1,224) and Jephthah's daughter (5,266); cf. 9,43 where the cognate noun is used of the King of Moab's "consecrating his first-born son to God as a holocaust".

7. In thus precising the Biblical wording ("the abominations of *the nations*") by reference to a group that had long since ceased to exist ("the Cannanites"), Josephus avoids potential offense to his Gentile audience.

8. This verse has a parallel in Isa 7,1. In 2 Kgs 15,37 the coalition's attack on Jerusalem is dated to the reign of Jotham; see chap. XIII.

In this instance Josephus aligns himself – initially – with the shorter presentation of 16,5-6. He begins his version (9,244) of this sequence with a transitional formula, underscoring the wrong-headedness of Ahaz' just-cited cultic measures: "But, while he was thus acting like a madman (μεμηνότος)...⁹". Picking up next on the notice of 16,5 itself, Josephus speaks of the combined assault on Ahaz by "Arasēs (᾿Αράσης; compare MT Rezin, BL ῾Ρααασσών), the king of Syria *and Damascus*¹⁰" and "Phakeas" (Φακέας; see 9,234-235). Given the long history of conflict between their respective realms, the Bible's mention of such a joint venture on the part of the kings of Syria and Israel might well puzzle readers. With a view to counteracting such a response, Josephus interjects an explanatory aside, i.e. "for they ['Arasēs' and 'Phakeas'] were friends (φίλοι)¹¹". Josephus amplifies as well 2 Kgs 16,5's notice on the Syro-Israelite siege of Jerusalem: the allies "drive" Ahaz into Jerusalem which they besiege him "for a long time". 2 Kgs 16,5 ends up by noting the failure of the coalition's assault. In MT, B, TJ this failure is expressed by means of a rather indeterminate formula, literally "they were not able to fight"; L's rendition is more definite: "they could not take Jerusalem". The Josephan version of the conclusion of 16,5 with its interjection of the reason for the allies' lack of success seems to represent a further precision of L's wording: "... but *because of the strength of its walls* [they] accomplished nothing".

In accord with 2 Kgs 16,6 Josephus directly couples mention of the coalition's attack on Jerusalem with a notice on yet another incursion into Ahaz' territory. 2 Kgs 16,6 itself appears textually problematic. In the first half of the verse, Rezin king of Aram (Syria), i.e. Pekah's partner in 16,5, is credited with recovering "Elath" (MT) for Aram and expelling the Judeans from "Eloth" (MT). MT 16,6b (*ketiv*) then states that "the Aramaeans" came to Elath and dwelt there to this day, whereas the *qere*, BL and TJ make the *Edomites/Idumaeans* the subject here. Josephus (9,245a) appears to conflate the distinct indications of 16,6 in a formulation which, like MT *ketiv*, mentions only Syria, and not also the Edomites (so BL etc.). His version thus reads: "However, the king

9. Compare Josephus' designation of Ahaz' reprobate predecessor Joram of Judah as ἐμμανής in 9,98.
10. Josephus uses the above double title also in *AJ* 7,100 (reverse order) and 8,363.
11. Cf. the historian's (also inserted) explanatory note as to why Joram of Israel turned to Jehoshaphat for assistance in his projected campaign against Moab in *AJ* 9,30 (compare 2 Kgs 3,7 which lacks a corresponding indication): "since he [Jehoshaphat] had from the first been his [Joram's] father's friend (φίλος)".

of Syria took the city of Elathūs (᾽Ηλαθούς)¹² *and, after killing its inhabitants*¹³, settled Syrians therein¹⁴".

In his opening narration of the military events of Ahaz' reign (9,244-245a), Josephus, as we have just seen, follows 16,5-6. Thereafter, however, he leaves the sequence of Kings (which now proceeds, 16,7, to relate Ahaz' embassy to Tilgath-pileser), in order to accomodate the *Sondergut* of 28,5-21. As already noted, 28,5 represents an alternative account of the events narrated in 16,5 according to which Syria and Israel appear to attack Judah separately, rather than in concert. Josephus, who has already utilized the presentation of 16,5 (see above), now (9,245b-246) cites the content of 28,5 as well. The notice of 28,5a on the incursion of the (nameless) king of Syria opens with a theological affirmation about the Lord's giving Ahaz "into his hands"; the result is that "they" (the Syrians, so MT; he = the Syrian king, BL) smote him (Ahaz)". Josephus (9,245b) substitutes a transitional formulation which picks up on, while also generalizing, his previous reference to Rezin's measures at Elath, i.e. "... when he had in like manner done away with the Jews (τοὺς ᾽Ιουδαίους)¹⁵ *in the garrisons and in the surrounding country...*". 2 Chr 28,5a continues with mention of the Syrian king's taking numerous prisoners and then returning to Damascus. In Josephus, the king "carrying off much spoil, withdrew *with his army* to Damascus".

2 Chr 28,5b relates that Ahaz was also "handed over" to the king of Israel who "smote him (Ahaz) with great slaughter". In Josephus

---

12. In *AJ* 8,163 (= 1 Kgs 9,26 // 2 Chr 8,17), where the city in question is called "Ailanē" (Αἰλανῆς, t.e.), Josephus adds that it is "now called Berenikē". Recall that in his version of 2 Kgs 15,22 // 2 Chr 26,2 in 9,217, Josephus does not reproduce the sources' name "Elath/Eloth", but contents himself with mention of Uzziah's "founding a city on the Red Sea"; see chap. XII. In contrast to 16,6aβ (Rezin "expelled the men of Judah from Elath") Josephus does not specify from whom the Syrian king "took" the city (his omission of this specification holds together with the fact that in his version of 2 Kgs 15,22 // 2 Chr 26,2 in 9,217 he does not reproduce those verses' indication about Uzziah "restoring" Elath/Eloth "to Judah" which itself serves to set up what one reads in 16,6). Cf. n. 15 on 9,245b.

13. Compare 16,6aβ where Rezin acts rather to "expel the Judeans" from Elath; cf. previous note.

14. In 16,6b the Arameans (so MT *ketiv*) seem to establish themselves in Elath on their own; Josephus, in line with his characteristic tendency, attributes their doing so to a royal initiative. From 16,6b Josephus omits the concluding specification that the Arameans have dwelt in Elath "to this day", doubtless on the consideration that by his own time this was no longer the case.

15. This phrase might be regarded as Josephus' (delayed) reapplication of the notice of 16,6aβ about Rezin's "driving the men of Judah (so MT)/ the Jews (so BL: τοὺς ᾽Ιουδαίους)" from Elath. Josephus' having the Syrian king eliminate a collectivity ("the Jews"), rather than smiting Ahaz personally (so MT, BL 28,5a), has a counterpart in TC which states that the Syrians "killed some of his (Ahaz') troops".

(9,246) it is Ahaz who becomes the (unlucky) aggressor in the conflict between him and the Israelite ruler. Thereby, the onus of responsibility for unleashing civil war is shifted from the latter to the former who thus appears in a still more negative light, given Josephus' consistent highlighting of the wrongfulness of intra-Jewish violence throughout his writings[16]. In thus assigning the initiative in the conflict to Ahaz himself, Josephus likewise introduces a (double) motivation for the king's attack on Israel, notwithstanding the fact that he has just (9,245) been defeated by Syria. His formulation on the point reads: "But the king of Jerusalem[17], *on learning that the Syrians had returned home, and thinking himself a match* (ἀξιόμαχος) *for the king of Israel*[18], *led out his force against him and, after joining battle...*". Josephus then picks up the end of 28,5b in noting the outcome of Ahaz' advance: ".... he was defeated". To this notice he appends an anticipation of the theological comment of 28,6b ("because they [the Judeans] had forsaken the Lord...")[19]: "... because of the anger which God felt (κατὰ μῆνιν τοῦ θεοῦ)[20] at his many great impieties (ἀσεβήμασιν; cf. ἀσεβέστατος, 9,243)[21]".

2 Chr 28,6a records that 120,000 valorous Judeans were killed by Pekah of Israel in a single day. Josephus' parallel (9,247), more realistically, ascribes the slaughter, not to Pekah personally, but to "the Israelites". Having anticipated the "theological notice" of v. 6b (see above), Josephus proceeds immediately from the global casualty figures of v. 6a to v. 7's list of three prominent Judeans who were slain. In the Biblical list the one responsible for their deaths is a certain "Zichri" (B Ἐζεκρεί), "a mighty man of Ephraim"; his victims are Maaseiah (B Μαασαίαν, L Μαασσίαν), the king's son; Azrikam (B Ἐγδρεικάν, L

---

16. Compare, e.g., Josephus' rewriting of 2 Chr 13,3 in *AJ* 8,274 where he represents, not the good king Abijah (so Chronicles), but rather the reprobate Jeroboam as the aggressor in the conflict between them.

17. Literally: "of the Jerusalemites" (τῶν Ἱεροσολυμιτῶν); for this designation, see on 9,31.

18. Contrast 9,61 where Joram of Israel's shutting himself up in Samaria is attributed to his "not thinking himself a match (ἀξιόμαχον) for the Syrians".

19. Compare his non-utilization of the similar theological notice of 28,5a about God's "handing over" Ahaz to the Syrians.

20. On this formula see 9,104 where it is used in reference to the reprobate Joram of Judah.

21. In Chronicles the theological notice of 28,6b is attached to the Judean casualty list of 28,6a. Josephus links his equivalent notice rather to the mention of Judah's defeat itself (= 28,5bβ). Note further than while in Chronicles Judah's casualties come as punishment for the whole people's "forsaking" of the Lord, Josephus attributes the defeat of Judah to the personal "impieties" of Ahaz, once again underscoring the king's depravity. See n. 28.

ʼΕζρεικάμ), "commander of the palace"; and Elkanah (B ʼΕιλκανά, L ʼΕλκανάν), "next in authority to the king" (RSV). According to Josephus the Israelite "general" (στρατηγός) "Zacharias" (Ζαχαρίας)[22] actually "killed" only Ahaz' son "Amasias" (ʼΑμασίαν)[23], while he merely "took captive" (αἰχμάλωτον ἔλαβεν)[24] the two other Judean notables, i.e. "Erikam" (ʼΕρικάμ), "the governor (τὸν ἐπίτροπον) of the entire kingdom" (compare MT נְגִיד הַבַּיִת; BL ἡγούμενον τοῦ οἴκου αὐτοῦ) and "Elikan" (ʼΕλικάν), "the chief officer (τὸν στρατηγόν) of the tribe of Judah" (compare MT מִשְׁנֶה הַמֶּלֶךְ; B τὸν διάδοχον [L δεύτερον] τοῦ βασιλέως)[25].

The enumeration of Judah's losses continues in 28,8: the Israelites return to Samaria with 200,000 Judean captives (including women, sons [MT בָּנִים] and daughters), as well as considerable booty. Josephus' parallel at the end of 9,247 omits the implausibly high Biblical figure for the Judean captives[26]. In addition, in place of Chronicles' mention of captive "women, sons, and daughters", it speaks of "women and children *of the tribe of Benjamin*[27]".

The Chronicler's Ahaz *Sondergut* goes on in 28,9-15 which relates the eventual release of the Judean captives; Josephus' parallel is 9,248-251. Their release is set in motion by the intervention of a prophet of Samaria named "Oded" who confronts the returning army as it approaches the capital. Josephus (9,248a) specifies that "Odēdas" met the Israelites "before the walls" of Samaria and addressed them "in a loud voice". 2 Chr 28,9b-11 cites Oded's prophetic speech in direct discourse; here again, Josephus recasts in indirect discourse. The Biblical Oded begins (28,9b) by averring that whereas God in his wrath (BL

22. This is the conjecture of Coccejus which Dindorf and Marcus follow. Niese reads Ζαχάριν in the line of the codices, while Bekker and Naber give Ζάχαρις.

23. This is the reading adopted by Dindorf, Bekker, Naber, and Marcus. Niese reads ʼΑμασίας with the codices other than M (which has ʼΑμίας).

24. This is the reading adopted by Dindorf, Bekker, Naber (ἔλαβε), and Marcus. The codices ROS², followed by Niese, read the plural verb ἔλαβον which makes not "Zechariah" himself, but the whole Israelite force the subject of the action (as it is in the continuation of the text; see above).

25. MARCUS, *Josephus*, VI, p. 131, n. e explains the divergence between Josephus (9,247) and Chronicles regarding the fate of the last two Judean leaders cited in 28,7 ("taken captive" vs. "killed") in terms of Josephus' having been influenced by the reading in 28,8 where the Israelites are said to "take captive" 200,000 Judeans.

26. Contrast, however, his reproduction (9,247a) of the also high figure for the Judean slain (120,000) of 28,5.

27. MARCUS, *Josephus*, VI, p. 131, n. i suggests two possible explanations for Josephus' reference to "Benjamin" here. First, it might represent a misreading of the word בנים ("sons") of MT 28,8. Alternatively, the reference could be intended to prepare Josephus' parallel to 28,15 in 9,251 where the captives are escorted back to their kinsfolk at Jericho (a *Benjaminite* city according to Jos 18,11-12).

ὀργή) against *Judah* had handed it over to the Israelites, the latter slew the Judahites "in a rage (BL ἐν ὀργῇ) that reached up to heaven". Josephus eliminates this initial reproach of excess anger on the part of the Israelites from his version of Oded's words. Instead, he has the prophet begin (9,248b) with a general statement concerning the source of Israel's triumph: "... their victory had come about, *not through their own might* (ἰσχύν), but through the wrath which God felt (διὰ ... τὸν τοῦ θεοῦ χόλον; cf. κατὰ μῆνιν τοῦ θεοῦ, 9,246) at King Achaz[28]".

Oded's address proceeds in 28,10a with the prophet evoking the Israelites' reprobate intention of enslaving their kinsfolk; in v. 10b there follows his rhetorical question "have you not sins of your own against the Lord your God[29]?" Josephus leaves aside this latter element. His Oded denounces (9,249a) the Israelites, not for their past "sins", but for their present hubris: "he rebuked them *because they had not been content with their success* (εὐπραγίᾳ) against Ahaz[30], but had dared to take captive (αἰχμαλωτίσαι; cf. αἰχμάλωτον ἔλαβεν, 9,247) people of the tribes of Judah and Benjamin[31], who were their kinsmen (συγγενεῖς)[32]".

Oded concludes his discourse in 28,11 by urging his hearers to return their captives, motivating this appeal by reference to the divine "wrath" (B ὀργὴ [L θυμοῦ] Κυρίου) that hangs over them. Josephus (9,249b) has Oded call for the captives to be returned "unharmed" (ἀπαθεῖς). He likewise replaces the source mention of God's wrath with an allusion to the divine "punishment" (δίκην) the Israelites will bring upon themselves should they fail to heed the prophet's directive.

---

28. Here again (see n. 21 on 9,246 = 28,6) Josephus makes the object of the divine wrath, not Judah as a whole (so 28,8; see above), but Ahaz personally. In so doing, he underscores the heinousness of the king's misdeeds.

29. Thus RSV's rendering of MT. B reads "behold am I not with you to testify (μαρτυρῆσαι, a likely corruption of ἁμαρτῆσαι = MT) for the Lord your God"?

30. Note again the emphasis on the person of Ahaz. The reference to the Israelites' not being "content with their success" here recalls Josephus' comment in 9,196 that Amaziah of Judah "was not able to contain himself at his good fortune (εὐπραγίαις)". Unlike Amaziah, however, the Israelites will pay heed to the prophetic warning against hubris made them; see below.

31. In 28,10a the reference is to "the people of Judah and *Jerusalem*". Josephus' mention of "Benjamin" here in 9,249 picks up on his earlier (likewise "un-Biblical") reference to the "women and children of the tribe of Benjamin" in 9,247; see n. 27. Conceivably, his substitution of "Benjamin" for Chronicles' "Jerusalem" is due to the fact that earlier (see 9,244) he had stated, in dependence on 2 Kgs 16,5, that the Syrian-Israelite coalition had been unable to capture the city. Given that fact, for Josephus to reproduce the Chronicler's reference to *Jerusalemite* captives here in 9,249 would leave readers wondering how the Israelites had been able to acquire such captives.

32. Compare 28,10a where the captives are specified rather as (intended) "male and female slaves". With his qualification of them as "kinsmen" here, Josephus anticipates the designation of the Judean prisoners as "your brothers" (BL ἀδελφῶν) in 28,11.

In 28,12 Oded's words are immediately followed by the intervention of four named Ephraimite chiefs whose speech to the army is then cited in 28,13. The historian (9,250a) interposes the notice that "the people of Israel came together in assembly (εἰς ἐκκλησίαν) and deliberated about these matters". He may have found inspiration for this notice in the subsequent Biblical reference (28,14) – which his insertion serves to prepare – to the Israelites' depositing their captives and spoil "before the princes and all the assembly (BL ἐναντίον ... πάσης τῆς ἐκκλησίας)³³".

Coming now to recount the content of 28,12 (see above), Josephus (9,250b) mentions by name only the second of the four figures listed in the source, i.e. "Barachias" (Βαραχίας)³⁴. Whereas he then further accentuates Barachias' own stature by qualifying him as "one of the men most respected in the state", he reduces his Biblical colleagues to an anonymous "three others³⁵". Josephus' reproduction of the four-some's words from 28,13 begins in indirect discourse, but then shifts to direct discourse. The leaders speech in 28,13 comprises a prohibition ("you shall not bring the captives in here") and appended motivation (doing so will only increase Israel's already great guilt and the divine wrath that has been provoked). Josephus' parallel represents the leaders as forbidding that the captives be brought into the city. The negative motivation they append to this prohibition then reads: "… *lest we should all be destroyed by God*³⁶; for we have committed quite enough sins (ἐξαμαρτεῖν) against Him³⁷, *as the prophets say*³⁸, without committing

33. Elsewhere as well Josephus interjects references to a convening of an "assembly" into his retelling of Biblical history (see, e.g., *AJ* 5,105 = Jos 22,15 where he introduces mention of the Transjordanians' "convening an assembly" to hear the Israelite delegation that has been sent to them). This feature of Josephus' rewriting of the Bible might be regarded as an instance of "Hellenization", given the importance of the deliberative assembly in Greco-Roman political life (and history-writing).

34. This is the form of the name found in L; compare MT "Berechiah" and B Ζαχαρίας.

35. In the same line, see, e.g., his non-reproduction of the names of Joram's six broth-ers (2 Chr 21,2) in 9,95 or of the five commanders with whom Jehoiada parleys (2 Chr 23,1) in 9,143.

36. This threat of divine annihilation is Josephus' specifying/intensifying equivalent for the evocation of God's "wrath" at the end of the leaders' speech in 28,13. The threat picks up on Oded's warning that the disobedient Israelites will "suffer punishment at the hands of God" in 9,249 (recall that this formulation itself replaces the prophet's affirma-tion about the Lord's "fierce wrath" against Israel in 28,11b).

37. Compare 28,13bα: "for our guilt (BL ἡ ἁμαρτία) is already great".

38. With this insertion Josephus underscores the conformity between the leaders' words and those of the prophet Oded who has spoken just previously. The plural refer-ence to "prophets" likewise recalls the numerous earlier prophetic denunciations of the Northern Kingdom's ways cited by him in what precedes.

fresh impieties (ἀσεβήματα; cf. ἀσεβέστατος, 9,243; ἀσεβήμασιν, 9,246, both times of Ahaz himself) in addition[39]".

2 Chr 28,14 relates the outcome of the leaders' intervention: the returning Israelites "leave" captives and spoil "before the princes and all the assembly". Josephus (9,251a), likely under the influence of the source's subsequent presentation where the leaders take the initiative with regard to the prisoners (see 28,15a), depicts the Israelite army as simply turning matters over to them: "*On hearing these words*, the soldiers agreed to let them [the speakers of 9,250] do what they thought expedient". 2 Chr 28,15a describes, with considerable circumstantiality, the benefactions conferred on the Judeans by the Israelite leaders ("the men who have been mentioned by name", cf. 28,12): having "taken" the captives, they use the spoils to cloth them, just as they outfit them with sandals, give them food and drink, anoint them, and mount the feeble on asses. Josephus' parallel (9,251b) generalizes the source benefits catalogue: "And so the aforementioned men [see 9,250] took over the captives *and released them*[40]; and they treated them with care (ἐπιμελείας) and gave them provisions for their homeward journey, after which they sent them away unharmed (εἰς τὴν οἰκείαν ἀπέλυσαν ἀβλαβεῖς)[41]".

The Chronicler's story of the Judean captives (28,8-15) culminates in v. 15b with the notice that the leaders escorted the Judeans as far as Jericho, whereupon they themselves returned to Samaria. In reporting this development, Josephus (9,251c) substitutes the notation that Jericho is "not far from Jerusalem" for the Biblical qualification of the former site as "the city of palm trees".

At this juncture, following the long *Sondergut* segment 28,(5-6)7-15, the Chronicler rejoins the sequence of Kings to relate (28,16) Ahaz' appeal to Tilgath-pileser of Assyria (// 2 Kgs 16,7). In Kings this appeal is motivated by the previously cited assaults of Syria-Israel and Edom upon Judea (16,5-6). Chronicles, on the other hand, links Ahaz' diplomatic initiative (28,16) with attacks on Judah by the Edomites and the Philistines which it proceeds to relate in 28,17-18 to which itself is appended a "theological motivation" for these threats, 28,19. Josephus

39. Compare 28,13aβ: "you propose to bring upon us guilt against the Lord in addition to our present sins (BL ταῖς ἁμαρτίαις) and guilt".
40. This indication lacks a source parallel; Josephus mentions the matter in first place, thereby making clear that the captives were, in fact, granted their liberty by the leaders.
41. Compare Oded's directive to the Israelites as cited in 9,249: "let the captives go and return to their homes unharmed (ἀπολῦσαι ... εἰς τὴν οἰκείαν ἀπαθεῖς)". By means of the verbal echo Josephus underscores that the Israelites did indeed do as directed by the prophet.

(9,252a) goes his own way with respect to both these presentations[42]. Specifically, he introduces Ahaz' appeal with a transitional phrase that harks back to the long preceding account (9,246-251 // 28,7-15) of Israel's victory over Judah and its sequels: "But King Achaz, *after suffering this defeat at the hands of the Israelites*, sent to Thaglathphallasrēs (see 9,235) the king[43] of Assyria...". 2 Chr 28,16 states merely that Ahaz sent to the Assyrian king(s) "for help". 2 Kgs 16,7b gives a more expansive account of his appeal: "I am your servant and your son (the L MS 93/e₂ lacks this sequence). Come up and rescue me from the hand of the king of Syria and from the hand of the king of Israel, who are attacking me". In this instance Josephus aligns himself with the presention of Kings, while, once again, substituting indirect for direct discourse: "... asking him to give aid as an ally (συμμαχίαν)[44] in the war against the Israelites, the Syrians *and Damascenes*...[45]".

2 Kgs 16,8 (// 2 Chr 28,21a)[46] relate how Ahaz backed up his verbal appeal with a monetary "contribution" which he drew from the holdings of Temple and palace. According to Josephus (9,252b) Ahaz both promised to give Tiglath-pileser "much money" and also actually sent him "spendid gifts". At this juncture, the historian says nothing about the "source" of either the (promised) money or the "gifts"; see, however, 9,254 below.

The Biblical narratives diverge in their description of the sequels to Ahaz' appeal. According to 16,9 Tiglath-pileser responded affirmatively to the appeal by seizing Damascus, deporting its people "to Kir" (so MT; BL lack this specification)[47] and killing its king, Rezin. 2 Chr 28,20, by contrast, states that the Assyrian "came against him [Ahaz]

---

42. In so doing he leaves aside the notice of 2 Chr 28,18 (as also the attached theological remark of 28,19) on the Philistine invasion of Judah (no parallel in Kings) completely. He likewise passes over the Chronicler's reference to the Edomite incursion of 28,17, having given his version – in which the people in question are the Syrians – of this in 9,245 in dependence on (BL) 16,6; see above.

43. Josephus' use of the singular here corresponds to the reading of 2 Kgs 16,7 and BL 28,16; MT 28,16 reads "the king*s* of Assyria".

44. This element of the Josephan Ahaz' request might be seen as his equivalent to the king's declaration about his being the Assyrian's "servant and son", i.e. a virtual ally, in 16,7.

45. With this added element compare Josephus' designation of Rezin ("Arasēs") as "king of Syria (literally: the Syrians) and Damascus (literally: of the Damascenes)" in 9,244.

46. In Chronicles the sequence of 2 Kgs 16,7 (// 28,16, Ahaz' embassy) and 16,8 (// 28,21a, Ahaz' "gifts") is interrupted by the *Sondergut* segment 28,17-20 on which see above.

47. VL 16,9 takes MT's place name ("Kir") as that of a Syrian king, i.e."Core" who, along with a second such king, i.e. "Ason", it represents as having been seized by Tiglath-pileser; see FERNÁNDEZ, *Scribes & Translators*, pp. 66-67.

and afflicted him instead of strengthening him[48]". Here too, Josephus clearly opts to follow Kings' account (although see below for a possible indication of his use also of 28,20). In so doing, however, he introduces his version (9,253) of 16,9 with a long expansion which reads: *"and so, after the envoys had come to him* [Tiglath-pileser], *he went to the help of* (σύμμαχος; cf. συμμαχίαν, 9,252) *Achaz, and, marching against the Syrians, ravaged* (ἐπόρθησε) *their country...".* Thereafter, he reproduces the source verse's content as follows: "... he took Damascus *by storm* (τὴν Δαμασκὸν κατὰ κράτος εἷλε)[49], and killed their king Arasēs (= Rezin; see 9,244). He then transported (ἀπῴκισεν) the Damascenes to upper Media (Μήδιαν)...[50]". Just as he elaborates on the opening of 16,9, Josephus also expands that verse's conclusion. In particular, he fills its "lacuna" as to what became of the land emptied by the Assyrian deportation of the Damascenes with his notice "... and (Tiglath-pileser) brought over some of the Assyrian tribes and settled them in Damascus (εἰς τὴν Δαμασκὸν κατῴκισε)[51]". Having filled this lacuna, Josephus goes on to introduce a further expansion of 16,9, one designed to respond to yet another question left unanswered by the Biblical account. In 2 Kgs 16,7b (= 9,252b), it will be recalled, Ahaz asks for Assyria's assistance, not only against the king of Syria, but also against the king of Israel. Surprisingly, however, the description of Tiglath-pileser's (affirmative) response to the appeal in 16,9 says nothing about any measures undertaken by him against Israel. Josephus' concluding expansion

48. A further difference between Kings and Chronicles regarding the Ahaz-Tiglath-pileser interaction should be noted here: in the former the Assyrian king's initiatives are described only after mention of Ahaz' tribute to him (16,8), whereas in the latter the sequence is: Assyrian advance (28,20), followed by the notice on Ahaz' contribution (28,21).

49. This phrase is very similar to that used by Josephus in his notice on Shalmaneser's capture of Samaria in 9,278 (= 2 Kgs 17,6): εἷλε κατὰ κράτος τὴν Σαμάριαν.

50. This is Josephus' substitution for the unknown site "Kir" of MT 16,9. His mention precisely of "Media" as the deportees' place of exile might have been inspired by 2 Kgs 17,6 where the Assyrians exile the Israelites, *inter alia*, to "the cities (LXX mountains) of *the Medes*" (the Josephan parallel in 9,278 reads "[Shalmaneser] transported [μετῴκισεν] all its [Israel's] people to Media [Μηδίαν] and Persia"). Cf. the previous note for another verbal link between Josephus' accounts of Assyria's dealings with Damascus and Samaria.

51. This phrase corresponds to that employed by Josephus in 9,279 (= 2 Kgs 17,24) in reference to the resettlement of peoples from the east in the former territory of Israel: κατῴκισεν εἰς τὴν Σαμάρειαν. Given the other verbal links between Josephus' accounts of the Assyrian measures first against Damascus and later against Samaria (see nn. 49,50), I would suggest that, in complementing 16,9's notice on the depopulation of Damascus with mention of a repopulating of the city with settlers from the east here, Josephus was inspired by the account of Samaria's fall in 2 Kings 17 where one hears of both a deportation of the original inhabitants (17,6) and the "importation" of new ones (17,24).

(9,254a) of 16,9 remedies this deficiency with its notice "… he also did much damage (κακώσας) to the country of the Israelites and took many of them captive (αἰχμαλώτους συνέλαβε)⁵²".

In the sequence of 2 Kings 16 (with which Josephus has aligned himself in 9,252-254a), the notice of Tiglath-pileser's initiatives (v. 9) is followed immediately by a lengthy *Sondergut* account (vv. 10-17) concerning an altar which Ahaz has built in Jerusalem on the model of the one he had seen in Damascus. At this juncture, however, Josephus seems to turn from Kings in order to base himself, once more, on the narrative of Chronicles. As pointed out above (see n. 48), the Chronicler recounts Tiglath-pileser's (negative) response to Ahaz' appeal (28,20) before mentioning (28,21a) the latter's tribute, i.e. the reverse of Kings' sequence in 16,8-9. Josephus, as we have seen, follows Kings in mentioning Ahaz' tribute before detailing the Assyrian measures taken in response to this; see 9,252-254a. On the other hand, with his inserted reference to Ahaz' "promising" to give Tiglath-pileser "much money" (9,252b; compare 16,8), he does set up expectations of subsequent additional contributions by the former. That expectation is, in fact, fulfilled now in 9,254b, Josephus' parallel to 28,21a, where Ahaz' tribute seems to come in response to moves already taken by the Assyrians against himself; see 28,20. At the same time, however, the historian adapts the content of 28,21 to his own previous, Kings-based presentation in which the Assyrian initiatives are directed, not against Judah (so 28,20), but rather against Syria (and Israel), just as he also incorporates the *Sondergut* remark on a meeting between Ahaz and Tiglath-pileser in Damascus from 2 Kgs 16,10aα. His resultant combination (9,254b) of 28,21 and 16,10aα runs: "*after he* [Tiglath-pileser] *had inflicted these things on the Syrians* [see 9,253], King Achaz took all the gold that was in the royal treasuries and the silver that was in the temple of God⁵³ *and the*

---

52. This phrase ironically echoes 9,247 where it is the Israelite general Zacharias who "took captive" (αἰχμάλωτον ἔλαβεν) two Judean leaders; now it is the Israelites' turn to be made captives. The whole above sequence further calls to mind Josephus' notice in 9,235 concerning Tiglath-pileser's seizure of Israelite territory and deportation of the inhabitants; this notice, in turn, itself represents his version of 2 Kgs 15,29, the "displaced" Biblical account of Assyria's response to the appeal of Ahaz cited in 16,7; see chap. XIII.

53. With Josephus' specification here about the double source of Ahaz' tribute, compare 16,8 ("the silver and the gold that was found in [BL + the treasuries of] the house of the Lord and in the treasuries of [> BL] the house of the king") // 28,21 ("he took from the house of the Lord and the house of the king and of the princes"). With its explicit mention of "gold and silver" Josephus' version stands closer to Kings than to Chronicles (although he likewise diverges from Kings in assigning a separate "source" for the two commodities).

finest dedicatory-offerings (ἀνάθημα)⁵⁴, *and carrying them with him,* came to Damascus [see 16,10aα] *and gave* (ἔδωκε) *them to the Assyrian king*⁵⁵, *in accordance with their agreement* (κατὰ τὰς ὁμολογίας)⁵⁶, *and, after acknowledging his thanks* (χάριν ἔχειν ὁμολογήσας) *for everything*⁵⁷, returned to Jerusalem⁵⁸".

3. *Ahaz' Cultic Measures*

Following their respective narrations of military developments under Ahaz (16,5-9 // 28,5-21 = 9,244-254), all three narratives return (16,10-18 // 28,22-25 = 9,255-257a) to the topic of the king's (reprobate) cultic measures, already broached by them in their introductions of Ahaz; see above.

In 2 Kgs 16,10-16 the opening allusion to the Damascus meeting (v. 10aα; see above) serves to lead into an account of the Ahaz' "Damascene" altar. Josephus opts not to utilize Kings' expansive (and rather obscure) treatment of the latter subject as one which would hardly likely be of much interest to Gentile readers. Instead, he elects to make use, at this juncture, of the Chronicler's negative reinterpretation of the neutral/positive account of Ahaz' Damascene altar of 16,10-16 according to which the king was guilty of worshipping "the gods of Damascus", 28,22-23. Both the Chronicler and Josephus introduce their respective notices on Ahaz' worship of the Syrian gods with a negative comment

---

54. Josephus' inserted mention of these items underscores the extent of Ahaz' tribute (and his willingness to hand over objects belonging to God to a pagan king). The insertion likewise accentuates the parallelism between Ahaz' initiative and that of his ancestor Joash who in *AJ* 9,170 (= 2 Kgs 12,18) "takes down the dedicatory offerings (ἀναθήματα)", using these to buy off the invading Syrian king.

55. This inserted reference to Ahaz' "giving" the items enumerated to Tiglath-pileser evidences the fulfillment of the Judean's promise (9,252), i.e. "to give" (δώσειν) the Assyrian "much money" should he attack the Israelites and Syrians – something which Tiglath-pileser has in fact done in the interval.

56. In neither Biblical source is there mention of an actual "agreement" between Ahaz and Tiglath-pileser. Josephus' use of the term recalls, however, his earlier, reciprocal use of "ally" terminology for the two kings; see 9,252 (Ahaz asks the Assyrian "to give aid as an ally [συμμαχίαν]") and 253 (Tiglath-pileser "goes to the help [as an ally, σύμμαχος] of Achaz"). The employment of such terminology serves to underscore the extent of Ahaz' willingness to associate himself with a pagan king.

57. With his use of the verbal form ὁμολογήσας here Josephus introduces a word-play with the noun ὁμολογίας used by him just previously in 9,254. The inserted reference to Ahaz' "thanking" Tiglath-pileser "for everything" here supplies a content for their Damascus meeting lacking in the source, 16,10.

58. Josephus' inspiration for this concluding reference is the double allusion to the king's "coming from Damascus", i.e. back to Jerusalem in 16,11-12.

about that royal initiative. Whereas, however, 28,22 speaks of Ahaz "becoming still more faithless to the Lord", Josephus (9,255) refers, "un-theologically", to his being "so stupid (ἀνόητος)[59] and unmindful of his own good (τοῦ συμφέροντος ἀσυλλόγιστος)[60]... that...".

According to 28,23a Ahaz sacrificed to the gods of Damascus who had "defeated him" in hopes that these would "help" him, as they had helped the kings of Syria. Josephus, on the other hand, represents Ahaz' worship of the Syrian gods as transpiring "even while he was at war with the Syrians" (διετέλει τούτους σεβόμενος)[61]. Ahaz acted thus, Josephus editorializes, "as if they [the Syrian gods] would grant him victory[62]". With this adaptation of the Biblical presentation, Josephus underscores Ahaz' "stupidity" (see above): without waiting to see if the Syrian gods were capable of assisting their own people (compare 28,23), the king takes to worshipping them[63].

2 Chr 28,23 ends up with the statement that, contrary to Ahaz' expectations, the Syrian gods "were the ruin of him and all Israel". This formulation fails to indicate the nature and agent of the "ruin" that befell Ahaz and his people. A like indeterminacy characterizes the continuation of Josephus' parallel to 28,23bß at the beginning of 9,256. There, the historian refers to Ahaz' "being defeated a second time" without specifying by whom. I suggest that Josephus' mention of this "second (i.e. subsequent to the ones earlier inflicted on him, back-to-back, by the Syrians and Israelites; see 9,245-247) defeat" suffered by Ahaz has in view the Chronicler's reference (28,20) to Tiglath-pileser's "coming against and afflicting" Ahaz by way of response to the latter's appeal to him for help. As will be recalled, Josephus earlier (9,253-254a) passed over this Chronistic notice on the negative outcome of Ahaz' appeal in

---

59. Josephus employs this same term in his summarizing judgment on Ahaz' predecessor Rehoboam in *AJ* 8,264. Compare his reference to Ahaz himself as "acting like a madman (ἔχοντος ... μεμηνότος) in 9,244.

60. Josephus uses the above construction only here. In its three other occurrences in his writings (*AJ* 4,161; 8,171; 12,40), the term ἀσυλλόγιστος has the meaning of "countless, huge".

61. The above phrase echoes that used by Josephus in 9,194 (= 2 Chr 25,14) in reference to the reprobate initiative of Ahaz' ancestor Amaziah who "persisted in worshipping the gods (τούτους σεβόμενος διετέλει) of the Amalekites" whom he had earlier defeated.

62. In 28,23 the equivalent phrase "(I will sacrifice to them) that they may help me" is formulated as a word of Ahaz himself.

63. MARCUS, *Josephus*, VI, p. 136, n. a comments concerning Josephus' notice of Ahaz' worship of the Syrian gods in 9,255 that the historian "freely paraphrases the scriptural account (2 Kings xvi. 10-11) of the altar at Damascus...". It seems, clear, however, that for his above presentation Josephus is rather directly dependent on 2 Chr 28,22-23 (which itself might be regarded as a "free paraphrase" of 2 Kgs 16,10ff.).

favor of the account of the assistance rendered Ahaz by Tiglath-pileser as found in 16,9. Here in 9,256, however, he appears to make delayed (and allusive) utilization of the alternative presentation of 28,20[64]. Confirmation of the above suggestion may be found in the continuation of 9,256 where Josephus states that, subsequent to his "second defeat", Ahaz "began to honour (τιμᾶν) the gods of the Assyrians...". This item has no equivalent as such in either of Josephus' sources. As Marcus[65] suggests, however, it is "probably based on 2 Kings xvi. 18 which says that Ahaz made certain changes in the temple 'for the king of Assyria'". Thus in 9,256 Josephus would be combining the data of 28,20 and 16,18 into a new, distinctive statement about Ahaz' worshipping the gods of the Assyrians who, like the Syrian deities before them, had "defeated" him. To this statement he appends a generalizing remark that underscores the extent of Ahaz' apostasy: "... he seemed ready to honour (τιμήσων) any god rather than his fathers' God, the true one (τὸν πατρῷον καὶ ἀληθῶς θεόν)[66], who in His wrath (ὀργιζόμενος)[67] had been the cause (αἴτιος) of his defeat (ἥττης; cf. ἡττηθείς at the start of 9,256)".

In his subsequent cataloguing of Ahaz' cultic misdeeds in 9,257a Josephus continues to follow the presentation of Chronicles (28,24-25a) in preference to the account of 16,17-18 which relates measures taken by Ahaz with regard to various components of the Temple fabric "because of the king of Assyria[68]". 2 Chr 28,24-25a "credits" Ahaz with the following four offenses: 1) cutting up the Temple vessels, 2) closing the doors of the Temple, 3) building altars throughout Jerusalem, and 4) constructing high places in every Judean city on which to burn incense to other gods. Of these four items, Josephus has already utilized the third in his introduction of Ahaz in 9,243b; see above. Here in his parallel to 28,24-25a in 9,257a, he takes over only item two of the Chronicler's list, leaving aside both one and four. In place thereof he substitutes two alternative charges against Ahaz, introducing the whole with a condemnatory comment on the

64. Compare Josephus' mention of Ahaz' tribute-paying both before (so 16,8 = 9,252) and after (so 28,21 = 9,254b) Tiglath-pileser's advance in response to his appeal.

65. *Josephus*, VI, p. 136, n. b.

66. The above adjectival collocation occurs only here in Josephus. Its word πατρῷον echoes the historian's introduction of Ahaz in 9,243 where the king is charged with "violating his country's (πατρίους) laws".

67. This participial form echoes Josephus' previous mentions of God's "anger" against Ahaz; see 9,246 (κατὰ μῆνιν τοῦ θεοῦ) and 248 (διὰ ... τὸν τοῦ θεοῦ χόλον).

68. On Josephus' adaptation of this formulation in his reference to Ahaz' worship of the Assyrian gods in 9,256, see above.

king's initiatives. His version reads: *"To such lengths of contempt* (ὀλιγωρίας) *and despite (of God)* (καταφρονήσεως)[69] did he go that[70] he shut up the temple completely (τέλεον ἀποκλεῖσαι τὸν ναόν; cf. B 28,24 ἔκλεισεν τὰς θύρας οἴκου Κυρίου) *and forbade the offering of the customary sacrifices* (τὰς νενομισμένας ... θυσίας ἐπιφέρειν)[71], *and stripped it of its dedicatory-offerings* (ἀναθημάτων)[72]".

4. *Closing Notices for Ahaz*

The three Ahaz narratives end up with a series of standard closing remarks (16,19-20 // 28,26-27 = 9,257b) for the king. From the Biblical sequences Josephus, as always elsewhere, leaves aside the source notices of 16,19 // 28,26. Conversely, he prefaces his reproduction of the data of 16,20 // 28,27 with a final characterization of Ahaz's kingship that is perhaps inspired by the phrase of 28,25b ("provoking to anger the Lord..."), appended to the list of Ahaz' cultic transgressions in 28,23-25a: "after outraging God (ὑβρίσας τὸν θεόν)[73] in this way...".

2 Kgs 16,20aα // 2 Chr 28,27aα relate that Ahaz "slept with his fathers". To his corresponding, non-figurative notice Josephus attaches several chronological items inspired by 16,2 // 28,1, i.e. Ahaz "... died

69. Elsewhere Josephus uses the noun καταφρόνησις in reference to a "scorning" of God in *AJ* 1,113 (the builders of the Tower were incited to "insolent contempt of God" by Nimrod); 6,264 (those who, like Saul, rise to high station "assume contempt for things human and divine"); 10,38 (in his "contempt of God" Manasseh killed all the righteous among the people). Cf. also *AJ* 4,190 (Moses warns the people against being carried away by wealth into "a contempt and disdain for virtue") where, as in 9,257, καταφρόνησις is collocated with ὀλιγορία. Josephus' use of the term ὀλιογορία with reference to Ahaz serves to connect the king with his ancestor Amaziah whose "contempt (ὀλιγωρίας) of God" he cites in 9,204.

70. Compare Josephus' introductory transition to his notice on Ahaz' worship of the Syrian gods in 9,255 (cf. 28,22): "so stupid and unmindful of his own good was this king that...".

71. This item might be seen as a vague reminiscence of 2 Kgs 16,12-15 where Ahaz "removes" the Temple's existing bronze altar and directs that henceforth sacrifices are to be offered on the "Damascene altar" he had had constructed. With the above measure Ahaz "negates" the directive given by the high priest Jehoaida in 9,155: "he ordered them [the priests and Levites] to offer the customary sacrifices (ἐπιφέρειν τὰς νενομισμένας ... θυσίας)".

72. This charge echoes the mention – likewise inserted by Josephus – about Ahaz' handling over "the finest dedicatory offerings (ἀνάθημα)" to Tiglath-pileser in 9,254.

73. The use of this phrase serves to associate Ahaz with the notorious Jeroboam I; see *AJ* 8,277 where Josephus has Abijah of Judah refer to "the insults (τῶν ὕβρεων) which he [Jeroboam] has never ceased to offer Him [God] (εἰς αὐτὸν ὑβρίζων)".

at the age of thirty-six years[74], of which he had reigned sixteen (so 16,2 // 28,1)". The Biblical verses 16,20 // 28,27 proceed to mention Ahaz' burial and the succession of his son Hezekiah. Josephus passes over the former point[75], moving directly to the accession of "Ezekias" (Ἐζεκίαν; cf. BL Ἐζεκίας).

5. *Hoshea's Reign*

Having jointly cited the accession of Hezekiah as the final element of their respective accounts of Ahaz, the Biblical narratives, once again, diverge thereafter. The Chronicler proceeds directly to his expansive presentation of Hezekiah (2 Chronicles 29-32), while the author of Kings first recounts (2 Kings 17) the final years of the Northern Kingdom which paralleled the first period of Hezekiah's reign, and only then gives his story of Hezekiah himself (2 Kings 18-20). Josephus follows Kings' sequence here – at least to the extent of relating the rule of Israel's final king, Hoshea (9,258-259 = 2 Kgs [15,30] + 17,1-3), before taking up Hezekiah's great cultic reform in 9,260-276 (= 2 Chronicles 29-31); see chap. XV.

In narrating Hoshea's reign Josephus first presents (9,258a) his parallel to 2 Kgs 15,30, the notice on this figure's assassination of his predecessor Pekah, earlier passed over by him (see chap. XIII). MT and B 15,30 date Hoshea's regicide "in the twentieth year of Jotham", a problematic indication given the fact that according to 15,33 Jotham himself ruled only sixteen years, and so not surprisingly without equivalent in L. Josephus, for his part, has (9,258a) the happening occur "at the same time", i.e. as the death of Ahaz, cited by him just beforehand in 9,257, a dating which makes it appropriate for him to mention Hoshea's deed at precisely this point. As he did with the earlier Northern regicides Shallum (9,228) and Pekahiah (9,234), he introduces the specification that "Oseos" (Ὠσήου; BL Ὠσῆε) was a "friend" (φίλου) of his victim[76].

74. Josephus obtains this figure by combining the Biblical indications (16,2 // 28,1) that Ahaz was 20 years old at his accession and ruled 16 years.

75. His doing so may reflect the divergence between the sources concerning Ahaz' burial. 2 Kgs 16,20 states that he "was buried with his fathers in the city of David", whereas 2 Chr 28,27 avers "they buried him in the city, in Jerusalem, for they did not bring him into the tombs of the kings of Israel". Compare the historian's non-mention of Hezekiah's burial (for which the Biblical indications likewise diverge); see p. 436 and n. 77 on *AJ* 10,36.

76. On this recurrent feature to Josephus' retellings of Biblical royal assassinations, see p. 203, n. 75.

Having thus reproduced the content of 15,30, Josephus proceeds immediately to append his version of 2 Kgs 17,1-3, the continuation of the Biblical account of Hoshea commenced in 15,30 but then interrupted by the sequence on the Southern kings, Jotham and Ahaz (15,32-16,20)[77]. Specifically, from 17,1 he draws his notice (9,258b) that Hoshea ruled nine years[78], while from 17,2 he takes over its negative evaluation of the king. The latter verse notably qualifies its charge about Hoshea's "doing evil in the Lord's sight" with the appended phase "yet not as the kings of Israel who were before him". Josephus disregards this qualification of Hoshea's depravity[79] in his own formulation which reads simply "he was a wicked man (πονηρός; cf. τὸ πονηρόν, BL 17,2) and contemptuous of his duty to God (τῶν πρὸς τὸν θεόν ὀλίγωρος)[80]". That Josephus does not make use of the Bible's qualification of Hoshea's evildoing is understandable given the fact that 17,2 itself fails to provide any basis for its statement concerning the king[81].

In 9,259 Josephus presents an expanded version of the account of 17,3 concerning Hoshea and the new Assyrian ruler, Shalmaneser. It reads: "And there came (στρατεύει) against him [Hoshea] Salmanassēs (Σαλμανάσσης; cf. L Σαλμανάσσαρ), the king of Assyria, *who defeated him – for Oseos did not have God propitious* (τὸν ... θεὸν οὐκ εἶχεν ... εὐμενῆ)[82] *or as his ally* (σύμμαχον; see

77. Josephus leaves aside the source notice for Pekah of 15,31.

78. This is the only datum of 17,1 utilized by him. Left aside are the synchronism of Hoshea's coup with Ahaz' twelfth year (which would conflict with the dating of both 15,30 and that of 9,258a according to which Hoshea seized power at the time of Ahaz' death after the latter's sixteen year reign; see p. 332), the name of the regicide's father (Elah, MT), and the precision that Hoshea ruled "over Israel in Samaria".

79. Compare his like omission of the qualification attached to the negative evaluation of King Jehoram of Israel of 2 Kgs 3,2 in his assessment of that ruler in 9,27; see chap. III.

80. This is Josephus' only use of the above phrase which does, however, echo his reference to Ahaz' "contempt (ὀλιγωρίας) and despite of God" in 9,257.

81. As might be expected, the Rabbis did attempt to answer the question of what distinguished Hoshea (*in bonam partem*) from the other kings of Israel. Their response, which recurs in a whole series of Talmudic and midrashic contexts (see, e.g., *b. B. Bat.* 121a; *b. Git.* 88a; *b. Ta'an.* 30b-31a; *Lam. Rab.*, Proem 33 [A. Cohen, tr., *Midrash Rabbah Lamentations*, London-New York, Soncino, 1983, p. 60]) is that Hoshea removed the guards whom Jeroboam I had posted to keep his people from going to Jerusalem. On the whole question see further H.G. VON MUTIUS, *Hosea, der letzte König des Nordreiches bei Josephus und im Talmud*, in Henoch 2 (1980) 31-36; A. VAN DER KOOIJ, *Zur Exegese von II Reg 17,2*, in ZAW 96 (1984) 109-112.

82. With the above construction compare 9,199 where the army of Amaziah is overtaken by a sudden panic "such as God inspires when He is not propitious" (θεὸς οὐκ εὐμενὴς ὤν).

9,252.253)[83] – and made him subject and imposed a fixed tribute on him[84]".

2 Kgs 17,4-6 continues with the story of Hoshea's fatal defection from his Assyrian overlord and its sequels. Josephus, by contrast, "interrupts" Kings' sequence in order to tell of Hezekiah's great cultic reform (9,260-276 = 2 Chronicles 29-31), a happening which he dates (9,260a) to Hoshea's fourth year. Thereafter, he resumes his account of the North's demise, itself precipitated by Hoshea's revolt, in 9,277.

Conclusions: Josephus' Rewriting of 2 Kings 16
(+ 15,30; 17:1-3) // 2 Chronicles 28

In the case of Ahaz for whom two, rather divergent Biblical presentations were extant, Josephus' version evidences an alternating use of both of these. Indeed, his concern for "inclusivity" goes so far that he several times "duplicates" narrative elements for which Kings and Chronicles give somewhat differing accounts, i.e. the Syrian/Israelite assault(s) on Judah (2 Kgs 16,5-6 = AJ 9,244; 2 Chr 28,5 = 9,245-246), Ahaz' tribute-paying both before (so 16,8 = 9,252) and after (so 28,21 = 9,254) the Assyrian advance, and Tiglath-pileser's initiative as directed against Judah's foes (16,9 = 9,253-254a) and Judah itself (so 28,20 = 9,256).

The question of the Biblical text-form(s) used by Josephus in 9,243b-259 remains without a clear-cut answer. Still, we did note various indications of the historian's familiarity with distinctive readings of MT 2 Kings 16 and 2 Chronicles 28. Thus, e.g., in agreement with MT 16,6 (and against BL and TJ), Josephus attributes (9,245) the whole of what befell "Elath" in Ahaz's reign to (the king of) the Syrians. Similarly, his reference to Ahaz' offering his son as "a whole burnt offering" (9,243c)

---

83. Josephus' one other use of the collocation "propitious and an ally" (also in reference to the Deity) is in AJ 4,296 where Moses speaks of the Israelites' being blest with "God's gracious favour and support" (εὐμενῆ τὸν θεὸν καὶ σύμμαχον). With the above inserted sequence Josephus fills in the "gap" in 17,3 where Shalmaneser's advance (v. 3a) and Hoshea's tribute-paying (v. 3a) are directly juxtaposed without the connection between the two happenings being spelled out. In Josephus it is Shalmaneser's "defeat" of Hoshea – itself due to God's displeasure with the Israelite king – which leads to the latter's tribute-paying. Given the above stress on God's lack of support for Hoshea one further sees why it would not have been appropriate for Josephus to reproduce the qualification of 17,2 concerning Hoshea's wickedness which would have led one to expect that he, of all the Israelite kings, would have a claim on the divine favor which, Josephus here affirms, was denied him.

84. Compare 17,3b where Hoshea takes the initiative in subjecting himself to Shalmaneser and offering him tribute. Josephus' formulation underscores the dominance of the Assyrian who leaves the defeated Hoshea no room to act on his own.

seems to presuppose the reading "he burned" of MT 28,3 in contrast to the more indeterminate "he caused to pass through the fire" shared by all witnesses for 16,3, as well as by BL and TC 28,3. Again, in common with MT 16,9, but *contra* BL, Josephus supplies (9,253) a terminus for the Damascene exile, albeit one ("upper Media") quite different from that cited in the source ("to Qir"). Conversely, in having Ahaz sacrifice "to the idols" Josephus (9,243) uses the same term employed in BL 28,2 whereas MT speaks more specifically of "the Baalim". Here again, then, the (sparse) relevant indications suggest that Josephus had available various text-forms of 2 Kings 16 // 2 Chronicles 28 in composing 9,243b-257(258-259).

Josephus' standard types of rewriting techniques are much in evidence throughout 9,243b-259. Thus, he interjects a variety of *additions/ expansions*. Of these, some are primarily stylistic in nature; see, e.g., the interjected transitional phrase "on hearing these words" introducing his notice on the army's response to the Israelite leaders' exhortation (9,251; cf. 28,14) and the formula "after he had inflicted these things on the Syrians" (9,254) with which he shifts from Tiglath-pileser's measures to Ahaz' (second) tribute-paying. Another group of additions provides explanations of some matter that is simply recorded as a fact in the source(s) and/or answers a question that might suggest itself to readers of the Biblical account(s). Thus, the allies' failure to take Jerusalem (16,5) is due to "the strength of its walls" (9,244), just as the cooperation between Rezin and Pekah spoken of in 16,5 is rooted in their being "friends" (9,244). Again, in 9,253-254a Josephus offers responses on several matters left without such in the narration of 16,9 (i.e., what became of the territory vacated by the exiled Syrians and did Tiglath-pileser, in fact, take action also against Israel as Ahaz had requested?). In the same line, he (9,259) inserts a theological motivation for Shalmaneser's success in subjugating Hosea (compare 2 Kgs 17,3). Still other Josephan additions in our segment serve to prepare some subsequent element of his presentation (e.g., the interjected mention of Ahaz' promise of "much money" to Tiglath-pileser in 9,252 [compare 16,8] "sets up" the notice of his [second] tribute-praying in 9,254 [compare 28,21]). Finally, the non-Biblical specification that Pekah's assassin Hosea was a "friend" of his victim introduced by Josephus in 9,259 (compare 2 Kgs 15,30) functions to heighten the pathos of that happening.

Josephus' account of Ahaz and Hoshea in 9,243b-259 also *omits*, for a variety of reasons, quite a number of Scriptural items. These include: the "source notices" of 16,19 // 28,26 (Ahaz) and 15,31 (Pekah); the mention of Ahaz' burial (16,20aβ // 28,27aβ); the synchronism for his accession (16,1); the cultic particulars of 16,10-18; the 200,000 Judeans taken prisoner by the Israelites (28,8); the names of three of the four Israelite leaders cited in 28,12 (compare 9,250); several of the specific benefactions conferred on the Judean captives as cited in 28,15 (compare 9,251), the Philistine invasion of Judah (28,18) and the appended theological comment of 28,19; Ahaz' cutting up of the cultic vessels and building of high places throughout Judah (28,24a.25a; compare 9,257); and the "qualification" attached to 2 Kgs 17,2's negative assessment of Hoshea (compare 9,258).

Likewise noteworthy in 9,243b-259 are Josephus' *modifications/ adaptations* of source elements. Stylistically, he several times replaces the Bible's direct with indirect discourse (see 9,248-249 = 28,9-11, Oded's address; 9,252 = 2 Kgs 16,7, Ahaz' appeal to Tiglath-pileser). Terminologically, the potentially offensive phrase "according to the abominable practices of the nations" (16,3 // 28,3) is reworded (9,243) as "according to the Canaanite custom". On the contentual level, Ahaz' age at accession (16,2 // 28,1) becomes his age at death (9,257), while Hoshea's coup is dated, neither to the 20th year of Jotham (so 15,30 MT B) nor to the 12th year of Ahaz (so 17,1), but rather "at the same time", i.e. of Ahaz' death in his 16th regnal year (9,258). Ahaz is the aggressor rather than the "victim" in the conflict between Judah and Israel (9,246; compare 28,5b); the Northern hero kills, not three (so 28,7), but only one of the Judean notables, leading the other two captive (9,247); the Israelites' prisoners are taken from "Judah and Benjamin" (9,249), not "Judah and Jerusalem" (so 28,10); Jericho is qualified as "not far from Jerusalem" (9,252) rather than as "a city of palm trees" (so 28,15); Ahaz sacrifices to the Syrian gods while still at war with Syria (9,254) instead of after his defeat by them (so 28,22); and Shalmaneser imposes tribute on Hoshea (9,259) in place of the latter offering this on his own initiative (so 2 Kgs 17,3).

Josephus' Ahaz-Hoshea segment is, finally, also not lacking in *re-arrangements* of the Biblical sequence: The chronological indications for Ahaz are given, not at the start (so 16,2 // 28,1), but rather at the end of his Ahaz account (9,257b). By contrast, the notice of 28,24 about Ahaz' erection of altars in Jerusalem is anticipated to the historian's opening evaluation of the king (9,243c). The references to Hoshea's ascent to power, which in the source stand in two different contexts (2 Kgs 15,30 and 17,1-3) are combined by him in 9,258-259, even while the immediate continuation of the Biblical Hoshea story (17,4-6) is delayed until after his account of Hezekiah's reform (9,260-276).

Josephus' employment of the foregoing rewriting techniques eventuates in a presentation of Ahaz and Hoshea with various distinctive features. The "cultic matter" prominent in both 2 Kings 16 and 2 Chronicles 28 is reduced in favor of a concentration on military and political developments. Both kings featured in the segment come across even more negatively in the Josephan presentation than they do in the sources. Thus, Hoshea is depicted as unqualifiedly evil (9,258; compare 17,2), while Ahaz, e.g, twice pays tribute to the Assyrians (9,252.254a) rather than only once (so 16,8 and 28,21), gives Tiglath-pileser also the "finest dedicatory offerings" (9,254a), "thanks" that pagan king "for everything" when he meets him in Damascus (9,254b; compare 16,10), is explicitly said to have worshipped, not only the Syrian (so 28,23), but also the Assyrian gods (9,256) and indeed to have been "ready to honour any god rather than his fathers' God, the true one" (9,256, no Biblical parallel). Distinctive too is Josephus' version of Tiglath-pileser's measures against Syria (9,253 = 2 Kgs 16,9) which seems to have been formulated as a *Vorspiel* of Shalmaneser's subsequent dealings with Samaria as he will relate these (see nn. 48-50). Under this heading mention might also be made of a negative finding with regard to the distinctiveness of Josephus' presentation of Ahaz and Hoshea, i.e. in contrast to his procedure in other contexts, he does not notably "de-theologize" the Biblical accounts of these two kings. Indeed in the case of Hoshea, he goes beyond 2 Kgs 17,3 in attributing (9,259) his defeat by Shalmaneser to God's not being "propitious to him" or his "ally".

For Gentile readers Josephus retells the story of Ahaz and Hoshea highlighting the political and military events that such readers would find particularly congenial, likewise taking care not to tax their credulity (e.g., he omits the implausibly high figure of 28,8 for the number of captives taken by the Israelites) or to cause them gratuitous offense (see his rewording [9,243] of the source allusions to the "abominations of the nations", 16,3 // 28,3). At the same time, Josephus underscores, for the benefit of his co-religionists, the reprehensibility and potentially disastrous consequences of intra-Jewish violence in his rendition of the story of the Judean captives (2 Chr 28,8-15) in 9,248-251 where, e.g., "Oded" explicitly threatens his Israelite hearers with divine "punishment" should they not release their prisoners "unharmed" (9,249; compare 28,10-11). Thereby, he presents contemporary Jewish readers with an implicit warning to desist from their recent intra-mural conflicts lest the punishment their ancestors had adverted by heeding Oded's word (continue to) befall them.

XV

HEZEKIAH'S BEGINNINGS
(9,260-276)

In 9,258-259 Josephus, basing himself on 2 Kgs 15,30-31; 17,1-3, briefly records the overthrow of Pekah of Israel by Hoshea and the latter's own subjugation by Shalmaneser. Whereas, however, 2 Kings continues immediately (17,4ff.) with its account of the later period of Hoshea's rule under which the Northern Kingdom came to an end, and only then (chaps. 18-20) relates the reign of Hezekiah of Judah, Josephus reverses this sequence, narrating first the beginnings of Hezekiah's kingship (9,260-276) and thereafter the demise of Israel (9,277-291)[1]. For his presentation of Hezekiah's beginnings[2], Josephus had available two Biblical sources, i.e. 2 Kgs 18,1-8(9-12) and 2 Chr 29,1-31,21. Of these, the latter provides a detailed account of the king's cultic initiatives to which the former devotes but a single verse (see 18,4). As will emerge, Josephus, in 9,260-276, does clearly base himself on the Chronicler's more expansive portrayal of Hezekiah the cultic reformer, even while notably reducing its level of detail.

I divide up the material to be studied in this chapter into three main segments: 1. Hezekiah's Personalia (*AJ* 9,260ab = 2 Kgs 18,1-3 // 2 Chr 29,1-2); 2. Hezekiah's Cultic Initiatives (9,260c-274 = 2 Kgs 18,4[5-6] // 2 Chr 29,3-31,21); and 3. Military Developments (9,275-276 = 2 Kgs 18,7-8). At the appropriate point, I shall further sub-divide the second of these segments.

---

1. There is a chronological "justification" for this reversal in that Hezekiah's accession is dated (2 Kgs 18,1; cf. 9,260b) to the third year of Hoshea's reign, i.e. prior to the events that culminated in the annihilation of Israel as related in 2 Kgs 17,3-6 // 18,9-12 (see 18,9 [= 9,277] which dates the start of Shalmaneser's siege of Samaria to the seventh year of Hoshea). Recall that in accord with 2 Kgs 16,20b // 2 Chr 28,27b, Josephus makes an initial reference to Hezekiah's accession at the end of *AJ* 9,257.

2. I use this expression to designate the complex of events in Hezekiah's earlier reign which precede Sennacherib's assault on Jerusalem in the former's 14th regnal year as recounted in 2 Kgs 18,13-19,37 (// 2 Chr 32,1-23). For the Josephan treatment of Hezekiah overall, see FELDMAN, *Studies*, pp. 363-374 (= ID., *Josephus' Portrait of Hezekiah*, in *JBL* 111 [1992] 597-620) and HÖFFKEN, *Hiskija und Jesaja, passim*.

1. *Hezekiah's Personalia*

As do his sources, Josephus commences (9,260a) his narration of Hezekiah's beginnings with a series of personal data for the king. The first of these items constitutes a version of the synchronization notice of 2 Kgs 18,1 (no parallel in Chronicles): "in the fourth[3] year of the reign of Osēos, Hezekiah began to reign in Jerusalem...". Both Biblical sources (18,2a // 29,1a) include among their opening data for Hezekiah indications on his age at accession (25 years) and length of reign (29 years). In accord with his usual practice, Josephus reserves his rendition of these figures until the conclusion of his account of Hezekiah; see 10,36. Proceeding then to Hezekiah's parentage, Josephus replaces mention of the king's maternal grandfather ("Zechariah," 18,2b // 29,1b) with a reference to his mother's hometown: "he was the son of Achaz and of Abia (Ἀβίας)[4], *a native* (ἀστῆς) *of that city*[5]". The sources' introductory evaluations of Hezekiah (18,3 // 29,2) laud him as one who "did what was right (BL Rgns and Par τὸ εὐθές) in the eyes of the Lord, according to all that his David his father had done[6]". Josephus (9,260b) substitutes a triad of positive adjectives: "His character was that of a kindly (χρηστή), upright (δικαία) and pious (εὐσεβής)[7] man[8]".

3. In MT B L* TJ 18,1 Hezekiah accedes rather in Hoshea's *third* year. Josephus' figure does, however, agree with that given by the L MS 127/ c_2. That figure might have in view the chronological indications of 2 Kgs 16,1 (= 9,257: Ahaz reigned *16* years) and 17,1 (Hoshea began to reign in Ahaz' *12th* year) which, taken together, might be understood to mean that Ahaz expired and Hezekiah acceded in Hoshea's 4th rather than 3rd year.

4. This is the declined form of the name as found in L 2 Chr 29,1, i.e. Ἀβιά; see VL "Abia". Compare "Abi" (MT 18,2), Ἀβού (B 18,2), Ἀβούθ (L 18,2), "Abijah" (MT 29,1), Ἀββά (B 29,1).

5. Josephus' – Biblically unparalleled – identification of Hezekiah's mother as a Jerusalemite here corresponds to his procedure with regard to the mother of King Jotham in 9,236, see p. 298, n. 5.

6. In 2 Kgs 18,5b this judgment is supplemented as follows: "... there was none like him among all the kings of Judah after him, nor among those who were before him". Neither the Chronicler nor Josephus has an equivalent to this supplementary evaluation, perhaps due to its seeming conflict with the very similar statement made concerning the later King Josiah in 2 Kgs 23,25.

7. This is the reading of ROZon followed by Niese and Marcus. MSPE have θεοσεβής (a reading followed by Dindorf, Bekker, and Naber); cf. Lat religiosa. As FELDMAN, *Studies*, pp. 368-370 (= ID., *Hezekiah*, 604-606) points out, it is above all the king's quality of "piety" which Josephus will accentuate throughout his presentation of him.

8. In the above formulation Josephus leaves aside the sources' comparison of Hezekiah with David as such. On the other hand, the three qualities which he ascribes to the former are all ones which figure in his evaluative remarks concerning the latter. See AJ 7,391 (David is eulogized as "... kind [χρηστός] to those in trouble, just [δίκαιος]..."); 7,110 (David was "of a just [δίκαιος] nature"); 7.130 (David "by nature a righteous [δικαίῳ] and godfearing [θεοσεβεῖ, so the variant reading in 9,260; cf. n. 7]

2. *Hezekiah's Cultic Initiatives*

Having introduced Hezekiah, the Biblical narratives proceed to recount the cultic initiatives undertaken by him, 2 Kgs 18,4 doing so quite summarily, 2 Chr 29,3-31,21 at much greater length. In terms of its extent Josephus' version of this element of Hezekiah's beginnings (9,260c-274) stands midway between the two Biblical accounts, although it is clearly more in line with the latter than the former. For convenience, I subdivide the material of 2 Chr 29,3-31,21 and *AJ* 9,260c-274 into six parallel sections: a) Hezekiah's Speech (9,260c-262 = 29,3-11); b) Hezekiah's Directives Accomplished (9,263a = 29,12-19); c) Hezekiah's Passover Summons (9,263b-267 = 30,1-12); d) Sacrifices Offered (9,268-270 = 29,20-36); e) Passover Observed (9,271-272 = 30,13-27); and f) Additional Cultic Initiatives (9,273-274 = 31,1-21).

a) *Hezekiah's Speech*. The Chronicler has the new king Hezekiah commence his cultic reforms with a rather lengthy discourse to the assembled cultic personnel (2 Chr 29,4-11). The report of the royal speech is itself preceded (29,3) by the following narrative notice: "In the first year of his reign, in the first month, he opened the doors of the house of the Lord, and repaired them". Josephus has no equivalent as such to this preliminary notice[9]. In place thereof he inserts an elaborate transition (9,260c) that serves to make a causal connection between his preceding "eulogy" of Hezekiah (9,260b) and the king's subsequent discourse: "And *therefore*, on his first coming into power[10], he considered nothing more necessary or profitable (ἀναγκαιότεραν οὔτε συμφορώτερον)[11]

man"); cf. 6,160 (God informs Samuel that the king he is seeking – who, in fact, will turn out to be David – is "one adorned with piety [εὐσεβείᾳ], justice [δικαιοσύνῃ]..."). Thus, Josephus' "eulogy" of Hezekiah here in 9,260b might, in its own way, well put readers in mind of *AJ*'s David.

9. Perhaps, his motivation for omitting it was a concern that the non-priest Hezekiah not appear to be usurping priestly prerogatives in handling the Temple doors (in this connection recall that one of the charges against the reprobate King Ahaz is precisely that he took upon himself to "shut up the doors of the house of the Lord", 2 Chr 28,24 = 9,257). He will, however, make use of the verse's reference to an "opening (of the doors) of the house of the Lord" in his version of Hezekiah's actual speech in 9,262; cf. 9,263.

10. This chronological indication takes the place of the more definite wording of 29,3: "in the first year of his reign, in the first month".

11. This precise collocation occurs only here in Josephus. Compare, however, the related phrase ἀναγκαίαν ... καὶ συμφέρουσαν in *AJ* 16,379. Note too the positive echo here of 9,255 where Ahaz is said to be "stupid and unmindful of his own good (συμφέροντος)".

to himself and his subjects than the worship of God (τοῦ θρησκεύειν τὸν θεόν)[12] and so...".

2 Chr 29,4-5aα depicts Hezekiah assembling priests and Levites "in the square on the east" where he speaks to them. Josephus omits the Biblical place indication, while also expanding the king's addressees with an additional group: "... he called together (συγκαλέσας) *the people* (τὸν λαόν)[13] and the priests and the Levites, and addressed (ἐδημηγόρησεν)[14] them in the following words...".

Within Hezekiah's actual discourse as recorded in 29,5aβ-11 on may distinguish the following elements: address to the Levites (v. 5aβ); exhortation to purification of their persons and of the Temple (v. 5b); motivation of exhortation (vv. 6-9), itself consisting of a retrospective featuring the ancestors' misdeeds (vv. 6-7) and God's punishing response (vv. 8-9); Hezekiah's statement of his intention of making a covenant with the Lord so as to turn away the divine anger (v. 10); and renewed exhortation to the assembled clergy (v. 11). In rendering the royal discourse Josephus takes considerable liberties with both its content and sequence. Thus, whereas the Chronicler has Hezekiah single out the Levites as his addressees and exhort them in first place, the historian (9,261) represents the king as speaking to all three of the groups previously assembled by him (see 9,260c)[15] and commencing with a retrospective parallel to that of 29,6-9. In addition, in contrast to vv. 6,10 where Hezekiah evokes what "our father*s*" did and suffered, respec-

12. Josephus' other uses of the above phrase are in *AJ* 3,49; 8,282 (350); 9,289.290; 10,63; 12,32 (the Deity); 19,297.

13. Also elsewhere in his account of Hezekiah's reforms, Josephus goes beyond the Bible in highlighting the presence/activity of the people as a whole; see below.

14. Josephus' other uses of the verb δημηγορέω are in *BJ* 2,619; *AJ* 8,226; 13,406; 19,333; *Vita* 92. Of these uses that of 8,226 is of particular interest since there it is conjoined with the participle συγκαλέσας just as it is here in 9,260. The verbal parallelism between 8,226 and 9,260 underscores the contrast between speakers and the content of their respective exhortations in the two passages: in the former it is the reprobate Jeroboam who is calling on the Israelites to abandon the service of the Jerusalem Temple, while in the latter Hezekiah summons the people of Judah to re-initiate worship at the Temple.

15. Throughout his rendition of 2 Chronicles 29-31, Josephus repeatedly leaves aside material that highlights the Levites over against the priests. On the point, see FELDMAN, *Hezekiah*, 601, n. 10 who explains his procedure in this regard in terms of Josephus' own status as a priest (see *Vita* 1) who, as such, would have found offputting the Chronicler's efforts at promoting a clerical grouping other than (and sometimes a rival to) his own. See further GLESSMER, *Leviten*, pp. 148-149 and C.T. BEGG, *David's Transfer of the Ark according to Josephus*, in *BBT* 7 (1997) 1-26, p. 14, n. 74 who calls attention to the similar *Tendenz* operative in Josephus' version of the story of the bringing of the ark to Jerusalem by David in *AJ* 7,78-89 vis-à-vis the Biblical sources, i.e. 2 Samuel 6 and, in particular, 1 Chronicles 13-16. Cf. chap. I on Josephus' downplaying of the Levites' role as featured in 2 Chronicles 19-20 in his version of these chapters in *AJ* 9,1-17.

tively, the Josephan speaker refers more specifically to the misdeeds of his own "father", Ahaz, thereby linking Hezekiah's address of 9,261-262 more closely to the preceding Ahaz story of 9,243-257. The Josephan Hezekiah thus begins (9,261) his address[16] as follows:

> You are not ignorant (οὐκ ἀγνοεῖτε) that it is on account of the sins (ἁμαρτίας) of my father, who transgressed against (παραβάντος)[17] the religion and worship (ὁσίαν καὶ[18] τιμήν)[19] of God[20], that you have experienced many and great misfortunes (ἐπειράθητε ... κακῶν)[21], *having been corrupted in mind* (διαφθαρέντες ... τὴν διάνοιαν)[22] *by him and persuaded to bow down* (προσκυνεῖν) *to those beings which he himself admitted as gods*[23].

Following his anticipation of the motivating retrospective of 29,6-9 in 9,261, Josephus next (9,262a) has the king deliver a version of his opening

16. Somewhat exceptionally, Josephus retains the direct address of the original throughout his rendition of Hezekiah's speech.

17. This term echoes the form παραβάς used of Ahaz' "violating his country's laws" in 9,243.

18. This conjunction is absent in the codices MSP; it is omitted by Dindorf, Bekker, and Naber (who likewise bracket the following term τιμήν).

19. The above collocation is hapax in Josephus. The noun τιμή as used here of Ahaz echoes the verbal forms employed of him in 9,256: "... he began to honour (τιμᾶν) the gods of the Assyrians, and seemed ready to honour (τιμήσων) any god rather than his fathers' God...".

20. The above accusation represents both a compression/generalization and a "re-application" to the individual Ahaz of Hezekiah's charges against the "ancestors" in 29,6-7: "For our fathers have been unfaithful, and have done what was evil in the sight of the Lord our God; they have forsaken him, and have turned away their faces from the habitation of the Lord and turned their backs. They also shut the doors of the vestibule and put out the lamps, and have not burned incense or offered burnt offerings in the holy place to the God of Israel". Here again, one may see Josephus' tendency to avoid or abridge Biblical "cultic specifics" at work; see further n. 36.

21. The expression "suffer (no) evils" recurs in *AJ* 4,132; 6,39.156; 7,84; 10,39.128; 11,155. Here in 9,261, it represents Josephus' generalization of Hezekiah's extended statement concerning the consequences of the "fathers'" transgression (29,6-7) in 29,8-9: "Therefore the wrath of the Lord came on Judah and Jerusalem, and he has made them an object of horror, of astonishment, and of hissing, as you see with your own eyes. For lo, *our fathers* have fallen by the sword and our sons and our daughters and our wives are in captivity for this". The foregoing words might well seem to (anchronistically) presuppose the actual destruction of Jerusalem and the exile of 587 B.C. as a *fait accompli* on Hezekiah's part. Josephus' substitute language has Hezekiah, in "historically" more appropriate terms, look back rather to the disasters Judah experienced under his father Ahaz; see 9,247.255-256.

22. For this phrase see p. 279, n. 16 on 9,222.

23. The reference here is to Ahaz' "sacrificing to idols" (9,243), as well as to his "worshipping" (σεβόμενος) the Syrian "gods" (θεούς) (9,255) and "honouring" (τιμᾶν) those of the Assyrians (9,256). Hezekiah's speech in 29,6-11 has no equivalent to the above sequence in which the king evokes his father's bad influence upon the people as a whole. The addition reflects the heightened importance given to the people in Josephus' version of the speech; see n. 13.

exhortation to the Levites (29,5): *"But now that you[24] have learned by experience how terrible a thing impiety* (δεινὸν τὸ ασεβεῖν)[25] *is*[26], *I urge* (παραινῶ) *you to put it out of your minds* (λήθην ποιήσασθαι)[27] *from now on*[28] and to purify (καθᾶραι) yourselves from your former pollutions (μιασμάτων)...[29]".

Up till this point, the Josephan Hezekiah has (9,261-262a) been address-ing himself to all those assembled by him in 9,260c without differentiation. In concluding his discourse, the king finally lays down specific directives (9,262b) for the two clerical groups making up part of his audience: "and in this manner let *the priests and* Levites[30] come together and open the tem-ple (ἀνοῖξαι τὸ ἱερόν)[31] and, by purifying (καθάραντας; see καθᾶραι, 9,262a) it *with the customary sacrifices* (ταῖς ἐξ ἔθους θυσίαις)[32], *restore*

24. As in what precedes, the addressee here continues to be the people as a whole (along with the priests and Levites); see 9260c and compare 29,5.

25. The phrase "terrible impiety" occurs only here in Josephus. Its verbal form ἀσεβεῖν echoes the adjective ἀσεβέστατος and the noun ἀσεβήμασιν used of Ahaz in 9,243 and 246, respectively (cf. ἀσεβήματα, of the Israelites, 9,250).

26. The above italicized sequence constitutes a motivating transition to Hezekiah's following exhortation to the people. It picks up on the king's earlier (see 9,261) evocation of their having "experienced many great misfortunes".

27. This phrase occurs twice elsewhere in Josephus: *AJ* 7,270; 17,353.

28. Also this element of Hezekiah's speech has no counterpart in the royal exhortation to the Levites of 29,5. It harks back to the king's reference to his father's corrupting influ-ence upon the minds of the people in 9,261.

29. The phrase "purify from pollution" recurs in *BJ* 6,48; *AJ* 5,42; 9,273; 12,286. In 2 Chr 29,5 Hezekiah's equivalent command "sanctify yourselves (B ἁγνίσθητε, L ἁγιάσθητε)" is addressed to the Levites (see v. 5αβ) whereas Josephus extends it here to encompass the entire populace; see nn. 13,23.

30. Hezekiah's speech as cited in 29,5-11 nowhere mentions the priests – who, along with the Levites, make up his audience according to 29,4 – as such. Josephus' insertion of an explicit reference to them here accords with his general tendency to "right the bal-ance" between priests and Levites throughout his reworking of material derived by him from Chronicles; see n. 15.

31. This phrase represents Josephus' "re-application" of the notice of 29,3 that Hezekiah himself "opened (BL ἀνέῳξε[ν]) the doors of the house of the Lord". See n. 9.

32. The above construction recurs in 9,263a and also in *BJ* 1,153. In 29,5 Hezekiah's command to the Levites is that they "sanctify (B ἁγνίσατε, L ἁγιάσατε) the house of the Lord", nothing being said of "sacrifices" as the means of effecting this. Josephus' men-tion of such sacrifices in conjunction with the previous royal directive about "opening the temple" constitutes a verbal echo/reversal of what he reports concerning Ahaz in 9,257: "he shut up the temple (τὸν ναόν) completely and forbade the offering of *the customary sacrifices* (νενομισμένας ... θυσίας – this last item, like Hezekiah's reference to "sacri-fices" in 9,262b, has no equivalent in the Chronicler's account of Ahaz; compare 28,24 which does speak of his closing the Temple's doors). See n. 43.

Josephus' royal speech has no parallel as such to the concluding directive given the Levites by Hezekiah in 29,5, i.e. "carry out the filth (BL τὴν ἀκαθαρσίαν) from the holy place". One might, however, see the king's earlier exhortation (9,262a) to the people as a whole to "purify yourselves from your former pollutions (μιασμάτων)" as a reminis-cence of this item.

it to the ancient service of our country (εἰς τὴν ἀρχαίαν καὶ πάτριαν[33] ... τιμήν [see 9,260])...[34]". Finally, Josephus rounds off the royal speech with mention, inspired by the king's concluding words according to 29,10, of the purpose behind the measures Hezekiah has just enjoined: "... for in this way we might make (ποιήσαμεν) God put aside His anger (ἀφέντα τὴν ὀργήν)[35] *and become gracious* (εὐμενῆ)[36]".

b) *Hezekiah's Directives Accomplished.* 2 Chr 29,12-19 relates, with considerable circumstantiality, the carrying out by the priests and Levites of the orders given them by Hezekiah in 29,4-11. Josephus drastically abridges the former account[37]. In place thereof he presents

33. The above terms are associated as well as in *AJ* 10,72; 12,280.301; cf. 18,11. The adjective ἀρχαῖος constitutes a kind of *Leitwort* in Josephus' account of Hezekiah's reforms, recurring in 9,264.274. See FELDMAN, *Studies*, p. 372 (= ID., *Hezekiah*, 607). As for the other component of the above collocation, i.e. πάτριον, this echoes, *in bonam partem*, language used by Josephus of Ahaz in negative fashion; see 9,243 (Ahaz "violated his country's [πατρίους] laws") and 257 (Ahaz "seemed ready to honour any god rather than his fathers' [πατρῷον] God").

34. This indication as to the intended effect/outcome of the prescribed purificatory sacrifices has no counterpart as such in the Biblical Hezekiah's speech. It does, however, serve to introduce a key emphasis of the historian's entire version of the royal reforms, i.e. the return to ancient (and legitimate) religious ways; see previous note.

35. The phrase "leave (off) anger" recurs in *BJ* 1,665; *AJ* 6,304; 7,184.186. Only here in 9,262, however, does it have God as subject. The noun ὀργή here echoes the participle ὀργιζόμενος used of God's being "wrathful" towards Ahaz in 9,256.

36. The expression "make God gracious" used above has a counterpart in 10,59 where Josiah enjoins the delegation he dispatches to Huldah to have her "attempt to win His (God's) favour (ποιεῖν εὐμενῆ)". The term "gracious" employed of God here in 9,262 likewise echoes – now positively – the statement made of Hoshea in 9,259, i.e. "he did not have God propitious (εὐμενῆ) to him": what Hoshea lacked, Hezekiah hopes to obtain through his reform initiatives.

With the above concluding words of 9,262 compare those attributed to Hezekiah in 29,10b: "... that his (God's) fierce anger (BL ὀργήν, so 9,262b) may turn away from us". Josephus' version of the royal speech passes over what precedes in 29,10a, i.e. Hezekiah's statement of intention: "Now it is in my heart to make a covenant with the Lord, the God of Israel". This omission is perhaps inspired by the consideration that, in the continuation of the Chronicler's account, we hear nothing, as such, about the realization of this intention (note further that whereas in 29,10 it is Hezekiah's personal initiative of covenant-making which will lead to the turning away of God's anger ["it is in *my heart*... that..."] in 9,262b this same result is to be achieved via the effort of the entire community ["in this way *we* might make God put aside His anger..."] – yet another indication of the importance accorded the people in Josephus' rewriting of 29,4-11). Josephus likewise leaves aside the concluding exhortation of 29,11, addressed to "my sons", wherein Hezekiah urges the Levites (see 29,5aβ) (and priests?) not to be negligent in carrying out their various, God-given cultic responsibilities. This further omission goes together with the historian's non-reproduction of the (negative) cultic particulars enumerated in 29,7; see n. 20.

37. In particular, he leaves aside the "Levitical unit" 29,12-15 which features the names of 15 Levites (and the groupings to which they belong) who responded to Hezekiah's summons (cf. 29,5aβ). This omission is in line both with Josephus' tendency to

(9,263a) a summary "execution notice" whose wording closely parallels that of Hezekiah's directives to the priests and Levites as cited by him in 9,262b: *"When the king had spoken these words,* the priests[38] opened the temple (ἀνοίγουσι ... τὸ ἱερόν; compare ἀνοῖξαι τὸ ἱερόν, 9,262b)[39], and, *after opening it,* made ready the vessels of God (τὰ σκεύη τοῦ θεοῦ ηὐτρέπισαν[40])[41], and, having got rid of all the pollutions (τὰ μιάσματα ἐκβαλόντες; compare καθᾶραι ... ἐκ τῶν ... μιασμάτων, 9,262b)[42], *they offered up the accustomed sacrifices* (τὰς ἐξ ἔθους ... θυσίας; see 9,262b) on the altar (τῷ βωμῷ)[43]".

downplay the Levites' pre-eminent role in Hezekiah's reforms as reported by the Chronicler (see n. 15) and his more general practice of sparing Gentile readers extended Biblical lists of names. In the same vein, he passes over the mention made in 29,16bβ of the Levites' transporting to the brook Kidron the "uncleanness" which the priests had previously removed from the Temple (see 29,16abα). He likewise dispenses, as such, with the report given Hezekiah by the cultic personnel as cited in 29,18-19, perhaps because in that report the speakers refer to their having done things other than those which they are described as actually doing in the preceding 29,16-17 (he does, however, draw on the wording of that report in several instances; see below). Finally, Josephus makes no use of the chronological indications of v. 17 concerning the duration of the Temple cleansing process (recall that he earlier, 9,260b, substituted more general wording for the precise dating of Hezekiah's speech as given in 29,3; see n. 10).

38. Note that whereas Hezekiah's directives in 9,262b concern both the "priests and Levites", it is only the former group who are mentioned as carrying these out here in 9,263a. Once again, Josephus, the priest, reverses the Chronicler's own accentuation of the Levites at the expense of the priests (compare the extended "Levitical unit", 29,12-15, to which Josephus has no parallel; see previous note).

39. Compare 29,16a: "the priests went into the inner part of the house of the Lord...".

40. This verbal form is absent in ROM Lat and is not printed by Niese.

41. Josephus derives his mention of the priests' "preparation" of the cultic "vessels" from the report – not reproduced by him as such; see n. 37 – made to Hezekiah in 29,18-19 where there is threefold reference to the Temple "vessels" (BL τὰ σκεύη). In thus directly conjoining the priests' entry into the Temple (= 29,16a) and their preparing of the vessels (cf. 29,18-19), Josephus "delays" an item which in 29,16 follows immediately upon mention of the priests' entry, i.e. their removal of the Temple's "uncleanness" (see 29,16bα). In his presentation this item appears only after the intervening notice, drawn from 29,18-19, concerning the preparation of the vessels.

42. The above item represents Josephus' equivalent to the notice of 29,16bα: "and they (i.e. the priests; see 29,16a) brought out (BL ἐξέβαλον; cf. ἐκβαλόντες, 9,263a) all the uncleanness (BL ἀκαθαρσίαν) that they found in the house of the Lord *into the court of the house of the Lord*". To be noted is that, whereas both Hezekiah's directive (9,262b) and the notice of its execution (9,263a), in Josephus' presentation, do speak of an elimination of "pollutions", in the former it is the community as a whole which is to effect this, while in the latter it is the priests alone who actually do so.

43. The above reference to "sacrifice" has no counterpart in the narrative of 29,12-19 itself (although there are frequent mentions of such in what follows; see 29,20-36). On the other hand, the reference does correspond to Hezekiah's – likewise Biblically unparalleled – directive that the priests and Levites are to purify the Temple "with the accustomed sacrifices" in 9,262b; see n. 32. As for the added specification that the sacrifices were offered "on the altar" in 9,263a, Josephus may have found inspiration for this in the concluding words of the cultic officers' report to Hezekiah in 29,19, i.e.: "and behold they [the Temple vessels] are before the altar (BL τοῦ θυσιαστηρίου) of the Lord". On

c) *Hezekiah's Passover Summons*. The Chronicler continues his account of the cleansing of the Temple with a lengthy narration (29,20-36) of the various rituals that were performed subsequent to the cultic officers' report to Hezekiah that the edifice and its equipment had been restored to proper order (29,18-19). For reasons that will be discussed below, Josephus departs from the Chronicler's sequence at this juncture. In his own presentation, the brief description of the fulfillment of Hezekiah's directives in 9,263a is followed immediately by an episode which comes only later in Chronicles, i.e. Hezekiah's Passover summons and the response this evokes, 2 Chr 30,1-12, to which his parallel is 9,263b-267. Only thereafter, in 9,268-270, does he pick up the content of 2 Chr 29,20-36.

2 Chr 30,1 stands as a kind of title to the following narrative, stating that Hezekiah sent "to all Israel and Judah", urging their attendance at the Passover celebration to be held at the Temple in Jerusalem. Josephus (9,263b-264) elaborates this notice into a description of two separate "missions" dispatched by the king. Of these, the first – contrary to the sequence of 30,1 itself – is directed (9,263b) to Judah: "Then the king sent messengers throughout his realm, summoning the people to Jerusalem to celebrate the festival of Unleavened Bread (τὴν τῶν ἀζύμων ἑορτήν)[44], *which had for a long time been allowed to lapse through the lawless action* (παρανομίας) *of the kings previously mentioned*[45]". Hezekiah's other embassy has the population of the North as its designated recipients (9,264): "He also sent messengers to the Israelites...[46]". As for the content of the king's message to them, Josephus draws this from the envoys' address to the Israelites as cited in 30,6-9[47]. In his ren-

---

Josephus' usage of the two Greek words for "altar" (θυσιαστήριον and βωμός) and his differences with (various books of) the LXX in this regard, see BEGG, *Early Divided Monarchy*, p. 42, n. 209.

44. In 30,1 the people are summoned to observe "the *passover* to the Lord the God of Israel". Josephus draws his alternative name for the feast from the continuation of the Biblical account where this designation does occur; see 30,13.

45. This appended qualification concerning the feast to be celebrated has no equivalent in 30,1. It takes the place of the motivation given for the "late" observance of Passover cited in 30,3: "they could not keep it [the Passover] in its time because the priests had not sanctified themselves in sufficient number nor had the people assembled in Jerusalem"; cf. also 30,5: "... for they had not kept it [the Passover] in great numbers as prescribed". On Josephus' omission of the whole of 30,2-5; see n. 47.

46. Compare the more differentiated wording of 30,1a: "Hezekiah sent to all Israel... and wrote letters also to Ephraim and Manasseh".

47. In so doing he passes over the intervening material of 30,2-5 which has the following content: general decision to keep Passover in the second month (v. 2); motivation for this decision (v. 3); approbation of the plan by king and assembly (v. 4); king and assemble decide to issue a nation-wide summons to a Passover observance in Jerusalem (v. 5). Various reasons for Josephus' non-utilization of this material may be

dition, their appeal opens with a distillation, echoing language earlier used by Hezekiah himself in 9,261-262, of the sequence of generalized admonitions making up 30,6-8: "... exhorting them [the Israelites][48] to give up their present manner of life (ἀφέντας τὸν ... βίον)[49] and return to their ancient custom (εἰς τὴν ἀρχαίαν ἐπανελθεῖν συνήθειαν)[50] and reverence God (σέβειν τὸν θεόν)...[51]". He then has the messengers continue in more specific terms, these recalling the summons issued the Judeans in 9,263b: "... for, he said, he would permit them to come and celebrate the festival of Unleavened Bread and join in their festal assembly (συμπανηγυρίζειν)[52]". Thereafter, he concludes the envoys' address with a word

proposed. Since he has omitted the chronological indications of 2 Chronicles 29 (see vv. 3,17) dating the Temple cleansing over the course of the first month of the year, any need to have Passover celebrated, not in the normal first, but rather in the second month (so 30,2) disappears in his presentation of Hezekiah's initiatives. In addition, Rabbinic tradition (see b. Pesaḥ. 56a) records criticism of Hezekiah for calendar manipulation and Josephus might be trying to preclude such criticism by omitting all mention of a second-month date for Hezekiah's Passover, thereby also sparing Gentile readers details of Jewish observance that would not likely be either of interest or intelligible to them. A further factor operative in Josephus' omission of 30,2-5 would be the critique of the priesthood evident in the assertion of v. 3 that the Passover could not be celebrated on time due to the priests' failure to "sanctify themselves in sufficient numbers". Here, as throughout his rewriting of 2 Chronicles 29-31, Josephus deals with such denigrations of his own cultic order by simply eliminating them; see n. 9.

The overall effect of Josephus' omission of 30,2-5 is to accentuate the stature of Hezekiah who initiates the Passover "missions" entirely on his own, without consultation with/approval by the princes and the assembly (compare 30,4).

48. As so often elsewhere, Josephus recasts the direct address of 30,6-9 in indirect address.

49. This phrase occurs only here in Josephus. It contains a certain echo of the expression used by Hezekiah of God in 9,262, i.e. ἀφέντα τὴν ὀργήν.

50. This element of the messengers' word echoes Hezekiah's exhortation to the priests and Levites that they restore the Temple "to the ancient (ἀρχαίαν) service of our country" in 9,262b. Cf. n. 33. Josephus' one other use of the above expression "ancient custom" is in AJ 16,166.

51. This phrase has a (negative) counterpart in 9,261 where Hezekiah speaks of his father's having "transgressed against the religion (ὁσίαν) and worship (τιμήν) of God". It likewise echoes the notice of 9,255 that Ahaz "continued to reverence (σεβόμενος) these [the Syrian gods]". Compare the envoys' exhortations to the Israelites according to the Chronicler: "return to the Lord (30,6)... yield yourselves to the Lord... and serve (BL δουλέσατε) the Lord" (30,8).

From the envoys' exhortations in 30,6-9 Josephus omits the references to the disasters which the Northerners had already experienced at the hand of the Assyrians (see vv. 6-7,9) as a result of God's wrath against them (cf. v. 8) which seem to presuppose the calamity of 721 as a fait accompli. His omission of these elements likely has in view the fact that, according to the sequence of his own presentation, Israel has not yet succumbed to Assyria; see n. 53.

52. The verb συμπανγυρίζω is hapax in Josephus. The above formulation represents a specification, inspired by the wording of 30,1 (= 9,263b), of the envoys' exhortation "come to his (God's) sanctuary" (30,8).

of assurance by Hezekiah without parallel in 30,6-9[53], i.e. "This, he said, he was proposing (παραινεῖν), not that they might become subject (ὑποακούσωσιν) to him against their will, but because it was for their own good (συμφέροντος; cf. συμφορώτερον, 9,260b and 9,255 where Ahaz is said to be unmindful of his own good [συμφέροντος]) and would, he added, make them happy (μακαρίους)[54]".

2 Chr 30,10-11 describes the Israelites' response to the envoys' message as both negative (v. 10) and positive (v. 11). Josephus elaborates particularly on the former point. In so doing he begins (9,265a) by reproducing the content of 30,10: "However, when the envoys came and brought them this message from their king, the Israelites *were not only not persuaded* (οὐκ ἐπείσθησαν), but even laughed (ἐχλεύασαν) at his envoys *as fools* (ἀνοήτους)...[55]". To this notice he then adds, however, a reference to an – equally unsuccessful – attempt at seconding the envoys' words, this time by the Israelites' own prophets. This extended Josephan "appendix" (9,265b-266) reads:

(265) and when their prophets (προφήτας) exhorted (παραινοῦντας)[56] them in like manner and foretold (προλέγοντας) what they would suffer

53. In 30,9 the envoys conclude their speech with a motivating assurance concerning, not the king's intentions with regard to the Israelites (so Josephus; see above), but rather those of God himself: "... if you return to the Lord, your brethren and your children will find compassion with their captors, and return to this land. For the Lord your God is gracious and merciful, and will not turn away his face from you, if you return to him". Once again, one may observe Josephus' "de-theologizing" tendency at work here, as also his concern not to "get ahead of himself" by making use of source references to the Exile of 721 which, in his own presentation, has not yet been narrated; see n. 51.

54. The above affirmation is designed to allay any suspicions his Northern audience might have about Hezekiah's political designs on them, making clear that his concern is exclusively with their own (spiritual) well-being. The inclusion of such an assurance in the message given the Israelites heightens their guilt in summarily dismissing it, as the majority of them will do; see below. On Josephus' intent with his insertion of this assurance see further FELDMAN, *Studies*, p. 368 (= ID., *Hezekiah*, 604). The wording of the above assurance likewise establishes a contrast between Hezekiah and his ancestor Amaziah who in 9,196 is represented as commanding that Joash of Israel "submit (ὑποκούειν) to him with all his people, just as formerly they had submitted (ὑπήκουε) to his forefathers David and Solomon...".

55. There is an ironic wordplay between the use of this term here in 9,265 and its application in 9,255 to King Ahaz who is said to be so "stupid" (ἀνόητος) that he continued to worship the gods of the Syrians even when at war with them. Ahaz manifested his "foolishness" by worshipping gods other than the Lord; in their rejecting the envoys' appeal to "worship God" (9,264) as "foolish" (9,265), the Israelites show themselves to be the real "fools".

With the entire above sequence compare the wording of 30,10: "So the couriers went from city to city through the country of Ephraim and Manasseh, and as far as Zebulun; but they laughed them to scorn (BL καταγελῶντες αὐτῶν) and mocked them (BL καταμωκῶμενοι [L + καὶ μυκτηρίζοντες αὐτούς])".

56. This is the same verb used of Hezekiah's "proposing" (παραινεῖν) to the Israelites, via his envoys, that they amend their ways in 9,264b (cf. also παραινῶ used of

350   AJ 9,260-276

(πείσονται)⁵⁷ if they did not alter their course to one of piety toward God (μεταθέμενοι πρὸς τὴν εὐσέβειαν τοῦ θεοῦ)⁵⁸, they poured scorn (literally: spat, διέπτυον)⁵⁹ upon them and finally seized them and killed them⁶⁰. (266) And not stopping even at these acts of lawlessness (παρανομοῦσιν; see παρανομίας, 9,263), they devised things still worse than those mentioned, and did not leave off until God punished them for their impiety (ἀμυνόμενος τῆς ἀσεβείας [cf. τὸ ἀσεβεῖν, 9,262])⁶¹ by making them subject (ὑποχειρίους) to their enemies (πολεμίοις)⁶². But of these things we shall write farther on⁶³.

Hezekiah's "urging" his Judean hearers in 9,262). The verbal link underscores the identity of the message which the Israelites hear first from Hezekiah, then from their own prophets.

57. The above sequence "the prophets exhorted... and foretold what they would suffer" is echoed in 9,281 (= 2 Kgs 17,13-14): "To such an end then did the Israelites come because... they disregarded the prophets (προφητῶν) who foretold (προύλεγον) that this misfortune would come upon them...". It likewise finds a counterpart in the report of Huldah's response to Josiah's delegation as cited in 10,60 "... (the people had not repented) although the prophets exhorted (τῶν προφητῶν ... παραινούντων) them to act thus wisely and foretold (προλεγόντων) the punishment for their impious deeds...". (as in 9,265 Josephus' generalized mention of "prophets" here in 10,60 has no counterpart as such in the Biblical source(s), i.e. the citation of Huldah's discourse in 2 Kgs 22,15-20 // 2 Chr 34,23-28). Finally, with the above, interjected reference to the Northern "prophets", compare Josephus inserted reference "as the prophets say" in his version of the Israelite leaders' words of warning (2 Chr 28,13) in 9,250.

58. This construction occurs only here in Josephus. Recall the characterization of Hezekiah himself as εὐσεβής in 9,260b.

59. Josephus' one remaining use of the verb διαπτύω comes in AJ 1,166 which speaks of Abraham's "exposing" (διαπτύων) as false the arguments of the contending Egyptian parties.

60. The function of the above sequence is to accentuate the Israelites' guilt (and the resultant deservedness of the punishment that will subsequently befall them) in failing to heed Hezekiah's appeal: in rejecting that appeal, they disregard the words, not only of some "foreign" king, but even of their own prophets. Where, though, might Josephus have found inspiration for his mention of the Israelite prophets' warning message and the hearers' negative response to this? I suggest that he did so in the notice of 2 Kgs 17,13-15 (= 9,281) which itself constitutes part of a long reflection on the causes of the Northern Kingdom's demise, 17,7-23. The verses in question read: "The Lord warned Israel and Judah by every prophet and seer, saying 'turn from your evil ways and keep my commandments and my statutes...'. But they would not listen, but were stubborn, as their fathers had been... They despised his statutes and his covenant... and the warnings which he gave them...". In anticipating these statements of 2 Kings 17 here, Josephus makes them function as part of a foreshadowing aitiology of Israel's destruction, which happening he will relate in 9,277-291. See further the continuation of Josephus' "insertion" in 9,265b-266 below.

61. The construction "punish impiety" occurs only here in Josephus. Cf., however, the similar phrase ἀμυνεῖται τῆς ἀδικίας (here with "the Deity" as subject) in AJ 2,293.

62. Note the irony implicit in Josephus' wording here: the Israelites contemptuously reject Hezekiah's overture which had in view, not their being made "subject" (ὑπακούσωσιν) to him, but rather "their own good" (9,264). As a result, they end up becoming "subject" (ὑποχειρίους)"to their enemies" who certainly did not have "good" at heart (9,266).

63. The above sequence "and not stopping... we shall write farther on" of 9,266 serves to prepare Josephus' account of the Assyrian annihilation of the Northern Kingdom in 9,277-291.

Following his lengthy inserted appendix to 30,10 in 9,265b-266, Josephus picks up (9,267) the notice of 30,11 (the affirmative response to Hezekiah's response by some Northerners) accentuating its positive character: "However, many[64] of the tribes of Manasseh, Zabulon and *Issachar*[65] heeded (πεισθέντες)[66] the prophets' exhortations (οἷς οἱ προφῆται παρήνεσαν)[67] and were converted to piety (εἰς εὐσέβειαν μετεβάλοντο)[68]. And all these flocked (συνέδραμον)[69] to Jerusalem *that they might worship God* (ὅπως τῷ θεῷ προσκυνήσωσιν)[70]".

64. This indication concerning the numbers of those Northerners who respond positively to Hezekiah's appeal contrasts with the mention in 30,11 of "(some/a few) men" who did so.

65. Josephus' listing of three tribes, some of whose members responded positively to Hezekiah's appeal here, agrees with that given in 30,11 for what concerns Manasseh and Zebulun, whereas he replaces the Biblical mention of "Asher" with "Issachar". (Conceivably, this substitution is inspired by the back-to-back coupling of "Zebulun" and "Issachar" in Gen 49,13-14 and Deut 33,18.) This is Josephus' only mention of specific Northern names by Josephus in the context of his version of 2 Chr 30,1-12. Compare 30,1 (cf. 9,264) which cites "Ephraim and Manasseh" as recipients of Hezekiah's letters and 30,10 (cf. 9,265a) which relates that the royal messengers ranged over "Ephraim and Manasseh and as far as Zebulun".

66. The use of this term here in 9,267 introduces a positive contrast to 9,265a where Josephus states that the Israelites in general were "not persuaded (ἐπείσθησαν)" by the envoys' message.

67. This phrase echoes the wording of 9,265b: "their prophets exhorted (τοὺς προφήτας ... παραινοῦντας) them".

68. The above construction "convert to piety" occurs only here in Josephus. Also this formulation looks back to the wording of 9,265b where the prophets warn of what the Northerners will suffer "if they did not alter their course to one of piety (μεταθέμενοι πρὸς τὴν εὐσέβειαν) toward God". In accord with his earlier presentation (see 9,265b-266) with its interjected reference to the intervention of the Israelite prophets, Josephus thus has some Israelites' responding positively to the "prophets' exhortations". Contrast 30,11 where the Israelites' "self-humbling" is in response to the Judean envoys' appeal as cited in 30,10. The difference evidences, once again, Josephus' tendency to accentuate the prophetic role in his people's history.

69. Josephus' verb for the Israelites' initiative here is more dramatic than the nondescript "they came (BL ἦλθον)" of 30,11.

70. This specification concerning the purpose of the Northerners' coming to Jerusalem lacks a counterpart in 30,11. It does, however, echo contentually Hezekiah's appeal that the Israelites "reverence God (σέβειν τὸν θεόν)" of 9,264, thereby signifying that the king's appeal has had at least a partial success. It further evokes a contrast with Hezekiah's statement to the Judeans in 9,261, i.e. Ahaz had persuaded them "to bow down (προσκυνεῖν) to those beings which he himself admitted as gods".

Josephus leaves aside the "theological notice" of 30,12 which concludes the pericope on Hezekiah's Passover summons (30,1-12): "The hand of God was also upon Judah to give them one heart to do what the king and the princes [see 30,3] commanded by the word of the Lord". In addition to Josephus' general tendency to "de-theologize" (see n. 53), this omission might also be explained in terms of the historian's supposing that the Judeans' positive response to their own king's summons to them (see 9,263 = 30,1) would be a matter of course that, as such, would hardly require the divine intervention spoken of in 30,12.

d) *Sacrifices Offered*. Having completed his "anticipated" version of 30,1-12 in 9,263-267, Josephus now (9,268-270) presents his rendition of 29,20-36, the Chronicler's account of the sacrifices and accompanying rites that followed upon the purification of the Temple as described in 29,12-19 (= 9,263a). Within the segment 29,20-36 itself, one may further distinguish three subunits, i.e. vv. 20-24 (initial sacrifices), 25-30 (musical accompaniment), and 31-36 (additional sacrifices) to each of which Josephus has an (abridged) equivalent.

2 Chr 29,20-24 relates, in rather repetitious detail, the various categories of and figures for the victims offered by the priests at Hezekiah's direction. Josephus' compressed rendering of this material (9,268) opens with a notice, paralleling 29,20, concerning a general movement to the newly cleansed Temple: *"when they came*[71], Hezekiah went up to the temple (ἀναβὰς εἰς τὸ ἱερόν) with the chiefs (ἡγεμόνων) *and all the people* (λαοῦ)...[72]". He then continues with a enumeration, drawn from 29,21a, of four categories of victims that were offered at this juncture: "and [he, i.e. Hezekiah] sacrificed (ἔθυσεν) *as his own offering*[73] seven bullocks (ταύρους; BL μόσχους) and as many rams (κριούς = BL), and seven lambs (ἄρνας; BL ἀμνούς) and as many kids (ἐρίφους; BL χιμάρους, he-goats)[74]".

71. The subject of this transitional phrase is the responsive Israelites spoken of in 9,267. Perhaps, the reference – unparalleled in the source text 29,20 – to this group here at the opening of 9,268 intimates a rationale for Josephus' above-mentioned "reversal" of the sequence of 29,20-36 and 30,1-12, i.e. he desires to depict the rituals cited in the former text as carried out with the participation of both Judeans and Israelites, rather than of the former alone (as is the case in the Biblical presentation). Such a concern would be in line with the historian's preoccupation with the issue of Jewish (dis-)unity that is evident throughout his writings.

72. Compare 29,20: "Then Hezekiah the king rose early and gathered the officials of the city (BL τοὺς ἄρχοντας τῆς πόλεως) and went up to the house of the Lord (BL ἀνέβη εἰς οἶκον Κυρίου)". Josephus' inserted reference to the presence of the "people" at this juncture corresponds to his introduction of them as co-addressees of Hezekiah's opening discourse in 9,260b alongside the priests and Levites (so 29,4). Perhaps, Josephus was inspired to make mention of the "people" here at the start of his parallel to 29,20-24 in view of that passage's subsequent reference to "the assembly" (see v. 23).

73. In making Hezekiah (alone) the one to present the victims here Josephus agrees with BL 29,21 which use singular verbs (B ἀνήνεγκεν, L ἀνήγαγεν) in reference to the "bringing" of the sacrifices as against MT's plural "they [i.e. the king and officials, 29,20] brought" (so also *VL, TC*). At the same time, Josephus further accentuates the king's piety in personally providing the victims with his insertion of the phrase "as his own offering". See n. 86.

74. From 29,21 Josephus leaves aside its concluding specification that the "he-goats" were intended as "a sin-offering for the kingdom and for the sanctuary and for Judah", a specification re-iterated in vv. 23-24. Perhaps, he supposes that the purificatory "sacrifices", mention of which he introduces in 9,262-263 (see above), had already served as such "sin offerings". In any event, the omission here does correspond to his tendency to dispense with Biblical cultic details for the sake of Gentile readers. See n. 87.

The Biblical account continues in 29,21b-22 with the priests, at Hezekiah's direction (v. 21b), killing and offering the blood of (v. 22) the first three categories of victims cited in v. 21a. Thereafter, vv. 23-24a relate, first an imposition of hands upon, and then the ritual slaughter of the fourth category of v. 21a, i.e. the he-goats, while v. 24b rounds off the whole sequence with a renewed reference (see v. 21b) to the king's "commanding" the offering of the sacrifices. Josephus conflates (9,268b) the Bible's separate handling of the two sets of victims into a single notice: "Then the king himself and the chiefs (ἡγεμόνες; see 9,268a) placed their hands (ἐπιθέντες ... τὰς χεῖρας) *on the heads* of the victims (τῶν ἱερείων)[75] and allowed the priests to complete the sacrifice auspiciously (καλλιερεῖν)[76]".

The second sub-unit within 2 Chr 29,20-36 is vv. 25-30; here the focus shifts from the sacrificing priests to the Levites and their musical activity. Josephus (9,269) both shortens and re-arranges the (highly repetitious) content of this passage. He begins (9,269a) his rendition with a parallel to its core component, i.e. v. 27b, amplifying this with elements drawn from elsewhere in the pericope: "And so, while these [i.e. the priests, see 9,268b] sacrificed (ἔθυον; cf. ἔθυσεν [of Hezekiah], 9,268) and offered up whole burnt-offerings (ὡλοκαύτουν)[77], the Levites, who stood round about with their musical instruments (ὀργάνων)[78], sang hymns (ᾖδον ὕμνους) to God[79] and played their harps (ἔψαλλον) as

75. Compare 29,23: "Then the he-goats for the sin-offering were brought to the king and the assembly (BL τῆς ἐκκλησίας), and they laid their hands (BL ἐπέθηκαν τὰς χεῖρας) upon them". In Josephus' presentation all four groups of animals (designated collectively as "the victims" by him) have hands laid upon them, the ones doing so being the king and the "chiefs", rather than Hezekiah and "the assembly" (perhaps, given his opening mention of the presence of the "people" in 9,268, Josephus supposes that the chiefs act as their representatives for the imposition of hands procedure).

76. Josephus' other uses of the verb καλλιερέω are in *BJ* 7,155; *AJ* 8,108; 9,271; 10,64; 12,146. Compare 29,21b: "he [Hezekiah] commanded (literally: said) the priests the sons of Aaron to offer (BL ἀναβαίνειν) them [i.e. the four categories of victims cited in v. 21a] on the altar of the Lord". Josephus leaves aside the (repetitious) "execution notice" of v. 22 with its triple mention of the slaughtering of the various groups of victims and the throwing of their blood against the altar by the priests, as also that of v. 24a regarding the disposition of the he-goats.

77. The above collocation "sacrifice and offer whole burnt-offerings" recurs, in reverse order, in *AJ* 3,245.

78. This element conflates 29,26a: "The Levites stood with the instruments (BL ὀργάνοις) of David" and the concluding words of 29,27: "... (accompanying) the instruments (BL ὄργανα) of David king of Israel".

79. The above sequence represents a conflation of the double reference to the "song" accompanying the sacrifices in 29,27bα ("and when the burnt offering began [BL ὁλοκαύτωσιν], the song [BL ᾄδειν] of the Lord also began") and 28aβ ("and the singers sang [BL οἱ ψαλτῳδοὶ ᾄδοντες]").

they had been instructed (ἐδιδάχθησαν) by David[80], and the other [i.e. those not engaged in sacrificing] priests blew (ἐπεσάλπιζον)[81] the trumpets (βυκάνας)[82] they carried, and accompanied those who sang (ὑμνῳδοῦσι)[83]". Basing himself on vv. 28aα,29, he then (9,269b) describes the response of the remaining participants to the cultic offi- cers' activities as related in what precedes: "After this was done, the king and the people (τὸ πλῆθος; compare the designation λαός used in 9,268) threw themselves on their faces (ἐπὶ πρόσωπον ῥίψαντες)[84] and did obeisance to God (προσεκύνουν τὸν θεόν; compare ὅπως τῷ θεῷ προσκυνήσωσιν, 9,267)[85]".

The Chronicler rounds off his account of the Temple's restoration with a rather extended catalogue of additional sacrifices (compare vv. 20-24) that were offered on this occasion, 29,31-36. Here again, Josephus acts to compress the source's highly circumstantial presentation, likewise con- centrating attention on the figure of Hezekiah. Thus while 29,31-33 rep- resents the assembly as supplying sacrificial victims in abundance in response to the king's appeal, the historian has (9,270a) Hezekiah provide these himself for the benefit of his people: "Then he sacrificed (θύει)[86]

80. This item – unparalleled in 29,27b itself – is drawn rather from 29,25 which states that Hezekiah "stationed the Levites in the house of the Lord with cymbals, harps (BL νάβλαις) and lyres, according to the command (BL κατὰ τὴν ἐντολήν) of David". Jose- phus leaves aside the continuation of v. 25: "... (according to the command of David) and of Gad the king's seer, and of Nathan the prophet for the commandment was from the Lord through his prophets" – still another instance of his "de-theologizing" of the pro- ceedings.

81. Josephus' one other use of the verb ἐπισαλπίζω is in AJ 7,356.

82. Josephus uses the word βυκάνη twice elsewhere, i.e. AJ 3,291.294.

83. Elsewhere in the Josephan corpus, the verb ὑμνῳδέω occurs only as a variant reading in AJ 12,349; here, it echoes the noun ὕμνους used earlier in 9,269a. The above, single reference to the priest-trumpeters represents a conflation of the Chronicler's triple reference to them in 29,26-28, see vv. 26b ("the priests with their trumpets [BL σάλπιγξιν]"), 27b ("and the trumpets, accompanied by the instruments of David the king") and 28aγ ("and the trumpeters sounded [BL σάλπιζουσαι]").

84. This construction occurs only here in Josephus.

85. The above sequence conflates the notices of 29,28aα ("the whole assembly wor- shiped [BL προσεκύνει]") and 29 ("when the offering was finished, the king and all who were present with him bowed themselves and worshiped [BL προσεκύνησαν]"). Continuing to play down the Levites' role in Hezekiah's reforms, Josephus leaves aside the appended notice of 29,30 ("And Hezekiah the king and the princes commanded the Levites to sing praises to the Lord with the words of David and of Asaph the seer. And they sang praises with gladness and they bowed down and worshiped") with its repetition of what has been said previously in vv. 25-29.

86. The use of this verb with Hezekiah as subject echoes 9,268 where, again in con- trast to the source (see 29,21), the king alone is represented as the one to sacrifice (ἔθυσεν); see n. 73. Compare 29,31b-32: "and the assembly brought sacrifices and thank offerings; and all who were of a willing heart brought burnt offerings. The number of the burnt offerings which the assembly brought...".

seventy oxen (βοῦς; BL 29,32 μόσχοι), a hundred rams (κριούς; BL κριοί) and two hundred lambs (ἄρνας; BL ἀμνοί)[87], and *presented the people* (τῷ πλήθει [see τὸ πλῆθος, 9,269b]... ἐχαρίσατο) with six hundred oxen (βοῦς; BL 29,33 μόσχοι) and three thousand cattle (θρέμματα) of other kinds [compare BL πρόβατα, sheep], *for them to feast on* (πρός εὐωχίαν)[88]".

In 29,34 the Chronicler interjects a characteristic editorial comment into his account of the ritual proceedings: "But the priests were too few and could not flay all the burnt offerings, so until other priests had sanctified themselves their brethren the Levites helped them, until the work was finished – for the Levites were more upright in heart than the priests in sanctifying themselves [cf. 29,4.15]". As might be expected, the priest Josephus takes care to give (9,270b) this notice a quite other content – one wherein the Levites disappear completely: "And the priests performed all things in accordance with the law (ἀκολούθως ... τῷ νόμῳ)[89]".

The segment 29,31-36 concludes in v. 36a with mention of the "rejoicing" of king and people over what the Lord had done for the latter. In line with his earlier procedure (see on 9,268a.270a), Josephus (9,270c) focusses attention on the person of Hezekiah alone: "With this [i.e. the priests' performance][90] the king was well-pleased, *and feasted* (εὐωχεῖτο) *with the people* (τοῦ λαοῦ; see

---

87. Josephus leaves aside the specification of 29,32 that the three categories of victims cited there (and by himself here in 9,270) were intended as "burnt offerings". Compare his similar handling of the designation of the he-goats ("kids" in his presentation) as a "sin offering" (so 29,21.23-24) in 9,268; see n. 74.

88. Compare 29,33 where the two categories of animals mentioned are designated as "consecrated offerings" (BL οἱ ἡγιασμένοι) and where, these, like the "burnt offerings" of 29,32, seem to be supplied by the assembly itself. Josephus' reworking of this notice such that the king becomes the one to supply the victims to the people for feasting purposes perhaps stands under the influence of his account of Solomon's dedication of the Temple; see *AJ* 8,123: "... this was the first time that he [Solomon] gave the temple a portion of victims, and all the Hebrews with their women and children feasted (κατευωχήθησαν) therein". Cf. the reference to Solomon in 9,272 below. The above phrase πρὸς εὐωχίαν likewise echoes *AJ* 9,16 (following his victorious return to Jerusalem King Jehoshaphat "gave himself up to feasting [πρὸς εὐωχίας] for many days").

89. Compare his comparable handling of the Chronicler's account of the purification of the Temple, 29,12-19, in 9,263b, from which he eliminates any mention of the Levites' role in order to concentrate solely on the work done by the priests; cf. n. 15. With the above phrase "in accordance with the law" compare 9,187 where Amaziah is said to be "acting in accordance with the laws of Moses (ἀκόλουθα ... τοῖς ... νόμοις)" in executing his father's assassins while sparing their children.

90. Compare 29,36a where the object of the "rejoicing" is "what *God* had done".

9,268)⁹¹, acknowledging his thanks (χάριν ἔχειν ὁμολογῶν)⁹² to God⁹³".

e) *Passover Celebrated.* In 9,268-270, as we have just seen, Josephus interrupts his account of Hezekiah's Passover celebration, begun in 9,263b-267 (= 30,1-12: the royal summons to the feast) in order to conclude his description of the restoration of the regular Temple cult (= 29,20-36). That done, he now (9,271a) resumes his Passover narrative with his parallel to 30,13-27. Here again, the historian's rendition is notable above all for its abridgement of the source story. Thus, he leaves aside the bulk of the segment 30,13-22 in order to proceed immediately to the pericope's core content: *"Then, when the festival of Unleavened Bread came round⁹⁴, they sacrificed (θύσαντες) the Phaska (φάσκα)⁹⁵, as it is called, and offered the other sacrifices (θυσίας) for seven days⁹⁶".*

91. This inserted indication harks back to the notice of 9,270a about Hezekiah's "presenting the people" with the victims "for them to feast on (πρὸς εὐωχίαν)".

92. This expression echoes the phrase, used of Ahaz' "thanking" Tiglath-pileser for his help, in 9,254: χάριν ἔχειν ὁμολογήσας. In contrast to his father, Hezekiah directs his thanks to his true helper, God.

93. From the concluding material of 29,31-36 Josephus eliminates both the listing of the various sorts of offerings in v. 30 and the obscure motive clause ("for the thing came about suddenly", RSV) of v. 36b.

94. The above transitional phrase with its reference to "Unleavened Bread" serves to resume Josephus' Passover account of 9,263b-267 (see the mentions of "Unleavened Bread" in 9,263b.264) following the intervening material of 9,268-270.

95. This is the reading adopted by Niese and Marcus; MSP(Lat) have πάσχα, as do Dindorf, Bekker, and Naber.

96. The above sequence represents Josephus' conflation of the following components of 30,13-22: vv. 15 ("... they killed the passover lamb [BL ἔθυσαν τὸ φάσεκ]..."), 21a ("the people of Israel... kept the feast of unleavened bread seven days with great gladness"), and 22b ("so the people ate the food of the festival for seven days, sacrificing [BL θύοντες] peace offerings...").

From the segment 30,13-22 Josephus leaves aside all indications suggestive of the "irregular" character of Hezekiah's Passover: its celebration in the second, rather than in the prescribed first month (see vv. 13,15) and the cultic "uncleanness" of many of those who participate (vv. 17-18a), together with both the royal (vv. 18b-19) and divine (v. 20) "endorsement" of this state of affairs. In Josephus' presentation, then, Hezekiah's Passover appears as an observance that in no way deviates from the Law's prescriptions – just as what would be expected from one whose central concern is to restore Israel's "ancient custom" (see 9,264).

In his rendition of 30,13-22 Josephus likewise focusses attention on the people's role in the proceedings by passing over the source's recurring references to the doings of the cultic officials, the Levites in particular, see vv. 15-16,17b,21b-22a. (This omission further accords with Josephus' wider tendency to cut down on both the level of cultic detail and the Chronicler's emphasis on the Levites' involvement in his rendering of the Biblical account of Hezekiah's reforms.)

Finally, Josephus reserves to a later point (see 9,272b) the notice on the people's iconoclastic initiatives of 30,14.

2 Chr 30,23-27 records a "prolongation" of the Passover observance as described in 30,13-22. In the former passage, we hear of the assembly's decision to extend the Passover festivities another seven days (see v. 23). This popular decision has no legal basis as such, and perhaps for that reason Josephus leaves it unmentioned[97]. On the other hand, he does (9,271b-272a) make (selective) use of data drawn from 30,24-27, representing these, however, as pertaining to the Passover observance itself rather than its "extension". His re-application of the content of 30,24-27 commences (9,271b) with (an appropriately modified) enumeration of the "victim statistics" of v. 24a: "To the people (τῷ πλήθει; see 9,269.270), *beside the sacrifices which they themselves had brought as auspicious offerings* (ἐκαλλιέρησαν; see καλλιερεῖν, 9,268)[98], the king presented (ἐχαρίσατο)[99] *two* thousand bullocks (ταύρους; see 9,268) and seven thousand small cattle (θρέμματα; see 9,270); the chiefs (οἱ ἡγεμόνες; see 9,268 [*bis*]) *did the same* and gave (ἔδοσαν) them a thousand bullocks (ταύρους) and a *thousand and forty* small cattle (θρέμματα)[100]".

The account of 30,23-27 continues in vv. 24b-27 with a variety of further particulars: the priests' sanctifying themselves in great numbers (v. 24b), the various groups of participants and their joy (vv. 25-26a), the

97. His non-utilization of the references in 30,13-22 to the "irregularities" of Hezekiah's Passover itself (see previous note) would stand in the same line.

98. The above inserted parenthesis harks back to 9,271a which speaks of the people's various sacrifices.

99. Josephus's reference here to Hezekiah's "presenting to the people" closely echoes the formulation used by him in connection with the sacrifices offered subsequent to the purification of the Temple in 9,270a, i.e.: "he [Hezekiah] presented the people (τῷ πλήθει ... ἐχαρίσατο)" (recall that this notice involves a modification of the source account, 29,31-33, where it seems that the victims are supplied by the assembly itself; see above). This double mention of Hezekiah's "presenting his people" with abundant victims within the space of two paragraphs (9,270-271) underscores his generous solicitude for them.

100. Compare 30,24a: "Hezekiah gave the assembly (BL τῇ ἐκκλησίᾳ) a *thousand* bulls (BL μόσχους) and seven thousand sheep (BL πρόβατα)... and the princes (BL οἱ ἄρχοντες) gave the assembly (BL τῷ λαῷ) a thousand bullocks (BL μόσχους) and *ten thousand* sheep (πρόβατα)". Josephus' double modification of the figures cited in 30,24a serves to enchance Hezekiah's stature as a provider vis-à-vis that of the princes: he supplies the people with more of both categories of victims than do they, whereas in the Bible the opposite is the case. See FELDMAN, *Studies*, p. 369 (= ID., *Hezekiah*, 605).

It is further worthy of note that, notwithstanding his tendency, evident throughout his treatment of 2 Chronicles 29-31, to cut down on the source's cultic detail, Josephus does take over all the "victim statistics" furnished by these chapters (see 9,268 = 29,21; 9,270 = 29,32-33; 9,271 = 30,24). The large numbers of animals cited in these statistics would serve to highlight two attributes of his people (and their leaders) which Josephus is particularly concerned to impress on the minds of Gentile readers, i.e. their piety and their wealth.

observance as unprecedented since the time of Solomon (v. 26b), the blessing of the people by the Levitical priests (v. 27a), and God's hearing of their prayer (v. 27b). Continuing to abridge the source's abundant cultic detail, the historian limits himself (9,272a) to a single item from this entire complex: "And the festival [i.e. of Unleavened Bread (9,271a)] which had not been kept in this manner since the time of King Solomon[101], *was then for the first time splendidly and magnificiently* (λαμπρῶς καὶ φιλοτίμως)[102] *celebrated* (ἐπετελέσθη)[103]".

f) *Additional Cultic Measures.* The Chronicler rounds off his account of Hezekiah's religious reforms (2 Chronicles 29-31) with a catalogue of additional cultic measures (chap. 31) which were put into effect subsequent to the Passover observance described in chap. 30. Josephus gives his (greatly compressed) version of the former chapter in 9,272b-274.

The first matter to be cited in 2 Chronicles 31 concerns the elimination, effected by "all Israel who were present [i.e. at the preceding Passover celebration]" of assorted idolatrous items from the territory of both Judah and representative Northern tribes (v. 1). This notice, in turn, represents the Chronicler's equivalent to 2 Kgs 18,4 (where, however, the iconoclastic measures are attributed to Hezekiah himself), minus its reference (v. 4b) to the destruction of a Mosaic cult object, i.e. the bronze serpent Nehushtan to which the Israelites had been "burning incense". Josephus presents his highly generalized parallel to 31,1 // 18,4 in 9,272b: "After the observance of the festival had come to an end [compare the opening of 31,1: now when all this (i.e. the festivities recounted in chap. 30) was finished], they went throughout the country (τὴν χώραν)[104] and sanctified (ἥγνισαν) it[105]". To this item he attaches (9,273a) a notice of simi-

101. Compare 30,26b: "... since the time of Solomon the son of David king of Israel there had been nothing like it in Jerusalem".

102. For this collocation, see p. 79, n. 68 on *AJ* 9,59.

103. Josephus' above "appendix" to his version of 30,26b serves to spell out in what respect Hezekiah's Passover was an observance "unprecedented" since the time of Solomon, i.e. in the lavish manner of its celebration.

104. This general term takes the place of the separate mention of the affected areas in 31,1, i.e. "the cities of Judah... throughout all Judah and Benjamin, and in Ephraim and Manasseh".

105. Josephus' other uses of the verb ἀγνίζω are in *AJ* 1,341.342; 2,312; 3,197.199.258; 5,45; 10,42; 12,145.318; 18,44; *c. Ap.* 1,306; only here in 9,272, however, does it appear with "the country" as object. His reference to a "sanctifying of the country" takes the place of the much more specific wording of 31,1 // 18,4 in which the elimination of a series of particular idolatrous items, i.e. high places, pillars, Asherah/Asherim and altars (> 18,4) is recorded. In making a collectivity ("they") the subject of the cultic cleanup, Josephus agrees with 31,1 against 18,4 where Hezekiah functions in this capacity. He

lar content held over by him from 30,14 (where it figures, somewhat extraneously, within the account of the Passover celebration, 31,13-22): "And the city [i.e. Jerusalem] also they purified of all pollution of idols (παντὸς ἐκάθαραν μιάσματος εἰδώλων[106])...[107]".

With 31,2 the Chronicler begins enumerating a series of cultic measures initiated, in constrast to that of 31,1, by Hezekiah personally. The first such (v. 2) concerns the king's organizing priests and Levites according to their divisions and tasks. Given, perhaps, that these two groupings appear to know and act on their respective duties in what precedes, Josephus leaves this item aside. Instead, he moves (9,273b) immediately to the next royal measure cited by the Chronicler, i.e. Hezekiah's contributions to the on-going Temple cult: "... and the king decreed that the daily sacrifices (καθημερινὰς θυσίας)[108] should be offered (ἐπιτελεῖσθαι; see ἐπετελέσθη, 9,272) at his own expense in accordance with the law (κατὰ τὸν νόμον)...[109]".

Next (31,4) the Chronicler tells of Hezekiah's prescription concerning the dues to be given the priests and Levites and the motivation for their being supplied such. Josephus (9,273c) expatiates on the latter point: "... and (Hezekiah) ordained that the tithes (δεκάτας) and first-fruits (ἀπαρχὰς τῶν καρπῶν) should be given by the people (τοῦ πλήθους) to the priests and Levites in order that they might always apply themselves to their divine office (τῇ θρησεκίᾳ [see θρησκεύειν, 9,260]

---

likewise follows Chronicles *contra* Kings in making no mention of the smashing of Nehushtan by Hezekiah recounted in 18,4b (see above). In this connection, it should be noted that Josephus has no parallel either to the related narrative of Num 21,4-9 which narrates Moses' making of the bronze serpent in the desert. In both instances Josephus' concern would seem to be for the reputation of Moses which is to protected against any suggestion that he was involved in idol-making.

106. This formulation echoes the wording of Hezekiah's directive to the people in 9,262 that they "purify themselves from their former pollutions (καθᾶραι ... ἐκ τῶν ... μιασμάτων)"; cf. 9,263 where the priests "get rid of all the pollutions (τὰ μιάσματα ἐκβάλοντες)" from the Temple.

107. Compare 30,14: "they [i.e. those coming to Jerusalem for Passover, 30,13] set to work and removed the altars [i.e. those erected by Ahaz in every corner of Jerusalem according to 2 Chr 28,24] and all the altars for burning incense they took away *and threw into the Kidron valley*" (recall that in his version of the purification of the Temple in 9,263a, Josephus leaves aside the similar indication of 29,15 that the Levites "took it [the Temple uncleanness] and carried it out to the brook Kidron").

108. The above expression occurs also in *AJ* 3,238; 8,104; 11,297; 12,25; 14,477.

109. This phrase echoes the statement of 9,270 that "the priests performed all things in accordance with the law (ἀκολούθως ... τῷ νόμῳ)". With the above sequence "the king decreed... in accordance with the law" compare the much more detailed formulation of 31,3: "The contribution of the king from his own possessions was for the burnt offerings: the burnt offerings of morning and evening [cf. Josephus' daily sacrifices], and the burnt offerings for the sabbaths, the new moons, and the appointed feasts, as it is written in the law (BL ἐν τῷ νόμῳ) of the Lord".

παραμένωσι)¹¹⁰ and be uninterrupted (ἀχώριστοι)¹¹¹ in the service of God (τῆς θεραπείας ... τοῦ θεοῦ)¹¹²". Hezekiah's "dues directive" (31,4) finds its realization in 31,5 of which Josephus gives a shortened rendition at the opening of 9,274: "And so the people (τὸ πλῆθος) brought in to the priests and Levites all kinds of fruit (παντο-δαπόν)...¹¹³".

Josephus (9,273b-274a) has a parallel, as we have seen, for each of the items making up the complex 2 Chr 31,3-5. At this point, however, he passes over an entire, extended segment of the Chronicler's presenta-tion, i.e. 31,6-10¹¹⁴. Doing this, he links up his version (9,274b) of an additional cultic initiative by Hezekiah, this concerning storage facilities for the supplies (31,11), directly with his mention of those supplies' being assembled (= 31,5): "... for which the king built storerooms (ἀποθήκας)¹¹⁵ and chambers (ταμιεῖα)...¹¹⁶".

The Chronicler devotes an extended segment of chap. 31, i.e. vv. 12-19, to a detailed account of the distribution of the previously collected items; this features both the names of 21 Levites¹¹⁷ who had a part in the process (vv. 12b-15a) and elaborate specifications concerning the vari-ous groupings among the priests and Levites who benefited from the dis-tribution (vv. 15b-19). Continuing to compress, Josephus reduces (9,274c) this entire source passage to a single phrase: "... and [Hezekiah] dis-tributed them [the collected supplies] among the priests and Levites and

110. This phrase occurs only here in Josephus.
111. The one other occurrence of the adjective ἀχώριστος in Josephus is as a variant in *BJ* 1,388.
112. This phrase recurs in *AJ* 3,251 (4,70). With the wording of the above notice com-pare that of its source text, 31,4: "And he (Hezekiah) commanded the people who lived in Jerusalem to give the portion due [cf. Josephus' specification: the tithes and first-fruits] to the priests and Levites, that they might give themselves to the law of the Lord".
113. Compare the more detailed enumeration of the people's contributions in 31,5: "As soon as the command was spread abroad, the people of Israel gave in abundance the first fruits of grain, wine, oil, honey, and of all the produce of the field; they brought in abundantly the tithe of everything".
114. This segment has the following content: further cultic dues are collected by the people (v. 6) accumulating over a four month period (v. 7); seeing the heaps of supplies, Hezekiah and the priests bless the Lord and the people (v. 8), Hezekiah inquires about the heaps from the priests and Levites (v. 9), and is informed by Azariah, the chief priest, concerning their origin (v. 10). Undoubtedly, a desire not to burden Gentile readers with such cultic details prompted Josephus' omission of this material.
115. This word is hapax in Josephus.
116. Compare 31,11: "Then Hezekiah commanded them to prepare chambers (BL παστοφόρια) in the house of the Lord; and they prepared them". Josephus' formulation ("the king built") throws into relief Hezekiah's personal involvement in the construction process.
117. This enumeration recalls the 14 Levitical names cited in 29,12-14 to which Jose-phus has no counterpart either; see n. 15.

their children and wives [see 31,18][118]". Thereafter, he rounds off his entire "reform account" (9,260b-274) with a summary notice (9,274d) that, yet again, insists on the character of Hezekiah's measures as a *resourcement*: "And thus did they once more return to their ancient form of religion (ἀρχαίαν θρησκείαν [see τῇ θρησκείᾳ, 9,273] ἐπανῆλον)[119]".

3. *Military Developments*

Throughout 9,260b-274, Josephus has followed the Chronicler's *Sondergut* account of Hezekiah's reform initiatives. At this juncture, however, the historian, in bringing his presentation of Hezekiah's beginnings to a close, switches to another topic, i.e. the military events which transpired during the reign's earlier years. For the first of these events he draws on a notice peculiar to his other Biblical source, i.e. 2 Kgs 18,8, for its summary notice on Hezekiah's Philistine incursion. His amplified rendition (9,275a) of this item runs: "*When the king had arranged these things in the manner described above*, he waged war with the Philistines (Παλαιστίνους) and, after defeating them, seized *all* the enemy's cities (πόλεις) from Gaza (Γάζης) *to Gitta* (Γίττης)[120]".

2 Kings 18 continues, in vv. 9-12, with a segment which reads like a (displaced) summation of the content of 2 Kgs 17,5-23 concerning the fall of the Northern Kingdom and its causes. Like Chronicles, Josephus has no equivalent to this additional element of Kings' *Sondergut*. In

118. Once again (see n. 116), Josephus' formulation accentuates the personal initiative of Hezekiah here. In 31,12-19, by contrast, the distribution is carried out by Levites under the supervision of the head priest Azariah (v. 13).

119. Note the echoes here of 9,262 (Hezekiah calls on the priests and Levites to purify the Temple and so "restore it to the ancient [ἀρχαίαν] service of our country") and 9,264 (the royal envoys are to summon the Israelites to "return to their ancient custom [εἰς τὴν ἀρχαίαν ἐπανελθεῖν συνήθειαν]"). Compare the extended *laudatio* of Hezekiah with which the Chronicler concludes his reform account in 31,20-21: "Thus Hezekiah did throughout all Judah; and he did what was good and right before the Lord his God [see 29,2]. And every work that he undertook in the service of the house of God and in accordance with the law and the commandments, seeking his God, he did with all his heart, and prospered".

120. Josephus' wording seems to magnify the extent of the Biblical Hezekiah's Philistine conquests. Compare 2 Kgs 18,8: "He (Hezekiah) smote the Philistines (BL ἀλλοφύλους) as far as Gaza (BL Γάζης = Josephus), from watchtower to fortified city (BL πόλεως)". Cf. the similar formulation used of Samuel's victory over the Philistines in *AJ* 6,30 (= 1 Sam 7,14): "(he took the Philistine territory) extending from the borders of Gitta (ἀπὸ ... Γίττης = 9,275a) to the city of Akkaron". In Josephus' presentation then Hezekiah's successes against the Philistines are comparable to those of Samuel centuries before.

place thereof, he recounts (9,275b-276) a further military/political development of Hezekiah's early reign whose purpose clearly is to foreshadow later events which he will relate in 10,1-23, this following the interlude of 9,277-291 which deals with Israel's demise. What Josephus narrates in 9,275b-276 has, as such, no parallel in either of his Biblical sources, although its component elements may be seen as inspired by various features of 2 Kings 18 in particular. This segment, (more or less) peculiar to Josephus, reads thus:

(275) Thereupon the king of Assyria[121] sent and threatened (ἠπείλει) to subdue (καταστρέψεσθαι)[122] his entire realm (ἀρχήν)[123] unless he would render the tribute which his father had previously paid [on Ahaz' tribute to Tiglath-pileser of Assyria see 9,252.254 = 2 Kgs 16,8.18 // 2 Chr 28,21][124]. (276) But Hezekiah gave no thought to these threats (ἀπειλῶν [cf. ἠπείλει, 9,275b] οὐκ ἐφρόντισεν)[125], for he had confidence in his piety towards God (ἐθάρρει ... ἐπὶ τῇ πρὸς τὸ θεῖον εὐσεβείᾳ [see 9,265. 267; cf. the adjective εὐσεβής used of Hezekiah in 9,260a])[126] and in the prophet Isaiah[127], by whom he was accurately informed of future events

121. Josephus leaves him nameless; from the immediate context (see 9,277) he is apparently to be identified as Shalmaneser.

122. This is the conjecture of Niese which Marcus follows. The codices and E read the aorist infinitive καταστρέψασθαι which Dindorf, Bekker, and Naber retain.

123. 2 Kgs 18,13ff. (cf. 2 Chr 32,1-23, undated) seems to know only of a single Assyrian threat to Hezekiah's domain, i.e. that initiated by Sennacherib in the former's 14th year to which the Josephan parallel is 10,1-23. Conceivably, Josephus "invented" the earlier Assyrian menace spoken of here in 9,275b to fill a seeming lacuna in the account of 2 Kings 18 where we are told (v. 7) of a revolt against the king of Assyria by Hezekiah, this apparently antedating his fourth regnal year (see v. 9), which then remains without Assyrian response for at least ten years, i.e. until Hezekiah's 14th year (see 18,13). See next note.

124. The above sequence presupposes that Hezekiah had been withholding tribute from Assyria. As such, it seems to reflect the notice of 2 Kgs 18,7b according to which Hezekiah – apparently early on in his reign – "rebelled against the king of Assyria and would not serve him". This item, in turn, gave rise to Josephus' preceding notice on the (prompt, as would be expected) Assyrian response to such rebellion; see previous note.

125. The above construction occurs only here in Josephus. Hezekiah's "nonchalance" here at the beginning of his reign in the face of the Assyrian threat contrasts with his later response to Sennacherib's advance against Jerusalem as described in 10,5 where Josephus states that it was "out of cowardice" that Hezekiah sent his officials to parley with the Assyrians rather than going out to them himself. What follows here in 9,276 will help explain the king's earlier, more exemplary stance; see n. 127.

126. This precise construction occurs only here in Josephus; cf. the expression "have confidence in God" in AJ 2,60; 3,13; 6,181; 11,171. The historian's reference to Hezekiah's "confidence" here is likely inspired by 2 Kgs 18,5a: "He (Hezekiah) trusted (BL ἤλπισεν) in the Lord the God of Israel". In his "confidence in his piety towards God" Hezekiah stands in contrast to his ancestor Uzziah who (9,222) "became contemptuous of the power that its immortal and endures for all times, this is, piety towards God (ἡ πρὸς τὸν θεὸν εὐσέβεια)...".

127. The expression "have confidence in the prophet Isaiah" recurs in AJ 13,64 with the high priest Onias as subject. Mention of "Isaiah" already here in Josephus'

(ἀκριβῶς τὰ μέλλοντα ἐπυνθάνετο)[128]. And so, for the present, this is all that we have to say about this king[129].

Conclusions: Josephus' Rewriting of 2 Kgs 18,1–8 & 2 Chronicles 29-31

In this conclusion I confine myself to highlighting certain salient findings of the foregoing comparison between *AJ* 9,260-276 and its Biblical *Vorlagen*. It is clear, first of all, that in relating Hezekiah's beginnings, Josephus does draw on both available sources, i.e. 2 Chronicles 29-31 (for the details of the royal reforms, 9,260b-274) and 2 Kings 18,1-8 (for Hezekiah's Philistine incursion, 9,275a = 18,8). No such clear-cut answer is forthcoming on the further question of which text-form(s) of these sources Josephus employed. We did, however, note his affinities with L 29,2 for the name of Hezekiah's mother (9,260a; see n. 4) and with BL 29,21 in making the king alone, rather than king and princes (so MT), the one to provide the victims in question. Recall as well Josephus' agreement (9,260a) with the synchronism of Hezekiah's accession with Hoshea's fourth regnal year found in the L MS 127/c$_2$ of 2 Kgs 18,1 as opposed to the third year cited by the other witnesses (see n. 3).

Among the Josephan re-writing techniques in 9,260-276, it is above all his abbreviation of the extended Chronistic reform account which stands out. In fact, of the six subsections we distinguished within 2 Chr 29,3–31,21, Josephus (9,260b-274) significantly abridges all but one (i.e. the royal Passover summons and the response to this, 9,263b-267 =

presentation helps prepare for the prophet's role in the later Assyrian crisis which Josephus will relate in 10,1-23. By contrast the initial allusions to Isaiah as a key player at the time of Sennacherib's assault which one finds in 2 Kgs 19,14 and 2 Chr 32,20, respectively, surface without any such preparation.

The above reference to Hezekiah's "confident" disregard of the Assyrian danger might be seen as an anticipation/retrojection of 2 Chr 32,6-8 where, in the face of Sennacherib's advance, Hezekiah "speaks encouragingly" to the people, exhorting them not to "be afraid or dismayed" given God's presence with them with the result that the people "took confidence" from his words.

128. This qualification of Isaiah accords with Josephus' recurring emphasis on accurate prediction as the hallmark of the true prophet; it will be echoed in Josephus' closing remarks on Isaiah in 10,35; see there. On the historian's (rather meager) use of the material of the Book of Isaiah and the reasons for this, see FELDMAN, *Studies*, 376-392 (= ID., *Josephus' Portrait of Isaiah*, in C.C. BROYLES and C.A. EVANS [eds.], *Writing and Reading the Scroll of Isaiah: Studies of an Interpretative Tradition*, I,2 [VTSup, 70,2], Leiden, Brill, 1997, pp. 583-608).

129. This notice prepares readers for the resumption of Josephus' Hezekiah story which will come in 10,1, following the interlude of 9,277-291 focussed on the final fate of the Northern Kingdom. Compare his earlier foreshadowing notice at the end of 9,266: "But of these things [God's subjecting Israel to its enemies in punishment for its sins] we shall write further on".

30,1-12). On the other hand, he also amplifies the Biblical narrative of Hezekiah's beginnings in several instances. Noteworthy examples of this technique include: the inserted motivation for the king's reforms (9,260b; compare 29,3); the role of the Northern prophets in seconding the envoys' appeal (see 9,265b-267); and the foreshadowing of the Assyrian menace with which his account of Hezekiah's beginnings concludes (9,275b-276). Nor is 9,260-276 without a striking example of re-arrangement of the Biblical sequence: in 9,263b-270 Josephus reverses the order in which the Chronicler (see 29,20-30,12) relates, first the sacrifices offered subsequent to the Temple cleansing and then Hezekiah's Passover summons. Throughout his rendition the historian modifies/replaces source data as well, e.g., the name of Hezekiah's maternal grandfather (2 Kgs 18,2 // 2 Chr 29,1) yields to the qualification of his mother as a Jerusalemite (9,260a); references to the Judean "ancestors" are recast as allusions to Ahaz and the hearers themselves in Hezekiah's opening speech (9,261-262; compare 29,4-11); the priests' fulfillment of their duties is praised, rather than denigrated (9,270; compare 29,34); the figures for the victims supplied the people by the king and princes respectively are altered so as to highlight the former's greater generosity (9,271; compare 30,24); Hezekiah in person, not a Levitical commission (so 31,11-12), distributes the people's offerings to the priests and Levites (9,274); while the extent of the king's Philistine conquests is magnified (9,275a; compare 2 Kgs 18,8).

The utilization of the above re-writing techniques results in a Josephan story of Hezekiah's beginnings which evidences a variety of distinctive features. With the interest level of Roman Gentile readers in mind, he drastically streamlines the Chronicler's account of the king's cultic reforms, while also accentuating features of those reforms (concern for "piety", return to "ancient" religious ways) with which such readers would feel most sympathetic. The segment's integration within its context is enhanced by the introduction of verbal links with what precedes and follows (e.g., the Ahaz story, the account of Josiah's reforms) and the insertion of foreshadowing notices (see 9,266.276). The stature/roles of Hezekiah, the people, and the priests are all accentuated, *in bonam partem*, vis-à-vis those accorded their Biblical equivalents. Conversely, in line with his overall tendency in *AJ*, Josephus plays down the involvement of both the Levites and the Deity in the events of Hezekiah's early reign. Also in line with his general practice, he interjects another set of characters, unmentioned as such in the sources, into his version, i.e. the nameless Northern prophets (9,265b-267) and their Judean counterpart, Isaiah (9,276b). The irregularities surrounding

Hezekiah's Passover observance as recorded in 2 Chronicles 30 are eliminated in favor of a presentation that underscores the conformity of the king's measures to the Law's requirements. Finally, the particular attention given by Josephus to Hezekiah's call to (religious) unity and the implications of a negative response to this (9,263-267) likely is intended by the historian as an oblique commentary on his people's history with its recent internicine warfare that had contributed so largely to the failure of their revolt against Rome. Possibly too Josephus' (un-Biblical) depiction of Hezekiah "giving no thought" to the threats made against him by Assyria, the great imperial power of his day, because of his confidence in his own piety and the knowledge of the future furnished him by the prophet Isaiah (9,276) is also meant as a message for contemporary Jewish readers: they need have no fear of the "Assyria" of their time if, like Hezekiah, they devote themselves to piety and the prophets' message.

The Chronicler's long-running account of Hezekiah's reforms might not appear to have much to offer Josephus. Nonetheless, the above analysis makes clear that the historian has devoted considerable effort to making the material a fitting vehicle for the variety of messages he wishes to convey to his double audience.

XVI

THE END OF ISRAEL[1]
(9,277-291)

Having begun his account of events in Judah during the reign of King Hezekiah in 9,260-276, Josephus thereafter shifts attention back to the Northern kingdom whose demise he recounts in 9,277-291. In narrating Israel's end, he bases himself on 2 Kgs 17,4-41 (+ 18,9-12), at the same time expanding its content with much additional matter. I divide up the material of the segment into six subunits as follows: 1. Samaria's Subjugation & Deportation (*AJ* 9,277-278 = 2 Kgs 17,4-6 // 18,9-11); 2. Samaria Resettled (9,279 = 17,24); 3. Chronological Indications (9,280); 4. Causes of Israel's Fall (9,281-282 = 17,7-23 // 18,12); 5. Extra-Biblical Testimonies (9,283-287); and 6. The Ways of the Samaritans (9,288-291 = 17,25-41).

1. *Samaria's Subjugation & Deportation*

Josephus introduced the figure of the usurper Hoshea and his submission to the Assyrian ruler Shalmaneser in 9,258-259 (= 2 Kgs 15,30; 17,1-3); see chap. XIV. Now in 9,277a he resumes his presentation of that king under whom Israel came to an end. The process eventuating in the North's demise gets underway when Shalmaneser hears of Hoshea's "treacherous" dealings with the Egyptian King "So", 2 Kgs 17,4a. The Biblical narrative leaves indeterminate the motivation behind Hoshea's Egyptian overture. Josephus clarifies the matter, substituting this clarification for the source verse's reference to another rebellious initiative by Hoshea, i.e. his failure to pay tribute to his overlord: "Now when Salmanassēs (see 9,259), the king of Assyria, was informed that Osēēs, the king of Israel, had sent secretly (κρύφα)[2] to

---

1. This chapter represents an expanded reworking of the earlier discussion in my *Last Six Kings*, 381-383. It also draws on L.H. FELDMAN, *The Concept of Exile in Josephus*, in J.M. SCOTT (ed.), *Exile: Old Testament, Jewish, & Christian Conceptions* (JSJSup, 56), Leiden, Brill, 1997, pp. 145-172.
2. This indication concerning the "secret" nature of Hoshea's mission might be seen as Josephus' equivalent of the opening formulation of 17,4: "(Shalmaneser) found treachery (B ἀδικίαν, L ἐπιβουλήν) in Hoshea". His use of the above term might also help account for his leaving aside the subsequent reference to Hoshea's non-payment of trib-

368   AJ 9,277-291

Soas (Σώαν)³, *inviting him to make an alliance* (παρακαλῶν ... ἐπὶ συμμαχίαν)⁴ *against the Assyrian king...*".

According to 2 Kgs 17,4b Shalmaneser's initial reaction to Hoshea's "treachery" was to "shut him up (so MT; BL ἐπολιόρκησεν, besieged) and bind him in prison". The chronology of events implied by the placing of this notice raises the question of how the Assyrian, prior to his invasion of Israel and seizure of Hoshea's capital as described in what follows (17,5-6a), managed to get his hands on his recalcitrant vassal. Accordingly, Josephus reserves his parallel to 17,4b to a point subsequent to Samaria's fall (see 9,278 *in fine*). In proceeding then directly from 17,4a to 17,5, the historian (9,277b-278a) expatiates on the latter verse's content in several respects: "... (Shalmaneser) *was filled with wrath* (παροξυνθείς)⁵, and marched upon Samaria in the seventh year of the reign of Osēēs⁶. *But the Israelite king would not admit him⁷*, whereupon he besieged (πολιορκήσας; compare ἐπολιόρκει, BL 18,9, ἐπολιόρκησεν, B 17,5) Samaria for three years...".

The Assyrian siege of Samaria ends with the city's fall as stated in 17,6a // 18,10. In reproducing this datum Josephus (9,278b) aligns himself with 18,10's double dating of the happening: "... (Shalmaneser) took it by storm⁸ in the ninth year of the reign of Osēēs

ute in 17,4: Hoshea wishes his projected rebellion to remain "secret" for the moment – something that would be impossible once he began withholding tribute.

3. Thus the reading of the *editio princeps* (followed by Dindorf, Bekker, Niese, Naber, Weill, Marcus, and SCHALIT, *Namenwörterbuch*, p. 117); the codices and E have Ὤαν. In MT 2 Kgs 17,4 Hoshea's confederate is called אסו, B designates him Σηγώρ, while in L he appears as "'Αδραμέλεχ, the Ethiopian dwelling in Egypt". On the problem of the identity of this figure, see P.T. CROCKER, *Recent Discussion on the Identity of King "So" of Egypt*, in *Buried History* 29 (1993) 68-74; B.U. SCHIPPER, *Wer war 'Sō,' König von Ägypten (2 Kön 17,4)?*, in *BN* 92 (1998) 71-84.

4. This construction occurs also in *AJ* 5,50; 13,376. This reference to Hoshea's desire for an "alliance" with "Soas" introduces an ironic wordplay with 9,259 where Josephus states that Hoshea did not have God as "his ally (σύμμαχον)". Given that state of affairs, Hoshea's attempts at enlisting a human "ally" in his effort to regain independence from Assyria is, one senses already now, foredoomed to failure.

5. With this interjected reference to Shalmaneser's emotional state, compare the same term used of King Ahaziah's reaction to the destruction of his men by Elijah in 9,24.

6. This chronological indication concerning the date of Shalmaneser's advance has no equivalent in 17,5. Josephus draws it from the parallel account of the North's fall in 18,9-12; see v. 9.

7. This notice concerning Hoshea's response to the Assyrian advance upon Samaria has no equivalent in 17,5a. It serves to explain how it came to the protracted siege spoken of in 17,5b: Shalmaneser had to lay siege to the capital because of Hoshea's refusal to open it to him. The insertion likewise helps account for the severity of the Assyrians' treatment of the city once they finally conquer it as described in what follows.

8. Like the Bible itself, Josephus seems unaware that the actual capture of Samaria occurred only under Shalmaneser's successor Sargon II. See the Assyrian documentation on the point cited and discussed by B. BECKING, *The Fall of Samaria: An Historical and*

[so 17,6a and 18,10] and in the seventh year of Hezekiah, king of Israel...⁹".

Josephus' Biblical sources both move immediately from Shalmaneser's capture of Samaria (17,6a // 18,10) to his deportation of the city's inhabitants (17,6b // 18,11). Josephus pauses (9,278c) to make explicit a point about the consequences of Samaria's fall to the Assyrians which Scripture leaves only implicit: "... and he utterly destroyed the government (ἡγεμονίαν ... ἠφάνισε)[10] of Israel...".

The deportation notice of 17,6b // 18,11 enumerates five place names (Assyria, Halah, the Habor, the river of Gozan, the cities of the Medes) as the sites where Samaria's survivors ended up. As is his wont, Josephus recasts in more general terms this abundance of geographical data: "... and [Shalmaneser] transported (μετῴκισεν; BL 17,6b // 18,11 ἀπῴκισε)[11] all its people [the Israelites, 17,6b // 18,11] to Media (εἰς τὴν Μηδίαν)[12] and Persia (Περσίδα)... [13]". To this notice, he attaches, at the very end of 9,278, mention of the personal fate of

Archaeological Study (Studies in the History of the Ancient Near East, 2), Leiden, Brill, 1992, pp. 21-45.

9. 2 Kgs 17,6a lacks such a synchronism. The witnesses to 18,10 differ as to the year in question: in MT BL* it is Hezekiah's sixth regnal year, in the L MS 127/c₂ his tenth, while MS 700 (r) reads simply "in the year of Hezekiah". Josephus' reference to Hezekiah's seventh year might have in view the preceding chronological data of 2 Kgs 18,9-12 according to which the siege commenced in Hezekiah's *fourth* year (so v. 9) and was successfully terminated "at the end of *three* years" (so v. 10), i.e. in Hezekiah's seventh (rather than his sixth, so 18,10) regnal year. On the other hand, it should be noted that Josephus' figure here in 9,278 does not seem to agree with those given previously in his own account where Hezekiah accedes in Hoshea's *fourth* year (9,260), while the siege of Samaria begins in the latter's *seventh* year (9,277) i.e. Hezekiah's *third* year. If then, as Josephus states in 9,278, Samaria fell in Hoshea's *ninth* year, one would expect this event to be correlated rather with Hezekiah's *sixth* (so 18,10) year. The problem illustrates the difficulty Josephus had in "keeping straight" the relevant Biblical chronological data from one part of his work to the next.

10. This construction occurs only here in Josephus.

11. On Josephus' above term ("transport") for the Assyrian initiative with regard to the Samaritan survivors which avoids the language of "exile" or "dispersion" for that happening, see FELDMAN, *Exile*, p. 154 who points out that the historian's usage here reflects his predominantly positive view of the Diaspora phenomenon.

12. Compare 17,6b // 18,10: "to the cities (so MT; B 17,6b // 18,11 Ὀρή; L 17,6b ἐν ὁρίοις [L 18,11 ἐν ὅροις]) of the Medes (BL Μήδων)". Recall Josephus' earlier reference to Tiglath-pileser's "deporting" the surviving Damascenes to "upper Media" in 9,253 – an indication which takes the place of the site "Kir" mentioned in the source text, 2 Kgs 16,9 (MT B) as the Syrians' place of exile.

13. Josephus' substitution of this place name for those of the sources likely is intended to prepare his subsequent reference to the river "Chūthos" located "in Persia" (see 9,279) as the site from which the replacement population of Samaria was drawn by Shalmaneser. Later on in *AJ* he will repeatedly return to the origins of the "Samaritans" in (Media and) Persia (see *AJ* 10,184; 11,9.114; 12,257) and the uses to which they put that origin.

Hoshea, here making use of the datum of 17,4b previously passed over by him (see above): "... and along with them carried off Osēēs alive".

2. Samaria Resettled

In the presentation of 2 Kings 17 the converse of the Assyrian deportation of Samaria's inhabitants (v. 6b), i.e. the resettlement of the site with peoples brought from elsewhere, comes only in v. 24, following the extended interlude of vv. 7-23 (cf. 18,12) devoted to the causes of the North's demise. Josephus, by contrast, opts to keep together in a continuous sequence his account of Shalmaneser's two-fold initiative subsequent to Samaria's capture. Thus, having cited the deportation of the population of Samaria as spoken of in 17,6b // 18,11 at the end of 9,278, he proceeds immediately to his version of 17,24 in 9,279: "And, after removing (μεταστήσας)[14] other nations (ἔθνη) from a region called Chūthos (Χούθου)[15] – there is a river (ποταμός) by this name in Persia (see 9,278; cf. n. 13)[16] –, he settled them in Samaria and in the country of the Israelites[17]".

3. Chronological Indications

In contrast to Kings, Josephus, as noted above, employs his version of 17,24 to round off his account (9,277-279) of measures taken by Shalmaneser in retaliation for Hoshea's disloyalty, 17,4-6. Thereafter, he fur-

---

14. In MSPE Zon (vid.) this word is followed by the phrase ἐκ ταύτης which is lacking in RO and not reproduced by Marcus and Niese. Dindorf, Bekker, Naber, however, do print the phrase as part of their texts.

15. Compare MT "Cuthah", B Χουνθά, L Χωθά. Of the five place names cited in 17,24 (Babylon, Cuthah, Avva, Hamath, and Sephar-vaim), this is the only one to be taken over by Josephus here in 9,279 (subsequently, however, he will evidence his familiarity with the five-fold listing of 17,24; see 9,288). His reason for singling out this particular name for mention is the fact that it gave rise to the later, alternative name for the Samaritans, i.e. the "Chūthaioi"; see 9,290.

16. 2 Kgs 17,24 itself makes no such association of "Cuthah" with "a river in Persia" – or anywhere else. MARCUS, Josephus, VI, p. 147, n. f suggests that Josephus' mention of a "river" here might be inspired by the wording of 2 Kgs 17,5 which speaks of "the Habor, the river (so MT, BL has ποταμοῖς, rivers) of Gozan".

17. Compare 17,24: "(the king of Assyria)... placed them [the five peoples mentioned previously] in the cities of Samaria instead of the people of Israel; and they took possession of Samaria, and dwelt in its cities". Josephus' version eliminates the repetitiousness of the source verse with, e.g., its double mention of the newcomers' occupation of the cities of Samaria.

ther departs from his Bibical source by delaying the continuation (17,25-28[29-41]) of the story of the newcomers to Samaria begun in 17,24 (= 9,279) to a much later point in his own presentation (see 9,288-291), interposing an extended segment, 9,280-287, having to do with a variety of other matters. Within 9,280-287 itself, one can distinguish a first, Biblically unparalleled sub-unit 9,280, which features a two-fold chronological indication regarding the Israelite catastrophe. The initial such datum (9,280a) dates Israel's end by reference to the Exodus. In the reading/ translation of Marcus this runs: "So the ten tribes of Israel emigrated (μετῴκησαν, see μετῴκισεν, 9,278; cf. n. 11) from Judaea ('Ιουδαίας)[18] nine hundred and forty-seven years after their forefathers went out (ἐξελθόντες)[19] of Egypt and (τήνδε) occupied this country (τὴν χώραν) under the command of Joshua (στρατηγοῦντος 'Ιησοῦ[20])[21]". As Marcus himself notes, the text here is uncertain, with the alternative reading adopted by Niese yielding an additional figure for the time between the Exodus/Conquest and the North's demise[22]. In addition, however, as both Weill[23] and Marcus[24] point out, the 947-year figure cited above does not correspond to the total – which would come to 908 years – of the dating indications given elsewhere (see AJ 8,61.211; 9,280b) by Josephus himself for the interval in question. Thus, we would have one more instance here of the "chronological incoherence" that marks Josephus' work – as it does the Bible itself – on occasion. On the other hand, the second figure given by him in 9,280, i.e. for the time from the breakup of the United Monarchy down to the end of the Northern Kingdom tallies precisely with the data supplied previously in AJ 8-9 on the reigns of the Northern kings from Jeroboam I through Hoshea. The historian's statement (9,280b) on the matter reads: "and from the time when they revolted (ἀποστάντες)[25]

18. Here "Judaea" appears to be used in a comprehensive sense, i.e., as an equivalent for "the Holy Land", "Palestine".

19. Naber tentatively suggests the emendation ἐκλιπόντες here.

20. Cf. 9,207 where the reference is to "the general Joshua (ὁ στρατηγός 'Ιησοῦς)" and his "defining" the boundaries of the Promised Land.

21. The above translation corresponds as well to that given by WEILL, ad loc.

22. MARCUS, Josephus, VI, p. 148, n. a renders Niese's text of 9,280a as follows "(So the ten tribes of Israel emigrated from Judaea) after 947 years. From the time when their forefathers went out (ἐξῆλθον, RO) of Egypt and (ὅν δε, RO) they occupied this country (τὴν χώραν ταύτην) under the command of Joshua it was (an interval) of 800 years (ἔστιν ἐτῶν ὀκτακοσίων)". The concluding reference to "800 years" here is found in the Greek codices, but is absent in E Lat. Weill, Josèphe, II, p. 299, n. 6 designates the figure as a "marginal correction" of the preceding one (i.e. 947).

23. Josèphe, II, p. 300, n. 6.

24. Josephus, VI, p. 148, n. a.

25. The use of this derogatory term to characterize the Israelites' initiative echoes the same usage in AJ 8,221.276. We will be noting other terminological links between

from Roboamos, the grandson of David, and gave the kingdom over to Jeroboam, as I have previously related[26], it was an interval of two hundred
and forty years, seven months and seven days[27]".

4. Causes of Israel's Fall

The second of the segments making up the "interlude" of 9,280-287
(see above), i.e. 9,281-282, constitutes Josephus' version of the extended
reflection on the causes of the North's demise set out in 2 Kgs 17,7-23
(cf. 18,12). Here, the historian both compresses the source text's extent
and shifts the emphasis from the sins against the Lord committed by the
people as a whole featured in 17,7-18(19-20), to the Israelites' defection
from the Davidids and their involvement in the sin of Jeroboam, a point
treated much more summarily in 17,21-23[28].

Summing up on the content of 17,7-18[29], Josephus commences his
aitiology of Israel's catastrophe with the statement (9,281): "To such
an end, then, did the Israelites come because they violated the laws
(παραβάντας τοὺς νόμους)[30] and disregarded the prophets (παρακούσαντας τῶν προφητῶν)[31] who foretold (προύλεγον) that this
misfortune (συμφοράν)[32] would overtake them if they did not cease

Josephus' wording in 9,280-281 and his account of the beginnings of the Northern Kingdom under Jeroboam in AJ 8,212-224.

26. This *Rückverweis* points back to Josephus' account of the North/South split in AJ
8,212-224. He will return to the subject in 9,282b.

27. On the correlation between this figure and those given by Josephus for the reigns
of the Northern kings, see MARCUS, *Josephus*, VI, p. 149, n. c.

28. In his version of 17,7-23 in 9,281-282 Josephus leaves aside entirely the parenthetical reference to Judah's going astray as well so that the entire people ended up being
rejected by the Lord found in vv. 19-20.

29. Josephus' reduction, in 9,281, of the catalogue of Israel's cultic crimes enumerated in 17,7-18, to a two-part, generalized accusation (see above) is in line with his overall tendency to cut down on the Bible's cultic detail.

30. This expression echoes Josephus' editorial comment concerning Jeroboam's preceding speech to the Israelites in AJ 8,229: "By these words he misled the people and
caused them... to transgress the laws (παραβῆναι τοὺς νόμους)". It will recur in Huldah's judgment speech against Judah as cited in AJ 10,60; see also the reference to King
Ahaz' "violating his country's laws" (πατρίους παραβὰς νόμους) in 9,243. The phrase
represents Josephus' parallel to the accusations made against the Israelites in 17,15 ("they
despised his statutes and his covenant...") and 16 ("they forsook all the commandments
[BL ἐντολάς] of the Lord...").

31. With this phrase compare AJ 6,141: "So Saul, as though he had neglected
(παρακούσας) none of the injunctions which the prophet (ὁ προφήτης, i.e. Samuel) had
given him...".

32. The phrase "foretell misfortune" occurs only here in Josephus. Compare, however, the similar expression "the prophets foretold the punishment (τιμωρίαν προλεγόντων)" used by Huldah in her speech to Josiah's envoys in 10,61.

from their impious actions (παυσαμένοις τῶν ἀσεβημάτων³³)³⁴". He then continues (9,282) with a more expansive rendition of the content of 17,21-23: "The beginning of their troubles (ἦρξε ... τῶν κακῶν)³⁵ was the rebellion they undertook (ἡ στάσις ἣν ἐστασίασαν)³⁶ against Roboamos, the grandson of David, when they chose as their king (ἀποδείξαντες βασιλέα)³⁷ his servant (δοῦλον)³⁸ Jeroboam³⁹, who sinned against the Deity (εἰς τὸ θεῖον ἐξαμαρτών)⁴⁰ and thereby made Him their enemy (ἐχθρὸν ... τοῦτ' ἐποίησε)⁴¹, for they imitated his lawless conduct (μιμησαμένοις τὴν ... παρανομίαν)⁴². But

33. This precise expression occurs only here in Josephus. One does, however, find analogous phrases involving the verb "to cease" + a noun denoting wrongful behavior in *AJ* 8,277; 9,167. The term ἀσέβημα recurs in Huldah's judgment speech – a text having several verbal contacts with 9,281, see nn. 30,32 – in 10,60: "(the prophets foretold the punishment) for their impious deeds (ἀσεβήμασι)".

34. The above accusation about the Israelites' failure to heed their prophets is inspired by 17,13-14 ("Yet the Lord warned Israel... by every prophet and seer, saying, 'Turn from your evil ways and keep my commandments and my statutes...'. But they would not listen [BL οὐκ ἤκουσαν; cf. παρακούσαντας, 9,281a], but were stubborn..."). It further echoes Josephus' "anticipation" of 17,13-14 in 9,265b "... and when their [the Israelites'] prophets (προφήτας) exhorted them... and foretold (προλέγοντας) what they would suffer if they did not alter their course to one of piety toward God, they [the Israelites] poured scorn upon them..."; see there.

35. Compare Josephus' editorial comment appended to his account of Jeroboam's speech to the people and its deleterious effect upon them (8,227-229a) in 8,227b: "this was the beginning of the Hebrews' misfortunes (ἀρχὴ κακῶν)...". Cf. n. 30.

36. The above paronomasia occurs only here in Josephus.

37. Compare *AJ* 8,221: "(the Israelites) proclaimed (ἀπέδειξε) Jeroboam head of the state".

38. This same designation for Jeroboam in reference to Rehoboam is used by Abijah of Judah in his appeal to the Northern army in *AJ* 8,276.

39. The above sequence "the rebellion... Jeroboam" represents a *Wiederaufnahme* of Josephus' chronological indication in 9,280b: "from the time when they revolted from Roboamos, the grandson of David, and gave the kingdom over to Jeroboam...". Compare 17,21a: "When he (the Lord) had torn Israel from the house of David, they made Jeroboam the son of Nebat king (BL ἐβασίλευσαν)". Josephus' rendition eliminates the allusion to the divine involvement in the split (compare *AJ* 8,218 where he does reproduce the notice of 1 Kgs 12,15 // 2 Chr 10,15 about the split being in accord with God's intentions as previously announced by the prophet Ahijah).

40. This precise phrase occurs only here in Josephus. The construction ἐξαμαρτάνω εἰς appears with God (him) as object in *AJ* 6,120; 8,207; 10,37; 13,71. Cf. the equivalent expression using the preposition πρός in 9,250 (of the people of Israel).

41. Josephus' one other use of this expression occurs in *AJ* 4,190 where Moses warns the people about the consequences of their "having made Him (God) your enemy (ποιήσαντες ... τοῦτον ἐχθρόν)". The phrase, underscoring the nefarious consequences of Jeroboam's behaviour, has no counterpart as such in 17,21-23.

42. This construction recurs in *AJ* 10,37 in connection with Manasseh who is there charged with "imitating the lawless deeds (μιμούμενος τὰς ... παρανομίας) of the Israelites" – who themselves, according to 9,282, imitated the reprobate behavior of their first king, Jeroboam. Cf. the related phrase used of Rehoboam's subjects in *AJ* 8,251: "they begin to imitate his unlawful deeds (μιμητὴν ... τῶν ἀνομημάτων)". The above

such was the punishment which he deservedly (ἄξιος δίκης) suffered[43]".

5. Extra-Biblical Testimonies

The longest component segment of the "interlude" of 9,280-287, i.e.
9,283-287, constitutes a clear digression within the flow of Josephus'
account. It features extra-Biblical testimonies, that of the Hellenistic historian Menander in particular, to the doings of an Assyrian king who
Josephus ends up (9,287 *in fine*) identifying with Shalmaneser, the con-
querer of Samaria according to 9,278. The digressive character of this
material is already apparent from the abruptness with which Josephus –
who is usually careful in making transitions from one topic to another –
introduces it in 9,283a following his remarks on the causes of the
North's fall in 9,281-282: "And the king of Assyria came with an army
and invaded Syria and all Phoenicia (ὁ ... τῶν Ἀσσυρίων βασιλεὺς
ἐπῆλθε πολεμῶν ... πᾶσαν ... Φοινίκην)[44]".

reference to the baleful effect of Jeroboam's example upon his people represents a conflation of the charges made in 17,21b-22: "And Jeroboam drove Israel from following the
Lord and made them commit great sin. The people of Israel walked in all the sins which
Jeroboam did; they did not depart from them". The reference further recalls Josephus'
own previous statements about the corrupting influence of Jeroboam upon the Israelites;
see 8,229a ("By these words he [Jeroboam] misled the people and caused them to abandon the worship of their fathers and transgress the laws"). 271 (the prophet Ahijah
informs the wife of Jeroboam "the people too shall share this [i.e. that to be meted out to
Jeroboam's line] punishment... because they have followed the impious ways of the king
[Jeroboam]"). 277 (Abijah affirms that Jeroboam "will end his transgressions and the
insults which he has never ceased to offer Him [God], persuading you [the Israelites] to
do the same"). 280 (Abijah alludes to Jeroboam with his affirmation that Judah worships
its own God whom "no wicked king has cunningly made to deceive the populace").

43. Both WEILL, *Josèphe*, II, p. 300, n. 1 and MARCUS, *Josephus*, VI, p. 149, n. d
express uncertainty as to whose "punishment" is being referred to in the above formulation. The former opines that the reference could be to either Jeroboam or Hoshea, while
the latter avers "apparently Jeroboam is meant". Given that Hosea has not been mentioned since 9,278, whereas Jeroboam is cited twice in what immediately precedes (see
9,280.282), the allusion is more likely to Jeroboam. That supposition is further supported
by the observation that the term "punishment" (δίκή) used in the above statement is one
that twice occurs in Josephus' account of Jeroboam; see *AJ* 8,266 ("these impieties and
the punishment [δίκην] attendent upon them... the Deity was... to visit upon... his own
[Jeroboam's] head..."). 277 (King Abijah refers to Jeroboam "paying God the penalty
[δίκην] for what he has done in the past"). In 17,23 it is the punishment of the entire
people which is mentioned: "(the Israelites persisted in sin; see 17,22) until the Lord
removed Israel out of his sight... So Israel was exiled from their own land to Assyria until
this day".

44. The above phrase is Josephus' imitation of the wording of Menander (ὁ τῶν
Ἀσσυρίων βασιλεὺς ἐπῆλθε ... Φοινίκην πολεμῶν ἄπασαν) which he will cite in
9,284; see n. 56.

In support of the foregoing affirmation about the initiative of the (anonymous) Assyrian king, Josephus next (9,283b) adduces, *en passant*, a first extra-Biblical source: "Now the name of this king is recorded in the Tyrian archives (ἐν τοῖς Τυρίων ἀρχείοις)[45], for[46] he marched upon Tyre in the reign of Elulaios ('Ελουλαίου)[47]". Thereafter, he invokes at more length the testimony of the historian Menander concerning the conflicts between Elulaios of Tyre and the Assyrian king. He introduces Menander's witness (9,283c) with the following formula: "This is also attested by Menander[48], the author of a book of Annals (τῶν χρονικῶν ... τὴν ἀναγραφήν) and translator of the Tyrian archives into the Greek language (τὰ τῶν Τυρίων ἀρχεῖα μεταφράσας εἰς τὴν Ἑλληνικὴν γλῶτταν)[49], who has given the following account...". Having thus introduced Menander Josephus proceeds to

45. Josephus uses this phrase also in *AJ* 8,144; 9,283c.287. Elsewhere he uses other designations for the Tyrian records alluded to by him: γράμματα δημοσία ("public records", *c. Ap.* 1,107); τῶν ἐπιχωρίων γραμματῶν ("the national records", *c. Ap.* 1,116).

46. In this part of his reference Josephus supplies a reason ("for") why the Assyrian king should have been mentioned by name in the Tyrian records, i.e. the fact of his having attacked Tyre.

47. Generally, the king of Tyre cited here by Josephus as "Elulaios" is identified with the "Luli, king of Sidon" mentioned in the inscriptions of Sennacherib; see, e.g., MARCUS, *Josephus*, VI, p. 150, n. a and F.C. EISELEN, *Sidon: A Study in Oriental History* (Columbia University Oriental Studies, 4), New York, Columbia University Press, 1907, pp. 50-52.

48. Josephus cites Menander in several other contexts of his writings: *AJ* 8,144-146 = *c. Ap.* 1,116-120 (on "Hirom", king of Tyre, the contemporary of Solomon); 8,324 (Menander's mention of the drought that befell Palestine in the reign of King Ahab of Israel; see 1 Kgs 17,1); and *c. Ap.* 1.121-125(126) (the succession of Tyrian kings from Balbazer, son of Hirom, to Pygamalion whose sister founded the city of Carthage). Menander's work has survived only in the foregoing quotations by Josephus. On the many questions surrounding its character (what was its relation to the "Tyrian archives" which, Josephus twice asserts [*AJ* 8,144; 9,283; see above], Menander translated into Greek from the original Phoenician?) and its utilization by Josephus (e.g., did he know Menander first hand or only via Nicolaus of Damascus or Alexander Polyhistor?; for what purpose(s) does Josephus invoke the testimony of such pagan authors as Menander?), see H.J. KATZENSTEIN, *The History of Tyre*, Jerusalem, The Schocken Institute for Jewish Research of the Jewish Theological Seminary of America, 1973, pp. 70-80; G. GARBINI, *Gli "Annali di Tiro" e la storiografica fenica*, in R.Y. EBIED and M.J.L. YOUNG (eds.), *Oriental Studies Presented to Benedikt S.J. Iserlin*, Leiden, Brill, 1980, pp. 114-127; J. VAN SETERS, *In Search of History*, New Haven-London, Yale University Press, 1983, pp. 195-199; and, more generally, J.E. BOWLEY, *Josephus's Use of Greek Sources for Biblical History*, in J.C. REEVES and J. KAMPEN (eds.), *Pursuing the Text: Studies in Honor of Ben Zion Wacholder on the Occasion of his Seventieth Birthday* (JSOTSSup, 184), Sheffield, Sheffield Academic Press, 1994, pp. 202-215.

49. Josephus uses very similar wording in his initial introduction of Menander in *AJ* 8,144: "... who translated the Tyrian records from the Phoenician language into Greek speech (ὁ μεταφράσας ... τὰ Τυρίων ἀρχεῖα εἰς τὴν Ἑλληνικὴν φωνήν)...".

allot three and-a-half paragraphs (9,284-287a) to the reproduction of his
testimony on the multi-phase interaction between Tyre and Assyria:

> (284) And Elulaios [see 9,283b], to whom they gave the name of Pyas
> (θεμένων αὐτῷ Πύας ὄνομα)[50], reigned thirty-six[51] years. This king, upon
> the revolt of the Kitieis (Κιτιεών)[52] (Cyprians), put out to sea
> (ἀναπλεύσας)[53] and again reduced them to submission (προσηγάγετο
> αὐτοὺς πάλιν)[54]. During his reign Selampsas (ἐπὶ τούτου Σελάμψας)[55],

50. The words θεμένων αὐτῷ Πύας as read by Marcus (as well as by Dindorf,
Bekker, Niese, and Naber) above have no counterpart in Lat and were omitted in the *editio princeps*. There is a further problem regarding the form of the proper name here, with
(M)SP reading Πύλας instead of Πύας. The former form is favored by a number of
authors who see it as the equivalent of the Babylonian name of the Assyrian king Tiglath-
Pileser, i.e. Pul (see 2 Kgs 15,19; cf. "Phūlos," 9,232) rather than as another name for the
Tyrian king Elulaios, thus: W. VON LANDAU, *Beiträge zur Altertumskunde des Orients*, I,
Leipzig, Pfeiffer, 1893, pp. 14-15 (he further proposes that the phrase originally stood
after the words "now the name of this king is recorded in the Tyrian archives" in
9,283b); H. WINCKLER, *Altorientalische Forschungen*, 2:1, Leipzig, Pfeiffer, 1898, p. 65;
EISELEN, *Sidon*, p. 48, n. 1 (both these authors adopt the transposition proposed by
von Landau as well), KATZENSTEIN, *Tyre*, pp. 221-222 (he restores the opening words of
Josephus' Menander quotation in 9,284 as follows: "And Eloulaios reigned [from the
days of Tiglath-Pileser] to whom they gave the name Pulas, thirty six years"). An alternative view takes Πύλας as the corrupted form of an original Λύλας, the latter being
equivalent to the "Luli king of Sidon" (= Eloulaios of Tyre) of the Assyrian inscriptions
(see n. 47), thus: G. Reisner (whose oral proposal of 1894 on the matter is reported
by C.F. LEHMANN, *Menander und Josephos über Salmanassar IV.*, in *Klio* 2 [1902], 126-
140, p. 130, n. 3 [commenting on this proposal, Lehmann offers yet another suggestion,
i.e. "Pulas" represents a corruption of the original name of Shalmaneser himself,
i.e. "Ulalai(a)]") and I. LÉVY, *Deux noms phéniciens altérés chez Josèphe*, in *Mélanges
Syriens offerts à Monsieur René Dussaud*, II, Paris, Librairie Orientaliste Paul Geuthner,
1939, 539-545, pp. 544-545 (without reference to Reisner or Lehmann). Finally to be
noted is the view of F.C. MOVERS, *Das phönizische Altertum*, I, Berlin, Dümmler, 1849,
p. 390 for whom the form Πύας is not a proper name (so Marcus), but rather the equivalent of the Hebrew word פֶּחָה, "governor, satrap", a title conferred on "Eulailos" by the
Assyrian king.

51. With reference to the chronology of the Assyrian records, WINCKLER, *Forschungen*, 2:1, p. 67 proposes emending this figure to twenty-six. His proposal is rejected by
KATZENSTEIN, *Tyre*, p. 223.

52. This is the conjecture of Niese which Marcus follows for the Κιτταίων of the
codices (retained by Dindorf, Bekker, and Naber); cf. Lat Cetuteis.

53. This is only occurrence of the verb ἀναπλέω in *AJ*; it appears four times in *BJ*:
2,641; 4,501.611.659.

54. With reference to Herodotus, *Histories*, II, 172, KATZENSTEIN, *Tyre*, p. 227 and n.
46 maintains that the above phrase should be rendered rather "and restored them to his
side".

55. For the above reading which he adopts "with hesitancy" (*Josephus*, VI, p. 151, n.
d), Marcus follows the conjecture of Niese (1886). The latter (see *Opera*, I, pp. xxxiii-
xxxiv) restores the proper name of the king of Assyria in 9,284 as "Selampsas" (which
would itself represent a form of the name Shalmaneser) with reference to Lat's "contra
quos denuo *Salamanassis*... insurgens" and the (damaged) reading of R, i.e. ἐπὶ τούτους
**άμψας where the first two letters of the third word cannot be made out in the MS (cf.
O's ἐπὶ τούτοις ἐλαμψάς). The codices MSPLaurV, for their part, have ἐπὶ τούτους
πέμψας, the reading generally followed by editors prior to Niese, e.g., by Dindorf (who

the king of Assyria, came with an army and invaded all Phoenicia[56] and, after making a treaty of peace (σπεισάμενος εἰρήνην)[57] with all (its cities), withdrew from the land. (285) And Sidon and Arke (Ἄρκη)[58] and

renders it by "contra hos misso exercitu" [the assertion of KATZENSTEIN, *Tyre*, p. 225, n. 39 that this reading is "only an emendation" by Dindorf is thus incorrect]) and Bekker.

Niese's reconstruction of the king's name here was anticipated some 35 years previously by MOVERS, *Altertum*, I, p. 384, n. 23, who, on the basis of Lat's reading (see above), introduces the name Σαλμανασάρης into the text of 9,284 cited by him. In constrast to Movers's proposed emendation that of Niese – made without reference to Movers – attracted immediate attention and widespread acceptance by Josephan scholars (e.g., Weill and Reinach), historians of the ancient Near East (e.g., von Landau, Winckler, Lehmann and Katzenstein; see n. 50), and biblicists, e.g., E. SCHRADER, Σελάμψας – *Salmanassar*, in *Zeitschrift für Assyriologie* 1 (1886) 126-27; J.F. KUAN, *Hosea 9.13 and Josephus*, *Antiquities IX, 277-287*, in *PEQ* 123 (1991) 103-108, p. 106 and p. 107, n. 7. Among the few to dissent in the post-1886 period are Naber, *Opera*, II, p. xxxiii who argues against it at length (and himself proposes a small modification of the MSPLaurV reading, i.e. ἐπὶ τούτου πέμψας) and F. JEREMIAS, *Tyrus bis zur Zeit Nebukadnezar's*, Leipzig, Teubner, 1891, p. 29 who calls it "fragwürdig". Finally, to be noted is the intermediate position on the question which holds that whereas Menander himself wrote "Sennacherib" as the name of the king of Assyria, that name reached Josephus in the corrupt form posited by Niese, thus EISELEN, *Sidon*, p. 49, and, without reference to Eiselen, LÉVY, *Noms*, pp. 543-544.

Beyond the text-critical problem of the reading here in 9,284 is the wider historical question of whether Josephus (and/or Menander himself) correctly connected the events recounted in 9,284-287 with the time of Shalmaneser V (727-722 B.C.). This latter question has divided scholars both before and after 1886. Some hold that this association is historically accurate (so, e.g., Lehmann [see n. 50] and more recently KUAN, *Hosea 9.13* [see above in this note]). On the other hand, J. ELAYI – A. CAVIGNEAUX, *Sargon II et les Ioniens*, in *Oriens Antiquus* 18 (1979) 59-75, pp. 66-67 date the happenings mentioned in 9,284-287 to the reign of Sargon II, others (e.g., Eiselen, Lévy, Katzenstein and E. MEYER, *Geschichte des Altertums*, II,II, Stuttgart-Berlin, J.G. Cotta'sche Buchhandlung Nachfolger, 1931², p. 127) to that of Sennacherib, while still others (e.g., von Landau and Winckler) maintain that events which, in fact, transpired under a whole series of Assyrian kings from Tiglath-pileser to Assurbanipal have all been wrongfully associated with Shalmaneser by Josephus. For a summary account of the controversy, see the article of Lehmann cited in n. 50 and KATZENSTEIN, *Tyre*, pp. 225-227.

56. Recall Josephus' utilization of Menander's language here in his own introductory formula in 9,283a; see n. 44.

57. This is the only occurrence of the above idiom (literally "libating peace") in the Josephan corpus. A related expression, consisting of the verb σπένδω + the noun φιλία as object, occurs in *AJ* 5,51; 17,68.

58. Two codices, i.e. Laur (ἀκὴ) and V (ἄκη) read another place name, i.e. the more southernly "Acco", the later Ptolemais here. Scholars have long been divided as to which reading is to be followed. The majority reading of the codices as adopted by Marcus ("Arkē") is espoused as well by, e.g., Niese, Weill, W. GESENIUS, *Commentar über den Jesaia*, Leipzig, Vogel, 1821, p. 710; I. BENZINGER, *Arka* in *PW* 3, 1895, cc. 1111-1112 (the site is situated in Lebanon, near Tripolis; see ST.J. THACKERAY, *Josephus*, IV, pp. 68-69, n. b [on *AJ* 1,139]). The alternative reading enjoys, however, a wide following, being endorsed, e.g., by E.W. HENGSTENBERG, *De Rebus Tyriorum*, Berlin, Oehmigke, 1832, pp. 14-15, n. *, MOVERS, *Altertum*, I, p. 384, n. 23; DINDORF, *ad loc.*; BEKKER, *ad loc.*; NABER, *ad loc.*; A. VON GUTSCHMID, *Kleine Schriften*, II (ed. F. RÜHL), Leipzig, Teubner, 1890, p. 68; E. SCHÜRER, *Geschichte des Jüdischen Volkes im Zeitalter Jesu Christi*, II, Leipzig, Hinrich, 1907, p. 142, n. 195; EISELEN, *Sidon*, p. 48; MEYER, *Geschichte*, II,II, p. 127, n. 1; LÉVY, *Noms*, pp. 539-534; and KATZENSTEIN, *Tyre*, p. 220,

Old Tyre (ἡ πάλαι Τύρος)[59] and many other cities also revolted from Tyre and surrendered to the king of Assyria. But, as the Tyrians for that reason would not submit to him, the king turned back and attacked them after the Phoenicians had furnished (συμπληρωσάντων)[60] him with sixty ships and eight hundred oarsmen (ἐπικώπους ὀκτακοσίους)[61]. (286) Against these the Tyrians sailed (ἐπιπλεύσαντες)[62] with twelve ships and, after dispersing the ships of their adversaries, took five hundred of their men prisoners. On that account, in fact, the price of everything went up in Tyre (ἐπετάθη δὴ [SP δ᾽ ἡ] πάντων ἐν Τύρῳ τιμὴ διὰ ταῦτα)[63]. (287) But the king of Assyria, on retiring, placed guards at the river and the aqueducts (ὑδραγωγείων)[64] to prevent the Tyrians from drawing water, and

n. 3.

59. On "Old Tyre" as the mainland site (called "Ushu" in Assyrian records) situated opposite the island on which Tyre originally stood and the latter's chief source of water, see KATZENSTEIN, Tyre, pp. 14-15.

60. The verb συμπληροῦσθαι recurs in AJ 3,119; 4,176 (both times with a "non-nautical" meaning; contrast its use in 9,285) and as a variant in 1,88.

61. The word ἐπίκωπος is hapax in Josephus. Through the years scholars have raised difficulties about the high figures given in the above reading for the Phoenician ships and crewmen in relation to the mere 12 ships credited to the Tyrians in what follows (and/ or the proportion between boats and men in the Phoenician contingent). Thus, MOVERS, Altertum, III, p. 174 proposes to read 16 rather than 60 ships, a proposal revived – without reference to Movers – by R. REBUFFAT, Une bataille navale au VIII⁹ siècle (Josèphe, Antiquités Judaïques, IX, 14), in Semitica 26 (1976) 71-79, p. 74. VON GUTSCHMID, Kleine Schriften, II, p. 66 and n. 3 adopts the reading ἐπικώπους ὀκτακοσίας of SP which he renders "800 Barken" (his editor, Franz Rühl, qualifies the reading of Niese [and Marcus; see above] as "unsinnig"). Finally, T. REINACH, Une passage incompris de Josèphe ou la vie chère à Tyr au temps de Sennachérib, in Revue des études grecques 37 (1924) 257-260, p. 258 and n. 3 maintains that one of the two figures given for the ships of the two contingents (i.e. 60 [the Phoenicians], 12 [the Tyrians]) is likely a scribal error (cf. WEILL, Josèphe, II, p. 301, n. 2 where it is the latter figure which is qualified as "probablement corrompu").

62. The verb ἐπιπλέω is hapax in Josephus; it echoes the term ἀναπλεύσας of 9,284.

63. The correct translation of the above Greek phrase has long been an object of controversy. Earlier editors rendered in the line of Lat ("unde honor Tyriorum propter haec crevit eximie"), thus HAVERCAMPUS, Opera, I, 507 and Dindorf ("itaque ob haec Tyrii omnes magno in honore esse coeperent"). In this understanding the phrase has in view the "glory" that accrued to Tyre in virtue of its naval victory mentioned just previously. An alternative interpretation was inaugurated by Grotius whose rendering is quoted by HAVERCAMPUS, ibid., as follows "aucta hinc Tyrios rerum omnia pretia vertit". Grotius's translation was revived (without reference to him) by REINACH, Passage, 259 ("à cause de cela le prix de toutes choses dans Tyr vint à renchérir"). Reinach further proposes that the phrase originally stood after the reference to the blocking of the Tyrian water supply by the Assyrians as mentioned in 9,287 (see below) where it served to spell out the consequences for Tyre of that Assyrian initiative (Reinach's suggested original placement of the phrase is adopted by WEILL, ad loc. who renders it "en raison de ces faits [the blocking of the city's water supply by the Assyrians], le prix de toutes les denrées renchérit à Tyr"; cf. Reinach's accompanying note, Josèphe, II, p. 304, n. 3). The above translation of Marcus (who does cite Grotius as its originator; see Josephus, VI, p. 151, n. g) stands in the same line. KAZTENSTEIN, Tyre, p. 229 cites both renderings, but leaves the choice between them open.

this they endured for five years, and drank from wells which they had dug (ὀρυκτῶν)[65].

Having quoted Menander at length in 9,284-287a, Josephus supplies his own conclusion to the digression of 9,283-287 as a whole in 9,287b. The language of this closing formulation constitutes an inclusion with his introductory statement of 9,283b ("Now the name of this king is recorded in the Tyrian archives"), although now with actual mention of the Assyrian ruler's name – which is nowhere cited as such in the Greek witnesses for the intervening 9,283c-287a (see, however, Lat 9,284 and n. 55): "This, then, is what is written in the Tyrian archives concerning *Salmanassēs* [see 9,277], the king of Assyria". In thus claiming that the allusion to/ quotation of the Tyrian archives and Menander given by him in 9,283b-287a have to do with "Shalmaneser", Josephus, finally, provides an implicit rationale for his lengthy digression, i.e. it supplies Gentile readers with extra-Biblical evidence concerning the Assyrian king whom he had earlier presented on the basis of the Bible (i.e. 2 Kings 17) itself (see further n. 94).

6. *The Ways of the Samaritans*

The long interlude of 9,280-287 completed, Josephus (9,288-291 = 17,25-28[29-41]) next picks up his story of the new settlers in Samaria and their ways begun by him in 9,282 (= 17,24). He makes the transition back to that earlier narrative by way of an extended notice (9,288a), without parallel as such in 17,24ff. concerning the etymology of the name received by the arrivals: "As for the Chūthaioi who were transported to Samaria (μετοικισθέντες εἰς τὴν Σαμάρειαν) – this is the name by which they have been called to this day because of having been brought over from the region called Chūtha, which is in Persia, as is a river (ποταμός) by the same name...[66]".

2 Kgs 17,25a sweepingly avers that the new inhabitants "did not fear the Lord". Josephus (9,288b) specifies the nature of their offense and

---

64. The word ὑδραγωγεῖον is hapax in Josephus.

65. Josephus' one remaining use of the word ὀρκυτός is in *AJ* 7,292. Scholars have tried to fill in, using, e.g., Assyrian material, the many missing pieces of Menander's skeletal account of the Tyrian-Assyrian hostilities in the time of King Elulaios as cited by Josephus above; for a representative such attempt see KATZENSTEIN, *Tyre*, pp. 226-230.

66. The wording of the above formulation harks backs to Josephus' introduction of Samaria's new population in 9,282 (I italicize the terminological contacts with 9,288) "... after removing other nations from a region called *Chūthos – there is a river* (ποταμός) *by this name in Persia –*, he [Shalmaneser] settled (κατῴκισεν) them *in Samaria* (εἰς τὴν

appends an indication concerning the Deity's emotional response to this:
"... each of their [i.e. the Chūthaioi's] tribes – there were five[67] –
brought along its own god (ἴδιον θεόν), and, as they reverenced (σεβό-
μενοι) them in accordance with the custom of their country (καθὼς ἦν
πάτριον)[68], *they provoked* (παροξύνουσι)[69] *the Most High God* (τὸν
μέγιστον θεόν; see 9,211)[70] *to anger and wrath* (ὀργὴν καὶ χόλον
[see 9,248])[71]".

The people's lack of "fear" of God (17,25a) calls forth (17,25b)
divine punishment, i.e. lions who are dispatched by him and kill some of
them. The historian (9,289a) employs more general terms in speaking of
the God-sent disaster: "For He visited upon them a pestilence (λοιμόν[72]
ἐνέσκηψεν)[73] by which they were destroyed (φθειρόμενοι)...[74]". The

Σαμάρειαν)...".

67. With this indication Josephus alludes to the five place names cited in 17,24; recall
that in his previous version of that verse in 9,282 Josephus had mentioned only one of
these, i.e. "Chūthos". Here in 9,288b he now gives (delayed) evidence of his familiarity
with the Biblical list in its entirety.

68. The above sequence takes the place of the negative statement of 17,25: "at the
beginning of their dwelling there, they [the new settlers] did not fear the Lord..." (on
Josephus' avoidance of this key Biblical expression, see p. 9, n. 25). It might also be seen
as Josephus' anticipation/ generalization of the segment 17,29-34a which speaks of the
new arrivals' syncretistic cult wherein, alongside worship of the Lord (so v. 33a), "each
nation still made gods of its own (BL τοὺς θεοὺς αὐτῶν)" – seven of which are mentioned by name in vv. 30-31 – and "served their own gods (BL τοῖς θεοῖς αὐτῶν) after
the manner (BL κατὰ τὸ κρίμα) of the nations from among whom they had been carried
away" (v. 33b).

69. This word echoes the participle used of Shalmaneser's emotional reaction to King
Hoshea's treachery in 9,277, i.e. παροξυνθείς: by their infidelity, the inhabitants of
Samaria contrive to "enrage" first their human and then their divine overlord.

70. Note the contrast here in 9,288b between "its own god", i.e. those brought along
by the five transported nations and "the most high God". It will soon emerge which of
these deities is worthy of the name.

71. Josephus' one other use of above collocation is in *AJ* 6,16 where he employs it in
connection with God's response to the lack of due respect shown the Ark by the people
of Beth-shemesh.

72. This is the reading adopted by Dindorf, Bekker, Niese, Naber, and Marcus.
MSPLat have λοιμός.

73. The above construction recurs in *AJ* 7,321 where the third choice offered David
by the prophet Gad is to have "pestilence... visited (λοιμὸν ἐνσκῆψαι) upon the
Hebrews for three days".

74. With reference to Josephus' substitution of a destroying "pestilence" for Scripture's "lions who killed some of them", MARCUS, *Josephus*, VI, p. 153, n. c comments:
"Josephus rationalizes, as usually" (compare RAPPAPORT, *Agada*, p. 63, #264 who suggests that Josephus was likely working with another *Vorlage*). It should, however, be
pointed out that elsewhere the historian does not hesitate to reproduce Scriptural mentions
of God's use of "lions" to accomplish his punishing purposes; see *AJ* 8,240-241 (= 1 Kgs
13,24: the man of God from Judah). 389 (= 1 Kgs 20,36: the man who refuses to strike
"one of the sons of the prophets" when ordered to do so). Why then should he not do so
here in 9,289 as well? I suggest that Josephus' procedure in this instance has to be seen

Bible's account moves directly from the lions' depredations (17,25b) to the Assyrian king's hearing of this (17,26), with no indication as to who brought him the news or how the informant(s) attained the theological insight about the divine source of the plague and God's reason for sending it attributed to them in the latter verse ("the nations... do not know the law of the god of the land; therefore he has sent lions among them..."). In view of such unanswered questions, Josephus amplifies (9,289a) the proceedings with several interjected elements: "... *and, as they could devise no remedy for their sufferings* (μηδεμίαν τῶν κακῶν θεραπείαν ἐπινοοῦντες)[75], *they learned from an oracle* (χρησμῷ ... ἔμαθον)[76] *that they should worship the Most High God* (θρησκεύειν τὸν μέγιστον θεόν [see 9,288])[77], *for this would bring them deliverance* (σωτήριον)[78]". Only thereafter, does he give (9,289b) his parallel to the report made to the king in 17,26, modifying this, however, with respect both to the identity of the royal informants and the content of what is told the king: "And so they [i.e. the afflicted settlers] sent envoys to the king of Assyria[79], asking him to send them some priest*s* (ἱερεῖς) from the captives he had taken in his war with the Israelites[80]".

in light of his overall presentation (see above) of the Samaritans' plight in which he accentuates both their helplessness in the face of it and, in addition to that of the Assyrian king (so 17,26-27), God's own role in providing a way for them to extricate themselves from this. Against such a background, however, mention of marauding lions by Josephus here might well provoke a sceptical question – could not the settlers have, in fact, devised their own defense against the beasts, without either God or the king having to get involved? By contrast, a God-sent "pestilence" would indeed overwhelm the settlers' capacities to counter it and so require the intervention of higher powers.

75. The expression "devise a remedy" recurs in *BJ* 1,657; *AJ* 6,166. The above indication underscores both the severity of the settlers' plight and the need for the divine direction concerning it which will be cited in what follows; cf. previous note.

76. The noun χρησμός occurs also in *BJ* 4,386; 6,109.312; *AJ* 2,241 (3,75); *c. Ap.* 1,307. The phrase "learn from an oracle" appears only here in the Josephan corpus; it answers the question of how the parties concerned came to realize what needed to be done (compare 17,26-27 where the king of Assyria's informants – and the king himself – seem to size up the situation on their own).

77. In connection with the "Samaritans" the title "the Most High God" of 9,288.289 recurs in 12,257 where their Temple on Mt. Gerizim is said to be dedicated to that Deity. The title represents a universalizing substitute for the phrase thrice used in 17,26-27, i.e. "the god of the land" which might suggest a geographical limitation to that God's power.

78. Like the preceding mention of the "oracle" itself, this statement of the oracle's content has no parallel in the story told in 17,25-28 as such (although its directive about the need to "worship the Most High God" might be seen as an anticipation – reattributed to the Deity himself – of the king of Assyria's injunction in 17,27 that the priest he sends to Samaria is to teach the inhabitants the "law of the god of the land").

79. As noted above, in 17,26 an unspecified "they" informs the king of the settlers' plight, this raising the question of how that "they" came to know of this.

80. Compare the content of the report given the king as cited in 17,26: "The nations which you have carried away and placed in the cities of Samaria do not know the law of the god of the land; therefore he has sent lions among them, and behold they are killing

The "lion story" of 17,25-28 concludes with an injunction by the
Assyrian king about the dispatch of a teaching priest (v. 27) and the
mention of its realization (v. 28). Josephus has already transposed the
king's directive into a request to him by the afflicted settlers (see above).
Thus, he now (9,290a) proceeds to relate the latter's favorable response
to the request and the consequences of this for the settlers: "Accordingly, he sent some priests [see 9,289b] and they [i.e. the settlers], after
being instructed (διδαχθέντες)[81] in the ordinances (νόμιμα; cf.
νόμους, 9,281) and religion of this God (τὴν περὶ τὸν θεόν ...
ὁσίαν)[82], worshipped (ἐθρήσκευον; see θρησκεύειν, 9,289) Him with
great zeal (φιλοτίμως)[83], *and were at once freed of the pestilence*
(λοιμοῦ; see λοιμόν, 9,289)[84]."

To his version of the story of 17,25-28 Josephus appends (9,290b-
291) a series of additional notices, without contentual parallel in 2 Kings
17 as such, concerning the Samaritans' practices down to his own time[85].

them, because they do not know the law of the god of the land". Josephus has already
anticipated this message in the "oracle" he has the settlers receive, 9,289a. Accordingly,
he represents them as themselves requesting of the king the thing which according to
17,27 he decides – without any such prompting – should be done, i.e. the dispatch of a
"priest" to them, this raising the question of how a pagan king would have come to such
insight on his own. (Josephus' mention of "priest*s*" in the plural here whereas in MT and
L 17,27 (>B) and 28 the reference is to "*one* of the priests" might have been inspired by
the use of several plural verbs in the continuation of the king's directive concerning the
"priest" (17,27αβ) in MT (and B) 17,27bα which reads "let them go and dwell there" [L
and Vulgate have singulars].) The wording of the settlers' appeal to the king as cited
above likewise seems to reflect the influence of 17,29 which refers to "one of the priests
whom they (the Assyrians) had carried away from Samaria".

    81. This is the reading of E Lat Zon (vid.) followed by Dindorf, Bekker, Niese, Naber,
and Marcus. The codices have ταχθέντες.
    82. On the term ὁσία ("religion"), see *AJ* (9,99).160.261; only here in Josephus is
it construed with the preposition περί. The above sequence represents a conflation of
the king's injunction of 17,27bβ (the priest is to "teach them the law [BL κρίμα] of the
god [> B] of the land") and the notice of 17,28b: (the returned priest) "taught (BL ἦν
φωτίζων) them the law of the god of the land". Josephus leaves aside the specification of
17,29 that the returnee priest settled "in Bethel".
    83. The above phrase "worship with zeal" occurs only here in Josephus. Compare *AJ*
11,85 where, in their address to the Jews, the Samaritans aver "we have been zealous in
His service (θρησκείας ... ἐπιθυμηταί) from the time when Salmanassēs... brought us
hither from Chuthia and Media".
    84. This concluding indication has no counterpart in the story of 17,25-28 which
leaves one wondering what became of the lion plague mentioned in v. 25. Josephus' clarification on the point underscores the trustworthiness of the oracle cited in 9,289a which
had promised just this result.
    85. This sequence takes the place of the long appendix to the lion story of 17,25-28
which one finds in 17,29-41, this comprising a series of further remarks on the Samaritans' cultic practices down to "this day" (vv. 34, 41). In substituting material of his own
for that of 17,29-41, Josephus both cuts down on the cultic detail of the source chapter
(compare his handling of the catalogue of the Israelites' offenses, 17,7-18, in 9,281b) and
eliminates the "contradiction" between 17,32-33 (the Samaritans did "fear the Lord",

The first of these (9,290b) has to do with the double name given the people(s) in question: "These same rites have continued in use even to this day[86] among those who are called Chūthaioi [see 9,288]... in the Hebrew tongue, and Samareitai (Σαμαρεῖται) by the Greeks...[87]".
Against these Chūthaioi/Samareitai he then (9,291) levels a charge of long-standing duplicity to which he will return in what follows:

> but they alter their attitude according to circumstance and, when they see the Jews ('Ιουδαίους) prospering, call them their kinsmen (συγγενεῖς)[88], on the ground that they are descended from Joseph and are related to them through their origin from him[89], but, when they see the Jews in trouble, they say they have nothing whatever in common with them nor do these have any claim of friendship or race (εὐνοίας ἤ γένους)[90], and they declare themselves to be aliens (μετοίκους)[91] of another race (ἀλλοεθνεῖς)[92]. Now concerning these people we shall have something to say in a more fitting place[93].

albeit in syncretistic fashion) and 34b (they did not "fear the Lord" *tout court*).

86. Compare 17,34: "To this day they do according to their former manner".

87. Compare the similarly-worded notice of 10,184: "Now when Salmanassēs removed the Israelites, he settled in their place the nation of Chuthaeans (Χουθαίων)... who were then, moreover, called Samaritans (Σαμαρεῖς) because they assumed the name of the country in which they were settled".

88. The codices ROSPV add καὶ συγγένειαν following the above word, which reading has also been inserted supralinearly in M. The plus is rejected by Dindorf, Bekker, Niese, Naber, and Marcus.

89. On the traditions of the Samaritans representing Joseph as their ancestor and associating him with their holy site, Mt. Gerizim, to which Josephus might be alluding here, see J. ZSENGELLÉR, *Gerizim as Israel. Northern Traditions of the Old Testament and the Early History of the Samaritans* (Utrechtse Theologische Reeks, 38), Utrecht, Faculteit der Godgeerdheid, Universiteit Utrecht, 1998, pp. 52-54.

90. This collocation is hapax in Josephus.

91. Josephus' one other use of the term μέτοικος is in 14,115. The word echoes the triple use of the verb μετοικέω in what precedes (see 9,278.279.288).

92. This term recurs in BJ 2,467; AJ 11,140.141.151; (12.141).241; 15,417; 19,330; 20,49. With the foregoing charge, compare the similar accusations in 11,340 ("When the Jews are in difficulties, they [the Samaritans] deny that they have any kinship [συγγενεῖς] with them, thereby admitting the truth, but whenever they see some splendid bit of fortune come to them, they suddenly grasp at the connexion with them, saying they are related to them and tracing their line back to Ephraim and Manasseh, the descendants of Joseph"); 12,257 ("But when the Samaritans saw the Jews suffering these misfortunes, they would no longer admit that they were their kin (συγγενεῖς)... thereby acting in accordance with their nature, as we have shown..."). 261 (the Samaritans in their address to Antiochus Epiphanes aver "... we are distinct from them [the Jews] both in race and customs [τῷ γένει καὶ τοῖς ἔθεσιν]...").

93. This *Vorverweis* points readers ahead to the recurring references to the Samaritans and their history in subsequent books of *Ant*. On Josephus' treatment of the Samaritans overall, see EGGER, *Josephus Flavius und die Samaritaner*; R.J. COGGINS, *The Samaritans in Josephus*, in L.H. FELDMAN & G. HATA (eds.), *Josephus, Judaism and Christianity*, Detroit, Wayne State University, 1987, pp. 257-273; L.H. FELDMAN, *Josephus' Attitude toward the Samaritans: A Study in Ambiguity*, in M. MOR (ed.), *Jewish Sects, Religious Movements, and Political Parties*, Omaha, Creighton University Press, 1992, pp. 23-45; J. ZANGENBERG, *ΣΑΜΑΡΕΙΑ. Antike Quellen zur Geschichte und Kultur der Samaritaner*

Conclusions: *Josephus' Rewriting of 2 Kings 17 (+ 18,9-12)*

Our study did not yield definite indications as to the text-form(s) of 2 Kings 17 (and 18,9-12) utilized by Josephus in *AJ* 9,277-291. On the other hand, the passage does offer noteworthy instances of Josephus' various rewriting techniques. Most conspicuous here are his additions to/expansions of source data. Large-scale additions occur at two junctures: the dating indications for the North's fall (9,280-281) and the extra-Biblical *testimonia* concerning Tyre and Assyria (9,284-287). Smaller elaborations abound as well, however. These have to do particularly with the overthrow of Samaria in 9,277-278 (Shalmaneser's "wrath"; Hoshea's refusal to "admit" him; the Assyrian destruction of Israel's government); and the "lion story" (2 Kgs 17,25-28) in 9,288-290a (i.e. the "reintroduction" of the "Chūthaioi" in 9,288a, God's anger at them, their powerlessness in the face of their affliction, the "oracle" received by them with its message of demand and promise, and the final removal of the pestilence).

AJ 9,277-291 is also, conversely, characterized by the abridgement of source material, most obviously its compression of the segment 17,7-18 into a single paragraph in 9,281, this coupled with the total omission of the "appendix" of 17,19-20. On a smaller scale, we noted too that of the five place names cited in 17,24 Josephus elects to mention expressly only the one that is necessary for the subsequent course of his narrative, i.e. "Chūthos" (9,279; see 9,288a). Josephus' account of the North's demise further evidences a conspicuous example of "re-arrangement", i.e. in its handling of the sequence 2 Kgs 17,24-28 (the initial religious situation among the Samaritans). He begins his reproduction of this sequence in 9,279 (= 17,24), but then "interrupts" it with a long interlude (9,280-287), after which he returns to it in 9,288b-290a (= 17,25-28) via the extensive *Wiederaufnahme* of 9,288a. Less dramatically, there is also an anticipation of the notices of 17,32-33 about the Samaritans "fearing the Lord" in the statement concerning their "worshipping Him with great zeal" of 9,290a.

Lastly, the Josephan version of the end of Israel also exhibits numerous modifications of/substitutions for source items. In 9,290b-291, at the very end of our pericope, he replaces the "appendix" (17,29-41) to the "lion story" of 17,25-28 with its additional charges about the Samaritans' cultic practices "to this day" with material of his own, i.e. the double name given the new settlers in Samaria and an accusation about the duplicity of the claims made by them concerning their (non-) relationship with the Jews. Many previous elements of the source account are replaced by him as well, however. Thus, for Hoshea's non-payment of tribute (so 17,4a) he has him inviting "Soas" of Egypt to enter an alliance (9,277). Samaria falls in Hezekiah's seventh (9,278) rather than his sixth year (so 18,10; cf. n. 9). The four place names of 17,6 other than "the cities of the Medes" yield to a reference to "Persia" as the Israelites' land of exile (9,278). Hoshea's seizure by the Assyrian king comes after (9,278), rather than before the fall of Samaria (so 17,4b). Subsequently, the divine role in the North/South split (see 17,21) is eliminated in Josephus' allusion to this happening (9,282), just as it is Jeroboam's punishment, not the people's as a whole, which is singled out for mention by him (9,282; compare 17,22-23b). Thereafter, the "lions" of 17,25-28 become a "pestilence" (9,289). It is the settlers themselves who, under the influence of the "oracle" received by them (9,289a), propose the sending of "priest(s)" (9,289b), instead of the Assyrian king devising this response to their plight (compare 17,26). That request of theirs, in turn, constitutes the content of the report given the king as opposed to the one cited in 17,26 where the royal informants display a degree of theological acumen that leaves one wondering how they could have attained it. In the same line, the king's directive that the settlers be taught by the priest (17,27) is transposed into an allusion to their having been, in fact, so "instructed" (9,290a). Going along with these contentual modifications of the Biblical "lion story" are terminological ones, references to the Samaritans' "(not) fearing the Lord" (17,25.28) and the "god of the land" (17,26 [bis].27) being replaced by alternative formulations.

The distinctive features of Josephus' narration of Israel's catastrophe and its sequels might be summed up under the following heads: 1) The Biblical focus on the cultic offenses, first of the Israelites (see 17,7-18) and then of the Samaritans (see 17,29-41), is played down, lest Gentile readers be put off. In place thereof, Josephus accentuates more congenial matters, i.e. political-military developments (the North/South split [see 9,280b.282] and the extended conflict between Tyre and Assyria [see 9,283-287])[94]. 2) Problems and unanswered questions posed by the source presentation (e.g., the moment of Shalmaneser's seizure of Hoshea [17,4b]; the location of "Cuthah" [17,24]; the royal informants'

---

in deutscher Übersetzung (TANZ, 15), Tübingen, Franke, 1994, pp. 44-91.

94. It might be noted here that the extra-Biblical "testimonies" on this subject cited in 9,283-287 have nothing to say about Israel itself. Josephus' inclusion of these testimonies is not then, as is usually the case with his quotations from/allusions to pagan sources, intended simply to provide "outside confirmation" of the Bible's own account (*in casu* its mention of Shalmaneser's campaign in the Syro-Palestinian region). Rather, in this instance, the quotation serves also, e.g., to underscore Josephus' wide reading as a historian and the range of his historiographical interests which are not limited to the fortunes of his own people. On this aspect of the historian's usage of pagan material, see BOWLEY,

knowledge of the source of the Samaritans' affliction [17,25] and the pagan king's realization concerning what must be done [17,26]; the "contradiction" between 17,32-33 and 24b on the Samaritans' "fear of the Lord") are resolved by the application of one or more of the foregoing rewriting techniques). 3) In accord with his tendencies elsewhere Josephus goes beyond the Bible in accentuating the perniciousness of the North's breakaway from the Davidids and its long-term negative consequences for Israel. 4) In the same line, he highlights Jeroboam's role as misleader of his people and his meeting of fitting punishment. 5) Josephus' "substitute appendix" on the future history of the Samaritans (9,290b-291; compare 17,29-41) serves to prepare matters which will recur in his subsequent account of them, i.e. the names used for them and their oscillating claims about their relationship with the Jews. 6) Somewhat surprisingly, in view of his overall depiction of them in his writings, Josephus' portrayal of the Samaritans in 9,288-290 shows itself to be more positive than does the source text, i.e. 17,25-28(29-41). Specifically, he depicts them as the recipient of a divine oracle, themselves taking the lead in requesting that priests be sent to them, and as worshipping God "with great zeal" once they are instructed (compare the charges of Samaritan syncretism featured in 17,29-34a). This last point makes clear, yet again, that Josephus is not, in fact, as single-mindedly "tendentious" in his handling of sensitive topics as he is often made out to be.

Josephus's Use, pp. 209-211.

XVII

JERUSALEM DELIVERED
(10,1-23)

The Bible relates Jerusalem's miraculous deliverance from the forces of the Assyrian King Sennacherib in three separate contexts. Of these 2 Kgs 18,13-19,37 and Isa 36,1-37,38 largely parallel each other. 2 Chr 32,1-23, by contrast, is rather different with, e.g., its emphasis (see vv. 2-9) on the military preparedness measures undertaken by Hezekiah in the face of Sennacherib's assault. Josephus' version of the happening appears in *AJ* 10,1-23[1]. Already at first reading, it is apparent that he has elected to follow the parallel presentation of Kings/Isaiah in preference to that of Chronicles[2]. For comparative purposes I divide up the material into seven segments as follows: 1. Initial Royal Exchange (*AJ* 10,1-3 = 2 Kgs 18,13-16 // Isa 36,1 // 2 Chr 32,1); 2. Rabshakeh's Address (10,4-7 = 18,17-25 // 36,2-10 [compare 32,2-9]); 3. Request Rejected (10,8-10 = 18,26-35 // 36,11-20); 4. Isaiah's Assurance (10,11-14 = 18,36-19,7 // 36,21-37,7); 5. New Assyrian Threat (10,15 = 19,8-13 // 37,8-13); 6. Hezekiah & Isaiah's Response (10,16 = 19,14-34 // 37,14-35 // 32,20); and 7. Assyrian Withdrawal (10,17-23 = 19,35-37 // 37,36-38 // 32,21-23).

1. *Initial Royal Exchange*

The four accounts concerning Jerusalem's deliverance all begin with mention of Sennacherib's invasion of Judah[3]. Josephus' version (10,1)

---

1. Sennacherib's assault also figures in Josephus' address to the defenders of Jerusalem as reported by him in *BJ* 5,388.404-408.

2. Josephus' non-utilization of the *Sondergut* of 2 Chr 32,2-9 which focusses on Hezekiah's military preparedness measures likely reflects a concern not to provide a "precedent" for the actions of the Jewish rebels of his own time; see his speech to them as reported in *BJ* 5,362-419 whose central affirmation (5,390), i.e. "if they [the Jews] sat still they conquered, as it pleased their Judge, if they fought they were invariably defeated", is precisely that whenever in the past the Jews had taken up arms on their own behalf they suffered defeat.

3. In Isa 36,1 and 2 Chr 32,1 the Assyrian invasion appears unmotivated. In the presentation of 2 Kings 18 (see v. 13) it represents the delayed response to Hezekiah's revolt against "the king of Assyria" (v. 7b). Josephus has spoken previously (see 9,275) of a threat by an unnamed king of Assyria to subjugate Hezekiah's realm unless he pays tribute as his father (Ahaz) had done. One might then see the notice on Sennacherib's advance in 10,1 as his finally "making good on" this earlier Assyrian threat. See on 9,275-276.

reads: "Now Hezekiah, the king of the two tribes [see 9,142], had occupied the throne for fourteen years[4] when the king of Assyria (Ἀσσυρίων)[5], named Senacheirimos (Σεναχείριμος)[6], marched (στρατεύει)[7] against him *with a great armament*[8] and took (αἱρεῖ) by storm all the cities of the tribes of Judah *and Benjamin*[9]".

Following their joint mention of Sennacherib's invasion (18,13 // 36,1), 2 Kings and Isaiah diverge. The latter book moves immediately to the king's dispatch of the Rabshakeh to Jerusalem (36,2 // 18,17), while in the former there supervenes a *Sondergut* exchange between Sennacherib and Hezekiah (18,14-16)[10]. Josephus (10,2-3) elects to follow Kings' more expansive presentation, doing so, however, in quite free fashion. Thus, he preceeds his rendition of Hezekiah's appeal to Sennacherib (18,14a) with a transitional notice (10,2a) which provides a further motivation for the former's initiative: "And he was about to lead his force against Jerusalem also, but, before he could do so...". He likewise rewords the appeal itself ("I have done wrong; withdraw from me; whatever you impose on me I will bear", 18,14aβ), recasting it in indirect discourse as well: "... Hezekiah sent envoys to him[11]

4. Josephus shares this chronological datum with 2 Kgs 18,13 // Isa 36,1. 2 Chr 32,1 lacks an equivalent.

5. This is the reading adopted by Dindorf, Bekker, Naber, and Marcus. Niese reads Βαβυλωνίων with the codices RO.

6. This is the conjecture of Niese which Marcus follows (SCHLATTER, *Namen*, p. 83 proposes Σαναχηριβος as Josephus' original form, while SCHALIT, *Namenwörterbuch*, p. 110 suggests Σενναχήριβος). The Josephan textual witnesses attest to many variant forms of the name (see the listing in MARCUS, *Josephus*, VI, p. 156, n. 2), as do those of the LXX. In his allusion to the king's assault in the context of his speech to the defenders of Jerusalem in *BJ* 5,388 Josephus calls him Σενναχηρείμ.

7. With this historic present form compare the ἀνέβη of BL 2 Kgs 18,13 // LXX Isa 36,1 [for LXX Isaiah I use J. ZIEGLER (ed.), *Isaias* (Septuaginta, XIV), Göttingen, Vandenhoeck & Ruprecht, 1985] and the ἦλθε(ν) of BL 2 Chr 32,1.

8. This indication has no equivalent in the respective opening verses of the three Biblical accounts. It does, however, have a counterpart in Rabbinic tradition (see, e.g., *b. Sanh.* 95b; *E.R.* §7(45), BRAUDE and KAPSTEIN, *Tanna děbe Eliyyahu*, p. 105) which affirms that Sennacherib's army numbered 2,599,999 men, among whom were 45,000 princes.

9. In 18,13 // 36,1 the reference is to Sennacherib's seizure of "all the fortified cities of Judah". Josephus' mention also of "Benjamin" picks up on his previous designation of Hezekiah as "king of the *two* tribes". In the presentation of 2 Chr 32,1 Sennacherib is said to encamp against the Judean cities, "thinking to win them for himself", rather than actually capturing them.

10. The absence of the material of 2 Kgs 18,14-16 in Isaiah 36 (and 2 Chronicles 32) might be explained in terms of its rather unflattering portrayal of Hezekiah who (so vv. 15-16) "pays off" the Assyrian with the Temple's gold and silver (recall in this connection that scholars generally regard Isaiah 36-39 as literarily dependent on 2 Kgs 18,13-20,19).

11. 2 Kgs 18,14aα specifies that Sennacherib was then at Lachish.

and promised to submit to him[12] and pay whatever tribute he should impose[13]".

Sennacherib responds to Hezekiah's message in 18,14aβ by demanding three hundred talents of silver and thirty of gold from him. Josephus elaborates on (10,2b) this development considerably, likewise turning the Assyrian's demand into mention of his actually receiving the sums in question: "When Senacheirimos *heard what the envoys had to say, he decided not to continue with the war* (πολεμεῖν), *but acceded to the request*[14] *and, on receiving* (λαβών) three hundred talents of silver and thirty of gold[15], *agreed* (ὡμολόγει) *to withdraw amicably* (φίλος), *and gave sworn pledges* (πίστεις δοὺς ... ἐνόρκους; see 9,145) *to the envoys that he would do him no harm* (ἀδικήσας) *at all but would retire under these terms* [i.e. Hezekiah's earlier promise (10,2a) to pay whatever tribute Sennacherib would impose]".

2 Kgs 18,15-16 enumerates the various "sources" whence Hezekiah assembled the tribute imposed by Sennacherib (18,14b): silver from the Temple and palace treasuries (v. 15), plus gold from the overlay of the Temple doors (v. 16). Josephus' rendition (10,3) eliminates any explicit mention of a despoliation of the Temple by Hezekiah[16], while

12. This "promise" takes the place of Hezekiah's two opening statements in 18,14aβ, i.e. "I have done wrong; withdraw from me". The first of these statements lacks a clear preparation in Josephus' own previous account (compare 18,7b which mentions Hezekiah's "revolt" against Assyria), while the following "command" ("withdraw from me") might appear presumptuous on Hezekiah's part (subsequently, however, Josephus presumes that Hezekiah did, in fact, make a "request" of Sennacherib *à la* that reported in 18,4aβ; see 10,2b and n. 14). The historian's substitute language (see above) underscores the Judean king's submissiveness to his overlord.

13. With the above item Josephus reproduces this concluding element of the Biblical Hezekiah's three-part message ("whatever you shall impose on me I shall bear", 18,14) since it will play a role in the continuation of the story.

14. In Josephus' version of Hezekiah's message in 10,2a, no "request" is made as such by the king. The reference to it here in 10,2b seems, however, to reflect Hezekiah's appeal as reported in 18,14aβ, i.e. "withdraw from me". See n. 12.

15. In 18,14b these are the sums which Sennacherib demands that Hezekiah dispatch to him. In Josephus' presentation above they seem to become a kind of propitiatory initial "gift" which accompanies Hezekiah's verbal message (compare Ahaz' overture to King Tiglath-pileser as reported in 2 Kgs 16,7-8 = *AJ* 9,252). The Assyrian's satisfaction with receiving this "gift" would, in turn, help account for Sennacherib's "un-Biblical" response to Hezekiah's message as reported by Josephus, i.e. his promise to end hostilities.

16. This "omission" is in line with Josephus' accentuation of Hezekiah's piety throughout his portrayal of the king; see FELDMAN, *Studies*, p. 369 (= ID., *Hezekiah*, 605). Compare *b. Pesaḥ.* 56a where Hezekiah's stripping of the Temple doors of their gold as reported in 2 Kgs 18,16 is censured by the Rabbis. In other instances, by contrast, Josephus does not hesitate to follow the Biblical indications concerning various Judean kings dispatching the Temple treasures to foreign rulers: Asa (*AJ* 8,304 = 1 Kgs 15,18 // 2 Chr 16,2); Joash (*AJ* 9,170 = 2 Kgs 12,18); Ahaz (*AJ* 9,254 = 2 Kgs 16,8 // 2 Chr 28,21).

also citing the king's "expectations" in dispatching the tribute: "So Hezekiah, *being persuaded* (πεισθείς)[17] *by this offer*, emptied his treasuries (κενώσας τοὺς θησαυρούς)[18] and sent (πέμπει) the money (χρήματα) *in the belief that he would be rid of the war* (ἀπαλλαγήσεσθαι τοῦ πολέμου)[19] *and the struggle for his throne* (τῆς βασιλείας ἀγῶνος[20])[21]".

2. Rab-shakeh's Address

The sequence of 2 Kgs 18,14-16 and 17ff. poses a problem: Hezekiah meets Sennacherib's demands for his withdrawal, but the latter responds, not by retiring, but rather by sending his officers to Jerusalem to demand the city's surrender[22]. Josephus – who, in contrast to Isaiah 36, does reproduce the content of 18,14-16 (see n. 22) – disposes of the problem by invoking (10,4) Sennacherib's "duplicity": "*But, when the Assyrian received* (λαβών, so 10,2) *the money, he paid no regard to the agreement* (ὡμολογημένων; cf. ὡμολόγει, 10,2)[23]; *instead, while he himself took*

17. The verb πείθω and its noun cognate constitute a *Leitwort* in 10,1-23; see 10,6.9.16.

18. Compare 18,15b: "And Hezekiah gave him all the silver that was found... in the treasuries (BL θησαυροῖς) of the king's house".

19. This construction recurs in *AJ* 7,305; 13,246; cf. the nominal equivalent in 7,337. It picks up on the reference to Sennacherib's "deciding not to continue the war (πολεμεῖν)" in 10,2.

20. The above phrase occurs only here in Josephus.

21. Josephus' above appendix concerning Hezekiah's "thinking" serves to set up the contrast between his *bona fides* in dealing with Sennacherib – cf. also the reference to the Judean king's "being persuaded by the Assyrian's offer" at the opening of 10,3 – and the latter's subsequent treachery; see 10,4.

22. Historical-critical scholarship resolves the difficulty by positing that 18,14-16 and 18,17ff. derive from different hands/sources; see the commentaries. Note that in the parallel text of Isaiah 36 the difficulty does not exist in that there its equivalent to 18,13 (i.e. 36,1: Sennacherib's invasion of Jerusalem) is followed directly by its parallel to 18,17 (36,2: the sending of the officers to demand Jerusalem's surrender). The problem is likewise absent in the account of 2 Chronicles 32 which has no parallel to 18,14-16.

23. The above formulation throws into relief the contrast between "trusting" Hezekiah and duplicitous Sennacherib (Josephus' inserted reference to the latter's bad faith would further serve to legitimate in the eyes of Roman readers, mindful of the *fides punica* with which their own ancestors had to contend, the severe divine retribution that will befall him and his force). The whole sequence of 10,2-4 concerning the interaction between the two kings with its divergences from the account given in 2 Kings 18 perhaps also stands under the influence of Josephus' own earlier evocation of the episode in his speech to the defenders of Jerusalem in *BJ* 5,405: "Did not he [Sennacherib] accept money (χρήματα [see 10,3]... λαβών [see 10,2.4]) from our king [Hezekiah] on the condition that he would not sack the city, and then come down, in violation of his oaths (ὅρκους; see ἐνόρκους, 10,2), to burn the sanctuary..."?

the field against the Egyptians and Ethiopians[24], he left behind *his general* Rapsakēs (ʿΡαψάκην)[25] with a large force (μετὰ πολλῆς ἰσχύος)[26], and also *two other commanding officers, to sack Jerusalem*[27]. *The names of these men were* Tharata (Θαρατά)[28] and Aracharis (Ἀράχαρις)[29]".

Both 18,17b and 36,2b specify in some detail the site of the upcoming exchange between the Rab-shakeh and Hezekiah's envoys ("the conduit of the upper pool, which is on the highway to the Fuller's Field"). Josephus' rendition (10,5a) dispenses with these precisions (which, in fact, play no role in what follows). Instead, he constructs a transitional sequence making use of items peculiar to 18,17b-18 as opposed to 36,2b-3 ("And they [the three officers of 18,17a] went and came to Jerusalem. When they arrived, they came... and when they called for the king..."): "When they arrived, *they encamped before the walls*[30] and sent to Hezekiah *and asked him to parley with them*[31]".

The sources (18,18 // 36,3) enumerate three Judean officials who "go out" to the Rab-shakeh at this juncture. Josephus (10,5b) intro-

---

24. This insertion serves to prepare Josephus' subsequent account (10,17-20), inspired by a report of Herodotus, of Sennacherib's campaign against Egypt which was itself countered by an advance of the Ethiopians against him. It further provides an implicit answer to a question raised by the Biblical narratives, i.e. why did Sennacherib not come to conduct negotiations at Jerusalem in person?

25. This form corresponds to that found in LXX 18,17 // 36,2 (in the former text it appears together with the definite article τόν); compare MT "the Rab-shakeh". As his preceding qualification of "Rapsakēs" as a "general" indicates, however, Josephus (mis-)understood the Assyrian title ("cup-bearer") as a proper name, just as he will do with the two additional designations used in 18,17; see above and cf. n. 29.

26. Cf. the – inserted – reference to Sennacherib coming against Hezekiah "with a great armament (μετὰ πολλῆς παρασκευῆς)" in 10,1. Just as he did in 10,2 (compare 18,14), Josephus here in 10,4 leaves aside the reference (18,17 // 36,2) to "Lachish" as Sennacherib's headquarters from which he dispatches the Rab-shakeh. His mention of Sennacherib's "leaving behind" the three officers suggests, in fact, that the Assyrian monarch had previously stationed himself in close proximity to Jerusalem.

27. This clarification concerning the task assigned by Sennacherib to his officers has no equivalent in 18,17 // 36,2.

28. SCHLATTER, *Namen*, p. 114 proposes to read an original Θαρτας here. Compare "Tartan" (MT 18,17); (τὸν) θανθάν (B); (τὸν) Τανθάν (L).

29. SCHLATTER, *Namen*, p. 102 proposes Ἀραψαρις, while SCHALIT, *Namenwörterbuch*, p. 15 calls the χ in the above form a "paläographische Verschreibung". Compare "Rab-saris" (MT 18,17); (τὸν) ʿΡαφείς (B); (τὸν) ʿΡαψείς (L). In mentioning two officers in addition to the Rabshakeh here, Josephus goes together with 18,17 against 36,2 which cites only the latter. At the same time, Josephus reverses the order in which the Rabshakeh and his two associates appear in 18,17, just as he (mis-) understands all three source titles as proper names; see n. 25.

30. Neither 18,17b nor 36,2b makes mention of the city "walls". Josephus anticipates the reference to them from 18,36 // 36,11 where Hezekiah's envoys ask that the Rabshakeh not speak in Hebrew "within the hearing of the people who *are on the wall*".

31. Josephus appends this indication as to why the officers summon Hezekiah to the mention of their doing so as found in 18,18.

duces explanations as to why the king himself does not go out (when he himself had been summoned, 10,5a) and why the three officials in question were selected to go in his place: "*He, however, out of cowardice* (ὑπὸ δειλίας)[32] *did not himself come out but sent out three of the friends who were closest* (ἀναγαιοτάτους φίλους)[33] *to him*[34], the steward of the kingdom (τὸν τῆς βασιλείας ἐπίτροπον)[35], named Eliakias (᾽Ελιακίαν)[36] and Sūbanaios (Σουβαναῖον)[37] and Jōachos (᾽Ιώαχον)[38], who was in charge of the records (τὸν ἐπὶ τῶν ὑπομνημάτων)[39]".

2 Kgs 18,19 // Isa 36,4 introduce the Assyrian commander's discourse with the simple formula "and the Rab-shakeh said to them [i.e. Hezekiah's three envoys]". The historian (10,6a) provides a more much expansive transition: "*So these three came forward and stood facing the commanders* (ἡγεμόνων) *of the Assyrian army; and, when the general Rapsakēs saw them, he told them...*[40]". The Rab-shakeh's discourse begins in 18,19bβ-20 // 36,4bβ-5 with a series of three questions, all asking on whom or what Hezekiah "relies" in rebelling against Sen-

32. On this motivation for Hezekiah's not responding in person to the Assyrian summons, see FELDMAN, *Studies*, p. 367 (= ID., *Hezekiah*, 603) who notes that it is part of the historian's overall tendency to downplay the Biblical king's courage and military stature. The *Wortfeld* of "fear" which Josephus interjects into his account of the siege of Jerusalem here will figure prominently in what follows; see 10,8.

33. The phrase "close(st) friend(s)" recurs in *AJ* 7,350; 10,59.229; 11,208. The designation of the three envoys with this title serves to explain why they in particular were chosen by Hezekiah to represent him.

34. In place of the sequence αὐτῷ ἐξέμπεμψε ("to him [Rab-shakeh]... he sent out") read by Dindorf, Bekker, Niese, and Marcus in 10,5b Naber conjectures ἀντεξέπεμψε. With his reference to Hezekiah's "sending out" the envoys Josephus makes clear the king's control of the process, whereas in 18,18 // 36,3 the three seem to act on their own initiative in "going forth".

35. For this title see on 9,247. In 18,18 // 36,3 Eliakim is called he "who was over the house (BL/LXX ὁ οἰκονόμος)".

36. Compare MT 18,18 // 36,3 "Eliakim"; BL 18,18 ᾽Ελιακείμ; LXX 36,3 ᾽Ελιακιμ. In common with L 18,18, Josephus does not mention the name of Eliakim's father, i.e. "Hilkiah".

37. Thus the RO reading of the name followed by Niese and Marcus (Dindorf, Bekker, and Naber read Σοβναῖον; cf. Lat Sobnaeam). Compare "Shebna" (MT 18,18 // 36,3); Σόμνας (BL 18,18, LXX 36,3). Josephus omits the title used of him in the sources, i.e. "the scribe" (RSV "the secretary").

38. This is the reading of the name adopted by Dindorf, Bekker, Niese, Naber, and Marcus; the witnesses have a series of variants. Compare "Joah" (MT 18,18 // 36,3); ᾽Ιωσαφάτ (B 18,18); ᾽Ιωάχ (L 18,18 // LXX 36,3). As he did with "Eliakim", Josephus leaves aside the name of this figure's father, i.e. "Asaph".

39. This title recurs in *AJ* 7,110.293. Compare ὁ ἀναμιμνήσκων (BL 18,18); ὁ ὑπομνηματογράφος (LXX 36,3).

40. This extended transition serves to highlight the import of the general's speech that follows.

nacherib. Josephus (10,6b) compresses the officer's triple question into a single, indirect discourse one, which, for its part, expatiates on Hezekiah's "offenses" against his overlord. This runs: "... he told them to go back to Hezekiah and say that the great king (βασιλεὺς μέγας)[41] Senacheirimos was inquiring of him on what he so confidently relied (θαρρῶν καὶ πεποιθώς; see πεισθείς, 10,3)[42] that *he avoided his master* (δεσπότην) *and was unwilling to listen to him and would not admit* (δέχεται) *his army into the city*[43]".

The Rab-shakeh proceeds in 18,21aα // 36,6aα to answer his own previous questions about the basis of Hezekiah's confidence, doing so by accusing him of "relying" on Egypt. Josephus (10,6c) first turns the Biblical general's initial statement ("you are now relying on Egypt") into a double, indirect discourse question: "Was it perhaps, he asked, because of the Egyptians, *and in the hope* (ἐλπίζων) *that the Assyrian army had been beaten* (καταγωνίσασθαι)[44] *by them*[45]"? To his accusation about Hezekiah's reliance on Egypt, the Rab-shakeh appends (18,21aβb // 36,6aβb) a derogatory reference to Egypt's unreliability as a "broken reed of a staff". The Josephan general expatiates (10,7a) on the stupidity of Hezekiah's relying on Egypt and the harmful consequences of his doing so: "*If this was what he expected*[46], *they should, he said, make clear* (δηλοῦν) *to him that he was very foolish* (ἀνόητος; see 9,255 of Ahaz) *and like a man* who leans upon a broken reed (καλάμῳ[47]

---

41. Compare BL 18,19 // LXX 36,4: ὁ βασιλεὺς ὁ μέγας.

42. Compare BL 18,19: τίς ἡ πεποίθησις αὕτη ἥν πέποιθας; and LXX 36,4 τί πεποιθώς εἶ;.

43. The above three "charges" spell out what is (purportedly) involved in the "rebellion" against Sennacherib of which Hezekiah is accused in 18,20b // 36,5b. Given that in what precedes Hezekiah has shown himself submissive in every respect to Sennacherib, it would appear that Rab-shakeh's charges here in 10,6b are to be understood as false ones, intended only to supply a fictive justification for Sennacherib's seizure of the city, notwithstanding his having agreed to withdraw (see 10,2). As such, the charges reflect that same "perfidity" earlier displayed by Sennacherib in disregarding his previous promises (10,2) by advancing against Jerusalem (10,4).

44. The verb καταγνωίζομαι occurs also in *AJ* 4,153; 7,53; 13,169; 16,8.

45. This interjected element picks up on Josephus' – likewise inserted – reference to Sennacherib himself "taking the field against the Egyptians and Ethiopians" while leaving the three officers behind in Jerusalem of 10,4. In addition, it provides a positive reason as to why, as Rab-shakeh charges, Hezekiah would have put his confidence in the Egyptians.

46. This hypothetical formulation prolongs the question formulation used by Rab-shakeh in 10,6c (compare 18,21aα // 36,6aα): "Was it perhaps... because of the Egyptians..."?

47. Josephus' one other use of the word κάλαμος is in *AJ* 3,190 where it designates an incense ingredient.

ἐπερειδόμενος τεθλασμένῳ[48]) *and not only falls* but also has his hand pierced (διαπαρείς)[49], *and feels the hurt*[50]".

Josephus has Rab-shakeh terminate his speech with a theological argument (10,7b) drawn from 18,25 // 36,10 into which he inserts a reference to the recent demise of the North: "They should know, he said, that by the will of God (βουλήσει θεοῦ)[51], *who had granted him to overthrow* (καταστρέψασθαι) *the kingdom of the Israelites also*[52], he had made this expedition against Hezekiah in order that he might in the same way destroy (διαφθείρῃ)[53] those ruled by him[54]". In thus moving directly from his parallel (10,6c-7a) to 18,21 // 36,6 to his counterpart (10,7b) to 18,25 // 36,10, Josephus leaves aside Rab-shakeh's evocation of Hezekiah's earlier "iconoclastic" measures which would – purportedly – preclude his being able to rely on the Lord, 18,22 // 36,7 (see also 2 Chr 32,12)[55]. He likewise reserves to a later point (see 10,9b) the general's "horse wager" of 18,23-24 // 36,8-9.

3. *Request Rejected*

At this juncture in the source accounts, Hezekiah's envoys interrupt Rab-shakeh's discourse with a request to him (18,26 // 36,11), a request which the latter rejects (18,27 // 36,12), thereafter resuming his threatening discourse (18,28-35 // 36,13-20). Josephus' parallel to this new sequence is 10,8-10.

48. The verb θλάω is hapax in Josephus.

49. Josephus' remaining uses of the verb διαπείρω are in *BJ* 3,231.526; 5,313; *AJ* 5,208. Only here is it employed with the "hand" as object.

50. Compare 18,21aβb // 36,6aβb: "(Egypt) that broken reed of a staff (BL 18,21 // LXX 36,6 τὴν ῥάβδον τὴν καλαμίνην τὴν τεθλασμένην ταυτήν), which will piece (στηριχθῇ, B 18,21; ἐπιστηρισθῇ, L 18,21 // LXX 36,6) the hand of any man who leans on it. Such is Pharoah... to all who rely on him".

51. For this key Josephan concept, see p. 156, n. 125 on 9,132.

52. This evocation of Israel's demise, recounted by Josephus in 9,277-291 (= 2 Kings 17 // 18,9-12), has no parallel in the Biblical Rab-shakeh's initial speech. It might, however, be seen as an anticipation/modification of his later word as cited in 18,34bβ // 36,19bβ: "Have they (the gods of the nations) delivered *Samaria* out of my hand"?

53. The verb διαφθείρω is a *Leitwort* in Josephus' account of Jerusalem's deliverance; see further 10,14.15.21.

54. Compare 18,25 // 36,10: "Moreover is it without the Lord that I have come up against this place to destroy (διαφθεῖραι, BL 18,25a; πολεμῆσαι, LXX 36,10a) it? The Lord said to me, 'Go up against this land and destroy (BL 18,25b διάφθειρον) it'". (LXX 36,10 has no equivalent to MT 36,10b = 18,25b).

55. His omission of this item might be due to the consideration that it presupposes an implausibly detailed knowledge of cultic developments in the minor kingdom of Judah on the part of the pagan general. The omission likewise reflects Josephus' general tendency to eliminate or reduce the Bible's cultic details.

In reporting the request made of Rab-shakeh, Josephus (10,8a) abridges the request itself, while conversely prefacing it with an extended explanation as to why it was made by the envoys: "*As Rapsakēs spoke these words in Hebrew* (ἑβραϊστί)[56], *with which language he was familiar* (γλώττης εἶχεν ἐμπείρως)[57], *Eliakas was afraid* (φοβούμενος) *that the people might overhear them and be thrown into consternation* (εἰς ταραχὴν ἐμπέση)[58], and so asked him to speak in Aramaic (συριστί)[59]".

The sources represent Rab-shakeh as first replying – seemingly privately – to the envoys (18,27 // 36,12), and only then addressing himself to the city's defenders (18,28 // 36,13). Josephus (10,8b) conflates the two moments of the Assyrian's response such that his initial (private) reply becomes a word that is intended to be (over)heard by the "people" as well. He likewise supplies an explicit motivation for Rab-shakeh's reacting to the embassy's request as he does: "But the general, *perceiving what was in the back of his* [Eliakas'] *mind and the fear* (δέος)[60] *that held him*, spoke in a very loud and clear voice (μείζονι καὶ διατόρῳ τῇ φωνῇ)[61] and replied that he was speaking to him [Eliakas][62]

---

56. In 18,26.28 // 36,11.13 the reference is to "the language of Judah" (MT יְהוּדִית, LXX Ἰουδαϊστί). Josephus substitutes a more current designation, found also, e.g., in John 20,16.

57. This construction is hapax in Josephus. The historian "deduces" that Rab-shakeh had been speaking "in Hebrew" from the fact of the Biblical envoys' asking him to switch languages. He further counters the question, which readers might well ask, i.e. would an Assyrian general have known the language of a small, unimportant people of the time by assuring us that Rab-shakeh was, in fact, "familiar" with it.

58. This construction occurs also in (*BJ* 4,301; 5,91); *AJ* 4,293; 6,250; 13,30 (*Vita* 409). With the above insertion Josephus spells out the motive behind the request made of Rab-shakeh by the Biblical envoy(s).

59. This is the same term used in BL 18,26 and LXX 36,11 as their Greek rendering of MT's אֲרָמִית. Note that in the source verses all three envoys named in 18,18 // 36,3 make the request of Rab-shakeh; Josephus focusses attention on "Eliakim" by having him alone do so.

60. Compare the term φοβούμενος used of Eliakas in 10,8a, as well as the reference to Hezekiah's not venturing forth from Jerusalem "out of cowardice" (ὑπὸ δειλίας) in 10,5; see n. 32.

61. The adjective διάτορος is hapax in Josephus. The above reference to the manner of Rab-shakeh's speaking represents an anticipation of 18,28 // 36,13: "he called out in a loud voice" (B 18,28 ἐβόησεν μεγάλῃ; L 18,28 // LXX 36,13 ἐβόησε φωνῇ μεγάλῃ). Cf. 2 Chr 32,18: "and they [the Assyrians] shouted it [their words of contempt for the Lord] with a loud voice...".

62. In 18,27 // 36,12 Rab-shakeh's reply is addressed rather to all three envoys and seems, as noted above, to have a "private" character (contrast Josephus for whom it is delivered "in a very loud and clear voice"). Josephus leaves aside as well the "vulgar" content of the general's words as cited in the source verses: "Has my master sent me to speak these words to your master and to you, and not to the men sitting on the wall, who are doomed with you to eat their own dung and to drink their own urine?" See FELDMAN, *Hezekiah*, 608.

in Hebrew (ἑβραϊστί)[63] *'in order that all might hear* (ἀκούσαντες)[64] *the king's commands and choose a course to their advantage* (τὸ συμφέρον [see 9,233.251.255.264] ἕλωνται)[65] *by surrendering* (παραδόντες)[66] *to us*[67]*'".

The Biblical Rab-shakeh begins his address to the city's defenders with a four-fold warning to them about what they should not let Hezekiah "do" in their regard (18,29-31aα,32b // 36,14-16aα,18a; see also 2 Chr 32,10-11): "do not let Hezekiah deceive you... do not let Hezekiah make you rely on the the Lord... do not listen to Hezekiah... do not listen to Hezekiah when he misleads you...". Josephus' rendition (10,9a) reduces this four-fold admonition to a single, more indirect one[68] which, at the same time, he extends to encompass the envoys' (potential) deception of the people as well: "For it is clear (δῆλον)[69] that *both you and* the king are beguiling (παρακρουόμενοι; cf. BL 18,30 μὴ ἐπελπιζέτω, LXX 36,14 μὴ ἀπατάτω, i.e. Hezekiah) the people with vain hopes (ἐλπίσι [see ἐλπίζων, 10,6]... ματαίαις)[70] in persuading (πείθετε; see πεισθείς of Hezekiah's being "persuaded" by Sennacherib's offer, 10,3) them to

---

63. See n. 56. In the sources (18,27-28 // 36,12-13) the language used by Rab-shakeh in responding to the envoys is not specified, and it only when he begins addressing the men on the wall that he is said to do so in "the language of Judah" (see also 2 Chr 32,18).

64. This verb ironically echoes the notice on Eliakim's "fearing that the people might overhear (ἐπακούσαν)..." of 10,8a: Disregarding the envoy's request, Rab-shakeh deliberately acts to bring about the thing Eliakim had "feared".

65. This construction recurs in *BJ* 3,536 and *AJ* 12,273.

66. The verb παραδίδωμαι is another *Leitwort* of Josephus' account of Sennacherib's assault; it recurs in 10,10 together with the noun cognate.

67. Rab-shakeh's above words have no equivalent as such in those attributed to him in 18,27-35 // 36,12-20. They might, however, be seen as the historian's adapted combination of the general's rhetorical questions to the envoys in 18,27 // 36,12 ("Has my master sent me to speak these words to your master and to you, and not to the men sitting on the wall...?") and his summons to the defenders in 18,31 // 36,16 "([thus says the king of Assyria] 'Make your peace with me and come out to me; then every one of you will eat of his own vine...'"); see nn. 68,78,79. One might also see in Josephus' formulation here an influence from the side of 2 Chr 32,18: "And they [the Assyrians] shouted it [their mockery of the Lord] with a loud voice in the language of Judah to the people of Jerusalem who were on the wall to frighten and terrify them, *in order that they might take the city*". Throughout his version of Rab-shakeh's second speech in 10,8b-10, Josephus, rather exceptionally, reproduces the direct address of the sources.

68. From the complex of Rab-shakeh's warnings making up 18,29-32 // 36,14-18a, Josephus eliminates as well all the "motivations", both negative (see 18,29b // 36,14b) and "positive" (see 18,31aβb-32 // 36,16aβb-17) which the general employs in trying to win over his hearers (cf., however, his anticipated allusion to the latter via his phrase "in order that... they may a choose a course to their advantage..." which he places on Rab-shakeh's lips in 10,8b; see n. 67).

69. This adjective echoes the verbal form δηλοῦν used by Rab-shakeh in his initial word to the envoys in 10,7.

70. The phrase "vain hopes" is hapax in Josephus.

resist (ἀντέχειν)". To this "abbreviation" of Rab-shakeh's Biblical "warning" Josephus then (10,9b) appends his "delayed" version of the "horse wager" of 18,23-24 // 36,8-9: *"If, however, you are confident* (θαρρεῖτε; see θαρρῶν, 10,6) *and think you can repulse our force*[71], I am ready to furnish you with two thousand of the horses *that are with me,* in order that you may mount on them the same number (ἰσαρίθμους)[72] of riders (ἐπιβάτας δόντες)[73] *and so show your strength* (ἐμφανίσατε ... δύναμιν)[74]. *But you cannot furnish* (τούτους δοίητε[75]) *riders whom you do not have*[76]".

The Biblical Rab-shakeh concludes his speech to Jerusalem's defenders in 18,33-35 // 36,18b-20 (see also 2 Chr 32,13-15) with a series of rhetorical questions calling attention to the failure of the nations' "gods" to defend their peoples against Assyria's might. Josephus leaves aside this entire sequence[77]. In place therefore, he has (10,10a) the Assyrian draw a practical conclusion for his hearers' benefit from their inability – as just asserted by him – to meet his challenge: "Why, then, do you hesitate to surrender (παραδιδόναι; see παραδόντες, 10,8b) *to those who*

71. Compare 18,23a // 36,8a: "Come now, make a wager with my master the king of Assyria". Rab-shakeh's reference to "our force (δύναμιν)" here picks up on the historian's inserted reference to Sennacherib's leaving his officers at Jerusalem "with a large force (ἰσχύος)" in 10,4; see n. 26.

72. Elsewhere in the Josephan *corpus* the adjective ἰσάριθμος occurs as a variant in *AJ* 16,51; 19,365.

73. The term ἐπιβάτης recurs in *Vita* 165,167 in the meaning "forces, crew". With Rab-shakeh's wording above, compare his offer as cited in 18,23b // 36,8b: "I will give you two thousand horses, if you are able on your part to set riders (BL 18,23 δοῦναι ... ἐπιβάτας [see Josephus]; LXX 36,8 δοῦναι ἀναβάτας) on them". Note further that, whereas in the sources the "I" who offers to supply the Judeans with horses is Sennacherib himself (see the *Botenformel* in 18,23a // 36,8a), Josephus represents Rab-shakeh as making the offer in his own name.

74. The above indication concerning the purpose of the challenge issued by Rab-shakeh to his hearers has no Biblical equivalent. For the phrase "show strength" see on 9,55. Note too the wordplay between "show your [the Judeans'] strength (δύναμιν)" and the phrase "... and think you [the Judeans] can repulse our [the Assyrians'] force (δύναμιν)" earlier in 10,9b.

75. This is the conjecture of Dindorf which Bekker, Naber, and Marcus follow. Niese retains the δῷητε of the codices. Note the wordplay between the phrase τούτους δοίητε here and the phrase ἐπιβάτας δόντες earlier in 10,9b.

76. This affirmation takes the place of the rhetorical question ascribed to the Rab-shakeh in 18,24 // 36,9: "How then can you repulse a single captain among the least of my master's servants, when you rely on Egypt for chariots and horses"? Josephus' "substitution" more clearly brings out the intended point of the Assyrian's challenge, i.e. the hearers are unable to meet that challenge.

77. His doing so is in line with his statement in various contexts (see *AJ* 4,207; *c. Ap.* 2,237) that Jews are forbidden to "blaspheme" the gods of other peoples out of respect for the word "god"; cf. FELDMAN, *Hezekiah*, 607-608. In adhering to this principle Josephus even refrains here from reproducing the derogatory language of a pagan general about other "gods". See n. 118.

are stronger than yourselves and will take you whether you like it or not[78]?" Thereupon, he terminates (10,10b) Rab-shakeh's second speech with a final statement by him concerning the choices facing his hearers and their respective consequences: "Nevertheless a voluntary surrender (τὸ ... ἑκούσιον τῆς παραδόσεως)[79] means safety (ἀσφαλές) for you[80], *while an involuntary one* (τὸ ἀκούσιον) *after your defeat will prove to be dangerous* (ἐπικίνδυνον)[81] *and the cause of misfortunes* (συμφορῶν [see 9,101.103.226,281] αἴτιον)[82]".

4. *Isaiah's Assurance*

The fourth section which I distinguish within the accounts of Sennacherib's assault on Jerusalem (18,36-19,7 // 36,21-37,7 = *AJ* 10,11-14) focusses on the word of assurance delivered by Isaiah in response to an appeal made him by Hezekiah. Within this new segment, one may further identify an opening sub-unit dealing first with what the city's defenders and then the royal envoys and/or the people as a whole did in response to Rab-shakeh's second speech: the former keep silent as instructed (18,36 // 36,21), while the latter report back to Hezekiah with their clothes rent (18,37 // 36,22). Once again, Josephus (10,11a) conflates and abridges: "When the people and the envoys *had heard* (ἀκούσαντες, see 10,8b) *these words of the Assyrian general*, they reported them to Hezekiah[83]".

78. The above question might be seen as Josephus' re-utilization of Rab-shakeh's summons as cited in 18,31 // 36,16 ("make your peace with me and come out to me"), and, as we have suggested (see n. 67), earlier anticipated by him in 10,8b. The phrase of 10,10a italicized above lacks an equivalent in the sources; it underscores both the disparity between the two parties and the Assyrian's hubristic self-confidence.

79. With this construction compare the reference to Jehoiachin's having "voluntarily surrendered (παραδόντι ... ἑκουσίως) to Neubuchadnezzar in 10,230. The noun παράδοσις here in 10,10b echoes the verbal form παραδίδωμι used in 10,8b,10a; see n. 66.

80. The above assurrance might be seen as Josephus' (compressed) version of the conditional promises which Rab-shakeh attaches to his summons to the defenders to surrender to him in 18,31-32a // 36,16-17. See also the general's allusion to "a course to their [the defenders'] advantage" in 10,8b; cf. n. 67.

81. Josephus' other uses of the term ἐπικίνδυνος are in *BJ* 2,207; *AJ* 17,139; 18,227.298.

82. The above phrase recurs in *AJ* 6,290; 13,417; cf. the related expression in *AJ* 2,60. The threat with which Rab-shakeh counterbalances his promise to the hearers here in 10,10b has no equivalent in the sources as such. It serves to underscore what is at stake in their choice.

83. The above rendition of 18,36-37 // 36,21-22 leaves aside a whole series of source particulars: the "people's" keeping "silent" before Rab-shakeh as they had been instructed by Hezekiah (recall that there has been no previous mention – in either the Bible or Josephus – of any such royal instruction), the names of the envoys, and their

The next sub-unit within the present segment concerns Hezekiah's reaction to the news brought him by the envoys. The king's initial response as described in 19,1 // 37,1 is to rend his clothes, don sackcloth and go into the Temple. The historian's rendition (10,11b) modifies both the first and third elements of this source sequence: "And he thereupon *took off his royal garments* (βασιλικὴν ... ἐσθῆτα)[84], put on (ἀμφιασάμενος; BL 19,1 // LXX 37,1 περιεβάλετο)[85] sackcloth (σάκκους; BL 19,1 // LXX 37,1 σάκκον) *and assumed an attitude of humility* (σχῆμα ταπεινόν)[86]; *then, falling on his face in the manner of his country* (τῷ πατρίῳ νόμῳ)[87], *he supplicated God* (τὸν θεὸν ἱκέτευε)[88] *and entreated* (ἠντιβόλει) *Him to help* (βοηθῆσαι) *one who had no other hope of salvation* (ἐλπίδα [see 10,6.9] ἔχοντι σωτηρίας)[89]".

2 Kgs 19,2 // Isa 37,2 relate a further reaction on the king's part, i.e. his dispatch of a mission to the prophet Isaiah made up of Eliakim, Shebna, and the "senior priests", all "clothed with sackcloth". In contrast to his handling of Hezekiah's initial reaction in 10,11b, Josephus (10,12a) compresses this item: "He [Hezekiah] also sent some of his friends (φιλῶν)[90] and some of the priests to the prophet

"rending" of their clothes (by omitting this last item, Josephus highlights the penitential gestures attributed in what follows to Hezekiah who, in his presentation, becomes the first – and only – Judean to engage in these).

84. This phrase occurs also in *BJ* 1,465; 2,444; *AJ* 6,330. In having Hezekiah remove his royal vesture prior to donning sackcloth (see above), Josephus eliminates the peculiarity of the sources' presentation wherein the king seems to put sackcloth on over his (rent) ordinary garments.

85. Elsewhere Josephus employs the verb ἀμφιάζω in *BJ* 7,131; *AJ* 19,314 – in neither case with "sackcloth" as object as here in 10,11.

86. This phrase has a counterpart in *BJ* 1,132; *AJ* 5,115; 11,225; 13,415. As used of Hezekiah here, it accentuates both the extent of his dismay and of his self-abasement before God.

87. On this phrase, see SCHRÖDER, *Gesetze*, p. 79; cf. 9,243 where Ahaz is charged with "violating his country's laws (πατρίους ... νόμους)".

88. On Josephus' uses of this formula, see BEGG, *Early Divided Monarchy*, p. 48, n. 251.

89. The phrase "have hope of salvation" recurs in *BJ* 1,390; 5,335; 6,160; *AJ* 7,158; 16,389; cf. "no (other) hope of salvation" in *BJ* 4,338; *AJ* 6,24; 13,399. The foregoing reference to Hezekiah's prostration and prayer takes the place of the notice of his going into the Temple of 19,1b // 37,1b. The replacement may have in view the consideration that as a layman Hezekiah would not have had access to the Temple (see p. 341, n. 9 on 9,260). It may further be inspired by the Biblical accounts of Hezekiah's later prayer for deliverance (19,15-19 // 37,15-20), which Josephus will not reproduce *in extenso*; see in particular 19,19a // 37,20a ("save [BL 19,19 // LXX 37,20 σῶσον; cf. σωτηρίας, 10,11b] us from his [Sennacherib's] hand").

90. This generalizing replacement for the mention of Eliakim and Shebna by name and office in 19,2 // 37,2 echoes Josephus' qualification of the three envoys sent by Hezekiah to Rab-shakeh as "three of the friends (φίλους) who were closest to him" in 10,5.

Isaiah...⁹¹". The message delivered to Isaiah by the delegation in Hezekiah's name is cited at some length in 19,3-4 // 37,3-4. That message consists of three elements: poetic lament over the situation (19,3b // 37,3b), expression of hope that God has heard and will rebuke Rab-shakeh's blasphemous words (19,4a // 37,4a) and appeal for Isaiah's intercession (19,4b // 37,4b). Omitting the first of these elements⁹², Josephus recasts what the delegation says to Isaiah in terms of the instructions given them by the king, these having the character of an appeal to the prophet to act on the people's behalf: "... and asked him [Isaiah] to pray to God (δεηθῆναι τοῦ θεοῦ)⁹³ *and, when he had offered sacrifices* (θυσίας) *for the common safety* (κοινῆς σωτηρίας)⁹⁴, to exhort (παρακαλεῖν) Him to show His wrath (νεμεσῆσαι)⁹⁵ at the hopes (ἐλπίσιν)⁹⁶, of the enemy, but to take pity (ἐλεῆσαι) on His own (αὐτοῦ)⁹⁷ people".

91. From his above reproduction of 19,2 // 37,2 Josephus omits the qualification of the priests as "senior", the reference to the whole delegation's being clad in "sackcloth", and the name of Isaiah's father ("Amoz"). Recall that Josephus has earlier provided an implicit motivation for Hezekiah's sending the delegation precisely to Isaiah via his Biblically unparalleled notice in 9,276: "But Hezekiah gave no thought to these [i.e. Assyrian] threats, for he had confidence... *in the prophet Isaiah, by whom he was accurately informed of future events*".

92. His reason for this omission is likely the obscurity of the messengers' metaphorical opening words which read (RSV): "This day is a day of distress, of rebuke, and of disgrace; children have come to birth, and there is no strength to bring them forth" (19,3b // 37,3b).

93. For this construction see on 9,67. Compare LXX 37,4b: δεηθήσῃ πρὸς κύριον τὸν θεόν.

94. The phrase "common safety" recurs in (*BJ* 1,332); *AJ* 3,297; 11,137; *c. Ap.* 2,196. The word σωτηρίας of Hezekiah's appeal here in 10,12 echoes the same term used in 10,11 where Hezekiah affirms that he has no other hope of "salvation" than God.

The words of the messengers as cited in 19,3-4 // 37,3-4 say nothing about the prophet Isaiah's "sacrificing". Conceivably, Josephus introduces the reference as a reminiscence of the "sacrifice" (θυσίαν) offered by the prophet Samuel on the people's behalf in the face of the Philistine threat in *AJ* 6,25 = 1 Sam 7,9 (note that the context of this passage contains wording that recalls that used in 10,11, see ἐλπὶς ... ἡμῖν οὐκ ἄλλη σωτηρίας [6,24]; compare μηδεμίαν ἄλλην ἐλπίδα ἔχοντι σωτηρίας [10,11] and τοῦ θεοῦ ἱκευθέντος [6,24]; compare τὸν θεόν ἱκέτευε [10,11]). On the assimilation – paralleled elsewhere in Josephus' portrayal of key characters of his narrative (himself included) – of the prophetic and the priestly roles effected by the inserted reference to Isaiah's "sacrificing" here in 10,12, see further FELDMAN, *Studies*, p. 381 (= ID., *Isaiah*, 591-592) and HÖFFKEN, *Hiskija und Jesaja*, 40.

95. The word νεμεσάω recurs in *BJ* 1,431.467; 6,57; *AJ* 3,42; 13,415. Only here in 10,12 is it used with God as subject.

96. With this word Hezekiah picks up on a term used earlier by Rab-shakeh; see 10,9 where the general accuses the king and his envoys of "beguiling the people with vain hopes (ἐλπίσι)". Hezekiah now asks that God render vain the Assyrian's own "hopes".

97. This is the reading adopted by Dindorf, Bekker, Naber, and Marcus for the αὐτοῦ of the codices which Niese retains. The above sequence "to exhort Him... to take pity on

The unit 18,36-19,7 // 36,21-37,7 culminates in 19,5-7 // 37,5-7 with Isaiah's reassuring response to the royal appeal. By way of introduction to the prophet's words, Josephus (10,13a) replaces the brief transitional phrase of 19,5 // 37,5 ("when the servants of King Hezekiah came to Isaiah...") with a more elaborate one of his own: "... when the prophet had done these things and received an oracle (χρηματίσαντος)[98] from God...[99]". To his (indirect discourse) reproduction of prophet's words from 19,6-7 // 37,6-7 in 10,13b-14 Josephus appends an additional promise which looks ahead to the later course of his own account:

> (13)... he encouraged (παρεθάρρυνεν)[100] both the king himself *and the friends* (φίλους; see 10,12) *who were with him*[101] by foretelling (προλέγων) that the enemy would be defeated without a fight (ἀμαχητὶ ... ἡττηθέντας)[102] and retire *ignominiously* (αἰσχρῶς), *with none of the self-confidence* (θράσους) *which they now showed*, (14) for God would see to it (προνοεῖν)[103] that they should be destroyed (διαφθαρῶσαι)[104]; *and he*

His own people" might be seen as Josephus' rendition of Hezekiah's hope as reported to Isaiah by the delegation in 19,4a // 37,4a: "It may be that the Lord... will rebuke the words which the Lord... has heard". In his version that hope becomes a matter for which the king requests Isaiah's intercession.

98. Josephus' other uses of the verb χρηματίζω are in *AJ* 3,212; 5,42; 11,327. Compare Josephus' − likewise inserted − reference to the new settlers in Samaria "learning from an oracle (χρησμῷ)" about what they needed to do to appease God in *AJ* 9,289.

99. The above formula, indicative of the inspired character of Isaiah's following words, takes the place of the *Botenformel* of 19,6 // 37,6 "thus says the Lord" which Josephus regularly avoids.

100. Josephus' one remaining use of the verb παραθαρσύνω/ παραθαρρύνω is in 10,128. Cf. θαρρέω/θαρσέω in 10,6.9.

101. Compare 19,6 // 37,6: "Isaiah said to them [the delegation], 'Say to your master... "do not be afraid because of the words that you have heard..."'".

102. This construction recurs in *AJ* 12,312.

103. God appears as subject of the verb προνοέω also in *AJ* 2,280; 3,23; 4,194; 7,65.93; 10,272; 11,231.327; *Vita* 327.

104. This term ironically echoes the same word as used by Rab-shakeh in 10,7 where he avers that Sennacherib has made his expedition against Hezekiah "in order that he might destroy... (διαφθείρῃ) those ruled by him [Hezekiah]". God now makes clear that Sennacherib's expedition will end, on the contrary, in his own "destruction". The above sequence "... the enemy... should be destroyed" represents Josephus' version of the announcement of 19,7 // 37,7: "Behold I [God] will put a spirit (BL 19,7 // LXX 37,7 πνεῦμα − on Josephus' tendency to avoid this term, see p. 16, n. 53 on 9,10) in him, so that he shall hear a rumor [Josephus' non-utilization of this element might be due to the fact that subsequently, see 19,35-36 // 37,36-37, Sennacherib's withdrawal seems to be attributed, not to a "rumor" that he hears, but to the actual destruction of his forces] and return to his own land; and I will make him fall by the sword in his own land". In reproducing the prophet's announcement Josephus accentuates the shamefulness which will surround the now so confident Assyrian's withdrawal, doing so, perhaps, under the influence of 2 Chr 32,21bα which states that Sennacherib "returned *with shame of face* (BL μετὰ αἰσχύνης προσώπου) to his own land". In any event, Josephus will pick up on the sources' specification about the circumstances of Sennacherib's end (in his own land, by

also foretold that Senacheirimos, the king of Assyria, would himself fail (διαμαρτόντα) *in his attempt against Egypt* [see 10,4][105] and on his return (ἐπανερχόμενον)[106], to his own land would perish by the sword (ἀπολεῖσθαι σιδήρῳ)[107].

5. *Renewed Assyrian Threat*

2 Kgs 19,8-13 // Isa 37,8-13 tell of a renewed Assyrian threat, this featuring Sennacherib's warning message to Hezekiah (vv. 9b-13) subsequent to Rab-shakeh's "return" and Sennacherib's hearing of the advance of Tirhakah of Ethiopia (vv. 8-9a). Given the fact that Sennacherib's new threats are largely repetitious of those already made by Rab-shakeh in what precedes[108], it is not suprising to find Josephus (10,15) drastically compressing the whole sequence. In particular, for the series of developments cited in 19,8-9a // 37,8-9a (Rab-shakeh's return; his finding his master engaged against Libnah, having left Lachish [see 18,17 // 36,3; not cited by Josephus]; the news of Tirhakah's advance whose connection with Sennacherib's sending messengers to Hezekiah in 19,9b // 37,9b remains unclear), he substitutes[109] a single, vague chronological indication linking the Assyrian's initiative with what precedes: "now it happened that about this time...".

In 19,9b // 37,9b the reference is to Sennacherib's dispatching "messengers" to Hezekiah. With an eye to the account of 19,14 // 37,14 where Hezekiah is said to take the "letter(s)" from the hand of the Assyrian envoys, Josephus introduces mention of "letters" already at the outset: "... the king of Assyria had written a letter (ἐπιστολάς)[110] to

the sword) at the end of 10,14, following his inserted prediction about the Assyrian's failed Egyptian campaign; see above in the text.

105. This insertion within the announcement of 19,7 // 37,7 looks ahead to the extra-Biblical account Josephus will relate about Sennacherib's Egyptian campaign in 10,17-20. Inclusion of a prediction of its failure here accentuates Isaiah's stature as a true prophet.

106. This is the conjecture of Ernesti which Niese, Naber, and Marcus all follow. The codices and E have παρερχόμενον (cf. Lat remearet), as do Dindorf and Bekker.

107. Compare BL 19,7 (καταβαλῶ αὐτὸν ἐν ῥομφαίᾳ) // LXX 37,7 (πεσεῖται μαχαίρᾳ).

108. 2 Kgs 18,17-19,9a (+ 19,36-37) and 19,9b-35 are, in fact, widely held to represent two versions of the same episode; see the commentaries.

109. Josephus will, however, make use of the reference to Tirhakah's advance of 19,9a // 37,9a in 10,18.

110. Literally "letters". Josephus' plural form agrees with that of MT B (τὰ βιβλία) 19,14 and MT 37,14 against the singular (τὸ βιβλίον) of L 19,14 and LXX 37,14. A further influence on Josephus' formulation here might be 2 Chr 32,17: "and he [Sennacherib] wrote letters (so MT; BL βιβλίον)...".

Hezekiah...". The content of Sennacherib's letter(s) as reported by Josephus represents a generalized composite of elements drawn from 19,10-13 // 37,10-13: "... in which he said that he was foolish (ἀνόητον)[111] to suppose that he would escape being made his servant (διαφεύξεσθαι δουλείαν[112])[113], since he had subdued many great nations (ἔθνη)[114], and he threatened (ἠπείλει) to destroy (διαφθερεῖν)[115] utterly and completely (πανωλεθρία)[116] after capturing him[117], *unless he opened the gates* (τὰς πύλας ἀνοίξας) *and willingly* (ἑκών; cf. ἑκούσιον, 10,10) *admitted his army* (δέξεται τὴν στρατιάν) *into Jerusalem*[118]".

6. Hezekiah & Isaiah's Response

2 Kgs 19,14-34 // Isa 37,14-35 devote an extended section to describing the responses by Hezekiah and Isaiah to Sennacherib's threatening

111. This term echoes Rab-shakeh's earlier directive to the envoys that they should make clear to Hezekiah that he was being "very foolish (ἀνόητος)", 10,7.

112. This construction occurs also in *AJ* 6,69 where it is used in connection with the treatment meted out to the Transjordanian Jewish cities by the Ammonite king Nahash.

113. Compare Sennacherib's opening warning in 19,10 // 37,10: "Do not let your God on whom you [Hezekiah] rely deceive you by promising that Jerusalem will not be given into the hand of the king of Assyria".

114. This motivation ("since") for Sennacherib's warning represents Josephus' compressed version of 19,11a // 37,11a: "Behold, you have heard what the kings of Assyria have done to all lands [L 19,11 // LXX 37,11 land], destroying them utterly".

115. This is the reading proposed by Niese and followed by Naber and Marcus for the διαφθείρειν of the codices and E, read also by Dindorf and Bekker. On this *Leitwort* of 10,1-23, see n. 104.

116. This term occurs elsewhere in Josephus only in *AJ* 3,60.

117. The above "threat" has no equivalent as such in Sennacherib's message as cited in 19,10-13 // 37,10-13. It might, however, be seen as the historian's adaptation of 19,11 // 37,11 where the king speaks of Assyria's having "utterly destroyed" (B 19,11 ἀναθεματίσαι; L 19,11 ὡς ἐξωλόθρευσαν; LXX 37,11 ὡς ἀπώλεσαν) "all the lands (L 19,11; LXX 37,11 land)", and then goes on to ask rhetorically "and shall you be delivered (> LXX 37,11)?". Josephus would thus have Sennacherib reapply the "destruction" previously inflicted on the lands to the fate awaiting Hezekiah himself. Sennacherib's "threat" here in 10,15 likewise has a counterpart in the words which Josephus places on the lips of Rab-shakeh – here too without Biblical basis as such – in 10,10: "... an involuntary (surrender) after your defeat will prove to be dangerous and the cause of misfortunes". The effect of both interjected threats is to accentuate the perilous situation facing Hezekiah.

118. This conclusion to the Josephan Sennacherib's message introduces a reminiscence of Rab-shakeh's words as cited in 10,6 where he questions Hezekiah about his being "unwilling to admit his [Sennacherib's] army (τὴν στρατιὰν οὐ δέχεται) into the city". It takes the place of the rhetorical questions, citing various nations and kings whose gods were unable to protect them against Assyria's might, with which Sennacherib's message concludes in 19,12-13 // 37,12-13 (cf. also 2 Chr 32,13-15). Josephus likely felt that the Biblical catalogue of long-vanished peoples would prove offputting to Gentile readers. Such readers might also take offense at the derogatory reference (19,12 // 37,12) to "the gods of the nations" – even though this is placed on the lips of a pagan king; see nn. 77, 123.

words to the former. As he did in the case of the Assyrian's threat itself, Josephus notably reduces this sequence, his version of which is limited to a single paragraph, i.e. 10,16[119].

The sources commence (19,14 // 37,14) their new section with an elaborate description of Hezekiah's handling of the Assyrian "letter(s)": he takes this from the Assyrian messengers, reads it, and proceeds to the Temple where he "spreads it before the Lord". Josephus' version introduces several notable changes: "When Hezekiah read these words, *he made light* (καταφρονεῖ) *of them because of his confidence* (πεποίθησιν)[120] *inspired by God*[121], but *he folded up the letter(s) and laid it away within the temple*[122]".

There now follows Hezekiah's prayer to which the sources devote five verses (19,15-19 // 37,15-20). In line with his tendency to abridge Biblical prayers[123], Josephus compresses the whole into a single, generalized transitional allusion (10,16b): "And, when he offered a second (πάλιν)[124] prayer to God (τῷ θεῷ τὰς εὐχάς αὐτοῦ ποιησαμένου; compare προσηύξατο ... πρὸς κύριον, L 19,15 //

119. His reduction of the sources' content here is undoubtedly prompted by fact that the words attributed to Hezekiah and Isaiah in 19,14-34 // 37,14-35 appear repetitious of what they have already said in 18,36-19,7 // 36,21-37,7. Josephus' abridgement here has a certain counterpart in the Chronicler's treatment of 19,14-34 // 37,14-35 which he compresses into the notice: "Then Hezekiah the king and Isaiah the prophet... prayed because of this [i.e. the Assyrian threats cited in 2 Chr 32,9-19] and cried to heaven" (32,20).

120. This noun echoes earlier uses of the verb πείθω in 10,3.6.9. In particular, it sets up a contrast with 10,3 where Hezekiah is (wrongfully) "persuaded" (πεισθείς) by Sennacherib's promises; now he (rigthfully) exhibits a "confidence" inspired by God.

121. This notice on Hezekiah's emotional response to Sennacherib's letter has no counterpart in 19,14 // 37,14. It does, however, call to mind Josephus' editorial comment in 9,276 (also no Biblical parallel) that Hezekiah gave "no thought" to the Assyrian threats "for he had confidence (ἐθάρρει) in his piety towards God". It likewise sets up a contrast with the mention of the king's "cowardice" which causes him to sent others to parley with the Assyrian envoys rather than going out to them himself in 10,5. By this point (10,16), under the influence of Isaiah's earlier message to him as reported in 10,13-14, Hezekiah has regained his *sang froid* in the face of the Assyrian threat.

122. As noted above, in 19,14 // 37,14 Hezekiah spreads out the letter(s) before the Lord in the Temple. Josephus' modification on this point might be designed to counter the sources' seeming implication that the Deity would not have known the content of the letter unless Hezekiah "showed" it to him. In Josephus' version the king simply "files" the letter in the Temple.

123. For this tendency, see, e.g., the historian's handling of Jonah's lengthy prayer (Jonah 2,2-10) in 9,214. Another reason for Josephus' not reproducing Hezekiah's prayer *in extenso* might be its derogatory references to the gods of the nations and their impotence, see 19,18 // 37,18-19; and cf. nn. 77, 118.

124. This term recalls the fact that there has already been mention of an earlier supplication by Hezekiah in 10,11.

37,15) *on behalf of the city* and the safety of all (τῆς ἁπάντων σωτηρίας)...[125]".

The highpoint of the present section comes in 19,20-34 // 37,21-35 where Isaiah delivers a series of assurances in response to Hezekiah's preceding appeal. In line with his previous treatment of the royal appeal itself, Josephus drastically abridges the prophet's announcements as well (10,16c): "... *the prophet* Isaiah told him that He had hearkened (ἐπήκοον)[126] to his prayer[127], and that *at the present time* he would not be besieged (πολιορκηθήσεσθαι) by the Assyrian (τοῦ Ἀσσυριοῦ)[128], *while in the future* (τῷ δὲ μέλλοντι)[129] his subjects (τοὺς ὑπ᾽ αὐτῷ[130] γενομένους[131]), relieved of all apprehension (ἀδεεῖς)[132], would till their land (γεωργήσειν)[133] in peace (μετ᾽ εἰρήνης) and look after their own possessions (ἐπιμελήσεσθαι ... κτημάτων) without fear of anything (οὐδὲν φοβουμένους[134])[135]".

125. The above phrase picks up the appeal "save us (σῶσον ἡμᾶς, B 19,19 // LXX 37,20; ῥῦσαι ἡμᾶς, L 19,19) from his [Sennacherib's] hand" of the Biblical Hezekiah's prayer. It likewise echoes Hezekiah's confession in 10,11 that he has no other hope of "salvation" (σωτηρίας) than God.

126. For the use of this term in reference to the Deity, see on 9,55.

127. Josephus draws this opening component of Isaiah's announcement from 19,20 (MT B): "your prayer to me... I have heard (B ἤκουσα)".

128. This is the reading of the codices MSP which Dindorf, Bekker, Naber, and Marcus follow. The remaining codices read Σύρου as does Niese; Lat has "Assyriis". The above announcement represents Josephus' compressed version of 19,32 // 37,33: "Therefore thus says the Lord concerning the king of Assyria: 'He shall not come into this city, or shoot an arrow there, or come before it with a shield or cast up a siege mound against it'"; cf. 19,33b // 37,34b: "... he shall not come into this city...".

129. This is the reading of the codices MSP which Dindorf, Bekker, Naber, and Marcus follow; the codices ROLaur have simply μέλλοντι. Niese conjectures μέλλειν τε.

130. This is the conjecture of Niese which Naber and Marcus follow. The codices have τῶν ὑπ᾽ αὐτοῦ (as do Dindorf and Bekker).

131. This is the reading of codex M which Niese, Naber, and Marcus follow. The other codices have γενομένων (as do Dindorf and Bekker).

132. This is the reading adopted by Dindorf, Bekker, Niese, Naber, and Marcus. Compare ἀνείς (RO), ἄν εἶναι ἀδεεῖς (SP), ἀνεῖναι (LaurV); cf. Lat).

133. This is the reading adopted by Niese and Marcus. The codices SPVLaur follow – as do Dindorf, Bekker, and Naber – the word with a plus (τε), while RO read ἀοργητί.

134. Contrast 10,6 where Eliakim is said to be "afraid (φοβούμενος) that the people might overhear" the Assyrian officers and themselves "be thrown into consternation".

135. The concluding segment of Josephus' version of Isaiah's annnouncements above seems loosely inspired by the prophet's "agricultural predictions" in 19,29-30 // 37,30-31: "And this shall be a sign for you: this year you shall eat what grows of itself, and in the second year what springs of the same; then in the third year, sow, and reap, and plant vineyards, and eat their fruit. And the surviving remnant of the house of Judah shall again take root downward, and bear fruit upward".

It thus appears that in his use of complex 19,20-34 // 37,21-35, Josephus reproduces (elements) of 19,20 // 37,21; 19,32 // 37,33; 19,29-30 // 37,30-31 in that order. He makes no utilization of the segment 19,21-28 // 37,22-29 with, e.g., its derogatory image of the foreign king Sennacherib as a beast which the Lord will lead by the nose (19,28 // 37,29); cf. FELDMAN, *Studies*, p. 372 (= ID., *Hezekiah*, 608).

7. *Assyrian Withdrawal*

Having related the Assyrian threats against Jerusalem and the inhabitants' response to these in great detail, the Biblical accounts conclude the whole episode of Sennacherib's assault with notable brevity in 19,35-37 // 37,36-38 (cf. 2 Chr 32,21). By contrast, Josephus (10,17-23) greatly expands on the circumstances surrounding Sennacherib's overthrow. Specifically, he precedes his parallel (10,21-23) to 19,35-36, etc. with a lengthy section concerning the Assyrian's Egyptian misadventure which lacks a Biblical counterpart as such, 10,17-20. The historian commences this *Sondergut* passage, for which he draws on Herodotus and Berosus (see 10,18b-20), by telling of Sennacherib's ill-fated incursion into Egypt in his own words in 10,17-18a, likewise incorporating here the allusion to the threatening advance of King Tirhakah of Ethiopia from 19,9a // 37,9a which he had earlier passed over; see above. The segment reads:

> (17) A little while after this[136] the king of Assyria failed (διαμαρτών)[137] in his attack (ἐπιβολῆς)[138] upon the Egyptians [see 10,4] and returned home (ἀνεχώρησεν ἐπ' οἴκου) without accomplishing anything[139] for the following reason. After he had spent a great deal of time on the siege (πολιορκίαν; cf. πολιοκηθήσεσθαι, 10,16) of Pelusium[140] and the earthworks (χωμάτων) which he was raising against the walls had already reached a great height, and he was on the point of attacking[141], he heard (ἀκούει) that Tharsikēs (Θαρσικήν)[142], the king of the Ethiopians, was

136. With this vague chronological indication compare that used in 10,15: "now it happened that about this time".

137. This word echoes the same term used in the prediction Josephus attributes to Isaiah in 10,14b: "(he also foretold that Senacheirimos) would himself fail (διαμαρτόντα) in his attempt against Egypt...". See n. 105.

138. This is the conjecture of Dindorf, based on Lat's "bello" and followed by Niese, Bekker, Naber, and Marcus. The codices read ἐπιβουλῆς.

139. Also this indication (see n. 137) has a counterpart in the predictions previously made by Josephus' Isaiah; see 10,13b-14: "the enemy would retire (ἀναχωρήσειν) ignominiously... and on his return to his own land (ἐπανερχόμενον εἰς τὴν οἰκείαν) would perish by the sword". Sennacherib's actual "return home" will be related by Josephus only in 10,22, following the extended segment, 10,17-21, devoted to the disasters that befall his forces, first in Egypt and then in Palestine.

140. According to WEILL, *Josèphe*, II, p. 306, n. 2 and MARCUS, *Josephus*, VI, p. 165, n. c this site on Egypt's eastern border represents the historian's substitute, based on the account of Herodotus which he will adduce in 10,18, for the city of Libnah against which Sennacherib is said to be "fighting" in 19,8 // 37,8.

141. The above references to the progress of the siege appear to represent Josephus' own embellishments of Herodotus' account of Sennacherib's siege of Pelusium which he will quote subsequently; see 10,18b-19.

142. Compare "Tirhakah" (MT 19,9 // 37,9); Θαρά (B 19,9); Θαρθάκ (L 19,9); Θαρακά (LXX 37,9). For the form of the king's name as read by Marcus above, SCHLATTER, *Namen*, p. 114 proposes an original θαρεικην, while SCHALIT, *Namenwörterbuch*, p. 53 suggests θαρσίκης.

coming *to the aid* (ἐπὶ συμμαχίᾳ) *of the Egyptians with a large force and had decided to make the journey through the desert and fall upon the Assyrians suddenly.* (18a) *And so, being alarmed* (ταραχθείς; cf. εἰς ταραχήν, of Jerusalem's defenders, 10,8) *at this news, King Senacheirimos left Pelusium and withdrew* (ἀνεχώρησε), *as I said* [see 10,17a], *without accomplishing anything* (ἄπρακτος)[143].

Having given his own version of the Assyrians' Egyptian fiasco in 10,17-18a, Josephus next adduces the confirmatory evidence of two non-Biblical historians to this same happening. Of these, the first to be cited is Herodotus whose testimony he features in 10,18b-19:

(18b) Concerning this Senacheirimos, Herodotus also tells us, in the second book of his History[144], that this king came against the king of Egypt, who was a priest of Hephaestus[145], and besieged (πολιορκῶν) Pelusium[146], but he abandoned the siege for the following reason. The king of Egypt prayed to God (ηὔξατο ... τῷ θεῷ)[147], and God hearkened (ἐπήκοος) to his prayer[148] and visited a plague (πληγὴν ἐνσκήπτει; cf. λοιμὸν ... ἐνέσκη-

---

143. The sequence italicized above might be seen as Josephus' elaboration of the background to and consequences of the enigmatic, passing reference to Sennacherib's "hearing", while fighting against Libneh, that Tirhakah had "set out to fight against" him in 19,8-9a // 37,8-9a.

144. More specifically in 2.141 (where the Assyrian's name appears in the accusative form of Σαναχάριβον; see A.D. GODLEY (ed. and tr.), *Herodotus*, I, (LCL), London, Heinemann; Cambridge, MA, Harvard University Press, 1946, pp. 446-449. For the above sequence "without accomplishing anything... in the second book of his history" which renders the reading of the codices SPLaurV, RO (cf. Lat) have simply "(and so being alarmed at this news King Senacherimios) to march against the priest of Hephaestus; he says (ἐπὶ τὸν ἱερέα τὸν Ἡφαίστου στρατεῦσαι ἔλεγεν)". The latter reading is printed by Niese (who further holds that the reading adopted by Marcus represents a scribal effort to fill a lacuna in the text (see *Opera*, I, pp. xliii, xlviii), but is emphatically rejected ("mihi... minime persuasit") by NABER, *Opera*, II, p. xxxiv.

145. Herodotus at the opening of 2.141 gives the king's name as "Sethos".

146. Josephus' rendition of Herodotus here echoes his own formulation in 10,17, i.e. "after he (Sennacherib) had spent a great deal of time on the siege (πολιορκίαν) of Pelusium...". In 2.141 it is rather the Egyptian king "Sethos" (see n. 145) who "encamps (στρατοπεδεύσασθαι) at Pelusium... for here is the road to Egypt...". Once he does so, the Assyrians assemble at the site as well. Josephus leaves aside Herodotus' further detail that Sethos was accompanied to Pelusium only "by hucksters and artificers and traders".

147. This phrase echoes Josephus' description of Hezekiah as τῷ θεῷ τὰς εὐχὰς ... ποιησαμένου in 10,16: in the face of their common peril from the side of Sennacherib, the Jewish and the pagan kings both "pray" to "the [one, true] God". Herodotus' own account is more detailed: "Sethos" goes into the temple shrine (presumably that of the deity, Hephaestus, whose priest he was according to the historian) "and there bewailed to the god's image the peril which threatened him".

148. Here again (see previous note), Josephus conforms his rendering of Herodotus' account of "Sethos" to his own earlier presentation of Hezekiah; see 10,16 where Isaiah informs the king that "God had hearkened (ἐπήκοον) to his prayer". Herodotus' own statement on the matter is considerably more expansive: "In his lamentation he [Sethos] fell asleep, and dreamed he saw the god (τὸν θεόν) standing over him and bidding him take courage, for he should suffer no ill by encountering the host of Arabia [see 10,19 and n. 150]: 'Myself', said the god, 'will send you champions'".

ψεν, i.e. the settlers in Samaria, 9,289) upon the Arab (τῷ ῎Αραβι)[149] – (19) at just this point he is in error (πλανᾶται), calling him king of the Arabs instead of king of the Assyrians[150] – for, he says, in one night (μιᾷ νυκτί; this same phrase is used in *BJ* 5,404 where Josephus is referring to Sennacherib's overthrow in his address to Jerusalem's defenders) a host of mice (μυῶν … πλῆθος)[151] ate through (διαφαγεῖν)[152] the bows (τόξα) and other weapons of the Assyrians[153], and, as the king on that account had no bows, he withdrew his army from Pelusium[154]. This, then, is the account which Herodotus gives[155].

At least in our extant text, Josephus' second witness for Sennacherib's Egyptian adventure is much briefer, this reading (10,20): "But Berosus, who wrote the *History of Chaldea*[156], also mentions King Senacheirimos

149. This notice is Josephus' (loose) transposition into narrative of Herodotus' report that "Sethos" was informed by the god that "he should suffer no ill by encountering the host of Arabia ('Αραβίων)"; see previous note.

150. As MARCUS, *Josephus*, VI, p. 167, n. a points out, Josephus' claim about Herodotus' "error" here is itself misleading in that previously in 2.141 Herodotus had, in fact, mentioned Sennacherib coming against Egypt "with a great host of Arabians *and Assyrians*" (cf. also his subsequent reference to the mice overrunning the *Assyrian* camp, as quoted in n. 153). (Compare, however, the view of NIESE, *Opera*, I, p. xlix who maintains that the words τε καὶ 'Ασσυρίων in the extant text of 2.141 are a later insertion made under the influence of the Biblical accounts of Sennacherib such that Josephus' claim about Herodotus' "error" would hold; NABER, *Opera*, II, p. xxxiv is inclined to accept this view.) On a similar case of an (apparently inaccurate) critique of Herodotus by Josephus for an alleged error (*AJ* 8,260-262), see BEGG, *Early Divided Monarchy*, pp. 79-82 and, more generally, BOWLEY, *Josephus's Use*, pp. 211-212 on criticism of Herodotus' "errors" as an standard procedure of later Greek historians.

151. This expression recurs in Josephus' account of the God-sent plague that befell the Philistine captors of the Ark in *AJ* 6,3.

152. The verb διαεσθίω is hapax in Josephus.

153. With the above sequence, compare the wording (2.141) of Herodotus himself: "… one night (νυκτός) a multitude of fieldmice (μῦς ἀρουραίους) swarmed over the Assyrian camp and devoured (φαγεῖν) their quivers and their bows (τόξα) and the handles of their shields likewise…".

154. Herodotus' own notice (2.141) on the point reads: "… insomuch that they (the Assyrians) fled the next day unarmed and many fell". Josephus leaves aside completely the statement with which 2.141 concludes: "And to this day a stone statue of the Egyptian king [Sethos] stands in Hephaestus' temple, with a mouse in his hand, and an inscription to this effect, 'Look on me, and fear the gods'". It might be noted here as well that the reason for Sennacherib's withdrawal from Pelusium which Josephus, in dependence on Herodotus, gives here in 10,19 (his army's lack of bows which the mice had consumed) differs from the one earlier adduced by him in 10,17 under the influence of the Biblical passages 19,8-9a // 37,8-9a, i.e. the advance of the Ethiopian king Tirhakah.

155. This closing formula would suggest that Josephus has given us a faithful reproduction of the content of Herodotus' testimony. In fact, however, as we have been noting, he presents a very loose rendering of 2.141 (this, of course, on the supposition that his text of Herodotus was essentially the same as that found in our printed editions) – looser even than his retellings of Biblical material.

156. On the Hellenized Babylonian priest Berosus, and Josephus' use of his *History*, see: H. BLOCH, *Die Quellen des Flavius Josephus in seiner Archäologie*, Leipzig, Teubner, 1879, pp. 62-65.

and tells how he ruled over the Assyrians and how he made an expedition against all Asia and Egypt (καὶ τῇ ᾿Αἰγύπτῳ)[157]; he writes as follows (λέγων οὕτως)...[158]".

Following the long extra-Biblical interlude of 10,17-20, Josephus finally reverts to his Scriptural sources in 10,21. In 2 Kgs 19,35 the calamity that befalls the Assyrian camp is introduced with the brief temporal phrase "and that night" (37,36 and 2 Chr 32,21 have no equivalent). Josephus' transition (10,21a) is more elaborate, linking the following happening with Sennacherib's earlier misfortune as just related by him: "When Senacheirimos returned to Jerusalem from his war with Egypt, he found (κατέλαβεν)[159] there the force (δύναμιν) under Rapsakēs[160] in danger from a plague (διὰ λοιμοῦ [see 9,289.290] κινδυνεύουσαν)[161], for (γάρ)...[162]".

To the foregoing transitional phrase Josephus attaches (10,21b) his version of 19,35a // 37,36a (cf. 32,21): "... God[163] had visited

157. These words are absent in the codices RO; Niese prints them within brackets.

158. These words, indicative of a lacuna in the extant text of Josephus – as was posited by J. Hudson, seconded by Dindorf and Niese (see *Opera*, I, p. xxxi) and which Marcus (*Josephus*, VI, p. 167, n. e) regards as the more likely possibility – are absent in the codices LaurV (as likewise in the text printed by Bekker and Naber).

159. This is the reading of Zon which Dindorf, Bekker, Naber, and Marcus follow. Niese reads the participle καταλαβών with the codices and E.

160. This reference to the force at Jerusalem under Rapsakēs' command harks back to 10,4 where Josephus mentions Sennacherib's "leaving behind his general Rapsakēs with a large force (ἰσχύος)"; cf. also 10,9 where the general refers to the Judeans' thinking they can "repulse our force (δύναμιν)". Recall that Josephus leaves aside the notice of 19,8a // 37,8a about Rab-shakeh's "returning and finding the king of Assyria fighting against Libnah": in his presentation Rab-shakeh has remained at Jerusalem ever since he was first positioned there by Sennacherib.

161. The above three words have no equivalent in the codices; they represent a retroversion, first proposed by J. Hudson and followed by Dindorf, Bekker, Naber, Weill [within parentheses]; and Marcus of Lat's "in periculo pestilentiae constitutam." Niese does not include the words in the text printed by him. The reference to Rab-shakeh's army being "in danger" (κινδυνεύουσαν) here in 10,21 ironically echoes the general's warning to the Jerusalemites in 10,10 that involuntary surrender after defeat "will prove to be dangerous (ἐπικίνδυνον)" to them. Now the tables have been turned by God.

162. This particle is lacking in the Greek witnesses. It is inserted by Hudson, followed by Dindorf, Bekker, Naber, Weill ("en effet"), and Marcus on the basis of Lat's "enim". Niese omits the word in the text printed by him.

163. In 19,35 // 37,36 // 32,21 the one smiting the Assyrians is the "angel" of/sent by the Lord (for a similar instance of the historian's replacing a Biblical mention of an "angel of the Lord" with a reference to God himself, see 9,20). Josephus' non-mention of God's angel here in 10,21 is generally seen as an instance of the historian's rationalizing tendencies, thus RAPPAPORT, *Agada*, p. 63, # 265; WEILL, *Josèphe*, II, p. 367, n. 5; MARCUS, *Josephus*, VI, pp. 168-169, n. c; FELDMAN, *Studies*, p. 374 (= ID., *Hezekiah*, 609). At the same time, these authors also note that in his evocation of the incident in his address to the defenders of Jerusalem in *BJ* 5,388 Josephus does follow the Bible in attributing the Assyrians' demise to "God's angel". It would appear that Josephus' substitute wording in 10,21 – which, it should be noted, does not in fact eliminate a super-natural cause

(ἐνσκηψαντος)¹⁶⁴ a pestilential sickness (λοιμικὴν ... νόσον)¹⁶⁵ upon his army, *and on the first night* (νύκτα) *of the siege* (πολιορκίας; see 10,17.18)¹⁶⁶ one hundred and eighty-five thousand men had perished (διαφθείρονται)¹⁶⁷ *with their commanders and officers* (ἡγεμόσι [cf. ἡγομόνων, 10,6] καὶ ταξιάρχοις¹⁶⁸)¹⁶⁹".

for the army's destruction – reflects the fact that he is recounting the happening here in *AJ*, in first place, rather for a Gentile audience which would not have shared current Jewish beliefs about angels (as would the defenders of Jerusalem to whom he is speaking in *BJ* 5,388).

In contrast to Josephus' procedure in 10,21, other post-Biblical Jewish writings develop the sources' reference to the destroying angel in various respects. That angel, for one thing, is given a variety of names: Gabriel (so *b. Sanh.* 95b), Michael (so TC 2 Chr 32,21 – in some MSS of this Targum both Gabriel and Michael are mentioned), Ramiel (*Apocalypse of Baruch* 63.6; see R.H. CHARLES – L.H. BROCKINGTON, trs., *The Syriac Apocalypse of Baruch*, in H.F.D. SPARKS [ed.], *The Apocryphal Old Testament*, Oxford, Clarendon, 1984, 841-895, p. 879). These documents likewise also offer a number of suggestions as to how the killing of the Assyrians was accomplished. Thus *b. Sanh.* 95b lists three such possiblities: the angel blew out the men's breath, clapped so loudly that they expired in fright, or caused them to hear the celestial living creatures singing their songs of praise with the result that they died; cf. *Apocalypse of Baruch* 63.8 which affirms that the angels burned the inside of the soldiers' bodies while leaving their outsides intact.

164. This is the reading of M Zon which Dindorf, Bekker, Niese, Naber, and Marcus all follow. Compare ἐκπέμψαντος (ROSPLaurV), πέμψαντος (Ε).

165. The above phrase recurs in *AJ* 7,326; 10,(116).132. With the sequence τοῦ θεοῦ λοιμικὴν ἐνσκήψαντος ... νόσον here in 10,21 compare the formulation used by Josephus in his rendition of Herodotus' testimony in 10,18 ὁ θεὸς πληγὴν ἐνσκήπτει. What befell Sennacherib's army in Egypt according to Herodotus is now repeated with the Assyrian force besieging Jerusalem. The phrase of 10,21 likewise echoes Josephus' notice in 9,289 that "God visited a pestilence (λοιμὸν ... ἐνέσκηψεν) on the new settlers in Samaria.

166. Josephus may have found inspiration for this temporal indication in the opening plus of 19,35: "and that night (BL νυκτός)...". Recall as well that the equipment of the Assyrian army in Egypt was consumed "in one night (μιᾷ νυκτί)" according to Josephus' citation of Herodotus in 10,19.

167. With the use of this term Josephus harks back to Isaiah's announcement in 10,14: "God would see to it that they (the Assyrians) should be destroyed (διαφθαρῶσι)". That prediction has now found its realization. See nn. 170,171,173 for further instances of Josephus' ironic reapplication of language used earlier of/against the Jerusalemites to the Assyrians themselves.

168. This is the emendation of Dindorf followed by Bekker, Naber, and Marcus for the ταξιάρχαις of the codices which Niese retains.

169. According to 19,35a // 37,36a the total of the Assyrian casualties came to 185,000 men. Josephus' reference to the loss of officers in addition to these might be inspired by 32,21 where there is mention of elimination of "mighty warriors *and commanders* (BL ἄρχοντα) *and officers* (BL στρατηγόν)", no figure for the casualties being given. Elsewhere in Jewish tradition one meets the statement that the 185,000 cited in 19,35 // 37,36 consisted solely of the Assyrian officers killed – not the (far more numerous) ordinary soldiers who died as well, thus *b. Sanh.* 95b; *Apocalypse of Baruch* 63.7 (CHARLES and BROCKINGTON, *Apocalypse*, p. 879); *E. R.* §7(45) (BRAUDE and KAPSTEIN, *Tana dĕbe Eliyyahu*, p. 104). Josephus leaves aside the (superfluous) notice of 19,35b // 37,36b: "and when men arose early in the morning, behold, these were all dead men".

2 Kgs 19,36 // Isa 37,37 (cf. 2 Chr 32,21aβ) relate the sequel to the angel's destruction of Sennacherib's army: the king returns home, taking up residence in Nineveh. In line with his psychologizing tendency, Josephus interjects (10,22) a reference to Sennacherib's state of mind which prompts his withdrawal: *"By this calamity* (συμφορᾶς)[170] *he was thrown into a state of alarm* (φόβον)[171] *and terrible anxiety* (δεινὴν ἀγωνίαν)[172], *and fearing* (δείσας)[173] *for his entire army*, he fled (φεύγει)[174] *with the rest of his force*[175] to his own (αὐτοῦ)[176] realm, called the kingdom of Ninos (τὴν ... βασιλείαν τὴν Νίνου)[177]".

The Biblical accounts conclude (19,37 // 37,38; cf. 32,21b) their narration of Sennacherib's failed assault on Jerusalem with mention of his assassination by two of his sons who thereupon make their escape while another son, Esarhaddon, succeeds his father. Josephus elaborates on these summary source data in 10,23a:

> *And, after remaining there a short while*, he was treacherously attacked (δολοφονηθείς)[178] by his *elder* sons Andromachos (Ἀνδρομάχου)[179] and

170. This term represents another (see n. 167) ironic echo of the language used earlier (see, 10,10) by Rab-shakeh in addressing the Jerusalemites whom he warns that their defeat and (involuntary) surrender will be "the cause of misfortunes (σομφορῶν)" for them. In fact, however, such "misfortunes" end up befalling the Assyrians themselves.

171. Compare 10,8 where it is Hezekiah's envoy Eliakas who "fears" (φοβούμενος) lest Rab-shakeh's words be overheard by the people. See n. 173.

172. This phrase occurs also in *AJ* 8,373, there in reference to King Ahab.

173. This term bespeaks the reversal God's initiative (see 10,21) has brought about: whereas in 10,8 Eliakas is perceived by Rab-shakeh to be in the grip of "fear" (δέος), it is now Sennacherib himself who is "fearing" (δείσας). There is likewise here in 10,22 an echo of 10,5 where Hezekiah's remaining in Jerusalem when summoned to a parley with the Assyrians is attributed to the king's "cowardice" (δειλίας) – a cowardice which has now taken hold of Sennacherib himself.

174. Compare 19,36 // 37,37: "he departed (BL 19,36 ἀπῆρε(ν); LXX 37,37 ἀπῆλθε). Josephus' verb accentuates the precipitous character of the Assyrian withdrawal, just as it ironically echoes the taunting question which Rab-shakeh poses in Sennacherib's name, i.e. why is Hezekiah "avoiding/ fleeing" (φεύγει) his master in 10,6. Now it is Sennacherib himself who is the one to "flee".

175. This phrase has no counterpart in the sources; it does, however, pick up on the mention of Sennacherib's fearing "for his entire [remaining] army" in what precedes. The reference would seem to be the troops who had been on Sennacherib's Egyptian expedition (10,4) and who would have accompanied the king to Jerusalem following his withdrawal from Pelusium (see 10,17.19.21).

176. This is the conjecture of Dindorf, Bekker, Niese, Naber, and Marcus for the αὐτοῦ of the codices and E.

177. This is the same phrase used by Josephus in 9,208 in reference to Jonah's God-ordained destination. In 19,36 // 37,37 Sennacherib takes up residence "at Nineveh" (BL 19,36 // LXX 37,37 Νινευή).

178. This same verb, δολοφονέω was used by Josephus in 9,228 in connection with the assassination of Pekahiah by Pekah; see there.

179. Compare "Adramelech" (MT 19,37 // 37,38); Ἀδραμέλεχ (BL 19,37 // LXX 37,38; cf. LaurV Ἀδρμαελέχου, Lat Adramelech).

Seleukaros (Σελευκάρου)[180] and so died (τελευτᾷ τὸν βίον)[181]; and
he was laid to rest (ἀνετέθη)[182] in his own temple, called Araskē
('Αράσκη[183])[184]. *And these two were driven out* (φυγαδευθέντες)[185] *by
their countrymen* (πολιτῶν) *for the murder* (φόνῳ)[186], and went away
(ἀπῆραν) to Armenia[187]; and the successor to the throne was Asarachod-
das ('Ασαραχόδδας)[188], *who disregarded the rights of the sons of
Senacheirimos next in line* (τῶν μετ' αὐτοὺς καταφρονῶν [see
καταφρονεῖ of Hezekiah, 10,16] τοῦ Σεναχειρίμου)[189].

180. Compare "Sharezer" (MT 19,37 // 37,38); Σαράσαρ (BL 19,37 // LXX 37,38;
cf. LaurV Σαρασάρου, Lat Seleusaro). 2 Chr 32,21b leaves the two parricides nameless.
    181. The Biblical sources speak of Sennacherib's sons "slaying/ striking him down
with the sword". It seems odd that Josephus does not make use of this language since in
10,14 he himself has Isaiah announce that Sennacherib will "perish *by the sword*". Like
the Biblical accounts Josephus gives no motivation for the sons' killing of their father.
Such motivation is, however, supplied elsewhere in Jewish tradition; see *b. Sanh.* 96a
which relates that their doing so was occasioned by their overhearing their father pledg-
ing to a plank from Noah's ark which he had discovered that, should he be successful in
future battles, he would sacrifice his sons to the plank.
    182. This is the reading adopted by Dindorf, Bekker, Niese, Naber, and Marcus
in preference to the ἀνῃρήθη ("he was slain") of the codices LaurV and Zon (which
Marcus, *Josephus*, VI, p. 169, n. g. calls a probable scribal assimilation to the Biblical
wording). MARCUS, ibid., points out that the verbal form read by him (ἀνετέθη) might
also be rendered "his image was set up".
    183. Compare the names of the deity in whose temple Sennacherib is assassinated
according to the various Biblical textual witnesses, i.e. "Nisroch" (MT 19,37 // 37,38);
'Εσδράχ (B 19,37); 'Ασράχ (L 19,37); Νασαραχ (LXX 37,38). 2 Chr 32,21b speaks
simply of "his [Sennacherib's] god".
    184. Josephus' mention above of Sennacherib's being "buried" in a temple involves
a modification of the sources' account according to which Sennacherib is murdered in the
temple and nothing is said of his burial. The modification entails a "toning down" of the
sons' deed which in the Bible is not only patricide/regicide, but also a sacrilege given the
place where it occurs.
    185. The verb φυγαδεύω occurs six times in *BJ*, but only one additional time in *AJ*,
i.e. 12,399.
    186. This noun echoes the participle δολοφονηθείς used earlier in 10,23. The Bibli-
cal accounts say nothing of such a response by the populace to Sennacherib's assassins;
rather they (19,37bα // 37,38bα) represent the sons simply as "escaping" following their
deed.
    187. This designation for the sons' destination corresponds to that found in LXX
37,38 (cf. *AJ* 1,90 where for the reference in Gen 8,5 [MT and LXX] to the ark's ending
up on "the mountains of *Ararat*", Josephus speaks of "a mountain-top in *Armenia*").
Compare "Ararat" (MT BL 19,37, MT 37,38; "Kardu" (TJ 19,37); see n. 191. 2 Chronicles 32 does not mention what become of the assassin sons.
    188. Compare "Esarhaddon" (MT 19,37 // 37,38); 'Ασορδάν (B 19,37 // LXX 37,38);
'Αχορδάν (L 19,37). Esarhaddon's succession is not mentioned in 2 Chronicles 32.
    189. This concluding sequence of 10,23a has no equivalent in Lat. MARCUS, *Josephus*,
VI, pp. 170-171, n. b points out that we do not know where Josephus found the extra-Biblical indications about Sennacherib's sons (the two assassins being "elder" sons, Esarhaddon's disregard for the claims of those sons next in line) – might it have been in Berosus
whom he has cited just previously in 10,20 (cf. n. 191)? Marcus further notes that Josephus is, in any case, historically correct in depicting Esarhaddon as a younger son of Sennacherib.

Thereafter, he rounds off (10,23b) the whole complex of 10,1-23 with one of his characteristic closing formulas: "To such an end was the Assyrian expedition against Jerusalem fated (συνέβη) to come".

Conclusions: Josephus' Rewriting of 2 Kgs 18,13-19,37 // Isa 36,1-37,38 // 2 Chr 32,1-23

I shall now attempt to sum up on my findings regarding the lengthy passage AJ 10,1-23. Vis-à-vis the three Biblical accounts concerning Sennacherib's assault on Jerusalem, Josephus clearly gives preference to the parallel presentations of 2 Kgs 18,13-19,37 and Isa 36,1-37,38 as opposed to the distinctive, shorter narrative of 2 Chr 32,1-23[190]. As between the Kings and Isaiah versions themselves, Josephus appears to align himself more with the former's, somewhat more expansive account (see, in particular, his utilization of the *Sondergut* passage 2 Kgs 18,14-16 in 10,2-4 and his mention of Rab-shakeh's two colleagues, 10,4 = 18,18, > 36,2). Beyond this, our passage yielded few indications concerning the text-form(s) of the Biblical sources used by Josephus in composing his version. One relevant item in this connection is, however, his identification (10,23a) of the assassins' place of refuge as "Armenia" (so LXX Isa 37,38) as opposed to the "Ararat" of MT BL 19,37 // 37,38[191].

On the other hand, AJ 10,1-23 does provide noteworthy examples of the historian's various rewriting techniques. Thus, he expands the Biblical accounts of Sennacherib's doings with a lengthy section concerning the king's Egyptian misadventure (10,17-20), relating this first in his own words (10,17-18a) and thereafter adducing the relevant testimonies of Herodotus and Berosus (10,18b-21). He further interjects a number of particulars into his rendition of the summary source notices on

190. We did, however, encounter several instances where Josephus' formulations reflect a possible influence from the side of the Chronicler's version; see nn. 67,104,119.

191. See n. 187. Given, however, that, as mentioned there, Josephus substitutes "Armenia" for the "Ararat" of Gen 8,5 in AJ 1,90, it is possible that Josephus came to his identification of the parricides' refuge site in 10,23 without knowledge of the LXX reading in 37,38, perhaps doing so under the influence of Berosus (cf. 10,20), see AJ 1,93, where, after mentioning the ark's coming to rest in Armenia in 1,90, Josephus quotes that historian's statement about a portion of the flood-time vessel still surviving "*in Armenia*".

In this connection it might also be noted that Josephus' version, AJ 10,1-36, of the events related in Isaiah 36-39 etc. does not seem to evidence any use by him of the (occasional) peculiar readings of the two major Qumran MSS, i.e. 1QIs[a] and IQIs[b]. On the former MS, see O.H. STECK, *Die erste Jesajarolle von Qumran (1QIs^a)* (SBS, 173/1-2), Stuttgart, KBW, 1997.

Sennacherib's assassination and its sequels (10,23). Repeatedly as well, the historian inserts indications concerning the psychological states of the story's characters: Hezekiah's trust in Sennacherib's promises (10,3) and his "cowardice" (10,5), Eliakas' "fearing" (10,8) and Rab-shakeh's perceiving this (10,8), Hezekiah's "making light of" the Assyrian threats due to his God-inspired "confidence" (10,16), and Sennacherib's "alarm and terrible anxiety" for the remainder of his army (10,22). Others of his elaborations of the Biblical data are intended to clarify matters or answer questions that might arise, see, e.g., the status of the three envoys as Hezekiah's "closest friends" (10,5), or Rab-shakeh's familarity with Hebrew (10,8). Still others serve to make connections with the wider or proximate context: the foreshadowings of Sennacherib's Egyptian fiasco (10,17-20) in 10,4 (his expedition against Egypt and Ethiopia) and 10,14 (Isaiah predicts the king's failure in Egypt); and Rab-shakeh's allusion to the earlier Assyrian overthrow of the Northern Kingdom (10,7).

Over against the foregoing additions/ expansions stand Josephus' omissions/abridgements in *AJ* 10,1-23. He markedly compresses (10,15) both Sennacherib's second warning message (19,8-13 // 37,8-13) and, above all, the source reports on the response to that message by Hezekiah and Isaiah (10,16 = 19,14-34 // 37,14-35). He also, however, leaves aside, condenses, or conflates a number of smaller-scale Biblical items which he found problematic, not in accord with his own purposes in presenting the episode, or excessively detailed/ verbose: Hezekiah's despoiling, not only the royal treasuries, but also the Temple (18,15-16; compare 10,3); the precisions concerning the site where the Assyrian officers position themselves (18,17 // 36,2; cf. 10,5); Rab-shakeh's three-fold question about the source of Hezekiah's confidence (18,19-20 // 36,4-5; compare 10,6); the latter's iconoclastic measures (18,22 // 36,7); Rab-shakeh's double reply to the envoys' request of him (18,27ff. // 36,12ff.; compare 10,8b-9); the general's "vulgar" warning about the fate awaiting the city's defenders (18,27 // 36,12); his quadruple exhortation to the Jerusalemites about what they ought not let Hezekiah "do" (18,29-31aα.32a // 36,14-16aα.18a; compare 10,8b-9a); his (conditional) promises to them should they surrender (18,31abα-32a // 36,16abα-17; compare 10,8b); and his rhetorical questions pointing up the impotence of the gods of the nations (18,33-35 // 36,18b-20; cf. 32,13-15); the "silence" on the part of Rab-shakeh's hearers in accord with Hezekiah's previous instructions to them (18,36 // 36,21); the rent clothes of the envoys (18,37 // 36,22; compare 10,11); the sackcloth worn by the delegation that goes to Isaiah (19,2 // 37,2; compare 10,12); and Hezekiah's metaphorical statements about the current "day" (19,3 // 37,3; compare 10,12).

Josephus re-arranges the sources' sequence as well. Specifically, he makes Rab-shakeh's "horse wager" which in 18,23-24 // 36,8-9 is part of his first address an element rather of his second speech (10,9). Similarly, he situates mention of Tirhakah's advance against the Assyrians as an element of his account of Sennacherib's Egyptian fiasco (10,17), rather than a component of the introduction to the king's warning message to Hezekiah, as in 19,9a // 37,9a.

The historian further modifies/adapts source data. Sennacherib does not simply demand gold and silver from Hezekiah (so 18,14b), but actually "receives" these from him (10,2). The Assyrian titles (Rab-shakeh, Tartan, Rab-saris) of 18,17 are (mis-) understood as proper names, 10,4. Not only the three envoys (so 18,37 // 36,22), but the people as a whole bring word of Rab-shakeh's threats to Hezekiah (10,11). In contrast to the sources which speak initially of Sennacherib's dispatching "messengers" to Hezekiah (19,9 // 37,9) and then of a letter(s) received by the latter (19,14 // 37,14), Josephus (10,15) refers to royal "letters" from the start. Hezekiah does not spread out the Assyrian's letter(s) before the Lord (19,14 // 37,14), but "lays it away within the temple" (10,16; see n. 122). The city besieged by Sennacherib in person is not "Libnah" (19,8 // 37,8), but "Pelusium" (10,17), as in Herodotus; see 10,18, cf. n. 140. The one responsible for the destruction of Sennacherib's army at Jerusalem is God himself (10,21) as opposed to the "angel of the Lord" (19,35 // 37,36). On a stylistic level, Josephus converts all but one (i.e. the words of Rab-shakeh quoted in 10,8b-9 = 18,27-35 // 36,13-20) of the many speeches cited in the sources into indirect discourse. Terminologically, the historian's use of *Leitworte* (e.g., the verb διαφθείρω; see n. 104) and verbal echoes of his own speech to the defenders of Jerusalem (*BJ* 5,362-419) are especially noteworthy.

What now is distinctive about Josephus' account of Sennacherib's failed assault on Jerusalem? Most obviously, he presents the episode in streamlined fashion, dispensing, e.g., with a good deal of the contentual repetitiousness and the catalogues of long-gone nations (see 18,33-35 // 36,18-20 // 32,13-15; 19,11-13 // 37,11-13) whose gods had been unable to defend them against Assyria's might which characterize the sources' presentations. Such streamlining, in turn, "makes room" in Josephus' rendition for the extended insertion concerning Sennacherib's Egyptian misadventure (10,17-20) which itself allows him to display, yet again, his familiarity with – and even ability to correct (see 10,19) – a range of non-Jewish authors and the wider, international context of Biblical happenings as recorded by them (compare the similar case of of the Tyrian-Assyrian conflict in Shalmaneser's time concerning which he adduces the Tyrian archives and Menander's history in 9,283b-287a). Questions and problems suggested by the sources' narration (e.g., why did Hezekiah not go out to parley with Rab-shakeh himself?, did the latter know Hebrew?) are adverted to and/or resolved via the application of one or other of the re-writing techniques discussed above. More elaborate transitions between the narrative's component parts (see, e.g., 10,21a) as well as a final concluding formula for the whole (see 10,23 *in fine*) are provided. Much greater attention is given to characters' psychology than is the case in the *Vorlagen*. Various nuances are introduced by Josephus into the portrayal of the story's main personages as well. Hezekiah's stature as a political/ military leader is downplayed (he is all too ready to submit to Sennacherib and unduly credulous with regard to the latter's promises; see 10,2-4, just as he displays "cowardice" by remaining in Jerusalem when summoned forth by Rab-shakeh, 10,5). On the other hand, his piety is accentuated both negatively (he does not – it would seem – hand over the Temple treasures to Sennacherib, 10,3; compare 18,15-16), and positively (he alone engages [10,11] in the penitential practices which are ascribed by the sources to his first [see 18,37 // 36,22] and second [19,2 // 37,2] delegations as well; similarly, his self-abasement before God is itensified via several extra-Biblical details, i.e. his adopting an "attitude of humility" and "prostrating" himself, ibid.). As for Hezekiah's antagonist Sennacherib, Josephus introduces reference to his *mala fides* – this in contrast to Hezekiah's own trust in his promises (10,4). He likewise underscores the threat posed by the Assyrian, his hubristic self-confidence, and the ultimate, all-encompassing disaster which he brings up himself thereby. Lastly with regard to the prophet Isaiah, one might speak of a certain diminuation by Josephus of his Biblical role in the episode given the historian's drastic compression of his lengthy second discourse (19,20-34 // 37,21-35) in 10,16b. On the other hand, the Josephan Isaiah's status is accentuated by his being asked, not only to pray for Jerusalem's deliverance (so 19,4b // 37,4b), but also to "make sacrifices" (10,12) as well as by his additional, veracious prediction of Sennacherib's failure in Egypt (10,14).

Josephus' retelling of Jerusalem's deliverance from Sennacherib's assault is intended, I suggest, to appeal to both cultivated Gentile and contemporary Jewish readers. For the benefit of the former audience, Josephus eliminates the sources' vulgarities (people eating their own dung and drinking their own urine, 18,27 // 36,12) and derogatory references to the impotence of the nations' "gods". Gentile readers might also be expected to appreciate Josephus' inserted references to non-Jewish authorities as well as his version's heightened attention to the wider historical context of the Biblical episode and the hubris thematic. To Jewish readers, Josephus' version offers, between the lines, the same lesson he had (vainly) attempted to convey in his speech to the defenders of Jerusalem, i.e. God can and does repulse the assaults of the mightest of foes upon his people whenever they "commit their cause to him and sit still" (*BJ* 5,390), whereas their own efforts to ward off enemy threats lead only to disaster. With regard to the further question of the appropriate Jewish response to the "Assyria" of Josephus' own day, that message offers both a hope (God is capable of dealing with Rome as he did with Sennacherib's overwhelming force) and a warning (like their ancestors in Hezekiah's time, contemporary Jews should not have recourse to arms in the face of the threat posed by a great imperial power)[192].

192. See further HÖFFKEN, *Hisjika und Jesaja*, 46-48.

XVIII

THE FINALE OF HEZEKIAH'S REIGN[1]
(10,24-36)

The three Biblical segments (2 Kgs 18,13-19,37 // Isa 36,1-37,38 // 2 Chr 32,1-23 = *AJ* 10,1-23) treated in chap. XVII ("Jerusalem Delivered") all focus on the central event of Hezekiah's reign, i.e. the city's miraculous escape from seemingly certain Assyrian capture. Each of them then continues (2 Kgs 20,1-21 // Isa 38,1-39,8 // 2 Chr 32,24-33) with mention of further events of the reign, these terminating with Hezekiah's own death. The Josephan parallel to this new source sequence is 10,24-36. I divide up the material into three segments: 1. Hezekiah's Illness (*AJ* 10,24-29 = 2 Kgs 20,1-11 // Isa 38,1-22 // 2 Chr 32,24); 2. The Babylonian Embassy (10,30-35 = 20,12-19 // 39,1-8 // 32,25-31); and 3. Hezekiah's Demise (10,36 = 20,20-21 // 32,32-33).

1. *Hezekiah's Illness*

The two more extensive Biblical accounts of Hezekiah's illness (2 Kgs 20,1-11 // Isa 38,1-22)[2] introduce the episode with an identical notice (20,1a // 38,1a) that is both rather jejune and only tenuously linked with what precedes, i.e. the description of Assyria's repulse in 19,35-37 // 37,36-38. That notice reads: "in those days Hezekiah became sick and was at the point of death". Josephus, for his part, develops the sources' half-verse into a sequence of two whole paragraphs, 10,24-25. His elaboration begins by addressing a point about which the Biblical presentation(s) is oddly silent, i.e. the king and people's response to their dramatic deliverance from the Assyrian threat[3]. *AJ*

---

1. This chapter represents a revision of my article *Hezekiah's Illness and Visit according to Josephus*, in *EstBíb* 53 (1995) 365-385 and is used by permission. My revision has benefited greatly from the above-cited article of HÖFFKEN, *Hiskija und Jesaja*.

2. The Chronicler devotes a single, allusive verse (32,24) to the happening. It reads: "In those days Hezekiah became sick and was at the point of death, and he prayed to the Lord; and he answered him and gave him a sign".

3. Indeed, Rabbinic tradition (see, e.g., *Songs Rab.* 4.8.3, M. SIMON, tr., *Midrash Rabbah Song of Songs*, London-New York, Soncino, 1983, pp. 209-211) takes note of this point, censuring Hezekiah for his failure to give due thanks to God for his rescue,

10,24 fills this lacuna with the following statement: "Having been thus wonderfully (παραδόξως) delivered from the fate which he feared (τῶν φόβων)[4], King Hezekiah together with all the people offered sacrifices of thanksgiving to God (χαριστηρίους ... θυσίας ἐπετέλεσε τῷ θεῷ)[5], for the destruction (διαφθειράσης)[6] of some of the enemy and the removal of the rest from Jerusalem[7] had no other cause (αἰτίας) than the aid given by their ally (συμμαχίας)[8] God". Such a statement serves to accentuate the piety of Hezekiah, as does the following phrase (10,25a) with which Josephus makes his transition to the source notice (see above) on the royal sickness: "But, though he showed all zeal and devotion in the worship of God (σπουδῇ καὶ φιλοτιμίᾳ περὶ τὸν θεόν)...[9]". Given this emphasis, the "shock effect" of what Josephus now goes on to report is all the greater, i.e. "he was smitten by a severe illness (νόσῳ[10] χαλεπῇ)". In fact, Josephus plays up still further the unexpected juxtaposition of the two items (the king's piety, his falling severely ill) via his embellishments regarding the malady itself: "... and

with the result that God revoked his earlier decision to designate Hezekiah as the Messiah. For an overview of the Rabbinic traditions on Hezekiah's sickness and the subsequent Babylonian embassy to him, see GINZBERG, *Legends*, IV, pp. 272-276; VI, pp. 366-368.

4. This reference to the king's "fear" harks back to 10,5 where Hezekiah's failure to treat with the Assyrian envoys in person is (extra-Biblically) attributed to his "cowardice" (ὑπὸ δειλίας); it also echoes the reference to Eliakim's "fearing" (φοβούμενος) that the defenders of Jerusalem would overhear Rab-shakeh's speech (10,8).

5. The entire above sequence recurs in *AJ* 5,114; 6,151. In addition the phrase "(offer) thanksgiving sacrifices" occurs in *BJ* 7,72; *AJ* 2,269; 3,228; 11,110; 12,349; 19,293; 20,49. The mention of communal sacrifices here in 10,24 following the Assyrian withdrawal recalls the insertion made by Josephus within his version of Hezekiah's appeal (see 2 Kgs 19,7 // Isa 37,4) to Isaiah during the siege itself, i.e. that the prophet offer "sacrifices (θυσίας) for the common safety" (10,12).

6. This form echoes the *Leitwort* διαφθείρω of Josephus' account of the Assyrian siege of Jerusalem; see 10,7.14.15.21.

7. Marcus's above translation of 10,24 fails to render a portion of the text dealing with the "removal" of the remaining Assyrians from Jerusalem. This reads in Greek φόβῳ τῆς ὁμοίας τελευτῆς which WEILL, *ad loc.* renders "par crainte d'une fin semblable". Note in this phrase the wordplay with the reference, earlier in 10,24, to Hezekiah's own "fears" (τῶν φόβων).

8. For Josephus' use of this term in reference to God, see on 9,15. The above formulation "no other (μηδεμιᾶς ἄλλης) cause than the aid given by their ally God" echoes 10,11 where Hezekiah entreats God "to help one who had no other (μηδεμίαν ἄλλην) hope of salvation"; see HÖFFKEN, *Hiskija und Jesaja*, 48.

9. The collocation "zeal and devotion" recurs in *AJ* 6,292; 7,380; 12,83.134; 14,154; 15,312. For the phrase "devotion in the worship of God" see on 9,157 (of Joash of Judah).

10. Note that this is the very same term which Josephus uses to refer to the "pestilential sickness (νόσον)" with which God visits the impious Assyrians in 10,21. The effect of the verbal echo here in 10,25 is to the highlight the mystery as to why the pious king should be himself "smitten" with illness. See n. 14.

all hope for him was given up the physicians[11], nor did his friends (φίλοι)[12] have any expectation (προσεδόκων)[13] of a change for the better (χρηστόν) in his condition". The historian's accentuation of the severity of the disease that so unexpectedly befell the pious king continues (10,25b) in his Biblically un-paralleled notice on Hezekiah's emotional response to it. This runs: "And the illness was aggravated by the dreadful despair (ἀθυμία δεινή)[14] of the king himself when he considered his childlessness (ἀπαιδίαν)[15] and that he was about to die leaving his house and his realm unprovided with a legitimate successor (γνησίας διαδοχῆς)[16]". This component of Josephus' elaboration of the source datum about the Hezekiah's illness is of special interest given its affinity with the Rabbinic tradition (see, e.g., *b. Ber.* 10a; *y. Sanh.* 10.28b; *E.R.* §8(46) [BRAUDE and KAPTSTEIN, *Tanna děbe Eliyyahu*, p. 107]) which also represents Hezekiah as childless at the moment of his falling sick[17]. On the other hand, whereas the Rabbis represent the king's childlessness as due to a deliberate and culpable decision on his part[18], Josephus depicts it as simply an inexplicable misfortune that has befallen the pious king[19].

Following their brief notices on the king's illness (2 Kgs 20,1a // Isa 38,1a), the Biblical accounts (20,1b // 38,1b) report – with similar brevity – an appearance by the prophet Isaiah who informs Hezekiah in

11. Conceivably, Josephus' mention of these figures here in 10,25 was inspired by the reference to King Asa's "seeking (help) from physicians" when afflicted by a severe foot-disease in 2 Chr 16,12.

12. This term harks back to 10,5 where "Eliakim" *et al.* are designated as "three of the friends (φίλους) who were closest to him (Hezekiah)".

13. This is the reading of LaurV (and perhaps Lat) which Naber and Marcus adopt. Dindorf, Bekker, and Niese read προσδοκῶν with the remaining codices.

14. Josephus' two remaining uses of this phrase are in *BJ* 3,182 and *AJ* 5,36; it echoes the phrase δεινὴν ἀγωνίαν used (10,22) of Sennacherib's reaction to the loss of his men due to a "pestilential sickness" (10,21); cf. n. 10. The noun ἀθυμία is used of the "despondence" of the leper king Uzziah in 9,227.

15. Josephus' three remaining uses of the noun ἀπαιδία are in *AJ* 5,276.343; 7,184.

16. This phrase recurs in *BJ* 1,545 (pl.); 4,596 (pl.); *AJ* 5,276.

17. The origin of this tradition seems to lie in the notice of 2 Kgs 21,1 // 2 Chr 33,1 that Manasseh, presumably Hezekiah's eldest son, was twelve years old at the moment he succeeded his father. Given this datum Manasseh would have been born – as Hezekiah's first-born son – during the "extra" fifteen years of life which God granted his father (see 2 Kgs 20,6 // Isa 38,5) at the time of the latter's illness.

18. See *b. Ber.* 10a where, when Isaiah affirms that the king's imminent death which he has just announced (Isa 38,1b) is in punishment for his failure to beget children, Hezekiah responds that he had adopted this course as a result of a divine revelation informing him that any offspring he might have would turn out degenerate. (Hezekiah's "excuse", in turn, is disallowed by Isaiah who tells the king that he should have done his duty of raising up descendants and left the consequences in God's hands.)

19. On this point, see S.S. KOTTEK, *Medicine and Hygiene in the Works of Flavius Josephus* (Studies in Ancient Medicine, 9), Leiden, Brill, 1994, p. 32, n. 21.

the Lord's name that he is certain to die. Josephus, who has just previously significantly embellished the sources' notice on the royal illness,
passes over this (initial) prophetic intervention entirely. His reason for
doing so is not difficult to discern. In the Biblical presentation(s), Isaiah's annnouncement of 20,1b // 38,1b – made as it is in the Lord's name
– is subsequently countermanded by the Lord who (20,4-6 // 38,4-6)
sends Isaiah back to inform Hezekiah that he will, rather, be given fifteen extra years of life. Thereby, his earlier announcement might well
appear to be an instance of false prophecy[20]. For Josephus, however, the
(true) prophet is above all the one who delivers accurate predictions
which are likewise consistent both with other announcements of that
prophet and those of his (true) contemporary colleagues[21]. The historian's "solution" to the difficulty thus posed is simply to eliminate the
prophet's initial, problematic announcement.

In the sources, Isaiah's announcement (20,1b // 38,1b) causes
Hezekiah to address an anguished appeal to God (20,2-3 // 38,2-3) in
which he begs him to "remember" his good deeds[22]. Josephus, as we
have noted, has no parallel to the former item. Accordingly, in his presentation (10,26) the sick king prays on his own initiative, without this
being "instigated" by the prophet's announcement. Josephus likewise
re-formulates the content of the royal prayer (which he recasts in indirect

20. The Bible itself leaves this problem unaddressed. Compare, however, *Eccl. Rab.*
5.6.1 (COHEN, *Midrash Rabbah Ecclesiastes*, p. 136) where Isaiah protests about being
sent by God to bring Hezekiah contradictory messages. In response to this protest the
Deity soothes Isaiah by telling him that the humble king will accept the new, different
message and furthermore that the earlier, now revoked one had not yet become public.

21. See, e.g., Josephus' (extra-Biblical) characterization precisely of Isaiah in *AJ*
10,35: "As for the prophet, he was acknowledged to be a man of God and marvellously
possessed of truth, and, as he was confident of never having spoken what is false..." –
a characterization that would not seem to accord with the presentation of Isaiah as the
bearer of contradictory messages in 2 Kgs 20,1b-6 // Isa 38,1b-6. Cf. FELDMAN,
Prophets, 407-411. In contrast to Josephus' "suppression" of Isaiah's initial announcement to the king, Rabbinic tradition (e.g., *b. Ber.* 10a; *y. Sanh.* 10.28b; *Eccl. Rab.* 5.6.1
[COHEN, *Midrash Rabbah Ecclesiastes*, p. 135]) elaborates on the opening scene between
them. According to these texts, Hezekiah responds to the prophet's initial announcement
that he will not recover by stating that he cannot accept it as definitive and that he
intends rather to follow the teaching/example of his ancestors (Solomon, Jehoshaphat),
i.e. that even in seemingly hopeless circumstances one should never cease to pray and
fear God.

22. In *b. Sanh.* 104a Hezekiah's invocation of his own good deeds in the above texts
is represented as an act of boasting which sets in motion a whole series of further offenses
by the king with the final result that his offspring are condemned by God to go into exile
(see 2 Kgs 20,18 // Isa 39,8). Compare *b. Ber.* 10b where the principle is enunciated that
when a petitioner invokes his own merits (as does Hezekiah in 20,3 // 38,3), God, when
granting the petition, makes clear that he does so on the merit of someone else (cf. 20,6
where Hezekiah, by way of answer to his prayer, is told that God will deliver Jerusalem
"for my own sake and for my servant David's sake").

discourse as well), making this center on the "progeny issue" introduced by him in what precedes; see above. His formulation of the prayer thus reads: "And so, suffering chiefly from this thought [i.e. that he would die without issue] and lamenting (ὀδυρόμενος) it, he supplicated God (ἱκέτευε τὸν θεόν)[23] to give him a little longer time to live, until he should beget children, and not let him depart this life before becoming a father[24]".

As noted above, in the Biblical sequence(s) Hezekiah's prayer (20,2-3 // 38,2-3), itself inspired by the prophetic announcement of doom (20,1b // 38,1b), is followed (20,4-6 // 38,4-6) by God's sending Isaiah back to the king with a new, very different word of promise for his future. In Josephus' version, Isaiah has not yet made an appearance in connection with the royal sickness, so that when he does so now (10,27b), subsequent to the king's prayer, it is for the first time. In addition, however, Josephus inserts between prayer (10,26) and the divine dispatch of Isaiah (10,27b) a long explanation (10,27a) as to why God did grant Hezekiah's appeal a favorable hearing, this – like the prayer itself – featuring the matter of the king's childlessness. It runs: "Then God took pity (ἐλεήσας) on him and granted his request[25], since he bewailed (ὠδύρετο; see ὀδυρόμενος, 10,26)[26] the death of which he had a presentiment (ὑπονοηθεῖσαν)[27], and had prayed (δεηθείη) to Him to give him yet a little while to live, not because he was about to be deprived of the benefits (ἀγαθῶν) of the kingship, but

23. This phrase echoes its occcurence in 10,11 in connection with Hezekiah's appeal to God in the face of the Assyrian threat; see there.

24. Note the greater definiteness concerning what Hezekiah is actually asking of the Lord here as compared with that of his Biblical counterpart who merely asks (20,3 // 38,3) that God "remember" his good works. With Josephus' version of the king's prayer, compare also the remarks of Jerome in his commentary on Isa 38,2-3 (PL 24, c. 390): "Flevit autem fletu magno propter promissionem Domini ad David, quam videbat in sua morte perituram... Ergo iste omnis est fletu, quod desperabat Christum de suo semine nasciturum".

25. This notice might be seen as Josephus' anticipation/ transposition into narrative of the opening word which God directs Isaiah to convey to the king in 20,5 // 38,5, i.e. "I (God) have heard your prayer"; see next note. Its use of the verb ἐλεέω in reference to God echoes 10,12 where Hezekiah asks Isaiah to exhort God to "take pity (ἐλεῆσαι) on His own people".

26. With this reference to God's having taken note of the king's "bewailing" his state, compare the announcement Isaiah is sent by God to bring to the king in 20,5 // 38,5: "I have seen your tears" which itself harks back to the mention of Hezekiah's "weeping bitterly" in 20,3 // 38,3. Cf. previous note for another instance of Josephus' anticipation/ transposition into editorial comment here in 10,27 of elements of the message entrusted by God to the prophet in 20,5 // 38,5.

27. This reference to Hezekiah's premonition of his coming death reflects the fact that in Josephus' presentation the king's prayer is "self-inspired", rather than being evoked by Isaiah's announcement that he is die as in the Biblical accounts; see above.

because he wished sons to be born to him who should succeed to his royal power...[28]".

Following the above, extra-Biblical interlude, Josephus finally (10,27b) comes to present his version of 20,4 // 38,4, i.e. the divine dispatch of Isaiah to the king. Whereas, however, the Biblical notices introduce this development by way of a *Wortereignisformel* ("the word of the Lord came..."), Josephus, as is his wont, avoids this phrase. In place thereof, he simply states: "and so He sent the prophet (τὸν προφήτην)[29] Isaiah and told him...[30]".

Josephus likewise markedly modifies the content of the message Isaiah is commissioned to bring the king according to the sources. Specifically, he first compresses the introductory words of that message ("... say to Hezekiah 'thus says the Lord the God of David your father: I have heard your prayer [see n. 25], I have seen your tears [see n. 26]...'") which becomes simply: "(He told him) to inform the king that...". In next citing the divine promise of recovery for Hezekiah, Josephus does utilize (the opening element of) the announcement of 20,5b ("I will heal you; on the third day you shall go up to the house of the Lord") which has no parallel in Isaiah 38[31]. His indirect discourse version of the item runs: "... within three days he should be free of his illness (νόσον; cf. νόσῳ, 10,25)". In common with both 20,6a and 38,5b he then has Isaiah being directed to announce that Hezekiah will "live another fifteen years". The Biblical announcement given Isaiah by the Lord ends up (20,6b // 38,6) with God promising to deliver Jerusalem from the Assyrian threat (+ "for my own sake and for my servant David's sake", 20,6b). Josephus leaves this element – which reads oddly in the current sequence of Kings and Isaiah where the withdrawal of the Assyrians has already been described prior to the account of

28. With the above wording, Josephus accentuates the "unselfishness" of Hezekiah's prayer: the king is concerned, not with his personal fate, but rather with that of his dynasty.

29. This is the fourth of seven instances in which Josephus goes beyond the Biblical sources in applying explicit "prophet terminology" to Isaiah; see on 9,276.

30. Like Isa 38,4 Josephus has no equivalent to the chronological specification of 2 Kgs 20,4 according to which the divine word came to the prophet "before Isaiah had gone out of the middle court". The absence of this item in his presentation is, however, only to be expected given that he has previously omitted the sources' notices on Isaiah's appearance before Hezekiah to which the plus of 20,4 harks back (the prophet is stopped by God before he can exit the courtyard of the palace where he had just spoken to Hezekiah). Thus the lack of an equivalent to the item in Josephus' version is no proof as such of his dependence on the text of Isaiah 38 as opposed to that of 2 Kings 20.

31. He reserves the further announcement of 20,5bβ about Hezekiah's "going up to the house of the Lord" to a later point (see 10,29), likewise transposing it there into a statement of what the king did following his cure.

Hezekiah's illness – aside. In its place, he introduces an alternative closing promise, one which picks up on his previous emphasis on the problem of Hezekiah's childlessness: "(Isaiah is to inform the king) that sons would be born to him".

The Biblical accounts diverge in their respective immediate continuations to God's giving of his announcement to Isaiah, 20,4-6 // 38,4-6. In 20,7 the prophet directs that a cake of figs be applied to Hezekiah's "boil" that he might recover, whereupon the king (20,8) asks for a "sign" that he indeed will be healed. By contrast, in Isaiah 38 the sequence corresponding to 20,7-8 comes only at the very end (vv. 21-22) of the episode of Hezekiah's sickness where it appears as a kind of afterthought. As its own direct follow-up to the divine announcement of 38,4-6 (// 20,4-6), Isaiah 38 gives rather, in v. 7, its parallel to 20,9, i.e. Isaiah's announcement of a "sign" for Hezekiah. Josephus (10,28) goes his own way with respect to both these divergent Biblical sequences. In particular, he dispenses completely with Isaiah's command about the figs (20,7 // 38,21), likely out of a concern that his cultivated readers might find such a remedy too primitive[32] (and also perhaps given the fact that this command constitutes a "blind motif" of which nothing further in said in the Biblical accounts). In place thereof, he follows his parallel (10,27b) to 20,4-6 // 38,4-6 with an elaborate transition of his own devising to the king's demand for a sign as reported in 20,8 (cf. 38,22). This inserted sequence, with its highlighting of the psychological factors behind the royal demand, reads: "when the prophet at God's command told him these things[33], he would not believe (ἀπιστῶν; see 9,73) him because of the severity of his illness and because the news brought to him (τῶν ἀπηγγελμένων[34]) surpassed belief (τὸ παράδοξον)[35], and so…". Following this extended insertion Josephus picks up on Hezekiah's sign request as related in 20,8. The source verse formulates this

32. See further FELDMAN, Studies, p. 390 (= ID., Isaiah, 606) and HÖFFKEN, Hiskija und Jesaja, 40-41.

33. This notice has no parallel in the sources which simply presuppose that the divine message of 20,4-6 // 38,4-6 was, in fact, delivered by the prophet.

34. This is the reading adopted by Marcus as well by Dindorf, Bekker, and Niese. M and Lat read ἐπηγγελμένων; this reading is followed by Naber, while Marcus comments "fort. recte" concerning it.

35. This term echoes the reference to Hezekiah's being "wonderfully (παραδόξως) delivered" from the Assyrians in Josephus' transition to the episode of the king's illness in 10,24. The verbal echo underscores the wrongfulness of Hezekiah's "unbelief" here in 10,28: having just recently experienced God's "paradoxical" overthrow of the Assyrians, he should have been all the more ready to believe that God could, as he has just been informed, do something equally "paradoxical" with regard to his own current illness. See further HÖFFKEN, Hiskija und Jesaja, 44.

request as a question in direct address which itself draws on the language of Isaiah's message in 20,5-6 (see above): "what shall be the sign (BL τὸ σημεῖον) that the Lord will heal me, and that I shall go up to the house of the Lord on the third day"? Josephus' (indirect discourse) version (10,28b) shifts attention from the person of Hezekiah to that of the prophet. It runs: "... he asked Isaiah to perform[36] some sign or miracle (σημεῖόν [so BL] τι καὶ τεράστιον)[37], in order that he might believe (πιστεύσῃ; compare ἀπιστῶν, 10,28a) in him when he said these things, as in one who came from God[38]". He then proceeds (10,28c) to have the king further explain his motivation in asking for a sign: "For, he said, things that are beyond belief (παράλογα; cf. τὸ παράδοξον, 10,28a) and surpass our hopes are made credible (πιστοῦται)[39] by acts of a like nature".

In 2 Kgs 20,9 Isaiah responds to Hezekiah's request for a sign by presenting him with a choice between having the Lord advance or turn back "the shadow" (BL ἡ σκιά) ten "steps" (B βαθμούς). Isaiah 38, which cites the king's request only at the very end of its account in v. 22 (// 20,8; see above), has no equivalent to the prophet's offer of a choice of signs to the king. Here again, Josephus (10,29a) follows the presentation of Kings, even while representing Isaiah as offering Hezekiah, not a choice between two specified alternatives, but rather a completely open-ended one: "when the prophet inquired what sign (σημεῖον; see 10,28) he wished to have performed...[40]". According to 20,10, Hezekiah, in making his choice between the two alternatives presented, opts for a

36. This formulation accentuates Isaiah's status as a (potential) miracle-worker; in 20,8 the king leaves unspecified by whom the asked-for sign is to be effected.

37. Josephus' only other use of the term τεράστιος is in *AJ* 10,232 where he speaks of the hand-writing on the wall at Belshazzar's feast as "a wonderful and portentous (τεράστιον) vision". On Josephus' terminology for "miracles" in relation to pagan and NT usage, see H. REMUS, *Does Terminology Distinguish Early Christian from Pagan Miracles?*, in *JBL* 101 (1982) 531-551, pp. 543-544.

38. Here too, note the accentuation of Isaiah's status which is what is to be "vindicated" by the "sign". With the above association of a "sign" and "belief", compare Josephus' phrase introducing the prophet's announcement of the imminent overthrow of Jeroboam's altar (= 1 Kgs 13,3) in *AJ* 8,232: "... that these people may believe (πιστεύσωσιν) that so it will be, I shall foretell to them a sign (σημεῖον) that will be given". Conceivably, in his use of "belief" and "sign" terminology in relation to Hezekiah and Isaiah here in 10,28 Josephus was inspired by story of the encounter – which he does not reproduce as such – between the prophet and Hezekiah's father Ahaz in Isaiah 7 where that terminology figures so prominently (see vv. 9-14).

39. This is the third use of a form of the πιστ – stem in 10,28.

40. By leaving the choice thus open-ended, Josephus magnifies Isaiah's stature as one who is confident of his ability to provide Hezekiah with any sign he might think to request. Compare Isa 7,11 where Isaiah instructs Ahaz "Ask a sign of the Lord... let it be deep as Sheol or high as heaven".

regression of the shadow rather than the "easy" advancement of it. Isaiah 38 relates no such royal choice; rather, in its vv. 7-8, the prophet simply informs the king of the sign that will be given him, i.e. the turning back of the shadow ten steps. Once more, Josephus aligns himself with Kings' account. His Hezekiah, however, makes his choice completely on his own, no prior limitations having been placed on this by Isaiah (see above): "... he asked him to cause the sun (τὸν ἥλιον), which in declining (ἀποκλίνας) had already cast a shadow (σκιάν) of ten degrees (δέκα βαθμούς, so B 20,10) in the house (ἐν τῇ οἰκίᾳ)[41], to return (ἀναστρέψαι; BL ἐπιστραφήτω) to the same place and again cast one there".

2 Kgs 20,11 // Isa 38,8b relate the realization of the sign requested by Hezekiah. Given the diversity among their respective witnesses, both verses pose difficult textual and translational problems; see the commentaries. Josephus' version (10,29b) is much less problematic. It begins with a clear reminiscence of 20,11a ("and Isaiah the prophet cried [BL ἐβόησεν] to the Lord"; no parallel in 38,8): "and when the prophet exhorted (παρακαλέσαντος) God *to show this sign* (σημεῖον; see 10,28.29a) *to the king*...[42]". He then summarily notes the outcome of the prophetic appeal: "... he [Hezekiah] saw what he wished...", leaving it to the reader to fill in the "what" that Hezekiah saw on the basis of the wording of the royal request as cited earlier in 10,29.

Josephus, at the end of the long paragraph 10,29, rounds off his account of Hezekiah's illness with two narrative notices which have no equivalent as such in the accounts of either 20,1-11 or 38,1-22 where they might well have been expected. In first place he states that Hezekiah was in fact "... at once freed (λυθείς)[43] from his illness"; compare the heading to the "Psalm of Hezekiah" (Isa 38,10-20) in 38,9, "a writing of Hezekiah... after he had... recovered from his sickness". Thereafter, Josephus reports the king's response to his healing: "then he went up to the temple and did

---

41. In the above formulation the reference to "the *sun's* having declined" has no equivalent either in Hezekiah's request of 20,10 or in the fulfillment notice of 20,11 (in MT L 20,11 [> B] what "declines" is "the shadow"). On the other hand, LXX Isa 38,8 does contain the phrase (οὕς) κατέβη ὁ ἥλιος (MT "the shadow... which had declined"). As to the above reference to "the [i.e. Hezekiah's, presumably] house" this too has no equivalent in either the MT or BL 20,10-11. The phrase does, however, have a counterpart in LXX 38,8: "the ten steps of the house (τοῦ οἰκοῦ) of your father" (MT: on the steps of Ahaz). There are thus indications that, in formulating his version of 20,10, Josephus also drew on a text like that of LXX 38,8.

42. With this addition to the wording of 20,11a Josephus provides a content for the prophet's appeal to the Deity as cited there.

43. This is the reading adopted by Niese and Marcus. Dindorf, Bekker, and Naber read λυθείσης with SPLaur.

obeisance to God and offered prayers to Him[44]". In formulating this last notice Josephus may have been inspired by several source elements. Thus, in 20,5 Isaiah tells Hezekiah that after his cure the king will "go up to the house of the Lord" on the third day. Josephus, as noted above, does not reproduce this prophetic announcement in his version of Isaiah's word in 10,27. Here in 10,29, however, he appears to transpose the announcement into a narrative statement of its fulfillment (something not cited in the source itself). As for the following reference to Hezekiah's "doing obeisance to God and offering prayers to him", this might be seen as an allusion to the "Psalm of Hezekiah", i.e. the prayer of thanksgiving which the king addresses to God following his cure in Isa 38,9-20[45].

2. Babylonian Embassy

2 Kgs 20,12 // Isa 39,1 vaguely date Hezekiah's visitation by the Babylonian envoys "at that time", i.e. of the king's sickness and recovery. Josephus (10,30a) presents a more elaborate chronological indication at the juncture between the two episodes: "now it happened at this time that the empire (ἀρχήν) of the Assyrians was destroyed (καταλυθῆναι; cf. λυθείς, of Hezekiah's being "freed" from his illness, 10,29) by the Medes, but I shall write about this in another place". This Josephan notice appears problematic in several respects. First of all, historically, the Assyrian empire did not, of course, fall during the reign of Hezekiah, but rather during that of his great-grandson Josiah, approximately a century later. In addition, its demise came at the hands, not merely of the Medes, but also (and primarily) of the Babylonians – as Josephus himself mentions in his subsequent brief allusion – foreshadowed here in 10,30 – to this event in AJ 10,74: "(Neco marched against) the Medes *and the Babylonians* who had overthrown the Assyrian empire" (κατέλυσαν ... ἀρχήν)[46]". In addition, there is the question of

44. With this inserted notice on the king's reaction to his healing compare the likewise interjected reference to Hezekiah and his people "offering sacrifices to God" following the elimination of the Assyrian threat in 10,24. Both insertions – which constitute a kind of inclusion around Josephus' version of Hezekiah's cure – serve to underscore the king's exemplary piety and thankfulness.

45. Josephus' "reduction" of the Isaian Hezekiah's lengthy "psalm" to a (possible) brief allusion here is in line with his handling of Jonah's prayer (Jonah 2,2-10) in 9,214 and Hezekiah's own earlier prayer of 2 Kgs 19,15-19 // Isa 37,15-20 in 10,16b; see above.

46. This passing allusion is, in fact, Josephus' only subsequent mention of Assyria's fate. As such, it does not seem to meet the expectation of a fuller account of this development awakened by the historian's wording ("I shall write about this in another place") here in 10,30; cf. MARCUS, *Josephus*, VI, p. 175, n. b.

why Josephus should introduce the above parenthetical aside on Assyria's overthrow precisely at this point where the Biblical sources have nothing at all equivalent. With regard to this last point, I suggest that Josephus mentions the matter here in order to account for the fact – presupposed but not explained by the Biblical "embassy stories" – that at this moment there was a king ruling in Bablyon, i.e. in what had been territory belonging to the Assyrian empire: this was the case, Josephus' insertion has it, because "at this time" that empire was "destroyed by the Medes"[47].

The Babylonian ruler whose envoys call on Hezekiah is differently designated in the Biblical textual witnesses. MT 20,12 names him Berodach-baladan, son of Baladan, MT 39,1 Merodach-baladan, son of Baladan; compare B 20,12 Μερωχβαλδὰν υἱὸς Βαλαάν, L 20,12 Μαρωδὰχ Βαλδὰν υἱὸς Βαλαδάν, LXX 39,1 Μαρωδαχ υἱὸς τοῦ Λααδαν. Josephus leaves aside the patronymic of the Babylonian king; his name for the king himself, i.e. "Baladas" (Βαλάδας) seems to reflect the second component ("Baladan") of the name as found in MT L 20,12 // MT 39,1.

According to 20,12 // 39,1 what the Babylonian monarch sent Hezekiah were "letters" (LXX 39,1 adds "and envoys", πρέσβεις) and a "gift(s)" (MT 20,12 // 39,1 מִנְחָה; B 20,12 μαναάν, L 20,12 // LXX 39,1 δῶρα). Josephus omits mention of the king's "letters"[48]; in line with the LXX's plus in 39,1 he has Baladas sending "envoys" (πρέσβεις) who themselves bear "gifts" (δῶρα, see L 20,12 // LXX 39,1).

47. On the question see further HÖFFKEN, Hiskija und Jesaja, 42-44 who argues that Josephus makes a distinction between Assyria's earlier loss of its dominion over Asia in the time of Hezekiah (see 10,30), this in accordance with the prophecy of Jonah (9,208.214), and the later destruction of the city Nineveh itself (see 10,74) in Josiah's time in fulfillment of Nahum's prediction which, Josephus states, came to realization "after a hundred and fifteen years" (see 9,239-242; and cf. p. 309, n. 66). I would note, however, that 10,74 does not, in fact, speak of the fate specifically of Nineveh, but rather, quite in the line of 10,30 ("the empire of the Assyrians was destroyed by the Medes"), of the "overthrow of the Assyrian empire" by the Medes and Babylonians. It would appear that in both passages Josephus has the same event in view, i.e. the destruction of the Assyrian empire at the hands of the Medes (and Babylonians). See further on 10,74.

48. By contrast, Songs Rab. 3.4.2 (SIMON, Midrash Rabbah Song of Songs, p. 150) expatiates on the content of the Babylonian king's letter(s), noting that he originally formulated the saluation with Hezekiah being mentioned before God. Becoming conscious of his mistake, the king rose from his throne and took three steps to retrieve the letter which he then rewrote so that the name of God appeared first. In reward for his initiative, God promised him three successors on the throne of Babylon who would rule the world, i.e. Nebuchadnezzar, Evil-merodach, and Belshazzar. b. Sanh. 96a gives a variant of this tradition according to which the "mistake" was due to the absence of Merodach-Baladan's scribe, i.e. Nebuchadnezzar, who, upon his return, went in pursuit of the letter-carrier, only to be halted by the angel Gabriel after having taken four steps.

The opening Biblical verses of the "embassy episode" conclude by noting the occasion for the Babylonian king's sending to Hezekiah, i.e. his hearing that "he (Hezekiah) had been sick (MT 39,1 + "and recovered [וַיֶּחֱזָק; cf. IQIsᵃ ויחיה]; L 20,12 // LXX 39,1 + καὶ ἀνέστη)". Josephus turns the Babylonians' courtesy call on the recovered king into an explicitly political overture by "Baladas":... he invited (παρεκάλει) him to become his ally and friend (συμμαχόν⁴⁹ ... καὶ φιλόν)⁵⁰".

The Biblical descriptions of Hezekiah's response to the Babylonians' visitation begin with mention of his "hearing of them" (וַיִּשְׁמַע עֲלֵיהֶם, MT 20,13)/ "rejoicing over them" (וַיִּשְׂמַח עֲלֵיהֶם, MT 39,1 = ἐχάρη ἐπ᾽ αὐτοῖς BL 20,13 // LXX 39,2). Josephus' version (10,31) of Hezekiah's initial reaction aligns itself with that of the witnesses other than MT 20,13, i.e. "thereupon he gladly received (ἡδέως ἀποδεξάμενος) the envoys (πρεσβευτάς; cf. πρέσβεις, 10,30)...". To this indication he appends a further one, i.e. "... and feasted them". This item has no equivalent in either Biblical account⁵¹. It does, on the other hand, cohere

49. This term echoes the reference in 10,24 to the aid given Hezekiah and his people by their "ally" (συμμαχίας) God. Now Hezekiah is being asked to look to an "ally" other than God. The above formulation likewise echoes 9,277 where Josephus states that Shalmaneser heard that King Hoshea of Israel had sent to Soas king of Egypt "inviting (παρακαλῶν) him to make an alliance (συμμαχίαν) against the Assyrian king". Given the disastrous outcome of that earlier overture, Josephus' similar wording here in 10,30 interjects an ominous note into his story of the Babylonian embassy right from the start.

50. The above notice might appear a more plausible motivation for the Babylonian mission than that alleged in the Bible – why should Merodach-Baladan go to the trouble of sending a delegation to a far-away king (with whom, moreover, he had no earlier contact as far as the Biblical documentation records) simply because that king had recovered from an illness? Such "disinterestedness" might strike Josephus' readers as highly unlikely, whereas they would readily appreciate the political motivation for the visit adduced by him.

In 2 Chr 32,32 there is a summary allusion to the Babylonian visitation of Hezekiah. Here, the Chronicler gives his own rationale for the mission, i.e. it was "to inquire about the sign that had been done in the land", i.e. the regression, it would appear, of the shadow as described in 2 Kgs 20,11 // Isa 38,8 (cf. the designation of this happening as a "sign" in 20,8-9 // 38,22). Rabbinic tradition picks up on the Chronicler's presentation, see, e.g., *Songs Rab.* 3.4.1 (SIMON, *Midrash Rabbah Song of Songs*, pp. 149-150) where Merodach-baladan lies down for a brief afternoon nap and wakes up in the morning. Thinking that his attendants have let him oversleep right into the next morning, he is ready to execute them. They, however, inform the king that the God of Hezekiah had turned back the course of the (same) day from afternoon to morning. Thereupon, the king recognizes the Lord as greater than his own god (the sun) and so dispatches a gift-bearing delegation to Hezekiah. See also *b. Sanh.* 96a where R. Johanan is cited as averring that the Babylonian visitation was prompted, not simply by news of Hezekiah's recovery, but also by the wonder of the day's having been lengthened.

51. The item does, however, have parallels in Rabbinic tradition, see *E. R.* §(8)9(47) (BRAUDE and KAPSTEIN, *Tanna děbe Eliyyahu*, p. 109) and *b. Sanh.* 104a where Hezekiah is censured for having "sat at table" with the envoys.

with Josephus' own apologetical purposes in its portrayal of a Jewish notable extending munificent hospitality to non-Jews[52].

2 Kgs 20,13 // Isa 39,2 continue with an extended enumeration of the items which Hezekiah displayed to the envoys, i.e. his treasure house (MT בֵּית נְכֹתֹה; B 20,13 // LXX 39,2 τὸν οἶκον τοῦ νεχωθά)[53], silver, gold, spices, precious oil, armory (MT 20,13 // 39,2 בֵּית כֵּלָיו; BL 20,13 τὸν οἶκον τῶν σκευῶν, LXX 39,2 τοὺς τῶν σκευῶν τῆς γάζης), and finally "all that was found in his storehouses" (MT 20,13 // 39,2 בְּאוֹצְרֹתָיו; BL 20,13 // LXX 39,2 ἐν τοῖς θησαυροῖς [αὐτοῦ]). The source verses then conclude with the generalizing affirmation "there was nothing in his house or in all his realm that Hezekiah did not show them". Josephus considerably shortens (and modifies) the sources' "display list": "... he also showed (ἐπιδείξας)[54] them his treasures (θησαυρούς) and his array of arms (ὅπλων) and the rest of his wealth (πολυτέλειαν), all that he had in precious stones (λίθοις)[55] and in gold (χρυσῷ)". Thereafter, however, he rounds off his account of Hezekiah's encounter with the envoys by way of the notice "... then, having given them gifts (δῶρα)[56] to bring to Baladas, he sent them back to him". Like his earlier reference (10,31a) to Hezekiah's "feasting" the envoys, this element has no equivalent in the sources. The first part of the "addition" does, however, reinforce the image of a preeminent Jewish figure who is generous to non-Jews which Josephus wishes to hold up to Gentile readers[57].

52. On the importance of this apologetic concern throughout *AJ*, see FELDMAN, *Studies*, p. 373 (= ID., *Hezekiah*, 607-608).

53. Rabbinic tradition proposes a variety of understandings for (the (second element of) the above MT expression (which B 20,13 and LXX 39,2 simply transliterate; see above), see *Songs Rab.* 3.4.2 (SIMON, *Midrash Rabbah Song of Songs*, pp. 150-151) which cites the following possibilities: the spoil taken by Hezekiah from Sennacherib, weapons of varying capabilities, ivory palaces that appeared to have been poured in wax, honey firm as a stone, and the Ark of the Covenant (the envoys are stated to have seen this last object without suffering harm thereby also in TC 2 Chr 32,31). Compare *b. Sanh.* 104b where three alternative renditions of the above phrase are suggested: Hezekiah's wife (who is further said to have mixed drinks for the envoys; cf. n. 51), his treasury, and weapons with the capability to destroy other weapons.

54. This term echoes the same verb used of Isaiah's request that God show (ἐπιδεῖξαι) Hezekiah the sign he had asked for in 10,29. Now it is Hezekiah's turn to "show (off)" the signs of his own power.

55. This is the one element of Josephus' listing which has no parallel at all in the Biblical enumerations. Conversely, Josephus has no counterpart to three source items, i.e. silver, spices, and precious oil.

56. This is the same term used in 10,30 of the "gifts" brought to Hezekiah by the envoys. The repetition of the term here in 10,31 underscores the reciprocity/ equality of the relationship between Hezekiah and the Babylonian king.

57. Compare Josephus' introduction of a similar element in *AJ* 8,368 where in his rewriting of 1 Kgs 20,34 he inserts mention of Ahab's "presenting him [the defeated Syrian king] with many gifts (δωρήσαμενος)" prior to releasing him.

The addition's second component, for its part, provides explicit closure to the exchange between Hezekiah and the Babylonians by noting that the king did, in fact, eventually sent the envoys on their way – a point which the Bible leaves readers to fill in on their own[58].

The second (and final) component of the Biblical "visit episode" is the exchange between Isaiah and Hezekiah regarding the envoys' coming (20,14-19 // 39,3-8 = 10,32-34a). This opens (20,14a // 39,3a) with the prophet approaching Hezekiah with a double question, i.e. what had the envoys said?, and whence had they come? Here, Isaiah poses his questions in an order which is the reverse of what might have been expected; moreover, it is only the second of them which Hezekiah will actually answer (20,14b // 39,3b). Josephus (10,32a) accordingly reduces the prophet's interrogation to a single (indirect discourse) query: "but the prophet [see 10,27] Isaiah came to him and inquired where the visitors were from...". In reproducing the king's answer to this question from 20,14b // 39,3b the historian leaves aside the (self-evident) qualification of Babylon as a "far country[59]". Instead, he has Hezekiah simply state that the callers "had come from Babylon on behalf of their master...".

In 20,15 // 39,4 Isaiah proceeds to ask Hezekiah what the Babylonians had seen in his house, whereupon the latter affirms that he had shown them everything. Continuing to compress the Biblical exchange, Josephus passes over the prophet's further question. Thus, in his presentation, Hezekiah, having mentioned whence the envoys had come, proceeds immediately (10,32b) to volunteer the further information that "... he had showed (ἐπιδεῖξαι; see 10,31) them everything". Josephus likewise has the king adduce a motivation for his action without counterpart in the Bible: "... in order that they might surmise his power (δύναμιν) from what they saw of his wealth and be able to report it to their king". This motivation, it will be noted, picks up on Josephus' earlier "un-Biblical" reference to the political purpose of the Babylonian king's mission to Hezekiah, i.e. "to invite him to become his ally and friend" (10,30). By means of his display, Hezekiah is here informing Isaiah, he had made clear to the envoys that he would indeed represent a suitable partner for Babylon.

---

58. Compare Josephus' – likewise inserted – explicit mention that Hezekiah was indeed healed as the prophet had announced to him (20,5 // 38,5) in 10,29.

59. Compare *Num. Rab.* 20.6 (J.J. SLOTKI, tr., *Midrash Rabbah Numbers*, II, London-New York, Soncino, 1983, p. 791) where Hezekiah's invocation of Babylon as a "far-away country" is taken as indicative of his pride. Instead of replying in this way, the Midrash avers, Hezekiah ought to have pointed out to Isaiah that, as a prophet, he (Isaiah) should be the one to have questions asked of him, rather than vice versa.

2 Kgs 20,16-18 // Isa 39,5-7 constitute Isaiah's announcement to Hezekiah about what awaits his wealth and descendants, i.e. deportation to Babylon. Given the negative content of this announcement, it is surprising that it is not accompanied by any explicit accusation of the king (e.g., for pride). Josephus (10,33a) too presents – here for once retaining the sources' direct address – a "truncated" judgment speech by Isaiah which avoids censuring the king as such[60]. He further leaves aside the prophetic call to attention of 20,16 // 39,5 with its reference to the divine "word" which he customarily avoids. The Biblical prophet "dates" his predictions (20,17 // 39,6) only very indeterminately in "the coming days". Josephus' Isaiah is more specific (and imminent) about his which are to occur "in a short time[61]". What will happen then, according to Isaiah, is, first, that all Hezekiah's "wealth" will be removed to Babylon (= 20,17 // 39,6 with omission of the sources' reference to "all that which your fathers have stored up to this day"). 2 Kgs 20,18a // Isa 39,7a go on to speak of a deportation also of some of Hezekiah's "sons". Josephus, once again compressing, passes over this item, in order to come immediately to his version of 20,18b // 39,7b, the announcement that Hezekiah's sons will be "eunuchs (MT 20,18 // 39,7 סָרִיסִים; B 20,18 εὐνοῦχοι; L 20,18 // LXX 39,7 ποιήσουσι σπάδοντας) in the palace of the king of Babylon". His formulation of this portion of Isaiah's prediction reads: "... your offspring (ἐκγόνους) shall be made eunuchs (εὐνουχισθησομένους)[62] and, after losing their manhood (ἀπολέσαντας[63] τὸ ἄνδρας)[64], *be servants*

60. Compare *Num Rab.* 20.6 (see n. 59) where Isaiah's announcement is represented as having been called forth by the pride manifest in Hezekiah's earlier response about the envoys having come so far to visit him. Cf. also *E.R.* §(8)9(47) (BRAUDE and KAPSTEIN, *Tanna děbe Eliyyahu*, p. 109) where Isaiah censures the king for his pride in displaying everything to the envoys (including the Temple treasures).

61. According to HÖFFKEN, *Hiskija und Jesaja*, 42-43 Josephus, with this modified chronological indication, has in view an initial, short-term realization of Isaiah's prophecy, i.e. the deportation of Hezekiah's son Manasseh to Babylon as related in 2 Chr 33,11 (= *AJ* 10,40). The prediction's long-term, full realization will come only much later, i.e. in the time of Nebuchadnezzar; see 10,186 and n. 64.

62. This is the only occurrence of the verb εὐνουχίζω in the Josephan corpus.

63. This is the reading adopted by Dindorf, Bekker, Niese, and Marcus. Naber reads rather ἀπολέσοντας with ROLaur, commenting (*Opera*, II, p. xxxv) concerning the above reading: "quod miror quomodo Niesio placere potuerit".

64. Note Josephus' insistence on the demeaning detail of the offspring's castration, compare ποιήσουσι σπάδοντας in L 20,18 // LXX 39,7. In *AJ* 10,186 Josephus recounts – though without the *Rückverweis* that might have been expected – the realization of Isaiah's announcement here in 10,33: "Nebuchadenezzar... took the Jewish youths... making some of them eunuchs (ποιήσας τινὰς αὐτῶν ἐκτομίας)". In so doing, he goes beyond the source text, i.e. Dan 1,3-4, which does not mention such a castration of (some of) the Jewish youths selected to be trained for Nebuchadnezzar's court service.

(δουλεύσοντας)[65] to the king of Babylon". Josephus then rounds off Isaiah's whole announcement with the formula (10,33b): "For God, he said, foretold (προλέγειν τὸν θεόν)[66] these things". This formula represents his "delayed" version of the expression "says the Lord" (LXX 39,6 God) which in the sources (20,17bβ // 39,6bβ) comes between the prophet's predictions concerning the fate of Hezekiah's wealth and that of his sons.

The visit episode ends in 20,19 // 39,8 with Hezekiah's response to Isaiah's predictions. That response does not appear to put the king in a very good light. In it, he begins by calling the Lord's foregoing word to him "good". This odd reaction is then explained in terms of Hezekiah's reflecting that, whatever might come later, he himself would enjoy "peace and security" (> B 20,19). One is thus left with the image of a king who is quite unconcerned about what will happen to his kingdom and his own descendants as long as he himself suffers no harm. Josephus (10,34a) markedly modifies this portrayal in the interest of presenting a more sympathetic, exemplary Hezekiah. He begins by informing us that Hezekiah was "grieved" (λυπηθείς) by what he had just heard – rather than finding it "good" as does his Biblical counterpart. Next, he has the king tell Isaiah that "he would be unwilling to have his nation (τὸ ἔθνος)[67] meet with such misfortunes". Having thus expressed a sense of solidarity with his people, Hezekiah, in Josephus' version, then continues with words of both resignation and appeal: "... but, since it was not possible to alter God's decrees (οὐκ ... δυνατὸν τὰ τῷ θεῷ δεδογμένα μεταβαλεῖν)[68], he prayed that there should be peace (εἰρήνην; cf. εἰρήνη, L 20,19b // LXX 39,8b) during his own lifetime". As will be noted, it is only the very end of this Josephan version of Hezekiah's

Josephus' above notice on the point is, however, comparable to the statement of Rab cited in *b. Sanh.* 93b and Jerome's comment on Isa 39,7 (PL, c. 399) that Daniel and his three companions were made eunuchs in fulfillment of Isaiah's announcement (note that Josephus himself does not explicitly state that Daniel *et al.* were among those Jewish youths made eunuchs; see too 10,188 where the former are introduced only after the reference to the latter in 10,186).

65. The Josephan Isaiah's mention of Hezekiah's descendants "serving" the king of Babylon here represents an amplification/specification of the Biblical predictions which speak merely of their being eunuchs in his palace. The wording used here in 10,33 likewise foreshadows that which Josephus places on the lips of another prophet, i.e. Jeremiah, during the siege of Jerusalem in *AJ* 10,122: "we shall be slaves (δουλεύσομεν) to him [Nebuchadnezzar] and his descendants for seventy years".

66. On this formula see on 9,189.

67. This is the reading adopted by Niese, Naber, and Marcus. Dindorf and Bekker read τὸ γένος with M[1]SP; cf. Lat's gentem.

68. Compare the (likewise "un-Biblical") words which Josephus attributes to the prophetess Huldah in *AJ* 10,60: "the Deity had already given His sentence against them and no one could make it ineffective (ἄκυρον) even by supplication...".

reaction which has a counterpart in the sources. Even this element, however, is transformed by him from a matter of smug self-assurance on the
king's part ("there will be peace and security in my days") into a prayer
that God will indeed grant him such "peace". Hezekiah's last word in
his presentation thus becomes something quite different (and much more
edifying) than that of his Biblical namesake.

Josephus rounds off (10,34b-35) his version of the Babylonian
embassy's visit with a series of appended notices which lack any parallel in the sources. This *Sondergut* sequence begins (10,34b) with Josephus calling attention to the fact that "Baladas" of Babylon, Hezekiah's
counterpart in 10,30, also figures in extant extra-Biblical literature, i.e.
the *History of Chaldea* of Berosus[69]. Thereafter, he proceeds to present
(10,35a) a summary eulogy for Isaiah:

> As for the prophet, he was acknowledged to be a man of God (θεῖος)[70] and
> marvellously possessed of truth (θαυμάσιος τὴν ἀλήθειαν)[71], and, as he
> was confident of never having spoken what was false (ψευδές), he wrote
> down in books all that he had prophesied and left them to be recognized as
> true (γνωρισθησόμενα) from the event by men of future ages[72].

To this eulogy for Isaiah Josephus, in turn, appends (10,35b) a final,
generalizing remark about the veracity also of the twelve other recognized "prophets"/ prophetic books of Judaism: "And not alone this
prophet, but also others, twelve in number[73], did the same, and whatever
happens to us whether for good or ill comes about in accordance with
their prophecies. But of each of these we shall give an account hereafter".

69. For Josephus' utilizations of Berosus, see on 10,20.

70. On Josephus' use of this term in reference to human figures, see BEGG, *Early
Divided Monarchy*, p. 59, n. 334 and the literature cited there. See further FELDMAN, *Studies*, p. 389 (= ID., *Isaiah*, 605)

71. This phrase occurs only here in Josephus.

72. As noted above, it is this emphasis on Isaiah's veracity as articulated by Josephus
here in 10,35 which prompted him to omit mention of the prophet's – subsequently countermanded – announcement about Hezekiah's imminent death of 20,1b // 38,1b. The
above notice likewise harks back to Josephus' initial reference (9,276) to Isaiah as one by
whom Hezekiah "was accurately informed of future events".

73. On the difficulties surrounding the referent of this figure (which apparently has in
view the 13 "historical books" in addition to the Pentateuch, each purportedly authored
by a prophet, to which Josephus alludes – though without naming them – in *c. Ap.* 1,40),
see MARCUS, *Josephus*, VI, pp. 176-177, n. c. (in this note Marcus points out that the continuation of Josephus' above statement with its reference to the account of the prophets
other than Isaiah he will *subsequently* give, would, on the foregoing understanding
of it, have to be regarded as "inexact" since he has actually already treated a number
of the post-Pentateuchal "prophetic" books, e.g., Joshua, Jonah, Nahum, prior to this
point).

3. Hezekiah's Demise

Josephus' two Biblical narrative sources round off their extensive treatments of Hezekiah with a series of concluding notices (2 Kgs 20,20-21 // 2 Chr 32,32-33) for this king. Of the items making up this complex, Josephus omits, in line with his invariable practice, the source references of 20,20 // 32,32. He likewise replaces (10,36) the summary, figurative reference to Hezekiah's "sleeping with his fathers" of 20,21a // 32,33aα with an elaborated "death notice" of his own: "*Now Hezekiah lived on for the length of time we stated above*[74] *and passed all of it in peace* (ἐν εἰρήνῃ)[75], and died *after completing the fifty-fourth year of his life*[76] *and reigning for twenty-nine years* [= 2 Kgs 18,2 // 2 Chr 29,1]". Having thus elaborated on the fact of Hezekiah's death, Josephus leaves unmentioned the king's burial[77], just as he makes the accession of his son Manasseh (20,21b // 32,33b) the opening (10,37) of a new segment, 10,37-46 devoted to that king; see next chapter.

Conclusions: Josephus' Rewriting of 2 Kings 20 // Isaiah 38-39 // 2 Chr 32,24-33

Our reading of *AJ* 10,24-36 has, first of all, brought to light varying indications concerning which of the available Biblical presentations (and text-forms of these) Josephus followed in composing his account of Hezekiah's later reign. On the one hand, we noted a number of instances where he agrees with Kings against Isaiah: the promise of healing within

---

74. This inserted indication harks back to Isaiah's announcement as cited in 10,27 that Hezekiah would live an additional fifteen years. As such it constitutes an implicit fulfillment notice for that announcement which, in turn, serves to accentuate Isaiah's veracity. Compare Josephus' explicit mention, interjected by him in 10,29, that Hezekiah was indeed "freed from his illness", just as Isaiah had announced to him in 10,27.

75. With this further insertion Josephus informs us that Hezekiah's prayer that "there should be peace (εἰρήνην) during his own lifetime" (10,34) was indeed heard by God – just as was his earlier prayer (10,27) about being allowed to live yet a while longer.

76. This indication concerning Hezekiah's age at death represents the historian's characteristic (delayed) adaptation of the opening Biblical mentions (2 Kgs 18,2 // 2 Chr 29,1) of the king's age at accession (25) and length of reign (29 years).

77. In his non-mention of this happening Josephus agrees with MT and B 20,21 against L 20,21 and MT BL 32,33. Given Hezekiah's status as a "good" king – who as such would certainly deserve a proper burial – (as well as the historian's tendency to embellish the burials of Biblical heroes like Elisha; see on 9,182), Josephus' lack of a corresponding notice might indicate that he was using a text(s), like that of MT B 20,21, in which such a notice was absent. On the other hand, it should also be recalled that Josephus has no equivalent either to the burial notice, jointly attested by all textual witnesses of 2 Kgs 16,20aβ // 2 Chr 28,27aβ, for the "bad" king Ahaz, Hezekiah's father.

three days (10,27 = 20,5, > 38,5); placing of Hezekiah's sign request prior to the notice on the "shadow miracle" (10,28-29 = 20,8-11; compare 38,8.22); and Isaiah's offering the king a choice of signs (10,29 = 20,9; compare 38,7-8 where Hezekiah is simply informed of the sign the Lord intends to give him). On the other hand, we also encountered indications of Josephus' familiarity with readings peculiar to the Isaiah version of the royal illness story. Thus whereas neither MT or BL 20,10 speak explicitly of "the sun" in connection with Isaiah's "sign", Josephus (10,29), like 38,8 (MT 1QIsa^a and LXX), does do so. Likewise, his explicit mention of Hezekiah's being cured and subsequently "offering prayers" in 10,29 might be seen as a summary allusion to the "Psalm of Hezekiah" (38,10-20) and its heading (38,9) which has no parallel in 2 Kings 20. We further noted various (minor) pointers towards Josephus' familarity with distinctive LXX readings in Isaiah and/or Kings, i.e. his reference to "the house" (i.e. palace) in connection with the regression of the shadow in 10,29 (// LXX 38,8) and the explicit mention of the castration of Hezekiah's progeny in 10,33 (so L 20,18 and LXX 39,7). Finally, in 10,36 we encountered a "negative agreement" between Josephus and MT B 20,21 *contra* L 20,21 // MT BL 32,33, i.e. the former's lack of a burial notice for Hezekiah as found in the latter witnesses. In sum, here again it appears that Josephus did not confine himself to one of the relevant Biblical sources (or to a single text-form of these) in developing his account of Hezekiah's final years. In fact, Josephus' presentation in this instance draws on extra-Biblical sources as well. He himself (10,34b) notes that Berosus too cites the figure of "Baladas". The many points of contact between the Josephan account and Rabbinic tradition concerning the sickness and embassy episodes, e.g., the fact of Hezekiah's "childlessness" at the moment his sickness befell him, further suggests Josephus' acquaintance with these traditions in some (prior) form.

Of the standard Josephan rewriting techniques, the one that comes most to the fore in 10,24-36 is his *elaboration* of source data. Such elaboration concerns the following points: the circumstances surrounding Hezekiah's falling sick (10,24-25; compare 20,1a // 38;1a); the rationale for God's hearing of the king's prayer (10,27a); the promise he would have sons (10,27b; compare 20,5-6 // 38,5-6); Hezekiah's disbelief of God's promise as the motivation for his requesting a sign (10,28; compare 20,8 // 38,22); the notice on the overthrow of the Assyrian empire prefacing the report of the Babylonian envoys' visit (10,30a; compare 20,12 // 39,1); Hezekiah's "feasting" of the envoys, giving them gifts of his own, and sending them back to their master (10,31; compare 20,13 //

39,2); the king's statement about his reason for showing the envoys everything (10,32; compare 20,15b // 39,4b), the extended "appendix" (10,34b-35) attached to the notice of Hezekiah's response (20,19 // 39,8 = 10,34a) to Isaiah's preceding announcement; and the more expansive death notice for Hezekiah of 10,36 (compare 20,21a // 2 Chr 32,33a).

At the same time, Josephus also *omits/ compresses* elements of the sources' presentation, e.g., Isaiah's initial approach to the king (20,1b // 38,1b); the "extraneous" divine promise to deliver Jerusalem from the Assyrians (20,6b // 38,6); Isaiah's directive about the application of the cake of figs to Hezekiah's boil (20,7 // 38,21); the enumeration of the things shown by Hezekiah to the envoys (10,31; compare 20,13 // 39,2); Isaiah's questions about what the envoys had said (20,14 // 39,3) and what they had seen in the king's house (20,15 // 39,4); and the source reference of 20,20 // 32,32.

AJ 10,24-36 likewise evidences noteworthy instances of Josephan *modification/ adaptation* of the sources' account, these bearing on, e.g., the content of Hezekiah's prayer (10,26; compare 20,2-3 // 38,2-3); the "sign offer" made Hezekiah (10,29; compare 20,8; cf. 38,7-8); the motivation for the Babylonian king's embassy (10,30; compare 20,12 // 39,1); Hezekiah's response to Isaiah's distressing announcement (10,34a; compare 20,19 // 39,8); and the substitution of Hezekiah's age at death for his age at accession (10,36; compare 2 Kgs 18,2 // 2 Chr 29,1). Finally, in making (10,37) Manasseh's accession the opening of a segment focussed on that king rather than the conclusion to the account of his father (so 20,21b // 32,33b), Josephus effects a certain *re-arrangement* of the sources' sequence. Another such instance occurs in connection with the promise of 20,5bβ (cf. 20,8) that Hezekiah will go up to the Lord's house on the third day; Josephus' narrative transposition of this item stands as a sequel to the king's actual healing in 10,29.

Josephus' application of the above rewriting techniques yields a depiction of the key figures Hezekiah and Isaiah that is not without its distinctive features. In general, it might be said that, overall, the Josephan Hezekiah of 10,24-36 is a considerably more sympathetic and admirable figure than is his Scriptural counterpart, this notwithstanding the fact that Josephus goes beyond the Bible (10,28; compare 20,8 // 38,22) in accentuating the king's disbelief of the divine promise of healing[78]. In particular, Josephus markedly transforms the self-centered egoism that characterizes the Biblical Hezekiah's responses in both

78. This Josephan emphasis does, at the same time, of course, serve to accentuate the greatness of the divine power manifest in Hezekiah's healing, the king's incredulity notwithstanding.

episodes making up this segment. Rather than appeal to his own merits (so 20,3 // 38,3) in the face of his imminent demise, Josephus' Hezekiah (10,27) is concerned above all with assuring his kingdom a proper successor prior to his death. Similarly, the smug and *degagé* king who calls Isaiah's word of doom for his nation's wealth and his own descendants "good" (20,19 // 39,8) since he himself is confident of escaping unscathed yields, in Josephus' presentation (10,34a), to one who expresses sorrow at the prospect of his people's pending misfortune, while also voicing resignation in the face of what God has decided in this regard, and who prays that at least he may be granted "peace" in his lifetime. Elsewhere too in our segment Josephus accentuates Hezekiah's piety: he responds to his deliverance from the Assyrians with thanksgiving sacrifices (10,24; no Biblical parallel) and pays homage to God following his cure (10,29; cf. 20,5 and 38,9-20). In addition, Josephus' king appears more open and forthcoming in his exchange with Isaiah following the envoys' visit. Thus whereas in 20,14 // 39,3 Hezekiah avoids answering the prophet's question about what the envoys had said to him, and has to be asked (20,15 // 39,4) what he had shown them, Josephus (10,32) leaves aside Isaiah's unanswered question and has Hezekiah volunteer the information about what he had let his visitors see and his rationale for doing so. Finally, Josephus also plays up the king's hospitality to his foreigner callers whom he both "feasts" and sends off with gifts for their sender (10,31), neither item having a Biblical equivalent[79].

In comparison with the sources, Josephus somewhat diminishes the "quantitative" presence of Isaiah in the two episodes, passing over several of the words/ questions which the Biblical accounts attribute to him. On the other hand, these very omissions reflect his primary concern throughout his portrayal of Isaiah, i.e. to accentuate his status as a true predictor. It is in accord with this aim that, e.g., he leaves aside Isaiah's initial "false" announcement about the outcome of the royal illness (20,1b // 38,1b), as well as the embarassing divine countermanding of this (20,4-6 // 38,4-6). In the same line, he introduces his own concluding eulogy for the prophet (10,35a) as one who "was confident of never having spoken what was false". Subsequently (10,186) the Josephan Isaiah's predictive veracity is again underscored when, in accordance with his statement about some of Hezekiah's offspring being castrated

---

79. This wide-going Josephan ameliorization of the sources' portrait of Hezekiah in the two episodes is all the more remarkable given the Rabbinic strictures – to which we have called attention above – on many aspects of the king's conduct during them, i.e. his willed failure to beget an heir, invocation of his own merits, disbelief in Isaiah's promise, and pride that caused him to consort with pagans.

(10,33), Nebuchadnezzar does "make eunuchs" of certain noble Jewish youths, whereas in the Bible (compare Dan 1,3-4) no such statement is found as such. Moreover, Josephus highlights Isaiah's status as a miracle-worker by having him (10,29) offer Hezekiah an "open-ended" choice of signs, rather than (so 20,9) one limited to two possibilities.

Josephus' retelling of the Biblical account of the Babylonian embassy to the revived Hezekiah sets before Gentile readers the picture of a Jewish leader whom the ruler of mighty Babylon sought out as an "ally and friend" (10,30) – and rightly so given the "power" and wealth Hezekiah was able to display to his envoys (10,32). As such, the embassy story gives the lie to contemporary claims about Jewish poverty and insignificance, just as the historian's accentuation of the hospitiality extended the envoys by Hezekiah (10,31) counteracts charges of Jewish xenophobia.

To Jewish readers Josephus' rendition of the stories of Hezekiah's recovery and the embassy that followed this has perhaps even more to offer. It reminds such readers, first of all, of the veracity, not only of Isaiah himself, but of the whole body of prophets whose writings can be looked to for reliable indications of what awaits the Jewish nation (10,35). The emphasis in Josephus' version on Hezekiah's state of childlessness, for its part, might have in view the recent decimation of the Jewish population in the war with Rome. To Jewish readers anxious over the continuation of their depleted race, Josephus offers the hope-inspiring story of childless Hezekiah whose prayer for progeny, made in a seemingly hopeless situation of his own imminent death, was heard by God. Finally and conversely, the Josephan Hezekiah of the embassy story presents Jewish readers with a warning about putting one's confidence, as Hezekiah himself did, in foreign "allies" (10,30) when, in fact, he (and they) had all the "ally" they needed in God himself (see 10,24).

AJ 10,24-36 stands then as another notable instance of Josephus' reutilizing Biblical stories to highlight significant lessons for both the work's audiences.

XIX

MANASSEH AND AMON[1]
(10,37-48)

The parallel chapters 2 Kings 21 and 2 Chronicles 33 feature the figures of Hezekiah's son Manasseh (21,1-18 // 33,1-20) and grandson
Amon (21,19-26 // 33,21-25). In their presentations of the former
monarch, the Biblical accounts differ dramatically: Kings portrays
Manasseh as unrelievedly evil, while 2 Chr 33,11-17 tells of his repentance in exile and eventual divine restoration. Josephus' story of
Hezekiah's two immediate successors comes in *AJ* 10,37-48. I divide
up the material into seven sections, basing myself on the sequence of
AJ which, as we shall be seeing, diverges to some extent from that of
both sources: 1. Manasseh Introduced (*AJ* 10,37a = 2 Kgs 21,1-2 // 2
Chr 33,1-2); 2. Manasseh's Cultic Crimes (10,37b = 21,3-9 // 33,3-9);
3. Manasseh's Bloodletting (10,38a = 21,16); 4. Prophetic Message
Unheeded (10,38b-39 = 21,10-15 // 33,10); 5. Exile, Repentance,
Restoration (10,40-45 = 33,11-17); 6. Closing Notices for Manasseh
(10,46 = 21,17-18 // 33,18-20); and 7. Amon (10,47-48 = 21,19-26 [+
22,1] // 33,21-25 [+ 34,1]).

1. *Manasseh Introduced*

The sources begin their presentation of Manasseh with mention
(21,1b // 33,1) of his age at accession and length of reign. In accord
with his fixed practice, Josephus holds over his corresponding indications until the end of his account of the king; see 10,46. So doing, he
commences (10,37a) his own introduction of Manasseh with a notice on
the queen mother (= 21,1b, no equivalent in Chronicles): "But on succeeding to his throne, his son Manasseh (Μανασσῆς)[2], whose mother,

---

1. For this chapter I draw on FELDMAN, *Studies*, pp. 416-423 (= ID., *Josephus' Portrait of Manasseh*, in *JSP* 9 [1993] 3-20) and my above-cited article *Jotham and Amon*,
10-13.
2. This is the same Greek form of the name as found in L 21,1 and BL 33,1; B 21,1
has Μανασσῆ.

a native of that city (πολίτιδος ... γεγονώς)³, was named Epsiba ('Εψίβας)...⁴".

The Biblical evaluations of Manasseh come in 21,2 // 33,2: he did what was evil in the Lord's eyes, acting in accord with "the abominable practices of the nations whom the Lord drove out before the people of Israel". Josephus' judgment on the king (10,37b) is equally negative, but makes use of alternative language to express it: "(Manasseh) broke away from his father's practices (ἀπέρρηξεν ... ἐπιτηδευμάτων)⁵ and took the opposite course (τὴν ἐναντίαν ἐτράπετο)⁶, exhibiting every form of wickedness (πᾶν εἶδος πονηρίας ἐπιδειξάμενος)⁷ in his conduct and leaving no impious act undone (μηδὲν ἀσεβὲς παραλιπών)⁸, but imitating the lawless deeds (μιμούμενος τὰς ... παρανομίας)⁹ of the Israelites¹⁰ wherein (αἷς)¹¹ they sinned against God (εἰς τὸν θεὸν ἐξαμαρτόντες¹²)¹³ and so perished (ἀπώλοντο)¹⁴".

3. The above indication has no equivalent in 21,1b; compare 9,260 where Josephus states – likewise without Biblical warrant – that Abi, the mother of Hezekiah, was a "native (ἀστῆς τὸ γένος) of that city", i.e. Jerusalem. For Josephus' uses of the form πολίτις, see on 9,186.
4. This is the conjecture of Marcus; SCHLATTER, *Namen*, p. 50 and SCHALIT, *Namenwörterbuch*, p. 47 also propose this as Josephus' original form, corresponding to the 'Εψιβά of L 21,1b. Niese reads 'Εχιβᾶς in accord with codex V (cf. Lat Echib), while Weill gives "Achiba" in line with MSP's 'Αχίβας (read also by Dindorf, Bekker, and Naber). Compare "Hephzibah" (MT 21,1b); 'Οψειβά (B).
5. This construction occurs only here in Josephus.
6. This construction is hapax in Josephus.
7. The above construction (as also the expression "form of wickedness") is hapax in Josephus. Its verb ἐπιδείκνυμι echoes a *Leitwort* of Josephus' account of the finale of Hezekiah's reign; see 10,29,31.32.
8. Also this expression is hapax in Josephus; the above four-part formulation represents Josephus' embellishment of/ replacement for the stereotyped (and anthropromorphic) reference to Manasseh's "doing what was evil in the sight (eyes) of the Lord" of 21,2a // 33,2a which he regularly avoids.
9. This construction occurs only here in Josephus.
10. Josephus' allusion to the "lawless deeds (παρανομίας) of the Israelites" here echoes his notice in 9,266 that the Israelites of Hezekiah's day did not stop even at these "acts of lawlessness (παρανομοῦσιν)".
11. This is the reading of SPLaurVLat which Dindorf, Bekker, Naber, and Marcus follow. Niese reads οἵ with ROM, this making the Israelites, rather than their "lawless deeds", the referent.
12. Niese reads ἁμαρτόντες with codex R here.
13. For the above construction, see on 9,280.282.
14. In 21,2b // 33,2b the reference is to the "abominable practices of *the nations*" which prompted the Lord to expel them before the Israelites. FELDMAN, *Studies*, p. 419 (= ID., *Manasseh*, 11) suggests that Josephus' reformulation – according to which it is the Israelites themselves whose sin brought divine retribution upon them – reflects the historian's concern not to lend credence to charges of Jewish xenophobia (he further notes that Josephus likewise leaves aside other derogatory references to the nations found in 21,9 // 33,9 and 21,11). Perhaps, Josephus found inspiration for his mention of the "Israelites" (i.e. the people of the Northern Kingdom) here in 2 Kgs 21,3 which speaks of Manasseh's building an Asherah "as Ahab king *of Israel* had done".

2. *Manasseh's Cultic Crimes*

The sources provide detailed evidence for their negative evaluation of Manasseh (21,2 // 33,2) in the form of a catalogue of the king's cultic violations in 21,3-9 // 33,3-9. Josephus, in line with his tendency to abridge such cultic particulars, reduces this entire sequence to a single, all-encompassing statement (10,37b): "He even dared (ἐτόλμησε) to pollute the temple (μιᾶναι ... τὸν ναόν)[15] of God[16] as well as the city (πόλιν) and the entire country (χώραν)[17]".

3. *Manasseh's Bloodletting*

2 Kings 21 extends Manasseh's crimes to the social sphere, its v. 16a accusing him of "filling" Jerusalem with innocent blood. The Chronicler lacks a parallel to this item. Josephus, for his part, does present an equivalent to the item (10,38a), which, however, he juxtaposes directly with the foregoing cultic accusation (10,37b), rather than, as in 2 Kgs 21,10-15, having the interlude of the prophets' speech supervene. In addition, he expatiates considerably on the brief allusion of 21,16a itself: "For, *setting out with a contempt of God* (τῆς εἰς τὸν θεὸν

15. The verb μιαίνω with the Temple/sanctuary as object occurs also in *AJ* 9,152 (see there); 11,297.300.

16. The above reference to Manasseh's "pollution of the Temple" represents Josephus' "synthesis" of the various illegitimate measures taken by the king with respect to the Temple as enumerated by the sources, i.e. his "building altars" both "in the house of the Lord" (21,4a // 33,4a) and in "the two courts of the house of the Lord" (these for "all the host of heaven", 21,5 // 33,5), as well as his placing "the graven image of Asherah" (21,7a)/ "the image of the idol" (33,7a) "in the house of the Lord". In contrast to Josephus' compression of the cultic details of the sources, other Jewish traditions elaborate on these, giving particular attention to Manasseh's "image" which they represent as having four (or five) faces in blasphemous imitation of the four-faced living creatures supporting God's throne according to Ezek 1,5-10. On the relevant texts, see the discussion by P. Bogaert, *Apocalypse de Baruch*, I (SC, 144), Paris, Cerf, 1969, pp. 304-310.

17. The list of Manasseh's cultic crimes in 21,3-9 // 33,3-9 does not speak specifically of these being perpetrated in Jerusalem and the surrounding "country". Josephus' indication on the matter might have in view the reference to Manasseh's "rebuilding the high places" in 21,3 // 33,3 which would have been situated outside the Temple (and Jerusalem) itself. In addition, his mention of a three-fold polluting activity by Manasseh echoes – negatively, the sequence of Hezekiah's reform measures as related in *AJ* 9,260ff. where, once "all the pollutions" have been removed from the Temple (9,263), the people go through "the country (χώραν) and sanctify it" (9,272), likewise "purifying the city (πόλιν)" (9,273). See also his account of Josiah's cultic reforms which extend to city and "the entire country" (10,52), as well as to the Temple itself (10,65). Manasseh thus appears in Josephus' presentation as the negative pendant to Hezekiah and Josiah – like theirs, his "reforms" encompass all three entities making up the kingdom of Judah.

καταφρονονήσεως)[18], he killed all (πάντας)[19] the righteous men (δικαίους) among the Hebrews[20], *nor did he spare even the prophets* (προφητῶν), *some of whom he slaughtered daily*[21], so that Jerusalem ran with blood (αἵματι ῥεῖσθαι)[22]".

4. Prophetic Message Unheeded

Both 21,10-15 and 33,10 relate a divine "speaking" in response to Manasseh's cultic aberrations (21,3-9 // 33,3-9). In contrast to the latter,

18. This indication as to the interior "source" of Manasseh's social crimes has no parallel in 21,16a. The expression "contempt of God" recurs in *AJ* 1,113 (of Nimrud); cf. 6,264 ("contempt of things human and divine", of Saul).

19. This is the reading adopted by Niese, Naber, and Marcus. Compare πάντας ὠμῶς (MSPExc, Dindorf and Bekker), καὶ πάντας (LaurV).

20. The above phrase might be regarded as Josephus' equivalent to the reference in 21,16aα to the "very much innocent blood" shed by Manasseh. Josephus' formulation has a noteworthy parallel in *Apocalypse of Baruch* 64.2 (CHARLES and BROCKINGTON, *Syriac Apocalypse of Baruch*, p. 880) which states "he [Manasseh] killed the righteous". In Josephus' above text "Hebrews" has the limited sense of "Judeans"; see HARVEY, *True Israel*, pp. 127-128 (who further holds that the term as used here in 10,38 has the nuance of "traditional", "conservative", "non-innovative").

21. 2 Kgs 21,16 says nothing about Manasseh's killing of "prophets" in particular. Josephus' notice on the point does, however, have a certain parallel elsewhere in Jewish tradition which reports that Manasseh had the prophet Isaiah sawn in two; see, e.g., *Ascension of Isaiah* 5.1 (R.H. CHARLES and J.M.T. BARTON, trs., *The Ascension of Isaiah*, in H.F.D. SPARKS [ed.], *The Apocryphal Old Testament*, Oxford, Clarendon, 1984, 784-812, p. 793) and the discussion by B.H. AMARU, *The Killing of the Prophets: Unraveling a Midrash*, in *HUCA* 54 (1983) 153-180, pp. 170-173. On the other hand, it is not necessary to presuppose that Josephus actually knew the tradition in question. Rather, his mention of Manasseh's massacring of prophet*s* could well be his own "invention," inspired by his personal interest in these figures together with the mention of them in 21,10 ("and the Lord said by his servants the *prophets*") itself (in this connection note too his earlier, likewise "un-Biblical", statement that King Saul massacred "three hundred priests *and prophets*" at Nob [*AJ* 6,268; compare 1 Sam 23,18 which mentions only slain priests], as well as his – also inserted – reference to the Israelites' "killing" their prophets at the time of Hezekiah's appeal in 9,265; compare 2 Chr 30,10 which makes no mention of prophets). Cf. the statement of RAPPAPORT, *Agada*, p. 64, n. 267 who, after noting that Josephus' reference to Manasseh's killing of the prophets is "perhaps" to be compared with the above mentioned tradition, goes on to remark: "Die Angabe des Jos. ist aber möglicherweise nur [i.e. his own self-devised] Erweiterung". Finally, with Josephus' specification that Manasseh killed the prophets "daily", compare *b. Sanh.* 103b according to which at the end of each day Manasseh put to death the workers who had been involved in the transport of his idolatrous "image" (cf. 21,7 // 33,7) during that day.

22. This expression recurs in *BJ* 3,249; *AJ* 9,39 (the Moabites falsely suppose the river is "running with the blood" of the invading armies). Compare 21,16aβ: "... till he [Manasseh] filled [i.e. with innocent blood, see 21,16aα] Jerusalem from one end to the other". Josephus has no equivalent to the summarizing notice of 21,16b with its repetition of language used in 21,2.6b.9, i.e. "... besides the sin which he made Judah to sin so that they did what was evil in the sight of the Lord".

the former passage provides a content to the divine speech, just as it specifies that this was mediated through "prophets". 2 Chr 33,10 on the other hand, makes mention of the double audience for the divine communication (king and people), just as it explicitly notes that God's word remained without effect upon them[23]. Josephus' rendition draws on elements of both sources. Thus in 10,39a he presents a compressed version of the prophetic word as "quoted" in 21,10-15[24]: "Thereupon God, *being wrathful* (λαβὼν ... ὀργήν) *at these things*[25], sent (πέμπει) prophets[26] to the king and the people (τὸ πλῆθος)[27], and through these threatened them with the same misfortunes (ἠπείλησε ... συμφοράς)[28] which had befallen their Israelite brothers (ἀδελφούς)[29] when they outraged Him (εἰς αὐτὸν ἐξυβρίζοντας[30])[31]". Having thus abridged the prophetic message itself, Josephus (10,39b) expatiates on its (non-) effect as reported in 33,10b: "They, however, were not persuaded (οὐκ ἐπίστευον) by these words[32], *from which they might so have profited as*

23. In 21,9a the phrase "they did not listen" relates to an earlier divine word, i.e. the one addressed to David and Solomon and cited in vv. 7-8.

24. From the prophetic word of 21,10-15 Josephus leaves aside in particular the reference (v. 11) to the "Amorites" who were "before" the Israelites and whose wrong-doing Manasseh had exceeded; see n. 14.

25. This introductory notice about God's emotional state as he dispatches the prophets has no equivalent in 21,10. It might, however, be seen as Josephus' transposition into narrative of the divine word as cited in 21,15 "(because they have done what was evil in my sight) and have provoked me to anger (BL ἦσαν παροργίζοντες με)...". Compare Josephus' transitional formula in 9,167 (unparalleled in the source, i.e. 2 Chr 24,19): "Thereupon God, being displeased (δυσχεράνας) at this change of heart in the king [Joash of Judah] and the others, sent the prophets...".

26. Compare 21,10: "and the Lord said by [literally: through the hand of] his servants the prophets".

27. Compare 33,10a: "The Lord spoke to Manasseh and to his people (BL τὸν λαόν)".

28. This construction occurs only here in Josephus. Compare, however, the similar formulation in 9,281 (the Israelites disregarded their prophets) who "foretold that this misfortune (προύλεγον ... συμφοράν) would overtake them...".

29. This is one of the relatively rare instances where Josephus employs the term "brothers" in reference to his people's relationship to one another; on the point see SCHLATTER, *Theologie*, p. 80.

30. This is the reading of the codices which Dindorf, Bekker, Niese, and Marcus follow. Naber adopts the aorist participle ἐξυβρίσαντες read by Exc. For the above construction, see on 9,186. Note too its echo of the phrase used of the Israelites in 10,37, i.e. εἰς τὸν θεὸν ἐξαμαρτόντες.

31. The above summation of the content of the prophets' message to king and people represents Josephus' prosaic version of the figurative language of 21,13: "And I (God) will stretch over Jerusalem the measuring line of Samaria and the plummet of the house of Ahab; and I will wipe Jerusalem as one wipes a dish, wiping it and turning it upside down".

32. Compare 33,10b: "they gave no heed (οὐκ ἐπήκουσεν, B; οὐκ ἤκουσαν, L)". Cf. also 9,265 where Josephus states of the Northerners' response to Hezekiah's appeal to

not to experience any misfortune (κακοῦ), *but had to learn* (ἔμαθον) from deeds the truth (ἀληθῆ)[33] *of what the prophets said*[34]".

5. *Exile, Repentance, Restoration*

It is at this juncture, subsequent to their mention of the divine word evoked by Manasseh's crimes (21,10-15 // 33,10), that the most conspicuous divergence between the sources in their respective presentations of Manasseh occurs. 2 Kings 21 continues with a reference to his shedding of blood (v. 16; see above) and then gives its closing notices for Manasseh (vv. 17-18). The Chronicler, as noted, has no equivalent to 21,16, while his parallel to 21,17-18 comes only in 33,18-20, following a long *Sondergut* segment devoted to the king's imprisonment and its sequels (33,11-17). In this instance, Josephus – who has already made use of the data of 21,16 in 10,38b – elects to follow the Chronicler's account.

Chronicles' special material begins in 33,11 with the statement "The Lord brought upon them [Manasseh and his people; see 33,10a] the commanders of the army of the king of Assyria, who took Manasseh with hooks and bound him with fetters of bronze and brought him to Babylon". Josephus' rendition (10,40) goes its own way in several respects: *"For, as they persisted in their ways*[35], God stirred up (ἐκίνει)[36] the king of Babylonia and Chaldea[37] *to make war*

them that they "were not persuaded (οὐκ ἐπείσθησαν)" by this. His reference to Manasseh and the Judeans not "believing" (ἐπίστευον) here likewise echoes his triple use of the πιστ – stem in connection with Hezekiah's reaction to the announcement made him by the prophet Isaiah concerning his cure in 10,28.

33. This term, used of the prophets' message here in 10,39 echoes Josephus' characterization of Isaiah in 10,35 as "marvellously possessed of truth (ἀλήθειαν)" and "confident of never having spoken what was false".

34. The above "appendix" to Josephus' rendition of 33,10b on the hearers' (non-) response to God's word to them serves a variety of purposes: to underscore the foolishness of their response, to foreshadow the coming disaster, and to reaffirm *the* distinguishing feature of "true" prophets for Josephus, i.e. they deliver accurate announcements about what is to come.

35. This transitional phrase has no equivalent in 33,11. It underscores, once again, the king and people's failure to heed the prophets' warnings; see 10,39b. It likewise provides an explanation ("for") about how the Judeans came "to learn from deeds the truth of what the prophets said" as spoken of there.

36. The verb κινέω occurs with the Deity as subject also in *AJ* 2,292; 3,311 (cf. 11,55). Compare 33,11: "The Lord brought upon them...".

37. In 33,11 the Lord's agents in punishing Manasseh are designated as "the commanders of the army of *the king of Assyria*". Josephus' substitute terminology is likely intended to resolve the seeming anamoly of the source verse in which the *Assyrian* offi-

(πόλεμον)³⁸ upon them, *and, sending an army into Judaea, he ravished their country* (τὴν ... χώραν ... ἐλεηλάτησε)³⁹ *and got their king, Manasseh, who had been captured by cunning* (δόλῳ) *and brought to him, into his power to punish in whatever way he wished⁴⁰*".

Manasseh's misfortune led to his appealing to the Lord and humbling himself before him according to 33,12. Josephus (10,41a) supplies both an éxplicit motivation for and a content to the reprobate king's recourse to prayer at this moment: "*Then at last did Manasseh realize in what a bad plight* (κακοῖς)⁴¹ *he was, and, believing himself to be the cause of it all⁴²,*

cers take the captive Manasseh, not to Nineveh – as would be expected – but rather to *Babylon*. Faced with this apparent inconsequence, Josephus has Manasseh, not simply being imprisoned in Babylon, but actually captured by the Babylonian king. In so doing, he likewise aligns his presentation here in 10,40 with his own earlier mention (see 10,30) of the destruction of the Assyrian empire by the Medes during the reign of Manasseh's father Hezekiah. Manasseh's removal to Babylon further provides an initial (implicit) fulfillment of Isaiah's prediction to Hezekiah that "*in a short time*, the latter's "offspring" would be "servants to the king of Babylon" (10,33). See HÖFFKEN, *Hiskija und Jesaja*, 42 and our discussion of 10,30.33 in chap. XVIII.

The above double title for Manasseh's captor, i.e. "king of Babylonia and of Chaldea" (literally: of the Babylonians and Chaldeans; compare "king of Babylon [of the Babylonians]", 10,30; "the Babylonian king", 10,33) recurs in 10,183; 11,91; *c. Ap.* 1,133 (here in reverse order; in all these instances the reference is to Nebuchadnezzar). Josephus likely derived the title from Berosus; see *c. Ap.* 1,133 where it appears in the context of a long passage (1,128-153) in which he is citing or summarizing relevant passages of that historian.

38. The above phrase "stir up to war" occurs also in *BJ* 2,354.362.408 (620).

39. This notice on the devastation of Judaea has no counterpart in 2 Chr 33,11 which concentrates exclusively on the personal fate of Manasseh. Josephus' insertion of the notice makes clear that, not only the king, but also the guilty people (see 10,39) suffered fitting punishment. It likewise introduces a foreshadowing of Judah's final fate at the hand of the Babylonians; see 10,109 where Josephus speaks of Nebuchadnezzar's responding to Zedekiah's treachery by "ravaging his country (τὴν χώραν ... κακώσας)".

40. The above sequence "and got their king... he wished" represents Josephus' reworking of 33,11b: "(they) took Manasseh with hooks and bound him with fetters of bronze and brought him to Babylon". Into his version Josephus inserts an intimation on how the enemy was able to capture Manasseh – without, it would appear, having gained possession of Jerusalem itself – i.e. "by cunning". Conversely, he drops both the source's mention of the place to which Manasseh is taken (see n. 35) and the degrading details of his being carried off weighed down with "hooks" and "bronze fetters". By contrast, the Biblical mention of Manasseh's "bronze fetters" gave rise to notable embellishments concerning the tortures suffered by the captive elsewhere in Jewish tradition (e.g., TC 33,12) which speaks of his being confined in a bronze mule/horse/bull/kettle to which fire was applied from beneath. On the relevant material, see BOGAERT, *Apocalypse de Baruch*, I, pp. 310-319.

41. This term echoes the same word used in 10,39b where Josephus makes mention of the king and people's failure to heed the prophets' words "from which they might so have profited as not to experience any misfortune (κακοῦ)".

42. The above sequence might be seen as Josephus' anticipation/ reapplication of the notice attached to the mention of Manasseh's restoration in 33,13b: "then Manasseh knew that the Lord was God". It likewise draws on the opening words of 33,12, i.e. "when he [Manasseh] was in distress".

he prayed to God (ἐδεῖτο τοῦ θεοῦ)[43] *to make* (παρέχειν)[44] *the enemy* (πολέμιον; cf. πόλεμον, 10,40) *humane and merciful* (φιλάνθρωπον καὶ ἐλεήμονα)[45] *to him*[46]".

The climax to the Chronicler's *Sondergut* story of Manasseh comes in 33,13a where God, responding to the king's appeal, restores him to Jerusalem. Josephus (10,41b) elaborates on the way in which Manasseh's restoration was accomplished: "And God hearkened (ἐπακούσας; cf. ἐπήκοον, also of God, in 10,16) to his supplication (ἱκεσίας) and granted this[47], *and so Manasseh was set free by the king of Babylonia*[48] and was safely restored (ανασώζεται) to his own land[49]".

2 Chr 33,14-17 relates the sequels of Manasseh's return to Jerusalem, i.e. his (defensive) military initiatives (v. 14) and his (partial) cultic reform (vv. 15-17). The historian's version accentuates (10,42-43) the

43. This phrase takes the place of the anthropromophic formulation of 33,12aβ with its reference to Manasseh's trying to mollify the Lord's "face".

44. This is the reading adopted by Marcus and Niese; MSPLaurVE Exc have παρασχεῖν, as do Dindorf, Bekker, and Naber.

45. Josephus' one other use of this collocation is in *AJ* 8,335 where the servants of the defeated king of Syria inform their master that the Israelite kings have these qualities. The historian's wording here in 10,41 likewise echoes his language in 10,12 where Hezekiah sends a delegation to Isaiah to request that the prophet "pray to God (δεηθῆναι τοῦ θεοῦ)... to take pity (ἐλεῆσαι) on His own people".

46. The summary content which Josephus supplies here for Manasseh's prayer has a more extensive counterpart in the apocryphal work, "The Prayer of Manasseh". Elsewhere in Jewish tradition as well one finds the Bible's passing allusion to the fact of Manasseh's praying being elaborated upon. Thus, e.g., TC 33,12; *Pesik. Rab. Kah.* 24.11 (BRAUDE and KAPSTEIN, *Pěsikta dě-Rab Kahāna*, pp. 375-376); *E. Z.* §9(188) (BRAUDE and KAPSTEIN, *Tanna děbe Eliyyahu*, pp. 400-401) *y. Sanh.* 10.2; *Deut. Rab.* 2.20 (J. RAB-BINOWITZ, tr., *Midrash Rabbah Deuteronomy*, London-New York, Soncino, 1983, p. 48); *Ruth Rab.* 5.6 (L. RABINOWITZ, tr., *Midrash Rabbah Ruth*, London-New York, Soncino, 1983, p. 63); *Lev. Rab.* 30.3 (J. ISRAELSON and J.J. SLOTKI, trs., *Midrash Rabbah Leviticus*, London-New York, Soncino, 1983, p. 385); *Num. Rab.* 14.1 (SLOTKI, *Midrash Rabbah Numbers*, II, p. 561); *Pirqe R. El.* 43.3 (PÉREZ FERNANDEZ, *Los capítulos de Rabbí Eliezer*, p. 304) all state that the king first turned to his idols for help. When these all failed to respond, he finally, in desperation and thinking he had nothing to lose, addressed himself to the Lord.

47. Compare 33,13aβ: "God received his entreaty (BL ἐπήκουσεν) and heard his supplication (BL ἐπήκουσε τῆς βοῆς αὐτοῦ)". The Jewish writings mentioned in n. 46 (e.g., TC 33,13) elaborate on the circumstances of God's hearing of Manasseh's prayer: when the angels blocked the entrances of heaven to keep the king's prayer from reaching him, God personally made an opening beneath his throne, thereby showing his willingness to receive the pleas of even the most sinful of penitents.

48. Josephus' explicit mention of this figure here – unparalleled in 33,13 where God himself is the subject of Manasseh's "bringing" to Jerusalem – picks up on the reference to God's "stirring up the king of Babylonia and Chaldea" in 10,40.

49. According to the texts listed in n. 46 (e.g., TC 33,13), Manasseh's "return" was effected by means of a God-sent "wind". Josephus has no equivalent as such to the appended notice of 33,13b about the restored Manasseh finally "knowing that the Lord was God"; see, however, nn. 42,50.

king's new-found piety, both by mentioning his cultic measures in first place and by introducing affirmations peculiar to himself about the extent of Manasseh's conversion[50]:

(42) When he came to Jerusalem, he strove (ἐσπούδαζεν) *to cast from his mind, if that were possible, the very memory* (μνήμην) *of his former sins* (ἁμαρτημάτων περὶ τὸν θεόν)[51], *of which he was anxious to repent* (ὧν μεταβουλεύειν[52] ὥρμησε) *and to show God the utmost reverence* (πάσῃ χρῆσθαι ... δεισιδαιμονίᾳ)[53]; *and he sanctified* (ἥγνισε) *the temple* (ναόν) *and purified* (ἐκάθηρε) *the city* (πόλιν)[54], *and thereafter his only care was to show his gratitude* (χαρῖν ... ἐκτίνειν[55])[56] *to God for having been saved* (τῆς σωτηρίας [see 10,11]; cf. ἀνασώζεται, 10,41) *and to keep His favour* (διατηρεῖν ... εὐμενῆ)[57] *throughout his whole life. (43) And he taught the people* (τὸ πλῆθος ἐδίδασκε) *to do the same[58], having*

50. On this point, see FELDMAN, *Studies*, pp. 420-423 (= ID., *Manasseh*, 15-17). Josephus may have found inspiration for his emphasis on Manasseh's conversion in the summary remark appended to mention of the king's restoration (33,13a) in 33,13b, i.e. "Then Manasseh knew that the Lord was God"; see previous note.

51. This construction occurs only here in Josephus; it echoes the expression used of the Israelites in 10,37, i.e. εἰς τὸν θεὸν ἐξαμαρτόντες. Note that Marcus's above rendition ("former sins") has no equivalent for the Greek words περὶ τὸν θεόν.

52. This is the reading of the *editio princeps* which Dindorf, Bekker, and Marcus adopt. In his text Niese reads ὧν ἐπιβουλεύειν with the codices (as does Naber); in his apparatus, however, he conjectures θεῷ δὲ δουλεύειν with reference to Lat. Josephus' only other use of the verb μεταβουλεύω is in 9,69 (see there).

53. This construction, "show reverence" occurs only here in the Josephan corpus; the noun δεισιδαιμονία is used a total of 15 times by the historian.

54. The above initiatives represent the reversal of Manasseh's measures as related in 10,37b: "he even dared to pollute the temple (ναόν) of God as well as the city (πόλιν)". The verbal combination "sanctify" and "purify" of 10,42b has a counterpart in 9,272-273 in connection with the reforms of Hezekiah; see there. Compare the more expansive and specific wording of 33,15 with its allusions to the catalogue of Manasseh's cultic crimes in 33,3-9 (likewise compressed and generalized by Josephus; see 10,37): "And he (Manasseh) took away the foreign gods and the idol from the house of the Lord, and all the altars that he had built on the mountain of the house of the Lord and in Jerusalem, and he threw them outside the city".

55. This is the reading of SPLaurV which Dindorf, Bekker, Naber, and Marcus follow. Niese opts for the ἐκτείνειν of ROM; E Exc have no equivalent for the infinitives read by the other witnesses.

56. This construction recurs in *AJ* 2,62 (6,353); 15,18; 18,162. On "gratitude" as a key trait of Josephus' Manasseh (after his restoration) as well as of his other Biblical characters, see FELDMAN, *Manasseh*, 18-19.

57. This construction occurs only here in Josephus. Compare 9,262 where Hezekiah avers that by cleansing the Temple his people will "make God become gracious (εὐμενῆ)".

58. Compare 33,16b: "(Manasseh) commanded Judah to serve the Lord". In the Chronicler's presentation, this notice follows upon mention of the king's restoring the altar and re-inaugurating sacrifices (v. 16a). Josephus reverses the order of the two royal initatives; see above. He likewise leaves aside the remark appended in v. 17 to mention of Manasseh's directive to the people (v. 16b) and suggestive of its limited efficacy, i.e. "Nevertheless the people still sacrificed at the high places, but only to the Lord their God". See FELDMAN, *Studies*, p. 421 (ID., *Manasseh*, 16). Josephus' reference here in

learned (μεμαθηκώς)[59] *how close he had been to disaster* (συμφορᾷ)[60]
because of following the opposite way of life (διὰ τὴν ἐναντίαν
πολιτείαν)[61]. He also repaired the altar (ἐπισκευάσας [see 9,162.165]...
τὸν βωμόν; cf. BL 33,16a κατώρθωσε[ν] τὸ θυσιαστήριον [+ τοῦ
κυρίου, L]) and offered up (ἐπετέλει) the customary sacrifices (νομίμους
θυσίας), *as Moses had ordained*[62].

Having anticipated the Chronicler's notices on Manasseh's cultic
reforms (33,15-17) in 10,42-43, Josephus now (10,44) supplies his "held-
over" version of 33,14, which deals with the king's military preparedness
initiatives. From this last verse, he eliminates the various proper Jerusalem
place names (Gihon, the Fish Gate, Ophel)[63] which would not have been
familiar to Gentile readers: *"And, when he had regulated the form of
worship* (διοικησάμενος ... τὰ περὶ τὴν θρησκείαν)[64] *in the proper
manner*[65], *he also provided for the security* (ἀσφαλείας προενόησεν)[66] *of*

10,43 to Manasseh's "teaching the people" echoes the language used by him of the like
"didactic" initiatives of King Jehoshaphat; see 8,395 (Jehoshaphat dispatches a delegation to "teach all the people [τὸν λαόν ... διδάξαι]") and 9,2 (Jehoshaphat undertakes a
circuit of his country "to teach the people thoroughly [τὸν λαόν ἐκδιδάσκειν]").
59. This term introduces a verbal reminiscence/ reversal of 10,39 where Josephus
states that the prophets' (non-) hearers had to "learn (ἔμαθον) from deeds the truth of
what the prophets said".
60. Also this term constitutes a verbal echo of Josephus' preceding account of Manasseh; see 10,39a where the prophets "threaten" their hearers with the same "misfortunes" (συμφοράς) as had befallen the Israelites.
61. Compare τὴν ἐναντίαν ἐτράπετο, 10,37. The above sequence "having learned...
way of life" provides a (Biblically unparalleled) motivation for the king's urgent concern
with teaching his people. Josephus' emphasis on Manasseh's thorough-going repentance
in 10,42-43a which goes far beyond the Chronicler's statements on the matter has a certain counterpart in Rabbinic tradition with its extensive discussions of whether or not
Manasseh, in virtue of his repentance, attained to a portion in the world to come; see, e.g.,
m. Sanh. 10.2; *y. Sanh.* 10.2; *b. Sanh.* 103b, and BOGAERT, *Apocalypse de Baruch*, I,
pp. 297-303 (in *Apocalypse of Baruch* 63.8 [CHARLES and BROCKINGTON, *Syriac Apocalypse of Baruch*, p. 880] it is definitely affirmed that Manasseh ultimately ended up in
everlasting fire, this after being delivered by God from his torments in the bronze horse;
see n. 40).
62. The above expression "customary sacrifice(s)" recurs in *AJ* 3,258; 5,266; 11,76;
12,253 (*c. Ap.* 2,48). Compare 33,16αβ: "(Manasseh) offered (BL ἐθυσίασεν) upon it
[the altar] sacrifices (BL θυσίας) of peace offerings and of thanksgiving". The above
concluding words of 10,43 echo both 9,257 (Ahaz forbade "the offering of the customary
sacrifices [τὰς νενομισμένας ... θυσίας ἐπιφέρειν]") and 263 (at Hezekiah's direction
the priests "offered up the accustomed sacrifices [τὰς ἐξ ἔθους ... θυσίας ἐπέφερον]").
63. Cf. his similar treatment of the comparable indications found, e.g., in 2 Chr 25,23
(= 9,201); 26,9 (= 9,218); and 27,3 (= 9,237).
64. This construction occurs only here in Josephus.
65. The above transitional phrase has no equivalent in 2 Chronicles 33 where Manasseh's military constructions are mentioned prior to his cultic reforms; it highlights the
restored king's stature as an exponent of right religion.
66. This construction recurs in *BJ* 2,620; 5,316 (487); 7,94; *AJ* 2,280; 12,16; *Vita*
(268), 283 (317).

*Jerusalem*⁶⁷, and so repaired (ἐπισκευάσας)⁶⁸ the old walls with great care (σπουδῆς)⁶⁹ and added a new one to them; he also erected very high (ὑψηλοτάτους) towers (πύργους; see 9,219.237)⁷⁰ and made the fortresses (φρούρια) *before the city* stronger (ὀχυρώτερα) in various ways, especially by bringing in (συγκομιδῇ)⁷¹ provisions and (καί)⁷² all sorts of things needed in them⁷³".

Josephus rounds off his parallel to 33,14-17 (10,42-44) concerning Manasseh's measures subsequent to his restoration with a notice peculiar to himself (10,45) which, once again, highlights the extent of the king's transformation. This reads: "In fact he underwent such a change of heart (μεταβολῇ; cf. μεταβουλεύειν, 10,42) in these respects and lived the rest of his life in such a way as to be accounted (λογιζό-μενος)⁷⁴ a blessed and enviable man (μακαριστὸς καὶ ζηλωτός)⁷⁵ after the time when he began to show piety towards God (τὸν θεόν εὐσεβεῖν)⁷⁶".

67. The above italicized phrase has no counterpart in 33,14a which begins immediately with the enumeration of Manasseh's constructions; it spells out the intention behind the king's initiatives.
68. The re-use of this verb, employed in 10,43 of Manasseh's "repairing (ἐπισκευάσας)" of the altar, serves to link more closely together the king's cultic and building initiatives following his restoration. See next note.
69. Also this term echoes the wording of Josephus' account of Manasseh's religious initiatives; see the reference to his being "anxious (ἐσπούδαζεν) to repent" in 10,42. Compare previous note.
70. 2 Chr 33,14a seems to speak of a single Jerusalem building initiative by Manasseh, i.e. his construction of an outer wall for Jerusalem which "he raised to a great height (BL ὕψωσεν)". Josephus, by contrast, credits him with three distinct building activities (repair of the city's old walls, addition of a new wall, and the erection of "high towers"); see above. Thereby he underscores the king's all-encompassing solicitude for the city's security – a concern accentuated in Josephus' portrayal of Manasseh's predecessors Uzziah (see 9,218-219) and Jotham (see 9,237) as well.
71. This word is inserted into the text of 10,44 by Niese and Marcus, but not by Naber. Following Coccejus, Dindorf and Bekker – the latter within brackets – insert an alternative verb, i.e. εἰσκομιδῇ.
72. This word is inserted by Niese and Marcus, but not by Dindorf, Bekker, and Naber.
73. In 2 Chr 33,14b the reference is rather to Manasseh's stationing "commanders in all the fortified cities in Judah". Josephus apparently felt that the provisioning of these sites would have been the more urgent matter.
74. This is the reading of the codices and Exc which Dindorf, Bekker, Naber, and Marcus follow. Niese conjectures the genitival form λογιζομένου which would yield the translation "... (in such a way) as to be blessed and enviable, *counting* from the time...". Cf. MARCUS, *Josephus*, VI, p. 182, n. b.
75. This collocation occurs only here in Josephus.
76. Josephus uses the verb εὐσεβέω with God/the Deity as object also in *BJ* 2,139; *AJ* 2,152; 10,68 (12,290); *Vita* 113; *c. Ap.* 2,125. The reference to Manasseh's "showing piety toward God" here in 10,45 constitutes a kind of inclusion with the mention of his "showing God the utmost reverence (δεισιδαιμονίᾳ)" in 10,42.

6. Closing Notices for Manasseh

The two Biblical Manasseh accounts reconverge for their closing
notices on the king, 21,17-18 // 33,18-20. As is his wont, Josephus leaves
aside the opening component of this complex, i.e. the "source reference"
of 21,17 // 33,18-19. In its place he (10,46a) introduces – likewise in
accord with his usual practice – a version of the sources' opening chronological data of 21,1a // 33,1, combining this with mention of Manasseh's
death anticipated from 21,18aα // 33,20aα: "And so he departed this life
at the age of sixty-seven years[77], after reigning fifty-five". He then proceeds to reproduce the content of 21,18aβb // 33,20aβb on the king's burial and successor: "And he was buried (θάπτεται) in his own gardens
(παραδείσοις)[78], and the kingdom passed to his son Ammon
('Αμμῶνα)[79], whose mother, named Emaselmē ('Εμασέλμης)[80], was a
native of the city of Jatabatē ('Ιαταβάτης)[81]".

7. Amon

As an appendix to their extended accounts of Manasseh, 2 Kgs 22,19-
25 // 2 Chr 33,21-25 = AJ 10,47-48 devote a few lines to the brief, ill-
fated reign of his successor Amon. The sources begin with the standard
chronological indications concerning the new monarch (21,19a // 33,21)

77. Josephus calculates Manasseh's age at death here by combining the Biblical data
on his age at accession (12) and length of reign (55).

78. The wording of Josephus' notice on Manasseh's burial has its closest equivalent
in BL 33,20 (ἔθαψαν αὐτὸν ἐν παραδείσῳ οἴκου αὐτοῦ). Compare MT 33,20 ("they
buried him in his house") and 21,18 ("he was buried in the garden [BL κήπῳ] of his
house, in the garden [BL κήπῳ] of Uzza"). Recall that Josephus has no equivalent to the
Biblical burial notices for either Manasseh's (wicked) grandfather Ahaz or his (righteous)
father Hezekiah. The fact of Manasseh's getting such a notice thus confers a heightened
stature upon him.

79. Compare "Amon" (MT 21,18 // 33,20); 'Αμών (L 21,18 // 33,20); 'Αμώς (B
21,18 // 33,20 [cf. codex M "Αμωσον]).

80. This is the form of the queen mother's named adopted by Niese and Marcus;
Dindorf, Bekker, and Naber read 'Εμαλσέμης with M. SCHLATTER, Namen, p. 77 proposes an original Μασελ(ε)μη, a proposal seconded by SCHALIT, Namenwörterbuch,
p. 44. Josephus anticipates the name from the opening notices of 21,19b where the
woman is called "Meshullemeth" (MT)/ Μεσολλάμ (BL). As in the case of Manasseh,
the Chronicler does not mention the name of Amon's mother.

81. This is the reading of the codices OLaurV which Marcus adopts. Niese reads
'Ιαζαβάτης with R, Dindorf, Bekker, and Naber 'Ιαβάτης with MSP. SCHLATTER, Namen,
p. 62 and SCHALIT, Namenwörterbuch, p. 57 suggest Ιαταβη as Josephus' original reading.
Compare "Jotbah" (MT 21,20b), 'Ιεσεβάλ (B), 'Ετεβαθά (L). In accord with his usual
practice, Josephus leaves aside the name of Amon's maternal grandfather, i.e. "Haruz".

and, in the case of Kings, mention of his mother (21,19b; no parallel in Chronicles). Josephus has already anticipated the latter item when citing Amon's accession in 10,46 (see above). Following his usual procedure, he conversely "delays" the source chronological data for Amon until the point where he relates the king's death. Accordingly, he moves immediately (10,47a) to present his parallel to the negative judgment notices regarding Amon of 21,20-22 // 33,22-23, while at the same time shortening and generalizing these: "This king [Amon] imitated (μιμησά-μενος)[82] those deeds of his father which he had recklessly committed (ἐτόλμησεν)[83] in his youth[84]".

Following his foregoing negative evaluation of Amon, Josephus next (10,47b) relates the king's assassination (= 21,23 // 33,24), appending to this the chronological indications of 21,19a // 33,21 earlier passed over by him: "... and, after a plot was formed (ἐπιβουλευθείς) against him by his own servants (οἰκετῶν), (he) was put to death (ἀπέθανεν)[85] in his house (οἰκίας)[86] at the age of twenty-four years[87], of which he reigned for two". The assassins' designs are quickly foiled, according to 21,24 // 33,25 by "the people of the land" who put them to death and raise Amon's son Josiah to the throne. Josephus (10,48) works into this sequence an anticipation of the notice of 21,26a on Amon's burial (no parallel in Chronicles): "But the people (τὸ πλῆθος)[88] punished

82. This term echoes the charge leveled against Manasseh himself in 10,37, i.e. his "imitating (μιμούμενος) the lawless deeds of the Israelites...". See next note.

83. This term constitutes an additional verbal reminiscence of 10,37 where Manasseh is said to have "even dared (ἐτόλμησε) to pollute the temple of God". See previous note.

84. Compare 21,20 // 33,22a: "he (Amon) did what was evil in the sight of the Lord as Manasseh his father had done". Josephus' appended qualification of Manasseh's misdeeds as those "done in his youth" acknowledges, as the source formulations do not, the fact of Manasseh's eventual conversion. Josephus, in line with his habit of reducing Biblical cultic detail, has no equivalent to the notice of 21,21b // 33,22b about Amon's "serving" his father's "images/idols". He likewise does not make use of the (repetitious) concluding judgment on Amon's behavior of either 21,22 ("he forsook the Lord... and did not walk in the way of the Lord") or 33,23 ("And he did not humble himself before the Lord, as Manasseh his father had humbled himself, but this Amon incurred guilt more and more").

85. The above construction "being conspired against... he died" recurs in AJ 7,46; 8,288 (9,203: Amaziah); 13,335. Compare 21,23 // 33,24: "And his servants (BL παῖδες) conspired (L 21,23 συνεστράφησαν ... καὶ ἐπεβούλευσαν) against him and killed (L 21,23 ἐθανάτωσαν) him in his house".

86. Note the above word-play, οἰκετῶν ... οἰκίας here which underscores the pathos of Amon's end: he is murdered by his household servants in his own house.

87. Josephus arrives at this figure by combining the indications of 21,19 // 33,21: acceding at age 22, Amon reigned two years.

88. This generalized designation for Amon's avengers takes the place of the phrase "the people of the land" used of them in 21,24 // 33,25. On Josephus' avoidance of the Biblical expression "the people of the land", see p. 184, n. 125 on AJ 9,156.

(μετῆλθε; cf. ἐπάτξεν, B 21,24 // BL 33,25; ἀπέκτειναν, L 21,24) his murderers (φονεῖς; compare: all those who had conspired against King Amon, 21,24 // 33,25) and buried (συνθάπτουσι)[89] Ammon with his father[90]; then they gave the kingship to his son Josiah (Ἰωσία)...[91]". Dispensing with the source reference of 21,25 for Amon (no parallel in Chronicles), Josephus appends to his mention of Josiah *personalia* drawn from 22,1 (cf. 34,1): "... a boy of eight years[92], whose mother, named Jedis (Ἰέδις)[93] came from the city of Bosketh (Βοσκέθ)[94]".

Conclusions: Josephus' Rewriting of 2 Kings 21 // 2 Chronicles 33

In composing 10,37-48 Josephus clearly made use of material peculiar to both Biblical accounts of Kings Manasseh and Amon, rather than adhering exclusively to the presentation of one of these. From 2 Kings 21 he draws the following *Sondergut* items: the names of the queen mothers (10,37 = 21,1b; 10,46 = 21,19b), Manasseh's bloodletting (10,38 = 21,16), mention of "prophets" as those through whom God spoke and the content of their message (10,38b-39 = 21,10-15), a "garden" as the place of Manasseh's burial (10,46 = 21,18; compare 33,20 "in his house"), and explicit reference to Amon's burial (10,48 = 21,26). The historian's utilization of 2 Chronicles 33 is most obvious in his parallel (10,40-45) to its segment (vv. 11-17) concerning Manasseh's punishment, repentance, restoration, and subsequent military/cultic measures to which Kings has no counterpart. Much less clear is the further issue of which text-form(s) of the Biblical narratives Josephus had available to him. The one noteworthy indication in this regard surfaced by our reading concerns the place of Amon's burial: in his reference (10,48a) to the king being "buried with his father" Josephus goes

89. Josephus' only other use of the verb συνθάπτω is in *BJ* 1,551.
90. In having Amon be buried with his father, Josephus stands closest to the reading of L 21,26a: "they buried Amon in the tomb *of his father*, in the grave of Uzza" as opposed to MT B: "and they buried him in his [i.e. Amon's own] tomb in the garden of Uzza (see 21,18)".
91. BL 21,24 // B 33,25 Ἰωσείαν; L 33,25 Ἰωσίαν.
92. 22,1a // 34,1 further state that Josiah went on to rule for thirty-one years. As is his wont, Josephus reserves this datum until the end of his account concerning Josiah; see 10,77.
93. This is the reading adopted by Dindorf, Bekker, Niese, and Marcus. Compare "Jedidah" (MT 22,1b); Ἰεδειά (B); Ἰεδδειά (L). Josephus leaves aside mention of her father's name, i.e. "Adaiah" (MT).
94. So Marcus and Niese; Dindorf, Bekker, and Naber read Βοσκέθι with SPLaurV Lat. Compare "Bozkath" (MT 22,1); Βασουρώθ (BL). As in the case of his two predecessors, the Chronicler does not mention Josiah's mother.

together with L 21,2⌐b against MT and B which have him interred in his (own) tomb; see n. 90.

In dealing with the Biblical data on the two reprobate kings, Josephus makes, first of all, prominent use of elimination and abridgement. The source references of 21,17 // 33,18-19 (Manasseh) and 21,25 (Amon) are passed over, as are the Chronicler's notices on the people's continuing to sacrifice on the high places (33,17) even after the penitent Manasseh's "command" to them (33,16b) and the king's own iconoclastic measures (33,15). The historian significantly reduces the lengthy catalogue of Manasseh's cultic crimes (21,3-9 // 33,3-9; compare 10,37b); the related indictment of Amon (21,20-22 // 33,22-23; compare 10,47); and the content of the prophets' admonition (21,10-15; compare 10,39a). On the other hand, he also expatiates notably on a number of source items: Manasseh's murderous deeds (10,38; compare 21,16); the hearers' non-responsiveness to the prophets' words (10,39b; compare 33,10b); the punishment imposed by God for this (10,40; compare 33,11); the captive king's prayer (10,41a; compare 33,12); his restoration (10,41; compare 33,13a); thorough-going repentance (10,42.45; compare 33,13b.16a); admonishing of the people (10,43a; compare 33,16b); and building activities (10,44; compare 33,14).

Josephus' version further evidences re-arrangements of the sources' sequence. Chronological data for both Manasseh (21,1a // 33,1; compare 10,46) and Amon (21,19a // 33,21; compare 10,47b) are re-positioned by him to the end of their respective reigns. He anticipates the notice of Manasseh's shedding of blood (10,38 = 21,16a), placing this (10,39a) before, rather than after (so 21,10-15) the prophets' word. He likewise has Manasseh undertake his cultic reforms (10,42-43 = 33,15-17) prior to commencing his military building activities (10,44 = 33,14).

Finally, the historian modifies the Biblical content as well. Manasseh's (21,1a // 33,1) and Amon's (21,19a // 33,21) age at accession is turned into their age at death (10,46.47). The reprobate practices which Manasseh adopts are those, not of the earlier "nations" (so 21,2 // 33,2), but of the Israelites (10,37; see n. 14). God commissions "the king of Babylonia and Chaldea" (10,40), rather than the Assyrian officers (so 33,11), as his punishing agent, while Manasseh provisions the fortified cities (10,44) instead of appointing commanders over them (so 33,14b).

What now is distinctive about Josephus' account of Manasseh and Amon? His version, first of all, resolves various seeming anamolies of the sources' presentation, e.g., the after-thought mention of an additional crime by Manasseh, i.e. his shedding of blood (21,16) after judgment has already been pronounced upon him (21,10-15) and the oddness of

Assyrian officers taking the captive Manasseh to *Babylon* (33,11). The (negative) cultic particulars which figure so largely in both Biblical accounts assume a more general character. As so often elsewhere in *AJ*, the role of the prophets is accentuated: they no only denounce Manasseh's crimes (so 21,10-15 = 10,39a), but are singled out as victims of the king's persecution (10,38b; compare 21,16), even as the "truth" of their announcement is underscored (10,39b). Most of all, however, Josephus' version stands out in its emphasis on the positive transformation of the reprobate Manasseh and the salutary effects of this (he is "accounted a blessed and enviable man after the time he began to show piety towards God", 10,45).

To Gentile readers Josephus' rendition offers the Biblical stories of Manasseh and Amon in a form which plays down their focus on these kings' reprobate cultic practices and the association of such practices with the "nations" which such readers would find of no great interest and potentially offensive. Perhaps too his reference to Manasseh's prayer that God make the enemy "humane and merciful" (10,41), as well as his notice on the Babylonian king actually setting Manasseh free (10,42), is intended as an implicit plea to the contemporary Roman audience that they, the Jews' erstwhile "enemies", now adopt a like stance towards them. As for Jewish readers, especially those living in the Diaspora, Josephus, through his account of the captive Manasseh, presents them with a encouragement to repent as he did, in hopes that God would honor that repentance with the same restoration to the land he once granted Manasseh. Here again then, Josephus' version is designed to make the Bible's story both more palatable and more transparently instructive for his double audience.

XX

JOSIAH[1]
(10,49-80)

Josiah, the great reformer king who comes to a tragic, premature end, receives extensive coverage in 2 Kgs 22,1-23,30a // 2 Chr 34,1-35,27[2]. The two Biblical accounts evidence some noteworthy differences in the details of what they tell concerning the king. Accordingly, our examination of Josephus' account of Josiah (AJ 10,49-80) in this chapter will focus on how the historian deals with these source divergences. I divide up the parallel material as follows: 1. Evaluation (AJ 10,49 = 2 Kgs 22,2 // 2 Chr 34,2)[3]; 2. Josiah's Initial Reforms (10,50-56 = 34,3-7); 3. Discovery of the Book (10,57-62a = 22,3-20 // 34,8-28); 4. The People Obligated (10,62b-64 = 23,1-3 // 34,29-32); 5. Josiah's Later Reforms (10,65-69 = 23,4-20 // 34,33); 6. Josiah's Passover (10,70-73 = 23,21-23 [+ 23,24-28] // 35,1-19 // 1 Esdras 1,1-24); and 7. Josiah's Death (10,74-80 = 23,29-30a // 35,20-27 // 1 Esdras 1,25-33).

1. *Evaluation*

The Biblical evaluations of Josiah (22,2 // 34,2) consist of two elements: a stereotyped formula about his "doing right in the eyes of the Lord" and the affirmation of his thorough-going adherence to the ways of his ancestor David. Josephus (10,49), as usual, replaces the former item with alternative language, while retaining mention of David as Josiah's model: "He was of an excellent character (τὴν ... φύσιν ... ἄριστος)[4] and well-disposed to virtue (πρὸς ἀρετὴν εὖ

---

1. For this chapter I have drawn on the treatments of the Josephan Josiah by FELDMAN, *Studies*, pp. 424-436 (= ID., *Josephus' Portrait of Josiah*, in *LS* 18 [1993] 110-130) and SPILSBURY, *Image*, pp. 195-200.

2. The content of 2 Chr 35,1-27 (Josiah's Passover and death) itself recurs, with various differences, in 1 Esdras 1,1-33.

3. I have already treated, at the end of the previous chapter, the personal data on Josiah found in 2 Kgs 22,1 // 2 Chr 34,1 which Josephus presents as an appendix to his mention (= 2 Kgs 21,26b // 2 Chr 33,25) of Josiah's succeeding his father Amon at the end of 10,48.

4. This construction occurs only here in Josephus.

γεγονώς)[5] and emulous (ζηλωτής)[6] of the practices (ἐπιτηδευμάτων) of King David[7], whom he made the pattern and rule (σκοπῷ καὶ κανόνι)[8] of his whole manner of life (περὶ τόν βίον ἐπιτηδεύσεως)[9]".

2. Josiah's Initial Reforms

Following their respective, common evaluations of Josiah (22,2 // 34,2), Josephus' sources diverge significantly. 2 Kgs 22,3 begins immediately to recount what happened in Josiah's 18th (regnal) year, i.e. the finding of the book in the Temple and Josiah's response to this. The Chronicler's parallel to this notice (34,8) is preceded by a rather extended segment, 34,3-7, dealing with religious initiatives undertaken by Josiah previous to that year[10]. Confronted with this difference between his sources, Josephus (10,50-56) elects to make use of the Chronicler's *Sondergut* on events of Josiah's reign antedating the finding of the book. The Chronicler himself distinguishes two stages in the king's earlier religious endeavors, the first in his *eighth* regnal year (i.e. when he was sixteen), at which point "he began to seek the God of David his father", the second four years later, in his twelfth regnal year (i.e. when he was twenty years of age)[11], this involving an extensive

5. Also this phrase occurs only here in Josephus.

6. This term is supplied by Dindorf whom Bekker, Naber, Weill ("jaloux"), Marcus and FELDMAN, *Studies*, p. 426 and n. 2 (= ID., *Josiah*, p. 114 and n. 11) follow. Niese, in the same line, holds that there is a lacuna in the text of 10,49 prior to the word "David"; see above. The noun ζηλωτής is employed with considerable frequency by Josephus in *BJ* as a (negative) designation for the Jewish rebels; in *AJ* its only other occurrences are in 12,271; 20,47. Cf. the cognate adjective ζηλωτός ("enviable") applied by him to the repentant Mansseh in 10,45.

7. The above expression sets up a terminological contrast between Josiah and Manasseh at the outset of their respective reigns: the former is "emulous of David's practices", whereas the latter "broke away from the practices (ἐπιτηδευμάτων)" of his righteous father Hezekiah according to 10,37.

8. Josephus uses the term κανών only once elsewhere, i.e. *c. Ap.* 2,174.

9. With this construction compare ἡ ἐπιτήδευσις τοῦ βίου in 18,66.

10. The Chronicler's divergence from Kings here is usually explained in terms of his desire to enhance Josiah's reputation for piety by having him begin to manifest this, not more than halfway through his reign and then under the "external" impetus of the finding of the book (so Kings), but already much earlier and on his own initiative; see the commentaries. Cf. also n. 12.

11. The explicit specification that the second stage to Josiah's earlier religious initiatives came in the twelfth year *of his reign* is found only in BL 34,3b, not in MT. However, the sequence of 34,3 in MT itself which speaks first (v. 3a) of Josiah's personal religious awakening in his 8th regnal year/ 16th year of life, and then (v. 3b) of specific reform measures carried out by him in his 12th year suggests that also here the reference is implicitly to the king's regnal year, rather than a year of his life. Otherwise, the second half of v. 3 would be telling of reform initiatives that happened four years prior to Josiah's "beginning to seek the God of David" as related in v. 3a. On the point, contrast FELDMAN, *Studies*, p.

campaign of cultic purification (34,3b-7)[12]. Josephus, by contrast, dates (10,50a) all Josiah's religious initiatives prior to the discovery of the book (related by him in 10,57) to a single year: "Now, when he was twelve years old[13], he gave proof of his piety and righteousness (εὐσέβειαν καὶ ... δικαιοσύνην)...[14]".

Already in 34,3b and then throughout 34,4-7a, one finds mention of the iconoclastic measures undertaken by Josiah in his twelfth (regnal) year. Josephus' actual (compressed) parallel to this catalogue comes only in 10,52. Preceding it in his presentation is an extended segment (10,50b-51), essentially representing a free creation by him, whose purpose is to underscore the boy-king's all-sided precocity (see n. 13). It reads:

> (50)... for he sought to bring the people to their senses (ἐσωφρόνιζε) and urged them to give up (ἀποστάντας) their belief (δόξης) in idols (εἰδώλων), which he said were not really gods (θεῶν), and to worship (σέβειν) the God of their fathers (τὸν πάτριον θεόν)[15]; and, reviewing

426 (= ID., *Josiah*, 115) who supposes that MT 34,3b, in contrast to BL, is, in fact, speaking of Josiah's twelfth year of life. Note finally that in some MSS of TC 34,3b the reference is to Josiah's 16th year, rather than his 12th as in MT. Commenting on the Targum's reading, LE DÉAUT, *Targum*, I, pp. 171-172, n. 2 notes that in it both parts of 34,3 refer to one and the same date, i.e. Josiah's 16th year of life (so v. 3b) which was likewise his 8th regnal year (so v. 3a), given that he acceded at the age of eight (so 34,1). See n. 13.

12. For the specifics of his account of this campaign, the Chronicler draws on/anticipates the description of Josiah's reform measures subsequent to the finding of the book as recounted in 2 Kgs 23,4-20 (of which he himself gives only a highly truncated version in 34,33). See the commentaries and cf. further below.

13. This indication corresponds, as such, to the datum found in MT 34,3b (MARCUS, *Josephus*, VI, p. 185, n. e calls it an apparent "misunderstanding" of the latter). I have suggested, however (see n. 11), that the intended reference there is actually to Josiah's 12th *regnal* year = his 20th year of life (so explicitly BL), rather than to his year of life (so Josephus here). Thus, Josephus would be dating the series of Josiah's religious reforms related by him in 10,50-56 to a moment four years earlier even than the king's initial religious awakening spoken of in 34,3a and dated (so MT BL) to his 8th regnal year = his 16th year of life. Thereby, he highlights Josiah's (religious) precocity, just as elsewhere he accentuates, e.g., the precocity of the boy Moses. On the point, see FELDMAN, *Studies*, pp. 426-427 (= ID., *Josiah*, 114-116).

14. This general formulation might be viewed as Josephus' equivalent to the mention of Josiah's "beginning to seek the God of David his father" in 34,3a. On the historian's regular ascription of the above pair of qualities to his Biblical heroes, see H.W. ATTRIDGE, *The Interpretation of Biblical History in the* Antiquitates Judaicae *of Flavius Josephus* (HDR, 7), Missoula, MT, Scholars, 1976, pp. 115-116. Terms of the ευσεβ – and δικαιοσ – stems constitute *Leitworte* in Josephus' account of Josiah; for the former see 10,53.61; for the latter, see 10,51.56. The reference to Josiah's "piety" (εὐσέβειαν) here likewise echoes the mention of the repentant Manasseh beginning "to show piety (εὐσεβεῖν) toward God" in 10,45.

15. For this phrase, see on 9,154. Via the above notice, Josephus introduces a distinctive feature of his portrait of Josiah, i.e. the king as a (persuasive) teacher of his people; see further 10,53.68 and cf. FELDMAN, *Studies*, pp. 428-429. Compare Josiah's initiative as cited here in 10,50 with that attributed to Hezekiah in 9,264: "He sent messengers to the Israelites, exhorting them to give up (ἀφέντας) their present manner of life... and reverence God (σέβειν τὸν θεόν)".

the acts (ἐπισκοπῶν ἔργα)¹⁶ of his forefathers, he wisely (συνετῶς)¹⁷ corrected the errors they had made (ἁμαρτηθέντα διώρθου)¹⁸, just as if (ὡσανεί)¹⁹ he were a very old man and quite competent to see (νοῆσαι ... ἱκανώτατος)²⁰ what needed to be done; but whatever practices he found that were good (εὖ γεγονότα)²¹ and in place he kept and imitated (ἐμιμεῖτο)²². (51) These things he did by using his natural (τῆς φύσεως; cf. τὴν φύσιν, 10,49) wisdom and discernment (σοφίᾳ καὶ ἐπινοίᾳ)²³ and being guided by the counsel and traditions of the elders (καὶ τῇ τῶν πρεσβυτέρων πειθόμενος²⁴ συμβουλίᾳ καὶ παραδόσει²⁵)²⁶; for it was by following the laws (τοῖς ... νόμοις κατακολουθῶν)²⁷ that he succeeded (εὐοδεῖν)²⁸ so well (οὕτως)²⁹ in the ordering of his government (περὶ τὴν τάξιν τῆς πολιτείας³⁰)³¹ and in piety (εὐσεβείας; see εὐσέβειαν, 10,50a) toward the Deity, and also because (διὰ τό)³² the lawlessness

16. Josephus' one other use of the above phrase "review act(s)" is in *BJ* 5,503.

17. Note Josephus' (terminological) emphasis on the intellectual acumen of the young Josiah: "wise" himself, he further endeavors to bring the people "to their senses".

18. This construction occurs only here in Josephus.

19. This is the conjecture of Niese which Marcus adopts. Dindorf, Bekker, and Naber read ὡς ἄν with the codices other than ROM (which have ὡς ἄν ὁ).

20. The phrase "competent to see" recurs in *AJ* 3,49; 7,391 (here in Josephus' eulogy of David, Josiah's exemplar); *Vita* 11; *c. Ap.* 1,287.

21. This phrase echoes the mention of Josiah himself being "well-disposed (εὖ γεγονώς) to virtue" in 10,49.

22. The same term "imitate" is used of both Josiah's grandfather Manasseh (10,37) and his father Amon (10,47), albeit *in malam partem*: the former "imitated the lawless deeds of the Israelites", while the latter "imitated" the reprobate acts committed by Manasseh in his youth.

23. Josephus' only other use of this collocation is in *AJ* 6,69, there in reference to the stratagems of the brutal king Nahash of the Ammonites.

24. The above sequence is absent in the codices ROLaurV, but is retained by Dindorf, Bekker, Niese, Naber, Marcus, as well as by FELDMAN, *Studies*, p. 427, n. 5 (= ID., *Josiah*, 117, n. 18) who affirms that without "some such phrase the Greek is unidiomatic".

25. The above collocation "counsel and tradition(s)" occurs only here in Josephus.

26. On the above phrase "(guided by) the traditions of the elders" which would make Josiah a "prototype of the Pharisees", its parallels in the Synoptics (see Mk 7,3 // Matt 15,2), and analogous expressions elsewhere in Josephus, see FELDMAN, *Studies*, pp. 427-428 (= ID., *Josiah*, pp. 117-118). Compare S. SCHWARTZ, *Josephus and Judean Politics* (Columbia Studies in the Classical Tradition, 18), Leiden, Brill, 1990, p. 181, n. 34 who avers "the language of 51 has a Pharisaic ring to it... but the text is so poor [see n. 24] as to render speculation about it unwise".

27. This precise expression occurs only here in Josephus. Compare τῆς ἀρετῆς τῶν νόμων οἷς κατακολουθοῦσιν in *AJ* 5,73 and ἀκόλουθα ... τοῖς Μωυσέος νόμοις (of Amaziah at the outset of his reign, 9,187). With regard to the above reading NABER, *Opera*, II, p. xxxvi, *ad loc.* tentatively suggests: "an forte κατακολούθως et (κολάσεως) μὴ τυγχάνειν".

28. The verb εὐοδέω is hapax in Josephus.

29. This is the reading of codex M which Marcus adopts. Niese reads ὡς with ROLaurV, while Dindorf, Bekker, and Naber give οὕτω.

30. This is the reading of the codices MSP which Dindorf, Bekker, Naber, and Marcus follow. Niese adopts the reading πόλεως of ROLV; cf. Lat civitatis.

31. This phrase occurs only here in Josephus.

32. Niese reads simply διά with RO here.

(παρανομίαν)³³ of the former (πρώτων)³⁴ (kings) no longer existed, but had been rooted out (ἐξηφανίσθαι)³⁵.

Following the above "interlude" of his own composition, Josephus (10,52) finally presents his version of the youthful Josiah's iconoclastic measures in Jerusalem and Judah as cited in 2 Chr 34,3b-5: "Going round the city and the entire country (τὴν πόλιν καὶ τὴν χώραν ἄπασταν)³⁶, the king cut down the groves (ἄλση ... ἐξέκοψε)³⁷ dedicated to foreign gods (ξενικοῖς ... θεοῖς)³⁸ and razed their altars (βωμοὺς ... κατέσκαψεν)³⁹,

33. This term echoes the notice that Manasseh "imitated the lawless deeds (παρανομίας) of the Israelites" in 10,37.

34. This is the reading of ROM which Marcus adopts. Dindorf, Bekker, and Naber follow SPLaur'V's τούτων, while Niese conjectures τῶν προγόνων.

35. The phrase "root out lawlessness" occurs only here in Josephus. It serves to make the transition to the list of Josiah's iconoclastic measures that follows in 10,52.

It is generally recognized that the text of 10,51b is not in order ("misere corrupta", NABER, Opera, II, p. xxxvi). L.K. ENTHOVEN, Ad Flavii Iosephi Antiquitates Iudaicas, in Mnemosyne 22 NS (1894), 15-22, pp. 20-21 ventures a far-reaching reconstruction, i.e. τοῖς γὰρ νόμοις κατακολουθοῦντι αὐτῷ περὶ τὴν τάξιν τῆς τε πολιτείας καὶ τῆς περὶ τὸ θεῖον εὐσεβείας εὐοδεῖν συνέβαινε διὰ τὸ τὴν πολιτῶν παρανομίαν μὴ ἀνεῖναι ἀλλ' ἐξαφανίσαι. He renders this reconstructed sequence "nam leges observans felici eventu et civitatem et cultum divinum licentia civium non neglecta sed exstirpata".

36. This is the same phrase used, in malam partem, of Manasseh in 10,35 who "(even dared to pollute the temple of God as well as) the city and the entire country". Compare 34,3b: (Josiah) "began to purge Judah and Jerusalem..." and the corresponding 34,5b: "... he purged Judah and Jerusalem".

37. This phrase occurs only here in Josephus. According to SPOTTORNO, Chronicles, p. 387, Josephus derives his compound form ἐξέκοψε in 10,52 from L 34,7 where it is used with "all of the high places" of the North as object (in B one finds rather the simple form ἔκοψεν). It is not so clear to me, however, that, already here in 10,52, Josephus is drawing on the account of 34,6-7 concerning Josiah's iconoclastic measures in the North; rather, in line with 2 Kgs 23,15-20, he appears to reserve his parallel to that segment to a later point in his presentation, i.e. 10,66-67; see below. In any event, with the above reference Josephus compresses into one the Chronicler's double reference to "the groves" (τὰ ἄλση, so BL/ MT: "the Asherim") which Josiah alternatively "purges" (BL 34,3b καθαρίσαι) and "breaks in pieces" (BL 34,4bα ἔκοψεν). On Josephus' standard following of the LXX rendition "grove(s)" where MT has "Asherah/Asherim", see further BEGG, Early Divided Monarchy, p. 153, n. 998 and the literature cited there.

38. On this phrase, see 9,27.96.133; the expression "groves dedicated to foreign gods" occurs only here in Josephus.

39. Josephus' only other use of this phrase is in c. Ap. 1,193 where he draws on the testimony of Hecataeus of Abdera concerning the Jews' destruction of pagan "temples and altars" constructed in their country by various invaders. Josephus' phrase τοὺς βωμούς corresponds to the L plus καὶ τῶν βῶμων in 34,3b to which neither MT nor B have an equivalent, as is noted by SPOTTORNO, Chronicles, p. 387. SPOTTORNO, ibid., further points out that the verbal form κακέσκαψεν which Josephus uses with "the altars" as object here corresponds to the κατέσκαψε employed by L 34,4aα of Josiah's action against "the altars (θυσιαστήρια) of the Baals and the high places upon them", whereas B reads κατέσπασεν (note, however, that Josephus will make subsequent use of this B form – absent from L 34,4, although it does appear in L (and B) 34,7 – in relating the king's treatment of the royal "dedicatory offerings"; see below).

and whatever dedicatory-offerings (ἀνάθημα) to them had been set up by his forefathers (προγόνων)[40] he treated with contempt (περιυβρίζων)[41] and pulled down (κατέσπα)[42]".

2 Chr 34,6-7 continues the "iconoclastic catalogue" begun in 34,3b-5 with mention of further such measures carried out by Josiah, particularly in the territory of the former Northern Kingdom. The former segment itself seems to represent the Chronicler's equivalent to the notices on Josiah's cultic purification of the North subsequent to the finding of the book as related in 2 Kgs 23,15-20. Josephus will give his equivalent to 2 Kgs 23,15-20 in connection with his account of the events of Josiah's 18th year; see 10,66-69. In order then to avoid a duplication of content he leaves aside the material of 2 Chr 34,6-7 here in his account of Josiah's earlier reign. In place thereof, he introduces a series of remarks (10,53-56) concerning "positive" reform initiatives undertaken by the youthful Josiah, these both complementing his iconoclastic measures as described in 10,52 and further underscoring the king's all-sided precocity. As we shall be seeing, Josephus found his (apparent) inspiration in attributing these additional initiatives to Josiah in the Biblical accounts of earlier Judean reform kings whose deeds Josiah, as the culminating such figure in Judah's history, now recapitulates.

The historian begins (10,53a) the series with mention of the affect of Josiah's elimination of the reprobate cultic objects upon his people: "And in this way he turned the people away from their belief in these gods (τῆς περὶ αὐτοὺς δόξης) to the service of God (τὴν τοῦ θεοῦ θρησκείαν)...[43]". That "service of God" to which Josiah causes the people to return (10,53a) is then exemplified in the act Josephus next (10,53b)

40. Compare the reference to the "lawlessness of the former (πρώτων) (kings)" in 10,51.
41. In AJ 9,103 this verb is used of the contemptous treatment accorded the body of King Joram of Judah by the populace; see there.
42. Only here does Josephus use the verb κατασπάω with "dedicatory-offerings" (ἀνάθημα) as object. The Chronicler's catalogue of the reprobate cultic entities (34,3b-5) eliminated by Josiah in "Judah and Jerusalem" (cf. the inclusio in vv. 3b, 5b) does not mention such "dedicatory offerings". Conversely, Josephus' own list leaves aside a whole series of entities cited in the Biblical one, i.e. high places, graven and molten images (bis), "incense altars" (so RSV), and the "bones of priests" burned on their altars (so v. 5a; Josephus will, however, make subsequent use of this item in his rendition of 2 Kgs 23,15-20 in 10,66-67; see below) His compression of the source listing reflects his overall tendency to reduce Biblical cultic details.
43. This notice picks up on the wording of 10,50: "(Josiah) sought to bring the people to their senses and urged them to give up their belief in (τῆς περὶ ... δόξης) idols... and to worship the God (θεόν) of their fathers". Here in 10,53 Josiah's earlier exhortations are now shown to have had their desired affect upon the people. As an efficacious religious teacher of his people, Josiah recalls his great-grandfather Hezekiah whose exhortations (see 9,264) resulted in the people returning to "their ancient form of religion" (θρησκείαν, 9,274; see 10,53).

attributes to the king: "... and he offered up (ἐπέφερε)⁴⁴ on His altar (αὐτοῦ τῷ βωμῷ)⁴⁵ the customary sacrifices (συνήθεις ... θυσίας)⁴⁶ and the whole burnt offerings (ὁλοκαυτώσεις [see 9,43.155])⁴⁷".

In 10,53c Josiah's reform measures extend beyond the cultic sphere itself: "He also appointed (ἀπέδειξε) certain judges (κριτάς) and overseers (ἐπισκόπους)⁴⁸ who, in administering the affairs of individuals, were to put justice (τὸ δίκαιον)⁴⁹ above everything else and treat it no less carefully than their own lives⁵⁰".

The last of the "supplementary measures" which Josephus – going beyond both Biblical accounts of him – attributes to the boy Josiah con-

44. This singular form with Josiah as subject is the reading adopted by Niese and Marcus. Dindorf, Bekker, and Naber reads the plural ἐπέφερον (subject: the people as a whole) with MSP.

45. Note the contrast with 10,52 where Josiah "razes their [the groves'] altars (τοὺς βωμοὺς αὐτῶν)".

46. This expression occurs only here in Josephus.

47. The sacrifical initiative attributed to Josiah here echoes measures attributed – whether positively or negatively – to a whole series of earlier Judean kings, i.e. Jehoshaphat (see 9,3: "the king betook himself to giving thanks and offering sacrifices [θυσίας] to God" [like 10,53b, this notice has no equivalent in the source account, i.e. 2 Chr 19,4-11, of Jehoshaphat's reforms]); Ahaz (see 9,257: "he forbade the offering of the customary sacrifices [τὰς νενομισμένας ... θυσίας ἐπιφέρειν]"); Hezekiah (see 9,263: at his direction the priests "offered up the accustomed sacrifices on the altar [ἐξ ἔθους τῷ βωμῷ θυσίας ἐπέφερον]"); and the repentant Manasseh (see 10,43: "he offered up the customary sacrifices [τὰς νομίμους θυσίας ἐπετέλει]"). See n. 50.

48. Josephus' one other use of the noun ἐπίσκοπος is in 12,254; cf. the participle ἐπισκοπῶν used of Josiah himself in 10,50.

49. Cf. 10,50 where the twelve-year old Josiah "gives proof of his righteousness (δικαιοσύνην)". Thus, the king is here asking his officials to evidence the same quality already manifest in his own life.

50. Neither Biblical account of Josiah says anything about such a judicial initiative by the king. MARCUS, Josephus, VI, p. 186, n. c raises the possibility that Josephus may have "confused" Josiah with Jehoshaphat to whom such an initiative is attributed in AJ 9,3-6 on the basis of 2 Chr 19,4-11. This proposal is dismissed by SCHWARTZ, Josephus, p. 181, n. 34 who opines: "more likely Josephus thought a thorough reform of the Judahite constitution would have involved a reform of the judicial system as well". FELDMAN, Studies, p. 431 (= ID., Josiah, p. 124), seconds the view of Schwartz, likewise noting that mention of Josiah's appointment of judges and his charge to them about the preeminence of the concern for justice serves to further the historian's picture of the king as an exemplar of the Greek cardinal virtue of justice. While not rejecting the remarks of Schwartz and Feldman on the point, I nevertheless think that Marcus's surmise ought not to be written off completely. Rather than it being a question, however, of Josephus' "confusing" Josiah with Jehoshaphat (so Marcus), I would suggest that the historian has applied to the former king an activity the Bible ascribes to the latter with a view to making Josiah appear as an all-sided reform king who recapitulates the whole range of reforms undertaken by his predecessors; see above. In this connection, I would call attention to the verbal contacts between 9,3-6 (i.e. ἀποδείξας [9,3], τοῦ δικαίου [9,3], κριτάς [9,4]) and 10,53c. I would further note that in Josephus' presentation – as opposed to that of the Bible itself – the two kings are credited with both sacrificial activity (see 9,2 and 10,53b; cf. n. 47) and the appointment of judicial officers.

cerns the king's organizing of a collection for the repair of the Temple
and its disimbursement for that purpose, 10,54-56. I would point to two
likely sources of inspiration for Josephus in composing this sequence.
On the one hand, it represents an application to Josiah of an activity
associated with yet another of Judah's earlier reform kings, i.e. Joash,
whose efforts on behalf of the Temple's renovation are described in similar terms in AJ 9,161-165 (= 2 Kgs 12,5-16 // 2 Chr 24,4-14). A second
such inspiration for Josephus' presentation in 10,54-56 would be the
subsequent Biblical narratives concerning the finding of the book in the
Temple which, e.g., make reference (2 Kgs 22,4 // 2 Chr 34,9) to monies
that had been previously collected from the people, this notwithstanding
the fact that there has been no mention, in either Kings or Chronicles,
of any such collection since the time of Joash many years before. Josephus' presentation, by contrast, sets up his own subsequent reference to
previously collected monies (see 10,57) by telling of such a collection
earlier in the reign of Josiah himself, crediting the initiative for it to the
king, whose piety is thereby duly enhanced. His account of the matter
reads:

> (54) Then he sent (διαπέμψας)[51] throughout the entire country (κατὰ
> πᾶσαν τὴν χώραν; cf. τὴν χώραν ἅπασαν, 10,52), bidding (ἐκέλευε)[52]
> those who wished to bring gold and silver (ἄργυρον) for the repair of
> the temple (εἰς ἐπισκευὴν τοῦ ναοῦ) to do so, each according to his
> inclination or ability (ἢ προαιρέσεως ἢ δυνάμεως)[53]. (55) When the
> money was brought, he gave the superintendence of the temple (τῆς
> ἐπιμελείας τοῦ ναοῦ)[54] and the expenses connected with it (τῆς εἰς

51. This aorist form is read by ROM followed by Niese and Marcus. Dindorf, Bekker,
and Naber adopt the form διαπεμψάμενος of SPLaurVE.

52. This is the form read by Niese and Marcus; Dindorf, Bekker, and Naber read the
aorist ἐκέλευσε of MSP.

53. This collocation is hapax in Josephus. The above notice seems to have been formulated with 2 Chr 34,9 (cf. 2 Kgs 22,4) in mind, i.e. "the money (BL ἀργύριον) which
the Levites... had collected from Manasseh and Ephraim and from all the remnant of
Israel and from all Judah and Benjamin and from the inhabitants of Jerusalem". (Josephus' non-mention of the Levites' role in the collection process is characteristic of his
downplaying of the Chronicler's emphasis on them). The notice likewise evidences noteworthy similarity with Josephus' own statement about King Joash in 9,161 (// 2 Chr 24,4-
5): "As for Joas... he was seized by a strong desire to renovate the temple of God, and
summoning the high priest Jōdas, he commanded (ἐκέλευσε) him to send (πέμψαι) the
Levites and priests throughout the entire country (εἰς ἅπασαν ... τὴν χώραν) to ask a
half shekel of silver (ἀργύρου) for each person for the repairing and renovation of the
temple (εἰς ἐπισκευὴν ... τοῦ ναοῦ)". Note, however, that while Josephus' Joash specifies the amount to be collected from each individual, Josiah leaves the sum up to each
person's "inclination or ability". In so doing the latter shows himself more prescient than
his predecessor whose (initial) scheme for collecting funds came to naught (see 9,162).

54. This expression occurs only here in Josephus; cf. the analogous phrases in AJ
9,155 (τὴν ... ἐπιμέλειαν καὶ φυλακὴν τοῦ ἱεροῦ); 14,90.

τοῦτο δαπάνης)⁵⁵ in charge to Amasias ('Αμασίαν)⁵⁶, the governor of the city (τόν τ' ἐπὶ τῆς πόλεως)⁵⁷, Sapha (Σαφᾶν)⁵⁸, the scribe (τὸν γραμματέα)⁵⁹, and Jōatēs ('Ιωάτην)⁶⁰, the keeper of the records (τὸν γραφέα τῶν ὑπομνημάτων)⁶¹, and the high priest (τὸν ἀρχιερέα)⁶² Eliakias ('Ελιακίαν)⁶³, (56) who, without allowing any postponement or delay (μηδὲν ὑπερθέσει μηδὲ ἀναβολῇ)⁶⁴, took hold of the work by providing master-builders (ἀρχιτέκτονας)⁶⁵ and all things necessary for the repairing (πρὸς τὴν ἐπισκευήν; cf. εἰς ἐπισκευήν, 10,54)⁶⁶. And so the temple, having been repaired (ὁ ναός ... ἐπισκευασθείς)⁶⁷ made clear (φανερὰν ἐποίησαν)⁶⁸ the piety (εὐσέβειαν) of the king⁶⁹.

55. Variations of this phrase occur in AJ 11,14.100.126; 13,57.

56. SCHLATTER, Namen, p. 75 calls this form "corrupt", while SCHALIT, Namen-wörterbuch, p. 9 suggests that it is due to metathesis of an original Μαασίας. Josephus draws the name from 34,8 where "Maaseiah" (MT; Μαασά, B; Μαασίαν, L) is one of three officials whom Josiah – in his 18th year – sends to the Temple to hand over monies to the high priest.

57. In BL 34,8 Maaseiah's title is ἄρχοντα τῆς πόλεως.

58. This form of the name agrees with that found in L 22,3 and BL 34,8. Compare "Shapan" (MT 22,3 // 34,8); Σαφφάν (B 22,3). Josephus omits the name of Shaphan's father ("Azaliah", MT 22,3 // 34,8) and grandfather ("Meshullam", MT 22,3).

59. In the list of the three persons dispatched by Josiah in 34,8 "Shaphan" has no title. Josephus supplies it from 22,3 where BL designate him with the same Greek phrase.

60. According to SCHLATTER, Namen, p. 59 this form is the corruption of an original shorter Ιωαν. The name corresponds to the "Joah" of MT 34,8 (B 'Ιουάχ; L 'Ιωάς). Josephus omits the name of the figure's father, i.e. "Joahaz" (MT).

61. This phrase occurs only here in Josephus; compare BL 34,8 τὸν ὑπομνη-ματογράφον αὐτοῦ (i.e. Josiah).

62. In BL 22,4 // 34,9 the Greek title for Hilkiah is τὸν ἱερέα τὸν μέγαν; Josephus substitutes a more current designation.

63. SCHLATTER, Namen, p. 48 holds that Josephus' original form was 'Ελκιας. In MT 22,4 // 34,9 the name is חִלְקִיָּהוּ; compare Χελκείαν (BL 22,4 // B 34,9); Χελκία (L 34,9). Note that Josephus turns the three-man delegation (2 Chr 34,8) who go to the high priest Hilkiah (34,9) in the king's name into a four-man commission, this including Hilkiah himself, which takes the repair of the Temple in hand.

64. This collocation occurs only here in Josephus.

65. Josephus' three remaining uses of this term are in AJ 3,104; 19,9; Vita 156.

66. This notice represents an anticipation/simplification of the complicated process described in 2 Chr 34,9-11 where Josiah's delegation (see 34,8) delivers the monies collected to the "workmen who had oversight of the Lord" who, in turn, distribute it to those working on the repair of the Temple, i.e. the carpenters and the builders, so that these may buy "quarried stone and timber for binders and beams for the buildings..." (in the parallel text of 2 Kgs 22,5-6 these same measures are presented as instructions which Josiah gives to Shaphan when dispatching him to Hilkiah). From his version of Josiah's temple repair initiative (= 2 Chr 34,8-13), Josephus characteristically omits all source mentions of the Levites' role therein (compare 34,9.12-13).

67. This phrase echoes that used of Joash's Temple renovation initiative in 9,165 (ἐπισκευασθέντος ... τοῦ ναοῦ).

68. The phrase "make clear" recurs in AJ 2,238; 7,307; 8,170.174.

69. The above conclusion to Josephus' account of the boy Josiah's solicitude for the Temple echoes his remark in 10,50 that at age twelve the king "gave proof of his piety (εὐσέβειαν) and righteousness", constituting an inclusion with that remark, prior to the account of events of Josiah's 18th regnal year which opens in 10,57. By having Josiah

3. Finding of the Book

The pivotal moment in both the Biblical and the Josephan accounts of Josiah's reign comes with the discovery of a book in the Temple, this occurring in the king's 18th regnal year. The circumstances surrounding the episode are related in some detail in 2 Kgs 22,3-20 // 2 Chr 34,8-28 = AJ 10,57-62a.

In the sources, the book-finding episode is set in motion when Josiah dispatches an official(s) to the Temple to see to the distribution of monies to those involved in its repair. As we have seen, Josephus (10,54-56) anticipates the king's temple repair initiative to an earlier point in his reign. Accordingly, it now becomes necessary for him to devise another "occasion" for the book's finding. In so doing, he seems to have drawn inspiration from the cultic initiative recorded of a previous Judean king, i.e. Joash, the presentation of whom he has already utilized in 10,54-56 itself; see above. In 9,165 (= 2 Chr 24,14; contrast 2 Kgs 12,14) one reads that, once Joash's Temple repair has been completed, the funds remaining from that project were spent on procuring a variety of cultic vessels. Inspired by this datum (see further n. 73), Josephus (10,57) relates the same thing as happening under Josiah, the new Joash:

> Now he had already been reigning eighteen years[70], he sent (πέμπει; compare BL 22,3 // 34,8 ἀπέστειλεν)[71] to the high priest Eliakias (Ἐλιακίαν τὸν ἀρχιερέα; see τὸν ἀρχιερέα Ἐλιακίαν, 10,55; cf. n. 62), telling him (κελεύων)[72] to melt (χωνεύσαντα)[73] *what was left over of the money* (τὸ

undertake his Temple repair at a much earlier age than in the Bible (i.e. 12 vs. 26), Josephus disposes of a question that might suggest itself to Scripture readers, i.e. why did the pious king wait till more than halfway through his reign before doing something about the condition of the Temple?

70. In specifying that the book-finding episode took place in Josiah's 18th *regnal* year, Josephus agrees with 34,8 (MT BL) against 22,3 (MT BL) which lacks that specification. In addition, he has no equivalent to the BL plus in 22,3 dating the episode more precisely to the "8th month" of Josiah's 18th year.

71. Unlike the sources, Josephus does not identify the one(s) sent by Josiah on this occasion. Compare 22,3 (Shaphan the secretary) // 34,8 (Shaphan, Maaseiah, Joah, MT). Recall that he has "anticipated" the three names of 34,8 in 10,55.

72. The above sequence πέμπει ... κελεύων echoes that used of Josiah in 10,54 διαπέμψας ... ἐκέλευε. Compare 22,3-4: "(Josiah) sent Shapan... saying, 'Go up to Hilkiah the high priest, that he may reckon...'". (In 34,8 the three officials are "sent" by Josiah "to repair the house of the Lord"; they thereupon, 34,9, are said to "come to Hilkiah the high priest").

73. This term has a counterpart in L 22,4 where Josiah issues the directive χωνεύσατε [Β σφράγισον] τὸ ἀργύριον; see further BL 22,9 in which Shaphan reports to Josiah "your servants have (s)melted (ἐχώνευσαν) the money". On the basis of the latter usage, MARCUS, *Josephus*, VI, p. 188, n. c suggests that the historian's whole pre-

περισσὸν τῶν χρημάτων)[74] *and with it make mixing-bowls* (κρατῆρας) *and libation-cups* (σπονδεῖα) *and bowls* (φιάλας)[75] *for the temple service* (εἰς τὴν διακονίαν), *and in addition, bring out* (προκομίσαντα)[76] *whatever gold and silver* (χρυσὸς ... καὶ[77] ἄργυρος; see 10,54) *might be in the treasuries and spend it* (δαπανῆσαι; cf. τῆς ... δαπάνης, 10,55)[78] *similarly for mixing-bowls* (κρατῆρας) *and such vessels* (σκεύη)[79].

After their extended preliminaries concerning Josiah's directives to his official(s), the Biblical accounts relate Hilkiah's (announcement of) the finding of the book itself rather briefly, 22,8 // 34,14. Josephus' version (10,58a) makes use of several items peculiar to the Chronicler's report of the happening: "But, in bringing out (προκομίζων; see προκομίσαντα, 10,57; cf. n. 76) the gold (τὸν χρυσόν; see 10,57), the high priest Eliakias came upon the sacred books (ταῖς ἱεραῖς βίβλοις) of Moses[80], *which had been placed in the temple*[81], *and he brought them*

sentation in 10,57 concerning the making of cultic vessels from the remaining Temple monies "may be based on a misunderstanding of 2 Kings xxii.9". As noted above, I see another (or further) source of inspiration for Josephus' presentation here in the account of the making of the Temple vessels under Joash in 9,165 = 2 Chr 24,14. In any case, note that the readings of the other witnesses in both of the above verses of 2 Kings 22 are quite different: in v. 4 MT has וְיַתֵּם (RSV: "that he may reckon"; alternatively, one might translate "he will give"), B σφράγισον ("let him seal"), and TJ ויטיק ("he will count out"), while in v. 9 MT reads הִתִּיכוּ (RSV: "[your servants] have emptied out"), and TJ טקיסו ("[your servants] have counted out"; see TJ 22,4).

74. This phrase establishes a link back to 10,55: "when the money (τῶν χρημάτων) was brought...", making clear that some of that earlier collected money still remains at this point and so is available for the further project now to be described.

75. The above triad of objects recurs in *AJ* 8,89; 12,40.117.

76. This is the conjecture of Bekker which Naber and Marcus follow. Dindorf and Niese read the plural accusative participle προσκομίσαντας with SPLaurV. In having Josiah command the "bringing out" of the Temple's gold and silver here in 10,57, Josephus sets up his following reference to Hilkiah's "bringing out the gold" in 10,58 (= 34,14a).

77. This is the reading adopted by Niese and Marcus; Dindorf, Bekker, and Naber read ἤ with MSPLaurV and Lat.

78. MARCUS, *Josephus*, VI, p. 188, n. b proposes "use it" as an alternative translation for the above rendering of δαπανῆσαι.

79. Note the verbal affinities between the above sequence and Josephus' account of what happened under Joash in 9,165a: "(and, when, the temple was repaired [see 10,56]), they spent the money (χρυσὸν καὶ ἄργυρον) that was left over... for bowls (κρατῆρας) and pitchers and cups and other vessels (σκεύη)...".

80. In the sources the reference is to a single "book": "the/a book (BL βιβλίον) of the law" (22,8)/ "the book (BL τὸ βιβλίον) of the law of the Lord given through Moses" (34,14; see Josephus above). MARCUS, *Josephus*, VI, p. 189, n. d maintains that Josephus' plural designation for the "find" indicates that he understood this to have been "the entire Pentateuch".

81. This qualification concerning the "book(s)" has no counterpart in 22,8 // 34,14; it serves to account for the books' presence in the Temple where Hilkiah finds them. The whole above transitional phrase of 10,58 corresponds to the opening plus of 34,14: "While they were bringing out the money that had been brought into the house of the Lord, Hilkah the priest (MT B, > L) found the book of the law of the Lord given through Moses...".

out (προκομίσας) and gave (δίδωσι) them to Sapha, the scribe (τῷ γραμματεῖ)[82]". The Biblical stories next shift attention to Shaphan and what he does subsequent to receiving the book from Hilkiah (22,8bβ-10 // 34,16-18). In line with his previous modification of the source presentations, Josephus eliminates the secretary's specific announcement to Josiah (22,9 // 34,17) that the monies had been distributed to the workmen as commanded by the king (see 22,5-6). Instead, he (10,58b) has Shaphan deliver a more general report to Josiah: "And, when he (Shaphan) had read (ἀναγνούς) them, he came (παραγίνεται) to the king[83] and informed him that[84] everything which he had ordered (κελεύσειε; cf. κελεύων, 10,57) to be done had been brought to completion. Then he also read the books aloud (παρανέγνω[85]... τὰς βίβλους[86]) to him[87]".

The segment 22,11-13 // 34,19-21 features the king's double reaction to what he hears, i.e. his rending of his clothes (vv. 11 and 19) and dispatch of a delegation to "inquire of the Lord concerning the words of the book" (vv. 12 and 20), both these measures being inspired by his consciousness of the divine wrath threatening the people because of their non-compliance with the book's requirements (vv. 13 and 21). Josephus' rendition (10,59) goes its own way in several respects, most notably in having Josiah also specify whom it is the delegation is to approach, instruct them to request her intercession, and spell out the implications of the people's disregard of the laws contained in the book. It runs:

> When the king had heard them [the books] read, he rent his garments (περιρρηξάμενος τὴν ἐσθῆτα)[88] and, calling the high priest Eliakas, sent

82. This is the LXX's designation for Shaphan; compare 10,55 where the title used of him is τὸν γραφέα. The above notice corresponds to 22,8bα // 34,15b: "And Hilkiah gave (BL ἔδωκε[ν]) the book to Shaphan". Josephus has no equivalent to the announcement attributed to the high priest in 22,8a // 34,15a: "Then Hilkiah said to Shaphan the secretary, 'I have found the book of the law in the house of the Lord'". See n. 87.

83. This sequence corresponds to that of MT B 22,8bβ-9aα: "And he [Shaphan] read (B ἀνέγνω) it. And Shaphan the secretary came (B εἰσῆλθεν) (+ in the house of the Lord, B) to the king...". Compare 34,16 (and L 22,9): "And Shaphan brought the book to the king".

84. Besides modifying the content of the Biblical Shaphan's report (see above), Josephus also recasts this in indirect discourse in accord with his frequent practice.

85. The verb παραναγινώσκω occurs twice elsewhere in Josephus: *BJ* 4,617; *Vita* 260.

86. The codices add αὐτῶν which Naber retains. Following J. Hudson, Dindorf, Bekker, and Marcus omit the word, while Niese prints it within brackets.

87. Compare 22,10b // 34,18b: "And Shaphan read (BL ἀνέγνω) it before the king". Josephus has no equivalent to the secretary's announcement in 22,10a // 34,18a: "Then Shaphan the secretary told the king, 'Hilkiah the priest has given me a book'". See his like omission of the priest's own announcement of his find in 22,8a // 34,15a; cf. n. 82.

88. For this construction, see on 9,67. Compare BL 22,11b // 34,19b: διέρρηξεν τὰ ἱμάτια αὐτοῦ.

him and the scribe himself [22,12 // 34,20: Shaphan the scribe] *and some of his closest friends* (ἀναγκαιοτάτων φίλων)[89] to the prophetess (προφῆτιν)[90] Oolda ('Οολδά)[91], the wife of Sallūmos (Σαλλούμου)[92], *a man of high repute* (ἐν δόξῃ) *and illustrious family* (δι' εὐγένειαν ἐπιφανοῦς[93])[94], *commanding them to go to her* and tell her *to appease God* (ἱλάσκεσθαι τὸν θεόν)[95] *and attempt to win His favour* (ποιεῖν εὐμενῆ)[96], for, he said, there was reason to fear that, since their fore-fathers (τῶν προγόνων; see 10,52) had transgressed against the laws of Moses (παραβάντων τοὺς Μωυσέος νόμους)[97], *they themselves*

89. This phrase echoes 10,5 where Hezekiah "sends out three of the friends who were closest to him (τοὺς ἀναγκαιοτάτους φίλους)" to parley with the Assyrian general. The phrase takes the place of the names of the three additional members of Josiah's delega-tion cited in 22,12 // 34,20, i.e. Ahikam, the son of Shaphan; Achbor/ Abdon, the son of Micaiah/ Micah; and Asaiah, "the king's servant".

90. Apart from 10,60 where it is used again in reference to Huldah, this title appears elsewhere in Josephus' works only in *AJ* 5,200 (of Deborah).

91. This is the form of the name read by Niese and Marcus. Dindorf, Bekker, and Naber read 'Ολδάν with LaurVEZon (cf. Lat Oldam), while SCHLATTER, *Namen*, p. 48 and SCHALIT, *Namenwörterbuch*, p. 93 propose 'Ολδάν. Compare "Huldah" (MT 22,14 // 34,22); "Ολδαν (BL 22,14 // B 34,22); "Ολδαν (L 34,22).

92. This is the reading adopted by Dindorf, Bekker, Niese, Naber, and Marcus. Com-pare "Shallum" (MT 22,14 // 34,22); Σελλήμ (BL). Josephus omits the name of his father (Tikvah/Tokhath) and grandfather (Harhas).

93. This expression occurs only here in Josephus.

94. Josephus' above double qualification of "Shallum" takes the place of the desig-nation of him as "keeper of the wardrobe" in 22,14 // 34,22. As a substitute for the latter phrase it suggests more of a rationale for the delegation's going specifically to Huldah, i.e. her being married to such a pre-eminent figure (in Rabbinic tradition one finds con-siderable speculation as to why the delegation approached Huldah rather than Jeremiah; see *b. Meg.* 14b). On Josephus' frequent highlighting – in accord with a standard feature of Hellenistic biographies and historiographies – of the "good birth" of Biblical figures, see FELDMAN, *Studies*, p. 546; ID., *Interpretation*, pp. 87-90.
Josephus' "anticipates" his mention of Huldah and her husband here in 10,59 from 22,14 // 34,22 where the delegation acts on the commission given it by Josiah in 22,12-13 // 34,20-21. In so doing, he resolves a difficulty suggested by the Biblical presenta-tions, i.e. the delegation seems to "know" whom they are to approach, even though Josiah has only told them "to inquire of the Lord" for him. In the historian's version the anamoly disappears with Josiah identifying the intended recipient of the inquiry by name. From the wording of 22,14 // 34,22 Josephus omits the (extraneous) detail of Huldah's place of residence, i.e. "in Jerusalem בְּמִשְׁנֶה (RSV: "in the Second Quarter" which TJ/TC understand as בבית אלפנא, "in the house of instruction").

95. Josephus' other uses of this construction are in *AJ* 6,124; 8,112; *c. Ap.* 1,308 (object "gods").

96. For this phrase, see on 9,162. Josiah's double call for Huldah's intercession above takes the place of the king's words in 22,12a // 34,20a where the delegation is told "inquire of the Lord for me… concerning the words of the book that has been found". Josephus' replacement seems better in place at this juncture in that the import of the book would seem already clear to Josiah and the need would be rather for an attempt at propi-tiating God – a matter which is conspiciously lacking in the words of both Josiah and Huldah as cited by the Bible.

97. For this phrase, see on 9,153. Recall the designation of Hilkiah's find as "the sacred books of Moses" in 10,58.

(αὐτῶν)[98] *might be in danger of being driven away* (ἀνάστατοι), *and, after being cast out of their own country* (τῆς οἰκείας ἐκπεσόντες)[99] *into a foreign land where they would be destitute of all things, might there miserably end their lives* (κακαστρέψωσιν οἰκτρῶς τὸν βίον)[100].

2 Kgs 22,14-20 // 2 Chr 34,22-28 relate the interaction between Huldah and the royal envoys. This new segment opens (22,14 // 34,22) with re-mention of the five members of the delegation and then a detailed presentation of the one to whom they go. Josephus, having anticipated the data concerning Huldah in Josiah's commission (see above), reduces (10,60) his sources' introduction to the following transitional phrase "when the prophetess [see 10,59] heard these things from the men through whom (αὐτῶν δι' ὧν)[101] the king had sent the message (ἐπέστειλεν)[102] [cf. 22,14bβ // 34,22bβ where the reference is to the delegation's speaking to Huldah]...".

Huldah's actual words (22,15 // 34,23) begin with a *Botenformel*, followed by the commission "tell *the man* who sent you to me". Characteristically avoiding the former element, Josephus recasts the latter (and what follows) in indirect address: "... she told them to go back to *the king*[103] and say that...". Huldah's initial message for Josiah is that the Lord intends to bring "evil" on Jerusalem (22,16 // 34,24). The historian interjects a preliminary statement by Huldah underscoring the certainty of the doom she is about to announce: "... the Deity had already given His sentence (ψῆφον)[104] against them, and that no one could make it

98. This is the reading adopted by Dindorf, Bekker, and Marcus. Niese, followed by Naber, conjectures αὐτοί.

99. This phrase occurs only here in Josephus.

100. This phrase occurs only here in Josephus. The above conclusion to Josiah's commission represents Josephus' rendition of the king's words in 22,13b // 34,21: "for great is the wrath of the Lord that is poured out on us, because our fathers have not kept the words of the Lord, to do according to all that is written concerning us [22,13]/ in this book [34,21]". The Josephan version accentuates the prescience of the king who foretells quite concretely (and accurately) what the divine "wrath" will entail for the people's future. See FELDMAN, *Studies*, pp. 453-454 (= ID., *Josiah*, 128).

101. This is the reading of M corr. which Marcus follows. Dindorf, Bekker, Niese, and Naber read δι' αὐτῶν ὧν with the remaining codices. For δι αὐτῶν, ENTHOVEN, *Antiquitates*, 22 conjectures ἀδυνατῶν, the reference being to the "impossibility" of Huldah's making the intercession Josiah has sent to ask of her.

102. This is the reading which Dindorf, Bekker, Niese, and Marcus adopt. Naber reads ἀπέστειλεν with SPLaur.

103. In having Huldah use this designation for Josiah as opposed to "the man" of the sources (22,15 // 34,23) Josephus eliminates a feature which led Rabbinic tradition (see *b. Meg.* 14b) to censure Huldah for her haughty disrespect evident in her reference to the king as simply a "man".

104. Josephus uses ψῆφος of a divine "sentence" also in *BJ* 7,359; *AJ* 3,44; 4,217.225; 5,168.

ineffective (ἄκυρον) even by supplications (ἱκεσίαις)...¹⁰⁵". He then has her continue with a elucidation of the "evil" predicted by her Biblical counterpart¹⁰⁶: "... this sentence was to destroy the people (ἀπολέσαι τὸν λαόν) and drive them out of their country (τῆς χώρας ἐκβαλεῖν)¹⁰⁷ and deprive them of all the good things (ἀφελέσθαι ... ἀγαθῶν)¹⁰⁸ which they now had....¹⁰⁹".

Having made her announcement of doom for the people, Huldah goes on to motivate this by reference to their reprobate practices which have provoked the Lord's anger (22,17a // 34,25a). Josephus' version of this accusation (10,60b) introduces mention also of the succession of prophetic warnings the sinful people have disregarded: "... because they had transgressed against the laws (παραβάντας τοὺς νόμους)¹¹⁰ *and during so long an interval of time had not repented* (μετανοήσαντας), *although the prophets* (προφητῶν) *exhorted them to act thus wisely* (παραινούντων σωφρονεῖν¹¹¹)¹¹² *and foretold* (προλεγόντων) *the punishment* (τιμωρίαν) *for their impious deeds* (ἀσεβήμασι)...¹¹³".

105. With this statement Huldah makes clear that there is no point to her attempting the propitiation of God for which Josiah calls in 10,59.

106. Compare Josiah's own spelling out of the implications of the divine "wrath" invoked by the king in 22,13 // 34,21 in 10,59.

107. This construction occurs also in *BJ* 1,19; *AJ* 6,327; 12,286; 13,352.

108. This construction is hapax in Josephus.

109. Note the content similarity between Huldah's prediction above and the "fear" expressed by Josiah himself in 10,59, i.e. "... they themselves might be in danger of being driven away, and, after being cast out of their own country into a foreign land where they would be destitute of all things, might miserably end their lives". The effect of this agreement between king and prophetess in their respective premonitions is to underscore the certainty of the catastrophe awaiting the people.

110. Here again (see n. 109), Josephus' Huldah echoes words earlier attributed to Josiah; see the king's reference to "their forefathers' having transgressed the laws of Moses (παραβάντων τοὺς Μωυσέος νόμους)" in 10,59.

111. Niese, *ad loc.* qualifies this term as "fort. spurium".

112. Compare 10,50 where Josiah himself "seeks to bring the people to their senses (ἐσωφρόνιζε) and urges (παρήνει) them to give up their belief in idols...". By implication, then, Josiah appears to belong to the line of prophets alluded to by Huldah in 10,60.

113. The above interjected reference to the prophets' recurring exhortations and threats serves to accentuate the people's guilt (and the deservedness of their eventual punishment). The whole sequence "because they had transgressed... for their impious deeds" here in 10,60b is highly reminiscent of Josephus' editorial remark about the demise of the Northern Kingdom in 9,281: "To such an end, then, did the Israelites come because they violated the laws (παραβάντας τοὺς νόμους) and disregarded the prophets (προφητῶν) who foretold (προύλεγον) that this misfortune would overtake them if they did not cease from their impious actions (ἀσεβημάτων)". This verbal similarity intimates that Judah will indeed come to the same bad end that had already befallen the North. Compare also 9,265 where Josephus – here too without Biblical basis as such – alludes to the Northern prophets who "exhorted" (παρανοῦντας) their hearers and "foretold (προλέγοντας) what they would suffer if they did not alter their course to one of piety toward God", only to have "scorn poured upon them" by the audience. See n. 115.

The Biblical Huldah concludes (22,17b // 34,25b) her judgment speech against the people with a reiteration of her earlier word of doom (22,16 // 34,24). Josephus' prophetess appends (10,61a) rather an indication of the purpose of God's coming overthrow of the people: "... which, she said, He would certainly (παντῶς) inflict (ποιήσειν)[114] on them *in order that they might believe* (πεισθῶσιν)[115] *that He was God and was not speaking falsely* (ἐψεύδετο) *about any of these things which He had announced through the prophets*[116]".

In the Biblical accounts Huldah rounds off her speech with a message of consolation for the king who had responded with due penitence to the reading of the book (22,18-20a // 34,26-28a). The Josephan rendering (10,61b) abridges this element of the prophetess' word, even while accentuating the favor accorded the king by God: "However, she said, *for the sake of Josiah, who was a righteous man* (δίκαιον)[117], He would put off these calamities (ἐφέξειν... συμφοράς)[118] for a time, but after his death would sent down on the multitude the sufferings which he had decreed against them (τὰ κατεψηφισμένα πάθη[119]... ἐπιπέμψειν[120])[121]".

114. Naber conjectures the form ἐποίσειν here.

115. Compare 9,265 where Josephus states that the Northerners were "not persuaded (οὐκ ἐπείσθησαν)" by Hezekiah's messengers. Cf. n. 113.

116. The above indication concerning the purpose of God's coming punishing initiative picks up on Huldah's reference to the prophets and their disregarded warnings in 10,60b. In particular, it underscores Josephus' recurring emphasis that God-sent prophets do make accurate predictions which, over time, invariably are shown to be such. Compare 10,35 where Isaiah is said to be "confident of never having spoken what was false (ψευδές)".

117. This characterization of the king echoes the reference to his "giving proof of his (piety and) righteousness (δικαιοσύνην)" in 10,50; cf. 10,53 where he calls on the judges appointed by him to "put justice (τὸ δίκαιον) above all else". It takes the place of the extended evocation of the penitential gestures (see 22,11 // 34,19) undertaken by Josiah in response to his hearing of the book which is placed on the lips of Huldah in 22,19 // 34,27. The king's life-long virtue of "righteousness" would provide, Josephus may have thought, more of an incentive for God's granting him the favor Huldah is about to announce than would the one-time penitential acts ascribed to his Biblical counterpart.

118. This expression occurs only here in Josephus.

119. This phrase is hapax in Josephus. In place of the singular παθή Naber reads παθήματα with the codices LaurV.

120. The above phrase "sent down sufferings" is hapax in Josephus.

121. Compare Huldah's promise to Josiah in 22,20a // 34,28a: "Therefore, behold I [God] will gather you to your fathers, and you shall be gathered to your grave in peace, and your eyes will not see all the evil which I will bring upon this place [+ and its inhabitants, 34,28]". Josephus' version highlights the benefit, i.e. postponement of the catastrophe, which Josiah's righteousness will procure, not simply for himself, but for the whole people; see FELDMAN, *Studies*, p. 431 (= ID., *Josiah*, 124). It likewise disposes of the Biblical Huldah's problematic announcement that Josiah will "be gathered to his grave in peace" which might be seen as a "false" prophecy in that the king, in fact, did not die a natural/peaceful death. See n. 199.

The interview scene between Huldah and the delegation ends (22,20b // 34,28b) with the latter reporting back to the king. Josephus (10,62a) interjects a transitional phrase between the conclusion of Huldah's speech and the delegation's return to their sender: *"And so, after the woman had prophesied* (προφητευσάσης)[122], they came and reported her words to the king"*.

4. *The People Obligated*

Once he has received prophetic guidance concerning the book that has been found, Josiah next (23,1-3 // 34,29-32 = 10,62b-64) acts to enforce compliance with its terms. Pursuant to this end, he convenes the entire population at the Temple, as described in 23,1-2a // 34,29-30a. Josephus (10,62b) omits mention of the Temple as the scene of the convocation[123]: "Thereupon he sent round (περιπέμψας) to all parts, commanding (ἐκέλευε)[124] the people to gather in Jerusalem, as also the priests and Levites[125], and ordering those of every age[126] to be present".

The sources proceed to tell of a two-fold initiative undertaken by the king: he reads the book found by Hilkiah to the assembled people (23,2b // 34,30b) and then binds them by covenant to observe its terms (23,3 // 34,31-32a) Characteristically, Josephus' version (10,63) avoids the Bible's "covenant-language": *"When these had been assembled*, he *first* read (ἀνέγνω = LXX; cf. ἀναγνούς, 10,58) them the sacred books (τὰς

122. This verb echoes the double use of the noun προφῆτις in reference to Huldah in 10,59-60.
123. His reason for doing this might be the consideration that the Temple would be too small to hold the assembled multitudes whose accomodation would require rather an open-air setting in Jerusalem.
124. This is the reading adopted by Niese and Marcus; Dindorf and Naber read the aorist ἐκέλευσε with MSPLaurVE (Bekker has ἐκέλευσεν). With the above sequence περιπέμψας ... ἐκέλευε, compare διαπέμψας ... ἐκέλευε in 10,54 (in both instances the people as a whole are those to whom Josiah "sends" with his "command").
125. In mentioning this latter group Josephus goes together with 34,30 against 23,2 where the reference is to "the priests and *the prophets*". His doing so is noteworthy given the historian's overall tendency to highlight the role of the prophets in Israel's history, while downplaying that of the Levites. Perhaps, in this instance he is simply conforming himself to the Old Testament's more standard *Sprachgebrauch* ("priests and Levites" vs. "priests and prophets") as employed by the Chronicler. In any case, he leaves unmentioned a group of participants cited in both 23,1 // 34,29, i.e. "the elders of Judah and Jerusalem", perhaps not deeming them of sufficient stature to merit separate notice.
126. This phrase might be seen as Josephus' equivalent to/ clarification of the reference to "(all the people), both great and small" of 23,2a // 34,30a.

ἱερὰς βίβλους)[127] and then, standing on the tribune (στάς ἐπὶ τοῦ βήματος)[128] *in the midst of the people*, he compelled them to take an oath and pledge (ὅρκους … καὶ πίστεις)[129] that they would truly worship God (θρησκεύσειν[130] τὸν θεόν; cf. τὴν τοῦ θεοῦ θρησκειάν, 10,53)[131] and keep the laws of Moses (φυλάξειν[132] τοὺς Μωυσέος νόμους)[133]".

The Chronicler concludes his account of Josiah's covenant-making (34,29-32) with a plus concerning the affect of this upon the people's behavior ("and the inhabitants of Jerusalem did according to the covenant of God, the God of their fathers", v. 32b). Josephus (10,64) embellishes and particularizes this generalized notice: "And they [the people] eagerly assented (προθύμως … ἐπήνεσαν)[134] and undertook to

127. This phrase echoes 10,58's ταῖς ἱεραῖς βίβλοις. Compare the more expansive designation used in 23,2b // 34,30b: "… all the words of the book of the covenant (BL [τοῦ] βιβλίου τῆς διαθήκης) which had been found in the house of the Lord".

128. This phrase is used also in AJ 4,209 (of the high priest reciting the laws) and 7,370 (David's urging the people to aid Solomon in building the Temple; thus, the phrase serves to establish yet another link between Josiah and David). The Biblical textual witnesses differ as to the entity by which or on which Josiah "stands" for the following covenant-making. In 23,3 it is "by the pillar (MT עַל־הָעַמּוּד; BL πρὸς [B]/ ἐπὶ [L] τὸν στύλον); MT 34,31 has him standing "in his place" (עַל־עָמְדוֹ, BL ἐπὶ τὸν στύλον), while in TJ and TC the king is positioned "upon the balcony" (עַל אסטונא). Compare 9,151 (= 2 Kgs 11,14 // 2 Chr 23,13) where Josephus has Athaliah see the boy king Joash ἐπὶ τῆς σκηνῆς [RO στήλης] ἑστῶτα; see there.

129. This collocation recurs in AJ 7,24.40 (reverse order); 12,(8).382. In 23,3 // 34,31-32 Josiah first makes a "covenant" (BL διαθήκην) of his own before the Lord, into which the people as a whole enter thereafter. Josephus conflates this two-stage process into the single moment of the king's obligating his people, perhaps influenced by the consideration that there would be no need for the exemplary Josiah to pledge himself to "walk after the Lord", etc. at this point, as he is represented as doing in the source verses. See n. 133.

130. This future infinitive is the conjecture of Niese which Naber and Marcus follow. Dindorf and Bekker read the aorist infinitive θηρσκεῦσαι with the codices and E. See n. 132.

131. On the above verbal phrase see 9,27.

132. This future infinitive is the conjecture of Niese which Naber and Marcus follow. Dindorf and Bekker read the aorist infinitive φυλάξαι with the codices and E. See n. 130.

133. The above phrase represents the positive reverse of that used by Josiah in 10,59 in reference to his people, i.e. παραβάντων τοὺς Μωυσέος νόμους. In 23,3 // 34,31 the content of Josiah's (personal) covenant is as follows: "to walk after the Lord and to keep (BL φυλάσσειν) his commandments, and his testimonies, and his statutes, with all his heart and all his soul, to perform the words of the covenant that were written in this book". Josephus transfers the "obligation" in question from king to people; see n. 129. The double content of the "oath and pledge" imposed by the people as cited above is quite reminiscent of what Jehoshaphat's teaching mission is to inculcate according to AJ 8,395: "… the laws of Moses (τοὺς Μωυσέος νόμους) both to keep (φυλάσσειν) them and to be diligent in worshipping God (περὶ τὴν θρησκείαν τοῦ θεοῦ)". See next note and recall the previous echoes of Josephus' presentation of Jehoshaphat in his portrayal of Josiah cited in nn. 47 and 50.

134. This indication serves to accentuate Josiah's persuasive powers as religious educator of his people; see on 10,50. It further calls to mind the historian's – likewise inserted – notice (8,395) on the impact of Jehoshaphat's teaching mission upon the recip-

do what the king urged upon them, *and straightway sacrificed* (θύοντες) *and while singing the sacred hymns* (καλλιεροῦντες[135])[136], *supplicated God* (τὸν θεόν ἱκέτευον; see 10,11.26)[137] *to be favourable and gracious* (εὐμενῆ καὶ ἵλεων)[138] *to them[139]*".

5. *Josiah's Later Reforms*

Following their respective narrations of Josiah's covenant-making (23,1-3 // 34,29-32), the Biblical accounts diverge, with 2 Kgs 23,4-20 recounting Josiah's purification of the national cult at considerable length, while 2 Chr 34,33 gives this all of one verse[140]. In face of such a marked source discrepancy, Josephus follows a mediating course: he gives (10,65-69) the king's "iconoclastic" initiatives subsequent to his covenant-making considerably more attention than does the Chronicler, but still much less than the author of Kings[141].

ients: "And so much were all the people pleased with this that there was nothing for which they were so ambitious or so much loved as the observance of the laws". See previous note.

135. MARCUS, *Josephus*, VI, p. 193, n. b comments, with reference to the occurrence of the same verb in 9,268, that "the exact meaning" of the above form is "uncertain here". Compare WEILL, *ad loc.* "(ils) célèbrent les rites sacrés".

136. Neither of Josephus' sources mentions "sacrifice" and "hymn-singing" in connection with Josiah's covenant-making as he does here. His interjected mention of the former activity at any rate does have a counterpart in 10,53 where the historian goes beyond 2 Chr 34,3b-5 in citing the king's "offering up... the customary sacrifices and the whole burnt offerings". In both instances (10,52-53 and 10,64-65), as well, Josiah's iconoclastic measures are accompanied, in Josephus' presentation, by the more positive cultic activity of offering sacrifice to his own God.

137. Mention of such activity by the people here appears tragically "superfluous" given Huldah's statement in 10,60 that no one could render God's sentence against Judah "ineffective even by supplications (οὐχ ἱκεσίαις)". Via Huldah's announcement, readers know what the people apparently do not (or do not accept), i.e. that any appeal to God regarding Judah's decreed fate is simply pointless at this juncture.

138. This collocation – also in reference to God – recurs in *AJ* 4,243.

139. Josephus' wording here echoes – ironically – Josiah's request to Huldah as cited in 10,59, i.e. that she attempt to "win His [God's] favour (εὐμενῆ)". Huldah had dismissed that request as pointless in 10,60. Here in 10,64, the people do untertake the thing Josiah had asked for, but their effort will prove unavailing – just as Huldah had warned. Recall in this connection that while references to supplication as an (im-)possibility at this juncture of Judah's history are conspicuously lacking in the Biblical sources, Josephus highlights precisely this matter in his own version.

140. This difference relates, of course, to an earlier one between the two sources, i.e. the fact that the Chronicler has "anticipated" elements of the catalogue of 23,4-20 to an earlier point of Josiah's career (i.e. his twelfth year) in 34,3b-7.

141. His adopting this course is readily understandable given the historian's "anticipation" – *à la* 2 Chr 34,3-7 – of items from the catalogue of 23,4-20 in 10,52; see there.

Josephus' account of Josiah's later, purificatory reforms, in turn, consists of three segments, these corresponding to one or other portion of 23,4-20 (and/or 34,[5]6-7). The first of these segments (10,65) represents a highly selective "synthesis" of Kings' enumeration of the cultic reforms initiated by Josiah in Jerusalem and Judah, 23,4-14. In particular, Josephus limits himself – for the moment, but see 10,69b below – to reproducing vv. 4-5 of the source sequence: "Then he ordered the high priest to cast out (ἐκβαλεῖν)[142] any vessels (σκεῦος; cf. σκεύη, 10,57) *that were left* of those that had been set up in the temple by their forefathers (ὑπὸ τῶν προγόνων ... κατασταθέν; cf. ὑπὸ τῶν προγονῶν ἀνέκειτο, 10,52) to the idols and strange gods (τοῖς εἰδώλοις [cf. τῶν εἰδώλων, 10,50] καὶ ξενικοῖς θεοῖς; see 10,52)[143]. *And when many of these had been collected*[144], he burnt (καταπρήσας) them and scattered their ashes (σποδὸν ... διέσπειρε)[145]; he also killed (ἀπέκτεινε)[146] the priests of the idols (τοὺς ἱερεῖς τῶν εἰδώλων)[147] *who were not of the family of Aaron* (ἐκ τοῦ Ἀαρῶνος γένους)[148]".

142. In 10,60 this same form is used of the people's future being "driven out" of their country. By "expelling" the reprobate cult objects from the Temple now, Josiah hopes to keep this other "expulsion" from happening later.

143. The above notice is Josephus' version of 23,4a: "And the king commanded *Hilkiah*, the high priest, *and the priests of the second order, and the keepers of the threshold*, to bring out of the temple of the Lord *all* the vessels (BL σκεύη) made for Baal, for Asherah, and for all the host of heaven". Here too, one notes Josephus' tendency to reduce the Bible's level of cultic detail, *in casu* his omission of the source verse's list of lesser cultic officials and generalization of its specific names/ classes of pagan deities. Conversely, Josephus inserted qualification of the "vessels", i.e. "any that were left", reflects the fact that, following Chronicles, and unlike Kings, he has already narrated a thorough-going cultic "cleanup" by Josiah (see 10,52) which, in turn, would call for the clarifying remark/recognition that there were, nonetheless, still reprobate items left in the Temple at this point.

144. This transitional phrase has a certain equivalent in the plus of L 23,4b: καὶ ἐξήγαγον [i.e. the cultic officials to whom Josiah gives his order in v. 4a] αὐτά [i.e. the reprobate "vessels"].

145. This construction occurs only here in Josephus. His source for the above sequence is 23,4b: "he (Josiah) burned (BL κατέκαυσεν) them [the cultic vessels, v. 4a] *outside Jerusalem in the fields of Kidron* and carried their ashes (BL τὸν χοῦν) *to Bethel*", from which, however, he eliminates all specific geographical indications. See n. 149.

146. In MT 23,5 Josiah "deposes" (וְהִשְׁבִּית) the idolatrous priests, while in BL he is said to have "burned" (κατέκαυσε[ν], so also *VL* "combussit") them. Josephus' verb calls to mind his notice (9,165) that the people "killed" (ἀπέκτειναν) the Baal-priest Mattan.

147. This phrase occurs only here in Josephus. In MT 23,5 the figures in question are designated as הַכְּמָרִים (RSV: "the idolatrous priests"). B "transliterates" with τοὺς χωμαρείμ (compare TJ כמריא), while L "translates" by τοὺς ἱερεῖς (cf. Josephus).

148. On this phrase see 9,224. The phrase takes the place of the lengthy qualification of the "idolatrous priests" found in 23,5: "... whom the kings of Judah had ordained to burn incense in the high places at the cities of Judah and round about Jerusalem; those

The second segment making up his Josephus' account of Josiah's later reforms (10,66-67) constitutes his parallel to 23,15-18 which describes the king's eradication of the Bethel cultic installations dating back to Jeroboam I (see 1 Kgs 12,25-13,34 = AJ 8,225-245). The Biblical account begins (23,15) with specific mention of Josiah's destruction of the Bethel altar along with its associated "high place" and Asherah. Josephus, typically, generalizes (10,66a): "*When he had carried out these reforms in Jerusalem, he went into the country*[149] and utterly destroyed (ἠφάνισε; compare ἐξηφανίσθαι, 10,51 [object: the lawlessness of the former kings]) everything which had been built there by King Jeroboam to the honour of the foreign gods (τὰ κατασκευασθέντα ... ὑπὸ Ἱεροβοάμου τοῦ βασιλέως εἰς τιμὴν τῶν ξενικῶν θεῶν)...[150]". 2 Kgs 23,16 tells of a further iconoclastic measure undertaken by Josiah at Bethel, i.e. his profanation of the site's altar by burning upon it the bones extracted from nearby tombs, this fulfilling the prediction made by the Judean "man of God" as recorded in 1 Kgs 13,3. The historian's version (10,66b-67) compresses Josiah's actual deed, while elaborating on the fulfillment of the long-past prophetic announcement which it represents:

(66b)... and he burnt (κατέκαυσε; BL 23,16 κατέκαυσεν) the bones (τὰ ὀστᾶ = BL) *of the false prophets* (τῶν ψευδοποφητων)[151] upon the altar

also who burned incense to Baal, to the sun, and the moon, and the constellations, and all the host of heaven". His "replacement" for this sequence provides an additional "legitimation" for Josiah's "elimination" of these priests, i.e. their having arrogated an office vested by God solely in Aaron's descendants. See FELDMAN, *Studies*, p. 434 (= ID., *Josiah*, 128).

149. This transitional phrase, noting Josiah's movement from one scene of activity to another, has no counterpart in 23,15 which simply presupposes the king's presence at Bethel. Conversely, Josephus speaks more generally of Josiah's measures in "the country" rather than at the specific site "Bethel". Cf. n. 145.

150. The above formulation establishes a verbal parallel between Josiah's iconoclastic measures "in the country" and his earlier initiatives with regard to the elimination of the reprobate Temple "vessels" the latter being qualified in 10,65 as ὑπὸ τῶν προγόνων ... τοῖς εἰδώλοις καὶ ξενικοῖς θεοῖς κατασταθέν. Compare the more expansive wording of 23,15: "... that (Jeroboam's) altar with the high place he [Josiah] pulled down (B κατέσπασεν, L καθεῖλε) and he broke in pieces its stones [so RSV following BL; MT: he burned the high place], crushing them to dust; also he burned the Asherah".

151. 2 Kgs 23,16 does not indicate whose "bones" Josiah burnt on the Bethel altar as such. With Josephus' specification on the point compare his version of the Judean prophet's announcement of 1 Kgs 13,3 in AJ 8,232: "God has foretold that there shall be one of the line of David who will sacrifice upon you [Jeroboam's altar] the false priests (ψευδιερεῖς) living in his time and will burn (καύσει) upon you the bones (τὰ ὀστᾶ) of these misleaders of the people, these imposters and unbelievers". See also the allusion to this prediction in 8,242 (= 1 Kgs 13,32) where the Bethel "false prophet" (so 8,236.241) says of his Judean colleague (whose death he has just brought about) "... everything was true whch he had prophesied against... the false prophets (τῶν ψευδοπροφητῶν)". For Josephus' use of the term "false prophet(s)" see further on 9,133.

(ἐπι τοῦ βωμοῦ; BL ἐπὶ τὸ θυσιαστήριον)¹⁵² *which Jeroboam had been the first to build* (κατεσκεύασε)¹⁵³. *(67) Now a prophet* (προφήτην)¹⁵⁴ *had come* (κατελθόντα) *to Jeroboam and foretold* (προκαταγγεῖλαι)¹⁵⁵, *as he was sacrificing* (θυσιάζοντος) *and in the hearing of all the people* (ἀκούοντος τοῦ λαοῦ), *that these things would come to pass* (γενησό-μενα)¹⁵⁶, *namely that someone of the line of David* (ἐκ τοῦ Δαυίδου γένους), *named Josiah* (Ἰωσίας τοὖνομα), *would do the things described above*¹⁵⁷. *And, as it happened, these prophecies were fulfilled after three hundred and sixty-one years*¹⁵⁸.

152. In 8,230 Josephus uses both terms, θυσιαστήριον (so BL 23,16) and βωμός, in reference to Jeroboam's Bethel "altar" which Josiah desecrates here in 10,66. In begin-ning immediately with Josiah's "burning" of bones on the altar, Josephus dispenses with the preliminaries to the king's act as cited in 23,16aαβγ: "And as Josiah turned, he saw the tombs there on the mount; and he sent and took the bones out of the tombs". He like-wise leaves aside the source verse's following qualification concerning Josiah's burning of the bones, "and defiled (BL ἐμίανε[ν]) it [the Bethel altar]".

153. The above qualification of the Bethel altar has no equivalent in 23,16 (although cf. 23,15); it harks back to the notice of 8,230 "... Jeroboam... built (οἰκοδομεῖ) an altar (θυσιαστήριον) before the heifer...".

154. Compare "man of God", 23,16 (MT BL; TJ "prophet of the Lord"). This is the same designation used by Josephus for the figure who confronts Jeroboam in 8,231, as opposed to that of 1 Kgs 13,1, i.e. "man of God" (so MT BL; TJ has "prophet of the Lord"). In 8,231 Josephus, going beyond the Bible, gives a name to the prophet as well, i.e. "Jadōn" (Ἰάδων); see BEGG, *Early Divided Monarchy*, p. 44 and n. 219. Here in 10,67 the codices LaurV supply a different name for the prophet in question, i.e. "Achias" (Ἀχίαν); their reading is adopted by Dindorf and Bekker.

155. Josephus' other uses of the verb προκαταγέλλω are in *AJ* 1,219; 2,68.85.218; 10,243.

156. This is the conjecture of Coccejus which Dindorf, Bekker, Naber, and Marcus adopt. Niese retains the codices' τὰ γενησόμενα.

157. The above sequence ("now a prophet... would do the things described above") harks back to Josephus' account of the "Bethel confrontation" in 8,231: "But as he [Jer-oboam] was about to offer the sacrifices... there came... a prophet... and standing in the midst of the multitude... addressed the altar in these words: 'God has foretold that there shall be one of the line of David, named Josias (ἐκ τοῦ Δαυίδου γένους Ἰωσίαν ὄνομα) who will sacrifice upon you the false priests...'". It takes the place of the "fulfillment notice" ("... according to the word of the Lord which the man of God proclaimed, who had predicted these things") of 23,16bβ (Josephus' allusion the prophet's "foretelling" to Jeroboam as the king was "sacrificing" does have a certain counterpart in the distinctive ending of the fulfillment notice of 23,16 according to *VL*, i.e. [secundum verbum quod locutus est homo dei,] *cum staret Hieroboam in die festo ad aram*", as attested by Lucifer Calaritanus, "De non Parcendo in Deum Delinquientibus" 7.79, DIERCKS, *Opera*, p. 209). As usual, Josephus avoids reproducing source mentions of the (divine) "word".

158. With this "non-Biblical" specification concerning the length of time that elapsed between the prophet's prediction under Jeroboam and its realization by Josiah, compare 9,242 where Josephus interjects the statement "But all the things that had been foretold concerning Nineveh [i.e. by Nahum (and Jonah)] came to pass after a hundred and fifteen years". MARCUS, *Josephus*, VI, pp. 194-195, n. b points out that the figure given by Josephus here in 10,67 (*361* years) does not tally with his own earlier chrono-logical indications for the period from the accession of Jeroboam to the 18th year of Josiah (in which the king's fulfillment of the "Bethel prophecy" took place), these com-ing to a total of *337* years.

The "Bethel episode" of 2 Kgs 23,15-18 concludes (vv. 17-18) with Josiah sparing the common grave of the "man of God from Judah" and the Bethel (false) "prophet", their joint burial having been enjoined by the latter in 1 Kgs 13,31. Josephus, who does reproduce the Bethel false prophet's directive in 8,242 (and attaches thereto the following statement of expectation by him "... he himself would suffer no mutilation after death if he were buried together with the prophet [from Judah], as their bones could not be told apart"), has, suprisingly, no equivalent to the content of 23,17-18[159]. In place thereof he proceeds directly to the further reform measures undertaken by Josiah outside Bethel itself. Basing himself in part on 2 Kgs 23,19-20 (Josiah's "purification" of "the cities of Samaria") and its (anticipated) parallel, 2 Chr 34,6-7 (see above), Josephus relates a final series of post-book-finding reforms carried out by Josiah in 10,68-69. Whereas, however, the Biblical accounts speak of the king's iconoclastic measures throughout the territory of the former Northern Kingdom, Josephus, in line with a tendency evident throughout his portrayal of Josiah (see on 10,50), focusses rather on the royal educative endeavors with regard to the erstwhile Israelites. His notice on the point (10,68) states: "After these events, King Josiah went also to the other Israelites[160], those who had escaped from captivity and servitude (αἰχμαλωσίαν καὶ ... δουλείαν)[161] under the Assyrians[162] and persuaded (ἔπεισε; see πεισθῶσιν, 10,61) them to give up (ἀφεῖναι) their impious practices (ἀσεβεῖς πράξεις)[163] and abandon

159. His omission of the Biblical account on the matter might go together with the status of the Bethel prophet as a "false prophet" (so explicitly 8,236.241; contrast MT BL 1 Kings 13 where this expression is not used of him as such, as it is in TJ). Given that status, it might seem inappropriate for the Bethelite to have his "prediction" on the sparing of his grave, as cited by Josephus in 8,242 (see above) "validated" (as would be the case if the historian were to reproduce the content of 23,17-18). It would likewise be inappropriate to have such a miscreant ultimately left "in peace". Recall too Josephus' interjected specification that it was the bones "of the false prophets" which Josiah burned on the Bethel altar in 10,67. In light of his previous designation of the Bethel figure as a "false prophet", one is led to suppose that his bones were among those that suffered this indignity – contrary to the prediction made by him in 8,242.
160. With this reference to the (other) "Israelites" as those to whom Josiah now "goes", compare 2 Chr 34,7 where Josiah's (additional) iconoclastic measures are carried out "throughout all the land of *Israel*".
161. The above terms are collocated (in reverse order) also in 11,213.
162. The above qualification of the "Israelites" is apparently intended to account for the availability of such persons to whom Josiah may now "go", given the earlier deportation of Israel's (entire) population by the Assyrians (see 9,278 where Josephus states that Shalmaneser "transported *all* its [Israel's] people to Media and Persia"). Josephus' "solution" to the problem is to evoke a – Biblically unattested – "escape" by some of the deportees, such that they can now be visited by Josiah.
163. Josephus uses this expression twice elsewhere: *AJ* 8,245 (Jeroboam). 251 (Rehoboam). There is a verbal echo here of 10,61 where Huldah "foretold the punishment for their [the Judeans'] impious deeds (ἀσεβήμασι)".

the worship (τὰς τιμὰς ... ἐγκαταλιπεῖν)[164] of foreign gods (ἀλλοτρίους θεούς)[165] and, instead, to show piety towards the Almighty God of their fathers (τὸν ... πάτριον [see 10,50] καὶ μέγιστον [see 9,133.211.288.289][166] θεὸν εὐσεβεῖν[167]) and remain faithful to Him (τούτῳ προσανέχειν)[168]".

To his notice on Josiah's reform measures throughout the former territory of Israel in 10,68, loosely based on 23,19-20 // 34,6-7, Josephus (10,69a) appends mention of an enforcement initiative undertaken by the king which has no parallel in the Biblical sources, but which does find a certain counterpart elsewhere in Jewish tradition. The historian relates the matter as follows: "He [Josiah] also searched the houses and villages and cities, suspecting that someone might have some idolatrous (τῶν εἰδώλων; see 10,50.65 [bis]) object within[169]". Finally, Josephus ends (10,69b) his extended account of Josiah's later purificatory reforms with an item held over by him from the catalogue of 23,4-20: "Furthermore he removed the chariots (ἅρματα) *placed for the king's officers* (τοῖς βασιλευομένοις[170] ἐφεστῶτα[171]) which his forefathers had built (ἃ κατεσκεύασαν οἱ πρόγονοι)[172], and

164. This construction occurs only here in Josephus.
165. For this expression, see 9,20.98.
166. This adjectival collocation is hapax in Josephus.
167. For the above expression "show piety to God", see on 10,45 (the repentant Manasseh).
168. Elsewhere Josephus uses God as the (datival) object of the verb προσανέχω also in *AJ* 11,279; cf. 1,15. Josiah's exhortation to the "Israelites" here in 10,68 recalls that addressed by him at age twelve to "the people" in 10,50: "... (he) urged them to give up their belief in idols... and to worship the God of their fathers (σέβειν τὸν πάτριον θεόν)...". Cf. also 10,52 "... he turned the people away from their belief in these gods to the service of God...".
169. With the above notice compare the tradition recorded, e.g., in *Lam. Rab.* 1.53 (COHEN, *Midrash Rabbah Lamentations*, p. 143) according to which Josiah dispatched two disciples of the Sages to check the people's homes for idols [in 10,69 he appears to do this in person]. Those idols were, however, affixed to the doors of the houses in such a way that the envoys failed to find them [10,69 suggests that whatever idols may have been present were, in fact, discovered by the king]. This continued presence of idols among the people, notwithstanding Josiah's efforts to eliminate them, in turn, called forth the king's subsequent tragic end. See n. 220.
170. NABER, *Opera*, II, p. xxxvi cites the emendations for this sequence proposed by J. Hudson (ταῖς βάσεσι λιθίναις or τοῖς βαθυμοῖς τοῦ τεμένους) and J.H. Holwerda (ταῖς βασιλικαῖς τοῦ τεμένους), commenting "Dubito equidem". WEILL, *Josèphe*, II, p. 316, n. 3 suggests the emendation τοῖς βασιλείοις ("[dressés] devant le palais royal") which MARCUS, *Josephus*, VI, p. 195, n. d calls "unnecessary".
171. Lat lacks an equivalent to the three-word Greek sequence above.
172. This phrase echoes the qualifications used of reprobate cultic objects earlier in Josephus' account of Josiah; see "(the dedicatory-offerings) ὑπὸ τῶν προγόνων ἀνέκειτο" (10,52) and "(the vessels) ὑπὸ τῶν προγόνων ... κατασταθέν" (10,65). His recurrent use of this "forefathers formula" serves to accentuate the contrast between

many other such things which they worshipped (προσεκύνουν) as gods (ὡς θεῷ)¹⁷³".

6. *Josiah's Passover*

Both Josephus' Biblical sources relate a Passover observance conducted under Josiah's auspices subsequent to the king's (later) cultic reforms. Whereas, however, the author of Kings allots the former happening a mere three verses (23,21-23) the Chronicler gives it no less than nineteen (35,1-19), his version being itself paralleled in 1 Esdras 1,1-24. Faced with this source discrepancy, Josephus adopts a middle course, relating the episode in more detail than does Kings but far less expansively than in Chronicles, 10,70-73(74); compare his treatment of their respective accounts of Josiah's post-book-finding reforms above. In common with 23,21 // 35,1 Josephus (10,70a) opens this new segment with a general reference to the fact of Josiah's seeing to the observance of the festival: "... *and having thus purified the entire country* (καθαρίσας ... τὴν χώραν ἅπασαν [see 10,52])¹⁷⁴, *he called the people* (τὸν λαόν) *together at Jerusalem*¹⁷⁵, and there celebrated the festival of

Josiah and his royal predecessors, the former eliminating all the accumulated cultic deviations of the latter.
The above reference to Josiah's removal of "the chariots" constructed by the king's forebears appears to represent a conflation of the double notice found in 23,11: "And he removed (so MT [וַיַּשְׁבֵּת]; BL κατέκαυσε[v], he burnt) *the horses* which the kings of Judah had dedicated *to the sun, at the entrance to the house of the Lord, by the chamber of Nathan-melech the chamberlain, which was in the precincts*; and he burned the chariots (so MT [מַרְכְּבוֹת]; BL τὸ ἅρμα; compare *VL* fontem [Lucifer Calaritanus, "De non Parcendo in Deum Delinquientibus" 7.61, DIERCKS, *Opera*, p. 208]) *of the sun with fire*".
173. This expression might been seen as Josephus' generalizing replacement for the many other individual cultic objects/persons whose elimination by Josiah is recorded in 23,4-20. The phrase involves as well a certain echo of 10,50 where Josiah urges the people to "give up their belief in idols, which he said were not really gods (θεῶν)...".
In light of 23,11 as well as the reference to his (Josiah's) "forefathers" as their makers (compare the parallel expression used of the Temple vessels in 10,65), it would appear that the "chariots", etc. cited in 10,69b are to be understood as located in Jerusalem. In thus having Josiah's later reforms begin (10,65) and end (10,69b) in the capital, Josephus creates an inclusion around his account of those reforms (10,65-69) which highlights the status of Jerusalem. For this presentation, he might have been influenced by the notices with which the Biblical accounts of Josiah's "Northern reforms" conclude, i.e. "then he (Josiah) returned *to Jerusalem*", 23,20b // 34,7b.
174. This construction occurs only here in Josephus. The verb καθαρίζω ("to cleanse in a religious sense") recurs in 11,153; 12,286.313. As such it is a variant of the term καθαίρω used in the same sense of a "cultic purifying" in, e.g., 9,138.262 (*bis*). 273; 10,42.
175. The above transitional phrase has no equivalent as such in either 23,21 or 35,1 // 1 Esdras 1,1. It does, however, echo the formulation with which Josephus introduces his account of Josiah's obligating of the people to the terms of the book in 10,62: "Thereupon he sent round to all parts, commanding the people (τὸν λαόν) to gather in Jerusalem...".

Unleavened Bread (τὴν ἀζύμων ἑορτήν)[176] and that (καὶ τὴν)[177] called Passover (πάσχα[178])".

2 Chr 35,2-6 (// 1 Esdras 1,2-6) relate a series of preparatory directives issued by Josiah, first to the priests (v. 2) and then, at much greater length, to the Levites (vv. 3-6). Josephus passes over this whole segment, thereby, once again, contriving to play down the Levites' involvement in the proceedings. As a result of this "omission", the historian's presentation moves directly from mention of Josiah's observance of the feast(s) (10,70a = 35,1) to a listing of the victims provided on this occasion by the king, along with the civil and religious leaders (10,70b-71 = 35,7-9 // 1 Esdras 1,7-9). The first of the festival "donors" to be cited (10,70b) is Josiah himself: "He also presented gifts to the people for the Passover (εἰς τὸ πάσχα)[179] (consisting of) thirty thousand (τρισμυρίους)[180] young (νεογνούς)[181] kids and lambs (ἐρίφους καὶ ἄρνας; BL 35,7 πρόβατα καὶ ἀμνοὺς καὶ ἐρίφους), and three thousand oxen (βοῦς; BL 35,7 μόσχων) for the whole burnt offerings (εἰς ὁλοκαυτώματα[182])[183]". This royal largesse is itself (10,71) next emulated by the two clerical orders (= 35,8b-9 // 1,8-9)[184]:

176. This designation for Josiah's feast is not found in 2 Kgs 23,21-23. It does appear as a name of the "follow-up feast" subsequent to the nocturnal Passover festival in 2 Chr 35,17 (BL τὴν ἑορτὴν τῶν ἀζύμων) // 1 Esdras 1,19.

177. In this reading adopted by Niese, Naber, and Marcus, Josephus would distinguish between the Festivals of Passover and Unleavened Bread. LaurELat read simply τὴν, while Dindorf (followed by Bekker) proposes – "forte recte" according to MARCUS, *Josephus*, VI, p. 196, n. 1 – τὴν καὶ (= "also called"). On these alternative readings Josephus would identify the two feasts, as, in fact, he does in 20,106. See further MARCUS, *Josephus*, VI, pp. 196-197, n. a.

178. This is the Greek form of the name of the feast used in BL 23,21 and 1 Esdras 1,1 ([τὸ] πάσχα); compare BL 35,1 (τὸ φάσεχ). With the above sequence compare 9,271: "when the festival of Unleavened Bread (τῆς τῶν ἀζύμων ἑορτῆς) came round, they [Hezekiah's people] sacrificed the *Phaska* (τὴν ... φάσκα)"; and 9,263 "(Hezekiah summons the people to "celebrate the festival of Unleavened Bread (τὴν τῶν ἀζύμων ἑορτήν)". Cf. our discussion of these texts in chap. XV.

179. This is the conjecture of J. Hudson, inspired by the εἰς τὸ φάσεκ of BL 35,7, which Marcus adopts. Niese and Naber read simply τὸ πάσχα with the codices, which reading Dindorf and Bekker bracket.

180. This figure corresponds to that given in 35,7 // 1,7. The codices RO have δισμυρίους which reading Niese follows.

181. The word νεογνός is hapax in Josephus.

182. The codices SP, followed by Dindorf, Bekker and Naber, read εἰς ὁλοκαύτωσιν. Cf. τὰς ὁκολαυτώσεις, 10,53.

183. This indication concerning the intended use of the victims contributed by Josiah takes the place of the (self-evident) specification at the end of 35,7 // 1,7 according to which the beasts donated by Josiah were "from the king's possessions".

184. Josephus has no equivalent to 2 Chr 35,8a which speaks of contributions made "to the people, the priests, and Levites" by Josiah's "princes" (in 1 Esdras 1,7 it is Josiah's own gifts which are said to have been given by him to the three groups in question, and there is no mention of the "princes").

"And the chief priests (τῶν ἱερέων οἱ πρῶτοι)[185] as well furnished to the (other) priests for the Passover (διὰ τὸ πάσχα τοῖς ἱερεῦσιν)[186] two thousand six hundred lambs (ἄρνας)[187] and to the Levites their leaders (οἱ προεστῶτες; BL ἄρχοντες; 1 Esdras χιλίαρχοι)[188] gave five thousand lambs (ἄρνας)[189] and five hundred oxen (βοῦς; BL 35,9 // 1 Esdras 1,9: μόσχους)".

The Chronicler continues his account of Josiah's Passover with a lengthy description (35,10-17 // 1 Esdras 1,10-17) of the sacrificial proceedings, this giving special attention to the Levites' involvement therein. In view of the historian's tendency both to reduce Biblical cultic detail and to downplay the role of the Levites in Israel's history, it is not suprising to find him compressing this whole sequence into a single sentence (10,72a): "*And so, there being such an abundance of victims* (ἀφθόνου ... τῶν ἱερείων εὐπορίας)[190], they performed the sacrifices in accordance with the laws of Moses (τὰς θυσίας ἐπετέλουν τοῖς Μωυσέως νόμοις [cf. 10,59.63])[191], the priests[192] directing each step (ἑκάστῳ[193]...

185. The above is the reading of the codices which Marcus and Niese follow. In place of the word (τῶν) ἱερέων Lat has iudaeorum. J. Hudson, followed by Dindorf and Bekker, accordingly conjectures (τῶν) Ἰουδαίων as the original Greek reading, while Naber proposes Ἑβραίων. MARCUS, *Josephus*, VI, p. 197, n. c., with reference to the wording of 2 Chr 35,8 // 1 Esdras 1,8 (which, however, he seems to me to report in a somewhat misleading way) calls the above emendations "unnecessary". The reading of the codices espoused by Marcus himself takes the place of the three named priestly figures of 35,8 // 1,8, i.e. "Hilkiah, Zechariah, and Jehiel, the chief officers (BL 35,8 οἱ ἄρχοντες; LXX 1,8 οἱ ἐπιστάται) of the house of God (35,8)/ of the Temple (1,8)".

186. Compare L 35,8b: τοῖς ἱερεῦσιν εἰς τὸ φάσεχ.

187. In 35,8b // 1,8b the chief priests give the other priests 2,600 "rams (so MT; BL: sheep and lambs [ἀμνούς] and kids; 1 Esdras 1,8b: sheep) *and 300 oxen* (BL 35,8 and 1 Esdras 1,8: μόσχους)". Josephus' omission of the italicized item here is noteworthy in that its effect is to make his own group, the priests, appear less "generous givers" than the Levites whose claims he is generally concerned to play down; see below.

188. As he does in the case of the priests of 35,8b // 1,8 (see n. 185) Josephus leaves aside the names of the seven (so 35,9)/ six (so 1,9) Levitical leaders cited in the source(s).

189. MT 35,9 speaks of "rams", L and 1 Esdras 1,9 of "sheep" (B 35,9 reads simply 5000 without an accompanying noun).

190. This construction is hapax in Josephus. The above transitional phrase, interjected here by Josephus, picks up on the catalogue of victims contributed cited by him in 10,71, underscoring the generous beneficence of the various leadership groups mentioned there.

191. Note that Josephus leaves unspecified the subject of the "sacrificing" here; the immediately preceding context would suggest that it is the Levites. With the above notice compare 35,12 // 1,11 ("And they [the Levites?, cf. 35,11] set aside the burnt offerings... to offer to the Lord, as is written in the book of Moses") and 35,16 // 1,17 ("So all the service of the Lord was prepared that day, to keep the passover and to offer burnt offerings... according to the command of King Josiah").

192. In contrast to his procedure with the Levites (see previous note), Josephus here singles out the priests' role in the proceedings for explicit mention.

193. This is the reading adopted by Niese, Naber, and Marcus. Dindorf and Bekker read ἑκάστου with MSPVLat, this yielding the rendering "each of the priests...".

ἐξηγουμένων)¹⁹⁴ and ministering to the multitude (διακαονουμένων [cf. διακονίαν, 10,57] τοῖς ὄχλοις)¹⁹⁵".

The various source accounts of Josiah's Passover all take care to underscore the peculiar character of that observance (23,22-23 // 35,18 // 1,20-21). With its explicit evocation of the figure of Samuel in this connection, Josephus' equivalent notice (10,72b) aligns itself with the two latter Biblical witnesses against the first: "No other festival had been celebrated by the Hebrews in such a manner since the time of the prophet Samuel...¹⁹⁶". To this indication he appends a statement, without source parallel as such, spelling out wherein the unprecedent-edness of Josiah's festival consisted: "... which was due to the fact that everything was carried out in accordance with the laws (κατὰ νόμους) and with the observance (παρατήρησιν)¹⁹⁷ of the fathers' ancient customs (τῆς πατρίου συνηθείας [cf. τὰς συνήθεις ... θυσίας, 10,53])¹⁹⁸".

Thereafter, he rounds off his account of the events of Josiah's 18th year (10,57-73) with a notice (10,73) that highlights the benefits that accrued to the king from the initiatives taken by him in that year, even while it also points ahead to his coming, tragic end: "Now Josiah after this lived in peace (ἐν εἰρήνῃ)¹⁹⁹, and moreover, enjoyed wealth

194. MARCUS, *Josephus*, VI, p. 197, n. e mentions as an alternative rendering of the above Greek phrase "expounding to everyone" (cf. WEILL, *ad loc.* "expliquant à cha-cun"). He goes to suggest that the phrase in question is based on the Lucianic reading in 1 Esdras 1,10, i.e. κατὰ τὴν διαίρησιν.

195. In 35,12-13 it is rather the Levites (see v. 11b) who are depicted as "serving" the people with the burnt offerings the latter are to offer and with the passover lamb (in 1 Esdras 1,12-13 the subject of these actions remains more indeterminate; cf. the mention of both priests and Levites in the preceding 1,10).

196. Compare 35,18αα // 1,20: "No passover like it had been kept in Israel since the days of Samuel the prophet" (Josephus leaves aside the further specification of 35,18αβb // 1,21: "none of the kings of Israel had kept such a passover as was kept by Josiah, and the priests and the Levites, and all Israel and Judah who were present and the inhabitants of Jerusalem" which might seem to conflict with the account given of Hezekiah's Passover in 2 Chronicles 30 = AJ 9,271-272). By contrast 23,22 ("For no such passover had been kept since the days of the judges who judged Israel, or during all the days of the kings of Israel or of the kings of Judah") does not mention Samuel by name.

197. Josephus uses παρατήρησις twice elsewhere: BJ 1,570; AJ 8,96.

198. With the above collocation "according to the laws and... the fathers'... cus-toms", compare 12,303 κατὰ τοὺς νόμους καὶ τὴν πάτριον συνήθειαν. The phrase "fathers' custom(s)" occurs as well in AJ 13,121; 20,263. Josephus has no equivalent, at this juncture – though see 10,57 – to the chronological indication, dating Josiah's Passover to his eighteenth year, of 23,23 // 35,19 // 1,22.

199. This phrase echoes 10,36 where Hezekiah is said to passed all the last fifteen "added" years of his life "in peace (ἐν εἰρήνῃ)". It might likewise be seen as a trans-position into narrative (and at the same time a corrective modification) of Huldah's pre-diction in 22,20 // 34,28: "you shall be gathered to your grave in peace (BL ἐν εἰρήνῃ)"; see n. 121.

(πλούτῳ) and the good opinion (εὐδοξίᾳ)[200] of all men[201], but ended his life in the following manner[202]".

7. Josiah's Death[203]

The sources (23,29aα // 35,20a // 1,25a) relate the advance of Josiah's slayer-to-be, Pharoah Neco, with tantalizing brevity. Josephus (10,74) elaborates: "Nechaō (Νεχαώ)[204], the king of Egypt, *having raised* (ἐγείρας)[205] *an army*[206], marched towards the Euphrates river[207] to make war (πολεμήσων; L 35,20 πολεμῆσαι) on the Medes and the Babylonians[208]

200. The combination "wealth" and "good opinion" occurs only here in Josephus. Compare what is said of Jehoshaphat in 8,394: "... he amassed very considerable wealth (πλοῦτον) and acquired the greatest glory (δόξαν)".

201. The above formulation reads like a application to the case of Josiah of the general principle enunciated by Josephus in *AJ* 1,14: "... men who conform to the will of God, and do not venture to transgress laws that have been excellently laid down, prosper in all things beyond belief, and for their reward are offered by God felicity...". As such, the historian's statement further serves to heighten the shock effect of what follows in which the same Josiah will come to an unhappy end.

202. Like 2 Chronicles (and 1 Esdras), Josephus has no equivalent to the complex of notices (23,24-28) appended in Kings to its account of Josiah's Passover (23,21-23). The historian's non-utilization of this material is understandable on various grounds: Josiah's additional (negative) cultic measures as spoken of in 23,24 read like an afterthought and would not accord with Josephus' tendency to diminish such items. The notice on Josiah's preeminence in v. 25 appears as repetitive of what has already been said of him in 22,2 // 34,2 = *AJ* 10,50. Further, the indications in vv. 26-27 about the Lord's continued determination to destroy Judah due to Manasseh's sins, Josiah's endeavors notwithstanding, would not accord with Josephus' own earlier presentation, inspired by the alternative account in 2 Chronicles 33, of an eventually repentant Manasseh; see 10,41-45. Finally, Josephus dispenses, as usual, with the source notice of 23,28 (// 2 Chr 35,26-27).

203. The discussion in this segment represents a reworking of my article *The Death of Josiah: Josephus and the Bible*, in *ETL* 64 (1988) 157-163, pp. 159-163 which I use here by permission.

204. This is the form of the name found in SPLat (and corresponding to that of LXX) which Dindorf, Bekker, Naber, and Marcus adopt. Niese reads Νεχαῦς with O, while SCHLALIT, *Namenwörterbuch*, p. 90 opts for LaurV's Νεχαώς. In Rabbinic tradition the name "Neco" is understood to mean "the lame one" from the verb נָכָה (it is likewise so rendered in TJ 23,29 and TC 35,20); *Eccl. Rab.* 9.1 (COHEN, *Midrash Rabbah Ecclesiastes*, p. 226) explains his lameness as due to an injury inflicted on him by a lion when the Pharoah improperly attempted to mount Solomon's throne.

205. This is the reading of the codices (apart from P²) which Niese and Marcus follow. Dindorf, Bekker, and Naber read ἀγείρας with P² and Coccejus.

206. With this interjected indication Josephus, in contrast to the sources, makes clear, from the start, that Neco did not, in fact, advance into Palestine all by himself.

207. In common with 23,29 (as well as BL 35,20) Josephus has no equivalent to the specification as to the site on the Euphrates towards which Neco advances, i.e. Carchemish, as cited in both MT 2 Chr 35,20 and 1 Esdras 1,25.

208. In 2 Kgs 23,29 and BL 35,20 Neco's intended opponent to/ against (LXX ἐπί) whom he goes up (+ to fight him, L 35,20) is rather "the king of Assyria". MT 2 Chr 35,20 and 1 Esdras 1,25 have no corresponding specification.

who had overthrown the Assyrian empire (τὴν ... κατέλυσαν ἀρχήν)[209], *for he had the desire to rule Asia*[210]". Neco's advance prompts a counter-move by Josiah, as described in 23,29aβ // 35,20b // 1,25b. Here too, the historian (10,75a) embellishes: "When he [Neco] came to *the city of* Mendē (Μένδην)[211] – *this was in Josiah's kingdom*[212] – the latter came *with an army*[213] *to prevent him from marching against the Medes* [see 10,74] *through his country*[214]".

At this point in their respective accounts of Josiah's death the sources diverge. 2 Kgs 23,29b states laconically and enigmatically: "and Pharoah Neco slew him [Josiah] at Megiddo when he saw him". By contrast, 2 Chr 35,21 // 1 Esdras 1,26-27 first relate an overture by Pharoah to Josiah in which the former claims to be acting under divine auspices and urges his fellow king to desist from trying to impede him. Josephus too (10,75b) tells of such an appeal by the Egyptian, though recasting this in indirect discourse: "So Nechaō sent a herald to him (πέμψας δὲ κήρυκα; compare BL 35,21 ἀγγέλους πρὸς αὐτόν)[215], saying that he was not taking the field against him (οὐκ ἐπ' αὐτὸν στρατεύειν)[216], but was making for

209. This reference to the "overthrow" of Assyria by a Median-Babylonian coalition lacks a parallel in the sources which speak only of Egypt, Assyria, and Judah. The datum, does, however, accord with extra-Biblical historiography which records the coalition's capture of Nineveh, the Assyrian capital, in 612 B.C.; see MARCUS, *Josephus*, VI, p. 198, n. b. It likewise echoes Josephus' own earlier reference in 10,30 to the Medes' "destroying the empire" (ἀρχὴν ... καταλυθῆναι) of the Assyrians during the later reign of Hezekiah, see our discussion of this passage in chap. XVIII.

210. Also this "motivation" for Neco's advance towards the Euphrates has no equivalent in the sources.

211. This is the reading adopted by Dindorf, Bekker, Niese, Naber, and Marcus (who, however, *Josephus*, VI, pp. 198-199, n. c, views the reading as a scribal error for the "Megiddo" [cf. BL's Μαγεδ(δ)ώ] mentioned as the site of Josiah's wounding in 23,29b; so similarly SCHLATTER, *Namen*, p. 71; SCHALIT, *Namenwörterbuch*, p. 90). O reads Μήδην, Lat Medin.

212. This interjected localization of "Mendē" intimates a rationale for Josiah's meeting Neco precisely at this site and attempting to block his further passage there as described in the continuation of 10,75; see above.

213. This (interjected) reference to the "army" accompanying Josiah corresponds to the – likewise interjected – mention of Neco's army in 10,74, both making clear that the two kings did not confront one another alone.

214. With this notice Josephus goes beyond the sources in spelling out Josiah's intent in confronting Neco; compare his – also interjected – indication on the motivation behind Neco's own advance in 10,74 ("for he had the desire to rule Asia").

215. The above phrase is highly reminiscent of that used by Josephus in *AJ* 8,363 where Ben-hadad of Syria πέμψας δὲ κήρυκα πρὸς Ἄχαβον. We will be noting other contacts between Josephus' account of Josiah's death and his earlier story of Ahab's demise (*AJ* 8,398-420).

216. Compare Neco's negative affirmation in 35,21 ("I am not coming against you [Josiah] this day", so MT L [B: "I am not coming against you today to wage war", conflating with what follows, stands closer to Josephus' formulation; see above]) and 1,26 ("I was not sent against you by the Lord God"). Josephus leaves aside Pharoah's obscure

the Euphrates[217], and he bade Josiah not to provoke (παροξύνειν) him into making war on him by preventing (κωλύοντι) him from going where he had made up his mind to go[218]". Continuing their *Ausmalung* of Kings' summary notice on Josiah's slaying (23,29b), 2 Chr 35,22 // 1 Esdras 1,28 both recount the Judean's ignoring of the admonition given him by Neco. They do so, however, with several differences of detail. The former text speaks of Neco's words as coming "from the mouth of God", thereby making the Egyptian a virtual prophet[219]; it likewise mentions Josiah's "disguising himself" – *à la* the reprobate Ahab in 1 Kgs 22,30 – to fight with Neco. The 1 Esdras passage, by contrast, makes no reference to the royal "disguise", just as it has Josiah failing to heed, not the "prophet" Neco, but rather "the words of Jeremiah the prophet from the mouth of the Lord[220]". Josephus' rendition (10,76) agrees, negatively, with 1

opening question ("what have we to do with each other, king of Judah?") as cited in both 35,21 and 1,26.

217. Compare 35,21: "(I am coming) against the house with which I am at war [so MT L; B conflates this phrase with the preceding one; see previous note]. *And God has commanded me to make haste*" and 1,27aβα: "... my war is at the Euphrates [compare Josephus above]. And now the Lord is with me! The Lord is with me, urging me on". Note how Josephus' wording of Neco's statement of his positive intentions eliminates any claim to divine backing by the pagan king. TC 35,21 makes a somewhat similar move, having Neco evoke, not "God" (so MT), but rather "my idol" (טְעָוָתִי) as the one who has enjoined him to "make haste". See next note.

218. Compare Neco's closing admonition in 35,21 ("Cease opposing God, who is with me, lest he destroy you") and 1,27 ("Stand aside, and do not oppose the Lord"). Here again (see previous note), Josephus eliminates any reference to God on the lips of the pagan king (TC 35,21 does likewise, having Neco urge Josiah to "stay away from me and my idol").

219. So MT BL 2 Chr 35,22bα: "He did not listen to the words of Neco from the mouth of God". TC, in accord with its earlier recasting of Neco's invocations of "God" (see nn. 217,218), reformulates here as well: "he did not accept the words of the Lame One [Neco; see n. 204] who had spoken about his idol". Cf. too the plus at the start of TC 35,22: "And when he (Josiah) heard how he [Neco] mentioned his idol, he did not turn back".

220. *Lam. Rab.* 1.17-18, §53 (COHEN, *Midrash Rabbah Lamentations*, pp. 142-144) elaborates on Josiah's non-heeding of Jeremiah as alluded to in 1 Esdras 1,28. According to the Midrash, Jeremiah, on the occasion of Neco's advance, cited to Josiah the words of Isa 19,2 about the Lord's "spurring Egypt against Egypt", this implying that the king ought to leave the overthrow of Egypt to God. In response, Josiah appeals to the higher authority of Moses' word in Lev 26,6 ("neither shall the sword go through your land"). Given that word, Josiah conceives it to be his duty to prevent the "wicked" Neco from traversing his territory. Unbeknowst to Josiah, however, his people have rendered the promise of Lev 26,6 void by their failure to fulfill its condition, i.e. worship of the Lord alone (on the idolatry of Josiah's people and his unwitting failure in supressing this, see n. 169). Accordingly, when Josiah acts to uphold the Leviticus promise, he brings death upon himself at Neco's hands. Somewhat in the same line, though without explicit mention of Jeremiah, is the explanatory plus at the opening of TC 35,23: "Because Josiah had not sought instruction from before the Lord... the Lord of the universe punished him".

Esdras, in saying nothing of Josiah's disguising himself[221]. Over against both source texts, on the other hand, it does not associate Josiah's disastrous ignoring of the warning made him by Pharoah with a divine utterance, mediated either by Neco (so 35,21) or Jeremiah (so 1,28). Rather, the editorial remark Josephus attaches to his mention of the king's persistence in his original plan associates his doing so with an alternative supernatural power, i.e. "Fate"[222]:

> Josiah, however, paid no attention (προσίετο) to Nechaō's request, but acted as if he would not permit him to traverse his territory[223]; *it was Destiny* (τῆς πεπρωμένης)[224], *I believe* (οἶμαι), *that urged him on* (παρορμησάσης) *to this course, in order to have a pretext* (λάβη πρόφασιν)[225] *for destroying him*[226].

In a further amplification of the notice on Josiah's slaying of 2 Kgs 23,29b, 2 Chr 35,22bβ-23 // 1 Esdras 1,29-30 present a miniature battle scene in which the king suffers a mortal wound. Josephus' rendition (10,77a) elaborates with various items designed to accentuate Josiah's energetic, courageous military leadership at this critical moment[227]:

221. This communality does not necessarily entail Josephus' dependence on 1,28 as opposed to 35,22. Rather, the historian, in the interests of portraying the king as a man of courage – a concern that manifests itself in the continuation of his account of Josiah's death, see below – might, with the text of 35,22 before him, well have omitted its detail of Josiah's disguise of his own accord, all the more since he thereby avoids as well the Chronicler's paralleling of Josiah with the wicked Ahab who likewise disguised himself before battle (see above). On the point, see FELDMAN, *Studies*, p. 430 (= ID., *Josiah*, 122).

222. His doing this accords with Josephus' previous eliminations of Neco's invocations of "God" from his version of 35,21 // 1,26-27 in 10,75b; see nn. 217,218. On the import of Josephus' replacement of source references to God by "Fate" as an attempt to resolve the difficulty posed by the bad end of the good king Josiah for the historian's overarching thesis in *AJ* (cf. 1,14) about those who observe God's laws being rewarded with "felicity", see BEGG, *Josiah*, 160-162; FELDMAN, *Studies*, pp. 429-430 (= ID., *Josiah*, 120-121). God, Josephus would be intimating here, had nothing to do with the righteous Josiah's demise – that was the work of a malign "Fate". Of course, such an "explanation" raises problems of its own, i.e. concerning divine omnipotence and the relation between the two powers, God and "Fate". Josephus, however, seems content simply to suggest the above "explanation" without pursuing its implications.

223. The above statement represents an elaboration of the summary source indications on the point: "Nevertheless Josiah would not turn away from him" (35,22aα)/ "But Josiah did not turn back his chariot" (1,28aα).

224. The codices ROM add ἀλαζονείας, this yielding the rendering "fated boastfulness" which MARCUS, *Josephus*, VI, p. 199, n. d avers "hardly makes sense". The plus is left aside by Dindorf, Bekker, Niese, Naber, and Marcus. Josephus' other uses of the verb πόρω are in *AJ* 19,347; *c. Ap.* 1,247.266 (it also appears as a variant in *AJ* 10,89.246).

225. Josephus' one remaining use of this construction is in *AJ* 8,369 where it appears on the lips of Ahab.

226. Similar editorial comments, attributing what happens to an individual king to the operations of some higher power (Fate, God) occur in *AJ* 8,409 (Ahab); 9,199 (Amaziah; see there).

227. On the point, see FELDMAN, *Studies*, p. 430 (= ID., *Josiah*, 122-123).

"For, as he was marshalling his force (διατάσσοντος ... τὴν δύναμιν [cf. μετὰ δυνάμεως, 10,75])[228] *and riding in his chariot* (ἐφ' ἅρματος ... ὀχυμένου)[229] *from one wing to another, an Egyptian archer shot* (τοξεύσας) him[230] *and put an end to his eagerness for battle* (τῆς πρὸς τὴν μάχην σπουδῆς)[231], and, being in great pain from his wound (τῷ τραύματι ... περιαλγής)[232], he ordered the call to be sounded for the army's retreat (ἀνακληθῆναι τὸ στράτευμα)...[233]".

The sources evidence certain divergencies with regard to the immediate sequels to Josiah's "run-in" with Neco. According to 23,30a, the already dead Josiah is brought back from Megiddo in a chariot to Jerusalem where he is buried in his own tomb. 2 Chr 35,24abα has his servants transfer the wounded Josiah to a second chariot for the return to Jerusalem; there – rather than in Megiddo – he expires and is buried in the tombs (so MT, > BL) of his ancestors. Finally 1 Esdras 1,30b-31 adds a preliminary item to the data of 35,24, i.e. Josiah's removal from the line of battle by his servants (v. 30b). Josephus' presentation of these developments (10,77b) clearly follows the account of 35,24 // 1,31 against that of 23,30a, appending to this chronological data inspired by 2 Kgs 22,1 // 2 Chr 34,1 and (partially) "held over" by

228. The above construction occurs only here in Josephus.

229. This construction occurs also in *AJ* 8,186 where the reference is to Solomon. Josephus anticipates his mention of Josiah's "chariot" here from the continuation of the source accounts.

230. 2 Chr 35,23a speaks of "archers" (BL τοξόται) in the plural who "shoot" (BL ἐτόξευσαν) Josiah; elaborating on this datum, Rabbinic tradition (see, e.g., *Lam. Rab.* 1,18-19, §53 [COHEN, *Midrash Lamentations Rabbah*, p. 154] declares that the king was riddled with arrows "like a sieve"). Josephus' single "archer" implicitly assimilates Josiah's wounding to that of Ahab who is "shot" by a lone Syrian bowman according to 1 Kgs 22,34 // 2 Chr 18,33 = *AJ* 8,414 (here, in the line of TC 18,33, Josephus identifies Ahab's "shooter" [τοξεύσας = the form used in 10,77] as "Amanos" = Naaman, one of the pages of Ben-hadad of Syria). 1 Esdras 1,29, for its part, does not mention the actual wounding of Josiah as does 35,23a (= *AJ* 10,77). In place thereof it speaks of "the [Egyptian] commanders coming down against King Josiah".

231. This expression occurs only here in Josephus. His interjected reference to Josiah's (earlier) "eagerness for battle" serves to underscore the king's courage; see n. 227.

232. The term περιαλγής occurs also in *BJ* 1,644; 7,201; *AJ* 2,54; 7,171; 8,273; only here in 10,77, however, is it used in reference to a "wound". The above narrative indication about Josiah's "wound" is inspired by/anticipates the king's words to his retainers in 35,23b: "(Take me away, for) I am badly wounded [BL ἐπόνεσα σφόδρα])"; compare 1,28a: "I am very weak (ἠσθένσα ... λίαν)". It further recalls Josephus' reference to Ahab's "being in great pain" (ὀδυνώμενος) as a result of his arrow-wound in *AJ* 8,415.

233. Josephus' one other use of this phrase is in *AJ* 18,124. In 35,23 // 1,30 Josiah's command (see previous note) concerns his own removal from the battlefield in light of his injury. Josephus' version of the royal command accentuates the king's magnanimity: his concern is not in first place for himself, wounded and in pain as he is, but for his army.

him: "... he returned to Jerusalem²³⁴. There (ἐκεῖ)²³⁵ he died *from his wound* (πληγῆς)²³⁶ and was buried *magnificiently* (μεγαλοπρεπῶς)²³⁷ in the tombs of his fathers (ἐν ταῖς πατρῴαις θήκαις)²³⁸, having lived thirty-nine years²³⁹ of which he reigned thirty-one (so 22,1b // 34,1b)". 2 Kgs 29,30b immediately follows mention of Josiah's burial (v. 30aβ) with a notice on the accession of his son Jehoahaz. In the other two Biblical sources, there intervenes (35,24bβ-25 // 1,32[33]) references to the mourning to which Josiah's death gave rise. The historian reproduces this additional element of the latter witnesses, amplifying it still further. He begins his statements on the subject (10,78a) with allusion to the general mourning evoked by the king's tragic end: "*Great* (μέγα) *was the mourning* (πένθος)²⁴⁰ *observed for him by all the people, who bewailed him and lamented* (ὀδυρομένου [see 10,26.27, of Hezekiah] καὶ κατηφοῦντος)²⁴¹ *for many days*²⁴²". He then continues (10,78b) with a reference to the lament for Josiah authored by Jeremiah: "And the prophet²⁴³ Jeremiah (Ἱερεμίας = LXX)²⁴⁴ composed a song of lament for his funeral

234. Josephus omits the (superfluous) detail of 35,24a // 1,29a about the king's change of chariot which precedes his return to the capital.

235. This is the reading of ROM which Niese, Weill, and Marcus follow. Dindorf, Bekker, and Naber read ἐκείνης with SPLaurV(Lat), this yielding the rendering "(he died) from *that* wound".

236. This noun echoes the adjective περιαλγής used of Josiah's "wound" (τῷ τραύματι) in 10,77a.

237. For Josephus' use of this term in connection with the "burial" of key Biblical figures, see on *AJ* 9,182.

238. In his specification that Josiah was buried in his fathers' *tombs*, Josephus goes together with MT 35,24 and 1 Esdras 1,29b (ἐν τῷ πατρικῷ τάφῷ) against BL 35,24 which simply have him being buried "with his fathers".

239. Josephus arrives at this indication concerning Josiah's life-span by combining the data of 22,1 // 34,1 (Josiah acceded at age 8 [so also 10,48] and ruled 31 years).

240. Josephus' one other use of the phrase "great mourning" is in *AJ* 4,85 (here in connection with Aaron's death).

241. This collocation occurs only here in Josephus.

242. Compare the more summary wording of 35,24bβ ("All Judah and Jerusalem mourned [BL ἐπένθησαν] for Josiah") // 1,32a ("and in all Judea they mourned [ἐπένθησαν] for Josiah"). Josephus' embellishment of the matter serves to heighten the stature of Josiah whose death calls for such intense grieving by all the people. His amplification of the mourning for Josiah has a certain counterpart in *b. Meg.* 3a which cites the mourning for Ahab and Josiah as the two pre-eminent cases of such national grieving in Israel's history.

243. In using this title for Jeremiah Josephus goes together with 1 Esdras 1,32aβ against 35,25aα which mentions him simply by name.

244. This is the first mention of "Jeremiah" in *AJ*; on Josephus' treatment of this prophet and utilization of his book, see the summary discussion of C. WOLFF, *Jeremia im Frühjudentum und Urchristentum* (TU, 118), Berlin, Akademie Verlag, 1976, pp. 10-15 as well as P. PIOVANELLI, *Le Texte de Jérémie utilisé par Flavius Josèphe dans le Xᵉ Livre des Antiquités Judaïques*, in *Henoch* 14 (1992) 11-36, pp. 20-23.

(ἐπικήδειον[245]... μέλος θρηνητίκον[246]), which remains to this day[247]".

Having thus introduced the figure of Jeremiah on the basis of 35,25 // 1,32, Josephus now (10,79-80) appends an extended passage of his own composition providing further information concerning that prophet and his contemporary Ezekiel in preparation for his subsequent account. This reads:

> (79) This prophet [Jeremiah] also announced (προεκήρυξεν)[248] the misfortunes (δεινά) that were to come upon the city [Jerusalem], and left behind writings concerning the recent capture of our city[249], as well as the capture (αἵρεσιν) of Babylon[250]. And not only this prophet

245. This word is hapax in Josephus; it echoes the verb κηδεύεται used in 10,77.

246. This word is bracketed by Niese.

247. The above formulation keeps attention focussed on the prophet and his composition, while also making use of wording drawn from the wider context of the source verses. Compare 35,25aβb ("and all the singing men and singing women have spoken of Josiah in their laments to this day [see Josephus]. They made these an ordinance in Israel; behold they are written in the Laments") // 1,32b ("and the principle men, with the women, have made lamentation for him to this day; it was ordained that this should be done throughout the whole nation of Israel").
According to MARCUS, *Josephus*, VI, p. 200, n. b Josephus, in referring to Jeremiah's "lament" for Josiah as remaining "to this day" here, was basing himself on the mention of written "Laments" at the end of 35,25 which he took to be a reference to the Book of Lamentations, traditionally ascribed to Jeremiah (see *b. B. Bat.* 15a and the title of Lamentations in the LXX). The Chronicler's reference is so understood also in Rabbinic tradition; see GINZBERG, *Legends*, VI, p. 378, n. 122. See also the expanded version of MT 35,25bβ in TC: "behold they are written *in the book which Baruch wrote at Jeremiah's dictation*, in the laments". Further according to WOLFF, *Jeremia*, p. 11 Josephus' mention in *c. Ap.* 1,39 of the 22 books held sacred by the Jews, of which 13 would be the work of prophets, presupposes that the historian regarded our Books of Jeremiah and Lamentation as a single entity.

248. Josephus' two other uses of the verb προκηρύσσω are in *BJ* 4,508; 6,385.

249. MARCUS, *Josephus*, VI, pp. 200-201, n. c rejects the view of V. Ussani for whom the above reference in 10,79 to the Roman seizure of Jerusalem under Titus would be an interpolation. Against that view, Marcus comments: "This suspicion, however, is hardly justified. Josephus naturally thought of the book of Lamentations (which, like his contemporaries, he regarded as Jeremiah's work [see n. 247]) as a prophecy of the capture of Jerusalem by the Romans as well as that by the Babylonians". SCHLATTER, *Theologie*, p. 256, on the contrary, is inclined to view the words in question as an interpolation on the consideration that the extant sequence of 10,79 in which the recent capture of Jerusalem by the Romans is mentioned before the long past event of Babylon's overthrow is "anstössig". WOLFF, *Jeremia*, p. 11, n. 6 rejects this view as "unnecessary".

250. This allusion has in view, e.g., Jeremiah's oracles against Babylon as found in Jeremiah 50-51. The allusion is echoed in *AJ* 10,247 where Josephus states: "And not long afterwards, both he [Belshazzar, King of Babylon] and the city [Babylon] were captured (ἐλήφθη) when Cyrus, the king of Persia, marched against it. For it was in the time of Baltasaros that the capture (αἵρεσιν) of Babylon took place...". Several authors suggest another level of meaning to the allusion here in 10,79, i.e. "Babylon" would be a "code name" for Rome whose eventual overthrow had been predicted by Jeremiah, so SCHLATTER, *Theologie*, p. 256; WOLFF, *Jeremia*, p. 11; PIOVANELLI, *Texte*, 21, n. 40. On

predicted (προεθέσπισε)²⁵¹ these things to the multitude, but also the prophet Ezekiel (Ἰεζεκίηλος; LXX Ἰεζεκιελ)²⁵², who left behind two books (βίβλους)²⁵³ which he was the first (πρῶτος) to write about these matters²⁵⁴. (80) These two men were both priests by birth²⁵⁵, but Jeremiah lived in Jerusalem from the thirteenth year of Josiah's reign until the city *and the temple* were demolished (κατεσκάφη)²⁵⁶.

the whole subject of the use of "Babylon" in reference to Rome, see C.-H. HUNZINGER, *Babylon als Deckname für Rom und die Datierung des 1. Petrusbriefs*, in H.G. REVENT-LOW (ed.), *Gottes Wort und Gottes Land. Hans-Wilhelm Hertzberg zum 70. Geburtstag*, Göttingen, Vandenhoeck & Ruprecht, 1965, 67-77.

251. Josephus uses the verb προθεσπίζω also in *BJ* 4,387.626; 7,349.

252. The Book of Ezekiel itself never applies the title "prophet" to him. Josephus' doing so here is in line with his tendency to introduce "prophetic terminology" where the Bible lacks it.

253. This is the reading adopted by Niese and Marcus. Dindorf, Bekker, and Naber read βιβλία with MSPLaurVEZon.

254. On Josephus' enigmatic reference to Ezekiel's "two books" here, see MARCUS, *Josephus*, VI, p. 201, n. e who, following H.ST.J. THACKERAY, *The Septuagint and Jewish Worship: A Study in Origins*, London, Oxford University Press, ²1923, p. 37, affirms that the historian "probably thought of the book of Ezekiel as composed of two distinct parts of 24 chapters each" (in his *Josephus the Man and the Historian*, rpt., New York, Ktav, 1967, p. 89, St.J. Thackeray suggests another possibility, i.e. the two books in question were originally ascribed, not to Ezekiel, but to Jeremiah, i.e. his prophecy and Lamentations [see n. 247], a supposition which WOLFF, *Jeremia*, p. 12 calls "schlecht möglich" given that Josephus regarded the Book of Jeremiah and Lamentations as a single work [see n. 247]). SCHLATTER, *Theologie*, pp. 252-253, proposes that the reference to Ezekiel's two books might have in view the pseudepigraphical work known as the *Apocryphon of Ezekiel* (on this supposition the reference would constitute a later interpolation).

The above reference to Ezekiel's being the "first" to write about "these matters" is also problematic in that it does not accord either with the relative chronology for Jeremiah and Ezekiel indicated by the Bible (compare Jer 1,2; cf. 36,2 [Jeremiah began receiving divine communications in Josiah's 13th year] and Ezek 1,2 [Ezekiel received his call in the fifth year of Jehoiachin's exile) or with the historian's own statements in 10,93 (in the fifth year of Jehoiakim's rule Jeremiah read the book he had composed about Jerusalem's upcoming misfortunes) and 98 (the "boy" Ezekiel is among those carried into exile along with King Jehoiachin, this following the execution of Jehoiakim). Accordingly, SCHLATTER, *Theologie*, p. 253 questions whether the word "first" in 10,80 derives from Josephus himself. WOLFF, *Jeremia*, p. 12 calls the Ezekiel reference in 10,79b "unverständlich", while PIOVANELLI, *Texte*, 21, n. 40 remarks "nous ignorons comment Josèphe a pu parvenir à établir l'antériorité par rapport à Jérémie...".

In any event, Josephus' mention of the convergence between Jeremiah and Ezekiel in their respective announcements of Jerusalem's coming overthrow exemplifies an important feature of his "prophetology", i.e. its emphasis on the agreement among "true" prophets; see FELDMAN, *Prophets*, pp. 409-410 and *AJ* 10,106-107,141 below.

255. Josephus draws this datum from Jer 1,1 and Ezek 1,3. His singling out of the point for mention reflects his own pride in his priestly ancestry (see *Vita* 1 where that ancestry is the very first thing Josephus has to tell about himself).

256. The above verb κατασκάπτω recurs in connection with the Babylonian "demolishing" of Jerusalem in *AJ* 10,112.146.149. Josephus draws his chronological indications concerning the duration of Jeremiah's ministry here from Jer 1,2-3. In that source text, however, it is not explicitly stated (so Josephus) that Jeremiah lived "in Jerusalem" throughout the 40 years of his ministry. There is likewise no reference in 1,2-3 to the fate of the Temple; Josephus' interjection of such a reference here in 10,80 is in line with his

What happened to this prophet, however, we shall relate in the proper place[257].

Following the above, Biblically unparalleled interlude, Josephus finally comes in 10,81 to relate the accession of Josiah's son Jehoahaz in accord with 23,30b // 36,1 // 1,34. We shall treat this item in our next chapter.

Conclusions: Josephus' Rewriting of 2 Kgs 22,1-23,30a // 2 Chronicles 34-35 (1 Esdras 1,1-33)

A first finding that emerges clearly from the above reading of 10,49-80 is that, in recounting Josiah's reign, Josephus drew on the *Sondergut* of both Biblical presentations concerning it. His dependence on 2 Kings 22-23 can be seen especially in the particulars he supplies (10,65-69 = 23,4-20) regarding Josiah's later reforms, while his utilization of 2 Chronicles 34-35 is evident in his treatment of the king's earlier reforms in Judah and Jerusalem (10,52 = 34,3b-5), Passover observance (10,70-73 = 35,1-19; compare 23,21-23), and death (10,74-80 // 35,20-27; compare 23,29-30). A use by him also of the apocryphal book 1 Esdras (1,1-33) for the last two of these episodes is possible, though in no case does the evidence for this appear compelling (see nn. 194,216,221,238,243).

The indications concerning the text(s) of 2 Kings 22-23 and 2 Chronicles 34-35 employed by Josephus in 10,49-80 showed themselves to be rather meager. His familiarity with an MT-like text of the two passages might be suggested, respectively, by his having Josiah "remove" the "chariot" (10,69 = 2 Kgs 23,11 [compare BL where the king "burns" the chariots]; cf. n. 172) and by his "unspecified" reference to Josiah's twelfth year (10,50 = 34,3 [compare BL: 12th *regnal* year; cf. n. 13]). On the other hand, there are also pointers towards his having a BL-like text (L in particular) of the Biblical segments before him as well; see, e.g., his use of the BL rendering "groves" for MT's "Asherim" (10,52 = 34,3-4 [cf. n. 37]) or his designation of those whom Josiah kills as "priests" (10,65 = L 23,5 [compare MT's הַכְּמָרִים which B simply transliterates; cf. n. 147]); see further nn. 39,73,144.

---

insertion of announcements about the threat facing the Temple into his version of the Biblical Jeremiah's words in what follows; see below.

257. This characteristic Josephan *Vorverweis* looks ahead to the historian's portrayal of the prophet and his fate over the course of the segment AJ 10,89-180; see below. The above complex, 10,79-80, is Josephus' replacement for the "source notices" on Josiah of 35,26-27 // 1,33 (in 2 Kings the corresponding notice stands in 23,28, prior to its account of Josiah's death in 23,29). Josephus habitually leaves such notices aside.

Throughout his account of Josiah, Josephus adds to/expatiates on the sources' data. Instances of his doing so include the following: the opening evaluation of the king (10,49-51; compare 22,2 // 34,2); Josiah's initial reforms in and around Jerusalem (10,52-56; compare 34,3b-5); his charge to the delegation about the book (10,59b; compare 22,13 // 34,21); the opening of Huldah's response (10,60; compare 22,15 // 34,23); the people's reaction to Josiah's obligating of them (10,64); the time-lapse (361 years) between the prophecy made to Jeroboam and its realization (10,67b; compare 23,15-18); Josiah's search of the Israelites' homes for idolatrous objects (10,69a); the clarification concerning the uniqueness of Josiah's Passover (10,72b; compare 23,23 // 35,18); the summation regarding his reign (10,73); the amplification of Neco's advance and Josiah's counter-move (10,74-75a; compare 23,29 // 35,20); the interjected allusions to Josiah's battlefield courage (10,77; compare 23,29bβ // 35,22-23); and the sequence concerning the persons and messages of the prophets Jeremiah and Ezekiel (10,79-80).

The converse procedure, i.e. compressing or deleting source elements, is also much in evidence in Josephus' version of Josiah's reign. Such abridgements manifest themselves particularly in connection with the historian's handling of the king's later reforms (10,65-69; compare 23,4-20) and his Passover celebration (10,70-73; compare 35,1-19). They are also recognizable, however, e.g., in his conflating of the double chronological indication of 34,3 in 10,50; leaving aside the content of 34,6-7 in the interest of avoiding duplication of the parallel material of 23,15-20 (see n. 37); the sequence 23,24-27 (see n. 202), the source notices of 23,28 // 35,26-27; the pagan Pharoah's invocation of God (35,21-22; compare 10,75-76a); the wounded Josiah's transfer of chariots (35,24a); and the male and female singers who mourn the king "to this day" (35,25aβ).

Josephus also ventures to re-arrange the sequence of the source material used by him. He does so most conspicuously in 10,55-56 where the names of the three men whom Josiah, in his 18th year, dispatches to the Temple to see to its repair (34,8) are "anticipated" to the time of the king's 12th year (see 10,50) when he appoints them overseers of the Temple repair funds. Another noteworthy instance of this technique concerns the placement of his parallel to the notice on Josiah's elimination of the chariot(s); in his presentation this stands as the very last of the (later) royal cultic reforms, whereas in the catalogue of such measures in 23,4-20 it comes at midpoint, i.e. as v. 11.

Also prominent in 10,49-80 are the numerous modifications/adaptations of Biblical data. Terminologically, Josephus substitutes (10,63) alternative language for the uses of the key word "covenant" in 23,2-3 // 34,30-32. He adduces (10,57) a different "occasion" for the Temple mission of Josiah's 18th year than do 22,3 // 34,8, this inspired by developments in the time of King Joash. Hilkiah finds "sacred *books*" (10,58), not a single such "book" (compare 22,8 // 34,14). Reference to some of the king's "closest friends" (10,59) replaces the names of the three of the five-member royal delegation (compare 22,12 // 34,20), just as the qualification of Shallum as "a man of high repute and illustrious birth" (10,59) substitutes for the specification concerning his office and his wife's place of residence found in 22,14 // 34,22. The Josephan Josiah (10,59) directs his delegation to approach Huldah in particular rather than simply telling them to "inquire of the Lord" (compare 22,13 // 34,21). The prophetess herself refers to Josiah as "the king" (10,60), instead of "the man" (compare 22,15 // 34,23; cf. n. 103), and promises, not that he will be "gathered to his grave in peace" (so 22,20 // 34,28), but rather that God will delay the impending catastrophe itself for his sake (so 10,61; see nn. 121, 199). The historian specifies the identity ("false prophets") of those whose bones are burned on Jeroboam's altar (10,66); compare the indeterminate wording of 23,16 on the matter. Josiah's iconoclastic measures in "the cities of Samaria" (23,19-20a) are turned into a royal endeavor to persuade escapees from Assyrian exile to return to their ancestral religion (10,68).

Josephus' application of the above rewriting techniques to the Biblical material serves to generate a version of Josiah's reign with a variety of distinctive features. The sources' level of cultic detail is significantly reduced and generalized, this extending not only to Josiah's iconoclastic measures against reprobate religious objects, but also to the right worship manifest in his Passover observance. Throughout 10,49-80 the king's stature is accentuated, both positively and negatively. In particular, Josephus highlights Josiah's precocity, piety, concern for justice, persuasiveness as a teacher of his people, courage and energy on the battlefield, and solicitude for his men even at the point of death. Conversely, the Josephan Josiah is not guilty of disregarding a prophetic word, whether mediated by Neco (so 35,21-22) or Jeremiah (so 1 Esdras 1,28). As a still more preeminent king than his Biblical counterpart, Josiah, in the historian's version, receives as well a funeral and a mourning that surpass those described in the sources.

Josephus' version further stands out in its heightened attention to the prophetic role (see, e.g., the mentions of "prophets" which he interjects into his rendition of Huldah's speech in 10,60-61 and his appendix concerning the prophetic pair Jeremiah and Ezekiel in 10,79-80). Conversely, the Levites' role in the proceedings is generally played down (see nn. 53,66), albeit with occasional exceptions (see n. 125). The historian goes beyond his sources in working explicit references to the topic of intercession as a(n) (im)possibility at this moment of Judah's history into his version of Josiah's charge (see 10,59) and Huldah's word (see 10,60b). He likewise attempts – as the Bible itself does not – to provide some explanation for the good king Josiah's ending up as he does, i.e. by invoking the power of "fate" (10,77). Other unanswered questions and unresolved difficulties suggested by the source accounts are addressed by him as well, e.g., why did the pious king wait so long to begin his reforms (see on 10,50)? Where did the initiative for the collecting of the Temple funds which is presupposed as having taken place by 22,4 // 34,9 come from (see 10,54)? How did the delegation know they were to go to Huldah and why did Josiah sent them specifically to her (see on 10,59)? How could a "true" prophetess like Huldah make the "false" announcement that Josiah would die in peace as she seems to do in 22,20 // 34,28 (see on 10,61)? The passage's integration within its context is furthered by Josephus' introduction of (verbal and/or contentual) reminiscences of earlier happenings (e.g., Jehoshaphat's appointment of judges [10,53b; cf. n. 50]); Joash's initiatives on behalf of the Temple [10,54; cf. n. 67; 10,57; cf. n. 73]; and the confrontation at the Bethel altar in Jeroboam's time [10,67; cf. n. 157]). In the same line, the appendix concerning the prophets Jeremiah and Ezekiel in 10,79-80 sets up what follows which will feature those figures' activities during Judah's final years.

To Gentile Roman readers Josephus' version of Josiah's reign offers a figure who, to an even higher degree than his Biblical namesake, exemplifies the cardinal virtues so valued by them. The historian likewise caters to such readers by diminishing the plethora of cultic details which they would likely find both uninteresting and offensive, even while he elaborates on a matter more congenial to them, i.e. the military confrontration between Josiah and Neco and its political background. Equally congenial to Gentile readers would be Josephus' adducing the concept of "fate" (so 10,76), that figured so largely in their own literature, in explaining Josiah's death.

Josephus' version also has something to offer Jewish readers, however. In particular, its emphasis on the prophetic word as one that finds its sure realization even over the lapse of centuries (the Judean's prophet's message to Jeroboam [see 10,67], Jeremiah's announcement of the Roman overthrow of Jerusalem [see 10,79]) suggests a message of hope for Josephus' compatriots: just as the prophets' oracles of doom for their people had come about in due time, so also will their predictions of deliverance, if only the Jews will be content to wait patiently for this, instead of attempting to take matters into their own hands as they – like Josiah before them – had done recently with such disastrous results.

XXI

JEHOAHAZ, JEHOIAKIM, AND JEHOIACHIN
(10,81-102 + 229-230)

In the period of some 11 1/2 years between the death of Josiah and the accession of its last monarch, Zedekiah, Judah was ruled by three kings, Jehoahaz, Jehoiakim, and Jehoiachin, of whom the first and third both reigned far less than a year. The OT Historical Books provide summary accounts of these three kings in 2 Kgs 23,30b-24,17 (+ 25,27-30) and 2 Chr 36,1-10, the latter passage being largely paralleled in 1 Esdras 1,34-46a. In addition, one finds references to one or other of them in several Prophetic Books, i.e. Jeremiah (*passim*), Ezekiel (1,2; cf. 19:1-14), and Daniel (1,1-2). Josephus presents his composite version of this Biblical source material in 10,81-102 (+ 229-230). Within this segment of *AJ* (and its corresponding Scriptural sources) I distinguish the following units: 1. Jehoahaz (10,81-83a = 2 Kgs 23,30b-35 // 2 Chr 36,1-4 [1 Esdras 1,34-38]); 2. Jehoiakim's Earlier Reign (10,83b-88 = 2 Kgs 23,36-24,1 // 2 Chr 36,5 [1 Esdras 1,39] + Jer 46 [LXX 26],2); 3. Jeremiah under Jehoiakim (10,89-95 = Jeremiah 26 [LXX 33] and 36 [LXX 43]); 4. Jehoiakim's End (10,96-98b = 2 Kgs 24,2-7 // 2 Chr 36,6-8 [1 Esdras 1,40-43a] + Jer 22,19; 36 [LXX 43],30; 52,28 [MT]; cf. Dan 1,1-2); 5. Jehoiachin's Reign (10,98c-102 [cf. *BJ* 6,103-105] = 2 Kgs 24,8-17 // 2 Chr 36,9-10 [1 Esdras 1,43b-46a]) + Jer 52,29 [MT]; Ezek 1,2); and 6. Jehoiachin's Release (10,229-230 = 2 Kgs 25,27-30 // Jer 52,31-34).

1. *Jehoahaz*

Having appended an introductory, Biblically unparalleled notice on the persons and predictions of the prophets Jeremiah and Ezekiel (10,79-80) to his account of Josiah's death and burial (10,74-78) which he drew from 2 Chr 35,20-27 (cf. 2 Kgs 23,29-30a), Josephus resumes his narrative of the Judean succession in 10,81a. He does so by means of a transitional phrase which explicitly links up with the mention of Josiah's dying of his wound in Jerusalem made by him in 10,77b: "*When Josiah died* (τελευτήσαντος; see τελευτᾷ, 10,77b), *as we have already said*, his son, Jōachazos ('Ιωάχαζος)[1] by name, succeeded to

---

1. This is the reading of the codices LaurVE which Dindorf, Bekker, Naber, and Marcus adopt and which SCHALIT, *Namenwörterbuch*, p. 65 calls "quite possibly original". Niese

the kingdom[2] in his twenty-third year (so 23,31aα // 36,2a // 1 Esdras 1,34)[3]". He then continues (10,81b) with *personalia* for the new king, here evidencing his dependence on the more expansive 2 Kgs 23,31b-32 and/or BL 2 Chr 36,2aβ as against MT 2 Chronicles 36 and 1 Esdras 1 which lack an equivalent to the former witnesses' additional data. His version of these data reads: "And so he reigned in Jerusalem[4], his mother being Amitalē ('Αμιτάλης)[5] of (ἐκ)[6] *the city of* Lobanē (Λόβανης)[7]; he was of an impious and corrupt (ἀσεβὴς ... καὶ μιαρός)[8] nature[9]".

and SCHLATTER, *Namen*, 54 opt rather for the form Ἰώαζος of RO. Compare MT יְהוֹאָחָז; Ἰωαχάς (BL 23,30b, etc); Ἰωαχάζ (BL 36,1, etc.); Ἰεχονίαν (i.e. the same name as the later king Jehoiachin/Jechoniah, 1 Esdras 1,34). In Jer 22,11 (and, apparently, 1 Chr 3,15) he is called "Shallum", possibly his pre-regnal name. Note, however, that in *b. Hor.* 11b and *y. Šeqal.* 6.1 "Shallum" is identified with Zedekiah, while Jehoahaz is equated rather with the first of the sons of Josiah listed in 1 Chr 3,15, i.e. (the otherwise unknown) Johanan.

2. With this formulation Josephus leaves unmentioned the circumstances of Jehoahaz' succession as (summarily) reported in the Biblical accounts. Compare 2 Kgs 23,30b (and BL 2 Chr 36,1) which reports that "the people of the land took Jehoahaz... and anointed him and made him king in his father's stead" (in MT 36,1 the detail about the "anointing" of Jehoahaz is absent, as is also the case in 1 Esdras 1,34 which ascribes Jehoahaz' accession to the initiative of "the men of the nation"). Josephus' non-reference to the role of "the people of the land" here might reflect his "anti-democratic" tendency and/or the disrepute into which this phrase had fallen (see on 9,204; 10,48). On the reason for the exceptional "anointing" of Jehoahaz as reported in 23,30b, see, e.g., *Lev. Rab.* 10.8 [ISRAELSTAM and SLOTKI, *Midrash Rabbah Leviticus*, p. 132]: this was done in recognition of the "irregularity" of Jehoahaz' succession given that he was not, in fact, his father's eldest son – on this point see further below and n. 16. Compare *b. Hor.* 11b which asserts that Jehoiakim, Josiah's first-born, was passed over for the succession due to his "unworthiness".

3. In line with his standard practice, Josephus reserves his equivalent to the sources' immediately following mention (23,31aβ // 36,2b // 1 Esdras 1,35a) of Jehoahaz' length of reign to the end of his account of this king; see 10,83a.

4. Josephus derives this indication about where Jehoahaz reigned from the notices of 2 Kgs 23,31aβ // 2 Chr 36,2b (cf. 1 Esdras 1,35a which reads "he reigned three months in *Judah and* Jerusalem") concerning his length of reign. See previous note.

5. Compare חֲמוּטַל (MT 23,31; many MSS read חֲמִיטַל); 'Αμιτάλ (L 23,31 // 36,2a); 'Αμειταί (B 23,31); 'Αβειτάλ (B 36,2a). In line with his usual practice, Josephus omits the name of the queen mother's father, i.e. "Jeremiah" (so MT 23,31).

6. This is the conjecture of Niese, inspired by the "de" of Lat, which Naber and Marcus follow. Dindorf and Bekker retain the καί of the Greek codices.

7. This is the conjecture of J. Hudson, followed by Dindorf, Bekker, Niese (who further proposes to add γεγονώς after it), Naber, and Marcus for the various forms found in the witnesses, all of which have an initial τ (e.g., Tomanē, Tomianē). SCHLATTER, *Namen*, p. 70 regards the form Λάβανης as equally possible, while SCHALIT, *Namenwörterbuch*, p. 79 asks whether Lat's Thobana might not reflect a θωβανή (= Hebrew תְּבְנָה) in Josephus' *Vorlage*. Compare לִבְנָה (MT 23,31); Λημνά (B 23,31); Λοβενά (B 36,2a); Λοβεννά (L 23,31 // 36,2a).

8. Josephus' one other use of the above collocation is in *AJ* 13,316 where Aristobulus I recognizes that he was "not destined to escape the notice of God in committing such impious and unholy (ἀσεβέσιν ... καὶ μιαροῖς) crimes".

9. The above judgment notice takes the place of the stereotyped phrase of 23,32 (and BL 36,2b), i.e. "and he (Jehoahaz) did what was evil in the sight of the Lord, according to all that his fathers had done".

Jehoahaz' reign was quickly cut shut by Pharoah Neco who removed him from office. Josephus' rendition of this development – here too – aligns itself with the more elaborate account found in MT BL 2 Kgs 23,33a (and BL 36,2c) *contra* that of MT 36,3a and 1 Esdras 1,35b which simply state that (an unnamed) "king of Egypt disposed him [Jehoaz] (+ from reigning, 1 Esdras) in Jerusalem". At the same time, the historian (10,82a) also introduces several expansions regarding Jehoahaz' deposition peculiar to himself: "Now the king of Egypt[10], *returning from the battle* (τῆς μάχης)[11], *summoned Jōachazos to him*[12] *at the city called* Amatha ('Αμαθά) which is in Syria (τῆς Συρίας)[13], *and, when he came*[14], put him in chains (ἔδησε)...[15]".

As the sequel to Pharoah's deposition of Jehoahaz, Josephus' sources all relate, first, the Egyptian's imposition of tribute (23,33b // 36,3b // 1,36) and then his appointment of Jehoiakim as replacement king (23,34

10. 2 Kgs 23,33a and BL 36,2c give his proper name, i.e. "Neco" (Greek Νεχαώ), likewise using the title "Pharoah" for him. Josephus' designation corresponds to that of MT 36,3a and 1 Esdras 1,35; see above. Recall that he does cite Neco by name in 10,74-76; the king's proper name will recur in 10,85; see below.

11. It is not immediately clear which "battle" Josephus has in mind here – is it that between Neco and Josiah spoken of in 10,77 (where the wounded Judean is said to have lost his "eagerness for battle" [πρὸς τὴν μάχην]) or rather, the one between the former and the Medes and Babylonians against whom Neco is said to be advancing in 10,75 when intercepted by Josiah (but which is never related as such in Josephus' subsequent presentation)? The fact, however, that in the continuation of 10,82 (see above) the "returning" Neco summons Jehoahaz to himself at "Amatha" (= Biblical Hamath; see p. 486, n. 211) in Syria, i.e. a site far to the north of "Mendē" (= Biblical Megiddo?; see above) where the Neco-Josiah conflict took place according to 10,75, lends credence to the latter possibility. Such a battle between the Egyptians (along with the Assyrians) and the Babylonians at Haran (with the latter emerging victorious) is recorded in the "Babylonian Chronicle" for the year 610 B.C.; see *ANET* (1969²), p. 303.

12. With this insertion Josephus provides an answer to the question suggested by the Biblical accounts of Jehoahaz' deposition by Pharoah, how did Neco get Jehoahaz – who was reigning "in Jerusalem" (so 2 Kgs 23,31 // 2 Chr 36,2b = 10,81) – into his power in the first place?

13. In the Biblical witnesses the site where Jehoahaz is deposed is called variously "Riblah in the land of Hamath" (so MT 23,33); 'Αβαλαά ἐν γῇ 'Εμάτ (B 23,33); Δεβλαθά ἐν γῇ Αἱμάθ (L 23,33; cf. Αἱμαθ, L 36,2c); Δαβλαθά ἐν γῇ 'Ιεμάθ (B 36,2c). It appears that Josephus took the Biblical country name(s) as that of a city ("Amatha"), substituting this for the sources' "Riblah", etc., and then supplied a new country name ("Syria") of his own as its locale. Compare his handling of the Biblical mention of "Hamath" in 9,206.

14. This indication represents the continuation/completion of Josephus' earlier insertion about Neco's summoning Jehoahaz to himself; see n. 12.

15. Among the Biblical witnesses Jehoahaz' "binding" by Neco is mentioned only by MT 23,33 and BL 36,2c (the latter witnesses use the same aorist form in reference to this happening as does Josephus; see above). In contrast to all his sources Josephus does not speak of an actual "deposition" of Jehoahaz by Pharoah, this being obviously implied, however, by his immediately following notice on the Egyptian's appointment of a new king over Judah; see below.

// 36,4 // 1,37). Likely on the consideration that regulating the Judean succession would be a matter of greater urgency to Pharoah than fixing the tribute to be paid him, Josephus (10,82b) gives the former point prior mention: "... and gave the kingdom over to his [Jehoahaz'] *elder* brother[16] by the same father, after changing his name, which was Eliakeimos ('Ελιακείμῳ)[17], to Jōakeimos ('Ιωάκειμον)[18]". In thereafter relating the fine fixed by Pharoah, Josephus (10,82c) follows the figures given in MT 23,33b // 36,3b (MT BL) // 1 Esdras 1,36 (most MSS) in contrast to those of BL 23,33b: "He [Neco] also imposed on the country a tribute of one hundred talents of silver and one talent of gold[19]".

2 Kgs 23,34b-35 (and BL 36,4) relate two further sequels to Neco's deposition of Jehoahaz, i.e. his removal of the latter to Egypt (v. 34b) and Jehoiakim's payment of the tax imposed by him according to v. 33b (v. 35)[20]. Here too, Josephus (10,83a) reverses the source's sequence[21]: "And this sum of money [see 10,82c] Jōakeimos paid[22]. As for Jōachazos, he carried him off to Egypt, which was where he died after reigning three months *and ten days*[23]".

16. The sources do not mention the age relationship between Jehoiakim and Jehoahaz as such. Josephus derives the datum by way of a comparison of the princes' ages as given in 23,31, etc. (Jehoahaz was *23* at his accession) and 23,36 (Jehoiakim was *25* at his, three months later; cf. 23,31). E.g., *SOR* 24.7 (GIRÓN BLANC, *Seder 'Olam Rabbah*, p. 115) makes explicit reference as well to Jehoiakim's being Jehoahaz' older brother. See further n. 2.

17. This is the declined form of the name as found in BL 23,34 // 36,4, i.e. 'Ελιακείμ. Compare MT אֶלְיָקִים. 1 Esdras 1,37 does not mention Jehoiakim's pre-regnal name.

18. This is the declined form of the name as given in BL 23,34 // 36,4 // 1 Esdras 1,37, i.e. 'Ιωακείμ. Compare MT יְהוֹיָקִים.

19. In B 23,33b Neco stipulates *100* gold talents (i.e. the same figure as for the silver talents) while in L 23,33 (and one MS of 1 Esdras 1,36) he demands *10* of them.

20. MT 36,4b mentions only the former point (also omitting reference to Jehoahaz' "dying" in Egypt as cited in 23,34b and BL 36,4). 1 Esdras 1, for its part, says nothing of Jehoahaz' being deported to Egypt, while in place of Jehoiakim's payment to Neco as reported in 23,35, its v. 38 states "Jehoiakim put the nobles in prison, and seized his brother Zarius [Zedekiah?] and brought him up out of Egypt".

21. Thereby he keeps together the financial indications of vv. 33b and 35 which in 2 Kings 23 are separated by notices on the appointment of Jehoiakim and the deportation of Jehoahaz of v. 34.

22. With the above notice Josephus limits himself to the fact of Jehoiakim's paying the required tribute. He leaves aside the circumstantial indications of 23,35 as to how he contrived to do this, i.e. by taxing "the people of the land" (recall Josephus' non-mention of this group's role in the succession of Jehoahaz in his version of 23,30b // 36,1 in 10,81).

23. Josephus draws the datum about Jehoahaz' three month reign from 23,31b // 36,2b. The "extra" ten regnal days which he assigns to him seems to reflect the historian's "confounding" of Jehoahaz with his nephew Jehoiachin to whom 2 Chr 36,9 // 1 Esdras 1,44 (and Josephus himself; see 10,98); so WEILL, *Josèphe*, II, p. 318, n. 9 and following him MARCUS, *Josephus*, VI, p. 203, n. g. Given the similarity both in the names of Judah's final kings and the fates which befell them, such "confusion" is not surprising.

2. Jehoiakim's Earlier Reign

The (Biblical) narratives give their summary, overall indications concerning Jehoiakim in 23,36-37 // 36,5 // 1 Esdras 1,39, while 2 Kgs 24,1 appends mention of his submission to Nebuchadnezzar for a period of three years during the course of the Judean's 11-year reign[24]. Josephus' initial presentation of Jehoiakim (10,83b-88) is considerably more expansive, drawing, as it does, also on the wording of Jer 46 (LXX 26),2.

Reserving the chronological data of 23,36a // 36,5a on Jehoiakim for a later point (see 10,98), the historian limits himself at this juncture (10,83b) to mention of the king's mother (= 23,36b and BL 36,5; no parallel in MT 36,5 or 1 Esdras 1) and an evaluation of him (= 23,37 // 36,5b.8 ["the abominations which he did"] // 1 Esdras 1,39b.42 ["his uncleanness and impiety"]). He words these items as follows: "Now the mother of Jōakeimos was called Zabūda (Ζαβούδα)[25], and she came from *the city of Abūma* ('Αβουμᾶς)[26]. He proved to be unjust and wicked (ἄδικος καὶ κακοῦργος)[27] by nature, and was neither reverent towards God (πρὸς θεὸν ὅσιος)[28] nor kind to man (πρὸς ἀνθρώπους ἐπιεικής)[29]".

Compare, e.g., 1 Esdras 1,34 which speaks of "Jeconiah", rather than his uncle Jehoahaz, as Josiah's immediate successor (see n. 1). Compare the fragment of Eupolemus preserved in Eusebius' *Ecclesiastical History* 9.39.1, who, in his account of Judah's final years, appears to conflate the figures of kings Jehoiakim, Jehoiachin, and Zedekiah, giving to this composite ruler the name of "Jonachim". Cf. B.Z. WACHOLDER, *Eupolemus: A Study of Judaeo-Greek Literature*, Cincinnati, Hebrew Union College – Jewish Institute of Religion, 1974, pp. 227-228.

24. On the varying nuances to the portrayal of the "bad" king Jehoiakim in the different Biblical witnesses (and in Josephus), see S. DELAMARTER, *The Vilification of Jehoiakim (A.K.A. Eliakim and Joiakim) in Early Judaism*, in C.A. EVANS and J.A. SANDERS (eds.), *The Function of Scripture in Early Jewish and Christian Tradition* (JSNTSup, 154/ SSEJC, 6), Sheffield, Sheffield Academic Press, 1998, 190-204.

25. Compare זְבִידָה (*ketiv*, 23,36); זְבוּדָה (*qere*); Ἰελλά (B 23,36); Ἀμιτάλ (L 23,36 // 36,5); Ζεχωρά (B 36,5). Josephus' form stands closest to that of MT's *qere*. As in the case of Jehoahaz, Josephus omits mention of the king's maternal grandfather, i.e. Pedaiah (MT 23,36b).

26. SCHLATTER, *Namen*, p. 102 and SCHALIT, *Namenwörterbuch*, p. 3 maintain that the above form is the corruption of an original 'Αρουμᾶς. Compare רוּמָה (MT 23,36); Κρουμά (B 23,36); Λοβεννά (L 23,36 // 36,5); Ῥαμά (B 36,5). As MARCUS, *Josephus*, VI, p. 203, n. 1 points out, the L MSS in 23,31 // 36,2 and 23,36 // 36,5 make both Jehoahaz and Jehoiakim sons of "Amital, daughter of Jeremiou, from Lobenna".

27. Josephus' one other use of this collocation is in *Vita* 290 where it is applied to his opponent Ananias.

28. This precise expression occurs only here in Josephus; compare 14,257 where the people of Halicarnassus are quoted as affirming of themselves "(we at all times have a deep regard) for piety toward the Deity and holiness (τὸ πρὸς τὸ θεῖον εὐσεβὲς καὶ ὅσιον)".

29. The above construction is hapax in Josephus. With the historian's statement concerning Jehoiakim's stance towards God and his fellows here, compare what he says of the Davidid Jotham in 9,236, i.e. "he was pious towards God (εὐσεβὴς ... τὰ πρὸς τὸν

At this juncture Josephus pauses in his reproduction of the Historical Books' summary notices on Jehoiakim in order to make mention (10,84-86) of a first success achieved by Judah's future nemesis, Nebuchadnezzar, at the outset of the Babylonian's long career. In constructing this interlude, he draws on two disparate passages of the Book of Jeremiah, i.e. 25,1 (MT; here Jehoiakim's 4th year is identified with the first year of Nebuchadnezzar) and 46 (LXX 26),2 (Nebuchadnezzar defeats Neco in Jehoiakim's 4th year), as well as on 2 Kgs 24,7b (the Babylonian conquers all Egyptian territory "from the Brook of Egypt to the river Euphrates"). This new Josephan segment opens with mention (10,84) of an expedition undertaken by Nebuchadnezzar at the start of his reign: "In the fourth year of his [Jehoiakim's] reign someone (τις)[30] called Nebuchadnezzar (Ναβουχοδονόσορος)[31] became ruler of the Babylonians[32] and *at the same time went up with a great armament* (μετὰ μεγάλης παρασκευῆς)[33] *against the city of* Karchamissa (Καρχαμισσάν)[34] – this is on the Euphrates river (πρὸς τῷ Εὐφράτῃ

θεόν) and just towards men (δίκαιος ... τὰ πρὸς ἀνθρώπους)". The whole above evaluation takes the place of the stereotyped judgment formula of 23,37, etc. ("and he [Jehoiakim] did what was evil in the sight of the Lord, according to all that his fathers had done"). On the various specific offenses alleged against Jehoiakim in Rabbinic/ Christian tradition (e.g., wearing of prohibited mixtures, incest even with his mother, disguising of his circumcision, tatooing of his body in violation of the prohibition of Deut 14,1), see *Lev. Rab.* 19.6 (ISRAELSTAM and SLOTKI, *Midrash Rabbah Leviticus*, pp. 246-247); *Midr. Tanhuma (B)* 7.14 (J.T. TOWNSEND, tr., *Midrash Tanhuma*, I. *Genesis*, Hoboken, NJ, Ktav, 1989, pp. 188-189); Pseudo-Jerome on 2 Chr 36,8 (PL 23, cc. 1401-1402).

30. This term is absent in RO and omitted by Niese. According to MARCUS, *Josephus*, VI, p. 203, n. i: "Josephus appears to use τις 'someone' as a tacit apology to Greek readers for the uncouth form of the Babylonian king's name".

31. According to NIESE, *Opera*, I, pp. xx-xxi the above form of the king's name (which is also adopted by SCHALIT, *Namenwörterbuch*, p. 89) represents a scribal assimilation to the form found in the LXX (see below); Josephus himself would have written Ναβοκοδρόσορος. SCHLATTER, *Namen*, p. 78, proposes reading Ναβουχαδανασσαρος. Compare נְבוּכַדְרֶאצַּר (MT Jeremiah); נְבוּכַדְנֶאצַּר (MT Kings and Chronicles); Ναβουχοδονοσόρ (LXX Kings, Chronicles, and Jeremiah). On the figure of Nebuchadnezzar in Jewish, Christian, and Muslim tradition generally see: S.G. BERNSTEIN, *König Nebucadnezar von Babel in der jüdischen Tradition*, Berlin, Itzkowski, 1907.

32. In thus correlating the start of Nebuchadnezzar's reign with Jehoiakim's fourth regnal year, Josephus bases himself on the indication to that effect found in MT (but not LXX) Jer 25,1 (*SOR* 24.10 [GIRÓN BLANC, *Seder 'Olam Rabbah*, p. 116) makes the same correlation, likewise dating Nebuchadnezzar's conquest of Nineveh to the year in question). On this and subsequent correlations made by Josephus between the regnal years of Nebuchadnezzar and those of his Judean counterparts, see H. GRAETZ, *Das Datum der Schlacht bei Kharkhemisch und der Beginn der chaldäischen Herrschaft über Judäa*, in *MGWJ* 23 (1874) 289-308; PIOVANELLI, *Texte*, 24-27.

33. This is the same phase used in *AJ* 10,1 in connection with Sennacherib's invasion of Judah; the verbal echo here in 10,84 serves to underscore the parallelism between Sennacherib and Nebuchadnezzar as the two greatest threats to Judah's existence in its history.

34. Compare כַּרְכְּמִשׁ (MT 46,2); Χαρχαμις (LXX 26,2).

ποταμῷ[35])[36] – *with the determination to make war* (πολεμεῖν) *on the Egyptian king Nechaō, to whom all Syria was subject*[37]". To this statement he appends a corresponding notice (10,85), peculiar to himself, concerning Pharoah's counter-move: "When Nechaō [see 10,74-76; cf. n. 10) learned of the Babylonian king's purpose and the expedition against him, he himself did not show indifference but set out (ὥρμησεν)[38] for the Euphrates with a large force (σὺν πολλῇ χειρί; cf. μετὰ μεγάλης παρασκευῆς, 10,84) to oppose (ἀμυνούμενος)[39] Nebuchadnezzar[40]". Thereafter, the historian picks up again (10,86) on the wording of Jer 46,2 in narrating the rout of the Egyptians, the sequels to which he then proceeds to relate on the basis of 2 Kgs 24,7b (see n. 44): "In the engagement that took place he [Neco] was defeated (ἡττήθη)[41] *and lost many myriads in the battle*[42]. Then the Babylonian king *crossed the Euphrates* [see 10,84] and occupied all Syria [compare 10,84 where "all Syria" is said to be subject to Neco], *with the exception of Judaea*[43], as far as Pelusium [cf. 10,17-19: Pelusium as the Egyptian site from which Sennacherib was forced to withdraw according to Herodotus][44]".

35. This word is absent in the codices MSPLaurV and omitted by Dindorf, Bekker, and Naber.

36. Compare LXX 26,2 ἐπὶ τῷ ποταμῷ Εὐφράτῃ.

37. The italicized elements in the above sequence represent Josephus' embellishments of the notice of Jer 46,2, indicating, e.g., the purpose of Nebuchadnezzar's initiative. Josephus would have inferred that "all Syria" was indeed "subject" to Neco at the moment given the mention of his "binding" of Jehoahaz "at Riblah in the land of Hamath" (i.e. in Northern Syria) in 2 Kgs 23,33 (cf. 10,82). The wording of the above notice on the aim of Nebuchadnezzar's advance recalls – Josephus' likewise inserted – indication on the purpose of Neco's own march "towards the Euphrates river" in 10,74, i.e. "to make war (πολεμήσων) on the Medes and Babylonians…".

38. This is the reading of ROM which Niese and Marcus adopt. Dindorf, Bekker, and Naber read ἐξώρμησεν with SPLaurV.

39. This is the emendation of Coccejus which Dindorf, Bekker, Naber, and Marcus follow. Niese reads ἀμυνόμενος with the codices.

40. The effect of the above insertion, with its reference to Neco's vigorous response and the large force mobilized by him, is to heighten the magnitude of the victory which Nebuchadnezzar nonetheless wins over him in what follows. It likewise recalls the (unsuccessful) earlier effort made by Josiah to impede Neco's own advance (see 10,75). Now Neco's own attempt at "interception" will end in failure.

41. Compare Jer 46(26),2: "the army of Pharoah Neco… which Nebuchadnezzar… defeated (LXX ἐπάταξε)…".

42. The above phrase represents Josephus' *Ausmalung* of the notice of 46,2 ("About Egypt. Concerning the army of Pharoah Neco… which was by the river Euphrates at Carchemish and which Nebuchadenazzar… defeated in the fourth year of Jehoiakim…"). On the other hand, in line with his usual procedure regarding Biblical poetic texts, he makes no use, as such, of the "taunt song" of 46,3-12 to which 46,2 itself serves as title.

43. Josephus inserts this qualification concerning the extent of Nebuchadnezzar's conquests in view of what follows where Judah will appear as still independent.

44. The above notice on the immediate sequel to Nebuchadnezzar's victory would appear to constitute Josephus' anticipation/adaptation of the remark of 2 Kgs 24,7 that the

Josephus rounds off his opening presentation of Nebuchadnezzar with a (markedly expanded) version (10,87-88) of the notice of 2 Kgs 24,1 (+ 24,7a) concerning Jehoiakim's submission to Nebuchadnezzar and eventual defection from him. It reads:

> (87) *In the fourth year of Nebuchadnezzar's reign, which was the eighth year of Jōakeimos's rule*[45] *over the Hebrews*[46], the Babylonian king marched *against the Jews* ('Ιουδαίους)[47] *with a large force* (μετὰ πολλῆς δυνάμεως; compare μετὰ μεγάλης παρασκευῆς, 10,84)[48], *demanding tribute of Jōakeimos under threat* (ἀπειλῶν) *of war*[49]. And so he, *being alarmed at*

king of Egypt remained in his own land "for the king of Babylon had taken all that belonged to the king of Egypt from the Brook of Egypt [Pelusium, so Josephus, being located in general proximity to this at the northeastern boundary of Egypt] to the river Euphrates [i.e. thus encompassing all Syria; see 10,86]".

In *AJ* 10,220-221a and again in *c. Ap.* 1,135 Josephus cites the testimony of Berosus concerning the beginnings of Nebuchadnezzar's career. In the Babylonian historian's account "Neco" appears as "the satrap in charge of Egypt, Coele-Syria and Phoenicia" (compare 10,84 where the – historically accurate – title "king of Egypt" is used of him) who revolts against his overlord Nabopolassar, Nebuchadnezzar's father. Moreover, it is while he is still crown-prince, rather than when already king (so 10,83), that Nebuchadnezzar wins his victory – the site of which is not mentioned – and so brings the rebel Neco's territory under Babylonian rule. In this instance, Josephus does not see fit either to harmonize the Bible's (Jer 46,2) account of Nebuchadnezzar's first victory (followed by him in 10,84-86) with the report of this happening given by Berosus (and quoted by him in 10,220-221a and *c. Ap.* 1,135). Nor does he find it necessary, with the Biblical record in view, to call attention to the pagan historian's "mistakes" (see above) – as he does, e.g., with Herodotus (see *AJ* 8,260; 10,19).

45. 2 Kgs 24,1 provides only the vaguest of datings ("in his [Jehoiakim's] days") for the Babylonian advance which resulted in Jehoiakim's submission. In placing this development in Jehoiakim's 8th regnal year, Josephus seems to have in view the indications of 24,1aβ (Jehoiakim "served Nebuchadnezzar for *three* years") and 23,36aβ (he reigned a total of *eleven* years). On the assumption that the three years of Jehoiakim's "service" were the last ones of his eleven-year reign, Josephus thus dates the beginning of his service to the king's eighth regnal year. Having fixed this figure, he further proceeds to date the Judean's submission to Nebuchadnezzar's own fourth regnal year, here basing himself on his earlier mention (10,83) of the Babylonian's accession in Jehoiakim's fourth year, i.e. four years prior to Nebuchadnezzar's advance against Judah. Compare *Pirqe R. El.* 49.3 (PÉREZ FERNÁNDEZ, *Los capítulos de Rabbí Eliezer*, p. 342) which dates Nebuchadnezzar's subjugation of Jehoiakim to the year in which the former became king, correlating this with the Judean's *third* regnal year in accordance with Dan 1,1.

46. Here, "Hebrews" would seem to be used as a synonym for "Judeans", the nation over whom Jehoiakim, in fact, ruled. See next note.

47. Note the rapid shift of designation for the people in question from "Hebrews" just previously to "Jews" here; see previous note.

48. This inserted mention of the "large force" accompanying Nebuchadnezzar would help account for the alacrity with which Jehoiakim submits to him as related in 24,1.

49. By means of this added element Josephus provides an indication of the purpose behind Nebuchadnezzar's advance (i.e. exortion of tribute), which advance appears unmotivated in the source. The whole above sentence is the historian's amplified rendering of the summary wording of 24,1aα: "in his [Jehoiakim's] days the king of Babylon came up...". Cf. 9,275 where an unnamed Assyrian king "threatens" (ἠπείλει) to subjugate Hezekiah's realm unless he pays the tribute his father had.

this threat (δείσας τὴν ἀπειλήν)[50], *purchased peace* (τὴν εἰρήνην ἀντικαταλλαξάμενος)[51] by paying the money, and for three years brought him the tribute which he had imposed[52]. (88) *But in the third* (τρίτῳ)[53] *year, having heard that the Egyptians were marching against the Babylonian king*, he did not pay him tribute[54]. *However, he was disappointed of his hopes* (διεψεύσθη τῆς ἐλπίδος)[55], *for* the Egyptians did not venture to undertake the campaign[56].

50. This construction occurs also in *BJ* 1,200. With it Josephus provides a motivation, lacking in the source, for Jehoiakim's act of submission. It echoes the reference to Hezekiah remaining in Jerusalem "out of cowardice" (ὑπὸ δειλίας) in 10,5; cf. 8,259 where Rehoboam admits Shishak to Jerusalem "because he feared (διὰ τὸν φόβον) him". Contrast 9,276 where Hezekiah gives "no thought" to the Assyrian "threat" should he fail to pax tribute (see previous note).

51. The above construction is hapax in Josephus; he uses the verb ἀντικαταλλάσσομαι also in *BJ* 3,204; cf. 5,427 where it appears as a variant.

52. The above sentence is Josephus' elaboration/concretization of the more general language employed in 24,1aβ: "and Jehoiakim became his servant three years", spelling out what Jehoiakim's "service" primarily entailed, i.e. tribute-paying.

53. NIESE, *ad loc.* tentatively suggests emending this dating to τετάρτῳ (cf. the reference to Jehoiakim's *fifth* year in 10,93).

54. Here again, Josephus expatiates, while also modifying in accord with his own earlier presentation, the summary notice of 24,1b: "then he [Jehoiakim] turned and rebelled against him [Nebuchadnezzar]". In particular, he provides a motivation for Jehoiakim's deed (his hearing of the – false, see below – rumor of an Egyptian advance) and elucidates wherein his "rebellion" consisted. Various authors make a connection between Josephus' above notice about a (rumored) Egyptian advance against Nebuchadnezzar and various ancient references to an Egyptian military success. The references in question are found in the Bible, i.e. Jer 47,1 (LXX 29,1) ("the word of the Lord that came to Jeremiah the prophet concerning the Philistines, before Pharoah smote Gaza [so MT; the corresponding LXX 29,1 reads simply "concerning the Philistines"]), and in extra-Biblical literature, i.e. "The Babylonian Chronicle" (see D.J. WISEMAN, *Chronicles of Chaldean Kings (626-556 B.C.) in the British Museum*, London, British Museum, 1956, p. 71: here there is mention of a battle between the Babylonians and the Egyptians which caused severe losses to both sides with the result that the former returned to Babylon) and Herodotus, *Histories* 2.159 (GODLEY, *Herodotus*, I, pp. 472-473) who states that Neco "met and defeated the Syrians at Magdolus, taking the great city of Cadytis [= Gaza] after the battle". On the subject see E. LIPINSKI, *The Egypto-Babylonian War of the Winter 601-602 B.C.*, in *AION* 32 (1972) 235-241; H.J. KATZENSTEIN, *"Before Pharoah Conquered Gaza" (Jeremiah XLVII 1)*, in *VT* 33 (1983) 249-251; and B. HUWYLER, *Jeremia und die Völker. Untersuchungen zu den Völkersprüchen in Jeremia 46-49* (FAT, 20), Tübingen, Mohr Siebeck, 1997, pp. 142-145 (he leaves the question of what event is being referred to in the concluding words of MT Jer 47,1 – see above – open).

55. Elsewhere Josephus uses (a variant of) this construction one other time, i.e. in *AJ* 9,40; see there.

56. Josephus draws the above explanation ("for") of the reason for Jehoiakim's "disappointment" (and clarification concerning the falsity of what the king had "heard") by anticipation from the seemingly "stray" notice of 2 Kgs 24,7a ("and the king of Egypt did not come again out of his land") where it appears subsequent to the mention of Jehoiakim's demise in 24,6. Recall our suggestion that Josephus has already made use of the continuation of 24,7 ("for the king of Babylon had taken all that belonged to the king of Egypt from the Brook of Egypt to the river Euphrates") in 10,86b; see n. 44.

3. Jeremiah under Jehoiakim[57]

At this juncture Josephus "interrupts" his "king-centered" account of Judah's final decades in order to relate (10,89-95) two episodes from the Book of Jeremiah (chaps. 26 [LXX 33] and 36 [LXX 43]), both involving the endangerment of the prophet – last mentioned by him in 10,80 – and dated in the reign of Jehoiakim, the ruler who is the focus of attention in what precedes and follows. The first of these episodes, Jeremiah's "Temple trial", is dated (so Jer 26,1) to "the beginning of the reign of Jehoiakim". In that year, according to vv. 1-6, the prophet received an extended divine communication which he is instructed to deliver to the people assembled in the Temple (v. 2), and which culminates (v. 6) in a conditional threat against Temple and city to be uttered by him[58]. Josephus replaces this opening component of Jeremiah 26 with a composition of his own, one which links up with his previous reference (10,88) to the Egyptians' failure to meet the rebel Jehoiakim's expectations of support. His "substitution" (10,89) for Jer 26,1-6 reads then:

> And this [i.e. the Egyptians' failure to undertake their projected campaign against Nebuchadnezzar, 10,88] was what the prophet Jeremiah foretold (προύλεγεν) day after day, how that it was vain (μάτην) for them to cling to their hope (ταῖς … ἐλπίσι [cf. τῆς ἐλπίδος, 10,88] προσανέχουσι)[59] of help from the Egyptians and that the city was destined (δεῖ τὴν πόλιν)[60] to be overthrown by the king of Babylonia, and King Jōakeimos to be subdued by him.

The above prediction, made by Jeremiah during the reign of Jehoiakim according to Josephus, has, as such, no parallel in the Book of Jeremiah. On the other hand, the historian does seem to have formulated it on the basis of announcements found here and there in that book. In particular, the Josephan Jeremiah's designating the Egyptians as a "vain

57. This segment represents a reworking of my article *Jeremiah under Jehoiakim according to Josephus (Ant. 10.89-95)*, in *Abr-Nahrain* 33 (1995) 1-16 which I use here by permission. For the text of LXX Jeremiah I use: J. ZIEGLER (ed.), *Jeremias Baruch Threni Epistula Jeremiae* (Septuaginta, 15), Göttingen, Vandenhoeck & Ruprecht, 1957.

58. This divine word, in turn, itself constitutes a condensed version of the "Temple Sermon" confided to the prophet by the Lord in Jer 7,1-15.

59. The above expression "cling to hope" occurs only here in Josephus.

60. This is the reading of ROMSP which Dindorf, Niese and Marcus follow; Bekker and Naber adopt the reading πέπρωται τῇ πόλει of LaurVE. With the above "deterministic" formulation, reflecting the actual outcome of events, compare the conditional language of the Lord's word in Jer 26,2-6 itself with its invocation (v. 3) of the possibility that "it may be they will listen, and every one will turn from his evil way, that I may repent of the evil which I [the Lord] intend to do to them…". The above formulation likewise harks back to Josephus' initial mention of Jeremiah in 10,79: "this prophet also announced the misfortunes that were to come upon the city (τῇ πόλει)…".

hope" recalls the Biblical prophet's telling King Zedekiah that "Pharoah's army which came to help you is about to return to Egypt..." (Jer 37[44],7). In that same context Jeremiah twice informs the king that the "Chaldeans" will "burn" Jerusalem (37,8.10; see also the similiarly worded announcements in 21,10; 34[41],2; 38[45],18.23). As for the prediction that Jehoiakim himself will be "subdued" by Nebuchadnezzar here in 10,89, this reminds one of Jeremiah's statements concerning the personal fate of Zedekiah in, e.g., Jer 21,7; 34(41),3.21; 38(45), 18.23. What is remarkable, however, about these Biblical "parallels" to Jeremiah's words as cited in 10,89 is that, in the prophetic book itself, they are associated with the reign of Zedekiah, not Jehoiakim's as Josephus' version has it. In other words, Josephus has "retrojected" to an earlier point in Jeremiah's ministry elements of the prophet's later, more specific message from the time of Zedekiah[61]. That procedure, I further suggest, is reflected in Josephus' generalizing formula above, "... this was what... Jeremiah foretold *day after day*...". By means of this formula, Josephus is indicating that, over the whole course of his ministry from the days of Jehoiakim on, Jeremiah was predicting both the ultimate unreliability of the Egyptians, as well as the fate of Jerusalem and its king(s) at the hands of Nebuchadnezzar. Thereby, of course, he accentuates the extent of the prophet's foreknowledge.

The next main section of Jeremiah 26, i.e. vv. 7-19, deals with the reaction by various Judean groups to the prophet's word as pronounced by him in the Temple (v. 7). Josephus (10,90a) introduces his version of this new source section with a general remark concerning the (non-) affect of Jeremiah's just-cited announcement and the reason for this: "These things, however, he spoke[62] to no avail, since there were none

---

61. Josephus' "transfer" of Jeremiah's words from a later to an earlier reign might have been facilitated by the fact that the OT "historical books" record developments around the figure of Jehoiakim which are reminiscent of the prophet's announcements to and about Zedekiah in the Book of Jeremiah (see above) which Josephus then "repositions" to the time of Jehoiakim in *AJ* 10,89. Specifically, 2 Kgs 24,7 follows the notice on the death of Jehoiakim of 24,6 with the statement that "the king of Egypt did not come up out of his land" (compare Jer 34,7: Egypt's non-intervention in Zedekiah's time), while 2 Chr 36,6 (MT) speaks of Nebuchadnezzar "binding" Jehoiakim "to take him to Babylon" (compare Jer 34,3: Zedekiah's coming deportation).

62. In contrast to Jer 26,7, which has the priests, prophets and people hear Jeremiah speaking "in the house of the Lord", Josephus does not specify where Jeremiah did the "speaking" in question. His failure to do so may go together with the fact that his previous reference is not to a particular address by the prophet, but rather to his long-term preaching activity ("Jeremiah foretold day after day...", 10,89) which might well have transpired at a variety of locales. Both chronologically and "geographically" then Josephus' version of Jeremiah 26 evidences a generalizing character vis-à-vis its Biblical counterpart.

destined) to be saved (σωθησομένων)...". As a Biblical inspiration for the first part of this Josephan comment, one might think of Jer 37(44),2: "But neither he [Zedekiah] nor his servants nor the people of the land listened to the words of the Lord which he spoke through Jeremiah the prophet". Here again then, Josephus would be "reapplying" to the time of Jehoiakim notices which in the Book of Jeremiah itself have to do rather with the reign of Zedekiah. The appended, "deterministic" affirmation (compare δεῖ, 10,89 and see n. 60) about the audience's disregard of Jeremiah's words as due to their having been "predestined" to miss the possibility for "salvation" offered them reflects Josephus' awareness of how things ultimately turned out for Judah. In the context of *AJ* 10 the affirmation likewise functions as an initial foreshadowing of his subsequent account of Jerusalem's destruction.

The account of the interchange between Jeremiah and his hearers in Jer 26,7-19 is a quite complicated one, with a variety of groups making an apppearance: First, "the priests, the (LXX: false) prophets (TJ: scribes) and all the people" (vv. 7-8) pronounce the death sentence on Jeremiah (vv. 8bß-9). Thereupon, the "princes of Judah" (v. 10) intervene to secure a trial for the prophet at which he is accused by "the priests and prophets (TJ: scribes)" before "the princes and all the people" (v. 11). In vv. 12-15 Jeremiah then speaks in his own defense, likewise directing himself to "the princes and all the people". In response, princes and people declare to "the priests and prophets (TJ: scribes)" that Jeremiah is not deserving of death (v. 16) Here, "the people", who earlier (v. 8) had joined the priests and prophets in condemning Jeremiah to death, align themselves with the princes in countermanding that earlier decision of theirs. The segment concludes in vv. 17-19 with yet another, previously unmentioned group, i.e. "the elders of the land", coming forward to speak on Jeremiah's behalf.

Josephus drastically simplifies (and clarifies) the above sequence. In his presentation, the "priests and (false) prophets" who consistently oppose Jeremiah throughout the Biblical proceedings totally disappear[63]. Their place is taken in 10,90b by two comprehensive categories, i.e. "the people" (τὸ πλῆθος; LXX Jer 26[33],7ff. ὁ λαός) and "the rulers" (οἱ ἄρχοντες; thus LXX Jer 26 [33],10ff.), i.e. those groups who both end up as defenders of Jeremiah in the source; see 26,16. This noteworthy divergence from the source's account does, it will be noted, accord with

---

63. Their non-mention in this connection likely reflects Josephus' favorable view of and identification with both groups on whom the Biblical presentation reflects so negatively.

Josephus' previous remark (10,90a) about the general lack of response to Jeremiah's word, there being "none" destined for "salvation". Of "the people and rulers" Josephus then states in his "telescoped" version of 26,7-11:

> ... for both the people and their rulers disregarded what they heard[64]; and, *being angered* (πρὸς ὀργὴν λαμβάνοντες) by his words, they accused Jeremiah of having as prophet *used divination* (οἰωνιζομένου) *against the king*[65], and, bringing him to trial (ὑπάγοντες δίκη)[66], demanded that he be sentenced to punishment (καταψηφισθῆναι πρὸς τιμωρίαν ἠξίουν)[67].

Jer 26,12-15 cites the prophet's speech to princes and people in response to the charge made against him by the priests and prophets (v. 11), whereupon the two former groups pronounce his acquittal, 26,16. Josephus who, as noted above, makes no mention of the priests and prophets as Jeremiah's accusers, and associates both people and leaders in opposition to him, passes over this whole sequence. In place of it, he

64. Jer 26,7-11 mentions a double "hearing" of Jeremiah's words, first by priests, prophets and people (v. 7), then by the princes of Judah (v. 10) which Josephus compresses into single such "audition" here.

65. The above accusation against Jeremiah replaces those cited in Jer 26,9a and 11b, both of which concern the prophet's announcement of the Temple's destruction (26,6), a point not mentioned as such in Josephus' own version of Jeremiah's word in 10,89b; see above. Josephus has prepared the above charge about Jeremiah's attempt to do harm to Jehoiakim by attributing to him the prediction, likewise Biblically unparalleled, that the king will be "subdued" by Nebuchadnezzar in 10,89b.

The above verb οἰωνίζομαι is hapax in the Josephan corpus. On it, see FELDMAN, *Prophets and Prophets*, 413 who points out that the term refers specifically to the practice of "augury". Feldman further suggests that Josephus' use of the term here represents a "Hellenization" which would put Gentile readers in mind of the famous prophet-augurer Calchas of Homer's *Iliad* (1.69).

66. This indication has no equivalent in Jeremiah 26 as such; it could, however, be seen as an explication of the reference in v. 10 to the princes "taking their seat" at the Temple's New Gate in order to hear the accusation of the priests and prophets against Jeremiah (v. 11). Whereas, however, in the source the princes thus function as "judges" at the prophet's trial, Josephus represents them (along with the people) rather as his accusers.

67. The above formulation represents Josephus' version of the statement by the priests and prophets to the princes and people in 26,11: "This man deserves the sentence of death...". At this point in his presentation, Josephus leaves indeterminate to whom the people and leaders make their "demand" about Jeremiah's punishment; subsequently, the addressee will be identified as the "elders"; see below. The language of the above passage is echoed in Josephus' account of Jeremiah's arrest and its sequels during the siege of Jerusalem in the reign of Zedekiah (= Jer 37[44],11-15) in *AJ* 10,115: "(Jeremiah's arrester)... brought him to trial (ἤγαγεν εἰς δίκην; note that Jer 37,14 does not mention a "trial" as such) before the magistrates (ἄρχοντας, i.e. Josephus' designation for one set of Jeremiah's accusers in 10,90), at whose hands he... was kept under guard for punishment (πρὸς τιμωρίαν)". It would appear then that Josephus has formulated 10,90 as a foreshadowing of what befalls Jeremiah in Zedekiah's time.

substitutes (10,91) a transitional phrase leading into the intervention of
the elders (who in 26,17 make a rather abrupt appeararance following
the prophet's acquittal): "and so all the others cast votes against him,
thereby rejecting (the advice) of the elders (οἳ καὶ ἀπέγνωσαν τῶν
πρεσβυτέρων; compare LXX Jer 26[33],17: ἄνδρες τῶν πρεσβυτέρων τῆς γῆς = MT)...[68]". Josephus continues this initial reference to the "elders" with a series of notices concerning them which
likewise lacks any direct Biblical equivalent: "... but these being of
wise understanding (σοφῆς ... διανοίας)[69], released the prophet from
the prison-hall (τῆς αὐλῆς)[70] and advised the others to do Jeremiah no
harm". Via the motivation ("*for*, they [the elders] said...") which he
next appends to the elders' "advice" to princes and people, Josephus
(10,92a) rejoins the sequence of Jeremiah 26, i.e. its v. 18 where the
elders "quote" a word of the prophet Micah (Mic 3,12). Whereas, however, the elders of Jer 26,18 cite Micah's triple evocation of the coming fate of Zion, Jerusalem, and "the mountain of the house" verbatim,
Josephus' version of the quotation markedly reduces and generalizes
this. It reads: "... he [Jeremiah] was not the only one to foretell (προλέγειν) what would befall the city (τῇ πόλει τὰ μέλλοντα)[71], but

68. Marcus, *Josephus*, VI, p. 206, n. b calls "the text and meaning" of the above
phrase "uncertain". Niese, *ad loc.* conjectures κατέγνωσαν for the ἀπέγνωσαν of the
codices (retained by Dindorf, Bekker, and Naber); cf. Weill, *ad loc.*: "... hors quelques-
uns d'entre les Anciens qui le *disculpèrent* (?)...".

69. This expression is hapax in Josephus.

70. According to Marcus, *Josephus*, VI, p. 207, n. c. the inspiration for Josephus'
mention of "prison-hall" here would be Jer 32(39),2; this text relates that, during the
Babylonian siege of Zedekiah's time, the prophet was confined "in the court of the
guard" (LXX ἐν αὐλῇ τῆς φυλακῆς), itself located in the royal palace. In connection
with this proposal Marcus further remarks: "It should not be surprising that Josephus
seems to confuse some of the events of Jehoiakim's reign with those of Zedekiah's since
the chronology in both Heb. and Gr. texts of Jer. is confused, *e.g.*, the narrative of
Jehoiakim's reign [see Jeremiah 35-36 MT] is resumed after a passage dealing with that
of Zedekiah [see Jeremiah 34 MT]". Weill, *ad loc.*, on the contrary, renders the above
phrase "de la cour (du Temple)"; on this understanding, the above reference would
reflect Jer 26(33),2 where Jeremiah is instructed to "stand in the court (LXX ἐν αὐλῇ) of
the Lord's house". PIOVANELLI, *Texte*, 21, n. 42 adopts the view of Weill. For my part, I
would tend rather to accept Marcus's suggestion. For one thing, unlike Jeremiah 26 (see
vv. 2,7), Josephus does not explicitly situate the episode of Jeremiah's speech and the
resultant trial in the Temple precincts; see n. 62. In addition, I have called attention to
other "anticipations" by Josephus of elements which in the Book of Jeremiah itself are
associated with Zedekiah's time in 10,89-90 (given this last consideration, it would seem
better to speak, not of Josephus' "confusing" [so Marcus above] the reigns of Jehoiakim
and Zedekiah, but rather of his conscious "retrojection" of features of the latter's time
into that of the former).

71. Compare 10,89b: "Jeremiah foretold (προύλεγεν)... that the city (τὴν πόλιν) was
destined to be overthrown...". See also 10,79 where Josephus refers to Jeremiah's "announcing
the misfortunes that were to come upon the city (τὰ μέλλοντα τῇ πόλει δεινά)". Cf. n. 85.

Michaias (Μιχαίαν, so LXX)[72] before him had announced these things[73], *as had many others...*[74]".

In Jer 26,19abα the elders invoke the exemplary penitential response of King Hezekiah to Micah's word[75] and the Lord's resultant "repenting" of his intended "evil[76]". In his handling of this sequence, Josephus omits all mention of a divine "change of heart[77]". His own version (10,92b) of the Biblical notice on the human response to Micah's prediction (= 26,19a) likewise manifests the same "generalizing tendency" already evident in his citation of the prediction itself. It runs: "none of them [i.e. all those prophets who had spoken of Jerusalem's coming

72. This is Josephus' only mention of the "classical prophet" Micah. He leaves aside the further particulars of 26,18a concerning Micah and his word, i.e. his being from Moresheth (see Mic 1,1) and his having made his announcement "in the days of Hezekiah king of Judah... to all the people of Judah".

73. Josephus' avoidance of the actual wording of Mic 3,12 as cited in Jer 26,18b in favor of the above, highly general language might have been prompted by the consideration that, contrary to Micah's prediction "Zion" did not (definitively) end up being "plowed as a field", any more than "the mountain of the house" became "a wooded height". Such a consideration might well have influenced Josephus, given his prevailing concern with depicting the Biblical prophets as accurate predictors. As for the *Botenformel* with which Mic 3,12/ Jer 26,18b opens, Josephus consistently avoids this formula in his reproduction of Biblical prophecies.

74. This "un-Biblical" generalization provides added support for the elders' advice that Jeremiah not be harmed: his prophecy against the city has a precedent, not only in the words of Micah, but also in those of "many others". Josephus may have found inspiration for his generalization here in the context of Jeremiah 26 itself; see v. 20 (not reproduced by Josephus as such) which – following the reference to Micah as a precedent for Jeremiah's announcement about the Temple (26,18) – speaks of a certain "Uriah" who "prophesied against this city and against this land *in words like those of Jeremiah*". Cf. also the historian's own earlier notice in 10,79b: "And not only this prophet [Jeremiah] predicted these things [i.e. the misfortunes that were to come upon the city, 10,79a], but also the prophet Ezekiel". As mentioned in the previous note, Josephus is concerned to highlight the veracity of the Biblical prophets; he is further concerned to point up the agreement among "true" prophets in their predictions. The fact then that Jeremiah's prediction accords with those of "many others" (Micah, [Uriah], Ezekiel) would be singular evidence of its truth.

75. In MT Jer 26,19a Hezekiah is the subject throughout; the equivalent LXX 33,19 reads pl. verbs in v. 19aβ.

76. This mention of Hezekiah's response to Micah's word and the Lord's relenting in Jer 26,19 has no parallel either in the Book of Micah itself or in the accounts of Kings and Chronicles concerning Hezekiah.

77. His doing so is likely inspired by the consideration that, in fact, Jerusalem did eventually suffer the destruction announced by Micah and Jeremiah. The omission likewise accords with the "deterministic" language used by him in 10,89-90 (see above in the text), just as it avoids the seeming contradiction between the elders' statement about the Lord's "repentance" in 26,19 and the word of Samuel to Saul cited in 1 Sam 15,29 ("the Glory of Israel will not lie or *repent*; for he is not a man, that he should *repent*"; cf. Josephus' version of this statement in *AJ* 6,153: "God would abide by what He had decreed concerning him [Saul], as change and reversal of judgement were the part of human fraility and not of divine power").

overthrow prior to Jeremiah] had suffered anything at the hands of those who were then kings[78], but had received honour as prophets of God (προφήτης τοῦ θεοῦ)[79]". The Biblical elders' word concludes in 26,19bβ with their affirmation "But we are about to bring great evil upon ourselves". Thereafter, nothing, oddly, is said about a response by the hearers (i.e. the people, v. 17) to the elders' appeal in vv. 17-19. Josephus dispenses with the concluding element of the Biblical elders' discourse. In its place he introduces (10,93a) a notice, unparalleled in the source, on the impact of their words which itself picks up his earlier, likewise "un-Biblical", reference to the efficacy of their intervention (see 10,91): "With these words they mollified the people (τὸ πλῆθος; see 10,90) and saved Jeremiah from the punishment to which he had been condemned (κατεψηφισμένης; see καταψηφισθῆναι, 10,90)".

Jeremiah 26 appends to its quotation of the elders' discourse (vv. 17-19) a narrative concerning the execution of (an otherwise unknown) prophet Uriah by Jehoiakim (vv. 20-23) along with a notice about "Ahikam, son of Shaphan" protecting Jeremiah from death at the hands of "the people" (v. 24). This material appears to come rather abruptly and anti-climatically after the extended "trial account" of vv. 7-19 (neither Uriah or Ahikam has been mentioned in what precedes). In addition, the notice of v. 24 that it was Ahikam who rescued Jeremiah from the people might appear to conflict with Josephus' own statement in 10,93a that the elders "saved" the prophet. Accordingly, it is not suprising to find that he passes over the whole of Jer 26,20-24 without any direct trace (although see n. 74). In his presentation, on the contrary, mention of the elders' efficacious intervention (10,93a) finds its immediate continuation (10,93b) in the opening of Josephus' version of the events of Jeremiah 36 (which in the Book of Jeremiah are separated from those of chap. 26 by a 10-chapter span) as follows: "they saved Jeremiah... who wrote down all his prophecies...". Josephus' "juxtaposition" of the two Biblical chapters here is dictated by chronological as well as thematic considerations, i.e. those chapters both relate events of the reign of Jehoiakim which have various features in common (prophetic words of doom for Jerusalem, a resultant threat to Jeremiah's life, involvement by the "princes").

78. This is Josephus' generalizing replacement for 26,19a's reference to King Hezekiah. That king is thus nowhere mentioned by name in Josephus' version of 26,18-19. In making no reference to Hezekiah's personal response to Micah's word, Josephus disposes of the difficulty that neither Kings nor Chronicles, nor his own treatment of this ruler in AJ 9,260b-10,36, recount any such initiative by him (or make any mention of Micah himself).

79. For this designation see on 9,33.211.

As just noted, Josephus commences his version of Jeremiah 36 (LXX 43) with mention of Jeremiah's "writing down all his prophecies (προφητείας)". He adapts this item from Jer 36,4 where, however, it is rather Baruch who, at Jeremiah's dictation, writes "all the words (LXX: λόγους) of the Lord which he had spoken to him". In thus beginning his version of Jeremiah 36 with its v. 4, Josephus passes over the chapter's opening vv. 1-3 according to which, in the fourth year of Jehoiakim (v. 1), Jeremiah was instructed by the Lord to write down all the words he had received from the days of Josiah on (v. 2) in hopes that Judah might repent and be accorded divine forgiveness (v. 3)[80]. Thus, in his account, Jeremiah acts on his own initiative in setting down his earlier prophecies in writing.

In the Greek, *AJ* 10,93 constitutes one long, complicated sentence. That sentence concludes with a parallel to Jer 36,9-10, the reading of Jeremiah's words to the people assembled in the Temple on the occasion of a fast in the ninth month of Jehoiakim's fifth (so MT; LXX: eighth) year. Josephus' version of Jeremiah 36 thus passes from its v. 4 (= 10,93b) directly to v. 9 (= 10,93c) This additional (see above) omission on the historian's part is readily understandable given that the intervening vv. 5-8 relate Jeremiah's charge to Baruch to read his words to the people because he himself is "debarred from going to the house of the Lord" (v. 5), whereas Josephus will represent the prophet himself as reading the words (which he, rather than Baruch, had earlier written down; see above). Josephus' adaptation of Jer 36,9-10 in 10,93c thus reads: "… while the people (τοῦ δήμου; LXX 43,10: τοῦ λαοῦ)[81] kept a fast (νηστεύοντος; cf. LXX 43,9: [ἐξεκλησίασαν] νηστείαν]) and were assembled in the temple (ἐν τῷ ἱερῷ; cf. LXX 43,10a: ἐν οἴκῳ κυρίου)[82], in the ninth month of the fifth [so MT] year of the reign of Jōakeimos[83], he [Jeremiah] read (ἀνέγνω; 43,10a:

---

80. Josephus' omission of 36,3's reference to the possibility of the people's repenting and God's forgiving them accords with his previous passing over both the elders' invocation of Hezekiah's appeal to the Lord and the latter's repenting of his intended evil against the people (Jer 26,19; compare 10,92), as well as the conditional language of the Lord's word in 26,2-6 (compare 10,89 and see n. 60). For Josephus there is, at this point, no chance for Jeremiah's hearers to still be spared, see his reference to there being "none destined to be saved" in 10,90; cf. also the word of irrevocable doom for the people he attributes to the prophetess Huldah already in the reign of Josiah in 10,60.

81. In his version of Jeremiah 26 in 10,89-93a Josephus designates "the people" rather as τὸ πλῆθος; see 10,90.93a.

82. Josephus dispenses with the elaborate specification of 36,10b concerning the precise site within the Temple precincts where the reading takes place, i.e. "… in the chamber of Gemariah the son of Shaphan the secretary, which was in the upper court, at the entry of the New Gate of the Lord's house".

83. Josephus' reading here, while it does agree with MT (and many LXX MSS, e.g., A) of Jer 36,9 (B has the 8th year) seems, in light of the preceding context in *AJ* 10, to

ἀνεγίνωσκε[84]) the book (τὸ βίβλιον; LXX: 43,10a: ἐν τῷ βιβλίῳ) which he had composed *concerning the things which were to befall the city* (τῶν μελλόντων ... τῇ πόλει)[85] *and the temple* (τῷ ναῷ) *and the people[s]* (τοῖς ὄχλοις)[86]".

Jer 36,11-21a is a lengthy transitional piece relating how the scroll read by Baruch in the Temple (v. 10a) finally reached the king. It begins with a certain Micaiah reporting to a group of "princes" (five of whom are mentioned by name, v. 12) about the words he had heard Baruch read. Next, in vv. 14-15, these princes summon Baruch who reads the scroll to them at their direction. Upon hearing the reading, the princes first resolve to report its words to the king (v. 16) and then ascertain from Baruch the circumstances of his writing the book, i.e. at Jeremiah's dictation (vv. 17-18). The princes then enjoin both Baruch and Jeremiah to hide themselves (v. 19), whereupon they themselves go off to make their report to the king after depositing the scroll in the chamber of the secretary Elishama (v. 20). Jehoiakim, in turn, dispatches "Jehudi" to retrieve the scroll (v. 21a). As he does with Jer 26,7-16, Josephus

involve him in a chronological difficulty. In MT Jeremiah the date in question is the fifth of Jehoiakim's eleven-year reign (see 2 Kgs 23,36). Prior to 10,93 Josephus has referred (10,87) to Jehoiakim's submission to Nebuchadnezzar in his (Jehoiakim's) eighth year and of his continuing as a Babylonian vassal for "three years" (thus 2 Kgs 24,1), i.e. into his eleventh (and final) regnal year. Thereafter (10,88) he dates Jehoiakim's revolt to "the third year", i.e. of his vassalship (= the eleventh of his reign). Read in conjunction with these previous indications, the "fifth year" of 10,93 would then naturally be understood as referring to a date two years after the revolt of Jehoiakim's eleventh year, i.e. in the thirteenth year of his reign which, however, according to the Bible (and Josephus himself; see 10,98) only lasted eleven years. Otherwise, one would have to suppose that, here in 10,93, Josephus is suddenly reverting to a much earlier point in Jehoiakim's reign, i.e. three years prior to his submission to Nebuchadnezzar in his eighth regnal year as cited in 10,87 – a supposition against which the narrative flow of 10,87-93 clearly militates, however. The difficulty is a by-product of Josephus' attempt to make room for the varying chronological indications of both the Books of Jeremiah and Kings/ Chronicles.

84. The subject of LXX's verb (as in MT) is Baruch rather than Jeremiah; see above in the text.

85. Note the echo here of the phrase Josephus attributes to the elders in 10,92 and earlier (10,79) to Jeremiah himself, i.e. τῇ πόλει τὰ μέλλοντα; cf. n. 71.

86. Marcus, *ad loc.* (mis-)translates this pl. form as "the people". The above threefold specification concerning the content of the book read in the Temple has no parallel as such in Jer 36,9-10. It can, however, be seen as Josephus' "delayed" specification/ adaptation of 36(43),2 where Jeremiah is instructed to write down the words the Lord had spoken to him "against Israel (so MT; LXX Jerusalem) and Judah and all the nations (LXX τὰ ἔθνη)". Specifically, Josephus' formulation takes over the first and third elements of the Biblical triad (the former according the LXX reading, his "the city" corresponding to its "Jerusalem"), while substituting a reference to the Temple for the source's middle item, i.e. "Judah" (recall that in his version of Jeremiah 26 in 10,89-93a, Josephus leaves aside that chapter's announcements of the Temple's fate – a subject which he now, in this later prediction, has the prophet address and to which he will have him return many times hereafter, as we shall be seeing).

(10,94a) markedly abbreviates and simplifies the above sequence, e.g., eliminating all the proper names of the royal officials as well as the place indications with which it is replete. His version reads: "But, when the leaders (οἱ ἡγεμόνες; LXX 43,12: οἱ ἄρχοντες) heard (ἀκούσαντες)[87] it, *they took the book* (τὸ βιβλίον, so 10,93)[88] *from him* [Jeremiah][89] and ordered both him and his scribe (τὸν γραμματέα)[90] Baruch (Βαροῦχον)[91] to take themselves off and not let themselves be seen by anyone (μή τισι δῆλοι γένωνται; LXX 43,19bβ: ἄνθρωπος μὴ γνώτω ποῦ ὑμεῖς); as for the book, they carried it off and gave it to the king[92]".

The last major segment in Jeremiah 36, vv. 21b-26, recounts the reading of the book to the king and Jehoiakim's reaction to this. Josephus' parallel (10,94b-95) evidences the same tendency to abridgement which marks his treatment of the entire source chapter. In 36,21b "Jehudi" reads the scroll Jehoiakim had sent him to retrieve (v. 21a) to the king and "the princes" (LXX: τῶν ἀρχόντων) who are standing around him. Josephus (10,94b) words as follows: "and he [Jehoiakim], in the presence of his friends (τῶν φίλων)[93], ordered his scribe (γραμματέα) to take it and read it aloud (ἀναγνῶναι; LXX 43,21b: ἀνέγνω)[94]".

87. Compare οἱ ἄρχοντες ἀκούοντες, 10,90. In Josephus' presentation the leaders themselves thus "hear" the initial reading of the book in the Temple by Jeremiah; there is thus no need for a separate reading of it to them by Baruch as in Jer 36,15.

88. This is Josephus' consistent designation for "the document" of Jeremiah 36(43) where it is called alternatingly "the book" (LXX τὸ βιβλίον; see, e.g., 43,10) and "the scroll" (LXX τὸ χαρτίον; see, e.g., 43,14).

89. This notice has no equivalent as such in the source where it is rather *Baruch* who is instructed to bring "the scroll" with him to the princes (36,14) who themselves subsequently "put" it in the chamber of Elishama (v. 20) whence it is retrieved by Jehudi at Jehoiakim's direction (v. 21a).

90. PIOVANELLI, *Texte*, 27 points out that Josephus' use of this title for Baruch here and in 10,95 is evidence of his acquaintance with an MT-like form of Jeremiah 36 as opposed to a LXX text-form seeing that the former twice (vv. 26,32) designates Baruch as הַסֹּפֵר, both times without parallel in the latter. See n. 99.

91. LXX reads the undeclined form Βαρουχ throughout the chapter. In contrast to the source where Baruch has already figured prominently in the production and reading of the book, Josephus here makes his first mention of Jeremiah's secretary.

92. Here again, Josephus simplifies the Biblical account, passsing over its mention of the princes' preliminary deposit of the scroll in the chamber of Elishama (36,20) as well as the king's dispatch of Jehudi to bring it from there (36,21a).

93. The substitution of this term for the source's "the princes" is in line with Josephus' characteristic tendency according to which he interjects mention of royal "friends" where the Bible itself does not use this designation; see, e.g., on 10,5.59.

94. Compare 36,21b where the reader of the scroll is mentioned by name, i.e. "Jehudi" rather than by title (Josephus' designation of the nameless reader as "his [Jehoiakim's] scribe" sets this figure in contrast to Jeremiah's "scribe" Baruch cited in 10,94a). Likewise in the source verse, "Jehudi", after being sent by Jehoiakim to retrieve the book (v. 21a, no parallel in Josephus), reads it without, as such, being directed to do so by the king; Josephus, as frequently elsewhere, reformulates here so as to underscore the royal authority/initiative.

Jer 36,22-26 narrates, rather circumstantially, the king's reaction to what he hears. The segment comprises the following components: 1) indications of time and place (the ninth month [see 36,9]; the winter house with a fire burning before the king, v. 22); 2) Jehoiakim destroys the scroll, cutting off its pieces as they are read and tossing these into the fire (v. 23); 3) Jehoiakim and his "servants" neither "fear" nor rend their garments (v. 24); 4) the king ignores the appeals of three named individuals not to burn the scroll (v. 25); and 5) Jehoiakim directs three (so MT; LXX two) named persons to apprehend Baruch and Jeremiah who, however, the Lord is said to "hide" (v. 26, MT; LXX: "they were hidden [κατεκρύβησαν]"[95]). Of these source elements, Josephus passes over the first, third and fourth completely. His abbreviated version (10,95) of the second and fifth reads:

> But, when he heard what was in the book, the king became angry (ὀργισθείς)[96] and destroyed (ἠφάνισε; cf. LXX 43,23: ἕως ἐξέλιπε) it by tearing it apart (διέρρηξε)[97] and throwing it into the fire (βαλὼν εἰς πῦρ; LXX 43,23: ἔρριπτεν εἰς τὸ πῦρ).[98] Then he ordered (ἐκέλευσεν; LXX 43,26: ἐνετείλατο) that a search be made for both Jeremiah and his scribe (γραμματέα)[99] Baruch and that they be brought to him[100] for

95. This form might, of course, be understood, in the line of MT, as a "divine passive".

96. The above transitional phrase has no parallel in Jer 36,22-26 as such. Its reference to Jehoiakim's "anger" at what he hears echoes Josephus' (likewise "un-Biblical") mention of the emotional reaction of people and leaders to Jeremiah's words in 10,90 (πρὸς ὀργὴν λαμβάνοντες τὰ λεγόμενα).

97. Compare Jer 36,23 where Jehoiakim "cuts off" (LXX ἀπέτεμνεν) the columns of the scroll as Jehudi finishes reading these. Interestingly, the verb διαρρήγνυμι used above by Josephus in reference to the king's "dismemberment" of the book is the same one employed by LXX 43,23 in speaking of the failure of Jehoiakim and his entourage to "rend" their garments upon hearing the scroll read. Josephus has no equivalent to the latter notice; rather, he "reapplies" its verb to designate the king's action with the book.

98. Josephus omits the specification of Jer 36,23 that the fire was "in the brazier" (just as he also leaves aside the "preparation" of this item in 36,22; see above in the text).

Rabbinic tradition goes its own way with regard to the identity of the "scroll" destroyed by Jehoiakim. According to b. Mo'ed Qat. 26a this would have contained the text of Lamentations. The king, taking its words to be directed against him, proceeded to cut out all occurrences of the divine name from the text and consign these to the flames. In Lam. Rab. 3.1 (COHEN, Midrash Rabbah Lamentations, p. 188) what Jehoiakim thus destroys was a scroll bearing the text of Lamentations 1; when Jeremiah subsequently reconstructed the scroll (see Jer 36,32) he "added" chaps. 2-5 of that book.

99. In his use of this title for Baruch Josephus follows MT Jer 36,26 (הַסֹּפֵר) against LXX which lacks it; see n. 90.

100. In contrast to 36,26 where three (LXX two) named individuals are directed to "seize" (LXX συλλαβεῖν) Jeremiah and Baruch, Josephus leaves the addressee of Jehoiakim's arrest command unspecified.

punishment (κολασθησομένους)[101]. So then they escaped *his wrath* (τὴν ὀργήν; see ὀργισθείς, 10,95a)[102].

Jeremiah 36 concludes in vv. 27-31 with an account of the Lord's response to Jehoiakim's provocation in burning the scroll: Jeremiah is directed to reconstitute the burned scroll (vv. 27-28) and to pronounce a word of doom over the king (vv. 29-31). Thereafter, v. 32 cites the prophet's execution (via dictation to Baruch, compare v. 4) of the first of these directives. Josephus, by contrast, breaks off his version of the chapter with the above notice on the escape of Jeremiah and Baruch, this seeming to suggest that his interest in the story of Jeremiah 36 was less with the fate of the prophetic scroll(s) than with that of the prophet himself.

4. *Jehoiakim's End*

Following the above interlude focussed on the figure of Jeremiah, 10,89-95, Josephus, in 10,96, returns to the point at which he left off in 10,88 in order to now relate the Babylonian response to Jehoiakim's rebellion as recounted there. In narrating this new development he draws on 2 Chr 36,6a (// 1 Esdras 1,40) which states: "Against him [Jehoiakim] came up Nebuchadnezzar king of Babylon[103]". To his mention of this he appends,

101. With this term Josephus explicates Jehoiakim's intention in commanding the "apprehension" of Jeremiah and Baruch. The term likewise echoes the use of κολάσεως in his version of Jeremiah 26 in 10,93a. In the fragment of Eupolemos (see n. 23), King "Jonachim" threatens to "burn Jeremiah alive" in retaliation for the latter's announcement of coming punishment for the Jews' sacrificing to an image named "Baal". The punishment in question would seem to be inspired by the king's action with the book as described in Jer 36,23 (and 10,95); see N. WALTER, *Fragmente jüdisch-hellenistischer Historiker* (JSHRZ, 1,2), Gütersloh, Mohn, 1976, pp. 106-107, n. 3a.

102. On this conclusion to Josephus' version of Jeremiah 36, MARCUS, *Josephus*, VI, p. 209, n. b comments: "The form of this last sentence (οὗτοι μὲν οὖν) suggests that the account of their [Jeremiah and Baruch's] escape has been lost from Josephus's text or perhaps was omitted by him because of his doubt as to the meaning of the bibl. phrase… 'And the Lord hid them' [MT 36,26; LXX: and they were hidden]". In any case, like LXX, Josephus' formulation lacks MT's explicit indication about God's involvement in the pair's deliverance.

103. In 36,6a (as well as in 1 Esdras 1,40a) Nebuchadnezzar's advance against Jehoiakim lacks an explicit motivation. Josephus has previously (10,88) supplied such a motivation, itself based on 2 Kgs 24,1, i.e. the Judean's cessation of tribute to his overlord. In thus linking the data of 24,1 and 36,6a, Josephus leaves aside the sequence of 2 Kgs 24,2-4 which tells of a divine intervention subsequent to Jehoiakim's revolt (24,1), i.e. the Lord's sending marauders against him in fulfillment of the word of doom pronounced over Judah at the time of Manasseh (see 2 Kgs 21,10-15). Josephus' omission of this sequence is understandable given his general tendency to de-theologize as well as the fact that, in accord with the Chronicler's presentation of Manasseh's repentance and restoration, he does not represent Judah as being irrevocably doomed already in that

however, an item of his own creation, this concerning Jehoiakim's response to the Babylonian initiative: *"But not long after*[104], when the king of Babylonia brought an army against him (στρατευόμενον ἐπ' αὐτόν)[105], *Jōakeimos, in fear* (κατὰ δέος)[106] *of what had been foretold by this prophet*[107], received (δέχεται)[108] *him, thinking that he would suffer* (πείσεσθαι) *no harm* (δεινόν)[109], *as he had neither shut him out nor made war on him*[110]*".

2 Chr 36,6b (MT) narrates that Nebuchadnezzar "bound" Jehoiakim with a view to taking him to Babylon (in BL and 1 Esdras 1,40b he is represented as actually conveying him there). Josephus (10,97a) amplifies and adapts the Chronicler's datum: *"On entering* (εἰσλθών)[111] *the city* (εἰς αὐτήν[112]), the Babylonian king (ὁ

king's time; see above. Recall too his non-utilization of the earlier reminiscence of 2 Kgs 21,10-15 found in 2 Kgs 23,26-27. Also to be noted here is that Josephus, in accord with his invariable practice, leaves aside the source notices for Jehoiakim found in 24,5 // 36,8 // 1 Esdras 1,42.

104. This vague chronological indication makes a connection with what precedes, dating Nebuchadnezzar's advance to shortly after Jehoiakim's destruction of the book in his "fifth year" (10,93). On the chronological problem involved, see n. 83.

105. This phrase echoes that used of Nebuchadnezzar's earlier advance in 10,87: στρατεύει ... ἐπὶ τοὺς Ἰουδαίους.

106. This inserted reference to Jehoiakim's "fear" serves to motivate the action which Josephus will attribute to him in what follows, i.e. opening the city to Nebuchadnezzar. It likewise echoes the motivation supplied by Josephus in 10,87 for Jehoiakim's earlier submission to Nebuchadnezzar spoken of 2 Kgs 24,1, i.e. "being alarmed (δείσας) at the threat". See n. 50.

107. This portion of Josephus' "appendix" to 36,6a spells out the grounds for Jehoiakim's "fear". It likewise serves as another (see n. 104) link with the preceding segment concerning Jeremiah; see in particular 10,89 where the prophet is cited as announcing that "King Jōakeimos [was destined] to be subdued by him [Nebuchadnezzar]".

108. Basing himself on Lat's "foederis iure suscepit", NIESE, *ad loc.* proposes to read δέχεται ὁμολογίᾳ here. With this initiative by Jehoiakim, compare Josephus' notice in *AJ* 9,278 that Hoshea "would not admit (οὐ δεξαμένου)" Shalmaneser to Samaria. See also 8,258 where Rehoboam "admits" (δεξαμένου) Shishak to Jerusalem "because he feared him (διὰ τὸν φόβον)" and 10,6 (Rab-shakeh asks why Hezekiah will not "admit" [δέχεται] the Assyrian army into Jerusalem).

109. This term ironically echoes Josephus' initial reference to Jeremiah's "announcing the misfortunes (δεινά) that were to come upon the city" in 10,79. The verbal echo points up Jehoiakim's delusion in thinking that he would "suffer no harm" by opening to the Babylonians.

110. The above reference to Jehoiakim's "thinking" as he opens to Nebuchadnezzar rounds off Josephus' appendix to 36,6a. That whole appendix is designed to respond to a question provoked by the Chronicler's account which Josephus is following at this point, i.e. how did Nebuchadnezzar get the Judean into his power – as 36,6b records – given that nothing is said previously either of a capture of Jerusalem by him or of its surrendering to him?

111. This is the reading of MLaur (cf. Lat's intrasset) which Dindorf, Bekker, Naber, and Marcus follow. Niese reads ἀπέλθών with the remaining codices.

112. This is the reading of MSPV which Dindorf, Bekker, Naber, and Marcus adopt; Niese opts for the αὐτόν of ROLaur².

Βαβυλώνιος)[113] *did not keep his pledges* (οὐκ ἐφύλαξε τὰς πίστεις)[114] *but killed the most vigorous* (ἀκμαιοτάτους) *and best favoured* (κάλλει διαφέροντας)[115] *of the inhabitants of Jerusalem*[116] together with King Jōakeimos[117], whom he ordered to be cast out unburied before the walls (ἄταφον[118]... ῥιφῆναι πρὸ τῶν τειχῶν)[119]".

113. This specfication of the subject is absent in MSPLaurV and omitted by Dindorf, Bekker, and Naber.

114. This inserted reference to Nebuchadnezzar's "treachery" recalls that ascribed by Josephus to other foreigner besiegers of Jerusalem earlier in *AJ*, i.e. Shishak (see 8,258) and Sennacherib (10,4) – also in these instances without Biblical warrant as such. The above phrase likewise has a counterpart in 10,229 which states that Nebuchadnezzar "did not keep faith (τὴν πίστιν οὐκ ἐφύλαξεν)" with Jeconiah; see our discussion of this passage below.

115. This phrase recurs in *BJ* 1,147; *AJ* 3,166; 6,130; 8,176; 11,199; 20,144; *c. Ap.* 2,167. The above collocation ("vigorous and best favored") is hapax in Josephus.

116. None of Josephus' Biblical sources mentions such a massacre of the Jerusalemites by Nebuchadnezzar in Jehoiakim's reign. The item does underscore the extent of the Babylonian's "treachery" (and of Jehoiakim's mistaken "thinking") spoken of in what precedes. Conceivably, Josephus found inspiration for the notice in the account of the execution of the city's notables subsequent to its capture in the reign of Zedekiah as related in 2 Kgs 25,18-21 // Jer 52,24-27 (cf. *AJ* 10,149-150). In his presentation Nebuchadnezzar's deed, now already in Jehoiakim's time, would thus foreshadow the Babylonian's later handling of Jerusalem's elite. (The comment by MARCUS, *Josephus*, VI, p. 210, n. a on this item appears misplaced; it would make better sense as part of his n. d on p. 211.)

117. None of the relevant Biblical accounts explicitly mention such a "slaying" of Jehoiakim by Nebuchadnezzar. In 2 Chr 36,6b (and 1 Esdras 1,40b) the Babylonian simply "binds" him (cf. Dan 1,2 where the Lord "gives Jehoiakim into his [Nebuchadnezzar's] hand"), while the formulation of 2 Kgs 24,6a ("So Jehoiakim slept with his fathers") could suggest that he actually died a natural death. Josephus' statement on the point provides the necessary preparation for the continuation of his account which speaks of Nebuchadnezzar's directive concerning Jehoiakim's corpse, this presupposing both that Jehoiakim is dead and that his remains are in the Babylonian's power; see below. Rabbinic tradition too cites Jehoiakim's death at Nebuchadnezzar's hands; see, e.g., *Lev. Rab.* 19.6 (ISRAELSTAM and SLOTKI, *Midrash Rabbah Leviticus*, p. 246) and *SOR* 25.3 (GIRÓN BLANC, *Seder 'Olam Rabbah*, p. 188; here, 2 Chr 36,6b on the "binding" of Jehoiakim by Nebuchadnezzar is cited and it is then added that the former "soon died in his captivity"). Compare Jerome who, in his commentary on Jer 22,19 (S. REITER, ed., *S. Hieronymi Presbyteri Opera*, I, 3 (CCSL, 74), Turnhout, Brepols, 1960, p. 208, avers that Jehoiakim was killed rather by the bands of marauders whom the Lord sent against him (see 2 Kgs 24,2 and cf. n. 103). For more on the question of the circumstances of Jehoiakim's demise, see E.J. SMIT, *So How did Jehoiakim die?*, in *Journal for Semitics* 6 (1994) 46-56; C.T. BEGG, *The End of King Jehoiakim: The Afterlife of a Problem*, in *Journal for Semitics* 8 (1996) 12-20 (used here by permission of the publisher).

118. This is the only occurrence of this term in *AJ*; elsewhere Josephus employs it in *BJ* 2,465; 3,377; 4,317 (here in conjunction with the verb "throw" as in 10,97). 385; *c. Ap.* 2,211.

119. 2 Kings 24 (MT B) // 2 Chronicles 36 (MT) // 1 Esdras 1 say nothing about what happened to Jehoiakim's body subsequent to his death (according to L 24,6 he was "buried in the garden of Oza"; cf. BL 36,8 ἐν γανοζαή; see DELAMARTER, *Jehoiakim*, 196-198). Josephus' notice on the point represents a transposition into narrative of the announcements recorded in Jer 22,19 ("with the burial of an ass he [Jehoiakim] shall be buried, dragged and cast forth [LXX ῥιφήσεται] beyond the gates of Jerusalem") and

Josephus rounds off his account of Jehoiakim's ignominious death (10,97a) with a series of additional notices (10,97b-98b). He draws the first of these (10,97b) from 24,6b // 36,8b // 1 Esdras 1,43a: "... and [Nebuchadnezzar] appointed his son Jōachimos ('Ιωάχιμον)[120] as king of the country and the city[121]". Next, he cites (10,98a) an item, i.e. a deportation of Jerusalem's elite, already at this transition point between the end of Jehoiakim's reign and the beginning of that of Jehoiachin, unattested in the Historical Books, but seemingly inspired by MT Jer 52,28 (no parallel in LXX) and Ezek 1,2, i.e.: "Those in power (τοὺς ... ἐν ἀξιώματι)[122], three thousand in number (ἀριθμόν[123])[124], he took captive and carried away to Babylon. Now among them was the prophet

36(43),30b ("his [Jehoiakim's] dead body shall be cast out to the heat by day and the frost by night"; recall that in his rendition of Jeremiah 36 in 10,93-95 Josephus makes no use of this item). *Lev. Rab.* 19.6 (ISRAELSTAM and SLOTKI, *Midrash Rabbah Leviticus*, p. 246), e.g., embellishes further, relating that when the skull of Jehoiakim was found many centuries later it would not stay buried and ended up being burned. For more details on the matter, see the articles of Smit and Begg cited in n. 117.

120. Niese and SCHALIT, *Namenwörterbuch*, p. 65 read 'Ιωάκειμον here with RO and Zon, i.e. the same form used for Jehoiachin's father in what precedes. Subsequently (see 10,229) Josephus will use the name 'Ιεχονίας for Judah's penultimate king; see n. 163. Compare יְהוֹיָכִין (MT); 'Ιωακείμ (B 24,6 // 1 Esdras 1,43); 'Ιωακείν (L 24,6); 'Ιεχονίας (BL 36,8). As is his custom, Josephus leaves aside the concluding "source notices" of 24,5a // 36,8a // 1 Esdras 1,42 for Jehoiakim.

121. Josephus' sources speak simply of Jehoiachin's becoming king without mention of Nebuchadnezzar's role in the process. Josephus' specification on the point – which is paralleled in *Lev. Rab.* 19.6 (ISRAELSTAM and SLOTKI, *Midrash Rabbah Leviticus*, p. 247) and *y. Šeqal.* 6.2 – reflects the fact that in his presentation (see 10,97a) the Babylonian had already gained entrance into Jerusalem prior to Jehoiakim's demise and so would be in a position to dictate who his successor would be. He may likewise have been inspired by 24,17 // 36,10b // 1 Esdras 1,46b where Jehoiachin's own successor, Zedekiah, is designated by Nebuchadnezzar.

122. Jer 52,28 calls those deported by Nebuchadnezzar simply "Jews/Judeans". Josephus' specification may be inspired by the references to Judean notables as those whom Nebuchadnezzar led away following his deposition of Jehoiachin himself in 2 Kgs 24,11-16.

123. RO, followed by Niese, adds αὐτοῦ which MARCUS, *Josephus*, VI, p. 211, n. d, suggests might be "a scribal note indicating that the number [3,000] is an addition to Scripture made by Josephus".

124. This figure represents a rounding off of that given in 52,28 (MT, > LXX), i.e. 3,023. Josephus leaves aside the chronological indication of 52,28 dating the deportation to "the seventh year", i.e. of Nebuchadnezzar which would be the 11th (and final) year of Jehoiakim according to the correlation established in Jer 25,1 (and 10,84); see above. Hippolytus in the Preface to his "Commentary on Daniel" mentions Nebuchadnezzar's exiling 11,000 men to Babylon along with Jehoiakim; see G.N. BONWITSCH and H. ACHEILIS (eds.), *Hippolytus Werke*, II,1 (GSC), Leipzig, Hinrichs, 1897, pp. 7-8. See also RAPPAPORT, *Agada*, pp. 64-65 (# 270) and p. 134, n. 265 who quotes *Midr. 'Eser Galuyyot* 10, according to which in Jehoiakim's fourth year Nebuchadnezzar carried off 3,320 people from the tribes of Judah, Ephraim and Benjamin. Likewise *SOR* 25.4-6 (GIRÓN BLANC, *Seder 'Olam Rabbah*, pp. 118-119) appears to associate the deportations spoken of in Jer 52,28 and in 2 Kgs 24,14-16 with the punishment of Jehoiakim, rather than that of Jehoiachin; cf. GINZBERG, *Legends*, VI, pp. 379-380, n. 132. See n. 144.

Ezekiel [see 10,79], *then a boy* (παῖς)[125]". The last of the historian's concluding notices for Jehoiakim are the chronological indications he gives in 10,98b, basing himself for these on the data of 23,36 // 36,5 (cf. 1 Esdras 1,39): "Such, then, was the end that overtook King Jōakeimos at the age of thirty-six years[126], of which he had reigned eleven (= 23,36aβ // 36,5aβ)".

5. *Jehoiachin's Reign*

Josephus introduces the short-reigned Jehoiachin in 10,98c with a selective use of the data of 24,8-9 // 36,9 (cf. 1 Esdras 1,44-45): "Jōachimos [see 10,97b], who succeded him [Jehoiakim] on the throne, had a mother named Noostē (Νοόστης)[127], a native of the city (πολίτι-δος, see 9,186; 10,37; compare "of Jerusalem", 24,8b), and reigned three months and ten days[128]".

125. The title of the Book of Ezekiel (1,1-3) does not, as such, specify either the date at which or at what age Ezekiel went into exile. The reference to the "exile of King Jehoiachin" in 1,2 might suggest that it was along with this king – rather than his father Jehoiakim (so Josephus) – that Ezekiel's deportation occurred. WEILL, *Josèphe*, II, p. 321, n. 5 points out that the form of the king's name in the LXX, i.e. Ἰωακ(ε)ίμ, could have led to a confusion of the two kings on Josephus' part. As for the historian's indication concerning Ezekiel's age when exiled, he might have inferred this from the mention of "the thirtieth year" in Ezek 1,1: supposing this to be the year of Ezekiel prophetic call – which came to him when he was already in exile (see Ezek 1,2-3); on this basis, Josephus would have concluded that he must have still been a "boy" when exiled. In any event, the above "deportation notice" takes the place of the reference to Nebuchadnezzar's (partial) despoliation of the Temple vessels found in 36,7 // 1 Esdras 1,42 subsequent to his seizure of Jehoiakim; compare Dan 1,1-2 where this happening is dated to Jehoiakim's "third year". (2 Kings 24 does not mention such a despoliation prior to the exile of Jehoiakim either). As we shall be seeing, Josephus likewise passes over the despoliation that follows the capitulation of Jehoiachin himself in 24,13 // 36,10b // 1 Esdras 1,45b. Thus in his presentation, the Babylonian removal of the Temple treasures is reserved to a single climactic moment, i.e. subsequent to Jerusalem's fall in Zedekiah's day; see 10.145; cf. n. 150. On the whole subject of the various Babylonian despoliations of the Temple vessels in the Bible itself and in subsequent Jewish tradition, see I. KALIMI and J.D. PURVIS, *King Jehoiachin and the Vessels of the Lord's House in Biblical Literature*, in *CBQ* 56 (1994) 449-457.

126. Josephus calculates this figure by adding together the source indications concerning Jehoiakim's age at accession (25 years) and length of rule (11 years).

127. SCHALIT, *Namenwörterbuch*, p. 91 calls this an Aramaic-influenced form which stood already in Josephus' *Vorlage*. Compare נחֻשְׁתָּא (MT 24,8b); Νεσθά (B); Νεσσθάν (L). In line with his usual practice, Josephus omits the name of the queen mother's father, i.e. "Elnathan" (MT).

128. This figure for Jehoiachin's length of reign corresponds to that given in 36,9 (and 1 Esdras 1,44a); compare 24,8aβ (MT and BL) which reads the round figure "three months". (Recall that in 10,83 Josephus assigns Jehoahaz a reign of three months and ten days likely under the influence of that ascribed to Jehoiachin in 36,9; see n. 23).

Having introduced Jehoiachin, the sources (24,10-11 // 36,10a // 1 Esdras 1,45a) proceed immediately to mention Nebuchadnezzar's move against him, without, however, indicating a motivation for the Babylonian's initiative against Judah's new – and personally blameless – king. Josephus' version (10,99) supplies such a motivation, one which picks up on his own earlier mention of Nebuchadnezzar's personally appointing Jehoiachin king (see 10,97b)[129]: *"But after the Babylonian had given the kingdom to Jōachimos, a sudden fear* (δέος) *seized him*[130], *for he was afraid* (ἔδεισε)[131] *that Jōachimos might bear him a grudge* (μνησικακήσας) *for the killing* (ἀναιρέσεως) *of his father* [see 10,97a], *and lead his country to revolt* (ἀποστήσῃ τὴν χώραν αὐτοῦ). He *therefore* sent a force (δύναμιν) which besieged (ἐπολιόρκει) Jōachimos in Jerusalem[132]".

Of the remaining source *personalia* for Jehoiachin, Josephus leaves aside his age at accession, perhaps in view of the discrepancy on the matter between 24,8aα (MT and BL); 1 Esdras 1,43b; and L 36,9a all of which have 18 years, and MT B 36,9a which read a mere 8. *SOR* 25.7 (GIRÓN BLANC, *Seder 'Olam Rabbah*, p. 119) "resolves" the discrepancy by asserting that the figure "eighteen" gives Jehoiachin's actual age at accession, whereas the "eight" refers to the number of years which had elapsed since the definitive divine sentence of doom on Judah had been pronounced in the fourth year of Jehoiakim's eleven-year reign; see *SOR* 24.11; ibid., p. 116. As for the (negative) judgment notice on Jehoiachin ("he did what was evil in the sight of the Lord") of 24,9 // 36,9b // 1 Esdras 1,44b, Josephus reserves his modified version of this until a later point; see on 10,100.

129. Given that earlier notice (on which see n. 121), it was particularly incumbent on Josephus to provide an explanation as to why Nebuchadnezzar would now move against the one whom he himself had designated king just previously. Rabbinic tradition too addresses the question of what prompted Nebuchadnezzar's immediate advance against Jehoiachin. According to *Lev. Rab.* 19.6 (ISRAELSTAM and SLOTKI, *Midrash Rabbah Leviticus*, p. 247) he was induced to do so by the warning proverb quoted him by his people when he informed them of his execution of Jehoiakim and his appointment of his son Jehoiachin in his place, i.e. "Do not rear a gentle cub of a vicious dog, much less a vicious cub of a vicious dog". *SOR* 25.7 (GIRÓN BLANC, *Seder 'Olam Rabbah*, p. 119) attributes to Nebuchadnezzar himself a similar reflection with regard to Jehoiachin: "good pups cannot come from a bad dog".

130. This phrase echoes the reference to Jehoiakim's opening Jerusalem to Nebuchadnezzar "in fear (δέος) of what had been foretold by the prophet" in 10,96; it also recalls the mention of the "state of alarm and terrible anxiety" into which an earlier great king, i.e. Sennacherib, was reduced by the destruction of his army before Jerusalem; in both instances a mighty Gentile ruler who had inspired terror in Judah's kings ends up experiencing such fear himself. See next note.

131. Josephus' emphasis on the all-powerful Nebuchadnezzar's "fear" here in 10,99 seems rather odd – what did he have, in fact, "to fear" from a minor king whose father, just previously (10,96), had, "out of fear" himself, opened his capital to him? That oddness, in turn, points up the contrived nature of the historian's "explanation" of Nebuchadnezzar's move against his own appointee, Jehoiachin, here.

132. The above formulation reflects 24,10: "at that time the servants of Nebuchadnezzar... came up to Jerusalem and the city was besieged (BL ἦλθεν ... ἐν περιοχῇ)". (In the telescoped presentations of 36,10a // 1 Esdras 1,45a Nebuchadnezzar simply

In the account of 2 Kings 24, Jehoiachin responds (v. 12) to the Babylonian siege by surrendering himself and his entourage to Nebuchadnezzar[133]. Just as he did with Nebuchadnezzar's initiative itself, Josephus (10,100) expatiates considerably on Jehoichin's response to this:

> But he, being kind and just (χρηστὸς ... καὶ δίκαιος)[134], did not think it right to suffer the city to be endangered on his account, and removed (ἀπάρας)[135] his mother and his relatives (συγγενεῖς)[136] and delivered (παραδίδωσι) them to the commanders sent by the Babylonian king[137],

deports Jehoiachin to Babylon with nothing being said of an intervening siege.) On the other hand, Josephus leaves aside the mention (24,11) of Nebuchadnezzar's coming in person to Jerusalem during the course of the siege.

133. 2 Chronicles 36 and 1 Esdras 1 have no parallel to this item; see previous note.

134. This double characterization of Jehoiachin – employed previously of the High Priest Jehoiada (9,166) and of King Hezekiah (9,260) – represents Josephus' version/reversal of the negative evaluation of him given in 24,9 // 36,9b // 1 Esdras 1,44b; compare his like reversal of the unqualifiedly negative Biblical judgment (2 Kgs 13,11) on King Joash of Israel (9,177). On the grounds for the historian's altered view of Jehoiachin (i.e., as a Biblical precedent for his own attempt to persuade Jerusalem to surrender to the Romans), see FELDMAN, Studies, 437-449, pp. 442-444 (= ID., Josephus' Portrait of Jehoiachin, in Proccedings of the American Philosophical Society 139 [1995] 11-31, pp. 25-27). In his study, Feldman also provides a detailed treatment of Josephus' overall usage of the above collocation, "kind and just" (Studies, pp. 441-442 = Jehoiachin, 19-25). He further notes that Josephus' "rehabilitation" of Jehoiachin has a certain parallel in Rabbinic tradition (see, e.g., Lev. Rab. 19.6 [ISRAELSTAM and SLOTKI, Midrash Rabbah Leviticus, pp. 248-249]; Songs Rab. 8.6.2 [SIMON, Midrash Rabbah Song of Songs, pp. 306-307]) where, however, the king is presented as initially, in fact, a sinner (so the Bible) who, however, repented during his long captivity (Studies, pp. 444-448 = Jehoiachin, 27-31). On the question, see further BOGAERT, Apocalypse de Baruch, II, pp. 7-9 and RAPPAPORT, Agada, p. 65 (# 272) who opines that the discrepancy between the Bible on the one hand and the haggadic tradition on the other in their respective evalutions of Jehoiachin might derive from a concern on the part of the latter to "defend" one who became the grandfather of Zerubabel (see 1 Chr 3,17; Hag 1,12), the repository of Davidic hopes. (FELDMAN, Studies, p. 448 = Jehoiachin, 30, noting the absence in Josephus of any mention, like that found in the Rabbis, of Jehoiachin's (post-deposition) "repentance", suggests that if he had made such a mention, this would have called to mind the divine promise of 2 Sam 7,11-16 that God would punish sinful Davidids but never reject the line definitively, a promise that could not but be a source of provocation to his Roman readers. A simpler explanation of the phenomenon would seem, however, to lie in the observation that since, right from the start, Josephus presents Jehoiachin as a "good" king, there would have been nothing for him to "repent" of subsequently – as the Rabbis depict the previously sinful king as doing).

135. This is the reading of RO which Niese, Naber, and Marcus follow. Dindorf and Bekker read ἐπάρας with MSPLaurVE; cf. Lat sumens.

136. This term represents Josephus' generalization for the three groups of persons with whom Jehoiachin "goes out" to the Babylonians according to 24,12, i.e. "his servants, and his princes and his palace officials (BL εὐνοῦχοι)". In contrast to the source verse, Josephus does not mention a self-surrender by Jehoiachin at this point.

137. In 24,12 Jehoiachin and his entourage go out to "the king of Babylon" himself (recall that Josephus does not reproduce the reference in 24,11 to Nebuchadnezzar's own presence at the siege of Jerusalem; see n. 132). Josephus' mention of the Babylonian "commanders" here was perhaps inspired by the notice on their presence at the later siege of Jerusalem in Zedekiah's time of Jer 39,2 (= AJ 10,135).

after receiving their oath (ὅρκους) *that neither these nor the city would
suffer* (παθεῖν) *any harm*[138].

2 Kgs 24,12b-17 tells, quite circumstantially and repetitiously, of
the various measures undertaken by Nebuchadnezzar subsequent to
Jehoiachin's self-surrender (24,12a)[139]. In particular it devotes considerable attention to the various categories of persons who are removed
to Babylon by him (see vv. 12b, 14-16; cf. the similar listing in Jer
29[36],2). Josephus compresses the source's multiple listings of Nebuchadnezzar's captives. At the same time, he prefaces his mention of
these (10,101-102a) with a notice that underscores the Babylonian's
continued treachery (see 10,97) in his dealings with the Jews:

> (101) *But their pledge was not kept for even so long as a year*[140], *for
> the Babylonian king did not observe it* (ἡ πίστις ... οὐ ... ἐφύλαξεν
> αὐτήν)[141], but *commanded his men* [literally "commanders", στρατηγοῖς,
> as in 10,100][142] to take captive *all the young men* (νέους τὴν ἡλικίαν)[143]

138. 2 Kings 24 makes no mention of this precautionary measure by Jehoiachin (the
wording of which echoes Josephus' comment about Jehoiakim's deluded thinking "he
would suffer [πείσεσθαι] no harm [δεινόν]" from the Babylonians in 10,96). Such a
precautionary measure on Jehoiachin's part would, however, indeed be well in place
given Nebuchadnezzar's recent "treachery" as described by Josephus – there too without
Biblical parallel – in 10,96.
  With the above notice on Jehoiachin's response to the Babylonian threat, compare
Josephus' reminiscence of the king's meritorious deed in his address to John of Gischala,
leader of the Jerusalem resistance, in *BJ* 6,103-105: "Yet, be sure, John, that it is no disgrace to repent of misdeeds, even at the last; and, if you desire to save your country, you
have a noble example (καλὸν ὑπόδειγμα) set before you in Jeconiah, king of the Jews.
He, when of old his conduct had brought the Babylonian's army upon him [compare the
alternative explanation of Nebuchadnezzar's advance given in 10,99] of his own free will
left the city before it was taken, and with his family (γενεάς; cf. συγγενεῖς, 10,100)
endured voluntary captivity, rather than deliver up these holy places to the enemy and see
the house of God in flames [in 10,100 there is no mention of Jehoiachin's concern specifically for the Temple]. Therefore, is he celebrated in sacred story by all Jews, and memory, in a stream that runs down the ages ever fresh, passes him on to posterity immortal".
139. By contrast, the account in 36,10 // 1 Esdras 1,45 limits itself to mention of Nebuchadnezzar's deportation of Jehoiachin and the Temple vessels to Babylon and his
installation of Zedekiah as substitute king.
140. This chronological indication takes the place of the notice that Nebuchadnezzar
took Jehoiachin captive "in the eighth year of his [Nebuchadezzar's] reign" of 24,12b. It
harks back to the statement of 10,98c that Jehoiachin reigned a total of "three months and
ten days".
141. This formulation clearly echoes Josephus' notice on Nebuchadnezzar's dealings
with Jehoiakim in 10,97a: οὐκ ἐφύλαξε τὰς πίστεις; see n. 114.
142. Here, as in what precedes (see above), Nebuchadnezzar continues to act through
agents, rather than in person. Contrast 24,12b-16 where he personally is the subject of the
various deportation measures cited.
143. This particular category is not, as such, cited among the various groups of those
taken into captivity by the Babylonians enumerated in 24,12b-16. Conceivably, Josephus
found inspiration for his mention of them in 2 Chr 36,17 where, in Zedekiah's time, the

and craftsmen (τεχνίτας)[144] *and bring them in chains* (δεδεμένους)[145] to him[146] – these came to ten thousand eight hundred and thirty-two in all[147] – as well as Jōachimos with his mother and friends (φίλων; see 10,94, Jehoiakim's "friends")[148]. (102) *And, when they have been brought to him, he kept them under guard...*[149]

Chaldeans slay "the young men" (BL νεανίσκους) in the Temple and "had no compassion on the young man" (so MT; in BL the reference is to Zedekiah himself). Also *b. Sanh.* 92b makes explicit mention of "young men" exiled by Nebuchadnezzar, though leaving it indeterminate when this happened (the Talmud's reference to them further states that these youths were executed by Nebuchadnezzar when the Babylonian husbands complained to him that their looks inspired passionate desire on the part of their wives; subsequently, however, their bones were brought back to life by the prophet Ezekiel; see Ezekiel 37).

144. 2 Kings 24 twice mentions (vv. 14,16) the deportation of this group (designated in BL with the singular τέκτονα), each time associating it with another category, i.e. the "smiths". Rabbinic tradition (see e.g., *Lev. Rab.* 11.7 [ISRAELSTAM and SLOTKI, *Midrash Rabbah Leviticus*, p. 146]; *b. Git.* 88a; *b. Sanh.* 38a) regards the terms "craftsmen and smiths" as designations for the outstanding "scholars" who were exiled with Jehoiakim; according to *SOR* 25.5-6 (GIRÓN BLANC, *Seder 'Olam Rabbah*, pp. 118-119) and *Midr. 'Eser Galuyyot* 10, this exile of the "scholars" took place rather at the end of Jehoiakim's reign; see n. 124). Josephus' non-mention of several additional categories, i.e. the "princes and mighty men of valor" (v. 14) as well as the royal "officials and the chief men of the land" (see v. 15) who were likewise carried off to Babylon at this moment according to 2 Kings 24 may reflect the fact that in 10,98 he has already cited an earlier deportation of "those in power" by Nebuchadnezzar subsequent to the execution of Jehoiakim; see above.

145. This term echoes the reference to Neco's "binding" (ἔδησε) Jehoahaz in 10,82.

146. Here in 10,101 Josephus leaves unspecified the whereabouts of Nebuchadnezzar to whom his generals are instructed to "bring" the captives; see n. 149. Contrast 24,12b-16 where Nebuchadnezzar is represented as carrying them off to Babylon himself.

147. As MARCUS, *Josephus*, VI, p. 213, n. d points out, this figure for the captives differs from those given in 24,12b-16 which speaks of 10,000 persons in v. 14, a further 8,000 in v. 16, plus an additional contingent made up of the king, his mother, wives, officials (see v. 15), the whole coming to a total of well over 18,000 deportees. Josephus derives his own figure (10,832) by combining the datum 10,000 of 24,14 with the mention, in MT Jer 52,29 (> LXX), of Nebuchadnezzar's carrying off 832 persons. In thus associating the deportation of the 832 with the exile of *Jehoiachin*, Josephus, as Marcus further notes, disregards the indication of 52,29 that they were carried off in Nebuchadnezzar's *18th* year, i.e. subsequent to the fall of Jerusalem in *Zedekiah's* reign. Recall here that in 10,98a Josephus drew on the reference in Jer 52,28 to a deportation in Nebuchadnezzar's 7th year in recounting the Babylonian's removal of 3000 of "those in power" subsequent to his execution of Jehoiakim and the Jerusalemite elite (10,97); see above.

148. The above phrase picks up on the reference in 10,100 to Jehoiachin's turning over "his mother and relatives (συγγενεῖς)" to the Babylonian generals. Compare 24,15: "(Nebuchadnezzar) carried away Jehoiachin to Babylon; the king's mother..., his officials (BL εὐνούχους)...". (The listing of 24,15 also mentions Jehoiachin's "wives". Josephus makes no reference to these figures here in 10,101; he will, however, cite them, along with Jehoiachin's "children", in his reprise of the list of those exiled with the king in 10,230; see n. 167.)

149. This indication concerning the execution of Nebuchadnezzar's "command" to his generals as cited in 10,101 continues to leave the king's whereabouts at the moment unspecified; see n. 146.

From his catalogue of Nebuchadnezzar's measures at this moment Josephus leaves aside the item common to 24,13 // 36,10a // 1 Esdras 1,45b (cf. also Jer 28[35],3), i.e. the king's removal of Temple vessels[150]. Instead, he couples his list of Nebuchadnezzar's captives (10,101-102a) directly with a notice (10,102b) on the Babylonian's designation of a substitute king for Judah (= 24,17 // 36,10b // 1 Esdras 1,46): "... and [he] appointed Jōachimos's uncle (θεῖον)[151] Sacchias (Σαχχίαν)[152] as king, after receiving his oath (ὅρκους παρ' αὐτοῦ λαβών)[153] *that he would surely keep the country* (φυλάξειν ... τὴν χώραν)[154] *and attempt no*

---

150. His doing so is in line with his non-mention of an earlier such measure by Nebuchadnezzar as part of his punishment of Jehoiakim as cited in 2 Chr 36,7 // 1 Esdras 1,41 (and Dan 1,2); see n. 125. Subsequently, however, Josephus, as appears from the version of Jer 28,3 (where the prophet Hanniah announces the Lord's intent to bring back the Temple vessels earlier carried away by Nebuchadnezzar along with Jeconiah/Jehoiachin himself) which he places on the lips of Jeremiah in 10,111, does presuppose the Babylonian despoilation of the Temple spoken of in the above texts; see next chapter.

151. In specifying the relationship of Zedekiah to Jehoiachin with this term Josephus aligns himself with MT 24,17 (דֹּד) as well as L 24,17 // BL 36,10b (ἀδελφὸν τοῦ πατρὸς αὐτοῦ) *contra* MT 36,10b which makes Zedekiah Jehoiachin's "brother" (so also 1 Chr 3,16) and B 24,17 according to which he was his predecessor's "son". 1 Esdras 1,46 does not mention the familial relationship between the two kings.

152. On this form of the king's name as reflecting Aramaic influence (cf. the Targums' צִדְקִיָּה), see SCHALIT, *Namenwörterbuch*, p. 108 (who regards it as the Greek translation of an Aramaic זַכָּאי) and PIOVANELLI, *Texte*, 31. Compare צִדְקִיָּהוּ (MT); Ζεδεκία(ς)/ν (BL; the reading of the codices Laur² V as well as Lat in 10,102, i.e. Ζεδεκίαν represents an assimilation to this form). Like 36,10b and 1 Esdras 1,46 Josephus does not mention Zedekiah's pre-regnal name, i.e. "Mattaniah" (so MT 24,17) or Nebuchadnezzar's changing of this name (contrast 10,82 where he does reproduce the notice of 23,34 // 36,4 [> 1 Esdras 1,37] on Neco's changing Eliakim's name to Jehoiakim). Compare *P.R.* 26.3 (W.G. BRAUDE, tr., *Pesikta Rabbati*, II, New Haven-London, Yale University Press, 1968, pp. 528-529) which, in commenting on the name change, states that Zedekiah assumed his new name supposing it to be a portent that "righteous" men would be born to him, whereas, in fact, however, the name intimated the divine intention of "justly" punishing Jerusalem in his time. Hippolytus in his "Preface to Daniel" (see n. 124) 3 conflates Jehoiakim's two successors, having Nebuchadnezzar appoint in his place "his uncle Jechonia *whom he also named Zedekiah*".

153. This phrase ironically echoes that used in 10,100 where Jehoiachin ὅρκους παρ' αὐτῶν λαβών, i.e. Nebuchadnezzar's commanders. The Babylonian king, who had no hesitation about violating his own "oaths" (so 10,101), nevertheless is ready to impose them on another (and, of course, expect them to be kept by him). Josephus found inspiration for the above "oath reference" in 2 Chr 36,13 which speaks of Zedekiah's rebelling against Nebuchadnezzar "who had made him swear (BL ὥρκισεν) by God [1 Esdras 1,48: by the name of the Lord]"; see also Ezek 17,13; cf. n. 157. 2 Kings has no equivalent. In *P.R.* 26.3 (see previous note) Zedekiah is made to swear by the scroll of the Law which Nebuchadnezzar places on his knees, while in *Eccl. Rab.* 9.2 (COHEN, *Midrash Rabbah Ecclesiastes*, p. 227) Zedekiah has to swear by the covenant of circumcision and by the altar.

154. Compare 10,99 where there is reference to Nebuchadnezzar's fear that Jehoiachin would "lead his country to revolt (ἀποστήσῃ τὴν χώραν αὐτοῦ)". Note too the wordplay between 10,101 (Nebuchadnezzar "did not keep [οὐ ἐφύλαξεν] his pledge") and 102 (he requires Zedekiah to "keep [φυλάξειν] the country for him").

uprising (νεωτερίσειν)[155] *nor show friendliness* (εὐνοήσειν)[156] *to the Egyptians*[157]".

6. *Jehoiachin's Release*

Like the author of 2 Kings (see 25,27-30 // Jer 52,31-34)[158], Josephus relates (10,229-230) the deposed Jehoiachin's ultimate fate at the hands of Nebuchadnezzar's successor only after he has narrated the (definitive) fall of Jerusalem and its immediate sequels, thereby preserving the chronological order of events[159]. The source accounts of Jehoiachin's eventual release commence (25,27 // 52,31) with an elaborate dating of this event, i.e. "and in the thirty-seventh year of the captivity of Jehoiachin... in the twelfth month, on the twenty-seventh (so 25,27; twenty-fifth, 52,31)[160] day of the month...". Josephus (10,229) substitutes a simple reprise of his previous mention (10,219) of Nebuchadnezzar's demise: "After the death of Nebuchadnezzar, *his son*[161] Abilmath-

155. On this term, see on 9,195. On the foregoing content of Zedekiah's "oath", compare *P.R.* 26.3 (see previous note) where Zedekiah is made to swear that he will not rebel against Nebuchadnezzar.
156. On this verb, see on 9,153.
157. MARCUS, *Josephus*, VI, p. 213, n. f points out that Josephus' above explication of the "oath" imposed on Zedekiah has no parallel in 2 Chr 36,13 which merely alludes to the fact of his being placed under oath by Nebuchadnezzar. I would suggest, however, that Josephus does have a Biblical basis for the item, i.e. the allegory of the cedar sprig (= Zedekiah) and the two eagles (= Babylon and Egypt, respectively) in Ezekiel 17 (see esp. vv. 13 [Nebuchadnezzar's putting Zedekiah "under oath" and 15 [Zedekiah rebels against Nebuchadnezzar "by sending ambassadors to Egypt"]).
158. Neither 2 Chronicles nor 1 Esdras mention the incident of Jehoiachin's eventual release.
159. In Josephus' presentation his version of 2 Kgs 25,27-30 (10,229-230) is preceded as well by the following items: account of Daniel's activities during the reign of Nebuchadnezzar (10,186-218); mention of Nebuchadnezzar's death after a 43-year reign (10,219a, a point not recorded in the Bible itself); citation of the testimony of Berosus concerning this king (10,219b-226), and allusion to what various other extra-Biblical historians have told of him (10,227-228).
160. In *SOR* 28.2 (GIRÓN BLANC, *Seder 'Olam Rabbah*, p. 129) and *'Abot R. Nat.* (Version B) 17.2 (M.A. NAVARRO PEIRÓ, tr. *Abot de Rabbí Natán* [Biblioteca Midrásica, 5], Valencia, Institución S. Jerónimo, 1987, p. 319) this discrepancy is resolved as follows: Nebuchadnezzar died on the 25th of the month and was buried on the 27th. See further n. 169.
161. The Biblical sources do not mention the family relationship between Nebuchadnezzar and his successor. Josephus derives the datum from Berosus whose account of the latter he cites in *c. Ap.* 1,146; see next note. Also Rabbinic tradition (e.g., *Targum Esther Sheni* 1.2 [B. GROSSFELD, tr., *The Two Targums of Esther* (The Aramaic Bible, 18), Collegeville, Liturgical Press/Michael Glazier, 1991, p. 98]; *SOR* 28.4 [GIRÓN BLANC, *Seder 'Olam Rabbah*, p. 130]; *Pirqe R. El.* 49.3 [PÉREZ FERNÁNDEZ, *Los capítulos de Rabbí Eliezer*, p. 344]) designate Evil-merodach as Nebuchadnezzar's son.

adachos (Ἀβιλμαθαδάχος)[162], who took the royal power, at once released Jechonias (Ἰεχονίαν)[163] from his chains (τῶν δεσμῶν)...[164]".

The Biblical accounts (25,28-30 // 52,32-34) proceed to enumerate a series of benefits accorded the released Jehoiachin: he is spoken kindly to by Evil-merodach, is granted a seat higher than those of the other kings resident in Babylon, can doff his prison garments, dines daily with his overlord, and receives an allowance from him as long as he lives. Josephus reduces the five items of this enumeration to three, likewise substituting other wording for all but one of them, the whole serving to accentuate the favor to which Jehoiachin finally attains "... and kept him as one of his closest friends (τοῖς ἀναγκαιοτάτοις τῶν φίλων; see 10,5.59), giving him many gifts (πολλὰς αὐτῷ δωρεὰς δούς)[165] and setting him above the kings in Babylonia[166]".

To his account (10,229) of Evil-merodach's initiative, drawn from 2 Kgs 25,27-30 // Jer 52,31-34, Josephus appends (10,230) a motivation for that act which is entirely his own creation, even while it does hark back to his mention of Nebuchadnezzar's "treachery" in his dealings with Jehoaichin in 10,101. This reads:

> For his father [Nebuchadnezzar] had not kept faith (τὴν πίστιν οὐκ ἐφύλαξεν; cf. ἡ πίστις ... οὐ ... ἐφύλαξεν αὐτήν, 10,101) with

162. This is the conjecture of Niese which Marcus follows for the varied readings of the codices (for these see MARCUS, *Josephus*, VI, p. 284, n. 2); SCHLATTER, *Namen*, p. 11 and SCHALIT, *Namenwörterbuch*, p. 2 opine that the original form was likely Ἀβιλμοραδαχος. In *c. Ap.* 1,146, Josephus, quoting Berosus, calls the king "Evilmaraduch" (Εὐειλμαράδουχος). Compare אֱוִיל מְרֹדַךְ (MT); Εὐειαλμαρωδέκ (B 25,27); Εὐϊλὰδ Μαρωδάχ (L 25,27); Ουλαιμαραδαχ (LXX 52,31).

163. On this form, see NIESE, *Opera*, I, p. xxxi who views it as a (one-time) scribal assimilation to that read by BL 2 Chr 36,8, i.e. Ἰεχονίας (this is likewise the form of the name found in *BJ* 6,104). Recall that in 10,97-101 Josephus designates the king rather as Ἰωάκιμος (thus the reading adopted by Niese and Marcus; see n. 120). Compare Ιωακείμ (B 25,27); Ιωακιμ (LXX 52,31); Ἰωακείν (L 25,27).

164. This term echoes the mention in 10,101 of Nebuchadnezzar's order that the Judean captives, including Jehoiachin, be brought to him "in chains" (δεδεμένους); here in 10,229 Josephus intimates that Jehoiachin had remained "enchained" throughout the intervening period. With the above notice on Jehoiachin's release compare the figurative language of MT 25,27 which reads literally "he [Evil-merodach] lifted up the head of Jehoiachin [+ and he brought him forth, BL TJ Jer 52,31] from the prison-house".

165. This item might be seen as Josephus' embellishment of the wording of 25,30 (cf. 52,34): "and for his allowance, a regular allowance was given him (BL ἐδόθη αὐτῷ) by the king, every day a portion, as long as he lived".

166. Compare 25,28b // 52,32b: "... and gave him a seat above the seats of the kings who were with him in Babylon". With the Biblical and Josephan catalogues of the favors done Jehoiachin by Evil-merodach, compare that of *Targum Esther Sheni* 2.1 (GROSS-FELD, *The Two Targums of Esther*, p. 98). Here, at the urging of Daniel, Evil-merodach releases, not only Jehoiachin, but all his fellow prisoners. Having done so, he proceeds to bathe and anoint Jehoiachin, put a royal garment upon him, and have him eat with him regularly as long as he lives.

Jechonias when he had voluntarily surrendered (παραδόντι) himself with his wives and children and all his relatives (συγγενείας)[167] for the sake of his native city (τῆς πατρίδος), that it might not be taken by siege and razed (κατασκαφείη ληφθεῖσα ὑπὸ τῆς πολιορκίας)[168] as we have said before[169].

Conclusions: Josephus' Rewriting of 2 Kgs 23,30b-24,17 (+ 25,27-30), etc.

Josephus' account of the three Judean kings Jehoahaz, Jehoiakim, and Jehoiachin in 10,81-101 (+ 229-230) is notable, first of all, for its recurrent insertion of elements drawn from the Book of Jeremiah (as also that of Ezekiel; see on 10,98 and 102b) into a narrative line which he takes over from the Historical Books, in particular the more expansive presentation of 2 Kgs 23,30b-24,17 (itself, partially reproduced in the BL plusses of 2 Chronicles 36; see, e.g., on 10,81.83.87.101-102a) as opposed to its summary parallels in MT 2 Chr 36,1-10 and 1 Esdras 1,34-46a[170]. With regard

167. In 10,101 the reference is to Jehoiachin's "delivering up (παραδίδωσι) his mother and his relatives (συγγενεῖς)". Josephus derives the reference to the king's "wives" as also among the captives here in 10,230 from 2 Kgs 24,15; see n. 148. The enumeration of the exiles in 24,12b-16 makes no mention of Jehoiachin's "children".

168. With this sequence compare Jeremiah's announcement to Zedekiah as cited in 10,112 that Nebuchadnezzar would "besiege (πολιορκήσει) Jerusalem... and raze (κατασκάψει) the city". It was to keep this calamity from happening that Jehoiachin had sacrificed himself.

169. This concluding *Rückverweis* is designed to remind readers of Josephus' statements in 10,99: "He [Nebuchadnezzar] therefore sent a force which besieged (ἐπολιόρκει) Jōachimos in Jerusalem. But he [Jehoiachin], being kind and just, did not think it right to suffer the city to be endangered on his account...". With Josephus' notice on Evil-merodach's undoing his father's treatment of Jehoiachin; compare *SOR* 28.2 (see n. 160) (cf. *Lev. Rab.* 18.2, ISRAELSTAM and SLOTKI, *Midrash Rabbah Leviticus*, p. 229) which relates that, in conjunction with his release of Jehoiachin, Evil-merodach exumed his father's remains as a sign that he was abrogating the latter's decrees against the Judean. In so doing he brought to fulfillment the announcement of Isa 14,19 concerning the "king of Babylon" (see 14,1): "but you are cast out, away from your sepulchre, like a loathed untimely birth". Compare the somewhat divergent presentation found in *'Abot R. Nat.* (Version B) 17.2-3 (NAVARRO PEIRÓ, *Abot de Rabbí Natán*, pp. 319-320). Here Evil-Merodach enters the prison on the 27th day (so 2 Kgs 25,27) and questions the jailors about their captives. The former inform him that whereas the other kings imprisoned there had been guilty of rebelling against Nebuchadnezzar's decrees, Jehoiachin had done nothing to deserve his incarceration. Thereupon, Evil-merodach exumes and drags about his father's remains as the prerequisite for annulling his decree against Jehoiachin. This Midrash further elucidates the "good words" which Evil-merodach spoke to Jehoiachin (2 Kgs 25,28) in terms of his telling the latter not to fear given that although his father had afflicted him, he himself would not do so, and had in fact dishonored his father's remains.

170. On occasion, however, Josephus does make use of a peculiarity of (MT) 2 Chronicles 36 *contra* 2 Kings; see, e.g., his reference to Nebuchadnezzar's coming against Jehoiakim (10,96 = 36,6a; cf. 1 Esdras 1,40a) and to the former's putting Zedekiah under oath (10,102 = 36,13; cf. 1 Esdras 1,48).

to the text-form(s) of his sources employed by Josephus in this segment, we noted recurrent affinities between his presentation and the longer MT-text of Jeremiah (see nn. 54,82,89,98,124,147), although indications of his familiarity also with the shorter LXX-text of the book were not totally lacking (e.g., his reference to Jeremiah's book as dealing with the fate of "the city" in 10,93 corresponds to the mention of "Jerusalem" in the source verse LXX 43,3 as opposed to MT 36,3's "Israel"; see n. 86). On the other hand, we failed to find significant pointers regarding the text-form(s) of Kings and Chronicles utilized by the historian for his narrative of the royal trio.

Throughout 10,81-102 (229-230), Josephus does notably reduce his sources' level of detail; see, e.g., his handling of both Jeremiah 26 and 36 (10,89-95) as well as his compression of the deportee list of 2 Kgs 24,12b-16 in 10,101-102a. By contrast, he markedly expands on a whole series of source items: the Carchemish confrontation (10,84-85; compare Jer 46[26],2), Nebuchadnezzar's initial subjugation of Jehoiakim (10,87; compare 2 Kgs 24,1), the former's subsequent advance against the latter (10,96; compare 2 Chr 36,6a; cf. 1 Esdras 1,41a), the Babylonian's threat against Jehoiachin and the latter's response (10,99-100; compare 2 Kgs 24,10-12a // 2 Chr 36,10a; cf. 1 Esdras 1,45a); see too his appended notice, unparalleled in either 2 Kgs 25,27-30 or Jer 52,31-34, on the rationale for Evil-Merodach's release of Jehoiachin (10,230).

Josephus also rearranges the sources' sequence. Thus, e.g., he reverses the order of the sequels to Neco's seizure of Jehoahaz as reported in 2 Kgs 23,33b-35 in 10,82b-83a, "repositions" the elements of 2 Kgs 24,7 (see 10,86 and 88b), and "anticipates" the reference to Nebuchadnezzar's putting Zedekiah under oath (2 Chr 36,13; cf. 1 Esdras 1,48) in 10,102b. Modifications/ adaptations of source data are likewise frequent in 10,81-101 (+ 229-230): Jehoahaz reigns an extra ten days (10,83; compare 2 Kgs 23,31bα // 2 Chr 36,2b // 1 Esdras 1,35: a round three months). Jeremiah's message in Jehoiakim's reign (Jer 26,1-6) is reformulated in terms reminiscent of his preaching in Zedekiah's time as reported in the Book of Jeremiah and given a "deterministic" slant as well (see 10,89). The prophet's accusers and judges/protectors (10,90) are both different from those cited in 26,7-16. The elders' invocation of Micah's word and the reaction to this by Hezekiah takes on a more general character (10,92; compare 26,18-19). Jeremiah writes his prophecies on his own volition rather than at God's direction (10,93b; compare Jer 36,2), just as he himself, not Baruch (so 36,2) publicly reads the book containing these (10,94). Nebuchadnezzar is explicitly stated to have "killed" Jehoiakim (10,97.99; compare 2 Kgs 24,6a //

2 Chr 36,6b // 1 Esdras 1,40b), and to have appointed the latter's successor Jehoiachin (10,97; compare 2 Kgs 24,6b // 2 Chr 36,8b // 1 Esdras 1,43b). The sources' unqualifiedly negative evaluation of Jehoiachin (2 Kgs 24,9 // 2 Chr 36,9b // 1 Esdras 1,44b) becomes a commendation of the king as "kind and just" – qualities which, in turn, motivate his surrender to Nebuchadnezzar (10,100). The figure given for "the exile of Jehoiachin" in 2 Kgs 24,12b-16 (i.e. 18,000+) is reduced (see 10,101) to 10,832 via a combination of 2 Kgs 24,14 and MT Jer 52,29. Nebuchadnezzar acts through his "commanders" rather than in person when dealing with Jehoiachin and the Jerusalemites (10,100-101; compare 2 Kgs 24,10-16). Finally, the reference to Evil-merodach's making Jehoiachin one of his "closest friends" (10,229) has no equivalent in the catalogue of the former's beneficences to the latter in 2 Kgs 25,28-30 // Jer 52,32-34.

Overall, the historian's application of the foregoing rewriting techniques in 10,81-102 (+ 229-230) results in a streamlined version of the period covered, with a noteworthy diminuation of minor proper names and specifications of place. The divine role in the course of events is sharply played down via elimination (see 2 Kgs 24,2-4; cf. n. 102) or reworking (see 10,89; compare Jer 26,1-6; 10,93b; compare Jer 36,1-3) of source passages that mention God's initiatives. Conversely, Josephus repeatedly interjects allusions to personages' motives/emotional responses; see 10,87 (Jehoiakim). 88 (Jehoiakim). 89-90 (the people in their reaction to Jeremiah's prophesying). 95 (Jehoiakim). 96 (Jehoiakim and Nebuchadnezzar). 100 (Jehoiachin). and 230 (Evil-merodach). The historian's characterizations of the period's players likewise appear distinctive – especially for what concerns Jehoiachin and Nebuchadnezzar. The former figure, as noted above, appears no longer as a bad – as in the Bible – but a good king with a selfless concern for the city's survival, whereas the "treachery" of the Babylonian monarch is repeatedly accentuated (see 10,97.99.100.230) in a way that goes far beyond the Bible's portrayal of him. Also to be noted under this heading is Josephus' "scrambling", throughout 10,81-102, of source data, such that what the Bible tells of one figure or time is reported by him in connection with a different personage or period (see, e.g., nn. 61,70,115,116,142,147). Thereby, he underscores the common (negative) character of the entire epoch from the death of Josiah through the fall of Jerusalem under Zedekiah.

This leaves the question of what message(s) Josephus' presentation in 10,81-102 (+ 229-230) might be intended to offer *AJ*'s double audience. Roman readers would, doubtless, find appealing the segment's height-

ened attention to politico-military matters and, above all, the summons
to submission to the *force majeure* of the regnant Empire implicit in the
words of Jeremiah (10,89) and the deed of the "kind and just"
Jehoiachin (10,100). That same summons, of course, likewise has in
view Jewish readers, to whom Josephus' prophet and king would further
function as Biblical precedents/warrants for his own conduct during the
War[171]. On the other hand, there is also the above-cited matter of Josephus' accentuation of the "treachery" displayed by Nebuchadnezzar in
his dealings with the Jews to which the hapless Jehoiachin fell victim.
Given the natural, obvious association of Nebuchadnezzar's Babylon
with contemporary Rome as fellow destroyers of Jerusalem[172] that
would suggest itself to contemporary Jews, Josephus' highlighting of
this point would seem intended to signal to his compatriots the need for
upmost caution and circumspection in their dealings with the new Babylon and its (deceitful) assurances[173]. Here again, then, one encounters the
willed ambiguity which characterizes Josephus' handling of the "Roman
theme" throughout *AJ*.

171. On Jehoiachin as a vehicle for Josephus' self-*apologia*, see FELDMAN, *Studies*,
pp. 442-444 (= ID., *Jehoiachin*, 25-27). On the similar role assumed by Jeremiah in Josephus' portrayal of him, see: D. DAUBE, *Typology in Josephus*, in *JJS* 31 (1980) 18-36,
pp. 26-27.
172. On the equation of Rome with Babylon in (later) Jewish literature, see BERN-
STEIN, *Nebucadnezar*, pp. 52-53; GINZBERG, *Legends*, VI, pp. 280, 419, 426; cf. pp. 491-
492, n. 250.
173. See nn. 114,141. Recall in this connection that Josephus interjects a like emphasis on the "treachery" of an earlier imperial power, i.e. Assyria, in his retelling of the
Biblical accounts of Sennacherib's assault on Jerusalem; see on 10,2-4.

XXII

ZEDEKIAH AND JEREMIAH[1]
(10,103-130)

The Biblical historical complexes follow their summary accounts of the short-reigned Jehoiachin with an equally summary narrative of the accession of his successor Zedekiah, that king's rebellion against his Babylonian overlord, and the extended siege of Jerusalem which that rebellion called forth (2 Kgs 24,18-25,1 [= Jer 52,1-4] // 2 Chr 36,11-17a). Josephus expatiates on these developments, doing so on the basis of material found in the Book(s) of Jeremiah (and Ezekiel), in 10,103-130. This segment, in turn, may be divided into three somewhat parallel sequences, each involving an intervention by the prophet at a given moment during Judah's final decade: 1. First Intervention (at beginning of Zedekiah's reign, 10,103-107); 2. Second Intervention (during a break in the Babylonian siege of Jerusalem, 10,108-115); and 3. Third Intervention (towards the end of the siege, 10,116-130).

1. *First Intervention*

Josephus precedes his account of the initial exchange between Zedekiah and Jeremiah with various notices concerning the former which he draws from 2 Kgs 24,17b-19 // 2 Chr 36,10b-12a // 1 Esdras 1,46b-47a (cf. Jer 37 [LXX 44],1-2; Ezek 17,13) in 10,103a. Here, Josephus informs us of four points: Zedekiah's age at accession (21 years)[2], his being a

---

1. This chapter represents a reworking of my articles *Josephus' Zedekiah*, in *ETL* 65 (1989) 89-104, pp. 96-101; *Jeremiah under King Zedekiah according to* ANT. *10.102-130*, in *REJ* 156 (1997) 1-36 which I use here by permission. It draws as well on the treatment of Zedekiah by FELDMAN, *Studies*, pp. 450-461 (= ID., *Josephus' Portrait of Zedekiah*, in Y. ELMAN & J.S. GUROCK (eds.), *Hazon Nahum: Studies in Jewish Law, Thought, and History Presented to Dr. Norman Lamm on the Occasion of his Seventieth Birthday*, Hoboken, NJ, Ktav, 1997, 69-92).

2. The historian's reproduction of this source item (see 24,18 // 36,11 // 1 Esdras 1,46b) here at the start of his account of Zedekiah is unusual in several respects, his ordinary procedure being to mention a king's age at death rather than at accession, and to do this at the end of his presentation of the given king. Perhaps, in handling the item as he does, Josephus intends to highlight the fact of Zedekiah's youth at the moment of his becoming king; his age, in turn, would serve to attenuate the wrongdoing which both Josephus and the Bible will attribute to him.

brother of "Jōakeimos"[3], his having the same mother as the latter[4], and, finally, his being "contemptuous of justice and duty" (τῶν ... δικαίων καὶ τοῦ δέοντος ὑπερόπτης)[5]. This complex concludes with a statement (10,103b) which mitigates the king's just-mentioned personal "depravity" by ascribing it to the influence of his courtiers and people ("*for* those of his own age about him were impious [ἀσεβεῖς] and the entire multitude (ὄχλος) had licence to act as outrageously [ὕβριζεν][6] as it pleased") and which itself seems inspired by 2 Chr 36,14a ("all the leading priests [BL: the nobles of Judah and the priests] and the people [+ of the land, BL] likewise were exceedingly unfaithful...")[7]. It is to this last notice that Josephus (10,104) attaches his presentation of Jeremiah's initial confrontation with Judah's last king: "it was for this reason that the prophet Jeremiah came to him [Zedekiah] and solemnly (πολλάκις)[8] protested...". Nowhere in the Biblical sources does one hear, as such, of Jeremiah appearing before Zedekiah at the beginning of the latter's reign to "protest" as Josephus represents him as doing here. On the other hand, Josephus may well have found indirect inspiration for his presentation in

3. And so *uncle* of the deposed Jehoiachin (as stated in 10,102). As MARCUS, *Josephus*, VI, p. 214, n. a points out, the sources differ with regard to Zedekiah's relationship with his two immediate predecessors. The historian's indication on the matter agrees with that given in MT L 2 Kgs 24,17 // BL 2 Chr 36,10. By contrast, B 24,17 makes Zedekiah the *son* of the deposed Jehoiachin, while in MT 36,10 he appears as Jehoiachin's *brother*.

4. MARCUS, *Josephus*, VI, pp. 214-215, n. b points out that the above indication involves a discrepancy between Josephus' earlier notice on the name of Jehoiakim's mother, i.e. Zabudah (10,83; compare 23,36: Zebidah) and the mention of "Hamutal" as Zedekiah's own mother in 24,18b, these data entailing that Jehoiakim and Zedekiah were half – rather than (so 10,103) – full brothers. Marcus goes on to suggest that Josephus here in 10,103 has confused Jehoiakim with his half-brother Jehoahaz who in 2 Kgs 23,31 is assigned the same mother as is Zedekiah in 24,18, i.e. Hamutal (in Josephus' parallel to 23,31 in 10,81 the name of Jehoahaz' mother is "Amitalē").

5. This accusation against Zedekiah echoes the one made against Jehu in his later reign in 9,160: "he became careless (ὑπερόπτης) of his duties towards the Deity and contemptuous of holiness and the laws". Compare the stereotyped formulas used of Zedekiah in 24,19 ("he did what was evil in the sight of the Lord according to all that Jehoiakim had done") and 36,12a // 1 Esdras 1,47a ("he did what evil in the sight of the Lord his God"). The above substantivized adjectival collocation "justice and duty" occurs only here in Josephus; in calling Zedekiah "contemptuous of justice (τῶν δικαίων)" the historian establishes a terminological contrast between him and his predecessor Jehoiachin whom 10,100 calls "kind and just (δίκαιος)".

6. This is the reading adopted by Dindorf, Bekker, Niese, Naber, and Marcus. ROLaurV read ἐξύβριζεν.

7. On Josephus' recurrent tactic of exculpating Zedekiah by highlighting the reprobate character of those around him, see FELDMAN, *Studies*, pp. 455-461 (= ID., *Zedekiah*, 84-91). Rabbinic tradition takes a somewhat similar line; see, e.g., *b. 'Arak.* 17a (which contrasts the two kings Zedekiah – who was virtuous whereas his generation was not and Jehoiakim – under whom the opposite state of affairs prevailed) and *b. Sanh.* 103a (the righteousness of Zedekiah placated God's anger at the wickedness of his generation).

8. On the translation of this term, see MARCUS, *Josephus* VI, p. 215, n. e.

various Scriptural contexts. Thus the Chronicler immediately follows his introductory notices on Zedekiah (2 Chr 36,10b-12a) with the remark (36,12b = 1 Esdras 1,47b) that the royal evil-doer (see 36,12a) "did not humble himself before Jeremiah the prophet, who spoke from the mouth of the Lord". Similarly, Jer 37,1-2 directly juxtaposes mention of Zedekiah's accession with the affirmation that the king, his officials and people, all disregarded Jeremiah's words. Finally, in some Hebrew MSS of Jer 27,1 the prophet's address to Zedekiah urging submission to the Babylonian "yoke" (27,12-15) is dated to "the beginning of the reign of Zedekiah[9]". It is these Biblical indications, I suggest, that might have given Josephus the idea of having Jeremiah confront Zedekiah right at the start of his reign. The remainder of 10,104 is Josephus' (indirect discourse) "citation" of Jeremiah's word to Zedekiah on this occasion. It commences: "... (he bade) him leave off his various impieties and lawless acts (ἀσεβείας καὶ παρανομίας)[10], and watch over justice (προνοεῖν ... τοῦ δικαίου)[11] and neither pay heed to the leaders (ἡγεμόσι), because there were wicked men (πονηρούς) among them...". This admonition has no actual equivalent in the Biblical record (in the words of Jeremiah to/ against Zedekiah cited in the Book of Jeremiah the king is never charged as such with cultic misdeeds or law-breaking). On the other hand, the rebuke does appear quite appropriate in its Josephan context where it picks up on the statements concerning Zedekiah's personal "contemptuousness of justice (τῶν δικαίων; cf. n. 11) and duty" and his contemporaries' "impiety" (ἀσεβεῖς; cf. n. 10) of 10,103. In addition, Jeremiah's reference to the "leaders" here serves to introduce into the story a group which, throughout his account of Zedekiah's reign, will function as the prophet's primary enemy and rival; see below.

Josephus' Jeremiah next proceeds to warn Zedekiah about a second influential group: "... nor put faith (πεπιστευκέναι)[12] in the false prophets (ψευδοπροφήταις)[13] who were deceiving (ἀπατῶσιν) him...".

---

9. The opening of Jer 27,1 is textually problematic. Most Hebrew MSS read "in the beginning of the reign of *Jehoiakim*". The minority Hebrew reading "Zedekiah" (see above) is found also in TJ and is advocated by BHS. LXX Jeremiah 27(34) lacks an equivalent to MT's v. 1.

10. This collocation occurs only here in Josephus. Cf. the adjective ἀσεβεῖς (of the people) in 10,103.

11. For this construction see on 9,93; cf. the reference to Zedekiah's being "contemptous of justice (τῶν δικαίων)" in 10,103.

12. The verb πιστεύω (and its cognates) is a *Leitwort* in Josephus' presentation of Zedekiah; see 10,105.106.107.114.119.124. Compare the similar concentration of "belief terminology" in Josephus' version of the story of Hezekiah's illness in 10,24-29, as noted in our chap. XVIII.

13. On the term "false prophet" in Josephus, see on 9,134.

This added warning does have a counterpart in the Biblical Jeremiah's exhortation to Zedekiah in Jer 27(34),14: "Do not listen to the words of the prophets who are saying to you" (so MT[14]; recall that this word is dated to "the beginning of the reign of Zedekiah" in some Hebrew MSS of 27,1); cf. also 37(43),9, where the Jerusalemites are warned "do not *deceive* yourselves" (LXX: μὴ ὑπολάβητε ταῖς ψυχαῖς ὑμῶν) and 38(45),22 "your [Zedekiah's] trusted friends have deceived (ἠπάτησαν, i.e. the same verb used in 10,104; see above) you". As does Jer 27,14, Josephus has Jeremiah go on to "quote" the deceptive words of Zedekiah's "prophets". The content of their cited words diverges, however. In the Biblical verse, the prophets urge Zedekiah "not to serve the king of Babylon". In 10,104, by contrast, their words comprise a double promise: "the Babylonian king would never again make war on the city and... the Egyptians would take the field against the Babylonian king and conquer him". Of the two components of the Josephan (false) prophets' promise here, the first does have a counterpart in Jer 37(44),19 where Jeremiah asks the king: "where are your prophets who prophesied to you saying, 'The king of Babylon will not come up against you and against this land'"? To be noted, however, is the fact that this evocation of the prophets' assurance by the Biblical Jeremiah of chap. 37(44) comes only during the Babylonian siege of Jerusalem at the end of Zedekiah's reign (see vv. 5, 7, 11) and in the context of a secret interview between king and prophet following the latter's imprisonment (see vv. 16-17). Here in 10,104 then Josephus "anticipates" the item to the start of Zedekiah's reign. The prophets' second promise in 10,104, i.e. of an effective Egyptian intervention against Babylon lacks a Biblical equivalent. It can, however, be seen as Josephus' transposition into (quoted) prediction of the references to the Egyptian advance and subsequent withdrawal during the siege of Jerusalem in Jer 37,5.7.11[15]. By thus noting here in 10,104 that the false prophets actually made such a prediction early in Zedekiah's reign, Josephus provides a motivation for Zedekiah's eventual defection to Egypt such as he will subsequently relate; see 10,108. Jeremiah's warning about the false prophets concludes at the end of 10,104 with his affirmation concerning their just –

14. This element has no counterpart in the LXX text of Jer 27(34),14(11) printed by Ziegler.

15. The wording of this "quotation" (Αἰγύπτιοι στρατεύσουσιν ἐπ' αὐτόν [i.e. Nebuchadnezzar]) here in 10,104 likewise echoes that of the (false) rumor heard by Jehoiakim as cited in 10,88 (στρατεύειν τοὺς Αἰγυπτίους ... ἐπὶ τὸν Βαβυλώνιον). The verbal similarity between the two passages points up both the unreliability of the Egyptians and the fatal consequences of Judah's kings putting their trust in them for help against Babylon.

cited promises: "… in this… they spoke falsely (οὐκ ἀληθῆ)[16] and these things were not to be". This statement echoes that pronounced by Jeremiah in Jer 27(34),14 regarding the prophets' promise as quoted by him there (see above), i.e. "it is a lie (MT שֶׁקֶר, LXX ἄδικια) which they are prophesying to you". Note, however, that what is being called "false" by Jeremiah differs in Jer 27,14 and *AJ* 10,104: in the former text it is the prophets' urging Zedekiah not to submit to the Babylonians, while in the latter it concerns the double prophetic (false) promise as cited above. The effect of this shift is to enhance Jeremiah's credibility as a prophet: already at the start of Zedekiah's reign he predicts in detail how things will (not) turn out at its end. Taking Jeremiah's speech in 10,104 as a whole, we might then designate it with P. Piovanelli as a *montage*[17] of elements drawn by Josephus from different contexts of the Book of Jeremiah, i.e. 27,14; 37,19; cf. also 37,5.7.11. In addition, however, Josephus amplifies the Biblical components of the prophet's speech with other elements of his own, i.e. Jeremiah's opening admonition to Zedekiah to desist from wrong-doing and to disregard the "leaders". We shall see the same compositional principle operative also in the subsequent portions of Josephus' account of Jeremiah under Zedekiah.

Having presented Jeremiah's speech to the king at the start of his reign in 10,104, Josephus next (10,105) relates the latter's response. That response unfolds in two moments, the first positive, the second negative. "So long", we are told initially, "as he listened to the prophet saying these things", Zedekiah "believed (ἐπείθετο) him and agreed to everything as true (ἀληθεύουσι; compare 10,104 οὐκ ἀληθῆ) and that it was to his interest (συμφέρον)[18] to have faith (πεπιστευκέναι; compare 10,104 [μήτε] πεπιστευκέναι) in him". Subsequently, however, "his friends (οἱ φίλοι) once more corrupted (διέφθειραν)[19] him and, winning him away from the prophet, led him wherever they pleased (ἤθελον)[20]". How might Josephus have come to this depiction of Zedekiah's two-stage response to Jeremiah's word? In having the king

16. Note the prevalence of falsehood terminology in Jeremiah's address as cited above in 10,104 ("false prophets", "deceiving", "untruly"). This terminology (and its positive counterpart) permeates the whole of Josephus' account of Zedekiah.

17. PIOVANELLI, *Texte*, 23.

18. This is the reading adopted by Niese, Naber, and Marcus. Dindorf and Bekker read συμφέρειν with MSP Exc.

19. This is the reading adopted by Bekker, Niese, and Marcus. Dindorf and Naber read the imperfect διέφθειρον with RO.

20. This indication concerning the friends leading Zedekiah where they "pleased" echoes Josephus statement in 10,103 about the "entire multitude having licence to act outrageously as it pleased (ἤθελεν)". The echo underscores Zedekiah's ineffectuality in the face of the (reprobate) desires of all segments of the population.

ultimately disregard the prophet's warning, he was likely influenced by the generalizing statements of 2 Chr 36,12b (Zedekiah failed to "humble himself" before Jeremiah) and Jer 37,1 MT (the king "did not listen" to the Lord's words spoken through Jeremiah); see above. There is as well a possible Biblical basis for Josephus' further attribution of Zedekiah's eventual rejection of Jeremiah's message to the machinations of the royal "friends" in particular. Thus, in Jer 38(45),22, in the context of the final interview between them just prior to the fall of Jerusalem, Jeremiah quotes to Zedekiah the words of a lament the palace women will pronounce over him, i.e. "your trusted friends (MT literally"the men of your peace", LXX: ἄνδρες εἰρηνικοί σου) have deceived you...". As with 37,14 (see above on 10,104) Josephus has then "anticipated" to the start of Zedekiah's reign the formulation of 38,22 which in the Bible itself is dated to its end. Josephus' notice on the king's spontaneous positive reaction to Jeremiah's words in 10,105, on the other hand, has no obvious Biblical precedent. That Josephan "creation" does, however, accord with the historian's overall endeavor to portray Zedekiah in a more favorable light. It likewise foreshadows the king's subsequent response to Jeremiah's words to him as recounted in 10,127; see below.

In 10,106-107 Josephus has still more to say on the question of why Zedekiah (ultimately) disregarded Jeremiah's (initial) warning to him. In this ("un-Biblical") appendix to his account of the first interaction between king and prophet (10,104-105), Josephus begins (10,106a) by noting that Jeremiah's announcements of doom were seconded by Ezekiel, who, in his exile in Babylon[21], "prophesied the misfortunes that were to befall the people and wrote them down (γράψας)[22] and sent them to Jerusalem". Nonetheless, he goes on to say (10,106b) Zedekiah "disbelieved" (ἠπίστησεν; compare πεπιστευκέναι, 10,105) the combined word of the two prophets. He did so in view of a single (apparent) discrepancy within their joint announcement about Jerusalem's coming fall and Zedekiah's own capture. The discrepancy that thus occasions Zedekiah's "unbelief" concerns the king's post-capture fate; its Biblical basis lies in the (seeming) contrast between the predictions of Ezek 12,13 and Jer 34(41),3. In the former text the Lord states that he will bring the captured "prince" of Jerusalem (see vv. 10-12) to Babylon which, however, the prince will "not see" (LXX οὐκ

21. Josephus has already cited Ezekiel as one who corroborated the message of Jeremiah in 10,79. In 10,94 he further mentions (compare Ezek 1,1-3) that the "boy" Ezekiel was among those deported to Babylon as a sequel to Nebuchadnezzar's execution of Jehoiakim.

22. This is the reading of O Zon and adopted Niese, Naber, and Marcus. Dindorf and Bekker read ἀκούσας with RMSPLaurV; E Lat have no equivalent.

ὄψεται). The divine address to Zedekiah Jer 34(41),3b[23], for its part, announces: "you shall see (LXX ὄψονται) the king of Babylon eye to eye... and you shall go to Babylon". In other words, although there is no direct contradiction between them – Zedekiah could have been blinded after his "seeing" of Nebuchadnezzar (so Jeremiah) and before his deportation to Babylon – the two prophets might appear to diverge on the question of whether or not Zedekiah will "see" his place of exile. In Josephus' (abridged) citation of their respective words the purported "contradiction" between them does not, it might be said, emerge all that clearly, however. It reads: "... Ezekiel in saying that Sacchias would not see (οὐκ ὄψεται = LXX Ezek 12,13) Babylon, differed from Jeremiah who told him that the king of Babylon would take him there *in chains* (δεδεμένον)[24]". The above formulation leaves readers to infer the intended contrast with Ezekiel's announcement for themselves, i.e. according to Jeremiah Zedekiah would, in fact, "see" his place of exile, Ezekiel's announcement to the contrary. In any event, it was due to this "disagreement", Josephus ends up informing us (10,107a), that Zedekiah "condemned" (καταγνούς) the two prophets' words as "untrue" (οὐδ'... ἀληθῆ; note the ironic contrast here where 10,104 where Jeremiah qualifies the false prophets' words as οὐκ ἀληθῆ) "and refused to believe (ἠπίστησε; compare ἠπίστησεν, 10,106a)[25] them".

As Josephus now hastens (10,107b) to add, Zedekiah's disbelief was a fatal mistake on his part: "nevertheless everything happened to him in accordance with their prophecies, as we shall show in a more fitting place". The *Vorverweis* at the the end of this statement look ahead to 10,140b-141 which relates:

23. Jer 34,1 dates this word to the time of the siege of Jerusalem at the end of Zedekiah's reign. Josephus' presentation seems to "antedate" the announcement to the start of his rule, thereby accentuating Jeremiah's predictive capacities; see above on his use of Jer 37,14 in 10,104. On the varying conceptions of what ulitimately happened to Zedekiah in the Book of Jeremiah itself, see J. APPLEGATE, *The Fate of Zedekiah: Redactional Debate in the Book of Zedekiah*, in *VT* 48 (1998) 137-160, 301-308.

24. This specification has no equivalent in Jer 34(41),3. It would seem to be inspired by the notice of 2 Kgs 25,7 // Jer 52,11: (the Babylonians) "bound Zedekiah in fetters (LXX ἐν πέδαις) and took him to Babylon". Thus here too (see previous note), Josephus magnifies Jeremiah's predictive powers: already years in advance, he foretells in detail the circumstances of Zedekiah's capture/deportation. Note too that the above participle echoes 10,101 where there is mention of Nebuchadnezzar's order that the Jerusalemite youth and craftsmen be brought to him "in chains (δεδεμένους)".

25. The Greek sequence καταγνοὺς ἠπίστησε in 10,107a represents the conjecture of J. Hudson which Dindorf, Bekker, and Marcus adopt. That conjecture combines the separate readings of SP (καταγνούς) and E (ἠπίστησε). Niese and Naber simply follow SP. Compare ROMLaurV's γνούς.

(140)... having put out Sacchias's eyes, he [Nebuchadnezzar] bound him in chains (δήσας; compare δεδεμένον, 10,106) and took him off to Babylon. (141) And thus there befell him what both Jeremiah and Ezekiel had prophesied to him, namely that he would be captured and brought to the Babylonian king and speak to him to his face and with his own eyes look into his eyes, which is what Jeremiah had said; furthermore, being blinded *and taken to Babylon*[26], he did not see it, as Ezekiel had foretold.

As noted above, the sequence of 10,106-107 is a Josephan "creation", one inspired by his adverting to the apparent discrepancy between the predictions of Ezek 12,13 and Jer 34,3. At the same time, however, the sequence (along with its "conclusion" in 10,140b-141) evidences certain characteristic emphases of Josephus' "prophetology", i.e. prophecy understood as above all a matter of accurate prediction and the agreement among true prophets in their announcements, even when these might, *prima facie*, appear to diverge.

2. *Second Intervention*

The next segment that might be distinguished within Josephus' account of Jeremiah under Zedekiah is 10,108-115 which deals with the beginnings of the Babylonian siege and the "interlude" of the Egyptian intervention. This new segment opens with mention of Zedekiah's revolt against Babylon. Josephus draws this item from the historical notices of 2 Kgs 24,20b // Jer 52,3b, embellishing their wording with elements likely inspired by the allegory of Ezekiel 17. His formulation thus reads: "after maintaining his alliance (συμμαχίαν) with the Babylonians[27] *for eight years*[28], Sacchias broke his treaty (διέλυσε ... πίστεις) with them[29] and

---

26. In his earlier "citation" of Ezek 12,13 in 10,106 Josephus does not have the prophet specifically predicting Zedekiah's removal to Babylon; see above in the text.

27. Compare Ezek 17,13: "He (Nebuchadnezzar) took one of the seed royal [the reference is to Zedekiah] and made a covenant (LXX διαθήκην) with him...".

28. This chronological specificiation concerning the duration of Zedekiah's fidelity to Babylon has no counterpart in the Biblical sources. It is likely inspired by the notice in 2 Kgs 25,1 // Jer 52,4 that it was in Zedekiah's *ninth* year that Nebuchadnezzar advanced against Jerusalem in response to the Judean's preceding revolt (2 Kgs 24,20b // Jer 52,3b).

29. Compare Ezek 17,16: "... the king [Nebuchadnezzar] who made him [Zedekiah] king... of whom he broke his [so MT; LXX my = the Lord's] covenant (LXX διαθήκην) with him..." See n. 27. The above formulation is likewise notable for its verbal echo of 10,97 which states that Nebuchadnezzar himself "did not keep his pledges (τὰς πίστεις)", i.e. those made by him to King Jehoiakim. FELDMAN, *Studies*, p. 459 (ID., *Zedekiah*, 89) calls attention to this terminological link between 10,97 and 108 and suggests that it is intended to play down the culpability of Zedekiah's "oath-breaking" in that the Judean thereby would simply have been imitating his overlord's own earlier action.

went over to the Egptians, hoping to overthrow the Babylonians if he joined (εἰ ... γένοιτο)³⁰ the other side³¹" (10,108).

In next relating the Babylonian response to Zedekiah's revolt, Josephus (10,109) draws on 2 Kgs 25,1 // Jer 52,4 though omitting – for the moment – their chronological precisions about the start of the Jerusalem siege (see, however, on 10,116 below). His version runs: "*and, when the Babylonian king heard of this,* he marched against him (ἐστράτευσεν ἐπ' αὐτόν)³² and, *after ravaging his country and taking his fortresses* (φρούρια)³³, he came against the city of Jerusalem itself to besiege (πολιορκήσων) it". Neither 2 Kings nor its parallel Jeremiah 52 make any mention of an attempted Egyptian intervention during the siege of Jerusalem. Josephus, who has just previously cited, on the basis of Ezek 17,15 (see n. 31), Zedekiah's hope of Egyptian assistance as the motivation for his revolt, naturally moves to fill this lacuna. He does so (10,110a) by utilizing, while also embellishing, the reference in Jer 37(41),5 to Pharoah's army "coming out of Egypt" in the course of the siege of Jerusalem: "*But, when the Egyptian king heard of the plight of his ally* (σύμμαχος)³⁴ Sacchias, *he raised a large force* (πολλὴν δύναμιν)³⁵ and came to Judaea to end the siege (πολιορκίαν; see

30. This is the conjecture of Coccejus which Dindorf, Bekker, Naber, and Marcus follow. The codices read αἵ ... ἐγένοντο – as does Niese. Lat has no equivalent to the phrase's verb.

31. Compare Ezek 17,15: "But he [Zedekiah] rebelled against him [Nebuchadnezzar] by sending ambassadors to Egypt, that they might give him horses and a large army". With the above reference to Zedekiah's "hope" inspired by Ezek 17,15, Josephus provides a rationale for his revolt which in 2 Kgs 24,20b // Jer 52,3b remains without explicit motivation.

32. This phrase ironically echoes 10,104 where Jeremiah quotes the false prophets' claim that the Egyptians "would take the field against him" (στρατεύσουσιν ἐπ' αὐτόν), i.e. Nebuchadnezzar. What, in fact, happens is that Nebuchadnezzar now "takes the field against" Zedekiah himself.

33. This Josephan plus underscores the damage Zedekiah brought upon his kingdom by his ill-conceived revolt. Possibly, its reference to the Babylonian taking of "fortresses" outside Jerusalem is inspired by Jer 34(41),7: "... the army of the king of Babylon was fighting against Jerusalem and all the cities of Judah that were left, Lachish and Azekah; for these were the only fortified cities (LXX πόλεις ὀχυραί) that were left". Cf. also the notice of 10,1 on the earlier invasion of Sennacherib who "marched against him (στρατεύει ... ἐπ' αὐτὸν, i.e. Hezekiah)... and took by storm all the cities of the tribes of Judah and Benjamin". In both instances Jerusalem is left isolated by the enemy's devastation of its surrounding territory.

34. Compare 10,108 where the related term συμμαχία is used of Zedekiah's "alliance" with the Babylonians. The terminological reminiscence underscores Zedekiah's treachery; he became an "ally" of Egypt by violating his "alliance" with Babylon.

35. This indication concerning the size of the Egyptian expedition has no equivalent in Jeremiah 34. It might, however, represent an additional echo of Ezek 17,15, previously used by Josephus in his formulation of 10,108 (see n. 25), which speaks of Zedekiah's request for a "large army" (LXX λαὸν πολύν) from Egypt.

πολιοκήσων, 10,109)³⁶". In Jer 37(44),5.11 the Babylonians simply "withdraw" from Jerusalem upon hearing of the Egyptian advance, no indication of their destination/purpose being given. Conversely, 37,7 predicts that the advancing Egyptians will themselves return to their own land without supplying a reason for their doing so (note further that the actual fulfillment of this latter prediction is nowhere cited in the Book of Jeremiah). Josephus' formulation in 10,110b clarifies both points (as well as the causal link between them), likewise noting the realization of the prediction of 37,7: "Thereupon the Babylonian king left Jerusalem *and went to meet the Egyptians and, encountering them in battle, defeated* (νικᾷ) *and put them to flight and drove them out of the whole of Syria* [compare the reference to "all Syria" being subject to Neco in 10,84 and to Nebuchadnezzar's "occupying all Syria..." in 10,86]". At the start of 10,111 Josephus reprises his earlier (see 10,110) mention of Nebuchadnezzar's withdrawal from Jerusalem in order to set the stage for a "prophetic contest" that will transpire during the Babylonian's absence. This contest – which has no direct counterpart in the Bible – is initiated by "false prophets" who "deceived" (ἐξηπάτησαν οἱ ψευδο-προφῆται) Zedekiah during the break in the siege. Josephus' above wording concerning these figures here in 10,111 clearly echoes the allu-sion to them he attributes to Jeremiah in 10,104, i.e. τοῖς ψευδοπροφή-ταις ἀπατῶσιν. As will be recalled, Josephus found his inspiration for that earlier, "anticipated" language in Jer 37(44),9 ("do not deceive yourselves"; cf. 38[45],22) and 19 ("where are your prophets"?), verses set Biblically in the context of the (temporary) lifting of the siege. Now here in 10,111 he re-utilizes that language in a context corresponding to its Biblical one, the siege interlude.

To the "false prophets" who operate upon Zedekiah at this point Jose-phus attributes a double word of assurance. Their first promise is that "... the Babylonian king would not make war (πολεμήσειν) on him again". This announcement harks back to Jeremiah's "quotation" of the false prophets at the start of Zedekiah's reign in 10,104: "they were say-ing that the Babylonian king would never again make war (πολεμήσει) on the city...". The Biblical basis for the Josephan prophets' earlier and current claim is Jer 37(44),19: "(where are your [Zedekiah's] prophets who prophesied to you saying) 'the king of Babylon will not come against you and this land'"?; see above. The false prophets further

---

36. For this concluding indication (unparalleled in the notice of Jer 37,5 itself) con-cerning the purpose of the Egyptian advance Josephus may have based himself on Jer 37(44),7 where the prophet is instructed by the Lord to inform Zedekiah that "Pharoah's army *which came to help you* is about to return to Egypt...".

assure Zedekiah at this juncture that "his countrymen (ὁμοφύλους) whom the king [i.e. Nebuchadnezzar] had removed (οὓς ἀναστή-σειεν)[37] from their own land to Babylonia, should come back (ἥξειν)[38] with all the vessels of the temple (πάντων ... τῶν τοῦ ναοῦ σκευῶν) of which the king had despoiled it[39]". This additional promise clearly echoes the word of Hananiah the prophet as cited in Jer 28(35),3-4: "... I [the Lord will bring back to this place all (MT [and Josephus; see above], > LXX) the vessels of the Lord's house (LXX τὰ σκεύη οἴκου κύριου) which Nebuchadnezzar... took away from this place and carried to Babylon (so MT [and Josephus], > LXX). I will also bring back to this place Jeconiah (> Josephus)... and all the exiles who went to Babylon...". At the same time, Josephus' version modifies the source text in a variety of respects: e.g., the announcement is attributed, not to the named individual Hananiah, but to an anonymous collectivity ("the false prophets"); the promise is delivered not early on in Zedekiah's reign (so Jer 28(35),1)[40], but during the siege at its end, just as the Biblical sequence of the announcement (first vessels, then deportees) is reversed by him. In sum, the two-fold promise Josephus ascribes to the false prophets in 10,111 represents another of his "*montages*" (Piovanelli) in which he draws together elements extracted from two distinct Biblical contexts, i.e. Jer 37(44),19 and 28(35),3-4.

The false prophets' claims inspire a new initiative by Jeremiah who (10,112) "coming forward (παρελθών)[41] prophesied the truth (ἀληθῆ)[42] which was the contrary of this...". The "contrary" truth which Josephus

37. This is the emendation of Niese, which Naber and Marcus follow, based on Lat's quos demigraverat. Dindorf reads οὔτε ἀναστήσειν with the codices. NIESE, *Opera*, I, pp. lvii-lviii cites this as an instance where only Lat has preserved the original reading.

38. This is the reading proposed by Naber and adopted by Marcus. Dindorf and Bekker follow the δὲ (LV δ') ἥξειν of the codices, while Niese conjectures ἀνήξειν.

39. In Josephus' presentation this announcement of a return of the Temple vessels comes as something of a surprise in that in what precedes the historian did not reproduce the Biblical references to a despoilation of those vessels as part of his measures against either Jehoiakim (so 2 Chr 36,7 // 1 Esdras 1,41 // Dan 1,2) or Jehoiachin (so 2 Kgs 24,13; cf. Jer 28,3). See our discussion of 10,97-101 in chap. XXI.

40. MT and LXX Jer 28,1 differ in their respective datings of Hananiah's word; the former ascribes it to "the same year [i.e. the first regnal year of Zedekiah (or Jehoiakim, 27,1; see n. 9)], at the beginning of the reign of Zedekiah... in the fifth month of the fourth year", whereas the latter reads simply "in the fourth year of Zedekiah...". Both MT and LXX, however, have Hananiah deliver his announcement considerably prior to the siege of Jerusalem starting in Zedekiah's ninth year, the moment at which Josephus situates his (generalized) version of Hananiah's predictions.

41. This is the reading of MSPLaurVE which Dindorf, Bekker, Naber, and Marcus follow. Niese reads προελθών with RO.

42. Compare 10,104 where Jeremiah avers that the false prophets have spoken "falsely" (οὐκ ἀληθῆ) to Zedekiah.

now places on the lips of Jeremiah begins with a statement about his (false) colleagues: "... they were doing the king a wrong and deceiving (ἐξαπατῶσι; see ἐξηπάτησαν, 10,111) him⁴³". Thereafter, Jeremiah proceeds to predict developments whose (initial) realization Josephus has already narrated in 10,110b: "... no good would come to them from the Egyptians, but that, when the Babylonian king had defeated (νικήσας; see νικᾷ, 10,110) them, he would lead an army against Jerusalem and besiege it and destroy the people by famine (τῷ λιμῷ)...". This prediction represents the Josephan version of the announcement delivered by Jeremiah during the siege interlude as cited in Jer 37(44),7-8 (see also 34[41],21): "behold, Pharoah's army... is about to return to Egypt...⁴⁴ And the Chaldeans shall come back and fight against this city; they shall take it and burn it with fire⁴⁵". Jeremiah's above reference to the "famine" which will befall Jerusalem during the siege has no counterpart in Jer 37(44),7-8 itself. Elsewhere in the Book of Jeremiah one does find such a reference, however; see 38(45),2 where the prophet's announcement is that those who remain in the city will die "by the sword, by famine (LXX ἐν λιμῷ), and by pestilence (MT, > LXX)"; see also 21,7.9.

AJ 10,112 continues with Jeremiah's predictions concerning the immediate sequels to Jerusalem's coming capture: "... (Nebuchadnezzar will) carry off the survivors into captivity, plunder their possessions and, after carrying off the wealth in the temple, burn (ἐμπρήσει) this itself and raze (κατασκάψει) the city...". Each of the items making up this sequence has its counterpart, whether in the prophet's announcements in the Book of Jeremiah and/or in the narratives of Kings and Chronicles. In particular, the initial prediction concerning the exiling and plundering of the Jerusalemites is paralleled in Jer 20,4b-5: "(I [the Lord] will give all Judah into the hand of the king of Babylon); he shall carry them captive to Babylon.... Moreover I will give all the wealth of the city, all its gains, all its prized belongings... into the hand of their enemies who shall plunder, and seize them (so MT, > LXX), and carry

43. With this charge against the "false prophets" compare Jeremiah's statement to Hananiah (whose own word of 28(35),3-4 Josephus has just "quoted" in 10,111; see above) in 28(35),15: "you have made this people trust in a lie (MT שֶׁקֶר; LXX ἐπ᾽ ἀδίκῳ)".

44. By having Jeremiah announce a Babylonian "defeat" of the Egyptians in 10,112 Josephus provides a motivation for the latter's retreat which Jer 37,7 itself leaves unexplained. Recall that, already previously, Josephus has introduced this same clarification in his narrative notice on the Egyptian rout in 10,110b.

45. Josephus reserves this element of the prediction of Jer 37(44),8 for a later moment within Jeremiah's prediction in 10,112; see above.

them to Babylon[46]". With the following announcement concerning the despoliation of the Temple, compare the prophet's announcement in Jer 27(34),21-22 (MT; LXX lacks v. 21 and most of v. 22): "the vessels which are left in the house of the Lord... shall be carried to Babylon...[47]". The numerous predictions concerning Jerusalem's fate in the Book of Jeremiah itself do not speak as such, as does the Josephan prophet of 10,112, of a "burning" of the Temple (in, e.g., Jer 21,10; 34,2,22; 37,10; 38,19 it is rather the city which is to be "burned"). Josephus' introduction of this particular prediction into Jeremiah's prophetic catalogue is understandable, however, given the fact that 2 Kgs 25,9 and 2 Chr 36,19 both explicitly mention the Babylonians' "burning" of the Temple. Inspired by these historical notices and with a view to enhancing Jeremiah's predicative capacities, Josephus has him foretell this particular as well here[48]. As just noted, the Book of Jeremiah represents the prophet as repeatedly announcing that Jerusalem will be "burned" by the Babylonians. Josephus here in 10,112 makes him speak rather of a "razing" of the city. Once again, his inspiration lies in the Biblical narrative material, *in casu* 2 Kgs 25,10 (MT = Jer 52,14; > LXX) and 2 Chr 36,19 which recount a "breaking down" (BL 36,19 κατέσκαψεν; see κατασκάψει, 10,112) of *the walls* of Jerusalem[49].

The predictions of 10,112 terminate with Jeremiah's announcement "we shall be slaves (δουλεύσομεν)[50] to him [Nebuchadnezzar] and his descendants for seventy years". For this prediction as well Josephus had available a variety of Biblical "inspirations". Thus, Jer 25,11 cites the

46. Compare also the narrative notices of 2 Chr 36,18b: "(Nebuchadnezzar brought to Babylon) the treasures of the king and his princes" and 2 Kgs 25,11 "(Nebuzaradan carried into exile) "the rest of the people who were left in the city...".

47. See also 2 Kgs 25,14-15 which enumerates those Temple "vessels" carried off by the Babylonians and 2 Chr 36,18a ("all the vessels of the house of God... he [Nebuchadnezzar] brought to Babylon").

48. Compare *BJ* 5,392 where, in his reminiscence of Jerusalem's earlier destruction during his address to the city's defenders, Josephus refers to Zedekiah's seeing the Temple "leveled to the ground" (κατασκαπτόμενον, i.e. the verb used in *AJ* 10,112 for the "razing" of the *city*). FELDMAN, *Isaiah*, p. 586 and n. 9 points out that, in a whole series of other instances as well, Josephus interjects a specific prediction by Jeremiah concerning the fate of the Temple. He sees the historian's doing this as reflective of his solicitude, as a priest himself, for the Temple.

49. The same sequence (burning of the Temple, razing of the city) found in the prophetic prediction of 10,112 recurs in 10,146 where Josephus recounts Nebuzaradan's initiatives that serve to fulfill Jeremiah's announcement in the former text: "he set fire (ἀνῆψε) to the temple... and demolished (κατέστρεψεν) the city". See there.

50. Note the switch to the first person plural here, following the third person singular forms (subject Nebuchadnezzar) in the preceding portion of Jeremiah's word in 10,112. Compare 10,33 where Josephus has Isaiah announce that Hezekiah's descendants "will be servants (δουλεύσαντας) to the king of Babylon".

prophet announcing a seventy-year "serving" (LXX δουλεύσουσιν) of the king of Babylon by "these nations", while in 25,12 and 29(36),12 he predicts a divine "visitation" of the exiles once Babylon's seventy years of domination are up. The Chronicler, for his part, appears to utilize these Jeremian predictions in formulating his notice in 2 Chr 36,20b-21: "they [the exiles] became servants (BL εἰς δούλους) to him [Nebuchadnezzar] and his sons... to fulfill seventy years". As will be noted, Josephus' own formulation of Jeremiah's announcement of the people's seventy years of servitude to the Babylonian kings above stands closest to the Chronicler's notice of which it represents a kind of "predictive transposition[51]".

In 10,113 Josephus rounds off Jeremiah's long series of predictions with the statement "At that time [i.e. the end of the seventy years of the Judeans' enslavement], by overthrowing the Babylonians, the Persians and Medes will free us from servitude to them, and, when we have been sent back by them to this land, we shall once more build (οἰκοδομήσομεν) the temple and restore Jerusalem". The Book of Jeremiah itself has no equivalent to this concluding announcement/ promise by the prophet. Josephus bases himself for it rather on the Chronicler's narrative. Specifically, the opening reference to the eventual overthrow of the the Babylonians by "the Persians and the Medes" draws on 2 Chr 36,20 where the exiles' Babylonian servitude (see above) is said to have lasted "until the establishment of the kingdom of Persia" (so MT; BL of the Medes). In attributing Babylon's demise to both the Persians and the Medes rather than to the Persians (so MT) or the Medes (so BL) alone, Josephus likely has in view yet another Biblical context, i.e. Dan 5,28 (= AJ 10,244) where Daniel announces to the final Babylonian ruler, Belshazzar: "your kingdom is divided and given to the Medes and the Persians". Jeremiah's further prediction that under Persian and Median rule[52] the exiles would be sent back to their land where they will rebuild the Temple and city, in turn, draws on the Cyrus edict cited in 2 Chr

---

51. The wording of the concluding segment of Jeremiah's predictions as cited in 10,112 (Nebuchadnezzar "will raze the city, and we shall be slaves to him and his descendants") is clearly echoed in Josephus' introduction to his account of Cyrus' release of the Jews in AJ 11,1-2: "... God had foretold to them through the prophet Jeremiah before the city was demolished (κατασκαφῆναι τὴν πόλιν, 10,112 κατασκάψει τὴν πόλιν), that, after they had served (δουλεῦσαι, 10,112 δουλεύσομεν) Nebuchadnezzar and his descendants (τοῖς ἐκγόνις, so 10,112) and endured this servitude for seventy years...".

52. Josephus' ascription of the Jews' return also to the Medes has no Biblical basis (in 2 Chr 36,22-23 // Ezra 1,1-4 the initiative for this comes solely from "Cyrus, king of Persia"). It is, however, in line with his previous attribution – itself based on Dan 5,28, see above – of Babylon's overthrow to the Persians and Medes acting in concert.

36,23 // Ezra 1,2-4; see, in particular, Ezra 1,3 (Cyrus enjoins the Jews "whoever is among you... let him go up to Jerusalem... and rebuild (LXX οἰκοδομησάτω) the house of the Lord..."). Taken in its entirety, the prospective survey of events from the repulse of the Egyptian relief expedition through the rebuilding of the Temple seventy years later which the historian puts on the lips of Jeremiah in 10,112-113 thus represents a remarkable instance of a Josephan *montage*. In compiling the sequence he made use, as we have seen, not only of many different contexts of the Book of Jeremiah, but also of the narratives of 2 Kings 25 and 2 Chronicles 36 (Ezra 1,1-4) as well as the prediction of Dan 5,28.

Josephus, it will be recalled, rounds off his account of Jeremiah's initial intervention at the start of Zedekiah's reign by noting (10,105) the king's reactions to the prophet's word, both positive and negative. Having now related Jeremiah's subsequent intervention during the siege interlude (10,112-113) in parallel to Jer 37(44),3-10, Josephus (10,114a) pauses to recount, once again, the divergent responses evoked by that new intervention. His notice on the matter (which has no counterpart in Jeremiah 37 as such) reads: "in saying these things Jeremiah was believed (ἐπιστεύετο)[53] by most of the people, but their leaders (ἡγεμόνες)[54] and the impious men (οἱ ἀσεβεῖς)[55] ridiculed (ἐξεφαύλι-ζον) him as though he were out of his mind (ἐξεστηκότα τῶν φρενῶν)[56]". Where now might Josephus have found inspiration for this notice on the divided reaction to Jeremiah's intervention during the siege break (which, as noted, has no parallel in Jeremiah 37 itself)? As a possible "source" for the notice's second, "negative" half, I would call attention to 2 Chr 36,16: "they [the people of Judah as a whole; see v. 15] kept mocking the messengers of God, despising his words and scoffing (BL ἐμπαίζοντες) at his prophets...". In speaking of the impious leaders' "ridiculing" Jeremiah in particular, Josephus, I suggest, has further specified this generalizing remark of the Chronicler – doing so under the additional influence of 2 Chr 36,12 where king Zedekiah fails to "humble himself before Jeremiah the prophet". As for the characteriza-

53. Compare 10,105 where Zedekiah is said (initially) to have "believed" (πεπισ-τευκέναι) Jeremiah.
54. See 10,104 where this term designates those against whom Jeremiah warns Zedekiah at the start of his reign.
55. Note the echo of 10,103: "those of his [Zedekiah's] own age were impious (ἀσεβεῖς)" here. Thus in his formulation in 10,114 Josephus re-utilizes two terms ("leaders", "impious") employed in 10,103-104 to designate those with whom Jeremiah is in opposition at the start of Zedekiah's reign; thereby, he intimates that their opposition perdured down to the time of the siege which ended Zedekiah's rule.
56. This is Josephus' only use of the above construction.

tion of the ridiculed Jeremiah as "out of his mind", this might reflect the word of Shemaiah to the priest Zephaniah concerning Jeremiah as quoted in MT Jer 29(36),26, i.e. "the Lord has made you priest... to have charge in the house of the Lord over every madman (MT לְכָל־אִישׁ מְשֻׁגָּע; compare LXX παντὶ ἀνθρώπῳ) who prophesies...". In addition to the above Biblical "inspirations" for Josephus' presentation in 10,114 one might also look to the historian's account of the reaction to his own speech to the defenders of Jerusalem (BJ 5,362-419), a speech which itself explicitly evokes the figure of Jeremiah (5,391-392) and whose content parallels that prophet's announcement of the city's certain fall in AJ 10,112. There, in the course of an extensive self-quotation of his words to the defenders, Josephus pauses (5,375) to note their (non-) affect upon his hearers in terms that do, in fact, put one in mind of his comment on the leaders' "ridiculing" Jeremiah in 10,114: "Josephus, during this exhortation, was derided (ἔσκωπτον) by many from the ramparts, by many execrated (ἐβλασφήμουν), and by some assailed with missiles[57]". That Josephus may indeed have formulated his (Biblically unparalleled) notice in 10,114 concerning the leaders' dismissal of Jeremiah's exhortations under the influence of his own experience of being derided by his own hearers (as he describes this in BJ 5,375; see above) is indeed plausible in view of the many indications that Josephus in BJ casts himself as a second Jeremiah, just as, conversely, his Jeremiah in AJ appears as a "type" of Josephus to come[58]. In this connection it is further of interest to note that Josephus' mention of the two contrasting responses to Jeremiah's words in 10,114 ("belief" by the many, "ridicule" by the leaders) has an analogue in the notice with which he concludes the account of his own speech before the walls of Jerusalem in BJ 5,420: "... the insurgents (οἱ στασιασταί, i.e. the "leaders" of the resistance) neither yielded nor deemed it safe to alter their course. The people (ὁ ... δῆμος), however, were incited [i.e. by Josephus' previous appeal] to desert...[59]". Both Jeremiah and Josephus, as the latter tells it, did then win the confidence of the multitude by their words, even as both met with total rejection by the city's political and military leadership.

57. See also Josephus' account of his subsequent delivery of Titus' message to the defenders and their response to this in BJ 6,96-113. Note in particular 6,98 ("the tyrant" John hurls "many invectives and imprecations upon Josephus" as he begins his speech) and 108 (Josephus says to John: "once again you are indignant and shout your abuse at me...").

58. On the point, see p. 534, n. 171.

59. Cf. also Josephus' notice on the contrasting reactions to his later address to the defenders which he delivers on Titus' behalf (on this see n. 57) in BJ 6,112: "John and his followers were only the more exasperated against the Romans, being eager to get Josephus also into their power. Many, however, of the upper class were moved by the speech".

Josephus' notice on the "leaders'" ridiculing of Jeremiah in 10,114a serves as a lead-in to the story he goes on to relate (10,114b-115), in dependence on Jer 37(44),11-15, concerning the punitive measures taken by those same leaders against the prophet. Jer 37(44),11 dates the incident in question to the period of the Babylonian withdrawal from Jerusalem (see 37,5). Josephus' chronological indication is much vaguer: "now once...", his equivalent to the dating of 37,11 having already been cited by him at the opening of 10,111. The happening is set in motion by the prophet's attempt to leave Jerusalem. According to Jer 37(44),12 his motive for this initiative was "to go to the land of Benjamin to receive his portion there among the people". As the RSV note points out, the Hebrew phrase which it renders "to receive his portion there" (לַחֲלִק מִשָּׁם; compare LXX: τοῦ ἀγοράσαι ἐκεῖθεν) is "obscure". Perhaps for this reason then, Josephus substitutes a different indication concerning Jeremiah's intention in leaving the city, i.e. one that draws on the notice of Jer 1,1 (not previously cited by him) about "Anathoth" as the prophet's home-town: "(now once), when he had decided to go to his native place called Anathoth (Ἀναθώθ, so LXX)...". To this mention of Jeremiah's destination, he appends, for the benefit of readers unfamiliar with Palestinian geography, the specification that the town is located "twenty stades distant from Jerusalem...".

In Jer 37(44),13 Jeremiah is confronted at the "Benjamin gate" by a sentry named Irijah (so MT; LXX: Sarouia) who accuses him of deserting to the Babylonians. Josephus modifies this account in several respects: First, the confrontation (apparently) occurs when Jeremiah is already outside Jerusalem ("there met him on the road..."). In addition, the named Biblical guardsman becomes anonymous, even while he takes on a higher stature as "one of the magistrates (ἀρχόντων)...[60]". Finally, in citing the accusation made against Jeremiah by the one who "seizes" (συλλαβών; LXX: συνέλαβε) him from 37(44),13b, Josephus transposes direct into indirect discourse, while also explicitly qualifying the charge as baseless: "... *falsely charging* (συκοφαντῶν)[61]

60. Note the switch to this collective designation for Jeremiah's opponents from the ἡγεμόνες used previously in 10,104.114 (see also 119). The terminological shift here at 10,114b might reflect Josephus' reading of Jer 37(44),14-15 where LXX twice employs the designation (οἱ) ἄρχοντες (MT הַשָּׂרִים; RSV "the princes") of the group before whom Jeremiah is brought following his arrest.

61. Josephus "anticipates" this specification concerning the accusation from Jer 37(44),14 where Jeremiah replies to "Irijah's" preceding charge (see 37,13b): "It is false (LXX ψεῦδος)". The verb συκοφαντέω occurs only here in the whole of *AJ*; elsewhere Josephus uses it 3 times (*BJ* 1,11; *Vita* 52; *c. Ap.* 2,42).

him with deserting (αὐτομολοῦντα[62]; LXX: σὺ φεύγεις) to the Babylonians".

Jer 37(44),14a records the prophet's laconic rejoinder to Irijah's
charge: "It is false (LXX: ψεῦδος); I am not deserting to the
Chaldeans". Josephus (10,115a) expands: "But Jeremiah said that he
was bringing a false (ψευδῆ) accusation against him *and asserted that
he was travelling to his home*[63]". Jer 37(44),14b next relates the negative
outcome of Jeremiah's attempt at self-defense: refusing to listen to
him, Irijah (LXX: Sarouia) hustles him off to the "princes" (LXX:
ἄρχοντας). Josephus' parallel (10,115b) specifies the purpose behind
the prophet's nameless interlocutor taking him before his fellow "magistrates" (see 10,114b; cf. n. 60): "The other, however, was not con-
vinced and took (λαβών)[64] him and brought (ἤγαγεν) him *to trial* (εἰς
δίκην)[65] before the magistrates (πρὸς τοὺς ἄρχοντας)[66]".

The episode of Jer 37(44),11-15 reaches its negative culmination in v.
15 which recounts the princes' anger at Jeremiah, their beating him, and
imprisoning him "in the house of Jonathan the secretary" which had
been converted into a prison. Josephus' version (10,115c) of these happenings is more generalized, passing over, e.g., the site of Jeremiah's
confinement. It reads: "... (at the hands of the magistrates) he suffered
every form of indignity and ill-treatment (αἰκίαν καὶ βασάνους)[67] and
was kept under guard for punishment (πρὸς τιμωρίαν)[68]. And for some

---

62. The verb αὐτομολέω (along with its various related noun forms) occurs with
some frequency in Josephus' account of Jewish "desertions" to the Romans during the
Jewish War (see, e.g., the above-cited *BJ* 5,420 where "the people are incited [i.e. by
Josephus' preceding address] to desert [πρὸς αὐτομολίαν]"); cf. RENGSTORF, *Concordance*, I, s.v. The use of the verb here in *AJ* 10,114 (it recurs in 10,127: "those who had
deserted [αὐτομολήσαντας] to the Babylonians") serves to underscore the parallelism
between the first and second great sieges of Jerusalem's history (and the similar roles
exercised during these by Jeremiah and Josephus, respectively).

63. The wording of this addition (βαδίζειν... αὐτὸν... εἰς τὴν πατρίδα) to the Biblical prophet's reply echoes Josephus' editorial statement in 10,114b: (Jeremiah decided)
εἰς τὴν πατρίδα παραγενέσθα. The effect is to underscore the veracity of the prophet's
"assertion" and the falseness of the charge against him.

64. This is the reading of RO which Niese and Marcus follow. Dindorf, Bekker, and
Naber read συλλαβών (i.e. the form found in 10,114b; see above) with MSPLaurV.

65. The above phrase "brought to trial" echoes Josephus' account of a similiar experience of the prophet's, occasioned by his "Temple Speech", during the reign of
Jehoiakim; see *AJ* 10,90 (the priests and the people) "bringing him [Jeremiah] to trial"
(ὑπάγοντες δίκῃ), demand that he be punished (= Jer 26(33),8 where, however, there is
no mention of a "trial" as such). Cf. our discussion of this passage in chap. XXI.

66. This identical phrase occurs at the end of LXX Jer 44,14.

67. The above collocation recurs, in reverse order, in *AJ* 16,389; cf. *BJ* 3,321.

68. Compare Josephus' account of the outcome of Jeremiah's earlier "trial" (see n.
65) during the reign of Jehoiakim. Then (see 10,90) "the people and their rulers (οἱ ἄρχοντες)" had "demanded that Jeremiah be sentenced to punishment (πρὸς τιμωρίαν)". In

time (χρόνον ... τινα)[69] he remained thus, suffering the unjust (ἀδίκως)[70] treatment here described".

Jer 37(44),16-21 relates a secret interview between Jeremiah and Zedekiah which results in the latter's being assigned a new place of confinement ("the court of the guard") as well as a ration of bread; see v. 21. Josephus passes over this sequence at this juncture (see, however, on 10,124-129 below). In its place he proceeds immediately to narrate (10,116) the resumption of the Babylonian siege, commenced already in 10,109, but then broken off in 10,110 due to the Egyptian advance. The notices of 10,116, in turn, serve to introduce Jeremiah's third and final intervention during Zedekiah's reign, 10,117-130. Accordingly, I treat 10,116-130 as a section on its own; see below.

3. Third Intervention

As just mentioned, Josephus in 10,116 (momentarily) breaks off his narrative of Jeremiah's experiences in order to re-introduce the subject of the (renewed) Babylonian siege of Jerusalem as foretold by the prophet in 10,112. In formulating his account in 10,116 Josephus draws initially on 2 Kgs 25,1 // Jer 39(46),1 // 52,4. In his earlier (10,109) use of this Biblical material, it will be recalled, the historian passed over its chronological precisions concerning the beginning of the siege, i.e. the tenth day of the tenth month of Zedekiah's ninth year[71]. Now, however, he does (10,116a) supply this three-fold dating indication. To it he then attaches mention of Nebuchadnezzar's "marching (στρατεύει) a second time" against Jerusalem[72] which he

response, "the elders" (10,91) "released the prophet from the prison-hall". Here in 10,115, however, there is no one to prevent Jeremiah "being kept under guard for punishment" by his long-term opponents, the ἄρχοντες.

69. Josephus likely drew this chronological indication from Jer 37(44),16 which speaks of the prophet remaining in prison "many days" (LXX ἡμέρας πολλάς).

70. Note the wordplay between this adverb and the nominal phrase εἰς δίκην earlier in 10,115.

71. MT and LXX Jer 39(46),1, as well as BL 2 Kgs 25,1, lack mention of the day on which the siege began.

72. MARCUS, Josephus, VI, p. 221, n. j affirms that with the above reference to Nebuchadnezzar's second advance against Jerusalem, Josephus "forgets" that he has already recounted two earlier such happenings, i.e. the first in Jehoiakim's time (see 10,96), the other under Jehoiachin (see 10,99). It seems, however, more likely that his mention of Nebuchadnezzar's second, i.e. "resumed" march on Jerusalem here in 10,116 is simply intended to refer back, following the hiatus of the Egyptian intervention (10,110-115), to 10,109 where he employs the same verb (in the aorist form ἐστράτευσεν) of the Babylonian's initial move against the rebel Zedekiah.

"besieges" (πολιορκεῖ)[73] "with utmost energy (μετὰ πάσης ... φιλο-
τιμίας)[74] for eighteen months[75]".

Having related Nebuchadnezzar's initiatives against Jerusalem in
10,116a, Josephus next (10,116b) describes their impact upon the population: "and, as the inhabitants of Jerusalem were under siege, they were
attacked by two of the greatest of calamities, famine (λιμός; cf. τῷ
λιμῷ, 10,112) and pestilence (φθορὰ λοιμική), which fell upon them
severely". In speaking here of the combined ravages of "famine" and
"pestilence" upon besieged Jerusalem, Josephus likely has in view the
prophetic announcements of these forthcoming calamities as cited in Jer
21,7.9; 38(45),2[76]; see above on 10,112. After the "national interlude"
of 10,116 Josephus reverts to the figure of Jeremiah, relating (10,117-
130) in extenso the story of the prophet's doings during Jerusalem's
final days as found in Jeremiah 38(45). The Biblical source text begins
(38,1) with mention of three (MT; LXX: two) named persons who
"hear" Jeremiah deliver the exhortation cited in vv. 2-3. Josephus
(10,117) passes over the listing of 38,1 – the figures enumerated there do
not recur by name in the further course of the episode – in order to focus
attention immediately on Jeremiah himself. His amplified (re-) introduction of the prophet reads: "The prophet Jeremiah, however, who was in
prison (ἐν ... τῇ εἱρκτῇ)[77], did not remain quiet but cried his message

73. The wording of Josephus' notice on Nebuchadnezzar's initiative here in 10,116
(στρατεύει ... ἐπὶ τὰ Ἱεροσόλυμα ... πολιορκεῖ) closely echoes the announcement he
places on the lips of Jeremiah at the time of the Babylonian withdrawal in 10,112 (ἐπισ-
τρατεύσειν εἰς τὰ Ἱεροσόλυμα μέλλει, καὶ πολιορκήσει). Thereby, he underscores
the prophet's veracity as a predictor.

74. This phrase, insisting on Nebuchadnezzar's resoluteness in prosecuting the siege,
has no equivalent in Josephus' sources as such. He could, however, have readily deduced
the point from the length of the siege itself; see above. On Josephus' use of the phrase
"utmost energy" in reference to the energetic building activities of Solomon (AJ 8,85)
and Herod's famine relief (15,312), see FELDMAN, Studies, p. 460, n. 10 (= ID., Zedekiah,
91, n. 60).

75. As MARCUS, Josephus, VI, p. 221, n. k points out, Josephus arrived at this figure
for the total duration of the siege by tallying the Biblical indications (see 2 Kgs 25,1-3
and parallels) that Jerusalem, which came under siege in the tenth month of Zedekiah's
ninth year, had run out of bread by the fourth month of his eleventh year.

76. Each of the above three texts also speaks of "the sword" as an instrument of
destruction for the besieged city. LXX 21,9; 45(MT 38),2 lack an equivalent to MT's
"pestilence". Compare 2 Kgs 25,3 // Jer 52,6 which refer solely to the severe "famine"
in Jerusalem.

77. Jeremiah 38 does not specify where Jeremiah was at the moment he delivered the
words cited in vv. 2-3 and "heard" by the trio listed in v. 1. Recall that previously
(10,115) Josephus has only mentioned the fact of Jeremiah's being "kept under guard"
(ἐφυλάττετο) by the leaders without indicating where this took place. His reference here
in 10,117 to Jeremiah's "being in prison" seems to reflect Jer 37(44),16 which speaks of
Jeremiah's remaining many days "in the dungeon cells" (so RSV; LXX: εἰς οἰκίαν τοῦ
λάκκου καὶ εἰς τὴν χερεθ).

aloud (ἐκεκράγει καὶ ἐκήρυσσε)[78] and urged the people (παραινῶν τῷ πλήθει; LXX 45,1: ἐλάλει ἐπὶ τὸν ὄχλον)...[79]".

In Jer 38(45),2 Jeremiah places his hearers before two eventualities: if they remain in the city they will perish by sword, famine or pestilence (MT; LXX lacks the last of these three items), whereas the life of anyone who goes out to the Babylonians will be spared. Josephus has the prophet begin his exhortation by calling, not for mere desertion to the Babylonians – so 38(45),3b – but for an actual surrender of the city to them: "... (he urged the people) to open the gates and admit the Babylonian king (δέξασθαι τὸν Βαβυλώνιον ἀνοίξαντας τὰς πύλας)[80]". Should they do this, Jeremiah goes on to assure them, "they would be saved (σωθήσεσθαι)[81] together with their families, but if not, they would be destroyed (διαφθαρήσεσθαι)[82]". Only after the above sequence (which lacks a parallel as such in the citation of Jeremiah's discourse given in 38(45),2-3), does Josephus (10,118) come to utilize the alternative propositions put forward by the prophet in 38,2. His version of that verse runs: "He also foretold that anyone who remained in the city would certainly perish in one of two ways, being made an end of either by famine (λιμῷ; LXX: ἐν λιμῷ) or by the sword (σιδήρῳ; LXX: ἐν ῥομφαίᾳ)[83] *of the enemy*, but that anyone who fled (φύγοι) to

78. Josephus' emphasis on the "vehemence" with which Jeremiah delivers his message here has its counterpart in his own speech to the Jerusalemites in *BJ* 5,392 where he evokes the Biblical prophet's "loudly proclaiming" (βοῶντα γοῦν) to his contemporaries.

79. Josephus does not seem to have adverted to the problem which the above presentation might suggest, i.e. how could Jeremiah, being "in the prison", make himself heard by "the people"?

80. Jeremiah's exhortation here strikingly echoes the demand made by the pagan king Sennacherib in Hezekiah's time as cited by Josephus in *AJ* 10,15 (Hezekiah is threatened with destruction) "unless he opened the gates and willingly admitted (τὰς πύλας ἀνοίξας ... δέξεται)" the Assyrian army into Jerusalem. Given that parallelism, one can understand the subsequent negative response of Jeremiah's audience who are being urged by him to do the very thing Hezekiah – properly in the event, given the eventual divine intervention on Jerusalem's behalf – had refused to do. See n. 82.

81. Compare *BJ* 5,393 where, following his evocation of Jeremiah in 5,391-392, Josephus complains that the Jerusalemites are "assailing with abuse and missiles me who exhort you to *save yourselves* (πρὸς σωτηρίαν)...".

82. The above verb, i.e. διαφθείρω, is the same used in *AJ* 10,15 where Sennacherib threatens "to destroy (διαφθερεῖν) Hezekiah utterly and completely" should he fail to surrender to him. Here too then (see n. 80) Jeremiah appears as a second (Judean) Sennacherib.

83. Josephus' sequence "famine and sword" above is the reverse of that of Jer 38(45),2. Like LXX, he makes no mention of the third destructive agent cited in MT 38,2, i.e. "pestilence". PIOVANELLI, *Texte*, 28 points out that this is one of the very few instances where Josephus seems to follow the shorter text of LXX Jeremiah in preference to the longer MT one. He also notes, however, that Josephus' wording ("they were attacked by... famine and *pestilence*") just previously in 10,116 does suggest his familiarity with the MT reading in 38,2.

the enemy [Bible: the Chaldeans][84] would escape death (διαδράσεται
τὸν θάνατον)[85]".

The Biblical Jeremiah rounds off his address to the people in 38(45),3
with an affirmation of Jerusalem's certain fall to the Babylonians. Josephus (10,119a) passes over, for the moment (but see on 10,119b below)
this concluding element, replacing it with mention of the negative emotional reponse on the part of Jeremiah's prominent listeners to his words
which will lead them (so 38,4) to denounce him to Zedekiah: "nevertheless not even though they were in these straits (δεινοῖς)[86] did those of the
leaders (ἡγεμόνων)[87] who heard (ἀκούοντες)[88] his words believe (ἐπίστευον)[89] him, but went in anger (μετ' ὀργῆς)...[90]". Thereafter, he picks
up the narrative thread at 38(45),4 where the "princes" call on Zedekiah
to have Jeremiah put to death on the grounds that he is "weakening the
hands" of the city's defenders through his words, and seeking the
people's harm rather than their welfare. Josephus expatiates (10,119b)
considerably on the leaders' address to the king:

84. Josephus' double use of the term "enemy" in 10,118 as opposed to the neutral
designation "the Chaldeans" of Jer 38,2 underscores the paradox that, notwithstanding
the state of war that exists between them, the Babylonians are potentially the "saviors" of
Jerusalem's population.

85. This phrase occurs only here in Josephus.

86. With this introductory indication, Josephus highlights the folly of the leaders'
response as he will subsequently describe it: the desperateness of their situation does not
at all prompt the leaders to reconsider their earlier negative reaction to Jeremiah's message. The term δεινοῖς as used here in 10,119 to qualify the Jerusalemites' situation represents an implicit fulfillment of Jeremiah's initial prediction as cited in 10,79, i.e. "(he
announced) the misfortunes (δεινά) that were to come upon the city".

87. Note the recurrence of this collective designation for Jeremiah's opponents of
10,104.114 after the switch to ἄρχοντες in 10,114-115 (it is this latter term which LXX
45(MT 38),4 employs of those who denounce Jeremiah to Zedekiah for his speech in
45(MT 38),2-3).

88. This verb echoes Jer 38(45),1 – earlier passed over by Josephus, see above –
where the figures mentioned are said to "hear" (LXX ἤκουσε) Jeremiah's words to the
people.

89. Compare 10,106 where Zedekiah is said to "disbelieve" (ἠπίστησεν) the prophecies of Jeremiah and Ezekiel. Josephus has previously stated (10,117) that Jeremiah
addressed his final admonitions during the siege to "the people" as a whole. Here in 10,119,
however, it is only "the leaders" among his hearers who are explicitly said to "disbelieve"
him. This might suggest that the remaining hearers did believe him; cf. the contrasting
responses of people and leaders to Jeremiah's earlier warnings as cited in 10,114.

90. This reference to the leaders' emotional state as they approach the king has no
equivalent in Jer 38(45),4. It might, however, be seen as Josephus' delayed utilization of
37(44),15 where the "princes" are said to have been "enraged" (LXX ἐπικράνθησαν) at
Jeremiah. The indication likewise echoes the references to the negative emotions evoked
by Josephus' earlier announcements in 10,90 (the people and their rulers are "angered
[πρὸς ὀργήν]" by Jeremiah's warnings about the unreliability of Egypt in Jehoiakim's
day) and 95 (Jehoiakim himself "becomes angry" [ὀργισθείς] at the reading of the
prophet's book).

... (the leaders) denouncing (κατηγοροῦντες) Jeremiah, asked (ἠξίουν)[91] him [Zedekiah] to put the prophet to death (κτεῖναι τὸν προφήτην)[92] *as a madman* (ὡς μεμηνότα)[93] *who was breaking down their spirit beforehand* (τὰς ψυχὰς αὐτῶν προκατακλῶντα)[94] and by his predictions *of disaster* was weakening the ardour of the people (ταῖς τῶν χειρόνων καταγελλίαις τὸ πρόθυμον ἐκλύοντα τοῦ πλήθους)[95], *who, they said, were ready to risk* (κινδυνεῦσαι)[96] *their lives for him* [Zedekiah] *and their country*[97], while the prophet was urging (παρήνει; cf. παραινῶν, 10,117)[98] *them to flee to the enemy* (πρὸς τοὺς πολεμίους φεύγειν)[99], *saying that the city would be taken and they would all perish* (ἀπολεῖσθαι; cf. ἀπολεῖται, 10,118)[100].

91. Thus the conjecture of Niese which Marcus follows, inspired by Lat's *poscebant* (this would be another instance according to NIESE, *Opera*, I, p. lviii, where Lat alone has preserved the original reading; see n. 37). Dindorf, Bekker, and Naber read κατητιῶντο (as does Niese in the text printed by him). ROM have καὶ ᾐτιῶντο. The form read by Marcus above (ἠξίουν) is the same as that used by Josephus in recounting Jeremiah's "Temple trial" in 10,90 where the people and rulers, "angered by his words" (see n. 90) "demand" (ἠξίουν) that the prophet be "sentenced to punishment".

92. Compare Jer 38(45),4: "let this man be put to death" (LXX: ἀναιρεθήτω δὴ ὁ ἄνθρωπος ἐκεῖνος).

93. In using this designation for Jeremiah the leaders echo Josephus' editorial statement concerning them in 10,114: (the leaders and impious men) "ridiculed him [Jeremiah] *as though he were a madman* (ὡς ἐξεστηκότα τῶν φρενῶν)". The leaders' abusive term here in 10,119 likewise recalls that used of the youthful disciple of the prophet Elisha who has just anointed Jehu king in *AJ* 9,110 (= 2 Kgs 9,11: "you know the fellow and his idle talk"): "... when they [Jehu's fellow officers] questioned him [Jehu] and urged him to tell them why the youth had come to him, adding that he was a madman (μαίνεσθαι), he replied, 'You have, indeed, guessed right, for the words he spoke were those of a madman (μεμηνότος)'".

94. The verb προκατακλάω is hapax in Josephus.

95. Compare Jer 38(45),4: "he is weakening (LXX: ἐκλύει)... the hands of all the people (LXX: τοῦ λαοῦ), by speaking such words (LXX: λόγους) to them". Note here again Josephus' substitution of alternative phraseology for the Bible's mention of (prophetic) "words".

96. This is the conjecture of Niese which Naber and Marcus follow. Dindorf and Bekker read κινδυνεύσειν with SPLaurV. Lat has *pugnare*, while ROM lack an equivalent.

97. This Biblically unparalleled element of the leaders' speech serves to underscore the enormity of Jeremiah's initiative in their view – he is seeking to demoralize those who otherwise would be quite ready to fight. It likewise functions to remind the king of the personal implications of the prophet's activity for himself – Jeremiah's aim is to deprive Zedekiah of his defenders.

98. This is the conjecture of Niese, followed by Naber and Marcus and inspired by Lat's *moneret*. Dindorf and Bekker read ἀπειλεῖ with the codices.

99. This phrase of the leaders' report echoes that attributed to Jeremiah himself in 10,118, i.e. (εἰ ...) φύγοι πρὸς τοὺς πολεμίους.

100. Also this element – which provides Zedekiah with an indication of the actual content of Jeremiah's "predictions of disaster" – has no equivalent in the leaders' speech of 38(45),4. The leaders' report of Jeremiah's pronouncement that "the city would be taken" here in 10,119b does, on the other hand, have a parallel in Jer 38(45),3 ("this city shall be given into the hand of the army of the king of Babylon and be taken") which Josephus earlier (10,117b-118) passed over when citing Jeremiah's own words; see above.

Jer 38(45),5 reports Zedekiah's *degagé* response to the leaders: "Behold, he [Jeremiah] is in your power; for the king can do nothing against you (LXX: them)". Josephus (10,120), in line with his overall attempt to "rehabilitate" Zedekiah, introduces an extended introductory comment which aims to cast the king's eventual yielding to the leaders in a more favorable light. This reads: *"Now the king himself, because of his goodness and sense of justice* (χρηστότητος καὶ δικαιοσύνης)[101], *was in no way personally resentful* (οὐδεν ... παρωξύνθη)[102] *but, in order not to incur the hostility of the leaders* (ἡγεμόσιν; see 10,119) *by opposing their wishes as such a time*, he gave them leave to do as they liked (ἄν θέλωσιν)[103] with the prophet".

Jer 38(45),6 describes the princes' acting on the free hand given them by Zedekiah: using ropes they drop Jeremiah into a mud-filled cistern located in the court of the guard. Once again, Josephus (10,121) embellishes: *"as soon as the king had given them this leave, they went into the prison* (εἰς τὴν εἰρκτήν)[104], *took him away and let him down by ropes into a pit* (εἴς τινα λάκκον; LXX: εἰς τὸν λάκκον)[105] full of mud (βορβόρου

101. This collocation echoes that applied to another of Josephus' rehabilitated kings, i.e. Jehoiachin whom he states (10,100) – likewise without Biblical warrant – to have been "kind and just (χρηστὸς καὶ δίκαιος) by nature". On the other hand, Josephus' characterization of Zedekiah here seems to contradict his own earlier (Biblically-based) estimate of him (10,103) as "contemptuous of justice (δικαίων) and duty". There, however, it will be recalled, Zedekiah's moral deficiencies are attributed to the influence of ("for") his "impious" entourage. Accordingly, one might understand Josephus' positive qualification of Zedekiah here in 10,120 in the sense that, like Jehoiachin, he was indeed "by nature good and just", though also susceptible to the contrary, reprobate influences of those around him. See FELDMAN, *Studies*, pp. 455-456 and n. 6 (= ID., *Zedekiah*, 85-86 and n. 31).

102. In thus qualifying Josephus' stance towards Jeremiah, Josephus (positively) differentiates him from several previous kings whom he charges with being "resentful" towards the prophets of their times, i.e. Jeroboam I (*AJ* 8,223, of Jadon), Ahab (8,392, of Micaiah), Ahaziah (9,24, of Elijah); cf. 9,199 (Amaziah's "resentment" at King Joash's letter to him).

103. This phrase echoes those used previously of the free hand Zedekiah's subjects had during his reign in 10,103 ("the entire multitude had licence to act outrageously as it pleased [ἄ ἤθελεν]") and 10,105 (Zedekiah's friends "led him wherever they pleased [ἄπερ ἤθελον]"). Here again, then, Josephus underscores the king's inability to keep his subjects under control.

104. This phrase picks up the reference in 10,117 to Jeremiah's "being in prison" (ἐν ... τῇ εἰρκτῇ) from whence he delivers the address to the people that so outrages the leaders. Jeremiah 38(45) itself fails to specify either the site of the prophet's speech to the people (see vv. 1-3) or whence he was "taken" (see v. 4) to be conveyed to the cistern.

105. The term used by Josephus (and the LXX) for Jeremiah's "cistern", i.e. λάκκος is the same one employed by him to designate his own hiding place following the fall of Jotapata in *BJ* 3,341: (Josephus was) "plunged into a deep pit (εἰς τινα βαθὺν λάκκον)". It is likewise the term used by Josephus (following LXX Gen 37,24) of the "pit" into which Joseph – another Biblical figure with whom Josephus seems particularly to have identified – is cast by his brothers (*AJ* 2,31); see G.L. JOHNSON, *Josephus – Heir*

πλήρη)[106] *in order that he might suffocate* (πνιγείς)[107] *and die by his own hand* (ἰδίῳ[108] θανάτῳ) *as it were*[109]. And so he remained (ἦν) there, held fast in the mud (ὑπὸ τοῦ πηλοῦ[110] up to (πρό)[111] his neck[112]".

In Jer 38(45),7-9 one hears of an intervention on Jeremiah's behalf by "Ebed-melech, the Cushite, a eunuch" (so MT v. 7)[113] who reports to Zedekiah concerning the prophet's parlous situation. Josephus (10,122a) introduces Jeremiah's deliverer as follows: "But one of the king's servants (τῶν ... οἰκετῶν τις), an Ethiopian by race, *who enjoyed his favour* (ἐν τιμῇ τυγχάνων)...[114]". He then continues with an indirect discourse version of the Ethiopian's word as cited in 38(45),8-9[115]: "he reported the sad plight (τὸ ... πάθος; cf. πάσχων, 10,115) of the prophet to the king and argued that his friends (φίλους)[116] and the leaders (ἡγεμόνας; see

Apparent to the Prophetic Tradition?, in *SBL Seminar Papers 22*, Chico, CA, Scholars, 1983, 337-346, pp. 341-342.

Here in 10,121b Josephus omits the additional particulars of Jer 38(45),6 regarding the cistern, i.e. that it belonged to "Malchiah, the king's son" and was located "in the court of the guard".

106. Compare Jer 38(45),6bα: "There was no water in the cistern, but only mire (LXX βόρβορος)".

107. Josephus' remaining uses of the verb πνίγω are in *BJ* 2,327; 5,471; *AJ* 20,248.

108. Naber tentatively proposes emending this reading of the codices to βιαίῳ; the above reading echoes the term ἰδία used of Zedekiah's not being "personally" resentful towards Jeremiah in 10,120.

109. This added specfication concerning the leaders' intent underscores the enormity of their deed.

110. This is the emendation, inspired by Lat's luto, of Coccejus (whom Dindorf, Bekker, Niese, Naber, and Marcus all follow) for the obviously corrupt reading of the codices and E, i.e. πλήθους.

111. This is the conjecture of Bekker and Naber which Marcus adopts, inspired by Lat's usque ad. Dindorf follows the conjecture of Coccejus, i.e. πρός, while Niese proposes ἀπό.

112. Compare Jer 38(45),6bβ: "and Jeremiah sank (MT; LXX: "was," ἦν, so Josephus) in the mire (LXX: ἐν τῷ βορβόρῳ)".

113. LXX speaks rather of "Αβδεμελεχ the Ethiopian" and omits the qualification of him as "a eunuch". Tg. Jeremiah renders: "the servant of the king, Zedekiah [sic!; on the Targum's name for Jeremiah's rescuer, see R. HAYWARD, *The Targum of Jeremiah* (The Aramaic Bible, 12), Wilmington DE, Glazier, 1987, p. 153, n. 5], a mighty man (גבר רב)".

114. In the above formulation, Josephus, unlike MT, LXX and TJ, gives no name to Jeremiah's rescuer. In place of MT's designation "a eunuch" (> LXX) he speaks rather of the figure's "being held in honor" by Zedekiah – a characterization which serves to explain how a mere "servant" could have exercised such influence upon the king and which is further comparable to the Targumic description of him as "a mighty man"; see HAYWARD, *Targum*, p. 153, n. 5.

115. Josephus omits the (parenthetical) place indication of Jer 38(45),7b: "the king was sitting in the Benjamin Gate".

116. Recall that in 10,105 Zedekiah's (eventual) disbelieving of the prophecy of Jeremiah at the start of his reign is attributed to the bad influence of this same group: "his friends (φίλοι) once more corrupted him [Zedekiah] and, winning him away from the prophet, led him wherever they pleased".

10,119.120) had done wrong (οὐκ· ὀρθῶς ... πεποιηκέναι)[117] to sink (καταποντίσαντας)[118] the prophet in mud [MT: by casting him into the cistern; > LXX] *and devise for him a death that would be so much more painful* (πικρότερον) *than one by imprisonment in chains*[119]".

Zedekiah's response to the Ethiopian's appeal is briefly cited in Jer 38(45),10: he commands the latter to take thirty[120] men and raise the prophet from the cistern before he dies. Josephus, with a view to underscoring Zedekiah's positive and provident concern for Jeremiah embellishes (10,123): "*when the king heard this, he repented* (μετανοήσας; see 9,168 [Joash's associates fail to repent]; 10,60 [the Judeans had not repented over a long period of time]) *of having delivered the prophet to the leaders* (ἡγεμόσιν; see 10,119.120.122), and ordered the Ethiopian to take thirty [see n. 120] of the king's men *with ropes and whatever else he might think* (ἐπινοεῖν)[121] *of use in rescuing* (τὴν ... σωτηρίαν)[122] *the prophet*[123], and draw up Jeremiah *with all haste* (μετὰ σπουδῆς)[124]".

117. The above formulation in which it is the "friends" and leaders who are said to have "done wrong" in their treatment of Jeremiah corresponds to MT Jer 38,9 ("these men have done evil [הֵרֵעוּ] in all that they did to Jeremiah...") as against LXX 45,9 ("you [sg., Zedekiah] have done wrong [ἐπονηρεύσω ἃ ἐποίησας] in sentencing this man to die..."). On this and other such differences between MT and LXX in their respective portrayals of Zedekiah, see H.-J. STIPP, *Zedekiah in the Book of Jeremiah: On the Formation of a Biblical Character*, in *CBQ* 58 (1996) 627-648. Josephus' following of the MT reading here in preference to that of LXX – supposing him to have known both – is understandable given his overall concern to exonerate Zedekiah. Note as well the verbal echo of Jeremiah's own earlier word to Zedekiah concerning the "false prophets", i.e. "they were doing the king a wrong (ποιοῦσι ... κακῶς)" in 10,112 in the Ethiopian's affirmation about the royal entourage here in 10,122, i.e. "they had done wrong (οὐκ ὀρθῶς ... πεποιηκέναι)".

118. Josephus' two remaining uses of the verb καταποντίζω are in 10,170 and *c. Ap.* 2,245.

119. This conclusion to the Ethiopian's address is Josephus' replacement for the closing words of Jer 38(45),9: "he will die there of hunger, for there is no bread left in the city". Note how Josephus' version insists on the responsibility and culpability of Jeremiah's enemies who have abandoned him to the most "painful" death imaginable.

120. This is the reading of all but one Hebrew MS, LXX and TJ. BHS, RSV and many commentators follow, however, the reading "three" (שְׁלֹשָׁה) of that single MS. Josephus, in any case, does reproduce the reading "thirty" in his version of Jer 38(45),10; see below.

121. This is the reading adopted by Niese, Naber, and Marcus. Dindorf and Bekker read ἐπινοεῖ with MSP.

122. This is the reading of the *ed. pr.* which Dindorf, Bekker, Niese, Naber, and Marcus follow; the codices have τῇ σωτηρίᾳ. Josephus' noun here in 10,122 echoes the verbal form σωθήσεσθαι used by him in 10,117. See n. 148.

123. The words italicized above have no counterpart in the Biblical Zedekiah's brief directive to Ebed-melech, Jer 38(45),10. They can be viewed, however, as an anticipation of 38(45),11 where Ebed-melech, acting on his own initiative, is said to "take old rags and worn-out clothes" and to let these down "by ropes" (so MT, > LXX) to Jeremiah in the cistern. This "anticipation" serves to underscore the image of a more provident and directive king who "thinks of everything" in his concern for Jeremiah's rescue that Josephus is concerned to present.

124. This concluding element of the Josephan Zedekiah's speech replaces the "before he dies" (MT) / "lest he die" (LXX) with which the Biblical king's directive ends up in

Josephus' version (10,117-123a) of Jer 38(45),1-10, as we have been seeing, consistently elaborates on the various components of its Biblical parallel. In 10,123b, on the contrary, Josephus drastically reduces the account of Jeremiah's actual rescue by Ebed-melech as found in Jer 38(45),11-13[125]. His condensed version reads: "so the Ethiopian took the men *as instructed*[126] (= 38(45),11aα) and pulled the prophet up out of the mud (= 38(45),13a)[127] *and released him from confinement*[128]".

The second half of Jeremiah 38(45) relates a final conversation between the newly freed prophet and Zedekiah (vv. 14-26) and the immediate sequels to this (vv. 27-28) which Josephus reproduces in detail in 10,124-130. The new Biblical sequence opens in 38(45),14 with Zedekiah summoning Jeremiah to "the third entrance of the temple of the Lord" where he says to him "I will ask you a question; hide nothing from me". As has been pointed out by Piovanelli[129], Josephus opts to replace this introduction to the last recorded interview between king and prophet with one drawn from their earlier exchange as related in Jer 37(44),16-20(21) and previously passed over by him; see above on 10,115. That the historian is, in fact, making "delayed" utilization of 37(44),17a here in 10,124a is clear from a comparison of the two texts. The former passage reads: "King Zedekiah sent for him, and received him. The king questioned him secretly (LXX: κρυφαίως) in his house, and said 'Is there any word (LXX: λόγος) from the Lord'"? The Josephan parallel

38(45),10. By having Zedekiah call on the Ethiopian to rescue the prophet "with haste", Josephus accentuates his concern for Jeremiah's safety.

125. In thus compressing the account of Ebed-melech's own activity in Jeremiah's deliverance while, conversely, amplifying Zedekiah's directive concerning the enterprise, Josephus heightens the king's own (positive) role in the prophet's rescue at the expense of that of his servant.

126. This phrase has no counterpart in Jer 38(45),11. It underscores the fact that the ultimate "source" of Jeremiah's rescue was Zedekiah himself.

127. Josephus' version thus moves directly from the opening phrase of Jer 38(45),11 to v. 13a, passing over the whole of vv. 11aβb (Ebed-melech procures old clothes and rags and lets these down to Jeremiah by means of ropes [recall Josephus' anticipation of this sequence in his version of Zedekiah's directive of 38(45),10 in 10,123a]) and 12 (Ebed-melech instructs Jeremiah about what to do with the items that have been lowered down to him and the prophet complies).

128. This concluding notice of Josephus' (abbreviated) version of Jeremiah's rescue, with its seeming suggestion that the prophet was set fully free, goes beyond the source text Jer 38(45),13b which merely states "and Jeremiah remained in the court of the guard". In this connection, it might be recalled that Josephus passed over previous Biblical references to "the court of the guard" as the place of Jeremiah's initial confinement (see 37(44),21; compare 10,115 *in fine*) and the site of the cistern into which he was subsequently cast (see 38(45),6; compare 10,121). Thus his avoidance of 38(45),13b's reference to the guard-court here in 10,123b is only to be expected.

129. *Texte*, 23, n. 58.

runs as follows: "Now, when the king sent for him secretly (κρύφα)[130] and asked him what message he could give him from God[131] *and what course he could indicate in the present circumstances...*[132]".

The narration of the final royal-prophetic encounter (Jer 38(45),14-26) continues in v. 15 with Jeremiah asking whether Zedekiah will not put him to death if he answers his question (see v.14) and further asserting that "you [Zedekiah] will not listen" to his counsel should he give it. In his version of the prophet's reply Josephus (10,124b) combines elements drawn from both 37(44),17bα and 38(45),15, even while characteristically toning down the latter verse's pointed personal attack on Zedekiah. This reads: "... the prophet replied that he had something to say [compare 37(44),17bα: "and Jeremiah (> LXX) said, 'There is'".], but would not be believed (πιστευθήσεσθαι)[133] if he spoke nor would his advice (παραινέσας)[134] be listened to (ἀκουσθήσεσθαι)[135]".

In Jer 38(45),18 Zedekiah replies immediately to Jeremiah's preceding accusatory questions (v. 17) by swearing that he will not put the prophet to death or hand him over to "these men" who "seek his life" (so MT, > LXX). Josephus (10,124b), by contrast, first interjects a further series of questions by Jeremiah drawn from 37(44),18-19, shifting from indirect to direct discourse for his citation of these. Jeremiah's question to the king in 37(44),18 asks: "what wrong have I done (LXX: ἠδίκησα) to you or to your servants or this people that you have put (MT pl.; LXX: sg. δίδως, i.e. Zedekiah)[136] me in prison"? Josephus compresses, character-

130. Note that Josephus here leaves aside the specification of Jer 37(44),17 that the interview took place in Zedekiah's "house". Compare the analogous case of 10,120 where Josephus passes over the indication of 38(45),7 regarding the locale of the Zedekiah-Ebed-melech exchange (i.e. "the Benjamin gate").

131. In the above version of Zedekiah's question, note Josephus' characteristic replacement of the references to both the (divine) "word" and to "the Lord" found in Jer 37(44),17a.

132. This element represents a further specification of Zedekiah's opening question about Jeremiah's ability to provide "a message from God"; it has no counterpart in Jer 37(44),17a.

133. Note the recurrence of this *Leitwort* of 10,102-130.

134. This verb echoes its double previous use in reference to Jeremiah's speaking in 10,117 (παραινῶν) and 119 (παρῄνει).

135. Compare LXX 45(MT 38),15: οὐ μὴ ἀκούσῃς μου. Josephus' substitution of a passive form of the verb "hear" (which itself picks up on his reference to the leaders "hearing" [ἀκούοντες] Jeremiah from prison in 10,119; cf. also the allusion to Zedekiah's "hearing" [ἀκούσας] the Ethiopian's report in 10,123) – as well as his previous interjection of the likewise passive phrase "he would not be believed" – both times with an unspecified subject serves, in line with his overall aim of rehabilitating Zedekiah, to downplay the Biblical Jeremiah's direct verbal assault on the king. See, however, 10,124 *in fine* below where Josephus does re-utilize Jeremiah's initial question of 38(45),15 in a way that highlights Zedekiah's own (potential) culpability in the case at hand.

136. On the difference between MT and LXX here as reflective of the latter's heightened animus against Zedekiah, see STIPP, *Zedekiah*, 638-640.

istically eliminating any suggestion of Zedekiah's own culpability for Jeremiah's plight: "'But what wrong have I done (τί ... κακὸν εἰργασμένον; compare Jeremiah's charge against the false prophets in 10,112: ποιοῦσι ... κακῶς)', he asked, 'that your friends (φίλοι) have determined to destroy (ἀπολέσαι) me...[137]'"? Jeremiah's further query to the king in Jer 37(44),19 is a sarcastic rhetorical question: "Where are your prophets who prophesied to you, saying, 'The king of Babylon will not come against you (so MT, > LXX) and against this land'"? As will be recalled, Josephus has already utilized the language of this question in the warning (10,104) he attributes to Jeremiah at the start of Zedekiah's reign, i.e. (he bade the king not to credit) "the false prophets who were deceiving (ἀπατῶσιν) him [for this element, unparalleled in 37(44),19, see 38(45),22] by saying that the Babylonian king would never again make war on the city...". Here in 10,124 he now has Jeremiah echo that earlier warning of his in the continuation of his question to the king: "... and where now are those who asserted that the Babylonian king would not march against us[138] again, and so deceived (ἀπατῶντες) you (pl. ὑμᾶς)[139]?" Finally, Josephus (10,124 in fine) rounds off Jeremiah's extended reply to Zedekiah with an admission by the prophet inspired by his initial question to Zedekiah as cited in 38(45),15, i.e. "If I tell you, will you not be sure to put me to death[140]"? He formulates the prophetic "confession" as follows: "I am, indeed, afraid (εὐλαβοῦμαι)[141] now to

137. In the above formulation the blame for Jeremiah's unjust treatment is assigned exclusively to the royal "friends" (see further 10,105.122 on their nefarious role throughout Zedekiah's reign). By contrast, in MT 37,18 Zedekiah is included among those responsible for the prophet's wrongful imprisonment, while in the LXX of that verse he alone is accused of such abuse. In Josephus' rewording of Jer 37(44),18 note too the accentuation of the friends' culpability vis-à-vis the blameless Jeremiah; whereas in the source verse Zedekiah et al. are merely stated to have put the prophet in prison, in 10,124 the friends are charged with having decided to "destroy" (ἀπολέσαι, i.e. the very verb used by Jeremiah himself in 10,118.119 of the city's impending doom) him.

138. Note Jeremiah's self-identification with his people via his use of this pronoun here. Compare 10,112 where, in the course of his extended prediction of Jerusalem's fate, the prophet avers "we shall be slaves to him (Nebuchadnezzar) and his descendants for seventy years".

139. Compare 10,104 where the false prophets' are said to deceive only Zedekiah himself ("him"). Note too that in the Biblical source for the charges of "deception" by those around the king which Josephus attributes to Jeremiah in both 10,104 and 124, i.e. Jer 38(45),22, the lament cited there speaks of Zedekiah's "trusted friends deceiving you (sg.)". Thus, Josephus' generalization in 10,124 might suggest that by this point the false prophets cited in 10,104 have succeeded in "deceiving" not only the king, but also the entire people.

140. Already previously in 10,124 Josephus has presented his adaptation of the prophet's double question in 38(45),15; see above in the text and cf. n. 135.

141. This admission of "fear" which Josephus attributes here (without Biblical basis as such) to Jeremiah is noteworthy; it serves to underscore the danger which he is currently facing. Note too that the wording of Jeremiah's statement echoes the (likewise "un-

speak the truth (ἀλήθειαν εἰπεῖν)[142] lest you condemn me to death (μή
με κατακρίνης θανάτω; compare LXX 45(MT 38),15: οὐχὶ θανάτω με
θανατώσεις;)".

In 10,125a Josephus comes finally to relate the royal pledge cited in
Jer 38(45),16: "But, as the king gave him his oath (ὅρκους ... δόντος;
LXX: ὤμοσεν)[143] that he himself would neither put him to death (αὐτὸς
αὐτὸν ἀναιρήσει; LXX: εἰ ἀποκτενῶ σε) nor deliver him to the leaders (τοῖς ἡγεμόσιν ἐκδώσει; LXX: εἰ δώσω σε εἰς χειρας τῶν
ἀνθρώπων τούτων)...[144]". Jer 38(45),17 has the prophet begin his
counsel to Zedekiah immediately upon receiving the royal oath. Josephus – who had just previously (10,124) introduced mention of Jeremiah's "fear" – first pauses to note the emotional affect of the king's
pledge upon him: "... he was encouraged (θαρσήσας) by the pledge
thus given (δεδομένη)[145] and advised him...".

Jer 38(45),17-18 cites the two hypothetical alternatives which Jeremiah sets before the king: if he "goes out" to the Babylonians, he is
assured that they will spare his life, the city, and his family, whereas if
he fails to do so, the city will be destroyed and he himself will fall into
the Babylonians' hands. Josephus' version (10,125b-126) presents a
more directive Jeremiah who, dispensing with the hypothetical wording
of his Biblical counterpart, immediately and directly "advises" Zedekiah
"to surrender (παραδοῦναι)[146] the city to the Babylonians".

Biblical") notice introduced by Josephus in *AJ* 6,157 regarding the prophet Samuel's reaction
to the divine directive that he repair to Bethlehem and there anoint one of Jesse's sons:
"Samuel replied that he was fearful (εὐλαβεῖσθαι) lest Saul on learning of this [directive]
should slay him by ambush or even openly..." (in both cases as well the object of the
prophets' "fear" is the possibility that a king, Zedekiah or Saul, will inflict death upon them).

142. Compare 10,112 where during the siege interlude Jeremiah "came forward and
prophesied the truth (ἀληθῆ ... προεφήτευσεν)...".

143. Jer 38(45),16 goes on to cite the wording of Zedekiah's oath formula ("as the
Lord lives, who made our souls"). Josephus, as is his wont, confines himself to mention
of the royal act of "swearing" itself.

144. Josephus' above substitution of "the leaders" for the Bible's vaguer "these men"
(MT + "who seek your life") is in line with his use of the former term as *the* collective designation for Jeremiah's opponents throughout 10,102-130. The reference to Zedekiah's
pledge not to turn Jeremiah over to the leaders here in 10,125 both echoes and reverses
Josephus' earlier formulations concerning the king-prophet-leaders triangle; see 10,120
("... in order not to incur the hostility of the leaders [τοῖς ἡγεμόσιν]... he [Zedekiah]
gave them leave to do as they liked with the prophet") and 10,123 (Zedekiah "repents of
having handed over the prophet to the leaders [παραδοῦναι ... τοῖς ἡγεμόσιν]").

145. Thus the emendation of Niese which Naber and Marcus follow; the codices read
λεγομένη (as do Dindorf and Bekker).

146. Compare the vaguer verbal phrase of 38(45),17: "if you go out (LXX: ἐάν
ἐξελθὼν ἐξελθῆς) to the princes of the king of Babylon...". The infinitival form παραδοῦναι used here in 10,125 of the "surrendering" of Jerusalem to the Babylonians is the very
same one employed in 10,123 of Zedekiah's "handing over" Jeremiah to the leaders.

Having given this advice, Josephus' Jeremiah goes on to present motivations for it, both positive (= 38,17) and negative (= 38,18). Specifically, Jeremiah first represents the advice just given as of divine origin for the case that Zedekiah is indeed genuinely concerned for his own welfare and that of everything under his care: "This, he said, God prophesied (τὸν θεὸν ... προφητεύειν) to the king through him[147], if indeed he wished to be saved (σώσεσθαι)[148] and to escape the impending danger (κίνδυνον διαφυγεῖν)[149] and not have the city brought down to the ground (τὴν πόλιν εἰς ἔδαφος πεσεῖν)[150] *and the temple burned* (τὸν ναὸν ἐμπρησθῆναι)...[151]". Thereafter, the prophet proceeds to adduce what will happen should Zedekiah disregard God's "prophecy" to him: "for, if he disobeyed (μὴ πεισθέντα)[152] (this warning), he would be the cause of these calamities (κακῶν) *to the inhabitants of the city* (τοῖς πολίταις)[153] and of the disaster to himself and all his house (πανοικί; compare LXX Jer 45(MT 38),17: καὶ ἡ οἰκία σου)".

Jer 38(45),19 cites Zedekiah's reply to Jeremiah in which the king expresses his "fear" of being handed over to those Jews who have deserted to the Chaldeans and of being abused by them. Josephus

147. The above formulation is Josephus' replacement for the elaborate *Botenformel* with which Jeremiah's words to Zedekiah in Jer 38(45),17 begin: "Thus says the Lord, the God of hosts, the God of Israel (so MT; LXX reads only thus says the Lord)...". For Josephus' uses of προφητεύω with God/the Deity as subject, see on 9,145.

148. This verb echoes the wording of Jeremiah's earlier warning as cited in 10,117 (if the people admitted Nebuchadnezzar) "they would be saved (σωθήσεσθαι)...", as well as the reference to Jeremiah's "rescue" (σωτηρίαν) in Zedekiah's directive to the Ethiopian a cited in 10,123; see n. 122.

149. Cf. 10,118 where Jeremiah affirms that "anyone who fled to the enemy would escape death (διαδράσεται τὸν θάνατον)". Note too the echo of 10,119 where the leaders, in their address to Zedekiah, evoke the people's readiness to "risk (κινδυνεῦσαι) their lives" for the king.

150. Compare 10,144 where Nebuchadnezzar, in fulfillment of Jeremiah's (unheeded) warning here in 10,126, orders his general "to raze the city to the ground (τὴν ... πόλιν εἰς ἔδαφος καθελεῖν)".

151. In Jer 38(45),17 Jeremiah says nothing of the Temple's fate, it being the city itself which, he assures Zedekiah, "will not be burned with fire" (LXX: οὐ μὴ κατακαυθῇ ἐν πυρί) should Zedekiah surrender (whereas, conversely, it will be so "burned" if he does not, 38,18). Recall that in the earlier prophecy he attributes to Jeremiah during the siege interlude in 10,112, Josephus already has him announce the fate threatening, not only the city (as in Jer 38,17-18, etc.) but also the Temple: Nebuchadnezzar will "burn" (ἐμπρήσει; compare ἐμπρησθῆναι, 10,126) the Temple itself and "raze the city" (κατασκάψει τὴν πόλιν). See also n. 49.

152. The above words are absent in the Greek codices. Dindorf, Bekker, Naber, and Marcus follow J. Hudson's restoration of them on the basis of Lat which reads "quod si non fieret". Niese conjectures (ἐμπρησθέντα) ἐπιδεῖν.

153. Jer 38(45),17-18 speaks only of the possible outcomes awaiting Zedekiah and his family. With the above insertion Josephus has Jeremiah remind the king that upon his decision hangs as well the fate of a much larger group of people.

(10,127) prefaces his version of the royal statement with a word which shows Zedekiah in a more favorable light, i.e. as one who clearly recognizes the rightfulness of Jeremiah's preceding counsel. His expanded parallel to 38,19 thus reads: *"The king, upon hearing this, said* (λέγει) *that he himself wished to do what Jeremiah advised* (παραινεῖ; see n. 134) *and what he said it would be to his interest* (συνοίσειν αὐτῷ) *to have done*[154], but that he was afraid (δεδιέναι; LXX: λόγον ἔχω)[155] of those of his own people who had deserted (τοὺς αὐτομολήσαντας [see αὐτομολοῦντα, of Jeremiah himself, 10,114] τῶν ὁμοφύλων; LXX: τῶν Ἰουδαίων τῶν πεφευγότων) to the Babylonians, for he might be denounced by them to the king and punished (κολασθῇ)[156]".

Jeremiah begins his response to Zedekiah in 38(45),20a with a rather brusque dismissal of the king's fears: "you shall not be given to them". Josephus (10,128a) elaborates, making Jeremiah appear more sympathetic to the anxious king: "The prophet, however, bade him take courage (παρεθάρσυνε)[157] and said that his apprehension of punishment (τὴν τιμωρίαν)[158] was groundless...". The Biblical Jeremiah's reply continues (38,20b) with an appeal to Zedekiah to "obey now the voice of the Lord (LXX: λόγον κυρίου)", coupled with the promise that if he does so, "it shall be well with you and your life shall be spared". Josephus' version, in line with his usual practice, omits the source reference to the "voice/word of the Lord". In its place he (10,128b) works into the prophet's assurance a specification as to what it is Zedekiah is being asked to do at the moment: "... for he should suffer no harm (κακοῦ)[159] *by surrendering* (παραδόντα)

154. Compare Josephus' notice on Zedekiah's immediate reaction to Jeremiah's admonition to him at the beginning of his reign in 10,105: "Now Sacchias, so long as he listened to the prophet saying these things, believed him and agreed to everything as true and that it was to his interest (συμφέρον αὐτῷ) to have faith in him...".

155. Zedekiah's admission of "fear" here echoes Jeremiah's own similar statement in 10,124: "I am, indeed, afraid (εὐλαβοῦμαι) now to speak the truth lest you condemn me to death". There is irony in the prophet's being "afraid" of a king who is "fearful" himself.

156. Compare Jer 38(45),19b where Zedekiah foresees the Babylonians handing him over to the Jewish deserters to be abused by them. Josephus reverses the procedure envisaged: the deserters will take the initiative in denouncing Zedekiah to the Babylonians who will then themselves execute punishment upon him. Such a scenario does seem more plausible than the Biblical one where one is left wondering why the Babylonians would not reserve the punishment of the chief culprit to themselves (as they indeed do in 2 Kgs 25,6-7 // Jer 52,9-10).

157. This directive picks up on the mention of Jeremiah himself being "encouraged" (θαρσήσας) by Zedekiah's assurances in 10,125.

158. With this term Jeremiah picks up on Zedekiah's previous statement about fearing that he would be "punished" (κολασθῇ) by the Babylonians in 10,127. The term also echoes 10,115 where it is Jeremiah himself who is kept under guard "for punishment" (πρὸς τιμωρίαν) by the magistrates.

159. Note the echo of 10,126 where Jeremiah warns that Zedekiah risks being "the cause of these calamities (τῶν κακῶν)...".

to the Babylonians[160], neither he himself, *nor his children nor his wives*[161], *and that the temple, moreover, should remain unharmed*[162]".

Jeremiah's reply to Zedekiah ends up in 38(45),21-23 with an extended warning about the consequences of his disregarding the divine directive to surrender. Josephus passes over this negative continuation of the prophet's address, thereby having Jeremiah's last word to the king end up on a positive note of promise; see above[163]. In its place he proceeds immediately to relate (10,129) Zedekiah's termination of the interview (= 38(45),24-26). The source (38,24) commences its account on the point with Zedekiah telling Jeremiah "let no one know of these words and you shall not die". Given that Josephus has already reproduced (10,125) Zedekiah's promise from Jer 38(45),16 to spare the prophet's life, here in 10,129 he passes over, for the moment, this opening royal statement. In its stead, he introduces the narrative remark "and so, after Jeremiah had spoken in this way, the king dismissed him...". Thereafter, he cites a double directive by the king. The first component of this directive ("ordering him not to divulge to any of the citizens [τῶν πολιτῶν][164] what they had decided on...") might be viewed as an adaptation of the initial portion of Zedekiah's assurance (38,24) previously left aside by Jeremiah, i.e. "let no one know of these words...". Its second element is, in any case, clearly inspired by 38(45),25-26 where

160. This phrase too echoes Jeremiah's earlier word to Zedekiah; see 10,125: "he advised him to surrender (παραδοῦναι) the city to the Babylonians"; cf. n. 146.

161. This expansion of the Biblical promise (38,20b) of safety for Zedekiah himself picks up on Jeremiah's warning in 10,126 that if he fails the surrender the king will be the cause of disaster to himself "*and all his house*". The added reference here in 10,128b further underscores how much is at stake in Zedekiah's decision about whether or nor to surrender, just as it appeals to the king's feelings as father and husband. Biblical inspiration for the addition was available to Josephus in Jer 38(45),23 (a verse not subsequently utilized by him as such; see above) which reads "all your wives and children" (LXX: τας γυναῖκας σου καὶ τὰ τέκνα σου; compare 10,128 οὔτε τὰ τέκνα οὔτε τὰς γυναῖκας). See also n. 163.

162. Also this promise has no equivalent in that of Jer 38(45),20b. It does, however, echo previous announcements about the Temple's fate which Josephus introduces into his version of Jeremiah's words during Zedekiah's reign; see 10,112.126.

163. In fact, Josephus does, as we have seen, utilize one or other element of Jer 38(45),21-23 elsewhere in his presentation in 10,102-130. Thus, the opening words of the palace women's lament over Zedekiah of 38,22 ("your trusted friends have *deceived* you") are incorporated into the Josephan Jeremiah's references to those "deceiving" Zedekiah in 10,104.124. We likewise pointed out (n. 161) that Jeremiah's promise of safety for the king's children and wives in 10,128b might have been derived by Josephus from 38(45),23 where the prophet warns that these persons will be led out to the Chaldeans.

164. With this specifying designation (compare 38,24: "[let no] man [LXX: ἄνθρω-πος]...") the Josephan Zedekiah picks up on Jeremiah's invocation of the fate of "the inhabitants of the city (τοῖς πολίταις)" in his address to the king in 10,126.

Zedekiah instructs the prophet as to how he is to answer the "princes" if they should ask what was said at the interview. Thus, the Josephan Zedekiah enjoins Jeremiah "not even to say anything about these matters to the leaders (τοῖς ἡγεμόσιν; LXX: 45,25 οἱ ἄρχοντες) if they should learn (μάθοντες, LXX: ἀκούσωσιν) that he had been summoned by the king (ὑπ' αὐτοῦ μετάπεμπτον; see 10,124 μεταπεμψαμένου ... τοῦ βασιλέως) and should ask what Jeremiah had said to him *when he was called*[165], but should *pretend* (σκήπτεσθαι)[166] to them that he had pleaded not to be kept in chains (ἐν δεσμῷ) and under guard[167]".

Jer 38(45),27-28 constitutes the sequel to the interview between king and prophet recounted in 38,14-26. In the former sequence Jeremiah is approached by the princes (v. 27aα) to whom he responds as directed by Zedekiah (v. 27aβ), with the result that they abandon the conversation (v. 27b), while Jeremiah himself remains in the court of the guard (see 38,13) until the day of Jerusalem's capture (v. 28). Josephus (10,130) presents the component elements of 38,27a in reverse order (thereby accentuating Jeremiah's adherence to Zedekiah's directive): "And this, in fact, was what he did tell them. For they [38,27 specifies "all the princes (LXX: οἱ ἄρχοντες)] came to the prophet and asked *what sort of story he had made up* (σκήπτεσθαι; the codices LaurV [as well as Dindorf and Bekker]): σκέπτεσθαι)[168] *about them when he came to the king*[169]".

165. Josephus omits the further hypothetical query of the princes cited in 38(45),25, i.e. "(tell us) what the king said to you". Thereby, he accentuates the status of Jeremiah whose side of the exchange seems to be the only one of interest to the "leaders" – understandably so given their previous success in browbeating the king himself into following their wishes.

166. Compare Jer 38(45),26 where Jeremiah is simply instructed "say to them...". Zedekiah's directing Jeremiah to "pretend" in his answer to the "leaders" introduces a note of irony into Josephus' version in that these same leaders have, according to Jeremiah, themselves been guilty of "deceiving" the king (see 10,104.124). Zedekiah is now about to "turn the tables" on his "deceivers" through the agency of Jeremiah. See n. 168.

167. This conclusion to the answer Jeremiah is to give the leaders represents a generalization of the wording of 38(45),26 where the prophet's prescribed (fictive) plea is that he not be sent back "to the house of Jonathan to die there". Josephus' replacement of this formulation with a more general one is understandable given that earlier (see 10,115) he left aside the mentions, found in 37(44),15 and 20, of "Jonathan's house" as Jeremiah's place of imprisonment. In its use of the phrase ἐν δεσμῷ the plea echoes the Ethiopian's reference to Jeremiah's facing "a death that would be so much more painful than one by imprisonment in chains (τῶν δεσμῶν) in 10,122.

168. This same verb was used just previously in Zedekiah's directive to Jeremiah in 10,129 that he "pretend" (σκήπτεσθαι) to have begged not to be kept in confinement. Here too (see n. 166), there is irony to Josephus' presentation: the leaders insinuate that Jeremiah has falsely represented them to the king, whereas, in fact, on Zedekiah's orders, he is now going to falsely represent himself to them.

169. With the above notice Josephus supplies a content to the leaders' question as mentioned in Jer 38(45),27a. The sarcastic tone of the query he attributes to them here underscores the leaders' unabated hostility to the prophet.

Josephus dispenses with the content of Jer 38,27b-28, i.e. the breaking off of the exchange between Jeremiah and the leaders and Jeremiah's remaining in the court of the guard for the duration of the siege[170]. In place thereof, he rounds off his whole account (10,116-130) of Jeremiah during the later period of the siege with a reiteration of his notice on the prophet's response to his interlocutors (see above): "this, then, is what was said (ἐλέχθη)[171]". Thereafter, in line with Jeremiah 39, he begins (10,131) his narration of Jerusalem's fall and its sequel; see chap. XXIII. Jeremiah will not be mentioned again until 10,141 where the fulfillment of both his and Ezekiel's prophecies concerning Zedekiah's fate (see 10,106-107) is cited.

Conclusions: Josephus' Rewriting of Jeremiah 37-38, etc.

Josephus' presentation of "Zedekiah and Jeremiah" (10,103-130) is remarkable above all for its assembling and interweaving of a wide variety of Biblical passages, drawn primarily, of course, from the Book of Jeremiah itself[172], but also from Kings, Chronicles, Ezekiel, and Daniel, into a series of three longer "montages" (10,103-107, 108-115, 116-130)[173]. These "assemblages" attest both to the historian's detailed knowledge of the relevant source material and his synthetic powers.

The above three scenes likewise evidence a certain parallel movement. Each begins with a complex of "historical" notices concerning, respectively, the start of Zedekiah's reign (10,103), the onset and temporary lifting of the Babylonian siege (10,108-111), and its resumption and worsening impact (10,116). There follows, in all three complexes, an intervention by Jeremiah in which, *inter alia*, he pronounces a warning

---

170. Josephus' omission of this latter item is in line with his passing over of earlier Biblical mentions of this site, i.e. Jer 37(44),16 (compare 10,115); 38(45),6 (compare 10,121).13 (compare 10,123). The omission is comparable as well with his non-utilization of the source references to "the house of Jonathan"; see n. 167.

171. Compare Lat "sunt gesta".

172. In this connection I would note that the foregoing detailed comparison between *AJ* 10,103-130 and the materials of the Book of Jeremiah utilized therein confirms Piovanelli's finding that Josephus employed a text of Jeremiah that was clearly closer to the longer form of our MT than to LXX's shorter version. In the course of this study we have identified many instances of Josephus' aligning himself, throughout 10,103-130, with the distinctive readings of MT Jeremiah, whereas we have encountered no clear-cut case of his dependence on a reading peculiar to LXX.

173. A noteworthy instance of the above-cited process is Josephus' working together of elements taken from the Biblical accounts of the two separate interviews between Zedekiah and Jeremiah (Jer 37,16-21; 38,14-26) into a single such interview narrative in 10,124-129.

about the Babylonian threat (10,104.112-113.117.125-126). Finally, each scene ends up by noting the mixed response that Jeremiah's words called forth from their various hearers: the new king Zedekiah is initially inclined to believe them, but eventually falls into disbelief (10,105-107); during the siege interlude Jeremiah's predictions are credited by the majority of the people but laughed off by the leaders (10,114); ultimately, his admonitions as the siege nears its end meet with continued unbelief by the leaders (10,119), whereas Zedekiah recognizes their validity (10,127). In addition, the language of "truth" and "falsity" (often with ironic connotations) permeates the segment from start to finish. At the same time, however, the three scenes also evidence a clear dramatic progression, and that in several respects. At the beginning of Zedekiah's reign, Jeremiah's announcement is simply that, contrary to the false prophets' claims, Nebuchadnezzar will return to war against Jerusalem and will defeat the advancing Egyptians (10,104). Although Zedekiah (ultimately) fails to believe this announcement (10,105-107), the prophet himself suffers no ill effects for having made it. Next, during the siege interlude, Jeremiah delivers a much longer prediction on Jerusalem's fate, now affirming that the city will be, not simply besieged, but actually destroyed by the Babylonians, eventually to be rebuilt under the Persians and Medes (10,112-113). For such statements he is ridiculed as a madman by the leaders (10,114) who, this time, act to place him under confinement (10,115). In the later course of the siege, Jeremiah takes his message a step further, now calling for actual surrender to the Babylonians, given the inevitability of the city's fall (10,117-118.125-126). In response, the leaders demand of Zedekiah that he be done away with (10,119) and themselves intensify the prophet's tribulations by casting him into the muddy pit (10,121) where he faces a "death that would be so much more painful than one by imprisonment in chains" (10,122). This parallelism with progression in the development of the three main scenes making up 10,103-130 bespeaks Josephus' literary skill.

What now of the segment's characters in relation to their Biblical prototypes? First, Josephus accords more explicit (and positive) attention to the people as whole than does his source material. Jeremiah's predictions during the siege interlude (10,112-113) are believed by "the majority (of the people)" (10,114). In his final exhortation to Zedekiah, Jeremiah invokes the fate facing Jerusalem's "citizens" (10,126), while the king himself makes allusion to their subsequent possible questioning of the prophet in his reply (10,129). Over against the people stand Jeremiah's rivals and enemies; these include the "leaders" (ἡγεμόνες, 10,104, etc.), the "magistrates" (ἄρχοντες, 10,114-115), the "false prophets" (10,104.111), and the royal "friends" (10,105.124). In the Book of Jeremiah itself many of these opponents have names; Josephus leaves them all as anonymous members of threatening collectivities (even Jeremiah's arrester – "Irijah" according to MT 37,13 – is simply [10,114] called "one of the magistrates"). Thereby, his presentation of these figures takes on a "de-particularized", more universal character that reminds one of the Johannine use of "the Jews" for Jesus' antagonists[174]. In developing his portrait of Jeremiah's opponents, Josephus further accentuates certain (negative) aspects of the Biblical depiction of them: their success in influencing the king against Jeremiah[175], their failure to believe the prophet's announcements when the people as a whole does so (10,114), their ridicule of him (10,114), their persistence in unbelief even as the city's plight worsens (10,119), this manifesting itself in their final sarcastic question to Jeremiah (10,130), and their determination to bring about his death evident in their casting him into the pit (10,121; compare Jer 38,6; cf. 10,122). Above all, however, it is the opponents' "mendacity" both in what they themselves assert about the course of events and in their words to and about Jeremiah which Josephus goes beyond the Bible in underscoring at every turn[176]. As noted above, Josephus ends up giving this theme a final ironic twist in 10,130 where he has the "leaders" who sarcastically (and groundlessly) query Jeremiah concerning the story he has "made up about them" to the king themselves "stymied" by the fictive account of his interview with Zedekiah which the prophet proffers them at the king's behest. Of the other minor actors in Josephus' account, Jeremiah's Ethiopian rescuer (Ebed-melech in MT Jer 38,7-13) is, like the leaders, relegated to namelessness. Josephus does supply an explanation of his influence upon the king in terms of his being a royal "favorite" (10,122), even while he de-emphasizes the figure's independent initiative in the rescue operation so as to under-

174. Such "de-particularization" also manifests itself in Josephus' sustained avoidance of the many specific place indications provided by Jeremiah 37-38 (e.g., the Benjamin Gate [37,13; 38,7], the house of Jonathan [37,15.20], the court of the guard [37,21; 38,13.28], and the "third entrance of the Temple" [37,14]) in his version of these two chapters.

175. See, e.g., his *Sondergut* notice about Zedekiah's "friends" (10,105) who "once more corrupted him and, winning him away from the prophet, led him wherever they pleased".

176. See, e.g., Jeremiah's characterization of those advising Zedekiah at the outset of his reign as *"false* prophets who were *deceiving* him" (10,104; compare the source text Jer 37,19 where Jeremiah alludes simply to "your [Zedekiah's] prophets"). See also 10,114 where Josephus, in reporting the charge of desertion which "one of the magistrates" addresses to Jeremiah, qualifies it as "a false accusation" (compare the "neutral" mention of Irijah's charge in Jer 37,13).

score Zedekiah's own control of the proceedings (see above on 10,123). Josephus introduces one additional, minor, but named character into his account of Zedekiah's reign who is nowhere mentioned in the historical narratives of Kings, Chronicles, or Jeremiah concerning that period, i.e. Ezekiel (see 10,106-107). He does so obviously under the influence of his reading of the Book of Ezekiel with its record of predictions made by the prophet in the years just before the fall of Jerusalem (see its chaps. 12 and 17 in particular). The Josephan Ezekiel clearly, however, takes second place to Jeremiah himself, serving basically as a "long-distance echo" of the latter's message, rather than as the purveyor of his own distinctive word.

Given the anonymity of the opponents (and of Ebed-melech) in Josephus' version, the named figures of Zedekiah and Jeremiah assume an even higher profile in *AJ* 10,103-130 than they do in the Biblical source material. For what concerns Zedekiah, Josephus has made Judah's last king both a more complex and a more sympathetic figure than his Scriptural counterpart. Zedekiah's first, instinctual reactions to Jeremiah's words to him are invariably the right ones, i.e. realization of their truth and belief in them (10,105.127). In comparison with the presentation in Jer 38,7-13, he appears more "in charge" of the process that leads to Jeremiah's rescue from the pit. Similarly, in a *Sondergut* notice (10,120) that clearly aims to relativize the negative evaluation of Kings and Chronicles earlier reported by him (10,103), Josephus explicitly credits Zedekiah with "goodness and a sense of justice". Ultimately, however, all these positive touches which Josephus introduces into his portrayal of the king are negated by his "tragic flaw", i.e. his inability to stand up to and impose his will upon the court circles opposing Jeremiah's message, even when he recognizes the validity of that message[177].

It remains to sum up on Josephus' portrayal of Jeremiah himself in 10,103-130 as compared with the Biblical *Vorlagen*. Here, I would call attention particularly to two distinctive characteristics of the Josephan Jeremiah in the segment studied. First, and above all, in contrast to his

---

177. Josephus' (partially) rehabilitative depiction of Zedekiah has a certain counterpart in a recently published Qumran text in which this king – if, in fact, its mention of a "Zedekiah" is a reference to him – is invited into a "covenant" under the auspices of (the angel?) Michael. For a discussion of this text see: E. LARSON, *4Q470 and the Angelic Rehabilitation of King Zedekiah*, in *DSD* 1 (1994) 210-28; idem., *4QText Mentioning Zedekiah*, in M. BROSHI et al. (eds.), *Qumran Cave 4. XIV: Parabiblical Texts, Part 2* (DJD, 19), Oxford, Clarendon, 1995, pp. 235-244. By contrast in various secondary (mostly LXX) readings of the Book of Jeremiah, one finds a tendency to accentuate Zedekiah's personal, active contribution to Jeremiah's "passion"; see the article of Stipp cited in n. 117.

mendacious opponents, Jeremiah is represented as a *true* prophet, i.e. one who delivers accurate predictions. The truth of his message is highlighted in a variety of ways. Already at the start of Zedekiah's reign he foretells the Babylonian defeat of the Egyptian expedition (10,104; compare Jer 37,7 where a like announcement is made by Jeremiah only during the Egyptian advance itself). His initial predictions under Zedekiah are seconded by another prophet, Ezekiel (10,106a), and although there appears to be a divergence of detail in their respective messages regarding Zedekiah's ultimate fate (10,106b-107), the veracity of both is eventually vindicated by the course of events (10,141). Subsequently, during the siege interlude Jeremiah's predictive prowess is further demonstrated by his detailed "prospectus" of the coming 70+ years of Jewish history, extending down to the overthrow of the Babylonians by the Persians and Medes and the latter's release of the exiles – points which the Biblical record nowhere represents Jeremiah predicting as such (10,112-113). Among the specific happenings foreseen by Jeremiah here is the "burning" of the Temple. Whereas the Book of Jeremiah itself frequently cites the prophet's prediction of a burning of the city, it does not depict him as announcing this fate for the Temple in particular. Given that the Temple did in fact get burned down (see 2 Kgs 25,9), Jeremiah's "advance notice" on the matter redounds to his credibility as a prophet. Subsequently as well, the Josephan Jeremiah returns to the question of what awaits the Temple (see 10,126.128), again without Biblical parallel. At the same time, these repeated expressions of concern for the fate of Temple on the part of Josephus' Jeremiah exemplify the other noteworthy feature of his portrayal of the prophet's career under Zedekiah, i.e. the parallels adumbrated by Josephus between himself and the revered prophet of old. Specifically, in his own addresses to the defenders of Jerusalem, Josephus, like the Jeremiah of his own – though not the Bible's – presentation, repeatedly invokes the danger hanging over the Temple (see *BJ* 5,362.391.411.417; 6,98-99.105.110), that danger being precisely the one of which Jeremiah warns for the Temple of his day, i.e. destruction by fire[178]. We have noted as well other communalities between Josephus' self-portrait in *BJ* and his picture of Jeremiah in *AJ* 10,103-130: the words of both meet with invective and murderous hostility from those leading the resistance in Jerusalem (*AJ* 10,114.119.130; *BJ* 5,375; 6,98.112); both, on the other hand, find a protector/releaser in their respective kings (i.e. Zedekiah [see 10,122-123.125]/Vespasian [see *BJ* 3,408; 4,622]), just as both spend time in a "pit" (λάκκος [see

178. On this point, see DAUBE, *Typology*, 26-27.

AJ 10,121 and *BJ* 3,341). Such parallels between himself and the great prophet of Judah's final days would help legitimate Josephus' own conduct during the Revolt in the eyes of his compatriots; no wonder then that he gives Jeremiah far more attention than, e.g., Isaiah, who advocated a stance towards those threatening Jerusalem quite different from that assumed by the two of them.

XXIII

JERUSALEM'S FALL
(10,131-154)

The Bible offers no less than four tellings of the Babylonian capture and destruction of Jerusalem along with the deportation of its population. Of these, the detailed narratives of 2 Kgs 25,2-21 and Jer 52,5-27 largely coincide. The versions of Jer 39 (= LXX 46 which has no equivalent to MT's vv. 4-13),2-10 and 2 Chr 36,17-21 (itself paralleled in 1 Esdras 1,52-58) are shorter, lacking an equivalent to much of the detailed content of the two former accounts. Josephus gives his rendition of Jerusalem's catastrophe in *AJ* 10,131-154. I divide up this portion of *AJ* and its Biblical parallels into six sub-units: 1. Jerusalem's Resistance (10,131-134, no Scriptural equivalent; see below); 2. Jerusalem Captured (10,135 = 2 Kgs 25,2-3 // Jer 39,2-3 // 52,5-6); 3. Zedekiah's Punishment (10,136-143 = 25,4-7 // 39,4-7 [MT] // 52,7-11); 4. Jerusalem Destroyed (10,144-148 = 25,8-17 // 39,8-10 [MT] // 52,12-23 // 2 Chr 36,17-21; cf. 1 Esdras 1,52-58); 5. Leaders Executed (10,149-153 = 25,18-21 // 52,24-27); and 6. Zedekiah & the Temple Vessels (10,154; cf. Jer 34,5).

1. *Jerusalem's Resistance*

In *AJ* 10,116 (2 Kgs 25,1 // Jer 39[46],1 // 52,4) Josephus, as we saw in our preceding chapter, makes summary reference to the onset and course of Nebuchadnezzar's 18-month siege of Jerusalem that began towards the end of Zedekiah's tenth regnal year. Thereafter, basing himself on the biographical material of the Book of Jeremiah, he focusses on the interactions among the besieged Jerusalemites, their prophet and king in particular (10,117-130). Now with 10,131-134 he redirects attention to the Babylonian threat and the people's attempt to counter it. This last passage lacks a Biblical equivalent as such; on the other hand, it likely has in view the historian's own memories and previous account of the Romans' siege of Jerusalem (as well as their earlier attack on Jotapata at which he himself was the commander of the Jewish forces, see *BJ* 3,145-339)[1]. It reads:

---

1. So WEILL, *Josèphe*, II, p. 327, n. 1; MARCUS, *Josephus*, VI, p. 230, n. b. FELDMAN, *Studies*, pp. 460-461 (= ID., *Zedekiah*, 90-91) additionally proposes that Josephus'

(131) Now the Babylonian king applied himself very strenuously and zealously (ἐντεταμένως ... καὶ προθύμως)² to the siege (πολιορκίας)³; he built towers (πύργους) on great earthworks (χωμάτων) from which he kept back those stationed on the walls, and also erected round the whole circuit (of the city) many earthworks (χώματα) equal in height to the walls. (132) But those within bore the siege with courage and spirit (καρτερῶς ... καὶ προθύμως)⁴, for they did not weaken (ἔκαμνον) under either famine (λιμόν) or disease (νόσον ... λοιμικήν), but, although plagued internally by these afflictions (ἐλαυνόμενοι τῶν παθῶν)⁵, opposed stout hearts (τὰς ψυχὰς ἔρρωντο)⁶ to the war; neither (μηδέ)⁷ were they dismayed (καταπληττόμενοι; see 9,16) at the devices (ἐπινοίας) and engines (μηχανήματα) of their foes, but on their side devised (ἀντεπινοοῦντες)⁸ engines to check (ἀντιμηχανήματα)⁹ all those used by the enemy, (133) so that the contest (ἀγῶνα) between the Babylonians and the people of Jerusalem was wholly one of cleverness and skill (τῆς¹⁰ ὀξύτητος καὶ συνέσεως)¹¹, one side thinking the capture (αἵρεσιν)¹² of the city could be more easily

"creation" in 10,131-134 with its emphasis on the intensity with which the siege was conducted by both sides is intended as an implicit refutation of current canards about Jewish cowardice and lack of military distinction. I would further suggest that this Josephan insertion serves to answer reader questions about what happened militarily during the 18 months of the siege and how it was that the siege lasted so long. In any case, we will be noting specific verbal contacts between Josephus' accounts of the Roman sieges of Jotapata and Jerusalem in *BJ* and his narrative of Jerusalem's fall to the Babylonians here in *AJ* 10,131-154 over the course of our discussion of the latter passage.

2. This is Josephus' only use of the above collocation; he uses the adjective ἐντεταμένως twice elsewhere: *AJ* 11,96; 18,262.

3. Josephus' opening notice above picks up on the wording of 10,116 ("the king of Babylon... besieged [πολιορκεῖ] it [Jerusalem] with the utmost energy [πάσης... φιλοτιμίας]...") after the interlude of 10,117-130; see above.

4. This collocation occurs only here in Josephus. Note that its second component, the adverb προθύμως, is the same term applied to the besieger Nebuchadnezzar himself in 10,131; the use of the identical word for both sides underscores their equal "zeal" for the fight, this, in turn, helping to explain, the protracted duration of the siege (see n. 1). As for its first element, this has an equivalent in Josephus' reference to Jerusalem's defenders "stubbornly (καρτερῶς) holding out" in *BJ* 5,296; cf. the use of the related verb in *BJ* 3,316 ("the defenders of Jotapata were still holding out [καρτερούντων]...").

5. This construction is used by Josephus one other time, namely, in *AJ* 6,6 where he employs it of the afflictions which the ark brought upon the Philistines. Also the above sequence in 10,132 (see n. 3) echoes the wording of 10,116: "(the Jerusalemites) were attacked by two of the greatest calamities (παθῶν), famine (λιμός) and pestilence (φθορὰ λοιμική)...". Cf. *BJ* 3,316 (the defenders of Jotapata "were beyond all expectation bearing up under their miseries [τοῖς δεινοῖς]...").

6. This construction is hapax in Josephus.

7. This is the conjecture of Dindorf which Bekker, Naber, and Marcus adopt. Niese retains the μήτε of the codices.

8. Note the wordplay between this verbal form and the noun ἐπινοίας used just previously of the Babylonians' "devises".

9. This term in hapax in Josephus.

10. Niese and Naber regard this article as "spurious".

11. The above collocation occurs only here in Josephus.

12. This is the reading of ROLaurV which Dindorf, Bekker, Naber, and Marcus follow. Niese reads ἀναίρεσιν with MSP.

effected in this way, while the other placed its hope of deliverance (σωτηρίαν)[13] solely in not wearying (καμεῖν; cf. ἔκαμον, 10,132) or giving up the search for counter-devices (ἀντεφευρίσκοντας)[14] by which the engines (μηχανήματα; see 10,132) of their foes might be rendered useless (μάταια ... ἀπελεγχθήσεται[15])[16]. (134) And thus they held out for eighteen months[17] until they were exhausted by the famine (λιμοῦ; cf. λιμόν, 10,132) and by the missiles (βελῶν, see 9,118.181) which the enemy hurled (ἠκόντιζον) from the towers (πύργων; cf. πύργους, 10,131)[18].

2. Jerusalem Captured

In relating now the outcome of the long siege, Josephus draws (10,135a), in first place, on the data of 25,2-3 // 39,2 // 52,5-6 concerning the fact and date of Jerusalem's fall: "The city was taken (εἱρέθη)[19] in the eleventh year of the reign of Sacchias, on the ninth day of the fourth month". He then proceeds to expatiate on the identity of those to whom the city fell, basing himself for this on an item peculiar to Jer 39(46),3 among the Biblical witnesses. In so doing, he begins (10,135b) with a more general reference to the figures in question: "And those

13. This noun, referring to the "deliverance" hoped for by the defenders from their military initiatives against the besiegers, echoes, while also contrasting with the cognate verb employed by Jeremiah in his affirmations that the only way to ensure the city's "salvation" was for the inhabitants to surrender to the Babylonians; see 10,117 (σωθήσεσθαι). 126 (σωζεσθαι).

14. The verb ἀντεφευρίσκω is hapax in Josephus.

15. This is the reading which Dindorf, Bekker, Niese, Naber, and Marcus follow. RLaurV have ἀπελεγχθήσεσθαι with L.

16. The above construction is hapax in Josephus. On the wiles and stratagems evidenced by the Jews during the Roman siege of Jerusalem; see, e.g., BJ 5,109.121; 6,152.177.

17. This indication on the duration of the siege echoes Josephus' mention of Nebuchadnezzar's zealous prosecution of the siege "for eighteen months" in 10,116.

18. The conclusion to the above sequence ("they held out until...") makes the transition to the following account (10,135) of the city's fall. Josephus "anticipates" his reference to the population becoming "exhausted by the famine" from 25,3 // 52,6 ("on the ninth day of the fourth month the famine [LXX ὁ λιμός] was so severe in the city that there was no food for the people of the land"). On the Romans' use of "missiles" of various sorts during their siege of Jotapata, see BJ 3,167-168.240-248.285-287.

19. Dindorf and Naber read ἡρέθη with RO. In referring specifically to the "taking" of the city Josephus echoes the concluding phrase of Jer 38(45),28: "until the day Jerusalem was taken (LXX συνελήμφθη)". In 39,2 (cf. 25,4; 52,7) the event that occurs on the ninth day of the fourth month of Zedekiah's eleventh year (so Josephus' dating above) is "the breaching of the city", the subject of this action being left unspecified (in P.R. 26.6 [BRAUDE, Pesikta Rabbati, p. 534] it is an "angel of the Lord" who breaches Jerusalem's walls, calling the Babylonians to enter the Temple as he does so; see also Apocalypse of Baruch 7-8 [CHARLES and BROCKINGTON, Syriac Apocalypse of Baruch, p. 844]).

who captured it were the commanders (ἡγεμόνες) of the Babylonian army [literally of the Babylonians][20], *to whom Nebuchadnezzar had entrusted the siege*[21], *for* he himself was staying in the city of Arablatha (Ἀραβλαθᾷ[22])[23]". Thereafter (10,135c), he supplies the proper names of five of these commanders. His source for this catalogue continues to be Jer 39(46),3 where, however, MT and LXX diverge sharply with regard to the reading of the names. MT lists a total of four names (one of these appearing twice), plus two titles thus: Nergal-sharezer, Samgarnebo, Sarsechim the Rab-saris, and Nergal-sharezer the Rab-mag (RSV). LXX, for its part, takes MT's titles also as proper names and divides up MT's consonants differently in several cases, this generating a total of six proper names (one of which is virtually repeated): Nagalsarasar, Samagōth, Nabousarsachar, Naboussaris, Nargalsaraser, and Rabamag. Josephus' listing contains five proper names, avoiding the "repetition", common to both MT and LXX, of the name "Nergalsharezer" (MT): "*As for the names of the commanders* (ἡγεμόνων) *to whom the sack* (πορθήσαντες; see 9,253; 10,4) *of Jerusalem was assigned, if anyone should desire to know them, they were*[24] Nēre-

20. Jer 39(46),3 designates the group as "all the princes (LXX οἱ ἡγεμόνες) of the king of Babylon". Josephus reserves to a later point (see 10,136) the source verse's mention of the site where these princes position themselves.

21. This further specification about the identity of the Babylonian "princes" has no equivalent in 39,3 which speaks of "all" Nebuchadnezzar's "princes" taking their positions in Jerusalem.

22. This is the conjecture of Niese which Marcus adopts for the various readings of the codices, e.g., Ἀραβαθᾶ (RMSLaurV). Dindorf, Bekker, and Naber read Ῥεβλαθᾷ, while SCHLATTER, *Namen*, p. 102 proposes Ἀριβλαθα as the oldest recoverable Josephan form of the city's name. Compare רִבְלָתָה (Riblah, MT); Ἱερεβλάθαν (B 25,6); Δαβλαθά (L 25,6 // LXX 52,9). See following note.

23. Josephus "anticipates" this indication concerning Nebuchadnezzar's whereabouts at the moment of Jerusalem's fall from 25,6 // 39,5 // 52,9 where the captive Zedekiah is brought before him at "Riblah" for sentencing (Josephus has no equivalent to the specification of MT 39,5 // 52,9 that this site was situated "in the land of Hamath"). See on 10,82. With the above indication that Nebuchadnezzar was not present in person for the siege and fall of Jerusalem Josephus implicitly corrects, under the influence of 25,6, etc., his own earlier presentation (see 10,16.131) which would seem to suggest the opposite; see n. 45. *b. Sanh.* 96b (cf. *Exod Rab.* 46.4) calls attention to the seeming discrepancy between Jer 52,12 which concludes "he [Nebuzaradan] stood before the king of Babel in Jerusalem", this implying Nebuchadnezzar's presence in the city and 52,9 which speaks of Zedekiah's being brought to Nebuchadnezzar at Riblah, this placing the latter at a great distance from Jerusalem. The discrepancy is "resolved" via alternative suppositions: Nebuzaradan's chariot bore an inscribed portrait of his master, thereby making the king "present" in Jerusalem, his physical absence notwithstanding, or Nebuzaradan had such great respect for his overlord that it was as though he were standing in his presence (so 52,12) even when physically separate from him in Jerusalem.

24. The above transitional phrase echoes the wording of 10,135b; it further offers an implicit explanation of/ apology for Josephus' subsequent mention of the Babylonians' "outlandish" names, i.e. the consideration that there might be someone who, in fact,

galsaros (Νηρεγάλσαρος)²⁵, Aremantos ('Αρέμαντος)²⁶, Semegaros (Σεμέγαρος)²⁷, Nabōsaris (Ναβώσαρις)²⁸ and Acharampsaris ('Αχαράμψαρις)²⁹".

3. Zedekiah's Punishment[30]

In line with the sequence of 2 Kgs 25,4-7 // Jer 39,4-7 (MT, no parallel in LXX chap. 46) // 52,7-11, Josephus follows his notice of Jerusalem's fall (10,135) with an extended account of the flight, capture, and sentencing of Zedekiah, 10,136-143. In introducing the latter developments, the historian bases himself (10,136a) on the wording of 39,3-4 (MT) regarding the motivation behind the king's attempted escape: "Now the city was taken (ἀλούσης ... τῆς πόλεως; cf. εἱρέθη ... ἡ πολίς, 10,135a) about midnight[31] and when Sacchias

would "desire to know them". Here then Josephus departs from his usual tendency to omit the names of minor characters in the interests of making his account more readable for a Gentile audience. At the same time the citation of the names does allow him to convey an impression of himself as a historian who is in a position to provide such precise, detailed information about his people's past.

25. Thus the conjecture of Marcus; Dindorf, Bekker, and Naber read Νηργελέαρος, Niese 'Ρεγλάσαρος, while SCHLATTER, Namen, p. 81 proposes Νηργαλασσαρος. This first name on Josephus' list is his (single) equivalent to that one which MT and LXX 39,3 mention twice, i.e. Nergal-sharezer/ Nargalsarasar.

26. Thus the form read by Niese and Marcus; Dindorf, Bekker, Naber, and SCHALIT, Namenwörterbuch, p. 15 read 'Αρέμμαντος with SPLaurV. This second name on Josephus' list would appear to derive ultimately from the title "Rabmag" which appears at the end of MT's listing and which LXX renders as a proper name, i.e. "Rabamag". On the paleographical process which eventuated in Josephus' form(s), see SCHALIT, ibid.

27. So also Dindorf, Bekker, Naber, and Niese. This third name in Josephus' enumeration corresponds to LXX's second name, i.e. Σαμαγωθ which, in turn, represents the initial element of MT's "Samgar-nebo" (whose second component, "Nebo", LXX reads as part of its following name; see next note).

28. So Niese, Naber, and Marcus; Dindorf and Bekker read Ναθώσαρις. This fourth name on Josephus' list is his equivalent of LXX's fourth name, i.e. Ναβουσαρις. The latter form, in turn, seems to represent a conflation of the (concluding element of the) second proper name and first title in MT's listing, thus: Samgar-nebo (see previous note) and Rab-saris.

29. Thus Niese, Marcus and SCHALIT, Namenwörterbuch, p. 21. Dindorf, Bekker, and Naber read 'Εχαραμψαρίς with MV, while SCHLATTER, Namen, p. 106 reconstructs an original Χαραψαρις. This fifth and final name on Josephus' list seems to go back ultimately to MT's second proper name and its associated title thus: Sarsechim rab-saris; compare LXX Ναβουσαχαρ in which elements of two distinct MT names, i.e. Samgarnebo and Sarsechim are apparently conflated. Josephus limits his listing to the above five names, leaving aside the further reference, with which both MT and LXX 39,3 conclude, to "all the rest of the officers of the king of Babylon".

30. This section represents a reworking of my article Josephus' Zedekiah, 102-103.

31. Josephus anticipates/reapplies this chronological indication about the moment of Jerusalem's fall from 25,4 // 39,4 // 52,7 which speak of Zedekiah and his entourage fleeing the city "by night".

learned that[32] the enemy commanders (ἡγεμόνων; see 10,135) had entered the temple...[33]".

In describing Zedekiah's actual flight, Josephus both expatiates on the sources' reference to those who accompany him and adapts their indications on his escape route: "... he took his *wives and children* (γυναίκας καὶ ... τέκνα; see 10,128) and his officers (ἡγεμόνας) *and friends* (φίλους)[34] and fled (φεύγει) with them[35] from the city through the fortified valley (διὰ τῆς καρτερᾶς φάραγγος)[36] and through the wilderness (καὶ διὰ τῆς ἐρήμου)[37]".

32. Compare MT 39,4: "when Zedekiah... *and all the soldiers* saw them [i.e. the Babylonian generals cited in 39,3]...".

33. This phrase represents an adapation of 39,3 which has the Babylonian generals "sitting in the second gate", Josephus understanding the reference to be specifically to a Temple gate. On the significance of Josephus' presentation here as yet another positive retouching of the Biblical portrait of Zedekiah, i.e. as one whose "primary concern was for the Temple", see FELDMAN, *Studies*, pp. 459-460 (= ID., *Zedekiah*, 90). Compare *P.R.* 26.6 (BRAUDE, *Pesikta Rabbati*, p. 535): having penetrated the city, the Babylonians construct a platform on the Temple Mount at the spot which Solomon once planned the adornment of the Temple; there they take their seats, discussing how they will now burn the Temple.

34. The sources speak only of military personnel accompanying Zedekiah on his flight, i.e. "the men of war (B 25,4 πάντες οἱ ἄνδρες τοῦ πολέμου)". In mentioning Zedekiah's taking of his family members as well, Josephus heightens the stature of king who thinks not only of his own safety but also of theirs (reference to the royal children accompanying the king here likewise prepares the continuation of both the Biblical and Josephan narratives in which Zedekiah's "sons" will be put to death; see 10,140). As for the "friends" who are also said to be part of the fugitive party, their inclusion both harks back to their key role in Josephus' earlier presentation (see previous chapter), and sets up the notice on their execution which he will introduce in 10,140. That Zedekiah takes along the "leaders" and "friends" who had so consistently misled him is another mark of the king's magnimity. See FELDMAN, *Studies*, p. 460 (= ID., *Zedekiah*, 90).

35. Compare MT 39,4: "they [i.e. Zedekiah and all the men of war] fled".

36. WEILL, *ad. loc.* translates in the same way ("à travers le ravin fortifié"). MARCUS, *Josephus*, VI, p. 232, n. a points out that the Greek phrase might also be rendered "through the *steep* valley". He opts for the above translation on the consideration that it is more in line with the source indications concerning Zedekiah's escape route; see next note.

37. Compare the source indications (25,4 // 39,4 // 52,7) on Zedekiah's escape route: "by way of the gate between the two walls, by the king's garden, though the Chaldeans were around the city [Josephus, like Jer 39,4 (MT), has no equivalent to this self-evident notice]; and they went towards the Arabah (B 25,4 and LXX 52,7 transliterate; L 25,4 renders ὁδὸν τὴν ἐπὶ δυσμάς)". Rabbinic tradition (see, e.g., *P.R.* 26.6 [BRAUDE, *Pesikta Rabbati*, p. 535) speaks of Zedekiah attempting to escape via a water-tunnel that extended all the way to Jericho. The above sequence on Zedekiah's flight is reminiscent of the proposition made to Titus by Jerusalem's defenders towards the end of the siege as cited in *BJ* 6,351 "they asked permission to pass through his line of circumvallation with their wives and children (μετὰ γυναικῶν καὶ τέκνων), undertaking to retire to the desert (εἰς τὴν ἔρημον)...". In Josephus' presentation neither group is successful in its effort to escape Jerusalem to the "desert": Titus rejects the proposal made him (*BJ* 6,352), while Zedekiah is captured during his flight through it (see above).

Zedekiah's flight ends (25,5a // 39,5a // 52,8a) with his being "overtaken" by the Babylonians in "the plains of Jericho". The Josephan version (10,137a) interjects an explanation as to how the besiegers became aware of the royal flight: *"But, when some of the deserters* (αὐτομόλων) *told the Babylonians of this*[38], they started out *at dawn*[39] in pursuit (διώκειν; cf. ἐδίωξεν, B 25,5) of him and overtook (καταλαβόντες; cf. κατέλαβον, BL 25,5 // LXX 52,8) him not far from Jericho, *where they surrounded him"*. 2 Kgs 25,5b // Jer 52,8b add a detail not mentioned in Jer 39,5, i.e. "and all his [Zedekiah's] army was scattered (διεσπάρη, B 25,5b; διεσπάρησαν, L 25,5b // LXX 52,8b) from him". Josephus (10,137b) elaborates on this item, thereby both heightening the pathos of the scene and his ongoing negative portrayal of the king's associates: "And when the friends and officers (οἱ ... φίλοι καὶ οἱ ἡγεμόνες; compare τοὺς ἡγεμόνας καὶ τοὺς φίλους, 10,136) of Sacchias *who had fled with him saw the enemy close upon them*[40], *they abandoned* (καταλιπόντες) *him* and scattered (διεσπάρησαν, so L 25,5b // LXX 52,8b) *in different directions* (ἀλλαχοῦ)[41], *each one determined to save* (σώζειν; cf. σωτηρίαν, 10,133) *himself*[42]".

The Biblical story continues with the actual capture of Zedekiah and his being haled before Nebuchadnezzar at Riblah (25,6a // 39,5bα // 52,9a). The historian (10,138a) embellishes here as well: *"So Sacchias was left with only a few men round him*[43], and the enemy captured him alive (ζωγρήσαντες; compare συνέλαβον, BL 25,6 // LXX 52,9) and

---

38. The above notice reads like a realization of the fear expressed by Zedekiah to Jeremiah in 10,127 (= Jer 38[45],19): "... he was afraid of those who had deserted (αὐτομολήσαντας) to the Babylonians, for he might be denounced by them to the king [Nebuchadnezzar] and punished". (In 10,128 Jeremiah assures Zedekiah that if he surrenders to the Babylonians, he, along with his children and wives [cf. 10,136], will suffer no harm. Because, however, the king failed to do what the prophet urged him, he now, 10,137, experiences the realization of the very fear expressed by him in 10,127.) Also to be mentioned in this connection is Josephus' notice in *BJ* 3,344 of his own comparable experience, i.e. his hiding place subsequent to the fall of Jotapata was "betrayed by a woman of the party, who was captured".

39. Cf. the reference to the city's being taken "about midnight" in 10,136.

40. The above interjected reference to Zedekiah's retainers "seeing" the Babylonians' proximity serves to account for their dispersal as cited in 25,5b // 52,8b.

41. This is the reading of RO which Niese and Marcus follow. Dindorf, Bekker, and Naber read ἀλλαχόσε with MSPLV.

42. Note Josephus' denigrating insistence above on the deliberateness with which Zedekiah's retainers separate themselves from him, motivated solely by a concern for their own self-preservation. In the sources, by contrast, the "scattering process" appears to be more an involuntary one, set in motion by the advent of the pursuers.

43. With this interjected phrase Josephus points up the result of the general "abandonment" of Zedekiah by his retainers as described in 10,137b, thereby heightening the scene's pathos.

brought (ἤγαγον = B 25,6 // LXX 52,9) *with his children and wives*[44] to the king[45]". The sources next proceed (25,6b // 39,5bβ // 52,9b) to make summary reference to Nebuchadnezzar's "passing sentence" (BL 25,6: ἐλάλησεν ... κρίσιν) on the captive Zedekiah. Josephus develops (10,138b-139) this item into an extended condemnatory speech by the Babylonian ruler:

> (138) *And, when he came before him,* Nebuchadnezzar began to denounce him as an impious wretch (ἀσεβῆ)[46] and a violator of treaties (παράσπονδον)[47] who had forgotten (ἀμνήμονα)[48] the words which he had spoken earlier (πρόσω)[49] when he had promised to keep the country safely for him (σώζειν[50] αὐτῷ τὴν χώραν)[51]. (139) He also reproached him for his ingratitude (ἀχαριστίαν)[52] in having first received the kingdom from him – for Nebuchadnezzar had taken it away from Jōacheimos ('Ιωαχίμου)[53], to whom it belonged and given it to him[54] – and then used his power against the one who had bestowed it upon him. 'But', he said[55], 'great is God (μέγας ... ὁ θεός)[56] who in His abhorrence (μισήσας)[57]

44. This reference picks up on Josephus' – likewise interjected – mention of Zedekiah's taking these two groups with him in 10,136. In *P.R.* 26.6 (BRAUDE, *Pesikta Rabbati*, p. 535) as well one finds explicit mention of the Babylonian capture of Zedekiah's *ten* "sons" along with their father (in what precedes they are said to have walked in advance of the exhausted Zedekiah during the flight attempt).

45. Josephus leaves aside the sources' specification of Nebuchadnezzar's whereabouts ("at Riblah") at this moment. Recall, however, that he has anticipated this datum in 10,135 where he speaks of the king remaining at "Arablatha" throughout the siege of Jerusalem; see n. 23. Josephus presumes then that readers will fill in the site of Nebuchadnezzar's headquarters here in 10,138 on the basis of that previous indication.

46. In 10,104 this term is applied to "those around" the new king Zedekiah.

47. This term is hapax in Josephus.

48. This is the reading followed by Dindorf, Bekker, Niese, Naber, and Marcus. SPLaurV have ἀγνώμονα ("ignored").

49. This is the reading of the codices which Dindorf, Niese, and Marcus follow. Bekker and Naber adopt the conjecture of Coccejus, i.e. πρὸ τοῦ.

50. Niese conjectures σώσειν here. The present infinitival form read by Marcus is the same used in 10,137 of the determination on the part of Zedekiah's entourage to "save" themselves.

51. Nebuchadnezzar's word here echoes the content of Zedekiah's accession oath to him as reported in 10,102: φυλάξειν αὐτῷ τὴν χώραν.

52. Josephus' other uses of the word ἀχαριστία are in *BJ* 1,237; *AJ* 4,41; 16,209; 19,272.

53. This is the reading of the name found in SP and adopted by Dindorf, Bekker, Naber, and Marcus. Niese reads 'Ιωακείμου with ROE.

54. The reference in the above *Rückverweis* is to 10,102a: "(Nebuchadnezzar) appointed Jōachimos's uncle Sacchias as king...".

55. Note the shift to direct discourse here for the continuation of Nebuchadnezzar's speech.

56. Nebuchadnezzar's "acclamation" here echoes Josephus' own exhortation to readers to "acknowledge the greatness of the Deity (μέγα ... τὸ θεῖον)" in *AJ* 8,418. On the historian's use of the term "great" as a qualification for God, see SCHLATTER, *Theologie*, p. 247.

57. Elsewhere Josephus uses the verb μισέω with God as subject in *BJ* 3,376; *AJ* 6,138; 8,129.314; 20,166.

of your conduct has made you fall into our hands (ὑποχείριον ... ἔθηκε)⁵⁸'.

Following the above "interlude" Josephus picks up (10,140) the sources' presentation (25,7 // 39,6-7 // 52,10-11) of the various moments of Zedekiah's punishment: *"After addressing Sacchias in these terms, he ordered his sons and his friends* [see 10,136.137]⁵⁹ *to be put to death on the spot*⁶⁰ *while Sacchias himself* (αὐτοῦ)⁶¹ *and the other captives* (αἰχμαλώτων)⁶² *looked on, and then having put out Sacchias's eyes* (τοὺς ὀφθαλμοὺς ἐκκόψας)⁶³, *he bound him in chains and took him off to Babylon* (δήσας ἤγαγεν εἰς Βαβυλῶνα)⁶⁴".

58. (Variants of) the above expression with God as subject appear in *AJ* 1,181; 6,183; 8,161. Like Josephus, *P.R.* 26.6 (BRAUDE, *Pesikta Rabbati*, pp. 535-536) cites an extended address by Nebuchadnezzar to the captive Zedekiah. This reads: "Tell me, Zedekiah, what made you rebel against me? By what law shall I judge you? If by the law of your God, you deserve the death penalty, for you swore in His name falsely; if by the laws of the state, you deserve the death penalty, for he who violates his oath to the king deserves the death penalty" (In contrast to Josephus this document goes on to record a response by both Zedekiah and his sons, each of whom pleads to be the first to be put to death so as not to have witness the death of the other.) One might also see the Josephan Nebuchadnezzar's speech to Zedekiah as intended as a parallel to the reproaches Titus addresses to the rebel leaders Simon and John of Gischala in *BJ* 6,328-350 just prior to the Roman sacking of the city.

59. At this moment, Zedekiah's "friends" – who have repeatedly misled him and have ended up abandoning him (10,137) – finally get their just desserts. (In thus mentioning a second group of Judean victims alongside Zedekiah's sons here, Josephus agrees with Jer 39,6[MT] // 52,10 which speak also of a slaying of the "nobles/princes [LXX 52,10: ἄρχοντας] of Judah" at this time, as against 25,7 which lacks this indication.)

60. The above translation reflects the reading of RO adopted by Marcus and Niese. Dindorf, Bekker, and Naber follow the variant of MSPLaurVE (τοὺς υἱοὺς) ἐκέλευσε παραχρῆμα καὶ τοὺς φίλους θύσαι which yields the translation "he ordered his sons (to be put to death) and his friends to be slaughtered [literally sacrificed] on the spot"; see MARCUS, *Josephus*, VI, p. 235, n. b. In speaking of Nebuchadnezzar's "ordering" the execution of Zedekiah's sons (and friends), Josephus assimilates the divergent presentations of Jer 39,6 // 52,10 (Nebuchadnezzar kills the sons in person) and 2 Kgs 25,7 (an unspecified "they" kills the sons).

61. In the codices SPLaurVE this word is preceded by ὁρῶντος (LaurV likewise read αὐτούς in place of αὐτοῦ) which Dindorf and Bekker retain but which Niese and Marcus omit in accordance with ROM. Naber hesitatingly suggests that the word be emended to παρόντος.

62. It is not immediately clear to whom Josephus is referring with this designation. Given the mention of Zedekiah's "wives" being brought to Nebuchadnezzar along with the king in 10,138, one might suppose that it is they, i.e. the mothers of the executed princes, who are in view (along with the "officers" who are also said to accompany Zedekiah in his flight in 10,136). On such a reading the pathos of the scene is heightened as both father and mothers behold their sons' death. Josephus returns to the fate of the "captives" in 10,150, there noting Nebuchadnezzar's taking them off to Babylon.

63. Josephus uses the above phrase in connection with the blinding of Samson by the Philistines in *AJ* 5,313 and of the Transjordanians by Nahash, king of Ammon in 6,69. Compare BL 25,7 // LXX 52,11 τοὺς ὀφθαλμοὺς ... ἐξετύφλωσεν where the subject, as in Josephus, is Nebuchadnezzar in person.

64. Compare B 25,7b // LXX 52,11b: καὶ ἔδησεν αὐτὸν ἐν πέδαις καὶ ἤγαγεν εἰς Βαβυλῶνα. Like 25,7 and 39,7 Josephus lacks an equivalent to the concluding words of

Josephus follows his Biblically-based notice on Zedekiah's punishment (10,140) with a series of appended notices (10,141-143) of his own
creation. The first of these (10,141), in accord with the *Vorverweis* of
10,107 (see there), calls attention to the realization of the – seemingly
divergent – prophecies of Jeremiah and Ezekiel effected in the circumstances of Zedekiah's punishment as described just previously. The
sequence reads:

> And thus there befell him what both Jeremiah and Ezekiel had prophesied
> (προεφήτευσαν) to him, namely that he would be captured and brought to
> the Babylonian king and speak to him to his face and with his own eyes
> look into his eyes which is what Jeremiah had said [see Jer 34(41),3]; fur-
> thermore being blinded (τυφλωθείς)[65], he did not see it, as Ezekiel had
> foretold [see Ezek 12,13][66].

The preceding remark, in its turn, inspires Josephus to a more general
reflection (10,142) on the certain, inescapable realization of prophecy
and the disastrous consequences of disregarding it:

> These things, then, which we have related should make sufficiently clear to
> those who do not know, how varied and manifold (ποικίλη … καὶ
> πολύτροπος)[67] is the nature of God (τὴν τοῦ θεοῦ φύσιν)[68] and how

52,11 i.e. "… and [Nebuchadnezzar] put him [Zedekiah] in prison till the day of his
death" at this juncture; although see 10,154. In *P.R.* 26.6 (BRAUDE, *Pesikta Rabbati*,
p. 536) Zedekiah is said to have been put in "an oven of brass (בתנור)" by Nebuchadnezzar before being taken to Babylon (compare the fate of the prisoner Manasseh as
described in Rabbinic tradition; see p. 447, n. 40). GINZBERG, *Legends*, VI, pp. 382-383,
n. 6 proposes emending this reference to "in a cage (בכלוב)".

65. Josephus' two remaining uses of the verb τυφλόω are in *AJ* 8,30 (metaphorical
sense) and *c. Ap.* 2,132.

66. The above reproduction of the prophecies of Jer 34,3 and Ezek 12,13 in fact provides a more accurate rendition (and so a clearer contrast between them) than does the
version of the two passages given in 10,107 to which Josephus is alluding here; see there.
Josephus' highlighting of the eventual fulfillment of the prophecies of both Jeremiah and
Ezekiel here in 10,141 has a counterpart in *AJ* 8,417 where he points out that the circumstances of Ahab's death realized the predictions of Elijah and Micaiah, notwithstanding
the claim (8,407-408) of the false prophet Zedekiah that these were contradictory (compare 10,106-107).

Also *P.R.* 26.6 (BRAUDE, *Pesikta Rabbati*, p. 536 connects the account of Zedekiah's
punishment with an allusion to the fulfillment of a prophecy made earlier about his
fate: (upon arriving in Babylon the blinded Zedekiah keeps crying out) "Come and see,
all you children of men, that Jeremiah [given the content of the prophecy which
Zedekiah goes on to cite, GINZBERG, *Legends*, VI, p. 383, n. 8 proposes emending to
Ezekiel here] prophesied truly about me when he said to me: 'You will go to Babylon
and in Babylon you will die, but your eyes will not have seen Babylon [see Ezek
12,13]'. I would not listen to his words. And here I am in Babylon, and my eyes do not
see it".

67. Josephus' one remaining use of this collocation is in *AJ* 15,179.

68. On Josephus' references to the divine "nature", see BEGG, *Early Divided Monarchy*, p. 175, n. 1145.

those things which He foretells (προλέγει; see 10,33) must come to pass, duly taking place at the appointed hour, and should also make clear the ignorance and disbelief (ἄγνοιαν καὶ ἀπιστίαν)[69] of these men[70], by which they were prevented from foreseeing (προϊδεῖν) any of these future events and, when they were delivered over to disaster, were taken off their guard (ἀφύλακτοι)[71], so that any attempt to escape from it was impossible (ἀμήχανον; see 9,65.73) for them[72].

The last (10,143) of the appended notices making up the complex of 10,141-143 supplies statistical/chronological information concerning the succession of the Davidic kings (compare the similar data given by Josephus in connection with the demise of the Northern Kingdom in *AJ* 9,280-282) now at the moment that succession has reached its end with the deposition of the last of them. The notice runs:

> Thus, then, did the kings of David's line end their lives; there were twenty-one of them[73] including the last king, and they reigned altogether for five hundred and fourteen years, six months and ten days[74]; for twenty years of which time their first king Saul held the royal power though he was not of the same tribe[75].

69. This collocation is hapax in Josephus. Its term "unbelief" echoes a *Leitwort* of Josephus' account of Jeremiah's ministry under Zedekiah; see preceding chapter.

70. The identity of those designated by this phrase is not immediately evident. The reference is likely, however, to Zedekiah and the Jerusalem leadership, both of whom are represented as "disbelieving" the prophecies of Jeremiah; see 10,106.107 (Zedekiah). 114 (the leaders). Cf. previous note.

71. In 10,123 this term is used of Jeremiah's being "released from confinement" by Zedekiah.

72. With the foregoing reflection compare the similar remarks which Josephus appends to his account of Ahab's death in accordance with the prophecy of Micaiah (and Elijah) in *AJ* 8,418-420 and the discussion of those remarks in BEGG, *Early Divided Monarchy*, pp. 266-268.

73. As MARCUS, *Josephus*, VI, p. 235, n. d points out, this figure for the Davidic kings excludes the queen Athaliah who ruled Judah for six years, but who was not of the Davidic house.

74. Laur and Zon make this sixteen *days*.

75. MARCUS, *Josephus*, VI, pp. 236-237, n. b points out that including Saul's twenty-year reign (in *AJ* 6,378 Josephus assigns him a reign of *40* years) in the total length of the (Judean) monarchical period as in the above rendering ("for twenty years of which time...") results in an figure, not of 514, but rather of 534 years for this period. Accordingly, Marcus suggests that we read πάρεξ ὧν εἴκοσι ("exclusive of the twenty years" in place of the sequence ἐξ ὧν εἴκοσι actually printed by him (WEILL, *Josèphe*, II, p. 329, n. 3, for his part, raises the possibility that the reference to Saul here in 10,143 might be an interpolation). Marcus goes on to note that even if we thus do exclude Saul's reign from the total figure (514+ years) for the succession of Davidic kings here in 10,143, that figure still does not agree with the actual sum of the years Josephus assigns the 21 kings David-Zedekiah inclusive over the course of *AJ* 7-10 which comes to 507 years, 6 months, and 20 days, i.e. seven years less than the figure cited by him in 10,143.

4. *Jerusalem Destroyed*

The "appendixes" of 10,141-143 completed, Josephus reverts (10,144-148) to the Biblical story line (see 2 Kgs 25,8-17 // Jer 39,8-10 // 52,12-23 // 2 Chr 36,17-21; cf. 1 Esdras 1,53-58) in relating the punitive measures taken by the Babylonians against conquered Jerusalem. This new sequel to the city's fall is set in motion with the arrival of the general Nebuzaradan at Jerusalem (25,8 // 39,8 // 52,12). Josephus prefaces his parallel to this item (10,145a) with mention of the instructions given the officer by Nebuchadnezzar (10,144): *"Then the Babylonian king sent his general (στρατηγόν)[76] Nabūzardanēs (Ναβουζαρδάνην)[77] to Jerusalem to despoil the temple (συλήσοντα τὸν ναόν), and ordered him at the same time to burn down (καταπρῆσαι; see 10,65) both it and the palace (τὰ βασίλεια) and to raze (καθελεῖν) the city to the ground (εἰς ἔδαφος; see 10,126) and transplant (μεταστῆσαι; see 9,279) the people to Babylonia[78]. And, when he came to Jerusalem in the eleventh year of Sacchias's reign...[79]"*.

According to 25,8 // 39,8 // 52,12, Nebuzaradan's first act upon arrival in Jerusalem was to fire the city's Temple and great houses; only later (see 25,13-17 // 52,17-23, no parallel in Jeremiah 39) did he proceed to carry off the Temple's treasures. 2 Chronicles 36 (as also 1 Esdras 1), by contrast, has *Nebuchadnezzar* – these sources make no mention of Nebuzaradan – burning Jerusalem's edifices (see v. 19) only after he had removed the Temple vessels (v. 18)[80]. In accord with the sequence of Nebuchadnezzar's directives to his general as cited by him in 10,144 (see above), Josephus (10,145b) follows the Chronicler's

76. MT designates Nabuzaradan as רַב־טַבָּחִים which BL 25,8 // LXX 52,12 render by ὁ ἀρχιμάγειρος.

77. This form represents a declined version of the name as read by B 25,8 // LXX 52,12, i.e. Ναβουζαρδάν; compare MT נְבוּזַרְאֲדָן.

78. The above insertion makes clear, first of all, Nebuchadnezzar's direction of the proceedings (in 2 Kgs 25,8, etc. Nebuzaradan appears to come to Jerusalem – and act there – on his own initiative, although note the qualification of him there as "servant of the king of Babylon"). The passage likewise serves to prepare the sequence of events in Jerusalem as these will be related by Josephus in what follows. Finally the wording of the paragraph recalls the warnings attributed to Jeremiah in 10,112.126 (see there), thus underscoring that the prophet's words did indeed find their realization through the agency of Nebuchadnezzar.

79. This dating indication echoes that given for the capture of Jerusalem in 10,135. In 25,8 // 52,12 Nebuzaradan's arrival is dated to the seventh (so 25,8; tenth, 52,12) of the fifth month of Nebuchadnezzar's 18th regnal year. Josephus will make (partial and adapted) use of these Biblical indications in 10,146; see there.

80. This latter act is itself preceded in 2 Chr 36,17 // 1 Esdras 1,53 by mention of Nebuchadnezzar's butchering of the city's inhabitants, an item which has no parallel in 2 Kings/ Jeremiah or Josephus.

order in making Nabuzaradan's initial measure the plundering of the Temple[81]: "... he despoiled the temple (συλᾷ ... τὸν ναόν; see συλη-σοντα τὸν ναόν, 10,144) and carried out the gold (χρυσᾶ) and silver (ἀργυρᾶ) vessels of God (σκεύη τοῦ θεοῦ; see 9,263)[82], in particular the great laver (τὸν μέγαν λουτῆρα)[83] which Solomon had set up (cf. 25,16 // 52,20) and even the bronze pillars (στύλους) and their capitals (κεφαλάς)[84], *as well as the golden tables* (χρυσᾶς τραπέζας)[85] and the lampstands (λυχνίας)[86]".

Continuing to execute Nebuchadnezzar's directives in the order given, Nebuzaradan next (10,146) disposes of Jerusalem's edifices (25,9-10 // 39,8 // 52,13-14 // 2 Chr 36,19; cf. 1 Esdras 1,55): "*And, when he had carried these out* [i.e. the Temple fixtures; see 10,145], he set fire (ἀνῆψε; compare καταπρῆσαι, 10,144) to the temple[87] on the new moon (τῇ νουμηνίᾳ)[88] of the fifth month (so 25,8 // 52,12) *in the eleventh year of*

81. This sequence in fact would appear to be more logical than that of 2 Kings 25 // Jeremiah 52 in that, prior to burning the Temple, Nebuzaradan would first have needed to secure its furnishings if these are to survive the conflagration.

82. The above sequence represents Josephus' version of 25,15b // 52,19bβ: "what was of gold (LXX 52,19 χρυσᾶ) the captain of the guard took away as gold, what was of silver (LXX 52,19 ἀργυρᾶ), as silver". He leaves aside the extended catalogue of assorted Temple "vessels" taken by Nebuzaradan as cited in 25,14-15a // 52,18-19aba. Elsewhere in Jewish tradition, one finds statements that the Temple vessels, instead of being confiscated by the Babylonians (so 2 Kgs 25,13-17, etc. and Josephus), were rather hidden prior to the city's fall, this either by angels (so *Apocalypse of Baruch* 7.7-10 [CHARLES and BROCKINGTON, *Syriac Apocalypse of Baruch*, pp. 843-844]; 80.2 [ibid., p. 845]) or by Jeremiah (and Baruch) acting at the Lord's direction (so 2 Macc 2,4-5; *Para-leipomena of Jeremiah* 3.7-14 [R. THORNHILL, tr., *The Paraleipomena of Jeremiah*, in H.F.D. SPARKS, ed., *The Apocryphal Old Testament*, Oxford, Clarendon, 1984, 821-833, pp. 822-823]). Cf. BOGAERT, *Apocalypse de Baruch*, II, p. 24.

83. This is Josephus' designation for the so-called bronze "sea" whose seizure by the Babylonians is cited in 25,13 // 52,17; cf. 25,16 // 52,20. The historian describes the appearance and function of the object in *AJ* 8,79-80.

84. Josephus describes these Temple fixtures in *AJ* 8,78-88. Their removal is mentioned in 25,13 // 52,17. Josephus leaves aside the specifications concerning the pillars' dimensions given in 25,17 (and in greater detail in 52,21-23).

85. These objects are not cited in the extended catalogue of Temple booty found in 25,13-17 // 52,17-23. Josephus inserts mention of them in order to make clear that all the larger fixtures of Solomon's Temple were carried off at this time (recall that, unlike the various Biblical accounts, he does not record a despoliation of the Temple at the time of either Jehoiakim or Jehoiachin; see chap. XXI). He provides a description of the Temple "tables" in *AJ* 8,89. Cf. *y. Šeqal.* 6.3 which lists 13 tables found in the sanctuary.

86. Josephus' mention of these objects among the Temple booty reflects the plus of 52,19 as against 25,14-15a which does not cite them. Josephus describes the Solomonic "lampstands" in *AJ* 8,90.

87. In the presentation of *P.R.* 26.6 the Babylonians who have occupied Jerusalem and are planning the burning of the Temple (see n. 33) witness four angels preclude their doing so by themselves setting fire to the edifice with their torches.

88. This indication concerning the day in question differs from those cited in MT B 25,8 (the seventh), L 25,8 (the ninth), MT LXX 52,12 (the tenth) for Nebuzaradan's

Sacchias' reign [see 10,145] the eighteenth[89] of Nebuchadnezzar's. He also burnt (ἐνέπρησε; see 10,112.126) the palace (τὰ βασίλεια; see 10,144)[90] and demolished the city (τὴν πόλιν κατέστρεψεν[91]; compare τὴν ... πόλιν εἰς ἔδαφος καθελεῖν, 10,144)[92]". To his foregoing mention of the burning down of the Temple, Josephus proceeds to append a series of chronological notices (10,147-148; cf. 10,143) inspired by this event:

> (147) Now the temple was burned (ἐνεπρήσθη; cf. ἐνέπρησε, 10,146) four hundred and seventy years, six months and ten days after it was built[93]; from the migration (μεταναστάσει)[94] of the people from Egypt it was an interval of one thousand and sixty-two years, six months and ten days[95]; from the flood (κατακλυσμῷ) to the sacking of the temple (τῆς

arrival in Babylon (recall that Josephus in 10,145 dates this event simply to the eleventh year of Zedekiah; see n. 79). It likewise diverges from Josephus' own statement in *BJ* 6,250 that the Second Temple was burned down on the same day, i.e. the tenth (see Jer 52,12), of the month as was its predecessor. For an effort to account for the discrepancy between the statements of *BJ* and *AJ* on the matter, see F.X. KUGLER, *Von Moses bis Paulus*, Münster, Aschendorff, 1922, pp. 474-477. Note too Josephus' statement in *BJ* 3,339 that Jotapata was taken "on the new moon (νουμηνίᾳ) of Panemus".

89. In all witnesses of 25,8 and 52,12 Nabuzaradan's coming to Jerusalem is dated rather to Nebuchadnezzar's *19th* regnal year. On Josephus' figure as an adjustment of the Biblical datum to his own overall chronological scheme for Nebuchadnezzar and the contemporary Judean kings, see PIOVANELLI, *Texte*, 25-26. Conceivably, Josephus found inspiration for the above figure in MT Jer 52,29 which dates a deportation of 832 Jerusalemites to Nebuchadnezzar's *18th* year (recall Josephus' previous utilization of this figure, though without the attached dating, in 10,101). In *SOR* 27.4 (GIRÓN BLANC, *Seder 'Olam Rabbah*, p. 126) the difference between the figures in 52,12 and 29, i.e. Nebuchadnezzar's 19th and 18th regnal years respectively, is resolved on the supposition that the former dating refers to the moment of the Babylonian's actual accession, while the latter alludes to the (later) time of Jehoiakim's submission to him.

90. The sources speak not only of a burning of the palace, as does Josephus here, but also of other "houses" in the city; see, e.g., 2 Kgs 25,8: "(Nebuzaradan burned)... all the houses of Jerusalem; every great house he burned down". Josephus' general follows the order given him by Nebuchadnezzar in 10,144 in burning only the royal palace.

91. Naber reads κατέσκαψεν with (Laur)VE.

92. Josephus' reference to the "demolishing of the city" here represents a generalization/intensification, in line with the order given Nabuzaradan in 10,144, of the sources' reference (25,10 // 39,8b // 52,14 // 36,19; cf. 1 Esdras 1,55b) to the Babylonians' breaking down the city's *walls*. Compare *BJ* 3,338 where Vespasian "orders the city [Jotapata] to be razed (κατασκάψαι)".

93. MARCUS, *Josephus*, VI, p. 238, n. b points out that in *AJ* 20,231-232 Josephus gives a slightly divergent figure for the duration of the Temple's existence, i.e. *466* years, six months, and ten days. FELDMAN, *Josephus*, X, p. 123, n. d, commenting on 20,232, remarks that the correct figure there would be 474 years, six months, and ten days. He further mentions that, according to *b. Yoma* 9a, the First Temple survived for 410 years.

94. Josephus' other uses of the noun μετανάστασις are in *AJ* 2,318; 19,3; *c. Ap.* 2,6 (here with "from Egypt" as in 10,147).

95. Josephus arrives at the above figure for the duration of the period from the Exodus to the destruction of the Temple by combining those given by him for the interval between the Exodus and the building of the Temple in *AJ* 8,61 (i.e. 592 years) and the length of time

τοῦ ναοῦ πορθήσεως) the whole period of time was one thousand nine hundred and fifty-seven years, six months and ten days[96]; (148) and from the birth of Adam to the time when these things happened to the temple it was an interval of four thousand (τετρακισχίλια)[97] five hundred and thirteen (δεκατρία)[98] years, six months and ten days[99]. This, then, is the number of years in question; as for the events that have taken place (during this time), we have related them severally, each in its place.

The sources include in their catalogue of measures taken against captured Jerusalem by the Babylonians the deportation of (elements of) its surviving population; see 25,11-12 // 39,9-10 // 52,15-16 // 36,20-21; cf. 1 Esdras 1,56b-58. Josephus links this item rather with his account of the execution of the Jerusalem leadership, thereby keeping together in a continuous sequence those Babylonian initiatives having to do with persons[100].

5. *Leaders Executed*

In the presentation of 2 Kings 25 // Jeremiah 52 the Babylonians' punishment of rebellious Jerusalem culminates (25,18-21 // 52,24-27) with Nabuzaradan's carrying off a group of the city's elite for execution at the hands of Nebuchadnezzar in Riblah. Josephus' version (10,149-153) of this happening opens (10,149a) with a transitional phrase which itself incorporates an allusion to the deportation of Jerusalem's population cited at an earlier point in the sources (see

from the latter happening to the Temple's destruction cited just previously in 10,147 (i.e. 470 years, six months, and ten days). Elsewhere, however (see *AJ* 20,230 and *c. Ap.* 2,19), he states that *612* years elapsed between the Exodus and the building of the Temple (in MT L 1 Kgs 6,1 the figure given for this period is 480 years, in B 440), this yielding a total of 1082 years (as opposed to the 1062 years of 10,147) for the time between the Exodus and the destruction of the Temple. See MARCUS, *Josephus*, VI, pp. 238-239, n. c.

96. This would yield an interval of 1487 years from the Flood to the building of the Temple; compare *AJ* 8,61 where the figure given for that period is 1440 years. See MARCUS, *Josephus*, VI, p. 239, n. d.

97. This is the reading adopted by Niese, Naber, and Marcus. Dindorf and Bekker read τρισχίλια with LaurVEZon; cf. Lat's tria millia.

98. RO, followed by Niese, read δέκα.

99. The above figure for the total interval from Adam to the destruction of the Temple (4513/ 3000 [this on the reading of Dindorf and Bekker; see n. 97] years) diverges notably from the number arrived at when one tallies the 3102 years from Adam to the building of the Temple cited in *AJ* 8,62 and the sum of 470 for the time from the Temple's construction to its destruction given in 10,147 (see above), i.e. 3572 years. See MARCUS, *Josephus*, VI, p. 239, n. g.

100. Contrast the sequence of 2 Kings 25 and Jeremiah 52 where the interlude concerning the removal of the Temple treasures (25,13-17 // 52,17-23) supervenes between the notices on the deportation of the population to Babylon (25,11-12 // 52,15-16) and the execution of the city's leadership (25,18-21 // 52,24-27).

above): "Now, when the general (στρατηγός, 10,144) of the Babylonian king had demolished (κατασκάψας; see 10,80.112; compare κατέστρεψεν, 10,146) Jerusalem and removed the people (τὸν λαὸν μεταναστήσας)...¹⁰¹". Thereafter, he enumerates those Nebuzaradan carries off for judgment by Nebuchadenezzar in accordance with 25,18-20 // 52,24-26: "... he took captive the high priest (ἀρχιερέα; compare [τὸν] ἱερέα τὸν πρῶτον, BL 25,18 // LXX Jer 52,24) Saraios (Σαραῖον)¹⁰² and Sephenias (Σεφενίαν)¹⁰³, the priest next to him in rank (τὸν μετ' αὐτὸν¹⁰⁴ ἱερέα)¹⁰⁵ and the officers who guarded the temple (τοὺς φυλάσσοντας τὸ ἱερὸν ἡγεμόνας)¹⁰⁶ – there were three of these – and the eunuch in charge of the soliders (τὸν ἐπὶ τῶν ὁπλιτῶν εὐνοῦχον)¹⁰⁷ and seven¹⁰⁸ friends (φίλους; see 10,136.137.140) of Sacchias¹⁰⁹ and his scribe (τὸν γραμματέα)¹¹⁰ and sixty other officers

101. This phrase signifies Nebuzaradan's execution of the final component of Nebuchadnezzar's directives to him as cited in 10,144, i.e. τὸν λαὸν εἰς τὴν Βαβυλωνίαν μεταστῆσαι. Josephus will supply more details, inspired by 25,11-12, etc., about the composition of the group carried off by Nebuzaradan in 10,155; see there.

102. This is the reading of EZon; Dindorf, Bekker, and Naber read Σαρέαν (compare Lat Saream), Niese Σεβαῖον (so RO), SCHLATTER, Namen, pp. 105-106 Σαραια-ν, SCHALIT, Namenwörterbuch, p. 107 Σαραίας. Compare שְׂרָיָה (MT); Σαραίαν (BL 25,18; in LXX 25,24 the "first priest" lacks a name).

103. This is the reading adopted by Niese, Marcus; Dindorf, Bekker, and Naber read Σοφονίαν with LaurV. Compare צְפַנְיָה (MT); Σοφονίαν (B 25,18); Σαφανίαν (L 25,18). In LXX 52,24 the "second priest" lacks a name.

104. MSP, followed by Dindorf, Bekker, and Naber read αὐτοῦ, this yielding the designation "the priest with him" for the figure in question.

105. Compare υἱὸν τῆς δευτερώσεως (B 25,18); τὸν ἱερέα τὸν δευτερεύοντα (LXX 52,24); τὸν ἱερέα τὸν δεύτερον (L 25,18).

106. Compare the designations for this group found in the Biblical witnesses: שֹׁמְרֵי הַסַּף (MT 25,18 // 52,24; "keepers of the threshold", RSV); τοὺς φυλάσσοντας τὸν σταθμόν (BL 25,18); τοὺς φυλάττοντας τὴν ὁδόν (LXX 52,21); אמרכליא (TJ 25,18 [HARRINGTON and SALDARINI, ad loc., "cashiers"]) // (TJ 52,24 [HAYWARD, ad loc., "temple-officers"]). MARCUS, Josephus, VI, p. 241, n. d suggests that Josephus' designation may reflect the Targums' term.

107. In 25,19 // 52,25 the reference is "to an officer (εὐνοῦχον, BL 25,19 // LXX 52,25) who had been in command (ἐπιστάτης, B 25,19 // LXX 52,25) of the men of war" (so RSV).

108. This figure corresponds to that of MT LXX 52,25 as against the "five" of MT BL 25,19.

109. This is Josephus' characteristic replacement for the group cited in 25,19 // 52,25, i.e. "men of the king's council who were found in the city" (RSV). Zedekiah's surviving (false) "friends" (cf. 10,140) are now about to receive their deserved punishment.

110. Here Josephus simplifies the sources' reference to "the secretary (τὸν γραμματέα, BL 25,19 // LXX 52,25) of the commander of the army who mustered the people of the land" (RSV), making the figure Zedekiah's own "scribe/secretary" reminiscent of the one he assigns to Jehoiakim in 10,94. Note too the historian's characteristic non-utilization of the sources' mention of the "people of the land", see next note.

(ἡγεμόνας)¹¹¹, all of whom he carried off, *together with the vessels he had taken as spoil* (μεθ' ὧν ἐσύλησε σκευῶν)¹¹², to the king at Arablatha ('Αραβλαθάν)¹¹³, a city in Syria¹¹⁴".

2 Kgs 25,21 // Jer 52,27 relate the fate accorded Nebuzaradan's captives, and then rounds off the story of the nation's catastrophe as a whole with their common concluding formula "so Judah was taken into exile out of its land". Josephus' version (10,150) expatiates in several respects: "As for the high priest and the officers (ἡγεμόνων; see 10,149), the king ordered (ἐκέλευσεν)¹¹⁵ their heads to be cut off (τὰς κεφαλὰς ἀποτεμεῖν)¹¹⁶ there, while he himself took (ἤγαγεν)¹¹⁷ all the captives (αἰχμαλώτους; see 10,140)¹¹⁸ and Sacchias to Babylon¹¹⁹; *he also carried off in chains* (δέσμιον) *the high priest Jōsadakos* ('Ιωσάδακον)¹²⁰, *a son of the high priest Saraios, whom the Babylonian king*

111. This group represents Josephus' substitute for the "sixty men of the people of the land" of 25,19 // 52,25; see previous note. On the "friends" and "leaders" combination introduced by Josephus here in 10,149, see 10,136-137.

112. This inserted reference to the Temple "vessels" picks up on the mention of Nabuzaradan's "carrying out the gold and silver vessels of God" (10,145) in accord with Nebuchadnezzar's order to him (10,144). Thereby, Josephus makes clear that the vessels were not simply left behind in Jerusalem once they had been removed from the Temple.

113. This is the emendation of Niese which Marcus follows in line with their like emendation in 10,135; see n. 22. Dindorf, Bekker, and Naber read 'Ρεβλαθάν. Compare "Riblah" (MT); Δεβλάθα (BL 25,20 // LXX 52,26). See n. 122.

114. Josephus anticipates this localization of the city from 25,21 // 52,27 where "Riblah" is said to lie "in the land of Hamath".

115. In 25,21 // 52,27 Nebuchadnezzar is represented as executing the prisoners in person. Josephus' reference to his "ordering" their execution echoes 10,140 where the king "ordered" (ἐκέλευσεν) Zedekiah's sons and friends to be put to death forthwith.

116. Compare 25,21// 52,27: "the king of Babylon smote them and put them to death..."; see, however, n. 121. (In *P.R.* 26.6 [BRAUDE, *Pesikta Rabbati*, p. 535] the [unnamed] high priest is butchered by the Babylonians in Jerusalem itself at the altar of sacrifice, whereupon the priests and the Levites, along with the virgins who wove the Sanctuary curtain, hurl themselves into the flames that are consuming the Temple.)

117. This word is absent in RO and omitted by Niese.

118. The reference here would seem to be to "the people", i.e. those Jerusalemites other than the leaders – whose execution has just been described in 10,150a – whom Nebuzaradan is said to "remove" in 10,149. Cf. the mention – not previously utilized by Josephus (see above) – of Nebuzaradan's deporting "the rest of the people who were left in the city and the deserters who had deserted to the king of Babylon, together with the rest of the multitude" in 25,11 (similarly 39,9 and 52,15). The "captives" in question here would also, one might suppose, include those "captives" (10,140) earlier brought before Nebuchadnezzar following their apprehension near Jericho, but not executed by him then, i.e. Zedekiah's "wives" and "officers" (10,136); see n. 62. Josephus will return to the fate of this group in 10,155.

119. Josephus seems to forget here that he has already related the carrying off of Zedekiah to Babylon by Nebuchadnezzar in 10,140.

120. Marcus' reading here (which he shares with Dindorf, Bekker, and Naber) reflects Lat's "Iosadach"; Niese reads 'Ιωσάδακον with SP. In *AJ* 20,231 Josephus calls this figure "Josadakes" ('Ιωσαδάκην), while in 20,234 he appears as "Josedek" ('Ιωσεδέκ).

had killed (ἀπέκτεινεν)[121] *in Arablatha* (᾽Αραβλαθᾷ)[122], *a city in Syria, as we have already related*[123]".

Just as he did in connection with the deposition of the Davidic dynasty (see 10,143) and the destruction of the Temple (see 10,147-148), Josephus appends to his preceding account of the fate of the high-priestly line (10,149-150) a series of notices on that line, 10,151-153. This appendix reads:

(151) Since we have enumerated those who were of the royal line and have told who they were and what were the years (of their reigns)[124], I have thought it necessary (ἀναγκαῖον ἡγησάμην; see 9,208) also to give the names of the high priests and tell who founded (καταδείξαντες)[125] the high priesthood (ἀρχιερωσύνην) in the period of the kings[126]. (152) The first to become high priest of the temple which Solomon built was Sadok (Σάδωκος)[127]; after him his son Achimas (᾽Αχιμᾶς)[128] succeeded to the office and after Achimas, Azarias (so BL 1 Chr 5,35; compare אֲזַרְיָה, MT), then his son Jōramos (᾽Ιώραμος)[129], next Jōramos's son Iōs (῎Ιως)[130], after him Axiōramos (᾽Αξιώραμος)[131], (153) then Axiōramos's son Phideas

Compare יְהוֹצָדָק (MT 1 Chr 5,41); ᾽Ιωσαδακ (B); ᾽Ιωσεδέκ (L). The various Biblical accounts of the fall of Jerusalem and its sequels do not mention such a deportation of the priest Jehozadak. Josephus draws the item from 1 Chr 5,41 (MT; Eng. 6,15).

121. With this formulation Josephus appropriates the wording of 25,21 // 52,27 where Nebuchadnezzar in person is said to have "smote and put to death" the Jerusalem leadership, including the high priest. Compare 10,150a according to which Nebuchadnezzar "ordered" that the leaders' "heads be cut off"; cf. n. 116.

122. This is the reading adopted by Marcus in line with the emendation ᾽Αραβλαθάν proposed by him in 10,149 (see n. 113). Dindorf, Bekker, and Naber read ῾Ρεβλαθᾷ in accord with the *ed. prin.*, while Niese conjectures ᾽Αριβλαθᾶ.

123. This concluding *Rückverweis* reminds readers of the information concerning Jehozadak's father and his fate presented just previously in 10,149-150a.

124. With this formulation Josephus harks back to his appendix concerning the Davidids in 10,143.

125. Josephus' other uses of the verb καταδείκνυμι are in *AJ* 11,80; 15,371. Coccejus proposes κατασχόντες (cf. Lat qui... habuerunt). MARCUS, *Josephus*, VI, p. 241, n. h, while retaining the above reading, designates both it and his rendering thereof by "founded" as "doubtful".

126. Josephus bases (the first part of) the list that follows on 1 Chr 5,34-41 (MT; Eng. 6,7-15). See further below.

127. In MT 1 Chr 5,34 the name is צָדוֹק (B Σαδωκ; L Σαδδούκ). Josephus' above indication about Zadok being the first high priest of Solomon's Temple would appear to conflict with 1 Chr 5,36 according to which it was Zadok's great-grandson, i.e. Azariah who "served as priest in the house that Solomon built...". (In *AJ* 8,12; cf. 7,110, Josephus speaks of Sadok as "the first to become high priest in the *reign of David*".)

128. Compare אֲחִימַעַץ (MT 1 Chr 5,35); ᾽Αχιμάας (BL).

129. Beginning with this great-grand son of Zadok, the names on Josephus' list diverge markedly from those enumerated in 1 Chr 5,34ff.; see n. 138.

130. Dindorf, Bekker, and Naber read ῎Ισος with Laur. SCHLATTER, *Namen*, p. 54 reconstructs an original form Ιωαζος; SCHALIT, *Namenwörterbuch*, p. 68 rejects this proposal.

131. SCHLATTER, *Namen*, p. 54 reconstructs Ιωραμος as the original form here.

(Φιδέας), then Phideas's son Sūdaios (Σουδαίας)[132], then Sūdaios's son Jūēlos ('Ιουῆλος)[133], then Jūēlos's son Jōthamos ('Ιώθαμος), then Jōthamos's son Ūrias (Ούρίας), then Ūrias's son Nērias (Νηρίας), then Nērias's son Ōdaias ('Ωδαίας)[134], then Odaias's son Sallūmos (Σαλλοῦμος)[135], then Sallūmos's son Elkias ('Ελκίας), then Elkias's son Azaros ("Αζαρος)[136] and finally Azaros's son Jōsadakos[137], who was taken captive to Babylon[138]. In each case the son (παῖς)[139] succeeded his father in the high priesthood[140].

6. *Zedekiah & the Temple Vessels*

Following the extended insertion of 10,151-153, Josephus picks up on the "deportation notices" of 10,149-150 in 10,154. The various items

132. Dindorf, Bekker, and Naber read Σουδέας with MLaurVE. SCHLATTER, *Namen*, p. 42 traces the name back to a Hebrew חוֹדִיָה, a proposal which SCHALIT, *Namenwörterbuch*, p. 115 rejects.

133. This is the reading of MSP which Dindorf, Bekker, Niese, Naber, and Marcus follow.

134. This is the reading adopted by Niese and Marcus. Dindorf, Bekker, and Naber read 'Ωδέας with SPVE.

135. This is the reading of SP which Dindorf, Bekker, Naber, and Marcus follow. Niese reads Σαλοῦμος with M.

136. Dindorf, Bekker, and Naber read Σαρέας here as does WEILL, *ad. loc.*; see nn. 137 and 140.

137. The above indication concerning "Azaros" as Jōsadakos' father is problematic given that in 10,150 Josephus has cited "Saraios" as the latter's father; see above. Accordingly, NIESE, *ad loc.* proposes that there is a lacuna in the text after the name "Azaros", while Dindorf, Bekker, Naber, and Weill read "Sareas" in place of this form (see previous note) so as to bring the name into line with that given in 10,150 (and the "Seriah", father of Jehozadak, cited in 1 Chr 5,40).

138. Josephus lists a total of 13 high priests between "Azariah" and "Jōsadakos" in 10,152b-153. By contrast, 1 Chr 5,36-40 enumerates nine priests between the corresponding names of its list, none of which remotely corresponds to those given by Josephus who, it seems clear, it drawing here on a special tradition which, in the case of Jōsadakos' father he has not bothered to harmonize with his own statement in 10,150. For purposes of comparison I give here the Hebrew and Greek forms of the nine names of 1 Chr 5,36-40 which diverge from those cited by Josephus: (1) יוֹחָנָן/ 'Ιωανάς (B)/ 'Ιωανάν (L); 2) אֲזַרְיָה/ 'Αζαριά (B)/ 'Αζαρίας (L); 3) אֲמַרְיָה/ 'Αμαριά (B)/ 'Αμαρίας (L); 4) אַחִיטוּב/ 'Αχειτώβ (B)/ 'Αχιτώβ (L); 5) צָדוֹק/ Σαδώκ (B)/ Σαδδούκ (L); 6) שַׁלּוּם/ Σαλώμ (B)/ Σελλούμ (L); 7) חִלְקִיָּה/ Χελκείας (B)/ Χελκίας (L); 8) עֲזַרְיָה/ 'Αζαρίας (BL); and 9) שְׂרָיָה/ Σαραιά (B)/ Σαραίας (L). Compare too the list of Aaronide high priests in the genealogy of Ezra given in Ezra 7,1-5 which has only 15 names between those of Aaron and the Seriah executed by Nebuchadnezzar as opposed to the 20 names of 1 Chr 5,30-40.

139. This is the reading of LaurVE (cf. Lat filius) which Niese, Naber and Marcus follow. Dindorf and Bekker read παῖδες with ROMSP.

140. MARCUS, *Josephus*, VI, p. 243, n. e points out that in *AJ* 20,231 Josephus states that there were a total of *18* high priests during the period in which the First Temple stood (*b. Yoma* 9a gives the same figure). By contrast the list of the high priests of the First Temple furnished by him here in 10,152-153 contains only *17* names. This observation, in turn, leads Marcus to the surmise that the name of Jōsadakos' father, i.e. "Saraias" (cf. "Seraiah", MT 1 Chr 5,40) as cited by Josephus himself in 10,150 may have fallen out after the name Azaros in 10,153 given the similarity between them in the Greek; see nn. 136-137.

making up the content of the latter paragraph are drawn by him from a variety of Biblical contexts. The first component element in 10,154 relates the ultimate fate of Zedekiah: "Now, when the king [Nebuchadnezzar] came to Babylon, he kept Sacchias in prison (ἐν εἰρκτῇ) until he died[141] and then buried him royally (θάψας... βασιλικῶς)...[142]". The second matter recounted in 10,154 concerns Nebuchadnezzar's disposition of the confiscated Temple vessels: "... after which he dedicated to his own gods (ἀνέθηκε τοῖς ἰδίοις θεοῖς)[143] the vessels taken as spoil (τὰ σκεύη τὰ ... συληθέντα; see 10,144.145.149) from the temple in Jerusalem... [144]". Finally, Josephus rounds off his catalogue of

141. This indication seems inspired by Jer 52,11bβ: ("[Nebuchadnezzar] put him in prison [LXX εἰς οἰκίαν μυλῶνος] till the day of his death"), a passage previously passed over by Josephus. Cf. the references to Nebuchadnezzar's "taking Sacchias to Babylon" in 10,140.150. The term for Zedekiah's "prison" used here in 10,154 (εἰρκτή) is the same employed for Jeremiah's place of confinement in 10,117.121. Having allowed the prophet to be "imprisoned" by his enemies, Zedekiah ends up in the same place himself.

142. The phrase "bury royally" occurs only here in Josephus. In noting this development, he provides an implicit fulfillment for another of Jeremiah's Biblical prophecies (compare on 10,141), i.e. that cited in Jer 34[41],4-5 in which the prophet, having previously announced that the king is destined to be taken to Babylon (34,3), informs Zedekiah: "You shall not die by the sword. You shall die in peace. And as spices were burned for your fathers, the former kings who were before you, so men shall burn spices for you and lament for you, saying 'Alas, lord'". (Note how in Josephus' presentation the "kingliness" of Zedekiah's burial is accentuated in that it is Nebuchadnezzar himself who is responsible for giving him a "royal burial".) Also Rabbinic tradition goes beyond the Bible itself by mentioning that Zedekiah did in fact receive the fitting burial predicted by Jeremiah; see, e.g., b. Mo'ed Qat. 28b (here, this happening is the recompense for Zedekiah's good deed in delivering Jeremiah from the mud; see Jer 38,6) and SOR 28.3 (GIRÓN BLANC, Seder 'Olam Rabbah, p. 129; this text dates Zedekiah's death contemporaneously with the release of Jehoiachin and cites an elaborated version of the "lament" of Jer 34,5 in which Zedekiah is mourned as one who had to bear the punishment to which all previous generations had made themselves liable). Cf. 'Abot R. Nat. (Version B) 43.15 (NAVARRO PEIRÓ, Abot de Rabbí Natán, p. 414) which affirms that Zedekiah was one of four Biblical personages who died in "a good old age", the others being Abraham, Gideon, and David (in the case of these other three figures, there is explicit Scriptural warrant for the Midrash's statement, whereas the Bible supplies no indication concerning Zedekiah's age at death, apart from Jeremiah's above announcement about his dying "in peace" which might be taken to entail the promise that he would die at a ripe old age).

143. This is the only reference in Josephus to the "dedication" of something to "gods" in the plural.

144. Josephus' Biblical inspiration for the above item would seem to be Dan 1,2 (cf. also Dan 5,2; Ezra 1,7) which mentions Nebuchadnezzar's seizing "some of the vessels of the house of God", bringing these "to the house of his god" and placing them in "the treasury of his god". Josephus' (apparent) utilization of this Biblical verse involves, however, a "reapplication" of it in that Dan 1,2 itself concerns a happening – previously passed over by Josephus, (see on 10,98) – dated (so 1,1) to the third year of Jehoiakim's rule – rather than subsequent to the death of Zedekiah (so 10,154). Another possible Scriptural source (so MARCUS, ad loc.) for Josephus' indication about the vessels could be 2 Chr 36,7 (at the time of his seizure of Jehoiakim Nebuchadnezzar carried off "part of

Nebuchadnezzar's deeds subsequent to his return to Babylon at the end of 10,154 with the notice: "... and settled (κατῴκισεν) the people in the territory of Babylon[145], *while he released the high priest from confinement* (τῶν δεσμῶν; see δέσμιον, used of the high priest Jōsadakos in 10,150)[146]".

Conclusions: Josephus' Rewriting of 2 Kings 25, etc.

In composing his account of Jerusalem's overthrow in 10,131-154 Josephus drew primarily on the expansive narrative of 2 Kgs 25,2-21 // Jer 52,5-27[147] as opposed to the more summary presentations of Jer 39,2-10; 2 Chr 36,17-21 (// 1 Esdras 1,52-58). Into that narrative's material he also inserts, however, elements derived from a number of other Biblical contexts, i.e. the *Sondergut* sequence Jer 39,3-4aα (the names of the Babylonian officers and Zedekiah's "seeing" these; see 10,135-136a), the high priest list of 1 Chr 5,34-41 (MT)[148], and his transposition into narrative (10,154a; see n. 142) of the prophecy of Jer 34(41),5 concerning the circumstances of Zedekiah's death (see also the reference to Nebuchadnezzar's installing the temple vessels in the "treasury of his god" of Dan 1,2 [cf. 2 Chr 36,7] as the possible inspiration for the comparable notice of 10,154b; see n. 144). Once again, our investigation

the vessels of the house of the Lord to Babylon and put them *in his palace* in Babylon"). Here too, however, a chronological reapplication of the Biblical reference (as also a difference as to the use made of the vessels) would be involved.

145. There is no direct Biblical parallel to this particular initiative by Nebuchadnezzar; cf., however, 2 Chr 36,20: "He [Nebuchadnezzar] took into exile in Babylon those who had escaped from the sword, and they became servants to him and his sons until the establishment of the kingdom of Persia".

146. Also this notice lacks Biblical warrant. It does, however, provide closure to the story of "Jōsadakos" whose being taken into captivity in Babylon Josephus has mentioned twice previously (10,150.153) on the basis of 1 Chr 5,41 (see above). The above positive note with which Josephus' account of Jerusalem's catastrophe closes does, it might be noted, have a certain counterpart in 2 Chr 36,21 (cf. 1 Esdras 1,58) with its indication that the Jews' servitude to Babylon did have a fixed end-point, i.e. the rise of the kingdom of Persia.

147. There are a number of indications that Josephus based himself specifically on the Jeremiah 52 form of this parallel text; see his explicit mention of the "lampstands" among the Temple booty (10,145 = 52,19; > 25,14); the group of seven captives (10,149 = 52,25 vs. five, 25,19) carried off by Nebuzaradan, and the reference to Nebuchadnezzar's keeping Zedekiah in prison until the day of his death (10,154 = 52,11bβ; > 25,7). Cf. also his allusion to persons other then Zedekiah's own sons being executed before the king's eyes in 10,140 as in 52,10b (> 25,7) though this also has a parallel in 39,6b (MT).

148. Recall, however, that for the latter part of his list in 10,152b-153, Josephus diverges completely from the Biblical names cited, this suggesting that he was making use, for that portion of the list, of an alternative series of names; see n. 138.

failed to turn up much evidence regarding the text-form(s) of the Biblical passages employed by Josephus in this segment. We did, however,
note that his list of the Babylonian generals in 10,135 stands closer to
what finds in LXX Jer 46,3 than to its MT counterpart 39,3; on the other
hand, his version of the opening words of Jer 39,4 in 10,136 betrays his
utilization of a MT-like text seeing that LXX chap. 46 has no equivalent
to MT's 39,4-13.

As a retelling of the story of Jerusalem's fall, Josephus' version is
characterized above all by its massive expansions of the Biblical record.
These include the following larger-scale items: the sequence on the
intensity of the siege and the city's resistance thereto (10,131-134);
Nebuchadnezzar's denunciation of Zedekiah (10,138b-139); the fulfillment notice of 10,141 and the attached reflection of 10,142; the indications on the Davidic succession (10,143); Nebuchadnezzar's directives
to Nebuzaradan (10,144); the dating of the Temple's destruction in relation to key events of earlier Biblical history (10,147-148); and mention
of Nebuchadnezzar's settling of the deportees in Babylon while also
releasing the high priest (10,154c).

The historian's omissions/ compressions of the Biblical record are not
nearly so conspicuous in 10,131-154. One such instance is his streamlining of the catalogue of the Babylonians' Temple booty (25,13-17 //
52,17-23); see 10,145. In this same context, Josephus likewise effects a
re-arrangement of the sources' sequence, mentioning the despoliation of
the Temple prior to its being burnt (see 10,145-146; compare 25,9.13-17
// 52,13.17-23; although cf. 2 Chr 36,18-19) and likewise prior to Nebuzaradan's carrying off, as his final measure, various groups of persons
to their respective fates (see 10,149; and compare 25,11-21 // 52,15-27
where the order is first removal of those who will go Babylon, then
despoliation of the Temple, and finally the leading away of the officials
whom Nebuchadnezzar will execute). Again, the allusion to Nebuchadnezzar's being at a site ("Riblah", MT) far removed from Jerusalem
during the city's siege and capture (25,6 // 39,5 // 52,9) is anticipated by
him in 10,135.

The historian further modifies/adapts the Biblical presentation(s) of
Jerusalem's fall. He gives a different description of Zedekiah's escape
route ("through the fortified valley", 10,136) then do the Scriptural
accounts (see 25,4 // 39,4 // 52,7). Nebuzaradan acts on orders issued
him by Nebuchadnezzar (10,144) rather than, seemingly, on his volition
(thus 25,8ff. // 39,9f. // 52,12ff.) and "demolishes the city" (10,147)
instead of "breaking down its walls" (so 25,10 // 39,8b // 52,14). The
Babylonian general carries off to execution seven "friends" of Zedekiah

(10,149) as opposed to seven "men of the king's council" (so 52,25; cf. 25,19 which speaks of five of these) along with the king's own "scribe" (10,149), instead of one attached to the officer responsible for mustering the people as in 25,19 // 52,25. In his dealings with the Jerusalem elite Nebuchadnezzar orders their decapitation (10,150), whereas his Biblical namesake "smites and puts them to death" (25,21a // 52,27a).

Josephus' application of the foregoing rewriting techniques in 10,131-154 results in a version of Jerusalem's fall which appears distinctive in a variety of respects. He highlights the circumstances of the catastrophe as fulfilling earlier prophecies (see 10,141-142.152). Nebuchadnezzar's directive role in the proceedings is accentuated (see his address to Zedekiah, 10,138b-139 and orders to Nebuzaradan, 10,144, neither of which has a Biblical counterpart as such). Reminiscences of Josephus' descriptions of the Roman sieges of Jotapata and Jerusalem in *BJ* are introduced throughout. The notices attached by him to the deposition of Zedekiah (see 10,143), the destruction of the Temple (10,147-148) and the disruption of the high priestly succession (10,151-153) all serve to underscore the ephochal import of Jerusalem's fall.

To Roman readers, Josephus' account with its reminiscences of Rome's recent conquests of Jotapata and Jerusalem might well function as a source of pride: Rome's military achievements, accomplished against so tenacious a foe (see 10,131-134), equal those of the mighty Babylonians of old. To such readers the account would likewise convey, via the words Josephus places on the lips of Nebuchadnezzar in 10,138b-139, a gratifying sense of the justice of Rome's cause: God had punished the treacherous Jews through their agency in the present, just as he had done, through the hand of the Babylonians, in the case of those Jews' equally perfidious ancestors in Zedekiah's time. As for Jewish readers, Josephus' version of Jerusalem's first destruction would supply a reason for pride on their part as well, i.e. the heroism of their forebears as portrayed by him in the interjected segment 10,131-134. At the same time, the historian's presentation would remind his Jewish audience that the earlier catastrophe of their holy city – as also, they might infer, its recent, similar calamity – was not a matter of inexplicable misfortune, but the fulfillment of the announcements of God-sent prophets. In addition and finally, however, the still unrealized predictions of those ancient prophets, including that of the eventual demise of Babylon = Rome – as that audience may further infer – are equally certain of realization. As such they deserve, from the side of contemporary Jews, the attention and credence which Zedekiah's generation had so disastrously failed to accord the words of Jeremiah and Ezekiel upon their first delivery.

XXIV

THE GOVERNORSHIP OF GEDALIAH AND ITS AFTERMATH[1]
(10,155-185)

The Books of Kings and Jeremiah both round off their accounts of Jerusalem's fall with mention of the brief, promising governorship of Gedaliah, its tragic end, and the consequences of this for the surviving Judeans in the land. Whereas, however, the former work relates this whole sequence of events in a mere five verses (2 Kgs 25,22-26), the latter devotes a five-chapter segment to them, i.e. Jeremiah 40-44 [LXX 47-51]. Josephus' own account of the happenings in question, in *AJ* 10,155-185, occupies a middle position between the minimalistic narrative of Kings and the maximalistic version found in Jeremiah. I divide up the material into seven parallel segments: 1. Nebuzaradan's arrangements (*AJ* 10,155-158 = Jer 40,1-6 [MT] // 2 Kgs 25,22); 2. Mizpah assemblies (10,159-163 = 40,7-12 // 25,23-24); 3. Gedaliah warned (40,13-16 = 10,164-167); 4. Gedaliah murdered (10,168-169 = 41,1-3 // 25,25); 5. Immediate Sequels (41,4-18 // 10,170-175); 6. Flight to Egypt (10,176-179 = 42,1-43,7 // 25,26); and 7) God's Word in Egypt (10,180 [181-185] = 43,8-44,30).

1. *Nebuzaradan's Arrangements*

Josephus begins his narrative of events subsequent to Jerusalem's fall and devastation (10,131-154) by recounting (10,155-158) various measures undertaken by the Babylonian general Nebuzaradan ("Nabūzar-danēs", see 10,144) with regard to the surviving Judeans. Of these, the first is his appointment (10,155 = 40,5 // 25,22) of a native governor

---

1. This chapter represents a reworking of my article *The Gedaliah Episode and its Sequels in Josephus*, in *JSP* 12 (1994) 21-46 and it is used here by permission. It likewise draws on FELDMAN, *Studies*, pp. 463-472 (= ID., *Josephus' Portrait of Gedaliah*, in *Shofar* 12 [1993] 1-10).

It might be mentioned here that Jeremiah 40-44 is the only portion of the Biblical book used by Josephus which has any extended parallel in the Qumran finds (the text of which does not differ significantly from that of MT). Thus, MS 2QJer contains portions of Jer 42,7-11.14; 43,8-11; 44,1-3,12-14 (see BAILLET, *Les 'Petites Grottes'*, pp. 63-65), while 4QJer^d preserves part of Jer 43,2-10 (see E. TOV, in ULRICH *ed. al.*, *Qumran Cave 4, X. The Prophets*, pp. 203-205).

(ἡγεμονα) for them, i.e. "Gadalias" (Γαδαλίαν)[2], son of "Aïkamos" (Ἀϊκάμου)[3]. Josephus combines this "appointment notice" with a reference to the general's leaving behind two groups of persons as Gedaliah's "subjects", i.e. "the poor (πένητας) and the deserters (αὐτομόλους; see 10,127.137)". For his mention of the former group, he could draw on 2 Kgs 25,12 // Jer 39,10 which speak of Nebuzaradan leaving behind "the poorest (LXX τῶν πενήτων) of the land" to till the soil as well as Jer 40,7 which cites "the poorest of the land" (so MT; > LXX) as among those repairing to the new governor. As for the second group of Gedaliah's subjects, i.e. the "deserters", Josephus may have derived these from 2 Kgs 25,11 // Jer 39,9 where "those who had deserted" are mentioned among the persons whom Nebuzaradan carries off to Babylon[4]. In any event, Josephus goes beyond both his sources in providing an initial characterization of Nebuzaradan's appointee which helps to account for the Babylonian's choice of him: "he was of noble birth (τῶν εὖ γεγονότων)[5] and kind and just (ἐπιεικῆ καὶ δίκαιον)[6]". Finally, Josephus rounds off his "appointment notice" with allusion to the "the payment (τελεῖν)[7] of a fixed tribute to the king from the

2. This is the reading adopted by Niese, Marcus and SCHALIT, *Namenwörterbuch*, p. 30, s.v. Dindorf, Bekker, Naber, and Weill read Γοδολίαν with LaurVEZon and Lat. Compare וּדְלִיָהוּ (MT), Γοδολίας (LXX = the variant in Josephus).

3. This is the reading of the *ed. pr.* which Dindorf, Bekker, Niese, Naber, Marcus, and SCHALIT, *Namenwörterbuch*, p. 6 all follow. Compare MT אֲחִיקָם; LXX Jer 40,5: Αχικαμ (cf. L 2 Kgs 25,22 Ἀχικάμος).

4. Note the difference between the Bible and Josephus regarding the fate of the "deserters": in the former they end up in Babylon, while in the latter they are allowed to remain in the land. The difference may reflect the historian's consideration that it would be this group whom the Babylonians would especially wish to "reward" – recall that in 10,137 (no Biblical parallel) it is they who report Zedekiah's flight to the Babylonians – by permitting them to stay on in the land. Note further that in the Bible (25,11-12 // 39,9-10) Nebuzaradan's dealings with the two groups (the poor, the deserters) are mentioned at an earlier point, i.e. in connection with the measures taken against Jerusalem following its capture, than they are in Josephus who integrates these items into his account of the (later) appointment of Gedaliah as governor.

5. On Josephus' characteristic emphasis on the distinguished ancestry of the figures cited in his works – himself included – see FELDMAN, *Studies*, p. 464 (= ID., *Gedaliah*, 2-3). Of course, in the case specifically of Gedaliah, Josephus' statement on the point does have a Biblical basis in the recurring references to the high offices and influential roles assumed by his various relatives found in 2 Kgs 22,3-14; Jer 26,24; 29,3; 36,10.12.25.

6. Significantly, Josephus' only other use of this collocation is in reference to David in his eulogy for the king in *AJ* 7,391. The above inserted characterization of Gedaliah is intended to indicate to readers, right from the start, how they are to view his appointment by the Babylonians and his subsequent, "pro-Babylonian" utterances, which might otherwise very well appear in a negative light; see further below.

7. This is the reading of VE which Bekker, Niese, Naber, and Marcus follow. Dindorf reads τελέσειν with ROMSP; Laur lacks an equivalent.

cultivation of the soil" which Nebuzaradan "imposes" on those he leaves behind in the land[8].

In 10,156-158 Josephus, drawing (loosely) on 40(47),1-6, proceeds to speak of Nebuzaradan's provisions for Jeremiah[9]. According to 40,1b[10], Nebuzaradan "let Jeremiah go from Ramah" (so MT; LXX ἐκ Δαμα) whither he had been taken "in chains", while in 40,4 the general informs the prophet "I release you today from the chains on your hands". By contrast, Josephus (10,156) simply has Nebuzaradan take Jeremiah "out of the prison" (ἐκ τῆς εἰρκτῆς). Here, it would seem, the historian is drawing on an earlier passage in the Book of Jeremiah concerning the prophet's "release", one not previously utilized by him, i.e. 39(46),13-14a where Nebuzaradan and his Babylonian colleagues "sent and took Jeremiah from the court of the guard" (i.e., in Jerusalem where he had been confined during the siege; see 38,22); cf. also the reference to Jeremiah's prison (εἰρκτή) in 10,117.121. Thus in Josephus nothing is said of Jeremiah having being taken "in chains" to Ramah by Nebuzaradan subsequent to the city's fall – a first indication of the historian's accentuation of the good treatment accorded the prophet by the Babylonians throughout the episode; see below.

Josephus further passes over Nebuzaradan's opening statement to the prophet (40,2b-3) about Judah's disaster as being due to divine retribution. That statement, which articulates what Jeremiah himself had been saying all along, is, one might suppose, not something the prophet was in any need of hearing. Accordingly, Josephus leaves it aside, doing so all the more appropriately in that he has already (see 10,139) had Nebuchadnezzar address a version of Nebuzaradan's statement of 40,2b-3 to King Zedekiah – a more fitting recipient of its sentiments, given his calamitous role in the city's overthrow.

In (re-) formulating the alternative Nebuzaradan offers Jeremiah according to 40,4b, Josephus has him underscore that Jeremiah's future is a matter of concern to Nebuchadenzzar himself: the king had

---

8. In Jer 40,9 // 2 Kgs 25,23 a comparable, though less determinate, directive is attributed, not to Nebuzaradan, but to Gedaliah himself when addressing the assembled survivors: "serve (so MT BL 25,23 // MT 40,9; compare LXX 40,9: ἐργάσασθε) the king of Babylon". In transferring the directive to Nebuzaradan, Josephus represents the general as taking care, in the midst of the other measures taken by him, to personally regulate the key matter of "tribute".

9. In placing this item after his notice on Gedaliah's appointment by Nebuzaradan, Josephus reverses the sequence of 40,7 (allusion to Gedaliah's appointment) and 40,1-5(6) (measures regarding Jeremiah). In the version of the happenings subsequent to Jerusalem's fall found in 2 Kgs 25,22-26 there is no mention of Jeremiah at all.

10. In 40,1a one finds an anacoluthic *Wortereignisformel* to which Josephus has no equivalent.

"ordered" his general "to provide him [Jeremiah] with everything",
while the prophet's decision about where he will settle is also to be
reported to the king. Once again then, Josephus highlights both the
stature of Jeremiah and the Babylonians' solicitude for him vis-à-vis the
Bible where Nebuzaradan makes no mention of his overlord in presenting the prophet's alternatives.

In the sequence of Jer 40,4-5 Nebuzaradan first addresses Jeremiah
and then releases him, without anything being said directly of the latter's
reaction to the choices given him (i.e. to go to Babylon or to remain
whereever he wills in the land, v. 4b). Josephus (10,157a) fills this
lacuna with an explicit evocation – itself inspired by the narrative notice
of 40,6 (Jeremiah "dwelt... among the people who were left in the
land") – about the prophet's thinking with regard to the choices offered
him. This inserted indication reads: "he neither wished to accompany
him [i.e. to Babylon] nor to dwell anywhere else [cf. Nebuzardan's closing word in 40,5: or go whereever you think it right to go], but was content to live on among the ruins of his native land and its miserable
remains (ταλαιπώροις ... λειψάνοις)[11]". With this notice Josephus
underscores the devotion of the prophet – who had earlier been accused
of being a traitor (see 10,119) – to his country.

In 40,5a Nebuzaradan tells Jeremiah that he may join Gedaliah
(whose appointment is mentioned as an accomplished fact for the first
time here; compare Josephus' sequence in 10,155-156 above) should he
decide to remain in the land. We are not, however, told of the governor
himself being given instructions concerning the prophet's (eventual)
reception. Josephus (10,157b) portrays a more provident general who,
once he learns of Jeremiah's decision (see above), "commanded
Gadalias... forthwith to take all possible care of him [Jeremiah] and provide him with everything he might need...". Josephus' continuing
accentuation of the Babylonian solicitude for Jeremiah finds further
expression in the fact that while 40,5b simply has Nebuzaradan give the
prophet a gift (MT, LXX δῶρα) when releasing him, the historian cites
the "*valuable* gifts" (δωρεαῖς πολυτελέσιν) bestowed on him by the
general.

Josephus (10,158) follows 40,6 in noting Jeremiah's settling with
Gedaliah at the latter's captial which MT calls "Mizpah" (LXX
Μασσηφα) and which he designates as "Masphata" (Μασφαθᾷ)[12]. To

---

11. This phrase occurs only here in Josephus.
12. This is the reading of codex O which Dindorf, Bekker, Naber, Marcus and
SCHALIT, *Namenwörterbuch*, p. 84 s.v. follow. Niese reads Μοσφοθᾶ with RSP. Josephus has mentioned the site previously in *AJ* 6,22.60; 8,306. In the codices ROM the

this item he then appends the following, extra-Biblical notice: "[Jeremiah] urged Nabūzardanēs to release, at the same time as himself, his disciple (μαθητήν)[13] Baruch... who came of a very distinguished family (ἐξ ἐπισήμου σφόδρα οἰκίας)[14] and was exceptionally well instructed in his native tongue[15]". Here again (see on 10,157) Josephus focusses attention on Jeremiah's side in the exchange between himself and Nebuzaradan, whereas in the source (Jer 40,1-6) it is the latter alone who has an active role. By means of the insertion he likewise accounts for the (Biblically unmotivated) subsequent presence of Baruch alongside Jeeremiah (see 43,2 // 10,178). At the same time, the item seems to represent a transposition into narrative of the divine prediction of 45,5 (not as such cited by Josephus), i.e. "I will give you [Baruch] your life as a prize of war in all the places to which you may go". Finally, the notice also constitutes an element of that two-way process whereby Josephus portrays himself and his hero-exemplar Jeremiah in one another's image[16]; see *Vita* 418 where the historian records his own "requesting Titus for the freedom of some of my countrymen" following the fall of Jerusalem[17].

2. *Mizpah Assemblies*

Jer 40,7-12 (= 10,159-163)[18] records a double coming of the Judean survivors to Gedaliah at Mizpah: first the leaders "from the open country" (40,7-10), then refugees returning from the neighboring countries (40,11-12). In each instance, the group's coming to Mizpah is moti-

word κατέμεινεν in Josephus' notice of 10,158a that "Jeremiah *remained* in the country" is followed by the phrase εἰς Δάναν (compare εἰς Δανάν, SP; εἰς ῎Αδαναν, LaurV) which MARCUS, *Josephus*, VI, p. 246, n. b suggests reflects the LXX reading (ἐκ Δαμα; compare MT: "from Ramah") in Jer 40(47),1; see above.

13. In his two previous mentions of Baruch (10,94.95) Josephus follows the Bible (Jer 36,26.32, MT) in calling him Jeremiah's "scribe". On the historian's use of the term μαθητής, see on 9,33.

14. This phrase echoes that used of Gedaliah's noble birth in 10,155 (although in Baruch's case Josephus had no Biblical basis for making it – as he did for Gedaliah; see n. 5). Its characterization of Baruch provides the Babylonians with a rationale for according him the special treatment requested by Jeremiah.

15. Also this indication (see previous note) lacks a Biblical basis as such. It is, however, likely inspired by the depiction of Baruch writing Jeremiah's words and reading these to others in Jeremiah 36 (compare *AJ* 10,93-95).

16. On this process see the conclusion to chap. XXII, pp. 573-574.

17. Likewise the previous mention of Nebuzaradan's giving Jeremiah's "valuable gifts" (10,157) has its pendant in what Josephus tells of the Romans' dealings with himself; see *BJ* 3,408 where Vespasian favors the captive Josephus with "precious gifts".

18. In 2 Kgs 25,22-26 there is mention only of the leaders coming to Gedaliah and his address to them (25,23-24 // 40,7-10).

vated by its "hearing" of Gedaliah's appointment (vv. 7,11). Josephus makes the transition to the first of these "assemblies", while also rounding off the preceding episode, via the opening words of 10,159: "Then Nabūzardanēs, having disposed of these matters, set out for Babylon[19]". He likewise provides a more expansive motivation (compare 40,7) for the first gathering at Mizpah: the Jews dispersed in the country "hear" of the Babylonians' withdrawal and their leaving behind a remnant to cultivate the land.

Jer 40,8 cites by name four[20] individual leaders who approach Gedaliah. Of these, the first is Ishmael, Gadaliah's future assassin who, at this point, remains simply one name among several, not distinguished from his fellows in any way. Josephus (10,160), on the contrary, reserves mention of him until the end of his listing; to the name he appends as well an extended characterization which recalls, while it also contrasts with, that previously supplied by him for Gedaliah. Ishmael, in Josephus' formulation, is "from the royal family... a wicked (πονηρός) and very crafty (δολιώτατος)[21] man, who had fled from Jerusalem during the siege to Baaleim (Βααλείμ)[22], the king of the Ammanites, and had stayed with him during all that time". For this characterization Josephus (once again) anticipates elements from the later course of the Biblical narrative: Ishmael's royal descent is drawn from 41,1, his link with the Ammonite king from 40,14. The historian's further indication that Ishmael had taken refuge with "Baaleim" during the siege of Jerusalem has no Biblical basis as such; it does, however, provide an explanation as to how the royal Ishmael escaped the fate of Zedekiah's sons (and other prominent

19. The Bible itself simply presupposes the fact of Nebuzaradan's return.

20. In fact, most MSS of MT have a fifth name, i.e. "Jonathan" which is absent in a few MSS, LXX 47,8 and a Targum MS (as well as in the parallel text 2 Kgs 25,23); its omission in these witnesses might be due to dittography with the preceding name, "Johanan". In any case Josephus lacks an equivalent to "Jonathan" following the four names which he has (10,160) in common with – though in a different order than – all witnesses to 40(47),8 // 25,23, i.e. Jōadēs, the son of Karias (= Johanan, son of Kareah, MT; Ιωανάν, etc., LXX), Sareas (= Seraiah, MT; Σαραια, etc., LXX), Jōazanias (= Jezaniah, MT; Ἰεζονιας, etc., LXX) and Ismaēlos (in the Bible "Ishmael" stands at the head of the list, while in Josephus he appears as the last of the four leaders named). He likewise leaves unmentiond the (otherwise unknown) group of "the sons of Ephai the Netophathite" of 40(47),8; cf., however, his phrase "and some others in addition to these" attached to his list of the four leaders which could be an allusion to these.

21. Both of the above terms are applied several times by Josephus to his arch-rival John of Gischala of whom the Josephan Ishmael appears as the "type"; see FELDMAN, *Studies*, p. 466 (= ID., *Gedaliah*, 5-6).

22. In MT 40,14 the name is "Baalis", while LXX 47,14 has Βεελιας, etc. In 10,164 Josephus will call the same king "Baalimos".

Jerusalemites) following the fall of Jerusalem (see 2 Kgs 25,7.18-25). Finally, the two terms used by Josephus of Ishmael here ("wicked, very crafty") obviously have in view this figure's later actions. At the same time they introduce an element of foreboding into the narrative, one that is completely lacking in the Bible's own initial, neutral mention of Ishmael.

Contentually, Josephus (10,161-162) essentially reproduces the speech of assurance and exhortation to the leaders which 40,9-10 attributes to Gedaliah. He does, however, make the governor's promise to the leaders somewhat more expansive and definite[23]. Thus, for 40,10a's "I will dwell at Mizpah, to stand before the Chaldeans who will come to us", he has Gedaliah "tell them that they should have him as their protector, so that, if anyone molested them, they would find him ready to help". A note of irony characterizes Josephus' formulation here seeing that in what follows Gedaliah will fail to "protect" even himself – much less anyone else – against the "molestor" Ishmael. Josephus further introduces into the governor's words a call for the leaders to summon "others" to assist their own forces in "rebuilding on the foundations", just as he provides a rationale for his urging them to lay in stores (see 40,10b), i.e. "in order to have food throughout the winter". He likewise takes care (10,162b) to round off the first "audience scene" with mention of Gedaliah's dismissal of the leaders[24].

Jer 40,11-12a narrates a general gathering at Mizpah on the part of Jews from the "diaspora", this (compare v. 7) occasioned by their "hearing" of Gedaliah's appointment, while v. 12b cites the harvest collected by them. Josephus leaves aside the latter notice, perhaps on the consideration that the rapid course of subsequent events would not have allowed time for such harvesting. Conversely, he (10,163) supplies a distinctive motivation for this second, more comprehensive assembly, one that itself recalls both his earlier characterization (10,155) of Gedaliah as "kind" and the wording of the governor's speech to the leaders in 10,161-162. This reads: "Now, when a rumour was spread among the nations (ἔθνη) round Judaea that Gadalias *had received with friendliness* (φιλανθρώπως)[25] *those of the fugitives who came to him, and had permitted them to settle down* (κατοικεῖν; see 10,162, *bis*) *and work the land* (γεωργοῦσι; cf.

---

23. On the point, see FELDMAN, *Studies*, p. 469 (= ID., *Gedaliah*, 9).

24. In Jeremiah 40 it is left unclear whether or not they are on hand for the following "assembly".

25. Josephus will twice subsequently use this term – or the cognate noun – in reference to Gedaliah; see 10,164.168. His application of it to the governor is of special interest given the fact that he employs the same language of his Roman patrons Vespasian and Titus with some frequency, see FELDMAN, *Studies*, pp. 464-466 (= ID., *Gedaliah*, 3,5).

γεωργοῦντας, 10,161) *on condition of paying* (τελεῖν)[26] *tribute to the Babylonian king*[27], they[28] too came together to Gadalias and settled on the land".

3. Gedaliah Warned

Jer 40,13-16 (= 10,164-167)[29] narrates Johanan and the other leaders' (unavailing) attempt to convince Gedaliah of the need to take measures against Ishmael, who, they charge, is bent on his destruction. In introducing the leaders' word, Josephus (10,164a) interjects a motivation for their attempt which further accentuates the positive image of the governor he has been developing: "when they observed (the nature of) the land (χώραν)[30] and the kindness and friendliness (χρηστότητα [see χρηστός of Jehoiachin, 10,100] καὶ φιλανθρωπίαν [cf. φιλανθρώπως, 10,163][31], [they] came to feel a very great affection (ὑπερηγάπησαν)[32]

26. This is the conjecture of Niese which Naber and Marcus follow. Dindorf and Bekker read τελέσειν with ROMSPE. See the similar case in 10,155 as cited in n. 7.

27. The Biblical basis for this component of what the Jews "hear" is Gedaliah's word to the leaders in 40,9, i.e. "serve (MT; LXX work for) the king of Babylon". In his reproduction of Gedaliah's speech to the leaders in 10,161-162 Josephus does not reproduce this reference to "serving" the Babylonian king as such. As we have seen, however, he does "anticipate" that item in his account of Nebuzaradan's measures in 10,155, using for it wording quite similar to that employed by him here in 10,163.

28. The grammatical subject here is "the nations" spoken of at the start of 10,163; see above. As MARCUS, *Josephus*, VI, p. 249, n. b remarks: "Josephus's language is decidedly careless; by 'they' he means the Jewish fugitives among the surrounding nations, not these nations themselves". Compare 40,11-12a (MT): "... when all the Jews who were in Moab and among the Ammonites and in Edom and in other lands heard... all the Jews returned from all the places to which they had been driven...".

29. The account in 2 Kgs 25,22-26 has no equivalent to this sequence. There, Gedaliah's address to the leaders (25,23-24 // 40,7-10) is followed directly by mention (25,25 // 41,1-3) of Ishmael's assassination of him.

30. This is the reading of the codices which Dindorf, Bekker, Niese, and Marcus follow. Naber does print the word in his text but tentatively (*Opera*, II, p. xxxix) suggests emending to χαρίν; cf. the translation of WEILL, *ad loc.*: "(Jean et les chefs... apprécièrent tant) *cette faveur*". With reference to Lat's plus ("provinciam in pace regi"), following its equivalent to the words τὴν χώραν, SCHALIT, *ad loc.* proposes to read τὴν χώραν εἰρηνικῶς διακειμένειν which he renders (את הארץ כי שלוה היא).

31. Compare AJ 8,214 where the people are said to look for "kindness and friendliness" (τὸ χρηστὸν καὶ φιλάνθρωπον) from Rehoboam. Rehoboam's subsequent failure to display these qualities in his dealings with the Israelites alienates them from him, whereas Gedaliah's evidencing of them causes the Jewish leaders to "feel a very great affection for him"; see above.

32. Elsewhere, Josephus uses ὑπεραγαπάω of the "great love" which one character has for another also in AJ 1,222 (Abraham for Isaac); 12,195 (Hyrcanus for his son Joseph); cf. 2,224 (Pharoah's daughter Thermuthis is "enchanted at the size and beauty" of the infant Moses). In 11,132 the verb has the sense "be greatly pleased".

for him". The Biblical source-passage (40,13-16) comprises a double exchange between leaders and governor in which Gedaliah twice reacts negatively to what is proposed to him. Josephus (10,164b-167), first of all, re-arranges matters so that all words of both speakers stand together in a continuous sequence. In so doing, he avoids the anomaly that Johanan's proposal of a pre-emptive strike against Ishmael (40,15) comes as his response to Gedaliah's "disbelief" (40,14b) of the leaders' previous accusation of Ishmael (40,14a), whereas one would expect Johanan rather – in first place at least – to attempt to substantiate his charge in face of the governor's incredulity. In formulating the leaders' words Josephus further introduces several modifications of their Biblical content. For one thing, he goes beyond 40,14 in supplying a rationale for "Baalimos's" (compare "Baaleim", 10,160) (alleged) commissioning of Ishmael to murder Gedaliah – one itself grounded in the reference to Ishmael's royal ancestry as cited in 41,1 (and already anticipated by Josephus in 10,160; see above): "… *in order that Ismaēlos might rule over the Israelites*[33], *for* he was of the royal line". In addition, he has the whole group of leaders instead of "Jōannēs" (Ἰωάννης)[34] alone (so 40,15) offering to eliminate Ishmael – a more plausible scenario.

Like 40,14b, Josephus (10,166) cites as Gedaliah's first response to the leaders' charge against Ishmael his "not believing" (ἀπιστεῖν; LXX 40,14: οὐκ ἐπίστευσεν) them. He proceeds, however, to attribute to the governor the following extended explanation of/ rationale for his "disbelief":

> … for, he said, it was not likely that a man who had not wanted for anything… should be found so base (πονηρόν) and ungrateful to his benefactor (εἰς τὸν εὐεργετήσαντα … ἀνόσιον)[35] as to seek to kill him with his own hands when it would be a wicked thing (ἀδίκημα) in itself for Ismaēlos not to be anxious (σπουδάζειν) to save (σῶσαι) him if he were plotted against by others.

Via this formulation Josephus once again accentuates his positive depiction of Gedaliah: the governor has been a generous "benefactor" to Ishmael, cf. his granting him, along with the other leaders, leave to

33. This designation for the surviving *Judeans* reflects Josephus' seemingly promiscuous manner of designating his people at various points in their history; compare his referring to the same group as "the Hebrew people" in 10,155.

34. Here in 10,164 Josephus uses this form of the leader's name which stands closer to the source's "Johanan" (MT)/ Ιωαναν (LXX) than does the form earlier employed by him in 10,160, i.e. "Jōadēs". Compare the difference regarding the name of the Ammonite king in 10,160 ("Baaleim") and 164 ("Baalimos").

35. With the above collocation "base and ungrateful" compare *AJ* 2,22 where Reuben tells his brothers that their plan to kill Joseph is πονηρὸν … καὶ θεῷ καὶ ἀνθρώποις ἀνόσιον.

settle where they choose in 10,162. At the same time, however, the
above wording constitutes an ironic verbal echo of the historian's own
previous characterization of Ishmael: Gedaliah finds it "not likely" that
Ishmael could be so "base" (πονηρόν) as the leaders allege, whereas
Josephus himself has already informed us that, in fact, Ishmael is a
"wicked" (πονηρός) man, 10,160.

   In 40,16 Gedaliah ends up forbidding Johanan to proceed against Ishmael on the grounds that he had "spoken falsely" of him. Josephus does
not represent Gedaliah thus formally prohibiting the leaders from acting
on their plan (see 10,165) to do away with Ishmael. Rather, he makes
(10,167) the governor affirm that even should their allegations be true,
"... it was better for him to die by the hands of Ismaēlos than to put to
death a man who had taken refuge with him and entrusted (πισ-
τεύσαντα; cf. ἀπιστεῖν, 10,166) his very life (σωτηρίαν; cf. σῶσαι,
10,166) into his hands for safe keeping". This statement too serves to
point up Gedaliah's nobility of mind: even while acknowledging – as
his Biblical counterpart never does – that the charges against Ishmael
may conceivably be true, he is, nonetheless, ready to die himself rather
than to do harm to one who had come to him as a suppliant[36].

4. *Gedaliah Murdered*

   In Jeremiah 40-41 (LXX 47-48) Gedaliah's last word to the leaders
(40,16) and the arrival of Ishmael at Mizpah (41,1) stand in such abrupt
juxtaposition that for the moment one is left uncertain as to whether the
leaders were on hand for the governor's assassination or not; only subsequently (see 41,11) does it emerge that, in fact, they were not on hand.
Josephus (10,168a) clarifies matters with yet another of his conclud-
ing/transitional notices[37]: "And so Jōannēs [see 10,164] and those of the
leaders who were with him went away without being able to convince
Gadalias". In his presentation, then, any ambiguity concerning the leaders' whereabouts at the time of the Mizpah massacre is removed; they
have departed the site in advance – and so will neither be able to prevent
it nor be among those murdered there by Ishmael – just as the Bible's
subsequent account presupposes, of course.

   36. FELDMAN, *Studies*, pp. 466-467 (= ID., *Gedaliah*, 6-7) points out that Josephus'
portrayal of Gedaliah's stance towards Ishmael here in 10,166-167 is "clearly reminiscent" of the historian's account of John of Gischala's plot against himself in *Vita* 85-88.
   37. Compare his appended mention of Gedaliah's dismissal of the leaders who had
come to him at the end of 10,162.

Jer 41,1 // 2 Kgs 25,25 date, without further specification, Ishmael's coming to Mizpah "in the seventh month", i.e. apparently of Zedekiah's eleventh regnal year in the fourth month of which Jerusalem's walls were breached (2 Kgs 25,3 // Jer 39,2 // 52,6) and in whose fifth month the city was devastated (25,8 // 52,12). Josephus (10,168b) gives an alternative dating for the villain's arrival: "when a period of thirty days had elapsed (i.e. a month after the leaders' warning of Gedaliah)[38]". From 41,1 // 25,25, Josephus further excises mention of Ishmael's royal ancestry, having already cited this twice previously (see 10,160.164)[39]. According to Jer 41,1b-2 Ishmael and his ten companions murdered[40] Gedaliah and those with him at Mizpah "as they ate bread together[41]". Josephus expatiates on this "context" for the assassination: Gedaliah "entertained" Ishmael and his suite "with a splendid banquet and presents (λαμπρᾷ τραπέζῃ καὶ ξενίοις) and, in his cordial reception (ὑποδεξάμμενος ... φιλοφρονούμενος [see 10,163.164])[42]... went so far as to become drunk (εἰς μέθην προήχθη)". This embellishment serves a variety of purposes in Josephus' version of the episode. It accentuates, one final time, the magnanimity of Gedaliah, who, warned as he has been about Ishmael's intent, still shows himself a generous and trusting host. At the same time, it also points up the governor's suicidal

38. MARCUS, *Josephus*, VI, p. 251, n. d points out that likewise Kimchi speaks of Ishmael's appearing at Mizpah one month after the departure of Johanan. Conceivably, Josephus' (and Kimchi's) alternative dating of Ishmael's arrival reflects the consideration that the chronology of events in Zedekiah's 11th year as found in 2 Kings 25 would not allow enough time – a mere two months – for all the happenings subsequent to the devastation of Jerusalem in the fifth month recounted in Jeremiah 40 (Nebuzaradan's initiatives, the double Mizpah assembly, the warning of Gedaliah by the leaders). Josephus' formulation, accordingly, is designed to allow for the possibility that more time would have elapsed between the destruction of Jerusalem and Ishmael's arrival at Mizpah. While neither the Bible nor Josephus specify the day of the month on which Ishmael came to Mizpah and murdered Gedaliah, *b. Roš. Haš.* 18b fixes this as the third day of the seventh month.

39. Like LXX Jer 48,1 (and MT BL 25,25) Josephus has Ishmael accompanied only by "ten men". In MT (and Targum) Jer 41,1 there is mention likewise of "officers of the (which?) king" (וְרַבֵּי הַמֶּלֶךְ) as part of Ishmael's entourage. On this and other differences between MT and LXX Jer 41(48),1-3(+7), see P.-M. BOGAERT, *La libération de Jérémie et le meutre de Godolias: le texte court (LXX) et la rédaction longue (MT)*, in D. FRANKEL *et al.* (eds.), *Studien zur Septuaginta: Robert Hanhart zu Ehren* (MSU, 20), Göttingen, Vandenhoeck & Ruprecht, 1991, 312-322, pp. 320-321.

40. In B 2 Kgs 25,25 the subject of this action is Ishmael alone, while MT and L read "they smote" in accordance with 41,2.

41. 2 Kgs 25,25 lacks this specification about the circumstances in which the massacre took place.

42. This elaboration of the datum of 41,1 about the parties "eating bread together" recalls a variety of similar contexts where Josephus goes beyond the Bible in depicting Jewish figures as exemplars of munificient hospitality; see on 9,25.

imprudence and indifference to the safety, not only of himself, but also of those to whom he had promised to be a "protector" (see 10,161). It is one thing not to allow a pre-emptive strike against a suspicious character, but quite another to totally drop one's guard in that character's presence. Finally, the historian's inserted reference to Gedaliah's "intoxication" provides an implicit answer to a question suggested by the Biblical account: How was it that Ishmael with a mere ten men (41,1 // 25,25; cf. n. 39) was able to assassinate Gedaliah and then butcher those staying with him without any resistance being offered? He could do so, Josephus' insertion intimates, because Gedaliah had rendered himself *hors de combat* in advance.

Thereafter (10,169) Josephus picks up the foregoing reference to the governor's "drunkenness" with a further insertion on Ishmael's recognizing the opportunity this afforded him: "seeing him in this condition, sunken into unconsciousness and a drunken sleep...". In thus launching his assault only when its intended victim has been rendered totally defenseless, Ishmael exemplifies both qualities previously attributed to him by Josephus (10,160), i.e. "wickedness" and "hyper-craftiness". Faced with the helplessness of his host, he experiences not a moment's hesitation or misgiving about exploiting the chance thus offered him. Thereafter, Josephus expands the source list (the Jews and the "Chaldean" soldiers residing at Mizpah, 41,3 // 25,25bβ) of Ishmael's victims with an additional category inspired by his preceding mention of the "banquet" put on by the governor: "(along with Gedaliah Ishmael killed) *those reclining with him at the banquet table* (ἐν τῷ συμποσίῳ); *after slaying them he went out by night*[43] and murdered all the Jews (᾽Ιουδαίους = BL 25,25 // LXX 48,3)[44] in the city and the soldiers[45] who had been left there by the Babylonians".

43. Also this chronological indication has no equivalent in 41,3 // 25,25. It underscores the "craftiness" of Ishmael who takes advantage of the surprise night would provide to attack Gedaliah's supporters.

44. Compare 10,164.165 where the reference is rather to "the Israelites". As we have been seeing, such oscillations in the designations used by him for his people are a characteristic feature of Josephus' presentation.

45. This specification concerning the identity of the Chaldeans/Babylonians slain by Ishmael corresponds to the phrase used of the Chaldeans in MT Jer 41,3, i.e. "the men of war" (אֵת אַנְשֵׁי הַמִּלְחָמָה) has no equivalent in the LXX parallel text (48,3) or in 2 Kgs 25,25. (Compare, however, BOGAERT, *Libération*, p. 321 for whom, taking MT's initial את in the sense of "with", the plus of MT 41,3 refers rather to Ishmael's own henchmen who assist him in dispatching the Chaldeans present at Mizpah.)

5. *Immediate Sequels*

Jer 41,4-18 (= 10,170-175; no parallel in 2 Kings 25) relates the immediate sequels to Ishmael's massacre. The first such sequel involves an additional slaughter perpetrated by him on the day after Gedaliah's murder (41,4-9). Jer 41,4-5 presents Ishmael's new victims as "eighty men... from Shechem, Shiloh and Samaria with their beards shaved and their clothes torn, and their bodies gashed, bringing cereal offerings and incense to present at the temple [literally house] of the Lord" who arrive at Mizpah on the next day. This description raises various questions: what are pilgrims from the reprobate North (Samaria!) doing bringing offerings to the Temple in Jerusalem[46] which itself no longer stands? What is the occasion for the mourning practices to which they have submitted themselves? Why too, do they appear in Mizpah if their destination is Jerusalem? Josephus' response to such questions is to drastically rework (10,170a) the Biblical portrayal of the eighty, doing so in such a way as to highlight – once again – the general esteem enjoyed by Gedaliah[47]. The travelers are spoken of by him in global terms as "of the country," with no reference to the three specific sites from which 41,5 has them proceed. The purpose and destination of their journey is likewise recast: they are headed, not to Jerusalem with offerings for the Temple, but rather to Mizpah itself, bearing "gifts" for Gedaliah. Finally, Josephus omits mention of the mourning practices Jer 41,5 ascribes to the travelers; in his presentation, wherein the 80 are headed to Mizpah to see Gedaliah (of whose death they know nothing, so 41,4) rather than to the devastated Temple (so 41,5), such practices on their part would have no *raison d'être*.

Like 41,6 Josephus has Ishmael (10,170b) invite the arrivals in "to Gedaliah". He does, on the other hand, eliminate the source verse's reference to the assassin's "weeping" as he approaches the 80 (so MT; in LXX 48,6 it is the travelers themselves who weep); in his version such an action by Ishmael would not make sense as an expression of sympathy for the visitors (whom he does not depict as in mourning themselves; see above), and might indeed be a cause of alarm for them. In then relating Ishmael's "disposing" of the hapless visitors (see 41,7),

---

46. This is the usual understanding of the reference to the "house of the Lord" as their destination. Some, however, identify the "house" in question as the sanctuary of Mizpah itself. See J. BLENKINSOPP, *The Judean Priesthood during the Neo-Babylonian and Achaemenid Periods: A Hypothetical Reconstruction*, in *CBQ* 60 (1998) 25-43, pp. 25-30.

47. On the point, see FELDMAN, *Studies*, pp. 469-470 (ID., *Gedaliah*, 9).

Josephus adds that he first "closed the gates of the court[48]". He further supplies a rationale for Ishmael's tossing their corpses into the pit/cistern as mentioned in 41,7, i.e. "that they might not be seen". Conversely, he passes over the (extraneous) historical notice of 41,9 about the Mizpah cistern having been constructed by King Asa.

In line with 41,8 Josephus recounts (10,171) Ishmael's sparing some of the eighty who tell him of goods they had hidden away. He leaves the precise number of the escapees unspecified, however (41,8 speaks of ten), and allots them a wider range of concealed commodities with which to bargain for their lives, i.e. not simply foodstuffs (compare 41,8: "wheat, barley, oil and honey"), but also "implements and clothing".

Jer 41,10 rounds off the account of Ishmael's initiatives with mention of his flight to the Ammonites with assorted captives in tow. Josephus (10,172) follows the source in its singling out the daughters of Zedekiah as among Ishmael's prisoners. Whereas, however, 41,10 speaks in a general way of the "people" remaining in Mizpah whom Ishmael takes with him, Josephus appends to his mention of "the people (λαόν, so LXX 48,10) left in Masphatha" whom Ishmael carries off a reference, anticipated from 41,16 where they are cited expressly, to his kidnapping of "their [the people's] wives and young children".

In Jer 41,11-12 Johanan and the other leaders "hear" of Ishmael's deeds, whereupon they set out in pursuit, overtaking his party "at the great pool which is in Gibeon" (v. 12b). Josephus (10,173) interjects a notice on the "indignation" (ἠγανάκτησαν) the news of Gedaliah's assassination causes the leaders (cf. the reference to their "great affection" for him in 10,164). Josephus' designation for the site where the two forces encounter each other differs, in any case, from the Biblical one ("Gibeon"), with RO (followed by Niese and Marcus) reading "Ibrōn" (Ἰβρῶνι), SPLaurV (followed by Dindorf, Bekker, and Naber) rather "Hebron" (Χεβρῶνι). Apparently, Josephus (or, alternatively, the manuscript tradition after him) misread a Hebrew "Gibeon" (or Greek Γαβαών) as one or other of these two place names – see the analogous case of 8,22 where for the "Gibeon" (LXX Gabaōn) of 2 Chr 1,3 our *AJ* codices read "Hebron" (which Thackeray/ Marcus emend to "Gibron")[49].

---

48. Literally: "closed off the court" (ἀποκλείσας τὴν αὐλήν [Niese reads αὔλειον]); see Marcus, *Josephus*, VI, p. 253, n. d.

49. So Weill, *Josèphe*, II, p. 335, n. 1 who calls the reading given by him in his translation of 10,173 (i.e. "Hebron") "une inadvertance de Josèphe". Schlatter, *Namen*, p. 34, and following him Schalit, *Namenwörterbuch*, p. 30, conjecture Γεβεωνι in 10,173.

Following 41,13-15 Josephus (10,174) proceeds to narrate the "rejoicing" (εὐθύμως διετέθησαν, so MT 41,13; LXX lacks an equivalent) which the approach of Johanan occasions Ishmael's captives who thereupon make their way to him, even while Ishmael himself gets off to the Ammonites with eight of his men. The Josephan version of these developments supplies an explicit motivation for the captives' "joy": this is due to their "thinking that they [the leaders] had come to help them". In Jer 41,16-18 the leaders and those just rescued by them end up at "Geruth Chimham" (LXX Γαβηρωθ Χαμααμ, v. 17) whence they envisage a flight to Egypt out of fear of Babylonian retribution for Gedaliah's murder. From 41,16 Josephus (10,175) takes over its list of the three categories of persons delivered by Johanan, i.e. "eunuchs and women and young children" (recall his earlier, anticipated mention of the two latter groups in 10,172). On the other hand, he leaves aside the Biblical mention of a fourth group of those rescued, i.e. "soldiers", perhaps in view of his own earlier reference (10,169 = MT Jer 41,3b) to Ishmael's killing "the soldiers who had been left there [in Mizpah] by the Babylonians". Here too (see 10,173), the localization given by Josephus for the events being recorded by him differs from the Biblical one. Thus, in place of 41,17's "Geruth Chimham near Bethlehem", he has the survivors assemble at "a certain place called Mandra (Μάνδρα)". Josephus' Greek form here has a first meaning of "fold, stable", etc; authors generally suggest that the word derives from the historian's reading the Hebrew consonantal form גרות (vocalized as גֵּרוּת in MT) as גְּדרֹות, "cattle pens[50]". Finally, in common with 41,17b-18 he makes (10,175b) the transition to the subsequent account of the Judeans' going to/ time in Egypt (Jeremiah 42-44 // 2 Kgs 25,26 = AJ 10,176-185) by noting that they were contemplating such a move out of fear of the Babylonians. At the same time, Josephus spells out what it is the survivors "fear" from the side of the Babylonians, i.e. "they might kill them, if they remained in the country, in their wrath over the murder of Gadalias...".

6. Flight to Egypt

2 Kgs 25,26 makes very summary mention of the Judean survivors betaking themselves to Egypt; Jer 42,1-43,7 tells of the circumstances

---

50. Thus SCHLATTER, Namen, p. 39, s.v. גֵּרוּת; THACKERAY, Josephus, The Man, p. 89, n. 1; SCHALIT, Namenwörterbuch, p. 82, s.v. Μάνδρα; PIOVANELLI, Texte, 31 and n. 68. WEILL, Josèphe, II, p. 335, n. 2 hesitatingly suggests that Josephus' form may rather represent a Greek transcription of the Aramaic word מגדרא ("hôtellerie"), itself a translation of Hebrew גרות (according to PIOVANELLI, ibid., the Aramaic word adduced by Weill "ne figure dans aucun lexique araméen").

surrounding their move in considerable detail. Josephus' acccount of the
happening (10,176-179) represents the mean between these extremes as
far as its length is concerned.

In Jer 42,1-6 there is a double address by leaders and people to the
prophet (vv. 2-3,5-6), between which stands a reply by the latter[51]. In a way
analogous to his treatment of the double exchange between the leaders and
Gedaliah of 40,13-16 in 10,164-167 (see above), Josephus (10,176) re-
arranges so that all the leaders'[52] words stand together in a continuous
sequence wherein his parallel to their "oath of obedience" (42,5-6) is
directly appended to his rendering of their appeal for Jeremiah's prophetic
offices (42,2-3) as an inducement for the prophet to do as requested by
them. At the same time, the historian also supplies a transition to this new
development: "while they were considering this plan (βουλῆς, i.e. of
going to Egypt, see 10,175]...". He likewise provides a motivation – which
he introduces within the leaders' speech itself – for the fact of their appealing to Jeremiah: "(they ask him to provide a divine directive about what
they should do) for they were unable to decide this". Conversely, in line
with his standard practice, he passes over the actual wording of the
oath/promise cited in 42,5-6, limiting himself to the notice "... they swore
they would do whatever Jeremiah told them". Josephus compresses
(10,177a) as well the prophet's reply (42,4) from which he eliminates Jeremiah's (presumptuous) statement of confidence that he will indeed have
something to say to them in the Lord's name ("... whatever the Lord
answers you I will tell you; I will keep nothing from you", v. 4b). His summary rendering of Jeremiah's response at the opening of 10,177 reads simply: "the prophet thereupon promised to use his good offices with God on
their behalf (διακονήσειν αὐτοῖς πρὸς τὸν θεόν)[53]".

The second unit within Jeremiah 42, i.e. vv. 7-22, cites the lengthy
divine response to Jeremiah's "inquiry". This is introduced in v. 7 with
a *Wortereignisformel*, coupled with the dating indication "at the end of
ten days". Josephus retains (10,177b) the latter item, but in accord with
his standard practice, uses substitute language for its "word happening

51. Jeremiah resurfaces rather abruptly in 42,1, nothing have been said of him since
40,7. A similar situation ordains in Josephus' account which has not mentioned Jeremiah
since 10,158. In both presentations one is left wondering where Jeremiah was at the time
of Ishmael's attack on Gedaliah and those with him at Mizpah, seeing that according to
40,6 = 10,158 the prophet had taken up residence there with Gedaliah.
52. In Jer 42,1 it is not only the two leaders Johanan and Azariah (so LXX/ MT Jezaniah), but also "all the people from the least to the greatest" who address Jeremiah. Josephus
(10,176) designates the prophet's interlocutors simply as "Jōannēs... and the leaders with
him", thereby echoing 10,164 where the same phrase is used of those addressing Gedaliah.
53. This is Josephus' only use of the construction διακονέω + πρός with "(the) God"
as object.

formula": "After ten days it happened that God appeared (φανέντα)[54] to him and told him to announce…". Thereafter, leaving aside the notice of 42,8 on Jeremiah's summoning of leaders and people, he gives a drastically shortened version of the prophet's word to them as reported in 42,9-22. In his rendition, that word consists simply of two conditional announcements which Jeremiah has been instructed by God to convey to leaders and people. Of these, the first (promise of God's protection of the people from the Babylonians if they remain in the land) has its protasis drawn from 42,10a, its apodosis from v. 11(12). The Josephan prophet's second, negative announcement, for its part, derives its conditional element ("if they set out to Egypt") from the double protasis in 42,13-14 and 15. To this Josephus appends a divine threat, not as such paralleled among those of 42,16-22, which he formulates as the negative counterpart to the preceding (conditional) promise (God "would be with them"), i.e. "he [God] would abandon them…". This generalized warning is then amplified with what reads like a version of 42,18 ("as my anger and my wrath were poured out on the inhabitants of Jerusalem, so my wrath will be poured out on you…"). It runs: "… in His anger (ὀργισθείς) [he would] visit upon them the same treatment 'which, as you know[55], your brothers (ἀδελφούς) suffered (πεπονθότας)[56] before you'". In limiting himself to the above two conditional formulations, Josephus avoids the anomaly of Jeremiah's words as cited in 42,19-22 where, even before the people have responded to the divine message, the prophet accuses them of disregarding it (see v. 21).

To his transitional notice (10,178) that Jeremiah did, in fact, deliver the word confided to him by God, Josephus then appends his parallel to 43,1-3, the leaders and people's reaction. He opens his report of their response with a verbal echo of his earlier reference (10,166) to Gedaliah's "not believing" (ἀπιστεῖν) the leaders' salutary warning concerning Ishmael. Now the roles are reversed with Jōannēs and the people themselves "not believing" (οὐκ ἐπιστεύετο) Jeremiah's equally urgent admonition. The hearers "unbelief" finds expression in

54. On Josephus' penchant for introducing references to a divine "appearance" where the Bible speaks only of the operation of God's "word", see on 9,20.

55. Note the switch from indirect to direct address here at the end of the prophet's discourse.

56. This is the reading of ROM which Niese and Marcus follow. Dindorf, Bekker, and Naber read παθόντας with SPLaurV. The above warning echoes that which Josephus attributes to the prophets of Manasseh's time in 10,39a who threatened their hearers "with the same calamities which had befallen their Israelite brothers (ἀδελφούς)". (In both contexts as well the prophetic admonition is disregarded by the hearers; see 10,39b.178, respectively.) On Josephus' relatively infrequent use of the term "brothers" as a collective term for his people, see p. 445, n. 29.

a series of assertions made by them and drawn by Josephus from
43,2b-3: "(They did not believe that) it was at God's command (κατ'
ἐντολὴν τὴν ἐκείνου) he bade them remain in the country, but that
to please Baruch, his own disciple (μαθητῇ; see 10,158)[57], he was
belying God (καταψεύδεσθαι ... τοῦ θεοῦ)[58] and trying to persuade
them to remain there in order that they might be destroyed by the
Babylonians".

Jer 43,4 rounds off the hearers' response with the statement "they did
not obey the voice of the Lord". Josephus (10,179) formulates equivalently: "... the people and Jōannēs disregarded (παρακούσας) the counsel (συμβουλίας)[59] of God, which He had given them through the
prophet...". Thereafter, he compresses the source's elaborate notice
(43,5-7) on the move to Egypt by various groups of Gedaliah's surviving protégés (see v. 6a) and its specification of "Tahpanhes" as their
arrival point (v. 7b) into the concise remark "... (they) departed for
Egypt, taking both Jeremiah and Baruch (see 43,7aβ.6b)".

7. God's Word in Egypt

The lengthy segment Jer 43,8-44,30 features divine communications to Jeremiah upon his arrival in Egypt. Within this complex 43,8-
13 comprises "the word which came to Jeremiah in Tahpanhes" (v. 8;
cf. v. 7b), itself consisting of a "sign" which the prophet is directed to
carry out, this involving the hiding of "large stones" in front of
Pharoah's palace in the city (v. 9) and an appended announcement
(vv. 10-13) regarding the coming Babylonian occupation of Egypt.
Leaving aside the obscure Biblical "sign of the stones", Josephus
(10,180) reformulates the *Wortereignisformel* of v. 8 (see on 10,177
above) as: "the Deity revealed (σημαίνει)[60] to the prophet that...".

---

57. This reference to Baruch's presence alongside Jeremiah is, as we noted above,
prepared by Josephus' (inserted) mention of the prophet's request for his disciple's
release in 10,158. By contrast, the allusion to Baruch in 43,3 itself appears rather unexpected in that nothing has been said of him since Jer 36,32.

58. Josephus employs the above genitival construction "belie God" also in *BJ* 6,228
(subject: the false prophets at the time of the Roman siege of Jerusalem) and *AJ* 8,404
(Micaiah affirms that "it is not possible for him to *tell falsehoods in God's name*").

59. This is the reading adopted by Dindorf, Bekker, Niese, Naber, and Marcus. The
codices SP read συμμαχίας. The above genitival phrase "disregard counsel" recurs in *AJ*
14,436 (Machera had "disregarded the counsel" of Herod). Note its echo of the opening
words of 10,176: "while they [the leaders] were considering this plan (βουλῆς)...".

60. Elsewhere, Josephus uses God/the Deity as subject of the verb σημαίνω also in
AJ 2,276; 6,50.92.271; 8,294.405.409; 10,238.

He extracts the content of God's revelation to Jeremiah from 43,11, while disregarding what precedes (i.e. v. 10: Nebuchadnezzar will set his throne on the stones hidden by Jeremiah; see v. 9, likewise left unused by Josephus) and follows (i.e. the Babylonian's king's future measures against the Egyptian cult, 43,12-13). His parallel to 43,11 itself reads: "... the king of Babylonia was about to march against the Egyptians... and Egypt would be taken and... the Babylonian king would kill some of them and would take the rest captive *and carry them off to Babylon*[61]".

Josephus passes over (although see n. 64) the whole extended exchange between Jeremiah and the people in Egypt concerning the latter's continuing idolatry as narrated in Jeremiah 44 with its concluding reiteration of the doom awaiting the Judean refugees there (44,27-30; compare 43,11)[62]. In place thereof he appends (10,181-182) to the foregoing divine announcement a notice on its fulfillment. He commences this latter item by picking up on the mention, found in Jer 52,30, of a third Babylonian deportation of (745) Jews in Nebuchadnezzar's 23rd regnal year. In the Biblical verse the general Nebuzaradan is the subject of this action, and it is not specified whence or where he carried off his Jewish captives. Josephus turns this reference to what Nebuzaradan did in Nebuchadnezzar's 23rd year into an enumeration of three successive conquests effected by the king himself in that year, i.e. of Coele-Syria, the Moabites and Ammonites[63], and finally Egypt. In recounting (10,182) the last of these Babylonian conquests (and its sequels)[64], Josephus uses wording reminiscent of the divine announcement cited by him in 10,180 (see above): "... (Nebuchadnezzar) invaded Egypt in order to subdue it, and, having killed (κτείνει) the king who was then reigning and appointed another[65], he

61. This specification concerning where the Judeans who have come to Egypt will be taken as "captives" has no counterpart in 43,11 itself. It does, however, correspond to Josephus' own "fulfillment notice" in 10,182; see below.

62. In leaving this segment aside Josephus eliminates a Biblical passage which reflects quite poorly on his people; see, in particular, the Judeans' assertion of their intention to resume their worship of the "queen of heaven" in vv. 15-19. Compare his similar non-utilization of the "Golden Calf" passage, Exodus 32(33-34).

63. MARCUS, *Josephus*, VI, p. 259, n. a suggests that Josephus found inspiration for his mention of Nebuchadnezzar's subjugation of these two peoples in the oracles against Moab and the Ammonites of Jeremiah 48 and 49,1-6 (MT), respectively.

64. The Bible itself does not, as such, relate a conquest of Egypt by Nebuchadnezzar. MARCUS, *Josephus*, VI, 259, n. a proposes that the historian "probably used Berosus as a source" for his notice on the matter. Jeremiah's oracles against Egypt in 46,2-26 (as also in 43,11-13; 44,30) might be an alternative/additional such source.

65. This element of Josephus' "fulfillment notice" has no precise counterpart in the divine announcement of 10,180 itself which speaks in more general terms of Nebuchadnezzar's "killing (ἀποκτενεῖ) some of them [i.e. the Egyptians]". It does, however, have

again[66] took captive the Jews who were in the country and carried them to Babylon (see n. 61)[67]".

To his mention, 10,181-182, of the Babylonian deportation of Jews from Egypt (distantly) inspired by Jer 52,30 (see above), Josephus appends, 10,183-185, a series of summarizing indications which have, as such, no Biblical counterpart, but which are reminiscent of the notices with which he rounds off his accounts of the fall of Samaria and of Jerusalem in 9,280-287.290b-291 and 10,143.147-148.151-153, respectively. The complex reads:

> (183) And so, as we have learned from history, the Hebrew race (τὸ ... Ἑβραίων γένος) twice came (δὶς ἐλθόν)[68] to such a pass as to go beyond the Euphrates. For the people of the ten tribes were driven out (ἐξέπεσεν) of Samaria by the Assyrians in the reign of Osēēs [see 9,278], and once again, the people of the two tribes who survived the capture of Jerusalem were driven out by Nebuchadnezzar, the king of Babylonia and Chaldaea [see 10,150] (184) Now, when Salmanassēs (Σαλμανάσσης)[69] removed (ἀναστήσας) the Israelites, he settled in their place the nation of the Chuthaeans (τὸ τῶν Χουθαίων ἔθνος), who had formerly lived in the interior of Persia and Media and who were then, moreover, called Samaritans because they assumed the name of the country in which they were settled[70]. But the king of Babylonia, when he carried off the two tribes, did not settle any nation in their place, and for this reason all of Judaea and Jerusalem and the temple (ναός)[71] remained deserted for seventy years[72]. (185) Now

a (partial) Biblical basis in Jer 44,30 where the Lord announces through the prophet: "... I will give Pharoah Hophra king of Egypt into the hand of his enemies and into the hand of those who seek his life...".

66. With this term Josephus refers back to his mentions of Nebuchadnezzar's earlier capture/ deportation of Jews; see AJ 10,98.101.150.

67. Note that in the above formulation Josephus, in contrast to the notice of Jer 52,30, does not specify the number (745 according to 52,30) of Jews taken captive in Nebuchadnezzar's 23rd year.

68. This is the reading adopted by Dindorf, Bekker, Niese, Naber, and Marcus. Compare διελθών, ME; εἰσελθὼν δέ, RO; transisse, Lat; μετενεχθέν, Zon.

69. This is the reading adopted, on the basis of Lat's Salamanassis, by Niese and Marcus. Dindorf, Bekker, and Naber read Σαλμανασαρής with ROMPVE. Josephus' account of this king and his dealings with the Israelites is found in 9,277-287; see chap. XVI.

70. This formulation harks back Josephus' notices on the Chuthaeans/Samaritans in 9,278-279.288.290. (In 9,279.288 Josephus gives a somewhat different indication concerning the original homeland of the Chuthaeans than here in 10,184 [the interior of Persia and Media], i.e. the area around a river in Persia called "Chūtha".)

71. This is the reading adopted by Dindorf, Bekker, Niese, Naber, and Marcus. ROMSP read λαός.

72. The above notice concerning the "deserted status" of Judea, etc. seems inspired by 2 Chr 36,21 which speaks of the land "enjoying its sabbaths" and "lying desolate for seventy years", this as the fulfillment of the word of Jeremiah (see 25,11-12; 29,10) about the 70 years of Babylonian hegemony. Recall that Josephus has made previous use of the prophet's "70-year word" in the speech which he attributes to Jeremiah in 10,112. Note further that 2 Chr 36,21 itself makes no mention of the on-going devastation of the

the entire interval of time from the captivity of the Israelites until the deportation (ἀνάστασιν; cf. ἀναστήσας, 10,184) of the two tribes amounted to (διεληλύθει)[73] one hundred and thirty years, six months and ten days[74].

Conclusions: Josephus' Rewriting of Jeremiah 40-44 // 2 Kgs 25,22-26

Following his usual practice, Josephus, in 10,155-185, bases himself for his account of Gedaliah's governorship and its aftermath, not on the summary narrative of 2 Kgs 25,22-26, but rather on the more expansive presentation of Jeremiah 40-44, even while significantly abridging the latter's text content. As for the text-form of Jeremiah 40-44 (LXX 47-51) utilized by Josephus, we noted instances of his agreement with distinctive readings of both MT and LXX for the five chapters in question. With the latter he has in common, e.g., his reference to the "gifts" Nebuzaradan gives Jeremiah (10,158 = LXX 47,5b) and, negatively, his non-mention of "the officers of the king" (so MT 41,1) accompanying Ishmael and his ten men (10,168 = LXX 48,1; see n. 39). Like MT and against LXX, on the other hand, Josephus makes explicit reference to Babylonian "soldiers" slain by Ishmael (10,169 = 41,3), just as he notes, in line with MT's plus, the "rejoicing" of Ishmael's captives on seeing the approach of their rescuers (10,174 = 41,13).

The segment 10,155-185 displays noteworthy examples of Josephus' various rewriting techniques. His numerous *additions to/expansions of* source data include: the inserted characterization of Nebuzaradan's appointee, Gedaliah (10,155; compare 25,22 // 40,7); Jeremiah's thinking with regard to the choices offered him (10,157a) Nebuzaradan's directive to Gedaliah about the care of Jeremiah (10,157b); the prophet's request for Baruch's release (10,158b); Nebuzaradan's return to Babylon (10,159a), Ishmael's qualities and his whereabouts during the siege

Temple; Josephus' specific mention of the matter is in line with the recurrent references to the fate of the Temple which he introduces into the words of Jeremiah as cited by him; see p. 547, n. 48.

73. This is the conjecture of Niese which Naber and Marcus adopt. Dindorf and Bekker read ἐληλύθει with the codices and E.

74. As MARCUS, *Josephus*, VI, pp. 260-261, n. a points out, the above figure for the length of time (130+ years) from the fall of Samaria in Hezekiah's 7th year (so 9,278) to the deportation that occurred in the 11th year of Zedekiah/ 18th of Nebuchadnezzar (10,146) (or, alternatively the latter's 23rd year, see 10,181) does not tally with the chronological indications given by him between 9,278 and 10,146/10,181 which would total 132 or 137 years, respectively. For a similar case of chronological discrepancy, see on 9,280.

of Jerusalem (10,160; compare 40,8); Gedaliah's dismissal of the leaders (10,162 *in fine*); the leaders' "affection" for the "gracious" Gedaliah (10,164; compare 40,13); the reason for Baalis' dispatching Ishmael to kill Gedaliah (10,164b; compare 40,14a); the elaboration of Gedaliah's reply to the leaders (10,166-167; compare 40,14b.16); the leaders' withdrawal (10,168a); Gedaliah's bounteous entertaining of Ishmael (10,168b; compare 25,25 // 41,2); Ishmael's recognizing his opportunity and killing also those at table with Gedaliah (10,169a); the reason for the "joy" of Ishmael's captives (10,174; compare 41,13); the survivors' apprehension of Babylonian "wrath" (10,175; compare 41,18); the motivation behind the leaders' consultation of Jeremiah (10,176; compare 42,1); and the entire segment 10,181-185 with its fulfillment notice (10,181-182) for the announcement made to Jeremiah by God in Egypt (10,180), and the appended indications about the various deportations suffered by the Jews (10,183-185).

Conversely, Josephus also markedly *compresses* the source segment Jeremiah 40-44, especially its chapters 42-44. He does so, e.g., in connection with the following Scriptural data: Nebuzaradan's opening word to Jeremiah (40,2-3); the harvest notice of 40,12b; the mourning practices of the eighty who approach Ishmael (41,4; compare 10,170); the origin of the cistern into which Ishmael casts the bodies (41,9), the "soldiers" rescued by the leaders (41,16; compare 10,175); the leaders' appeal to Jeremiah (42,2-3.5-6; compare 10,176) and the prophet's reply to this (42,4; compare 10,177a); the divine message that comes to Jeremiah after ten days (42,7-22; compare 10,177b); the description of the flight to Egypt, ending up in Tahpanhes (43,4-7; compare 10,179); the initial divine communication to Jeremiah in Egypt (43,8-13; compare 10,180), and the entire passage 44,1-30 with its additional prophetic announcements to the people in Egypt and their response to these.

This sequence of *AJ* 10,155-185 is further marked by several *rearrangements* of the Biblical sequence. Thus, e.g., the matter of Ishmael's royal ancestry is "anticipated" (10,160.164; compare 41,1), as is his carrying off also of women and children (10,172; compare 41,16). Similarly, Gedaliah's directive about the survivors' serving the king of Babylon (25,24 // 40,9) gets repositioned as a prior measure emanating from Nebuzaradan himself (10,155). By contrast, the Bible's earlier references to the fate of the "poor" and the "deserters" (see 2 Kgs 25,11-12) are integrated into Josephus' account of a later development, i.e. the appointment of Gedaliah (10,155). Likewise, Josephus' listing of the leaders who call on Gedaliah (10,160) mentions Ishmael in last rather than first place (so 25,23 // 41,8).

Also prominent throughout 10,155-185 are Josephus' *adaptations/ modifications* of the source account(s). He consistently replaces references to the divine "word/voice" with alternative language (10,177; compare 42,7; 10,179; compare 43,4.7; 10,180; compare 43,8). For the references (40,1b.4a) to Nebuzaradan's freeing Jeremiah from the "chains" he had earlier imposed on him, the historian substitutes (10,156) wording seemingly inspired by another context of the Book of Jeremiah, i.e. 39,13-14a. The Jews from the neigbhoring countries come to Gedaliah having heard, not of his appointment as governor (so 40,11), but rather of the graciousness exhibited by him (10,164). The leaders *en bloc* – not Johanan alone (so 41,15) – offer to eliminate Ishmael (10,165). The assassin's coming to Mizpah is dated "after thirty days" (10,168), instead of "in the seventh month" (so 25,25 // 41,1). The eighty persons who run afoul of Ishmael were coming with "gifts for Gedaliah" (10,170) rather than with "offerings for the house of the Lord" (41,5). Josephus' names for the sites where the leaders overtake Ishmael (Ibron/ Hebron [10,173] vs. Gibeon 41,12] and where they assemble the survivors ("Mandra" [10,175] vs. "Geruth-Chimham" [41,17]) both differ from those given in the Bible. Lastly, the measures taken in Nebuchadnezzar's 23rd regnal year are attributed to the king himself (10,182), as opposed to his general Nebuzaradan (so Jer 52,30) and involve, not just the deportation of a group of Jews, but the conquest of a whole series of nations.

Josephus' utilization of the above rewriting techniques makes of 10,155-185 an account of events subsequent to Jerusalem's fall and devastation with a variety of distinctive features. He drastically streamlines the lengthy series of divine and human discourses cited in Jeremiah 42-44 in 10,176-180. On the other hand, in a whole of series of instances, he spells out matters that the Bible leaves readers to fill in for themselves, i.e. Nebuzaradan's return to Babylon (10,169); Gedaliah's dismissal of the leaders (10,162); their subsequent departure prior to the coming of Ishmael (10,168); and the fulfillment of the divine words of doom for Egypt and the Jews who had taken refuge there (10,181). He goes beyond the Bible as well in supplying explicit evaluations of characters (see 10,155 [Gedaliah]; 10,160 [Ishmael]), and in evoking figures' feelings and motivations (the leaders' "affection" for Gedaliah [10,164] and their "anger" at his murder [10,173]). The "assassination scene" is related in considerably more dramatic fashion in 10,169 than in the source text(s), 25,25 // 41,3. The whole complex of events from Gedaliah's appointment through the divine words of doom pronounced in Egypt receives more emphatic closure via the expansive appendix of 10,181-185.

Especially noteworthy are the distinctive "retouchings" evidenced by Josephus' portrait of the story's four main (human) characters. Nebuzaradan, as the representative of Babylon, appears more respectful and solicitous vis-à-vis Jeremiah, who, for his part, takes on a more assertive posture in Josephus' presentation. The historian further gives us a Gedaliah whose all-inclusive hospitality (see 10,163-164.169) and high-mindedness is accentuated (see on 10,166-167), even as is his imprudence in the face of the threat posed by Ishmael (10,169), this notwithstanding the "protector" role he had assumed (10,161)[75]. Over against him stands his nemesis, Ishmael whom Josephus portrays in still more unrelievedly negative colors than the source(s), doing so with wording employed elsewhere by him of his own arch-enemy, John of Gischala (see nn. 21, 36).

Josephus' retelling of the events commencing with Gedaliah's appointment has something to offer both his intended audiences. To Gentile readers it presents the sympathetic figure of the Jewish leader Gedaliah who dies upholding the requirements of hospitality, evidences a willingness to work constructively with Babylon, the Rome of his day, and who is, finally, a recognizably tragic figure reminiscent of the protagonists of Greek drama. His rewriting likewise withholds from his Gentile public the unedifying fact about his people reported in Jeremiah 44 (see vv. 15-19; cf. n. 62), i.e. their stated intention of resuming their idolatrous worship which would militate against the image of the Jews as a people singularly devoted to its God and his Law that Josephus is concerned to convey to that public (see, e.g., c. Ap. 2,179-181). As for Jewish readers, Josephus' portrayal of the conflict between Gedaliah and Ishmael is designed to intimate the rightness of his own Gedaliah-like stance towards the occupying power and the wrongfulness of the efforts to thwart this on the part of John of Gischala, the Ishmael of the day. Thus, also in this instance, Josephus' rewriting of Scripture shows itself to be one intended to convey a double message.

---

75. More clearly than in the Bible itself Gedaliah thus appears in Josephus' presentation as a good man with a tragic flaw. As such he reminds one of the Josephan Zedekiah; see the conclusion to chap. XXIII.

CONCLUSIONS

By way of conclusion to this study I shall now attempt to bring together its more salient findings on the overarching questions concerning *AJ* 9,1–10,185 posed in the introduction. I do this following the sequence in which those questions were cited there.

Sources

The (written) sources utilized by Josephus in *AJ* 9,1–10,185 pertain to three main categories: the Biblical Historical Books; the Biblical Prophetic Books (i.e. the Latter Prophets); and extra-Biblical writings. Of these categories, the first provides the basis and organizational framework for Josephus' account of the later monarchy. The category itself comprises the paralllel segments 2 Kings 1–25 and 2 Chronicles 19–36. Josephus clearly drew on both these segments, as appears from the presence in his narration of *Sondergut* from each of them; see, e.g., Kings' material on the Northern rulers and the Chronicler's lengthy report of Hezekiah's cultic reforms (2 Chronicles 29–31 = *AJ* 9,260-276; compare the single verse notice of 2 Kgs 18,4 on the topic). In those instances where one of his two biblical historical sources provides a notably more elaborate account of a given king, Josephus generally follows this in preference to the other source's shorter presentation; see, e.g., 9,105-139 where he bases himself on 2 Kgs 8,25–10,31 versus 2 Chr 22,2-9 in relating Jehu's bloody revolt and, conversely, 9,243b-259 where he goes together with 2 Chronicles 28 against the more summary 2 Kings 16 for his treatment of Ahaz. Where the two sources generally run parallel to each other, but differ in details, Josephus typically oscillates between them, utilizing items now from one, now from the other as can be seen, e.g., in his version of Josiah's reign, 10,49-80, in comparison to 2 Kgs 22,1–23,30 and 2 Chr 34,1–35,27. In all these cases Josephus evidences his intention of making maximal use of the data of both his historical sources – in so far as these do not militate against other of his authorial purposes (see under "omissions" below).

Into the "royal framework" provided him by the Biblical Historical Books Josephus incorporates, over the course of 9,1–10,185, material drawn from five of the (Latter) Prophetic Books, i.e. Jonah, Nahum, Isaiah, Jeremiah, and Ezekiel; cf. also the allusions to Zech 14,4-5 worked into his account of Uzziah's punishment in 9,225 (= 2 Chr 26,19). Thereby, first of all, he goes beyond both Kings and Chronicles, in accentuating the "prophetic presence" in the period of the later monarchy[1]. In all but one instance, he inserts this prophetic material within his account of that/ those king(s) to whose reign(s) Biblical tradition dates the prophet in question (e.g., Jonah under Jeroboam II, see 9,205-215; cf. 2 Kgs 14,27). Biblical tradition fails to provide such a dating for the prophet Nahum. Accordingly, Josephus, on his own, places Nahum in the reign of Jotham of Judah (9,236-243a), doing this perhaps with the intent of making Nahum's prophecy of Assyria's overthrow come in close proximity to the similar prophecy of Jonah (see chap. XI). As for Josephus' principle(s) of selection in his use of the above five (six) prophetic books[2], he concentrates, as we have noted, on the "true" predictions which he found recorded therein, while leaving aside, e.g, the call narratives of Isaiah, Jeremiah, and Ezekiel, the wording of Jonah's prayer (Jonah 2,2-10; compare 9,214), as well as the "confessions" of Jeremiah. He does, on the other hand, also make use of some of the narrative material associated with the words attributed to Jonah and Jeremiah in their respective books. His procedure in both these instances was, we suggested, influenced by "apologetic" considerations: the story of Jonah at sea recounted in Jonah 1 (= 9,209-212) depicts a sympathetic interaction between a Jew and Gentiles, just as the narratives of Jeremiah's tribulations at the hands of his opponents, the Jerusalem "resistance party", incorporated by him throughout 10,89-180 provide a Biblical "precedent" for the persecution experienced by Josephus himself during the Jewish War. In addition, Josephus makes use of the Book of Jeremiah to supplement the Historical Books' own rather meager notices on the siege of Jerusalem and its immediate aftermath; see 10,135b (= Jer 39,3: the names of the Babylonian commanders who took possession of Jerusalem). 155-185 (= Jer 40,1–44,20 [compare 2 Kgs 25,22-26]: the governorship of Gedaliah and the subsequent flight to Egypt of the surviving Judeans).

In line with his aim of showing Gentile readers that the figures and events spoken of in the Bible may be corroborated by the testimony of

---

1. Josephus also, of course, makes extensive use, in 9,1–10,185, of the material concerning the various "pre-classical" prophets (e.g., Elijah and Elisha in particular) found in Kings and/or Chronicles. Under this head we might recall too his references to Isaiah in 10,1-36 for which he had available both the "historical" segment 2 Kgs 18,13–20,19 and its "prophetic" parallel, Isa 36,1–39,8 (see chaps. XVII-XVIII).

2. Recall that Josephus leaves aside completely the "preexilic" prophetic figures/books of Hosea, Amos, Zephaniah, and Habakkuk, while he cites Micah only as part of his version of Jeremiah 26 in *AJ* 10,92.

non-Jewish historians as well, Josephus further thrice explicitly cites or alludes to extra-Biblical sources over the course of 9,1–10,185. The three instances of his doing so are 9,283-287 (the Tyrian annals and their translator Menander concerning the assault on Tyre undertaken by "Salmaneser", the conqueror of Samaria; see 9,277-282); 10,18b-20 (the accounts by Herodotus and Berosus of Sennacherib's failed campaign against Egypt, cf. 10,17-18a; compare 2 Kgs 19,9b); and Berosus' mention of "Baladas" (10,34c), the Babylonian king who sent envoys to Hezekiah according to 2 Kgs 20,12-19 // Isa 39,1-8. Also to be mentioned in this connection are the notices on Damascene traditions reported by the historian in 9,93b-94a which may derive from Nicolas of Damascus; see there. By means of such (ultimately rather limited) references to extra-Biblical historians Josephus imparts a more cosmopolitan flavor to his account of the later Israelite/Judean monarchy.

Under the sources heading, reference should, finally, be made as well to Josephus' apparent utilization – in whatever form he made have known these – of post-Biblical Jewish midrashic traditions concerning various figures and events; see, e.g., his reference to Hezekiah's childlessness at the moment of his life-threatening sickness (10,27) and his specification that Manasseh's persecution numbered prophets among its victims (10,38).

Biblical Text-form(s)

A whole range of factors militates against one's drawing assured conclusions concerning Josephus' Bible text(s) in 9,1–10,185 (as throughout AJ 1–11), i.e. uncertainties about the Josephan text itself, the wide degree of (content) agreement among the Biblical textual witnesses for the particular book/passage being used by him, and above all, the historian's tendency to paraphrase the wording of his sources. Nonetheless, we have, over the course of this study, encountered noteworthy points of contact between Josephus' presentation and the distinctive readings of MT[3], LXX (BL)[4], and the Targums[5] for his two primary sources, i.e. 2 Kings 1–25 and 2 Chronicles 19–36. He likewise seems to have had several text-forms of the Books of Jonah and Nahum available to him (see chaps. XI and XIII, respectively). We noted as well (isolated) instances

---

3. See, e.g., on 9,42-43.62.98.102.125.218; 10,50.69.
4. See, e.g., on 9,1.27.43.122.149. On Josephus' affinities with readings peculiar to L 2 Kings, see on 9,27.176.185; 10,48a.65.
5. See, e.g., on 9,47.117.227.

of his apparent acquaintance with LXX readings in the Books of Isaiah (see 10,23 = LXX Isa 37,38: "Armenia" as the place of refuge of Shalmaneser's assassins) and Zechariah (see 9,225 = LXX Zech 14,5: the roads obstructed by pieces of the mountain that had been broken off by the earthquake). Finally, as P. Piovanelli has argued, and this study has confirmed, Josephus made predominate -albeit not exclusive – use of the longer MT/Targumic text of the Book of Jeremiah as opposed to the shorter form represented by LXX[6]. Overall, then, it seems possible to conclude that Josephus did know the Biblical books utilized by him in 9,1–10,185 in a variety of text-forms[7]

Rewriting Techniques

In summing up here on the rewriting techniques employed by Josephus in 9,1–10,185, I shall make use of the same four (overlapping and interconnected) categories distinguished throughout this study, i.e. additions/expansions; omissions/ abridgements; re-arrangements; and modifications/adaptations.

1) *Additions/ Expansions.* All through his narrative of the later monarchy, Josephus does not hesitate to add to or expatiate on what he found in his sources. Instances of this phenomenon differ greatly in extant, however, ranging from a inserted word or phrase to sequences of several paragraphs. They also serve a range of functions. Oftentimes, the historian's elaborations of source wording are stylistic in nature. Thus, by way of interjected *Rückverweise* (see, e.g., on 9,1), foreshadowings (see, e.g., on 9,3.13.105.275b-276), *Wiederaufnahmen* (see, e.g., on 9,228a), and the use of verbal/content "echoes" of his own earlier presentation (see, e.g., 9,31: Jehoshaphat's ["un-Biblical"] entertaining of Joram of Israel recalls Ahab's earlier feasting of the former) he smooths the transitions between different segments of his narrative and gives it a higher degree of overall unity. Similarly, he provides clearer closure to the story's individual episodes via the closing notices which he appends to many of these (see, e.g., 9,50,183a; 10,23 [*in fine*]). At times, he introduces remarks on his own editorial procedures (see, e.g., 9,208a.214b [his inclusion of the Jonah story). 242 [his abbreviation of

---

6. For indications of his (secondary) use of LXX Jeremiah, see, e.g., on 10,93.158.
7. This conclusion with regard to Josephus' Bible text(s) for 9,1-10,185 coincides with the one reached by me concerning the Biblical text-form(s) utilized by him in *AJ* 8,212-420; see BEGG, *Early Divided Monarchy*, pp. 271-276.

Nahum's words). Frequently too the added elements inform us of the emotions and motivations of the story's characters (see, e.g., Josephus' spelling out of the reason for Hezekiah's lament [2 Kgs 20,2-3 // Isa 38,2-3] in 10,25b-26). In the same line he introduces explicit evaluations of Biblical personages and their actions (e.g., Gedaliah is "kind and just", 10,155; Ishmael "wicked and very crafty", 10,160; cf. also the epithet for Elisha in 9,182). Points of interest about various Biblical sites are noted as is that site's position in relation to another location (see, e.g., 9,7: Engadē lies a hundred stades from Jerusalem and produces "the finest palm-trees and opobalsamum"). In a number of instances contemporary equivalents for Biblical weights and measures are supplied (see, e.g., 9,86). The roles of both priests (see, e.g., 9.144,148,150) and prophets (see 9,265b-267;10,38a.79-80.106b-107.141) in the unfolding of events receive additional (positive) mention. Certain of Josephus' insertions are designed to answer questions left unanswered by the source(s) (see, e.g., 9,74; compare 2 Kgs 7,3: what are the lepers doing outside the walls of besieged Jerusalem?) or to resolve their apparent contradictions/ implausibilities (see, e.g., 9,60; compare 2 Kgs 6,23-24: the cessation, followed by immediate resumption of the Syrian attacks on Israel). Occasionally (and somewhat uncharacteristically; see below), he inserts references to the "higher power" at work in various occurrences (God provokes Amaziah to venture against Joash of Israel, 9,199; "Destiny" inspires Josiah's fatal challenge to Neco, 10,76). A number of Josephus' other elaborations impart a greater drama/pathos to the events narrated (see, e.g., his *Ausmalung* of the summary notice on Ishmael's killing Gedaliah as they "ate bread together" of Jer 41,1-3 in 10,168-169 or his expatiation on the jejune siege notice of 2 Kgs 25,1 etc. in 10,131-134, this last itself likely inspired by Josephus' own military experiences at Jotapata and Jerusalem). Interjected fulfillment notices call attention to the realization of the prophets' predictions (see, e.g., 10,141 [Zedekiah's fate is in accordance with the announcements of both Jeremiah and Ezekiel; cf. 10,106]. 181 [Jeremiah's prophecy about the Babylonian invasion of Egypt comes about]). Finally, the complex of chronological statistics, name-lists, and reflections which Josephus appends his accounts of the fall of Samaria (9,280-282), the capture and destruction of Jerusalem (10,142-143.147-148.151-153), and the final Babylonian deportation of the Jews (10,183-185) all serve to underscore the import of those events as key moments in Jewish history.

2) *Omissions/ Abridgements*: AJ 9,1–10,185 also evidences numerous instances where Josephus leaves aside or compresses source data; these too

vary considerably in extent and the sort of items affected by them. Overall, he tends to dispense with Biblical elements that appear repetitious, self-evident, contexually misplaced (e.g., God's promise to the sick Hezekiah that he will be delivered from the Assyrians [2 Kgs 20,6b // Isa 38,6] notwithstanding the fact that in the sequence of the Biblical accounts that delivery has already been narrated), unsubstantiated (e.g., the claim about King Hoshea of Israel being not as evil as his predecessors, 2 Kgs 17,2), difficult to understand (e.g., Jeremiah's "stones sign" and God's elucidation of this, Jer 44,8-13), or "functionless" (see, e.g., the "blind motif" of Joram's wearing sackcloth mentioned in 2 Kgs 6,30). Minor proper and place names are often omitted (see, e.g., the list of Joram's brothers, 2 Chr 21,2; compare 9,95 and that of Jehoiada's co-conspirators, 2 Chr 23,1; compare 9,143; the two Jerusalem gates cited in 2 Kgs 14,13 // 2 Chr 25,23). Josephus routinely compresses source cultic details – whether the practice, object, etc. in question be legitimate (see, e.g., the plethora of sacrificial initiatives attributed to Hezekiah in 2 Chronicles 29–30; compare 9,260-274, cf. chap. XV) or illegitimate (see, e.g., his elimination of the bulk of the particular iconoclastic measures attributed to Josiah following the promulgation of the law-book by 2 Kgs 23,4-20 in his version of this development, 10,65-69). In the same line he several times abridges the prayers which the Bible places on characters' lips (e.g., those of Hezekiah [2 Kgs 19,15-19 // Isa 37,15-20; compare 10,16] and Jonah [Jonah 2,2-10; compare 9,214]). Under the heading of "cultic omissions" one might also recall Josephus' practice of cutting back on the Chronicler's recurrent positive mentions of the Levites and their activities (compare in this regard his rendering of the reforms of Hezekiah [9,260-276] and Josiah [10,49-80] with 2 Chronicles 29–31 and 34-35, respectively). Biblical notices that do not accord with the view of things the historian wants to present are likewise rather frequently jettisoned by him (see, e.g., the entire segment Jonah 3,5-4,11 with its depiction of an unfulfilled prediction and an *en masse* Gentile "conversion"; Isaiah's initial "false" prophecy and the Lord's countermanding of this, 2 Kgs 20,1b // Isa 38,1b; compare 10,24ff.; and the Judeans' declaration of their idolatrous intentions, Jer 44,15-19; compare 10,180). He invariably drops Kings' and Chronicles' "source notices" for the Israelite and Judean rulers, just as he does all but one of the "synchronic formulae" found in 2 Kgs 15,8–18,1 (i.e. that for Hezekiah, 18,1 = 9,260). Likewise omitted by him are 2 Kings' recurrent references to the people's continuing to sacrifice on the high places even during the reigns of "good" Judean rulers (see 2 Kgs 12,2, etc.)[8]. The miraculous element so

---

8. Recall that Josephus has a "precedent" for this particular omission in Chronicles which itself has no equivalent to them.

prominent in 2 Kings is significantly downplayed with Josephus reducing the expansive story of Elijah's translation (2 Kgs 2,1-18) to a brief allusion (9,28); passing over a number of Elisha's miracles (e.g., those recounted in 2 Kgs 2,19-25; 8,1-6); and making no mention of the "cake of figs" prescribed by Isaiah for Hezekiah's cure (2 Kgs 20,7 // Isa 38,21). More generally, the historian eliminates various source references to God's role in events (e.g., Jeremiah and Baruch's "escape" from Jehoiakim is not attributed to God's "hiding" of them [so Jer 36,26; compare 10,95]), even while, conversely, he inserts a number of such indications of his own (see above on 9,199). In like fashion he markedly reduces as well the extended "theological commentary" concerning Israel's (and Judah's) fall, 2 Kgs 17,7-23, in his rendition of this in 9,281-282.

3) *Re-arrangements*: Josephus also takes recurrent liberties with the sequence of the Biblical materials, both on the micro (i.e. within a given text) and the macro (i.e. between texts) levels. His re-arrangements are likewise motivated by a variety of considerations. Thus, he regularly repositions the chronological indications for the kings from the initial mention of them (where one finds these in both Kings and Chronicles) to the conclusion of his own account. He cites Gedaliah's appointment as governor before recounting Nebuzaradan's dealings with Jeremiah (10,155-158; compare Jer 40,1-6). Whereas in the Bible ten chapters separate the two stories of Jeremiah's travails in the reign of Jehoiakim related in Jeremiah 26 and 36, Josephus directly juxtaposes his version of these happenings in 10,89-95, given both their shared dating and common character as stories of the hostile reception Jeremiah's preaching encountered. A number of Josephus' re-arrangements are possibly inspired by the Bible's own chronological indications which themselves appear to run counter to the sequence of its presentation. Thus, in contrast to the order of 2 Kings 17–18, e.g., he relates the initial events of the reign of Hezekiah (9,260b-276) prior to the demise of the Northern Kingdom (9,277-291), a happening which 2 Kgs 18,9 dates to Hezekiah's *sixth* year. Likewise diverging from the Biblical sequence, he disjoins the conclusion of Jehu's reign (9,159-160 = 2 Kgs 10,34-36) from the remainder of his account of this king (9,105-139 = 2 Kgs 9,1–10,30), interpolating the story of the overthrow of Athaliah and the accession of Joash (9,140-158) – events which occurred in Jehu's *seventh* year according to 2 Kgs 12,1 – between them. Another factor influencing the historian's re-arrangements seems to have been his desire to keep together related materials which he found separated in his sources. So, he reproduces *en bloc* (9,258-259) the notices on Hosea's coup and sub-

jugation by the Assyrians, the Biblical parallels to which stand in two different contexts, i.e. 2 Kgs 15,30-31 and 17,1-3, respectively. Various of Josephus' re-arrangements reflect a concern with giving a more "logical" sequence of events; see, e.g., 9,214 where he has Jonah make his prayer of thanksgiving after, rather than before (so Jonah 2), his delivery from the fish. Via his application of the re-arrangement technique Josephus then, *inter alia*, endeavors to "improve" on the Bible's presentation in various respects.

4) *Modifications/Adaptations*: Finally, throughout 9,1–10,185, Josephus freely modifies the data of his sources in all sorts of ways. Stylistically, e.g., he employs hypotaxis for the Bible's parataxis, often recasts direct as indirect discourse, and introduces historic present forms where the corresponding text of LXX has a verb in the past tense. On the terminological level, he substitutes alternative formulations for terms and expressions not current in non-LXX Greek or otherwise problematic, e.g., "(the) Lord", as a divine title, διαθήκη in the sense of "covenant", references to God's "word" and "spirit", the *Botenformel*, the designation "man of God", the expression "fear of God", and the allusion to Jehu's "zeal" (see 2 Kgs 10,16; compare 9,133). The actual wording of the oaths attributed to Biblical characters is avoided (see on 9,35). Scripture's figurative language is often replaced with a prosaic equivalent and its anthropomorphisms reformulated. At the same time, Josephus regularly employs *Leitworte* of his own as a way of furthering the internal coherence of a given episode; see, e.g., his repeated interjection of terms of the πιστ-stem in his version of Hezekiah's cure 10,24-29 or his fourfold use of the term "prophet" in his retelling of the Jonah story in 9,209-214. Terminology is likewise used by him to establish connections between Biblical characters and contemporary figures, i.e. himself and his opponents as portrayed in *BJ* (e.g., verbal echoes link Gedaliah's assassin Ishmael with Josephus' own foe, John of Gischala; see chap. XXIV). In addition he takes care to vary the stereotypical language employed in the Biblical "judgment notices" on the Israelite and Judean kings as also the other sorts of verbal repetitions that one so often meets in the Scriptural accounts (see, e.g., 9,86 in comparison with 2 Kgs 7,18-20).

Josephus' contentual modifications of Biblical data concern a variety of matters and serve an array of authorial purposes. Some represent implicit corrections of problematic source indications (see, e.g., 9,216 vs. 2 Kgs 15,1: the chronologically "incorrect" synchronic notice for Amaziah's accession; 10,61 vs. 2 Kgs 22,20 // 2 Chr 34,28: Huldah's "false" announcement of Josiah's peaceful end; 10,170 vs. Jer 41,4: Ishmael's visitors bringing gifts to a Temple that no longer stands). On occasion, he adapts a Biblical datum in light of his own presentation elsewhere: 2 Chr 33,11 has Manasseh being carried off to Babylon by the king of Assyria; Josephus, who has mentioned the destruction of Assyria's power already at the time of Manasseh's father Hezekiah (see 10,30), designates the former's captor rather as "the king of Babylonia and Chaldaea" (10,40). A like phenomenon occurs in 10,17 where he replaces "Libnah" as the city besieged by Sennacherib (so 2 Kgs 19,8 // Isa 37,8) by "Pelusium" in view of the fact that he will subsequently quote (see 10,18) Herodotus' testimony on the Assyrian's unsuccessful assault on the latter city. Again, he sometimes rewrites the presentation of his Scriptural historical sources in light of what he found in the prophetic books. A case in point is Josephus' depiction of Jehoiakim's end in 10,97 where Nebuchadnezzar's orders his corpse to "be cast out unburied before the walls". No such order is reported in either 2 Kgs 24,6 (Jehoiakim simply "sleeps with his fathers") or 2 Chr 36,6 (Nebuchadnezzar "binds Jehoiakim to take him to Babylon"). The order does, however, represent a transposition into narrative of the predictions concerning the king's fate found in Jer 22,19 and 36,30 (see chap. XXI).

Other of Josephus' modifications have to do with his procedure regarding the (non-)naming of Biblical characters. Sometimes he supplies names for figures who remain anonymous in a given source context (see, e.g, on 9,51), while at others he substitutes collectivities (the "leaders", etc.) for the named individuals of his *Vorlage* (see, e.g., on 10,102-130). Biblical imagery undergoes modification at his hands, e.g., perhaps under the influence of Ezek 19,2, the reference to the lions' "pasture" of Nahum 2,11 is turned into an allusion to their "mother" (9,241). Source cultic particulars are frequently generalized (see 9,1; compare 2 Chr 19,2 and cf. the omissions heading above). Biblical weights, measures, and monetary denominations are given equivalents that would be better known to Gentile readers (see 9,232 vs. 2 Kgs 15,20: Menachem pays his tribute in talents rather than shekels). In like manner, the sources' place names are updated (see, e.g., 9,207 vs. 2 Kgs 14,25: "the Sea of the Arabah" becomes "Lake Asphaltitis"). At times times the historian simplifies the Bible's presentation (see 9,164 vs. 2 Kgs 12,11 // 2 Chr 24,11: Jehoiada and King Joash hire the Temple workers directly rather than going through overseers) or resolves its ambiguities (see 9,90 vs. 2 Kgs 8,11a as to the identity of the one "making a face"). In still other instances he actually contradicts or reverses the Bible's statements: e.g., his Jehoiachin is not the "evildoer" of 2 Kgs 24,9 // 2 Chr 36,9, but rather a "kind and just" ruler (10,100), while the priests are praised (so 9,270) rather than denigrated (so 2 Chr 29,34) for their role in the renewal of the cult under Hezekiah's auspices. Josephus likewise variously modifies Scripture's mentions of the supernatural agency that prompts characters' actions. His Elijah is dispatched to King Ahaziah, not by an "angel" (so 2 Kgs 1,3), but by God himself who appears to him (so 9,20). Subsequently, however, where 2 Kgs 1,15 speaks of an angel directing the prophet to accompany the third captain, Josephus (9,26) has Elijah go with the latter on his own initiative; see further 9,139b; 10,21. In place of the kings' age at accession as reported in the sources, he mentions how old they were at death. He supplies a (intended) destination ("Pontus and the trading stations of Thrace", 9,17) different from that given in either 1 Kgs 22,48 (Ophir) or 2 Chr 20,35 (Tarshish) for Jehoshaphat's ill-fated trading venture. He adduces as well seemingly more plausible motivations for events than those cited in the Bible, e.g., the Babylonian envoys come from afar to Hezekiah, not as a simple courtesy call on the recovered king (so 2 Kgs 20,12 // Isa 39,1) or to "inquire about the [sundial] sign" (so 2 Chr 32,31), but to invite him to become Baladas' "ally and friend" (10,30). His highlighting of the Amalekites, Israel's *Erbfeind*, as the primary target of Amaziah's campaign (see 9,188-195) is perhaps intended to make more palatable to Gentile readers the Biblical account of an unprovoked and exceptionally brutal Judean attack upon the Edomites (so 2 Kgs 14,7 // 2 Chr 25,5-16). Finally, Josephus' modifications not infrequently involve a retouching of the Biblical portrayal of a given figure. He avoids, e.g., having Elisha urge Hazael to lie to his master (so 2 Kgs 8,10; compare 9,90); reformulates (10,34) the egotistical words attributed to Hezekiah in 2 Kgs 20,19 // Isa 39,8; and makes Josiah begin displaying his piety already at age 12 (10,50), rather than first at 16 (so 2 Chr 34,3).

Distinctiveness

Given the preceding review of Josephus' rewriting techniques in 9,1–10,185, what now can be said in summary about the distinctiveness of his account of the later monarchy? First of all, by basing himself on a range of Biblical and extra-Biblical sources, Josephus provides a presentation of the period that is substantially fuller, richer, and more comprehensive than what finds in either Kings or Chronicles taken alone. His rendering, with its interjected hypotaxis, verbal variation, transitional formulae, closing remarks, and foreshadowings/ preparations of what will follow, etc., represents a more elegant and smoother-reading version of its Biblical models. Vis-à-vis those models, Josephus' rendition often shows itself to be a streamlined one. Questions suggested by the Biblical presentation receive an answer, and source problems of all sorts are "resolved" in some way or other. The irony surrounding various happenings is highlighted (see, e.g., 10,130 where Jeremiah, at the behest of Zedekiah, responds to the leaders' query about the "made-up" story he had told the king with a made-up story of his own). There is an evident concern to give a more dramatic turn to events (e.g., Gedaliah's assassination; see chap. XXIV). Source cultic, miraculous, theological and Levitical features are all downplayed to some extent. Conversely, the story's prophetic, priestly, and political/military element is amplified, as are the active roles assumed by both kings (see, e.g., Zedekiah's taking charge of Jeremiah's rescue, 10,123) and the people as whole (see, e.g., the inserted reference to their "eagerly assenting" to Josiah's directives, 10,64). Jewish history is situated within its wider international context as known from extra-Biblical sources. Finally, the Biblical characterizations of many figures undergo various sorts of retouchings in Josephus' depiction of them, whether *in bonam* or *malam partem*. The evil-doer Jehoiachin becomes a good king; see above. By contrast, the depravity and senselessness of rulers like Joram and Ahaz of Judah is still further accentuated. The sources' "neutral" portrayal of Gedaliah yields to one in which a series of explicitly positive terms are applied to him (see 10,155.164). The ambiguity surrounding kings like Jehoram of Israel, Hezekiah, and Zedekiah already in the Bible itself is highlighted via inserted items and/or modifications of source data regarding both their virtues (e.g., Hezekiah's piety and thankfulness; see 10,24.34) and defects (e.g., the same king's "cowardice", 10,5)[9].

Message for Audience(s)

In both what he tells and refrains from telling of the Biblical record of the later monarchy, Josephus aims to appeal to, instruct, and dissipate

9. It might be recalled here that in a number of cases where Josephus' presentation goes beyond or differs from the Bible's own it does have parallels elsewhere in Jewish/ Christian tradition; see, e.g., the identification of the late husband of the widow who appeals to Elisha as Ahab's steward "Obedias" (9,47; compare 2 Kgs 4,1) or Hezekiah's being "childless" at the moment of his severe sickness (10,25-26; compare 2 Kgs 20,2-3 // Isa 38,2-3). On the point as suggesting Josephus' familiarity with a stream of tradition which reached fixed written form often only centuries after his time, see FELDMAN, *Hezekiah*, 597, n. 1.

the prejudices of his primary audience, i.e. cultivated Gentiles. Pos- tively, he presents those readers with a series of leading Jewish figures from the period in question who exemplify a range of congenial, famil- iar values, attainments, and behavior patterns: they, e.g., embody the Greek cardinal virtues, have mysterious ends to their earthly lives (Eli- jah; see 9,28), are hospitable, compassionate towards Gentiles in distress (see 9,43: the kings' reaction to the sacrifice of the Moabite crown prince), wealthy, generous towards foreign visitors (see 10,31: Hezeki- ah's gifts to the Babylonian envoys), militarily successful, heroic, resourceful defenders of their besieged capital (see 10,131-134), but likewise ready to seek reasonable accomodation with the great powers of their time (so Hezekiah, Jeremiah, Jehoiachin, Zedekiah, and Gedaliah), even as a number (e.g., Amaziah, Uzziah) of them also fall victim to the fateful temptation of hubris which had brought to ruin so many of the great men of Greco-Roman mythology and history. More generally, Josephus' version presents the Jews, in their better moments, as mirror- ing the Romans' own self-image as a people devoted to their law and ancestral customs[10]. His inserted references to Greek historians (i.e. Herodotus; see 10,18-20a) and allusions to such Roman institutions as the triumph (see 9,194,200) would help cultivated Gentile readers feel more "at home" with the Biblical story. At the same time Josephus takes care to play down, eliminate entirely, or explicitly condemn those features of the Biblical narrative likely to render it less appealing to his Gentile audience, i.e. the insubordination of certain Jewish elements (e.g., Jeremiah's opponents) to earlier imperial powers, the divine promise of an everlasting dynasty for David (see 9,96 and compare 2 Kgs 8,19 // 2 Chr 21,7), Jewish aggressivity and violence towards non- Jews and their cults, derogatory Biblical references to the "nations" (see 9,243 and compare 2 Kgs 16,3 // 2 Chr 28,3; 10,37 and compare 2 Kgs 21,2 // 2 Chr 33,2: "the abominable practices of the nations"), and the practice of proselytism (see his retelling of the Jonah story).

For his Jewish readers, Josephus' account in 9,1–10,185 also has a variety of implicit messages. His emphasis on the reliablity of ancient prophecy intimates a word of hope for his compatriots' future: just as the prophets' words of doom for their people were fulfilled, so will also their announcements of God's eventual overthrow of the Jews' oppres- sors – whoever these may be and however invincible they may now appear. As for the present, Josephus' version of the later monarchy sug- gests a program for Jewish life both *ad intra* and *ad extra*, as also an

---

10. On this point see the summary remarks of SPILSBURY, *Image*, pp. 221-223.

apologia for the historian's own career. Specifically, by casting the long-running interaction between Israel and Judah in a more positive light than does the Bible itself, he calls contemporary Jews with their own splits and antagonisms to a like harmony. In their dealings with Rome those same Jews should at the same time – like Josephus himself during the recent War – follow the line of accomodation (and respect for God's prerogatives as the maker and unmaker of empires) espoused by the Josephan Jehoiachin, Jeremiah, and Gedaliah rather than the militant stance of their opponents (Zedekiah's false prophets, Ishmael), the proto-types of the Zealot leaders, Josephus' own antagonists. In so doing, Jews must also, however, act with due circumspection given the empires' long history of treachery in their regard (see on 10,4.97.99.100,230), and above all not allow themselves to be captivated by "foreign" fashions in religion.

A Final Remark

As just noted, Josephus makes his retelling of the history of the later monarchy an effective, purposeful vehicle for the messages he wishes to convey to his double (and antagonistic) publics. On the other hand, however, he also manages to provide all his readers with what is (for the most part) a quite faithful reproduction of the story told by the Bible itself, as promised by him in *AJ* 1,17. Such a multi-facetted achievement calls, I think, for both admiration and respect. Throughout the segment studied here – as in *AJ* overall – Josephus shows himself a literary juggler of no little skill.

INDEXES

ABBREVIATIONS

I. Ancient Writings, Manuscripts, Editions, etc.

A	Codex Alexandrinus of LXX
b. 'Abod. Zar.	Tractate 'Aboda Zara, Babylonian Talmud
'Abot R. Nat.	'Abot de Rabbi Nathan
AJ	Antiquitates Judaicae
c. Ap.	Contra Apionem
b. 'Arak.	Tractate 'Arakin, Babylonian Talmud
B	Codex Vaticanus of LXX
b. B. Bat.	Tractate Baba Batra, Babylonian Talmud
b. Ber.	Tractate Berakot, Babylonian Talmud
y. Ber.	Tractate Berakot, Jerusalem Talmud
BHS	Biblia Hebraica Stuttgartensia
BJ	Bellum Judaicum
Deut. Rab.	Deuteronomy Rabbah
E	Epitome, AJ
Eccl. Rab.	Ecclesiastes Rabbah
Ed. pr.	Editio princeps of AJ
E. R.	Eliyyahu Rabbah
Esth. Rab.	Esther Rabbah
Exc	Excerpta Peiresciana, AJ
Exod. Rab.	Exodus Rabbah
E.Z.	Eliyyahu Zuta
Gen. Rab.	Genesis Rabbah
b. Git.	Tractate Gittin, Babylonian Talmud
b. Hor.	Tractate Horayot, Babylonian Talmud
b. Ker.	Tractate Keritot, Babylonian Talmud
L	Lucianic MSS of LXX
Lam. Rab.	Lamentations Rabbah
Lat	Latin version, AJ
Laur	Codex Laurentianus, AJ
Lev. Rab.	Leviticus Rabbah
LXX	Greek version of OT
M	Codex Marcianus, AJ
m.	Mishnah
b. Meg.	Tractate Megillah, Babylonian Talmud
Mek.	Mekilta
Midr.	Midrash (on a Biblical book)
b. Mo'ed Qat.	Tractate Mo'ed Qatan, Babylonian Talmud
MT	Masoretic Text
b. Ned.	Tractate Nedarim, Babylonian Talmud
N.S.	New Series
Num. Rab.	Numbers Rabbah

O	Codex Oxoniensis, *AJ*
P	Codex Parisinus, *AJ*
Par	Paralipomena
b. Pesaḥ.	Tractate *Pesaḥim*, Babylonian Talmud
P.R.	*Pesikta Rabbati*
Pesik. Rab. Kah.	*Pesikta de Rab Kahana*
Pirqe R. El.	*Pirqe Rabbi Eliezer*
R	Codex Regius Parisinus, *AJ*
Rgns	(I-IV) Reigns
b. Roš. Haš.	Tractate *Roš Haššana*, Babylonian Talmud
S	Codex Vindobonensis, *AJ*
b. Šabb.	Tractate *Šabbat*, Babylonian Talmud
b. Sanh.	Tractate *Sanhedrin*, Babylonian Talmud
y. Sanh.	Tractate *Sanhedrin*, Jerusalem Talmud
y. Seqal.	Tractate *Šeqalim*, Jerusalem Talmud
Songs Rab.	*Song of Songs Rabbah*
b. Sot.	Tractate *Sotah*, Babylonian Talmud
SOR	*Seder 'Olam Rabbah*
b. Suk.	Tractate *Sukkah*, Babylonian Talmud
y. Suk.	Tractate *Sukkah*, Jerusalem Talmud
b. Ta'an.	Tractate *Ta'anit*, Babylonian Talmud
TC	Targum of Chronicles
t.e.	textus emendatus
TJ	Targum Jonathan of the (Former) Prophets
V	Codex Vaticanus, *AJ*
VL	*Vetus Latina*
VP	*Vitae Prophetarum*
b. Yeb.	Tractate *Yebamot*, Babylonian Talmud
b. Yoma	Tractate *Yoma*, Babylonian Talmud
Zon	Zonaras, *Chronicon*

II. JOURNALS, MONOGRAPH SERIES, DICTIONARIES, ETC.

AB	The Anchor Bible
ABR	*Australian Biblical Review*
AGJU	Arbeiten zur Geschichte des antiken Judentums und des Urchristentums
AJSL	*American Journal of Semitic Languages and Literature*
ALGHJ	Arbeiten zur Literatur und Geschichte des hellenistischen Judentums
AnBib	Analecta Biblica
ANET	Ancient Near Eastern Texts Relating to the Old Testament (1969[2])
ANRW	Aufstieg und Niedergang der römischen Welt
Anton	*Antonianum*
AO	*Aula Orientalis*
ATSAT	Arbeiten zu Text und Sprache im Alten Testament
Aug	*Augustinianum*

AUSS	*Andrews University Seminary Studies*
BBR	*Bulletin for Biblical Research*
BEATAJ	Beiträge zur Erforschung des Alten Testaments und des Antiken Judentums
BETL	Bibliotheca Ephemeridum Theologicarum Lovaniensium
BFCT	Beiträge zur Förderung christlicher Theologie
Bib	*Biblica*
BibOr	Biblica et Orientalia
BIOSCS	*Bulletin of the International Organization for Septuagint and Cognate Studies*
BJRL	*Bulletin of the John Rylands University Library of Manchester*
BK	*Bibel und Kirche*
BN	*Biblische Notizen*
BZAW	Beiträge zur ZAW
CBC	Cambridge Bible Commentary
CBL	Collectanea Biblica Latina
CBQ	*Catholic Biblical Quarterly*
CC SL	Corpus Christianorum, Series Latina
CRINT	Compendia Rerum Iudaicarum ad Novum Testamentum
DJD	Discoveries in the Judean Desert
DSD	*Dead Sea Discoveries*
ErIsr	Eretz Israel
EstBíb	*Estudios Bíblicos*
EstEcl	*Estudios Eclesiásticos*
ETL	*Ephemerides Theologicae Lovanienses*
ETS	Erfurter Theologische Studien
FAT	Forschungen zum Alten Testament
FB	Forschung zur Bibel
FS	*Festschrift*
FRLANT	Forschungen zur Religion und Literatur des Alten und Neuen Testaments
GCS	Die griechischen christlichen Schriftsteller der ersten drei Jahrhunderte
HDR	Harvard Dissertations in Religion
HSM	Harvard Semitic Monographs
HTR	*Harvard Theological Review*
HUCA	*Hebrew Union College Annual*
ICC	International Critical Commentary
JBL	*Journal of Biblical Literature*
JEOL	*Jaarbericht Ex Oriente Lux*
JETS	*Journal of the Evangelical Theology Society*
JJS	*Journal of Jewish Studies*
JNES	*Journal of Near Eastern Studies*
JQR	*Jewish Quarterly Review*
JSHRZ	Jüdische Schriften aus hellenistisch-römischer Zeit
JSJ	*Journal for the Study of Judaism in the Persian, Hellenistic and Roman Periods*
JSNT	*Journal for the Study of the New Testament*
JSOTSup	Journal for the Study of the Old Testament Supplement Series

JSP	*Journal for the Study of the Pseudepigrapha*
JSPSup	Journal for the Study of the Pseudepigrapha Supplement Series
JTS	*Journal of Theological Studies*
LCL	Loeb Classical Library
LS	*Louvain Studies*
LSB	La Sacra Bibbia
LSJ	LIDDELL-SCOTT-JONES, *Greek-English Dictionary*
MGWJ	*Monatschrift für Geschichte und Wissenschaft des Judentums*
MTS	Münchener Theologische Studien
MSU	Mitteilungen des Septuaginta Unternehmens
NCB	New Century Bible
NovT	*Novum Testamentum*
NovTSup	Novum Testamentum, Supplements
NTOA	Novum Testamentum et Orbis Antiquus
NTS	*New Testament Studies*
NTTS	New Testament Tools and Studies
OBO	Orbis Biblicus et Orientalis
OLZ	*Orientalische Literaturzeitung*
OTL	Old Testament Library
OTP	Old Testament Pseudepigrapha
OTS	Oudtestamentische Studiën
OTWSA	Ou-Testamentiese Werkgemeenskap in Suider-Afrika
PAAJR	*Proceedings of the American Academy of Jewish Research*
PAPS	*Proceedings of the American Philosophical Association*
PEQ	*Palestine Exploration Quarterly*
PG	Patrologiae Cursus Completus, Series Graeca
PL	Patrologiae Cursus Completus, Series Latina
PW	PAULY-WISSOWA, *Real-Encyclopädie der klassischen Altertums-wissenschaft*
RAC	Reallexicon für Antike und Christentum
RB	*Revue biblique*
REJ	*Revue des études juives*
SANT	Studien zum Alten und Neuen Testament
SBLMS	SBL Monograph Series
SBLSCS	SBL Septuagint and Cognate Studies
SBS	Stuttgarter Biblische Studien
SC	Sources chrétiennes
SCI	*Scripta Classica Israelica*
SE	Studia Evangelica
Sef	*Sefarad*
SF	Studia Freiburgensia
SJOT	*Scandinavian Journal for the Old Testament*
SPB	Studia Post-Biblica
SSEJC	Studies in Scripture in Early Judaism and Christianity
ST	*Studia Theologica*
TANZ	Texte und Arbeiten zum neutestamentlichen Zeitalter
TECC	Textos y Estudios "Cardenal Cisneros"
TLZ	*Theologische Literaturzeitung*
TRE	Theologische Real-enzyklopädie

TSAJ	Texte und Studien zum Antiken Judentum
TU	Texte und Untersuchungen
TWNT	KITTEL - FRIEDRICH (eds.), *Theologisches Wörterbuch zum Neuen Testamentum*
TZ	*Theologische Zeitschrift*
UUÅ	Uppsala Universiteits Årsskrift
VT	*Vetus Testamentum*
VTSup	Vetus Testamentum, Supplements
WBC	Word Biblical Commentary
WMANT	Wissenschaftliche Monographien zum Alten und Neuen Testament
WUNT	Wissenschaftliche Untersuchungen zum Neuen Testament
ZAW	*Zeitschrift für die alttestamentliche Wissenschaft*

BIBLIOGRAPHY

I. Texts, Translations, Tools

J.M. Allegro and A.A. Anderson (eds.), *Qumrân Cave 4. I. (4Q158-4Q186)* (DJD, 5), Oxford, Clarendon, 1968.

M. Baillet *et al.* (eds.), *Les 'Petites Grottes' de Qumrân. Textes* (DJD, 3), Oxford, Clarendon, 1962.

I. Bekker (ed.), *Flavii Josephi Opera Omnia*, Leipzig, Teubner, 1855-1856.

S.A. Berman (tr.), *Midrash Tanhuma-Yelammedenu*, Hoboken, NJ, Ktav, 1996.

P. Bogaert (tr.), *Apocalypse de Baruch*, I-II (SC, 144), Paris, Cerf, 1969.

G.N. Bonwitsch and H. Achelis (eds.), *Hippolytus Werke*, II,1 (GSC), Leipzig, Hinrichs, 1897.

W.G. Braude (tr.), *The Midrash on Psalms*, New Haven, Yale University Press, 1959.

— (tr.), *Pesikta Rabbati*, New Haven-London, Yale University Press, 1968.

— and I. J. Kapstein (trs.), *Pĕsiḵta dĕ-Raḇ Kahăna*, Philadelphia, Jewish Publication Society of America, 1975.

— (trs.), *Tanna dĕḇe Eliyyahu: The Lore of the School of Elijah*, Philadelphia, Jewish Publication Society of America, 1981.

A.E. Brooke, N. MacLean, H.St.J. Thackeray (eds.), *The Old Testament in Greek according to the Text of Codex Vaticanus*, II/II *I and II Kings*, Cambridge, Cambridge University Press, 1930; II/III *I and II Chronicles*, 1932.

K.J. Cathcart and R.P. Gordon (trs.), *The Targum of the Minor Prophets* (The Aramaic Bible, 14), Wilmington, DE, Glazier, 1989.

R.H. Charles and J.M.T. Barton (trs.), *The Ascension of Isaiah*, in H.F.D. Sparks (ed.), *The Apocryphal Old Testament*, Oxford, Clarendon, 1984, 784-812.

— and L.H. Brockington (trs.), *The Syriac Apocalypse of Baruch*, in H.F.D. Sparks (ed.), *The Apocryphal Old Testament*, Oxford, Clarendon, 1984, 835-895.

B.D. Chilton (tr.), *The Isaiah Targum* (The Aramaic Bible, 11), Wilmington, DE, Glazier, 1987.

A. Cohen (tr.), *Midrash Ecclesiastes Rabbah*, London / New York, Soncino, 1983.

— (tr.), *Midrash Lamentations Rabbah*, London/New York, Soncino, 1983.

F.H. Colson and G.H. Whitaker (eds. and trs.), *Philo* (LCL), London, Heinemann; Cambridge, MA, Harvard University Press, 1929-1963.

R. Le Déaut and J. Robert (eds. and trs.), *Targum des Chroniques* I-II (AnBib, 51), Roma, P.B.I., 1971.

G. Diercks (ed.), *Luciferi Calaritani Opera Quae Supersunt* (CC SC, VIII), Turnhout, Brepols, 1978.

G. Dindorf (ed.), *Flavii Josephi Opera*, Paris, Didot, 1845-1847.

Y.-M. Duval (ed. and tr.), *Jérôme Commentaire sur Jonas* (SC, 323), Paris, Cerf, 1985.

K. ELLIGER and W. RUDOLPH (eds.), *Biblia Hebraica Stuttgartensia*, Stuttgart, Württembergische Bibelanstalt, 1977.

J.C. ENDRES et al., *Chronicles and its Synoptic Parallels in Samuel, Kings, and Related Biblical Texts*, Collegeville, MN, The Liturgical Press/Michael Glazier, 1998.

I. EPSTEIN (ed.), *The Babylonian Talmud*, London, Soncino, 1935-1948.

L.H. FELDMAN, *Josephus and Modern Scholarship (1937-1980)*, Berlin - New York, de Gruyter, 1984.

—, *Josephus: A Supplementary Bibliography*, Berlin - New York, de Gruyter, 1986.

N. FERNÁNDEZ MARCOS and J.R. BUSTO SAIZ (eds.), *Theodoreti Cyrensis Quaestiones in Reges et Paralipomena. Editio critica* (TECC, 32), Madrid, Instituto de Filología del C.S.I.C., 1984.

— (eds.), *El texto antioqueno de la Biblia Griega. I. 1-2 Samuel* (TECC, 50), Madrid, Instituto de Filología del C.S.I.C., 1989; II. *1-2 Reyes* (TECC, 53), 1992; III. *1-2 Crónicas* (TECC, 60), 1996.

B. FISCHER (with the collaboration of E. ULRICH and J.E. SANDERSON), *Palimpsestus Vindobonensis: A Revised Edition of L 115 for Samuel-Kings*, in *BIOSCS* 16 (1983) 13-87.

J.A. FITZMYER, *The Dead Sea Scrolls: Major Publications and Tools for Study* (SBL Resources for Biblical Study, 20), Atlanta, GA, Scholars, 1990 (rev. éd.).

H. FREEDMAN and M. SIMON (eds.), *The Midrash Rabbah*, London, Soncino, 1977.

L. GINZBERG, *The Legends of the Jews*, Philadelphia, Jewish Publication Society of America, 1909-1925.

L.-F. GIRÓN BLANC (tr.), *Seder 'Olam Rabbah El Gran Orden del Universo. Una cronología judía* (Biblioteca Midrásica, 18), Estella (Navarra), Verbo Divino, 1996.

A.D. GODLEY (ed. and tr.), *Herodotus*, I (LCL), London, Heinemann; Cambridge, MA, Harvard University Press, 1946.

J. GOLDIN (tr.), *The Fathers According to Rabbi Nathan*, New Haven/London, Yale University Press, 1955.

R.M. GREER (ed. and tr.), *Diodorus of Sicily*, X (LCL), Cambridge, MA, Harvard University Press; London, Heinemann, 1954.

B. GROSSFELD (tr.), *The Two Targums of Esther* (The Aramaic Bible, 18), Collegeville, MN, The Liturgical Press/Michael Glazier, 1991.

D.R.A. HARE (tr.), *Lives of the Prophets*, in J.H. CHARLESWORTH (ed.), OTP 2, Garden City, NY, Doubleday, 1985, 379-399.

D.J. HARRINGTON and A.J. SALDARINI (trs.), *Targum Jonathan of the Former Prophets* (The Aramaic Bible, 10), Wilmington, DE, Glazier, 1987.

R. HAYWARD (tr.), *The Targum of Jeremiah* (The Aramaic Bible, 12), Wilmington, DE, Glazier, 1987.

J. HUDSON and S. HAVERCAMPUS (eds.), *Flavii Josephi Opera Omnia* I-II Amsterdam, apus R. & G. Wetstenios, 1726.

J. ISRAELSTAM and J.J. SLOTKI (trs.)., *Midrash Rabbah Leviticus*, London/New York, Soncino, 1983.

G. KITTEL and G. FRIEDRICH (eds.), *TWNT*, Stuttgart, Kohlhammer, 1933-1973.

E. LARSON, *4QText Mentioning Zedekiah*, in M. BROSHI et al. (eds.), *Qumran Cave 4. XIV Parabiblical Texts, Part 2* (DJD, 19), Oxford, Clarendon, 1995, 235-244.

J.Z. LAUTERBACH (tr.), *Mekilta De-Rabbi Ishmael*, Philadelphia, Jewish Publication Society of America, 1933-1935.

S.M. LEHRMAN (tr.), *Exodus Rabbah*, London/New York, Soncino, 1983.

H.G. LIDDELL, R. SCOTT and H. S. JONES, *A Greek-English Lexicon*, Oxford, Clarendon, 1968.

S.A. NABER (ed.), *Flavii Josephi Opera omnia*, Leipzig, Teubner, 1888-1896.

M.A. NAVARRO PEIRÓ (tr.), *Abot de Rabbí Natán* (Biblioteca Midrásica, 5), Valencia, Institución San Jerónimo, 1987.

B. NIESE (ed. and tr.), *Flavii Josephi Opera*. Editio maior, Berlin, Weidmann, 1955² (= 1885-1895)

E. NODET (ed.), *Flavius Josèphe, Les Antiquités juives*. *I:A. Livres I à III. Introduction et texte; II:B. Traduction et notes*, Paris, Cerf, 1990; *Livres IV-V* (1995).

J. NEUSNER (ed. and tr.), *The Talmud of the Land of Israel*, Chicago and London, University of Chicago Press, 1982.

C.H. OLDFATHER (ed. and tr.), *Diodorus of Sicily*, I (LCL), Cambridge, MA, Harvard University Press; London, Heinemann, 1933.

A. PELLETIER (ed. and tr.), *Lettre d'Aristée à Philocrate* (SC, 89), Paris, Cerf, 1962.

M. PÉREZ FERNÁNDEZ (tr.), *Los capítulos de Rabbí Eliezer* (Biblioteca Midrásica, 1), Valencia, Institución San Jerónimo, 1984.

J. RABBINOWITZ (tr.), *Midrash Rabbah Deuteronomy*, London/New York, Soncino, 1983.

— (tr.), *Midrash Rabbah Ruth*, London/New York, Soncino, 1983.

H. RACKHAM, (ed. and tr.), *Pliny Natural History*, II (LCL), Cambridge, MA, Harvard University Press; London, Heinemann, 1947.

T. REINACH (ed.), *Textes d'auteurs grecs et romains relatifs au Judaïsme*, Paris, P.U.F., 1895.

—, J. WEILL *et al.* (trs.), *Œuvres complètes de Flavius Josèphe*, Paris, Leroux, 1900-1932.

S. REITER (ed.), *S. Hieronymi Presbyteri Opera*, 1,3 (CCSL, 74), Turnhout, Brepols, 1960.

K.H. RENGSTORF (ed.), *A Complete Concordance to Flavius Josephus*, Leiden, Brill, 1973-1983.

A. SCHALIT (tr.), *Joseph ben Mattatijjahu Kadmoniot ha-jehudim* I-III, Jerusalem, Bialik Institute, 1944-1963.

—, *Namenwörterbuch zu Flavius Josephus* (A Complete Concordance to Flavius Josephus, Supplement I), Leiden, Brill, 1968.

A. SCHLATTER, *Die hebräischen Namen bei Josephus* (BFCT, 17:3), Gütersloh, Bertelsmann, 1913.

A.M. SCHWEMER (tr.), *Vitae Prophetarum* (JSHRZ, I.7), Gütersloh, Gütersloher Verlagshaus, 1997.

F. SIEGERT (tr.), *Drei hellenistisch-jüdische Predigten*, I (WUNT, 20), Tübingen, Mohr Siebeck, 1980.

M. SIMON (tr.), *Midrash Rabbah Song of Songs*, London/New York, Soncino, 1983.

J.J. SLOTKI (tr.), *Midrash Rabbah Numbers*, I-II, London/New York, Soncino, 1983.

H.F.D. SPARKS (ed.), *The Apocryphal Old Testament*, Oxford, Clarendon, 1984.

A. Sperber (ed.), *The Bible in Aramaic*, Leiden, Brill, 1959.

O.H. Steck, *Die erste Jesajarolle von Qumran (1QIsᵃ)* (SBS, 173.1-2), Stuttgart, KBW, 1997.

M. Stern (ed.), *Greek and Latin Authors on Jews and Judaism*, I, Jerusalem, The Israel Academy of Sciences and Humanities, 1974.

H.St.J. Thackeray, R. Marcus, A. Wikgren and L.H. Feldman (eds. and trs.), *Josephus* (LCL), London, Heinemann; Cambridge, MA, Harvard University Press, 1926-1965.

R. Thornhill (tr.), *The Paraleipomena of Jeremiah*, in H.F.D. Sparks (ed.), *The Apocryphal Old Testament*, Oxford, Clarendon, 1984, 821-833.

E. Tov (ed.), *The Greek Minor Prophets Scroll from Naḥal Ḥever (8HevXII gr) (The Seiyâl Collection)* (DJD, 8), Oxford, Clarendon, 1990.

—, *Jeremiah*, in E. Ulrich et. al. (eds.), *Qumran Cave 4, X. The Prophets*, 145-208.

J.T. Townsend (tr.), *Midrash Tanhuma*, I. *Genesis*, Hoboken, NJ, Ktav, 1989.

E. Ulrich et al. (eds.), *Qumran Cave 4, X. The Prophets* (DJD, 15), Oxford, Clarendon, 1997.

C. Vercellone (ed.), *Variae Lectiones Vulgatae Latinae Bibliorum Editionis*, II, Romae, Spithöver, 1864.

N. Walter (tr.), *Fragmente jüdisch-hellenistischer Historiker* (JSHRZ, 1.2), Gütersloh, Mohn, 1976.

R.Weber (ed.), *Les anciennes versions latines du deuxième livre des Paralipomènes* (CBL, 8), Rome, Abbaye Saint-Jérôme/Liberia Vaticano, 1945.

R. Willems (ed.), *Tertulliani Opera, II* (CC SL, II:II), Turnhout, Brepols, 1954.

A. Wünsche (tr.), *Aus Israels Lehrhallen*, I, Leipzig, Pfeiffer, 1907.

J. Ziegler (ed.), *Ezechiel* (Septuaginta, 16,1), Göttingen, Vandenhoeck & Ruprecht, 1952.

—, *Jeremias Baruch Threni Epistula Jeremiae* (Septuaginta, 15), Göttingen, Vandenhoeck & Ruprecht, 1957.

—, *Duodecim prophetae* (Septuaginta, 13), Göttingen, Vandenhoeck & Ruprecht, 1967².

—, *Isaias* (Septuaginta, 14), Göttingen, Vandenhoeck & Ruprecht, 1983³.

II. Studies

F.-M. Abel, *AṢAL dans Zecharie XIV, 5*, in *RB* 45 (1936) 385-400.

L. Allen, *The Greek Chronicles I-II* (VTSup, 25), Leiden, Brill, 1975.

N. Allen, *Jerusalem and Shechem*, in *VT* 24 (1974) 353-357.

B.H. Amaru, *Land Theology in Josephus' Jewish Antiquities*, in *JQR* 71 (1980-1981) 201-221.

—, *The Killing of the Prophets: Unraveling a Midrash*, in *HUCA* 54 (1983) 153-180.

J. Applegate, *The Fate of Zedekiah: Redactional Debate in the Book of Jeremiah (Parts I and II)*, in *VT* 48 (1998) 137-160, 301-308.

A. Arazy, *The Appelations of the Jews (Ioudaios, Hebraios, Israel) in the Literature from Alexander to Justinian*, Diss., New York University, 1977.

H.W. Attridge, *The Interpretation of Biblical History in the Antiquitates Judaicae of Flavius Josephus* (HDR, 7), Missoula, MT, Scholars, 1976.

—, *Josephus and his Works*, in CRINT 2:3, pp. 185-232.

D.E. AUNE, *The Use of ΠΡΟΦΗΤΗΣ in Josephus*, in *JBL* 101 (1982) 419-421.

E. BAMMEL, *φίλος τοῦ καίσαρος*, in *TLZ* 77 (1952) 205-210.

J. BARR, *Seeing the Wood for the Trees? An Enigmatic Ancient Translation*, in *JSS* 13 (1968) 11-20.

D. BARTHÉLEMY, *Les Devanciers d'Aquila* (VTSup, 10), Leiden, Brill, 1963.

W.W. GRAF BAUDISSIN, *Kyrios als Gottesname im Judentum und seine Stelle in der Religionsgeschichte*, II (ed. O. EISSFELDT), Giessen, Töpelmann, 1929.

B. BECKING, *The Fall of Samaria: An Historical and Archaeological Study* (Studies in the History of the Ancient Near East, 2), Leiden, Brill, 1992.

C.T. BEGG, *The Death of Josiah: Josephus and the Bible*, in *ETL* 64 (1988) 157-163.

—, *The "Classical Prophets" in Josephus' Antiquities*, in *LS* 13 (1988) 341-357.

—, *Josephus' Zedekiah*, in *ETL* 65 (1989) 96-104.

—, *Constructing a Monster: The Chronicler's Sondergut in 2 Chronicles 21*, in *ABR* 37 (1989) 35-51.

—, *Josephus' Portrayal of the Disappearances of Enoch, Elijah and Moses: Some Observations*, in *JBL* 109 (1991) 691-693.

—, *Josephus' Account of the Early Divided Monarchy (AJ 8,212-420): Rewriting the Bible* (BETL, 108), Leuven, Leuven University Press/Peeters, 1993.

—, *Josephus' Version of Jehu's Putsch*, in *Anton* 64 (1993) 450-484.

—, *Filling in the Blanks: Josephus' Version of the Campaign of the Three Kings, 2 Kings 3*, in *HUCA* 64 (1993) 89-109.

—, *Joram of Judah according to Josephus (Ant. 9.45,95-104)*, in *JSQ* 1 (1993/1994) 323-339.

—, *Joash and Elisha in Josephus, Ant. 9.177-185*, in *Abr-Nahrain* 32 (1994) 28-46.

—, *The Gedaliah Episode and its Sequels in Josephus*, in *JSP* 12 (1994) 21-46.

—, *Uzziah (Azariah) of Judah according to Josephus*, in *EstBíb* 53 (1995) 5-24.

—, *Ahaziah's Fall (2 Kings 1): The Version of Josephus*, in *Sef* 55 (1995) 25-40.

—, *Hezekiah's Illness and Visit according to Josephus*, in *EstBíb* 53 (1995) 365-385.

—, *Amaziah of Judah according to Josephus (Ant. 9.186-204)*, in *Anton* 70 (1995) 3-30.

—, *Josephus' Portrait of Jehoshaphat Compared with the Biblical and Rabbinic Portrayals*, in *BN* 78 (1995) 39-48.

—, *Josephus and Nahum Revisited*, in *REJ* 154 (1995) 5-22.

—, *Jehoshaphat at Mid-Career according to AJ 9,1-17*, in *RB* 102 (1995) 379-402.

—, *Jehoahaz, King of Israel according to Josephus*, in *Sef* 55 (1995) 227-238.

—, *Jotham and Amon: Two Minor Kings of Judah according to Josephus*, in *BBR* 6 (1996) 1-13.

—, *Ahaz, King of Judah according to Josephus*, in *SJOT* 10 (1996) 28-52.

—, *Athaliah's Coup and Overthrow according to Josephus*, in *Anton* 71 (1996) 191-210.

—, *Elisha's Great Deeds according to Josephus (AJ 9,47-94)*, in *Henoch* 18 (1996) 69-110.

—, *The Last Six Kings of Israel according to Josephus*, in *ETL* 72 (1996) 371-384.

—, *The End of King Jehoiakim: the Afterlife of a Problem*, in *Journal for Semitics* 8 (1996) 12-20.

—, *Joash of Judah according to Josephus*, in M.P. GRAHAM *et al.* (eds.), *The Chronicler as a Historian* (JSOTSup, 238), Sheffield, Sheffield Academic Press, 1997, 301-320.

—, *Solomon's Apostasy (1 KGS. 11,1-13) according to Josephus*, in *JSJ* 28 (1997) 294-313.

—, *Israel's Battle with Amalek according to Josephus*, in *JSQ* 4 (1997) 201-216.

—, *David's Transfer of the Ark according to Josephus*, in *BBR* 7 (1997) 1-26.

I. BENZINGER, *Arka*, in *PW* 3 (1895), cc. 1111-1112.

E. BEN-ZVI, *The Authority of 1-2 Chronicles in the Late Second Temple Period*, in *JSP* 3 (1988) 59-88.

S.G. BERNSTEIN, *König Nebucadnezar von Babel in der jüdischen Tradition*, Berlin, Itzkowski, 1907.

E. BEST, *The Use and Non-use of Pneuma by Josephus*, in *NovT* 3 (1959) 218-225.

O. BETZ, *Offenbarung und Schriftforschung in der Qumransekte* (WUNT, 6), Tübingen, Mohr Siebeck, 1960.

—, *Das Problem des Wunders bei Flavius Josephus im Vergleich zum Wunderproblem bei den Rabbinen und im Johannesevangelium*, in O. BETZ, K. HAACKER, M. HENGEL (eds.), *Josephus-Studien. FS O. Michel*, Göttingen, Vandenhoeck & Ruprecht, 1974, 23-44.

—, *Miracles in the Writings of Flavius Josephus*, in L.H. FELDMAN and G. HATA (eds.), *Jesus, Judaism and Christianity*, Detroit, Wayne State University, 1987, 212-235.

E. BICKERMAN, *Four Strange Books of the Bible*, New York, Schocken, 1967.

P. BILDE, *Flavius Josephus between Jerusalem and Rome* (JSPSup, 2), Sheffield, Sheffield Academic Press, 1988.

B. BLACKBURN, *Theios Anēr and the Markan Miracle Traditions* (WUNT 2,40), Tübingen, Mohr Siebeck, 1991.

S.H. BLANK, *The Death of Zechariah in Rabbinic Literature*, in *HUCA* 12-13 (1937-1938) 327-346.

J. BLENKISOPP, *Prophecy and Priesthood in Josephus*, in *JJS* 25 (1974) 239-263.

—, *The Judean Priesthood during the Neo-Babylonian and Achaemenid Periods: A Hypothetical Reconstruction*, in *CBQ* 60 (1998) 25-43.

H. BLOCH, *Die Quellen des Flavius Josephus in seiner Archäologie*, Leipzig, Teubner, 1879.

P.-M. BOGAERT, *La libération de Jérémie et le meutre de Godolias: le texte court (LXX) et la rédaction longue (MT)*, in D. FRANKEL *et al.* (eds.), *Studien zur Septuaginta. Robert Hanhart zu Ehren* (MSU, 20), Göttingen, Vandenhoeck & Ruprecht, 1991, 312-322.

T.M. BOLIN, *Freedom beyond Forgiveness: The Book of Jonah Re-examined* (JSOTSup, 236), Sheffield, Sheffield Academic Press, 1997.

J.E. BOWLEY, *Josephus's Use of Greek Sources for Biblical History*, in J.C. REEVES and J. KAMPEN (eds.), *Pursuing the Text: Studies in Honor of Ben Zion Wacholder on the Occasion of his Seventieth Birthday* (JSOTSup, 184), Sheffield, Sheffield Academic Press, 1994, 202-215.

B. BRÜNE, *Flavius Josephus und seine Schriften in ihrem Verhältnis zum Judentume, zur griechisch-römischen Welt und zum Christentume*, Gütersloh, Bertelsmann, 1913.

C.F. BURNEY, *Notes on the Hebrew Text of the Book of Kings*, London, Revington, 1903 (rpt. New York, Ktav, 1970).

J.R. BUSTO SAIZ, *On the Lucianic Manuscripts in 1-2 Kings*, in C. COX (ed.), *VI Congress of the International Organization for Septuagint and Cognate Studies* (SBLSCS, 23), Atlanta, Scholars, 1987, 305-310.

—, *El Texto Luciánico en el Marco del Pluralismo textual. Estado de la Cuestion y Perspectivas*, in *EstEcl* 65 (1990) 3-18.

K.J. CATHCART, *Nahum in the Light of Northwest Semitic* (BibOr, 26), Roma, P.B.I., 1973.

S. CHOW, *The Sign of Jonah Reconsidered: A Study of its Meaning in the Gospel Traditions* (ConBNT, 27), Stockholm, Almqvist & Wiksell, 1995.

M. COGAN and H. TADMOR, *II Kings* (AB, 11), Garden City, NY, Doubleday, 1988.

R.J. COGGINS, *The Samaritans in Josephus*, in L.H. FELDMAN and G. HATA (eds.), *Josephus, Judaism and Christianity*, Detroit, Wayne State University Press, 1987, 257-273.

S.J.D. COHEN, *Josephus in Galilee and Rome. His Vita and Development as a Historian* (Columbia Studies in the Classical Tradition, 8), Leiden, Brill, 1979.

—, Ἰουδαῖος τὸ γένος *and Related Expressions in Josephus*, in F. PARENTE and J. SIEVERS (eds.), *Josephus and the History of the Greco-Roman Period: Essays in Memory of Morton Smith* (SPB, 41), Leiden, Brill, 1994, 23-38.

J.N. COLLINS, *Diakonia. Reinterpreting the Ancient Sources*, Oxford/New York, Oxford University Press, 1990.

P.T. CROCKER, *Recent Discussion on the Identity of King "So" of Egypt*, in *Buried History* 29 (1993) 68-74.

S. DANIEL, *Recherches sur le vocabulaire du culte dans la "Septante"* (Études et commentaires, 61), Paris, Klinksieck, 1966.

D. DAUBE, *Typology in Josephus*, in *JJS* 31 (1980) 18-36.

S. DELAMARTER, *The Vilification of Jehoiakim (A.K.A. Eliakim and Joiakim) in Early Judaism*, in C.A. EVANS & J.A. SANDERS (eds.), *The Function of Scripture in Early Jewish and Christian Tradition* (JSNTSup, 154/ SSEJC, 6), Sheffield, Sheffield Academic Press, 1998, 190-204.

E.K. DIETRICH, *Die Umkehr (Bekehrung und Busse) im Alten Testament und im Judentum*, Stuttgart, Kohlhammer, 1936.

R.B. DILLARD, *2 Chronicles* (WBC, 15), Waco, TX, Word, 1987.

F.G. DOWNING, *Redaction Criticism: Josephus'* Antiquities *and the Synoptic Gospels* (I), in *JSNT* 8 (1980) 46-65; (II) 9 (1981) 29-48; rpt. in S.E. PORTER & C.A. EVANS (eds.), *New Tetament Interpretation and Methods: A Sheffield Reader* (The Biblical Seminar, 45), Sheffield, Sheffield Academic Press, 1997, 161-189.

A.J. DROGE, *Josephus between Greeks and Barbarians*, in L.H. FELDMAN and J.R. LEVISON (eds.), *Josephus'* Contra Apionem: *Studies in its Character & Context with a Latin Concordance to the Portion Missing in Greek* (AGJU, 34), Leiden, Brill, 1996, 115-142.

H. DRÜNER, *Untersuchungen über Josephus*, Marburg, Hamel, 1896.

Y.-M. DUVAL, *Le livre de Jonas dans la littérature chrétienne grecque et latine*, Paris, Études augustiniennes, 1973.

R. EGGER, *Josephus Flavius und die Samaritaner* (NTOA, 4), Freiburg, Universitätsverlag; Göttingen: Vandenhoeck & Ruprecht, 1986.

F.C. EISELEN, *Sidon: A Study in Oriental History* (Columbia University Oriental Studies, 4), New York, Columbia University Press, 1907.

S. EK, *Herodotismen in der Jüdischen Archäologie des Josephus und ihre textkritische Bedeutung* (Kungl. Humanistiska Vetenskapssamfundet i Lund, Årsberåtellelse 1945-1946), Lund, C.W.K. Gleerup, 1946, 27-62, 213.

J. ELAYI and A. CAVIGNEAUX, *Sargon II et les Ioniens*, in *Oriens Antiquus* 18 (1979) 59-75.

L.K. ENTHOVEN, *Ad Flavii Iosephi* Antiquitates Judaicae, in *Mnemosyne* 22 N.S. (1894) 15-22.

K. ERIKSSON, *Das Präsens historicum in der nachklassischen griechischen Historiographie*, Diss., Lund, 1943.

L.H. FELDMAN, *Josephus as an Apologist to the Greco-Roman World: His Portrait of Solomon*, in E. SCHLÜSSER FIORENZA (ed.), *Aspects of Religious Propaganda in Judaism and Early Christianity*, Notre Dame, IN, Notre Dame University Press, 1976, 69-88.

—, *Josephus' Portrait of Saul*, in *HUCA* 53 (1982) 45-99.

—, *Flavius Josephus Revisited: The Man, his Writings, and his Significance*, in H. TEMPORINI and W. HAASE (eds.), ANRW II:21:2, Berlin-New York, de Gruyter, 1984, 763-862.

—, *Josephus as a Biblical Interpreter: the 'AQEDAH*, in *JQR* 75 (1985) 212-252.

—, *Josephus' Portrait of Deborah*, in A. CAQUOT *et al.* (eds.), *Hellenica et Judaica. FS V. Nikiprowetzky*, Leuven-Paris, Peeters, 1986, 115-128.

— and G. HATA (eds.), *Jesus, Judaism and Christianity*, Detroit, Wayne State University Press, 1987.

—, *Use, Authority and Exegesis of Mikra in the Writings of Flavius Josephus*, in M.J. MULDER and H. SYSLING (eds.), *Mikra* (CRINT, 2:1), Assen, van Gorcum, 1988, 455-518.

—, *Josephus' Version of Samson*, in *JSJ* 19 (1988) 171-214.

—, *Josephus' Portrait of Noah and its Parallels in Philo, Pseudo-Philo's Biblical Antiquities and Rabbinic Midrashim*, in *PAAJR* 55 (1988) 31-57.

— and G. HATA (eds.), *Josephus, The Bible and History*, Leiden, Brill, 1989.

—, *Josephus' Portrait of Jacob*, in *JQR* 79 (1989) 101-151.

—, *Josephus' Portrait of David*, in *HUCA* 60 (1989) 129-174.

—, *Josephus' Portrait of Joshua*, in *HTR* 82 (1989) 351-376.

—, *Prophets and Prophecy in Josephus*, in *JTS* 41 N.S. (1990) 386-422.

—, *Josephus' Portrait of Manasseh*, in *JSP* 9 (1991) 3-20.

—, *Josephus*, in D.N. FREEDMAN (ed.), *The Anchor Bible Dictionary*, Vol. 3, New York, Doubleday, 1992, 981-998.

—, *Josephus' Portrait of Moses*, in *JQR* 82 (1992) 285-328.

—, *Josephus' Portrait of Joseph*, in *RB* 99 (1992) 379-417.

—, *Josephus' Portrait of Hezekiah*, in *JBL* 111 (1992) 597-610.

—, *Josephus' Attitude towards the Samaritans: A Study in Ambivalence*, in M. MOR (ed.), *Jewish Sects, Religious Movements, and Political Parties*, Omaha, Creighton University Press, 1992, 23-45.

—, *Josephus' Portrait of Josiah*, in *LS* 18 (1993) 110-130.

—, *Josephus' Portrait of Jehoshaphat*, in *SCI* 12 (1993) 3-33.

—, *Josephus' Portrait of Gedaliah*, in *Shofar* 12 (1993) 1-10.

—, *Josephus' Portrait of Jeroboam*, in *AUSS* 31 (1993) 29-52.

—, *Josephus' Portrait of Elisha*, in *NovT* 36 (1994) 1-28.

—, *Josephus' Portrait of Jehoram, King of Israel*, in *BJRL* 76 (1994) 3-20.

—, *Josephus' Portrait of Elijah*, in *SJOT* 8 (1994) 61-86.

—, *Josephus' Portrait of Jehoiachin*, in *PAPS* 131 (1995) 11-31.

—, *Josephus' Portrait of Solomon*, in *HUCA* 66 (1995) 103-167.

—, *The Concept of Exile in Josephus*, in J.M. SCOTT (ed.), *Exile: Old Testament, Jewish & Christian Conceptions* (JSJSup, 56), Leiden, Brill, 1996, 145-172.

—, *Josephus' Portrait of Isaiah*, in C.C. BROYLES & C.A. EVANS (eds.), *Writing and Reading the Scroll of Isaiah: Studies of an Interpretative Tradition* (VTSup, 70,2), Leiden, Brill, 1997, 583-608.

—, *Josephus' Portrait of Jehu*, in *JSQ* 4 (1997) 12-32.

—, *Studies in Josephus' Rewritten Bible* (JSJSup, 58), Leiden, Brill, 1998.

—, *Josephus's Interpretation of the Bible* (Hellenistic Culture and Society, 27), Berkeley, University of California Press, 1998.

—, *The Importance of Jerusalem as Viewed by Josephus* (International Rennert Guest Lecture Series, 2), Bar-Ilan, Bar-Ilan University, 1998.

N. FERNÁNDEZ MARCOS, *The Lucianic Text in the Book of Kingdoms: From Lagarde to the Textual Pluralism*, in A. PIETERS and C. COX (eds.), *De Septuaginta. FS J.W. Wevers*, Mississauga, Ont., Benben Publications, 1984, 161-174.

—, *Literary and Editorial Features of the Antiochene Text in Kings*, in C. COX (ed.), *VI Congress of the International Organization for Septuagint and Cognate Studies* (SBLSCS, 23), Atlanta, Scholars, 1987, 287-304.

—, *Some Reflections on the Antiochian Text of the Septuagint*, in D. FRAENKEL et al. (eds.), *Studien zur Septuaginta. FS Robert Hanhart* (MSU, 20), Göttingen, Vandenhoeck & Ruprecht, 1990, 219-229.

—, *Scribes & Translators: Septuagint & Old Latin in the Book of Kings* (VTSup, 54), Leiden, Brill, 1994.

—, *The Old Latin of Chronicles between the Greek and the Hebrew*, in B.A. TAYLOR (ed.), *IX Congress of the International Organization for Septuagint and Cognate Studies* (SBLSCS, 45), Atlanta, Scholars, 1997, 123-136.

M.J. FIEDLER, Δικαιοσύνη *in der diaspora-jüdischen und intertestamentlichen Literatur*, in *JSJ* 1 (1970) 120-143.

T.W. FRANXMAN, *Genesis and the "Jewish Antiquities" of Flavius Josephus* (BibOr, 35), Rome, Biblical Institute Press, 1979.

G. GARBINI, *Gli "Annali di Tiro" e la Storiografia Fenica*, in R.Y. EBIED and M.J.L. YOUNG (eds.), *Oriental Studies. FS B.S.J. Isserlin*, Leiden, Brill, 1980, 114-127.

G. GERLEMAN, *Studies in the Septuagint*, II. *Chronicles*, Lund, C.W.K. Gleerup, 1946.

W. GESENIUS, *Commentar über den Jesaia*, Leipzig, Vogel, 1821.

C.H.J. DE GEUS, *Idumaea*, in *JEOL* 26 (1979-1980) 53-74.

J.G. GIBBS and L.H. FELDMAN, *Josephus' Vocabulary for Slavery*, in *JQR* 76 (1986) 281-310.

U. GLESSMER, *Leviten in spät-nachexilischen Zeit. Darstellungsinteressen in den Chronikbüchern und bei Josephus*, in M. ALBANI and T. ARNDT (eds.), *Gottes Ehre erzählen. Festschrift für Hans Seidel zum 65. Geburtstag*, Leipzig, Thomas Verlag, 1994, 127-151.

R.K. GNUSE, *Dreams & Dream Reports in the Writings of Josephus: A Traditio-Historical Analysis* (AGJU, 36), Leiden, Brill, 1996.

H. GRAETZ, *Das Datum der Schlacht bei Kharkhemisch und der Beginn der chaldäischen Herrschaft über Judäa*, in *MGWJ* 23 (1874) 289-308.

J. GRAY, *I and II Kings* (OTL), Philadelphia, Westminster, 1970².

A.R. GREEN, *The Fate of Jehoiakim*, in *AUSS* 20 (1982) 103-109.

A. VON GUTSCHMID, *Kleine Schriften*, II (ed. F. RÜHL), Leipzig, Teubner, 1890.

A. HALDAR, *Studies in the Book of Nahum* (UUÄ, 1946:7), Uppsala, A.B. Lundequistska Bokhandeln; Leipzig, Harrassowitz, 1946.

M. HARDING, *Making Old Things New: Prayer Texts in Josephus's* Antiquities *1-11: A Study in the Transmission of Tradition*, in J.H. CHARLESWORTH et al. (eds.), *The Lord's Prayer and Other Prayer Texts from the Greco-Roman Era*, Valley Forge, PA, Trinity Press International, 1994, 54-72.

R.S. HAUPERT, *The Relation of Codex Vaticanus and the Lucianic Text in the Book of Kings from the Viewpoint of the Old Latin and Ethiopic Versions*, Diss., University of Pennsylvania, 1930.

M. HENGEL, *Die Zeloten* (AGJU, 1), Leiden, Brill, 1961.

E.W. HENGSTENBERG, *De Rebus Tyriorum*, Berlin, Oehmigke, 1832.

A. HILLHORST, *"Servir Dieu" dans la terminologie du judaïsme hellénistique et des premières générations chrétiennes de langue grecque*, in A.A. BASTIAENSEN et al. (eds.), *Fructus Centesimus. FS G.J.M. Bartelink* (Instrumenta Patristica, 19), Steenbrugis, In Abbatia S. Petri; Dordrecht, Kluwer, 1989, 177-192.

P. HÖFFKEN, *Hiskija und Jesaja bei Josephus*, in *JSJ* 29 (1998) 37-48.

—, *Weltreiche und Prophetie Israels bei Flavius Josephus*, in *TZ* 55 (1999) 47-56.

G. HÖLSCHER, *Josephus*, PW 9², 1916, cc. 1934-2000.

L.P. HOGAN, *Healing in the Second Temple Period* (NTOA, 21), Freiburg, Universitätsverlag; Göttingen, Vandenhoeck & Ruprecht, 1992.

C.H. HOLLADAY, *Theios Aner in Hellenistic Judaism* (SBLMS, 40), Missoula, MT, Scholars, 1977.

K. HUBER, *"Zeichen des Jona" und "Mehr als Jona". Die Gestalt des Jona im Neuen Testament und ihr Beitrag zur bibeltheologischen Fragestellung*, in *Protokolle zur Bibel* 7 (1998) 77-94.

P. HUMBERT, *Nahoum II, 9*, in *REJ* 83 (1927) 74-76.

C.-H. HUNZINGER, *Babylon als Deckname für Rom und die Datierung des 1. Petrusbriefes*, in H.G. REVENTLOW (ed.), *Gottes Wort und Gottes Land. Hans-Wilhelm Hertzberg zum 70. Geburtstag*, Göttingen, Vandenhoeck & Ruprecht, 1965, 67-77.

B. HUWYLER, *Jeremia und die Völker. Untersuchungen zu den Völkersprüchen in Jeremia 46-49* (FAT, 20), Tübingen, Mohr Siebeck, 1997.

A. JAUBERT, *La notion d'alliance dans le Judaïsme aux abords de l'ère chrétienne*, Paris, Seuil, 1963.

S. JELLICOE, *The Septuagint and Modern Study*, Oxford, Clarendon, 1968.

F. JEREMIAS, *Tyrus bis zur Zeit Nebukadnezar's*, Leipzig, Teubner, 1891.

G.L. JOHNSON, *Josephus – Heir Apparent to the Prophetic Tradition?*, in *SBL Seminar Papers* 22, Chico, CA, Scholars, 1983, 337-346.

I. KALIMI & J.D. PURVIS, *King Jehoiachin and the Vessels of the Lord's House in Biblical Literature*, in *CBQ* 56 (1994) 449-457.

H.J. KATZENSTEIN, *The History of Tyre*, Jerusalem, The Schocken Institute for Jewish Research of the Jewish Theological Seminary of America, 1973.

—, *"Before Pharoah Conquered Gaza" (Jeremiah XLVII 1)*, in *VT* 33 (1983) 249-251.

H.P. KINGDOM, *The Origins of the Zealots*, in *NTS* 19 (1972-1973) 74-81.

G. KITTEL, ἀκολουθέω κτλ, in *TWNT* 2 (1935) 210-216.

S. KLEIN, *Talmudische-midraschische Glossen zu Josephus*, in *Jeshurun* 7 (1920) 456-461.

A. VAN DER KOOIJ, *Zur Exegese von II Reg 17,2*, in *ZAW* 96 (1984) 109-112.

S.S. KOTTEK, *Medicine and Hygiene in the Works of Flavius Josephus* (Studies in Ancient Medicine, 9), Leiden, Brill, 1994.

K.-S. KRIEGER, *Geschichtsschreibung als Apologetik bei Flavius Josephus* (TANZ, 9), Tübingen/ Basel, Franke, 1994.

— *et al.*, *Flavius Josephus*, in *BK* 53 (1998) 49-102.

J.K. KUAN, *Hosea 9.13 and Josephus*, Antiquities *IX,277-287*, in *PEQ* 123 (1991) 103-108.

F.X. KUGLER, *Von Moses bis Paulus*, Münster, Aschendorff, 1922.

C.J. LABUSCHAGNE, *Did Elisha Deliberately Lie? A Note on II Kings 8:10*, in *ZAW* 77 (1965) 327-328.

W. VON LANDAU, *Beiträge zur Altertumskunde des Orients*, I, Leipzig, Pfeiffer, 1893.

E. LARSON, *4Q470 and the Angelic Rehabilitation of King Zedekiah*, in *DSD* 1 (1994) 210-228.

C.F. LEHMANN, *Menander und Josephos über Salmanassar IV.*, in *Klio* 2 (1902) 126-140.

J.R. LEVINSON, *Josephus' Interpretation of the Divine Spirit*, in *JJS* 47 (1996) 234-255.

I. LÉVY, *Deux noms phéniciens altérés chez Josèphe*, in *Mélanges Syriens offerts à Monsieur René Dussaud*, II, Paris, Librairie Orientaliste Paul Geuthner, 1939, 539-545.

A. LEWINSKY, *Beiträge zur Kenntnis der religionsphilosophischen Anschauungen des Flavius Josephus*, Breslau, Preuss & Jünger, 1887.

D.R. LINDSEY, *Josephus and Faith: πίστις and πιστεύειν in the Writings of Flavius Josephus and the New Testament* (AGJU, 19), Leiden, Brill, 1993.

E. LIPINSKI, *The Egypto-Babylonian War of the Winter 601-600 B.C.*, in *AION* 32 (1972) 235-241.

G. LOHFINK, *Die Himmelfahrt Jesu* (SANT, 26), München, Kösel, 1971.

F. LUCIANI, *I Profeti Minori*, III (LSB), Torino, Marietti, 1969.

D. LÜHRMANN, *Epiphaneia. Zur Bedeutungsgeschichte eines griechischen Wortes*, in G. JEREMIAS *et al.* (eds.), *Tradition und Glaube. FS K.G. Kuhn*, Göttingen, Vandenhoeck & Ruprecht, 1971, 185-199.

M. MACH, *Entwicklungsstadien des jüdischen Engelglaubens in vorrabbinischer Zeit* (TSAJ, 34), Tübingen, Mohr Siebeck, 1992.

G.W. MACRAE, *Miracle in the Antiquities of Josephus*, in C.F.D. MOULE (ed.), *Miracles. Cambridge Studies in their Philosophy and History*, London, Mowbray, 1965, 129-147.

J. MAIER, *Amalek in the Writings of Josephus*, in F. PARENTE and J. SIEVERS (eds.), *Josephus & the History of the Greco-Roman Period: Essays in Memory of Morton Smith* (SPB, 41), Leiden, Brill, 1994, 109-126.

A. MARMORSTEIN, *The Doctrine of Merits in Old Rabbinic Literature*, New York, Ktav, 1968 (rpt.).

S. MASON, *Flavius Josephus on the Pharisees: A Composition-critical Study* (SPB, 39), Leiden, Brill, 1991.

—, *"Should Any Wish to Enquire Further" (ANT. 1.25): The Aim and Audience of Josephus's Judean Antiquities*, in MASON (ed.), *Understanding Josephus: Seven Perspectives* (JSPSup, 32), Sheffield, Sheffield Academic Press, 1998, 64-103.

G. MAYER, *Josephus Flavius*, in *TRE* 17, Berlin-New York, de Gruyter, 1988, 258-264.

M.K. MERCER, *Daniel 1:1 and Jehoiakim's Three Years of Servitude*, in *AUSS* 27 (1989) 179-192.

K. METZLER, *Der griechische Begriff des Verzeihens untersucht am Wortstamm συγγνώμη von den ersten Belegen bis zum vierten Jahrhundert n. Chr.* (WUNT, 2.44), Tübingen, Mohr Siebeck, 1990.

E. MEYER, *Geschichte des Altertums*, II,II, Stuttgart-Berlin, J.G. Cotta'sche Buchhandlung Nachfolger, 1931[2].

A. MEZ, *Die Bibel des Josephus untersucht für Buch V-VII der Archäologie*, Basel, Jaeger & Kober, 1895.

H.R. MOEHRING, *Rationalization of Miracles in the Writings of Flavius Josephus*, in E.A. LIVINGSTONE (ed.), SE VI = TU 112 (1973) 376-383.

J.A. MONTGOMERY, *The Religion of Flavius Josephus*, in *JQR* 11 N.S. (1920-1921) 277-305.

— and H.S. GEHMAN, *A Critical and Exegetical Commentary on the Book of Kings* (ICC), Edinburgh, Clark, 1951.

E. MOORE, ΒΙΑΖΩ, ΑΡΠΑΖΩ *and Cognates in Josephus*, in *NTS* 21 (1974-75) 519-543.

A. MORENO HERNANDEZ, *Las Glosas Marginales de Vetus Latina en las Biblias Vulgatas Españolas. 1-2 Reyes* (TECC, 49), Madrid, Instituto de Filología del C.S.I.C., 1992.

J. MORGENSTERN, *Amos Studies, II. The Sin of Uzziah, the Festival of Jeroboam, and the Date of Amos*, in *HUCA* 12-13 (1938) 1-53.

—, *The King-God among the Western Semites and the Meaning of Epiphanes*, in *VT* 10 (1960) 138-197.

F.C. MOVERS, *Das phönizische Altertum*, I, Berlin, Dümmler, 1849.

M. MULZER, *Jehu schlägt Joram. Text-literar- und strukturkritische Untersuchung zu 2 Kön 8,25-10,36* (ATSAT, 37), St. Ottilien, EOS Verlag, 1992.

— and K.-S. KRIEGER, *Die Jehuerzählung bei Josephus (Ant. Jud. IX, 105-109, 159f.)*, in *BN* 83 (1996) 54-82.

H.G. VON MUTIUS, *Hosea, de letzte König des Nordreiches bei Josephus und im Talmud*, in *Henoch* 2 (1980) 31-36.

S.A. NABER, *Observationes criticae in Flavium Josephum*, in *Mnemosyne* N.S. 13 (1885) 252-399.

E. NODET, *Le texte des Antiquités de Josèphe (l. 1-10)*, in *RB* 94 (1987) 323-375.

—, *Pourquoi Josèphe?*, in *Naissance de la méthode critique. Colloque du centenaire de l'École biblique et archéologique française de Jérusalem* (Patrimoines, Christianisme), Paris, Cerf, 1992, 99-106.

A.T. OLMSTEAD, *Source Study and the Biblical Text*, in *AJSL* 30 (1913) 1-35.

A. PADILLA MONGE, *Consideraciones sobre el Tarsis bíblico*, in *AO* 12 (1994) 51-71.

A. PAUL, *Flavius Josephus' "Antiquities of the Jews" : An Anti-Christian Manifesto*, in *NTS* 31 (1985) 473-480.

E. PAX, *ΕΠΙΦΑΝΕΙΑ. Ein religionsgeschichtlicher Beitrag zur biblischen Theologie* (MTS, 10), München, Zink, 1955.

—, *Epiphanie*, in *RAC* 5, 1962, 832-909.

A.S. PEASE, *Some Aspects of Invisibility*, in *Harvard Studies in Classical Philology* 53 (1924) 17-21.

A. PELLETIER, *Flavius Josèphe, adapteur de la lettre d'Aristée. Une réaction atticisante contre la Koine* (Études et commentaires, 45), Paris, Klincksieck, 1962.

E. PETERSON, *ΕΙΣ ΘΕΟΣ. Epigraphische, formgeschichtliche und religionsgeschichtliche Untersuchungen* (FRLANT, 41), Göttingen, Vandenhoeck & Ruprecht, 1926.

P. PIOVANELLI, *Le texte de Jérémie utilisé par Flavius Josèphe dans le Xe Livre des* Antiquités Judaïques, in *Henoch* 14 (1992) 11-36.

S. PISANO, *Additions and Omissions in the Books of Samuel* (OBO, 57), Freiburg, Universitätsverlag; Göttingen, Vandenhoeck & Ruprecht, 1984.

C. RAAB, *De Flavii Josephi Elocutione Quaestiones criticae et observationes grammaticae*, Erlangen, Junge, 1890.

A. RAHLFS, *Septuaginta-Studien, III. Lucians Rezension der Königsbücher*, Göttingen, Vandenhoeck & Ruprecht, 1911.

M. RAHMER, *Das biblische Erdbeben*, Magdeburg, Friese, 1881.

T. RAJAK, *Josephus and the "Archaeology" of the Jews*, in *JJS* 33 (1982) 465-477.

S. RAPPAPORT, *Agada und Exegese bei Flavius Josephus*, Wien, Alexander Kohut Memorial Foundation, 1930.

R. REBUFFAT, *Une bataille navale au VIIIe siècle (Josèphe,* Antiquités Judaïques *IX, 14)*, in *Semitica* 26 (1976) 71-79.

J. REILING, *The Use of ψευδοπροφήτης in the Septuagint, Philo and Josephus*, in *NovT* 13 (1971) 147-156.

T. REINACH, *Un passage incompris de Josèphe ou la vie chère à Tyr au temps de Sennachérib*, in *Revue des études grecques* 37 (1924) 257-260.

H. REMUS, *Does Terminology Distinguish Early Christian from Pagan Miracles?*, in *JBL* 101 (1982) 531-541.

J.D. SCHENKEL, *Chronology and Recensional Development in the Greek Text of Kings* (HSM, 1), Cambridge, MA, Harvard University Press, 1968.

B.U. SCHIPPER, *Wer war 'Sō,' König von Ägypten (2 Kön 17,4)?*, in *BN* 92 (1998) 71-84.

A. SCHLATTER, *Wie Sprach Josephus von Gott?* (BFCT, 14:1), Gütersloh, Bertelsmann, 1910.

—, *Die Theologie des Jüdentums nach dem Bericht des Josephus* (BFCT, 2. Reihe, 26), Gütersloh, Bertelsmann, 1932.

G. SCHMIDT, *De Flavii Iosephi Elocutione Observationes criticae*, in *Jahrbücher für classische Philologie, Supplementband* 20 (1894) 345-550.

E. SCHRADER, *Σελάμψας – Salmanassar*, in *Zeitschrift für Assyriologie* 1 (1886) 126-127.

H. SCHRECKENBERG, *Einige Vermutungen zum Josephustext*, in *Theokratia* 1 (1967-1969) 64-75.

—, *Rezeptionsgeschichtliche und textkritische Untersuchungen zu Flavius Josephus* (ALGHJ, 10), Leiden, Brill, 1977.

B. Schröder, *Die 'väterlichen Gesetze'. Flavius Josephus als Vermittler von Halachah an Griechen und Römer* (TSAJ, 53), Tübingen, Mohr Siebeck, 1996.

E. Schürer, *Geschichte des Jüdischen Volkes im Zeitalter Jesu Christi*, II, Leipzig, Hinrich, 1907.

R.J.H. Schutt, *Studies in Josephus*, London, SPCK, 1961.

—, *The Concept of God in the Works of Flavius Josephus*, in *JJS* 31 (1980) 171-189.

S. Schwartz, *Josephus and Judean Politics* (Columbia Studies in the Classical Tradition, 18), Leiden, Brill, 1990.

A.M. Schwemer, *Studien zu den frühjüdischen Prophetenlegenden* Vitae Prophetarum, *I-II* (TSAJ, 49), Tübingen, Mohr Siebeck, 1995.

J. Van Seters, *In Search of History*, New Haven-London, Yale University Press, 1983.

J. Sievers, *Michea Figlio di Imla e la profezia in Flavio Giuseppe*, in *Ricerche Storico Bibliche* 11 (1999) 97-105.

E.J. Smit, *Josephus and the Final History of the Kingdom of Judah*, in W.C. Van Wyk (ed.), *Studies in the Chronicler*, in OTWSA 19 (1976) 53-56.

—, *So How Did Jehoiakim Die?*, in *Journal for Semitics* 6 (1994) 46-56.

J.A. Soggin, *Das Erdbeben von Amos i,1 und die Chronologie der Könige Ussia und Jotham von Juda*, in ZAW 82 (1970) 117-121.

C. Spicq, *La Philanthropie hellénistique, vertu divine et royale*, in *ST* 12 (1958) 161-191.

—, *Notes de Lexicographie Néo-Testamentaire* I (OBO, 22/1), Freiburg, Universitätsverlag; Göttingen, Vandenhoeck & Ruprecht, 1978; II (OBO, 22,1), 1978; III, Supplément (OBO 22/3), 1982.

P. Spilsbury, *The Image of the Jew in Flavius Josephus' Paraphrase of the Bible* (TSAJ, 69), Tübingen, Mohr Siebeck, 1998.

V. Spottorno, *Some Remarks on Josephus' Biblical Text for 1-2 Kings*, in C. Cox (ed.), *VI Congress of the International Organization for Septuagint and Cognate Studies* (SBLSCS, 23), Atlanta, Scholars, 1987, 277-285.

—, *The Book of Chronicles in Josephus' Jewish Antiquities*, in B.A. Taylor (ed.), *IX Congress of the International Organization for Septuagint and Cognate Studies, Cambridge, 1995* (SBLSCS, 45), Atlanta, Scholars, 1997, 381-390.

L.R. Stachowiak, *Chrestotes. Ihre biblisch-theologische Entwicklung und Eigenart* (SF, N.S., 17), Freiburg, Herder, 1957.

G. Stählin, *Das Schicksal im NT und bei Josephus*, in O. Betz, K. Haacker, M. Hengel (eds.), *Josephus-Studien. FS O. Michel*, Göttingen, Vandenhoeck & Ruprecht, 1974, 319-343.

G.E. Sterling, *Historiography and Self-Definition. Josephos, Luke-Acts and Apologetic Historiography* (NovTSup, 64), Leiden, Brill, 1992.

H.-J. Stipp, *Zedekiah in the Book of Jeremiah: On the Formation of a Biblical Character*, in CBQ 58 (1996) 627-648.

H.St.J. Thackeray, *The Septuagint and Jewish Worship* (The Schweich Lectures, 1920), London, Oxford University Press, 1923².

—, *Josephus, the Man and the Historian*, rpt., New York, Ktav, 1967 (original: New York, Jewish Institute of Religion, 1929).

B. Thérond, *Discours au style indirect et discours au style direct*, in A. Caquot et al. (eds.), *Hellenica et Judaica. FS V. Nikiprowetzky*, Leuven/Paris, Peeters, 1986, 139-152.

E.R. Thiele, *The Mysterious Numbers of the Hebrew Kings*, Chicago, University of Chicago Press, 1951.

E. Tov, *Lucian and Proto Lucian. Towards a New Solution of the Problem*, in *RB* 79 (1972) 101-113.

—, *Jeremiah Scrolls from Qumran*, in *Revue de Qumran* 14 (1989-90) 189-206.

—, *Textual Criticism of the Hebrew Bible*, Minneapolis, Fortress; Assen/Maastricht, Van Gorcum, 1992.

J.C. Trebolle Barrera, *Salomon y Jeroboán. Historia de la recensión y redacción de 1 Reyes 2-12,14* (Bibliotheca Salmanticensis Dissertationes, 3), Salamanca/Jerusalem, Institución San Jerónimo, 1980.

—, *Jehú y Joás. Texto y composición literaria de 2 Reyes 9-11*, Valencia, Institución San Jerónimo, 1984.

—, *Catena in Libros Samuelis et Regum: Varientes textuales, y Composición literaria en los Libros de Samuel y Reyes* (TECC, 47), Madrid, Instituto de Filología del C.S.I.C., 1989.

—, *Crítica textual de 1 Re 22,35. Aportación de una neuva lectura de la* Vetus Latina, in *Sef* 52 (1992) 235-243.

E.C. Ulrich, *The Qumran Text of Samuel and Josephus* (HSM, 19), Missoula, MT, Scholars, 1978.

—, *Josephus' Biblical Text for the Books of Samuel*, in L.H. Feldman and G. Hata (eds.), *Josephus, the Bible and History*, Leiden, Brill, 1989, 81-96.

R. De Vaux, *Les Philistins dans la Septante*, in J. Schreiner (ed.), *Wort, Lied und Gottespruch. Beiträge zur Septuaginta. FS J. Ziegler*, I (FB, 1), Würzburg, Echter, 1972, 185-194.

P. Villalba i Varneda, *The Historical Method of Flavius Josephus* (ALGHJ, 19), Leiden, Brill, 1986.

B.Z. Wachholder, *Nicolaus of Damascus*, Berkeley-Los Angeles, University of California Press, 1962.

—, *Eupolemus: A Study of Judaeo-Greek Literature*, Cincinnati, Hebrew Union College/Jewish Institute of Religion, 1974.

—, *Josephus and Nicolaus of Damascus*, in L.H. Feldman and G. Hata (eds.), *Josephus, the Bible and History*, Leiden, Brill, 1989, 147-172.

J. Weill, *Nahoum, II, 9-12 et Josèphe (Ant. IX, XI, ## 239-241)*, in *REJ* 76 (1923) 96-98.

H.F. Weiss, *Pharisäismus und Hellenismus. Zur Darstellung des Judentums im Geschichtswerk des jüdischen Historikers Flavius Josephus*, in *OLZ* 74 (1979) 421-433.

F. Westberg, *Die biblische Chronologie nach Flavius Josephus und das Todesjahr Jesu*, Leipzig, Deichert, 1910.

J.W. Wevers, *Principles of Interpretation Guiding the Fourth Translator of the Kingdoms (3 K. 22:1 - 4 K. 25:30)*, in *CBQ* 14 (1952) 40-56.

M.J. Wilkens, *The Concept of Disciple in Matthew's Gospel* (NovTSup, 59), Leiden, Brill, 1988.

H.G.M. Williamson, *1 and 2 Chronicles* (NCB), Grand Rapids, Eerdmans, 1982.

H. Winckler, *Altorientalische Forschungen*, 2,1, Leipzig, Pfeiffer, 1898.

C. WOLFF, *Jeremia im Frühjudentum und Urchristenum* (TU, 118), Berlin, Akademie-Verlag, 1976.

L.S. WRIGHT, mkr *in 2 Kings xii 5-17 and Deut xviii 8*, in *VT* 39 (1989) 438-448.

J. ZANGENBERG, *ΣAMAPEIA. Antike Quellen zur Geschichte und Kultur der Samaritaner in deutscher Übersetzung* (TANZ, 15), Tübingen/Basel, Franke, 1994.

A. ZERON, *Die Anmassung des Königs Uzia im Lichte von Jesajas Berufung. Zu 2. Chr. 26,16-22 und Jes. 6,1ff.*, in *TZ* 33 (1977) 65-68.

J. ZSENGELLÉR, *Gerizim as Israel. Northern Tradition of the Old Testament and the Early History of the Samaritans* (Utrechtse Theologische Reeks, 38), Utrecht, Faculteit der Godgeleerdheid, Universiteit Utrecht, 1998.

MODERN AUTHORS

JOSEPHAN PASSAGES

Antiquitates Judaicae (AJ)

1

5	255
14	157 187 224 301
	485 488
15	480
17	635
43	192 208
57	235
73	192
85	43
86	230
88	378
90	412 413
93	413
100	237
103-109	235
106	219
110	256
113	331 444
114	9 14
116	307
125	24
127	24 258
129	75
143	303
154	256
164	124
166	350
174	12
176	84
181	583
184	256
187	256
194	316
202	76 233
203	307
219	478
223	230
224	317
226	175
229	230
233-235	31

233	230
258	144
259	256
279	80
313	22
324	292
341	358
342	358
346	219

2

3	49
6	228 234
22	607
31	558
41	39
54	489
60	362 398
62	449
68	478
82	91
85	478
117	263
122	606
139	93
152	451
156	266
163	230
177	308
209	40
218	478
224	606
229	144
235	103
238	465
241	381
253	85
269	420
276	616
278	75
279	256

280	401 450
292	446
293	15 350
294	58
312	358
323	256
334	124
337	256
339	80
345	80
381	588

3

1	20
13	362
15	208
16	192
19	245
23	401
30	78
40	229 232 234
42	400
44	470
45	230
49	342 460
56	252
57	232 235
59	253
60	403
75	381
104	465
119	378
166	521
190	393
195	290
197	358
199	183 358
210	61
212	401
213	116
218	199

228	420	216	9	276	230 421
238	359	217	470	313	583
243	280	218	9	339	316
245	353	225	470	343	421
250	181	237	230		
251	360	243	475		
258	358 450	288	230	**6**	
261	90	289	227		
291	354	293	395	2	230
294	354	296	334	3	408
297	400	299	56	6	576
309	14	309	229	10	181
310	80	323	43	16	380
311	446	324	253	22	602
321	93	326	43	24	100 399 400
		318	181	25	400
				30	361
				35	212
4				38	230
		5		39	343
8	124			47	36
13	237	14	199	50	616
14	8	31	237	54	133
41	582	36	284 421	56	54
46	256	42	344 401	60	602
55	256	45	358	61	182
66	133	50	368	63	237
70	360	51	377	69	403 460 583
82	232	63	241 292	76	54
85	490	65	256	83	132
93	20	73	460	84	253
99	252	80-89	253	86	157
107	199	96	92	87	54
111	240	105	323	90	199
112	256	114	420	91	199
118	85	115	399	92	616
126	233	162	21	117	240
127	82	168	470	120	373
130	181	179	245	124	240 469
132	343	182	42	130	521
153	393	198	104	136	114 153
161	329	200	469	138	582
165	253 256	201	85	139	256
176	378	205	77	141	372
181	192	208	394	146	116
190	245 331 373	212	82	150	192
194	401	230	256	151	104 420
207	397	251	239	153	513
209	474	265	104	156	343
215	192 208	266	317 450		

9,1–10,185

9		26	**39-40** 45 46 632	
		27-28	215	
1-17	**5-28** 29 342	27	**40-42** 43 45 47 51 62 133 333	
1	**5-7** 19 24 25 26 27 30 42 48		461 474 625	
	625 631	28	29 41 **43-44** 45 46 48 52 68 75	
2-6	5 **7-11** 26		86 103 119 629 634	
2	**7-8** 17 19 21 26 279 450 463	29-45	**47-65** 119 219	
3-6	463	29-43	23	
3	**8-9** 26 27 463 626	29-31	**47-51**	
4-6	25	29	30 **47-48** 62 64	
4	**9-10** 25 27 463	30	23 **48-50** 63 116 117 126 228	
5	**10**		318	
6	**10-11**	31-32	47	
7-8	5	31	23 **50-51** 57 63 64 79 320	
7	**11-12** 16 19 26 27 253 627	32	47 **51** 54 57 63 64	
8-9	5 **13-15** 26	33-36	47 **52-56** 67	
8	**13** 15 20 21 27	33	**52** 54 63 64 86 216 514 603	
9	**13-15** 16 27	34	36 47 **53-54** 55 63 64 214	
10-11	5 **15-17**	35	52 56 64 65 630	
10	**15-16** 17 27 44 201 401	36	**55-56** 57 58 62 64	
11	**16-17** 19 25 27	37-43	47	
12-13	5 **17-20**	37-41	**56-59**	
12	**17-19** 25 26 27 63 576	37	**56-57** 63	
13	**19-20** 26 96 100 626	38	**57** 58 63 64	
14-16	5 **20-22**	39-40	64	
14	**20** 21 26 27 28 58 97	39	**57-58** 63 444	
15	**21** 22 420	40	**58** 64 97 507	
16	**21-22** 26 27 52 184 355	41	**58-59** 62 63 64	
17	5 **22-24** 25 26 28 29 48 50 632	42-45	47 59	
18-94	29 113	42-43	62 625	
18-28	23 27 **29-46**	42	**59** 63	
18-27	23	43	**59-61** 62 63 64 67 317 463 625	
18-19	**29-31**		634	
18	24 42	44-45	23 26 **61-62** 67 113	
19-27	31	44	5 63 119 245 316	
19	36 40 46 47 48	45	113 126 137 213	
20	29 **31-33** 34 35 38 42 45 118	46-94	**67-112** 113	
	409 480 615 632	46-50	**67-71**	
21-22	29 **33-34**	46	**67-68** 72 99 108 111 219	
21	40 45 46 80	47-94	99 108	
		47-50	**68-71** 108	
22-26	29 **34-39**	47	**68-69** 71 83 87 102 104 105	
22	35 46		106 134 625 633	
23	**35-36** 37 40 45 53 88	48	**69-70** 71 77 105 111	
24	**36-37** 38 45 46 368 558	49	**70-71** 74	
25	**37-38** 45 46 69 83 101 609	50	**71** 106 108 626	
26-27	29 **39-41**	51-94	99 104	

51-59	67 **71-79** 81	87-94	67 **99-104** 130 191
51-53	80	87-88	107
51	**71-72** 73 77 79 95 106 631	87	19 **99-100** 104 109 110 111
52	**73** 77 83		199
53	**73** 106	88	**100** 101 109 161
54	**73-74** 75 77 91 107	89	**101**
55	**74-76** 80 83 91 95 106 110 397	90-92	209
	405	90	**101-102** 103 106 210 631 632
56-58	216	91	**102** 107 191 209 210 288
56	**76-77**	92	**102-103** 210
57	**77** 78 91 109 110 111	93-94	**103-104** 109 625
58	**78-79** 80 85 109 111 220	93	111 210 537
59	**79** 106 358	94	113 129 144 213
60-86	67 **79-98**	95-104	62 104 **113-127** 146
60	34 **80** 83 109 110 111 218 627	95-96	**113-116** 120
61	**81-82** 83 84 110 320	95	24 50 103 119 120 122 126 127
62	**82** 84 88 89 90 98 105 106 108		140 213 323 628
	625	96	49 118 120 125 126 137 157
63	**83** 84 88 91 94 95 110 139		167 168 461 634
64	**83-84** 85 106 110	97-98	113 **116-118**
65-69	628	97	126
65-66	87	98-103	118
65	**84** 89 90 109 585	98	32 125 126 318 480 625
66	**84-85** 106	99-101	113 **119-121** 125 252
67	**85-86** 87 88 91 97 106 107 109	99	125 126 127 382
	110 468	100-101	126
68	**86** 94 106 132	100	122 125
69	**87** 449	101	123 126
70	**87-88** 94 97 99 110	102-104	113 **121-124**
71	**88** 89 97 98 105	102	125 126 155 162 625
72	**88** 89 97 98 110	103-104	125 126
73	**89** 94 98 110 143 291 425	103	126 462
	585	104	114 125 126 130 137 320
74	**90** 109 133 308 627	105-139	**129-166** 214 623 629
75	**90-91** 110	105-106	**129-131**
76-78	109	105	104 137 143 145 165 626
76	**91-92** 94 109	106-111	129 **131-136**
77-78	**92** 95 100	106	**131-132** 133 135 136 139 176
77	107 110		215
78	97	107	**133** 149 154 164
79-80	**92-94**	108	**133-134** 135 136
79	97 107 109	109	**134** 163
81	**94** 108 114	110	**135** 557
82-83	110	111	**135-136** 138 166
82	**94-95** 97	112-116	129 **136-140**
83	**95-96** 107 111	112	50 129 130 **136-137** 138 140
84	**96-97** 110		141 155 165
85	88 **97** 98 106 107 210	113	**138** 150
86	**98** 106 108 110 627 630	114	**138-139** 140 148

99-100   532
99   **524** 526 528 531 532 533 553
           635
100   157 524 **525-526** 528 533 534
           536 558 632 635
101-102   **526-528** 531
100-101   533
101   530 533 541 588 618
102-130   631
102   **528-529** 531 582
103-130   **535-574** 562 564 567
103-107   **535-542** 569
103-104   549
103   192 **535-536** 537 539 549 558
           569 572
104-105   540
104   8 42 **536-539** 540 541 543 544
           545 549 551 556 563 567 568
           570 571 573 582
105-107   570
105   537 **539-540** 549 558 559 563
           566 571 572
106-107   492 **540-541** 569 572 573 583
           627
106   537 542 556 573 585 628
107   537 583 585
108-115   535 **542-553** 569
108-111   569
108   538 **542-543**
109   447 **543** 544 553
110   **543-544** 546 553
110-115   553
111   528 **544-545** 546 551 571
112-113   549 570 573
112   492 531 **545-548** 550 553 554
           560 563 564 565 567 586 588
           590 618
113   **548-549**
114-115   551 556 570 571
114   537 **549-552** 557 566 570 571
           573 585
115   511 **552-553** 554 559 561 566
           568 569 570
116-130   535 **553-569**
116   410 543 **553-554** 555 569 575
           576 577
117-130   553 554 575 576
117-123   561
117-118   557 570

117   **554-555** 556 557 558 562 565
           570 577 601
118   **555-556** 557 563 565
119   537 **556-557** 560 562 563 570
           571 573 602
120   **558** 559 560 562 563 564 572
121   **558-559** 561 569 570 571 574
           601
122-123   573
122   434 **559-560** 563 568 570 571
123   **560-561** 562 563 564 565 572
           585 633
124-129   553 569
124   537 **561-564** 565 567 568 571
125-126   **564-565** 570
125   566 567 573
126   172 566 567 570 573 577 586
           588
127   540 552 **566** 570 572 581 600
128   343 **566-567** 573 580 581
129-130   561
129   **567-568** 570
130   **568-569** 571 573 633
131-154   **575-597** 599
131-134   **575-577** 596 597 628 634
131   569 578
132-133   81
132   410
133   581
135-136   595
135   525 575 **577-579** 580 582 586
           591 596 624
136-143   575 **579-585**
136-137   591
136   578 **579-580** 581 582 583 590
           596
137   **581** 582 583 590 600
138-139   **581-582** 596 597
138   583
139   601
140-141   **541-542**
140   580 583 590 591 594 595
141-143   584 585 586
141-142   597
141   492 569 **584** 596 627
142-143   627
142   **584-585**
143   **585** 588 592 596 597 618
144-148   575 **586-589**

144	565 586 587 588 590 591 594 596 597 599
145	523 **586-587** 588 591 594 595 596
146	492 547 586 **587-588** 590 619
147-148	**588-589** 592 596 597 618 627
147	589 596
149-153	575 **589-593**
149-150	521 592 593
149	492 **589-591** 592 594 596 597
150	583 **591-592** 593 594 595 597
151-153	**592-593** 597 618 627
152-153	595
152	597
153	595
154	245 575 **593-595** 596
155-185	**599-622** 624
155-158	**599-603** 629
155-156	602
155	590 591 **599-601** 603 605 606 607 619 620 621 633
156-158	601
156	**601-602** 621
157	**602** 603 619
158	**602-603** 614 616 619 626
159-163	599 **603-606**
159	**604** 619
160	**604-605** 607 608 609 610 620 621 627
161-162	**605** 606
161	606 610 622
162 .	608 620 621
163	**605-606** 609
163-164	622

164-167	599 **606-608** 614
164	604 605 **606-607** 608 609 610 612 614 620 621 633
165	608 610 621
166-167	608 620 622
166	**607-608** 615
167	**608**
168-169	599 **608-610**
168	79 605 **608-610** 619 620 621
169	**610** 613 620 621 622
170-175	599 **611-613**
170	560 **611-612** 620 621
171	**612**
172	**612** 613 620
173	**612** 613 621
174	**613** 619 620
175	**613** 614 620 621
176-185	613
176-180	621
176-179	599 **613-616**
176	**614** 616 620
177	61 **614-615** 616 620 621
178	230 603 **615-616**
179	**616** 620 621
180-185	599 **616-619**
180	**616-616** 620 621 628
181-185	620 621
181-182	**617-618** 620
181	619 627
182	621
183-185	**618-619** 620 627
183	447
184	369 383

10

		229	24 50 392 521 522 533	272	401
186-218	529	230	398 527 532 533 635		
186	433 434 439			**11**	
188	434	232	426		
195	103	238	616	1-2	548
214	78 316	241	182	3	157 240
215	219	242	103	9	369
219-226	529	243	478	14	465
219	529	244	548	50	182
220-221	506	246	488	55	343 446
227-228	529	247	491	62	17
229-230	499 **529-531**	264	219	76	450

80	592	146	353	277	82		
85	382	158	236	316	500		
90	157	177	39	335	453		
91	447	195	606	352	471		
96	230 576	205	235	376	368		
100	465	241	383	399	399		
110	420	245	308	406	342		
112	253	250	280	415	399 400		
113	182	252	6	417	398		
114	369	253	120 450				
126	465	254	463				
132	606	257	157 369 381 383	**14**			
137	400	261	383				
140	383	269	157	2	104		
141	19 383	271	458	22	219		
151	383	273	396	24	16		
153	481	280	345	41	181		
171	362	286	115 344 471 481	54	12		
174	19	290	451	90	464		
175	19	301	345	115	383		
183	157	303	484	154	420		
199	521	312	401	169	393		
208	392	313	481	254	252		
213	479	318	358	257	503		
225	399	323	181	292	93		
231	181 401	349	354 420	367	102		
279	480	357	192 208	436	616		
297	359 443	382	474	455	219		
300	237 443	385	6	475	82		
311	234	399	412	477	359		
327	401			491	267		
332	279						
340	383	**13**					
				15			
		30	395				
12		34	6	18	449		
		57	465	27	234		
4	158	64	157 362	96	12		
8	474	65	157	135	230		
16	450	71	373	138	54		
25	359	114	157	179	584		
32	342	121	484	181	265		
40	329 467	173	252	194	79		
76	116	186	234	243	124		
83	420	227	21	303	116		
117	467	243	148	312	420		
134	420	246	390	345	308		
141	383	275	82	371	592		
145	358	276	82	385	157		

417	383	**18**		293	420	
				297	342	
		11	345	307	233	
16		44	289 358	314	399	
		66	458	330	383	
8	393	124	489	332	100	
22	308	162	449	333	342	
42	181	175	86	347	488	
51	397	198	182	365	397	
55	181	204	136			
166	348	211	182			
167	182	227	398	**20**		
209	582	262	576			
233	305	286	80	47	267 458	
297	92	288	79	49	383 420	
363	288	298	398	100	8	
379	341	326	158	106	482	
389	399 552	328	182	144	521	
394	103	345	256	147	8	
				162	308	
				166	582	
17		**19**		230	589	
				231-232	588	
62	93	3	588	231	591 593	
68	377	9	465	232	588	
96	80 234	69	79	234	591	
139	398	88	39	248	559	
169	200	233	22	254	114	
207	39	237	260	263	484	
240	238	241	92			
353	344	272	582			

Contra Apionem (c. Ap.)

1		198	280	**2**	
		214	77		
3	104	234	265	4	308
39	491	242	14	6	588
40	435	247	488	19	589
107	375	253	265	42	551
116-120	375	266	488	48	450
116	375	273	265	125	451
121-125(126)	375	287	460	132	584
128-153	447	306	233 358	167	521
133	447	307	381	174	458
135	506	308	469	179-181	622
146	529 530			190	80
193	461			196	400

200	158	237	397	273	245
211	521	245	560		

Bellum Judaicum (BJ)

1		231	243	405	235
		296	576	408	573 603
3	261	327	559	427	265
11	551	354	447	523	260
20	102	362	447	525	263
65	82	408	447	526	394
69	40	434	102	536	396
138	12	444	399		
147	521	465	521		
153	344	467	383	**4**	
198	235	472	283		
200	507	538	78	27	234
237	582	619	342	33	54
271	102	620	447 450	42	234
331	219	641	376	93	235
332	400			128	154
341	558			131	104
361	12	**3**		162	233
388	360			228	157
390	399	9	234	233	118
428	88	74	92	238	235
431	400	145-339	575	317	521
465	399	167-168	577	338	399
467	400	182	421	385	521
492	91	204	507	386	381
501	235	231	394	387	492
545	421	240-248	577	388	54
551	454	249	444	405	154
570	484	285-287	577	459	253
628	235	316	576	460-464	44
644	489	321	552	475	310
657	381	337	263	476	12
665	345	338	588	501	376
		339	588	508	491
		341	574	591	116
2		344	581	596	421
		353	54	608	89
56	102	368	263	611	89 376
104	114	373	257	617	468
139	451	376	582	622	573
207	398	377	521	626	492
230	237	403	263	659	376

5

5	233
79	92
91	100
109	577
121	577
246	77
251	239
265	104
273	305
296	576
313	394
316	450
335	399
362-419	387 415 550
362	573
367	272
375	550 573
388	387 388 409 410
390	387 417
391-392	550 555
391	573
392	547 555
393	555
394	237
404-408	387
404	408

405	390
411	573
420	550 552
427	242 507
462	235
471	559
487	450
503	460
517	573
569	263

6

48	344
57	400
96-113	550
98-99	573
98	550 573
103-105	499 526
104	530
105	573
108	550
109	381
110	573
112	550 573
127	182
152	577
160	399

177	577
180	78
228	616
250	588
279	102
312	381
320	85
328-350	583
351	580
352	580
385	491
429	102

7

7	288
57	118
72	420
94	450
98	141
131	399
155	353
201	489
349	492
359	470
371	234

Vita

1	492
11	460
15	263
52	551
85-88	608
92	342
113	451
156	465

165	397
167	397
260	468
268	450
283	450
290	503
301	181

317	450
310	102
320	142
327	401
372	142
409	395
418	603

BIBLICAL REFERENCES

11,1	186	13,4-6	209 **210-212**	14,14	**242-243**	
11,4-12	167 **169-177**	13,4	208 212 224	14,15-16	243	
11,4	**169-172** 174 185	13,6	224	14,15	243	
11,5-8	**172-174** 186	13,7	207 **209** 210 211	14,16	223 243	
11,5	175		212 215 221	14,17-22	**244-246**	
11,9	**174-175**	13(8)9-13	207 **212-214**	14,17-19	**244**	
11,10-11	**175-176**	13,8-9	224	14,17	243 248	
11,10	185 186	13,8	212 223 254	14,18	247	
11,12	**176-177** 185 186	13,9-10	212 224	14,19	248	
11,13-16	167 **177-180**	13,9	212 224	14,20	**245** 247	
11,13	**177-178** 186 187	13,10-21	211	14,21	**245-246** 273	
11,14	**178-179** 474	13,10	207 208	14,22	244 **246** 273 275	
11,15	**179-180** 185	13,11	216 224 525		295	
11,16	**180**	13,12-13	222 243	14,23-29	**251-272** 269 270	
11,17-20	167 **180-185**	13,12	222 223 224		273	
11,17	**180-181** 183 187	13,13	222 223 243	14,23-25(26-27)	**251-254**	
11,18	**181-183** 186 187	13,14-21	67		269	
11,19	**183-184** 185 187	13,14-19	68 207 **214-218**	14,23-24	**251**	
11,20	**184-185** 185		224	14,23	269 285	
12,1-22	(Eng. 11:21-	13,14	**214-215** 216 223	14,24	252 269	
	12,20) 189	13,15-19	**216-218** 223-224	14,25	251 **252-254** 255	
12,1-4	**189-191**	13,15	215		266 269 301 302	
12,1-2	204	13,17	221 224		303 631	
12,1	169 629	13,19	224 253	14,26-27	253 254 269	
12,2	205 628	13,20-21	207 **218-220** 224	14,27	252 624	
12,5-17	189 **193-198** 464	13,20	223	14,28-29	251 **268-269**	
12,5-6	**193-194**	13,21	224	14,29	285	
12,7-8	**194**	13,22-23	209 221	15,1-29(30-31)	**273-296**	
12,7	206	13,22	211	15,1-7	273	
12,9	194	13,23	207 211 212 224	15,1-4	**273-274**	
12,10	**194-195**		254	15,1	293 295 630	
12,11	**195-196** 206 631	13,24-25	207 **221-223**	15,2	295 298	
12,12-13	**196-197**	13,25	209 214 218 223	15,3	295	
12,13	206		253 254	15,4	299	
12,14	197 466	13,26	(L) 222 223	15,5-6	294	
12,15	197	14,1-22	**225-249** 251	15,5	273 275 **281-284**	
12,16	197	14,1-4	**225-226**		294 298	
12,17	198	14,1	246	15,6-7	273 **284**	
12,18-19	189 198 **201-203**	14,2	243 248	15,7	295	
12,18	328 389	14,4	246 247	15,8-18,1	628	
12,20-22	189 **203-205**	14,5-6	225 **226-227**	15,8-31	285 294	
12,20-21	226	14,7	225 227 228	15,8-13	273 **285-286** 294	
12,20	205 206 227		**231-232** 246 247	15,14-22	273 **286-290**	
12,21	206		248 632	15,14	**286-287** 288 294	
13,1-25	**207-224**	14,8-14(15-16)	225	15,15	287	
13,1-10	209	14,8	**238** 246	15,16	**287-288** 294	
13,1-2	**207-208**	14,9	**238-239**	15,17-18	**288-289**	
13,1	192 213 215	14,10	234 **239** 246	15,19-20	**289-290**	
	224	14,11	234 **240** 247	15,20	631	
13,2	213 224	14,12	241 247 248	15,19	292 294 376	
13,3	209 210 211 215	14,13	234 **241-242** 247	15,21-22	**290**	
13,4-7	207 221		276 628	15,22	291 319	

694 BIBLICAL REFERENCES

OTHER ANCIENT WRITINGS

SUBJECTS (selective)

Additions to/embellishments of Biblical material by Josephus,
10 25-26 45-46 50 63 88 90 91 101 103-104 108-109 116 120 121 123-124 126 130 135 138 145 156-157 159 162 165 177 185-186 206 208 223 247 282-283 287-288 289 294 326 327 335 364 380 384 389 392 393-394 401-402 406-409 411-412 413-414 419-421 423-424 437-438 455 459-461 468-470 470-471 474-475 484 490 491-493 494 501 519-520 520-521 532 543-544 556-557 566 581 582-583 586 591-592 596 609-610 618-619 619-620 626-627

Ally, God as,
21 22 75 76 333-334 420

Amalakites,
228-229 234 248 632

Anamolies, Josephus' resolution/ correction of Biblical,
49-50 58 72 79-80 101 131 132 137 141 143-144 149 155 161-162 175 207-208 216-217 274 382 386 390 446-447 469 514 566 607 611

Angelology, Josephus',
31-32 38-39 46 409-410 632

Anthropmorphisms, Josephus' handling of,
54 55 64 210 257

Antiquity, Josephus' emphasis on Jewish,
104

Apologia, Josephus'self- as reflected in *AJ*,
525 534 550 555 558-559 573-574 603 608 622 635

Appearances, divine, Josephus' inserted references to,
32 75 80 615

Audience(s) of *AJ* and its messages for these,
2-3 28 46 64-65 111-112 127 166 248-249 271 296 313 337 364-365 416-417 440 456 496-497 533-534 597 622 633-635

Babylon, as code name for Rome,
491-492 534 598;
positive depiction of, 600 601 602 622

Belief terminology in Josephus,
18 88-89 98 425 426 445-446 472 537 539 540 549 556 562 607 615-616 630

Birth, noble, Josephus' attribution of to Biblical characters,
469 600 603

"Bold", Josephus' use of as epithet,
42

Botenformel, Josephus' avoidance of,
16 34 40 88 119 401 470 565

"Brethren", Josephus' tendency to avoid as designation for Jews,
10 45 445 615

Burials (royal), Josephus' treatment of,
61 219 332 436 452 490 594

Fate, role of,
488
Figures, Josephus' supplying of precise,
276
"Friends" (royal), Josephus' inserted references to,
48 89 94 152 156 203 227 244 286 291 318 332 392 399 469 527 530 539
559 563 580 590

Gratitude, as hallmark of Josephus' biblical characters,
449
Greek authors, Josephus' use of,
43 104 374-379

Hand (divine), Josephus' avoidance of Biblical references to,
54
Happiness/prosperity,
269 301
Hebrew (people) Josephus' use of designation,
31 261-262 506 607;
language, 395
Hellenizations of Biblical account,
35 278 291 511
"High Places notice", Josephus' omission of Biblical,
190 226 274 298 628
Historic present, Josephus' use of,
8 30 10 74 231 247-248 261
Hospitality, Josephus' accentuation of Jewish,
50 79 431
Hubris thematic,
235 237 240 245 247 279 283 322 416 634
Hypotaxis, Josephus' replacement of Biblical parataxis by,
27 33 34-35 247

"Idumaea", Josephus' use of,
49 116
Imagery, Josephus' handling of Biblical,
445
Imitation terminology, Josephus' use of,
61-62 119 208 316 373
Indirect discourse, Josephus' replacement of Biblical direct by,
7 27 36 105 194 205 235 239 248 321 388 393 415 422 432 470 551 559
Innovation theme, religious, Josephus' handling of,
237
inspiration (divine),
54-55
Irony, Josephus' use of,
51 53 98 203 241 242 283 327 368 409 410 411 475 528 541 566 568 571
605 608 633

Jeroboam I as prototype of wicked ruler,
30 42 116 118 127 192 252 373-374 385 386

Motivations/purposes, Josephus' supplying of,
   35 48 50-51 55 57 59 77 78 82-83 85 87 90 98 99-100 101-102 130 137
   138 144 150 153 160 168 171 176 179-180 202-203 215 228 287 320 388
   395-396 397 432 447 450 472 486 505 507 524 530-531 546 559 604 605-
   606 612 613 614 632

Nahum, Josephus' dating/placing of his activity,
   301-302;
reasons for including Biblical words of, 312-313
Names, personal, Josephus' tendency to omit Biblical lists of,
   62 170 204 205 323 336 345-346 483 517 554 571 578-579 628 631;
place, Josephus' tendency to omit, 144 145 154 155 191 204 205 240 286 292-
   293 299 303 358 369 450 628;
supplied by Josephus, 68 104 106 115 143 478 489 592-593 631
Nineveh, Josephus' names for, 256 266 303;
end of,
   309 428-429 486

Oaths (curses), Josephus' avoidance of wording of,
   54 83 85 106 614
Obscurities, Josephus' clarification of Biblical,
   38 53 58 73 101 106 109 116-117 119 139-140 147 218 367 544 631
Omissions/abridgement of Biblical material by Josephus,
   9 11 13 14 16 17 24 25 43-44 45 64 85 93-94 96 99 107-108 126 133 134
   140 143-144 147 148 149 150 151 152 153 156 158 159-160 162 165 186-
   187 223 247 266 268 270 285 286 294 312 321 330 335-336 345 347-348
   353 354 356 357 358-359 360 363 384 389 391 393 395 396 397 398 400
   402 404 405 409 414 422 425 431 433 438 445 455 468 479 494 500 511
   512 514 515 517-518 519-520 526 530 532 561 567 569 596 601 611 612
   615 617 620 627-629

Pagan religion, Josephus' attentuation of Biblical denigrations of,
   7 42 46 162 166 182 397 403 404 634
Peacefulness, Jewish, Josephus' emphasis on,
   104
(the) People, Josephus' highlighting of their active role,
   342 345 356
"People of the land", Josephus' handling of designation,
   184 453
Philistines, Josephus' terminology for,
   122
Piety, Josephus' accentuation of Jewish,
   357
Poetic texts, Biblical, Josephus' handling of,
   505
Prayer, Josephus' treatment of theme,
   15 36 266
Precocity of Biblical characters, Josephus' accentuation of,
   226 459 462

BIBLIOTHECA EPHEMERIDUM THEOLOGICARUM LOVANIENSIUM

SERIES I

* = Out of print

29. M. Didier (ed.), *L'évangile selon Matthieu. Rédaction et théologie*, 1972. 432 p. FB 1000.
*30. J. Kempeneers, *Le Cardinal van Roey en son temps*, 1971.

Series II

31. F. Neirynck, *Duality in Mark. Contributions to the Study of the Markan Redaction*, 1972. Revised edition with Supplementary Notes, 1988. 252 p. FB 1200.
32. F. Neirynck (ed.), *L'évangile de Luc. Problèmes littéraires et théologiques*, 1973. *L'évangile de Luc – The Gospel of Luke*. Revised and enlarged edition, 1989. x-590 p. FB 2200.
33. C. Brekelmans (ed.), *Questions disputées d'Ancien Testament. Méthode et théologie*, 1974. *Continuing Questions in Old Testament Method and Theology*. Revised and enlarged edition by M. Vervenne, 1989. 245 p. FB 1200.
34. M. Sabbe (ed.), *L'évangile selon Marc. Tradition et rédaction*, 1974. Nouvelle édition augmentée, 1988. 601 p. FB 2400.
35. B. Willaert (ed.), *Philosophie de la religion – Godsdienstfilosofie. Miscellanea Albert Dondeyne*, 1974. Nouvelle édition, 1987. 458 p. FB 1600.
36. G. Philips, *L'union personnelle avec le Dieu vivant. Essai sur l'origine et le sens de la grâce créée*, 1974. Édition révisée, 1989. 299 p. FB 1000.
37. F. Neirynck, in collaboration with T. Hansen and F. Van Segbroeck, *The Minor Agreements of Matthew and Luke against Mark with a Cumulative List*, 1974. 330 p. FB 900.
38. J. Coppens, *Le messianisme et sa relève prophétique. Les anticipations vétérotestamentaires. Leur accomplissement en Jésus*, 1974. Édition révisée, 1989. xiii-265 p. FB 1000.
39. D. Senior, *The Passion Narrative according to Matthew. A Redactional Study*, 1975. New impression, 1982. 440 p. FB 1000.
40. J. Dupont (ed.), *Jésus aux origines de la christologie*, 1975. Nouvelle édition augmentée, 1989. 458 p. FB 1500.
41. J. Coppens (ed.), *La notion biblique de Dieu*, 1976. Réimpression, 1985. 519 p. FB 1600.
42. J. Lindemans & H. Demeester (ed.), *Liber Amicorum Monseigneur W. Onclin*, 1976. xxii-396 p. FB 1000.
43. R.E. Hoeckman (ed.), *Pluralisme et œcuménisme en recherches théologiques. Mélanges offerts au R.P. Dockx, O.P.*, 1976. 316 p. FB 1000.
44. M. de Jonge (ed.), *L'évangile de Jean. Sources, rédaction, théologie*, 1977. Réimpression, 1987. 416 p. FB 1500.
45. E.J.M. van Eijl (ed.), *Facultas S. Theologiae Lovaniensis 1432-1797. Bijdragen tot haar geschiedenis. Contributions to its History. Contributions à son histoire*, 1977. 570 p. FB 1700.
46. M. Delcor (ed.), *Qumrân. Sa piété, sa théologie et son milieu*, 1978. 432 p. FB 1700.
47. M. Caudron (ed.), *Faith and Society. Foi et société. Geloof en maatschappij. Acta Congressus Internationalis Theologici Lovaniensis 1976*, 1978. 304 p. FB 1150.

48. J. KREMER (ed.), *Les Actes des Apôtres. Traditions, rédaction, théologie*, 1979. 590 p. FB 1700.

49. F. NEIRYNCK, avec la collaboration de J. DELOBEL, T. SNOY, G. VAN BELLE, F. VAN SEGBROECK, *Jean et les Synoptiques. Examen critique de l'exégèse de M.-É. Boismard*, 1979. XII-428 p. FB 1000.

50. J. COPPENS, *La relève apocalyptique du messianisme royal. I. La royauté – Le règne – Le royaume de Dieu. Cadre de la relève apocalyptique*, 1979. 325 p. FB 1000.

51. M. GILBERT (ed.), *La Sagesse de l'Ancien Testament*, 1979. Nouvelle édition mise à jour, 1990. 455 p. FB 1500.

52. B. DEHANDSCHUTTER, *Martyrium Polycarpi. Een literair-kritische studie*, 1979. 296 p. FB 1000.

53. J. LAMBRECHT (ed.), *L'Apocalypse johannique et l'Apocalyptique dans le Nouveau Testament*, 1980. 458 p. FB 1400.

54. P.-M. BOGAERT (ed.), *Le livre de Jérémie. Le prophète et son milieu. Les oracles et leur transmission*, 1981. *Nouvelle édition mise à jour*, 1997. 448 p. FB 1800.

55. J. COPPENS, *La relève apocalyptique du messianisme royal. III. Le Fils de l'homme néotestamentaire*. Édition posthume par F. NEIRYNCK, 1981. XIV-192 p. FB 800.

56. J. VAN BAVEL & M. SCHRAMA (ed.), *Jansénius et le Jansénisme dans les Pays-Bas. Mélanges Lucien Ceyssens*, 1982. 247 p. FB 1000.

57. J.H. WALGRAVE, *Selected Writings – Thematische geschriften. Thomas Aquinas, J.H. Newman, Theologia Fundamentalis*. Edited by G. DE SCHRIJVER & J.J. KELLY, 1982. XLIII-425 p. FB 1000.

58. F. NEIRYNCK & F. VAN SEGBROECK, avec la collaboration de E. MANNING, *Ephemerides Theologicae Lovanienses 1924-1981. Tables générales. (Bibliotheca Ephemeridum Theologicarum Lovaniensium 1947-1981)*, 1982. 400 p. FB 1600.

59. J. DELOBEL (ed.), *Logia. Les paroles de Jésus – The Sayings of Jesus. Mémorial Joseph Coppens*, 1982. 647 p. FB 2000.

60. F. NEIRYNCK, *Evangelica. Gospel Studies – Études d'évangile. Collected Essays*. Edited by F. VAN SEGBROECK, 1982. XIX-1036 p. FB 2000.

61. J. COPPENS, *La relève apocalyptique du messianisme royal. II. Le Fils d'homme vétéro- et intertestamentaire*. Édition posthume par J. LUST, 1983. XVII-272 p. FB 1000.

62. J.J. KELLY, *Baron Friedrich von Hügel's Philosophy of Religion*, 1983. 232 p. FB 1500.

63. G. DE SCHRIJVER, *Le merveilleux accord de l'homme et de Dieu. Étude de l'analogie de l'être chez Hans Urs von Balthasar*, 1983. 344 p. FB 1500.

64. J. GROOTAERS & J.A. SELLING, *The 1980 Synod of Bishops: «On the Role of the Family». An Exposition of the Event and an Analysis of its Texts*. Preface by Prof. emeritus L. JANSSENS, 1983. 375 p. FB 1500.

65. F. NEIRYNCK & F. VAN SEGBROECK, *New Testament Vocabulary. A Companion Volume to the Concordance*, 1984. XVI-494 p. FB 2000.

66. R.F. COLLINS, *Studies on the First Letter to the Thessalonians*, 1984. XI-415 p. FB 1500.

67. A. PLUMMER, *Conversations with Dr. Döllinger 1870-1890*. Edited with Introduction and Notes by R. BOUDENS, with the collaboration of L. KENIS, 1985. LIV-360 p. FB 1800.

68. N. LOHFINK (ed.), *Das Deuteronomium. Entstehung, Gestalt und Botschaft / Deuteronomy: Origin, Form and Message*, 1985. XI-382 p. FB 2000.

69. P.F. FRANSEN, *Hermeneutics of the Councils and Other Studies*. Collected by H.E. MERTENS & F. DE GRAEVE, 1985. 543 p. FB 1800.

70. J. DUPONT, *Études sur les Évangiles synoptiques*. Présentées par F. NEIRYNCK, 1985. 2 tomes, XXI-IX-1210 p. FB 2800.

71. *Recueil Lucien Cerfaux*, t. III, 1962. Nouvelle édition revue et complétée, 1985. LXXX-458 p. FB 1600.

72. J. GROOTAERS, *Primauté et collégialité. Le dossier de Gérard Philips sur la Nota Explicativa Praevia (Lumen gentium, Chap. III)*. Présenté avec introduction historique, annotations et annexes. Préface de G. THILS, 1986. 222 p. FB 1000.

73. A. VANHOYE (ed.), *L'apôtre Paul. Personnalité, style et conception du ministère*, 1986. XIII-470 p. FB 2600.

74. J. LUST (ed.), *Ezekiel and His Book. Textual and Literary Criticism and their Interrelation*, 1986. X-387 p. FB 2700.

75. É. MASSAUX, *Influence de l'Évangile de saint Matthieu sur la littérature chrétienne avant saint Irénée*. Réimpression anastatique présentée par F. NEIRYNCK. *Supplément: Bibliographie 1950-1985*, par B. DEHAND-SCHUTTER, 1986. XXVII-850 p. FB 2500.

76. L. CEYSSENS & J.A.G. TANS, *Autour de l'Unigenitus. Recherches sur la genèse de la Constitution*, 1987. XXVI-845 p. FB 2500.

77. A. DESCAMPS, *Jésus et l'Église. Études d'exégèse et de théologie*. Préface de Mgr A. HOUSSIAU, 1987. XLV-641 p. FB 2500.

78. J. DUPLACY, *Études de critique textuelle du Nouveau Testament*. Présentées par J. DELOBEL, 1987. XXVII-431 p. FB 1800.

79. E.J.M. VAN EIJL (ed.), *L'image de C. Jansénius jusqu'à la fin du XVIIIᵉ siècle*, 1987. 258 p. FB 1250.

80. E. BRITO, *La Création selon Schelling. Universum*, 1987. XXXV-646 p. FB 2980.

81. J. VERMEYLEN (ed.), *The Book of Isaiah – Le livre d'Isaïe. Les oracles et leurs relectures. Unité et complexité de l'ouvrage*, 1989. X-472 p. FB 2700.

82. G. VAN BELLE, *Johannine Bibliography 1966-1985. A Cumulative Bibliography on the Fourth Gospel*, 1988. XVII-563 p. FB 2700.

83. J.A. SELLING (ed.), *Personalist Morals. Essays in Honor of Professor Louis Janssens*, 1988. VIII-344 p. FB 1200.

84. M.-É. BOISMARD, *Moïse ou Jésus. Essai de christologie johannique*, 1988. XVI-241 p. FB 1000.

84ᴬ. M.-É. BOISMARD, *Moses or Jesus: An Essay in Johannine Christology*. Translated by B.T. VIVIANO, 1993, XVI-144 p. FB 1000.

85. J.A. DICK, *The Malines Conversations Revisited*, 1989. 278 p. FB 1500.

86. J.-M. SEVRIN (ed.), *The New Testament in Early Christianity – La réception des écrits néotestamentaires dans le christianisme primitif*, 1989. XVI-406 p. FB 2500.

87. R.F. COLLINS (ed.), *The Thessalonian Correspondence*, 1990. XV-546 p. FB 3000.

88. F. VAN SEGBROECK, *The Gospel of Luke. A Cumulative Bibliography 1973-1988*, 1989. 241 p. FB 1200.

89. G. THILS, *Primauté et infaillibilité du Pontife Romain à Vatican I et autres études d'ecclésiologie,* 1989. XI-422 p. FB 1850.
90. A. VERGOTE, *Explorations de l'espace théologique. Études de théologie et de philosophie de la religion,* 1990. XVI-709 p. FB 2000.
91. J.C. DE MOOR, *The Rise of Yahwism: The Roots of Israelite Monotheism,* 1990. *Revised and Enlarged Edition,* 1997. XV-445 p. FB 1400.
92. B. BRUNING, M. LAMBERIGTS & J. VAN HOUTEM (eds.), *Collectanea Augustiniana. Mélanges T.J. van Bavel,* 1990. 2 tomes, XXXVIII-VIII-1074 p. FB 3000.
93. A. DE HALLEUX, *Patrologie et œcuménisme. Recueil d'études,* 1990. XVI-887 p. FB 3000.
94. C. BREKELMANS & J. LUST (eds.), *Pentateuchal and Deuteronomistic Studies: Papers Read at the XIIIth IOSOT Congress Leuven 1989,* 1990. 307 p. FB 1500.
95. D.L. DUNGAN (ed.), *The Interrelations of the Gospels. A Symposium Led by M.-É. Boismard – W.R. Farmer – F. Neirynck, Jerusalem 1984,* 1990. XXXI-672 p. FB 3000.
96. G.D. KILPATRICK, *The Principles and Practice of New Testament Textual Criticism. Collected Essays.* Edited by J.K. ELLIOTT, 1990. XXXVIII-489 p. FB 3000.
97. G. ALBERIGO (ed.), *Christian Unity. The Council of Ferrara-Florence: 1438/39 – 1989,* 1991. X-681 p. FB 3000.
98. M. SABBE, *Studia Neotestamentica. Collected Essays,* 1991. XVI-573 p. FB 2000.
99. F. NEIRYNCK, *Evangelica II: 1982-1991. Collected Essays.* Edited by F. VAN SEGBROECK, 1991. XIX-874 p. FB 2800.
100. F. VAN SEGBROECK, C.M. TUCKETT, G. VAN BELLE & J. VERHEYDEN (eds.), *The Four Gospels 1992. Festschrift Frans Neirynck,* 1992. 3 volumes, XVII-X-X-2668 p. FB 5000.

SERIES III

101. A. DENAUX (ed.), *John and the Synoptics,* 1992. XXII-696 p. FB 3000.
102. F. NEIRYNCK, J. VERHEYDEN, F. VAN SEGBROECK, G. VAN OYEN & R. CORSTJENS, *The Gospel of Mark. A Cumulative Bibliography: 1950-1990,* 1992. XII-717 p. FB 2700.
103. M. SIMON, *Un catéchisme universel pour l'Église catholique. Du Concile de Trente à nos jours,* 1992. XIV-461 p. FB 2200.
104. L. CEYSSENS, *Le sort de la bulle Unigenitus. Recueil d'études offert à Lucien Ceyssens à l'occasion de son 90ᵉ anniversaire.* Présenté par M. LAMBERIGTS, 1992. XXVI-641 p. FB 2000.
105. R.J. DALY (ed.), *Origeniana Quinta. Papers of the 5th International Origen Congress, Boston College, 14-18 August 1989,* 1992. XVII-635 p. FB 2700.
106. A.S. VAN DER WOUDE (ed.), *The Book of Daniel in the Light of New Findings,* 1993. XVIII-574 p. FB 3000.
107. J. FAMERÉE, *L'ecclésiologie d'Yves Congar avant Vatican II: Histoire et Église. Analyse et reprise critique,* 1992. 497 p. FB 2600.

108. C. BEGG, *Josephus' Account of the Early Divided Monarchy (AJ 8, 212-420). Rewriting the Bible*, 1993. IX-377 p. FB 2400.
109. J. BULCKENS & H. LOMBAERTS (eds.), *L'enseignement de la religion catholique à l'école secondaire. Enjeux pour la nouvelle Europe*, 1993. XII-264 p. FB 1250.
110. C. FOCANT (ed.), *The Synoptic Gospels. Source Criticism and the New Literary Criticism*, 1993. XXXIX-670 p. FB 3000.
111. M. LAMBERIGTS (ed.), avec la collaboration de L. KENIS, *L'augustinisme à l'ancienne Faculté de théologie de Louvain*, 1994. VII-455 p. FB 2400.
112. R. BIERINGER & J. LAMBRECHT, *Studies on 2 Corinthians*, 1994. XX-632 p. FB 3000.
113. E. BRITO, *La pneumatologie de Schleiermacher*, 1994. XII-649 p. FB 3000.
114. W.A.M. BEUKEN (ed.), *The Book of Job*, 1994. X-462 p. FB 2400.
115. J. LAMBRECHT, *Pauline Studies: Collected Essays*, 1994. XIV-465 p. FB 2500.
116. G. VAN BELLE, *The Signs Source in the Fourth Gospel: Historical Survey and Critical Evaluation of the Semeia Hypothesis*, 1994. XIV-503 p. FB 2500.
117. M. LAMBERIGTS & P. VAN DEUN (eds.), *Martyrium in Multidisciplinary Perspective. Memorial L. Reekmans*, 1995. X-435 p. FB 3000.
118. G. DORIVAL & A. LE BOULLUEC (eds.), *Origeniana Sexta. Origène et la Bible/Origen and the Bible. Actes du Colloquium Origenianum Sextum, Chantilly, 30 août – 3 septembre 1993*, 1995. XII-865 p. FB 3900.
119. É. GAZIAUX, *Morale de la foi et morale autonome. Confrontation entre P. Delhaye et J. Fuchs*, 1995. XXII-545 p. FB 2700.
120. T.A. SALZMAN, *Deontology and Teleology: An Investigation of the Normative Debate in Roman Catholic Moral Theology*, 1995. XVII-555 p. FB 2700.
121. G.R. EVANS & M. GOURGUES (eds.), *Communion et Réunion. Mélanges Jean-Marie Roger Tillard*, 1995. XI-431 p. FB 2400.
122. H.T. FLEDDERMANN, *Mark and Q: A Study of the Overlap Texts*. With an *Assessment* by F. NEIRYNCK, 1995. XI-307 p. FB 1800.
123. R. BOUDENS, *Two Cardinals: John Henry Newman, Désiré-Joseph Mercier*. Edited by L. GEVERS with the collaboration of B. DOYLE, 1995. 362 p. FB 1800.
124. A. THOMASSET, *Paul Ricœur. Une poétique de la morale. Aux fondements d'une éthique herméneutique et narrative dans une perspective chrétienne*, 1996. XVI-706 p. FB 3000.
125. R. BIERINGER (ed.), *The Corinthian Correspondence*, 1996. XXVII-793 p. FB 2400.
126. M. VERVENNE (ed.), *Studies in the Book of Exodus: Redaction – Reception – Interpretation*, 1996. XI-660 p. FB 2400.
127. A. VANNESTE, *Nature et grâce dans la théologie occidentale. Dialogue avec H. de Lubac*, 1996. 312 p. FB 1800.
128. A. CURTIS & T. RÖMER (eds.), *The Book of Jeremiah and its Reception – Le livre de Jérémie et sa réception*, 1997. 332 p. FB 2400.
129. E. LANNE, *Tradition et Communion des Églises. Recueil d'études*, 1997. XXV-703 p. FB 3000.

130. A. DENAUX & J.A. DICK (eds.), *From Malines to ARCIC. The Malines Conversations Commemorated*, 1997. IX-317 p. FB 1800.
131. C.M. TUCKETT (ed.), *The Scriptures in the Gospels*, 1997. XXIV-721 p. FB 2400.
132. J. VAN RUITEN & M. VERVENNE (eds.), *Studies in the Book of Isaiah. Festschrift Willem A.M. Beuken*, 1997. XX-540 p. FB 3000.
133. M. VERVENNE & J. LUST (eds.), *Deuteronomy and Deuteronomic Literature. Festschrift C.H.W. Brekelmans*, 1997. XI-637 p. FB 3000.
134. G. VAN BELLE (ed.), *Index Generalis ETL / BETL 1982-1997*, 1999. IX-337 p. FB 1600.
135. G. DE SCHRIJVER, *Liberation Theologies on Shifting Grounds. A Clash of Socio-Economic and Cultural Paradigms*, 1998. XI-453 p. FB 2100.
136. A. SCHOORS (ed.), *Qohelet in the Context of Wisdom*, 1998. XI-528 p. FB 2400.
137. W.A. BIENERT & U. KÜHNEWEG (eds.), *Origeniana Septima. Origenes in den Auseinandersetzungen des 4. Jahrhunderts,* 1999. XXV-848 p. FB 3800.
138. É. GAZIAUX, *L'autonomie en morale: au croisement de la philosophie et de la théologie*, 1998. XVI-739 p. FB 3000.
139. J. GROOTAERS, *Actes et acteurs à Vatican II*, 1998. XXIV-602 p. FB 3000.
140. F. NEIRYNCK, J. VERHEYDEN & R. CORSTJENS, *The Gospel of Matthew and the Sayings Source Q: A Cumulative Bibliography 1950-1995*, 1998. 2 vols., VII-1000-420* p. FB 3800.
141. E. BRITO, *Heidegger et l'hymne du sacré*, 1999. XV-800 p. FB 3600.
142. J. VERHEYDEN (ed.), *The Unity of Luke-Acts*, 1999. XXV-828 p. FB 2400.
143. N. CALDUCH-BENAGES & J. VERMEYLEN (eds.), *Treasures of Wisdom. Studies in Ben Sira and the Book of Wisdom. Festschrift M. Gilbert*, 1999. XXVII-463 p. FB 3000.
144. J.-M. AUWERS & A. WÉNIN (eds.), *Lectures et relectures de la Bible. Festschrift P.-M. Bogaert*, 1999. XLII-482 p. FB 2400.
145. C. BEGG, *Josephus' Story of the Later Monarchy (AJ 9,1–10,185)*, 2000.
146. J.M. ASGEIRSSON, K. DE TROYER & M.W. MEYER (eds.), *From Quest to Q. Festschrift James M. Robinson*, 2000. FB 2400.
147. T. RÖMER, *The future of Deuteronomistic History*, 2000.
148. F.D. VANSINA, *Paul Ricœur. Bibliographie primaire et secundaire. Primary and Secondary Bibliography. 1935-2000*, 2000.
149. G.J. BROOKE & J.D. KAESTLI, *Narrativity in Biblical and Related Texts*, 2000.

PRINTED ON PERMANENT PAPER • IMPRIME SUR PAPIER PERMANENT • GEDRUKT OP DUURZAAM PAPIER - ISO 9706

ORIENTALISTE, KLEIN DALENSTRAAT 42, B-3020 HERENT